L'ENTENTE CORDIALE ♥
1915

L'Entente Cordiale, 1915

*A German poster showing how the German submarines were cutting the
web of British domination.*

From the Hoover War Library.

L'ENTENTE CORDIALE ♥
1915

L'ENTENTE CORDIALE, 1915

A German poster showing how the German submarines were cutting the
web of British domination.

(From the Hoover War Library.)

READINGS IN
EUROPEAN INTERNATIONAL
RELATIONS

SINCE 1879

SELECTED AND EDITED BY

W. HENRY COOKE, Ph.D.

AND

EDITH P. STICKNEY, Ph.D.

Assistant Professors of History
Pomona College

HARPER & BROTHERS PUBLISHERS
NEW YORK AND LONDON

READINGS IN

EUROPEAN INTERNATIONAL RELATIONS

CONTENTS

v

CONTENTS   xxi

ILLUSTRATIONS

EDITORIAL FOREWORD

Once before this series of Harper Histories was opened to a volume of selected readings. Speaking nominally as editor but really as a teacher and as one long concerned with the problems of a university library, I said in the foreword to that volume my brief say about the necessity of using some basic source material if we were to secure realism in the classroom and reality in our claims for the kind of training history is supposed to give. I also indicated that the bravest attempt to do these things, if sustained year after year, would be at the cost of valuable and often irreplaceable library material. The better the teacher succeeded who attempted to use collections and great series, the quicker he would exhaust the library's limited supply of this material and thus end the possibility of continuing his promising method of teaching. One answer, and apparently the best one, to the difficulties that confront teacher and librarian in discharging their joint and several obligations is in well-selected volumes of readings.

In no field is such a collection of readings more needed and therefore more justified than in the field of international relations during the last half century. We deal here with a period that has more than the normal complexity of an historical era; it has its special difficulties because the basic material is in many languages, and buried, except for the specialist, in the serried ranks of great government collections of diplomatic documents. It is a period that impinges directly on the life and interests of everyone who studies it and everyone who teaches or writes about it. There is some help and some liberation in letting the leading actors who are just passing off the stage they have set for us tell their own story, no matter what we may think of their acting. It is a great advantage to have them do it in the language we understand and that permits us most readily to concentrate upon their thought and real purpose. This volume serves these several purposes admirably.

There is something more that it clearly purposes to do and that is to make it possible—indeed, to make it necessary—for the student to form his own judgment. The selections embody a great deal of factual material better told than most histories; but in the restraint used in their notes and their skill in introducing on occasion parallel accounts, the editors enable the student to get a fresh and vivid view that is really his own. No text, no matter how good—and good ones are still too few for this period—can do this. Indeed, it seems to me quite possible that a skillful teacher could use such a collection as a basic text in a course on the recent history of international relations.

As an editor I think I am free to give my testimony to the care and thought the editors have used in making their selections, a very difficult task indeed, and to the pains that have been taken to make the text trustworthy.

GUY STANTON FORD

PREFACE

Readings in European International Relations Since 1879 is a collection of materials which the editors think valuable for use in teaching a college course in European history covering the half century since the Congress of Berlin. They have attempted to select items which will give the point of view of men who took an active part in international politics. In making extracts from memoir or biographical materials, the attempt has been made to cut the author's words so as to reduce the length of the selection and still keep his essential thought on a given subject. In several cases, reports of a negotiation as recorded by two or more of the principals have been included in order to present the situation the more vividly and also to furnish the basis for a study in historical evidence. These contrasting or even contradictory accounts are offered without editorial comment of a kind to suggest that one is nearer the truth than another.

The treaties and documents that are included among the selections have been chosen for the use that they may have in class room work. Most of them are to be found in the original languages in a well-supported university library, but not in sufficiently large numbers so that a class can be referred to them—and, moreover, most students are equipped with a mastery of English only. In a few instances, treaties, reports, or other papers that are not easily accessible to students have been included. Among these are the selections from the Peace Conference Reports and Minutes, the Supreme Economic Council's Reports and Minutes, excerpts from the British Foreign Press Review, clippings from the foreign press, the British report on propaganda literature, propaganda of national delegations at the Paris Peace Conference, Northcliffe propaganda, papers relating to Belgian Relief work, the George F. Herron report on the break-up of Austria-Hungary, the foreign war posters, and translations of French and German diplomatic exchanges. The editors have had the advantage of the unusual facilities offered by the Hoover War Library of Stanford University. They have made use of their opportunities by including selections from the unique materials which have come there as a result of Mr. Herbert Hoover's activities: especially the American Relief Administration and the Commission for Relief in Belgium archives. If they succeed in small measure in opening that veritable treasure-house to the college student, they will be well rewarded for their labors. The documents listed as Hoover War Library Manuscripts have been used with the express permission and through the courtesy of the Directors of the Hoover War Library.

The small number of selections bearing upon the history of the years before 1895 is explained by the fact that for this period the editors have thought it necessary and useful to include only the materials that have become public since the war. The problem of the immediate causes of the war has been handled by submitting diplomatic exchanges or reports from a variety of angles and with nothing more than a brief statement as to the general contents of each item. To learn to develop from these very contradictory bits of evidence some sort of a connected story is the task left for the student; furthermore, a full elucidation would make the notes unwieldy. Selections have been chosen with a view to making possible the consideration of various theses regarding the question of responsibility for the outbreak of the war. The growth of the League of Nations, something of a description of its organization, and reports concerning the more important of its activities are included. On this topic and on the Peace Conference, the problem of selection was solved by taking certain questions as types: a typical report of a commission to the Conference; an example of Minutes of the Council of Ten; a mandate question; a situation involving a plebiscite; an example or two of humanitarian effort; a difficulty for which the League found it hard to get a solution and one which was handled more successfully, etc. It is to be regretted that more space could not be given to these topics as to many others.

To include materials relating to the internal history of the several European states has seemed entirely impracticable in the present enterprise, for obvious reasons of space. All topics not relating directly to international relations have, accordingly, been rigidly excluded. The editors are conscious of many obvious omissions. Unanimity in choice cannot be hoped for in a work of this kind, consisting of selections from such a mass of materials; yet it is the hope of the editors that somewhere within the list of items that they themselves have wanted students to read, other teachers will find the satisfactions of their needs.

For the choice of materials, transcription, translation, and editing generally, the editors take joint responsibility. Their task has been materially lightened by the efficient services of Mrs. Charles A. Stickney, Mrs. R. N. Woodworth, Mrs. Jennie P. Cooke, Miss Ruth Yoder, Miss Mary June Burton, Miss Ina A. Nelson, and Mr. Homer P. Foster; and of Dr. Harold Deutsch of the University of Minnesota for a final checking and revision of many of the translations. The editors are very appreciative also of the willing coöperation and the counsel of Miss Nina Almond, Librarian of the Hoover War Library; Professors Percy A. Martin and Ralph H. Lutz of Stanford University; Professor Carl Becker of Cornell University; Professor Waldemar Westergaard of the University of California at Los Angeles; and Dr. Oswald Wedel of the University of Arizona. Their acknowledgments to publishers and authors who have coöperated appear in the footnotes.

W. H. C.
E. P. S.

PART I

DIPLOMATIC EUROPE

1879–1914

READINGS IN
EUROPEAN INTERNATIONAL RELATIONS

1. TREATY OF ALLIANCE BETWEEN AUSTRIA-HUNGARY AND GERMANY. OCTOBER 7, 1879[1]

[In view of the increasing hostility between Russia and Germany after the Congress of Berlin, Bismarck determined to form a defensive alliance with Austria before Andrássy should resign from control of foreign affairs. He would have preferred a promise of mutual support in case of attack by a third power, whether Russia, France, or Italy. It is instructive to compare with this aim the actual terms of the treaty as signed, and to see what each would gain under possible contingencies. Reuss was the German Ambassador at Vienna.]

Article I. Should, contrary to their hope, and against the loyal desire of the two High Contracting Parties, one of the two Empires be attacked by Russia, the High Contracting Parties are bound to come to the assistance one of the other with the whole war strength of their Empires, and accordingly only to conclude peace together and upon mutual agreement.

Article II. Should one of the High Contracting Parties be attacked by another Power, the other High Contracting Party binds itself hereby, not only not to support the aggressor against its high Ally, but to observe at least a benevolent neutral attitude towards its fellow Contracting Party.

Should, however, the attacking party in such a case be supported by Russia, either by an active coöperation or by military measures which constitute a menace to the Party attacked, then the obligation stipulated in Article I of this Treaty, for reciprocal assistance with the whole fighting force, becomes equally operative, and the conduct of the war by the two High Contracting Parties shall in this case also be in common until the conclusion of a common peace.

Article III. The duration of this Treaty shall be provisionally fixed at five years from the day of ratification. One year before the expiration

[1] *Die Grosse Politik der Europäischen Kabinette, 1871-1914.* Vol. III, p. 102ff., No. 485. Eng. trans. in A. F. Pribram, *The Secret Treaties of Austria-Hungary, 1879-1914,* Cambridge: Harvard University Press. 1920. Vol. I, pp. 25-31. Reprinted with the permission of the Harvard University Press, holders of the copyright.

of this period the two High Contracting Parties shall consult together concerning the question whether the conditions serving as the basis of the Treaty still prevail, and reach an agreement in regard to the further continuance or possible modification of certain details. If in the course of the first month of the last year of the Treaty no invitation has been received from either side to open these negotiations, the Treaty shall be considered as renewed for a further period of three years.

Article IV. This Treaty shall, in conformity with its peaceful character, and to avoid any misinterpretation, be kept secret by the two High Contracting Parties, and only communicated to a third Power upon a joint understanding between the two Parties, and according to the terms of a special Agreement.

The two High Contracting Parties venture to hope, after the sentiments expressed by the Emperor Alexander at the meeting at Alexandrovo, that the armaments of Russia will not in reality prove to be menacing to them, and have on that account no reason for making a communication at present; should, however, this hope, contrary to their expectations, prove to be erroneous, the two High Contracting Parties would consider it their loyal obligation to let the Emperor Alexander know, at least confidentially, that they must consider an attack on either of them as directed against both.

Article V. This Treaty shall derive its validity from the approbation of the two Exalted Sovereigns and shall be ratified within fourteen days after this approbation has been granted by Their Most Exalted Majesties.

In witness whereof the Plenipotentiaries have signed this Treaty with their own hands and affixed their arms.

Done at Vienna, October 7, 1879

ANDRÁSSY   H. VII v. REUSS
  L.S.   L.S.

2. LEAGUE OF THE THREE EMPERORS. BERLIN, JUNE 18, 1881[1]

[Bismarck declared that the new friendship of Germany and Russia sealed in this treaty would prevent an Austro-Russian war and a Franco-Russian coalition. The initiative was due to the Russian Sabouroff rather than to Bismarck. A "Ministerial Declaration of Policy on the Relation of the Dual Alliance to the League of the Three Emperors" stated that the German and Austrian governments recognize that the prospective agreement "can under no circumstances prejudice their treaty of alliance which continues to determine the relations of the two Powers." It was regarded as so secret that Bismarck did not entrust the negotiations to the chancery secretaries, but wrote out the

[1] *Die Grosse Politik*, Vol. III, p. 176ff. Eng. trans. in A. F. Pribram, *The Secret Treaties of Austria-Hungary, 1879-1914*, Vol. I, p. 37ff. Reprinted with the permission of the Harvard University Press, holders of the copyright.

documents in regard to it with his own hand. The treaty was renewed in 1884 and was terminated in 1887.]

The Courts of Austria-Hungary, of Germany, and of Russia, animated by an equal desire to consolidate the general peace by an understanding intended to assure the defensive position of their respective States, have come into agreement on certain questions which more especially concern their reciprocal interests. . . .

With this purpose the three Courts . . . have agreed on the following Articles:

Article I. In case one of the High Contracting Parties should find itself at war with a fourth Great Power, the two others shall maintain towards it a benevolent neutrality and shall devote their efforts to the localization of the conflict.

This stipulation shall apply likewise to a war between one of the three Powers and Turkey, but only in the case where a previous agreement shall have been reached between the three Courts as to the results of this war.

In the special case where one of them shall obtain a more positive support from one of its two Allies, the obligatory value of the present Article shall remain in all its force for the third.

Article II. Russia, in agreement with Germany, declares her firm resolution to respect the interests arising from the new position assured to Austria-Hungary by the Treaty of Berlin.

The three Courts, desirous of avoiding all discord between them, engage to take account of their respective interests in the Balkan Peninsula. They further promise one another that any new modifications in the territorial status quo of Turkey in Europe can be accomplished only in virtue of a common agreement between them.

In order to facilitate the agreement contemplated by the present Article, an agreement of which it is impossible to foresee all the conditions, the three Courts from the present moment record in the Protocol annexed to this Treaty the points on which an understanding has already been established in principle.

Article III. The three Courts recognize the European and mutually obligatory character of the principle of the closing of the Straits of the Bosporus and of the Dardanelles, founded on international law, confirmed by treaties, and summed up in the declaration of the second Plenipotentiary of Russia at the session of July 12 of the Congress of Berlin.

They will take care in common that Turkey shall make no exception to this rule in favor of the interests of any Government whatsoever, by lending to warlike operations of a belligerent Power the portion of its Empire constituted by the Straits.

In case of infringement, or to prevent it if such infringement should be in prospect, the three Courts will inform Turkey that they would regard her, in that event, as putting herself in a state of war towards the injured Party, and as having deprived herself thenceforth of the benefits of the security assured to her territorial status quo by the Treaty of Berlin.

Article IV. The present Treaty shall be in force during a period of three years, dating from the day of the exchange of ratifications.

Article V. The High Contracting Parties mutually promise secrecy as to the contents and the existence of the present Treaty, as well as of the Protocol annexed thereto.

Article VI. The secret Conventions concluded between Austria-Hungary and Russia and between Germany and Russia in 1873 are replaced by the present Treaty. . . .

SZÉCHÉNYI
v. BISMARCK
SABOUROFF

SEPARATE PROTOCOL ON THE SAME DATE TO THE CONVENTION OF BERLIN. JUNE 18, 1881

1. *Bosnia and Herzegovina.* Austria-Hungary reserves the right to annex these provinces at whatever moment she shall deem opportune.

2. *Sanjak of Novibazar.* The Declaration exchanged between the Austro-Hungarian Plenipotentiaries and the Russian Plenipotentiaries at the Congress of Berlin under the date of July 13/1, 1878, remains in force.

3. *Eastern Rumelia.* The three Powers agree in regarding the eventuality of an occupation either of Eastern Rumelia or of the Balkans as full of perils for the general peace. In case this should occur, they will employ their efforts to dissuade the Porte from such an enterprise, it being well understood that Bulgaria and Eastern Rumelia on their part are to abstain from provoking the Porte by attacks emanating from their territories against the other provinces of the Ottoman Empire.

4. *Bulgaria.* The three Powers will not oppose the eventual reunion of Bulgaria and Eastern Rumelia within the territorial limits assigned to them by the Treaty of Berlin, if this question should come up by the force of circumstances. They agree to dissuade the Bulgarians from all aggression against the neighboring provinces, particularly Macedonia; and to inform them that in such a case they will be acting at their own risk and peril.

5. In order to avoid collisions of interests in the local questions which may arise, the three Courts will furnish their representatives and agents in the Orient with a general instruction, directing them to endeavor to smooth out their divergences by friendly explanations between themselves in each special case; and, in the cases where they do not succeed in doing so, to refer the matters to their Governments.

6. The present Protocol forms an integral part of the secret Treaty

signed on this day at Berlin, and shall have the same force and validity. . . .

3. THE AUSTRO-SERBIAN ALLIANCE, JUNE 16/28, 1881[1]

[This treaty was part of Bismarck's system of insurance against a disturbance of the status quo by France or Russia. Serbia, though naturally pro-Russian, had been shocked by Russian support of Bulgaria in the treaty of San Stefano. In spite of the Austrian occupation of Bosnia, Serbia turned to Vienna because of Andrássy's services in securing Nish and Pirot for her. The signers of the treaty were the Austrian Minister at Belgrade and the Serbian Foreign Minister.]

Article I. There shall be stable peace and friendship between Austria-Hungary and Serbia. The two Governments engage to follow mutually a friendly policy.

Article II. Serbia will not tolerate political, religious, or other intrigues, which, taking her territory as a point of departure, might be directed against the Austro-Hungarian Monarchy, including therein Bosnia, Herzegovina, and the Sanjak of Novibazar.

Austria-Hungary assumes the same obligation with regard to Serbia and her dynasty, the maintenance and strengthening of which she will support with all her influence.

Article III. If the Prince of Serbia should deem it necessary, in the interest of His dynasty and of His country, to take in behalf of Himself and of His descendants the title of King, Austria-Hungary will recognize this title as soon as its proclamation shall have been made in legal form, and will use her influence to secure recognition for it on the part of the other Powers.

Article IV. Austria-Hungary will use her influence with the other European Cabinets to second the interests of Serbia.

Without a previous understanding with Austria-Hungary, Serbia will neither negotiate nor conclude any political treaty with another Government, and will not admit to her territory a foreign armed force, regular or irregular, even as volunteers.

Article V. If Austria-Hungary should be threatened with war or find herself at war with one or more other Powers, Serbia will observe a friendly neutrality towards the Austro-Hungarian Monarchy, including therein Bosnia, Herzegovina and the Sanjak of Novibazar, and will accord to it all possible facilities, in conformity with their close friendship and spirit of this Treaty.

Austria-Hungary assumes the same obligation towards Serbia, in case the latter should be threatened with war or find herself at war.

Article VI. In any case where military coöperation is considered

---

[1] A. F. Pribram, *The Secret Treaties of Austria-Hungary, 1879-1914*, Vol. I, pp. 51-55. Reprinted with the permission of the Harvard University Press, holders of the copyright.

necessary by the two Contracting Parties, the questions touching this coöperation, especially those of the superior command and of the contingent passage of troops through the respective territories, shall be regulated by a military convention.

Article VII. If, as a result of a combination of circumstances whose development is not to be foreseen at present, Serbia were in a position to make territorial acquisitions in the direction of her southern frontiers (with the exception of the Sanjak of Novibazar), Austria-Hungary will not oppose herself thereto, and will use her influence with the other Powers for the purpose of winning them over to an attitude favorable to Serbia.

Article VIII. The present Treaty shall remain in force for a period of ten years, dating from the day of the exchange of ratifications. Six months before its expiration the Contracting Parties shall, if there is occasion, take counsel together in regard to its prolongation or to the modifications which the circumstances of the moment may render desirable.

Article IX. The Contracting Parties undertake to keep the present Treaty secret, and not to communicate either its existence or its tenor to any other Government without a previous understanding.

Article X. The ratifications of the present Treaty shall be exchanged at Belgrade within a period of a fortnight, or sooner if may be.

In witness whereof the respective Plenipotentiaries have signed it and have affixed to it the seal of their arms.

Done at Belgrade, in duplicate, the twenty-eighth/sixteenth of June of the year 1881.

<table>
<tr><td>BARON DE HERBERT</td><td>CH. MIJATOVICH</td></tr>
<tr><td>L.S.</td><td>L.S.</td></tr>
</table>

4. FIRST TREATY OF ALLIANCE BETWEEN AUSTRIA-HUNGARY, GERMANY, AND ITALY. VIENNA, MAY 20, 1882[1]

[This alliance originated with Italy, not with Bismarck, who, when a treaty with Italy was first suggested to him, said: "You don't need to run after Italy if you want something of her; moreover, her promise will have no value if it is not in her interest to keep it." Its character was entirely defensive, but due to the secrecy maintained regarding its terms, exaggerated suspicions arose as to its offensive aims, particularly against France.]

Article I. The High Contracting Parties mutually promise peace and friendship, and will enter into no alliance or engagement directed against any one of their States.

[1] A. F. Pribram, *The Secret Treaties of Austria-Hungary, 1879-1914*, Vol. I, p. 65ff. Reprinted with the permission of the Harvard University Press, holders of the copyright.

They engage to proceed to an exchange of ideas on political and economic questions of a general nature which may arise, and they further promise one another mutual support within the limits of their own interests.

Article II. In case Italy, without direct provocation on her part, should be attacked by France for any reason whatsoever, the two other Contracting Parties shall be bound to lend help and assistance with all their forces to the Party attacked.

This same obligation shall devolve upon Italy in case of any aggression without direct provocation by France against Germany.

Article III. If one, or two, of the High Contracting Parties, without direct provocation on their part, should chance to be attacked and to be engaged in a war with two or more Great Powers nonsignatory to the present Treaty, the *casus foederis* will arise simultaneously for all the High Contracting Parties.

Article IV. In case a Great Power nonsignatory to the present Treaty should threaten the security of the states of one of the High Contracting Parties, and the threatened Party should find itself forced on that account to make war against it, the two others bind themselves to observe towards their Ally a benevolent neutrality. Each of them reserves to itself, in this case, the right to take part in the war, if it should see fit, to make common cause with its Ally.

Article V. If the peace of any of the High Contracting Parties should chance to be threatened under the circumstances foreseen by the preceding Articles, the High Contracting Parties shall take counsel together in ample time as to the military measures to be taken with a view to eventual coöperation.

They engage henceforward, in all cases of common participation in a war, to conclude neither armistice, nor peace, nor treaty, except by common agreement among themselves.

Article VI. The High Contracting Parties mutually promise secrecy as to the contents and existence of the present Treaty.

Article VII. The present Treaty shall remain in force during the space of five years, dating from the day of the exchange of ratifications.

Article VIII. The ratifications of the present Treaty shall be exchanged at Vienna within three weeks, or sooner if may be.

In witness whereof the respective Plenipotentiaries have signed the present Treaty and have affixed thereto the seal of their arms.

Done at Vienna, the twentieth day of the month of May of the year one thousand eight hundred and eighty-two.

KÁLNOKY   H. VII OF REUSS   C. ROBILANT
L.S.   L.S.   L.S.

[Additional Declaration of Italy that the provisions of the Alliance could not be regarded as directed against England. Rome, May 22, 1882.]

MINISTERIAL DECLARATION

The Royal Italian Government declares that the provisions of the secret Treaty concluded May 20, 1882, between Italy, Austria-Hungary, and Germany, cannot, as has been previously agreed, in any case be regarded as being directed against England.

In witness whereof the present ministerial Declaration, which equally must remain secret, has been drawn up to be exchanged against identic Declarations of the Imperial and Royal Government of Austria-Hungary and of the Imperial Government of Germany.

Rome, May 22, 1882

The Royal Minister of Foreign Affairs.

L.S.   MANCINI

5. ALLIANCE OF ROUMANIA WITH AUSTRIA-HUNGARY WITH GERMANY AND WITH ITALY, 1883 AND 1888[1]

[Like Serbia, Roumania was angry at Russia for her lack of reward for participating on the Russian side in the Turkish war of 1877. The first attempts at a *rapprochement* came from Vienna in 1880, but did not bear fruit till 1883, after long conversations of the Roumanian Bratianu with Bismarck and Kálnoky. The treaty was signed in Vienna by the Austrian Foreign Minister and the Roumanian Minister to Austria-Hungary. The treaty was again renewed February 5, 1913, between Austria-Hungary and Roumania. Germany and Italy signed within a month. King Carol signed reluctantly after threatening a new orientation of Roumanian policy. Austria-Hungary had little reason after this to count on Roumanian support of the Triple Alliance in case of war. *Ibid.*, Vol. I, pp. 261-265.]

Article I. The High Contracting Parties promise one another peace and friendship, and will enter into no alliance or engagement directed against any one of their States. They engage to follow a friendly policy and to lend one another mutual support within the limits of their interests.

Article II. If Rumania, without any provocation on her part, should be attacked, Austria-Hungary is bound to bring her in ample time help and assistance against the aggressor. If Austria-Hungary be attacked under the same circumstances in a portion of her states bordering on Rumania, the *casus foederis* will immediately arise for the latter.

Article III. If one of the High Contracting Parties should find itself threatened by an aggression under the abovementioned conditions,

---

[1] A. F. Pribram, *The Secret Treaties of Austria-Hungary, 1879-1914*, Vol. I, pp. 79-83. Reprinted with the permission of the Harvard University Press, holders of the copyright.

the respective Governments shall put themselves in agreement as to the measures to be taken with a view to coöperation of their armies. These military questions, especially that of the unity of operations and of passage through the respective territories, shall be regulated by a military convention.

Article IV. If, contrary to their desire and hope, the High Contracting Parties are forced into a common war under the circumstances foreseen by the preceding Articles, they engage neither to negotiate nor to conclude peace separately.

Article V. The present Treaty shall remain in force for a period of five years, dating from the day of the exchange of ratifications. If the present Treaty is not denounced one year before its expiration, or if its revision is not demanded by either of the High Contracting Parties, it shall be regarded as prolonged for a period of three years more.

Article VI. The High Contracting Parties mutually promise secrecy as to the contents of the present Treaty.

6. ANGLO-GERMAN UNDERSTANDING, 1879[1]

[An early suggestion of an Anglo-German alliance. Beaconsfield (Benjamin Disraeli), a Conservative, was at that time Prime Minister of England.]

Count Münster, German Ambassador in London, to Prince Bismarck
Private letter Very Secret

London, Sept. 27, 1879

Your Excellency:

I have the honor to inform you that I have just returned from Hughenden, Lord Beaconsfield's country house. I was entirely alone with him and had yesterday afternoon and evening and this morning opportunity to talk with him without interruption. He apologized for not being able to receive me sooner, but said that he had wished to be alone with me.

After I had explained in a few words the object of my visit and Lord Beaconsfield had promised me the greatest discretion and secrecy, he began by saying that he had given much consideration to the present situation in Europe. He could not deny that he saw with a certain satisfaction that Russia, blinded and entirely overcome by the senseless Pan-Slavism, was thrusting her old Allies from her and seemed to be giving up the League of Three Emperors which had been essentially profitable to Russia. England needed and wanted allies in order to be able to intervene in European affairs. The policy of non-intervention was unpracticable, and for a country which was conscious of its own power impossible in the long run. It had begun with Cobden and his

---

[1] *Die Grosse Politik*, Vol. IV, p. 7ff.

followers who had done as much harm in the field of politics with their "non-intervention at any price" as with their "free trade without reciprocity." The most natural allies for England were Germany and Austria. *He would enter an alliance with Germany with joy.* The principal questions in connection with this were France and the possibility of a Franco-Russian alliance. But just on this point he could give me the most definite assurances. France would never attack Germany as soon as she saw that England would consider this attack as a *casus belli*, and it was self-evident that Germany, who as against France had all she required for the safety of her borders, would never take the aggressive against France.

I replied to the Minister that I was very happy to hear this view, but that it was too serious an affair for us not to consider all eventualities carefully. Among these I reckoned the future position of the Crown and the Opposition and I asked for his opinion on this point.

"As far as the Crown is concerned, you may be quite easy," he continued. "Her Majesty knows but one enemy for England and that is Russia, and she wishes nothing more earnestly than a full understanding with Germany. From that side you are therefore quite safe."

"What of the Prince of Wales whose great sympathies for the French are known?" I remarked.

To this Lord Beaconsfield replied: "You are right. The Prince has certain sympathies for France, but even more," he said laughingly, "for French ladies. But these sympathies are less deeply rooted than his dislike, one can almost call it hatred, for Russia. Were it merely a question of the possibility of a war between France and Germany alone, he might, perhaps, side with France; but a war against Russia and France would certainly find the Prince on the side of Germany." [Bismarck's marginal note: "Austrian recipe."]

On the party question and that which concerned the Opposition Lord Beaconsfield's remarks were very interesting.

As for his Party, he could answer for its support so long as British policy pursued this path; in the political field, the Tories were the party of action and wished to uphold the influence of England in Europe and to resist the influence of Russia which alone they regarded as injurious. . . .

Lord Beaconsfield begged to be remembered to Your Excellency in the friendliest manner, and expressed his thanks that Your Excellency had commissioned me to speak to him so openly. "Write to the Prince," he told me on my departure this morning, "that if we come to an understanding, I consider European peace to be assured for a long time to come. If the Prince will help us in the East where the interests of England go hand in hand with those of Austria, we will guarantee to keep France from moving in case this policy should bring Germany into trouble with Russia. We will in that case keep France quiet [Bismarck's marginal note: "Nothing else?"], you may depend on us." . . .

I had assumed beforehand that Lord Beaconsfield would welcome our overtures by meeting us half-way, but I had hardly expected the definite and far-reaching assurances that he gave me. I am also convinced that in this case he is really sincere.

MÜNSTER

7. LETTERS EXPRESSING ENGLISH DESIRE FOR A GERMAN ALLIANCE, 1885[1]

[In 1885 Hatzfeldt was German Ambassador to England and Salisbury was the British Prime Minister. Randolph Churchill, a Cabinet Minister, was the leading advocate of an Anglo-German alliance. This time the initiative seems to have come from England (*cf.* doc. no. 6). The second letter well shows some of the obstacles to an Anglo-German alliance.]

Count Hatzfeldt to Count Herbert Bismarck

Private letter   London, December 5, 1885

Since I have no opportunity to see Lord Salisbury, who is in the country, before the departure of today's messenger, I am not in a position to send a report.

I was especially struck by my interview with Randolph Churchill, because of all those whom I have seen thus far, he alone sees into the future, has real ideas, be they right or wrong, and seems to pursue a settled policy. His desire is for an alliance with Germany, as you know, and he strongly deplores the fact that it has not come to pass. He spoke of the correspondence between the Chancellor and Lord Salisbury [July 2 and 8, 1885] as if it had been inspired by himself with this design in view. "À nous deux [Bismarck's marginal note: "Not enough"] nous pourrions gouverner le monde. Mais vous n'avez pas voulu [Bismarck's marginal note: "?"] I sought to make it clear to him that no German statesman could thoughtlessly run the risk of stirring up the enmity of Russia and with that bringing an attack by France. Our position was quite different from England's, and he must bear that in mind. In addition, the British Parliamentary institutions and the uncertainty which they caused were not able to offer a sufficient guarantee that an engagement entered upon by the Government would be respected by its successor. In what kind of a situation would we be if the Chancellor in the days when that correspondence with Salisbury took place had really entered into an alliance, and now at the elections Gladstone should again come to the head of the Government? Randolph Churchill replied with feeling that this very alliance with Germany, which would have been a colossal achievement for the Con-

---

[1] *Die Grosse Politik,* Vol. IV, p. 138ff.

servative Government, would have given it firmness for years and made Gladstone an impossibility. This lasting success of the Conservative Party would have given us the guarantee which we required. Today it was otherwise. Instead of success coming as the result of founding an alliance with us, the Conservative Government had to note that we had closed the Dardanelles against England, instead of opening them to her, and this failure was bound to injure the Government.

In reference to the Roumelian question R. Churchill does not see eye to eye with Lord Salisbury, in so far as the latter, in his opinion, has gone too far *en avant* in the question. Churchill has mainly India in mind and goes on the assumption that England still requires two years more to become unassailable there. (He urgently requested me to make no use of this information.) Therefore it is his idea that any conflict with Russia in the Balkans should be avoided, and he considers this easy, for England has no fundamental interests there and she could without anxiety leave Austria in charge of any she has there against Russia. Austria would eventually have to play this rôle whether or not she might wish to do so today. For these reasons Churchill would use his influence with Salisbury, that one would in principle indeed maintain the assumed standpoint, namely respect for national aspirations, which was necessary on account of public opinion, but actually let Russia do as she pleases.

This again agrees with a remark of Lord Salisbury's, who told me a short time ago that if the Turks really advanced into Eastern Roumelia, England would naturally maintain her standpoint, also insisting on her advisory rights, but would naturally not put up a single man to prevent it.

He has already exercised, and not without success, I think, these advisory rights when he forcefully warned Rustem Pasha [Turkish Ambassador in London] to prevent bloodshed in Eastern Roumelia. I gather from some rather confused utterances of the Turkish Ambassador that it has been suggested to him that the best way to arrive at an understanding would be by direct negotiations between the Porte and Prince Alexander.

So long as I lack instructions to the contrary, I shall continue to work quietly to the end that Lord Salisbury coöperate with the rest of the powers on the basis of some formula or other. This, I think, is to our interest. Not only is England a useful counterweight, and her presence at the green table would make one-sided decisions, which might be embarrassing, impossible, but—and this seems the most important to me—she will have to consider her interests herself and forego the idea of pushing Austria forward—as Churchill openly says and Salisbury thinks—thus forcing her into antagonism with Russia.

The perception sensed in Russian circles, that the sentiment has changed in favor of Prince Alexander, I have been able to confirm here

also. The gentlemen of the Russian embassy speak rather freely
about it.

P. HATZFELDT

Prince Bismarck to Count Hatzfeldt

Berlin, December 9, 1885

The reference made by Lord Churchill to an alliance with Germany
I do not understand, for there has never been any offer made to me
which I could have refused. The correspondence between Lord Salisbury and myself was limited to a single letter from each side. . . . In
mine there was not the slightest mention of a refusal. I cannot accept
Churchill's remark: "À nous deux nous pourrions gouverner le monde."
We two are not strong enough, but need a third power, which would
naturally be Austria. British policy has not understood this, or has
refused to understand it, and has frivolously estranged Austria.
Churchill's closing words "mais vous n'avez pas voulu" are a pure
invention, for the question of an alliance was never raised. If Your
Excellency should discuss this question with Lord Randolph Churchill
again, you should explain to him his error and tell him that the
conclusion of a lasting alliance with England would necessitate an act
of law, to which the English Parliament would probably not agree.
Otherwise only an alliance between cabinets would be reached with the
result that we would serve merely as leaders of the team as long as
we were needed. An alliance, moreover, cannot be made in this way, by
the proclamation that one would be ready to go through thick and
thin with the other party. Such a one can only be formed in actuality
by the pursuit of a common policy, particularly when made with a
country whose foreign policy depends upon changes of government.
Otherwise the idea of making a proclamation remains only an aircastle.
We could not enter such an alliance without risking an immediate break
with Russia and Austria; and then the enmity of France could not
be avoided. England seems to think that against such a coalition
Germany would play some such part as Churchill now assigns to
Austria, namely that of carrying out English policy at her own
expense. The exaggerated expectation which Churchill expressed to
you relative to Austria is really naïve and I cannot imagine that the
English Government really thinks Austria will be so foolish as to ruin
herself for England's sake; just this short-sightedness involved in this
sort of politics, namely that of employing the ally whose interests are
the same as one's own without supporting him and without knowing
how one afterward could operate without him, makes one very cautious
when considering a leaning toward England. If England had energetically supported Austrian politics in the direction of the latter's own
policy—that is, in the sense of protection of Constantinople against
Russia—Austria would probably have sought in preference the protection of her own interests in an alliance with England rather than

with Russia. Since there exists on the part of England the inclination first to use up Austria and then with a change of ministry in accordance with Gladstone's program, to have an understanding with Russia at the expense of Austria, I consider it a fine-spun but unfortunate management, and I cannot take part in it. If England had clear and stable aims and above all the courage to confess them publicly, she could find every alliance she might need; but if, in addition to her parliamentary changeableness, the lack of decision and honesty and an inclination to use the ally as if playing upon a certain egoistic, simple, rustic credulity, are to play a part, naturally everybody will be careful.

It will be appropriate if Your Honor will express yourself in this sense to other English statesmen also as opportunity arises and add that in the present parliamentary conditions of all countries the consideration for public responsibility makes the potentates of continental countries also more cautious than formerly, and limits them in the possibility of using the power of their respective countries according to the changing moods of their governments for other interests than those of their own nation. As long as England has no desire to fight for common interests without first sending the ally into the fire, just that long will it be hard to find an ally.

Lord Randolph Churchill is entirely in error when he anticipates that [English] foreign policy will make an impression on the new rural voters; and he forgets also that the Liberal ministry was in office when in the spring of last year the conflict between Russia and England threatened to become acute and the question of closing the Straits was discussed. In the time of Mr. Gladstone, if we had wanted to urge the Sultan to violate the Dardanelles agreement, we would indeed have come into conflict with Russia, but the Conservatives who at that time were not ruling in England would not have won the new communistic-radical class of voters, for these voters hardly know who [sic] the Dardanelles are. Austria is not strong enough to assume alone the protection of Constantinople against Russia, and we have no interest in this question as long as Russia withholds an attack on Austria.

If England had energetically and reliably supported Austrian policy in the direction of her own English policy, namely in the protection of Constantinople against the Russians, Austria would probably have tried to protect her interests by joining England rather than Russia.

There is no alternative for the Austrians, but to come to an agreement with Russia so long as they cannot from the first count on an English alliance in support of their resistance, as in the Crimean War. If Austria designs to fight for other purposes than in self-defense, she will not receive our help, as I say quite confidentially. But she could rightly claim that of England if she fights in defense of interests which are also those of England.

8. Notes Regarding Anglo-Italian Mediterranean Agreement, 1887, and Austria's Accession[1]

[In January, 1887, Italy asked for a treaty with Great Britain. Though Salisbury recognized that both governments had the same interests in the Mediterranean and the Near East, he preferred an understanding, because it could be kept secret and would be less binding. The arrangement was made with the encouragement of Bismarck. (See also doc. no. 11.)]

Italian Note to the British Government in regard to a Mediterranean Agreement, London, February 12, 1887. Dispatch of Count Corti to Lord Salisbury

The undersigned, Ambassador Extraordinary and Plenipotentiary of His Majesty the King of Italy, has received from his Government instructions to bring to the attention of His Excellency the Marquess of Salisbury, Principal Secretary of State of Her Britannic Majesty for Foreign Affairs, the following:

The Government of His Majesty the King, animated by the desire of establishing with that of Her Majesty the Queen an understanding upon various questions concerning their interests, is of the opinion that this object could be attained by the adoption of the following bases:

I. The status quo in the Mediterranean as well as in the Adriatic, the Aegean Sea, and the Black Sea shall be maintained so far as possible. Care must be taken in consequence to watch, and, if need be, to prevent any change, which, under form of annexation, occupation, protectorate, or in any other manner whatsoever, would affect the present situation to the detriment of the two Powers.

II. If the maintenance of the status quo becomes impossible, they shall so act that no modification whatsoever shall occur except after a previous agreement between the two Powers.

III. Italy is entirely ready to support the work of Great Britain in Egypt. Great Britain in her turn is disposed, in case of encroachments on the part of a third Power, to support the action of Italy at every other point whatsoever of the North African coast districts, and especially in Tripolitania and Cyrenaica.

IV. In general, and to the extent that circumstances shall permit, Italy and England promise one another mutual support in the Mediterranean in every difference which may arise between one of them and a third Power.

In expressing the confidence that these bases will receive the assent

---

[1] A. F. Pribram, *The Secret Treaties of Austria-Hungary, 1879-1914*, Vol. I, pp. 95-101. Reprinted with the permission of the Harvard University Press. holders of the copyright.

of the Government of Her Britannic Majesty the Queen, the undersigned avails himself, etc.

British Note to the Italian Government in regard to a Mediterranean Agreement, London, February 12, 1887. Answer of Lord Salisbury to Count Corti

Secret

The statement of Italian policy which is contained in your Exc.'s
dispatch of the 12th of February has been received by H. M.'s Government with great satisfaction, as it enables them to reciprocate
cordially Count Robilant's friendly sentiments and to express their
own desire to coöperate generally with the Government of Italy in
matters of common interest to the two countries. The character of
that coöperation must be decided by them, when the occasion for it
arises, according to the circumstances of the case.

In the interest of peace and of the independence of the territories
adjacent to the Mediterranean Sea, Her Majesty's Government wish
to act in the closest concert and agreement with that of Italy. Both
powers desire that the shores of the Euxine, the Aegean, the Adriatic
and the northern coast of Africa shall remain in the same hands as
now. If, owing to some calamitous events, it becomes impossible to
maintain the absolute status quo, both powers desire that there shall
be no extension of the domination of any other great Power over any
portion of those coasts. It will be the earnest desire of H. M.'s Government to give their best coöperation, as hereinbefore expressed, to the
Government of Italy in maintaining these cardinal principles of policy.

Accession of Austria-Hungary to the Agreement, London, March 24, 1887. Note of Count Károlyi to the Marquess of Salisbury

I have the honor, by order of my Government, to address to Your
Excellency the following communication:

It is with a lively satisfaction that the Cabinet of Vienna has taken
cognizance of the understanding reached between the British Cabinet
and that of Italy on the bases of a common policy to be followed in
the questions of the Mediterranean and of the adjacent seas.

I am charged with expressing to Your Excellency the deepest thanks
of the Imperial and Royal Government for having been apprised without loss of time of this important and eminently conservative
agreement.

Animated, above all things, by the desire to contribute so far as
possible to the maintenance of European public laws and of peace,
the Austro-Hungarian Government is happy to be able to note that
the fundamental principles and the political objects which are established by this understanding conform to those which guide the policy
of Austria-Hungary.

Moved by the conviction that these objects would best be assured by our coöperation, the Government of His Imperial and Royal Apostolic Majesty is ready to adhere to the declarations of friendship and of identity of political views such as are recorded in the notes exchanged between Your Excellency and Count Corti under date of February 12 of the current year.

In announcing this adhesion, the Austro-Hungarian Government congratulates itself particularly on the political rapprochement between England and Austria-Hungary and on the resulting consolidation of reciprocal relations. These relations will thereby be distinctly placed on a common basis looking to the pursuit of identical aims and the defence of common interests.

Although the questions of the Mediterranean in general do not primarily affect the interests of Austria-Hungary, my Government has the conviction that England and Austria-Hungary have the same interests so far as concerns the Eastern Question as a whole, and therefore the same need of maintaining the status quo in the Orient, so far as possible, of preventing the aggrandizement of one Power to the detriment of others, and consequently of acting in concert in order to insure these cardinal principles of their policy.

In expressing the confidence that these declarations will receive the cordial assent of the Government of Her Majesty the Queen, I avail myself, etc.

9. MEDITERRANEAN AGREEMENT BETWEEN ITALY AND SPAIN, 1887[1]

[The extension of the Mediterranean agreements to include Spain attached that country indirectly to Bismarck's coalition. Spain feared a possible French attempt to take Morocco, while Italy feared possible French designs on Tripoli.]

Spanish Note to Italy proposing a Mediterranean Agreement

Ministry of State
Madrid, May 4, 1887

The undersigned, Minister of Foreign Affairs of Spain, has the honor to bring the following to the knowledge of Marquis Maffei, Envoy Extraordinary and Minister Plenipotentiary of His Majesty, the King of Italy:

The Government of Her Majesty the Queen Regent, animated by the desire to seek an understanding with the Government of His Majesty the King of Italy for the purpose of fortifying more and more the monarchical principle and of contributing to the strengthen-

---

[1] A. F. Pribram, *The Secret Treaties of Austria-Hungary, 1879-1914*, Vol. I, pp. 117-121. Reprinted with the permission of the Harvard University Press, holders of the copyright.

ing of the peace, declares itself from the present time in favor of the acceptance of the following provisions:

1. Spain will not lend herself as regards France, in so far as the North African territories among others are concerned, to any treaty or political arrangement whatsoever which would be aimed directly or indirectly against Italy, Germany, and Austria, or against any one of these Powers.

2. Abstention from all unprovoked attack, as well as from all provocation.

3. In view of the interests involved in the Mediterranean, and for the principal purpose of maintaining there the present status quo, Spain and Italy will keep in communication with one another on this subject, by conveying to each other all information of a kind to enlighten each other concerning their respective dispositions, as well as those of other Powers.

In expressing the hope that these present and secret proposals will obtain the assent of the Government of His Majesty the King of Italy, the undersigned avails himself of this occasion to renew to Marquis Maffei the assurances of his most distinguished consideration.

Madrid, the fourth of May, one thousand eight hundred and eighty-seven.

(signed) Moret

Italian reply to Spanish Note

Royal Legation of Italy
Madrid, May 4, 1887

The undersigned, Envoy Extraordinary and Minister Plenipotentiary of His Majesty the King of Italy, has received the Note which His Excellency the Minister of Foreign Affairs of Spain has done him the honor to address to him under today's date, and he is authorized to respond thereto in the following terms:

The Government of the King gives its assent to the provisions enunciated in the aforesaid Note and pledges itself to reciprocity.

At the same time, it reserves to itself to examine, in full agreement with the Governments of Their Majesties the Emperor of Germany, King of Prussia, and the Emperor of Austria, King of Hungary, whether and to what extent there may be need, according to circumstances, to enter into further concert with the Cabinet of Madrid in order the better to assure the purpose which it too has in view.

In the meantime, the Government of His Majesty takes note of the abovementioned communication and regards the secret agreement established by the present exchange of Notes as entering into force from today, and for a period of four years.

The undersigned avails himself of this occasion to renew to His Excellency the Minister of Foreign Affairs of Spain the assurances of his most distinguished consideration.

Madrid, the fourth of May, one thousand eight hundred and eighty-seven.

(signed) MAFFEI

10. THE "REINSURANCE TREATY," 1887[1]

[When in 1887 the *Dreikaiserbund* (Three Emperors' League) expired, owing to hostility between Austria and Russia, Alexander III refused to renew it. Bismarck, however, was anxious to keep open the wire from Berlin to St. Petersburg. He regarded the new arrangement as of advantage to Austria, since Germany would retain a certain hold over Russia. Nevertheless, this treaty was not revealed to Austria, at the desire of Russia, although Bismarck expressed the wish that Russia would betray it. Its existence was revealed only after his fall by Bismarck himself. The treaty produced no outward result. It lapsed in 1890.]

TREATY BETWEEN GERMANY AND RUSSIA. BERLIN, JUNE 18, 1887

The Imperial Courts of Germany and of Russia, animated by an equal desire to strengthen the general peace by an understanding destined to assure the defensive position of their respective States, have resolved to confirm the agreement established between them by a special arrangement, in view of the expiration on June 15/27, 1887, of the validity of the secret Treaty and Protocol, signed in 1881 and renewed in 1884 by the three Courts of Germany, Russia, and Austria-Hungary.

To this end the two Courts have named as Plenipotentiaries:

His Majesty the Emperor of Germany, King of Prussia, the Sieur Herbert Count Bismarck-Schoenhausen, His Secretary of State in the Department of Foreign Affairs;

His Majesty the Emperor of All the Russias, the Sieur Paul Count Schouvaloff, His Ambassador Extraordinary and Plenipotentiary to His Majesty the Emperor of Germany, King of Prussia, who, being furnished with full powers, which have been found in good and due form, have agreed upon the following Articles:

Article I. In case one of the High Contracting Parties should find itself at war with a third great Power, the other would maintain a benevolent neutrality towards it, and would devote its efforts to the localization of the conflict. This provision would not apply to a war against Austria or France in case this war should result from an attack directed against one of these two latter Powers by one of the High Contracting Parties.

[1] *Die Grosse Politik*, Vol. V, pp. 253-255. Eng. trans. in A. F. Pribram, *The Secret Treaties of Austria-Hungary, 1879-1914,* Vol. I, pp. 275-281. Reprinted with the permission of the Harvard University Press, holders of the copyright.

Article II. Germany recognizes the rights historically acquired by Russia in the Balkan Peninsula, and particularly the legitimacy of her preponderant and decisive influence in Bulgaria and in Eastern Rumelia. The two Courts engage to admit no modification of the territorial status quo of the said peninsula without a previous agreement between them, and to oppose, as occasion arises, every attempt to disturb this status quo or to modify it without their consent.

Article III. The two Courts recognize the European and mutually obligatory character of the principle of the closing of the Straits of the Bosphorus and of the Dardanelles, founded on international law, confirmed by treaties, and summed up in the declaration of the second Plenipotentiary of Russia at the session of July 12 of the Congress of Berlin (Protocol 19).

They will take care in common that Turkey shall make no exception to this rule in favor of the interests of any Government whatsoever, by lending to warlike operations of a belligerent power the portion of its Empire constituted by the Straits. In case of infringement, or to prevent it if such infringement should be in prospect, the two Courts will inform Turkey that they would regard her, in that event, as putting herself in a state of war towards the injured Party, and as depriving herself thenceforth of the benefits of the security assured to her territorial status quo by the Treaty of Berlin.

Article IV. The present Treaty shall remain in force for the space of three years, dating from the day of the exchange of ratifications.

Article V. The High Contracting Parties mutually promise secrecy as to the contents and the existence of the present Treaty and of the Protocol annexed thereto.

Article VI. The present Treaty shall be ratified and ratifications shall be exchanged at Berlin within a period of a fortnight, or sooner if may be.

In witness whereof the respective Plenipotentiaries have signed the present Treaty and have affixed thereto the seal of their arms.

Done at Berlin, the eighteenth day of the month of June, one thousand eight hundred and eighty-seven.

(L. S.)   COUNT BISMARCK
(L. S.)   COUNT PAUL SCHOUVALOFF

ADDITIONAL PROTOCOL. BERLIN, JUNE 18, 1887

In order to complete the stipulations of Articles II and III of the secret Treaty concluded on this same date, the two Courts have come to an agreement upon the following points:

1. Germany, as in the past, will lend her assistance to Russia in order to reëstablish a regular and legal government in Bulgaria. She promises in no case to give her consent to the restoration of the Prince of Battenberg.

2. In case His Majesty the Emperor of Russia should find himself under the necessity of assuming the task of defending the entrance of the Black Sea in order to safeguard the interests of Russia, Germany engages to accord her benevolent neutrality and her moral and diplomatic support to the measures which His Majesty may deem it necessary to take to guard the key of His Empire.

3. The present Protocol forms an integral part of the secret Treaty signed on this day at Berlin, and shall have the same force and validity.

In witness whereof the respective Plenipotentiaries have signed it and have affixed thereto the seal of their arms.

Done at Berlin, the eighteenth day of the month of June, one thousand eight hundred and eighty-seven.

Count Bismarck
Count Paul Schouvaloff

11. England's Rôle in the Triple Alliance[1]

[These notes are selected from a group which constitute a second Mediterranean agreement between Austria, Italy, and England. Rumors of the accord led to a question in the British Parliament, but the reply merely stated that the Government had concluded no agreement which bound the country to undertake military action.]

Secretary for Foreign Affairs, Count Herbert Bismarck, to the Ambassador at London, Count Hatzfeldt

Secret   Berlin, November 8, 1887

While in Berlin you were told of the secret negotiations for an understanding between England, Austria, and Italy on the basis of the maintenance of peace and the status quo in the East, and also of our attitude concerning them. For your added personal information and with an urgent request for strict secrecy in handling it, I send you a copy of the "8 Points" which are a result of the ambassadorial conferences in Constantinople. . . .

With reference to our conversation and to the instructions given you at Friedrichsruh, I request again that you use your influence to try to bring Lord Salisbury to conclude an agreement in some form with Austria and Italy on the above basis.

If, as you expected, you find that Lord Salisbury proposes certain alterations in the drafting, his Austrian and Italian colleagues will without doubt agree. The Constantinople Points are described by the ambassadors themselves as merely "bases d'un accord" and are in any case not drawn up in the form of an agreement. Obviously they still require final editing.

It is of the greatest significance not only that an entente be arrived at between Austria and Italy, but that England should join

---

[1] *Die Grosse Politik,* Vol. IV, p. 365f.

it in some binding form. The entente between the two former powers will begin to have effectiveness and permanency only when England joins it. Germany could form without England a lasting alliance with Italy, but to hold Austria and Italy firmly together English cement is necessary.

In addition, the Sultan will put more trust in the group of three than in a mere entente between Austria and Italy which England remains out of. English prestige is greater in Turkey and more influential than that of the remaining powers, and the Sultan pays more attention to the movements of the British fleet than to the numerical strength of the armies of the rest. . . .

ANNEX: EIGHT-POINT BASIS OF ACCORD À TROIS[1]
(England, Austria, and Italy)

Secret   October, 1887

1. Maintenance of peace by the exclusion of all policy of aggression.

2. Maintenance of the status quo in the East founded on the treaties by the exclusion of all policy of compensations.

3. Maintenance of local autonomies established by the same treaties.

4. Independence of Turkey, trustee of important European interests (independence of the Caliphate, freedom of the Straits, etc.) of all preponderating foreign influence.

5. As a consequence, the Porte may neither cede nor delegate its suzerain rights over Bulgaria to any other power, nor intervene to establish there a foreign administration, nor tolerate any acts of coercion, undertaken for this last purpose, under a form, be it military occupation, be it by the dispatch of volunteers, which would constitute not only an infraction of the legal status quo but would be injurious to the interests of the three Powers.

6. The desire of these Powers to associate Turkey with them for the common defense of these principles.

7. In case of resistance on the part of the Porte to the illegal enterprises above indicated, the three Powers will immediately advise with each other on the support to be given it.

8. In case, however, the Porte should be in connivance with an illegal enterprise of the kind indicated, or even in case she should not oppose such with serious resistance, the three Powers shall unite in the provisional occupation by their land or sea forces of certain points of Turkish territory, with the aim of reëstablishing such political and military equilibrium as is necessary to safeguard the principles and interests above mentioned.

[Bismarck's note: "It is not to our interest to fight for the program and equally so not to oppose it. We can fight only for *Germany's interests*, and they are not concerned here."]

---

[1] *Ibid.*, Vol. IV, p. 354.

12. BISMARCK'S SUGGESTION OF AN ANGLO-GERMAN ALLIANCE, 1889[1]

[Another attempt of Bismarck to draw England within the sphere of continental alliances which he controlled. Hatzfeldt was the German ambassador to Great Britain.]

Prince Bismarck to Count Hatzfeldt

Berlin, January 11, 1889

During your recent visit to Friedrichsruh I requested you to make use of the next opportunity for a private conversation with Lord Salisbury to express my conviction that peace, which England and Germany equally desire, or even the respite required by them in order to arm suitably for the magnitude of the dangers of the next wars, could not be more certainly obtained than through the conclusion of a treaty between England and Germany in which both Powers bind themselves for a limited period to combined resistance against a French attack upon either of them. Such a secret treaty, if it should be possible, would give to both Powers considerable security against the result of such a war, while an impediment to war might possibly come from its mere publication.

England and Germany are not threatened with an attack by any Power other than France. Only through Russian-Austrian difficulties could Germany be brought into a war with Russia, and as there would be no acceptable reward for Germany as a result of such a war, we must do our utmost to keep Austria from being involved in war.

The only threatening element for the two friendly Powers, England and Germany, is their sole common neighbor, France. England possesses divergent interests with North America and Russia, as well as with France. But a war with one of those Powers, even with both at once, can only be threatening for England if France is allied with England's enemies. And the behavior of America would be more prudent toward England than it was on the Canadian and Sackville questions, if America were made to realize that a break with England would leave her without material or moral aid from France. The most practical means to prevent America from counting on France in a quarrel with England is the certainty that France would not be able to make an attack upon England without at the same time having to face a German army of more than a million men. America will not be inclined to emphasize by war the chauvinistic tendencies of her future government and of her former unfriendliness towards England unless she is assured of eventual French support. British foreign policy would enjoy freedom of movement in all directions only if she were fully

[1] *Die Grosse Politik*, Vol. IV, p. 400ff.

protected from the French war danger by adequate alliances. Even
then, if such alliances are only concluded for the short period required
by England for the restoration of her fighting power on the sea, it
would seem to me that the absolute certainty of peace for one or more
years thus created might be of great service to all peace-loving Powers.
It is not a question of being stronger in case of war, but of the prevention of war. Neither France nor Russia will break the peace if
they are officially told that they will certainly find England against
them if they do so. They will break it only if they may hope that they
might be able to attack the peace-loving nations of Europe in succession. When once it is clearly understood that England would be
protected against a French attack by a German alliance and Germany
against a French attack by an English alliance, I hold that European
peace would be assured for the duration of such a publicly announced
alliance.

It is a question whether the conviction that European peace can be
considered as assured for a given time may not be bought too dearly
at the price of taking an open and parliamentary position in favor
of a defensive alliance in the interests of the maintenance of peace.

My idea is that, if His Majesty consents, an alliance should be
concluded between the English and the German Governments through
which both should bind themselves to support each other in case the
French should attack either of them in the next 1, 2, or 3 years, and
that this treaty, which would be binding on Germany even without
the consent of the Reichstag, should be submitted to the English
Parliament for approval and publicly communicated to the German
Reichstag.

I think that the effect of such an open and manly step in this
direction would be an easing and a calming of feeling not only in
England and Germany, but all over Europe, and would secure for the
English cabinet the reputation of being the Protector of World
Peace. . . .

13. THE FRANCO-RUSSIAN ALLIANCE, 1891-1894

[In spite of the many obstacles, chief among which was the fundamental one of republicanism in France in contrast with absolutism in
Russia, a Franco-Russian entente was the natural result of the isolation and suspicions of both countries against Germany and the Triple
Alliance. The vague terms at first, which indicate a divergence of views,
should be noticed. A formal treaty was not signed, owing to the fear
of Cabinet discussion disclosing the secret; a military convention
signed only by military officers did not have to be submitted to the
French Parliament for ratification. The text of the military convention was kept in an envelope on which the French President, Faure,
had written: "The Military Convention is accepted by the letter of
M. de Giers giving to the Convention the force of a treaty." It was

not made public till 1918, though Viviani had been prepared to read its terms when asking for war credits on August 4, 1914, had anyone demanded it. Its defensive character should be noted.]

(a) *Definition of the Russo-French Understanding*[1]

M. de Mohrenheim, Ambassador of Russia at Paris, to M. Ribot, Minister of Foreign Affairs of France, communicating the instructions of M. de Giers, Russian Minister of Foreign Affairs

Paris, August 15/27, 1891

During my recent sojourn in St. Petersburg, whither I was ordered by my August Sovereign, it pleased the Emperor to provide me with special instructions, set forth in the letter, subjoined in copy, which His Excellency, M. de Giers, Minister of Foreign Affairs, addressed to me, and which His Majesty has deigned to direct me to communicate to the Government of the Republic.

In execution of this Supreme order, I am making it my pressing duty to bring this document to the knowledge of Your Excellency, in the firm hope that its contents, previously concerted and formulated by common agreement between our two Cabinets, will meet with the full approbation of the French Government; and that you will be kind enough, Mr. Minister, in conformity with the wish expressed by M. de Giers, to honor me with a reply testifying to the perfect agreement fortunately established from this time on between our two Governments.

The ulterior developments, of which the two points thus agreed upon not only are susceptible, but which will form their necessary complement, may be made the subject of confidential and intimate conferences at the moment judged opportune by either Cabinet, when they believe they can proceed to it at a good time.

Holding myself for this purpose at the entire disposition of Your Excellency, I am happy to be able to take advantage of such an occasion to ask you to be kind enough to accept the renewed homage of my highest consideration and of my most unalterable devotion.

Mohrenheim

ANNEX

Letter of M. de Giers, Minister of Foreign Affairs of Russia, to M. de Mohrenheim, Ambassador of Russia at Paris

Petersburg, August 9/21, 1891

The situation created in Europe by the open renewal of the Triple Alliance and the more or less probable adhesion of Great Britain to the political aims which that alliance pursues, has, during the recent sojourn here of M. de Laboulaye, prompted an exchange of ideas be-

---

[1] France. Ministère des affaires étrangères. *Documents diplomatiques. L'Alliance franco-russe.* Paris, Imprimerie nationale, 1918. No. 17, p. 15.

tween the former Ambassador of France and myself, tending to define the attitude which, as things now stand and in the presence of certain eventualities, might best suit our respective Governments, which, having kept out of any league, are none the less sincerely desirous of surrounding the maintenance of peace with the most efficacious guaranties.

It is thus that we have been led to formulate the two points below:

1. In order to define and consecrate the cordial understanding which unites them, and desirous of contributing in common agreement to the maintenance of the peace which forms the object of their sincerest aspirations, the two Governments declare that they will take counsel together upon every question of a nature to jeopardize the general peace;

2. In case that peace should be actually in danger, and especially if one of the two parties should be threatened with an aggression, the two parties undertake to reach an understanding on the measures whose immediate and simultaneous adoption would be imposed upon the two Governments by the realization of this eventuality.

Having submitted to the Emperor the fact of this exchange of ideas as well as the text of the conclusions resulting therefrom, I have the honor to inform you today that His Majesty has deigned to approve completely these principles of agreement, and would view with favor their adoption by the two Governments.

In informing you of these Sovereign dispositions, I beg that you be kind enough to bring them to the knowledge of the French Government and to communicate to me the decisions which it may take on its side.

GIERS

M. Ribot, French Minister of Foreign Affairs, to M. de Mohrenheim, Russian Ambassador at Paris, in reply to the preceding [1]

Paris, August 27, 1891

You have been kind enough, by order of your Government, to communicate to me the text of the letter of the Minister of Foreign Affairs of the Empire, wherein are set forth the special instructions with which the Emperor Alexander decided to provide you in pursuance of the last exchange of ideas to which the general situation of Europe had given rise between M. de Giers and the Ambassador of the French Republic at St. Petersburg.

Your Excellency was instructed to express at the same time the hope that the contents of this document, previously concerted and formulated in common agreement between the two Cabinets, would meet with the full assent of the French Government.

I hasten to thank Your Excellency for this communication.

The Government of the Republic can only take the same view as does the Imperial Government of the situation created in Europe by

---

[1] *Ibid.*, No. 18, p. 17.

the conditions under which the renewal of the Triple Alliance has come to pass, and believes with it that the moment has arrived to define the attitude which, as things now stand and in the presence of certain eventualities, might seem best to the two Governments, equally desirous of assuring the guaranties for the maintenance of peace which result from the European balance of power.

I am, therefore, happy to inform Your Excellency that the Government of the Republic gives its entire adhesion to the two points which form the subject of the communication of M. de Giers and which are formulated as follows: [See points 1 and 2 in preceding letter.]

I furthermore hold myself at your disposal for the examination of all questions which, under present political conditions, make more particular demand upon the attention of the two Governments.

Conversely, the Imperial Government will doubtless appreciate, as do we, the importance of confiding to special delegates, who should be designated as soon as possible, the practical study of measures designed to meet the eventualities foreseen by the second point of the agreement.

In begging you to bring the reply of the French Government to the knowledge of the Government of His Majesty, I wish to emphasize how much I cherish the opportunity to participate in the consecration of an understanding which has been the constant object of our common efforts.

RIBOT

(b) The Military Convention[1]

DRAFT OF MILITARY CONVENTION

France and Russia, being animated by an equal desire to preserve peace, and having no other object than to meet the necessities of a defensive war, provoked by an attack of the forces of the Triple Alliance against the one or the other of them, have agreed upon the following provisions:

1. If France is attacked by Germany, or by Italy supported by Germany, Russia shall employ all her available forces to attack Germany.

If Russia is attacked by Germany, or by Austria supported by Germany, France shall employ all her available forces to fight Germany.

2. In case the forces of the Triple Alliance, or of one of the Powers composing it, should mobilize, France and Russia, at the first news of the event and without the necessity of any previous concert, shall mobilize immediately and simultaneously the whole of their forces and shall move them as close as possible to their frontiers.

[1] Ibid., No. 71 (extract), p. 92.

3. The available forces to be employed against Germany shall be, on the part of France, 1,300,000 men, on the part of Russia, 700,000 or 800,000 men.

These forces shall engage to the full, with all speed, in order that Germany may have to fight at the same time on the East and on the West.

4. The General Staffs of the Armies of the two countries shall coöperate with each other at all times in the preparation and facilitation of the execution of the measures above foreseen.

They shall communicate to each other, while there is still peace, all information relative to the armies of the Triple Alliance which is or shall be within their knowledge.

Ways and means of corresponding in times of war shall be studied and arranged in advance.

5. France and Russia shall not conclude peace separately.

6. The present Convention shall have the same duration as the Triple Alliance.

7. All the clauses above enumerated shall be kept rigorously secret.

Signature of the Minister:

Signature of the Minister:

General Aide-de-Camp,
    Chief of the General Staff,
    Signed: Obrucheff

General of Division,
    Councillor of State,
    Sub-Chief of the General
    Staff of the Army,
    Signed: Boisdeffre

(c) *General de Boisdeffre's interview with the Tsar regarding the Military Convention. "Mobilization is a declaration of war"*[1]

Saint Petersburg, August 18, 1892

This morning, Tuesday, I received from the Minister of War a letter dated August 5/17, in which . . . he made known to me that the Emperor had approved in principle the project as a whole. [The draft of the Military Convention.] . . . The Emperor had evidently held that the basis of the entente would have to be precisely and officially fixed before his audience.

We have now, awaiting the exchange of ratifications with ministerial signatures, an official basis for a definite convention, a basis that can be considered as absolutely sure and decisive when one knows the reserve and the prudence of the Russian Government and the firmness of the Emperor in his engagements.

At eleven o'clock, I was received by the Emperor. His Majesty declared to me immediately that he had read, re-read, and studied the project of the convention, that he gave it his full approbation, taking

[1] *Ibid.,* No. 71 (extract), p. 94ff.

it as a whole, and that he thanked the French Government for accepting some changes of wording that he had requested.

His Majesty added that the convention contained, to his mind, some political articles which he desired to have examined by the Minister of Foreign Affairs; that there might be, as a result, some minor changes of wording to be made. Finally, His Majesty repeated that the project gave him entire satisfaction and that everything seemed to him to be adjusted to the best interests of the two countries.

I did not believe it necessary to take up again the defence of the first text, since the new text had received the approval of the Government. I only said to the Emperor that the French Government had wished to testify once more through this concession to its confidence in him. The Emperor did not fail to tell me of his strong desire that we guard the secret absolutely. . . .

The Emperor spoke of his desire for peace. I remarked to him that we were no less pacific than His Majesty. "I know it," he responded. "You have given proof of it for twenty-two years." I believe, moreover, that at this moment, peace is not threatened. The German Emperor has enough internal troubles, and England has as many. Moreover, with our convention, I estimate that our situation will be favorable. I surely desire to have at least two more years of peace, for it is necessary for us to complete our armament, our railways, and to recover from want and from the cholera. In fine, it is necessary to hope that peace will be maintained for a long time yet, and let us wish for it.

The Emperor then spoke of mobilization under Article 2. I ventured to remark that mobilization was the declaration of war; that to mobilize was to oblige one's neighbor to do so also; that the mobilization entailed the execution of strategic transportation and of concentration. Without that, to allow the mobilization of a million men on one's frontier without doing the same simultaneously was to deny to one's self all possibility of stirring later. It would be like the situation an individual would be in if he had a pistol in his pocket and would allow his neighbor to point a gun at his forehead without drawing his own. "That is the way I understand it," the Emperor responded. . . .

(d) *Approval of the Convention*[1]

M. de Giers, Russian Minister of Foreign Affairs to M. de Montebello, French Ambassador at St. Petersburg

St. Petersburg, December 15/27, 1893

Very secret

After having examined, by Supreme order, the draft of a military convention drawn up by the Russian and French General Staffs in August, 1892, and after having submitted my estimate thereof to the Emperor, I esteem it my duty to inform Your Excellency that the text

---

[1] *Ibid.,* No. 91, annex, p. 128.

of this arrangement, as approved in principle by His Majesty and signed by Aide-de-Camp General Obrucheff and General of Division de Boisdeffre, may be regarded henceforth as having been definitively adopted in its existing form.—The two General Staffs will thus have the faculty of taking counsel together at any time and of reciprocally communicating any information which might be useful to them.

GIERS

(e) *Exchange of Letters Modifying the Convention of 1893*[1]

Count Mouravieff, Russian Minister of Foreign Affairs, to M. Declassé, French Minister of Foreign Affairs

St. Petersburg, July 28/August 9, 1899

The few days that Your Excellency has just spent among us will, I hope, have permitted you to note once more the solidity of the bonds of lively and unchanging friendship which unite Russia to France.

In order to give fresh expression to these sentiments and to respond to the desire that you have expressed to His Majesty, the Emperor has deigned to authorize me, Mr. Minister, to propose to you an exchange of letters between us which shall establish that:

The Imperial Government of Russia and the Government of the French Republic, ever solicitous for the maintenance of the general peace and of the European balance of power,

Confirm the diplomatic arrangement formulated in the letter of August 9/21, 1891, of M. de Giers, that of August 15/27, 1891, of Baron Mohrenheim and the letter in reply of M. Ribot, likewise bearing the date of August 15/27, 1891.

They decide that the draft of a military convention which was the complement thereof and which is mentioned in the letter of M. de Giers of December 15/27, 1893, and that of Count de Montebello of December 23, 1893/January 4, 1894, shall remain in force as long as the diplomatic agreement concluded for the safeguarding of the common and permanent interests of the two countries.

The most absolute secrecy as to the tenor and even as to the existence of the said arrangements must be scrupulously observed on either side.

In addressing this communication to you, Mr. Minister, I avail myself of the opportunity it offers me to renew to you the assurance of my high consideration.

COUNT MOURAVIEFF

14. FRANCO-GERMAN COÖPERATION IN AFRICA, 1894[2]

[On May 12, 1894, a treaty between Great Britain and the Congo Free State leased the Bahr-el-Ghazel district, in central Africa, re-

---

[1] *Ibid.*, No. 93, p. 129.
[2] *Die Grosse Politik*, Vol. VIII, p. 450ff.

garded by England as a British sphere of influence, to Leopold, King of Belgium. In return for this recognition of Belgian occupation of certain districts, Leopold leased to Great Britain a strip of territory west of Tanganyika for the proposed Cape to Cairo railway. This lease was inconsistent with the Congo-German treaty of 1884. France protested against the former part of the pact, since the Bahr-el-Ghazel territory was not England's to give, while the German protest against the latter led to its annulment. Discussion in the French Chamber of Deputies led to the unanimous adoption of the following resolution: "France, relying on the fact that the Anglo-Congolese Convention is in manifest contradiction to the Berlin Act and that it threatens the integrity of the Ottoman Empire, considers it contrary to law and null." The French discussions clearly foreshadowed the later Marchand expedition which resulted in the Fashoda crisis. The Anglo-Congolese treaty was torn to shreds, but the following memorandum shows the drawing together of France and Germany over their common enmity to England's proposed action.]

Memorandum of the Secretary of State for Foreign Affairs, Baron Marschall

Berlin, June 13, 1894

I told the French Ambassador today the following:

It was known to the Ambassador that Sir Edward Grey had declared in a recent session of the Lower House that England and the Congo State had answered the German objections to the agreement of May 12th of this year in a manner completely satisfactory to Germany. Also the Ambassador himself had informed me yesterday that Lord Dufferin had made a similar declaration regarding the status of the German-English differences. On the converse, they seem inclined in London to make us believe that the negotiations pending between England and France are making the very best progress. These tactics are transparent. France is being played off against Germany and *vice versa* in order to awaken distrust and to hinder every common action. Finally it is hoped to satisfy one party through some kind of concessions and to isolate the other. Whether these tactics should not be counteracted is a question. German and French interests were not identical, to be sure, in matters of detail. We could not expect France to get excited over the strip of land from Albert Edward Lake to Tanganyika and we ourselves had no interest in the question as to who is to govern the Province of Bahr-el-Ghazel. But the meaning of the agreement of May 12 was of the nature of a principle and touched the basis upon which the international legal condition of Central Africa is founded. In so far the interests of France and Germany, and indeed of other European States, were common. The fact that the Congo State claims international recognition of its neutrality on the ground of Article X of the Congo Act would allow a state privileges and rights at the cost of other states or permit it to do as it pleases and

15088

would create a precedent the meaning of which would extend beyond
the details of the present matter at issue. The Government of the
Congo State has not as yet given us a substantial answer, presumably
because directions from London are awaited. In case of complications
the Congo State would probably expect military protection from England, since it alone is too weak. Thereby a condition would be created
contrary to the purposes of the parties to the Congo Act.

These conditions raise the question if it would not be well for France
and Germany—without binding themselves as to details—to take as a
common point of departure for negotiations with England the maintenance of status quo relative to the legal condition created by the
Congo Act. A conference of the Powers which are parties to the Congo
Act has been mentioned in the papers. I did not know what the French
Government thought of that—presumably there will be a very extensive program to be submitted to such a conference; but even if only
France and Germany should prove their agreement well founded in
the direction conceived above, and act accordingly, the effect in London would not be absent.

M. Herbette received my communications with a lively interest and
promised to report to Paris regarding them. He launched forth into
bitter complaints of the British policy in Egypt. France did not wish
to occupy Egypt, nor recreate the condominium, nor overturn anything, but in the long run the occupation of Egypt by England was
not endurable. Still less could France now allow England also to dispose of regions in the Sudan which belong to Egypt.

MARSCHALL

15. LORD SALISBURY'S PROPOSAL TO PARTITION TURKEY, 1895[1]

[The following report gives considerable insight into the motives and
methods of pre-war European diplomats, as well as illustrating the
problem which a tottering Turkey presented to imperialist powers.
Salisbury was again British Prime Minister in 1895.]

*The Ambassador in London, Count Hatzfeldt, to the Reporting Coun-
cillor in the Foreign Office, von Holstein*

London, July 31, 1895

When I saw Lord Salisbury yesterday, whom I found in a happy
and loquacious mood, I introduced the proposed communication of
Blanc's mémoire with the remark that this time I had come especially
relying upon his long proved reserve to commit an indiscretion which
the interests of the matter at hand seemed to demand. At any rate, it
would interest him to read the manuscript of Baron Blanc's designated
as secret and to infer what objectives Italy is pursuing, what disposition prevails within the present Italian Government—well dis-

---

[1] *Die Grosse Politik,* Vol. X, p. 10ff.

posed toward the Triple Alliance and also toward England—and what conclusions relative to the further development of Italian policy can be drawn.

Lord Salisbury, who read through the mémoire with the greatest attention, interrupted himself only once to remark smiling: "C'est une femme légitime qui demande à être payée." When he was through his reading, he thanked me for my confidential communication, adding that he would answer my "indiscretion" by a similar indiscretion with reference to his views and purposes in the matter. First of all he developed rather thoroughly the thought that the Italian undertaking in the part of Africa in question was a failure which no one even with English help could carry to a profitable conclusion. But it was excluded by the circumstances that even though this help would be given with the greatest willingness to accommodate Italy, it could not go as far as the Italians had demanded; for England could not give up the possession of Zeila because it is needed by her to secure her own interests in the Red Sea.

Lord Salisbury then told me in a strictly confidential way that he was thinking of showing himself agreeable to the Italians at another point, which in his thought was far more important for Italy than the sterile undertaking in Africa. It concerned Albania and Tripoli, two provinces the possession of which the Italians had long desired and which would really be valuable to them. His idea was to bind the Italians by a really advantageous assurance and at the same time to bring about what he would designate "une division des reclamations à Constantinople." I asked various questions in order to make clear what he meant by it, but I must confess that I succeeded but imperfectly. Either of two things can be meant: (1) that if England continues her course of protests, begun in the Armenian question, against the shortcomings of the Turkish administration in certain parts of the Turkish Empire, Italy would take over the same rôle with reference to other parts of Turkey; or (2) that this is a plan by which England will strengthen herself in Constantinople, now checked by Russian and French reserves, and will thereby assure herself of active Italian cooperation. I should like to assume that Lord Salisbury has *both* in view and that he certainly has the purpose of binding Italy's future action more closely to English interests in the Mediterranean by assigning her two Turkish provinces bordering on the Mediterranean and giving her an active rôle in Constantinople.

Just in this connection it was of signal interest that Lord Salisbury, in the course of the conversation, perhaps not unintentionally, developed the theory that, even if the Armenian question should temporarily come to rest, Turkey was nevertheless, by and large, too rotten [*trop pourrie*] to be able to last long. When I casually asked what would happen if Turkey fell and in what manner he believed that an amicable division among the interested Powers could be brought about, the Minister answered that this latter would indeed be no easy undertaking, but that the difficulty would not now exist had not England made the mistake before the Crimean War of turning down the offer made by Tsar Nicholas—Egypt to England, Saloniki to Austria, etc. —a mistake which he, Salisbury, would not have made. Upon my reference to another historical reminiscence, namely the negotiations between Napoleon I and Tsar Alexander, which had in the main failed chiefly because Napoleon would at the most concede Constantinople, but in no case the Dardanelles in addition, Lord Salisbury grew thoughtful and at last remarked that the matter would indeed offer great difficulties, as it could hardly be doubted that Russia would always be in a position, in combination with France, to endanger English interests in the Mediterranean most seriously if she succeeded in getting possession of the Dardanelles.

In my opinion, it follows from the above that Lord Salisbury recognizes the value of an understanding with Italy and is by no means indisposed to make in return certain concessions if by so doing he can bind Italy to English policy in the Mediterranean and secure her support in the Orient. I believe that it would be very much worth our while to consider seriously whether we will encourage this understanding (which would at the same time mean a strengthening of the Triple Alliance) and bring it to the speediest possible conclusion. Towards me Salisbury showed, as you will observe, the same confidence and frankness as formerly.

In the second place, it unquestionably follows from the remarks of the Minister that his views regarding the preservation of Turkey have undergone an essential change and that he is now thoroughly convinced that England, in order not to lose out, must reckon with the possibility of the fall, and must keep in mind the matter of partition. The presumptions regarding the developments of European politics with which we would have to reckon will thereby also be quite different— perhaps more advantageous—since there is the possibility of a peaceful division of spheres of interest between Russia and Austria for which Prince Bismarck long strove, while the main ground for the Russian unfriendly mood toward us would disappear and French friendship would become very much less valuable for Russia. That I may not be too prolix, I confine myself to these suggestions all the more so since all this is at least as well known to you as to me.

I have to remark in closing that I feel that Salisbury has no objections to our privately encouraging his ideas in Rome. . . .

HATZFELDT

16. German Policy in Eastern Asia Discussed, 1895[1]

[Diplomatic discussions of the partitioning of China were frequent among the great powers. This document throws considerable light on the aims and methods of imperialism.]

---
[1] *Die Grosse Politik,* Vol. IX, p. 253ff.

The Imperial Chancellor, Prince von Hohenlohe, to Emperor William II

Berlin, March 19, 1895

Apropos the telegram submitted to Your Majesty in which the Emperor of China has sought Your Majesty's support in bringing about peace with Japan, I beg Your Imperial and Royal Majesty's permission to present the following regarding our position relative to the Chinese-Japanese conflict:

Conformable to the previous decision of Your Majesty, our attitude hitherto was one of strict neutrality. Even before it came to real hostilities Your Majesty's representatives in Peking and Tokio were empowered to join in the common efforts of the other Great Powers for the peaceful settlement of differences, and later after the outbreak of hostilities we declared ourselves ready to coöperate in common measures of the Powers insofar as these were restricted to the protection of persons and property.

On the other hand, the repeated requests from England and also from China that we participate in intervention were rejected on the ground that such a step seemed premature.

The following were the essential considerations: England and Russia are especially interested in the development of things in the Far East to the extent that the former would like to see China maintained as far as possible unweakened as a buffer state to protect India against the advance of Russia and the latter does not wish to see its possible claims upon Korea, or at least upon portions of that country, prejudiced by further Japanese progress. But Germany, for the present at any rate, has not at stake any interests of like importance in Eastern Asia. German commerce especially has not suffered noticeably under war conditions. On the contrary, our manufacturers, merchants, and ship owners have had a good opportunity to make profit by supplying and transporting war materials. With our participation in the intervention undertaken by England and Russia merely for the restoration of peace, we would serve the interests of those States and indeed probably with considerable sacrifice for us, for it is obvious that against a victorious Japan only an armed intervention or at least the display of preponderant forces upon the theater of war would offer prospect of success.

It already follows from these considerations that our attitude would be altered if there were a prospect of special advantages as compensation for the sacrifices on our part. And indeed the gaining of several places on the Chinese coast might be considered as such an advantage of first rate importance, which could serve as points of support for the navy and for our commerce, a need which has already been felt for some decades. [Kaiser's note: "Right."]

Naturally it cannot be the affair of Germany, relatively the least directly interested, to come forward with claims of this sort and thereby give a signal to a certain extent for the first partition of the Chinese Empire. Rather we should have to wait until other powers set about to realize similar purposes.

Whether or not it comes to this will depend on the peace negotiations. Japan holds back for the time being the conditions which it will set up and appears to be willing to reveal its final demands only gradually. There are in the meantime indications that these will be very hard for China. The Japanese Ambassador here spoke a few days ago in strictest confidence and with the request for secrecy of an exchange of views between the Russians and his Government at the end of last month whereby Japan would acquiesce in the Russian demand for the complete independence of Korea and in return Russia will accord its benevolent support in the peace negotiations in the sense of procuring war indemnity, surrender of territory, and new regulations of commercial relations between Japan and China. In harmony with this is the fact that according to the announcement of Your Majesty's Ambassador in London, Russia and England have agreed that the independence of Korea is to be maintained.

Mr. Aoki added the confidential communication that Japanese military men consider the cession of Port Arthur with a part of the hinterland as indispensable while in their eyes the surrender of an island, for example Formosa, would be only of lesser significance. [Kaiser's note: "We might claim that then."]

Now, in my opinion, Port Arthur in Japanese hands would signify the domination of the Gulf of Chili and hence a standing menace to the Chinese capital. It may be assumed therefore that the Chinese will resist such a cession to the utmost.

To be sure, China's position in a military way is almost hopeless. Your Majesty's minister in Peking answered to questions sent by telegraph to the effect that he did not believe that the Chinese forces could hold the enemy back from Peking; that the capture of the capital would not necessarily result in the dissolution of the existing political order; but that nevertheless Li-Hung-Chang considers the withdrawal of the Court from Peking as no longer possible. On the other hand, Baron von Gutschmid telegraphs from Tokio that Japan can continue the war till next winter without fearing exhaustion of man power, financial means or materials of war. Moreover, that the war enthusiasm of the Japanese nation was undiminished.

Likewise, it seems not impossible that the disposition which has thus far prevailed among Chinese statesmen to deceive themselves regarding the true situation reaches even to the extent of renewing the unequal struggle if Japan will not let drop its demand regarding Port Arthur and be satisfied possibly with Formosa.

In this case it might indeed come to an intervention of the powers in spite of existing differences of interests among them and so precipitate for us as well the Chinese question.

In this situation it follows in my humble opinion as a criterion of our policy that on the one hand we must avoid allowing ourselves to be drawn prematurely into action to serve primarily foreign interests, but on the other hand we must hold open to ourselves the participation in such undertakings as could lead to dislocations in the relative strength of the great European powers in Eastern Asia. [Kaiser's note: "Right."]

I ask Your Majesty, accordingly, to authorize me to direct the Imperial Ambassador in London, who is for the time being generally informed regarding the above-mentioned viewpoint, to give the Government there to understand at this time orally and without committing ourselves that Your Majesty's Government is not essentially opposed to the idea of a common intervention, and indeed would not hesitate, in the face of essential alterations in the situation in Eastern Asia, to take an emphatic stand for German [Kaiser's note: "Yes, but not Chinese"] interests.

England seems urgently to desire our participation to have at least a counterweight against France and Russia, judging from the utterances thus far of the statesmen there, and will undoubtedly meet our wishes to a certain extent at any rate. [Kaiser's note: "But we must sell ourselves very dearly."]

What and how much we shall ask for our co-operation can scarcely at this time be determined and will depend among other things upon what the other powers claim. In this connection there is the statement of the English Ambassador, Sir F. Lascelles, at Petersburg, and reported by Your Majesty's Ambassador there, indicating that England would have no objections to Russia's annexing a part of Northern China on account of her railway and perhaps a harbor in Korea. What England would take for herself is not known. [Kaiser's note: "Shanghai!"] Past experience suggests among other possibilities the Island of Chusan opposite Ningpo, which was once occupied by her.

In the meantime I have asked the Secretary of State for the Imperial Navy for a statement as to which points in Eastern Asia might perhaps be desirable for Germany in the interest of her Navy. I still await this statement.

In this connection, the Island of Formosa could hardly be considered. Among other things, Baron von Richthofen, the Professor at the University here and a distinguished authority on China, warns against the acquisition of this place. So far as is known, it has no harbors suitable for large vessels; on account of its relatively dense and wild population it is unsuited for colonization; and on account of its extent it is hard to defend. [Kaiser's note: "Not quite pertinent."] An effort to secure Formosa would bring us into conflict not only with Japan but probably also with France who has herself asserted claims to it since 1885. [Kaiser's note: "Formosa must be considered again."] On the other hand, it would not be disadvantageous to us if Japan with England's and Russia's support would make claims to Formosa because in that way France would be brought into a certain opposition to Russia.

Finally, as regards the Chinese Emperor's telegram mentioned at the beginning, I humbly ask permission to say to the Chinese envoy that Your Majesty has taken cognizance thereof and authorized him to report to his Imperial Master that Your Majesty has the most complete sympathy with his and his Empire's hard lot and also that Your Majesty's most fervent wishes are directed to the early success of the approaching peace negotiations. Your Majesty is ready and glad to have renewed expression of these wishes given to the Japanese Government. [Kaiser's note: "Yes"; and to the whole note: "Agreed."]

PRINCE V. HOHENLOHE

17. AUSTRO-RUSSIAN BALKAN AGREEMENT, 1897[1]

[The author of this document is Goluchowski, Austrian Foreign Minister. The agreement, ratified by Nicholas II for Russia and Francis Joseph for Austria, was made by the two foreign ministers on the occasion of a complimentary visit of the Austrian Emperor to the Tsar. The Russian Foreign Minister, Muraviev, replied in a note to the Russian Ambassador in Vienna approving the statement of principles but objecting to some of the concrete proposals. Among these were the annexation of Bosnia and Herzegovina, which he said would raise a more extensive question requiring special scrutiny at the proper times and places; the question of the Sanjak of Novibazar, the boundaries of which were undefined; the formation of an independent Albania, and the equitable partition of all the territory to be disposed of between the Balkan states. Penetrating comments, the truth of which the future was to show! This entente formed the basis of Austro-Russian policy in the Balkans up to 1908.]

Dispatch from the Austrian Government to the [Austrian] Ambassador in St. Petersburg containing the agreement reached between Austria-Hungary and Russia in regard to Balkan affairs. Copy of a secret dispatch to Prince Liechtenstein at St. Petersburg, dated Vienna, May 8, 1897

On my return from St. Petersburg it seems to me useful to set down in a short summary the cardinal points of the understanding which has so happily resulted from the exchange of views and ideas which I have had with Count Mouravieff and of which the conclusions have been ratified by Their Majesties the Emperor and King, our August Master, and the Emperor Nicholas.

The conference which the two Sovereigns, accompanied by Their

[1] A. F. Pribram, *The Secret Treaties of Austria-Hungary, 1879-1914,* Vol. I, pp. 185-191. Reprinted with the permission of the Harvard University Press, holders of the copyright.

Ministers of Foreign Affairs, held at the Winter Palace has had for its practical result the establishment of a common line of conduct in the affairs of the Orient, which, while taking account of the security and of the vital interests of the two Empires, and while eliminating the danger of a rivalry disastrous to the peace of Europe on the seething soil of the Balkan Peninsula, permits us now and henceforward to view with more calm and quiet the political complications which, at a given moment, may present themselves in our immediate neighborhood.

Based on a principle of reciprocal confidence and loyalty, this understanding includes all the elements necessary to an efficacious coöperation; and thus understood, as I have every reason to believe it is, by the two Cabinets, it offers at the same time solid guaranties for the pacific solution of the Oriental problem.

This established, I wish to bring to notice, in the first place, that, having come to an agreement as to the *necessity of maintaining* the present status quo as long as circumstances will permit, we, Count Mouravieff and I, were pleased to record that there existed between Austria-Hungary and Russia no divergence of principle of a nature to preclude the possibility of an understanding between our two countries to guard against eventualities which, in a perhaps near future, might, even against our inclination, occur in the Balkan Peninsula. Quite the contrary. After having maturely examined the question in all its details, we had no difficulty in convincing ourselves that it would be easy to reconcile the interests of the two great Empires, on the condition, however, of dissipating all spirit of mistrust in our relations and of explaining to one another in perfect frankness and loyalty the principles which are to regulate our conduct henceforth.

Imbued with these sentiments, we thenceforth applied ourselves to establishing the bases of an agreement between the Cabinets of Vienna and of St. Petersburg, which, approved without restriction by our August Sovereigns, is found in summary in the following points:

1. It was agreed that, in case the maintenance of the present status quo becomes impossible, Austria-Hungary and Russia discard in advance all idea of conquest in the Balkan Peninsula, and that they are decided to make this principle respected by every other Power which might manifest designs on the abovementioned territory.

2. It was equally recognized that the question of Constantinople and of the adjacent territory as well as that of the Straits (Dardanelles and Bosphorus), having an eminently European character, is not of a nature to be made the object of a separate understanding between Austria-Hungary and Russia.

Count Mouravieff did not hesitate to declare in this connection that, far from striving for any modification of the present state of things, sanctioned by the Treaty of Paris and the Convention of London, the Imperial Government held, on the contrary, to the complete maintenance of the provisions relative thereto, which gave full and entire satisfaction to Russia in prohibiting, by the closing of the Straits, access to the Black Sea to foreign war vessels.

In its inability to admit of concession on this point, the Cabinet of St. Petersburg was only guided by a principle of legitimate security, a principle the recognition of which was accorded by us from the outset.

3. On the other hand, the establishment of a new order of things in the Balkan Peninsula, outside Constantinople and the Straits, would, in case it should occur, give rise to a special stipulation between Austria-Hungary and Russia, who, being chiefly interested in the settlement of this question, declare themselves disposed to act in common accord in fixing henceforth the bases of their understanding, to wit:

a. The territorial advantages, accorded to Austria-Hungary by the Treaty of Berlin, are and remain acquired by her. In consequence, the possession of Bosnia, of Herzegovina, and of the Sanjak of Novibazar may not be made the object of any discussion whatsoever, the Government of His Imperial and Royal Apostolic Majesty reserving to itself the right of substituting, when the moment arrives, for the present status of occupation and of right of garrisoning that of annexation.

b. The part comprised between Janina to the south and the Lake of Scutari to the north, with a sufficient extension on the east side, shall form an independent state under the name of the principality of Albania, to the exclusion of every foreign domination.

c. The rest of the territory to be disposed of shall be the object of an equitable partition between the different small existing Balkan States, a partition on the subject of which Austria-Hungary and Russia reserve the right of being heard in good time. While inclined to take into consideration as far as possible the legitimate interests of the participants, they are resolved, on the other hand, to safeguard the principle of the present equilibrium, and, if need be by means of rectifications of frontiers, to exclude every combination which would favor the establishment of a marked preponderance of any particular Balkan principality to the detriment of the others.

d. Having finally recorded that our two Cabinets have no other objective in the Balkan Peninsula than the maintenance, the consolidation, and the pacific development of the small States established there, we agreed to pursue in future in this field a policy of perfect harmony, and to avoid in consequence everything which might engender between us the elements of conflict or of mistrust.

Such is, Prince, the summary of the conferences of St. Petersburg, which I believe I have reproduced as faithfully as possible.

I do not doubt for a moment that Count Mouravieff will confirm its exactness to you; and it is for that reason that I ask you to let him read my present despatch, a copy of which you should leave in his hands with the request that he acknowledge its receipt.[1]

Accept, etc.

---

[1] Turkish misrule in Macedonia encouraged Bulgaria, Serbia, and Greece to organize propaganda and massacres in hopes of establishing their claims when the Turkish

18. Proposed Anglo-Russian Entente, 1897-98

[In January of 1897 Great Britain was ill at ease in her European relations and made an endeavor to seek friendship in Russia. The address of the British Prime Minister, Salisbury, in the House of Lords on January 19, 1897, in which he suggests that Great Britain might have done better to have given support in the past to Russia instead of to Turkey, and that a change of policy in this regard may still be necessary, is here cited. A fuller explanation of his idea is revealed in his secret telegram to the British Ambassador at St. Petersburg. The English approach was at first given general approval in Russia, but was cut short by the Russian steps to take Port Arthur between December of 1897 and the following March, and by an agreement for an Anglo-German loan to China from which Russian participation was excluded (March 1, 1898). A reference to the English proposal to Russia is seen in the Tsar's letter to the Kaiser, June 3, 1898 (see doc. No. 21b).]

(a) Salisbury's speech, January 19, 1897[1]

. . . I am bound to say that if you call upon me to look back and to interpret the present by the past, to lay on this shoulder or on that the responsibility for the difficulties in which we find ourselves now, the parting of the ways was in 1853, when the Emperor Nicholas's proposals were rejected. Many Members of this House will keenly feel the nature of the mistake that was made when I say that we put all our money upon the wrong horse. [Laughter.] It may be in the experience of those who have done the same thing that it is not very easy to withdraw from a step of that kind when it has once been taken [Laughter]—and that you are practically obliged to go on. All that Lord Beaconsfield did was to carry out the policy which his predecessors had laid down. I was acquainted with Lord Beaconsfield's thoughts at that time; he was not free from misgiving, but he felt that unity of policy in this great country was something so essential, and that the danger of shifting from one policy to another without perfectly seeing all the results to which you would come, was so paramount that he

Empire should break up. A scheme of reform was proposed by Lansdowne, British Secretary of State for Foreign Affairs, and was adopted, known as the February Program. Bulgaria thereupon dissolved the Macedonian Committees and warned her agents in Turkey that she would render no assistance if an insurrection occurred. In July, 1903, however, the expected explosion occurred in Macedonia. On October 24, 1903, the two Powers most interested in the Balkans, who had agreed in 1897 to coöperate, Austria and Russia, drew up the Mürzsteg program for reform of the gendarmerie. Its failure was partly due to the lack of improvement in the financial and judicial methods of the Turkish administration. See H. W. Steed, *Through Thirty Years, 1892-1922,* Vol. I, pp. 209-210; G. P. Gooch, *History of Modern Europe, 1878-1919,* pp. 400-401.

[1] *Parliamentary Debates,* Series 4, Vol. XLV, pp. 28-31.

always said that the policy of Lord Palmerston must be upheld. He still entertained hopes which I did not entertain in quite the same degree. But those hopes have not been justified. I shall not describe the present condition of the Turkish Empire; it would not be decorous; besides, the noble Earl has done it for me. But that we are placed in a position of exceeding difficulty in consequence of those historic events is a matter that cannot be disputed, and the difficulty lies in this— neither our own feelings, nor the feelings of those we represent, nor the enlightened conscience of the day in which we live will allow us to look with absolute indifference to what is going on. And yet how small our power of modifying the results of those events must be! . . . My own conviction is strong that, unless some very essential reforms in the conduct of the government are adopted, the doom of the Turkish Empire cannot be very long postponed. [Cheers.] I think that many, and some of the most important of the other Powers do not differ materially from us in that respect. But if I said that they had pledged themselves to use force it might be thought that I had used a slightly too strong expression. The pledge is, of course, a matter of exceeding importance, and they have used care and circumspection in the language which they have employed. But they are all convinced that, unless the Powers can agree and the Sultan can agree with us as to introducing genuine and effective reforms in the extravagant autocracy which prevails in Turkey at this moment, the worst results must follow. ["Hear, hear!"]

(b) *The Marquess of Salisbury to Sir N. O'Conor*[1]

Tel. Secret   Foreign Office, January 25, 1898

Our idea was this. The two Empires of China and Turkey are so weak that in all important matters they are constantly guided by the advice of Foreign Powers. In giving this advice Russia and England are constantly opposed, neutralizing each other's efforts much more frequently than the real antagonism of their interests would justify; and this condition of things is not likely to diminish, but to increase. It is to remove or lessen this evil that we have thought that an understanding with Russia might benefit both nations.

We contemplate no infraction of existing rights. We would not admit the violation of any existing treaties, or impair the integrity of the present empires of either China or Turkey. These two conditions are vital. We aim at no partition of territory, but only a partition of preponderance. It is evident that both in respect to Turkey and China there are large portions which interest Russia much more than England and *vice versa*. Merely as an illustration, and binding myself to nothing, I would say that the portion of Turkey which drains into the Black Sea, together with the drainage valley of the Euphrates as far as Bagdad, interest Russia much more than England: whereas Turkish

---

[1] *British Documents on the Origins of the War, 1898-1914,* Vol. I, p. 8.

Africa, Arabia, and the Valley of the Euphrates below Bagdad interest England much more than Russia. A similar distinction exists in China between the Valley of the Hoango [sic] with the territory north of it and the Valley of the Yangtze.

Would it be possible to arrange that where, in regard to these territories our counsels differ, the Power least interested should give way to and assist the other? I do not disguise from myself that the difficulty would be great. Is it insuperable? I have designedly omitted to deal with large tracts in each Empire, because neither Power has shown any keen interest in them.

19. The Kaiser and the Boer War

[Throughout 1895 Great Britain and Germany stood in open antagonism in South Africa. Kruger was president of the Transvaal Republic, which the British were trying to absorb, since the discovery of gold there had led to the migration of many British who were not granted citizenship at once by the Boers. Despite the British Government's disapproval, in 1895 Jameson's troops crossed the frontier in a filibustering expedition. News came of the ignominious collapse of the raid before Germany could protest, and the next day the Kaiser dispatched his telegram. Conflicting versions are given as to the responsibility for the telegram, but with the Kaiser's *Memoirs* compare his letter to the Tsar: "The Transvaal Republic has been suddenly attacked in a most foul way, as it seems not without England's knowledge. I have used very severe language in London . . . come what may I will never allow the British to stamp out the Transvaal." Marschall explained to the *Times* correspondent that the telegram was a state action and that it was necessary to give England a lesson. Though applauded in Germany, it was bitterly resented in England; the British Government informed Kruger that Great Britain would at any price oppose foreign interference. The telegram Gooch calls "the most disastrous error of the early years of the reign of William II," while Salisbury observed in 1899: "The raid was folly, but the telegram was even more foolish."]

(a) *Emperor William to President Kruger, January 3, 1896*[1]

I express my sincere congratulations that, supported by your people, without appealing for the help of friendly Powers, you have succeeded by your own energetic action against armed bands which invaded your country as disturbers of the peace, and have thus been enabled to restore peace and safeguard the independence of the country against attacks from the outside.

WILHELM I.R.

---

[1] *Die Grosse Politik*, Vol. XI, p. 31. (Translation in Dugdale, *German Diplomatic Documents 1871-1914*, Harper & Brothers, 1929, Vol. II, p. 387.)

(b) *Baron von Marschall to Count Hatzfeldt, January 6, 1896*[1]

The British Ambassador mentioned today the unfavourable impression which His Majesty's telegram to President Kruger had made on British public opinion. I replied that I must decidedly take exception to the view adopted by the British Press, that the telegram implied hostility to England and an invasion of her rights. In the matter of rights the German was very sensitive; he had no wish to infringe foreign rights, but he demanded that his own should be respected. It could not possibly be called an act of hostility to England for the German Emperor to congratulate the Head of a friendly State on having beaten armed bands, which had entered his country illegally and had been declared "outlaws" by the British Government itself. Moreover, Germany had a right to speak of the independence of the South African Republic, since that had been recognised in the Convention concluded by England with that State in 1884, except for the minor restriction on Art. IV. I considered the British Press in the wrong in speaking of England's suzerainty over the South African Republic, after this had been formally and in essence removed by that Convention.

(c) *The Kaiser's account*[2]

Since the so-called Kruger dispatch made a big stir and had serious political consequences, I shall tell the story of it in detail.

The Jameson Raid caused great and increasing excitement in Germany. The German nation was outraged at this attempt to overpower a little nation, which was Dutch—and, hence, Lower Saxon-German in origin—and to which we were sympathetic because of racial relationship. I was much worried at this violent excitement, which also seized upon the higher classes of society, foreseeing possible complications with England. I believed that there was no way to prevent England from conquering the Boer countries, should she so desire, although I also was convinced that such a conquest would be unjust. I was unable, however, to overcome the prevailing excitement, and on account of the attitude I adopted, was even harshly judged by my intimates.

One day, when I had gone to my uncle, the Imperial Chancellor, for a conference, at which the Secretary of State for the Navy, Admiral Hollman, was present, Freiherr Marschall, one of the Secretaries of State, suddenly appeared in high excitement, with a sheet of paper in his hand. He declared that the excitement among the people—in the Reichstag, even—had grown to such proportions that it was absolutely necessary to give it outward expression, and that this could best be

---

[1] *Ibid.*, Vol. XI, p. 39. (Dugdale, *op. cit.*, Vol. II, p. 393.)

[2] Ex-Kaiser William II, *My Memoirs: 1878-1918.* Cassel, 1922, pp. 80-83. Reprinted with the permission of the McClure Newspaper Syndicate.

done by a telegram to Kruger, a rough draft of which he had in his hand.

I objected to this and was supported by Admiral Hollman. At first the Imperial Chancellor remained passive in the debate. In view of the fact that I knew how ignorant Freiherr Marschall and the Foreign Office were of English national psychology, I sought to make clear to Freiherr Marschall the consequences which such a step would have among the English; in this, likewise, Admiral Hollman seconded me. But Marschall was not to be dissuaded.

Then, finally, the Imperial Chancellor took a hand. He remarked that I, as a constitutional ruler, must not stand out against the national consciousness and against my constitutional advisers; otherwise, there was danger that the excited attitude of the German people, deeply outraged in its sense of justice and also in its sympathy for the Dutch, might cause it to break down the barriers and turn against me personally. Already, he said, statements were flying about among the people; it was being said that the Emperor was, after all, half an Englishman, with secret English sympathies; that he was entirely under the influence of his grandmother, Queen Victoria, that the dictation emanating from England must cease once for all, that the Emperor must be freed from English tutelage, etc. In view of all this, he continued, it was his duty as Imperial Chancellor, notwithstanding the fact that he admitted the justification of my objections, to insist that I should sign the telegram, in the general political interest, and above all else, in the interest of my relationship to my people. He and also Herr von Marschall, he went on, in their capacity of my constitutional advisers would assume full responsibility for the telegram and its consequences.

Sir Valentine Chirol, at that time correspondent of the *Times*, wrote in the *Times* of Sept. 11 that Herr von Marschall, directly after the sending of the dispatch, had stated to him that the dispatch did not give the personal opinion of the Emperor but was a governmental act for which the chancellor and himself assumed full responsibility.

Admiral Hollmann, appealed to by the Imperial Chancellor for corroboration of this point of view, and asked by him to uphold it to me, declined to do so with the remark that the Anglo-Saxon world would unquestionably attribute the telegram to the Kaiser, since nobody would believe that such a provocative act could come from His Majesty's elderly advisers and that all would consider it an "impulsive act of the youthful Emperor."

Then I tried again to dissuade the ministers from their project; but the Imperial Chancellor and Marschall insisted that I should sign, reiterating that they would be responsible for the consequences. It seemed to me that I ought not to refuse after their presentation of the case. I signed.

Not long before his death Admiral Hollman recalled the occurrence to me in full detail, as it is described here.

After the Kruger dispatch was made public the storm broke in
England, as I had prophesied. I received from all circles of English
society, especially from aristocratic ladies unknown to me, a veritable
flood of letters containing every possible kind of reproach; some of the
writers did not hesitate even at slandering me personally and insulting
me. Attacks and calumnies began to appear in the press, so that soon
the legend of the origin of the dispatch was as firmly established as the
"Amen" at church. If Marschall had but announced in the Reichstag
what he stated to Chirol, I personally would not have been drawn into
the matter to such an extent.

20. British Suggestions for an Alliance with Germany, 1898

[The British archives contain no mention of this proposal of Joseph
Chamberlain's for an alliance—an extraordinary fact which suggests
that this was his own personal venture rather than any official move
on the part of the British Cabinet. The German Secretary of State
for Foreign Affairs, Bülow, fearing public opinion in both countries
would not approve an alliance after the Kruger dispatch, directed
Hatzfeldt to deal with Chamberlain's offer in a dilatory manner, thinking that Germany and England might thus settle some of their colonial
problems without going so far as to risk an open alliance. Chamberlain,
then British Colonial Secretary, made a glowing speech at Leicester
in which he publicly proposed an alliance. Owing to anti-English feeling
in Germany, Bülow, speaking in the Reichstag December 11, declared
the alliance quite unnecessary for Germany. It has even been asserted
by Eckhardstein that the Leicester speech had been made at Bülow's
own suggestion; if so, this rude rebuff was treachery. At any rate, the
British Foreign Office became more suspicious of the German Foreign
Office as a result of these negotiations.]

(a) *The German Ambassador in London, Count Hatzfeldt, to
the German Foreign Office*[1]

Telegram
Private for Baron von Holstein   London, March 24, 1898
Alfred Rothschild asks me to breakfast with him next Saturday to
meet some of the Cabinet Ministers, perhaps Balfour and Chamberlain.
I have the impression that this is not merely Rothschild's undertaking;
but the controlling idea is confidentially to try to make an approach
to Germany.
In case it should come to this interview, I should be grateful for
timely indications by telegraph if and in what sense I should eventually
express myself, or whether to listen in silence.
According to my feeling, it might not be indelicate for me to express

---
[1] *Die Grosse Politik,* Vol. XIV, p. 193.

my personal view that they are acting here very unwisely in that we are being forced to the other side through unfounded and useless protests in Peking, while we if left in peace would have no desire to take any side at all in China. This temperateness on our part, according to my personal opinion, is all that one would desire and the only thing that we eventually could do. And Mr. Chamberlain, in case I could come in contact with him, I would give clearly to understand that I, in order to support *rapprochement* at all in Berlin, would have to win at first the conviction that we would have to expect from him greater willingness to advance toward us on certain colonial questions; for instance, on that of the Neutral Zone.

I advise you to present the above to the Secretary of State. The matter does not seem to be quite ripe for an official communication and inquiry.

HATZFELDT

(b) *The Secretary of State for Foreign Affairs, Bernard von Bülow, to the Ambassador in London, Count Hatzfeldt*[1]

Berlin, March 25, 1898

In reply to your interesting private communication of yesterday, I should like to submit that you call to the special attention of the English Ministers the fact that so far as you know Germany has come to the conclusion of its Chinese action without having anything to do with obligations to other powers in case of war. This fact, that we have carried through such a difficult diplomatic undertaking without limiting our freedom of action, together with the fact that—*as you positively know*—we had refused a Chinese offer of another port a little further to the south, besides a settlement in Kiaochow, make it plain that we would gladly avoid friction with England.

Our purpose to meet them should, then, be contrasted, as you suggest, with the unfriendly attitude of England and the natural consequences of the same pointed out. The express declaration that in principle we wish to remain neutral in China it would be better to avoid. BÜLOW

(c) *The Ambassador in London, Count Hatzfeldt, to the Foreign Office*[2]

London, March 25, 1898

Mr. Balfour sent word to me this morning that he would be prevented from meeting me tomorrow at Rothschild's and asked me to meet him there today. . . .

Baron Rothschild left us immediately alone and we had a confi-

---

[1] *Ibid.,* Vol. XIV, p. 194.
[2] *Ibid.,* Vol. XIV, p. 195.

dential interview lasting an hour and a half, in which Mr. Balfour throughout manifested the most friendly sentiments for Germany, traced back the present estrangement to unfortunate misunderstandings, repeatedly emphasized the thought that Germany and England in the great political questions had no contrary interests to maintain, and finally made clearly evident a wish for a *rapprochement* and better understanding. . . .

HATZFELDT

(d) *The Ambassador in London, Count von Hatzfeldt, to the Foreign Office*[1]

London, March 29, 1898

Quite private

For the Secretary of State personally

Mr. Chamberlain, whom I met today, explained for me in an exhaustive and very confidential interview that the political situation has now taken a turn which does not admit of England's maintaining her traditional policy of isolation. The British Government is confronted by the necessity of making far-reaching decisions and would now be able to count on the approval of public opinion if she were to give up the policy of isolation and look about for alliances which would make easier the maintenance of peace which she, too, desires. The situation is critical not only on account of the Chinese question relative to which the British Government will shortly have to make decisions which the Commons is expecting to hear next Tuesday, but there are also serious complications to be feared with France regarding West Africa. Assertions of M. Hanotaux, according to which the negotiations in Paris are taking a peaceful course, are without foundation in fact. Thus far no basis at all has been found upon which an understanding could be expected and he, Chamberlain, was firmly resolved not to give in further.

The Minister then came to the relations between England and Germany, briefly recapitulated the grounds which have led to estrangement, and remarked finally that according to his opinion both countries have the same political interests and that any small colonial differences which may perhaps exist can be compromised if at the same time an understanding could be reached regarding the large political interests. He added that the occupation of Kiaochow had not been liked here only because it admits of the assumption that Russia and France will follow on a larger scale, and that serious difficulties will thus arise. Otherwise he fully acknowledged that our procedure there does not threaten any English interest. If friendly relations between England and Germany were established and if they were reinforced by the political understanding which he had in view, England would not only

---

[1] *Ibid.,* Vol. XIV, p. 196ff.

refrain from opposition to us in China, but would support us there with all her might.

With regard to these hints I took the position that our affairs in China had been settled by our own initiative and without foreign help, so that, as far as I knew, we were not under obligation to anybody. We had given friendly consideration to England to the extent that we had rejected—as I knew for certain—the offers to occupy southerly points. It would not therefore be to English interests to make difficulties for us in Kiaochow since this, so far as I could form a personal judgment, must only drive us to reliance upon Russia. Moreover, I could, of course, express only purely personal views and assumptions regarding all these questions.

Chamberlain answered that he completely agreed and that we could consider our interview as merely an interchange of views between two private persons. But in order that it should lead to any satisfactory result the first condition would be that we treat perfectly frankly with each other. From this viewpoint he would say to me quite sincerely and without reservation that the British Government is in the presence of a compelling necessity of making serious decisions in the next few days and that it wishes upon giving up its erstwhile policy of isolation to achieve an understanding with us and our friends. In other words, if we would be on England's side, England would, in case of an attack upon Germany, be on Germany's side. This would be equivalent to the accession of England to the Triple Alliance and should be fixed by treaty, for which we should formulate our conditions.

With this opportunity, without expressing an opinion upon the proposal, I referred to the fact that England continually sent others into the fire and wanted to remain behind herself, as she had now attempted to do with Japan to her own harm. Chamberlain replied that it was Japan's fault if she had not gotten sufficient information regarding the intentions of England. Had the simple question been put by Japan as to whether and to what extent England would support her, she would have been given immediately a frank answer.

When I finally mentioned in a conversational way the rumors which are going about regarding the supposedly intended movements of the English fleet in Chinese waters and thereby let fall the name of Weihaiwei, Chamberlain answered smiling that he had heard of more serious things, naturally also only by rumor since as a minister he could not say what was known to him officially. When I pressed him somewhat, it came out that it appeared to be a question of sending the English fleet to Talienwan. It seemed to him very questionable whether the Russians would not raise objections. To my remark that it was not quite clear to me whether a visit by the ships or a landing was intended, Chamberlain answered merely by calling special attention to the fact, as it now appears, that the harbour of Port Arthur can be completely dominated from a height near Talienwan; if therefore the English occupy this height, Port Arthur would be controlled by them by land and water.

In this entire interview Chamberlain expressed himself quietly and decidedly and revealed with great frankness the wish for a binding agreement between England and the Triple Alliance. Again and again he said that there was no time to lose in the matter since it must be decided in the next few days.

In case Your Excellency should consider an official report regarding this matter advisable, I propose that the above should be designated an official telegram and provided with a number.

May I ask that the communications of Chamberlain be handled with the greatest discretion since everything made known, especially in Petersburg, would unquestionably destroy all confidence which the English Ministers have in me.

HATZFELDT

(e) *Chamberlain's Leicester Speech of November 30, 1899*[1]

. . . But there is something more which I think any far-seeing statesman must have long desired, and that is that we should not remain permanently isolated on the continent of Europe; and I think that the moment that aspiration was formed it must have appeared evident to everybody that the natural alliance is between ourselves and the great German Empire. [Loud cheers.] We have had our differences with Germany; we have had our quarrels and contentions; we have had our misunderstandings. I do not conceal that the people of this country have been irritated and justly irritated by circumstances which we are only too glad to forget, but at the root of things there has always been a force which has necessarily brought us together. What does unite nations? Interest and sentiment. What interest have we which is contrary to the interest of Germany? We have had, as I said, differences, but they have all been about matters so petty as regards the particular merits of the case that they have not really formed occasion for anything like serious controversy. These differences have, under Lord Salisbury's wise administration of foreign affairs [Cheers], been one by one gradually removed, until at the present time I cannot conceive any point which can arise in the immediate future which would bring ourselves and the Germans into antagonism of interests. [Cheers.] On the contrary, I can foresee many things in the future which must be a cause of anxiety to the statesmen of Europe, but in which our interests are clearly the same as the interests of Germany, and in which that understanding of which I have spoken in the case of America might, if extended to Germany, do more perhaps than any combination of arms in order to preserve the peace of the world. [Cheers.] . . .

It is with the German people [that we desire to have an understanding]; and I may point out to you that at bottom the character,

---

[1] The London *Times*, December 1, 1899, p. 7. Reprinted by permission.

the main character, of the Teutonic race differs very slightly indeed from the character of the Anglo-Saxon [Cheers], and the same sentiments which bring us into close sympathy with the United States of America may also be evoked to bring us into closer sympathy and alliance with the Empire of Germany. What do we find? We find our system of justice, we find our literature, we find the very base and foundation on which our language is established the same in the two countries, and if the union between England and America is a powerful factor in the cause of peace, a new Triple Alliance between the Teutonic race and the two great branches of the Anglo-Saxon race will be a still more potent influence in the future of the world. [Cheers.] . . .

21. Reactions to the Proposed Anglo-German Alliance

[The Kaiser revealed with exaggerations the British proposals, which had been strictly confidential, in letters written in English to the Tsar. It appears that he deliberately attempted to bid Russia and England against each other and to sow discord between them.]

(a) *Kaiser's Revelation of English Proposal in a Letter to the Tsar, May 30, 1898*[1]

Dearest Nicky   Berlin 30/v 98

With a suddenness wholly unexpected to me am I placed before a grave decision which is of vital importance to my country, and which is so far reaching that I cannot foresee the ultimate consequences. The traditions in which I was reared by my beloved Grandfather of blessed memory as regards our two houses and countries, have as you will own allways been kept up by me as a holy bequest from him, and my loyalty to you and your family is, I flatter myself, above suspicion. I therefore come to you as my friend and "confidant" to lay the affairs before you as one who expects a frank and loyal answer to a frank and loyal question.

In the beginning of April the attacks on my country and person, till then showered on us by the British Press and people, suddenly fell off, and there was, as you will have perceived, a momentary lull. This rather astonished us at home and we were at loss for an explanation. In a private inquiry I found out that H. M. the Queen herself through a friend of hers had sent word to the British Papers, that she wished this unnoble and false game to cease. This in the Land of the "Free Press"! Such an unwonted step naturally led us to the conclusion that something was in the air. About Easter a Celebrated Politician *propriomotu* suddenly sent for my Ambassador and *à brûle pour point*

---

[1] Isaac Don Levine, *Letters from the Kaiser to the Czar*, New York, Frederick A. Stokes Company, 1920, pp. 47-50. Reprinted with the permission of the author.

offered him a treaty of Alliance with England! Count Hatzfeldt utterly astonished said he could not quite make out how that could be after all that had passed between us since '95. The answer was that the offer was made in real earnest and was sincerely meant. My Ambassador said he would report, but that he doubted very much whether Parliament would ever ratify such a treaty, England till now allways having made clear to anybody who wished to hear it, that it never by any means would make an Alliance with any Continental Power whoever it may be! Because it wished to keep its liberty of action. In 1897 (Jubilee Year) this Principle was even put into verse, saying that England needed no Allies, that *le cas échèant* it could fight the whole world alone, with the refrain: "We've got the ships, we've got the men, we've got the money too"!—The Answer was that the prospect had completely changed and that this offer was the consequence. After Easter the request was *urgently* renewed but by my commands coolly and dilatorily answered in a colourless manner. I thought the affair had ended. Now however the Request has been renewed for the third time in such an unmistakable manner putting a *certain short term* to my definite answer and accompanied by such enormous offers showing a wide and great future opening for my country that I think it my duty to Germany duly to reflect before I answer. Now before I do it I frankly and openly come to you my esteemed friend and cousin to inform you, as I feel that it is a question so to say of life and death. We two have the same opinions, we want peace, and we have sustained and upheld it till now! What the tendence of the Alliance is, you will well understand, as I am informed that the Alliance is to be with the Triple Alliance and with the addition of Japan and America with whom pourparlers have allready been opened! What the chances are for us in refusing or accepting you may calculate yourself. Now as my old and trusted friend I beg you to tell me what you can offer me and will do if I refuse? Before I take my final decision and send my answer, in this difficult position I must be able to see clearly, and clear and open without any backthoughts must your proposal be, so that I can judge and weigh in my mind and before God, as I should, what is for the good of the Peace of my fatherland and of the world. You need not fear for your Ally in any Proposal you make should she be placed in a combination wished by you. With this letter dearest Nicky I place my whole faith in your silence and discretion to *everybody*, and write as in old times my Grandfather would have written to your Grandfather Nicholas I! May God help you to find the right solution and decision! It is for the next generation! But time is pressing so please answer soon!

Your devoted friend
WILLY

P.S. Should you like to meet me anywhere to arrange by mouth I am ready every moment at sea or on land to meet!

(b) *The Tsar's Reply to the Kaiser Regarding the English Proposal, 1898*[1]

Nicholas II of Russia to William II of Germany

Tsarskoe Selo, May 22/June 3, 1898

Dearest Willy,

I thank you heartily for your interesting and long letter, the contents of which greatly surprised me.

I am very grateful to you for the loyal and frank manner in which, as usual, before deciding a question you would like to know my opinion about it.

Three months ago, in the midst of our negotiations with China, England handed us over a memorandum containing many tempting proposals trying to induce us to come to a full agreement upon all points in which our interests collided with her's. These proposals were of such a new character, that I must say, we were quite amazed and yet—their very nature seemed suspicious to us, never before had England made such offers to Russia. That showed us clearly that England needed our friendship at that time, to be able to check our development, in a masked way, in the Far East. Without thinking twice over it, their proposals were refused. Two weeks later Port Arthur was our's. As you know we have arrived at an understanding with Japan upon Corea and we have been since a long time on the best of terms with North America.

I do not see any reason why the latter should suddenly turn against old friends—only for the "beaux yeux" of England's?

It is very difficult for me, if not quite impossible, to answer your question whether it is useful or not for Germany to accept these often repeated English proposals, as I have not got the slightest knowledge of their value.

You must of course decide what is best and most necessary for your country.

Germany and Russia have lived in peace since old times, as good neighbours, and God grant! they may continue so, in close and loyal friendship.

Our countries have luckily no political frictions and no where do our interests come into collision.

The story of Kiaotschau is a good example of what I have just said and I am perfectly sure, so it will also be in the future! You know my ideas and convictions and you can therefore rely fully on my country's peaceful and quiet attitude.

I thank you once more for writing to me at such a grave moment for you! God bless you my dearest Willy.

Believe me ever your loving cousin and trusting friend.

(signed) NICKY

[1] *Die Grosse Politik*, Vol. XIV, p. 250. (In English in the Tsar's handwriting.)

(c) *Proposal for including England within the Triple Alliance*[1]

This is a [German] proposal for including England within the bounds of the Triple Alliance. I understand its practical effect to be:

1. If England were attacked by two Powers—say France and Russia—Germany, Austria, and Italy could come to her assistance.

2. Conversely, if either Austria, Germany, or Italy were attacked by France and Russia, or, if Italy were attacked by France and Spain, England must come to the rescue.

Even assuming that the Powers concerned were all despotic, and could promise anything they pleased, with a full confidence that they would be able to perform the promise, I think it is open to much question whether the bargain would be for our advantage. The liability of having to defend the German and Austrian frontiers against Russia is heavier than that of *having to defend the British Isles against France*. Even, therefore, in its most naked aspect the bargain would be a bad one for this country. Count Hatzfeldt speaks of our *"isolation"* as constituting a serious danger for us. *Have we ever felt that danger practically?* If we had succumbed in the revolutionary war, our fall would not have been due to our isolation. We had many allies, but they would not have saved us if the French Emperor had been able to command the Channel. Except during his reign we have never even been in danger; and, therefore, it is impossible for us to judge whether the "isolation" under which we are supposed to suffer, does or does not contain in it any elements of peril. It would hardly be wise to incur novel and most onerous obligations, in order to guard against *a danger in whose existence we have no historical reason for believing*.

But though the proposed arrangement, even from this point of view, does not seem to me admissible, these are not by any means the weightiest objections that can be urged against it. The fatal circumstance is that *neither we nor the Germans are competent to make the suggested promises*. The British Government cannot undertake to declare war, for any purpose, unless it is a purpose of which the electors of this country would approve. If the Government promised to declare war for an object which did not commend itself to public opinion, the promise would be repudiated, and the Government would be turned out. I do not see how, in common honesty, we could invite other nations to rely upon our aids in a struggle, which must be formidable and probably supreme, when we have no means whatever of knowing what may be the humour of our people in circumstances which cannot be foreseen. We might, to some extent, divest ourselves of the full responsibility of such a step, *by laying our Agreement with the Triple Alliance before Parliament* as soon as it is concluded. But there

---

[1] Memorandum by Marquess of Salisbury, May 29, 1901. *British Documents on the Origins of the War, 1898-1914*, Vol. II, p. 68.

are very grave objections to such a course, and I do not understand it to be recommended by the German Ambassador.

The impropriety of attempting to determine by a *secret contract* the future conduct of a Representative Assembly upon an issue of peace or war would apply to German policy as much as to English, only that the German Parliament would probably pay more deference to the opinion of their Executive than would be done by the English Parliament. But a *promise of defensive alliance with England would excite bitter murmurs in every rank of German society*—if we may trust the indications of German sentiment, which we have had an opportunity of witnessing during the last two years.

It would not be safe to stake any important national interest upon the fidelity with which, in case of national exigency, either country could be trusted to fulfil the obligations of the Alliance, if the Agreement had been concluded without the assent of its Parliament.

Several times during the last sixteen years Count Hatzfeldt has tried to elicit from me, in conversation, some opinion as to the probable conduct of England, if Germany or Italy were involved in war with France. I have always replied that no English minister could venture on such a forecast. The course of the English Government in such a crisis must depend on the view taken by public opinion in this country, and public opinion would be largely, if not exclusively, governed by the nature of the *casus belli*.

(d) *Bülow's Advice to Delay Negotiations for a British Alliance*[1]

The Imperial Chancellor, Count von Bülow, to Emperor William II, temporarily at Osborne

Berlin, January 21, 1901

. . . .

Your Majesty is quite right in feeling that the English must come to us. In Africa they have lost much hair, America shows herself to be uncertain, Japan unreliable, France full of hate, Russia perfidious, public opinion in all countries antagonistic. In 1897 at the Diamond Jubilee English self-confidence reached its height, the English peacock spread out his proud tail and was pleased with its splendid isolation. In 1898 the first efforts toward *rapprochement* appeared in the letter of Her Majesty, the Empress Frederick. In December 1899 the English wishes took form in the Chamberlain addresses and now the English are gradually becoming aware that they will not be able to maintain their world dominion with their own strength against so many adversaries. It is now a matter of neither discouraging the English nor of letting oneself be prematurely pinned down by them. The embarrassment of the English will be enhanced in the next few months and thereby the price which we will be able to demand will increase. We must not show the English too great readiness—for that would increase the English

---

[1] *Die Grosse Politik*, Vol. XVII, p. 20f.

demands and curtail our prospects of advantages—but we must at the same time keep the English convinced that we desire the perpetuation of a powerful England, that we believe in the solidarity of German and English cultural, political and economic interests, and that we would eventually be ready with the proper conduct on the English side to come to some sort of an agreement with them.

In this connection, according to my humble opinion, a dilatory behavior is demanded on our part, partly because very little solid gain can be made until Lord Salisbury has retired. It is true that he is no longer our avowed enemy, but still he is distrustful, indecisive, and slow in pulling the trigger. With reference to the general world situation and also to our own vital interests, Your Majesty would make a master stroke if Your Majesty were to succeed in letting Englishmen in authority hope for future firm relations with us without Your Majesty's now being prematurely pinned down. The understanding which the English threaten to make with the Dual Alliance is only a bugbear for our intimidation, with which the English have been maneuvering for years. The sacrifices which such an agreement would impose upon England are so enormous that the English government, even at the time of greatest irritation between us and England, did not decide in its favor. This agreement, which through the sacrifices required would weaken England, would strengthen and encourage the Dual Alliance for further opposition to England; it could only delay for a short time England's decisive battle for existence and would therefore be not only useless but directly harmful for her. Your Majesty will certainly know how to make the English conscious of this in a friendly but evident manner.

It seems to me very important, too, to avoid everything that might give the British the idea that the political relations between us and Russia and the personal relations between Your Majesty and the Tsar are strained or indeed irremediably bad. If the English believed that, they would no longer make us serious concessions in the hope and expectation that by the force of things Germany would be forced into conflict with Russia and France, and England would thereby be relieved of the necessity of risking her own skin.

God grant that Your Majesty may not have any too painful impressions in Osborne!

Bülow

22. The Fashoda Crisis, 1898[1]

[At the time of the Fashoda crisis, Salisbury was British Prime Minister; Edmund Monson, the British Ambassador in Paris; Theophile Delcassé, the French Foreign Minister; Rennell Rodd, the British representative in Cairo, Egypt; Baron de Courcel, French Ambassador

---

[1] *British Documents on the Origins of the War, 1898-1914*, Vol. I, Nos. 188, 193, 194, 201, 222, 226, 228.

in London; and General Kitchener, the sirdar (British military representative in Egypt).

One of the cardinal points in Delcassé's policy was to bring about a *rapprochement* with England. On June 14, 1898, he concluded an agreement delimiting spheres of influence in West Africa, though the question of the Nile basin remained unsolved. Kitchener was advancing from Egypt up the valley in the Sudan, and on September 2 took Khartoum. Salisbury's instructions of August 2 to him stated that "nothing should be said or done which would in any way imply a recognition of a title to possession on behalf of France or Abyssinia to any portion of the Nile valley". The course of events and the ensuing diplomatic negotiations may be followed in the selections from the correspondence given below. Conversations between Courcel and Salisbury showed that the French Government realized that Fashoda must be evacuated, but wished to save its face. Delcassé declared in the Chamber: "A conflict would have involved sacrifices disproportionate to the object." France yielded to force. On November 4 the French Ambassador informed Salisbury that Fashoda would be evacuated. Marchand returned home through Abyssinia in preference to the short route through Egypt. Despite his deep humiliation, Delcassé said he wished to remain in office till he had brought about the restoration of good relations with England, which did not occur till 1904. Meanwhile an agreement was reached, March 21, 1899, by which the provinces falling to Britain (Darfur, Bahr-el-Ghazel, and Kardofan) formed a free commercial zone. France thus obtained commercial access to the Nile and was not required to recognize British claims in Egypt. Though Britain thus made no sacrifices, she recognized the French right to expand from West Africa toward the interior.]

(a) *Sir E. Monson to the Marquess of Salisbury*

F. O. France 3396
(No. 441.) Confidential

Paris, D. September 8, 1898
R. September 10, 1898

My Lord,

M. Delcassé, whom I had not seen for ten days, received the Diplomatic Body as usual yesterday.

His Excellency, without loss of time, congratulated me upon the Khartoum victory. He said that the differences of opinion which existed between the two countries about Egypt could not affect the judgment passed by France upon this brilliant feat of arms.

I thanked him, and he then went on to say that he presumed that the British flotilla would now push up the river as quickly as possible, and that he consequently wished to observe that the French expedition under Captain Marchand, undertaken in virtue of an understanding with the Congolese Government, might before long be met with by it, and that it was proper that Her Majesty's Government should know that the clearest instructions had been given to that gentleman as to his position and attitude. He had been distinctly told that he is nothing but an "emissary of civilisation," and that he has no authority to assume the decision of questions of right which appertain exclusively to the competence of the British and French Governments. He had been warned to take no steps whatever which may give rise to local conflicts, and his Excellency therefore begged me to communicate to your Lordship the foregoing information, together with the expression of his hope that Her Majesty's Government would, in transmitting it to the officers in command of the advancing expedition, give such instructions as would prevent a collision by reserving all questions of principle for direct discussion at home.

M. Delcassé referred to our last conversation, in which he had expressed his conviction that all outstanding differences between the two countries might be amicably arranged by the exercise of patience and conciliation. He repeated that the Government of the Republic held this view most strongly, and that they are consequently anxious to avoid local disputes.

I said that I would at once inform your Lordship of what he had said, but that as he had spoken of a possibility of a meeting between our gun-boats and Captain Marchand's expedition, I should like to know where that expedition is, and whether he had any recent news from Captain Marchand himself.

M. Delcassé replied that he had within the last forty-eight hours had news "of" (he did not say "from") Captain Marchand, but that it could not be said to be recent, as it had taken a long time to reach France. As for the position of the expedition at this moment, he could not tell me where it is, as he himself does not know.

The news which he had received had been satisfactory as regards the health and condition of its members, but the progress had been slow; and now the French Government had cause for anxiety as to the fate which might be reserved for it at the hands of the scattered and flying remnants of the Dervish army, whose attempt to find refuge in the south might create disturbance in other regions, to which the members of the French expedition might fall victims.

I put several tentative questions to M. Delcassé with the hope of eliciting something more definite, but without avail. Nevertheless, although he spoke with apparent frankness, I can hardly believe that he has not some more positive information than he was willing to disclose. He said, however, with a smile, that as the British forces were so admirably served by all the appliances of civilisation, he had no doubt that a telegraph line would soon be carried above the junction of the two Niles, and that he should have direct and speedy information of Captain Marchand's whereabouts.

M. Delcassé's language and manner were throughout very cordial.

. . . But in this M. Delcassé only reflects, I imagine, the deliberate judgment of the majority of his countrymen who had begun to recognise that there is nothing to be gained by blustering about Egypt, and that it will be more dignified for them to accept the inevitable. I do not mean to say that they are prepared to acquiesce without renewed remonstrance in the continuance of the British occupation, or that a great deal of abuse will not be showered upon us by the Parisian press. But while they very naturally try to argue that "logically" that occupation should now come to an end, they see clearly enough that the recent operations have simply clinched our hold upon Egypt more tightly, and that British "practice" cannot be assimilated to French "logic."

The moderation of M. Delcassé's tone and manner inspires me with a certain amount of hope that, if the French are going to discuss this question at once, they will do so with calmness. No doubt the Government will be questioned upon the subject when the Chamber meets, and will be forced to maintain in public that French policy does not and cannot vary in regard to it. But as the whole country is aware that under existing circumstances that policy must remain unsupported by action, I trust that there is no danger that the Government will compromise itself by any talk of entering upon impracticable engagements.

I have, etc.,
EDMUND MONSON

(b) *Mr. Rodd to the Marquess of Salisbury*

F. O. Turkey (Egypt) 4960   *Cairo, D. September 25, 1898*
Tel. (No. 244.) P.   R. *September 25, 1898*

I have received the following telegram this morning from Sir Herbert Kitchener:—

"I have just returned here from Fashoda where I found Captain Marchand, accompanied by eight officers and 120 men, located in the old Government buildings, over which they had hoisted the French flag; I sent a letter announcing my approach the day before my arrival at Fashoda. A small rowboat carrying the French flag brought me a reply from Captain Marchand on the following morning, the 19th September, stating that he had reached Fashoda on the 10th July, his Government having given him instructions to occupy the Bahr-el-Ghazal as far as the confluence of the Bahr-el-Jebel, as well as the Shilluk country on the left bank of the White Nile as far as Fashoda. He stated that he had concluded a Treaty with the Chief of the Shilluk tribe, whereby the latter placed his country under the protection of France, and that he had sent this Treaty to his Government for ratification by way of Abyssinia, as well as by the Bahr-el-Ghazal. Captain Marchand described the fight which he had had with the Dervishes on the 25th August, and said that, in anticipation of a second and more severe attack, he had sent his steamer south for reinforcements, but our arrival had averted this danger.

"When we arrived at Fashoda, Captain Marchand and M. Germain came on board, and I at once stated that the presence of a French force at Fashoda and in the Valley of the Nile was regarded as a direct infringement of the rights of the Egyptian Government and of that of Great Britain, and I protested in the strongest terms against their occupation of Fashoda and their hoisting the French flag in the dominions of His Highness the Khedive. In reply, Captain Marchand stated that he had precise orders to occupy the country and to hoist the French flag over the Government buildings at Fashoda, and that it was impossible for him to retire without receiving orders from his Government to that effect, but he did not expect that these orders would be delayed. On my pressing him to say whether, seeing that I had a preponderating force, he was prepared to resist the hoisting of the Egyptian flag at Fashoda, he hesitated and replied that resistance was impossible. I then caused the flag to be hoisted on a ruined bastion of the old Egyptian fortifications about 500 yards south of the French flag, and on the only road which leads to the interior from the French position, which is surrounded by impassable marshes on all sides. Before leaving for the south, I handed to Captain Marchand a formal protest in writing, on behalf of the British and Egyptian Governments, against any occupation by France of any part of the Nile Valley, such occupation being an infringement of the rights of these Governments which I could not recognise.

"I appointed Major Jackson to be Commandant of the Fashoda district, where I left a garrison consisting of one Soudanese battalion, four guns, and a gun-boat, after which I proceeded to the Sobat, where, on the 20th September, a post was established and the flag hoisted. We neither saw nor heard anything of the Abyssinians on the Sobat River, but we were told that their nearest post was situated some 350 miles further up. The Bahr-el-Jebel is completely blocked by the 'sudd,' and in consequence I ordered a gun-boat to patrol up the Bahr-el-Ghazal towards Meshra-er-Rek. On my way north, as I passed Fashoda, I sent a letter to Captain Marchand, stating that all transport of war material on the Nile was absolutely prohibited, as the country was under military law. The Shilluk Chief, with a large following, has come into Major Jackson's camp; the whole tribe are delighted to return to their allegiance to us, and the Chief absolutely denies having made any Treaty with the French.

"The position in which Captain Marchand finds himself at Fashoda is as impossible as it is absurd. He is cut off from the interior, and his water transport is quite inadequate; he is, moreover, short of ammunition and supplies, which must take months to reach him; he has no following in the country, and nothing could have saved him and his expedition from being annihilated by the Dervishes had we been a fortnight later in crushing the Khalifa.

"The futility of all their efforts is fully realised by Captain Marchand himself, and he seems quite as anxious to return as we are to facilitate his departure. In his present position he is powerless, but I hope that Her Majesty's Government will take the necessary steps for his removal as soon as possible, as the presence of a French force and flag on the Nile is manifestly extremely undesirable.

"Captain Marchand only lost four natives on the journey, and his expedition is all well.

"I am sending a complete despatch by Lord Edward Cecil, who is leaving with it for Cairo at once."

(c) *Mr. Rodd to the Marquess of Salisbury*

F. O. Turkey (Egypt) 5051   *Cairo, September 25, 1898*
Tel. (No. 245.)   D. 1 :30 P.M.
Further from Sirdar :—   R. 2 :30 P.M.

"If the French Government will at once give telegraphic instructions for the explorer M. Marchand and his expedition to leave Fashoda and come down Nile, I can now send special steamer with such orders to fetch them.

"I am quite sure that no one would be more pleased than M. Marchand and his officers to secure release from their unpleasant position."

He suggests taking over their boats and launch at a valuation.

(d) *The Marquess of Salisbury to Mr. Rodd*

F. O. Turkey (Egypt) 4959
Tel. (No. 92.) P.   *Foreign Office, October 1, 1898*
The following is secret :—

I request that you will inform the Sirdar that it has become clear that the French Government will not instruct M. Marchand to leave Fashoda. They expect that Her Majesty's Government will purchase his departure by large concessions of territory. This Her Majesty's Government will not do.

Under these circumstances, the question remains how M. Marchand is to be dealt with if he persists in remaining at Fashoda.

The Sirdar has already stated that he will not allow any reinforcements or munitions of war to pass upon the Nile. Nothing further remains to be done in this respect. The Sirdar has, no doubt, taken care that there is a sufficient force to secure that his declaration is carried into effect.

M. Marchand's position should be made as untenable as possible. If he is in want of food supplies, it will be very necessary to use circumspection in helping him to obtain them. Until he expresses his intention of going down the river, no such supplies should be furnished to him except in case of extreme necessity.

(e) *Sir E. Monson to the Marquess of Salisbury*

F. O. Turkey (Egypt) 5052
(No. 558.) Most Confidential   *Paris*, D. *October 29, 1898*
                                                           R. *October 31, 1898*

My lord,

I called without any appointment on M. Delcassé this morning, and found his Excellency more than a little irate at the "escapade" of M. Marchand. He could not, he said, understand how an officer in such a position could have believed himself at liberty to quit his post without permission.

He proceeded to inform me, after warning me that our conversation must, in view of his being a "Ministre démissionaire," be regarded as confidential and unofficial, that he was going to send M. Marchand at once back from Cairo; and that tonight Captain Baratier would have to start for Marseilles and Egypt, and convey his instructions to his Chief.

I was unprepared for this view of the case, and I said to M. Delcassé that it seemed to me natural that M. Marchand should think that he had best deliver his Report himself, and that he had doubtless been animated by the best intentions in starting on this trip.

M. Delcassé, however, reiterated that the step taken by M. Marchand was incredible and unpardonable, and that good intentions could be no excuse for it. Already all the journalists were attacking him (the Minister), and accusing him of having sent secret orders to M. Marchand to come away.

His Excellency stated further that his own continuance in office depended very much upon the definite answer to be given by Her Majesty's Government to his request that the French Government should, in some way or another, be assured that their order to M. Marchand to evacuate Fashoda would be followed by an undertaking that England will negotiate on the principle of the grant to France of an outlet for her commerce to the Nile. If this is not acceded to, a humiliation will be inflicted on France, which he, personally, cannot accept; and as a war with England, which is the only alternative, would be alike contrary to his avowed policy, and repulsive to his principles, he would be obliged to retire from his post as Minister of Foreign Affairs.

I did all in my power to persuade him that there would be no humiliation in his acknowledging that M. Marchand had no political mission, and had never been ordered by his Government to advance to the Nile, but had gone there on his own initiative and in an excess of zeal; but his Excellency replied that, much as he should have liked to do this, he was prevented from taking such a line by our declaration of our sole right, in partnership with Egypt, to appropriate the territories recently in the hands of the Khalifa.

I find it quite impossible to shake these obstinate views of M. Delcassé, and I confess that I was this morning disappointed at being able to make no impression upon him, as I had hoped that he would have hailed M. Marchand's excursion down the Nile without any orders from home as facilitating an absolute and entire retreat from an untenable position.

I have, etc.,

EDWARD MONSON

(f) Sir E. Monson to the Marquess of Salisbury

Paris, November 3, 1898

F. O. Turkey (Egypt) 5052   D. 6 P.M.

Tel. (No. 200.)   R. 7:30 P.M.

After the Cabinet Council this morning orders were telegraphed at once to French Ambassador to inform your Lordship that Fashoda would be evacuated with the least possible delay.

MM. Marchand and Baratier have been instructed to return to Fashoda to carry out this decision, and Foreign Minister has expressed to me his hope that Her Majesty's Government will give them every facility to accomplish this. The mission has ceased to have any political character and must henceforth be considered a simple inoffensive troop armed only for its own defence against native attack. Foreign Minister said he would lose no time in settling the route to be taken by the Mission, and is almost decided upon Eastern one via Jibouti or Obok.

23. FIRST HAGUE CONFERENCE

[Dillon was a well-informed British journalist. The Tsar's invitation was presented on August 24, 1898, and was accepted by all the Governments to which it was addressed, including every European state, the United States, and Japan. The conference opened May 18, 1899. The German veto of a reduction of armaments, as well as her refusal to consider arbitration, was a serious blow to the work of the conference. But (c) and (d) show that Germany was not alone in her opposition to disarmament. The achievements of the conference consisted, aside from an ineffective resolution favoring restriction of armaments, in conventions and declarations regarding the laws of warfare and a convention for the pacific settlement of international disputes.]

(a) Russia's motives in calling the conference[1]

One day, Count Muravieff, the most empty-headed of the Tsar's advisers who had succeeded M. Shishkin at the Foreign Office, called on Witte who, like a masculine Fate, was spinning the threads of

[1] E. J. Dillon, The Eclipse of Russia. London, Dent, 1918, pp. 272-278.

Russia's existence in his finance department. . . . Muravieff produced a document, waved it theatrically before his colleague, said that it had been drawn up by the War Minister, Kuropatkin, read with close attention by the Emperor, and sent on for the Finance Minister to peruse and report on.

"I suppose it is a demand for more money for war materials?" Muravieff smiled but said nothing. "Unless it is for something necessary I really cannot and will not give another rouble." Muravieff muttered something about the necessity of breaking the eggs if you wish to make an omelette. Witte took the paper. He had guessed aright: it was a roundabout demand for a very large sum of money. The form in which it was put seemed to him at first but the sugar-coating of the pill. Witte frowned as he read the report: France and Germany, Kuropatkin wrote, having stolen a march on the other powers by providing their armies with the improved guns, Austria and Russia could not and would not lag behind. But the cost was dèterrent, and was all the more to be dreaded that other and heavier expenses would have to be incurred very shortly, almost simultaneously. Neither Russia nor Austria is wealthy. The populations of both empires are heavily enough taxed already. They and their respective governments would therefore, no doubt, welcome any arrangement in virtue of which they could escape the taxation which the re-arming of the national forces would entail. But how could one devise an effective plan? Could not one hit upon some simple compromise that would commend itself to both governments all the more readily that the two empires belong, so to say, to opposite camps? Whether you multiply or divide both the divisor and the dividend by the same number, the quotient undergoes no change. Apply that proposition to the case in point. Whether Russia and Austria go to the expense of supplying their armies with the improved guns or leave their artillery as it is, the final result, if the two groups of powers went to war, would be the same. Why then should they not agree between themselves to keep the money in their respective treasuries? If we in Russia plunge into the expense, the Austrians will vie with us and neither they nor we shall have scored an advantage over the other, yet we shall both be much the poorer. The Minister of Finance, who is the money provider of the Empire and has an interest in keeping down its expenditure, may be able to utilise this suggestion.

That was the gist of Kuropatkin's message to the Emperor.

Witte replied with some warmth that the suggestion was not practical and ought not to have been made. "Just think it out," he said. "As an abstract proposition, Austria and Russia can well be imagined falling in with General Kuropatkin's expedient. But put the invitation in a concrete shape to the official representatives of the Austrian Government and try to picture to yourself what would follow. Suspicion would at once be aroused as to the real motive of the device. Do you fancy they would accept our explanation? Nowise. They would infer either that our impecuniosity bordered on insolvency, and therefore that they could not do better than intensify it by obliging us to invest in the improved artillery, or else they would conjecture that we were preparing to embark on some unavowed and unavowable enterprise directed against them for which funds were needed, and that one of our methods of raising them was by economising on the new ordnance. In neither case would they close with our offer, and in either we should have injured our credit abroad. These are some of the reasons why I cannot entertain General Kuropatkin's project favourably. I need hardly add that if the defences of the Empire really call for the outlay in question, the War Minister has only to say so and I, as Finance Minister, will find the money and eschew all dangerous expedients for getting it."

Witte while thus talking turned the subject over in his mind and contemplated it from various angles of vision, giving utterance to his thoughts as they arose. He was anxious to save as much of the public money as he could, but it was impossible to allow his government to approach the statesmen of the Ballplatz with a suggestion as puerile as that framed by Kuropatkin. That was self-evident. How then could the Tsar's wish to act upon that suggestion and his own desire to economise be realised? That was the problem, and it must be solved on the lines—considerably widened if needs were, but not otherwise changed—of the War Minister's scheme. "In other words," Witte explained to me, "I knew that what was wanted was some ruse by means of which we could get Austria to stay her hand and discuss disarmament in lieu of investing in the improved gun. Within these limits then I had to work. I walked up and down the room for some time in silence, pondering the different aspects of the matter and giving utterance to my half-formed thoughts as they emerged into the realm of consciousness. They centred naturally and necessarily around my old pet idea óf a league of pacific nations vying with each other in trade, industry, science, arts, inventions, and I said to myself that even if the opportunity had not yet come to draw nearer to that, there would be no harm in setting the powers talking about it. And that started me." . . .

Witte grudged every rouble he had to spend on armaments. He loathed the very name of war and was never weary of denouncing it. "It is my conviction," he wrote in my wife's album, "that the burden of armaments without limitations may become more irksome than war itself." To assert that the groundwork of his policy was the avoidance of war does not commit me to approval of his political aims, or of the means by which he would fain have accomplished them. His most vigorous exertions were made to safeguard peace, and the war that first marked his failure also ruined his career and undid his whole life-work.

Pursuing the train of reflections started by Kuropatkin's memorandum, the Finance Minister reflected that if in lieu of saving a few million pounds on their artillery for the benefit of two needy peoples it were possible, as it would be one day, to economise the countless sums of money that were being annually squandered on armaments generally, then the game would indeed be worth the candle. But all that could be done in his lifetime would be to prepare men's minds for the general reception of these notions, and in particular for the axiom that one deadly enemy to cultural advance is militarism. Witte did not deny the fine side of patriotism, nor would he have done aught to weaken the sentiment, neither would he leave his own country inadequately prepared for the war which he knew was coming. "But I often think," he said, turning to Muravieff, "that the unexampled prosperity of the United States of America is a direct effect of its immunity from militarism. Suppose each of the States there were independent as are those of Europe, would the revenue of North America exceed its expenditure as it does today? Would trade and industry flourish there as they now do? On the other hand, suppose Europe could contrive to disband the bulk of her land forces, do with a mere nominal army, and confine her defences to warships, would she not thrive in an unprecedented way and guide the best part of the globe? Can that ever be accomplished? Who knows?"

The conversation ended thus: "Does His Majesty wish the money for the new weapon to be provided, or is it on the War Minister's plan that he lays the chief stress?" "He desires that General Kuropatkin's scheme should be discussed in council. It has taken his fancy. And he asked me to get your general impression in advance. I am sure he means to carry out the idea in some shape, and he hopes you will design a practical one." "Well, in that case," Witte remarked with a smile, "say that I approve the principle underlying it, but I would apply it not to Austria and Russia only, but to all the nations of the globe. In this way we should avoid invidious distinctions and leave no ground for misgivings. A proposal of this kind might be addressed to all nations, great and small; it would be welcomed by many. Whether the few would put off ordering the new artillery is another matter. But if that be the theme to which I am to compose variations, you have them now. There can be none other."

Muravieff then left, and Witte said no more about the matter until he attended the special council at which Count Lamsdorff as Assistant Minister of Foreign Affairs appeared beside Count Muravieff. As soon as General Kuropatkin had read and explained his project, Witte criticised it sharply. A lively debate ensued in the course of which the two Ministers of Foreign Affairs endorsed Witte's view unreservedly, whereupon the scheme was negatived and dropped.

Then, to the amazement of those present, Muravieff calmly took out a sheet of paper and read the rough draft of a circular to the powers on the subject of the limitation of armaments. It was Witte's proposal put in diplomatic phraseology by the Foreign Office. It was approved unanimously by all present. Witte recognised the fruit of his suggestion, and smiled at the humanitarian wrappings which had thus been vouchsafed to Kuropatkin's simple ideas, for he knew that the whole scheme was a piece of hypocrisy and guile. That rough draft—in its finished form the work of Lamsdorff—was ratified by the Tsar and subsequently handed to all the foreign diplomatic representatives accredited to the Court of St. Petersburg. Soon afterwards Witte, when making his usual weekly reports to the Emperor, behaving like one of the sceptical Roman augurs, paid him a handsome tribute for the warmth with which he had taken up the great humanitarian idea. And Nicholas II accepted the tribute as well deserved. In this first circular the object of the conference was described as "a possible reduction of the excessive armaments which weigh upon all nations." And the way to effect it was "by putting a limit to the progressive development of the present armaments." But in view of the recent improvements in artillery, of the uncertain situation, and of disturbing elements which continued to agitate the political spheres, the Russian government took no further steps for a while. People hoped or feared that the matter would not be proceeded with further. But after some months' reflection and groping, the programme was modified, and instead of calling for a reduction of armaments, all that was now asked for was the maintenance of the budgetary sums allotted for them at a level which for a certain term of years must not exceed that of the year 1898-9.

There would in all probability have been no Hague Conference if General Kuropatkin had asked in the ordinary way for the necessary credit to enable him to follow the example of his German colleague and supply the Russian army with the new gun. It is equally probable that if Witte had simply accepted or rejected the War Minister's suggestion of a "deal" with Austria, the peace conference would not have been convoked or thought of. With a touch of that irony which generally accompanied his frank talks about the Tsar with an intimate friend like myself, Witte, who was sentimental rather than cynical, remarked that the Tsar's peace proposal was one of the greatest mystifications known to history, and at the same time a beneficent stimulus. However high we may rate the contributory causes of the peace movement inaugurated by Nicholas II, history will retain the decisive fact that the motive of its prime author was to hoodwink the Austrian government and to enable the Tsar's War Minister to steal a march on his country's future enemies.

(b) *German Objection to Arbitration*[1]

June 13, [1899]

This morning come more disquieting statements regarding Germany. There seems no longer any doubt that the German Emperor is opposing arbitration, and, indeed, the whole work of the conference,

---

[1] Andrew D. White, *Autobiography*, Century Company, 1906, Vol. II, pp. 298-299. Reprinted with the permission of the Century Company.

and that he will insist on his main allies, Austria and Italy, going with him. Count Nigra, who is personally devoted to arbitration, allowed this in talking with Dr. Holls; and the German delegates— all of whom, with the exception of Count Münster, are favorably inclined to a good arbitration plan—show that they are disappointed.

I had learned from a high imperial official, before I left Berlin, that the Emperor considered arbitration as derogatory to his sovereignty, and I was also well aware, from his conversation, that he was by no means in love with the conference idea; but, in view of his speech at Wiesbaden, and the petitions which had come in to him from Bavaria, I had hoped that he had experienced a "change of heart."

Possibly he might have changed his opinion had not Count Münster been here, reporting to him constantly against every step taken by the conference.

There seems danger of a catastrophe. Those of us who are faithful to arbitration plans will go on and do the best we can; but there is no telling what stumbling blocks Germany and her allies may put in our way; and, of course, the whole result, without their final agreement, will seem to the world a failure and, perhaps, a farce.

The immediate results will be that the Russian Emperor will become an idol of the "plain people" throughout the world, the German Emperor will be bitterly hated, and the socialists, who form the most dreaded party on the continent of Europe, will be furnished with a thoroughly effective weapon against their rulers.

Some days since I said to a leading diplomatist here, "The ministers of the German Emperor ought to tell him that, should he oppose arbitration, there will be concentrated upon him an amount of hatred which no minister ought to allow a sovereign to incur." To this he answered, "That is true; but there is not a minister in Germany who dares tell him."

(c) *French Position*[1]

The Ambassador in Paris, Count Münster, to the Imperial Chancellor, Prince von Hohenlohe

Paris, April 21, 1899

M. Delcassé directed the conversation to the disarmament conference [at the Hague] and expressed himself thereon very frankly. Above everything he desires that we come to an understanding and as far as possible work together. He said:

"We have quite the same interests in this Conference as you. You do not wish to limit your power of defense at this moment nor to have anything to do with proposals for disarmament. We are entirely in the same position.

"We mutually wish to spare the Tsar and to seek a formula to cir-

---

[1] *Die Grosse Politik,* Vol. XV, p. 186.

cumvent the question, but not to have anything to do with anything which could weaken our mutual power of defense.

"In order, however, to avoid a complete fiasco, we will possibly be able to make some concessions with reference to arbitration. [Kaiser's marginal note: "No."] But these may in no case limit the complete independence of the Great States.

"The Congress of Berlin has already concerned itself with the question. On a few less significant questions we will easily come to an understanding. We must consider in addition to the Tsar the public opinion of Europe, for this has been excited by the unconsidered step of Russia."

In further conversation he condemned in a manner that surprised me the thoughtless conduct of the Russian statesmen. The Conference was planned on far too grand a scale. I utilized the opportunity to turn the conversation to the invitation of the Pope to the Conference.

M. Delcassé maintained that he has purposely had nothing to do with it and that he did not know how the matter now stands.

Italy had offered opposition; Russia had played a doubtful rôle. The Dutch Government was in a difficult situation because the influence of the Catholics there was much greater than is generally assumed. . . . The word that the nuncio had left The Hague was false and covert negotiations seemed to be still proceeding.

According to his view it would do no harm if a delegate of the Pope were allowed to participate in the consideration of questions of the Court of Arbitration and the Red Cross. But he would not take the initiative. . . . Regarding the influence of the Jesuits I shall especially report.

MÜNSTER

(d) *British Report. A British Note on the Limitation of Armaments*[1]

The Peace Conference has closed one chapter of its deliberations with an expression of opinion that a reduction of the naval and military burdens, which weigh so heavily upon the world, is greatly to be desired in the interests of humanity.

If the work of this Assembly has been barren of results in what was at first the leading motive of its programme, it has at least shown clearly where we stand in relation to the whole matter, and how many long and difficult negotiations will have to be carried on before the next step in advance can be ventured with any prospect of success.

Germany is the military centre of gravity of Europe, and all ideas of effecting any reduction, small or great, in the present burden of armaments on land, must inevitably fail if they do not receive support from Berlin. They do not receive such support; on the contrary, they are met with the plain intimation that Germany will, under no circum-

[1] *British Documents on the Origins of the War, 1898-1914*, Vol. I, No. 282, pp. 229-231.

stances, be a party to any limitation and still less to any reduction of armaments: they consequently fall to the ground.

To this state of affairs, with all it entails both for Germany and for her neighbours, there is a corollary, namely, that the rivalry between the great military Powers of Europe will not allow any very great or very sudden increase of naval expenditure at the expense of army budgets, and that Russia herself will not be able to reduce her military expenditure, or to divert it either to the navy or to other uses.

England, as the greatest naval Power, has not taken up the same uncompromising attitude in relation to naval armaments, and the question naturally arises whether some agreement may not be possible, if not with all, at least with some of the greater naval Powers.

I have ascertained the views of the Naval Delegates here, and am compelled to admit, and to state my reasons for the belief, that there is not at present the slightest chance of any agreement of the kind.

Having asked the Russian Naval Delegate to state why Mr. Goschen's speech had not been even mentioned during the debates, I received an explanation in the following sense:—

England is the very last naval Power that Russia either considers or fears. The reason is a very simple one. She considers our fleet ten times more powerful than her own, and will never wage a naval war against us. If forced to declare or accept war, she will shut up her fleet in fortified ports and fight us on land in the East. If she did otherwise, and even sank five British ships for every three Russian, she would soon have no navy, and we should still remain strong. With no marine Russia would be in a bad posture in face of her continental rivals, who would not fail to take advantage of her weakness.

She could, it is true, attack our sea-borne trade, but the results accruing from such action have been exaggerated, and Russia has few cruisers and no coaling-stations; her ships would soon die of inanition in neutral ports, even if they escaped destruction, and her geographical position, as against the British Empire, is detestable in view of a naval war.

But, although anxious to meet us half-way, Russia cannot come to a separate understanding with England to limit naval armaments so long as there is no check upon the navies of Germany and Japan, with whose maritime strength Russia is mainly concerned, since she would gain nothing as against us, and lose all as against them.

But the German Naval Delegate has been as frank as his military colleague, and has made it quite clear that Germany will not hear of limiting naval armaments, while Japan, according to her Naval Representative, will only listen when she has reached the standard of the Great Naval Powers, that is to say, never.

Taking only the broad lines of the question, France is in many ways in a similar position to Russia, and is debarred from adhering to any agreement if the Triple Alliance stands aside. Neither can she afford to risk the military and political capital represented by her battle-ships against the heavy odds of a contest with England, since the loss of her fleet would expose what Colonies we might leave her to capture by her other rivals, and would gravely paralyse her power of defence in Europe by laying open her long coast-line to attack in the event of a continental war.

The two Powers, therefore, against whom our naval activity is confessedly directed will not singly fight us squarely at sea, since they cannot afford, as against other rivals, to lose their position as naval Powers, and they can refuse a naval combat with the greater equanimity since they know that our capacity for waging offensive war on the continent of Europe against their national armies is a quantity that may be neglected.

This situation is clearly and unmistakably bound up with the retention of our present maritime supremacy, and would change with any reduction in our standard of strength.

The Powers with whom France has to count are as resolute to refuse all compromise as are those that face Russia. The Italian Naval Delegate has informed me that his instructions were to agree to nothing in the shape or guise of limitation of armaments, and the Austrian Delegate was prepared to assume a similar attitude.

The difficulties in the way of naval disarmament are not at the top of the graduated scale of naval Powers, but at the bottom; they are none the less almost insuperable, and the crux of the problem lies in the fact that no Power can cry a halt while the one next below him on the scale continues to arm, and that the latter will not cease to arm until he has reached an equality with the rival above him.

Moreover, the new policy of America and the rapid growth of her fleet are bringing a fresh set of considerations to the front.

The American Delegates have, it is true, stated that they stand apart from Europe, and that their naval policy has no relation to, and can have no importance for, the Powers of Europe. Mr. White indeed made an eloquent speech in defence of the policy of protection for private property at sea, and laid stress on the sentimental side of American character; but it is difficult to get credit for good intentions, and the French Admiral remarked to me at the close of the speech that the Americans had destroyed the Spanish navy and commerce, and now wanted no one to destroy theirs.

Captain Mahan has not only stated that his Government will on no account even, discuss the question of any limitation of naval armaments; he has also informed me that he considers that the vital interests of America now lie East and West, and no longer North and South; that the great question of the immediate future is China, and that the United States will be compelled, by facts if not by settled policy, to take a leading part in the struggle for Chinese markets, and that this will entail a very considerable increase in her naval forces in the

Pacific, which again must influence the naval arrangements of at least five Powers.

It is understood that later on in the year a fresh attempt may be made to raise the question of limiting naval armaments.

The facts stated go to show that the success of such attempt is not to be counted on.

CHARLES À COURT, Lieutenant-Colonel,
Military Attaché

The Hague, July 29, 1899

24. ANGLO-PORTUGUESE SECRET DECLARATION, 1899 (SO-CALLED WINDSOR TREATY)[1]

[The occasion for renewing the old treaty of 1661 was the outbreak of the Boer war. The provision by which Portugal undertook not to issue any formal declaration of neutrality was aimed at the supplying of coal to British warships at Delagoa Bay. This treaty was regarded with suspicion by Germany in view of the Anglo-German Convention of August 30, 1898, for the contingent partitioning of Portuguese colonies.]

Anglo-Portuguese Secret Declaration, October 14, 1899

The Government of Her Majesty the Queen of the United Kingdom of Great Britain and Ireland, Empress of India, and the Government of His Most Faithful Majesty the King of Portugal and the Algarves, considering as of full force and effect the ancient treaties of alliance, amity and guarantee which subsist between the two Crowns, specifically confirm on this occasion Article I of the Treaty of the 29th January, 1642, which runs as follows:—

"It is concluded and accorded that there is, and shall be for ever, a good true and firm peace and amity between the most renowned kings, Charles King of Great Britain and John the Fourth King of Portugal, their heirs and successors, and their Kingdoms, Countries, Dominions, Lands, People, Liegemen, Vassals and Subjects whomsoever, present and to come, of whatsoever condition, dignity or degree they may be, as well by land as by sea and fresh waters, so as the said Vassals and Subjects are each of them to favour the other and to use one another with friendly offices and true affection, and that neither of the said most renowned Kings, their heirs and successors, by himself or by any other, shall do or attempt anything against each other, or their Kingdoms, by land or by sea, nor shall consent nor adhere unto any war, counsel, or Treaty, in prejudice of the other."

They equally confirm the final Article of the Treaty of the 23rd June, 1661, of which the first part runs as follows:—

---

[1] *British Documents on the Origins of the War, 1898-1914*, Vol. I, No. 118, p. 93f.

"Over and above all and singular agreed and concluded in the Treaty of Marriage between the Most Serene and Most Powerful Charles, the Second of that name, King of Great Britain and the Most Virtuous and Serene Lady Catherine, Infanta of Portugal, it is by the Secret Article concluded and accorded, that His Majesty of Great Britain, in regard of the great advantages and increase of dominion he hath purchased by the above-mentioned Treaty of Marriage shall promise and oblige himself as by this present Article he doth, to defend and protect all conquests or colonies belonging to the Crown of Portugal against all his enemies, as well future as present."

The Government of His Most Faithful Majesty undertakes not to permit, after the declaration of war between Great Britain and the South African Republic, or during the continuance of the war, the importation and passage of arms, and of munitions of war destined for the latter.

The Government of His Most Faithful Majesty will not proclaim neutrality in the war between Great Britain and the South African Republic.

Done, in duplicate, at London, this 14th day of October, 1899.

(L. S.)   SALISBURY.

(L. S.)   LUIZ DE SOVERAL.

25. THE ANGLO-GERMAN "YANGTZE AGREEMENT," 1900[1]

[The Yangtze Agreement led to Anglo-German friction because of a misunderstanding as to whether or not it applied to Manchuria, where Germany did not wish to antagonize Russia. The British regarded as of great value the understanding of Germany to defend the status quo against Russian aggression; consequently, they asked for no special rights in the Yangtze valley. Lamsdorff was the Russian Foreign Minister.]

(a) *Memorandum respecting the Relations between Russia and Great Britain, 1892-1904, by J. A. C. Tilley*

(Extract)   Foreign Office, January 14, 1905

Towards the end of 1899 the "Boxer" disturbance began, which led to the armed intervention of the Powers. In July 1900 the disturbances spread to Manchuria, and the Chinese attacked the railway line. The Russians thereupon occupied the province with an army, and, on the pretext of an alleged attack on the foreign quarter at Newchwang, seized that town on the 4th August, and took possession of the custom-house, and began to collect revenue.

Count Lamsdorff assured Her Majesty's Minister at St. Petersburgh that the steps taken by the military authorities could only be

[1] *British Documents on the Origins of the War, 1898-1914,* Vol. II, No. 1, p. 1.

of a temporary and provisional character. A little later the Russian Minister to London repeated the announcements, made at an earlier stage of the disturbances, of the principles on which Russia meant to act in China; these principles were:—

(1.) The maintenance of agreement between the Powers;
(2.) The maintenance of the existing system of government in China;
(3.) The exclusion of everything which might lead to a partition of the Empire; and
(4.) The establishment, by common effort, of a legitimate central authority, capable in itself of assuring order and security to the country.

They added that they would not fail to withdraw from Manchuria as soon as its pacification had been secured.

These principles did not prevent the Russians from making a speedy attempt to seize the whole of the line from Newchwang to Peking, or from claiming one section of that line "by right of conquest" or from contesting the claim of the British authorities to any share in the management of the line, and seizing 50 miles of railway material belonging to Messrs. Jardine, Matheson and Co. The interest of Her Majesty's Government in this matter was peculiar, inasmuch as the line from Peking to Shanhaikwan was mortgaged to British bond-holders, whilst the rolling-stock and the profits of the other section, from Shanhaikwan to Newchwang, formed the security of those bond-holders. The remonstrances of Her Majesty's Government led the Russians to hand the *intra-mural* portion of this line to Count Waldersee, the Commander-in-Chief of the allied forces, for restitution to the British.

With these examples of Russian policy before them, Her Majesty's Government responded favourably to a proposal by the German Emperor for an Agreement in regard to the future action of the two Powers in China: the principles laid down in the Agreement, which was signed on the 16th October, 1900, were that the ports on the rivers and littoral of China should remain open to trade throughout China, so far as the two Powers could exercise influence; that they would not make use of the present complication to obtain any territorial advantages for themselves, and would direct their policy towards maintaining undiminished the territories of China; that in the case of another Power making use of the complications in China in order to obtain territorial advantages, they would come to an understanding as to the steps to be taken to protect their own interests.

Austria, Italy and Japan accepted all these principles; the United States the first two, without expressing an opinion on the third; Russia and France expressed general concurrence in the two first clauses, but the Agreement as a whole produced a very bad impression in Russia, and Her Majesty's Chargé d'Affaires, Mr. Hardinge, reported that the Russian Government only accepted the principles in so far as they coincided with their own interpretation of them.

Mr. Hardinge was told that if any complaint were made of Her Majesty's Government having concluded the Agreement without previous consultation with Russia, he was to dwell on the perplexity caused to Her Majesty's Government by the conduct and language of Russian officers in respect to the Newchwang-Peking Railway, and by their dealings with the property of British subjects on the railway.

Early in 1901 rumours began to spread as to an Agreement between Russia and China in regard to Southern Manchuria, which would establish a virtual Russian Protectorate over that province. The Russian Government were profuse in denials, but Great Britain, Germany, and Japan, at the suggestion of the latter, made declarations to China warning her against Treaties with any individual Power of a territorial or financial character.

From that time on the relations between Great Britain and Russia in China have consisted mainly in a series of endeavours on the part of His Majesty's Government to bring about the evacuation of Manchuria. The Convention under which that evacuation was to take place was signed by Russia and China on the 8th April, 1902, and the date fixed for the commencement of the evacuation was the 8th April, 1903; but when the latter date came, Russia had further conditions to be fulfilled by China, one of which, providing that no nationals other than Russians were to be employed in the north of China, the Russian Ambassador at Washington admitted to be aimed against England and the Englishmen in the Chinese Customs service. Other conditions virtually handed over Newchwang, a Treaty port, where the trade was almost exclusively British, American and Japanese, to Russian administration.

From the date of the Russian occupation the Customs revenues of Newchwang have been retained by Russia, and no account of them even has ever been rendered to China.

Further protests followed from Her Majesty's Government, but before another year was over the war between Russia and Japan brought all negotiations to an end.

(b) Memorandum on the Present State of British Relations with France and Germany, by Sir Eyre Crowe[1]

[Extract]

Secret   Foreign Office, January 1, 1907

As if none of these things had happened, fresh German demands in another field, accompanied by all the same manifestations of hostility, were again met, though with perhaps increasing reluctance, by the old willingness to oblige. The action of Germany in China has long

---

[1] *British Documents on Origins of the War, 1898-1914*, Vol. III, pp. 412-413.

been distinctly unfriendly to England. In 1895 she tried to obtain from the Chinese Government a coaling station in the Chusan Islands, at the mouth of the Yang-tsze, without any previous communication with the British Government, whose preferential rights over the group, as established by Treaty, were of course well known. The manner in which Kiao-chau was obtained, however unjustifiable it may be considered by any recognized standard of political conduct, did not concern England more than the other Powers who professed in their Treaties to respect China's integrity and independence. But Germany was not content with the seizure of the harbour, she also planned the absorption of the whole of the large and fertile province of Shantung. The concession of the privileged rights which she wrung from the Chinese Government was obtained owing in no small degree to her official assurance that her claims had the support of England who, needless to say, had never been informed or consulted, and who was, of course, known to be absolutely opposed to stipulations by which, contrary to solemn British treaty rights, it was intended to close a valuable province to British trade and enterprise.

About this time Germany secretly approached Russia with a view to the conclusion of an Agreement, by which Germany would have also obtained the much desired foothold on the Yang-tsze, then considered to be practically a British preserve. These overtures being rejected, Germany wished at least to prevent England from obtaining what she herself had failed to secure. She proposed to the British Cabinet a self-denying Agreement stipulating that neither Power should endeavour to obtain any territorial advantages in Chinese dominions, and that if any third Power attempted to do so both should take common action.

The British Government did not conceal their great reluctance to this arrangement, rightly foreseeing that Germany would tacitly exempt from its operations her own designs on Shantung, and also any Russian aggression in Manchuria, whilst England would solemnly give up any chances she might have of establishing on a firm basis her well-won position on the Yang-tsze. That is, of course, exactly what subsequently did happen. There was no obvious reason why England should lend herself to this gratuitous tying of her own hands. No counter-advantage was offered or even suggested, and the British taste for these one-sided transactions had not been stimulated by past experience. Nevertheless, the policy of conciliating Germany by meeting her expressed wishes once more triumphed, and the Agreement was signed —with the foreseen consequences: Russian aggression in Manchuria was declared to be altogether outside the scope of the stipulations of what the German Chancellor took care to style the "Yang-tsze" Agreement, as if its terms had referred specially to that restricted area of China. And the German designs on Shantung continue to this day to be tenaciously pursued. . . .

26. Hay's Proposal for the Open Door in China[1]

[Andrew D. White was American Ambassador in Berlin. Secretary of State Hay's famous note was made while the European powers were engaged in the partition of China. It was not easy for other nations to formulate respectable reasons against his proposal for the "open door" policy. The Boxer uprising in 1900 brought American sincerity to the test. When the various nations were preparing for the relief expedition, Hay again stated the open door which was accepted by the coöperating powers as the aim of the invasion. This document may be regarded as containing the official definition of the open door.]

Mr. Hay to Mr. White

No. 927   Department of State,
Washington, September 6, 1899

Sir: At the time when the Government of the United States was informed by that of Germany that it had leased from His Majesty the Emperor of China the port of Kiao-chao and the adjacent territory in the province of Shantung, assurances were given to the ambassador of the United States at Berlin by the Imperial German minister for foreign affairs that the rights and privileges insured by treaties with China to citizens of the United States would not thereby suffer or be in anywise impaired within the area over which Germany had thus obtained control.

More recently, however, the British Government recognized by a formal agreement with Germany the exclusive right of the latter country to enjoy in said leased area and the contiguous "sphere of influence or interest" certain privileges, more especially those relating to railroads and mining enterprises; but as the exact nature and extent of the rights thus recognized have not been clearly defined, it is possible that serious conflicts of interest may at any time arise not only between British and German subjects within said area, but that the interests of our citizens may also be jeopardized thereby.

Earnestly desirous to remove any cause of irritation and to insure at the same time to the commerce of all nations in China the undoubted benefits which should accrue from a formal recognition by the various powers claiming "spheres of interest" that they shall enjoy perfect equality of treatment for their commerce and navigation within such "spheres," the Government of the United States would be pleased to see His German Majesty's Government give formal assurances, and lend its coöperation in securing like assurances from the other interested powers, that each, within its respective sphere of whatever influence—

---

[1] United States, Department of State. *Foreign Relations of the United States,* 1899, pp. 129-130.

First. Will in no way interfere with any treaty port or any vested interest within any so-called "sphere of interest" or leased territory it may have in China.

Second. That the Chinese treaty tariff of the time being shall apply to all merchandise landed or shipped to all such ports as are within said "sphere of interest" (unless they be "free ports"), no matter to what nationality it may belong, and that duties so leviable shall be collected by the Chinese Government.

Third. That it will levy no higher harbor dues on vessels of another nationality frequenting any port in such "sphere" than shall be levied on vessels of its own nationality, and no higher railroad charges over lines built, controlled, or operated within its "sphere" on merchandise belonging to citizens or subjects of other nationalities transported through such "sphere" than shall be levied on similar merchandise belonging to its own nationals transported over equal distances.

The liberal policy pursued by His Imperial German Majesty in declaring Kiao-chao a free port and in aiding the Chinese Government in the establishment there of a custom-house are [sic] so clearly in line with the proposition which this Government is anxious to see recognized that it entertains the strongest hope that Germany will give its acceptance and hearty support.

The recent ukase of His Majesty the Emperor of Russia declaring the port of Ta-lien-wan open during the whole of the lease under which it is held from China to the merchant ships of all nations, coupled with the categorical assurances made to this Government by His Imperial Majesty's representative at this capital at the time and since repeated to me by the present Russian ambassador, seem to insure the support of the Emperor to the proposed measure. Our ambassador at the Court of St. Petersburg has in consequence been instructed to submit it to the Russian Government and to request their early consideration of it. A copy of my instruction on the subject to Mr. Tower is herewith inclosed for your confidential information.

The commercial interests of Great Britain and Japan will be so clearly served by the desired declaration of intentions, and the views of the Governments of these countries as to the desirability of the adoption of measures insuring the benefits of equality of treatment of all foreign trade throughout China are so similar to those entertained by the United States, that their acceptance of the propositions herein outlined and their coöperation in advocating their adoption by the other powers can be confidently expected. I inclose herewith copy of the instruction which I have sent to Mr. Choate on the subject.

In view of the present favorable conditions, you are instructed to submit the above considerations to His Imperial German Majesty's Minister for Foreign Affairs, and to request his early consideration of the subject.

Copy of this instruction is sent to our ambassadors at London and at St. Petersburg for their information.

I have, etc.,

JOHN HAY

27. FRANCO-ITALIAN AGREEMENT OF 1900-1902[1]

[Italy represented her promise to France as merely a definition of her obligations to the Triple Alliance. Though not contrary to the letter, it was, nevertheless, contrary to the spirit of the Triple Alliance. Count Bülow, the German Chancellor, was worried at Italy's defection, but, putting up a good front, he declared in the Reichstag, January 8, 1902: "The Triple Alliance still enjoys the best of health. . . . In a happy marriage the husband must not get angry right off if his wife innocently takes an extra dance with another partner. The main thing is that she does not elope with him; but she will not elope, if she realizes that she is better off with her husband." The real situation, however, was shrewdly summed up by Poincaré to Izvolski, in 1912: "Neither the Triple Entente nor the Triple Alliance can count on the loyalty of Italy; the Italian Government will employ all its efforts to preserve the peace; and in case of war, it will begin by adopting a waiting attitude, and will finally join the camp toward which victory will incline."]

(a) *Exchange of Letters concerning Morocco and Tripolitania*

M. Barrère, Ambassador of the French Republic at Rome, to His Excellency the Marquis Visconti-Venosta, Minister of Foreign Affairs of Italy

Rome, December 14, 1900

Following the conclusion of the convention of March 21, 1899, between France and Great Britain, my Government, replying to your honorable predecessor, had the opportunity to give him through me explanations of a nature to dissipate all ambiguity as to the scope of that instrument.

Since then, Your Excellency has expressed the opinion that these assurances, reiterated in a more explicit manner, would contribute to strengthen the good relations between our two countries.

Consequently, I have been authorized by the Minister of Foreign Affairs to inform Your Excellency, in view of the friendly relations which have been established between France and Italy, and in the belief that this explanation will conduce further to improve them, that

---

[1] France. Ministère des affaires étrangères. *Documents diplomatiques. Les accords franco-italiens de 1900-1902*, pp. 3-4. Eng. trans. in A. F. Pribram, *The Secret Treaties of Austria-Hungary, 1879-1914*, Vol. II, pp. 241-245. Reprinted with the permission of the Harvard University Press, holders of the copyright.

the Convention of March 21, 1899, while leaving the vilayet of Tripoli outside of the partition of influence which it sanctions, marks for the French sphere of influence, in relation to Tripolitania-Cyrenaica, a limit which the Government of the Republic has not the intention of exceeding; and that it does not enter into its plans to interrupt communications by caravan from Tripoli with the regions contemplated by the aforesaid convention.

These explanations, which we are agreed to keep secret, will contribute, I have no doubt, to strengthen, on this as upon other points, the friendly relations between our two countries.

BARRÈRE

Marquis Visconti-Venosta, Minister of Foreign Affairs of Italy, to M. Barrère, Ambassador of the French Republic at Rome

Rome, December 16, 1900

The present situation in the Mediterranean and the eventualities which might occur there have been the subject of a friendly interchange of ideas between us, our two Governments being equally animated by the desire to eliminate, in this respect also, everything that would be susceptible of compromising, in the present and in the future, their mutual good understanding.

So far as concerns Morocco more particularly, it appeared from our conversations that the action of France has as its purpose the exercise and the safeguarding of the rights which are the result for her of the proximity of her territory with that Empire.

So defined, I recognized that such action is not in our view of a nature to prejudice the interests of Italy as a Mediterranean power.

It was likewise understood that, if a modification of the political or territorial status of Morocco should result therefrom, Italy would reserve to herself, as a measure of reciprocity, the right eventually to develop her influence with regard to Tripolitania-Cyrenaica.

These explanations, which we are agreed to keep secret, will contribute, I have no doubt, to strengthen the friendly relations between our two countries.

VISCONTI-VENOSTA

(b) *Autograph Note of M. Delcassé*[1]

June 4, 1902

Count Tornielli has just read me the following telegram, containing the declaration stated, and has left a copy with me at my request.

June 4, 1902. 4 P.M.

DELCASSÉ

---

[1] France. Ministère des affaires étrangères. *Documents diplomatiques. Les accords franco-italiens de 1900-1902*, pp. 5-6. Eng. trans. in Pribram, *The Secret Treaties of Austria-Hungary, 1879-1914*, Vol. II, p. 247. Reprinted with the permission of the Harvard University Press, holders of the copyright.

Copy left by Count Tornielli

I have been authorized by His Excellency, M. Prinetti, to communicate to Your Excellency a telegram in which the Minister of Foreign Affairs of Italy assures me that, in the renewal of the Triple Alliance, there is nothing directly or indirectly aggressive toward France, no engagement binding us in any eventuality to take part in an aggression against her, finally no stipulation which menaces the security and tranquillity of France.

M. Prinetti likewise desires that I should know that the protocols or additional conventions to the Triple Alliance, of which there has been much talk of late, and which would alter its completely defensive character, and which would even have an aggressive character against France, do not exist.

The Minister of Foreign Affairs of Italy expresses at the same time his firm confidence that this communication will have the effect of strengthening more and more the good relations existing between the two countries and of assuring the fruitful development thereof.

This communication is meant to remain secret.

(c) *Exchange of Letters Declaring that no Divergence Subsists between the Two Countries as to their Respective Interests in the Mediterranean*[1]

M. Prinetti, Minister of Foreign Affairs of Italy, to M. Barrère, Ambassador of the French Republic at Rome

Rome, November 1, 1902

In continuation of the conversations which we have had concerning the reciprocal situation of Italy and of France in the Mediterranean basin, and concerning more especially the respective interests of the two countries in Tripolitania-Cyrenaica and in Morocco, it seemed to us opportune to define the engagements which result from the letters exchanged on this subject, between Your Excellency and Marquis Visconti-Venosta, on December 14 and 16, 1900, in this sense, that each of the two Powers can freely develop its sphere of influence in the above mentioned regions at the moment it deems it opportune, and without the action of one of them being necessarily subordinated to that of the other. It was explained on that occasion that the limit of French expansion in Northern Africa contemplated in the abovementioned letter of Your Excellency of December 14, 1900, was fully understood to be the frontier of Tripolitania indicated by the map attached to the Declaration of March 21, 1899, additional to the Franco-English Convention of June 14, 1898.

---

[1] France. Ministère des affaires étrangères. *Documents diplomatiques. Les accords franco-italiens de 1900-1902*, pp. 7-9. Eng. trans. in Pribram, *The Secret Treaties of Austria-Hungary, 1879-1914*, Vol. II, pp. 249-255. Reprinted with the permission of the Harvard University Press, holders of the copyright.

We noted that this interpretation left no divergence still existing between our Governments as to their respective interests in the Mediterranean.

Profiting by the occasion of these conferences, and in order to eliminate in a definitive manner any possible misunderstanding between our two countries, I do not hesitate, in order to define their general relations, to make of my own accord to Your Excellency, in the name of the Government of His Majesty the King, the following declarations:

In case France should be the object of a direct or indirect aggression on the part of one or more Powers, Italy will maintain a strict neutrality.

The same shall hold good in case France, as the result of a direct provocation, should find herself compelled, in defence of her honor or of her security, to take the initiative of a declaration of war. In that eventuality, the Government of the Republic shall previously communicate its intention to the Royal Government, which will thus be enabled to determine whether there is really a case of direct provocation.

In order to remain faithful to the spirit of friendship which has inspired the present declarations, I am authorized further to confirm to you that on the part of Italy no protocol or military provision in the nature of an international contract which would be in disagreement with the present declarations exists or will be concluded by her.

I may add that—save as concerns the interpretation of the Mediterranean interests of the two Powers, which has a final character—in conformity with the spirit of the correspondence exchanged between Your Excellency and Marquis Visconti-Venosta, on December 14 and 16, 1900, as the preceding declarations are in harmony with the present international engagements of Italy, the Royal Government understands that they shall retain their full validity so long as it has not notified the Government of the Republic that these engagements have been modified.

I should be obliged if Your Excellency would be kind enough to acknowledge receipt of the present communication, which must remain secret, and to take note thereof in the name of the Government of the Republic.

PRINETTI

M. Barrère, Ambassador of the French Republic at Rome, to M. Prinetti, Minister of Foreign Affairs of Italy

Rome, November 1, 1902

By your letter of today's date, Your Excellency has been kind enough to recall to me that in the continuation of our conversations relative to the reciprocal situation of France and of Italy in the Mediterranean basin, and more especially to the respective interests of the two countries in Tripolitania-Cyrenaica and in Morocco, it seemed to us opportune to define the engagements which result from the letters exchanged on this subject between Marquis Visconti-Venosta and myself on December 14 and 16, 1900, in this sense, that each of the two Powers can freely develop its sphere of influence in the abovementioned regions at the moment it deems it opportune, and without the action of one of them being necessarily subordinated to that of the other.

It was explained on that occasion that the limit of French expansion in Northern Africa contemplated in my abovementioned letter of December 14, 1900, was fully understood to be the frontier of Tripolitania indicated by the map attached to the Declaration of March 21, 1899, additional to the English Convention of June 14, 1898.

This interpretation leaving, as we have noted, no divergence as to their respective interests in the Mediterranean still existing between our Governments, and with the purpose of eliminating in a definitive manner any possible misunderstanding between our two countries, you have been authorized by the Government of His Majesty to formulate of your own accord certain declarations intended to define the general relations of Italy towards France.

I have the honor to acknowledge receipt thereof to Your Excellency and to give you note of these declarations in the name of my Government.

I am authorized, in return, to formulate in the following manner the conditions under which France on her side intends, in the same friendly spirit, to order her general relations towards Italy.

In case Italy should be the object of a direct or indirect aggression on the part of one or more Powers, France will maintain a strict neutrality.

The same shall hold good in case Italy, as the result of a direct provocation, should find herself compelled, in defence of her honor or of her security, to take the initiative of a declaration of war. In that eventuality, the Royal Government shall previously communicate its intention to the Government of the Republic, which will thus be enabled to determine whether there is really a case of direct provocation.

I am authorized equally to declare to you that on the part of France no protocol or military provision in the nature of an international contract which would be in disagreement with the present declarations exists or will be concluded by her.

It is fully understood finally that—save as concerns the interpretation of the Mediterranean interests of the two Powers, which has a final character—in conformity with the spirit of the correspondence exchanged between Marquis Visconti-Venosta and myself, on December 14 and 16, 1900, as the declarations which precede, and which must remain secret, are in harmony with the present international engagements of Italy, they shall retain their full validity so long as the Royal

Government has not notified the Government of the Republic that these engagements have been modified.

BARRÈRE

(d) Recapitulation of the Negotiations

M. Barrère, Ambassador of the French Republic at Rome, to M. Poincaré, President of the Council, Minister of Foreign Affairs[1]

Rome, March 10, 1912

The recent incidents which have occurred between France and Italy, the press polemics to which they have given rise, have called attention to Franco-Italian relations and have awakened certain curiosities in regard to the understandings upon which they are based and of which the existence only is definitely known to the public. I have had occasion to indicate to Your Excellency, in reply to a question which you were kind enough to put to me, in what measure, in my opinion, the value and scope of these understandings, and more particularly of the one which bears the dates of November 1 and 2, 1902, could be publicly explained.

It seemed to me that it was opportune to recall the conditions under which this last agreement was conceived, negotiated, and concluded by French diplomacy. This examination, which will summarize long and often delicate conferences, will give the Department the opportunity to comprehend in a single survey the object pursued; it will moreover permit it, by placing the diplomatic instrument in question back in the circumstances which gave it birth, to assign to it its exact sense both as respects ourselves and as regards the position into which it has put the Kingdom in the Triple Alliance and consequently in the international political situation.

Without going too far back into the past, we may assign, as the point of departure for the conferences which were to result in 1902 in the secret agreement, the situation created between France and Italy by the visit which the Italian squadron commanded by the Duke of Genoa paid to Toulon in the spring of 1901. At that time the Franco-Italian rapprochement was an accomplished fact. The negotiations relative to Tunisia, the settlement in commercial matters, the delimitation of the possessions of the two countries on the Red Sea, and finally the agreement relative to Tripolitania and Morocco reached in December, 1900, had marked its stages. This last protocol was secret. But if its text was unrevealed, its existence was known. It was henceforth established that France and Italy had dispelled from between

---

[1] France. Ministère des affaires étrangères. *Documents diplomatiques. Les accords franco-italiens de 1900-1902*, pp. 11-14. Eng. trans. in Pribram, *The Secret Treaties of Austria-Hungary, 1879-1914*, Vol. II, pp. 231-241. Reprinted with the permission of the Harvard University Press, holders of the copyright.

them the causes of trouble and uneasiness, and put an end to Mediterranean rivalry by defining their respective interests. On this last point
there remained a further step for them to take by defining their interests in Tripoli and in Morocco, and by affirming more clearly their
mutual disinterestedness in the sense indicated in the agreement negotiated with Marquis Visconti-Venosta. It was one of the legitimate
desires of Italian policy to arrive at this complementary understanding.
French diplomacy, which on its part desired this so far as concerned
Morocco, deemed that at the moment of beginning the conversation
there was need of making in all friendliness mutual explanations concerning the future of the relations between the two countries. The
present was satisfactory. The existence, however, of the Triple Alliance
made its character precarious. In order to assure to the reëstablished
good relations a stability which should confer upon them their full
value, it was necessary to clear up the point of knowing whether the
Triple Alliance was, under the form which it then possessed, compatible with Franco-Italian friendship.

In 1901, the Triple Alliance was no longer what it was at its beginning. The actual text of the Treaty bearing the signature of Italy had
not been modified. The Alliance remained defensive. But it permitted a
very broad interpretation of the duties of the Allies: if France, openly
provoked, should declare war, could Italy regard this declaration as a
defensive step on our part? It was doubtful. What is more, nothing
prevented her from going beyond the actual text of the Treaty, if she
should judge that her political interests demanded it of her.

It is the knowledge of this state of affairs which led the Department
and this Embassy to conclude that, under defensive appearances, the
Triple Alliance implied an eventually offensive character, which ought
to be got rid of in the interest of our security and of the relations of
friendship between the two countries. It is along this line that conversations, pursued in parallel fashion, were entered into at Paris by
M. Delcassé with the Ambassador of Italy, and at Rome by myself with
M. Prinetti. The latter, exposed from the other side to German attacks
in view of the expiration of the Treaty, was nevertheless inclined to
take the side of France, to which his personal sympathies and a very
high conception of the future of his country impelled him. Encouraged
by declared partisans of Franco-Italian friendship, such as MM.
Luzzatti and Rattazzi, as also by the well-known sentiments of
M. Zanardelli, President of the Council, by the support which he received from M. Giolitti, Minister of the Interior, by the exhortations
of the Marquis di Rudini, who was strongly imbued with a sense of the
necessity of establishing on a solid basis the general political relations
of the two countries by consecrating them through a mutual agreement,
and by the attitude of Baron Sonnino, who from the ranks of the
Opposition counselled the strengthening of good relations with France,

the Minister of Foreign Affairs took a stronger stand and was in a position to talk with me of what remained to be done in order to establish mutual confidence.

The moment, moreover, was approaching when the question was going to become a burning one. A year had elapsed since our first conversations. M. Prinetti was to have a meeting at Venice with Herr von Bülow; they would certainly speak of the renewal of the Alliance. In a conversation I had with him in the month of March, 1902, he specifically broached the subject. M. Prinetti did not believe it possible to modify the actual text of the Treaty. He declared himself ready, on the other hand, to give us assurances of a nature to leave no doubt in our mind as to the character and as to the scope of this document. He wished, he said, that he could communicate it to us, but this would be impossible for him, because the Triple Alliance bears upon other points which do not interest or affect us. Moreover, it was not expressly in the text of the Treaty, properly speaking, that the thing figured with which France had a right to be concerned; it was in the documents annexed. "These," he added, "must fall and disappear, for they looked forward to conjunctures which could no longer occur."

In reporting this interesting conversation to the Department, I indicated that it would open the door to a negotiation and to an understanding. On his side, M. Delcassé seized the occasion of an interview with Count Tornielli to take note of the declarations of M. Prinetti relative to the eventual renewal of the Triple Alliance, and to indicate to him that only the execution of the assurances which he had given us could assure to the relations of the two countries a long and fruitful future.

Hereupon, the interview of Venice took place, in the course of which M. Prinetti tried to bring Prince von Bülow to modify the text of the Treaty. The Chancellor not having followed him in this path, M. Prinetti did not insist. It appeared to him thenceforth that it was in a direct understanding with us that he should find the means of fixing the interpretation with regard to us which Italy intended to give to her obligations as an ally. Moreover, had he succeeded, he could not have satisfied us by having the text thus modified communicated to us; it was necessary that a mutual written engagement should give us the certainty that the Italian Government would not undertake to modify anew the clause thus restricted. It was soon decided between M. Prinetti and myself that the moment had come to take up the discussion of the agreement, which was to come about, and I went to Paris to reach an understanding on this subject with M. Delcassé. Hereupon, as the approaching renewal of the Triple Alliance was becoming a matter of public notoriety, M. Prinetti, without waiting for our agreements to be concluded, felt impelled to instruct Count Tornielli to make to the Minister of Foreign Affairs of the Republic a declaration of a nature to reassure the French Government concerning the dispositions of Italy towards our country. This had the effect of enabling M. Delcassé, without divulging its text, which must remain secret, to enlighten the Parliament as to the scope of the renewal of the Alliance by alluding to a spontaneous declaration of the Royal Government intended to reassure us in this respect. Your Excellency is acquainted with this important document, which determines the purely defensive value of the Triple Alliance as respects us, and which records "that there does not exist" any protocol or annexed conventions of a nature to alter this character. The declaration looked to the *renewal* and not to the past. If, therefore, there had existed annexed documents disturbing to us, they had just disappeared.

On my return to Rome, I resumed the negotiations with M. Prinetti. They were soon to be concluded. The form of letters which covered this agreement was chosen in order not to give to this document the character of a counter-treaty. Italy took, it is true, no engagement in contradiction with her Alliances. We had never asked it of her. M. Prinetti always asserted that the Franco-Italian agreement must be in harmony with the Alliances, as he renewed them, and without military protocols. The agreement is in no way contradictory to the obligations of Italy. It confines itself to defining their character. In doing this, the Italian Government did not contravene its engagements towards its Allies; it defined them as regards us by interpreting them in a spirit suitable to its relations of friendship with us; it eliminated all ambiguity as to the *defensive* character of the Alliance by its definition of an act of provocation. At the same time, it precluded itself from modifying at will, from enlarging in the future, this interpretation in a sense unfavorable to us, without our being advised thereof under the conditions which the letters exchanged between M. Prinetti and myself determine.

According to the text of the two principal letters dated November 1, it is the Italian Government which took the initiative of putting the questions to us, my letter being a reply to its own. On the other hand, in the letters interpretative of a direct provocation, it is we who took the initiative of asking the Italian Government to define it.

Finally, the letters dated November 1 began by declarations relative to Morocco and Tripolitania. It was not without reason that these questions had been brought together with the interpretation of the Triple Alliance. It had been desired to justify this interpretation by the importance which this adjustment of their Mediterranean interests had for the two countries. Thus as regards Italy the motive was explained which had led her to give us assurances about her attitude in case of a Franco-German war. The agreement is not, I have said, a counter-treaty, but it is a *counterpart* of the Triple Alliance.

At the present hour, after about ten years of existence, what place do the agreements of 1902 occupy in Franco-Italian policy? It follows from the above that their value is more precious for us than ever. The text is so cogent, so explicit, that it leaves room only for a minimum of interpretation. Before 1902 it could have produced serious misunderstandings to raise on this side of the Alps the question of the interpretation or of the modification of the Alliance in a dangerous sense.

Such are, Mr. President of the Council, the considerations which spring from a careful examination of our mutual engagements of 1900-1902.

I must excuse myself for having made the exposition of them a little lengthy, but it has seemed to me that they deserve to be elucidated.

BARRÈRE

28. THE ANGLO-JAPANESE AGREEMENT, JANUARY 30, 1902[1]

[Both Japan and Great Britain had come to feel their isolation. When a satisfactory agreement with Russia proved impossible, Japan preferred an alliance with her rival. Negotiations were carried on by Lansdowne, British Secretary of State for Foreign Affairs, and Hayashi, the Japanese Ambassador in London. Japan was thus placed on equal terms with a great European Power and was practically assured of having only one enemy in case of war with Russia. Great Britain gained less, since Japan refused to include India within her sphere of obligations, but at least British isolation was ended.]

The Governments of Great Britain and Japan, actuated solely by a desire to maintain the *status quo* and general peace in the extreme East, being moreover specially interested in maintaining the independence and territorial integrity of the Empire of China and the Empire of Corea, and in securing equal opportunities in those countries for the commerce and industry of all nations, hereby agree as follows:—

The High Contracting Parties, having mutually recognised the independence of China and Corea, declare themselves to be entirely uninfluenced by any aggressive tendencies in either country. Having in view, however, their special interests, of which those of Great Britain relate principally to China, while Japan, in addition to the interests which she possesses in China, is interested in a peculiar degree politically as well as commercially and industrially in Corea, the High Contracting Parties recognise that it will be admissible for either of them to safeguard those interests if threatened either by the aggressive action of any other Power, or by disturbance arising in China or Corea, and necessitating the intervention of either of the High Contracting Parties for the protection of the lives or property of its subjects.

If either Great Britain or Japan, in the defence of their respective

[1] *British Documents on the Origins of the War, 1898-1914*, Vol. II, pp. 115-120.

interests as above described, should become involved in war with another Power, the other High Contracting Party will maintain a strict neutrality, and use its efforts to prevent other Powers from joining in hostilities against its Ally.

If in the above event any other Power or Powers should join in hostilities against the Ally, the other High Contracting Party will come to its assistance and will conduct the war in common, and make peace in mutual agreement with it.

The High Contracting Parties agree that neither of them will, without consulting the other, enter into separate arrangements with another Power to the prejudice of the interests above described.

Whenever, in the opinion of either Great Britain or Japan, the above-mentioned interests are in jeopardy, the two Governments will communicate with one another fully and frankly.

The present Agreement shall come into effect immediately after the date of its signature, and remain in force for five years from that date.

In case neither of the High Contracting Parties should have notified twelve months before the expiration of the said five years the intention of terminating it, it shall remain binding until the expiration of one year from the day on which either of the High Contracting Parties shall have denounced it. But if, when the date fixed for its expiration arrives, either ally is actually engaged in war, the alliance shall, *ipso facto*, continue until peace is concluded.

In faith whereof the undersigned, duly authorised by their respective Governments, have signed this agreement and have affixed thereto their seals.

Done in duplicate at London the 30th day of January, 1902

(L.S.) LANSDOWNE

(L.S.) HAYASHI

Diplomatic Note Accompanying the Agreement

In reference to the Agreement concluded by us today on behalf of our respective Governments, I have the honour to inform you that the British/Japanese Government recognises that the naval forces of Great Britain/Japan should, so far as is possible, act in concert with those of Japan/Great Britain in time of peace, and agrees that mutual facilities shall be given for the docking and coaling of vessels of war of one country in the ports of the other, as well as other advantages conducing to the welfare and efficiency of the respective navies of the two Powers.

At the present moment Japan and Great Britain are each of them maintaining in the Extreme East a naval force superior in strength to that of any third Power. Great Britain/Japan has no intention of relaxing her efforts to maintain, so far as may be possible, available for concentration in the waters of the Extreme East a naval force superior to that of any third Power.

29. The Anglo-French Entente, April 8, 1904[1]

[The Entente Cordiale was apparently initiated by Edward VII and Lansdowne, though Delcassé too was eager for a *rapprochement*. Both powers were anxious not to be involved in the Russo-Japanese War, as England was the ally of one of the belligerents and France of the other. Egypt had been one of the most acute sources of friction between the two powers. Morocco was of special interest to France because it was the origin of continual plundering raids into Algeria (French since 1830). To protect this important possession, it seemed essential to France to extend her control over Morocco. As the increasing weakness of the Sultan's régime coincided with a period of intense colonial rivalry, Morocco became the center of diplomatic interest. By 1904 Delcassé had bought off the claims of Italy (see doc. no. 27) and Spain. His failure to include Germany was partially responsible for the Moroccan crises of 1905 and 1911.]

Article 1. His Britannic Majesty's Government declare that they have no intention of altering the political status of Egypt.

The Government of the French Republic, for their part, declare that they will not obstruct the action of Great Britain in that country by asking that a limit of time be fixed for the British occupation or in any other manner, and that they give their assent to the draft Khedivial Decree annexed to the present arrangement, containing the guarantees considered necessary for the protection of the interests of the Egyptian bondholders, on the condition that, after its promulgation, it cannot be modified in any way without the consent of the Powers signatory of the Convention of London of 1885.

It is agreed that the post of Director-General of Antiquities in Egypt shall continue, as in the past, to be entrusted to a French *savant*.

The French schools in Egypt shall continue to enjoy the same liberty as in the past.

Article 2. The Government of the French Republic declare that they have no intention of altering the political status of Morocco.

His Britannic Majesty's Government, for their part, recognise that it appertains to France, more particularly as a Power whose dominions are conterminous for a great distance with those of Morocco, to preserve order in that country, and to provide assistance for the purpose of all administrative, economic, financial, and military reforms which it may require.

They declare that they will not obstruct the action taken by France for this purpose, provided that such action shall leave intact the rights

---

[1] Great Britain, *Parliamentary Papers*, 1911, Vol. CIII, Cmd. 5969. "Declaration Between The United Kingdom and France Respecting Egypt And Morocco Together With The Secret Articles Signed At The Same Time."

which Great Britain, in virtue of treaties, conventions, and usage, enjoys in Morocco, including the right of coasting trade between the ports of Morocco, enjoyed by British vessels since 1901.

Article 3. His Britannic Majesty's Government, for their part, will respect the rights which France, in virtue of treaties, conventions, and usage, enjoys in Egypt, including the right of Coasting trade between Egyptian ports accorded to French vessels.

Article 4. The two Governments, being equally attached to the principle of commercial liberty both in Egypt and Morocco, declare that they will not, in those countries, countenance any inequality either in the imposition of customs duties or other taxes, or of railway transport charges.

The trade of both nations with Morocco and with Egypt shall enjoy the same treatment in transit through the French and British possessions in Africa. An agreement between the two Governments shall settle the conditions of such transit and shall determine the points of entry.

This mutual engagement shall be binding for a period of thirty years. Unless this stipulation is expressly denounced at least one year in advance, the period shall be extended for five years at a time.

Nevertheless, the Government of the French Republic reserve to themselves in Morocco, and His Britannic Majesty's Government reserve to themselves in Egypt, the right to see that the concessions for roads, railways, ports, etc., are only granted on such conditions as will maintain intact the authority of the State over these great undertakings of public interest.

Article 5. His Britannic Majesty's Government declare that they will use their influence in order that the French officials now in the Egyptian service may not be placed under conditions less advantageous than those applying to the British officials in the service.

The Government of the French Republic, for their part, would make no objection to the application of analogous conditions to British officials now in the Moorish service.

Article 6. In order to ensure the free passage of the Suez Canal, His Britannic Majesty's Government declare that they adhere to the treaty of the 29th October, 1888, and that they agree to their being put in force. The free passage of the Canal being thus guaranteed, the execution of the last sentence of paragraph 1 as well as of paragraph 2 of article 8 of that treaty will remain in abeyance.

Article 7. In order to secure the free passage of the Straits of Gibraltar, the two Governments agree not to permit the erection of any fortifications or strategic works on that portion of the coast of Morocco comprised between, but not including, Melilla and the heights which command the right bank of the River Sebou.

This condition does not, however, apply to the places at present in the occupation of Spain on the Moorish coast of the Mediterranean.

Article 8. The two Governments, inspired by their feeling of sincere friendship for Spain, take into special consideration the interests which that country derives from her geographical position and from her territorial possessions on the Moorish coast of the Mediterranean. In regard to these interests the French Government will come to an understanding with the Spanish Government.

The agreement which may be come to on the subject between France and Spain shall be communicated to His Britannic Majesty's Government.

Article 9. The two Governments agree to afford to one another their diplomatic support, in order to obtain the execution of the clauses of the present Declaration regarding Egypt and Morocco.

In witness whereof his Excellency the Ambassador of the French Republic at the Court of His Majesty the King of the United Kingdom of Great Britain and Ireland and of the British Dominions beyond the Seas, Emperor of India, and His Majesty's Principal Secretary of State for Foreign Affairs, duly authorised for that purpose, have signed the present Declaration and have affixed thereto their seals. Done at London, in duplicate, the 8th day of April, 1904.

(L.S.) LANSDOWNE

(L.S.) PAUL CAMBON

SECRET ARTICLES

Article 1. In the event of either Government finding themselves constrained, by the force of circumstances, to modify their policy in respect to Egypt or Morocco, the engagements which they have undertaken towards each other by articles 4, 6, and 7 of the Declaration of to-day's date would remain intact.

Article 2. His Britannic Majesty's Government have no present intention of proposing to the Powers any changes in the system of the Capitulations, or in the judicial organisation of Egypt.

In the event of their considering it desirable to introduce in Egypt reforms tending to assimilate the Egyptian legislative system to that in force in other civilised Countries, the Government of the French Republic will not refuse to entertain any such proposals, on the understanding that His Britannic Majesty's Government will agree to entertain the suggestions that the Government of the French Republic may have to make to them with a view of introducing similar reforms in Morocco.

Article 3. The two Governments agree that a certain extent of Moorish territory adjacent to Melilla, Ceuta, and other *présides* should, whenever the Sultan ceases to exercise authority over it, come within the sphere of influence of Spain, and that the administration of the coast from Melilla as far as, but not including, the heights on the right bank of the Sebou shall be entrusted to Spain.

Nevertheless, Spain would previously have to give her formal assent to the provisions of articles 4 and 7 of the Declaration of to-day's date, and undertake to carry them out.

She would also have to undertake not to alienate the whole, or a part, of the territories placed under her authority or in her sphere of influence.

Article 4. If Spain, when invited to assent to the provisions of the preceding article, should think proper to decline, the arrangement between France and Great Britain, as embodied in the Declaration of to-day's date, would be none the less at once applicable.

Article 5. Should the consent of the other Powers to the draft Decree mentioned in article 1 of the Declaration of to-day's date not be obtained, the Government of the French Republic will not oppose the repayment at par of the Guaranteed, Privileged, and Unified Debts after the 15th July, 1910.

Done at London, in duplicate, the 8th day of April, 1904.

(L.S.) LANSDOWNE

(L.S.) PAUL CAMBON

30. "WILLY-NICKY" CORRESPONDENCE, 1904-1905, REGARDING AN ALLIANCE: BJÖRKÖ NEGOTIATIONS[1]

[The Kaiser and the Tsar habitually corresponded in English; these letters are accordingly not translations. The Kaiser obviously extorted the treaty, but it quickly lapsed. In the end Witte, newly appointed Prime Minister, wrote to Berlin that the pact was not binding because it did not bear the signature of the Foreign Minister; and the Russian Ambassador in Berlin declared that it could not come into force till Russia, Germany, and France could agree, but that the adhesion of France was for the present impossible and the pact was inconsistent with the Franco-Russian Alliance.]

(a) *Emperor William II to Emperor Nicholas II of Russia at the time in Tsarskoe Selo*

Telegram. Draft in his own handwriting (in English)

27. X. 1904

For some time English press has been threatening Germany, on no account to allow coals to be sent to your Baltic Fleet now on its way out. It is not impossible, that the Japanese and British Governments may lodge a joint protest against our coaling your ships coupled with a "sommation" to stop further work. The result aimed at by such a threat of war would be the absolute immobility of your fleet and inability to proceed to its destination from want of fuel. This new danger would have to be faced in community by Russia and Germany together, who would both have to remind your ally France of the obligations

[1] *Die Grosse Politik*, Vol. XIX, Pt. 1, p. 303ff, No. 6118.

she has taken over in the treaty of Dual Alliance with you, the casus
fœderis. It is out of the question, that France on such an invitation,
would try to shirk her implicit duty towards her ally. Though Delcassé
is an Anglophile "enragé," he will be wise enough to understand, that
the British fleet is utterly unable to save Paris! In this way a powerful
combination of 3 of the strongest continental Powers would be formed
to attack, whom the Anglo-Japanese group would think twice before
acting [sic]. The plaints of England against our coaling Russian ships
are all the more frivolous, as England since the beginning of the war—
after making a present of two ironclads "Nikin" and "Kasuga" under
British officers and crews to Japan—has constantly supplied the
Japanese fleet with their coals, selling them no less than 30 steamers.
The naval battles fought by Togo are fought with Cardiff coals. It
would of course be much more agreeable for us, if the British were wise
and, remembering all this, left us alone and in peace. But never will I
for a moment recede before an unjust threat. I am sorry for the mishap of the North Sea [Hull fisherman incident]. If the fleet are afraid
of night attacks, I think the use of the searchlights alone would suffice
to guard the ships from being surprised, if all the lights are turned on
the sectors outside the fleet. But the use of guns—especially in European waters—should be restricted as much as possible. My news from
London say, that the Press and mob make a noise, the Admiralty some
fuss, but that Government, Court and Society look with greatest calm
at the event as an unhappy accident, arising from to[o] great nervousness. I have sure news from Italy, that the "Terni Shipbuilding
Trust" are building 3 swift seagoing ironclads of 12 000 tons each
for a foreign unnamed Power,—probably Japan—; this reminds me
of my former suggestion, that you ought not to forget to order new
ships of the line also so as to be ready with some of them, when the
war is over. They will be excellent "persuaders" during the Peace
negociations; our private firms would be most glad to receive contracts.
I have attached Lamsdorff to your suite and person, as you kindly
did with Shebeko for me. I am deeply sensible for your kind appreciation of my action towards you and Russia, and assure, you can always
rely on my absolute and faithful loyalty. Best love to Alix.

WILLY

(b) *Emperor Nicholas II of Russia to Emperor William II*
(in English)[1]

[Tsarskoe Selo] 29. October 1904

Your telegram comes at a very serious moment. Of course you know
the first details of Northsea incident from our Admirals telegram.
Naturely it changes completely the character of the event. I have
not words to express my indignation with Englands conduct. It
seems that the continental powers in similar cases, have to confront

---

[1] *Ibid.*, No. 6119.

the danger of her public opinion overwhelming a more reasonable attitude of her Government. The latter has to follow. The Ministers of the
country take risky steps and sending shnodering notes with quite unacceptable conditions. That is the consequence of acting on the spur
of the moment! To-day I ordered Lamsdorff to send to my London
Ambassador a proposition to subject the whole question to an international commission of inquiry as laid down in the Hague-Conference-
Protocol. I agree fully with your complaints about England's behaviour
concerning the coaling of our ships by German steamers whereas she
understands rules of keeping neutrality in her own fashion. It is certainly high time to put a stop to this. The only way as you say would
be that Germany, Russia, and France should at once unite upon an
arrangement to abolish Anglo-Japanese arrogance and insolence.
Would you like to lay down and frame outlines of such a treaty and
let me know it? As soon as accepted by us France is bound to join her
ally. This combination has often come to my mind. It will mean peace
and rest for the world. Best love from Alix.

(signed) NICKY

(c) *Draft of a Letter of Emperor William II to Emperor Nicholas
of Russia (in English)*[1]

[No date]

My dear Nicky,
   Your kind telegram has given me the pleasure to feel, that I was
able in a serious moment to be of some use to you. I have at once
communicated with the Chancellor, and we both have drawn up the
3 articles of the treaty you wished. Be it as you say. Let us stand
together. Of course the alliance must be purely defensive and exclusively directed against the European aggressor or aggressors in the
form of an mutual fire insurance company against incendiarism. It is
very essential, that America should not feel threatened by our agreement. Roosevelt, as I know, owing to the innate American antipathy
against all coloured races, has no special partiality for Japan, although the English do their utmost to work upon American opinion
in favour of the Japanese. Besides the Americans have a clear perception of the indisputable fact, that a powerful Japanese Empire is a
lasting danger for the American Philippines.
   As for France, we both know that the radical or anti-christian
party, which for the moment appears to be the stronger one, inclines
towards England, Crimean tradition, but is opposed to war, because
a victorious General would mean certain destruction to this republic
of miserable civilians. The nationalist or clerical party dislikes England and has sympathies for Russia, but does not dream of throwing
in its lot with Russia in the present war. Between the two parties the
Republic will remain neutral and do nothing. The English count upon

---
[1] *Ibid.,* No. 6120, ANNEXES I AND II.

this neutrality and upon the consequent isolation of Russia. I positively know that as far back as last December the French Finance Minister Rouvier told the Finance Minister of another power, France would on no account join in a Russo-Japanese war, even though England sided with Japan. To make doubly sure, the English have handed Morocco over to France. The certainty, that France intends to remain neutral and even to lend her diplomatic support to England, is the motive, which gives English policy its present unwonted brutal assurance.

This unheard of state of things will change as soon as France finds herself face to face with the necessity of eventually choosing sides. As I said, the radical party, which gravitates towards England, abhors war and militarism, while the nationalist party while not objecting to war in itself, hates fighting for England and against Russia. Thus it will be in the interests of both parties to bring pressure to bear on and warn England to keep the peace. The main result will be, if you and I stand shoulder to shoulder, that France must formally and openly join us, thereby fulfilling her treaty-obligations towards Russia. That, I expect, will put an end to made up grievances about so called breaches of neutrality.—This consummation once reached, I expect to maintain peace and you will be left an undisturbed and free hand to deal with Japan.

Let me finally add that I sincerely admire your masterful political instinct, which caused you to refer the North-Sea-incident to your Hague tribunal. For this systematically distorted incident has been used by the French radicals, Clemenceau and all the rest of the tag-rag and bobtail, as a further argument against France fulfilling her treaty-obligations towards Russia.

I enclose the draft of an agreement that you desired.

Annex (*in French*)

Their Imperial Majesties, the Emperor of all the Russias, and the Emperor of Germany, in order to localise as much as possible the Russo-Japanese war, have agreed upon the following articles of a treaty of defensive alliance.

Article I. In case one of the two Empires is attacked by a European power, its ally will aid it with all its land and sea forces. The two allies, in that case will equally work toward the common end of re-calling to France the obligations that she assumed according to the terms of the Franco-Russian alliance.

Article II. The two high contracting parties engage not to conclude separate peace with any common adversary.

Article III. The engagement to aid one another is equally valuable in case some acts of one of the two high contracting parties during the war, such as the delivery of coal to a belligerent should be the occasion after the war of some claims made by a third power under the pretension that the rights of neutrals had been violated.

(d) *Emperor William II to Emperor Nicholas II of Russia (in English)*[1]

30. X. 1904

Best thanks for telegram. Have sent letter including draft of treaty you wished for, off by Imperial Feldjäger this evening. Heard from private source, that Hull fishermen have already acknowledged, that they have seen foreign steam craft among their boats not belonging to their fishing fleet, which they knew not! So there has been foul play! I think the British Embassy in Petersburg must know these news, which are kept from the British public till now, for fear of "blamage." Best love to Alix.

WILLY

(e) *Emperor Nicholas II of Russia to Emperor William II in his own handwriting (in English)*[2]

[No date]

My dear Willy,

Count Lamsdorff is the bearer of this letter from Suwalki. I thank You before hand for sending General v. d. Goltz and v. Moltke to greet me near our frontier. I have studied the "draft of Treaty" very carefully and have only shown it to my minister for Foreign Affairs. He and I composed this "Project" in answer to Your's, and it is written by himself. I on purpose underlined in red ink the lines which are changed or put in by us, so that it might be clearer when You read it. It seemed to me that the last article ought to be kept secret.

If You find it necessary please make the variations You think best; I only *insist* on keeping the wording of Art. I of our proposal, wh[ich] is very essential.

The day we sign this agreement a great result will be arrived at! The three countries may feel calm and confident that no one else shall dare threaten them after that.

The four officers of our squadron, sent here by Admiral Rojestvensky, have come. I saw the senior—Capt. Clado, a very able officer; he was on the bridge of the flagship "Suvoroff" that night and, like all around him, saw perfectly well two long torpedoboats coming rapidly towards them.

If we could only find out where they came from and where they are gone? One plausible suggestion about their possible place of shelter— that is a lonely Norwegian fiord! In any case my country firmly believes that there has been foul play and that the truth must come out sooner or later.

---

[1] *Ibid.*, No. 6121.
[2] *Ibid.*, No. 6124.

Alix sends You her fondest love.

Believe me dearest Willy ever Your devoted cousin and friend.

NICKY

ANNEX (in French)

Their Majesties, the Emperor of Germany and the Emperor of all the Russias, in order to localise as much as possible the Russo-Japanese war, have agreed upon the following articles of a treaty of defensive alliance.

Article I. In case one of the two Empires is attack by a European Power, its ally will aid it with all its land and sea forces. *His Majesty the Emperor of all the Russias will make the necessary overtures toward initiation France into this accord and of engaging her to associate as an ally.*

Article II. The high contracting parties engage not to conclude peace separately with any common adversary.

Article III (secret?) The high contracting parties agree to make common cause in case some acts on the part of one of them during the war, such as the delivery of coal to a belligerent should be the occasion after the war of some claims made by a third power under the pretension that the rights of neutrals had been violated.—*Their entente cordiale will be equally in force in the presence of possible difficulties during the period of the negotiation of the peace between Russia and Japan.*

(f) *Emperor Nicholas II of Russia to Emperor William II Telegram (transcript in Emperor William's hand, in English)*[1]

Tsarskoe Selo, 23. XI. 1904

Before signing the last draft of Treaty I think it advisable to let the French see it. As long as it is not signed one can make small modifications in the text; whereas if allready approved by us both, it will seem as if we tried to enforce the treaty on France. In this case a failure might easily happen, which I think is neither your wish. Therefore I ask your agreement to acquaint the Government of France with this project, and upon getting their answer I shall at once let You know by telegraph.

(g) *Draft of a Telegram from Emperor William II to Emperor Nicholas II of Russia*[2]

[no date]

Many thanks for your telegram. That you will not speak to France without my agreement is a new testimony of your perfect loyalty. That the French should be informed before an agreement has been concluded

---

[1] *Ibid.,* No. 6126, Annex.

[2] *Ibid.,* No. 6127, Annex (in German).

between You and me seems to me to be absolutely dangerous. According to my understanding, a premature approach to France would produce the opposite effect from that which we want. If France knows for a certainty that Russia and Germany are bound by treaty to support each other it will have the effect of urging England in the direction of peace in order not to get into an uncomfortable position. If France knows, however, that the German-Russian treaty is projected but not concluded, the French Government would be tempted, as long as there remains time, to give the English a tip. It is not impossible that the latter will then, as a prophylactic measure, together with Japan, attack me all along the line in Asia and Europe. Germany would then be temporarily crippled in the face of the naval superiority of the other two, and thereby the equilibrium of the World would be destroyed to my disadvantage and also to yours; and after the conclusion of peace, Japan and its friends would have quite the upper hand. My wish was and still is to maintain the equilibrium through agreement between Germany, Russia and France in the interests of peace. But I believe it to be possible only if we first come to an agreement in some form or other and make our treaty an actuality. To inform France beforehand could lead to a catastrophe. If, however, you find that you cannot conclude a treaty without the previous consent of France, then the less dangerous alternative for us both would be not to make a treaty. Naturally I shall keep the secret regarding our conversations as conscientiously as you. Just as you have let only Lamsdorff into the secret, so I have spoken only to Bülow about it and have taken pains to preserve absolute secrecy. Our attitude toward each other remains in any case as of old. I shall continue to try to be of service to you in so far as I can within the limits of my own security. The Emperor Franz Joseph communicated to me your neutrality agreement.[1] It is quite all right with me.

(h) *Emperor William II to Emperor Nicholas II of Russia*[2]

7 December, 1904

The British Government, as you will have seen in the English Press, seems to think the moment opportune for an action against the providing of your Baltic Fleet with coal.

Under pretext of its duty to maintain strictest neutrality it has forbidden the German vessels belonging to the Hamburg-American-Line to leave British ports.

Consequently my fears that this would happen—formerly written to you ——, have come true, and it is now incumbent upon me to take steps to fix the attitude, Germany has to take up vis-à-vis of this action. It is not my intention to hurry you in your answer to my last remarks about your proposal as to our defensive treaty. But you will,

---

[1] See Pribram, *op. cit.*, Vol. I, pp. 236-239.
[2] *Ibid.*, No. 6130 (in English).

I am sure, be fully alive to the fact, that I must now have absolutely positive guarantees from you, whether you intend leaving me unaided or not in case of a war, which England and Japan would declare against me on account of the coaling of the Russian Fleet by Germany.

Should you be unable to absolutely guarantee me, that in such a war you will fight loyally with me shoulder to shoulder, then I regret to be under the necessity of immediately forbidding German steamers continuing to coal your fleet.

Alvensleben is under orders to elucidate the coaling situation at once with Lamsdorff.

(signed) WILLY

(i) *Emperor Nicholas II of Russia to Emperor William II* [1]

Tsarskoe Selo, Nov. 24/Dec. 7, 1904

Dearest Willy,

First of all I beg Your pardon for not answering You at once, but I really had so much to do this week, that I could not find a free moment to sit down and write to You. Since I got Your telegram with Your opinion upon the possible consequences of letting France know about our treaty before it is signed, I have turned over the question often in my head. After long deliberations with Lamsdorff I have come to the conclusion of submitting to Your kind approval the following idea.

Finding it impossible not to warn our ally about a step, which we are intending to make and if she consents—with her together, we propose to acquaint France, I mean the President and Delcassé, with the reasons and *general ideas* of the future arrangement between the three countries. I send You this Notice as an example of the communication, that Nelidoff would be ordered to make, if You approved such a plan. As You can see, we do not want to let France know all the details and the wording of our "draft," but merely the main lines of the proposed agreement.

A few days ago I saw M. Bompard, the French ambassador here, who just came back from Paris. He told me that his government had been rather nervous these last months on account of different rumours: that people in Russia were dissatisfied with France's conduct during our war with Japan, that she was afraid of England and therefore kept too strict rules of neutrality, that I was no more sure of the government and did not believe in the stability of the dual alliance etc. etc. All this made me a rather good impression, because it proved to me how eager the French are "d'être en bonne grâce aux yeux de leurs alliées," which is exceedingly serious and necessary at the present moment before the whole world.

I must add, that France has never hidden from us *till* now the meaning of her flirtation across the Channel and of the "entente cor-

---

[1] *Ibid.*, No. 6131 (in English).

diale," which resulted therefrom. I have written all this to You, dear Willy, in full frankness, that You may be able to judge my point of view. Once more I beg You to answer me, whether you deem it possible for me, to let France know about the coming arrangement *so as it is shaped* in the Notice? In case of a negative answer—the second phrase of Art. I of the draft of treaty ought to be left out I think. . . .

NICKY

ANNEX (in French)

Notice

regarding some very confidential communications which might be made to the French Government.

The malevolent and even arrogant attitude that the British Government, dominated by a misled press and public opinion, believes possible to adopt more and more frequently with regard to the other Powers has inspired *us*, Emperor William and myself, with the belief that the peace of Europe can be troubled at any moment by any incident whatever relating to the question of contraband, of the rights of neutrals, or any other which English presumption may unfortunately cause to develop into a conflict. In order to avoid this danger, *we* would judge useful the conclusion of an *exclusively defensive* arrangement which would assure reciprocally to the two neighboring Empires forceful support—(the coöperation of the land and sea forces)—of the one if the other should be attacked by a third European Power—an agreement of this nature, the details of which would have to be fixed, would seem able to serve as an effective check, useful if not unique, for a Power which believes itself to be sheltered from all dangers even though it abuses the rights of others and does not consider itself obligated in any respect toward them. *We* have not wished, however, to effect this proposal without having previously initiated France in this combination, and having proposed to associate her in it.

This three-sided accord, the immense value of which would be particularly noticeable in the present circumstances, would create a political situation which would evidently not be unfavourable to France; it would be able to serve at the same time in the direction of the consolidation of the peace which Russia and her Ally are attempting to maintain in Europe in their own interest as well as in that of entire humanity.

The obligation of absolute secrecy is apparent.

(j) *Emperor William II to Emperor Nicholas II of Russia*[1]

(Telegram, in his own handwriting, without date or signature)

Your letter of the 7th., for which best thanks, has just crossed mine of same date. We must now however *before all* come to a permanent

---

[1] *Ibid.*, No. 6132.

agreement about coaling question. This question becomes *daily* more and more *urgent*. Today again serious news has reached me from Pt. Said and Cape Town; there is now no time to be lost any more. No third Power must hear even a whisper about our intentions, before we have concluded the convention about the coaling business, the consequences otherwise would be most dangerous; I of course place full reliance in Your loyalty.

(k) *Emperor Nicholas II of Russia to Emperor William II*[1]

Telegram. (*Copy, without date, in English*)   [Dec. 11, 1904]

Hearty thanks for your letter. Fully agree, that both our Governments *must now come* to a permanent understandi[n]g upon coaling question. Lamsdorff was to see Alvensleben this morning.

You may *fully rely* on my loyalty and on my wish to arrive at a speedy settlement of this serious question.

NICKY

(l) *Emperor William II to Emperor Nicholas II of Russia*[2]

(*Undated draft*) (*in English*)

Dearest Nicky,

I thank you for your letter and two telegrams, and also for ordering the coaling question to be regulated. We cannot to-day foresee, whether the declaration given by your Government will prove sufficient for every kind of complication, which may arise out of the present train of affairs. It is, however, not my intention, to press any sort of solution, which might appear undesirable to you. True and loyal friends we shall remain under all circumstances.

We cannot take France into our confidence, before we two have come to a definite arrangement. I look upon Loubet and Delcassé as statesmen of experience. But naturally I cannot place them on the same footing with you in a question of confidence. If therefore you think it imperative eventually to acquaint the French with our negotiations, before we have arrived at a settlement, then it is better for all parties, to continue in our present condition of mutual independence, and spontaneously to promote each others ends as far as the situation will permit. I trust that the hope of our being useful to each other may be realized not only during the war, but also during the peace-negotiations, for our interests in the far East are identical in more than one respect.

---

[1] *Ibid.*, No. 6133.
[2] *Ibid.*, No. 6141.

(m) *Final Text of the Björkö Treaty*[1]

Björkö 24/VII 1905 11/VII

Their Majesties the Emperors of all the Russias and of Germany, in order to assure the maintenance of peace in Europe have agreed upon the following articles of a Treaty of defensive alliance:

Article I. In case one of the two Empires is attacked by an European Power, its ally will aid it in Europe with all its land and sea forces.

Article II. The High Contracting Parties engage not to conclude separate peace with any common adversary.

Article III. The present treaty will be in force from the moment of the conclusion of peace between Russia and Japan, and may be denounced only by giving a year's previous notice.

Article IV. After this treaty has become effective, the Emperor of all the Russias will take the necessary steps to make its terms known to France and invite her to subscribe to it as an ally.

WILLIAM I. R.   NICOLAS
VON TSCHIRSCHKY and   A. BIRILEFF
BÖGENDORFF

(n) *Emperor Nicholas II of Russia to Emperor William II*[2]

(*In his own handwriting in English*)

Nov. 10/23, 1905

Six weeks have passed since I wrote to You last and many events have happened in this short space of time.

But first of all I must come back to the question of our Björkoe treaty. You remember that when it was signed, the war with Japan was continuing and it seemed that there would be ample time to prepare France to participate. Events of the last weeks have shown that there is not much chance of winning her over to our treaty "à trois" at least for the present.

Russia has no reasons to abandon her old ally suddenly nor to violate her.

Our influence must be cautious and persevering to become fruitful and certainly must take some time.

But a very serious difficulty would arise if France refused to join in our understanding. In that case Germany and Russia would remain alone and if the *secret* of Björkoe were to transpire, I am positively sure, a strong coalition will form itself against us two (Crimean al-

---

[1] *Ibid.*, Vol. XIX, Pt. 2, p. 465. (In the Kaiser's handwriting in French.) No. 6220, Annex.

[2] *Ibid.*, No. 6254.

liances etc.). [Kaiser's marginal note: "This has long been in existence. The 'Entente Cordiale' is certainly nothing else!"]

Nevertheless, as You rightly said, what is signed—is signed. The same loyalty imposes upon me to fulfil what was signed by my Father & cannot be struck off by a stroke of a pen.

Therefore in order to be able to fulfil just as *loyally* the clauses of the new treaty with Germany, Russia finds it necessary to complete the Björkoe understanding by the Declaration annexed.

This makes the whole affair clear [Kaiser's note: "Yes, very"] and I feel sure You will approve of my not wishing to change anything in our agreement itself.

May I mention a subject which does not concern me straightly. When Ct. Witte came back from Germany he told me that he had spoken to You of the Morocco question. Rouvier & Radolin were of the same opinion about the coming Conference. I have heard lately that Your minister at Tanger does not look calmly at things down there, with the same broadmindedness as does his Government & that of France.

I think it would not be quite the moment that complications [Kaiser's note: "Stamboul? Mazedonien? Flottendemonstrationen?"] were to happen anywhere in Europe or near it. Excuse me, but I find it my duty to warn You as a true friend ought to. Perhaps You will order Tattenbach to cool down.

England is trying hard to get us round for an understanding about Asiatic frontier questions and this directly after the renewed A[n]glo-Japanese alliance!

I [Kaiser's note: "Lamsdorff has allready?"] have not the slightest wish to open negociations with her & so it will drop of itself.

You know well enough the phases of our internal affairs. I thank You again for having sent four of Your torpedoboats with post despatches from Memel, this was of a very great use.

Now the railways are again working & the strikes are over for how long though?

It is a humiliating feeling not to be able to stop strikes which are a curse & a real danger to the whole country. Nearly $\frac{3}{4}$ of the army & all railway-troops are in Manchuria therefore it is difficult to cope with this movement at the present moment. I rely strongly upon Witte, but curiously enough his energy is not what I expected it would be. It is true a great number of russians are far from being his admirers and yet all understand there is *no one* but him to stand in his place.

I have often to egg Witte on, when he has to decide upon this or that measure.

This letter has become too long for me to dwell upon this subject, I will take it up in the next one. Alix and I send You our best love.

Believe me dearest Willy ever Your most loving & devoted cousin & friend & ally

NICKY

DECLARATION (in French)

In view of the difficulties which obstruct an immediate adhesion of the French Government to the treaty of defensive alliance signed at Björkoe the 11/24 July 1905—the adhesion envisaged in Article IV of said treaty—it is expressly understood that Article I of this treaty will not be able to have any application in the event of a war with France; and that the mutual engagements which unite France and Russia will be fully maintained until the extablishment of an accord "à trois."

Peterhof, the . . . October 1905.

(o) *Emperor William II to Emperor Nicholas II of Russia*[1]

(Draft in his own handwriting in English)

Telegram   26/XI, 1905

Thanks for letter. Shall reply after hearing Chancellor. Your information about Tattenbach incorrect. He has acted "en concert" with his French Colleague the whole time, & they both left Fez a while ago. I quite agree that complications should be avoided in or near Europe. There is no fear of any arising in or about Morocco. Macedonia & the Balkans are much more dangerous; & the Naval Demonstration against Turkey in this moment may lead to most unexpected consequences, should the "amour propre" of the Islamitic world resent the pressure brought to bear upon their master. The work of the "Crimean Combine" is recognisable here!

WILLY

(p) *Emperor William II to Emperor Nicholas II of Russia*[2]

(Unsigned draft, in English)

Neues Palais, 28 XI 1905

Dearest Nicky,

The Chancellor, to whom I read some parts of your letter, told me that our purely defensive agreement cannot possibly clash with the French treaty concluded by your father. For if it did the meaning would be that by the French treaty Russia is bound to support France even in a war of *aggression* against Germany! But such a contingency, i.e. Russia supporting France in an aggressive policy against us, we never till now looked upon as deserving even moments consideration, because your dear Father often told me he would at all times set his

---

[1] *Ibid.*, No. 6256.
[2] *Ibid.*, No. 6257.

face openly against any war of aggression, besides being in most friendly and intimate terms with me. This is illustrated by the fact that in 1891, at the manoeuvres near Narva, he openly expressed his aversion against the French Republican system, advocating a restoration of Monarchy in Paris for which undertaking he begged me to help him. If the French agreement is like ours, purely defensive, then there is no incompatibility between the two, and one does not exclude the other, so that no further declaration is required.

On the other hand I can understand that it may be opportune for you, not to proclaim yourself publicly as my ally, at the moment, when the international revolutionists are spreading the infamous lie of my having tried to influence you in favour of reaction. My fervent wish is that you may pass unharmed through the present crisis and that your people may fully grasp our noble intentions. Now you must wait and see how the institutions you called into life, work practically; only after this it will be possible to judge whether and how modifications would be required.

As for your opinion of Witte, I cannot of course pretend to know him as well as you do, but he certainly impressed me as a man much above the average. At the same time I am glad that you took your uncle Nicholas Nicholaiewitch into your confidence. He appears to me as representing an additional element of firmness, and firmness may be necessary to maintain order. Without order young liberty cannot live.

With regard to Tattenbach and Morocco your French information is not correct. I do not aim nor ever aimed at any special advantage for Germany, and Tattenbach never advocated a policy of his own. This is a thing unheard of in my service; my representatives in foreign countries only advocating one policy and that is mine! Germany only wishes to secure the Open Door, that is an interest we have in common with all the other sea faring and trading nations. There is no reason whatever why an equitable arrangement with France should not be arrived at on that ground; I trust that you whose permanent aim is to promote peace between all nations and good will all over the civilized world will lend your powerful help to bring the Conference to a general understanding, based on the maintenance of the Open Door. A word to your representative at the Conference in this direction would be most advantageous in lightening the task of my Minister.

(q) *Emperor Nicholas II of Russia to Emperor William II*[1]

Telegram (in English)

Tsarskoe Selo, 2 December 1905

Best thanks for your kind letter that gave me great pleasure. Our alliance with France is a defensive one. I think the declaration I sent

---

[1] *Ibid.*, No. 6258.

you could remain in force until France accept our new agreement. I will certainly do all in my power to bring the Morocco conference to a general understanding.

31. THE KAISER'S LANDING AT TANGIER, 1905[1]

[The German Foreign Office was disquieted by the Anglo-French agreement over Morocco of 1904, and rightly felt that two countries by secret agreement could not deprive third Powers of their rights in Morocco. They feared France would "Tunisify" Morocco by "peaceful penetration." Holstein said (June 3, 1904): "If we let our toes be trodden upon in Morocco without saying a word, we encourage others to do the same thing elsewhere." Kühlmann, the German *chargé d'affaires* in Tangier, secretly encouraged the Sultan of Morocco to resist the French program of police measures to curb the anarchy there. At this juncture in affairs, Bülow suddenly decided to have the Kaiser stop at Tangier on his trip to Corfu and greet the Sultan. He prevailed upon the Kaiser to do this by having a dispatch from Tangier printed in a German newspaper announcing his Majesty's intention, and then shrewdly pointing out that if the visit were abandoned it would appear to be at the insistence of the French. In his speech to the Sultan's uncle and plenipotentiary, the Kaiser said that his visit was to safeguard German interests in Morocco, and that, considering the Sultan as absolutely free, he wished to discuss the means of securing these interests; the reforms contemplated should consider the religious sentiments of the people, so that public order would not be troubled.]

As far as the Mediterranean trip is concerned, the proposed visit to Tangier was no longer a secret. It was often openly discussed, and more or less plainly spoken of as a serious warning to France, on account of the high hand she was taking in Morocco. It was also whispered that the Kaiser had only reluctantly agreed to such an unusual demonstration. As a matter of fact, I noticed in the course of the voyage that he was not looking forward to the Tangier adventure without some misgiving. He told me himself that he had not intended to let the trip assume the character of an important political demonstration; he had only wanted to give his numerous guests a passing glimpse of genuine Mussulman life, and thought of remaining on board himself at Tangier, as the East was not new to him. But the Chancellor, presumably influenced by Herr von Holstein, had so firmly insisted on the political side of the visit being accentuated, that, true to the constitutional principle, he had finally given way.

In addition to his doubts as to the political wisdom of the undertaking, the Kaiser was very much concerned because he had been told

---

[1] Schoen, *Memoirs of an Ambassador*. London, George Allen & Unwin, Ltd., 1922, pp. 19-23. Reprinted with the permission of George Allen & Unwin, Ltd.

in Lisbon that the streets were too narrow to drive through, and that he was consequently expected to ride a horse to which he was not accustomed from the harbour to the Legation on the far side of the town. He had also heard that in case of a fresh wind blowing from the east it might be difficult, if not impossible, to land, for lack of a sheltered harbour. Now and then the Kaiser seemed inclined to back out of the promise he had given the Chancellor, on the ground that he had not known of these difficulties beforehand. His vacillation placed me in rather an awkward position: on the one hand I was personally convinced of the political and other objections to the undertaking, and on the other it was not only my duty, as the representative of the Foreign Office, not to allow the Kaiser to waver, but special stress had been laid on the duty. It was made easier for me by the presence of Count Tattenbach, the Minister in Lisbon, who had been in Morocco before going there, and had fought diplomatic battles against French presumption. He was a firm advocate of the Tangier adventure, and was accompanying the Kaiser to Morocco both as being familiar with the matter in hand and with the place. For my part I thought it best to leave the God Aeolus to decide whether he would favour the enterprise or not.

When we arrived at the Tangier roadstead, sure enough a stiff east wind was blowing, so that landing in boats was out of the question. The Kaiser decided to wait for better weather, or to go to Gibraltar, if necessary, and come back from there. In the meantime the chargé d'affaires, Kühlmann, succeeded in reaching the *Hamburg* in a sailing boat with the pilot, and getting on board by means of the rope-ladder —the sea was too rough for the steps to be used—covered with spray, and in the full uniform of the Bamberg Uhlans. The senior Captain of the French cruisers anchored in the roadstead also arrived on board to pay his respects to the Kaiser, who drew him into a long conversation about the weather. When the wind had fallen a little, General von Scholl, an aide-de-camp, was told to try to land and find out for certain whether there was any possibility of getting to the Legation. When the General returned and reported that there was no great difficulty in landing, if one did not mind getting wet, that the horse provided for the Kaiser was excellent, and that in the town all the world was awaiting the Kaiser in feverish excitement, the landing was decided on and accomplished without any trouble.

According to the papers the Kaiser made speeches to the Sultan's aged uncle, and the representatives of the German colony who received His Majesty on shore, in which special stress was laid on the Sultan's independence and equality of right. The truth is that the Kaiser did not make any formal speeches, he merely replied to the addresses of welcome in a conversational strain, although indeed the purport of what he said was as stated.

We were within an ace of being prevented from carrying out the remainder of the programme, by the white Arab horse the Kaiser was to ride becoming restive at the unaccustomed sight of the helmet, and refusing to let him mount. The animal was reduced to obedience, however, and, followed by an escort of about twenty persons, all on horseback, the Kaiser rode into the town, where the narrow streets, filled with jubilantly noisy crowds, only allowed of a slow progress.

The flat roofs of all the houses were also packed with Moorish, Christian, and Jewish women, who hailed the Kaiser in a variety of keys, and scattered flowers. At last the cortège reached the Soko, the open space in front of the Legation garden. It was a seething mass of people, who displayed their enthusiasm by rending the air with deafening shouts, and shooting wildly in every direction. A military band sent by the Sultan, which vainly tried to drown the uproar made by the people, added to the confusion. The horse became so restive that I asked a French officer who seemed to be in command, whether he could not put a stop to the firing. He replied gloomily that he had some influence over the handful of regular troops which had been entrusted to him for training, but none whatever over the half savage Kabyles.

The Kaiser had an exhaustive conversation in the Legation with the Sultan's uncle, when he again promised to support the Sultan's claim to independence, and received other Moorish guests, as well as the Ministers of foreign countries. I now approached the Kaiser, pointing out that a historical event of an importance which could not yet be estimated had taken place, and urged his ordering a return to the ship. I was afraid that the longer the tension lasted, the more easily the excitement of the populace might lead to unpleasant incidents, and I also feared that, if the wind got up again, we might not be able to embark, and that the Kaiser would be detained in a Moorish town which was not controlled by any strong authority. Fortunately we managed to get on board without any misadventure. It was only some days later, when the Kaiser first heard in Naples of the tremendous sensation his visit to Tangier had made in the world, that he seemed to become fully aware of its great political importance. Although he did not say so, my impression was that he looked back on the event with a feeling that it would have been better to have adhered to his original opposition to it.

32. ALGECIRAS CONFERENCE, 1906

(a) *Roosevelt's account*[1]

[We possess an account of what Roosevelt said he did to arrange the Algeciras Conference of 1906, dictating the terms by which in his opinion war between France and Germany was averted. In a letter to Whitelaw Reid, then Ambassador in London, Roosevelt gave his own

---

[1] Joseph Bucklin Bishop, *Theodore Roosevelt and His Time, Shown in His Own Letters*, Vol. I, pp. 477-500 (*passim*). New York, Scribners, 1920. Reprinted with the permission of Charles Scribner's Sons.

narrative in full. His efforts as peacemaker, of which nothing was known at the time, were undertaken in response to the earnest and repeated appeals of the Kaiser. Though Germany won in principle at the Algeciras Conference, France won in practical results. The ultimate significance of the Morocco crisis of 1905-06 is that the bonds of the Entente were strengthened. The memorandum of Edward Grey, Secretary of State for Foreign Affairs, shows the effects of Germany's action upon British relations with France.]

It really did look as if there might be a war, and I felt in honor bound to try to prevent the war if I could, in the first place, because I should have felt such a war to be a real calamity to civilization; and in the next place as I was already trying to bring about peace between Russia and Japan, I felt that a new conflict might result in what would literally be a world-conflagration; and finally, for the sake of France. Accordingly, I took active hold of the matter with both Speck and Jusserand, and after a series of communications with the French Government, through Jusserand, got things temporarily straightened up. Jusserand repeated to his government substantially just what I said. I told him that as chief of state I could not let America do anything quixotic, but that I had a real sentiment for France; that I would not advise her to do anything humiliating or disgraceful; but that it was eminently wise to avoid a war if it could be done by adopting a course which would save the Emperor's self-esteem; that for such purpose it was wise to help him save his face. I urged upon the French Government, in the first place, the great danger of war to them, and the fact that British assistance could avail them very, very little in the event of such a war, because France would be in danger of invasion by land; and in the next place, I pointed out that if there were a conference of the Powers France would have every reason to believe that the conference would not sanction any unjust attack by Germany upon French interests, and that if all the Powers, or practically all the Powers, in the conference took an attitude favorable to France on such a point it would make it well-nigh impossible for Germany to assail her. I explained that I would not accept the invitation of the conference unless France was willing, and that if I went in I would treat both sides with absolute justice, and would, if necessary, take very strong grounds against any attitude of Germany which seemed to me unjust and unfair.

At last, the French Government informed me through Jusserand that it would agree to the conference.

*   *   *   *   *   *

There was, however, much higgling as to exactly what should be discussed at the conference; and both Jusserand and Speck came to me to say they were still on the verge of seeing the negotiations broken off. Finally I made a pencil memorandum as follows: "The two Governments consent to go to the conference with no program, and to discuss there all questions in regard to Morocco, save of course where either is in honor bound by a previous agreement with another power." I gave a copy of this memorandum to Jusserand and the memorandum itself to Speck, and after they had transmitted it to their respective governments, I received the assent of both governments to the proposition. I explained to both that I did not care to appear in the matter, and that no publicity whatever would be given by me or by any of our representatives to what I had done, and I thought it far better that it should take the shape of an agreement freely entered into by themselves. You may remember that not a hint of any kind got out throughout the whole of last summer as to my taking any part in this Morocco business.

.   .   .   .

Elihu Root to Baron Speck von Sternburg

No. 342   (L)   March 7, 1906

Excellency:

May I ask you to transmit to the German Emperor a message from the President which is as follows:

"I have given most earnest thought to Your Majesty's comments on the suggestion contained in Mr. Root's letter of February 19th, but I cannot bring myself to feel that I ought to ask France to make further concessions than the arrangement suggested in that letter would require. This being so, I would gladly drop the subject, in which our traditional policy of abstention from the political affairs of Europe forbids the United States to take sides. I feel, however, that the events which led to the Conference at Algeciras forbid me to omit any effort within my power to promote a settlement of differences.

"By the request of Germany I urged France to consent to the Conference, giving her very strong assurances of my belief that a decision would be reached, consonant with an impartial view of what is most fair and most practical. The nature, the strength and the justification of these assurances may be realized by referring to the terms of Baron Sternburg's letter to me of June 28, 1905, which said:

" 'The Emperor has requested me to tell you that in case, during the coming Conference, differences of opinion should arise between France and Germany, he, in every case, will be ready to back up the decision which you should consider to be the most fair and the most practical.

" 'In doing this, he wants to prove that the assistance which you have rendered to Germany has been rendered in the interest of peace alone, and without any selfish motives.'

"Under these circumstances, I feel bound to state to Your Majesty that I think the arrangement indicated in the above mentioned letter of February 19th is a reasonable one, and most earnestly to urge Your Majesty to accept it. I do not know whether France would accept it or not. I think she ought to do so. I do not think that she ought to be expected to go further. If that arrangement is made, the Conference will have resulted in an abandonment by France of her claim to the right of control in Morocco answerable only to the two Powers with whom she had made treaties and without responsibility to the rest of the world, and she will have accepted jointly with Spain a mandate from all the Powers, under responsibility to all of them for the maintenance of equal rights and opportunities. And the due observance of these obligations will be safeguarded by having vested in another representative of all the Powers a right to have in their behalf full and complete reports of the performance of the trust, with the further right of verification and inspection.

"I feel that if this arrangement be made, Germany will have accomplished the declared object for her intervention in the affairs of Morocco and for the Conference. I feel such arrangement would be in very fact the evidence of the triumph of German diplomacy in this matter. Looking at the subject as I do, from this standpoint of an observer friendly to both parties and having no possible interest in the result, except the interest of peace, I see grave reasons to apprehend that if the Conference should fail because of Germany's insisting upon pressing France beyond the measure of concession described in this proposed arrangement, the general opinion of Europe and America would be unfavorable, and Germany would lose that increase of credit and moral power that the making of this arrangement would secure to her, and might be held responsible, probably far beyond the limits of reason, for all the evils that may come in the train of a disturbed condition of affairs in Europe.

"As a rule, parties to a past controversy, looking back, can see that they have ascribed undue importance to matters of difference which were really unimportant. A disinterested spectator is often able to take such a view at the time. I believe that I am taking such a view; that if the suggested arrangement can be made none of the matters which Germany will not have secured by that are of any real importance to her, and I most sincerely hope that Your Majesty may take this view and throw upon France the responsibility for rejecting, if it is to be rejected, the suggested arrangement."

Accept, Excellency, the renewed assurances of my highest consideration.

ELIHU ROOT

.   .   .   .

Hotel Cambridge,
New York, March 19, 1906
Dear Mr. President:

I have the honor to inform you of the contents of a telegram, just received, which is the answer to my telegram, forwarded after the conversation I had with you on the situation at Algeciras:

Sincere regret is expressed that the attitude of Germany should have led to certain misunderstandings. The Kaiser had suggested the Conference so as to find a peaceful way to solve the question of Morocco.

He appreciates the fundamental idea of your proposal: coöperation of French and Spanish officers to be about equally divided in each of the ports.

He would readily join in any proposal at the Conference which would contain this mixed system and an inspector general to which France already has agreed in principle.

Germany abstains from entering into details, so as to prevent that these should obscure the main points. The telegram concludes in saying that the immediate removal of all misunderstandings is far more important to Germany than the whole Morocco affair.

Believe me, Mr. President, most

Sincerely yours,
STERNBURG

(b) *Terms on which France and Germany agreed to come to a Conference over the Moroccan Question*[1]

Prince Radolin, German Ambassador at Paris to M. Rouvier, President of the Council, and Minister of Foreign Affairs

Paris, July 8, 1905

The Government of the Republic, having agreed to be present at the conference proposed by the Sultan of Morocco, the Imperial Government has charged me to confirm to you its verbal declarations by the terms of which it will not pursue at the conference any end which would compromise the legitimate interests of France in Morocco; or which would be contrary to the rights of France resulting from her treaties or arrangements and in harmony with the following principles:

The sovereignty and independence of the Sultan;

The integrity of his empire;

Economic liberty, without any inequality;

Usefulness of police reforms and of financial reforms, the introduction of which shall be regulated for a short period by means of international agreement;

Recognition of the situation of France in Morocco resulting from the contiguity, over an extended area, of Algeria and the sherifian empire, and by the particular relations resulting therefrom between the two adjacent countries, as well as by the special interest which would ensue for France that order should reign in the sherifian empire.

This exchange of letters was followed by the following declaration:

The government of the republic and the German government agree:

---

[1] France. Ministère des affaires étrangères. *Documents diplomatiques: Affaires du Maroc, 1901-1905*, pp. 251-252; 306-307.

1. To recall to Tangier simultaneously their missions at present at Fez, as soon as the conference shall have convened;

2. To advise the Sultan of Morocco through their representatives by a common agreement, with a view to the determination of the program which he will propose at the conference, on the lines indicated in the letters exchanged under the date of July 8, 1905, between the President of the Council, Minister of Foreign Affairs, and the German ambassador in Paris. . . .

Agreement signed Sept. 28, 1905, by M. Rouvier, President of the Council, Minister of Foreign Affairs, and His Most Serene Highness, Prince Radolin, German ambassador at Paris.

The two governments have agreed to propose to the Sultan the following outline of a program elaborated in conformity with the principles adopted in the exchange of letters of July 8:

I. Organization, by means of international agreement, of the police beyond the frontier region;

Regulation organizing the surveillance and repression of contraband of arms.—In the frontier region, the application of this regulation will remain the exclusive concern of France and of Morocco.

II. Financial reform.

Financial coöperation given to the Maghzen by the creation of a state bank with the privilege of issue, being charged with the operations of the treasury and acting as a medium for the stamping of money of which the advantages will accrue to the Maghzen.

The state bank will proceed to reform the monetary situation.

The credits open to the Maghzen are to be used for equipping and paying the police troops and for certain urgent public works, notably for the improvement of the ports and their facilities.

III. The study of a better return from taxes and the creation of new revenues.

IV. Agreement by the Maghzen not to alienate any of the public services to the profit of particular interests.

The principle of award, without regard to nationality, for public works.

Done at Paris, Sept. 28, 1905.

signed: ROUVIER
RADOLIN

(c) *Memorandum by Sir Edward Grey*[1]

Private   February 20, 1906

The German Ambassador asked to see me yesterday for the purpose of telling me that his Government had met the last proposal of the French about police in Morocco with a point blank refusal.

---

[1] *British Documents on the Origins of the War, 1898-1914,* Vol. III, p. 266ff.

If the Conference breaks up without result the situation will be very dangerous. Germany will endeavour to establish her influence in Morocco at the expense of France. France to counteract this or even simply to protect herself and a neighbour from the state of disturbance, which is now chronic in Morocco, will be driven to take action in Morocco, which Germany may make a *casus belli*.

If there is war between France and Germany it will be very difficult to keep out of it. The *Entente* and still more the constant and emphatic demonstrations of affection (official, naval, political, commercial, Municipal and in the Press), have created in France a belief that we should support her in war. The last report from our naval attaché at Toulon said that all the French officers took this for granted, if the war was between France and Germany about Morocco. If this expectation is disappointed the French will never forgive us.

There would also I think be a general feeling in every country that we had behaved meanly and left France in the lurch. The United States would despise us, Russia would not think it worth while to make a friendly arrangement with us about Asia, Japan would prepare to reinsure herself elsewhere, we should be left without a friend and without the power of making a friend and Germany would take some pleasure, after what has passed, in exploiting the whole situation to our disadvantage, very likely by stirring up trouble through the Sultan of Turkey in Egypt. As a minor matter the position of any Foreign Secretary here, who had made it an object to maintain the *entente* with France, would become intolerable.

On the other hand the prospect of a European War and of our being involved in it is horrible.

I propose, therefore, if unpleasant symptoms develop after the Conference is over, to tell the French Ambassador that a great effort and if need be some sacrifice should in our opinion be made to avoid war. To do this we should have to find out what compensation Germany would ask or accept as a price of her recognition of the French claims in Morocco. There is also a point about Egypt, which might be worked in our behalf. I should myself be in favour of allowing Germany a port or coaling station, if that would ensure peace; but it would be necessary to consult the Admiralty about this, and to find out whether the French would entertain the idea, and if so what port?

The real objection to the course proposed is that the French may think it pusillanimous and a poor result of the *Entente*. I should have to risk this. I hope the French would recognize that in a war with Germany our liabilities would be much less than theirs. We should risk little or nothing on land, and at sea we might shut the German fleet up in Kiel and keep it there without losing a ship or a man or even firing a shot. The French would have a life and death struggle and that expenditure of blood and treasure with a doubtful issue. They ought therefore not to think it pusillanimous on our part to wish to avoid a war in which our danger was so much less than theirs.

I have also a further point in view. The door is being kept open by us for a *rapprochement* with Russia; there is at least a prospect that when Russia is re-established we shall find ourselves on good terms with her. An *entente* between Russia, France and ourselves would be absolutely secure. If it is necessary to check Germany it could then be done. The present is the most unfavourable moment for attempting to check her. Is it not a grave mistake, if there must be a quarrel with Germany for France or ourselves to let Germany choose the moment, which best suits her.

There is a possibility that war may come before these suggestions of mine can be developed in diplomacy. If so it will only be because Germany has made up her mind that she wants war and intends to have it anyhow, which I do not believe is the case. But I think we ought in our own minds to face the question now, whether we can keep out of war, if war breaks out between France and Germany. The more I review the situation the more it appears to me that we cannot without losing our good name and our friends and wrecking our policy and position in the world.

Notes by Sir C. Hardinge

If France takes action in Morocco to protect herself which Germany might resent it is not certain that Germany would declare war and attack France in Europe since such action would at once present a "casus fœderis" and bring Russia into line with France. If however it is understood by Germany that England is absolutely "solidaire" with France as far as the Moroccan question is concerned, without any limitations as to whether action by France in Morocco is aggressive or not, such knowledge would almost certainly deter Germany from provoking a conflict by which Germany must lose her whole foreign trade.

If France is left in the lurch an agreement or alliance between France, Germany and Russia in the near future is certain. This has been twice proposed during the last six years and is the Kaiser's ideal, France and Russia becoming satellites within the German system. There are many politicians in Russia in favour of such a scheme amongst them being Count Witte. These are in favour of the French alliance for purely economic reasons and of an *entente* with Germany from fear of her hostility.

If, as a result of the failure of the Conference, compensation is offered to Germany for her recognition of the French position in Morocco with the view of avoiding an almost certain war in the near future, it seems to me that our demand about Egypt should be kept entirely in the background and not be dependent on our assent to any agreement between France and Germany, since it would be interpreted in France as a self-seeking action on our part by which we would secure greater advantages in Egypt than those which we have already obtained from our agreement with France on Egypt and Morocco and from which the French Gov[ernmen]t have so far profited little.

C. H.

Feb. 23 [1906]

33. SECOND HAGUE CONFERENCE, 1907[1]

[The Kaiser stated to the British Ambassador in Berlin that if disarmament were to be brought up at the forthcoming Hague Conference he should decline to be represented, saying that each state must decide for itself what forces it required. The new British Liberal Cabinet strove to arrest armaments by announcing that one of the four battleships on the building program would be dropped, and by a promise to omit a second if others would do likewise. When this proposal was officially made, Germany, Russia, and Austria expressed a desire to postpone the question. Despite these objections, the British representative at the Conference, Edward Fry, opened the question. The resolution of 1899 to which he referred was: "That the limitation of military charges which weigh on the world is highly desirable for increasing the material and moral well-being of humanity." The achievements of the conference consisted in the reform of the laws of naval warfare and the approval of the establishment of an international prize court.]

The Limitation of Armament

Extract from the Minutes of the Fourth Plenary Session of the Conference Held August 17, 1907

His Excellency Sir Edward Fry: Mr. President, I have the honour to submit to you in behalf of the Government of His Britannic Majesty a proposal of the highest importance.

When His Imperial Majesty of Russia convoked the First Peace Conference at The Hague he proposed as the prime object of its work that "of seeking without delay means for putting a limit to the progressive increase of military and naval armaments, a question the solution of which becomes evidently more and more urgent in view of the fresh extension given to these armaments."

After having taken into consideration the report of the First Commission of the Conference, which had been charged with the examina-

---

[1] James Brown Scott, editor. *The Reports to the Hague Conferences of 1899 and 1907.* Carnegie Endowment for International Peace, Oxford, 1917, pp. 892-897. Reprinted with the permission of the Carnegie Endowment for International Peace and of the Oxford University Press.

tion of the question, the Conference unanimously adopted the following resolution:

"The Conference is of opinion that the restriction of military charges, which are at present a heavy burden on the world, is extremely desirable for the increase of the material and moral welfare of mankind."

Count Mouravieff, in his memorandum of August, 1898, addressed to Europe in the name of His Majesty the Emperor of Russia, said:

"The ever-increasing financial charges strike and paralyze public prosperity at its source; the intellectual and physical strength of the nations, their labour and capital, are for the most part diverted from their natural application and unproductively consumed; hundreds of millions are spent in acquiring terrible engines of destruction, which though today regarded as the last word of science are destined tomorrow to lose all value in consequence of some fresh discovery in the same field. National culture, economic progress, and the production of wealth are either paralyzed or perverted in their development.

"Moreover, in proportion as the armaments of each Power increase, so do they less and less attain the object aimed at by the Governments. Economic crises, due in great part to the system of amassing armaments to the point of exhaustion, and the continual danger which lies in this accumulation of war material, are transforming the armed peace of our days into a crushing burden, which the peoples have more and more difficulty in bearing. It appears evident, then, that if this state of affairs be prolonged, it will inevitably lead to the very cataclysm which it is desired to avert, and the impending horrors of which are fearful to every human thought."

These words, so eloquent and so true when they were first uttered, are today still more forcible and more true. For, Mr. President, since that date military expenditure upon armies as well as upon navies has considerably increased. Thus, according to the most exact information which I have received, this expenditure reached in 1898—that is to say, in the year which immediately preceded the First Conference at The Hague—a total of more than £251,000,000 for the countries of Europe—with the exception of Turkey and Montenegro (regarding which I have no information)—the United States of America, and Japan; while in the year 1906 the similar expenditure of the same countries exceeded a total of £320,000,000.

It will thus be seen that in the interval between the two Conferences annual military expenditure has been augmented by the sum of £69,-000,000 or more than 1,725 millions of francs, which is an enormous increase.

Such is this excessive expenditure, which might be employed for better ends; such, Mr. President, is the burden under which our popula-

tions are groaning; such is the Christian peace of the civilized world
in the twentieth century.

I will not speak of the economic aspect of the question, of the great
mass of men who are compelled by these preparations for war to leave
their occupations, and of the prejudicial effect of this state of things
upon the general prosperity. You know this aspect of the question
better than I do.

I am, therefore, quite sure that you will agree with me in the conclusion that the realization of the desire expressed by the Emperor of
Russia and by the First Conference would be a great blessing for the
whole of humanity. Is this desire capable of being realized? This is a
question to which I cannot supply a categorical answer. I can only
assure you that my Government is a convinced supporter of these
high aspirations, and that it charges me to invite you to work together for the realization of this noble desire.

In ancient times, Mr. President, men dreamed of an age of gold
which had existed on earth in the distant past; but in all ages and
among all nations poets, sibyls, prophets, and all noble and inspired
souls have always cherished the hope of the return of this golden
age under the form of the reign of universal peace.

> *Ultima Cumæi venit iam carminis ætas;*
> *Magnus ab integro sæclorum nascitur ordo.*
> *Iam redit et virgo, redeunt Saturnia regna.*

Such was the dream of the Latin poet for his age; but today the sense
of the solidarity of the human race has more than ever spread over
the whole world. It is this sentiment that has rendered possible the
convocation of the present Conference; and it is in the name of this
sentiment that I request you not to separate without having asked
that the Governments of the world should devote themselves very earnestly to the question of the limitation of military charges.

My Government recognizes that it belongs to the duty of every
country to protect itself against its enemies and against the dangers
by which it may be threatened, and that every Government has the
right and the duty to decide what its own country ought to do for this
purpose. It is, therefore, only by means of the good-will, the free-will,
of each Government, acting in its own right, for the welfare of its own
country, that the object of our desires can be realized.

The Government of His Britannic Majesty, recognizing that several
Powers desire to restrict their military expenditure, and that this
object can only be realized by the independent action of each Power,
has thought it to be its duty to inquire whether there are any means
for satisfying these aspirations. My Government has therefore authorized us to make the following declaration:

"The Government of Great Britain will be prepared to communicate
annually to Powers which would pursue the same course the programme

for the construction of new ships of war and the expenditures which this programme would entail. This exchange of information would facilitate an exchange of views between the Governments on the subject of the reductions which it might be possible to effect by mutual agreement.

"The British Government believes that in this way it might be possible to arrive at an understanding with regard to the expenditure which the States which should undertake to adopt this course would be justified in incorporating in their estimates."

In conclusion, therefore, Mr. President, I have the honour to propose to you the adoption of the following resolution:

"The Conference confirms the resolution adopted by the Conference of 1899 in regard to the limitation of military expenditure; and inasmuch as military expenditure has considerably increased in almost every country since that time, the Conference declares that it is eminently desirable that the Governments should resume the serious examination of this question."

The President: The British proposition that you have just heard, gentlemen, is supported by the United States of America, whose first delegate has addressed me the following letter:

"Mr. President,—In the course of the negotiations which preceded the present Conference the Government of the United States considered it to be its duty to reserve the right to bring forward here the important subject of the limitation of armaments, in the hope that they might advance in some small degree the lofty conception which inspired the Emperor of Russia in his first appeal.

"While regretting that more progress in the direction indicated by His Imperial Majesty cannot be made at this moment, we are happy to think that there is no intention on the part of the nations to abandon his endeavours, and we request to be allowed to express our sympathy for the views expressed by his Excellency the first delegate of Great Britain, and to support the proposal that he has just made."

"JOSEPH H. CHOATE."

His Excellency Mr. Léon Bourgeois: In the name of the French delegation I declare our support of the proposal formulated by his Excellency Sir Edward Fry and supported by our colleagues of the United States of America.

The first delegate of the French Republic, remembering that he was in 1899 the initiator of the *voeu* of the First Conference, will perhaps be allowed to express the confident belief that between now and the meeting of the next peace assembly the study to which the Conference invites the Governments in the name of humanity will be resolutely pursued.

The President: A similar communication has come to me **from the**

Spanish delegation in a letter from the first delegate, his Excellency Mr. de Villa Urrutia, worded as follows:

"Mr. President,—The Spanish Government, at the time of the convocation of the present Conference, expressed its desire to reserve the right to discuss the question of the limitation of armaments, which had already been submitted to the previous Conference through the generous initiative of His Majesty the Emperor of Russia.

"While regretting that existing circumstances have not permitted us to follow in the same efficacious manner the great and noble idea with which his Imperial Majesty was inspired, and while we express our sympathy with the views expounded by his excellency the first delegate of Great Britain, which are also those of the Spanish Government, we are happy to think that all nations will exert their efforts in this direction and that they will one day be crowned with success."

"W. R. DE VILLA URRUTIA."

The President: I have received a communication on the same subject from the delegates of the Argentine Republic and Chile also.

They acquaint the Conference with the fact that these two States have been the first to give effect to the wish expressed by the Conference in 1899 by concluding on May 28, 1902, a Convention on the limitation of naval forces which has been put into execution under a special protocol signed January 9, 1903. The communication reads:

"The delegations of the Argentine Republic and the Republic of Chile have the honour to present to the Peace Conference a treaty of May 28, 1902, and the supplementary agreement of January 9, 1903, treaties which have been faithfully observed by the two nations.

"By the terms of these protocols a part of the fleets of the two Governments was dismantled, armed cruisers in course of construction on account of the respective Governments were sold upon the docks, and the countries agreed to abstain for a period of five years from the acquisition of new vessels of war.

"In the belief that the annexed protocols may be of some use in a study of the proposal of Great Britain on the subject of the limitation of armaments, we beg you, etc., etc."

We can welcome, gentlemen, with the greater pleasure and satisfaction the communication of this Convention and protocol since the latter, which regulates the details of the limitations of the Chilean and Argentine naval forces, is the work of two of our most distinguished young colleagues, who were at that time, one the Minister for Foreign Affairs and the other the Envoy Extraordinary and Minister Plenipotentiary of their respective countries, Messrs. Drago and Concha, to whom it is my duty to offer, as well as to the delegations of the States that they represent, in the name of the Conference, our thanks and congratulations.

The eloquence of his Excellency the first British delegate, and the

proposal with which it concluded, as well as the communications with
which I have just acquainted you, cannot, it seems to me, fail to meet
with a sympathetic reception on our part. The idea of diminishing
the charges which weigh upon the populations owing to the fact of
wars, by seeking the means of putting an end to the progressive increase of armaments on land and on sea, constituted the chief motive
of the initiative taken by the Emperor of Russia in order to bring
about the meeting of the Peace Conferences. This thought has been,
so to speak, the corner-stone of that action. It formed the starting-
point of the Russian circular of August 12/24, 1898, and was placed
at the head of the programme which the Cabinet of St. Petersburg
proposed to the Powers in its circular of December 30, 1898/January
11, 1899. All the Governments gave their adherence, and the Conference, from the outset, had to occupy itself with a proposal of the
Russian delegation which aimed at preventing the increase of
armaments.

Contact with reality, however, was not long in revealing all the
practical difficulties which this generous thought involved when the
question of applying it arose. In the Commission which was entrusted
with the consideration of the subject very keen differences of opinion
soon broke out, and the debates assumed such a character that, instead of the desired understanding, there was a danger of a disagreement which might have proved fatal to the rest of the labours of the
Conference. It had to be acknowledged that the question was not ripe,
that it required further study on the part of the different Governments
at home; and it was in this sense that, after having unanimously
adopted the resolution which has just been recalled by the first delegate of Great Britain, the Commission expressed the wish that "the
Governments, taking into consideration the proposals made at the
Conference," should "examine the possibility of an agreement as to
the limitation of armed forces by land and sea, and of war budgets."

But here once more practical experience was not destined to correspond with the ideal nature of the wish. As I have just intimated,
only two States, the Argentine Republic and Chile, have been able
to give effect to that wish by concluding a convention of disarmament, which I have had the honour of reading to you. The majority
of the Powers of Europe had other preoccupations. Scarcely had the
Conference terminated its labours when troubles which arose in an
empire of eastern Asia obliged the Governments to intervene with
armed force. A short time afterwards one of the great European
Powers found itself engaged in South Africa in a struggle which
necessitated on its part a great military effort. Finally, during these
last years, the Far East was the theatre of a gigantic war, the liquidation of which is barely finished. Need I also mention the colonial
struggles and diplomatic difficulties which may have temporarily compelled one Power or another to increase its armaments? The result was
that the Governments, far from having been able to occupy them-

THE HAGUE
(HUIS TEN BOSCH)
TEMPLE·OF·DISARMAMENT

MODEL
DREADNOUGHT

THE TUG OF PEACE.

Everybody (to everybody else). "AFTER YOU, SIR!"

From *Punch*, March 13, 1907
(Reprinted by arrangements with the proprietors of *Punch*.)

selves, in conformity with the desire expressed by the Conference, with the means of limiting armaments, had, on the contrary, to increase their armaments to an extent which has just been shown you by the figures adduced by Sir Edward Fry.

It was in consideration of these circumstances, gentlemen, that the Russian Government this time refrained from placing the limitation of armaments upon the programme of the Conference which it proposed to the Powers. To begin with, it considered that this question was not ripe for fruitful discussion. In the second place, it did not desire to provoke discussions which, as the experience of 1899 showed, could only, in opposition to the aim of our common endeavours, accentuate a disagreement among the Powers by giving occasion for irritating debates. The Russian Government, for its part, was determined not to take part in such discussions, and it knew that this was likewise the determination of some other Great Powers.

Yet the seed sown at the time of the First Conference has germinated independently of the action of the Governments. A very emphatic movement of public opinion has arisen in different countries in favour of the limitation of armaments, and the Governments, whose sympathies for the principle have not diminished, in spite of the difficulties of carrying it out, find themselves confronted with manifestations which they are not in a position to satisfy. Thus it is, gentlemen, that the British Government, giving expression to its own preoccupations, and making itself the organ of public feeling, evinced its intention of nevertheless calling the attention of the Powers assembled in Conference at The Hague to the question of the limitation of armaments, and that its first delegate has just brought before us the wish which the cabinet of London would like to see adopted by us.

I for my part am unable to discover any other means of evincing the interest which the Powers take in this question. If the question was not ripe in 1899, it is not any more so in 1907. It has not been possible to do anything on these lines, and the Conference today finds itself as little prepared to enter upon them as in 1899. Any discussion which should in itself prove sterile could only be harmful to the cause which was in view by accentuating differences of opinion on questions of fact, while there exists unity of general intentions which might one day meet with their realization. It is for this reason, gentlemen, that the proposal now made to us by the British delegation, to confirm the resolution adopted by the Conference of 1899 by formulating anew the desire which was then expressed, is what best corresponds with the present state of the question and with the interest which we all have in seeing it directed into a channel where the unanimity of the Powers could alone constitute a guarantee of its further progress. And it will be an honour for the Second Peace Conference to have contributed to this end by its immediate vote.

I therefore can only applaud the English initiative, and recommend you to unite in accepting the resolution, as it has been proposed to us by Sir Edward Fry, with unanimous acclamation.

The unanimity of your acclamations appears to make it unnecessary to proceed to a vote.

The meeting adjourned at 4.15 p.m.

The President,

Secretaries General, NELIDOW

W. DOUDE VAN TROOSTWIJK
PROZOR

34. AGREEMENT BETWEEN RUSSIA AND JAPAN RESPECTING CHINA, 1907[1]

[The dangerous tension following the Russo-Japanese War was removed by treaties between the two parties: France and Japan, and Russia and Japan. In this latter treaty, cited below, the former enemies decided to pool their interests in exploiting Manchuria. In spite of the declaration in favor of the "open door," they excluded other nations and practically partitioned Manchuria between themselves. This arrangement increased the feeling of diplomatic isolation on the part of Germany, since it completed a basis for friendly coöperation in the Far East on the part of the members of the (future) Triple Entente. This agreement was signed by Izvolski and Motono.]

St. Petersburg, July 17/30, 1907

The Government of His Majesty the Emperor of Japan, and the Government of His Majesty the Emperor of All the Russias, desirous of consolidating the peaceful and neighbourly relations which have been happily reëstablished between Japan and Russia, and wishing to avoid for the future every cause of misunderstanding in the relations of the two empires, have agreed to the following clauses:

Article I. Each of the High Contracting Parties pledges itself to respect the actual territorial integrity of the other and all the rights accruing to each Party from the treaties, conventions, and contracts in force between them and China, copies of which have been exchanged by the contracting Parties (in so far as these rights are not incompatible with the principle of equal opportunity), from the Treaty signed at Portsmouth on August 23rd/September 5th, 1905, as well as from the special conventions concluded between Japan and Russia.

Article II. The High Contracting Parties recognize the independence and territorial integrity of China and the principle of equal opportunity as regards the commerce and industries of all the nations in that Empire, and pledge themselves to uphold and defend the maintenance

[1] R. B. Mowat, *Select Treaties and Documents to Illustrate the Development of the Modern European States System, 1815-1916*, pp. 32-33. Reprinted with the permission of the Oxford University Press.

of the *status quo* and the respect of that principle by all the pacific means at their disposal. . . .

35. The Anglo-Russian Entente, 1907[1]

[A proposal for an Anglo-Russian entente was apparently discussed by Edward VII and Izvolski during the Russo-Japanese War. Such an understanding was an obvious complement to the Anglo-French Entente of 1904. The two countries had interests in the Near and Middle East which had long conflicted. Draft proposals were worked out by Grey, and Arthur Nicolson, new British Ambassador in St. Petersburg. The provisions for spheres of influence in Persia were at first not approved by the Russians, who demanded that Persia must come entirely under Russian influence. The conclusion of an agreement was hampered also by the political differences between the two governments: English liberals criticized the oppression of the Tsar's absolutism, the suspension of the Duma, and the Russian pogroms. By this treaty England gained peace of mind in regard to the Indian frontier, but lost her freedom to protest against Russian imperialistic aggression upon defenseless Persia, since henceforth she did not dare endanger the solidarity of the Entente, and the Russians knew as much. The reason for the small British sphere of influence is found in the reply of Kitchener, commander-in-chief in India, to the effect that he could only defend the southeastern part of Persia. In Russia the treaty was criticized: Witte, remarking that it made it impossible for Russia to annex Persia, regarded it as a triumph of British diplomacy. The Afghan clauses, lacking the Ameer's assent, remained a dead letter.]

Agreement Concerning Persia

The Governments of Great Britain and Russia having mutually engaged to respect the integrity and independence of Persia, and sincerely desiring the preservation of order throughout that country and its peaceful development, as well as the permanent establishment of equal advantages for the trade and industry of all other nations;

Considering that each of them has, for geographical and economic reasons, a special interest in the maintenance of peace and order in certain provinces of Persia adjoining, or in the neighborhood of, the Russian frontier on the one hand, and the frontiers of Afghanistan and Baluchistan on the other hand; and being desirous of avoiding all cause of conflict between their respective interests in the above-mentioned provinces of Persia;

---

[1] Great Britain. *Parliamentary Papers*. 1908. Vol. CXXV. Cmd. 3750. "Convention between the United Kingdom and Russia relating to Persia, Afghanistan, and Thibet. Signed at St. Petersburgh, August 31, 1907." (Ratified Sept. 23, 1907.)

Have agreed on the following terms:—

I. Great Britain engages not to seek for herself, and not to support in favour of British subjects, or in favour of the subjects of third Powers, any Concessions of a political or commercial nature—such as Concessions for railways, banks, telegraphs, roads, transport, insurance, etc.—beyond a line starting from Kasr-i-Shirin, passing through Isfahan, Yezd, Kakhk, and ending at a point on the Persian frontier at the intersection of the Russian and Afghan frontiers, and not to oppose, directly or indirectly, demands for similar Concessions in this region which are supported by the Russian Government. It is understood that the above-mentioned places are included in the region in which Great Britain engages not to seek the Concessions referred to.

II. Russia, on her part, engages not to seek for herself and not to support, in favour of Russian subjects, or in favour of the subjects of third Powers, any Concessions of a political or commercial nature— such as Concessions for railways, banks, telegraphs, roads, transport, insurance, etc.—beyond a line going from the Afghan frontier by way of Gazik, Birjand, Kerman, and ending at Bunder Abbas, and not to oppose, directly or indirectly, demands for similar Concessions in this region which are supported by the British Government. It is understood that the above-mentioned places are included in the region in which Russia engages not to seek the Concessions referred to.

III. Russia, on her part, engages not to oppose, without previous arrangement with Great Britain, the grant of any Concessions whatever to British subjects in the regions of Persia situated between the lines mentioned in Articles I and II.

Great Britain undertakes a similar engagement as regards the grant of Concessions to Russian subjects in the same regions of Persia.

All Concessions existing at present in the regions indicated in Articles I and II are maintained.

IV. It is understood that the revenues of all the Persian customs, with the exception of those of Farsistan and of the Persian Gulf, revenues guaranteeing the amortization and the interest of the loans concluded by the Government of the Shah with the "Banque d'Escompte et des Prêts de Perse" up to the date of the signature of the present Agreement, shall be devoted to the same purpose as in the past.

It is equally understood that the revenues of the Persian customs of Farsistan and of the Persian Gulf, as well as those of the fisheries on the Persian shore of the Caspian Sea and those of the Posts and Telegraphs, shall be devoted, as in the past, to the service of the loans concluded by the Government of the Shah with the Imperial Bank of Persia up to the date of the signature of the present Agreement.

V. In the event of irregularities occurring in the amortization or the payment of the interest of the Persian loans concluded with the "Banque d'Escompte et des Prêts de Perse" and with the Imperial Bank of Persia up to the date of the signature of the present Agreement, and in the event of the necessity arising for Russia to establish control over the sources of revenue guaranteeing the regular service of the loans concluded with the first-named bank, and situated in the region mentioned in Article II of the present Agreement, or for Great Britain to establish control over the sources of revenue guaranteeing the regular service of the loans concluded with the second-named bank, and situated in the region mentioned in Article I of the present Agreement, the British and Russian Governments undertake to enter beforehand into a friendly exchange of ideas with a view to determine, in agreement with each other, the measures of control in question and to avoid all interference which would not be in conformity with the principles governing the present Agreement.

36. Bosnian Crisis, 1908-09

[On July 2, 1908, the Russian Foreign Minister, Izvolski, accepted the Turkish concessions to Austria for a railway through the Sanjak of Novi-bazar, to provide a non-Serbian route to Salonika; at the same time he announced his readiness to discuss changes, such as the annexation of Bosnia and Herzegovina, and the Sanjak by Austria, in return for the opening of the Straits to Russian warships. The Austrian Foreign Minister, Aehrenthal, determined to seize the first opportunity of carrying out this suggestion: the Young Turk Revolution of July, 1908, provided the occasion. In August he secured the consent of his allies, Germany and Italy, to the proposal, and made final arrangements with Izvolski at a meeting at Buchlau, Bohemia. As no written record was made of this conversation, which was without witnesses, we do not know just what occurred: both statesmen gave conflicting versions afterward. Before acting, Aehrenthal took pains to secure the connivance of Bulgaria by assurances that Austria would not object if King Ferdinand were to proclaim the independence of Bulgaria. Bulgarian independence was accordingly proclaimed October 5, and on October 6 Francis Joseph announced the formal annexation of Bosnia and Herzegovina and the evacuation of the Sanjak. Izvolski declared Aehrenthal had acted without his knowledge, and insisted upon a conference to ratify the action, hoping to secure compensations for Russia at the same time. He therefore went to London to gain British consent to this plan. Grey agreed that changes in the Treaty of Berlin (of 1878) required the assent of all signatories, but he made it plain that the question of the Straits must not be raised at the conference. As the months passed the idea of a conference lapsed, since Austria refused to attend without a preliminary agreement ruling out discussion of the annexation. Austria decided, in view of the Turkish boycott of Austrian goods, to pay Turkey monetary compensation. Serbia, however, was still insistent in her opposition to the Austrian incorporation of the provinces inhabited by so many of her fellow-Yugoslavs, but submitted, at the urgent advice of Russia, which desired to avoid being dragged into an Austro-Serbian War.

Serbia, accordingly, surrendered to Austrian demands: she undertook to cease from her attitude of protest and opposition, to live with Austria on neighborly terms, and to reduce her army. The outcome of the crisis was the apparent victory of the Central Powers, but the ultimate tightening of the bonds of the Triple Entente. Russia had been deeply humiliated; and henceforth Serbia was closely linked to her by resentment and desire for revenge upon Austria. This crisis has been aptly called the grand rehearsal for the World War.]

(a) *British Correspondence*[1]

Foreign Office
October 14, 1908

Sir Edward Grey to Sir Arthur Nicholson
Secret

Sir, Monsieur Iswolsky arrived in London on the 9th instant and called upon me at the Foreign Office on the 10th instant.

His Excellency began his conversation with me by a long explanation of what had passed between him and Baron d'Aerenthal.

It was, in substance, what I had already heard, but he spoke very frankly of Baron d'Aerenthal as being tortuous and insincere and always wishing to compromise the person with whom he was dealing. It was not true that he (Monsieur Iswolsky) had given his consent in advance to what Austria had done about Bosnia. He had simply exchanged views, and had intended to discuss in Paris and London, afterwards, the possibility of the annexation of Bosnia by Austria and the consequences of such an eventuality. Meanwhile, this had been sprung upon him.

He made the most of the compensation offered by Austria as regards Novi-Bazar. In Austrian hands this would have prepared the way for an advance, and have been a wedge driven into the Slav States.

He emphasised the fact that these breaches of the international Treaty should be dealt with by a Conference, and he proposed that a Conference should be announced as soon as possible with a definite programme to deal with Bulgarian independence, Bosnia, Herzegovina, Novi-Bazar and Montenegro.

But it would not be enough simply to ratify what had already been done; that would not secure enough compensation either for Turkey or the other Balkan States.

Bulgaria had shown, in this matter, no consideration for Russian wishes, and Russia was prepared to be stiff in dealing with her. It might be arranged at the Conference that Bulgaria should pay for the Eastern Roumelian Tribute and the Railway. Servia might have some rectification of her frontier, but it must not be at the expense of Turkey. There might also be a revision of the regulations about the

---

[1] *British Documents on the Origins of the War, 1898-1914*, Vol. V, No. 379; No. 801.

Danube which would put the Balkan States on a more favourable footing: this would be in the nature of compensation to them at the expense of Austria. For Turkey, the hope might be held out that, if things went well, the Financial Commission and joint right of superintendence given to the Powers with regard to Macedonia and Armenia by Treaty would be done away with; and that the Capitulations also would be altered, if the Turkish Government justified such a step.

Russia would not raise the question of the Straits at the Conference.

Monsieur Iswolsky urged very strongly that, if Russia could satisfy Turkey that an arrangement about the Straits was safe for Turkish interests, England should not oppose it. He told me that there had been great opposition in Russia to the Anglo-Russian Convention. He had had to spend great energy in getting it accepted in Russia. All the Liberal and advanced elements in Russia were in favour of an understanding with England; but the reactionary elements were against it, and would like to upset the Convention. The Emperor was by training and education not on the Liberal side. It was possible to keep him reconciled to reforms in Russia only by proving to him that things were going better: for instance, whereas, two years ago, there was a state of active revolution, the state of affairs was now much improved. In the same way it would be fatal to a good understanding with England if, when the question of the Straits were raised, it was found that England blocked the way and that no improvement followed from good relations with England.

His proposal to Turkey would be that ships of war belonging to the riverain Powers on the Black Sea should have a right of way through the Straits. They would not be allowed to remain in the Straits. There might be regulations that not more than three vessels should go through at a time, and that no other vessels should go through for 24 hours after the first. Such regulations would, of course, only apply in times when Turkey was at peace. In time of war, Turkey would be able to do as she pleased.

In other words, the closing of the Straits would be maintained, subject to a limited serviture of this kind, in favour of Russia and the riverain States.

Monsieur Iswolsky went on to say that the present was a most critical moment. It might either consolidate and strengthen the good relations between England and Russia, or it might upset them altogether. His own position was at stake, for he was entirely bound up with the policy of a good understanding with England, which he had advocated against all opposition.

I asked him to give me a draft of what he proposed with regard to the Conference, so that I might have something definite to put before the Cabinet: this he promised to do.

I said I realized how critical the moment was. We were most anxious to work with Russia. We were in favour of the new régime in Turkey, not in order that we might support Turkey against Russia, but because we regarded an independent and well-governed Turkey as the only alternative to anarchy and confusion.

Monsieur Iswolsky said the Russian desire now was to be friendly with Turkey. They did not wish to have Constantinople for themselves: it was not a place which could be held like Gibraltar, it had to be made a Capital, they could not make it their own Capital, and they would not wish to see it in any hands but those of Turkey. Therefore they wished to have a peaceful and well-governed Turkey, with whom they could be friendly.

I told him I recognised the Russian feeling about the Straits; but the proposal he had now put before me was not the same as that which Count Benckendorff had discussed with me at the time of the Anglo-Russian Convention. The proposal then had been that, while Russia should have egress from the Black Sea through the Straits, other Powers should have liberty to send their vessels of war into the Straits without going into the Black Sea.

Monsieur Iswolsky pointed out that as Russia would not ask for any right to stay in the Straits, it would be useless to grant a right of access to the Straits without staying there and without going on into the Black Sea. But he was not putting the proposal before me now on the ground that I had made any promise previously. He was putting it forward from the point of view of good relations.

If Russia did not make the proposal now, it might be blocked by Germany or Austria at some future time; and he hoped that if Russia could get the consent of Turkey voluntarily to an arrangement such as he had suggested we would not oppose it.

I told Monsieur Iswolsky I must have time to consult the Prime Minister and my Colleagues, who had seen the proposal made some time ago, but to whom this would be quite new.

I urged that some immediate proof of confidence in the new régime in Turkey and good will to it should be shown by offering a guaranteed loan if Turkey desired it. This would at once produce a general feeling of confidence and tranquillity.—I am, etc.

Minute by King Edward.   E. Grey
    App[rove]d.—E. R.

Sir A. Nicolson to Sir Edward Grey

St. Petersburgh,
March 29, 1909

Sir, It was only on the morning of the 27th instant that the general public became aware that the Russian Government had consented, if asked by Austria-Hungary, to the unconditional abrogation of Article 25 of the Berlin Treaty, or, in other words, to recognize the annexation by Austria-Hungary of Bosnia and Herzegovina. It had always been understood that the Russian Government were, in conjunction with the Governments of Great Britain and of France, maintaining the attitude, which had been announced on more than one occasion, both officially and publicly, that the modifications of an international Treaty by Austria-Hungary on her own initiative, as well as the arbitrary infractions of the same Treaty by Bulgaria, would not be recognized until the matter had been discussed and examined by all the Signatory Powers in conjunction with the compensations due to other states whose interests had been directly or indirectly affected by the acts of last autumn. It was therefore with surprise and indeed with bewildered consternation that the public learnt that the Russian Government, who were supposed to have under their especial care the interests of the smaller Balkan States, and whose influence in the Balkan Peninsula had been endangered, had consented suddenly to abandon the position which they had hitherto assumed and to sanction the act which Austria-Hungary had executed some months ago. It was considered not only in the press but also, so far as I have been able to observe and ascertain, in all classes of society, that Russia had suffered a deep humiliation, and had renounced the traditional part which she had hitherto played in South East Europe and in the prosecution of which she had made so great sacrifices in the past. Even among those who take but little interest in foreign affairs, and who do not feel much sympathy for the smaller Balkan States, whom they regard as troublesome and ungrateful younger brethren, there was a feeling of bitter resentment that, at a most critical moment for two of the minor Slav States, their natural protector had abandoned them to the mercy of a German Power; and that Russia had consented, without making any reservations in favour of those who had looked to her for assistance, if not material, in any case moral and diplomatic, to give her seal to an act which had been committed by Austria-Hungary to the detriment of Slav interests. I have been assured, by those who have witnessed many various phases in the recent history of Russia, that there has never previously been a moment when the country had undergone such humiliation; and though Russia has had her troubles and trials, both external and internal, and has suffered defeats in the field, she has never had, for apparently no valid cause, to submit to the dictation of a foreign Power.

As I am sending this despatch by post I do not like to enter into fuller details or to draw certain consequences which may possibly follow from the step which the Russian Government have taken. I will only notice that voices are being raised whether the ally and friend of Russia have proved sufficiently strong supporters at the hour of need. The "Golos Pravdy," the organ of the Octobrist party, has given expression of these doubts in no uncertain tones, and has drawn the attention of its readers to the fact that the combination of the three Powers was too weak to withstand the first shock which it sustained from the Central Powers. It is considered out of the question that Russia could have taken the recent step without previous consultation with her ally and her friend: and indeed it has been spread about that it was on the advice of Great Britain that the step was taken. When this version has come to my ears, I have naturally given it a direct denial. The whole truth will doubtless gradually be known, but when it is known it is hardly likely to mitigate the feeling of humiliation which at present is weighing so heavily on the public mind.—I have, etc.,

A. NICOLSON

Minutes

It is not the right deduction to say that the Triple Entente was too weak to resist the Central Powers in this matter. It was not worth their while to do so. If it had been, we could have prevented war. Russian public opinion will take a calmer view on reflection.

L.[ouis] M.[allet]

This is true and it is also true that M. Isvolsky did not give either us or France the chance of saying whether we should help him to make better terms.

E.[dward] G.[rey]

(b) A Russian View[1]

. . . .

From this political rivalry in the Balkans sprang a perpetual enmity between Vienna and St. Petersburg, fated to lead sooner or later to open war—the inevitable outcome of the irreconcilable antipathy. It was always improbable, on account of·the general European character which Balkan questions had long since assumed, that Russia and Austria-Hungary would be able to settle accounts with regard to the Balkans without drawing the other Powers into the struggle; but when Bismarck concluded an alliance with Austria in 1879 there was no longer any hope of confining the matter to a mere duel between the two rivals. This was recognized by all the European Cabinets. Nevertheless, up to 1909 Germany refrained from openly avowing her full solidarity with Austria-Hungary's Balkan policy; and, despite the fundamental change in her own policy, she had ostensibly adhered to Bismarck's advice concerning 'the bones of a Pomeranian Grenadier.' The Bosnia and Herzegovina crisis in 1908-9 revealed the true state of affairs to the whole of Europe. Aehrenthal's unscrupulous conduct in converting the actual control of Bosnia and Herzegovina, which entailed no danger for the Austro-Hungarian Monarchy, into a juridical possession by means of a gross infringement of all law, was a challenge to the whole Serbian people and also to Russia; not only

---

[1] Serge Sazonov. *Fateful Years 1909-1916*. London, Jonathan Cape. 1928; New York, Frederick A. Stokes Company, 1928, pp. 14-20. Reprinted with the permission of the publishers.

did it fail to evoke any expression of disapproval from the German Government—it actually received the support and protection of Germany's Imperial power. Europe was confronted with a *fait accompli*, and was forced either to accept it as such, or to engage in an armed struggle with Austria-Hungary, and possibly with the whole of the Triple Alliance.

The public opinion of Europe condemned the methods of Austrian diplomacy, recognizing in them a threat to the legal stability of international State life; but no one was eager to oppose them by force of arms. The direct interests of Western Europe were not affected by the Austrian *coup*, and the danger of provoking a European war, with its disastrous consequences, was apparent to all. Consequently neither France nor England could be expected to concern themselves with this question, beyond according their diplomatic support to the wronged party.

In Serbia and Russia, however, the Bosnia-Herzegovina crisis called forth very different feelings. For Serbia the absorption by Austria-Hungary of a considerable portion of the Serbian race was not only a heavy blow to her national pride, it was also an ominous forecast of the ulterior designs of the Viennese policy. Russia, although her interests were not directly affected, nevertheless felt insulted by the methods adopted by Count Aehrenthal in dealing with the Russian Minister for Foreign Affairs. By means of a palpable concealment he allowed himself to interpret certain general conversations between himself and Isvolsky as a consent on the part of the Russian Government to the immediate annexation of the occupied Turkish provinces. In the course of these conversations, which took place in Count Berchtold's house in Moravia, Isvolsky demanded appropriate compensation for Russia, should Austria-Hungary succeed in carrying out her aims.

There is no doubt that Isvolsky made a great mistake in reposing so much confidence in a diplomat whose character demanded special caution in all business dealings; indeed he had the courage to confess it. Aehrenthal's astonishing lack of conscience was only equalled by that of his trusted assistants, and the fact that none of them had the slightest hesitation in using deceit was abundantly demonstrated soon afterwards. But the harm was already done, and its consequences were soon apparent. I do not wish to imply that these consequences, which nearly led to a war between Austria and Serbia, in which Russia could not have remained neutral, would not still have occurred even if Isvolsky had employed the utmost circumspection in dealing with Viennese diplomacy. Aehrenthal, an unusually boastful man, was anxious to score an outstanding success, both for his personal credit, and in order to strengthen the position of the Austro-Hungarian Monarchy, which became more precarious with each succeeding year. It had long been understood in Vienna, that the awakening of national self-consciousness among the Slavonic subjects of the Hapsburg Empire, due to the emancipatory policy pursued by Russia in the Balkan

Peninsula, must ultimately bring Austria-Hungary to ruin. During the long reign of the Emperor Francis Joseph the administrative organization of the Dual Monarchy had, by reason of its injustice, depending for its existence upon the oppression of the majority by a tyrannous minority in both Austria and Hungary, begun to show indubitable signs of internal dissolution. Young Italy, rich in her youthful vigour, gave the first impetus to the dismemberment of the Austrian Empire; and although she did not achieve her aim of uniting all the Italian territories included in the decrepit Hapsburg Monarchy, this very fact constituted a standing menace to Austria, in spite of the formal alliance between the two countries. Austria-Hungary had another neighbour—Serbia: a still younger people, fated to attain to political freedom after ages of burdensome slavery. Up to the time of the last Balkan War the outstanding qualities of the Serbs had failed to obtain due recognition, not only from the Western European Powers, who were but little interested in them, but also from Russian public opinion. But they became an object of intense enmity and suspicion to the Austro-Hungarian Government from the moment when the Karageorgevich dynasty became established on the throne, and the period of political subservience which had prevailed during the reign of Milan passed away never to return. The Karageorgevich dynasty enjoyed the affection of the people, and all the Serbian hopes of national expansion were bound up with it. As the Hapsburg monarchy tended towards decrepitude, and its internal creative powers declined, Serbia became an increasing danger. Too weak to renew the rusty machinery of State, and to base it on a broader foundation more in accordance with the spirit of the times, Austria-Hungary had no choice but to come into open conflict with Serbia, relying upon the crushing superiority of her military forces and the powerful support of her German ally. In this unequal struggle Viennese diplomacy displayed complete indifference as to what means it employed to injure its antagonist. One of the measures adopted, and one that was most bitterly resented, was, as has already been mentioned, the establishment of sovereign rights over a considerable portion of the Serbian people domiciled in the Turkish provinces, and placed under Austrian administration by the Berlin Treaty. The rights of Turkey in Bosnia and Herzegovina, although they continued to exist in theory, became a mere fiction from the day when the Austrian military occupation began. The possibility of Turkish protests caused but little anxiety to Aehrenthal, who rightly judged that he would meet with no insuperable obstacles in setting them aside. Neither did Austria, in view of her military superiority, anticipate any counter-action on the part of Serbia; and she correctly calculated that the Western Powers would do nothing beyond making a diplomatic protest. There remained only Russia, to whom the brutal seizure of two Slavonic districts in the Balkan Peninsula constituted a direct challenge; it foreshadowed the possibility of further interference with the political equilibrium of the Balkans, in

a manner injurious to Russian interests. In order to paralyse any
active opposition on the part of Russia, it was necessary to have recourse to extreme measures; and Aehrenthal, not relying upon his own
strength, sought the aid of his ally Germany. Assistance was accorded
him without stint. . . . 'The sword of Germany thrown into the scale
of Europe's decision' quickly decided in favour of Austria-Hungary the
political dilemma which had threatened an international conflict.
Aehrenthal's immediate object was to obtain the assent of the Great
Powers to an abrogation of the 25th clause of the Treaty of Berlin—
defining the rights of Austria-Hungary in Bosnia and Herzegovina
—by a simple exchange of notes. Russia and the Western Powers desired an international conference; but this, the only legal method,
seemed too slow to Aehrenthal. It had also a further disadvantage in
his eyes: it offered no sufficient guarantee for the success of his plans,
in view of the opposition aroused in the European Cabinets by the
policy of Vienna. He had also another object; he sought to obtain
from the Belgrade Government, and in a manner galling to Serbian
self-respect, an admission that the demand for territorial compensation which it made after the seizure of Bosnia and Herzegovina was
in reality groundless. Thus Viennese policy displayed its contempt for
the sanctity of treaty obligations, and its petty malice towards a
neighbour whom Aehrenthal desired not only to weaken, but to humiliate—a desire characteristic of his unprincipled and short-sighted
policy. Yet this policy called forth no protest from Prince Bülow, but
rather earned his approval and his support. The Chancellor believed
that it should be the object of German diplomacy to eliminate Russian
opposition to Austria's Balkan plans; he therefore instructed the
German Ambassador in St. Petersburg to inform M. Isvolsky verbally,
but absolutely officially, that, should the Russian Government refuse
its consent to the unconditional abrogation of Clause 25 of the Treaty
of Berlin, Germany would have no alternative but to 'let events take
their course unimpeded,' laying upon us the responsibility for the consequences. 'Thus,' observes Isvolsky, in a telegram which he sent to
the Ambassadors in Paris and London on March 10/23, 1909, 'we
were compelled to choose between an immediate decision on the annexation question, and an irruption of Austrian troops into Serbia.'

It is evident that such an announcement bears the character of an
ultimatum. The Russian Government was called upon to choose between two weighty decisions: to sacrifice Serbia, or to renounce its
openly-expressed opinion as to the illegality of the Austrian seizure.
It chose the latter course, at the price of its own self-respect. Prince
Bülow and Count Aehrenthal gained a diplomatic victory over Russia
and Serbia and, indirectly, over the Powers of Western Europe. Little
did either of them suspect, at the time, that this victory would prove
to be the first nail in the coffin of Austria-Hungary, and would contribute indirectly to the overthrow of Germany from her commanding
position in Continental Europe. . . .

Great as was the sacrifice which the Russian Government made to preserve the peace of Europe, it was indispensable and therefore wise; and in spite of the painful position in which it placed him, Isvolsky took upon himself the whole burden of public censure. Less than five years had elapsed since the conclusion of our unsuccessful war with Japan, which caused those internal troubles which were the forerunners of the revolution of 1917. Our economic and financial position was still suffering from the strain of a war lasting eighteen months, and our military forces were in an unsatisfactory condition. Our reverses on the battlefields of Manchuria had deprived our Higher Command of that self-confidence which is indispensable to success, and had weakened the military discipline of the lower ranks. With regard to material the army was in the same condition as at the conclusion of the war. In order to complete the picture of Russia's internal condition in the spring of 1909, it must be added that Stolypin, who accepted the power that was falling from the weak hands of Witte and Goremykin, had as yet barely succeeded in pacifying the wide-spread revolutionary passions and in stemming the advancing wave of anarchy.

These facts serve to explain why Russia did not take up the challenge hurled at her by the Austro-German alliance. Although Serbia received no territorial compensation for her loss of prestige, her real interests did not, on this occasion, suffer through Austria-Hungary's predatory policy. Her territory remained untouched and her sovereign rights unaffected. There was consequently no alteration in the existing balance of power in the Balkans, such as would have threatened the vital interests of Russia, and compelled her to draw the sword in their defence. Serbia obeyed the friendly advice of Russia and the Western Powers, and prudently refrained from kindling a European conflagration under political circumstances unfavourable to her own future. The diplomatic incident was closed; but the bad seed sown by Aehrenthal bore poisonous fruit in the injured sense of national dignity of which the Serbs remained conscious.[1]

(c) German "Blank Check" to Austria, 1908[2]

Bülow to Aehrenthal, October 30, 1908

. . . I have complete confidence in your judgment. In this particular case, I tell myself, in addition, that you are in a much better position than I am to pass judgment on the Serbian question and its

---

[1] Italy, too, was concerned at this advance of her ally, Austria, in the Balkans, but did not feel called on to protest so long as no great power had increased its hold on the shores and islands of the Adriatic. See the speech of the Italian premier on December 3 and 4, 1908. Tommaso Tittoni, *Italy's Foreign and Colonial Policy*, pp. 125-147. London, 1914. A later version in T. Tittoni, *Who Was Responsible for the War?* pp. 86-98, Paris, 1918.

[2] *Die Grosse Politik*, Vol. XXVI, No. 9079, p. 227.

attendant circumstances. For that reason I will view whatever decision you eventually arrive at, as the one demanded by the circumstances.

(d) *Russian Advice to Serbia*[1]

Izvolski to the Russian Minister at Belgrade

February 14/27, 1909

In reply to the two communications which were sent us by the Serbian Minister on February 10 and 13, I beg to acquaint the Royal Government with the following:

We hear with satisfaction that the Serbian Government remains true to its resolution not to depart from the peaceful standpoint it has assumed, to avoid everything that might lead to an armed conflict between Serbia and Austria and to carry out no military measures at the frontier. We are convinced that the vital interest of Serbia, for whom we have always felt the greatest sympathy, necessarily imposes upon her this line of policy, which is also the only one which does justice to the general situation at the moment.

We have been able to convince ourselves through various sources that the Powers are not disposed to support the idea of a territorial aggrandizement of Serbia. The Royal Government must deduce from this that all efforts to move the Powers to support such demands would remain futile and that Serbia can be assured of the sympathies of the Powers only if she refrains from insisting upon demands which must lead to an armed conflict with Austria. We deem it necessary to warn the Royal Government against adopting any attitude which might expose it to such a danger. We hope that Serbia, as she has just declared, will remain true to her commitments to follow the advice of the great Powers. At the same time, we believe that the Serbian Government must, under the prevailing circumstances, clearly declare to these Powers, that it does not insist on its territorial demands and that it will rely upon the decision of the Powers in all pending questions. These could then devote all their efforts towards protecting Serbian interests.

A copy has been forwarded to Cettinje.

37. ANGLO-RUSSIAN RELATIONS: THE REVAL VISIT, 1908

[The Anglo-Russian Entente was followed the next year by a visit of Edward VII to Nicholas II. Germany feared designs against her security, though when Bülow made pointed inquiries, Izvolski assured him that no secret Anglo-Russian convention existed which could be directed against German interests. The true significance of the visit is

---

[1] B. De Siebert and George Abel Schreiner, editors. *Entente Diplomacy and the World. Matrix of the History of Europe, 1909-14.* New York, G. P. Putnam's Sons, 1921, No. 261, p. 235. Reprinted with the permission of George A. Schreiner.

THE HARMLESS NECESSARY CAT.

BRITISH LION (to Russian Bear) "LOOK HERE! YOU CAN PLAY WITH HIS HEAD, AND I CAN PLAY WITH HIS TAIL, AND WE CAN BOTH STROKE THE SMALL OF HIS BACK."

PERSIAN CAT. "I DON'T REMEMBER HAVING BEEN CONSULTED ABOUT THIS!"

From Punch, October 2, 1907
(Reprinted by arrangements with the proprietors of Punch.)

to be found in the tightening of the bonds between the two allies. Charles Hardinge, the former British Ambassador in St. Petersburg, in 1908 was Permanent Under Secretary of State for Foreign Affairs.]

(a) *Hardinge's Memorandum on the Visit to the Emperor of Russia at Reval in June, 1908*[1]

Secret

After a rough passage across the North Sea the King and Queen arrived at Kiel on Sunday, the 7th June. Their Majesties were there met by Prince and Princess Henry of Prussia, and after a short stay left again for Reval escorted by a division of German destroyers for some distance from the harbour.

The smart appearance of the whole of the German North Sea Fleet lying at anchor in the port gave food for reflection upon the recent German naval programme of construction, while the intricate evolutions of the torpedo flotilla, which excited the admiration of all the naval officers on board the Royal Yacht served as a useful object lesson of the efficiency of the German navy.

I may mention that the officers of the two British cruisers H.M.S.S. "Minotaur" and "Achilles" were, while waiting at Kiel to escort the King in the Baltic, entertained at dinner by Prince Henry of Prussia, who made a speech to them expressing friendship towards England, disclaiming any aggressive intentions on the part of the German navy, and asking them to make these views understood and spread throughout England. It is thought by those who know Prince Henry that he would not have spoken in this strain without direct instructions to do so.

I was able to ascertain during our short stay at Kiel that the work of enlarging the Canal has already been begun, and that a commission is this very week sitting at Kiel to arrange the details of the work.

The King and Queen arrived at Reval on the morning of the 9th instant, having had splendid weather in the Baltic, and there met the Emperor, the two Empresses, and members of the Imperial Family, with some of the Russian Ministers, on board the two Imperial Yachts and the cruiser "Almaz," the sole survivor of the large Russian fleet that took part in the battle of Tsushima. . . .

I had several opportunities of discussing with M. Isvolsky the various questions of foreign policy in which our two countries are chiefly interested, and I cannot help thinking that this direct exchange of views between the two Foreign Offices will be beneficial and facilitate the solution of most of our pending questions. . . .

The question of Macedonian reform entailed a considerable amount of discussion, and gave M. Isvolsky an opportunity of expounding the

---

[1] *British Documents on the Origins of the War, 1898-1914,* Vol. V, No. 195.

general policy of Russia towards England and Germany, which I will endeavour to describe as shortly as possible.

M. Isvolsky stated that the scheme of Macedonian reforms was one which he had deeply at heart, and upon which the Russian public opinion, as shown by the press, felt strongly. He personally would have gladly accepted the whole of the scheme as first developed by Sir Edward Grey if he had seen the slightest prospect of obtaining its adoption by the rest of the Powers and, lastly, by the Sultan. He knew for a fact, however, that this scheme would have met with the greatest opposition on the part of Germany and Austria, and even now he anticipated considerable difficulties if any further modifications of a drastic nature were to be introduced into the scheme as defined by his last note. He reminded me that Russia is always in a difficult position *vis-à-vis* of Germany, owing to the military supremacy of the latter Power on the frontier, that in Germany there is very great nervousness as to future political developments amongst the Powers, and that the age and indifferent health of the Emperor of Austria are a source of uneasiness as to the future. It was imperative therefore that Russia should act with the greatest prudence towards Germany, and give the latter Power no cause for complaint that the improvement of the relations of Russia with England had entailed a corresponding deterioration of the relations of Russia towards Germany. During the past two months the German Government had formally complained to him more than once of the hostility of the Russian press towards Germany, and although he greatly regretted the outspoken sentiments of the Russian press which he fully believed reflected their true feelings, he had been obliged to confess his impotence under the present system of liberty of the press to control their utterances. The visit of the French President to London, of the King to Reval, and the impending visit of the President to Russia had not tended to improve matters, and he foresaw that difficulties were to be expected from Germany and Austria, especially in the adoption of the scheme of Macedonian reforms. He therefore expressed the hope that his last note, which he had reason to believe the German Government might be induced to accept as it stands, would be adopted by Sir Edward Grey as the limit to which the rope could be strained without breaking, and that the King's visit to Reval might be consecrated by the announcement of the complete agreement of England and Russia upon the scheme of reforms to be adopted in Macedonia.

I told M. Isvolsky that when I left London the text of his last note had not been received by Sir Edward Grey. . . . As for the attitude of Germany towards England and Russia, and towards the recent improvement of relations between them, His Majesty's Government were inspired with no hostile feelings towards Germany, with whom they were anxious to maintain the most friendly relations, and they realised that every action should be avoided which would unnecessarily irritate or exasperate feeling in Germany. Such an attitude was prob-

ably even more necessary for Russia, but in the case of His Majesty's
Government this did not mean that they would be ready to sacrifice
their legitimate interests or those of humanity at large to escape the
ill-will of Germany, since this would be the course best calculated to
provoke it. Although the attitude of His Majesty's Government towards Germany was, and had been, absolutely correct, it was impossible to ignore the fact that, owing to the unnecessarily large increase
in the German naval programme a deep distrust in England of Germany's future intentions had been created. This distrust would be still
further accentuated with the progress of time, the realisation of the
German programme, and the increase of taxation in England entailed
by the necessary naval counter-measures. In seven or eight years' time
a critical situation might arise, in which Russia, if strong in Europe,
might be the arbiter of peace, and have much more influence in securing the peace of the world than at any Hague conference. For this
reason it was absolutely necessary that England and Russia should
maintain towards each other the same cordial and friendly relations
as now exist between England and France, which in the case of England and Russia are, moreover, inspired by an identity of interests of
which a solution of the Macedonian problem was not the least.

So, also, as regards the King's visit to Reval, which could not possibly be interpreted as a provocation to Germany, since it could not be
admitted that the Germany Emperor should enjoy a monopoly of State
visits to other Sovereigns, and Sir Edward Grey had been very explicit
in his statement in the House of Commons that it was not proposed to
negotiate any *new* treaty or convention at Reval. I explained that this
statement had been expressly made with a view to preventing any
trouble between Germany and Russia owing to the King's visit to the
Emperor of Russia. . . .

Considerable time was devoted to the discussion of Persian affairs.

M. Isvolsky said that he was much preoccupied with the condition
of affairs on the Russo-Persian frontier, that the delay granted for
the required satisfaction to be given by Persia was about to expire,
and that it might be necessary to exact compensation from the tribes.
I replied that it was not a matter in which we wished to interfere, that
since the conclusion of our Convention we had confidence in Russia's
intentions towards Persia, but that we earnestly hoped that a satisfactory and amicable solution of the difficulty could be found.

Turning to Persia generally, M. Isvolsky expressed his concern for
the general situation of that country and his anxieties as to the
intrigues of Germany. He strongly advocated a joint loan to Persia
as the only means of restoring order and of maintaining the Shah and
the present Government.

I observed that to give the present Persian Government a large loan
would be a simple waste of money; that in a very short time it would
be spent like all previous loans without any productive results, and it
would simply increase the indebtedness of Persia. . . .

M. Isvolsky then remarked that the railway convention would expire within the next two years and that it was very necessary that the British and Russian Governments should have a definite policy of railway construction in Persia. He reminded me that he had been waiting some time for the views of His Majesty's Government. I asked him what were the views of the Russian Government, and he replied that there were in his opinion only three possible through-routes from Russia to India, from Julfa through Tehran and Kerman to Nushki, from Askabad through Meshed to Seistan, and from Tashkend through Afghanistan to Peshawar.

I told M. Isvolsky in the plainest possible manner that all of these three lines were for the moment quite out of the question, that the idea of the junction of the Indian and Russian railway systems was at present premature although undoubtedly it would be made some day in the more or less remote future. I told him that His Majesty's Government would however approve of a line passing through Persia to the Persian Gulf at Mohammerah, from which place a British road concession as far as the Russian one at Khoremabad already exists. I pointed out that the advantages of this route from a Russian point of view, and, in view of his timidity of Germany, touched only lightly on the effect that the construction of this road would have on the Bagdad Railway.

M. Isvolsky studied the proposed route on the map with evident interest, and remarked that, although this route would have the undoubted advantage of neutralising the Bagdad Railway, he feared that it would be economically disadvantageous to Russia as it would facilitate the competition of foreign seaborne trade with that of Russian goods brought by rail. This, I observed, would be the same with all railways wherever they might lead to. He said that the matter was one which would require careful study, and that he would inform Sir Edward Grey later of his views. . . .

M. Isvolsky then asked me whether complete order had been restored on the Afghan border, and whether there was any possibility of a renewal of military operations. I told him that, as far as I knew, the military operations had been completely successful, and that there was no question of any further military measures. I pointed out to him that during the recent border troubles the advantages of the Anglo-Russian Convention had been put to the test, and that had it not been for this Convention, it might have been very difficult to prevent a punitive expedition being despatched into Afghanistan. There had also been no rumours, as was usual formerly in similar circumstances, of encouragement by Russian emissaries and intrigues with the tribes. These were the best proofs of a real improvement in Anglo-Russian relations, which there was every reason to hope would be fruitful of the best results, and the loyalty of the Russian Government in observing that part of the agreement relating to Afghanistan which had so far not been confirmed had been much appreciated by His Majesty's Government. . . .

In raising the question of the Balkan railways he complained bitterly of Baron Aehrenthal's action in springing upon him the Sanjak Railway concession without any warning whatever, a proceeding which had seriously disturbed the *status quo* in the Balkans, and had shaken his confidence in him. It was clear that in spite of Baron Aehrenthal having spent seventeen years in Russia, he had not grasped the real feeling in Russia towards the Slav population in the Balkans, since he had imagined that there could be only a short flare up in the Russian press, and that Austro-Russian relations would then return once more to their former groove. In this he was entirely mistaken, since the relations between Austria and Russia in connection with affairs in the Balkans could not be the same again. M. Isvolsky said that he felt considerable anxiety about the Balkan railway questions; he was convinced that the Sanjak Railway would be pushed by Austria with the utmost energy, and he considered it absolutely necessary that the Danube-Adriatic railway should be pushed forward *pari passu.* The Russian Government had only a very small financial interest in the proposed railway, but they realised that the completion of the Austrian schemes would mean the Germanisation of Macedonia. He had heard rumours of Austria having obtained a monopoly of railway construction in Macedonia, and if this rumour should be confirmed he would not hesitate to take strong measures to prevent what he would consider to be an infringement of the spirit of the Treaty of Berlin. Although he regretted that His Majesty's Government had been unable so far to support the Serbian railway scheme he appreciated their reasons for not doing so, but he hoped that, as soon as an agreement had been arrived at on the scheme of Macedonian reforms, His Majesty's Government would be able to lend their support to it.

I told M. Isvolsky that His Majesty's Government are not at all opposed in principle to the construction of railways in Macedonia, which must necessarily have a civilising influence, but that they had deprecated the opportuneness of the action of Austria at a moment when the Powers were devoting their whole attention to the question of reforms. I was, however, able to state that, as soon as the scheme of reforms had been put forward by the Powers at Constantinople, Sir Edward Grey would be ready to instruct His Majesty's Ambassador to impress upon the Porte the necessity for granting similar treatment to the Danube-Adriatic Railway as has already been granted to the Sanjak Railway. We were, I said, of the opinion that either no concession, or both concessions, should be granted.

M. Isvolsky entirely concurred, adding that the Russian Government would prefer that none should be granted.

The conversations which I had with M. Isvolsky, of which the above is a summary, lasted about three hours altogether, and although I have known M. Isvolsky personally for a great many years, they gave

me an interesting insight into the official side of his character which
I had not previously had an opportunity of seeing. He struck me as
very able and adroit, but extremely timid. Although he tried hard to
make me commit myself on the Macedonian question beyond the limit
of the authority which was given to me, any suggestion which I made
to him was at once set aside as requiring careful study. He was, however, very friendly throughout.

I had several opportunities of short conversations with the Emperor,
who looked extraordinary well and in the best possible spirits. On the
first occasion that His Majesty spoke to me he warmly praised Sir
Edward Grey's speech in the House of Commons which, he said showed
a remarkably true appreciation of the real political situation in Russia,
and which had made the best possible impression. . . .

The Emperor repeatedly expressed his great satisfaction at the
visit of the King and Queen which, he said, sealed and confirmed the
intention and spirit of the Anglo-Russian Agreement, and he expressed
his profound conviction that the friendly sentiments which now prevail between the two Governments could only mature and grow stronger
with the progress of time to the mutual advantage of both countries.
There might be occasional divergence of views in small matters, but
the identity of the national interests of England and Russia in Europe
and Asia would far outweigh any possible results from such trivial
differences of opinion. A glance at the Russian press of all shades and
opinions showed conclusively how extremely popular throughout Russia
the King's visit had become, and how it was welcomed as the visible
sign of a new era in Anglo-Russian relations. On my expressing my
surprise that such papers as the "Novoe Vremja," which I had always
regarded when in Russia as the bitterest foe of England, had now
become the ardent supporters of an Anglo-Russian understanding, His
Majesty admitted that he also was astonished at the rapidity with
which the feeling had spread, and that he had never been so surprised
as when he had read recently in a Chauvinistic "rag" called the "Sviet"
a warm article in praise of England, and urging closer relations between the two countries. Since the liberty of the press had been established in Russia, the press had really become the reflex of public
opinion, and it was astonishing to see the complete unanimity that
prevails as to the necessity of warm and friendly relations with England. The idea had taken firm root amongst the people and it only
required now to be carefully fostered to bear fruit in the future. The
Emperor admitted that from the point of view of the relations of
Russia to Germany, the liberty of expression now enjoyed by the
press had caused him and his Government considerable embarrassment,
since every incident that occurred in any distant province of the Empire, such as an earthquake or thunderstorm, was at once put down to
Germany's account, and serious complaints had recently been made to
him and the Government of the unfriendly tone of the Russian
press. . . .

I had but few opportunities of conversation with M. Stolypine, the Prime Minister, but he expressed himself in very friendly terms towards England, and warmly advocated a policy of *rapprochement* with our country. He gave me the impression of a very straightforward, strong, and courageous man. I was informed on the very best authority that when invited by the Emperor to accompany His Majesty to Reval he told the Emperor it must be distinctly understood that he went to meet a Constitutional Sovereign as the first Minister in a Government based on constitutional principles, to which His Majesty at once assented.

It is not for me to touch upon the private aspect of the effect of the King's visit upon the Emperor, and the manifest pleasure shown by the Emperor and the Empress at meeting again after so long an interval of trial and misfortune to some of their relations to whom they are most attached, but some of the members of the Emperor's suite commented upon the marked difference in the Emperor's spirits and attitude during the King's visit to Reval compared to what they were at the Emperor's recent visit to Swinemünde, where he felt anxiety all the time as to what might be unexpectedly sprung upon him.

On the second day of the visit, when the King was on board the Imperial yacht "Standart," His Majesty appointed the Emperor an Admiral of the Fleet in the British Navy. The Emperor was immensely pleased at the unexpected honour bestowed upon him by the King, and, at the official banquet on board the royal yacht in the evening, the King proposed the Emperor's health as a British Admiral of the Fleet, and the British cruisers saluted the Emperor.

It was a touching incident to all those who remember the arrogance and self-confidence of the large Russian Fleet which set sail for Japan in 1904, and of which the sole surviving ship lay at anchor at Reval alongside the Emperor's yacht, when the Emperor, rising to reply to the King's toast, with great modesty and apparent diffidence, paid the King a counter compliment by asking His Majesty to do him the honour of becoming an admiral "of our young and growing fleet," and as the King warmly accepted the honour, the guns of the Emperor's yacht saluted the new Russian Admiral of the Fleet.

It was a fitting ending to a satisfactory visit, which should be productive of the best possible results in the future.

June 12, 1908   CHARLES HARDINGE

(b) *Report of the Reval visit sent by the German Ambassador at St. Petersburg, Count von Pourtalès, to the Imperial Chancellor, Prince von Bülow*[1]

St. Petersburg, June 12, 1908

The meeting of the monarchs in Reval took place in fine weather according to program. The returning participants express great satis-

[1] *Die Grosse Politik,* Vol. XXV, No. 8807, pp. 451-454.

faction with the proceedings. It is probably too early to appraise rightly the political significance of the meeting. Official reference has thus far been principally to the objects which the visit of the English King did not have. On the Russian as well as upon the English side, it has been emphasized that there was no question of an extension of last year's agreement to an alliance and that the Russian-English agreement was not directed in hostility against anyone. Along with this negative side the interview probably had its positive results. M. Isvolsky has referred my colleague and me to the proposals for Macedonian reform as the principal object which he wished to discuss with Sir Charles Hardinge and expressed the hope of reaching an agreement with the London Cabinet. According to the wording of the official telegram regarding the outcome of the meeting of the monarchs, this hope appears not to have been fully realized. In the telegram it is said that it may be assumed that the negotiations regarding this question "almost" led to complete agreement.

Along with the Macedonian question, the situation in Persia may, as is generally assumed, have formed the object of discussion. At any rate a long discussion [Kaiser's note: "A regular conference!"] took place between the monarchs with the collaboration of Sir Charles Hardinge and M. Isvolsky as well as the two ambassadors, lasting, according to a creditable report, for two and a half hours.

The rather meagre accounts partially supported by apparent considerations, which I have thus far been able to obtain regarding the outcome of the interview, which, however, are probably not essentially supplemented by the communications given out by M. Isvolsky, nevertheless admit of the conclusion that, even if it did not come to new agreements in the harbor of Reval, the *rapprochement* between Russia and England has nevertheless been advanced a step on this occasion. Some observers claim to have noticed that England appeared more as the wooing party and Russia was very well pleased by the approach. It is not to be denied that the toast of the King of England struck a warmer note than the correct and well-considered words of the Tsar. Because the newspaper correspondents present were kept waiting a long time for the authentic version of the extemporaneous [Kaiser's note: "?!"] toast of the King of England while the prepared toast given by the Tsar was put at their disposal immediately, it is frequently concluded that the King must have said more than was made public. A passage upon which there has been much comment is one in which the King expressed the hope of another meeting "before long." This has been construed to mean that a return visit of the Tsar to England has been arranged, and indeed for this autumn. I may recall in this connection that M. Isvolsky recently told me that any foreign journey of the Tsar for this year was very improbable. At any rate, the King's expressed wish indicates that the personal relations between the royal and imperial families have grown very friendly during the time of the visit.

The attitude of the Russian press is also to be noted. If further proof were needed that the government here is by no means as powerless against the press as it claims in those moments in which certain press agitations are not disagreeable to it, such proof could be produced in the last few days. It was clearly perceivable that hostile attacks against Germany on the occasion of the English visit were not agreeable to the Government. Nowhere in the local press with the exception of a single sheet, the *Birschewyja Wjedomosti*, has there been contradiction of the "Rossija" article of last week in which suspicions of German policy were denounced. The anxiety frequently expressed by M. Isvolsky that by an official article he would only pour oil on the fire of agitation against us has thus been shown to be completely unfounded. [Kaiser's note: "He simply lied."] It is very noticeable that every article regarding the Reval interview is at pains to use moderate language regarding Germany and emphasizes the absence of any threat against Germany in the Anglo-Russian *rapprochement*.

When, moreover, the press gladly refers to the English-French-Russian grouping—said to be merely for promoting peace, but which might at any moment be changed into an alliance—I am inclined to believe that a train of thought not entirely foreign to the policy of the Russian Government is pursued. An alliance, so runs this argument, would be necessary only if the behavior of any power should make it necessary. [Kaiser's note: "Germany's, naturally."] By this, only Germany could be meant. The grouping in three is to form, a counterpoise to the assumed ascendency of German influence. Germany shall not be threatened; and the policy of "encirclement" is avoided; but wherever opportunity offers, it is desired to present a common diplomatic front, as was done at Algeçiras, to the supposed desire of Germany to achieve its position of world power. [Kaiser's note: "Only a veiling of an anti-German combination as before the Seven Years' War!"] This idea seems to be the cement of the ever-growing *rapprochement* between Russia and England. Russia can offer her hand all the more readily to this inasmuch as no sacrifice is demanded of her. The attitude of England toward Russia in recent months admits rather of the conclusion that a price is being offered to turn Russian policy into English channels. I cannot say in which field this concession may be sought, but I should not be surprised if Russia in the discussion of Persian matters had secured English diplomatic support against the assumed German advance of influence in Persia. So far, to be sure, I have no other evidence for this than the extreme nervousness which M. Isvolsky reveals every time he has occasion to speak of the behavior of our representation in Teheran.

Just as luck would have it, the English visit happened to follow immediately upon occurrences in the Duma the significance of which must be said to be the strengthening of constitutionalism in Russia. Further progress of Russia on this course will remove many obstacles which have thus far stood in the way of an Anglo-Russian understanding. [Kaiser's note: "Perhaps also the Tsar himself."] At any rate, we will in my opinion have to reckon in the near future with a growing intimacy between the cabinets of St. Petersburg and London [Kaiser's note: "Will be nice!"] of which the Reval interview is to be regarded as an expression. [Kaiser's closing note: "Very good and entirely correct. Therefore reform of the imperial finances! Many indirect taxes; strong fleet, strong army! Powder dry!"]

38. Franco-German Accord of February 8, 1909, Concerning Morocco[1]

[The Treaty of Algeciras did not make a final adjustment between France and Germany on the question of Morocco; incidents occurred which gave occasion for a reaffirmation of the principles upon which it was based. This 1909 convention, although favorably proclaimed from many sides at the time it was announced, proved to be of doubtful value because it, too, was hard to put into effect. The immediate causes for the friction which resulted in the Crisis of 1911, lay in the attempts at application of the following accord, which provided for the working out of schemes of Franco-German economic coöperation.]

The Government of the French Republic and the Imperial German Government, animated by an equal desire to facilitate the execution of the Act of Algeciras, have agreed to define the meaning that they attach to its clauses, in order to avoid all cause of misunderstanding between them in the future.

In consequence,

the Government of the French Republic, entirely attached to the maintenance of the integrity and independence of the Sherifian Empire, has resolved to safeguard the economic equality and consequently not to hinder the German commercial and industrial interests,

and the Imperial German Government, pursuing only economic interests in Morocco, recognising on the other hand that the particular political interests of France there are closely bound up with the consolidation of order and internal peace, and decided not to impede these interests,

declare that they will not pursue nor encourage any measure of a nature to create in their favor or in the favor of any other Power an economic privilege, and that they will endeavor to associate their citizens in the affairs for which they may obtain concessions.

---

[1] France. Ministère des affaires étrangères. *Documents diplomatiques: Affaires du Maroc. 1908-1910.* No. 114, *annexe*, p. 73.

39. Russo-Italian Accord at Racconigi, October, 1909[1]

[In the Franco-Italian reconciliation of 1902, France, it will be remembered, had agreed, in the event of a modification of the status of Morocco, not to oppose Italian influence in Tripoli. Accordingly, among the repercussions of the Moroccan crisis of 1911 was the Italian seizure of Tripoli. In 1905 Tittoni had declared that all interested Powers had recognized the prior rights of Italy in that province of Turkey. The bargain with Russia was part of this policy of gaining the consent of the Powers in advance to a deliberate war of aggression.]

Letter of Sazonov to Izvolski

To the Ambassador at Paris, A. P. Isvolsky
Very confidential

St. Petersburg, 15/28 Nov., 1912

M. Alexandre Petrovitch,

In my letter dated November 1, I explained to Your Excellency the reasons for my negative attitude as to the communication to the French Government of the text of our Treaty with Italy, concluded at Racconigi, although I understand perfectly how desirable is mutual information by the allies as to details of treaties existing between each of them and foreign powers.

The reasons which I gave continue to hold; nevertheless, in view of the declarations made to the French Minister of Foreign Affairs by the Italian Ambassador and communicated in your telegram no. 376, I am inclined now to satisfy your repeated demand to inform M. Poincaré confidentially of the terms of the treaty given below, in exchange for the communication to be made simultaneously to us through you, of the Franco-Italian Accord of 1902.

I consider it necessary, however, to hold strictly to the following conditions: you should make the communication to the Minister personally, verbally, without a written statement in any case. Having read the agreement, you must emphasize the fact that we have decided to make this communication only to M. Poincaré personally; we expect him to promise to keep silent in regard to it, not only in the French Council of Ministers, but even to his nearest colleagues.

On such conditions, you can read to M. Poincaré the enclosed copy of the accord concluded at Racconigi and which I beg Your Excellency to return to me by the next messenger, at the same time that you send the *memoire* of the text of the Franco-Italian treaty which you will have heard.

Believe me, etc.

Sazonof

---

[1] *Un Livre Noir.* Paris. Librairie du Travail (n. d.), Vol. I, pp. 356-358. Reprinted with the permission of the Librairie du Travail.

Russo-Italian Accord concluded at Racconigi [October, 1909]

1. Russia and Italy agree to act together, in the maintenance of the *status quo* in the Balkan Peninsula.

2. In any eventuality which may occur in the Balkans, they agree to support the application of the principle of nationality by the development of the Balkan States to the exclusion of all foreign domination.

3. They agree to oppose by common action all activity opposed to these ends; by "common action" is meant diplomatic action, all action of a different sort being simply reserved for a future understanding.

4. If Russia and Italy should wish to contract for Eastern Europe new agreements with a third power besides those which already exist, each would do so only with the participation of the other.

5. Italy and Russia engage themselves to consider with good will, the former, Russian interests in the question of the Straits, the latter, Italian interests in Tripoli and Cyrenaica.

40. RUSSO-GERMAN POTSDAM AGREEMENT, 1910

[In September, 1910, Izvolski became Russian Ambassador in Paris; whereupon Sazonov succeeded him as Russian Minister of Foreign Affairs. He favored Germany and thus welcomed the visit of the Tsar to the Kaiser in November, 1910, as affording an opportunity of reëstablishing cordial relations with Germany. The conversations were frank but were not confirmed in writing. When Bethmann-Hollweg, the German Chancellor, drew up a statement on general policy as a basis for his speech in the Reichstag, Sazonov avoided signing it. Accordingly, an agreement on the Middle East only was worked out and was finally signed on August 19, 1911. Meanwhile Bethmann's Reichstag speech (December 10, 1910) summed up the Potsdam conversations as an assurance that neither Germany nor Russia would enter any hostile combinations against the other. This view was regarded with consternation by Russia's allies, since the impression had prevailed in Paris and London that Persia and the Bagdad Railway were the only important questions that had been discussed.]

(a) *Sazonov's Report to the Tsar*[1]

I venture to submit to the benevolence of Your Imperial Majesty the account of the interviews which I have had with the Emperor William

---

[1] *Un Livre Noir,* Vol. II, pp. 331-334. Reprinted with the permission of the Librairie du Travail.

and the German statesmen at the time of the interview of Your Majesty with the German Emperor at Potsdam, last October.

St. Petersburg, Nov. 4, 1910

When I had the honor of talking with Emperor William at Potsdam, His Majesty touched on several political questions of the greatest importance.

The most interesting part of my interviews with the Emperor was that which concerned the question of Pan-Islamism and the development of the naval forces of Germany. On the subject of the first question, I have sought to draw the attention of His Majesty to the danger, from the point of view of the interests of Russia, which the expansion of panislamic propaganda coming from Constantinople and little by little diffused in all the countries where there are Moslems, presents. Inasmuch as this propaganda, I said to the Emperor, had for a base religious questions only, that is to say was only the expression of the religious idea of the califate, we have been able to view it with a calm eye, since the Mohammedan subjects of His Majesty the Emperor, according to our laws, enjoy liberty of conscience; but our attitude in regard to this propaganda has necessarily changed since it took on a political character, with revolutionary tendencies. I consider it my duty to say frankly to His Majesty that the rôle of protector of the Moslems can not be interpreted other than as an encouragement of this propaganda and inspires in us serious uneasiness. The creation of a new califate, "that of Berlin," I remarked, can not but make Russia uneasy, since it numbers more than twenty millions of Moslem subjects. This remark made the Emperor laugh; he replied to me that "the Califate of Berlin" did not exist and consequently did not present any danger to anyone. His Majesty added that he had had an interview on this subject with His Majesty the Emperor, in the course of which he had given the most satisfactory assurances as regards the rôle of Germany in the panislamic movement of which we are now witnesses. He is ready to repeat to me these assurances and begs me to accept them with confidence.

Then, after touching certain political questions, among others that of the danger to general peace and the stability of the monarchical principle presented by the activity of the Free Masons' lodges, the conversation passed to British and German naval armaments. The Emperor manifested on this question considerable irritation as regards the British Government which he accused of harboring secret designs against Germany, against which it was ready to act traitorously, as it had done in regard to the Low Countries, and, at the beginning of the 19th century, in regard to Denmark in destroying the fleet of that State in a brusque attack. "I have done my best," said the Emperor, "to avoid this danger, and it seems to me that the fleet which I have created is powerful enough not to suffer the fate of that of Denmark. That is what provokes the anger of the English against me and my

Government," added the Emperor. We should note the last remark made by Emperor William, when he declared that he would never permit the proportion between the naval forces of Germany and those of England, established by the program of German naval construction, to be changed, however little, to the detriment of the interests of Germany. "If," said the Emperor, "our program of constructions in 1912 is executed and England continues to increase her naval forces, we can only do likewise, and I assure you that we shall not remain behind."

In the course of my first interview with the German Secretary of State for Foreign Affairs, Herr von Kiderlen-Waechter spoke of our relations with Austria-Hungary and asked me where we stood on them. I replied that, in coming to Berlin, I had no intention of treating of this question, but from the moment when he touched upon it, I could only tell him what follows. Last winter, in renewing normal diplomatic relations, we had found a common point of view, which it had been necessary for us to adopt to maintain peace in the Balkan peninsula; the Austrian Government, while refusing to give to our declaration, as we had proposed, extensive publicity, accepted nevertheless the fundamental principles of policy that we had formulated concerning the Balkans, which policy has been confirmed by Count Aerenthal in his speech in the Assembly of Delegates. As far as I can see, if Austria does not change her point of view, there is nothing to menace European peace. "If, nevertheless," I said, "relations stamped with more confidence between Russia and Austria were becoming necessary in the interests of peace, relations which the recent past did not render possible, the Russian Government would not refuse to treat with Vienna through German statesmen, who in that case would serve as a link between us." M. Kiderlen-Waechter replied that Germany would accept that rôle and that Russia could count on her disinterested coöperation which would be lent in good faith with the aim of guaranteeing the peace equally necessary for the whole world.

The following day, during my interview with the Chancellor, Herr von Bethmann-Hollweg touched on the same question, but he did not confine himself to the declarations which had been made to me by the Secretary of State for Foreign Affairs; he told me on his own initiative, that in case Austria-Hungary did not remain faithful to the principles enunciated by Count Aerenthal and should manifest aggressive tendencies in the Balkans, she would not find from her ally a support which is not stipulated by any treaty and which does not conform to the interests of Germany. I told the Chancellor that I attached great importance to what he had just told me and that I would make it known to His Majesty the Emperor, to which the Chancellor replied that that conformed to his intentions and that he would be much obliged to me for it.

In the course of the Potsdam interview, there also arose the question of the Russian sphere of Persia. On this occasion the directors of

German policy confirmed once more the fact that Germany aspired to no political end in Persia, and that, disposed not to seek any territorial concession in our sphere, she only wished to guarantee to German products free importation into that country. I confirmed on my side the fact that we had no intention of violating the principle of free exchanges established by the Anglo-Russian entente of 1907 and of contravening in any way German commerce in Persia.

As concerns the question of the railway, I said that it was impossible to speak of it at present with precision, in view of the present circumstances in Persia, the difficulty of finding the necessary funds, of solving the question of guaranties, etc. But I added that in case we should construct a system of railways in the north of Persia, we should be more than ready to meet the desires of Germany to make a junction with the future Bagdad railway, at the place designated by Germany, notably at Khanekin, while agreeing not to impose on the Khanekin-Teheran line any condition unfavorable to German commerce, as differential tariffs, customs difficulties, etc. But we would wish in return that Germany should make a formal engagement not to construct any railway leaving the Bagdad line in the direction of the Russo-Persian frontier north of Khanekin and not to lend aid to anyone for similar enterprises, in view of the harm which such railways would cause us not only in an economic connection, but also from a strategic point of view. On this point, the directors of German policy expressed their perfect agreement.

The question of the Bagdad railway itself was not raised. Nevertheless, I judged it necessary to establish the view that in case of the partition of this line between the interested Powers, we could not remain with empty hands and that we would wish to have the Bagdad-Khanekin section. This declaration did not provoke any objection.

As to the encroachments of the Turks on the Persian frontiers, the most categorical assurances were given me that Germany was not concerned in them at all and that she was in no way disposed to encourage the Turks in their aggressive disposition. In particular, a propos of the declaration made last year by the Ottoman Minister of Foreign Affairs to our Ambassador at Constantinople that the Turkish troops had been sent into Ourmie on the demand of the German Government to protect a school of German missionaries there, M. de Kiderlen-Waechter denied the fact in the most categorical manner and added that there was no German school at Ourmie.

SAZONOF

(b) *Account of the negotiations by the British Ambassador to Russia*[1]

Though the Emperor was acting in perfect good faith, he failed to grasp the fact that the concessions which his Government were making

---

[1] George Buchanan, *My Mission to Russia*. London, Cassell, 1923. 2 vols. Vol. I, pp. 94-101. Reprinted with the permission of Little, Brown & Company.

to Germany with regard to the Bagdad railway were incompatible with the support which they were pledged to give their partners in the Triple Entente. It was not, as I subsequently endeavoured to impress on M. Sazonoff, that we had the slightest objection to Russia cultivating good relations with Germany, but that we were afraid that she was about to do so at our expense. Anxious as we were ourselves to come to an understanding with Germany on the subject of armaments, we should never, I assured him, think of taking any step that might entail the sacrifice of our friendship with Russia and France. We trusted, therefore, that the Russian Government would, in its dealings with Germany, show a like consideration for our interests.

In view of the historical interest attaching to them, I appended a short account of the long-drawn-out negotiations which ensued between the Russian and German Governments. They entailed constant intervention on my part, as, had not the former Government realized in time that there was a point beyond which they could not go, the latter would have succeeded in causing a serious split in the ranks of the Entente Powers.

At the beginning of December, 1910, Sazonoff had submitted to the German Ambassador a draft agreement embodying the substance of the Potsdam conversations. By the first of its articles Russia engaged not to oppose the realization of the Bagdad railway nor to put any obstacle in the way of the participation of foreign capital in that enterprise, on the condition that she would not be required to make any pecuniary or economic sacrifices. By the second, she undertook to link up the Bagdad railway with the future North Persian railway system. By the third, Germany engaged neither to construct nor to give her material or diplomatic support to the construction of any railway in the zone situated between the Bagdad line and the Russian and Persian frontier to the north of Khanikin; while, by the fourth, she declared that she had no political interests in Persia; that she would but pursue there objects of a commercial character; that she recognized Russia's special political, strategical and economic interests in North Persia, and that she would not seek for any concession of a territorial character to the north of a line running from Kasri Chirin by Ispahan, Yezd and Khakh to the Afghan frontier, in the latitude of Ghazrik.

The engagement taken by Russia in the first article was, Sazonoff contended, to apply only to the Koniah-Bagdad section of the railway, and left the Russian Government free, as far as the Gulf section was concerned, to coöperate with Great Britain in the future, as in the past. Early in January the *Evening Times* published the text of the draft agreement, and in order to prove that this version was unauthentic the two Governments agreed to recast the whole text. The negotiations now turned mainly on the question of the linking up of the two railway systems, as Germany was anxious to bind Russia to commence the construction of the linking-up line as soon as a branch line from Sadijeh had reached Khanikin. This question was complicated by the fact that Russian public opinion proved to be opposed to the expenditure of money on a railway that was to open the Persian markets to German trade, before provision was made for the construction of a railway from Enzeli to Tehran that would render a similar service to Russian goods. In order to get over this difficulty M. Sazonoff suggested that British and French financiers should finance the construction of both the Enzeli-Tehran and the Khanikin-Tehran lines; but in the absence of any guarantee from the Russian Government, this suggestion could not be entertained. The only other alternative—that of allowing the Germans to build the railway—was opposed by us on the ground that the Germans would then get the control of the railway into their own hands, with the result that they might use it for the transport of troops. On February 21 Sazonoff handed the German Ambassador a revised draft, under which Russia engaged to obtain a concession for the linking-up line as soon as the Sadijeh-Khanikin branch line had been completed, while the text of the first article of the original draft was modified so as to restrict Russia's engagement—not to oppose the realization of the Bagdad railway—to the Koniah-Bagdad section. Russia also stipulated that, in the event of her ceding her rights in the linking-up line to any third party, all the other clauses of the agreement should still remain in force.

The negotiations were interrupted, owing to the serious illness that incapacitated Sazonoff for over nine months, but were resumed later on by the acting Foreign Minister, M. Neratoff, who in July submitted a further amended draft.

The progress of the negotiations was now somewhat accelerated, as both Governments had special reasons for bringing them to a speedy conclusion. Germany, on the one hand, was engaged in a delicate conversation with France on the subject of Morocco, and considered the moment well chosen for the publication of an agreement which would, she hoped, demonstrate the intimate character of her relations with France's ally. Russia, on the other hand, was anxious—in view of the internal conflict that had broken out in Persia—to secure a declaration of Germany's *désinteressement* in that country, so that she might have a freer hand to deal with the situation should intervention become necessary. Germany declined to accept the restricted interpretation placed by Russia on the term "Bagdad Railway" or to consent to the retention in the agreement of Article III of the original draft, under which she was to engage not to construct any railway in the zone north of Khanikin. The German Ambassador did, however, give a categorical verbal assurance, on the part of the Emperor William, that Germany would only construct in that zone such railways as she was entitled to build under the Bagdad railway concession. She further claimed the right to obtain for herself the concession for the Khanikin-Tehran railway, should Russia, or the finance syndicate to whom she might cede her rights, fail to commence its construction within two years of the completion of the Sadijeh-Khanikin branch line. All her demands were, in the end, conceded, and the agreement as finally signed was a diplomatic victory for Germany. The initial mistake committed by Sazonoff, in allowing himself to be entrapped during his conversations with M. Kiderlen-Waechter into giving verbal assurances, of which he did not at the time realize the full significance, was never retrieved. He had pledged Russia, without previous consultation with Great Britain and France, to withdraw her opposition to the Bagdad railway scheme, and, though he subsequently endeavoured to restrict this engagement to the Koniah-Bagdad Section, it was clear from the outset that Germany would hold him to the strict letter of his bond.

Whether, in thus accelerating the final stage of these negotiations, the Russian Government were prompted or not by the desire to be relieved of all apprehensions as to Germany's attitude in the event of their embarking on a policy of active intervention in Persia, the signature of the Russo-German agreement was shortly followed by a change for the worse in their relations with that country. This change was primarily due to the fact that the Persian Government had, in spite of Russia's repeated remonstrances, taken Mr. Shuster and other American advisers into their service. One of Mr. Shuster's first acts was to entrust Major Stokes (at one time British military attaché at Tehran) with the task of organizing a treasury gendarmerie. The appointment of a British officer to the command of a gendarmerie, whose operations were to extend over the whole of Persia, including the Russian sphere in the north, was resented by the Russian Government as a violation of the Anglo-Russian understanding; and it was only by making strong representations at Tehran, which resulted in the appointment being left in abeyance, that we were able to convince them of our good faith.

But hardly had this incident been happily closed when Mr. Shuster's disregard of Russia's privileged position in Persia provoked a still more serious crisis. Bent, as he was, on securing for himself an absolutely free hand with regard to loans and railway concessions, he gave her serious offence by appointing an Englishman (Mr. Lecoffre) as treasury agent at Tabriz; and in November he brought matters to a head by seizing a property belonging to Shoa es Sultaneh that had been mortgaged to the Russian bank, and by replacing the Persian Cossacks on guard there by treasury gendarmes. The Russian Government at once presented an ultimatum demanding an apology and the reinstatement of the Persian Cossacks within forty-eight hours; and, as the Persian Government, in order to avoid compliance with these demands, resigned, orders were given for the despatch to Kaswin of a force sufficiently strong to enable a detachment being eventually sent to occupy Tehran.

It was in vain that I endeavoured to impress on the acting Minister for Foreign Affairs the serious consequences which an occupation of Tehran might have for the maintenance of the Anglo-Russian understanding. While assuring me that Russia had no intention of violating the principle of Persian integrity, he not only refused to cancel the orders already given, but told me that, unless the Persian Government complied with the terms of the ultimatum before the Russian troops landed on Persian territory, further demands would be presented. With M. Kokovtsoff, who had recently succeeded M. Stolypin as President of the Council, I was more successful; and after Neratoff's uncompromising language, I was agreeably surprised to receive from him the unqualified assurance that, as soon as the two original Russian demands had been conceded, the Russian troops would be recalled. M. Kokovtsoff, however, had counted without his colleagues in the Government. The Russian troops having, meanwhile, landed at Enzeli, a second ultimatum was despatched, demanding a refund of the cost of the military expedition, the dismissal of Mr. Shuster and Mr. Lecoffre, and an engagement that the Persian Government would not in future take any foreigners into their service without the previous consent of the Russian and British Governments.

The despatch of this second ultimatum, in the teeth of the categorical assurances given me by the President of the Council, naturally evoked a protest from His Majesty's Government; and in my conversations with M. Neratoff I once more endeavored to dissuade him from an occupation of Tehran, which would, as I reminded him, be regarded in England as a blow struck at the independence of Persia, and consequently at our understanding with Russia. Neratoff, notwithstanding, remained obdurate on this point, and at the same time declined to sanction a statement being made in the House of Commons to the effect that the two Governments had agreed under no circumstances to recognize the ex-Shah Mohammed Ali, who had recently returned to Persia. It was only after Sazonoff had, towards the middle of December, resumed the direction of foreign affairs that the tension between the two Governments relaxed and that the Russian demands, as the result of further negotiations, were toned down. They were accepted by the Persian Government before the end of the year, though, owing to the outbreak of serious disturbances in North Persia, the promised recall of the Russian troops from Kaswin had to be postponed.

I have recorded the above incidents in order to show how difficult it sometimes was for the two Governments to act in concert owing to the diametrically opposite standpoints from which the situation was viewed by public opinion in their respective countries. In Russia the despatch of troops to Kaswin and the contemplated occupation of Tehran were regarded as measures which it was incumbent on her to take for the vindication of her outraged honour. In England, on the contrary, they were condemned as an unjustifiable attempt to bring a weak country into subjection and as a violation of its integrity and independence. So acute was the divergence of views that, had not the Persian Government yielded before the order was given for an advance on Tehran, the Anglo-Russian understanding would with difficulty have

borne the strain. Fortunately, both Sir Edward Grey and M. Sazonoff
were statesmen endowed with the gifts of tact, patience and forbear-
ance, so necessary for the conduct of delicate negotiations; and, though
it is now the custom to depreciate the services of the Old Diplomacy,
I doubt whether the vaunted New Diplomacy would have been equally
successful in saving the Anglo-Russian understanding from the ship-
wreck with which it was more than once threatened.

41. The Moroccan Crisis of 1911

[Though the Franco-German Morocco agreement of 1909 was lived up
to at first, friction gradually developed. The French occupied Fez,
where reports of disorder gave them a pretext for securing a stronger
hold on Morocco, if it did not actually cause genuine fear of danger to
Europeans. German motives for sending the gunboat *Panther* to
Agadir are clearly shown in a memorandum drawn up by Kiderlen-
Waechter, the German Foreign Minister, on May 3: he saw that it
would do no good to protest against the French absorption of Morocco; Germany should therefore secure an object which would make
the French ready to give them compensations; just as the French protected their subjects in Fez, so Germany argued she could do the same
for German subjects at Mogador and Agadir by peacefully stationing
ships there, and then waiting to see if France would not offer compensations. But the English and the French saw more sinister designs in
the German action.

The Mansion House speech caused an outburst of feeling in Germany where it was regarded as a threat, but it did not prevent a peaceful settlement for Germany simultaneously informed England that, contrary to Grey's fear, she had no intention of establishing herself on
the Atlantic coast of Morocco, and perhaps by causing Germany to
moderate her demands. By the agreement of November 4, 1911,
Germany practically acknowledged that France might establish a protectorate over Morocco, and in return France ceded more than 100,000
square miles of the French Congo, thus giving Germany two river out-
lets to the Congo for the export of their Cameroon products, while
Germany, to enable the French Government to justify the agreement
to French public opinion, ceded to France the "duck's bill," a small
valueless tract of Cameroon territory east of Lake Chad. That there
was an even compromise on each side is shown by the bitter criticism of
both French and German nationalists.]

(a) *Lloyd George's "Mansion House Speech," July 21, 1911*[1]

. . . But I am also bound to say this—that I believe it is essential
in the highest interests, not merely of this country but of the world,

[1] The London *Times*, July 22, 1911.

that Britain should at all hazards maintain her place and her prestige amongst the Great Powers of the world. [Cheers.] Her potent influence has many a time been in the past, and may yet be in the future, invaluable to the cause of human liberty. It has more than once in the past redeemed Continental nations, who are sometimes too apt to forget that service, from overwhelming disaster and even from international extinction. I would make great sacrifices to preserve peace. I conceive that nothing would justify a disturbance of international good will except questions of the gravest national moment. But if a situation were to be forced upon us in which peace could only be preserved by the surrender of the great and beneficent position Britain has won by centuries of heroism and achievement, by allowing Britain to be treated where her interests were vitally affected as if she were of no account in the Cabinet of nations, then I say emphatically that peace at that price would be a humiliation intolerable for a great country like ours to endure. [Cheers.] National honour is no party question. [Cheers.] The security of our great international trade is no party question; the peace of the world is much more likely to be secured if all nations realize fairly what the conditions of peace must be. And it is because I have the conviction that nations are beginning to understand each other better, to appreciate each other's points of view more thoroughly, to be more ready to discuss calmly and dispassionately their differences, that I feel assured that nothing will happen between now and next year which will render it difficult for the Chancellor of the Exchequer in this place to respond to the toast proposed by you, my Lord Mayor, of the continued prosperity of the public purse.

(b) *Extracts from the speech delivered by Bethmann-Hollweg in the Reichstag, November 9, 1911*[1]

For the consideration of the agreements laid before you it will first of all be of value to inform you as to the latest phase of the Morocco question, and as to the important points of the agreements concluded. The Algeciras Act was intended to maintain the independence of Morocco with a view to the economic development of the country for the benefit of the trade of all the Powers parties to it. It was soon evident that one of the essential conditions was lacking, namely, a Sultan who was actual ruler of the country, and was in a position to carry out the reforms contemplated. Even Sultan Mulai Hafid could not do so in spite of his personal qualities. He became more and more dependent upon foreign influence, and came into constantly increasing conflict with the tribes of his own country in consequence. This led to ever-growing influence on the part of France, for, of the four Powers which

[1] Cited from Great Britain, *Parliamentary Papers.* 1911. Vol. CIII. Cmd. 5970, "Morocco, No. 1 (1911)."

since the seventies possessed treaty rights to maintain military missions at the Sultan's Court, only the French Mission had succeeded in establishing its position. In the same way France had for long supplied Morocco with money. The position of the Sultan, surrounded by hostile tribes and shut up in Fez, became eventually so precarious that France informed the Powers that grave apprehensions must be felt for the lives and property of her officers at the Sultan's Court and of the European colony.

France accordingly declared that she proposed to send troops to Fez, and to conduct the Europeans back to the coast. We had received no such threatening reports from Fez and, therefore, declared that our colony did not require foreign assistance. Since, however, we could naturally assume no responsibility for the lives of the French citizens who were apparently threatened, we raised no objection to the advance to Fez to bring back the threatened French citizens to the coast. We added the explicit reservation, however, which we also announced publicly, that we retained our liberty of action, should the French expedition go beyond its alleged object, even should such action be merely the result of circumstances arising out of the expedition. This occurred, as was to be expected. France exerted practically unlimited sway over the relieved Sultan in virtue of her influence, which had gradually become absolute. The independence of the Sultan assumed by the Algeciras Act thus ceased to exist. It has, indeed, been urged that the Sultan himself summoned the French to his assistance, but a ruler who summons foreign troops to his assistance and who relies solely upon the support of foreign bayonets, is no longer the independent ruler on whose existence the Algeciras Act was based. We let this be known and suggested to France an understanding, leaving, of course, the initiative to her. We indicated the general outlines only of our programme to the effect that we should be ready to take into account the altered position of France resulting from the changed conditions, but that in return we must demand more precise guarantees for the equality assured to us in the domain of commerce and industry, especially in regard to public works, besides compensations for the rights assumed by France without previous understanding with us and going beyond the letter and spirit of the Algeciras Act. At first we received no positive proposals from Paris, whilst the French military power continued to spread in Morocco, and the fiction began gradually to become established, not only in France but also with the other Powers, that France was acting in pursuance of a European mandate. When, therefore, German interests appeared to be threatened in consequence of the events in Morocco, we sent a war-ship to Agadir. The dispatch of this ship was primarily intended for the protection of the lives and property of our subjects. It represented at the same time a clear intimation of our right and our intention to defend our subjects in

Morocco just as independently as France protected hers, so long as she came to no understanding with us. This object of the dispatch of our war-ship and its limitation to this object were announced, immediately before the arrival of the ship, to the Powers through our Ambassadors and Ministers accredited to them. It is, accordingly, an untrue assertion if the dispatch of a ship to Agadir was represented in the press—in the foreign press—as a provocation and a threat. We provoke and threaten no one; but we protect our rights, and we shall not allow ourselves to be deterred or hindered by anyone.

The discussion with France then began. From a purely formal point of view we might have demanded the restoration of the *status quo ante*, that is to say, the status of 1906; theoretically that would have been correct, in practice it was impossible. It was hardly possible to clear Morocco again of foreign troops without incurring the danger of internal disturbances. The *restitutio in integrum* would, moreover, have been highly incomplete, since the lasting impression produced by the action of France would have continued to prevail even after the withdrawal of her troops. Finally we should have only come back to a situation, and that under circumstances unfavourable for us, which had resulted in constant friction to which both Governments desired equally to put an end. The assertion that the "Panther" was sent to Agadir with the object of acquiring territory in Morocco is incorrect. By the agreement of February 1909 the acquisition of territory in Morocco was already put out of the question. Our programme, which was drawn up long before the dispatch of the "Panther," was conceived on the same lines. The incorrectness of the assertion is also established by the declarations which we made to the foreign Powers immediately before the arrival of the ship at Agadir. It is also made evident by the declarations which the Imperial Government issued through the organs of the press simultaneously with the arrival of the ship at Agadir. It is highly regrettable that this incorrect assertion should have been unpatriotically made use of, even at home, in order to create the impression of a retreat of the Imperial Government and a humiliation of Germany.

In the negotiations with France the leading idea was that it had been shown to be impossible for the Moors to reëstablish and maintain order in their country by their own efforts, and that the intervention of a foreign Power was required. As regards the greater part of Morocco, this Power could only be France. The greater the freedom which France obtained, therefore, the better she was in a position to guarantee and assume responsibility for the maintenance of order. In return we have obtained far-reaching and detailed guarantees for the equal treatment of non-French trade and for the rights of non-French nationals resident in Morocco. The particulars may be seen in the treaty laid before you.

I come to the question of the compensations. In connection therewith I will speak first of all of the resignation of Herr von Lindequist. . . .

This brings me back to the real point. I have just explained why
our claims for compensation were directed towards a compact addition
to the Cameroons. I have further explained that the territory which
has fallen to us includes such tracts of land as those who know our
colonies told us were worth striving for. Their acquisition is of value
for the present, and at the same time it rounds off the Cameroons in a
satisfactory manner. But we had also to think of the value to us of
gaining access to Africa's greatest river, the Congo, and to its tributary, the Ubangi. On that point also we succeeded. I do not contest
the fact that in doing so we had also to take over countries which are
for the present of less value, and the administration of which will
give us some trouble. I need not tell you it was just as hard for me
as for the colonial administration to cede the territory on the Logóne.
But we could never have achieved what we wanted without some sort
of an exchange of territory. I admit that the new boundaries are to a
certain extent inconvenient and difficult for the administration to deal
with. Similar difficulties have, however, already existed on the old
southern boundary of the Cameroons and in the "Duck's Beak." In
order to lessen these difficulties a wide scope of action has been left to
the commission to be appointed for the delimitation of the frontiers.
They are to pay particular attention to the natural boundaries and
to the homogeneousness of the native tribes. For this purpose the
commission is to have the right to deviate from the boundary laid
down in general lines by treaty, here in favour of one of the parties,
there in favour of the other. They have only to be careful to see that
the net result constitutes a balance of deviations. Far-reaching conditions have been laid down for the transit traffic of both countries. We
have given one another mutual assurances respecting the extension
and the linking up of the railways, and we are thereby now in a position
to gain access by railway to the great rivers in case we should find it
necessary. We guarantee the French a military road to the Congo for
their North-East Congo territory similar to that granted to them by
England in the Niger basin, which has led to no difficulties on either
side.

The concluding article of the agreement does not become operative
at present, but it may do so in the event of territorial changes taking
place in the Congo basin, in which we should then have a voice.

Gentlemen, a regular storm of indignation has now been raised
against these acquisitions in the Congo by a large section of public
opinion. No expression is strong enough to condemn the work done by
the Government and to discredit it abroad. A correct opinion can only
be formed by not passing over either the bad or the good side of the
bargain. There certainly exist, I repeat, among these new acquisitions,
tracts of little value, perhaps of no value at all, but this is also the

case in our other colonies. The concessions are a heavy burden, but they are limited in point of time, and they will be subject to German jurisdiction and administration, which will protect us against abuses. The sleeping sickness which prevails in some districts is a sad burden.

On the other hand, we receive valuable strips of country, country which is conveniently situated as regards the Cameroons. No one can deny that, not even the gentlemen who wish to disturb me with their interruptions. We gain access to the Congo and Ubangi. The value of this access will only be realised in the future. But that it will be realised even you will not deny. We get, on the whole, quite a considerable new colonial territory. You should not reproach us with trying on this occasion to get what we can, because Germany has only now, unfortunately much too late, joined the ranks of colonial nations.

I am firmly convinced that the favourable manner in which the Cameroons have developed, thanks to the activity of our merchants and the energy of our governors and protectorate troops, will also find its echo in the newly acquired territory. Those who want to carry on a colonial policy should not forget future possibilities in considering present values. From a mere "sand-box" to what has South-West Africa grown? Who saw furthest into the future: those who laughed at Rhodesia or the man whose energy gave that country his name?

All the successes attained by the great colonial nations have only been won by the fact that these nations did not take short but very long views, and that they had the courage to make light of the difficulties of the present for the sake of successes to be awaited in the perhaps far-distant future.

Nor, gentlemen, is it true that the French are glad to be rid of a part of the Congo territory. The French statesmen have assessed at a high figure—and rightly so—the advantages they have gained in Morocco, but with no light heart did they give up for it wide stretches of a territory to which experienced and distinguished French explorers and officers had for a generation devoted the best efforts of their lives.

Such has been the sequence of events and such is the result.

Our programme from the outset was as follows:—Recognition of increased political rights for France, in return only for an increased guarantee of our economic interests in Morocco and for colonial acquisition. We never for a moment attempted to acquire territory in Morocco. Negotiations between ourselves and France alone, not before an international congress, nor with the participation of a third Power. This is the programme which we drew up and to which we have adhered. We have not allowed ourselves to be turned aside one single step from following it either by external or internal influences. All the reproaches of weakness which have been cast in our teeth during these last months, reproaches of weakness and of yielding, the talk of a "second Olmutz" and what not, all fall to the ground before the facts as they are. The negotiations between ourselves and France have been carried on without interruption on both sides in the endeavour to come to a working agreement acceptable to both parties. At no stage of the negotiations was any language used, any idea mooted, in any quarter which would have been incompatible with the honour of either party. There was never any occasion for the "banging on the table with the fist," which was recommended to us. Moreover, I do not hold with this sort of threatening gesture. I should prefer, at the appropriate moment, to act. We no longer live in the Homeric days when threatening and bragging was part of a soldier's outfit. Germany is strong enough to do without that sort of armour. She will know how to draw her sword if need be. Foreign policy is only possible on such a basis. I must here make it quite clear, in order to contradict the misleading statements of the foreign and also of our own press, that His Majesty the Emperor commanded that the programme, which was already drawn up in May last, should be adhered to throughout all the phases of the negotiations, fully realising that every political action of a Great Power can evoke the fateful question of war or peace, and fully prepared to draw the sword in defence of the nation's honour. On this point the Emperor knew that he was at one with the nation, which during this whole time has been imbued with the firm determination to defend its honour and its vital interests against all the world. As a matter of fact, there never at any moment existed the slightest doubt as to the complete readiness for war of the army and navy. The reports, which are now being spread abroad to the effect that at a confidential council our readiness for war, especially as regards the navy, was questioned, are pure inventions. They are belied by the facts.

Now it has been asserted—and this assertion has eaten deep into the people—that we retreated before England. A speech made at a banquet by the British Minister, Mr. Lloyd George, has specially served in this connection. [Laughter and cheers on the Left.]—Gentlemen, I am speaking of a grave matter, and I beg you to allow me to finish my speech without interruption.—One of our Conservative papers, indeed, by substituting "Germany" for "England" right through the speech, brought out clearly that the speech, taken by itself, might equally have been made by a German statesman without giving occasion for criticism. What gave significance to the speech was the fact that the whole of the French press, and a great portion of the English press, interpreted it in a chauvinistic sense and in a manner spiteful towards Germany, and that this interpretation was in no way repudiated from the English side. I found myself constrained to instruct the Imperial Ambassador in London to speak about the matter. My representation was to the effect that we were discussing the Morocco question with France; that England's interests were not so far affected thereby; and that if England should consider her interests to be affected by the result of the discussions, we expected the British Government to urge those interests upon the two contracting Governments only through the usual diplomatic channel. The British

Government, after this, intimated no more desire of any kind to take part in our negotiations with France.

For all that, the ill-effects of that after-dinner speech remained. Owing more particularly to the interpretation given to it by the French and English press, it produced in wide German circles a very bitter feeling, which naturally found expression in a more or less forcible manner in our press. To judge by its effect, this speech was, it must be admitted, not such as to further a good understanding with England. However sincerely I regret this, I must distinctly protest against the speech having been used as a justification for reproaching the Government with a weak and hesitating policy. As a matter of fact, our programme of a reasonable settlement with France has been carried out without interference on the part of a third Power and uninfluenced by irresponsible press manœuvres.

The English Minister, Sir Edward Grey, in an appeal to the press of both countries, gave utterance to serious words in the House of Commons the day before yesterday, and especially warned the press against spreading false news. I can only associate myself with this warning in order that ideas do not become established in the public opinion of both countries which in the long run could not but poison the relations between the two great countries to their mutual disadvantage, and, I may add, to the disadvantage of the whole world.

I have explained to you that we have carried through what we intended. In everyday life that is not usually called weakness. But, I take it, the reproach was really directed to another point, namely, that we ought to have tried for something else, something more; that was what the honour and prestige of Germany demanded: either Southern Morocco or the restitution of the Algeciras Act. In fact, one thing or the other. Yes, gentlemen, he who considers the possession of Southern Morocco to be a vital interest for Germany, he who thinks that failure to claim this possession meant jeopardising Germany's prestige, for him there cannot be any alternative; he must demand that we shall go to war in order to conquer Southern Morocco, for him the restitution of the Algeciras Act can be no real equivalent. There is nothing to be got out of this formula, from the point of view of Germany's honour and prestige; neither, however, will it yield anything from the point of view of *Realpolitik*.

Southern Morocco was not a desirable country for us, as its acquisition, protection, and defence would have entailed upon us sacrifices out of all proportion to the value of the country. That has been till the middle of last summer the general opinion. I will not speak of Bismarck, who, as is well known, expressed the desire that France might annex Morocco. You might perhaps reply that times have changed since then, but even since Bismarck's days the opinion has been continually upheld that we should not seek to acquire political rights in Morocco. This opinion was formally recognised by the agreement of February 1909, and all parties in the Reichstag assented to this recognition. In what way, then, is the situation thought now to have suddenly changed? Southern Morocco is doubtless a fine country; it is said to be very rich in minerals, to have a fertile soil on which German emigrants could settle. I will not argue this point, although there is much that might be said on the subject of a policy of colonisation in Morocco. I assume that it is in itself a very desirable piece of territory. But I must say that those who consider it to be Germany's duty to conquer desirable countries by war might just as well, in fact, perhaps, more readily, bethink themselves of other countries than Morocco. That, indeed, has actually happened even in regard to European countries.

These are mere phantasies, and I am only astonished that people can still be found abroad who attach importance to them in connection with German policy. Germany can only pursue a strong policy, in the sense of a *Weltpolitik,* if she keeps herself strong on the continent. It is only the weight which we exert as a continental Power which makes world commerce and colonial policy possible. Both collapse if we do not maintain our power at home; if we acquire outlying positions, to defend which we should be obliged to fritter away and weaken our continental power, then we should be sawing at the branch on which we sit. German policy in the last decades was therefore right in not pursuing political aims in Morocco, and therefore our present policy is also right in having from the very outset excluded all thought of the acquisition of territory in Morocco. It is, I claim, to the credit of our policy that we did not pursue the Utopia of the acquisition of Moorish territory. The complaints as to our bad policy do not, however, emanate only from those who wished to acquire a portion of Morocco. They have been raised in much wider circles. If these complaints have any other object than to put difficulties in the way of the Government's conduct of foreign affairs, then they ought to point to a tangible aim. I am not speaking of those who were simply bent on war this summer. There were such people. But their number was not so big as the words they used. Others wanted a preventive war, either against France, or against England, or against both at the same time. You all know what Bismarck thought of preventive wars. He has said that his advice would never be to go to war because a war was sooner or later inevitable; he had no means of seeing what a hand Providence was playing. Even a successful war he regarded as in itself an evil which it should be the aim of national statesmanship to prevent. Now, Gentlemen, these are the principles which have guided us too. No one can tell whether Germany will some day be fated to go to war with her neighbours. But on me who have now to bear the responsibility it is incumbent so to conduct affairs that a war which is avoidable, and which is not demanded by the honour of the country, shall be avoided. Such have been the principles on which the last phase of our Moroccan policy has been based.

Morocco was like a continually festering wound in our relations

not only with France but also with England. The French expedition
to Fez led to an acute stage and rendered an operation necessary.
We have performed this operation in order to heal the wound. We
should never have reached the result now before you, if both Governments had not steered for the same goal. I consider it a great gain
that it should have been possible for Germany and France to arrive
at a peaceful understanding on such a delicate question as that of
Morocco, involving as it did so many open and concealed dangers.
This fact is worth more than all discussions on disarmament and arbitration treaties. It can become the foundation for the development and
consolidation of relations in harmony with the true needs and progress
of the two great nations. It is true that only the future can build on
this foundation; but the present would have been guilty of a sin of
omission had it cast aside the corner-stone instead of putting it in
place.

I said just now that the Moroccan question also affected our relations with England. I would say one word more on this point. In virtue
of treaty stipulations England stood on the side of France, at least
diplomatically, in all differences between us and France respecting
Morocco. Our understanding with France accordingly also cleans the
slate in respect to our relations with England.

I return to the consideration from which I started. The depression
and pessimism evinced by our people, which sought to urge the Government to other deeds, ought to have indicated tangible aims, aims
which could have been achieved in solving the Morocco question. I have
explained why we did not attempt to secure a portion of Morocco.
Failing that, we were pressed with special urgency at least to break off
negotiations with France, to insist on the reversion to the Algeciras
Act. To break off negotiations would have been easy enough, still easier
perhaps not to begin them at all. But the reversion to the Algeciras
Act! Gentlemen, I see no advantage for Germany in the restoration of
a situation which suffered from the fiction, no longer tenable, of the
sovereignty of the Sultan of Morocco and the independence of the
Shereefian Empire. Surely we have got to know enough of this situation
since 1906. It was materially and morally unsatisfactory to us. The
desire for the reversion to the Algeciras Act was also to some extent
inspired by another motive: If we could not, or would not, have
Southern Morocco, then, at least, France must not have it. This was
frequently to be read in the press throughout this summer. In my
opinion, the value of a policy does not consist in the injury done to
others, but in the advantages gained for one's own country. A policy
which aims at injuring another without considering whether it benefits
oneself is a shortsighted one. The animosity which it engenders must
be paid for sooner or later. He, however, who sees in the increase of
power accruing to France from her protectorate over Morocco a
danger to Germany's existence, becomes an advocate of a preventive war.

Hence, Gentlemen, why this yearning for reversion to the Algeciras Act? Was this reversion, too, demanded by Germany's prestige? No, Gentlemen, our prestige as a Great Power demands that we should not suffer an international treaty like the Algeciras Act, which bears our signature, to be altered for the benefit of one party without our assent and to our disadvantage. For this we had to fight, if necessary with the sword. This has been our attitude, and our action has been successful.

In conclusion, let me sum up. How did things stand before Fez and Agadir? Nominally Morocco was independent; *de facto* it had fallen under French influence. After Tangier and Algeciras this complicated and nebulous situation was a standing menace to our relations with France. The "open door" existed indeed on paper, but it lacked the special guarantees which the obscurity of the internal situation rendered doubly urgent. Political aspirations in Morocco we had renounced.

And now? We have given up nothing in Morocco that we had not already given up before. In return we have obtained the economic guarantees which were hitherto lacking. We have besides acquired a considerable colonial possession, which will—of this I am certain—bear fruit under German administration. We have achieved this by means of a peaceful understanding with France. For the first time we have succeeded in solving by agreement with our western neighbours a grave and difficult political question which possibly contained the germs of great evil.

Such, Gentlemen, is the result. It is now for you to weigh the pros and cons of our policy. We do not expect praise; neither, however, do we fear reproach.

(c) *Extract from the speech of the German Foreign Secretary, Kiderlen-Waechter, before the Budget Committee of the Reichstag, November 17, 1911*[1]

. . . .

Germany's first direct relations with Morocco began in the year 1873 with the establishment of a post of Minister Resident; until then German interests had been represented by England.

Morocco had attained an international position in the year 1880, when the Madrid Conference took place at the instigation of England and on the invitation of Spain. The object of this conference was principally to bring about a limitation of the right to have protégés in Morocco. For France had at that time already begun to exercise a preponderating influence in Morocco, through the adoption of a very large number of protégés, whereby occasion had constantly been

---

[1] Cited from Great Britain. *Parliamentary Papers.* 1911. Vol. CIII. Cmd. 5992. "Morocco. No. 2 (1911)."

afforded for conflicts and intervention in the internal affairs of the country. To this the conference was intended to put a stop. France, on the other hand, aimed at the greatest possible extension of this right. Germany had at first adopted the attitude of the other Powers in opposition to France. Shortly before the conference, however, Prince Bismarck had, by a personal report to His Majesty the Emperor, brought about a departure from this attitude. Bismarck had advocated the view that it could only be desirable for Germany were France to establish herself as firmly as possible in Morocco.

In regard to Germany's alleged further negotiations relative to Morocco, all kinds of false accounts had now appeared in the press. Amongst others the "Germania" had asserted that portions of Morocco had been offered to us in the year 1899 and that negotiations had taken place in connection therewith. That was, however, not accurate. The British Minister of the Colonies, Chamberlain, had certainly at the time had views of partition in regard to Morocco. England was to receive Tangier, Germany a port on the Atlantic coast. It had, however, never come to formal negotiations. The then British Prime Minister, Lord Salisbury, had not pursued the idea further, and the matter had been allowed to drop.

It had then been asserted that negotiations had taken place in 1904. That also was not accurate. There was obviously a confusion with the year 1905. In the year 1905, after the German Emperor's journey to Tangier, M. Delcassé had made an attempt at direct negotiations, which, however, for want of any positive proposals, had not led to any result. Rouvier had then again both semi-officially and officially expressed a desire for an understanding. The word "Congo" had then been mentioned for the first time. The question had been whether we could not be indemnified on the Congo. Positive proposals had been demanded by us without leading to any result. In the meantime we had taken up the attitude that changes in Morocco could only be effected with the consent of the signatory Powers of the Conference of Madrid. We should then have been exposed to the danger that by direct negotiations with France we might detach ourselves from the other Powers and then fall between two stools if direct negotiations were wrecked by inacceptable proposals. Prince Bülow had therefore not been able to consider further the French desires for an understanding which had never been accompanied by positive proposals.

Later on negotiations were supposed to have taken place with Pichon. That was not correct. Pichon had never made a proposal.

In the meantime came the Algeciras Act. In spite of it, however, the influence of France in Morocco had continued to increase. The Sultan had no longer the power to maintain order. The events at Casa Blanca had afforded the first opportunity for a further advance. Europeans, among them Frenchmen, had been murdered there whilst engaged on work sanctioned by the Algeciras Act. France had, in consequence, taken the well-known measures and had notified them to the signatory

A MATTER OF DIGNITY.

GERMAN EAGLE (*to French Chanticleer*). "LOOK HERE, AS BIRD TO BIRD, IF I COME DOWN
A PERCH OR TWO, WILL YOU PROMISE NOT TO CROW AT ME?"

From *Punch*, September 20, 1911
(Reprinted by arrangements with the proprietors of *Punch*.)

Powers of the Algeciras Act. She had at the same time laid stress on the fact that it was merely a question of safeguarding her nationals; as soon as this had been accomplished the measures would be discontinued. This could not be contradicted.

On the occupation of Casa Blanca the surrounding country had, of course, also to be protected. Outposts and patrols had then been attacked; the places whence the attack had originated had to be punished and occupied. New measures had, it was alleged, constantly become necessary, and slowly but surely the power of France had spread over the Shawia like an oil stain. It would have been difficult to have lodged a protest on that score for violation of the Algeciras Act. One day the Sultan of Morocco, who had naturally been always doing his utmost to play off the two Powers, Germany and France, against each other, had protested in a most excited manner to the German consul at Fez against the occupation of a certain village on the borders of the Shawia territory, and asserted that the place lay outside the Shawia, and that the French were on the high road to Fez. Germany had for a long time considered what was to be done. Had it been said to the French that they were going too far, they were contravening the Algeciras Act, it would probably have been replied that the measures were absolutely necessary. Germany could then have only either given way or issued an ultimatum. What sort of impression would have been created, however, if the Imperial Chancellor had said in the Reichstag: "The French have occupied some village or other on the borders of the Shawia with an unpronounceable name, and His Majesty the Emperor has therefore declared war"?

The position had become difficult for Germany, because it was developing gradually and it had never been able to be said: "With this precise measure, at this moment, is the Algeciras Act violated, and we protest." The conviction was therefore come to that it would be wisest to wait and see how far the French measures would go, and, in the event of the continued violation of the Algeciras Act, to again claim complete freedom of action for ourselves also.

The French measures had then gone farther and farther. It had been asserted that the French colony in Fez was in danger. It had to be protected. Our reports, indeed, from Fez had not been so alarming; we had therefore declared that the protection of our colony was superfluous. But if France declared that the lives of her nationals were threatened we could still have undertaken no guarantee therefor, and consequently could also not have opposed an expedition to Fez.

This expedition was intended, according to the explicit declaration of the French Government, merely to bring the Europeans from Fez to the coast. We had therefore immediately declared, and announced the same in our press, that should France overstep the limits of the specified programme, even if she did so unintentionally, being compelled thereto merely by the force of circumstances, we should again claim our full freedom of action.

The French had then eventually reached Fez. They had, however, driven by the force of circumstances, established themselves more and more in the country, had extended their exclusive influence, and had also hereby behaved as the mandatory of Europe for the establishment of order in Morocco; at the same time, however, they had continued to maintain the assertion that it was a question of temporary measures which would later be again withdrawn, and that the Algeciras Act was not violated.

The other Powers, and particularly England, had been inclined to concur in the French view. Germany had stood alone in her resistance. At the same time Germany had never even so much as hinted that a part of Morocco would be claimed. All that was demanded the whole time was that France should come to an understanding with us with regard to the violation of the Algeciras Act, and that, as this violation had been committed by her, she must make positive proposals. This view had finally also been expressed in a conversation between the Imperial Chancellor and the French Ambassador in Berlin, and again in a conversation which had taken place at Kissingen between the speaker himself and the French Ambassador. It had been emphasised throughout that Germany was willing to allow France an entirely free hand politically, but must demand for herself in return better guarantees for the maintenance of the principle of the "open door" in Morocco, and in addition an indemnification in the colonial sphere as compensation for the fact that France had violated the Algeciras Act by establishing herself in Morocco without previous agreement. The French Ambassador had taken note of this. The positive proposals of the French Government were, however, not forthcoming. It was always merely stated that they would gladly come to an agreement later. Meanwhile France had established herself in Morocco ever more and more unceremoniously.

When, then, complaints of oppression and requests for protection were received from German subjects, especially from the Sus district near Mogador and Agadir, it was felt on the German side that France was in no way the mandatory of Europe and could therefore in no way be considered as the sole protecting Power. We were obliged to claim an equal right for ourselves to protect our subjects. It was in view of these considerations that a German ship was dispatched to Agadir.

Germany had acted thus in the first place in order to protect her nationals, but she certainly desired also at the same time to protect her own right in the face of the action of France, by the dispatch of the ship, a proceeding which was to a certain extent symptomatic. But the intention of taking a part of Morocco had never existed. This he, the Secretary of State, had also distinctly stated at the time to a well-known Pan-German. Unfortunately the gentleman in question had not believed him. But the German intentions had also from the outset been made clear to the Powers. If it had been represented in the press that German Ambassadors, Ministers, etc. had obtained knowledge of the

step taken by Germany through the perusal of newspapers, the one
with his morning coffee, the other at afternoon tea, this was a malicious
invention. . . .

During the Franco-German negotiations which followed the dispatch
of the German war-ship to Agadir certain discussions also took place
with the British Government. After the conversation which the Ambassador in London had on the dispatch of the ship to Agadir, no
question was asked from the British side either of our Ambassador in
London or here in Berlin. It was only on the 21st of July that Sir
E. Grey arranged to have a conversation with our Ambassador. The
impression which, in the meantime, Sir Edward Grey had gathered
respecting our attitude, and which was not in accordance with the
explanations given by our Ambassador at the time of the dispatch of
the ship, had been reflected in this conversation. This impression had
been caused by the suspicions purposely raised against our policy by
the French, and to a certain extent by the English press, and also,
indeed, by certain officials.

The Ambassador had reported on this conversation, which had taken
place on the 21st July, that Sir E. Grey had asked him for the interview. The Minister had expressed the wish to discuss the Morocco
question with him in an unofficial manner, as he had, since the first
démarche of the Ambassador, heard nothing further from him. The
Minister was compelled to touch now again on the Morocco question,
because he feared that a situation might arise when his taking up a
position on the Morocco question would have greater significance than
a preliminary expression of views in the present phase of the question.
He had from the very beginning never felt any doubt that in any
settlement of the Morocco question England, owing to her great
economic interests in that country, must take part. He had waited in
the hope of an understanding between Germany and France. Since,
however, as he now heard, our demands were so extensive that it was
obvious that France would not be able to accept them, there was
imminent danger that the negotiations would terminate without result;
and in that case the question would again come to the front: "What
was Germany doing in the closed port of Agadir and in its hinterland?"
He had no news of what was going on there—whether German troops
had been landed, or whether treaties were being concluded which might
be prejudicial to the economic participation of others. Agadir was very
suitable for a naval base; no one knew what Germany intended to do
there. Questions of this sort would be sure to be put to him in Parliament, and he was not in a position to give an explanatory answer.

If the Franco-German negotiations failed, which, in view of our
demands, appeared by no means unlikely, then the Agadir question, in
which British interests were also involved, would at once come into the
foreground. Therefore he believed that the time had come when England also should take part in the Franco-German negotiations. As long
as there had been a well-founded hope of a Franco-German understand-

ing outside Morocco, he had held aloof, as it would not disturb British policy if Germany and France endeavoured to reach a settlement on a colonial basis—for instance, by a rectification of the Cameroon frontier, as had at first been said. As France, however, could not accept the German demands, it was highly probable that the Morocco question proper would again be re-opened, a question in which British interests were involved in a high degree, and in that case the question as to what our intentions were with regard to the closed port of Agadir and its hinterland would again become acute.

He wished once more to declare that he had brought about this conversation only in the desire that he should not subsequently find himself face to face with facts which would oblige him too on his side to take up a definite position and whereby the already sufficiently complicated political situation might become still more difficult and serious.

The Ambassador had answered that he had no detailed information regarding the course of our negotiations with France, but that he could nevertheless not admit that our demands were, as the Minister had said, of course inacceptable, as otherwise we should not have put them forward. With this proviso the Ambassador could naturally only express his own personal views. Sir E. Grey had stated, though not officially, that, as British interests were involved, the time had now come for negotiations à trois, and he had based this pretension on the idea that we might eventually establish a naval base in Agadir and cut off the hinterland. These were suppositions of which the Ambassador had no knowledge, and on mere suppositions no claim could be founded. Should, however, British interests have been injured by our proceedings, perhaps the Minister would be so good as to name them. As he was not in a position to do so, it would be more correct to wait until he could show that an English interest or right was affected. The Ambassador repeated that we had not the slightest intention of injuring English rights or interests. He could not admit that this had been done by the dispatch of a German war-ship to Agadir. He had communicated to the Minister the object and intention of this act when he made his first statement to him on the subject, namely, the protection of the interests of German subjects by the presence of a war-ship until peace and quiet were restored. Hitherto it had been a generally recognised principle that a European nation is justified in personally undertaking the protection of her interests in a semi-barbaric country which does not belong to a third party. No third Power was bound by the Anglo-French convention of 1904. Since this convention Germany was only bound by the Algeciras Act and one treaty with France of 1909. Both the Act and our convention assumed as a condition for everything else the independence of the Sultan and the integrity of Morocco. After the lasting occupation of the Shawia and after the recent French expedition of conquest ("Eroberungszug") in a great part of Morocco, no one could seriously maintain that the territory

of Morocco had not been violated and that its Sultan was still independent. We made no complaint on this score, as the Ambassador had
already likewise stated in the first conversation. Owing to the course
events had taken, however, the moment had arrived when we were compelled to come to an understanding with France on the Moroccan
question. We had now undertaken this step. If, as Sir E. Grey assumed,
our proposals in other directions were considered inacceptable, this
merely showed that France appeared to attach less importance than
might have been expected to a free exercise of those pretensions of hers
in Morocco which had not obtained international recognition. The
presence of a foreign war-ship in a Moorish port had now to be taken
into account.

A glance at the map would show that a North African colonial
Empire, extending from the Tripolitan frontier to Senegambia, together with supremacy in Morocco, was no small thing. England had
obtained compensation from France in Egypt, which was also no small
thing; we, however, had obtained nothing. If France desired that we,
like England, but always subject to the protection of our commercial
interests, should step into the background in Morocco, she must offer
some compensation approximately equivalent in value to the great
goal she had in view. If not, we should know how to safeguard our
independent position in Morocco. The Minister appeared to attach
great importance to the fact that we had dispatched a war-ship to a
closed port of Morocco, and that this port should have been Agadir,
the appearance at which of a French war-ship last autumn had led us
to address an enquiry to the French Government. To this the Ambassador had to observe that last autumn the French expedition of conquest ("Eroberungszug") to Fez had not yet been entered upon. He
could not conceal from the Minister that he seemed to be applying two
standards, one standard for France and another for Germany. According to his (Sir E. Grey's) conception, a situation had arisen by the
dispatch of a German war-ship to Agadir which, looked at from the
standpoint of English interests, demanded an explanation. If he attached so much importance to the inviolability of Moroccan territory,
he should apply first and foremost to France for explanations. The
occupation of the Shawia territory, the fact that a French army was
spreading itself over the interior of Morocco, meant undoubtedly a
more active intervention in Moroccan affairs than the German action
so far as it went.

The Minister (Grey) replied that he would in no wise stand in the
way of an extension of German colonial possessions in the heart of
Africa; he could not, however, shut his eyes to the fact that English
interests might be most seriously affected by the Moroccan question
itself. He had therefore honestly hoped for an understanding between
France and Germany. It was only in view of the unwished-for possibility of the failure to arrive at such understanding that he was compelled forthwith to make it clear that the *démarche* in Agadir would

lead to an exchange of views between us and England. He considered that the situation would become less acute if an exchange of views took place between us before fresh events occurred at Agadir, which would compel England to take up a definite attitude in regard thereto. He had always hoped for an understanding between France and ourselves on Moroccan questions, and had therefore also welcomed our agreement with France of 1909.

The Secretary of State indicated that it appeared from the interview with Sir E. Grey that the Minister had obviously assumed that we intended to establish ourselves in Morocco, in spite of the communications made to him by the Ambassador immediately upon the dispatch of the "Panther" to Agadir. The telegram in regard to the interview had reached Berlin on the 22nd July, and the reply was dispatched from here forthwith. In this reply the Ambassador was instructed to inform the Minister that we had declared from the very beginning that our ship at Agadir was solely intended to protect German interests there. A special motive for this was, amongst other things, the attack by natives on a German firm. Nothing had occurred up till now to justify a belief that we had changed our intentions. Not a man had yet been landed. We regretted that people in England should seem to think that credence should be attached to insinuations in regard to our intentions which clearly emanated from a source hostile to us. We had never thought of procuring a naval harbour on the coast of Morocco, nor would we ever think of such a thing. These were hallucinations. We had also no design on Moroccan territory, though we had to demand that France should either observe strictly the Algeciras Act or, if she thought she could not do so, come to an understanding with us.

We had thought that the latter coincided more with French interests and made the proposal to the French—hitherto only in quite a general manner—to give us compensation in colonial territory for the renunciation of our right to protest against the action of France in Morocco.

The negotiations had begun; both parties had mutually promised to observe the strictest secrecy. We took this obligation seriously and did not even inform our allies. France adopted a different course and unfortunately communicated not only to the press but, it appears, also in part to her friends information which, inaccurate and incomplete as it was, was calculated to arouse suspicion as to our intentions. We therefore did not negotiate further for a time so long as the secrecy of the negotiations was not guaranteed. The negotiations could not be advanced by the chauvinistic tone of the French press, which also some English papers seemed recently to have adopted and which was especially directed towards threatening us with the intervention of France's allies and friends. If these negotiations should break down, we had still no designs on Moroccan territory. We should, however, in that event have been compelled to call on France with emphasis and determination to observe fully both the letter and spirit of the Algeciras Act.

As a Great Power we could not permit France to infringe our rights in contravention of written treaties. We continued to hope, however, that a friendly conversation à *deux* would prevent its going so far as this. We counted upon the support of the other Powers, especially on that of England, should the French not be willing to come to an understanding on the basis proposed by us and we had to demand the restoration of the *status quo ante* in Morocco.

The Secretary of State declared that, therefore, after the communication with regard to the dispatch of a ship had been made in the early days of July, no enquiry had been made by the British Government of the Imperial Government either in London or here. The first conversation which took place at the invitation of Sir E. Grey, after the communication respecting the dispatch of a ship, was on the 21st July, and our reply to it was already in London on the 23rd July. Therefore the assertion made by a portion of the German press that the German Government had for a fortnight returned no answer to a question addressed to them by the British Government fell to the ground. When the answer to the questions raised by Sir E. Grey had been dispatched to the German Ambassador, the text became known in Berlin of the speech delivered by Mr. Lloyd George at the Mansion House on the evening of the 21st July, that is to say, on the very day on which the interview took place between the Ambassador and the English Minister of Foreign Affairs. It had not been possible for us to comply with the request made in the meantime by the British Minister that we should authorise him to make use in Parliament of our notification that we had no designs on Moroccan territory. This would have made it appear as if the explanation had been given as a result of Mr. Lloyd George's speech.

On the 24th July the Ambassador in London was instructed to point out that the speech of the English Chancellor of the Exchequer, the text of which had just become known, had given rise to violent attacks against Germany on the part of a large portion of the English press and the whole of the French press. It might remain an open question as to how far the British Minister had intended to produce this effect. The British Government could not, in any case, fail to perceive that this effect of a speech delivered by one of its members was bound to produce a bad impression here.

We were negotiating with France for the removal of differences, which were the result of France having unceremoniously set aside the obligations arising from the International Treaty of Algeciras. Germany stated explicitly and repeatedly that she wished to come to a direct agreement with France in a peaceful and friendly manner without recriminations as to the past. France accepted this, and agreed with us to conduct the negotiations in secret for the present. Germany had made proposals to France which appeared to be entirely loyal and acceptable. They concerned territories in which English interests were neither directly nor indirectly involved. If, in spite of this, England considered it necessary to express wishes, it was open to her to convey such wishes through the usual diplomatic channel. If, instead of doing so, the English Government caused public declarations to be made by one of its members which could be interpreted at least as a warning addressed to us, and which were, as a matter of fact, interpreted by English as well as French papers as a warning bordering on a threat, it was difficult to recognise the reasons for such action. The English Government could not doubt that a friendly understanding between Germany and France, which they themselves professed to desire, would not be advanced thereby. In view of the tone adopted against Germany for some time past by a portion of the English press and by nearly all French papers, the English Government could not have been in doubt as to the result to be anticipated from the speech of the Chancellor of the Exchequer. If the English Government had intended to complicate and embroil the political situation and to bring about a violent explosion, they would certainly have chosen no better means than the speech of the Chancellor of the Exchequer, which took so little into account for us the dignity and position of a Great Power which was claimed by him for England.

The Ambassador reported thereupon that Sir E. Grey had indeed consented to make no parliamentary use of the communications in regard to the intention of Germany not to acquire any territory in Morocco, but that he had observed that he would then have no means of allaying the public anxiety as to our alleged designs on Agadir. The Minister had defended the speech of the Chancellor of the Exchequer as being moderate, and had maintained that it was thoroughly correct that it should have been delivered. It contained no threat against Germany. The Ambassador had then again pointed out that the Anglo-French press had represented the speech of the Chancellor as a threat against Germany.

The Minister had laid stress on the fact that Germany's contingent intention to undertake alone the restoration of the *status quo ante*, that is to say, to proceed independently even without the other signatory Powers, was calculated to give a still more serious significance to the Morocco question. The Minister had protested against the idea that the English Government did not desire a Franco-German agreement. He would also make it clear in Parliament that the English Government desired a Franco-German agreement; he must, however, at the same time point out that, should English interests be affected in the course of the Moroccan question, the English Government would be compelled to protect them.

The Ambassador observed on this that no one disputed England's right in this matter. We had never intended to dispose of English interests or rights. This intention existed only in English imagination.

The English Government had no ground for this suspicion, which also betrayed itself in the speech of the Chancellor of the Exchequer, and was the cause of its provocative effect. Should the occasion arise, Germany would welcome the coöperation of the other signatory Powers in the restoration of the *status quo*. Only in the event of such coöperation not being forthcoming would she enforce her rights unaided. The Ambassador was not able to conceal from the Minister that threatening warnings would only have the effect of encouraging Germany to uphold her rights.

An answer was thereupon sent to Sir E. Grey, by fresh instructions addressed to the Ambassador on the 26th July, to the effect that he must have seen from the official communications that British interests had not been touched upon in the negotiations with France; it was therefore expected of his proved loyalty that he would mention this in Parliament without going into the confidential details of our communication.

The Ambassador was further instructed to take note of the fact with satisfaction that Sir E. Grey had stated that he desired to see an understanding arrived at between France and Germany, and also to express the conviction that this would contribute in a high degree to the success of the negotiations. It was, however, difficult to reconcile this desire with the fact that, without any knowledge of what we were giving up in the way of political influence, our colonial demands were characterised in England as inacceptable.

As we had bound ourselves to secrecy *vis-à-vis* of France, we could not give further details; we thought also that where it was a question exclusively of the exchange of territories which were the absolute possessions of Germany and France the interests of a third party, and especially English interests, could not be affected, and that it must therefore be left entirely to the two contracting parties to balance against one another the value of the objects to be exchanged. Adverse judgments on the part of England on the subject of the German demands could only therefore impede the negotiations. On the other hand, an open declaration to the effect that England would welcome a Franco-German agreement could only have a favourable influence upon the attainment of our sincere desire for such an agreement. It was Germany's ardent desire to lessen or to do entirely away with the causes of friction with France on colonial, and more especially African, territory. Even if thereby intimate relations between ourselves and France were not established, we nevertheless promised ourselves as a result of this policy that countless causes for more or less serious tension would be removed. If England equally desired this she could only contribute to it by exercising a soothing influence on the very excited state of feeling then prevailing in France, a state of feeling which had been brought about by the dissemination of false reports and by semi-indiscretions.

(d) *Extracts from the speech of Grey, at that time Secretary of State for Foreign Affairs, in the House of Commons, November 27, 1911*[1]

The German Chancellor and the German Foreign Secretary have already disposed of one misapprehension with regard to the Moroccan question. It was imagined in some quarters, I think I have seen it on the Paper of this House in a question put, that Germany had protested against the French action in going to Fez at all, and that France had persisted in going there in the face of the German protest. The German Government have now explained what the German view of the French going to Fez really was, and I have no comment or criticism to make upon what they said. I therefore begin my narrative not with the French expedition to Fez, but with the 1st July. On that day the German Ambassador came to the Foreign Office and made the following communication:—

"Some German firms established in the south of Morocco, notably at Agadir and in the vicinity, have been alarmed by a certain ferment which has shown itself among the local tribes, due, it seems, to the recent occurrences in other parts of the country. These firms have applied to the Imperial Government for protection for the lives of their employés and their property. At their request the Imperial Government have decided to send a warship to the Port of Agadir to lend help and assistance in case of need to their subjects and employés, as well as to protect the important German interests in the territory in question. As soon as the state of affairs in Morocco has resumed its former quiet aspect, the ship charged with this protective mission shall leave the Port of Agadir."

That was accompanied by an explanation given to us at the same time which seemed to me much more important than the actual communication of the sending of the ship. The explanation given to us made it clear that the Moroccan question was being opened—the whole Moroccan question—by the sending of the ship to Agadir. It made it clear that the German Government regarded a return to the *status quo* in Morocco as doubtful, if not impossible, and that what they contemplated was a definite solution of the Moroccan question between Germany, France, and Spain. The whole question, or at least the kernel of the question, after that communication was received, was what was the definite solution of the Moroccan question which Germany contemplated? If a return to the *status quo* was doubtful, if not impossible, then the only alternative was a definite solution of the Moroccan question. What was the nature of that? What was clearly the objective Germany contemplated? Was it to be the partition of Morocco or what was it to be? That was what occupied our minds

---

[1] *Parliamentary Debates. Commons,* 1911, Vol. XXXII, pp. 45-54.

after receiving that communication. The communication was made to the Foreign Office on the Saturday. On the next Monday, the 3rd July, I asked the German Ambassador to come and see me. I informed him I had seen the Prime Minister, and that we considered the situation created by the dispatch of the "Panther" to Agadir as so important that it must be discussed in a meeting of the Cabinet. I would say no more pending the meeting of the Cabinet, but I wished the German Government to learn at once that, in our view, the situation was serious and important. The next day, the 4th July, I asked the German Ambassador to come and see me again, and said that I must tell him— this was after the Cabinet meeting—that our attitude could not be a disinterested one with regard to Morocco. We must take into consideration our Treaty obligations to France and our own interests in Morocco. We were of opinion that a new situation had been created by the dispatch of a German ship to Agadir. Future developments might affect British interests more directly than they had hitherto been affected, and, therefore, we could not recognise any new arrangements that might be come to without us. I made it quite clear to the Ambassador that this communication, and the exact words which I used, were those of His Majesty's Government sitting in Cabinet.

After that there was a period of silence. The German Ambassador was not instructed to make any comment to me with regard to my communication, and we received no information from the German Government as to what their aims or desires were, or as to what they had in mind when they spoke of a definite solution of the Moroccan problem. Some information reached us from other quarters, leading us to apprehend that the settlement contemplated by the German Government might be a partition of Morocco, arrived at by negotiations to which it was not intended we should be a party. I think, in the German mind, it has sometimes been assumed that our agreement made with France in 1904 entirely disinterested us with regard to Morocco, and if Germany wished to make a new settlement with regard to Morocco, it was going out of our way and intrusive for us, having given by our agreement of 1904 a free hand to France in Morocco, as far as we are concerned—it was going out of our way and intrusive to interfere with any other Power wishing to make her own arrangements. That does not take full account of the agreement of 1904 made by the right hon. Gentleman opposite. It is quite true we disinterested ourselves in Morocco politically, but we did it on conditions laid down—conditions both strategic and economic. What were the reasons of our being disinterested in Morocco? We have no jealousy of other Powers. It is obvious, if the Moroccan question was to be reopened and a new settlement made, unless we were consulted, unless we knew what was going on, unless we were in some way parties to the settlement, the strategic and economic conditions stipulated for between ourselves, France, and Spain in 1904 might be upset.

On the 12th July, the British Ambassador in Berlin had occasion

SOLID.

to see the German Foreign Secretary on some minor matters, and took
the opportunity to say that there had been at one time some mention
of a conversation *à trois* between Germany, France and Spain, the
inference being that we were to be excluded from it. The German Foreign Secretary told our Ambassador to inform us that there never had
been any idea of such a communication; and, except for this negative
communication, we had no information from the German Government
of their views. A little later it appeared in the Press that the German
Government—and indeed it was the case—that the German Government had made demands with regard to the French Congo of an extent
to which it was obvious to everybody who thought of it that neither the
French Government nor the French Chamber could agree. That at once
made me anxious as to the development of the situation. If Germany
was going to negotiate with France an arrangement by which Germany
received from France something in the French Congo and left France
in Morocco as she is under our agreement of 1904, then of course we
were prepared to stand aside and not to intrude, but if Germany,
starting negotiations on that basis with France, made demands not
for a portion, but for the greater part of the French Congo or anything of that kind, it was quite clear France must refuse those demands
and negotiations would be thrown back on some other basis and the
question of the possible partition would arise again. That is why I
became anxious.

I therefore asked the German Ambassador to see me again on the
21st July. I said to him, I wished it to be understood that our silence,
in the absence of any communication from the German Government—
our silence since the Cabinet communication of the 4th July, and since
the Prime Minister's statement of the 7th July in this House—our
silence since then must not be interpreted as meaning that we were not
taking in the Moroccan question, the interest which had been indicated
by our statement of the 4th of that month. We knew that a rectification
of the frontier of the French Congo had been proposed as a basis for
negotiations with France. We thought it possible that a settlement
might be come to between Germany and France on this basis without
affecting British interests. We would be very glad if this happened,
and in the hope that it would happen at a later stage we had hitherto
stood aside. But I had been made anxious by the news which appeared
the day before as to the demands which the German Government had
made on the French Government; demands which were in effect not a
rectification of the frontier, but a cession of the French Congo, which
it was obviously impossible for the French Government to concede. I
heard that negotiations were still proceeding, and I still hoped that
they might lead to a satisfactory result, but it must be understood that
if they were unsuccessful, a very embarrassing situation would arise.
I pointed out to the German Ambassador that the Germans were in the
closed port of Agadir; that according to native rumours they were
landing and negotiating with the tribes, so that, for all we knew, they

might be acquiring concessions there and that it might even be that the German flag had been hoisted at Agadir, which was the most suitable port on that coast for a naval basis. We could not say to what extent the situation might be altered to our disadvantage, and if the negotiations with France came to nothing, we should be obliged to do something to watch over British interests and to become a party to the discussion of the matter. The longer the Germans remained at Agadir the greater the risk of their developing a state of affairs which would make it more difficult for them to withdraw and more necessary for us to take some steps to protect British interests. I wished to say all this now while we were still waiting, in the hope that the negotiations with France would succeed, for, if I did not say this now, it would cause resentment later on if the German Government had been led to suppose by our previous silence—our silence since 4th July—that we did not take an interest in the matter.

The German Ambassador was not in a position to give me any information, but he deprecated the assumption that what I had sketched as the possible damage to British interests would be accomplished. He was sure that his Government had no intention of acquiring commercial monopolies, and unfairly prejudicing our interests. On this I observed that the fact that Germany remained in occupation of a closed port involved at least a monopoly of commercial opportunities. I had waited before saying anything further between the 4th July and the 21st July. I made that statement on the 21st July, because I was getting anxious because the situation seemed to me to be developing unfavourably.

The German Ambassador was still not in a position to make any Communication to me from the German Government. In the course of that day, the 21st July, the Chancellor of the Exchequer told me that he had to make a speech on an occasion of importance at the Mansion House the same evening. He consulted the Prime Minister and me as to what should be said. It was fourteen days since the last public statement about Morocco had been made here, and that had been only the very short statement made by the Prime Minister in the House. We were anxious as to the way in which things were developing, and we all three felt that for a Cabinet Minister of first-rate importance to make a speech on a formal occasion and to say no word about Foreign Affairs after that interview would be misleading to public opinion here and everywhere. What I had said to the German Ambassador that day as to Agadir and the negotiations with France was obviously suitable only—I read it to the House now because the German Foreign Minister has disclosed it, and there is no reason why it should not be said now— what I said to him that day as regards Agadir and the negotiations with France was obviously suitable only—for diplomatic channels and not for public statement. The Chancellor of the Exchequer therefore made his speech in quite general terms. What he said is on record. He claimed no preëminence, no predominance for us in international affairs. It contained no menace, such as the saying of "Hands off!" to anyone anywhere. It did not say that there was any particular demand or claim on the part of Germany that was inconsistent with British interests. Its purport and its point was that where British interests were affected, we must not be treated as if we were of no account. If the time ever comes when this cannot be said by a Minister speaking in the position the Chancellor of the Exchequer was in then, we shall have ceased to exist as a great nation.

As a matter of fact, the first German comments on this speech that I saw in the Press were such as naturally might have been expected. One German Conservative newspaper said that if the word "Germany" were substituted for the word "England," the speech might have been made by a German Minister. The words of the speech were soon forgotten, and a sort of legend has grown up about them. For instance, a few weeks ago, I heard of one German who protested to an English friend of his and of mine against the speech, and was given a report of the speech to read. Having read it, he said that what was objected to in Germany was, not the speech itself, but the fact that it had been made at a moment when France and Germany were coming to terms, and that it upset the negotiations. The exact contrary is the truth as to the particular circumstances of the negotiations existing at the time. I was afraid, and I spoke to the German Ambassador because I was afraid, that things were developing in a way that would bring up the Moroccan question, force the Moroccan negotiations back, not upon an arrangement between France and Germany about the Congo and Morocco respectively, but upon something in the nature of a partition of Morocco, or some sort of solution which might make the question of British interests to be directly affected, and which would certainly directly bring into operation our Treaty obligations with France.

On 24th July, three days after the speech of the Chancellor of the Exchequer, the German Ambassador came to see me. He informed me that the German intention in sending a ship to Agadir had not changed. Not a man had been landed there. The German Government regretted the credence which was given to the insinuations as to the intentions of Germany that came from hostile quarters. Germany had never thought of creating a naval port on the coast of Morocco, and never would think of it. Such ideas were hallucinations. As to the negotiations with France, if the German demands were rather high his Government were ready to make concessions in Morocco as well as in Colonial matters; but the Chauvinistic tone of the French Press and a part of the British Press, menacing Germany with the interference of the friends of France, did not tend towards a settlement. I said that I was likely to be asked in Parliament what was happening at Agadir, and I should like to know whether I might say that the German Government had informed me that not a man had been landed. The Ambassador asked me to make no public statement with regard to this communication until he had had time to communicate with his Government. The next day, 25th July, the German Ambassador came to see me again, and told me that the information that he had given me on the preceding day was confidential, and that the German Government could not consent to its being used in Parliament in view of the speech of the Chancellor of the Exchequer. He then made to me in regard to that speech a communication which has now been published by the German Government, and which I need not read in full to the House, because it has been in the Press here already, except to say about it that that communication was a strong criticism upon the effect of the speech upon the Press rather than upon the substance of the speech itself.

The communication, however, was exceedingly stiff in tone, and I felt it necessary—for, of course, I had not expected any communication of this kind—to say at once that as the speech of the Chancellor of the Exchequer seemed to me to give no cause for complaint, the fact that it had created surprise in Germany was in itself a justification of the speech, for it could not have created surprise unless there had been some tendency to think that we might be disregarded. The speech had not claimed anything except that we were entitled to be considered as one of the great nations. It had claimed no preëminence, and it had not even indicated that there was a crisis. It dealt in general terms with remote contingencies. The German Government had said that it was not consistent with their dignity, after the speech of the Chancellor of the Exchequer, to give explanations as to what was taking place at Agadir. I said to the Ambassador that the tone of their communication made it inconsistent with our dignity to give explanations as to the speech of the Chancellor of the Exchequer. Of course, by that I meant a public explanation. Explanations as to Agadir had already been given me by the German Ambassador, but it was the public explanation that the Government could not consent to. Then I thought it right to say further on the question generally, knowing that the interests of France were involved as well as our own, and that it was the desire of France that the negotiations should go smoothly—I said to the German Ambassador that it was not intended, by anything that had been said, or would be said here, to embroil the negotiations between Germany and France. On the contrary, we sincerely desired that they should succeed, but the tone of the German communication was unfavourable with regard to France as well as with regard to us, and made it more than ever evident that a very difficult situation would arise if the German negotiations with France should not succeed. There the matter was left by that conversation, and there it remained for two days, until the 27th July. Then the German Ambassador came to me again and made another communication from his Government, in conversation, so that I took down the words. The communication he made to me on the 27th July was this—I put it in the words I took down—

"We trust that Sir Edward Grey, by our very open and candid communication, has gathered the conviction that our pourparlers with France at the moment do not touch British interests. We trust to the Minister's great loyalty, that he has so often shown, that he will find it possible to state this fact in Parliament, without, however, giving any details of our confidential communication. We acknowledge with pleasure that the Minister has stated that he desires an agreement between Germany and France, and feel quite convinced that this will prove most helpful to the progress of the negotiations.

"But, having in view the wish expressed by Sir Edward, we cannot quite see how he can, in the present state of the pourparlers, describe our demands as obviously impossible, without knowing what we on our side have the intention to offer to France in the political and colonial territorial field. It is not possible in regard of the formal pledge of secrecy we have given—"

"We" means the German Government—

"to go into details; but as the territories to be eventually exchanged are exclusively German and French, we do not believe that special English interests could be touched, and that it seems advisable to leave it to the two parties immediately concerned to form an estimation of the value of the objects to be eventually exchanged.

"Adverse criticism from the English side must obviously render the negotiations more difficult. On the other hand, a public statement that England would be pleased to see a successful conclusion of the Franco-German pourparlers would have a most beneficial influence on an auspicious result, for which we most earnestly hope. We most seriously wish to diminish any points of friction we have with France in the colonial sphere, especially in Africa, and hope it may eventually be possible to make them disappear entirely. We could not look forward, even if this was done, to establishing intimate relations with France; but we believed that it would do away with a cause of frequently-recurring tension. If the wishes of England are in the same direction, the best way to help to bring about this result would be by having a calming influence on public opinion in France, which just now, by half-truths and inaccurate statements, has been brought to considerable excitement."

The House will observe that the tone of that communication was exceedingly friendly, not only to ourselves, but to France. I at once expressed appreciation of the friendly tone in which the communication was couched. The German Ambassador and myself then had some further conversation of a general and informal kind, in the course of which he expressed some regret at the way in which our public opinion had been misled to adverse conclusions as to German action. I asked, on that, what else could have been expected, when the German Government suddenly sent a ship to Morocco, to a closed port, which was said to be the most suitable place on the west coast of Morocco for a naval base. Of course, this action had mobilised British public opinion. I also pointed out that, after I had made to him on 4th July a declaration on behalf of the British Government, we had had no communication from the German Government until 24th July, and even then their denial of any intention to establish a naval base had been in a form which I could not use to allay the suspicions which had been roused here. I suggested to the Ambassador, and he received the suggestion very cordially, that we should not pursue this point. I expressed the hope that this latest German communication might be taken as a new point of departure, and that we need not go back upon things which might lead to mutual recriminations. In the afternoon of the same day the Prime Minister made a statement in the House. That statement is on record, and anyone who reads that statement will, of course, see that the spirit in which we discussed the thing in public here corresponded to the spirit in which we had then been approached. From that date onwards there were no further difficulties between the German Government and ourselves about the Moroccan negotiations.

(e) *The Justification of the Agreement with Germany by the French Premier, M. Caillaux*[1]

I will leave to the *Yellow Book* (The European War) the task of commenting upon the success of France, affirmed, since November 5, 1911, by the resounding resignation of the Secretary of State for the Colonial Empire, Herr von Lindequist: "I think," wrote in regard to this subject our Military Attaché to the Minister of War, November 5, 1911, "that you have been informed of the outburst of discontent which in Germany followed upon the news of the conclusion of the agreement. I had foreseen some such thing; but the event surpassed my expectations.

"In such a well-regulated country, and where it is inherent in the constitution that the secretaries of state are but functionaries without parliamentary responsibility, clerks for the chancellor, the resignation of Herr von Lindequist is an anarchical act. What astonishes me, what is most interesting to note, is that but yesterday *all* the Germans with whom I talked of it, even the officers, even a member of the *Bundesrat*, approved of Herr von Lindequist.

"Yesterday there was not a single voice to defend the chancellor. . . ."

[1] Joseph Caillaux, *Agadir. Ma Politique extérieure*. Paris, Albin Michel, 1919, pp. 235-243. Reprinted with the permission of Albin Michel.

On his part, M. Cambon sent me on November 3, the following letter, of which I give the entire text:

"Berlin, November 3rd

"M. PRESIDENT,

"I believe that I may at last congratulate you upon having by means of your perseverance and personal firmness, brought the work of our Moroccan agreement to a successful termination. I shall very likely sign the final documents tomorrow, after which I shall myself take them to you in Paris. Your Government will always have the honour of having concluded the task begun in Northern Africa by the Government of the Restoration, which is its greatest claim to fame in the eyes of history.

"I have complied with your instructions in concluding the matter yesterday. I do not know if delaying still longer would have enabled us to obtain more. I doubt it, for the offers of Germany were like Balzac's "Wild Asses' Skin," and grew smaller each day. The internal difficulties of the German Government were increasing: the colonial sentiment was in the ascendency and today it is announced that the Under-Secretary of State for the Colonies has tendered his resignation in order not to be associated with a policy which has yielded to us Morocco in exchange for portions of the Congo, which he considers of insufficient value.

"Also, a book on Equatorial Africa, by M. Rondet-Saint, has been sent to me; it is full of information of which I am very glad that the Germans had no knowledge.

"On the whole, the affair of the Belgian Congo was a fortunate one, which for the future ties Germany's hands. The formula, the author of which I somewhat suspect, was a very fortunate discovery.

"I hope to be able to pay you my respects in the near future, and beg you, M. President, to believe me always entirely yours,

Signed: JULES CAMBON."

Still more precious to me were the congratulations of our allies and of our friends throughout the world, particularly those that came from Russia and from England: "Tell M. Caillaux," repeated the Prime Minister of Great Britain, "that he comes back from Berlin like Lord Beaconsfield, bearing upon his flag: *Peace with Honor*." "M. de Kider-len is perfectly well aware," wrote M. Jules Cambon, on September 23rd, in a letter which I have already cited, "that from now on his cause is lost, but there will be time enough for us to triumph, if that be necessary, when we shall have won the stakes." On November 4th we won the stakes, and it was permissible to triumph. Why should we have done so? Realities only, count in the lives of nations as in those of men. Is it ever worth while to demonstrate to one's adversaries the extent of their failure? A statesman who sees beyond the political foreground, who makes himself look into the future, should strive to dull the glory of a diplomatic victory. What a blunder by boasting to provoke an immediate or a future revenge! What a criminal blunder when the one who so indulges himself is placed at the head of a country whose military preparedness is not yet achieved, and whose allies are either irresolute or in such a situation as M. Isvolsky exposed to me and which was confirmed by General Dubail! I hear that the legitimate pride of our country was offended by the gesture of Agadir. I understand that the odious pretension, entirely Germanic, to substitute brutality for discussion excited the indignation of French public opinion. But did not the Teutonic provocation find its punishment in the result of the diplomatic debates to which Germany has been subjected? In spite of her military power, the Empire succumbed beneath the load of her own arrogance; it had to renounce Morocco, which it had never ceased to covet; which it had ever, under different guises, *intended to control*; in exchange it received a portion of marshy land, which it had looked upon as its own until 1895. The lesson was severe. It was felt from the further bank of the Rhine where the discontent mentioned by Colonel Pellé, broke out. To answer this clamor of the Pan-Germanists, and of their chief, the Crown Prince, by modesty in our success, was to adorn France with her usual crown of Gallic finesse.

I did not hesitate to adopt this attitude. In addition I had presided at the negotiations, I had learned what I have related regarding our situation and that of our allies, I had verified the discord in the Ministry of Foreign Affairs, the frivolity and dangerous mentality of certain bureaus of the Quai d'Orsay, which more than once determined my attitudes and resolutions. Prudence was demanded of me; I was careful not to swerve therefrom. Frequently I took refuge in silence regardless of the cost, however difficult it might be at times not to destroy by a turn of the hand, the puerile or cynical lies, the miserable calumnies. I would have failed in my duty, if in order to avoid a downfall of the ministry, and to triumph over my adversaries, I had said that which, even to-day after the lapse of years, I still hesitate to write.

This prudence, this moderation have been used as a pretense for argument against me. It has been insinuated that I wished to change the direction of France's foreign policy, renounce our alliances and friendships, when I simply meant to return to, and to develop the traditions bequeathed to me by my great predecessors. Like them, I considered that our alliances or our ententes are infinitely precious, on condition that our country not be taken in tow by certain jingo parties. In my eyes France was the great nation, holding aloft the torch of Western civilization in the west; having a high ideal of realizations of the right which she should force herself to follow in peace and by peace, which she should cause to prevail by the developments of liberty and democracy with which some day or other she will *forcibly* penetrate Europe. At the positive, inevitable overthrow of the France of the Revolution, the feudal states which surrounded her were able to create obstacles; and against such action, the Republic should be fortified by material force. It is because I was conscious of such peril that

I sought and succeeded in extending our African empire from the Ocean to Tripoli, *to exclude the redoubtable menace of a Morocco half-Germanized by the agreement of 1909*, on the contrary, to assure to us, in that case, a reserve of Moroccan troops in addition to the Algerian and Tunisian. At the same time I ordered the construction, starting January 1, 1912, of heavy artillery which seemed to me indispensable. Increase of effective force which the modifications under consideration and preparation by my government in the recruiting in Northern Africa should render very considerable! The limit in war materials! France could meet eventualities not of her seeking! We could count upon ourselves! Could act alone! Could carry out our own policy of European conciliation, of a proud and dignified peace with a sense of our material as well as our moral strength! Could conserve carefully our alliances and friendships, but could keep our allies or our friends, even ourselves, from any adventure, any imprudence! Could have patience, prudence, calm! Give confidence to our age! These were the directions I wished to give to my country's foreign policy.

These were discarded soon after my fall from office. Imperceptibly a different policy was developed. New German provocations arose. France was led into the Great War. It will be the pride of my life that in spite of the obstacles accumulated along my way I prevented its breaking out in 1911.

J. CAILLAUX

Mamers, November 25, 1915

42. TURCO-ITALIAN WAR OF 1911[1]

[The Italian Premier's account of the outbreak of the war with Turkey gives a good survey of Italian foreign policy for some years preceding the actual war. The concluding paragraph of this selection is a classical example of the cynicism of secret diplomacy.]

As I have already indicated, a third point on the program with which I had assumed the government, was the solution of the Libyan problem—a problem that henceforth faced Italy for several years; that is to say, since the unexpected agreements between France and England, France and Germany, France and Spain, had—with our consent and that of the other Powers—solved in addition to the questions of Egypt and Morocco, the general problem of Mediterranean Africa, by recognizing Italy's predominant rights and interests in Tripoli and Cyrenaica. . . .

I had already proved, since my entrance into Parliament, how much importance I had attached to the problem of Mediterranean Africa and the necessity that Italy should not be excluded from its solution. And I had demonstrated this by giving my adherence to a group which

---

[1] Giovanni Giolitti. *Mémoires de ma vie*, Paris, Plon Nourrit et Cie, 1923, pp. 203-222, *passim*. Reprinted with the permission of Plon Nourrit et Cie.

had separated from the Left, simply because it reproached its head, Cairoli, with the Tunisian affair. I also blamed the Government for not having accepted England's invitation to share in her action in Egypt. After the agreements concluded with France and England, which recognized our original interests in Libya in exchange for our disinterestedness regarding Morocco and Egypt, I never lost sight of the diplomatic aspect of the question. Also, at the time of the Czar's visit to Racconigi, I had secured Russia's recognition of our rights in that zone. Furthermore, as regards Article 9 of the Triple Alliance, which referred to our eventual occupation of Tripoli "by right of legitimate compensation," at our demand there had been inserted into a further memorandum relative to the renewal of the Alliance, and dated May, 1902, a declaration pure and simple of disinterestedness on the part of Germany and Austria-Hungary, regarding the Libyan question, without any reservation of compensation in their favor.

During my preceding period of office I applied myself directly to the uncertainty for Italy of braving a war in Libya; and to establish a local preparedness and to profit by the conflicts and political dissensions of the local chiefs with the Turkish authorities, I had certain of my agents bring pressure to bear in Cyrenaica and Tripoli. Among these I name Mohamed Ali Elui Bey, an Egyptian who had already rendered services to Italy and who got in touch with the chief of the Senoussi. I also made use of other persons, whom it is best not to name, in order that they be not exposed to any vengeance; and who had also assimilated the Senoussi element of the Islamic University in Cairo. A military solution of the Libyan problem had not appeared necessary during the reign of Abdul Hamid, from whom one would have been able, it seemed, to obtain concessions of an economic and judicial character, such as would assure Italian interests against any designs whatsoever. Things had greatly changed with the coming of the régime of the Young Turks. These had everywhere aroused political and fanatical feeling among the people; directing it particularly against the nation that seemed to them most formidable within a given zone of their empire: and as regards Libya the suspected power was naturally Italy. In Tripoli and in Cyrenaica the Bank of Rome had in these last years established considerable interests which the Italian government was bound to protect; and if Turkey had had a clear vision of the situation she would have guarded against putting in the way of these interests the difficulties, obstacles, and menaces of rivalry which would sooner or later have the effect of obliging Italy to intervene. I remember that when we called the attention of the Porte to these things and to the necessity of favoring Italian interests in Libya, she replied evasively to us, making propositions which at first sight appeared absurd; thus once, she offered us very simply concessions in Mesopotamia while she refused them in Tripolitania. This was not an absurdity but a refined cunning, too refined to have any result. By such offers the Porte aimed at sowing discord and provoking dissensions and conflicts among the Powers variously interested in the different zones of the Ottoman Empire: in Mesopotamia we should in effect clash with German and English interests while the English and Germans in Libya would clash with Italian interests.

Such was in its general lines the state of the Libyan problem, when in 1911 I again came to power. That is to say, a situation growing worse and making henceforth a peaceful solution such as perhaps would have been acceptable heretofore, difficult if not impossible. . . .

When war was declared with Turkey, conjectures were made as to what reasons could have induced the government to make such a decision, one which would seem impulsive to those ignorant of what had preceded it. And it was said there were secret reasons which, at one time, had overcome my hesitation.

There is no truth in all this. The reasons that had convinced me of the necessity for action were of a general political nature. The Moroccan question once settled with the establishment of the French sway; and that of Egypt with diplomatic recognition of the English sway—long an established fact—the condition in which Libya remained under Ottoman rule was such that it could not continue. In effect, while Western Africa, from Tunis to Morocco, as well as Egypt, were under the ægis of European administrations, most backward conditions still prevailed in Libya; we need only recall that the traffic in negroes still persisted in Bengali, they being forcibly captured in the center of Africa to be sold in this market. It was impossible that such an infamy could be tolerated at the very doors of Europe. As for us, in the negotiations with France and England regarding Egyptian and Moroccan questions, we claimed rights which were recognized by the other Great Powers. And the moment should come—and for me it had come or was imminent—when we should find ourselves faced with the following alternative: either to exercise our rights without further ceremony or to renounce them. The existing state of things could not continue, and in view of the Young Turks' conduct, it was evident that if we had not gone into Libya, some other Power with political interests or knowing how to create economic interests, would certainly have done so. Furthermore, Italy, already so profoundly alarmed by the French occupation of Tunis, would certainly not have tolerated the repetition of a similar action in Libya, and we would thus have incurred the risk of a conflagration with some European power, a more serious thing than a conflict with Turkey. To persist in the situation where we now found ourselves of having a first claim on Libya—that prevented the other Powers from going there—without going in ourselves, would have been a slightly serious matter, and which besides would have created difficulties with all the other European questions, notably those of the Balkans. Another complication arose from the pro-Turkish policy in which our allies, above all Germany, were then engaged and which was contrary to the treatment which the government at Constantinople accorded to Italian interests. Hence San

Giuliano, in his communications to the governments of Berlin, and of Vienna, supported the apparently paradoxical theory, that the only way to reëstablish good-feeling between us and Turkey, and to make a harmonious policy of the Triple Alliance possible in the Ottoman Empire, would be for us to occupy Tripoli. . . .

In addition let me state that if, towards the end of the Moroccan problem, the question of Libya would have alone presented itself in the diplomatic field, it would have more easily obtained general assent. But if we were to act in such a manner as to show that another question of profound interest to certain of the greatest European powers was still open, consent would have been bargained for by various sides with the result of greatly complicating matters.

As the Moroccan question between France and Germany had been settled in a peaceful manner, I judged that the moment had come for me to act. During this time, the conduct of the Young Turk government, far from ameliorating the situation, had aggravated it. Notably at Tripoli the *vali*, urged on and supported by the local committee of "Union and Progress," multiplied the insults against Italian citizens, and sought for pretexts to do them injury, and to hinder their activities. To such a degree, that the Bank of Rome, which, in particular, had extended its commercial interests in Tripolitania seeing itself exposed to serious injuries, had, it seemed, opened negotiations to cede all its interests to a group of Austro-German bankers. In truth, one had to recognize the fact, that for two years past, the Porte had shown itself obstinately deaf to all our claims and protests. In this way she clearly showed the desire to uproot all Italian influence in Libya, while at the same time inciting the infiltration of other interests, especially those of Germany. This, with the evident intention of creating a situation which, in time, would have made a breach in our political rights, even in those which the other Powers had conceded to us. The decisive importance of the commercial element in determining the validity of the political interests, even those that are traditional, is one of the aspects of modern colonization. And the Ottoman government, in seeking to embarrass the affirmation of our economic supremacy in Libya, and in combatting it by offering concessions or promises to the citizens of other Powers, robbed us of the alternative of a pacific penetration. It also made an Italian military occupation inevitable, which it hastened by offering the best reasons in justification. Here is an example, among others, of these manoeuvres against Italian interests: at that time the government of Constantinople, having decided to accept bids for the important work of enlarging and adapting the port of Tripoli, had let it be known that it would go to any extreme to prevent the contract from being awarded to an Italian. Since the month of July we had been endeavoring through the medium of our allies to make the Turkish government understand how much, in continuing this policy, it would render radical decisions on our part inevitable. We notified them that, in order to improve the relations between the two countries, several changes would be necessary, among others, a change of the *vali*, the chief persecutor of our interests, who was too much involved in an anti-Italian policy for there to be any hope of a sincere and loyal transformation on his part. Aehrenthal, at that time head of the Austro-Hungarian government, and the German Chancellor, Kiderlen-Waechter, recognized the justice of our protestations and the legitimacy of our demands. But according to certain allusions of theirs, they appeared to believe that the Young Turks, having assumed the nationalist attitude, upon which they based their prestige, could make no real concessions without exposing this prestige to a serious blow, with the possible consequence of the fall of their régime. And a new and very serious diplomatic fact demonstrated how far the Turkish government, in place of recognizing the justice of our claims, believed it could go on taking liberties against us, outside of the Libyan question: being in need of funds, the Porte was about to negotiate with Germany and Austria-Hungary, an increase of four and a half per cent on the customs rates; and we were informed that its intention was —once the consent of the other nations was obtained—to face Italy with the *fait accompli*, and to apply the new rates to Italian merchandise, without any redress. As the assent of the other Powers had been obtained on the basis of indemnities and concessions, it was evident that the Turkish government proposed, not only to evade all discussion of indemnities or of concessions with Italy, but that it believed it possible openly to carry out against us an act of contempt, destined to lower our prestige in the Orient—according to the reports of our consuls in Tripoli—already well-shaken, thanks to the vexations to which our co-nations had been subjected.

The conclusion of the Moroccan question had had, moreover, considerable and inevitable repercussions in Italian public opinion expressed in the press, which was occupied largely with the question of Mediterranean Africa. And even the prudent and moderate journals did not hide the fact that the conclusion of the Franco-German accord on the subject of Morocco giving finally to France, without any reservation, that which had been recognized by her in the convention concluded with Italy, rendered hereafter imperative the necessity of defining clearly, and once for all, the interests and the rights which had likewise been recognized as ours. The definition could have been pacific, if, at Constantinople, they had had a clear idea of the situation, and if they had understood that the sole means of avoiding a conflict was that of coming loyally before Italy. On the contrary, letters and despatches from Tripoli brought constantly a detail of new vexations, which, though mediocre and secondary when taken separately, constituted as a whole grave economic and political obstacles, while the news from Constantinople, confirmed by the dispatches of our Embassy, and even by foreign press correspondents, represented the Porte in an attitude of misunderstanding and defiance towards us.

General consideration of our interests in Mediterranean Africa, joined to this news which showed the danger run not only by our economic interests, but also by our prestige and our national dignity, ended by determining a veritable compaign in a large section of our press, which demanded without delay the solution of the Libyan question. . . .

At Tripoli, the situation was more complicated. The reports of our consuls had already called our attention to the fact that the Turkish régime was not popular among the Arabs, who were continually annoyed; and there was no lack of influential chiefs, such as the mayor of Tripoli, Hassuna Pasha, descendant of the ancient royal family of the country, who had been disposed to be on good terms with us. Our consuls, nevertheless, never had excessive illusions on this subject; for they presumed that in case of war, the appeal to Islamic fanaticism and to nationalism would not have been in vain. In fact, the local committees of "Union and Progress" began at one time a nationalist campaign, convoking to the mosques the Arab chiefs and peoples for manifestations protesting against Italy. They obtained a mediocre success for this end, but nevertheless it increased in proportion their fervor.

The attitude of the Turkish Government was variable and changed with the development of events. It tried first the strong manner. The Turkish chargé d'affaires presented himself Aug. 4 at the Consulta, and in the absence of San Giuliano, complained with hauteur to the under-secretary of the hostility which was manifested against Turkey in public opinion and even in the lobbies of the Parliament; he complained above all that this hostility was not moderated by explicit and official declarations of the Italian Government. . . .

On the other hand, during all this preparatory period which lasted from June to September, I judged it opportune to manage diplomatic affairs well as regards those Powers in any way interested. This task was intensified when the occupation of Libya became for us an irrevocable decision and even an imminent realization.

Nevertheless, in this matter also it was necessary to proceed with great prudence, in order not to cause any alarms nor to provoke complications. It was necessary to solve the Libyan situation which could not be prolonged further without prejudice to our interests and our prestige, without alarming Europe on the subject of the Ottoman question, susceptible of provoking a general conflagration. There was then the danger, in case our intentions became too apparent, that some Power would have the idea of giving us advice, thus beginning a general discussion which could have compromised everything and given Turkey time to prepare herself strongly in the territory which we must occupy. Consequently, the diplomatic work necessary to create around our enterprise, when it should begin, a feeling of benevolence or to avoid at least too strong and too open aversions, must consist in holding the Powers *au courant* of the difficult situation in which the conduct of the Turkish Government placed us, and to let them understand that we could sooner or later be obliged to act, without being precise at all in this regard.

We then sent opportune instructions to our ambassadors in the great capitals. Our ambassador at London, Marquis Imperiali, found good will at the government to which he was accredited, while the attitude of the press was not equally favorable. Speaking with Sir Edward Grey, then Minister of Foreign Affairs, our ambassador put emphasis upon the truly exemplary length with which the Italian Government had given proof of its desire to avoid complications, without ever succeeding in persuading the Young Turks to change their conduct, either overtly or secretly hostile. This hostility was increased from day to day; to the point where soon our Government would be unable to resist public opinion, which demanded the safety of our interests and our national dignity. This communication was made July 25. Grey received it with cordiality. He declared that preceding statements had put him *au courant* of the difficulties of our situation, and that an examination of it had persuaded him that our complaints were well founded. If the failure of all possible attempts at a peaceful solution put Italy in the position of having to act to safeguard her disregarded interests, England would not oppose it, but she would give us the support of her sympathy, well understood to be moral only, while reserving for an opportune moment to make it understood at Constantinople that Turkey could expect a different treatment on the part of Italy in view of her incorrect procedure against the latter. Grey observed further—always friendly and personal advice—that our eventual action ought to be justified by a flagrant violation of our rights, or by flagrant proof of the intention of Turkey to put us in a condition of inferiority toward other nations. He insisted particularly on this point, desiring to avoid any appearance in our action of obtaining from Turkey an economic position based on particular interests; a thing which would have rendered difficult for Sir Edward Grey the task of supporting before Parliament the sympathy and moral approval which he was disposed to concede us, England having always maintained intact, in economic matters, the principle of the open door, even in her agreements with France on the subject of Morocco. This cordial and friendly disposition of England was due first to the old friendship between the two countries and to the accord established between them for Mediterranean Africa; then to the fact that the English Government—thanks to her experience of colonial matters—recognized the impossibility of any other solution. It was fully confirmed at the last moment. In fact, when, on September 26, when our action was imminent, the Turkish Ambassador at London presented himself by order of his Government at the Foreign Office, asking that England intervene in giving us counsels of moderation, Grey replied to him that, in a question exclusively between Italy and Turkey, the British Government did not intend to intervene in any manner, even in the case that, in the last extremity, Italy should occupy Tripolitania.

. . . Fully as cordial toward us was the attitude of France, for whom, furthermore, our rights in Libya must seem most legitimate and our action most justifiable. For the general situation of Mediterranean Africa and the particular position in which Italy found herself were in large part a direct consequence either of French policy on the subject of Morocco, or of stipulated agreements of long standing and always confirmed between Italy and France. The French Government understood perfectly that the definitive solution to which the Moroccan question had arrived by the last accords with Germany, opened the Libyan problem for Italy. Our ambassador, Tittoni, who, having been Minister of Foreign Affairs, had already taken a large share in the negotiations relative to our rights in Libya, had recently obtained from Ministers Pichon and Cruppi the most explicit and categorical statements on the fidelity of France to the engagements concluded in 1902. September 22, he had had a new conversation with the Minister of Foreign Affairs, de Selves, and the latter had assured him that, for our action in Tripolitania, we could count on the French Government's being unconditionally with us. And he added further that, as it was a question of launching eventually a new Turkish loan in France, the Government would only give its adhesion when the Tripolitan question was fully solved. Indeed, Delcassé declared to Tittoni that every wish and sympathy was with Italy. . . .

In consideration of the special situation of Germany and Austria— and especially the first quarrel in the alliance with Italy on one side and the friendship and the interests of Turkey on the other, San Giuliano and I were persuaded that we should delay as long as possible the moment of informing our allies of our intentions and of our eventual action. A reason which, consequently, we declared frankly, and which even Aehrenthal recognized as legitimate and just when, towards the end of September, we finally judged it opportune to inform them of it. We had wished to spare them serious embarrassment, and to guarantee us against interventions, which, however well intentioned and friendly, would have complicated our situation. Aehrenthal, informed by our Ambassador d'Avarna and put in touch with the reasons of our action, showed that he took very good account of it. He showed himself satisfied with our project of wishing to localize the question in the Mediterranean, and of abstaining as far as possible from actions likely to provoke repercussions in the Balkans. But he insisted on the danger that such repercussions could not be avoided, in view of the situation in the interior of Turkey and the disposition of the Young Turks. As a friend and ally of Italy, he believed it his duty to call the attention of our Government to this point, and begged it to consider the grave responsibility which it might run. For the rest, he demanded time to reflect before making his report to the Emperor, upon whom rested the power of decision, reserving the right of communicating to us the decisions which the Government might take. Austria was sur-

prised by a *fait accompli*. Count Aehrenthal, making the reply on
September 29, which he had reserved, declared that his Government
had first of all to express its regret that Italy had so quickly abandoned diplomatic ground. Nevertheless, the Austro-Hungarian Government considered that Italy, her friend and ally, had the right of
organizing as she liked the guardianship of her own interests, and that
he would not oppose any difficulty to our action in Tripolitania. And,
in conclusion, he again drew our attention to the eventual repercussions
of our action in the Balkans, and recalled that the treaty of the Triple
Alliance was based on the maintenance of the *status quo* in European
Turkey, expressing the hope that Italy would take all the necessary
precautions to localize her action in the Mediterranean and prevent
all perturbation in the Balkans. In making our communications to
Austria and Germany, we had bound, in a certain way, the question of
Tripolitania to the renewal, next time, of the Triple Alliance, to have
it understood at Vienna and Berlin that a hostile and hardly cordial
attitude toward us had gravely compromised the Alliance.

More even than that of Austria, the situation of Germany was complicated and delicate. For, having accomplished, during the last years
the assiduous labor, crowned with success, of drawing Turkey into the
orbit of the Triple Alliance, she now saw the imminence of a conflict
between Turkey and one of her allies. . . .

The secrecy which I considered necessary in the preparation of our
action and which was perfectly kept to the end, coincided with the
summer seasons, which, while withdrawing from Rome the ambassadors
of the different Powers, avoided indiscretions and those contacts in
which it is not always possible not to betray one's thought. Moreover,
I had agreed with San Giuliano that, under the pretext of vacations,
he should go to Fiuggi or Vollombrosa, while I should go to Cavour
and Bardonnèche, thus showing that there was nothing in the air.
I recall that the most fervent newspapers on the Libyan question reproached me severely for my absence from the capital, and my lack of
contact with the Minister of Foreign Affairs in such a time. But the
abuse which they addressed to me caused me great pleasure, for they
showed that my strategem had succeeded marvelously, while it dissi-
pated the suspicions of the Turkish Government, which was, in fact,
surprised by our ultimatum.

43. The Balkan Crisis, 1912-1913

[Nekludov was the Russian Minister at Sofia and Hartwig was the
Russian Minister at Belgrade. Danev was President of the Bulgarian
Sobranje (National Assembly) and, after Gueshov's resignation on
the eve of the Second Balkan War, he was the Prime Minister. Though
Gueshov, the Russo-phil Bulgarian Prime Minister, shows himself as
the author of the Balkan Alliance, Serbia had made—as he indicates—

earlier approaches, as a result of her humiliation in the Bosnian crisis. Milovanovitch was the Serbian Foreign Minister. When Sazonov showed Poincaré the text of the Serbo-Bulgarian pact, he was shocked, saying that it contained the germ of a war not only against Turkey but against Austria, and that it established the hegemony of Russia over the Slav kingdoms, since she was to arbitrate in all matters.

The agreement of the Powers that Austria and Russia should inform the Balkan states that the Powers condemned war and would allow no change in the *status quo*, came too late, for on October 8 Montenegro opened hostilities by attacking Turkey. The success of the Balkan states was rapid. The Conference of Ambassadors met in London throughout the winter. From December to March the danger of war among the Great Powers was acute. The Balkan war was reopened in February, when Adrianople fell under the attack of the Bulgars and Serbs, and Janina to the Greeks. When Serbia demanded revision of the partition treaty, Bulgaria signed an armistice with Turkey April 16. The diplomats returned to London and drafted a treaty in May, but progress was slow and Grey's pressure of May 28 was needed to get the treaty signed. June 29, by order of King Ferdinand and without the knowledge of the Bulgarian Premier, the Bulgarians treacherously attacked the Serbian forces in Macedonia. The Bulgarian Cabinet called off the troops, but it was too late. Roumania, resolved to prevent the predominance of Bulgaria in the Balkans, joined the allies. The war was quickly ended and, without the intervention of the Powers, the peace of Bukarest was imposed upon vanquished Bulgaria.]

(a) *The Serbo-Bulgarian Treaty*[1]

The Serbo-Bulgarian negotiations lasted from October, 1911, till February, 1912. The place chosen was Sofia, King Ferdinand being very persistent on this point: he pretended that Belgrade, owing to its geographical position, was infested with Austro-Hungarian spies; but the fact of the matter was that it flattered his vanity to see the Serbians coming, as it were, to him! The negotiations were to be conducted with the utmost secrecy, and only the respective Russian Ministers were allowed to know what was going on. In point of fact, Hartwig and I were the constant arbiters, continually consulted, and referred to in each difficulty, however small, by both parties.

The negotiations were soon concentrated almost exclusively on the defining of the spheres of influence in Macedonia, and finally four months were spent in fixing the future frontier between Serbia and

---

[1] A. Nekludoff, *Diplomatic Reminiscences before and during the World War, 1911-1917*. New York, E. P. Dutton & Co., Inc., 1921, pp. 52-56, *passim*. Taken by permission from Nekludoff's *Diplomatic Reminiscences before and during the World War*, published and copyright by E. P. Dutton & Co., Inc., New York City.

Bulgaria. In discussing the line of this frontier *in spe*, the two parties showed such an entire lack of any conciliatory spirit that I am still wondering how they ever arrived at any agreement! After long preliminary debates they at last agreed on the two extreme points of this famous frontier. These were: in the northeast the spot where at that period the frontiers of Turkey, Bulgaria and Serbia converged; in the southwest the northern point of Lake Ochrida.

But then the line between these two points had to be drawn. As it was manifestly impossible to send a commission to work on the spot (the Turks might have taken this amiss!), it was necessary to rely on the most detailed maps of the Russian, Serbian and Bulgarian General Staffs. The demarcation of the boundary-line gave rise to endless discussions; each elevation, each village, each stream was bitterly disputed, and to solve the question they sought now the interposition of the Russian Ministers, now the topographical authority of our military agents. Each side wished to mark the frontier by a curved line, curving outwards as far as possible into the future territory of the competitor; but by dint of arguing, a remarkably straight line was arrived at—and this in spite of the very uneven surface configuration of Macedonia— the result—well-known in physics—of two equal efforts working in an inverse sense!

On the Bulgarian side it was M. Gueshov and M. Todorov who were the most amenable and the most willing to arrive at a sincere agreement, whereas M. Danev and the military, as was moreover to be expected, displayed inflexible obstinacy. So far as the principal representative of Serbian interests—the Serbian Minister in Sofia, M. Spalaikovitch (later on Minister in St. Petersburg)—was concerned, his vehement nationalism was tempered by the sincere desire to cause Slav solidarity to triumph on this question. . . .

In the dispatches which I sent off every fortnight to St. Petersburg, to M. Neratoff and then to M. Sazonoff on his return from Davos, I related in detail the progress of the Serbo-Bulgarian negotiations; but each of my dispatches was accompanied by a private and confidential letter in which I did not omit to point out the danger of war which might be brought about by the Serbo-Bulgarian agreement. . . . I laid great stress on the facts that the negotiations were now exclusively concerned with territorial demarcation and with the defining of a frontier *in spe* between Bulgaria and Serbia; that throughout the conferences I could not observe a desire to arrive at a really cordial agreement between the two countries; that these conferences were assuming a character of mere political opportunism, and that the Italo-Turkish war which was going on meanwhile certainly incited the Balkan States to action. Each time the answer from St. Petersburg was to the effect that we certainly would not hear of an armed collision in the Balkans, and that everything must be done to prevent such a collision, but that, on the other hand, a Serbo-Bulgarian agreement would be particularly welcome and agreeable to us, because it would constitute an effectual barrier against Austro-German penetration in the Peninsula.

(b) *The Account of the Making of the Balkan Alliance by the Former Prime Minister of Bulgaria, M. Gueshov*[1]

No Bulgarian statesman, responsible for the future of the Bulgarian nation, could remain indifferent to such a condition of things, or ignore the open threats of the Turks to aggravate the measures aiming at the annihilation of the Bulgarians in Macedonia. My manifest duty was to examine how Bulgaria could best be enabled to stop these excesses. Among the various methods that suggested themselves, the most important consisted in an understanding, not with Turkey who had rejected our advances, but with our other neighbours. Such a policy was greatly facilitated by the unanimity with which public opinion in Bulgaria had recently greeted the meeting of the Serbian and Bulgarian economists and the visit of the Bulgarian students to Athens in April 1911. Matters were further simplified by the fact that in 1904 a secret agreement had been signed with Serbia, and that the latter country had since made repeated efforts, both while the Democratic party was in office and during the first six months of our administration, to conclude an offensive and defensive alliance with Bulgaria. . . .

We, M. Milovanovitch and myself, left Belgrade on October 11, at 11.30 p.m. and at 2.30 a.m. reached Lipovo, where the Serbian Ministerial carriage was detached and we had to part company. During the three hours which we spent together, we touched on all the questions affecting the interests of our countries, beginning from the Turco-Italian war and the Young Turkish régime.

Speaking on the latter topic, M. Milovanovitch said that Count Aehrenthal had despaired of the Young Turks being able to regenerate Turkey. A few months ago—last spring—he had spoken in favour of an autonomous Albania which would help to solve the great Balkan question. M. Milovanovitch again dwelt on the dangers which such an Albania, stretching to the Bulgarian frontiers and including the vilayets of Monastir and Uskub, would present for the Balkan Slavs. In his opinion the Albanians, most of whom are Mohammedans and afflicted with the common Moslem incapacity to form a civilised State, were condemned to the fate of the other Moslem nations—the fate of Algeria, Tunis, Morocco, and Tripoli. The only possible solution, when the time comes for a final settlement with Turkey, would be found in the annexation of northern Albania by Serbia and of southern Albania by Greece.

The liquidation of Turkey being mentioned, M. Milovanovitch en-

---

[1] I. E. Gueshoff, *The Balkan League*. London, John Murray, 1915, pp. 9-10, 15-17, 36-40, 48-50, 76-77, 81-82, 84-87, 91-93. Reprinted with the permission of John Murray.

tered into a long discussion on the present and the future of our two countries. He thinks that nothing can be done at this juncture, all the Powers being determined to localise the war and not to tolerate any Balkan complications. We must, therefore, remain quiet. Serbia will under no circumstances stir, the more so as he thinks that a war between Turkey and one of the Balkan States will consolidate rather than weaken the Young Turkish régime. We must wait until the end of the war, trying meanwhile to secure the support of Russia. Without such support nothing can or ought to be undertaken. But before turning to Russia we must come to an understanding among ourselves and conclude a treaty in three copies, one of which will be handed to Russia.

The main provisions of the *casus fœderis* should be as follows:

1. An absolute defensive alliance against whosoever attacks Bulgaria or Serbia;

2. A defensive alliance against whosoever attempts to occupy those parts of the Balkan Peninsula which shall be specifically mentioned: Macedonia, Old Serbia, etc.;

3. An offensive alliance against Turkey with the object: (*a*) of liberating Macedonia and Old Serbia in circumstances deemed favourable to both countries; (*b*) of putting an end to the anarchy or massacres in the Turkish provinces where the vital interests of either contracting party are at stake.

When I remarked to M. Milovanovitch that if our attempt at liberating Macedonia and Old Serbia takes the character of annexation, our task will be greatly complicated, owing to the touchiness of our neighbours, he agreed that it would be better to ask for autonomy, although that solution did not particularly appeal to him. He kept insisting on a partition of the territories liberated and said that for some of them there could be no discussion between us. Adrianople must revert to Bulgaria, in the same way as Old Serbia, to the north of Shar Mountain, must belong to Serbia. As regards Macedonia, the greater part of that province will fall to the Bulgarians. But a section of northern Macedonia must be given to Serbia, and the best way would be to reserve the partition for the arbitration of the Russian Emperor. Let us draw no dividing line at present, he added. By adopting that course you will spare yourselves the criticisms of having consented to a preliminary repartition of Macedonia. Later on, when your compatriots have secured the lion's part, no one would think of protesting that a small part of Macedonia has been awarded to Serbia by the Russian Emperor, under whose patronage and high sense of justice this great work will have been accomplished. Ah, yes! If the "winding-up" of Turkey coincides with the crumbling of Austria-Hungary, matters will be enormously simplified. Serbia will get Bosnia and Herzegovina, while Roumania receives Transylvania, and we shall then have no reasons for apprehending a Roumanian intervention in our war against Turkey.

[Gueshov gives the following account of the signing of the Greco-Bulgarian treaty.]

As early as May 1911, or two months after my advent to office, the question of an understanding with Greece had been raised by Mr. J. D. Bourchier, the well-known friend of Bulgaria and correspondent of *The Times* in the Balkan Peninsula. Mr. Bourchier wrote to me a letter from Athens in which he informed me that the Greek King and the Greek Government were anxious to arrive at an agreement with Bulgaria. The visit of the Bulgarian students to Athens, in the spring of 1911, the friendly reception which was accorded to them in Greece, had created an atmosphere highly propitious to an exchange of ideas, paving the path for an understanding, if not an alliance, between the two countries. Mr. Bourchier was given to understand that the Bulgarian Government was in no way opposed to such an exchange of views. Matters, however, remained at a standstill until the Turco-Italian war and the conduct of the Young Turks towards us, more especially their unprovoked mobilisation against Bulgaria at the beginning of October 1911, forced us to commence negotiations with Greece.

The first step in that direction was taken immediately after the said Turkish mobilisation. On October 16, 1911, M. Panas, Greek Minister in Sofia, came, as he expressed himself, to make an important communication on behalf of his Government. After recapitulating the history of his various conversations with me, before I left for Vichy, and with M. Theodoroff, while the latter was acting as my substitute, M. Panas concluded that if I could assure him of our willingness to intervene in the event of a Turkish aggression on Greece, he was authorised by his Government to declare to me that Greece, in her turn, will fight should Bulgaria be attacked by Turkey.

In view of the critical state of our relations with Turkey at the beginning of October 1911, this communication was of capital importance to us. Before Serbia had promised to fight on our side in the event of a war with Turkey, we were receiving such an assurance from Greece. The Greek proposal was communicated to the King and the Ministerial Council and accepted by them, I being authorised to tell M. Panas that Bulgaria will assist Greece in a war with Turkey, on conditions which must be specified in a defensive treaty. M. Panas agreed to that.

No project for such a treaty was, however, prepared, while our negotiations with Serbia went on. After we signed the treaty with Serbia, I had another conversation with M. Panas, and on April 27, 1912, received from him a note, enclosing the draft for a defensive alliance between the two countries.

In this preliminary project not only was nothing said about autonomy for Macedonia and Thrace, but even those privileges which had been granted to the Christian provinces of European Turkey by various international acts, particularly article 23 of the Treaty of Berlin, were passed over in silence. I told M. Panas that we could not accept their project so long as Greece did not declare explicitly that she would raise no objections to autonomy. With that object in view, I submitted to him the following formula:

Greece undertakes not to offer any opposition to an eventual demand by Bulgaria of administrative autonomy for Macedonia and the vilayet of Adrianople, guaranteeing equal rights to the nationalities there.

My suggestion, however, was not adopted. I again made it clear that it was impossible for me to sign a treaty which did not at least recognise our obligation to fight for those rights of the Christians in Turkey which were based on treaties. M. Panas replied that I was trying, in a roundabout way, to get back to autonomy, since I had in my mind article 23 of the Treaty of Berlin, about the application of which numerous meetings were just then being held throughout Bulgaria. People still remember the movement which spread rapidly all over the country, after the example was set by Sofia, where, on May 12, an imposing demonstration took place, under the chairmanship of Dr. Stambolski and the MM. Ivan Vazoff, Professor Iv. Shishmanoff, Dr. S. Sarafoff, Iv. Grozeff, G. Gueorgoff, Stanisheff, and many others. I did not disguise from M. Panas that I aimed at the carrying out of this article 23, but that in order to spare the susceptibilities of Greece I proposed to use in the preamble of our treaty and in article 2, which dealt with the rights of the Christian nationalities, the words "conceded" (by the Sultans) and "deriving from the treaties." Thereupon M. Panas entered into an excited discussion with me, and tried to convince me that, as I had in view article 23 of the Treaty of Berlin, my proposal would not be accepted. For a considerable time Athens remained silent. M. Panas came frequently to see me, under the pretext of telling me that he was still without instructions, his real object being to induce me not to press my formula. But I remained unmoved. Finally, about May 23, he informed me that the Greek Government had agreed to my formula concerning the privileges secured by international treaties. It being already decided that the King and the Queen would start on June 1 for Vienna and Berlin, where they were paying their first official visit, I hastened to sign the treaty with Greece before our departure. This was done by M. Panas and me on May 29, 1912. The ratification of the treaty by the two rulers followed after our return from Berlin. As for our military convention with Greece, its examination was entrusted to Generals Nikiphoroff and Fitcheff, but its signature was deferred until September 1912. I may mention at this place that, owing to lack of time, we were unable to conclude with Greece an agreement with respect to the future frontiers in Macedonia. Among the various other things, M. Panas had told me that Greece refused to treat with Austria because the latter had made it clear that she wanted Salonica for herself.

THE EVE OF THE BALKAN WAR

I need not dwell at great length on the first symptoms of the coming crash: agitations throughout Turkey against the Young Turks; the circular letter of Mahmoud Shevket Pasha forbidding the officers to occupy themselves with politics; the revolt of the garrison in Adrianople; the *pronunciamento* at Monastir; the revolt of the Albanians; the fall of the Young Turkish Cabinet; the battle near Mitrovitza after which the victorious Albanians became masters of the sandjaks of Ipek, Prizrend, and Prishtina; the Albanian ultimatum; the massacres at Kotchani and Berana; the occupation of Uskub by the Albanians. All these events, especially the last three, awoke a resounding echo in Sofia, Athens, Belgrade, and Cettigne, and it required no prophetic gift to foretell that they would not pass without far-reaching consequences. The European Chancellories were no less impressed than the Balkan Governments by what was happening, and on August 14 the Austrian Government, which was most amicably disposed towards Turkey, stepped forward with the famous proposals of Count Berchtold in favour of administrative decentralisation in European Turkey. If Austria was driven to such radical measures, was it likely that the Balkan States would remain indifferent to the fate of their co-nationalists? To this preoccupation in Athens and Belgrade was added the anxiety caused by the Albanian claims on Greek and Serbian districts, the Albanians openly demanding the entire vilayets of Uskub and Monastir. No such fears were entertained in Sofia as regards the Albanian danger, but in Bulgaria the massacre at Kotchani had produced even a deeper impression. What reason had we for being overpunctilious with an Empire already exhausted by the war with Italy, torn by internal feuds, with an undisciplined army and an empty treasury? On August 14 an impressive meeting was held in the Bulgarian capital, and ten days later the various brotherhoods, representing the Macedonian and Thracian districts, opened their congress. Both the meeting and the congress voted resolutions to the same effect: Bulgaria must immediately mobilise her army and demand autonomy in favour of Macedonia and Thrace, failing which, she must declare war on Turkey. Otherwise the country was threatened with troubles, bringing in their wake incalculable consequences.

The moment was one of solemn gravity and the pressure on the part of public opinion had become well-nigh irresistible. In the midst of the crisis arrived M. Kolusheff from Cettigne, with an offer on the part of the Montenegrin King of immediate action. We had either to accept this proposal or to decline it. On August 26 MM. Daneff, Theodoroff, General Nikiphoroff and myself, with the consent of the Ministerial Council, met the King at Tzarska Bistritza, near Tcham Kourya. I reported on the situation, after which followed prolonged deliberations on the most difficult problem which had confronted any Bulgarian

Government since the country was liberated. The unanimous decision at which we arrived did not differ from that already taken by the Ministerial Council—and was to accept the offer of Montenegro and to arrange with Greece and Serbia for an immediate intervention on behalf of the Christian populations in European Turkey.

. . . .

The Russian Minister of Foreign Affairs to the Russian Minister in Belgrade

Petrograd,
April 17, 1913

The Bulgarian Minister, acting on instructions from the Sofia Cabinet, has drawn our attention to the dangerous undercurrents which threaten the existence of the Balkan Alliance. For instance, not long ago the Serbian Finance Minister asked for suplementary military credits for a period from the conclusion of peace until the final repartition of the conquered territories among the allies. The Greek and Serbian armies are being reinforced against the Bulgarian troops. Besides, it appears that special negotiations have been opened between Serbia and Greece, it being seriously rumoured that an alliance between those two countries has been concluded. Please point out to the Foreign Minister how serious and regrettable are all these measures, which can only lead to a disruption of the Balkan Alliance.

SAZONOFF

From the Russian Minister in Sofia

April 19, 1913

The enmity between Bulgarians, on one side, and Greeks and Serbians, on the other, assumes threatening proportions. The Serbians are fortifying themselves at Monastir and are massing troops at Veles. The Greeks have sent reinforcements towards Negrita and other places. The Bulgarian press, especially the Opposition newspapers, are full of accusations and attacks upon the allies. People openly talk of an inevitable conflict with them, and confidence is expressed that the Bulgarians will in a few days defeat the allies, taking Salonica and southern Macedonia. The Bulgarian Headquarters are taking measures in the event of the outbreak of a fratricidal war.

NEKLUDOFF

The Russian Minister of Foreign Affairs to the Russian Minister in Belgrade

Petrograd,
June 19, 1913

The information received from various sources confirms the growing agitation in the Bulgarian army in favour of immediate war or demobilisation. If Serbia does not accept the arbitration of Russia *without reservation, as Bulgaria has done,* the Bulgarian Government refuses to wait any longer, and the proposed meeting of the Premiers will not take place.

An unconditional acceptance by Serbia of Russian arbitration can in no way be considered as a concession to Bulgaria.

The consent of Serbia for the purpose indicated is indispensable not only to Bulgaria, but to us also, because without an assurance that the two sides will accept arbitration unconditionally we cannot fulfil our mission as arbitrators.

Please invite M. Pashitch to give us a clear and definite reply without delay, and use all your influence for the purpose of obviating another ruinous conflict among the allies.

SAZONOFF

Reports to H. M. the Roumanian King by the Roumanian Minister for Foreign Affairs (Greek proposals for an alliance)

Bucharest,
May 15, 1913

At 11 o'clock this morning the Greek Minister, M. Papadiamanto-poulos, visited the Ministry of Foreign Affairs and, acting on instructions from his Government, made me the following oral communication:

1. The Greek Government will grant to all the Macedonian-Roumanian churches and schools in the territories annexed by Greece full liberty to carry on their work and to use the Macedonian-Roumanian language.

I replied that we expected that much after the declaration made by M. Venizelos to M. Take Ionesco in London, and requested him to give me the same declaration in writing and to add that Roumania will be allowed to subsidise these churches and schools, as under the Turkish rule, and that in accordance with the Eastern Orthodox canons the said Macedonian-Roumanian church will be entitled to have its own episcopate.

M. Papadiamantopoulos added that:

2. The Greek Government wishes to know whether we are prepared to conclude an alliance with Greece in view of the fact that the demands of Bulgaria are becoming more threatening.

I replied to him that I could not answer such a question before reporting the matter to H. M. the King and to the other Ministers, and that in my view Parliament must first finish with the question of the intervention in Petrograd, after which we could decide what conduct Roumania must follow in the event of a new Balkan crisis.

T. MAIORESCO

Bucharest,
Sunday, June 9, 1913

At 10 o'clock this morning the Greek Minister, M. Papadiamanto-poulos, again called on me to speak about an alliance with Greece against an excessive expansion of Bulgaria, adding that Turkey also might participate in such an alliance. I replied to him that as far as Turkey was concerned, it would be wiser to wait until her internal condition had been consolidated. With respect to a rapprochement with Greece, I postponed my reply until a later moment, when the friction between the allies should become greater.

T. MAIORESCO

Telegram of Sir Edward Grey to the British Ambassadors abroad (Requesting Balkan delegates to sign treaty)

London,
May 28, 1913

Sir Edward Grey has told the Balkan delegates that those of them who are willing to sign the preliminary treaty without any alterations should do so immediately. Those who are not disposed to sign had better leave London, as it is useless for them to remain and continue to engage in discussions of which the only result is indefinite delay. Those who do sign will have our moral support.

[Two days later the treaty was signed by all the delegates. This success of the Balkan Alliance was greeted with enthusiasm by all the friends of the allies.]

Gueshov's Account of the Second Balkan War

As to the motives of my resignation, they were well known to every one concerned. My policy of coming to an understanding with our allies without bloodshed, of keeping the Balkan Alliance intact, of having recourse to arbitration with Serbia and Greece, did not meet with approval. For this reason I thought it my duty to leave the head of the State to decide whether it would be necessary to call in fresh politicians for the settlement of our differences with the allies. I had been the first artificer of the Balkan Alliance and I became its first victim, not so much on account of the sacrifice I made in resigning the Presidency of the Ministerial Council, but because of the criticisms to which I exposed myself for leaving my post at a critical moment. But I was obliged to resign because I was not in unity with the Crown, and because I was of the opinion that such a critical situation imperatively called for a coalition Ministry on the broadest possible basis. I had a deep-rooted conviction that none of the other parties, once they were in office, would have undertaken the heavy responsibility of a second war. And as a matter of fact, M. Daneff's Cabinet which assumed office after the failure of an effort to form a large concentration Government, and which included members of two political parties, decided unanimously on June 22, 1913, that M. Daneff should go to Petrograd, and that our differences with Serbia and Greece should be submitted to arbitration.

Contrary, however, to the unanimous decision of the Bulgarian Government and without the knowledge of the Cabinet, on June 29 the Second and the Fourth Bulgarian armies, acting on order from the Headquarters, attacked our allies. Those who advised and ordered these attacks have been blamed by no one more implacably than by me. The text of the orders was published by the Carnegie Commission, which, in its report, rightly qualifies them as shifty and childish. But however much History may condemn this criminal act, she must acknowledge that the Bulgarian nation is not responsible for it. Every one knows how Bulgaria entered the Balkan war. After a mobilisation, approved by the Ministerial Council, the National Assembly was called to vote the war credits. The Sobranje approved of the mobilisation and voted the credits. After the Turks had declared war, a manifesto to the nation was issued, bearing the signatures of the King and the Ministers. Is it possible to make this same nation answerable for a *coup d'état*, a criminal folly, accomplished without the consent of the legislative body and even without the knowledge of the responsible Government? Bulgarian courts of law have publicly established that the Bulgarian Government did not decide to declare war on the allies.

(c) *Treaty of Friendship and Alliance between Bulgaria and Serbia*[1]

February 29, 1912 (O.S.)

His Majesty Ferdinand I, Tsar of the Bulgarians, and His Majesty Peter I, King of Serbia, being firmly convinced of the unity of interests and the identity of fate of their States and of the two kindred nations, the Bulgarian and the Serbian, and determined to defend those interests with united force and to work for their general advancement, have agreed upon the following:

Article 1.—The kingdom of Bulgaria and the kingdom of Serbia guarantee to each other their national independence and the integrity of their national territories, binding themselves absolutely and without reservation to succour each other with their entire forces, in the event of one of them being attacked by one or more States.

Article 2.—The two contracting parties also undertake to come to each other's assistance with all their forces in the event of any Great Power attempting to annex, occupy, or even temporarily to invade with its armies any part of the Balkan territories which are today under Turkish rule, if one of the parties should consider this as contrary to its vital interests and a *casus belli*.

Article 3.—The two contracting parties bind themselves not to conclude peace except jointly and after a preliminary understanding.

Article 4.—For the complete and most appropriate application of this treaty, a military convention will be concluded which will provide minutely for everything that may have to be undertaken by either side

---

[1] *Ibid.*, Appendix, p. 112ff.

in the event of a war, or that appertains to the military organisation, disposition, or mobilisation of the armies and the relations between the higher commands which must be settled in time of peace, as a preparation for the war and its successful prosecution. The military convention will form an integral part of the present treaty. Its formulation must begin at the latest fifteen days after the signature of the present treaty, and the convention must be ready within a maximum period of two months.

Article 5.—This treaty and the military convention will remain in force from the day of their signature to December 31, 1920 (old style), inclusive. They can be prolonged after that date through an additional understanding, explicitly ratified by the two parties. If, on the day when the treaty and convention expire, the contracting parties should be engaged in war, or should not yet have wound up the situation arising from a war, the treaty and convention will retain their force until the conclusion of peace, or until the situation resulting from a war has been definitely settled.

Article 6.—The treaty will be signed in two identical copies, both of them in Bulgarian and Serbian. They will be signed by the two Rulers and their Ministers of Foreign Affairs. The military convention, also in two copies, both of them in Bulgarian and Serbian, will be signed by the Rulers, the respective Ministers of Foreign Affairs, and by special military plenipotentiaries.

Article 7.—The treaty and the convention may be published, or communicated to other States, only after a preliminary agreement between the two contracting parties, and even then only jointly and simultaneously by the two sides.

In the same way, a third party may be admitted to join the alliance after a preliminary understanding between the two parties.

Made in Sofia, on February 29, 1912 (old style).

Iv. Ev. Gueshoff
I. Milovanovitch

Secret Annex to Treaty of Friendship and Alliance between the Kingdom of Bulgaria and the Kingdom of Serbia

Article 1.—In the event of internal troubles arising in Turkey which might endanger the State or the national interests of the contracting parties, or of either of them; or in the event of internal or external difficulties of Turkey raising the question of the maintenance of the *status quo* in the Balkan Peninsula, that contracting party which first arrives at the conclusion that in consequence of all this military action has become indispensable must make a reasoned proposal to the other party, which is bound immediately to enter into an exchange of views and, in the event of disagreement, must give to the proposing party a reasoned reply.

Should an agreement favourable to action be reached, it will be communicated to Russia, and if the latter Power is not opposed to it, military operations will begin as previously arranged, the parties being guided in everything by the sentiment of solidarity and community of their interests. In the opposite case, when no agreement has been reached, the parties will appeal to the opinion of Russia, which opinion, if and in so far as Russia pronounces herself, will be binding on both parties.

If, Russia declining to state an opinion and the parties still failing to agree, the party in favour of action should on its own responsibility open war on Turkey, the other contracting party is bound to observe towards its ally a friendly neutrality, ordering at once a mobilisation in the limits fixed by the military convention, and coming to its assistance in the event of any third party taking the side of Turkey.

Article 2.—All territorial gains acquired by combined action within the scope of articles 1 and 2 of the treaty, and of article 1 of this secret annex, shall constitute common property (condominium) of the two allies, and their repartition will take place immediately or, at the latest, within a period of three months after the restoration of peace, the following principles being observed:

Serbia recognises the right of Bulgaria to the territory east of the Rhodope Mountains and the River Strouma; while Bulgaria recognises a similar right of Serbia to the territory north and west of Shar Mountain.

As regards the territory lying between Shar Mountain and the Rhodope Mountains, the Archipelago and the Lake of Ochrida, if the two parties should become convinced that the organisation of this territory into an autonomous province is impossible, in view of the common interests of the Bulgarian and Serbian nationalities, or owing to other internal and external causes, in such a case the said territory will be disposed of in accordance with the following declarations: Serbia undertakes to ask for nothing beyond a line, drawn on the accompanying map. . . . Bulgaria undertakes to accept this line, if His Majesty the Russian Emperor, who will be requested to act as supreme arbitrator, pronounces in its favour. It is understood that the two parties bind themselves to accept as a definite frontier the line between the indicated frontiers which His Majesty the Russian Emperor will esteem to correspond best to the rights and the interests of the two parties.

Article 3.—A copy of the treaty and of the secret annex, as also of the military convention, will be jointly communicated to the Russian Government, which will be asked to take note of them, to show itself benevolent towards their aims, and to request His Majesty the Russian Emperor to accept and sanction the parts reserved by the treaty for His Majesty and the Imperial Government.

Article 4.—All disputes concerning the interpretation and the execution of any part of this treaty, of its secret annex, and of the military convention will be submitted to the final decision of Russia, as soon as one of the contracting parties declares that, in its opinion, an agreement by direct negotiations is impossible.

Article 5.—No disposition of the present secret annex shall be made public, or communicated to another State, without the previous consent of the two parties and the permission of Russia.

Made in Sofia, on February 29, 1912 (old style).

Iv. Ev. Gueshoff
M. Milovanovitch

(d) *Treaty of Defensive Alliance between Bulgaria and Greece. May 16, 1912*[1]

Taking into consideration that the two kingdoms strongly desire the maintenance of peace in the Balkan Peninsula and can, by means of a solid defensive treaty, better secure that end;

Bearing in mind that the peaceable existence of the various nationalities in Turkey, based on a real and genuine political equality and on the respect of all the rights of the Christian nationalities in the Empire, whether they derive from treaties or have been conceded to them in a different way, constitutes an indispensable condition for the consolidation of peace in the East;

Lastly, taking into account that the joint efforts of the two kingdoms in that direction would facilitate and strengthen the good understanding between Greeks and Bulgarians in Turkey, thereby helping their good relations with the Ottoman Empire;

The Government of His Majesty the Tsar of the Bulgarians and that of His Majesty the King of the Hellenes, promising not to impart to their purely defensive agreement any aggressive tendency and determined on concluding with each other a peaceable and mutually protective treaty, on the lines indicated hereafter, have appointed as their plenipotentiaries . . .

Who, after verifying their credentials, agreed upon the following:

Article 1.—If, notwithstanding the sincere wish of the two high contracting parties and efforts of their Governments to avoid all aggression or provocation against Turkey, one of the parties should be attacked by Turkey, either on its territory or through systematic disregard of its rights, based on treaties or on the fundamental principles of international law, the two contracting parties undertake to assist each other with all their armed forces, and not to conclude peace except by joint agreement.

Article 2.—The two high contracting parties promise each other to use their moral influence over their co-nationalists in Turkey so as sincerely to assist the peaceable existence of the nationalities forming the population of the Empire; they also promise to support each other and to act together, both as regards the Turkish Government and

---

[1] *Ibid.,* Appendix 7, pp. 127-130.

towards the Great Powers, in all actions having for object to secure the respect of the privileges deriving from treaties or otherwise conceded to the Greek and Bulgarian nationalities, and to obtain political equality and constitutional guarantees.

Article 3.—The present treaty will remain in force for a period of three years from the date of its signature, and will be tacitly prolonged for another year, unless previously denounced. The denunciation must take place at least six months before the end of the third year from the day of its signature.

Article 4.—The present treaty will be kept secret and may not be communicated to any third State, totally or in part, nor be published, totally or in part, except with the consent of the two contracting parties.

The present treaty will be ratified as soon as possible. The exchange of the ratifications will take place in Sofia (or in Athens).

In proof whereof, the respective plenipotentiaries have signed the present treaty and affixed their seals.

Made in Sofia, in two copies, on May 16, 1912 (old style).

Iv. Ev. Gueshoff
D. Panas

DECLARATION

The first article does not apply to the case of a war breaking out between Greece and Turkey in consequence of the admission in the Greek Parliament of the Cretan deputies, against the wishes of Turkey. In that event, Bulgaria is only bound to observe towards Greece a benevolent neutrality. As the settlement of the Eastern crisis, due to the events of 1909, and of the Cretan question harmonises with the general interest, and is even likely to consolidate the international situation favourably to peace, without upsetting the equilibrium in the Balkan Peninsula, Bulgaria (independently of any engagements assumed by the present treaty) promises in no way to embarrass any eventual action of Greece tending to solve this problem.

Iv. Ev. Gueshoff
D. Panas

(e) *The account of the crisis by the Russian Foreign Minister, M. Sazonov*[1]

When I passed through London on my way to Paris the Turkish Ambassador, Tewfik Pasha, came to see me. During our interview I more than once drew his attention to the desirability of concluding peace between the Porte and Italy at the earliest possible moment; it

---

[1] Serge Sazonov, *Fateful Years, 1909-1916*. London: Jonathan Cape, 1928; New York, Frederick A. Stokes Company, 1928, pp. 62-66; 68-70; 71-74; 82-84; 86-88; 90-93; 96-97. Reprinted with the permission of the publishers.

might then be possible at least to postpone the war that was relentlessly approaching in the Balkans, even if it could not be altogether averted. If these results were attained, I should have the satisfaction of knowing that governing circles abroad would appreciate more justly the efforts of Russian diplomacy to end the war in Tripoli, by the agreed action of the Great Powers, before it led to the outbreak of a conflagration in the Balkan Peninsula.

I received belated expressions of regret with regard to this matter from various quarters; but the time for the course we had proposed was already past, and it only remained to consider what measure could best be adopted to smother the flames which were already blazing.

For some time before my journey to England, the policy of the British Cabinet with regard to the Mahometan world had been controlled by a desire to gain the goodwill of the latter, in order to enlist the support of the Mussulman population in India against the growing revolutionary activity of the local Hindu elements. This anxiety explains the indifference which we observed in England with regard to the fate of the Christians in Turkey—an indifference contrary to the political tradition of English Liberal Cabinets. This fact was also responsible for the vacillations of British policy in Persia and Central Asia. In addition to this fundamental consideration there was probably another of a subsidiary character: the desire on the part of the English not to weaken the position of the Turkish Government at whose head stood the Anglophile Kiamil Pasha, and to prevent its replacement by a Young Turk Cabinet under Ferid Pasha, whose sympathies distinctly inclined towards Germany. These considerations explain the fact that England, despite her sincere desire to coöperate in the pacification of the Balkan Peninsula, more than once prevented the attainment of this object by refusing to participate in some diplomatic step directed to this end, for fear of producing an unfavourable impression in Constantinople. It became clear to me that we could not count upon the active assistance of England, should increased tension in the Balkans require the exercise of energetic pressure upon Turkey by the Great Powers.

My three days' stay in Paris was chiefly devoted to efforts made in concert with M. Poincaré, to retard the course of the rapidly developing events in the Balkans. To this end we employed all the resources of diplomacy, beginning with persuasion, and ending with the threat that we should not recognize the new territorial situation which would result if the war ended favourably for the Balkan Allies. All our efforts proved vain. The Allies recognized that circumstances so favourable to themselves were unlikely soon to recur, and decided to take advantage of their political and military preparedness in order to make an end of Turkish rule in the Balkans. It hampered the natural growth of these young nations and had long ago become a monstrous anachronism.

The one possibility of preventing war lay in adopting the course which I had proposed to our friends during the Tripolitan War: to bring united and vigorous pressure to bear upon the Turkish Government, in order to induce it to enter, without loss of time, on the path of radical reforms in the Macedonian vilayets; but this course was precisely the one to which it was most difficult to persuade the Great Powers to agree, for each of them was pursuing its own particular aims in Constantinople. If none of them desired a war in the Balkans in 1912, with all the possible consequences which it threatened, Germany and Austria-Hungary feared it least, for reasons which I will mention later; but not one of the Powers except Russia and perhaps France, was willing to expose its interests in Turkey to even temporary risks, for the sake of preventing this war. Russia and France would have taken this course only with the support of England; and this, as we have seen, was not to be expected.

The attitude of the French Government towards the Balkan crisis was fully defined from the very beginning. As I said above, M. Poincaré regarded it as the only possible source of European complications; and whatever his German opponents may afterwards have said as to his militarist attitude, he feared these complications more than anyone, and exerted all his strength to avoid them. The fate of the Balkan peoples, in itself, interested the French Government but little; it consequently did not adopt a benevolent attitude towards the Balkan Alliance. But although we regarded the matter from another point of view, we did not therefore feel justified in reproaching our Allies.

While I was in charge of the Ministry of Foreign Affairs, it fell to my lot to pay three visits to France. I made it a rule when returning to Russia from those visits, to remain a day in Berlin as I passed through, in order to meet the men who were directing Germany's foreign policy. I considered these halts useful, because, although brief, they afforded me an opportunity of satisfying myself as to the political outlook of the German Government at the moment. Apart from the interest of such a verification, my meetings with the Chancellor and the Secretary of State for Foreign Affairs were of some importance, because I was usually able to instil some measure of reassurance into German minds. Any manifestation of our friendship with our Ally France was always regarded with great suspicion by governing circles in Berlin, although on their side they made a point of emphasizing on every convenient occasion their solidarity with the Hapsburg Monarchy.

I knew that the German Government, despite its very real power, had suffered ever since Prince Bismarck's time from the delusion that it was persecuted, and was the constant object of hostile intentions on the part of its Western and Eastern neighbours. For this reason I esteemed it my duty, by means of a perfectly frank exchange of ideas on current political questions, to do all in my power to calm these morbid apprehensions.

On this occasion my fortnight's visit to England and my subsequent stay in Paris provided abundant food for German suspicion. Therefore to stop in Berlin seemed to me particularly opportune, apart from the fact that it was important that I should satisfy myself how far Berlin was inclined to exercise a moderating influence upon the Viennese Government. The peace of Europe depended upon the course of action pursued by Austro-Hungarian diplomacy, and it was dangerous to entertain too great hopes of its reasonableness with regard to Balkan problems.

Fortunately, I was able to assure myself without difficulty, when I visited Berlin, that on this occasion there existed no such desire to demonstrate, in the face of Europe, the invincible strength of the Austro-German Alliance as had prevailed in March, 1909; on the contrary some uneasiness was felt lest this Alliance might draw Germany into undesired international complication, at a moment not chosen by herself.

I was able to note with satisfaction that the attitude of Berlin approximated to that which I found in Government circles in Paris. Like France, Germany was ready to do anything in her power to prevent a Balkan war; or if this proved impossible, at least not to allow Europe to be drawn into it. With this as a starting point, German diplomacy honestly welcomed M. Poincaré's proposal to commit to Russia and Austria-Hungary the task of voicing, in the Balkan capitals, the 'will to peace' of the Great Powers of Europe. In this connection I was told several times in Berlin that Germany announced in advance her readiness to join in all the steps that might be agreed upon by Russia and Austria.

I subsequently learned that a strong hope, if not a firm belief, existed then in Vienna, that a conflict between the Balkan Allies and Turkey would end in the complete defeat of the former. It was felt that the danger of Serbia's acquiring a stronger position in the Peninsula would thereby be averted for a long time to come, without any efforts on the part of the Viennese Cabinet. This belief doubtless influenced the attitude which I found to prevail in Berlin.

This hope proved unjustified; but it served to maintain in Vienna and also through the influence of Vienna, in Berlin, that moral balance which rendered possible the combined efforts which all the Great Powers made in the autumn of 1912 to preserve mankind from the horrors of a European war. . . .

Warlike operations between the Balkan Allies and Turkey began with Montenegro's declaration of war against the Porte on October 8, 1912. This was the day of my arrival in Berlin on my return journey from London and Paris to St. Petersburg, which I reached on the 10th. Although the other parties to the alliance did not yet declare war against Turkey, mobilization proceeded with feverish haste in Bulgaria, Serbia and Greece, and everything pointed to an early armed conflict in Macedonia.

Before I left Paris I agreed with M. Poincaré upon the three following conditions to be laid down in the combined announcement to be made in the name of all the Great Powers in Belgrade, Sofia, Athens and Cettinje, by the Russian and Austro-Hungarian representatives acting as plenipotentiaries: (1) The Powers censure any action likely to lead to a breach of peace. (2) Basing themselves on clause 23 of the Treaty of Berlin, the Powers, in the interest of the Christian population, will themselves carry out the introduction of administrative reforms in European Turkey, while maintaining inviolate the rights of the Sultan and the territorial unity of the Ottoman Empire. (3) If nevertheless war should break out between the Balkan States and the Porte, the Powers will not allow any alteration in the territorial status of Turkey in Europe at its conclusion.

These three points, which the Great Powers accepted without objections of any kind, embodied our attempt to avert at the last moment the impending war in the Balkans, with all its incalculable consequences. I had but little faith in the success of our efforts to maintain peace. The complete military unity which the Balkan Allies had achieved, filled them with a burning desire to measure their strength with their immemorial enemy, and to settle accounts finally with him for his age-long and merciless oppression. To restrain their outburst by promises of a renewed attempt on the part of the Powers to compel Turkey to carry out at last the reforms which she had so often promised and never performed, was extremely difficult, especially in view of the fact that the Powers themselves had, out of regard for their own special interests, placed obstacles in the way of these reforms, sometimes openly and sometimes secretly. The die was cast, and it only remained for the friends of the Balkan nationalities to see that, if the war went unfavourably for these peoples, their bold attempt should not bring upon them too heavy consequences, and that the already insupportable lot of the Macedonian Christians should not be made still harder. In this respect the third of the conditions accepted by the Powers was to my mind the most important; for while giving satisfaction to Turkey, as the object of the aggressive policy of the Allies, it at the same time afforded a guarantee that the Balkan States, in the very possible event of their military defeat, would not be exposed to any risk of a diminution of their already sufficiently restricted territories.

In order further to ensure our Balkan friends against the dangers and risks attendant upon their attack on Turkey, on my return to Russia, I instructed our Ambassador in Paris to come to an agreement with the French Government with regard to combined intervention in the Balkan War by the Great Powers immediately after the first decisive battle, with a view to the earliest possible cessation of military operations. By this means I hoped, as I have said, to save the forces of the Allies from destruction, and to put an end to the state of extreme and dangerous tension which had prevailed in Russia and in Europe from the moment when it became plain that all the efforts of the Powers to delay the inevitable collision between the Balkan peoples and the Porte had failed. At the same time M. Isvolsky was instructed to inform M. Poincaré that the Imperial Government attached the greatest importance to its proposal; because, despite its firm intention not to allow itself to be drawn into a war, it would be very difficult for it to resist the demands of Russian public opinion, should the situation of the Balkan States become critical. France and England were undoubtedly interested in ensuring that Russia should not be forced to take part in the struggle; and the sooner the war came to an end, the easier it would be to prevent this. If it proved possible to stop the war before the resources of one or other of the adversaries were entirely exhausted, it would probably not prove difficult to find the means for settling the quarrel by a compromise acceptable to both sides.

My proposal was accepted in principle by all the Powers, disagreement being manifested only on the question of the moment for intervention. France proposed to summon an international conference immediately, to decide this point, but the other Powers, including Russia, advocated intervention only after the first serious battle had been fought. . . .

However agreeable to us the victories of the Allies might be, from the point of view of our Balkan interests, the outcome of the war necessitated certain changes in the policy pursued by Russia up to the beginning of the military operations. The new distribution of power in the Balkans which followed the victorious advance of the Allied troops almost to the very walls of the Turkish capital, demanded from us, and from the other members of the Triple Entente, a new attitude and new measures. Russia no longer had to fear for the existence of her friends in the Balkans; but nevertheless she had to face extremely complicated problems, demanding untiring vigilance on her part; the active support of France and England which were almost as much interested as ourselves, was also necessary for a successful solution. While the issue of the armed struggle between the Balkan States and Turkey remained uncertain, the necessity of preventing this war from assuming European dimensions exhausted all the efforts of the Entente Governments; the victory of the Balkan States not only afforded no guarantee to this effect, but perhaps even increased the danger arising from the new situation in the Near East. It was clear to all that it would be impossible now to use the same language to the victors as was employed when their own strength and the hopeless weakness of their antagonist had not yet been exposed. It was necessary to find new formulas corresponding to the new situation. The events which had produced this situation can only be compared, in their immense influence on Balkan history, with the battle of Kossovo; this disastrous defeat was at last avenged, and the new state of affairs represented the first triumph of emancipated Balkan Christianity over its Mussulman oppressors.

The formula concerning the territorial *status quo*, which had presented certain advantages when it was accepted by the Powers before the commencement of hostilities, had now to be abandoned. No one even in Vienna or Berlin could seriously think of enforcing it to preserve the inviolability of the Ottoman Empire. It was necessary to retain for Turkey only such portions of her Balkan territory as were indispensable to the defence of her capital. Macedonia, which the Allies had conquered, must be handed over to the victors, to divide as they pleased; and they must be allowed to profit by their victory to the greatest possible extent.

The untiring efforts of Russian diplomacy, and of the Governments friendly to Russia, were exerted to solve this problem which was fated during the next year to be the chief objective of the counter-efforts of our closely united political opponents, and to cause endless complications, and more than once to threaten the peace of Europe.

The Balkan Alliance, constituted with the good wishes of Russia, had brilliantly justified the hopes reposed in it. But it was still far from attaining the most valuable of all its objects from the Russian point of view: the strengthening of peace in the Balkans through the free national development of each member of the Alliance, with a mutual guarantee against unfriendly interference from without. The enslavers of the Christian peoples of the Balkan Peninsula were destroyed, and their power irretrievably shattered; but it was necessary to see that the new political existence of each of these peoples was allowed to develop on the ruins of Turkish rule in accordance with the principles of a just conception of its rights and interests. In aiming at this object, it was essential to bear in mind the fact that the enemies of Balkan Slavdom, embarrassed and angered by the unforeseen results of the war, would exert every effort to snatch from the conquerors the fruits of their victory. But as always, the most unsecure position was that of Serbia, over whom the threat of Austrian interference hung like the sword of Damocles. I have already mentioned the angry astonishment of the Viennese Government at the successes of the Serbian army against the Turks—an astonishment revealed in the conversation of its representatives abroad, and displayed with still less restraint in the opinion expressed by every organ of the Austro-Hungarian press, of whatever shade of political opinion. The successes of Serbia, however disagreeable in themselves to Austria, did not as yet afford her the desired occasion for interference; but this was not long in presenting itself, in connection with the political consequences which naturally resulted from the Serbian victories.

As early as the end of October, I was informed by our Minister in Belgrade of the intentions of the Allies as to the division of their conquests among themselves. Judging by what the Minister communicated to me, there was reason to fear that Austro-Hungarian diplomacy would find more occasion than it required for interference in the aspirations of Serbia, which were directed towards the Albanian coast bordering upon the Adriatic. Cut off by the unfavourable course of history from the Adriatic, whose shores were peopled along a considerable stretch by her Dalmatian and Croatian kinsmen, Serbia had not ceased to strive for free access to the sea since the first moment of her emancipation from Turkish rule. This gravitation towards the Adriatic is explained by the atavism of the Southern Slavonic tribes which were historically connected with this sea, and also by economic causes. The Serbs wished to escape from the endless restrictions upon their freedom of export across the frontier, which Austria-Hungary imposed whenever Vienna or Budapest became dissatisfied with the direction of Serbian policy.

The successes of the Serbs, which surpassed their own expectations, were naturally bound to intensify their impulse to reach the sea; and their attention was directed in the first place towards the coast of Albania. This coast did not in itself offer many advantages; but it could be made to serve the purpose of Serbia, by securing for her that complete freedom of export which she would never obtain until she had emancipated herself once and for all from the constantly recurring frontier restrictions imposed by her neighbours. There was consequently no cause for astonishment when M. Hartvig, our Minister in Belgrade, wrote to inform me that among the demands drawn up by the Allied Governments was one for the partition of Albania between Serbia, Montenegro and Greece; Serbia intended to take as her share of the spoil the northern portion of Albania (excluding the Province of Scutari which was to be ceded to Montenegro) with the sea-coast from San Giovanni di Medua right up to Skumbia, leaving Southern Albania to Greece. Hartvig wrote that the victorious Balkan States had decided to maintain these demands by force of arms.

It will be readily understood that Russia could offer no opposition to this partition of Albania among the Balkan States, in itself, owing to the fact that Russian interests were in no way concerned with the Adriatic littoral. Nevertheless, as soon as these demands were made known to me, it became my unpleasant duty to restrain the Serbian Government from being carried away by excessive zeal in pursuit of this enticing plan. I myself had no doubt that every encroachment by the Allies on Albanian territory would immediately call forth most determined opposition from Austria-Hungary and Italy, whose interests in that particular part of the Balkan Peninsula, unfortunately for Serbia, were identical. . . .

Meanwhile I continued to use every effort to obtain, by means of amicable conversations with the Austro-Hungarian Government, at least a partial satisfaction of Serbian desires, by securing for her an exclusively commercial port on the Adriatic; but all my endeavours, which were supported by our Allies, were unsuccessful, meeting with united opposition from the Powers of the Triple Alliance.

In the beginning of November it became absolutely clear that Serbia could be established in any port whatsoever on the Adriatic only by force of arms—that is to say, at the cost of a European war. The lack of proportion between the end desired by the Triple Entente and the means necessary to attain it was plainly apparent. I have already said that any idea of a European war for the sake of a Serbian port on the Adriatic was out of the question—neither we nor our Allies and friends entertained it. Meanwhile tension in Serbia did not decrease, and Serbian troops prepared to occupy Durazzo. In order to leave no shadow of doubt in Belgrade as to the realities of the situation and the intentions of Russia, I was obliged to instruct Hartvig to warn the Serbian Government in these terms: 'We will not go to war with the Triple Alliance for the sake of a Serbian port on the Adriatic. With regard to the decision of the Balkan Allies to divide up European Turkey among themselves without taking into consideration the interests of Austria and Italy, we warn Serbia against the consequences to which any rash policy might lead, by depriving her of the sympathy of France and England.' Finally I was obliged to caution our Serbian friends that we should be compelled to refuse them our support if they allowed themselves to go too far.

I have a lively recollection of how painful it was for me to play the part of an elder brother, and preach, to the Serbs, who enjoyed my full sympathy; but political considerations insistently demanded Russia's decisive intervention in the Serbian affair, which threatened to cause a national catastrophe that must at all costs be averted in the interests of the Serbs themselves. Moreover, if there was a Government in Europe from which they could accept friendly advice without any feeling of offence or suspicion, it was certainly the Russian Government; they had no reason to doubt our sincerity, and our sympathies were bound up with the fate of Balkan Slavdom by innumerable sentimental and material considerations.

The whole of the first half of 1913 was spent in conveying admonitions of this kind to the Serbian Government, and in conducting negotiations with Austria-Hungary and Italy, behind whom unwaveringly stood their ally Germany. These negotiations concerned the establishment of Albania and the attainment in one way or another of an outlet to the Adriatic for Serbia. In order to give weight to its opinion the Vienna Cabinet proceeded to take certain military measures along the Austro-Hungarian frontiers. Thus five or six army corps were concentrated near the Serbian frontier, and the three corps in Galicia were brought up to war strength. The Russian Government replied by suspending the discharge of the reservists, and by completing the war equipment of the frontier troops. Nevertheless these precautionary measures were not such as to embarrass the further course of the diplomatic negotiations carried on by the Council of Ambassadors in London.

The work of this Conference proceeded very slowly, and the representative of each of the Great Powers taking part in it set forth the proposal of his Government only with extreme caution, and after preparing the ground by preliminary conversations with the other members of the group of Powers with which his Government was associated. At that time not one of the European Governments desired to go to war, with the exception of the Austro-Hungarian, which was ready to attack Serbia in the hope of finding in this desperate course an antidote to the pitiful internal condition of the State; but this disposition did not meet with the necessary support from Germany. The other Powers were all averse to war, and each of them felt, not without alarm, that the danger of a European war might nevertheless arise suddenly at any moment. Even Austria-Hungary, although she adopted the attitude I have described, and continued to demand the establishment of an independent Albania, and to oppose the idea of allowing Serbia access to the Adriatic, did not go so far as to refrain from an outward display of conciliatoriness. Under the stress of circumstances, she consented to discuss with the other Powers the means for compensating Serbia for the injury occasioned her by the refusal of the Triple Alliance to allow her any territory whatsoever on the Adriatic littoral. . . .

Meanwhile there was added to the already confused and complicated situation a new political factor, with which the Powers, and especially Russia, had to reckon seriously. This factor was Rumania, to which up till now only an indirect reference has been made. She was not, in the strict sense of the word, a Balkan State; but on account of her geographical position she was keenly interested in the fate of the Balkan Peninsula.

At the very beginning of the Balkan War, the Rumanian Government had announced its intention not to intervene in the struggle unless it resulted in territorial changes in the Balkans which might have political consequences disadvantageous for Rumania. In that case she would feel obliged to demand corresponding compensation for herself. The rapid successes of the Bulgarian troops foreshadowed the establishment on her frontiers of a new Bulgaria, increased in size, and strengthened by the augmentation of her population. This indisputable fact moved the Rumanian Government to demand from Bulgaria the cession of certain territory in the Dobrudja, in order to protect Rumania's strategic position on the Danube. She demanded the cession to herself of the town of Silistria, and the rectification of her frontiers by the transfer of Bulgarian territory from a point south of this town right up to Baltchik on the Black Sea. This demand, in itself exaggerated, rendered the efforts of the Triple Entente in the interests of peace still more difficult. They sought a way out of the complications which had arisen on the Danube, by handing over the Rumano-Bulgarian dispute to the arbitration of the Great Powers. The Geshov Cabinet, which was then in power in Bulgaria, was friendly to Russia, and Rumania's confidence in the policy of the Russian Government was gradually increasing. These facts led to the choice of St. Petersburg by both parties as the meeting-place of the arbitral conference.

At my invitation the Ambassadors of Austria-Hungary, Great Britain, Germany, Italy and France proceeded, on April 1, 1913, to examine the claims of Rumania. Although at the very first meeting the usual disagreement between the representatives of the Powers of the Triple Entente and the Triple Alliance became apparent, the work of the Conference proceeded peacefully. It was clear that none of the Governments represented desired, in connection with a question not of primary political importance, to pour oil on the flames of Balkan dissension, which were burning brightly enough without any such assistance. The representatives of the Triple Alliance, who at first fully supported the Rumanian demands, soon changed their point of view, and gave their adherence to the proposal of the Russian Government and those who shared its views; these, while admitting the justice of Rumania's demand for a strategic rectification of her frontier, regarded the cession by Bulgaria of Silistria alone, without the transfer of any considerable portion of the Dobrudja, as a wholly sufficient guarantee in the respect. The labours of the Conference were completed by the 11th of April; the text of its decision was drawn up, and confirmed immediately afterwards by the Governments concerned, and was accepted without reservations by the contending parties. The town of Silistria, with a small extent of territory, was allotted to Rumania; the latter undertook to compensate all Bulgarians who expressed a desire to remove from the ceded district. Bulgaria accepted an obligation not to erect fortifications along her frontier up to the Black Sea, and agreed to the establishment of special bishoprics in the parts of the conquered Macedonia inhabited by Wallachians, and to ecclesiastical and educational autonomy for the Rumanian population in these districts.

This exhausted the results of the St. Petersburg Conference. They were not very effective, but should have been recognized as satisfactory, for they obviated the possibility of fresh complications at a time which was already sufficiently disturbing and dangerous. Nevertheless the arrangement made by the Conference proved to be of short duration. The Peace of Bucharest, which concluded the second Balkan War, removed every trace of it; and Rumania rewarded herself with interest for the moderation which she had previously shown. . . .

Although the Russian Government had firmly decided not to allow itself to be drawn into war on account of a secondary Balkan question, it was most important—for very comprehensible reasons—to prevent Austria-Hungary from taking the matter into her own hands and dealing separately with Montenegro. The great disparity between the forces of the Hapsburg Monarchy and those of the small Balkan kingdom would have lent an odious character to such a proceeding. It was impossible for Russia to take part in any coercive measures against Montenegro. All my efforts, therefore, were exerted to induce France and England to send warships to Antivari, and if necessary, to land troops there, in order to give an international character to the measures taken, and be less likely to wound the pride of a small State like Montenegro than action by a single Power. Such a course, moreover, would avert the danger of allowing Austria-Hungary to dispose without control of the fate of a Slavonic State that had enjoyed the friendship of Russia and the protection of our Sovereigns for over a century. It was very difficult to obtain agreement on this question, not only between the members of the Conference of Ambassadors in London, but even between the representatives of the Triple Entente, none of whom wished to take part in the inglorious enterprise of a naval demonstration in the waters of Antivari, forced upon Europe by the threat of separate action on the part of the Viennese Cabinet. On the 5th of May, after a fortnight of wearisome negotiations, King Nicholas at last declared that, in deference to the wishes of the Powers, he placed the fate of Scutari in their hands. This concluded an episode which had no intrinsic political importance, but which had for some time appeared to menace the peace of Europe. The only advantage which the Russian Government was able to obtain for the Serbs in return for the renunciation of the Montenegrin claim to Scutari, was the cession of Ipek, Diakovo, Prizrén, and Dibra to the Balkan States. I am bound in fairness to add that in this matter Russian diplomacy received the support of the Berlin Cabinet.

Meanwhile, the Balkan situation was growing more strained every day. It was evident that if the internal relations of the Balkan Allies did not assume a more favourable aspect, a rupture, followed by open war, was inevitable. The situation was the more serious, in that it was impossible to expect any practical results from negotiations between the Balkan Governments themselves, as they had now adopted an irreconcilable attitude with regard to their respective claims. The Bulgarians, the Greeks and the Serbs all concentrated considerable forces in those districts which they hoped to be able to retain, and the temper of the troops was strained to such a point that the slightest incident might have provoked hostilities. The Russian Government was therefore obliged to abandon its original intention of arranging a meeting between the Prime Ministers of the three Balkan States, with a view to effecting an accommodation. There remained but a faint hope of persuading them to submit to arbitration by the Powers of the Triple Entente. Bulgaria seemed disposed to agree to this; but the plan had soon to be jettisoned as impracticable, in view of the opposition it would inevitably arouse on the part of the Triple Alliance, who would have regarded it as an attempt to solve the Balkan problem without their assistance. On the other hand, nothing was to be gained by inviting the Cabinets of the Triple Alliance, and especially the Viennese, to take part in its solution; at the best, this would have meant indefinitely protracted negotiations, whereas rapid and decisive action was essential; at the worst, it would have hastened the approach of the catastrophe. One of these alternatives, however, seemed inevitable, for at the London Conference Sir Edward Grey had the greatest difficulty in dissuading Austria-Hungary from coming to separate decisions and taking independent action.

In these circumstances I thought it best to resort to a measure for which the text of the Serbo-Bulgarian Treaty of Alliance provided the opportunity. I hoped to relieve the tension of the general situation by bringing about a peace between at least two of the disputants, ignoring, for the time being, the quarrel between Greeks and Bulgarians.

I have already mentioned that the treaty between the Balkan Allies assigned the rôle of arbitrator to the Russian Sovereign, and I added that I had no very great confidence in the result. The intervention of Russia in this quarrel between two allies—a quarrel which was to be foreseen from the moment the alliance was formed—could only be of value if both sides had sufficient moral courage and political wisdom to submit willingly to arbitration. It was difficult to count upon such favourable conditions, whatever sympathy one might feel for the Slavs. Having the power to apply this measure, however, it was impossible not to resort to it at this critical juncture, when there was a grave risk of seeing the brilliant results attained by the Allies irretrievably forfeited.

It was inevitable that in proposing the Russian Sovereign as arbitrator to the Serbs and Bulgarians, the St. Petersburg Cabinet should make it a condition that the Emperor's decision must be accepted without reserve by both disputants. A further condition was added, namely the maintenance of the Balkan Alliance. It seemed at first that these conditions would meet with no opposition from the Allies. Soon, however, it became evident that neither the Bulgarians nor the Serbs were disposed to place their interests unreservedly in the hands of Russia; they preferred to count on other, more practical methods of safeguarding them than could be afforded by the most impartial arbitration. At the end of May the Greeks, who expected every moment that the Bulgars would attack them, in order to dislodge them from Salonika, held similar views. Although the treaty between the Allies, in so far as it concerned the Greeks, contained no reference to the possibility of arbitration, the Russian Government and the other Governments of the Entente tried to induce M. Venizelos to submit the Greeko-Bulgarian quarrel to the judgment either of Russia or of the Powers. Serbia seemed convinced that, whatever the Government of M. Pashich might do, no agreement could be reached with Bulgaria, and that war was inevitable. The news that reached us from Sofia indicated a state of extreme tension in military circles, with which MM. Geshov and Daneff, whose peaceful intentions could be relied on up to a certain point, would hardly be able to cope. In Bulgaria, moreover, the final decision lay with the King, whose real intentions no one ever knew. At the same time we were informed, from Vienna, that the Austro-Hungarian Cabinet was inciting Ferdinand of Coburg to hold out, and promising him support; while the German and Austro-Hungarian representatives in Bucharest were using their influence to prevent the Rumanian Government from complicating the Bulgarian situation. These conditions were very serious. I was thus driven to resort to the extreme course of intervention by the Emperor, in the form of a personal appeal to the Kings of Serbia and Bulgaria to cease their contest and leave the problem in his hands. I hesitated for some time before resolving to induce His Majesty to intervene personally in the conflict. I realized the responsibility I was taking upon myself, from the point of view of Russia's prestige abroad, in risking a rebuff from the Balkan Sovereigns. In spite of this considera-tion, knowing the Emperor well, I urged him to throw the weight of his personal influence into the scale, as the last hope of averting a fratricidal war between two Slavonic nations, on whose fate Russia had exercised a decisive influence. . . .

When the text of the Emperor's summons to peace and concord became known abroad, it produced a deep impression everywhere, especially in the Balkan States. Even the enemies of Russia were forced to acknowledge the sincerity and complete disinterestedness of this appeal, and its profoundly peaceful character. It revealed in the clearest light the whole Near-Eastern policy of the St. Petersburg Cabinet at this critical moment in Balkan history. There could be but one answer to such an appeal—the surrender of the problem into the hands of Russia, and an unreserved acceptance of her decisions. And, in outward form at least, this answer soon followed. The King of Bulgaria was the first to reply that he accepted Russia's mediation; at the same time he drew attention to Serbia's ambiguous attitude with regard to her obligations as ally, and to the indignation of the Bulga-rians at her attempt to deprive them of the fruits of victory.

After Ferdinand of Coburg's telegram came the reply of King Peter of Serbia, who also complained of the attitude of his allies with regard to his country's just demands; but he concluded by saying that he placed complete confidence in the justice and benevolence of Russia.

There is no doubt that the first of these answers expressed the King's consent to submit the Balkan quarrel to the Emperor's decision more categorically than the second. If my memory does not deceive me, there was no direct reference, in King Peter's reply, to arbitration by the Emperor. But in comparing the two answers we must bear in mind the fact that King Ferdinand's telegram was sent less than a fortnight before June 17, when the Bulgarian troops attacked the Serbian outposts at Bregalnitza, thus opening the second Balkan War. This war was not waged by the Allies against a common foe, but by two of them against Bulgaria, who wished to decide the Macedonian ques-tion in her own favour, and to establish her predominance in the Balkans by means of a treacherous attack on her allies. The Russian Government never obtained any direct proofs of the complicity of the Viennese Cabinet in these designs; but we had sufficient reason to believe that Ferdinand of Coburg had not taken the initiative in this matter without the knowledge and encouragement of the Austro-Hungarian Government. The moral responsibility of the Viennese

Cabinet for this treacherous attempt is all the more probable since Austrian diplomacy—as I have said before—could never reconcile itself to the fact that the first Balkan War had ended in a brilliant victory for the Allies. They had hoped for the annihilation of Serbia and the destruction of her army; whereas this victory led to a corresponding territorial enlargement of all the Balkan States, including Serbia, whose army had exhibited great fighting qualities and a splendid military organization. In supporting Ferdinand of Coburg, the Viennese diplomats hoped to atone for their previous lack of foresight, and wipe out their heavy moral defeat. Events ultimately proved, however, that their hopes and calculations were again mistaken. Serbia, whom they so virulently hated, emerged triumphant from this second ordeal, and her victories brought her considerably nearer to the realization of her Pan-Serbian ambitions.

(f) *Baron Rosen's account of the London Conference of Ambassadors*[1]

In the meantime events in the Balkan Peninsula had taken a turn little expected by the diplomacy of the Great Powers. The collapse of Turkey, weakened by the Young Turk Revolution and by the war with Italy, had been unexpectedly rapid and complete; and the victory of the four allied Balkan Powers, Serbia, Bulgaria, Greece and Montenegro, had given each of them more than they had dared to hope for —a result which was not at all to the liking of the Great Powers, whose solemn warning about the maintenance of the *status quo* had been thrown to the winds by the exultant victors. Besides, the division of the spoils threatened to become a problem difficult to solve.

The probabilities were, indeed, that a peaceful solution of the problem might have been found if the four victorious Balkan Powers had been left to settle it between themselves without any outside interference. But, of course, such a disinterestedness on the part of Russia and Austria-Hungary was not to be hoped for, although it was manifestly the only sensible policy to adopt. In both countries light-headed incompetence and dreamy conceptions of "manifest destiny" and "vital interests" had control of foreign policies. A solid and powerful federation of Balkan States would have stood in the way both of Russian ambitions in the direction of Constantinople and the Dardanelles and of Austro-Hungarian aims at reaching an outlet to the Ægean Sea at Salonika. Therefore such a simple and, indeed, the only rational solution of the vexed problem, even if the four Balkan Powers concerned had been found willing to sink their growing differences and to maintain and consolidate their alliance, would not have been attainable.

Considered separately, and in view of the needless antagonism be-

---

[1] Baron Rosen, *Forty Years of Diplomacy*. New York, Knopf, 1922, Vol. II, pp. 127-131. Reprinted with the permission of Alfred A. Knopf, Inc.

tween the two Empires unfortunately existing and cultivated on both sides by ambitious politicians, a too powerful Bulgaria would have been contrary to Russian policy, and on the other hand a greatly strengthened Serbia with access to the Adriatic would have been considered as a Russian outpost constituting a most serious menace to the very existence of the Dual Monarchy.

This Austro-Russian antagonism and rivalry gave the tone to the discussions of the London Conference of the Great Powers assembled to adjudicate the division of the spoils among the victors of the first Balkan War, and necessarily influenced its ultimate decisions. The result was that this grave problem, on whose equitable solution depended the establishment in the Balkan Peninsula of conditions which would, at least to some extent, have been a guarantee of lasting peace between the Balkan nationalities, was handled by the Conference not from the point of view of the vital interests of these nationalities, but exclusively with a view to bring about some settlement that would in a measure conciliate the conflicting pretensions of Russian and Austro-Hungarian diplomacy. I advisedly use the expression "conflicting pretensions" and avoid speaking of "conflicting interests" of Russia and Austria-Hungary, since there was not, nor could there be, any conflict between the real vital interests of both, which could only be the maintenance of peace and which therefore demanded the sinking of all differences based on rivalry of imperialistic policies and pretensions to supremacy in Balkan affairs.

It must be admitted, however, that such a policy of renunciation was rendered somewhat more difficult to Austria-Hungary than to Russia by the apparent predominance in Russia of Pan-Slavistic tendencies, which, indeed, presented a serious menace to an Empire the majority of whose population belonged to the Slav race. On the other hand, the predominance of Pan-Slavism in Russia, in the sense of its suspected controlling influence over the policy of the Government, was certainly more apparent than real, although it could not be denied that the activities of some of our diplomatic and consular agents were lending colour to such suspicions. The chief sinner in this respect was our Minister at Belgrade, Mr. Hartwig, a most honourable, capable and hardworking functionary but the last man to be entrusted with such a post at a time when the world's peace was hanging by the slenderest thread and depended on the avoidance of serious complications in the Balkans. He had ever since the beginning of his diplomatic career been in contact with Balkan policies and intrigues, and, like most ambitious diplomats, had become an adept of Slavophilism as the surest way to earn early promotion, a reputation of live patriotism and the powerful support of the Nationalist and Slavophile Press ensuring considerable latitude and impunity in the pursuit of lines of policy rather independent of, and even opposed to, the policies of the central authority for the time being. . . .

It is hardly to be wondered at that Austro-Hungarian statesmen, however cognizant of the absence of political discipline in Russian diplomatic circles, especially in the East, should have taken serious alarm at the attitude of Russia's representative at Belgrade, which they had every reason to consider as being, if not inspired, in any case openly tolerated, by the Russian Government.

Russia's case before the London Conference does not seem to have elicited sufficiently strong support from her friends and allies—maybe on account of their consciousness of its inherent weakness and of the not unreasonable nature of the Austro-Hungarian Government's apprehensions, maybe because they did not consider the time and occasion to be favourable for allowing the long-expected wind-up of the European drama to begin. Russian diplomacy had to submit with what good grace it could to letting her protégé, Serbia, be shorn of the principal fruit of her victories—access to the Adriatic; and Austria-Hungary was allowed to compel the evacuation by Serbia of Durazzo and the other ports conquered by her, as well as the abandonment by Montenegro of her conquest—Scutari. . . .

Not satisfied with having inflicted upon Serbia the humiliation of having to renounce the hard-earned access to the Adriatic, gallantly won by the victory of her arms, Austria-Hungary, with the support of her allies, obtained the Conference's sanction for the creation of an independent principality or Kingdom of Albania, with a scion of one of the minor German dynasties as Sovereign under the fantastic title of "Mpret." The creation of this new independent State was obviously directed against the interests and ambitions of Serbia as well as of Greece, the result being that both these Powers were eager to compensate themselves in Macedonia at Bulgaria's expense for what they had lost or missed in Albania. This situation could not but lead to an armed conflict between the former allies. Serbia and Greece joined hands, and with the help of the unprovoked intervention of Rumania, succeeded in inflicting on Bulgaria a crushing defeat, reflected in the terms of the treaty of peace which terminated the war and was negotiated at Bucharest—this time by the belligerents alone without assistance or interference by the Great Powers. It was one of those transactions which bear in themselves the germs of conflicts to come.

Whatever view one takes of the settlement of the second Balkan War by the Treaty of Bucharest, it was plain that it had left affairs in the Peninsula in a state of unstable equilibrium, which was bound to react on the general political situation in Europe. The greatly strengthened position of Serbia as a consequence of her victory in the war and the enhanced prestige she had thereby acquired in the eyes of Austria's Slav population, however gratifying to Russian diplomacy, could not but appear to the Vienna Government, for this very reason, in the light of a serious and growing menace to the safety of the Dual Monarchy. The resulting tension in Austro-Russian relations added a new element of danger to the all-pervading atmosphere of unrest which could bode no good to the cause of European peace.

(g) *A Review of the Conference of Ambassadors by the German Ambassador in England*[1]

Shortly after my arrival in London, at the end of 1912, Sir E. Grey proposed an informal conversation to prevent the Balkan War developing into a European one, after we had unfortunately refused, on the outbreak of the war, to agree to the French proposal of a declaration of disinterestedness. The British statesman from the very beginning took up the position that England had no interest in Albania, and had no intention of going to war over this question. He merely wished to mediate between the two groups as an "honest broker" and smooth over difficulties. He therefore by no means took sides with the Entente, and during the eight months or so of the negotiations his goodwill and his authoritative influence contributed in no small degree to the attainment of an agreement. We, instead of adopting an attitude similar to the English one, invariably took up the position which was prescribed for us by Vienna. Count Mensdorff was the leader of the Triple Alliance in London; I was his "second." It was my duty to support his proposals. That clever and experienced man Count Szögenyi was conducting affairs in Berlin. His refrain was "Then the *casus fœderis* will arise," and when I once ventured to doubt the truth of this conclusion I was severely reprimanded for "Austrophobia." . . .

On all questions we took sides with Austria and Italy—about Albania, a Serbian port on the Adriatic, Scutari, and also about the delimitation of the frontiers of Albania—while Sir E. Grey hardly ever supported the French or Russian claims. He mostly supported our group in order not to give a pretext like the one a dead Archduke was to furnish later on. Thus with his assistance it was possible to coax King Nikita out of Scutari again. Otherwise this question would already have led to a world war, as we should certainly not have ventured to induce "our ally" to give way.

Sir E. Grey conducted the negotiation with circumspection, calm, and tact. When a question threatened to become involved, he sketched a formula for agreement which was to the point and was always accepted. His personality inspired equal confidence in all the participants.

As a matter of fact we had again successfully emerged from one of those trials of strength which characterize our policy. Russia had been obliged to give way to us on all points, as she was never in a position to procure success for the Serbian aims. Albania was estab-

---

[1] Lichnowsky, *My Mission to London, 1912-1914.* New York, Doran, n. d., pp. 10-13. Reprinted with the permission of Doubleday, Doran & Company.

lished as a vassal state of Austria and Serbia was pressed back from the sea. Hence this conference resulted in a fresh humiliation for Russian self-esteem. As in 1878 and in 1908, we had opposed the Russian plans, although no *German* interests were involved. Bismarck was clever enough to mitigate the mistake of the Congress by the secret treaty and by his attitude in the Battenberg question; but we continued to pursue in London the dangerous path, upon which we had once more entered in the Bosnian question, nor did we leave it in time when it led to the precipice. . . .

At the same time the Balkan Conference was sitting in London and I had occasion to come into contact with the leaders of the Balkan States. M. Venizelos was certainly the most distinguished personality. At that time he was anything rather than anti-German, and visited me several times. . . . His prepossessing charm and ways of a man of the world secured him much sympathy. Next to him M. Daneff, at that time Bulgarian Premier and confidant of Count Berchtold, played a great part. He gave the impression of a subtle and energetic man, and it is probably only due to the influence of his Vienna and Budapest friends, of whose homage he often made fun, that he was induced to commit the folly of entering upon the second Balkan War and of refusing Russian arbitration.

M. Take Jonescu was also frequently in London and then visited me regularly. I knew him from the time when I was Secretary at Bucharest. He was also one of Herr von Kiderlen's friends. In London he was endeavouring to obtain concessions to Rumania from M. Daneff by means of negotiations, in which he was assisted by the very able Rumanian Ambassador Misu. It is known that Bulgarian opposition brought about the failure of these negotiations. Count Berchtold (and we of course with him) was entirely on Bulgaria's side, otherwise by putting pressure on M. Daneff we might have secured the desired satisfaction for Rumania and placed her under an obligation to us; she was finally estranged from the Central Powers by Austria's attitude during and after the second Balkan War.

The defeat of Bulgaria in the second Balkan War and the victory of Serbia, with the Rumanian invasion, naturally constituted a humiliation for Austria. The plan to rectify this by an expedition against Serbia seems to have been evolved in Vienna soon after. The Italian revelations prove this, and it may be assumed that Marquis San Giuliano, who described the plan—most aptly—as a *pericolosissima aventura*, saved us from being involved in a world war as early as the summer of 1913.

Owing to the intimacy of Russo-Italian relations, the Vienna plan was doubtless known in Petrograd. In any case, M. Sazonof openly declared at Constanza, as M. Take Jonescu told me, that an Austrian attack on Serbia would be a *casus belli* for Russia.

(h) *French Correspondence*

M. Briand, Minister of Foreign Affairs, to the French Ambassadors in St. Petersburg, London, Rome, Vienna, Berlin, Constantinople[1]

Paris, Aug. 14, 1912

The Austro-Hungarian *chargé d'affaires* has just told me of the uneasiness which the situation in the Balkans inspires in his government.

According to Count Berchtold, a strong emotion is shown among the Bulgarians, Serbs, and Greeks, who fear to see the Turkish government concede to Albania privileges incompatible with their national interests. There is danger of this agitation provoking soon a crisis dangerous for peace.

This is why the cabinet of Vienna wishes to know whether the Great Powers are disposed to enter into conversations with it with a view:

1. To advise the Porte to adopt a policy of progressive decentralization, which would procure for the Christian nationalities the guaranties which they can legitimately claim;

2. To urge the Balkan States to await pacifically the results of this policy.

I have replied to Count Somssich: "The government of the republic will examine with interest the suggestion of Count Berchtold. You can meanwhile declare to him now that the policy of France in the Near East has for its principal object the conservation of the general peace and the maintenance of the *status quo* in the Balkans. We are happy to agree, in this respect, with the views of the cabinet of Vienna."

BRIAND

M. du Halgouet, Chargé d'Affaires of France at Athens, to M. Raymond Poincaré, President of the Council, Minister of Foreign Affairs[2]

Athens, Oct. 1, 1912

The legations of Russia, Germany and Austria-Hungary have separately taken steps directed at preventing the sending of the note to Turkey. The Minister of Foreign Affairs has begged them to give a delay for a reply.

M. Venizelos this morning said to the Austrian Minister that the preparations of Greece would not be ended for twenty days, but that if, by that time, the Balkan States had not obtained sufficient guaranties for the application of reforms in Macedonia, a conflict must be expected.

DU HALGOUET

---

[1] France. Ministère des affaires étrangères. *Documents diplomatiques. Affaires Balkaniques.* 3 vols. 1912-1914; Vol. I, No. 50, p. 34.

[2] *Ibid.*, Vol. I, No. 115, p. 68.

M. Raymond Poincaré, President of the Council, Minister of Foreign Affairs, to the Ministers of France at Sofia, Belgrade, Athens, Cettigne[1]

Paris, Oct. 7, 1912

On the initiative of the government of the Republic, the Russian, British, Austro-Hungarian, German and Italian governments have adopted the following resolution:

"The Russian and Austro-Hungarian Governments will declare to the Balkan States:

1. That the Powers disapprove energetically of any measure likely to lead to the breaking of peace;

2. That, relying on article 23 of the Treaty of Berlin, they will undertake, in the interest of the populations, the realization of reforms in the administration of Turkey in Europe, it being understood that these reforms will not constitute any blow at the sovereignty of H.M. the Sultan and at the territorial integrity of the Ottoman Empire: this declaration, moreover, reserves the liberty of the Powers to collectively study further reforms;

3. That, if war nevertheless breaks out between the Balkan States and the Ottoman Empire, they will not allow, at the end of the conflict, any modification of the territorial *status quo* in Turkey in Europe.

The Powers will collectively take measures with the Sublime Porte in accordance with the preceding declaration."

Kindly put yourself at the disposal of your Russian and Austro-Hungarian colleagues for the support of their measures.

RAYMOND POINCARÉ

M. Raymond Poincaré, President of the Council, Minister of Foreign Affairs, to the French Ambassadors at Berlin, St. Petersburg, London, Rome, Vienna[2]

Paris, Oct. 8, 1912

I am informed that the *Chargé d'affaires* of Montenegro at Constantinople announces that he has to deliver at noon today the declaration of war and that he will leave immediately by the Roumanian boat. He has himself explained to M. Bompard that without doubt the Balkan States, disquieted by the measures which are being prepared with a view to stopping them, had probably found nothing better than to bring the *casus fœderis* into play by the opening of hostilities.

Kindly inform the government to which you are accredited and indicate the extreme urgency of the Austro-Russian measure.

For Berlin. Kindly advise M. Sazonoff.

RAYMOND POINCARÉ

[1] *Ibid.*, Vol. I, No. 168, p. 99.
[2] *Ibid.*, Vol. I, No. 169, p. 103.

Speech of the German Chancellor, Bethmann-Hollweg, in the Reichstag, December 2, 1912[1]

In the course of this year, the relations between Turkey and the Balkan States became so delicate that the maintenance of peace, in spite of the efforts of the Powers, became impossible. We had especially to expect an explosion of the conflict since we had learned, early in the summer, that the Balkan States had united in an alliance. When we saw that the conflict was inevitable, our effort was to localize it. We have succeeded up to the present, and I can doubtless express with precision the hope that we will succeed in the future.

The events in the Balkans do not immediately interest us. In many respects, the interests of the other Powers surpass ours. . . .

If . . . insoluble conflicts are set up—we hope that they will not be produced—it will be the business of the Powers directly interested to maintain, in this particular case, their claims.

This applies also to our Allies.

Nevertheless, if our Allies, at the moment when they should be maintaining their rights, were, contrary to all expectation, attacked on a third side and were menaced in their existence, we should, faithful to our duty, place ourselves resolutely at their sides.

We would then fight to protect our own situation in Europe and to defend our future and our security.

I am absolutely convinced that on this occasion we should have behind us the entire nation.

M. Paul Cambon, French Ambassador at London, to M. Raymond Poincaré, President of the Council, Minister of Foreign Affairs[2]

London, Dec. 3, 1912

I asked Sir Edward Grey today what he thought of the speech of Bethmann-Hollweg. He finds it inopportune and disquieting. The useless affirmation of the Austro-German solidarity in the case of a conflict can be taken at St. Petersburg as a menace and arouse Russian opinion. By a singular contradiction, the Chancellor, while recognizing that Germany has no special interest at stake and that the regulation of Balkan questions must be reserved for all the Powers after the war, says that Germany will put in the balance the weight of her influence for the benefit of her allies. But England, France and Germany are the only disinterested Powers; they can exercise a sort of mediation in acting each on their own side on their allies and friends; the declarations of the Chancellor made these interventions impossible. Sir Edward Grey ended by saying that the words of Bethmann cause him a feeling of uneasiness.

[1] *Ibid.*, Vol. I, No. 311, p. 185.
[2] *Ibid.*, Vol. I, No. 304, p. 176.

I drew his attention to the words of Kiderlen after those of the Chancellor. The German Minister of Foreign Affairs praises the good feeling of Germany and England, as if it was certain that this latter Power would disinterest herself in events on the continent.

Sir Edward Grey replied that he had asked my German colleague for an interview for tomorrow in order to speak to him on all these questions.

Sir A. Nicolson shares the opinion of the Secretary of State and shows himself still more uneasy because he knows Russia so well. He considers the words of the German Chancellor as of a nature to render vain all the efforts of M. Sazonoff to restrain opinion.

He inquires whether the military preparations of Austria, which are undeniable, do not indicate intentions of aggression or at least of menacing pressure on Serbia.

PAUL CAMBON

M. Paul Cambon, French Ambassador at London, to M. Raymond Poincaré, President of the Council, Minister of Foreign Affairs[1]

London, Dec. 17, 1912

The Conference of Ambassadors met today at the Foreign Office. Our conversations were prolonged for more than three hours.

Sir Edward Grey invited us to consider immediately the question of Albania and the access of Serbia to the Adriatic Sea. After a discussion in which our Austrian and Italian colleagues took part, we are in agreement on the following formula:

"Autonomy guaranteed and controlled exclusively by the six Powers under the sovereignty or the suzerainty of the Sultan."

We had to mention the sovereignty and the suzerainty of the Sultan, one or the other of these terms being employed in the instructions of one or the other of our colleagues.

A discussion was opened on the organization of this autonomy and Sir E. Grey observed that, Austria and Italy having taken the initiative on the proposition of autonomy, it devolved upon them to bring forward a proposal for organization. We then drew up the following resolution:

"The Austro-Hungarian and Italian governments are invited to indicate their general views on the future organization of this autonomy."

We then adopted an observation that: "autonomous Albania will be neutralized."

But Count Benckendorff, being authorized by his instructions to admit only the neutrality of the coast and the ports, has accepted this formula only *ad referendum*.

We considered then the question of the commercial access of Serbia to the Adriatic and we adopted the following formula:

---

[1] *Ibid.*, Vol. II, No. 20, p. 15.

"Commercial access shall be reserved for Serbia by an Albanian free and neutral port, reached by an international railroad under European control and under the guard of a special international force with freedom of transportation for all merchandise, including munitions of war."

This formula conforms to the instructions received by my colleague of Russia.

As to the delimitation of Albania, that led to a long discussion. My Russian colleague had received very precise directions from M. Sazonoff, which have been communicated to your Excellency; but it was agreed between us that he would confine himself today to speaking of the frontiers of the autonomous State to the north and to the south, in a fashion to assure Montenegro and Greece the means of rectifying their frontiers and to give Austria a guaranty against territorial access of Serbia to the sea. He accordingly proposed a formula which we accepted and which is thus conceived:

"The frontiers of autonomous Albania and of Montenegro on the north and of Greece on the south shall be in any case contiguous."

The words "in any case," which caused numerous objections on the part of the Austrian ambassador, look to an extension of Montenegro and of Greece on the Albanian coast.

But Count Mensdorf had orders from his government to make reservations on the subject of any modification of the present frontier of Montenegro and he read to us the part of his instructions relative to this point: "The Austrian government wishes to prevent any territory inhabited by Albanians from being detached from the future Albania." Developing his instructions he told us that Scutari and all the region bordering Montenegro as far as Ipek were peopled only by Albanians and that it would be impossible to admit any extension of Montenegro to the south. My Russian colleague and I replied to him that to discuss this question would be to inject ourselves into the negotiations at present pending between Turkey and Montenegro and that, if these two Powers agreed to certain rectifications of frontiers, no one ought to hinder them. Count Benckendorff in consequence made a reservation which he sent to our Austrian colleague and of which these are the terms:

"The Russian ambassador can not adhere to the point of view of his Austrian colleague because it implies an interference in the negotiations in progress between Montenegro and Turkey. He confines himself to acquainting his government with the opinion expressed by Count Mensdorf."

The German ambassador did not take part in this discussion and the Italian ambassador abstained, saying that he lacked instructions. The disagreement on this point is serious enough, for it shows on the part of the Austrian government the intention of preventing Montenegro from taking Scutari.

We adjourned till tomorrow to continue our conversations.

The negotiations between the Ottoman and Balkan delegates are suspended until Thursday to permit the Turkish delegates to receive instructions from Constantinople on the subject of the inclusion of the Greeks in the present negotiations.

PAUL CAMBON

M. Deville, French Minister at Athens, to M. Pichon, Minister of Foreign Affairs[1]

Athens, April 5, 1913

The Minister of Foreign Affairs has just sent us the following reply:

"The allied States express their gratitude to the Great Powers for their efforts to bring about the conclusion of peace, and, desiring sincerely to aid them in their task, accept their conditions for mediation under the following reservations:

1. As to the definitive fixing of the frontier with Thrace, the line indicated in the conditions formulated by the Powers shall be taken as a base and not as a definitive line.

2. The Aegean islands shall be ceded by Turkey to the Allies.

3. The Allies think that they ought first to recognize the projected frontiers of Albania, hoping that they will conform to those which they proposed at London.

4. The demand of a war indemnity ought to be accepted in principle, leaving the task of fixing its amount to a commission which will study the financial questions, a commission on which the allied States will be represented.

5. The allied States agree that operations of war shall stop when the above conditions shall have been favorably accepted and admitted."

I add, according to a sure source, that the situation is becoming grave, as Bulgarian troops are marching on Saloniki. I expect to have more details this evening.

DEVILLE

M. Pichon, Minister of Foreign Affairs, to M. Bompard, French ambassador at Constantinople, and to the ministers in Sofia, Belgrade, Athens, and Cettigne[2]

Paris, April 9, 1913

Will you, in agreement with your colleagues of the Great Powers, present the following declaration to the government to which you are accredited:

"The Powers, noting with satisfaction the disposition of the allies toward a cessation of hostilities, reply in the following manner to the four points in the note of the allies:

The first point raises no objection.

[1] *Ibid.*, Vol. II, No. 214, p. 138.
[2] *Ibid.*, Vol. II, No. 224, p. 144.

On the second point, the Powers observe that, the fate of the Aegean islands having been reserved for the decision of the Powers, this point can only be admitted with the reservation of the decision on certain of these islands.

On the third point, the Powers declare that they are ready to inform the allies now of the north and northeast delimitation of Albania and that that on the southeast and south will be communicated to them as soon as they shall have been established.

On the fourth point, the solution of all questions of a financial character having been reserved for the technical commission at Paris, in which the delegates of the belligerents will take part, the Powers think that there is no need of explanation, for the present, on the principle of the indemnity."

PICHON

(i) Treaty of Peace between Turkey and the Balkan Allies Signed at London, May 30, 1913[1]

Article 1. Upon the exchange of ratifications of the present treaty there shall be peace and amity between His Imperial Majesty the Sultan of Turkey, on the one hand, and Their Majesties the Allied Sovereigns, on the other hand, as well as between their heirs and successors, their respective states and subjects forever.

Article 2. His Imperial Majesty the Sultan cedes to Their Majesties, the Allied Sovereigns, all the territories of his Empire on the continent of Europe west of a line drawn from Enos on the Aegean Sea to Midia on the Black Sea, with the exception of Albania.

The exact line of the frontier shall be determined by a commission appointed by. . . .

Article 3. His Imperial Majesty the Sultan and Their Majesties the Allied Sovereigns declare that they submit to His Majesty the Emperor of Germany, His Majesty the Emperor of Austria and King of Hungary, the President of the French Republic, His Majesty the King of Great Britain and Ireland and Emperor of India, His Majesty the King of Italy, and His Majesty the Emperor of All the Russias the matter of arranging the delimitation of the frontiers of Albania and all other questions concerning Albania.

Article 4. His Imperial Majesty the Sultan declares that he cedes to Their Majesties the Allied Sovereigns the Island of Crete and renounces in their favor all rights of sovereignty and all other rights which he possessed over that island.

Article 5. His Imperial Majesty the Sultan and Their Majesties the Allied Sovereigns declare that they entrust to His Majesty the

[1] *American Journal of International Law*, Vol. VIII, No. 1. Supplement, Jan., 1914, pp. 12-13. Reprinted with the permission of the *American Journal of International Law*.

Emperor of Germany, His Majesty the Emperor of Austria and King of Hungary, the President of the French Republic, His Majesty the King of Great Britain and Ireland and Emperor of India, and His Majesty the Emperor of All the Russias the matter of passing upon the title to all the Ottoman Islands in the Ægean Sea (except the Island of Crete) and to the Peninsula of Mount Athos.

Article 6. His Imperial Majesty the Sultan and Their Majesties the Allied Sovereigns declare that they refer the matter of settling questions of a financial nature resulting from the war which is ending and from the above-mentioned cessions of territory to the international commission convened at Paris, to which they have sent their representatives.

Article 7. Questions concerning prisoners of war, questions of jurisdiction, of nationality and of commerce shall be settled by special conventions.

(j) *Treaty of Peace between Bulgaria and Roumania, Greece, Montenegro and Serbia*

Signed at Bukharest July 28-August 10, 1913; ratifications exchanged August 30, 1913[1]

Their Majesties the King of Roumania, the King of the Hellenes, the King of Montenegro, and the King of Servia, on the one part, and His Majesty the King of the Bulgarians, on the other part, animated by the desire to bring to an end the state of war at present existing between their respective countries and wishing for the sake of order, to establish peace between their long-suffering peoples, have resolved to conclude a definitive treaty of peace. Their said Majesties have, thereforce, appointed as their plenipotentiaries, to wit: . . .

Who, in accordance with the proposal of the Royal Government of Roumania, have assembled in conference at Bukharest, with full powers, which were found to be in good and due form, and who having happily reached an accord, have agreed upon the following stipulations:

Article I. Dating from the day on which the ratifications of the present treaty are exchanged there shall be peace and amity between His Majesty the King of Roumania, His Majesty the King of the Bulgarians, His Majesty the King of the Hellenes, His Majesty the King of Montenegro, and His Majesty the King of Servia, as well as between their heirs and successors, their respective states and subjects.

Article II. The former frontier between the Kingdom of Bulgaria and the Kingdom of Roumania, from the Danube to the Black Sea, is, in conformity with the *procès-verbal* drawn up by the respective military delegates and annexed to Protocol No. 5 of July 22 (August 4),

[1] *Ibid.*, pp. 13-19.

1913, of the Conference of Bukharest, corrected in the following manner:

The new frontier shall begin at the Danube above Turtukaia and extend to the Black Sea south of Ekrene.

Between these two extreme points the frontier line shall follow the route indicated on the 1/100,000 and 1/200,000 maps of the Roumanian General Staff, in accordance with the description annexed to the present article.

It is formally understood that within a period of not more than two years, Bulgaria shall dismantle existing fortifications and shall not construct new ones at Rustchuk, at Shumla, in the intervening country, and within a zone of twenty kilometers around Baltchik.

A mixed commission, composed of an equal number of representatives of each of the two high contracting parties, shall be charged, within fifteen days from the signing of the present treaty, with delimiting the new frontier in conformity with the preceding stipulations. This commission shall supervise the division of the lands and funds which up to the present time may have belonged in common to districts, communes or communities separated by the new frontier. In case of disagreement as to the line or as to the method of marking it, the two high contracting parties agree to request a friendly government to appoint an arbitrator, whose decision upon the points at issue shall be considered as final.

Article III. The frontier between the Kingdom of Bulgaria and the Kingdom of Servia shall follow, conformably to the *procès-verbal* drawn up by the respective military delegates, which is annexed to Protocol No. 9 of July 25 (August 7), 1913, of the Conference of Bukharest, the following line:

The frontier line shall begin at the old frontier, on the summit of Patarica, follow the old Turko-Bulgarian frontier and the dividing line of the waters between the Vardar and the Struma, with the exception of the upper valley of the Strumitza, which shall remain Servian territory; the line shall extend as far as the Belasica Mountain, where it will meet the Bulgaro-Greek frontier. A detailed description of this frontier and the 1/200,000 map of the Austrian General Staff, on which it is shown, are annexed to the present article.

A mixed commission, composed of an equal number of representatives of each of the two high contracting powers, shall be charged, within fifteen days from the signing of the present treaty, with delimiting the new frontier, in conformity with the preceding stipulations.

This commission shall supervise the division of the lands and funds, which up to the present time may have belonged in common to the district, communes or communities separated by the new frontier. In case of disagreement as to the line or as to method of marking it, the two high contracting parties agree to request a friendly government to appoint an arbitrator, whose decision upon the points at issue shall be considered as final.

Article IV. Matters relating to the old Serbo-Bulgarian frontier shall be settled in accordance with the understanding reached by the two high contracting parties, as set forth in the protocol annexed to the present article.

Article V. The frontier between the Kingdom of Greece and the Kingdom of Bulgaria shall follow, conformably to the *procès-verbal* drawn up by the respective military delegates and annexed to Protocol No. 9 of July 25 (August 7), 1913 of the Conference of Bukharest, the following line:

The frontier line shall begin at the new Bulgaro-Servian frontier on the crest of Belasica Planina and extend to the mouth of the Mesta on the Aegean Sea.

Between these two extreme points the frontier line shall follow the route indicated on the 1/200,000 map of the Austrian General Staff, in accordance with the description annexed to the present article.

A mixed commission, composed of an equal number of representatives of each of the two high contracting parties, shall be charged, within fifteen days from the signing of the present treaty, with delimiting the frontier in conformity with the preceding stipulations.

This commission shall supervise the division of the lands and funds, which up to the present time may have belonged in common to the districts, communes or communities separated by the new frontier. In case of disagreement as to the line or as to the method of marking it, the two high contracting parties engage to request a friendly government to appoint an arbitrator, whose decision upon the points at issue shall be considered as final.

It is formally understood that Bulgaria renounces from this time forth all claim to the Island of Crete.

Article VI. The headquarters of the respective armies shall be immediately informed of the signing of the present treaty. The Bulgarian Government engages to begin to reduce its army to a peace footing on the day after such notification. It shall order its troops to their garrisons, whence, with the least possible delay, the various reserves shall be returned to their homes.

If the garrison of any troops is situated in the zone occupied by the army of one of the high contracting parties, such troops shall be ordered to some other point in the old Bulgarian territory and may not return to their regular garrisons until after the evacuation of the above-mentioned occupied Zone.

Article VII. The evacuation of Bulgarian territory, both old and new, shall begin immediately after the demobilization of the Bulgarian army and shall be completed within a period of not more than fifteen days.

During this period, the zone of demarcation for the Roumanian army of operations shall be determined by a line running as follows:

Sistov-Lovcea-Turski-Isvor-Glozene-Zlatitza-Mirkovo-Araba-Konak-Orchania-Mezdra-Vratza-Berkovitza-Lom-Danube.

Article VIII. During the occupation of the Bulgarian territories, the various armies shall retain the right of requisition in consideration of cash payment.

Such armies shall have free use of the railroads for the transportation of troops and of provisions of all kinds, without compensation to the local authority.

The sick and wounded shall be under the protection of the said armies.

Article IX. As soon as possible after the exchange of ratifications of the present treaty, all prisoners of war shall be mutually surrendered.

The governments of the high contracting parties shall each appoint special commissioners to receive the prisoners.

All prisoners in the hands of any of the governments shall be delivered to the commissioner of the government to which they belong or to his duly authorized representative, at the place which shall be determined upon by the interested parties.

The governments of the high contracting parties shall present to each other, respectively, as soon as possible after all the prisoners have been returned, a statement of the direct expenses caused by the care and maintenance of the prisoners from the date of their capture or surrender to the date of their death or return. The sums due by Bulgaria to each one of the other high contracting parties shall be set off against the sums due by each of the other high contracting parties to Bulgaria, and the difference shall be paid to the creditor government in each case as soon as possible after the exchange of the abovementioned statements of expense.

Article X. The present treaty shall be ratified and the ratifications thereof shall be exchanged at Bukharest within fifteen days, or sooner if it be possible.

In witness whereof, the respective plenipotentiaries have hereunto affixed their names and seals.

Done at Bukharest the twenty-eighth day of the month of July (tenth day of the month of August) in the year one thousand nine hundred and thirteen.

(Signed)

For Roumania:	For Bulgaria:
(L. S.) T. MAOIRESCO	(L. S.) D. TONTCHEFF
AL. MARGHILOMAN	GENERAL FITCHEFF
TAKE IONESCO	DR. S. IVANTCHOFF
C. G. DISSESCO	S. RADEFF
GENERAL COANDA, Aide-de-Camp	LT. COLONEL STANCIOFF
COLONEL C. CHRISTESCO	

For Greece:

(L. S.) E. K. VENISELOS
D. PANAS
N. POLITIS
CAPTAIN A. EXADACTYLOS
CAPTAIN PALI

For Montenegro:

(L. S.) GENERAL SERDAR I. VOUKOTITCH
I. MATANOVITCH

For Servia:

(L. S.) MIK. P. PACHITCH
M. G. RISTITCH
M. SPALAIKOVITCH
COLONEL K. SMILIANITCH
LT. COLONEL D. KALAFATOVITCH

(k) *Grey's Speech in the House of Commons, August 12, 1913*[1]

". . . In the next place, I would like people to realise what it is that the meetings of the Ambassadors were called into existence to do. It has been an axiom of diplomacy for many a year past that if ever war broke out in the Balkans it would be impossible, or almost impossible, to prevent one or more of the Great Powers being dragged into the conflict. Suddenly, last October, we were confronted with that situation which had been regarded as so threatening and ominous to the peace of Europe, and the peace of the Great Powers themselves. Up to the time of the outbreak of that war in October there had been universal expectation that if war took place in the Balkans, the Great Powers, or some of the Great Powers, would be unable to keep out of it, and that, if one or more was brought in, it was impossible to say how many others would be brought in. I ought to say that the Great Powers at once set to work to see if they could not disappoint that gloomy expectation by localising the conflict, at all events, in the Balkans. They saw at once the necessity of keeping in touch with each other with that object. The ordinary method of diplomatic communication by which the Great Powers keep in touch with each other is that of telegrams between the different Capitals. That is a machinery which in the case of six Great Powers requires for its working six foreign Ministers and thirty Ambassadors—a personnel of thirty-six in all— necessarily a very cumbrous and slow-moving machine, and the meetings of Ambassadors in London were called into existence then as an emergency expedient by which, through a simpler machinery than the

[1] *Parliamentary Debates, Commons,* 1913, Vol. LVI, pp. 2283-2284.

ordinary diplomatic methods, the Great Powers might keep more constantly and more quickly in touch with regard to each difficulty as it arose. The object was to localise the war, and we found after surveying the ground that if Constantinople and Asiatic Turkey were not to be brought within the area of the war, and if these questions were not to be raised in the course of the war, then the Great Powers might find themselves in agreement, provided they came to an understanding with each other about Albania and the Aegean Islands. For that purpose we set to work to come to an understanding on these two points, taking Albania and the Aegean Islands as a matter of discussion between the Great Powers, on which it was essential to them to reach an agreement, if they were to keep in touch and friendship with each other, and to localise the war, and in this sense that with regard to the rest, provided Constantinople and Asiatic Turkey and the Straits were not touched the rest could be fought out among the combatants themselves without interference.

That was not the only difficulty that was referred to the Ambassadors in the course of the last few months. As other questions arose they were from time to time brought up for discussion between the Ambassadors, because I think I may claim for that meeting that it became in a short time trusted by all the Powers, to this extent: that it was regarded as an eminently safe place at which to raise questions for discussion, and that if we could not settle things we did not, at any rate, make anything worse which was brought before us. But our main work was to secure agreement between the Great Powers by dealing with the question of Albania, and in the question of Albania I include that of commercial access to Servia, to the Adriatic and the Aegean Islands. We have at last, after discussing many tedious details, reached an agreement which covers Albania and the Aegean Islands. I will not go into any details about what the actual agreement is. Roughly it is this, that an international commission of control is to be established with regard to Albania, with a *gendarmerie* under officers selected from one of the smaller neutral Powers, the object being to set up an autonomous State, eventually under a Prince selected by the great Powers. The difficulty of coming to an agreement about particular frontiers has been very great. . . ."

44. Churchill's Speech on the German Naval Bill of 1912[1]

[When the Haldane Mission failed to limit naval rivalry, the British Government in reply to the German Naval Bill (*Novelle*) introduced a Supplementary Estimate. In his speech on this topic in the House of Commons, July 22, 1912, the First Lord of the British Admiralty, Winston Churchill, gave the following account of the German Naval

---

[1] *Parliamentary Debates, Commons*, 1912, Vol. XLI, pp. 838-842.

Bill. To meet this situation he stated that a further concentration of
battleships in home waters would be necessary. (See doc. no. 49).]

I think it will be for the convenience of the Committee if first of
all this afternoon I proceed to examine in detail the scope and character of the new German Navy Law. The main feature of that law is
not the increase in the new construction of capital ships, though that
is an important feature. The main feature is the increase in the striking
force of ships of all classes which will be available, immediately available, at all seasons of the year. A Third Squadron of eight battleships
will be created and maintained in full commission as part of the active
battle fleet. Whereas, according to the unamended law, the active battle
fleet consisted of seventeen battleships, four battle or large armoured
cruisers, and twelve small cruisers, in the near future that active fleet
will consist of twenty-five battleships, eight battle or large armoured
cruisers, and eighteen small cruisers; and whereas at present, owing
to the system of recruitment which prevails in Germany, the German
fleet is less fully mobile during the winter than during the summer
months, it will, through the operation of this law, not only be increased
in strength, but rendered much more readily available. Ninety-nine
destroyers, torpedo-boat destroyers—or torpedo-boats, as they are
called in Germany—instead of sixty-six, will be maintained in full commission out of the total of 144. Three-quarters of a million pounds
had already been taken in the general estimate for the year for the
building of submarines. The new law adds a quarter of a. million to
this, and that is a provision which, so far as we can judge from a study
of the finances, would appear to be repeated in subsequent years.
Seventy-two new submarines will be built within the currency of the
law, and of those it is apparently proposed to maintain fifty-four with
full permanent crews.

Taking a general view, the effect of the law will be that nearly
four-fifths of the entire German navy will be maintained in full permanent commission—that is to say, instantly and constantly ready for
war. Such a proportion is remarkable, and, so far as I am aware, finds
no example in the previous practice of modern naval Powers. So great
a change and development in the German fleet involves, of course,
important additions to their personnel. In 1898 the officers and men
of the German navy amounted to 25,000. Today that figure has
reached 66,000. Under the previous Navy Laws, and various amendments which have preceded this one, the Germans have been working
up to a total in 1920, according to our calculations, of 86,500 officers
and men, and they have been approaching that total by increments of,
approximately, an addition of 3,500 a year. The new law adds a total
of 15,000 officers and men, and makes the total in 1920 of 101,500.
The new average annual addition is calculated to be 1,680 of all ranks,
but for the next three years by special provision 500 extra are to be
added. From 1912 to 1914, 500 are to be added, and in the last three

years of the currency of the law 500 less will be taken. This makes a total rate of increase of the German Navy personnel about 5,700 men a year. The new construction under the law prescribed for the building of three additional battleships—one to be begun next year, one in 1916, and two small cruisers of which the date has not yet been fixed. The date of the third battleship has not been fixed. It has been presumed to be later than the six years which we have in view. The cost of these increases in men and in material during the next six years is estimated as £10,500,000 above the previous estimates spread over that period. I should like to point out to the Committee that this is a cumulative increase which follows upon other increases of a very important character. The law of 1898 was practically doubled by the law of 1900, and if the expenditure contemplated by the law of 1900 had been followed the German estimates of today would be about £11,000,-000. But owing to the amendments of 1906 and 1908, and now of 1912, that expenditure is very nearly £23,000,000. The actual figures of the expenditure have been given by my right Hon. Friend the Chancellor of the Exchequer on a recent occasion in Committee of Supply. But the fact that personnel plays such a large part in this new amendment and that personnel is more cheaply obtained in Germany than in this country makes the money go further there than it would do over here.

The ultimate scale of the new German fleet, as contemplated by the latest Navy Law, will be forty-one battleships, twenty battle or large armoured cruisers, and forty small cruisers, besides a proper proportion—an ample proportion—of flotillas of torpedo-boat destroyers and submarines. [*An Hon. Member:* "By what year?"] By 1920. That is not on paper a great advance on the figures prescribed by the previous law, which gave thirty-eight battleships, twenty battle or large armoured cruisers, and thirty-eight small cruisers. That is not a great advance on the total scale. In fact, however, there is a remarkable expansion of strength and efficiency, and particularly of strength and efficiency as they contribute to striking power. The number of battleships and large armoured cruisers alone which will be kept constantly ready and in full commission will be raised by the law from twenty-one, the present figure, to thirty-three—that is to say, an addition of twelve, or an increase of about 57 per cent. The new fleet will in the beginning include about twenty battleships and large cruisers of the older type, but, gradually as new vessels are built, the fighting power of the fleet will rise until in the end it will consist completely of modern vessels. This new scale of the German fleet—organised in five battle squadrons, each attended by a battle or armoured cruiser squadron, complete with small cruisers and auxiliaries of all kinds, and accompanied by numerous flotillas of destroyers and submarines, more than three-fourths, nearly four-fifths, maintained in full permanent commission—the aspect and scale of this fleet is, I say, extremely formidable. Such a fleet will be about as numerous to look at as the fleet which was gathered at Spithead for the recent Parliamentary visit, but, of course, when completed it will be far superior in actual strength. This full development will only be realised step by step. But already in 1914 two squadrons will, so far as we can ascertain, be entirely composed of "Dreadnoughts," or what are called "Dreadnoughts," and the third will be made up of good ships like the "Deutschlands" and the "Braunschweigs," together with five "Dreadnought" battle-cruisers. It remains to be noted that this new law is the fifth in fourteen years of the large successive increases made in German naval strength, that it encountered no effective opposition in its passage through the Reichstag, and that, though it has been severely criticised in Germany since its passage, the criticisms have been directed towards its inadequacy.

Before I come to the measures which will be necessary on our part, perhaps the Committee will permit me to make a general observation. There are two points with regard to navies and naval war which differentiate them from armies and land war. The first is the awful suddenness with which naval warfare can reach its decisive phase. We see on the continent of Europe immense military establishments possessed by nations dwelling on opposite sides of political frontier lines; yet they dwell and have dwelt for a whole generation in peace and tranquillity. But between those armies and any decisive collision there intervenes an inevitable period of delay that acts as a great buffer, a cushion of security. I mean the vast process of mobilisation, the very first signs of which must be noticed, and which, once it begins, lays idle the industry of both countries and dominates the whole course of national life. So it is that through all these years nations are able to dwell side by side with their tremendous military establishments without being a prey to undue anxiety as to immediate attack. But none of these considerations apply to fleets. The Fleet which was assembled for the manoeuvres the other day was fully capable of going into action as soon as the ammunition could be brought up and put by the side of the guns. And that is true of all the great highly efficient navies of the world.

I am bound to say, looking far ahead, and farther than the purposes of this Vote, at the aspect which Europe and the world will present when the power of States, which has been hitherto estimated in terms of armies, will be estimated very largely in naval strength, and when we have a number of Great Powers all possessed of very powerful navies, the state of Europe and of the world would seem to contain many more germs of danger than the period through which we have been passing in our lifetime.

The second general point to which I would direct the attention of the Committee is the extreme slowness with which naval preparations can be made. Small ships take eighteen to twenty months to build; large ships take from two to three years, sometimes four years. Docks take more than four years to build. Seamen take from two to three years to train; artificers take much longer; officers take between six and seven years. The efficiency which comes from the harmonious com-bination of these elements is a plant of very slow growth indeed. Cool, steady, methodical preparation, prolonged over a succession of years, can alone raise the margin of naval power. It is no use flinging millions of money about on the impulse of the moment, by a gesture of impatience, or in a mood of panic. Such a course only reveals your weakness and impotence. Those who clamour for sensational expenditure, who think that the kind of danger with which we are faced needs to be warded off or can be warded off in that way, are either ignorant themselves of naval conditions or take advantage of the ignorance of others. The strain we have to bear will be long and slow, and no relief will be obtained by impulsive or erratic action. We ought to learn from our German neighbours, whose policy marches unswervingly towards its goal across the lifetime of a whole generation. The two general principles which I would deduce from these observations, and which will guide my remarks this afternoon, are, first, that we must have an ample margin of strength instantly ready; and, secondly, that there must be a steady and systematic development of our naval forces untiringly pursued over a number of years.

45. HALDANE MISSION, 1912

[Ballin was the head of the Hamburg-American Line, a man of influence who was on intimate terms with Tirpitz, the Kaiser, and Bethmann-Hollweg, and a friend of Ernest Cassel, a powerful London banker. On January 29, 1912, Cassel brought to Berlin a memorandum, approved by Grey, Churchill, and Lloyd George, which served as a basis for opening official negotiations. The German Chancellor suggested a visit by Grey to Berlin. Grey, distrusting Germany and fearing to alarm France, was unwilling to go in person, but sent Richard Haldane, the Minister of War. Grey desired the visit to be private and informal so that if nothing came of it the public would not be disappointed. He stated to Paul Cambon, French Ambassador in London, that Haldane was merely to find out whether Germany's recent overture were serious or not, but that he was not to enter upon negotiations but merely to inquire about German plans for a naval program. Grey's restricted view of the mission did not make its success likely, nor did Churchill's Glasgow address in reply to the Kaiser's speech at the opening of the Reichstag announcing that an increase in the German army and navy would be introduced later. Churchill said: "The British Navy is to us a necessity and, from some points of view, the German Navy is to them more in the nature of a luxury. . . . We shall make it clear that other naval Powers, instead of overtaking us by additional efforts, will only be more outdistanced in consequence of the measures which we ourselves shall take." This speech was received with indignation in Berlin, and offended some of the more pacific members of the British cabinet. Upon Haldane's return to London, the draft of the proposed German Naval Law was studied. It was seen by the naval experts that large expenditures would need to be made by the British to meet the proposed three new capital ships and the increase in personnel and expenditures. The British sent a memorandum to this effect to Berlin, and Grey told the German ambassador that it would be impossible to sign any political agreement when both countries were making increased naval expenditures. The Kaiser resented the change in England's attitude, though Bethmann-Hollweg (Chancellor) and Kiderlen-Waechter (Foreign Minister) still made efforts to satisfy Grey; but they were unable to persuade Tirpitz and the Kaiser to abandon the three extra ships and to postpone the publication of the Navy Law. Though the Haldane mission failed to achieve its primary purpose because of England's unwillingness to make an agreement about neutrality which might restrict her freedom to aid France and because of Germany's unwillingness to make sufficient reductions in the Supplementary Navy Law, it resulted eventually in the working out of agreements regarding colonial matters and the Bagdad Railway. (See doc. no. 52.)]

(a) *Haldane's Account*[1]

The Emperor therefore sent his message in the beginning of 1912, to the effect that feeling had become so much excited that it was not enough to rely on the ordinary diplomatic intercourse for softening it, and that he was anxious for an exchange of views between the Cabinets of Berlin and London, of a personal and direct kind. As the result of this intimation, the British Cabinet decided to send one of its members to Berlin to hold "conversations," with a view to exploring and, if practicable, softening the causes of tension, and I was requested by the Prime Minister and Sir Edward Grey and my other colleagues to go to Berlin and undertake the task. Our Ambassador there came over to London specially to discuss arrangements, and he returned to Berlin to make them before I started.

I arrived in the German capital on February 8, 1912, and spent some days in interviews with the Emperor, the Imperial Chancellor, the Naval Minister (Admiral von Tirpitz), and others of the Emperor's Ministry. The narrative of my conversations I have extracted from the records I made after each interview, for the preservation so far as possible of the actual expressions used during it.

My first interview was one with Herr von Bethmann Hollweg, the Imperial Chancellor. We met in the British Embassy, and the conversation, which was quite informal, was a full and agreeable one. My impression, and I still retain it, was that Bethmann-Hollweg was then as sincerely desirous of avoiding war as I was myself. I told him of certain dangers quite frankly, and he listened and replied with what seemed to me to be a full understanding of our position. I said that

---

[1] Haldane, *Before the War.* New York. Funk & Wagnalls. 1920, pp. 71-82. Reprinted with the permission of Funk & Wagnalls Co.

the increasing action of Germany in piling up magnificent armaments was, of course, within the unfettered rights of the German people. But the policy had an inevitable consequence in the drawing together of other nations in the interests of their own security. This was what was happening. I told him frankly that we had made naval and military preparations, but only such as defence required, and as would be considered in Germany matter of routine. I went on to observe that our faces were set against aggression by any nation, and I told him, what seemed to relieve his mind, that we had no secret military treaties. But, I added, if France were attacked and an attempt made to occupy her territory, our neutrality must not be reckoned on by Germany. For one thing, it was obvious that our position as an island protected by the sea would be affected seriously if Germany had possession of the Channel ports on the northern shores of France. Again, we were under treaty obligation to come to the aid of Belgium in case of invasion, just as we were bound to defend Portugal and Japan in certain eventualities. In the third place, owing to our dependence on freedom of sea-communications for food and raw materials, we could not sit still if Germany elected to develop her fleet to such an extent as to imperil our naval protection. She might build more ships, but we should in that case lay down two keels for each one she laid down.

The Chancellor said that he did not take my observations at all in bad part, but I must understand that his admirals and generals were pretty difficult.

I replied that the difficulty would be felt at least as much with the admirals and generals in my own country.

The Chancellor, in the course of our talk, proposed a formula of neutrality to which I will refer later on.

I left the Chancellor with the sense that I had been talking with an honest man struggling somewhat with adversity. However, next day I was summoned to luncheon with the Emperor and Empress at the Schloss and afterward had a long interview, which lasted nearly three hours, with the Emperor and Admiral von Tirpitz in the Emperor's cabinet room. The conversation was mainly in German, and was confined to naval questions. My reception by the Emperor was very agreeable; that by Tirpitz seemed to me a little strained. The question was, whether Germany must not continue her programme for expanding her fleet. What that programme really amounted to we had not known in London, except that it included an increase in battleships; but the Emperor handed me at this meeting a confidential copy of the draft of the proposed new Fleet Law, with an intimation that he had no objection to my communicating it privately to my colleagues. I was careful to abstain even from looking at it then, for I saw that, from its complexity and bulk, it would require careful study. So I simply put it in my pocket. But I repeated what I had said to the Chancellor, that the necessity for secure sea-communications rendered it vital for us to be able to protect ourselves on the seas. Germany was quite free to do as she pleased, but so were we, and we should probably lay down two keels for every one which she added to her programme. The initiative in slackening competition was really not with us, but with Germany. Any agreement for settling our differences and introducing a new spirit into the relations of the two nations would be bones without flesh, if Germany began by fresh shipbuilding, and so forced us to do twice as much. Indeed, the world would laugh at such an agreement, and our people would think that we had been fooled. I did not myself take that view, because I thought that the mere fact of an agreement was valuable. But the Emperor would see that the public would attach very little importance to his action unless the agreement largely modified what it believed to be his shipbuilding programme.

We then discussed the proposal of the German Admiralty for the new programme. Admiral von Tirpitz struggled for it. I insisted that fundamental modification was essential if better relations were to ensue. The tone was friendly, but I felt that I was up against the crucial part of my task. The admiral wanted us to enter into some understanding about our own shipbuilding. He thought the Two-Power standard a hard one for Germany, and, indeed, Germany could not make any admission about it.

I said it was not matter for admission. They were free and so were we, and we must for the sake of safety remain so. The idea then occurred to us that, as we should never agree about it, we should avoid trying to define a standard proportion in any general agreement that we might come to, and indeed say nothing in it about shipbuilding; but that the Emperor should announce to the German public that the agreement on general questions, if we should have concluded one, had entirely modified his wish for the new Fleet Law, as originally conceived, and that it should be delayed, and future shipbuilding should at least be spread over a longer period.

The Emperor thought such an agreement would certainly make a great difference, and he informed me that his Chancellor would propose to me a formula as a basis for it. I said that I would see the Chancellor and discuss a possible formula, as well as territorial and other questions with him, and would then return to London and report to the King (from whom I had brought him a special and friendly message) and to my colleagues the good disposition I had found, and leave the difficulties about shipbuilding and indeed all other matters to their judgment. For I had come to Berlin, not to make an actual agreement, but only to explore the ground for one with the Emperor and his ministers. I had been struck with the friendly disposition in Berlin, and a not less friendly disposition would be found in London.

The evening after my interview with the Emperor I dined with the Chancellor. I met there and talked with several prominent politicians, soldiers, and men of letters, including Kiderlen-Waechter (the then Foreign Secretary), the afterwards famous General von Hindenburg, Zimmermann of the Foreign Office, and Professor Harnack.

Later on, after dinner, I went off to meet the French Ambassador, M. Jules Cambon, at the British Embassy, for I wished to keep him informed of our object, which was simply to improve the state of feeling between London and Berlin, but on the basis, and only on the basis, of complete loyalty to our Entente with France. It was, to use a phrase which he himself suggested in our conversation, a *détente* rather than an *entente* that I had in view, with possible developments to follow it which might assume a form which would be advantageous to France and Russia, as well as to ourselves and Germany. He showed me next day the report of our talk which he had prepared in order to telegraph it to Paris.

I had other interviews the next day, but the only one which is important for the purposes of the present narrative is that at my final meeting with the German Chancellor on the Saturday (February 10), I pressed on him how important it was for public opinion and the peace of the world that Germany should not force us into a shipbuilding competition with her, a competition in which it was certain that we should have to spare no effort to preserve our margin of safety by greater increases.

He did not controvert my suggestion. I could see that personally he was of the same mind. But he said that the forces he had to contend with were almost insuperable. The question of a retardation of building under the proposed Fleet Law was not susceptible of being treated apart from that of the formula of which he and the Emperor had both spoken. He suggested that we might agree on the following formula:

"1. The High Contracting Parties assure each other mutually of their desire for peace and friendship.

"2. They will not, either of them, make any combination, or join in any combination which is directed against the other. They expressly declare that they are not bound by any such combination.

"3. If either of the High Contracting Parties become entangled in a war with one or more other powers, the other of the High Contracting Parties will at least observe toward the power so entangled a benevolent neutrality, and use its utmost endeavour for the localization of the conflict.

"4. The duty of neutrality which arises from the preceding article has no application in so far as it may not be reconcilable with existing agreements which the High Contracting Parties have already made. The making of new agreements which make it impossible for either of the Contracting Parties to observe neutrality toward the other beyond what is provided by the preceding limitations is excluded in conformity with provisions contained in Article 2."

Anxious as I was to agree with the Chancellor, who seemed as keen as I was to meet me with expressions which I might take back to England for friendly consideration, I was unable to hold out to him the least prospect that we could accept the draft formula which he had just proposed. Under Article 2, for example, we should find ourselves, were it accepted, precluded from coming to the assistance of France should Germany attack her and aim at getting possession of such ports as Dunkirk, Calais, and Boulogne, a friendly occupation of which was so important for our island security. Difficulties might also arise which would hamper us in the discharge of our existing treaty obligations to Belgium, Portugal, and Japan. The most hopeful way out was to revise the draft fundamentally by confining its terms to an undertaking by each Power not to make any unprovoked attack upon the other, or join in any combination or design against the other, for purposes of aggression, or become party to any plan or naval or military combination, alone or in conjunction with any other Power, directed to such an end.

He and I then sat down and redrafted what he had prepared, on this basis, but without his committing himself to the view that it would be sufficient. We also had a satisfactory conversation about the Bagdad Railway and other things in Turkey connected with the Persian Gulf, and we discussed possibilities of the rearrangement of certain interests of both Powers in Africa. He said to me that he was not there to make any immediate bargain, but that we should look at the African question on both sides from a high point of view, and that if we had any difficulties we should tell him, and he would see whether he could get round them for us.

I replied that I also was not there to make a bargain, but only to explore the ground, and that I much appreciated the tone of his conversation with me, and the good feeling he had shown. I should go back to London and without delay report to my colleagues all that had passed.

I entertain no doubt that the German Chancellor was sincerely in earnest in what he said to me on these occasions, and in his desire to improve relations with us and keep the peace. So I think was the Emperor; but he was pulled at by his naval and military advisers, and by the powerful, if then small, chauvinist party in Germany. In 1912, when the conversations recorded took place, this party was less potent, I think a good deal less, than it appears to have become a year and a half later, when Germany had increased her army still further. But I formed the opinion even then that the power of the Emperor in Germany was a good deal misinterpreted and overestimated. My impression was that the really decisive influence was that of the Minister who had managed to secure the strongest following throughout Germany; and it was obvious to me that Admiral von Tirpitz had a powerful and growing following from many directions, due to the backing of the naval party.

(b) A Statement of von Tirpitz about the Haldane Mission of 1912[1]

Von Tirpitz (retired) Secretary of State for the Imperial Navy, to Emperor William II

Berlin, October 9, 1917

I have the honor of submitting to Your Majesty the accompanying account of the interview with Haldane on February 9, 1912, which I have found among my private papers.

I should like to supplement this by the following statement:

From the negotiations which preceded the interview I definitely recall that at the end of January [Kaiser's note: "Cassel appeared accompanied by Ballin with a verbal note from the English Government to me. Thereupon in the presence of Bethmann, Tirpitz, Cassel, and Ballin, I drafted an answer to the verbal note brought by Cassel from the English Government"] or beginning of February a telegram was sent by way of Ballin and Sir Ernest Cassel to the English Foreign Office, and indeed with my knowledge and in complete agreement with Your Majesty as with me, which was somewhat to the effect that we could meet them in the question of the *Flottennovelle* [supplementary naval law] if we on our side were assured of a friendly direction in English policy. [Kaiser's note: "Right"]. Such an assurance we envisaged in an agreement according to which neither of the two powers should let itself be involved in complications directed against the other. On this basis we could negotiate further and come to an understanding regarding naval armaments [Kaiser's note: "Right"].

From the communications of Sir Ernest Cassel, which Ballin transmitted to Your Majesty, it could already be inferred, as I recall, that England was in no way willing to offer such assurance. The English Government wanted rather merely to declare that in return for our renunciation, she would remain neutral in case France should attack Germany; but if Germany should attack France, she wanted to preserve a free hand. [Kaiser's note: "Right! That was the bait upon which Bethmann bit! and on account of which he attempted to put aside the *Novelle* which led to the conflict between him and me, which was settled with the help of Dr. Burchards in the Bundesrat on March 22, after the Chancellor had received the English declination."]

Since to represent Germany as the aggressor would always have been easy for England in case of war, the worth of this promise therefore amounted to nothing, as July 1914 showed. In fact, England from the beginning offered us nothing but a part of the Portuguese colonial territory of relatively little value, which we might buy, and upon which, moreover, von Kiderlen, at the time Secretary for Foreign Affairs, set little economic worth.

At the same time Portugal had declared that it intended to sell none

---

[1] *Die Grosse Politik*, Vol. XXXI, pp. 221ff., No. 11426 with annex.

of its colonies and Churchill made a speech on the German luxury fleet. [Kaiser's note: "Haldane appeared in the negotiations as a result of a disagreement between Grey and Churchill as to who should go to Berlin; Haldane was chosen as a neutral person to prepare the treaty which Grey claimed to be willing to sign in Berlin."]

I definitely recollect further that Haldane had said in reply to a question of Your Majesty's that England could not speak of neutrality toward us with a view to its application to France. [Kaiser's note: "Right! In contrast to the verbal note by Cassel in which this neutrality was expressly offered."] This assertion of Haldane's, however, is not expressed so sharply in the annexed account.

Whether Haldane in his statements acted and spoke in good faith may be dismissed. The English Cabinet at any rate did not act accordingly. Rather, as soon as we had extended toward it our little finger, it made demands which far exceeded the originally discussed limits. [Kaiser's note: "Right!"]

The real purpose of the English Government to wrest Germany's sea defense out of her hands without any real counter concessions, became ever clearer. Your Majesty, if I remember rightly, demonstrated this in a letter in Your Majesty's own hand to King George about March 1912. [Kaiser: "?"] In a similar sense the Chief of the Naval Staff wrote to me on March 18, 1912: "The English proposal received yesterday is completely unacceptable. Their neutrality was hedged in by clauses [verkausulierte neutralität] on condition of our giving up the *Novelle*. [Kaiser's note: "Right."] The purpose of the whole action —the obliteration of the *Novelle*—has thereby been most clearly expressed. Naturally the English proposal will be rejected."

Without doubt Haldane's realization that almost anything could be had from the Chancellor of the time contributed to the enhancement of English demands.

Haldane himself had declared, first to Your Majesty and, as we came down from the Castle, to me and likewise to others, that he was "very satisfied" with the interview. [Kaiser's note: "Yes, also to Ballin."]

The Imperial Chancellor, Bethmann-Hollweg, to whom I said this in a conversation some time later, told me that Haldane had generally said that but had added that he did not know whether his Cabinet would declare itself entirely satisfied. [Kaiser's note: "Right, Ballin told me."] I could not refrain from presenting these details to Your Majesty now because I felt that Your Majesty might be able to utilize them politically in the present situation [1917]—perhaps by a suitable publication. [Kaiser's note: "Yes."]

As Your Majesty will remember, and as it must have been stated in a communication to Your Majesty from the Chief of Cabinet, I was quite ready to recommend that Your Majesty withdraw the entire

Flottennovelle in case a real counter concession on the part of England [Kaiser's note: "*id est* neutrality"], either in the form of a useful declaration of neutrality or in the form of a naval limitation on the part of England also, could be obtained. [Kaiser's note: "Yes."] For political reasons alone such a counter concession was absolutely essential because Your Majesty had already announced the *Novelle* in an address from the throne.

v. TIRPITZ

Annex to letter of Tirpitz to William II, October 9, 1917
Account of the Interview with Haldane on February 9, 1912

According to my knowledge and comprehension, there was nothing to justify letting it be assumed that the English would really give up the policy they had followed for years and undertake a complete change. In so far as there is no certainty on this point, a great mistrust on the part of Germany seems not only justified but necessary.

As a result of the objections and demands made by the Imperial Chancellor, the *Novelle* was so reduced in the course of the winter that it contained only the bare principle and hardly any additional material on which concessions could be made. In the negotiations with Haldane I could not go back to the *Novelle* in its original form ordered by Your Majesty so as to negotiate on this more favorable basis, since the contents of the *Novelle* in its final abbreviated form had already been communicated to Haldane by the Imperial Chancellor.

Contents of the Interview

Haldane declared at the beginning of the interview that he spoke "in the name of the English Cabinet and with the approval of His Majesty the King." (The Churchill address at Glasgow makes the unity of the cabinet seem doubtful.) Not quite in harmony with this declaration was the emphasis which Haldane, at the end of the interview and after we had apparently reached complete unity, put upon the remark that this negotiation was merely an inquiry of his own.

I explained at the beginning of the interview that we would welcome an understanding if it could be reached, that we had always desired such, and that our efforts had never been intended to lead to "supremacy" or to a naval rivalry with England. The preamble of our naval law had been translated in England in a way which quite distorted its meaning. At any rate, what we were striving for was a fleet which England could not simply defeat without injuring herself.

Haldane began by opening up the widest political perspectives. He promised all Angola, Zanzibar, Pemba, etc., assured us an equatorial colonial empire through the entire middle of Africa, hence also to a degree the Congo State; England would limit itself to the concession for the railroad which should lead from Egypt to Cape Town and which His Majesty the Kaiser had already discussed with Cecil Rhodes. To a question of His Majesty regarding the neutrality of England in a war between France and Germany, Haldane made lengthy explanations with comparisons of attacks by Germany upon Japan or England upon Austria, comparisons quite beyond the realm of probability. From this evasion of His Majesty's question I got the impression that our new relations with England would not alter the *de facto* entente between England and France, although Haldane said that they had no written treaties with France.

Haldane then explained that there was only a political agreement in question here and that England would not make any demands at all regarding "naval disarmament." [Kaiser's note: "Right."] He saw that we must have a third active squadron. Requirements for personnel and maintenance were immaterial to England. A slackening in the rate of building new ships would greatly facilitate the political agreement at home. Then he himself began with the two-power standard which they must maintain and designated it an essential "tradition" for England. Thereupon I explained that we could not recognize the principle involved in the "two-keel-to-one" standard—I purposely used this clear designation as applying to Germany. Another ratio, perhaps 2 : 3 might be a possible principle. All experts from Lord Vincent on, Mahan, McKenna in his more recent addresses, as well as Grey, had acknowledged that such a ratio would not imply aggressive intentions against England on the part of another nation. Haldane expressed the opinion that it would be possible to consider some such idea. For the moment it was not. England must be ready with a fleet for every possible combination. To my counter that our army must then be equal to every possible combination, while in numbers it was hardly as strong as those of each of our neighbours, he did not reply further but remarked that that was quite another matter. [Kaiser's note: "Right."]

In answer to His Majesty's question as to what he would entertain as a proposal, Haldane made very meagre demands. First he mentioned a certain slowing up of ship construction and asked if we could not distribute the increase over twelve years. He placed special value upon the year 1912. [Kaiser's note: "Right."]

To enhance the value of concession I endeavored to make clear the difficulties connected with a further change in the bill since we had already reduced our program by three ships as a consequence of the improved frame of mind in England. It was not really a matter of the enlargement of the fleet, but rather of change in organization to meet modern conditions (radio telegraphy, complications of newer ships) and the requirements of our system of defense. I reminded Haldane that he must also take into account that His Majesty had already committed himself to the *Novelle* in his address from the throne. This Haldane admitted, and repeated that we must have our third squadron.

He wanted merely "as a formality"—it was not a matter of an actual sum—an indication of our accommodating attitude.

He also admitted that the increase of the naval law by three ships in twenty years really did not matter.

It now had to be decided whether we would give a general approval of the concession in relation to the *Novelle* in case a political agreement could be achieved or whether the measure of the concession should be fixed in this conference. Since Haldane himself proposed only that the rate of increase should be reduced or at least a ship omitted, it seemed proper to take this course and to consent to his own proposals.

Haldane then expressed that proposal personally and on his own initiative and later wrote it down—the one that I myself had indicated as a possibility in the portfolio of the *Novelle*; viz., the first ship in 1913, the second in 1916, the third indefinite, at any rate after 1917. [Kaiser's note: "Yes."]

After Haldane had declared himself satisfied with this, and had thus secured this concession, he proceeded with his demands, and finally very carefully touched upon the question whether the naval law needed to be put into effect at all. Thereupon His Majesty the Kaiser said that it was law and must be executed. Haldane thereupon dropped this question. [Kaiser's note: "Yes."]

In spite of all, I have received the impression that the English action is directed not so much against the present, materially less significant *Novelle* as against our protective power on sea in general.

His Majesty the Kaiser has furthermore pointed out especially that we, only because of the enlarged fleet programs of our continental neighbors, are forced to keep the development of our fleet at its height. Haldane made certain remarks to the effect that England would see to it that the French and Russian fleet programs would not increase too much. To my concrete question, however, as to how France stood in this regard in that she is laying the keels of three big vessels for the year 1912 while we consider that we will eventually build only two, Haldane did not respond.

In reality the question, of course, is this: that each warship which is being built in the world makes the English monopolistic position more difficult, but under the present-day conditions this is favorable for us but unfavorable for England.

Haldane shows himself as a most able mediator. It was characteristic that whenever there was mentioned an instance in which Germany had been treated badly by England, he would always openly admit without self-defense that Germany rightly could complain about it.

Haldane said finally that he would hasten the political agreement as much as possible and that England would not make public its estimates until our *Novelle* was published. [The final remark of the Kaiser: "Right. W."]

46. Fifth Treaty of the Triple Alliance, Dec. 5, 1912[1]

[Though the Triple Alliance was not due to expire until 1914, talk of its renewal began as early as 1911. Italy favored its early renewal to make up to her allies for her war with Turkey, which was displeasing to them, while Germany always favored anything which would draw her two allies closer. Though Conrad was opposed, even urging war with Italy to crush irredentism, Aehrenthal and Francis Joseph secured Italian adherence to its renewal, which was finally made without modification. The alliance was no longer merely defensive, because it provided support for offensive Italian and Austrian action.]

Their Majesties the Emperor of Austria, King of Bohemia, etc., and Apostolic King of Hungary, the Emperor of Germany, King of Prussia, and the King of Italy, firmly resolved to assure to Their States the continuation of the benefits which the maintenance of the Triple Alliance guarantees to them, from the political point of view as well as from the monarchical and social point of view, and wishing with this object to prolong the duration of this Alliance, concluded on May 20, 1882, renewed a first time by the Treaties of February 20, 1887, a second time by the Treaty of May 6, 1891, and a third time by the Treaty of June 28, 1902, have, for this purpose, appointed as Their Plenipotentiaries, to wit: . . .

Article I. The High Contracting Parties mutually promise peace and friendship, and will enter into no alliance or engagement directed against anyone of their States.

They engage to proceed to an exchange of ideas on political and economic questions of a general nature which may arise, and they further promise one another mutual support within the limits of their own interests.

Article II. In case Italy, without direct provocation on her part, should be attacked by France for any reason whatsoever, the two other Contracting Parties shall be bound to lend help and assistance with all their forces to the Party attacked.

This same obligation shall devolve upon Italy in case of any aggression without direct provocation by France against Germany.

Article III. If one, or two, of the High Contracting Parties, without direct provocation on their part, should chance to be attacked and to be engaged in a war with two or more Great Powers nonsignatory to the present Treaty, the *casus fœderis* will arise simultaneously for all the High Contracting Parties.

Article IV. In case a Great Power nonsignatory to the present Treaty should threaten the security of the states of one of the High

---

[1] A. F. Pribram, *The Secret Treaties of Austria-Hungary, 1879-1914.* Vol. I, pp. 245-259. Reprinted with the permission of the Harvard University Press, holders of the copyright.

Contracting Parties, and the threatened Party should find itself forced on that account to make war against it, the two others bind themselves to observe towards their Ally a benevolent neutrality. Each of them reserves to itself, in this case, the right to take part in the war, if it should see fit, to make common cause with its Ally.

Article V. If the peace of one of the High Contracting Parties should chance to be threatened under the circumstances foreseen by the preceding Articles, the High Contracting Parties shall take counsel together in ample time as to the military measures to be taken with a view to eventual coöperation.

They engage, henceforth, in all cases of common participation in a war, to conclude neither armistice, nor peace, nor treaty, except by common agreement among themselves.

Article VI. Germany and Italy, having in mind only the maintenance, so far as possible, of the territorial status quo in the Orient, engage to use their influence to forestall on the Ottoman coasts and islands in the Adriatic and the Aegean Seas any territorial modification which might be injurious to one or the other of the Powers signatory to the present Treaty. To this end, they will communicate to one another all information of a nature to enlighten each other mutually concerning their own dispositions, as well as those of other Powers.

Article VII. Austria-Hungary and Italy, having in mind only the maintenance, so far as possible, of the territorial status quo in the Orient, engage to use their influence to forestall any territorial modification which might be injurious to one or the other of the Powers signatory to the present Treaty. To this end, they shall communicate to one another all information of a nature to enlighten each other mutually concerning their own dispositions, as well as those of other Powers. However, if, in the course of events, the maintenance of the status quo in the regions of the Balkans or of the Ottoman coasts and islands in the Adriatic and in the Aegean Sea should become impossible, and if, whether in consequence of the action of a third Power or otherwise, Austria-Hungary or Italy should find themselves under the necessity of modifying it by a temporary or permanent occupation on their part, this occupation shall take place only after a previous agreement between the two Powers, based upon the principle of a reciprocal compensation for every advantage, territorial or other, which each of them might obtain beyond the present status quo, and giving satisfaction to the interests and well founded claims of the two Parties.

Article VIII. The stipulations of Articles VI and VII shall apply in no way to the Egyptian question, with regard to which the High Contracting Parties preserve respectively their freedom of action, regard being always paid to the principles upon which the present Treaty rests.

Article IX. Germany and Italy engage to exert themselves for the maintenance of the territorial status quo in the North African regions on the Mediterranean, to wit, Cyrenaica, Tripolitania, and Tunisia. The Representatives of the two Powers in these regions shall be instructed to put themselves into the closest intimacy of mutual communication and assistance.

If unfortunately, as a result of a mature examination of the situation, Germany and Italy should both recognize that the maintenance of the status quo has become impossible, Germany engages, after a formal and previous agreement, to support Italy in any action in the form of occupation or other taking of guaranty which the latter should undertake in these same regions with a view to an interest of equilibrium and of legitimate compensation.

It is understood that in such an eventuality the two Powers would seek to place themselves likewise in agreement with England.

Article X. If it were to happen that France should make a move to extend her occupation, or even her protectorate or her sovereignty, under any form whatsoever, in the North African territories, and that in consequence thereof Italy, in order to safeguard her position in the Mediterranean, should feel that she must herself undertake action in the said North African territories, or even have recourse to extreme measures in French territory in Europe, the state of war which would thereby ensue between Italy and France would constitute *ipso facto*, on the demand of Italy, and at the common charge of Germany and Italy, the *casus fœderis* foreseen by Articles II and V of the present Treaty, as if such an eventuality were expressly contemplated therein.

Article XI. If the fortunes of any war undertaken in common against France by the two Powers should lead Italy to seek for territorial guaranties with respect to France for the security of the frontiers of the Kingdom and of her maritime position, as well as with a view to stability and to peace, Germany will present no obstacle thereto, and, if need be, and in a measure compatible with circumstances, will apply herself to facilitating the means of attaining such a purpose.

Article XII. The High Contracting Parties mutually promise secrecy as to the contents of the present Treaty.

Article XIII. The Signatory Powers reserve the right of subsequently introducing, in the form of a Protocol and of a common agreement, the modifications of which the utility should be demonstrated by circumstances.

Article XIV. The present Treaty shall remain in force for the space of six years, dating from the expiration of the Treaty now in force; but if it has not been denounced one year in advance by one or another of the High Contracting Parties, it shall remain in force for the same duration of six more years.

Article XV. The ratifications of the present Treaty shall be exchanged at Vienna within a period of a fortnight, or sooner if may be.

In witness whereof the respective Plenipotentiaries have signed the present Treaty and have affixed thereto the seal of their arms.

Done at Vienna, in triplicate, the fifth day of the month of December, one thousand nine hundred and twelve.

L.S.   BERCHTOLD

L.S.   VON TSCHIRSCHKY

L.S.   AVARNA

First Final Protocol concerning the mutual granting of commercial advantages, and concerning means of bringing about the accession of Great Britain to the Articles of the Treaty relating to Mediterranean questions. Vienna, December 5, 1912

Protocol

At the moment of proceeding to the signing of the Treaty of this day between Austria-Hungary, Germany and Italy, the undersigned Plenipotentiaries of these three Powers, thereto duly authorized, mutually declare themselves as follows:

1. Under reserve of parliamentary approval for the executory stipulations proceeding from the present declaration of principle, the High Contracting Parties promise each other, from this moment, in economic matters (finances, customs, railroads), in addition to most-favored-nation treatment, all of the facilities and special advantages which would be compatible with the requirements of each of the three States and with their respective engagements with third Powers.

2. The accession of England being already acquired, in principle, to the stipulations of the Treaty of this day which concern the Orient, properly so-called, to wit, the territories of the Ottoman Empire, the High Contracting Parties shall exert themselves at the opportune moment, and to the extent that circumstances may permit it, to bring about an analogous accession with regard to the North African territories of the central and western part of the Mediterranean, including Morocco. This accession might be realized by an acceptance, on the part of England, of the programme established by Articles IX and X of the Treaty of this day.

In witness whereof the three Plenipotentiaries have signed the present Protocol in triplicate.

Done at Vienna, the fifth day of the month of December, one thousand nine hundred and twelve.

BERCHTOLD

VON TSCHIRSCHKY

AVARNA

Second Final Protocol concerning North Africa, Albania, and Novi-Bazar. Vienna, December 5, 1912

Protocol

At the moment of proceeding to the signing of the Treaty of this day between Austria-Hungary, Germany, and Italy, the undersigned

Plenipotentiaries of these three Powers, thereto duly authorized, mutually declare themselves as follows:

1. It is understood that the territorial status quo in the North African regions on the Mediterranean mentioned in Article IX of the Treaty of June 28, 1902, implies the sovereignty of Italy over Tripolitania and Cyrenaica.

2. It is likewise understood that Article X of the same Treaty has for its basis the existing territorial status quo in the North African regions at the moment of the signing of the Treaty.

3. It is understood that the special arrangements concerning Albania and the Sanjak of Novi-Bazar agreed upon between Austria-Hungary and Italy on December 20, 1900/February 9, 1901, and on November 20/December 15, 1909, are not modified by the renewal of the Treaty of Alliance between Austria-Hungary, Germany, and Italy.

In witness whereof the three Plenipotentiaries have signed the present Protocol in triplicate.

Done at Vienna, the fifth day of the month of December, one thousand nine hundred and twelve.

L.S.   BERCHTOLD
L.S.   VON TSCHIRSCHKY
L.S.   AVARNA

47. THE GERMAN MILITARY MISSION TO TURKEY

[The arrangements for the German military mission to Turkey were made through military not diplomatic channels. This explains Bethmann-Hollweg's omission to mention it to Sazonov in October when he passed through Berlin and talked frankly with the German Chancellor. This apparent secrecy, however, was unfortunate in its effects on Russo-German relations. The Russian Government learned of the plan only through a rumor telegraphed by Giers, the Russian Ambassador at Constantinople. Sazonov's sense of injury was deepened by fears that the mission might ultimately block Russia's designs on the Straits in view of the importance he attached to Russia's "historic mission." The ultimate solution, worked out by the German Ambassador at Constantinople, brought the affair to a peaceful close without involving the danger of a test of strength between the two groups of powers. The affair shows how a serious crisis was settled by German willingness to make some concessions and by French and British restraint upon Russia. This crisis, however, caused German statesmen in July, 1914, to believe that Sazonov would not have England's support and that it was therefore probably safe to support Austria.

The account in (a) is by the former Governor of Constantinople and Imperial Ottoman Naval Minister.]

(a) *A Turkish Account*[1]

I doubt whether there is a single man in Europe or America who really knows the circumstances under which the German Military Mission came to Constantinople to reorganise the Turkish Army.

The numerous accounts published by our enemies always aver that this Mission arrived during Enver Pasha's term of office as War Minister and impute it as a crime against him. My revelations will show how the affair really came about.

When Mahmud Shefket Pasha had convinced himself that it was impossible to beat the Bulgarians, and signed the Peace preliminaries of London which gave us the Enos-Midia line as our frontier with Bulgaria, and the Islands of Imbros and Tenedos, he decided that the whole national energies must be husbanded for domestic reforms if the country, which was already very exhausted, was not to be weakened yet further. . . .

In his opinion what we needed most was money, and he was contemplating raising a substantial loan from one of the European Powers. First he applied to the Germans, but they pointed out that the Berlin money market was in no position to arrange a new Turkish loan, and they frankly advised us never to count on Germany in financial matters, but always to apply to France in that respect. Thereupon the Government decided to follow that advice and sent Djavid Bey to Paris. Djavid was not indeed a member of the Ministry, but he was regarded as the soul of the efforts being made by the party of "Unity and Progress" in the direction of organisation in the politico-financial sphere. . . .

Last but not least he took up the question of the reorganisation of the army and navy. A British Naval Mission was already at work. He got into personal touch with the head of that Mission and asked him to accelerate the reorganisation of the Navy. As regards the organisation of the Army I will now relate the facts, the details of which were given to me by Mahmud Shefket Pasha personally, so that their accuracy cannot be doubted.

During the Pasha's term of office as Grand Vizier he usually spent the night and slept at the Sublime Porte, and as I slept at the Military Governor's Headquarters he called me to the telephone after dinner on several evenings when he felt very tired after heavy work during the day and asked me to go round and see him. On these occasions he often told me of his ideas and plans and asked my opinion.

On one of these evenings he remarked:

"I believe that everything we have done hitherto with regard to the reorganisation of our army has been only half measures, if not bad measures. All the organisers whom we have had here, both during the

---

[1] Djemal Pasha. *Memories of a Turkish Statesman, 1913-1919.* New York, Doran. 1922. pp. 65-70. Reprinted with the permission of Doubleday, Doran & Company, Inc.

reign of Sultan Abdul Hamid and since the promulgation of the
constitution, have been selected quite casually and on no definite principle. We have never thought of inviting a serious mission. . . .

"Look at the Greeks, for example. They were much cleverer than
ourselves. They have entrusted the reorganisation of their navy to the
English, and that of their army to the French. . . . The result was
the creation of the Greek Army which we learned to respect during the
Balkan War, and of a fleet with which the old fleet of the Turco-Greek
War cannot be compared.

"In my view the greatest service Venizelos has rendered his country
was in organising the armed forces of the nation and thus presenting
the diplomatists with an effective argument—I might say the only
effective argument—for the realisation of the national ideal. I want
to perform the same service for my country. . . .

"As regards our army, I don't think we must hesitate any longer to
adopt the methods of the Germans. For more than thirty years we
have had German instructors in our army, our Corps of Officers is
trained entirely on German lines, and our army is absolutely familiar
with the spirit of German training and military education. It is quite
impossible to change all that now. I therefore intend to send for a
German military mission on the grand scale. . . . I will give the
Turkish world an army which will certainly be small but, on the other
hand, well organised and trained. In time of war it will not be difficult
to bring this army up to maximum strength by expanding the *cadres*.
I am now inquiring of the Germans on what terms they would be
prepared to send us some such mission, and consider it advisable to
leave the question of their conditions entirely to them."

Such are the circumstances under which General Liman von Sanders'
mission for the reorganisation of our army was invited to Constantinople. Enver Pasha had nothing to do with this affair and played no
part whatever in it.

After Mahmud Shefket Pasha's death his successor at the War
Office, Izzet Pasha, had the same idea, and took up the same line as
his predecessor. During his period of office the agreement with reference
to the mission was drawn up and concluded. On the day of the arrival
in Constantinople of Liman von Sanders and his officers they were met
at the station by Izzet Pasha and, in fact, it was a month or six weeks
after the arrival of the mission that Enver Pasha became War
Minister. . . .

The arrival of the mission in Constantinople was the signal for the
most violent attacks upon us by the Russians, French, and English.
The fact which the Russians put in the forefront of their grounds of
protest was that, if the troops appointed to guard the Straits were
commanded by German officers, the defence would be strengthened, and
that this step, adopted out of suspicion and specially directed against
Russia, would seem to ascribe ambiguous intentions to that Power.
. . . It was quite natural that the Russians should endeavour to

oppose the scheme, because they regarded themselves as the natural heirs to Constantinople, and were convinced that one day they would be engaged in a terrific struggle with the Turks on land and sea in the vicinity of Constantinople. Was their action, which meant intervention in the domestic affairs of a neighboring State, possible without the support and approval of England and France? Certainly not, I say! Under these circumstances, and remembering that in this affair the French and English shed even more tears than the Russians themselves, must we not assume that even then the Triple Entente had promised Constantinople to the Russians? Great Heavens! When I think of those days I go cold all over. I cannot describe the torments I had to go through in the discussions with the French Military Attaché (etc.). One day I ended up with the words:

"Just look how unreasonable you are, gentlemen! . . . Every country has armed forces of three kinds—first, the army, then the navy, and, thirdly, the police. We have entrusted the organisation of the first to the Germans, that of the second to the English, that of the third to the French. So where's the quarrel? . . ."

(b) *The Russian Ambassador at Berlin to Sazonov. Nov. 21, 1913*[1]

. . . Emperor William has described in detail, to the Secretary of State, the political situation in the Balkans arising from the most recent occurrences, which, according to His Majesty's view, might lead to still further complications, especially on the part of Bulgaria —"and of Greece," the Secretary of State added. The Emperor insisted on the necessity of preserving the Turkish Realm in its present form, to which both the Czar of Russia, as well as the King of England, had agreed during their last visit to Berlin. Emperor William then mentioned the request which the Turkish Government had addressed to Germany and England, asking them to send the necessary officials and instructors to Turkey in order to reorganize the administration.

King George declined this request, and merely consented to send English naval officers to Constantinople. "Whilst I have been compelled to give my assent to the despatch of army instructors," said the Emperor, "I was unable to act otherwise, even if it were only for the reason, that our former 20 years' activity has not met with success, and has resulted in many reproaches being levelled against Germany; and no less for the reason, that Turkey would have appealed to another Power, which no doubt would have granted the request of the Turkish Government."

The Emperor added, that it might possibly have been more advantageous for Russia if French officers had undertaken this task, but for Germany this would have meant too distinct a moral defeat. Kokowtzeff replied to this, that such a moral defeat of Germany would

---

[1] B. De Siebert and George Abel Schreiner, editors. *Entente Diplomacy and the World,* No. 781, pp. 676-7. Reprinted with the permission of George A. Schreiner.

not have corresponded with the interests of Russia, since she is linked to Germany by ties of traditional friendship. The Emperor expressed to him his sincere thanks for these words.

Thereupon Secretary of State Kokowtzeff sought to convince the Emperor, that the best way out of the present difficult situation would be to revert to the former idea of ordinary instructors, to which the Emperor replied with animation, that this would indeed be impossible for the reason that this kind of former experiment had been entirely unsuccessful.

At the present period, the instructors must have the necessary power to reëducate the Turkish officers, and to drag them out of the political mire in which they are so engrossed with politics as to forget the duties of their service.

Only the power of military command can accomplish this. You are already acquainted with the arguments of our Secretary of State against the concentration of a model troop detachment in Constantinople, as well as the perfectly sincere explanation of the Emperor that he had conceived the whole question from a totally different point of view, and that nothing was farther from his mind than to cause Russia any kind of difficulties whatsoever.

When Secretary of State Kokowtzeff mentioned that the German Military Mission might perhaps take up quarters at Adrianople, I ventured to point out to him, that this would probably cause great excitement in Bulgaria, and still further estrange this country from us; for this reason, Smyrna, or any other town in Asia Minor, at a certain distance from the Armenian frontier, would be a suitable place for the German officers.

(c) *The Russian Ambassador at Berlin to Sazonov. Dec. 2, 1913*[1]

A misunderstanding has arisen in the course of the exchange of telegrams between Paris and London. Grey has agreed with Pichon, that the enquiry in question is to be addressed to the Sublime Porte by all three Ambassadors in Constantinople,—those of Russia, England and France. Grey believes the notes must be identical, but that they must not be handed in simultaneously. Grey believes that it would be better if the negotiations in Berlin were for the time being conducted by us alone.

(d) *Sazonov to the Russian Chargé d'Affaires at London, Dec. 7, 1913*[2]

Urgent. Identical to Paris

We consider it desirable that the three Ambassadors should at once address themselves to the Turkish Government with the following

---

[1] *Ibid.*, No. 787, pp. 680-681.

[2] *Ibid.*, No. 788, p. 681.

identical note, which has been drawn up according to the English proposal. We have desisted from mentioning the Dardanelles, since it is clear from the Iradé [proclamation of the Sultan of Turkey] that they are not under command of the German general.

As to the compensations, we shall mention them only later, after having agreed as to their nature. Please, ask the Minister to send necessary instructions to the Ambassador in Constantinople.

Text of the Note:

"The fact that the command over the Turkish Army Corps in Constantinople has been entrusted to a German general would create for him a position which hitherto, neither a German, nor any other, officer has ever occupied in Constantinople. As a result, the whole diplomatic Corps would be in the power of Germany. Besides, the German General would be in a position to take military measures which might call the sovereignty of the Sultan in question. The actual guarantee of the integrity of the Turkish Realm, which consists in the balance of Powers, would have vanished. Indeed, if Germany should obtain such a privileged position in Constantinople, the other Powers would be forced to safeguard their interests in Turkey."

(e) *Paraphrase of a telegram from Sir E. Grey to the British Ambassador at Constantinople. Dec. 9, 1913*[1]

I have seen the Russian Ambassador, who informs me that Sazonoff is desirous of making a communication to the Sublime Porte concerning the German military command. I am of the opinion that every Ambassador should make this communication separately and verbally and that this communication should have the following contents:

We have heard that a German general has been given a very effective and far-reaching command in Constantinople; we hear that this command would create for him a position which hitherto has been occupied by no foreign officer in Turkey. We assume that Turkey would do nothing, by which the independence of the Turkish Government, or the safety of the Straits and Constantinople, would be brought into question. Other Powers, however, are very much interested in this question, and we should be glad to have the Sublime Porte communicate with us, concerning the agreement which has been concluded with the German general, in order to be able to define the function he is to perform and the position he is to occupy.

(f) *The Russian Ambassador at Constantinople to Sazonov. Dec. 15, 1913*[2]

The Grand Vizier has given me the following answer today. General Liman has been appointed Chief of the Military Mission, Member of

---

[1] *Ibid.,* No. 792, pp. 683-684.
[2] *Ibid.,* No. 805, p. 690.

the War Council, with the right to one voice only, Inspector of Schools and Commander of the First Army Corps.

The First Army Corps has been selected, because the Secretary of War intends to make it a model army corps, to which the officers of the other army corps are to be sent. Under these conditions, it will be more convenient to concentrate these school sections in the city. The Command over the Army Corps will be purely technical. The Straits, the Fortifications, and the preservation of order in the Capital, are not within the competency of the General. These, as well as the declaration of the state of siege, are directly dependent upon the Secretary of War. In the General's contract, it is not stated that in case of a state of war he will be appointed Commander of the city. Such an appointment will depend upon the Minister of War.

(g) *The Russian Ambassador at Constantinople to Sazonov.* *Dec. 20, 1913*[1]

Wangenheim told me, yesterday, in strict confidence that he had enquired at Berlin last evening, whether he might make me the following proposal. But as he had not received any answer as yet, he would request me not to make any use of this communication for the present. In consequence of this, I earnestly request you to regard this telegram as strictly personal and confidential.

After consulting upon the situation that has arisen, Wangenheim and Liman have come to the conclusion, that there is no necessity for the General to command the Army Corps, if there are only a sufficient number of troops to give the military schools an opportunity for practical exercises; a German general would command the army corps in Adrianople.

The technical details of a compromise of this sort could be arranged by the Russian military agent in conjunction with his German colleague, or with General Liman's Chief of Staff.

Wangenheim merely requests that a certain time be left him—about a month—so that public opinion in Germany, and in Turkey, does not receive the impression that Germany was forced to yield to us. He asserts, moreover, that he had twice proposed such a compromise to the Turks, but he had met a refusal on their part, and a certain time must elapse, before he would succeed in bringing them to a different frame of mind. I replied to the German Ambassador, that one must attempt to come to a solution as quickly as possible, as, otherwise, the excitement of public opinion might increase still further, and lead to new complications. I do not believe what the Ambassador says regarding the twofold refusal of the Turks. Personally, I consider the solution proposed as acceptable, if the number of troops placed at the disposal of Liman would be limited as much as possible. Should Wangenheim be

---

[1] *Ibid.*, No. 814, p. 694.

empowered to make a proposal of this sort, I would deem it desirable that our press should refrain from all too violent attacks upon Germany during the negotiations.

(h) *The Russian Ambassador at Berlin to Sazonov. Confidential letter, Jan. 16, 1914*[1]

As you may have already seen from my last telegram, the question of the German Military Mission is about to be solved, and if the rumour mentioned by the evening papers be correct: that General Sanders has been appointed a Turkish Field Marshall and Inspector General of the Turkish Army, his relinquishment of the command of the First Army Corps is already an accomplished fact. The point at issue will now be, to ascertain, whether we are to content ourselves with this concession.

I asked the Secretary of State for Foreign Affairs, whether the division stationed at Scutari was commanded by a Turkish General, and upon Jagow's remarking, that he had not occupied himself with this question, which would, moreover, signify a new demand on the part of Russia, I replied, that I had already directed his attention, previously, to the impossibility of leaving the command of so important a section of an army corps as a division, to a German officer, and that I was surely not in error in saying, that this was also the opinion of the Russian Government. The Secretary of State replied, with some animation, that, after the Berlin Cabinet had so plainly shown that it wished to meet the Russian demands, and after it had removed all the difficulties that stood opposed to it, he, Jagow, was not in a position to make any addition to the important concessions already made. Furthermore, nothing was known to him as to the division at Scutari.

It is possible, that in conjunction with the appointment of a Turkish Corps Commandant, the division mentioned will also be commanded by a Turkish officer. Perhaps, however, the German Government does not at once wish to yield to us in this question, after having already given us satisfaction in the question of the Corps Command. In any case, we shall hardly succeed in attaining more here in Berlin, and should the Russian Government, nevertheless, insist upon removing the German Divisional Commander, then I must repeat my opinion, that we must, for the time being, content ourselves with the yielding attitude displayed in Berlin, and might later on attempt to achieve our aims in Constantinople.

I must needs declare that the Berlin Cabinet has actually done everything in its power in order to fulfil our justifiable wishes, and this has not been easy for it, in view of the newspaper campaign directed against the Government. The appointment of General Sanders, as a General of Cavalry is, as I was told by the Secretary of State, a quite unusual occurrence, since he had no claims to an advance in rank

---

[1] *Ibid.*, No. 836, pp. 706-708.

before the expiration of a year. Jagow requested me to communicate this to you in strict confidence, as he does not wish his statements to get into the press.

One must, however, not lose sight of the fact that General Liman's relinquishment of the command of the First Army Corps is only a formal concession. The General retains his decisive influence upon the military questions of Turkey. But this was clear from the beginning, for according to my opinion, we have now to deal with the fact, that during von der Goltz Pasha's time, nobody in Turkey desired serious military reforms,—whereas now, after the failures of the last war, all have recognized the necessity of reorganizing the Turkish army, in order to protect Turkey in the future from further conquests and ultimate collapse.

If this, however, be the real sentiment of Turkey, then General Liman will naturally succeed, no matter what position he may occupy, in concentrating the entire military power in his hands.

On the other hand, it appears to me, that one must reckon with the unstable nature of the Turks, and their inborn hatred of Europeans. All Turkish generals and officers who are dissatisfied with the preferential position of the Germans—and their number has grown considerably since the days of Enver Pasha—will scarcely reconcile themselves to the new order of things, and it is possible, that, in the immediate future, events will occur in Turkey, which will not only jeopardize the position of the German Military Mission, but also the existence of the Turkish Empire.

(i) *Report of Kokovtsef, Russian President of the Council of Ministers and Minister of Finance, November 19, 1913*[1]

Russian View of the German Military Mission to Turkey

When I decided upon my trip to Berlin, I considered that my visit ought to have but a single object, as I have already informed Your Imperial Majesty, namely, to be presented to the German Emperor to offer him my thanks for having bestowed upon me the Superior Prussian Order of the Black Eagle.

In reality, it was necessary for me to take part in a matter on which Your Imperial Majesty had deigned to bestow most particularly His very High Attention. The day of my arrival at Berlin, the Minister of Foreign Affairs addressed to me, through our ambassador, a request. He wished to explain fully to me with the German Chancellor and even, if that was possible, with Emperor William, a project studied by the German Government of sending to Constantinople a special military mission with the purpose of organizing a Turkish select corps which would be under the command of the officers of the

[1]*Un Livre Noir*, Vol. II, pp. 411-416. Reprinted with the permission of the Librairie du Travail.

mission. The documents which were presented to me initiated me for the first time into this question. They showed from the first that the plan of the German Government had come to our knowledge at a very recent date, exactly at the moment of the presentation by our Minister of Foreign Affairs of a very humble report at Livadia, then that this plan, conceived according to every appearance long before, had not been the object of explanations between the Chancellor of the German Empire and the Foreign Minister Sazonof before the journey of the latter to Berlin.

The explanations exchanged on this subject, those with the Chancellor as much as those with the Emperor, left me under the impression that this project was born in the spring of the current year and that the Chancellor, according to his statement in a very frank conversation, had scarcely had knowledge of it. He had learned merely that the Turkish Government had addressed to Germany the request to undertake the instruction of the Turkish army, that this question had been touched upon by the German Emperor in a private conversation with Your Imperial Majesty at the time of his stay in Berlin in the month of May of last year, and that to the principle of this project Your Majesty had made no objection, in view of the fact that German officers had served as instructors in the Turkish army for twenty years without interruption; but finally the subsequent direction given this question in the sense of an organization of a select army corps under German command, with its headquarters in the capital of Turkey, had remained completely unknown to Herr von Bethmann-Hollweg and had been developed in the military institutions of the Empire.

The Imperial Chancellor did not hide from me in our repeated and quite sincere conversations how particularly distressing for him was the possibility of the thought that he had taken part in the preparation of a project which was disagreeable to Russia and that he had not informed our Minister of Foreign Affairs in time.

"In the four years I have held the office of Imperial Chancellor," Herr von Bethmann-Hollweg told me, "I have made every effort to avoid, in the relations of the two neighboring Empires, united by traditional bonds of friendship and confidence, every occasion of the least misunderstanding, and my honesty serves as a guarantee that I would never lend a hand to a disloyal act toward Russia." In the course of the conversation between the Imperial Chancellor and myself I had the impression that he was entirely sincere and I am not likely to fall into a mistake of judgment, if I may take the liberty of saying that the very idea of an army corps at Constantinople under the command of German officers was in reality unknown to Herr von Bethmann-Hollweg, at least until the last days before my arrival, or even in part by my own explanations.

As regards the principles of the question, I strove to throw light upon our point of view as far as I could. I drew the attention of the Chancellor to the fact that we took no offence at a German military mission for the instruction of the Turkish army. We understood very well that the appeal of Turkey, after the disasters she has sustained, to her former instructors, represented in itself for Germany a certain moral satisfaction and makes us understand that the German Government could not reply to Turkey by a refusal. It was still more comprehensible that Germany could not have tolerated the thought of being replaced in Turkey by French instructors, that such a request of Turkey to Austria-Hungary would have been still less desirable for us, that the English Government, having already undertaken to direct the rehabilitation of the Turkish navy, could not undertake the same rôle in the army also, and consequently it was evident that the continuation of the former relations between Germany and Turkey not constituting in itself anything essentially new, could not have been accepted by Your Imperial Majesty in other than a very benevolent fashion. I thereupon took the liberty of explaining in all sincerity that evidently Your Imperial Majesty had only had knowledge of the project to send a mission of instruction. But our point of view must completely change on the subject of command by Germany of an army corps at Constantinople. Without even approaching the question of knowing up to what point the formation of a select corps under German command could be regarded as a serious menace to Russia, I showed Herr von Bethmann-Hollweg that such a command could not fail to give rise to the most serious doubts on our part. In concert with Germany and the other Powers, we strove to preserve the remnants of the Turkish Empire in Europe with Constantinople within its power, at the moment when Bulgaria was on the point of triumphantly entering its walls. We regarded this as a delay in the solution of the Eastern question, and found that the relinquishment of the Straits in the hands of Turkey was, for the present, what was most desirable, not only for Russia, but for all Europe, and we grounded this view on the principle that Constantinople ought to remain a Turkish capital, in the maintenance of which all the great Powers are equally interested.

The formation of an army corps commanded by a German general and by officers dependent upon him gives to this question a totally different aspect. The ambassadors of the great Powers are thus placed under the protection of Germany alone. On the occasion of the least complications, the quelling of disorders is entrusted to this military force and Germany in fact seizes the rôle of maintaining order and security at Constantinople. I added to my reflections, that probably other Governments would not be less disturbed than Russia at this turn in the affair. And to the number of unsolved political conflicts is disastrously added still a new one second to no other in its intensity. In concluding my long conversations with the German Chancellor, I summed up all the reflections which I had presented to him under the form of a demand with an alternative: either to renounce completely the command of Turkish military forces, replacing the command by the organization of a supervision somewhat like the arrangement which existed before, or, if this should appear impossible because of the obligations of Germany toward Turkey, to concentrate the select corps not at Constantinople but at some other point, for example, at Adrianople, or in Asia Minor, but naturally neither on our frontier nor in the sphere of French special interests.

My explanations on this subject with the German Emperor began in quite a natural way and the initiative for them came not from me but from His Majesty.

. . . The Emperor William began his interview with me by showing that he regarded at present the restoration of Turkey and the maintenance of its integrity as one of the most important problems imposed on Europe. He then reminded me that at the time of the interview of May of the present year, Your Imperial Majesty as well as the King of England had deigned to share his point of view and had recognized the necessity of coming to the aid of Turkey, and of reëstablishing her disorganized military organization. With this end in view he had consented, upon the request of Turkey, to send a special military mission, at the head of which he had placed General Liman, one of the ablest generals of the German army. Such consideration for me on the part of His Highness gave me the opportunity of explaining in all sincerity all the arguments which I had developed in my two interviews with the Chancellor. I had the impression that my remarks were disagreeable to the German Emperor. He hastened to declare that he could in no way understand how one could even entertain the idea of any menace whatsoever for powerful Russia on the part of a Turkey profoundly shaken, that the previous system of instruction and inspection could only result in the most complete disasters and that he could in any case not consent to renew them. Finally, after I had repeated, with the greatest frankness, the conclusions on the subject of the position of the Russian Government on the question of the command of a corps at Constantinople, he told me that this idea did not originate with Germany, that it had been put forward by Turkey herself but that he was ready to reëxamine the question of the choice for this corps of another place than Constantinople. The last words of His Majesty gave me occasion to state that if such was the origin of the project of an army corps at Constantinople under German command, it seemed to me so much easier to admit a modification of this plan and to make a concession to so natural a desire on the part of Russia.

To remove all misunderstanding on this subject I transmitted to Herr von Bethmann-Hollweg all my remarks to the German Emperor and then I made known to the French Ambassador at Berlin, M. Cambon, all the details of my negotiations. Not without some astonishment on my part, I learned from the French Ambassador that the question of the military mission had been broached to him by the Turkish Ambassador, Mahmoud Moukhtar Pasha, but that the details relative to the army corps, and in particular to the choice of Constantinople as the general headquarters, were apparently unknown to M. Cambon.

What will be the further course of this affair I cannot indicate to Your Majesty further than that it should be the subject at an opportune time of reports of the Minister of Foreign Affairs, but I shall not hide from His Majesty that my explanations at Berlin have left me with a feeling of disquiet and give me reason think that the German Government will not easily yield, if it yields at all, the position which it has taken.

It is to be regretted in any case that we have been informed so lately of such an enterprise, to which it would have been easier to give another form at its inception than now when we have before us every appearance of a matter nearly concluded. In any case I believe that it is my just duty to bear witness again to Your Imperial Majesty that in all my exchanges of views, I have never found any reason to accuse the German Chancellor of ill-will and of lack of candor toward us.

48. AUSTRIAN POLICY IN THE BALKANS[1]

[A leading German statesman of Austria, Dr. Baernreither, wrote to his friend, Max Furstenberg (an intimate of Emperor William II), a report on his observations in Bosnia just after the beginning of the First Balkan War. A part of this letter and an entry from his diary are here reproduced.] . . . .

The pro-Austrian Prime Minister of Serbia, Milovanovitch, was in Vienna in 1909 to secure from Aehrenthal a concession for the importation of Serbian meat—in vain. I had a searching conversation with him at that time, and informed Aehrenthal of every word of it, meantime urging him to hold out some positive hope to Serbia. Milovanovitch sought some definite assurance from Austria in case things in Macedonia should come to a head—a definite word, a sign of good will. But Aehrenthal answered: "My policies deal only with the present; the future will take care of itself." When I came back from Belgrade a year later and pointed out to him the necessity of strengthening the pro-Austrian groups in Serbia by meeting them halfway, and of abandoning the timid policy of limiting meat importations, he replied: "Bulgaria means more to me than Serbia." He actually took it ill that I had gone especially to Belgrade. He was perpetually speaking of the Serbs in the tone Vienna used towards the Prussians before 1866: "they need a few good sound whacks." The monstrous error of his policy lay in the fact that while he did not come to grips with the Serbs and crush them—a course which might have produced some good—neither did he take the only other course remaining and come to an understanding with them as to what, under Prime Minister Milovanovitch, their desires really were.

[1] Josef Redlich, "Hapsburg Policy in the Balkans before the War," *Foreign Affairs,* July, 1928, Vol. VI, pp. 649-651. Reprinted with the permission of *Foreign Affairs.*

At that time the Serbians might have been ours, and by admitting a greater number of pigs and oxen we might have achieved a friendship that now we must go out and seek for. . . .

Vienna, December 21, 1912

Professor Masaryk hunted me up yesterday. He has been in Belgrade three times recently and called to tell me about his experiences. As I saw that what he was doing was important I asked him to describe everything to me from his notes, which he kindly consented to do.

The first time he went to Belgrade it was at the suggestion of the editor of the *Neue Freie Presse*, Moritz Benedikt. He talked with Finance Minister Pachu and came to Budapest, where the Delegation was still in session, charmed with the idea of a Serbian corridor. The second time he was in Belgrade was early in December, when he had several conversations with Pashitch. In the first place, both of them were in general agreement that relations between the Monarchy and Serbia must be improved. Pashitch spoke of his willingness to curb the Serbian press, but they came to no definitely formulated plan. Then just when Masaryk was getting ready to leave, on December 10, Pashitch had him come once more and developed a quite detailed plan, leaving it to Professor Masaryk's discretion whether or not to communicate it to Berchtold—by which he meant: "Please go to Count Berchtold and tell him what I am saying now."

According to Masaryk's notes, Pashitch declared himself as follows:

1. Serbia will and must remain completely independent both politically and economically, but we can enter into the best possible friendly relations with Austria.

2. We wanted to divide Albania, but we accommodate ourselves to Austria's desire for an autonomous state as proof of our willingness to meet Austria's wishes.

3. We are asking Austria for a harbor and for territory sufficient to provide a corridor to the harbor.

4. We are ready to give all possible guaranties and to pledge ourselves never to fortify it, not to place it at the disposal of any other Power, nor to cede it.

5. We are willing to make all possible economic concessions, to give Austria first consideration in everything, to conclude a commercial treaty in 1917, to give Austria first consideration in all loans, to abolish tariff discriminations, and to give favored treatment to Austria in deliveries. If matters cannot be adjusted along these lines we shall nevertheless maintain a correct attitude, wage no war to get the harbor, but create an outlet by way of Saloniki, attach ourselves economically to the Balkan Confederation, and buy nothing from Austria.

Pashitch will also be ready to consider Austria's prestige, is ready to come to Vienna and present his desires in person, and to negotiate with regard to them.

Masaryk came to Berchtold with these proposals on December 12. It is quite comprehensible that the latter assumed a reserved attitude and did not involve himself in the economic questions without further consideration. The main question, whether Pashitch should come to Vienna, he answered in the negative, while he went over with Masaryk the same ground that he went over with me a day later. Masaryk, however, was disappointed over the answer and did not know what to think. He came to my house but did not find me, as I was away from Vienna; talked with some South Slav friends and Wickham Steed, of the London *Times*; and then went off to Belgrade. He apprised Pashitch of the negative results of his journey and, it seems, disappointed him too. This final conversation with the Serbian Prime Minister took place on December 17. Meantime various papers printed the news—which, however, did not attract much attention—that Berchtold had deliberately discouraged a visit from Pashitch. This is the story as Masaryk told it to me yesterday.

49. Grey-Cambon Letters on Anglo-French Naval and Military Coöperation, 1912[1]

[To meet the increases in the German navy, the British fleet was concentrated in home waters. This was facilitated by the fact that France wished to concentrate her fleet in the Mediterranean to deal with the combined fleets of her prospective foes, Austria and Italy. Her Atlantic and Channel coasts thus left unguarded, France counted upon the British fleet to defend. A closer political, military, and naval understanding between France and England was deemed necessary under these new circumstances, and the entente was accordingly defined in an exchange of letters between the British Secretary of State for Foreign Affairs and the French Ambassador in London. Grey's repeated statements that Great Britain was left free have been seriously challenged; while literally true, perhaps, still as various members of the British Cabinet pointed out, the military conversations were dangerous in the encouragement they gave the French, while the new arrangement of the navies created for England a moral obligation to defend the French coast no matter how war should arise.]

Foreign Office,
November 22, 1912

My dear Ambassador,

From time to time in recent years the French and British naval and military experts have consulted together. It has always been understood that such consultation does not restrict the freedom of either

---

[1] France, *Ministère des affaires étrangères. Documents diplomatiques. 1914. La Guerre Européenne.* No. 159, pp. 167-9. For Eng. trans. see: Great Britain, Foreign Office. *Collected Diplomatic Documents relating to the Outbreak of the European War.* 1915, pp. 260-261.

Government to decide at any future time whether or not to assist the other by armed force. We have agreed that consultation between experts is not, and ought not to be regarded as, an engagement that commits either Government to action in a contingency that has not arisen and may never arise. The disposition, for instance, of the French and British fleets respectively at the present moment is not based upon an engagement to co-operate in war.

You have, however, pointed out that, if either Government had grave reason to expect an unprovoked attack by a third Power, it might become essential to know whether it could in that event depend upon the armed assistance of the other.

I agree that, if either Government had grave reason to expect an unprovoked attack by a third Power, or something that threatened the general peace, it should immediately discuss with the other whether both Governments should act together to prevent aggression and to preserve peace, and, if so, what measures they would be prepared to take in common. If these measures involved action, the plans of the General Staffs would at once be taken into consideration, and the Governments would then decide what effect should be given to them.

Yours, etc.,

E. GREY

To this letter our Ambassador, M. Paul Cambon, replied on the 23rd November, 1912:—

London, November 23, 1912

Dear Sir Edward,

You reminded me in your letter of yesterday, 22nd November, that during the last few years the military and naval authorities of France and Great Britain had consulted with each other from time to time; that it had always been understood that these consultations should not restrict the liberty of either Government to decide in the future whether they should lend each other the support of their armed forces; that, on either side, these consultations between experts were not and should not be considered as engagements binding our Governments to take action in certain eventualities; that, however, I had remarked to you that, if one or other of the two Governments had grave reasons to fear an unprovoked attack on the part of a third Power, it would become essential to know whether it could count on the armed support of the other.

Your letter answers that point, and I am authorised to state that, in the event of one of our two Governments having grave reasons to fear either an act of aggression from a third Power, or some event threatening the general peace, that Government would immediately examine with the other the question whether both Governments should act together in order to prevent the act of aggression or preserve peace. If so, the two Governments would deliberate as to the measures which they would be prepared to take in common; if those measures

involved action, the two Governments would take into immediate consideration the plans of their general staffs and would then decide as to
the effect to be given to those plans.

Yours, etc.,

PAUL CAMBON

50. FRANCO-RUSSIAN MILITARY CONFERENCE, 1913[1]

[This extract shows the close coöperation of the French and Russian
general staffs and the extent of their preparations for a war with
Germany.]

Ninth Franco-Russian Military Conference. August, 1913

. . . Preamble (Accepted without observation by the conferees).

The two chiefs of staff declare jointly that the words "defensive
war" should not be interpreted in the sense of "war which will be conducted defensively." They state on the contrary the absolute necessity
of the Russian and French armies taking a vigorous and as far as
possible simultaneous, offensive according to the text of article 3 of
the Convention, by the terms of which "the forces of the two contracting powers bind themselves fully and thoroughly."

Article I. The same observations as in the 1910 and succeeding conferences, thus stated: "The two chiefs of staff, in accordance with the
point of view of preceding conferences, are in perfect accord on the
point that the defeat of the German armies remains, whatever the
circumstances, the first and principal objective of the Allied armies."
Completed as follows: "And this still more than formerly, by reason
of the considerable increase of the relative military power of Germany
in the Triple Alliance."

Article II. Same observations as in the 1910, 1911, and 1912 conferences . . .

"Just as the Russian and French Governments recognized in 1911
and 1912, German mobilization obliges Russia and France to mobilize
immediately and simultaneously all their forces at the first news of the
event and without need of a previous agreement." *It will be the same
for every act of war of the German Army against one or the other of
the allied powers.* But in case of partial mobilization, or even general,
of Austria or Italy alone, this agreement is indispensable.

The italicized phrase has been added to cover the case of an unexpected attack of covering forces preceding the mobilization, with the
intention of seizing an important strategical point.

Article III. Sharing the opinion of their predecessors, the conferees,

---

[1]*Un Livre Noir,* Vol. II, pp. 432-433; 435. Reprinted with the permission of the
Librairie du Travail.

To Republicans

That there was sentiment in France in favor of an understanding with Germany is shown by the poster on the opposite page. *Le Bonnet Rouge* (The Red Cap) was an extreme revolutionary journal working for pacifism. The poster reads as follows:

To Republicans

A poisoned atmosphere hangs over the country. The French people have lost confidence even in themselves. Reaction again takes the offensive and the Republic knows anew the attack of the *Calottes*.

The reason?

The powerlessness of the Republic to make good its promises.

The Republic has an excuse: if it has not realized all the hopes that the people have placed in it and met all its engagements, it is because since its birth a terrible evil has depressed the world: the folly of armaments. Caught in the whirlwind, France has had to follow, and it can be said that the Republican régime has certainly prevented us going further into this madness, but the hour has come to put an end to it.

All, or nearly all, of the national wealth falls into the bottomless pit of the budget for war. Money for social reforms, money to insure internal development and prosperity is lacking. No progress is made. France suffers and is exhausted. A general uneasiness obstructs commercial and industrial activity. A crisis is near. A collapse is probable.

The solution to avoid catastrophe?

Peace, peace solidly and definitively established.

The means to assure the peace of the world?

Franco-German Understanding

For fear of Germany, France made the Triple-Entente.

For fear of the Triple-Entente, Germany arms herself ceaselessly.

To establish equilibrium France, Russia and England increase their armaments in proportion.

Menaced by these formidable forces, all the other countries enter the infernal round of armaments.

Thus is being prepared the most horrible slaughter the world has ever known.

Wisdom demands, then, the Franco-German understanding which will stop the nations in their race to death and will permit the redirecting toward productive ends a part of the sums absorbed in the preparation of war.

What Is It That Opposes This Understanding? Economic Antagonism? The Desire for Revenge?

It is proved that the economic interests of France and Germany are more and more closely bound together. It is equally proved that the idea of revenge is repellent to the French people as a whole, and that the Alsatians and Lorrainers themselves regard it as a monstrosity.

We have made the entente with England and only a dozen years ago. England was for the French the "hereditary enemy," "perfidious Albion," which it was necessary to attack and subjugate. Remember the cry of "Aoh Yes!" cast as a slur on the democrats suspected of dreaming of an understanding with England . . . Canada . . . Fashoda . . . Fashoda was a more serious injury for us than Agadir.

We have forgotten; in a few months opinion has been reversed, the entente-cordiale is made, and no one would dare maintain that it was not a great benefit.

Why should not forgetfulness develop in connection with our differences with the Germans?

It is not possible that the remembrance of the war of 70–71 should hang eternally over the policy of France. Those who by their incitements feed the discord between the two countries are either fools or miserable fishers in troubled water.

Peace is the essential condition of human development.

Nothing in the order of social reforms and of great industrial and commercial achievements will be made unless the peace of the world is assured.

World peace will be assured only by a Franco-German understanding.

Conclusion

The next French Chamber ought to have a majority favorable to a Franco-German *rapprochement*.

Republicans who are zealous for a great and noble Republic; Democrats who dream of giving to the workers greater well-being; merchants who hope to work in calm and security tomorrow; voters, all powerful by virtue of the ballot, force the candidates to show their position on the question, and vote only for those who will agree to bring about this great work of public safety.

Le Bonnet Rouge

[This poster was dated by locating the two articles advertised. It is reproduced by permission from the Hoover War Library.—Editors.]

AUX RÉPUBLICAINS

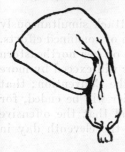

Une atmosphère empoisonnée pèse sur le pays. Le peuple français a perdu confiance jusqu'en lui-même. La réaction reprend l'offensive et la République connaît de nouveau l'assaut des Calottes.

La raison ?

L'impuissance de la République à réaliser ses promesses.

La République a une excuse ; si elle n'a pas réalisé toutes les espérances que le peuple avait mises en elle et tenu tous ses engagements, c'est que depuis sa naissance un mal terrible s'est abattu sur le monde ; la folie des armements. Prise dans le tourbillon, la France a dû suivre, et l'on peut dire que le régime républicain nous a certainement empêché d'aller plus avant dans la démence. Mais l'heure est venue d'en finir.

Toute la richesse nationale, ou presque, tombe dans le gouffre du Budget de la guerre. De l'argent pour les réformes sociales, de l'argent pour assurer le développement et la prospérité intérieurs, il n'y en a pas. Plus rien ne marche. La France souffre et s'épuise. Un malaise général entrave l'activité du Commerce et de l'Industrie. Une crise est prochaine. Une débâcle est probable.

La solution pour éviter la catastrophe ?

La Paix, la Paix solidement et définitivement établie.

Le moyen pour assurer la paix du monde ?

Le rapprochement franco-allemand.

Par peur de l'Allemagne, la France a fait la Triple-Entente.

Par peur de la Triple-Entente, l'Allemagne arme sans discontinuer.

Pour établir l'équilibre, la France, la Russie et l'Angleterre augmentent à mesure leurs armements.

Menacés par ces deux formidables états, tous les autres pays entrent dans la ronde infernale des armements.

Ainsi se prépare le plus épouvantable égorgement que le monde ait jamais connu.

La sagesse exige donc le rapprochement franco-allemand qui arrêtera les nations dans leur course à la mort et permettra de reporter sur des œuvres de vie une partie des sommes absorbées par la préparation à la guerre.

Qu'est ce qui s'oppose à ce rapprochement ? L'antagonisme économique ? Le désir de la revanche ?

Il est prouvé que les intérêts économiques de la France et de l'Allemagne sont de plus en plus étroitement liés. Il est également prouvé que l'idée de revanche est repoussée par l'ensemble du peuple français et que les Alsaciens-Lorrains eux-mêmes la regardent comme une monstruosité.

Nous avons fait l'entente avec l'Angleterre et pourtant il n'y a pas douze ans l'Angleterre était pour les Français l'ennemie héréditaire, la perfide Albion - qu'il fallait abattre et réduire. Rappelez-vous : Le cri de « Noh Yes ! » lancé comme un outrage aux démocrates soupçonnés de rêver un accord avec l'Angleterre... Le Canada... Fachoda... Fachoda fut pour nous une injure plus grave qu'Agadir.

Nous avons oublié ; en quelques mois l'opinion a été retournée, l'entente cordiale s'est faite, et nul n'oserait soutenir que ce ne fût pas un grand bienfait.

Pourquoi l'oubli ne se ferait-il pas sur nos différends avec les Allemands ?

Il n'est pas possible que le souvenir de la guerre de 70-71 pèse éternellement sur la politique de la France. Ceux qui par leurs excitations entretiennent la discorde entre les deux pays sont des fous ou de misérables pêcheurs en eau trouble.

La paix est la condition essentielle du développement humain.

Rien dans l'ordre des réformes sociales et des grandes réalisations industrielles et commerciales ne se fera tant que la paix du monde ne sera pas assuré.

La paix du monde ne sera assurée que par le rapprochement franco-allemand.

CONCLUSION

La prochaine Chambre française doit avoir une majorité favorable au rapprochement franco-allemand.

Républicains qui ambitionnez une République grande et généreuse; démocrates qui rêvez de donner aux travailleurs une large part de bien-être; commerçants qui aspirez à travailler dans le calme et la sécurité du lendemain : électeurs tout-puissants par la vertu du bulletin de vote, forcez les candidats à se prononcer sur la question et ne votez que pour ceux qui prendront l'engagement de réaliser cette grande œuvre de salut public.

LE BONNET ROUGE.

[February 21, 1914.]

in full agreement, think that Germany will direct the greatest part of her forces against France and will leave only a minimum of forces against Russia.

The putting into application of the German military law of 1913 will have for its principal consequence the reduction of delays in the mobilization of the German army. This army can then have more time than in the past to operate against France before returning against Russia.

The Allies' plan ought then to be to strive to attack simultaneously on both sides at once, while exercising the maximum of combined efforts.

General Joffre declares that France will engage on her northeastern frontier nearly all her forces, of which the number will exceed by more than 200,000 men that stipulated in the text of the Convention; that the concentration of the combatants on the frontier will be ended, for the most part, the tenth day of mobilization; and that the offensive operations of this group of forces will begin on the eleventh day in the morning.

General Gilinsky declares that Russia will engage against Germany a group of forces reaching 800,000 men at least, of which the concentration of combatants on the Russo-German frontier will be ended for the most part the fifteenth day of mobilization, and that the offensive operations of this group of forces will begin immediately after the fifteenth day. At the end of the year 1914 the end of concentration will be advanced about two days. . . .

As regards the conduct of operations, it is of supreme necessity that the allied armies obtain a decisive success as rapidly as possible. A repulse of the French armies at the beginning of the war would allow Germany to bring to her eastern frontier part of the forces which had been fighting against France. But if the French armies obtain a rapid success against the German forces, this success will greatly facilitate the operations of the Russian armies since the forces led by Germany to her western frontier cannot possibly be brought back towards the east.

It is then essential that the French armies should have a marked numerical superiority over the German forces in the west. These conditions will easily be realized if Germany is under the obligation of guarding her eastern frontier with more forces. . . .[1]

51. THE HOUSE MISSION, 1914

[On the eve of the war, a private American citizen, Edward House, whose only relevant title was "personal friend of the President," set out for Europe in an attempt to bring together the Great Powers, whom he saw clearly to be headed for the abyss. The following selections, the first from his diary (entry of June 1, 1914), and the second

---

[1] The picture of diplomatic alliances at this time (1913) is supplemented by doc. No. 5.

his letter to the Kaiser, give his account of the "Great Adventure," as he termed his mission. House was appalled by the militarism of Berlin. He reported: "Everybody's nerves are tense. It only needs a spark to set the whole thing off." The aim of his mission was to secure an understanding between England, Germany, and the United States to maintain peace.]

(a) *Extract from House's Diary*[1]

"Afterwards we adjourned to one of the larger drawing-rooms, where I was presented to the Empress. We talked of Corfu, the beauty of Germany in the spring, and other generalities. When this formality was over, the Kaiser's Aide-de-Camp came to say that His Majesty was ready to receive me on the terrace. . . .

"I found that he had all the versatility of Roosevelt with something more of charm, something less of force. He has what to me is a disagreeable habit of bringing his face very close to one when he talks most earnestly. His English is clear and well chosen and, though he talks vehemently, yet he is too much the gentleman to monopolize conversation. It was give-and-take all the way through. He knew what he wanted to say, so did I; and since we both talk rapidly, the half-hour was quite sufficient.

"Gerard and Zimmermann stood in conversation some ten or fifteen feet away, quite out of hearing. At first I thought I would never get His Majesty past his hobbies, but finally I drew him to the subject I had come to discuss. . . . I found him much less prejudiced and much less belligerent than von Tirpitz. He declared he wanted peace because it seemed to Germany's interest. Germany had been poor, she was now growing rich, and a few more years of peace would make her so. 'She was menaced on every side. The bayonets of Europe were directed at her,' and much more of this he gave me. Of England, he spoke kindly and admiringly. England, America, and Germany were kindred peoples and should draw closer together. Of other nations he had but little opinion. . . .

"He spoke of the impossibility of Great Britain being able to make a permanent and satisfactory alliance with either Russia or France. I told him that the English were very much concerned over his ever-growing navy, which taken together with his enormous army constituted a menace; and there might come a time when they would have to decide whether they ran more danger from him and his people making a successful invasion than they did from Russia, and the possibility of losing their Asiatic colonies. I thought when that point was reached, the decision would be against Germany.

---

[1] Charles Seymour, editor, *The Intimate Papers of Colonel House*, Boston, Houghton Mifflin. Vol. I, pp. 254-257. Reprinted by permission of, and by arrangement with, Houghton Mifflin Company.

"I spoke of the community of interests between England, Germany, and the United States, and thought if they stood together the peace of the world could be maintained. He assented to this quite readily. However, in my opinion, there could be no understanding between England and Germany so long as he continued to increase his navy. He replied that he must have a large navy in order to protect Germany's commerce in an adequate way, and one commensurate with her growing power and importance. He also said it was necessary to have a navy large enough to be able to defend themselves against the combined efforts of Russia and France.

"I asked when he would reach the end of his naval programme. He said this was well known, since they had formulated a policy for building and, when that was completed, there would be an end; that Great Britain had nothing to fear from Germany, and that he personally was a friend of England and was doing her incalculable service in holding the balance of power against Russia.

"I told him that the President and I thought perhaps an American might be able to better compose the difficulties here and bring about an understanding with a view to peace than any European, because of their distrust and dislike for one another. He agreed to this suggestion. I had undertaken the work and that was my reason for coming to Germany, as I wanted to see him first. After leaving Germany it was my purpose to go directly to England, where I should take the matter up with that Government as I had done with him.

"I explained that I expected to feel my way cautiously and see what could be accomplished, and, if he wished it, I would keep him informed. He asked me to do this and said letters would reach him through our friend Zimmermann here in the Foreign Office." . . .

(b) *House's Letter to the Kaiser*[1]

Colonel Edward M. House to Emperor William

London, July 8, 1914

Sir!

Your Imperial Majesty will doubtless recall our conversation at Potsdam, and that with the President's consent and approval I came to Europe for the purpose of ascertaining whether or not it was possible to bring about a better understanding between the Great Powers, to the end that there might be a continuation of peace, and later a beneficent economic readjustment, which a lessening of armaments would ensure. Because of the commanding position Your Majesty occupies, and because of your well-known desire to maintain peace, I came, as Your Majesty knows, directly to Berlin. I can never forget the gracious acceptance of the general purposes of my mission, the masterly exposition of the world-wide political conditions as they exist

---

[1] *Die Grosse Politik,* Vol. XXXIX, p. 113 (in English).

today, and the prophetic forecast as to the future which Your Majesty then made. I received every reasonable assurance of Your Majesty's cordial approval of the President's purpose, and I left Germany happy in the belief that Your Majesty's great influence would be thrown in behalf of peace and the broadening of the world's commerce. In France I tried to reach the thoughts of her people in regard to Germany and to find what hopes she nursed. My conclusion upon leaving was that her statesmen have given over all thought of revenge, or of recovery of the two provinces. Her people in general still have hopes in both directions, but her better-informed rulers would be quite content if France could be sure of her autonomy as it now exists. It was then, Sir, that I came to England and with high hopes, in which I have not been disappointed. I first approached Sir Edward Grey, and I found him sympathetic to the last degree. After a two hours' conference, we parted with an understanding that we should meet again within a few days. This I inferred to mean that he wished to consult with the Prime Minister and his colleagues. At our next conference, which again lasted for two hours, he had to meet me, the Lord Chancellor [Lord Haldane], Lord Crewe, and Sir William Tyrrell. Since then I have met the Prime Minister and practically every important member of the British Government, and I am convinced that they desire such an understanding as will lay the foundation for permanent peace and security. England must necessarily move cautiously lest she offend the sensibilities of France and Russia; but, with the changing sentiment in France, there should be a gradual improvement of relations between Germany and that country which England will now be glad to foster. While much has been accomplished, yet there is something still to be desired in order that there may be a better medium created for an easy and frank exchange of thoughts and purposes. No one knows better than Your Majesty of the unusual foment that is now going on throughout the world, and no one is in so fortunate a position to bring about a sane and reasonable understanding among the statesmen of the Western peoples, to the end that our civilization may continue uninterrupted. While this communication is, as Your Majesty knows, quite unofficial, yet it is written in sympathy with the well-known views of the President, and, I am given to understand, with the hope from His Britannic Majesty's Government that it may bring a response from Your Majesty which may permit another step forward.

Permit me, Sir, to conclude by quoting a sentence from a letter which has come to me from the President: "Your letter from Paris, written just after coming from Berlin, gives me a thrill of deep pleasure. You have, I hope and believe, begun a great thing and I rejoice with all my heart."

I have the honour to be, Sir, with the greatest respect, Your Majesty's very obedient Servant,

EDWARD M. HOUSE

52. ANGLO-GERMAN AGREEMENTS ON QUESTIONS IN THE NEAR EAST, 1914

[The Turkish Petroleum Agreement and the Bagdad Railway Convention form parts of a Near Eastern Anglo-German understanding of 1914. By the terms of the former the British were to control a large majority of the oil interests in Mesopotamia and the Germans to content themselves with a minority, for while the Deutsche Bank was a German institution, all of the others mentioned were British with the exception of the Royal Dutch, and that came under British oversight when Deterding was made a British subject in 1915. It will be noticed that the agreement was signed by governmental representatives as well as financial leaders. In December, 1918, British control was still further increased when the German interests were expropriated. By the San Remo Agreement of April 25, 1920 (see doc. no. 163), these German interests were handed over to France. Gulbenkian was a Turkish subject.

The Bagdad Railway convention, initialed on June 15, 1914, was a delimitation of interests in Asiatic Turkey and would have constituted a complete settlement of the controversy that had been waged for more than ten years over railway construction in Mesopotamia had there not come the crisis of July to interfere with the signing of the treaty.]

(a) *Turkish Petroleum Agreement, March 19, 1914*[1]

Agreements for Fusion of Interests in Turkish Petroleum Concessions of the d'Arcy Group and of the Turkish Petroleum Company

It is agreed that the interests shall be divided as follows:

Fifty per cent to the d'Arcy group,
Twenty-five per cent to the Deutsche Bank,
Twenty-five per cent to the Anglo-Saxon Petroleum Company,
  [A Subsidiary of the Royal Dutch and Shell Companies, controlling 60% and 40% of the shares, respectively.]
and that, in order to carry out this division,

1. The shares in the Turkish Petroleum Company now held by the National Bank of Turkey shall be transferred in equal moieties to the Deutsche Bank and the Anglo-Saxon Petroleum Company.

2. The capital of the Turkish Petroleum Company shall be increased to £160,000 by the creation of 80,000 new shares of £1 each of the same class as those now existing.

---

[1] Text in appendix to article by E. M. Earle, "The Turkish Petroleum Company," *Political Science Quarterly*, Vol. XXXIX, pp. 265-279 (1924). Reprinted with the permission of the *Political Science Quarterly* and of E. M. Earle.

3. These 80,000 new shares shall be allotted to the d'Arcy group on terms to be agreed upon between the parties.

4. The Board of the Company shall consist of eight members, of whom four will be nominated by the d'Arcy group, two by the Deutsche Bank, and two by the Anglo-Saxon Company.

5. The capital of the Turkish Petroleum Company shall be employed only in exploring, testing, and proving oil fields, a separate public company or companies being formed to work any field or fields the examination of which has proved satisfactory.

6. Such working company or companies shall issue to the Turkish Petroleum Company fully paid ordinary shares as consideration for the properties to be acquired; such ordinary shares shall carry full control of the working company or companies, which control shall in no circumstances be parted with by the Turkish Petroleum Company.

7. The working capital required by such working company or companies shall be raised by means of preference shares and (or) debentures which shall be offered to the public to such extent as the members of the Turkish Petroleum Company or any one of them shall elect not to subscribe for themselves.

8. The alterations in the memorandum and (or) articles of association of the Turkish Petroleum Company necessary to carry out the above conditions shall be made forthwith.

9. Mr. C. S. Gulbenkian shall be entitled to a beneficiary five per cent interest without voting rights in the Turkish Petroleum Company, this five per cent being contributed equally by the d'Arcy group and the Anglo-Saxon Company out of their respective holdings. The shares representing Mr. Gulbenkian's interest shall be registered in the names of nominees of the d'Arcy group and of the Anglo-Saxon Company, and shall be held by them, but undertakings shall be exchanged between these parties whereby

(1) Mr. Gulbenkian undertakes to pay the calls on the shares, and

(2) The d'Arcy group and the Anglo-Saxon Company undertake that Mr. Gulbenkian shall be [entitled to] all financial benefits of the shares.

(3) If Mr. Gulbenkian shall desire to dispose of this interest, and also in the event of his death, the d'Arcy group and the Anglo-Saxon Company shall have the option of purchasing the interests standing in their names as defined in Article 36 (b) of the articles of association of the Turkish Petroleum Company.

10. The three groups participating in the Turkish Petroleum Company shall give undertakings on their own behalf and on behalf of the companies associated with them not to be interested directly or indirectly in the production or manufacture of crude oil in the Ottoman Empire in Europe and Asia, except in that part which under the administration of the Egyptian Government or of the Sheikh of Koweit, or in the "transferred territories" on the Turco-Persian frontier, otherwise than through the Turkish Petroleum Company.

For the Imperial German Government
R. von Kühlmann
For His Britannic Majesty's Government
Eyre A. Crowe
For the National Bank of Turkey
H. Babington Smith
For the Anglo-Saxon Petroleum Company, Ltd.
H. Deterding
Walter H. Samuel
For the Deutsche Bank
C. Bergmann
For the d'Arcy Group
C. Greenway
H. S. Barnes

The Foreign Office (London)
19 March, 1914

(b) Bagdad Railway Convention, 1914[1]

[After the preamble, the convention runs:]

Article 1. (a) In recognition of the general importance which the construction of the Bagdad Railway possesses for international trade, His Britannic Majesty's Government binds itself not to adopt or to support any measures which might render more difficult the construction or management of the Bagdad Railway by the Bagdad Railway Company or to prevent the participation of capital in this enterprise.

(b) The Imperial German Government declares that it will use its best endeavors to have elected to the Board of Directors of the Bagdad Railway Company, as representatives of the British shareholders, two English members acceptable to His Britannic Majesty's Government.

Article 2. (a) Whereas the Bagdad Railway Company has entered into an agreement with the Imperial Ottoman Government on the following basis, the Imperial German and His Britannic Majesty's Governments declare, in so far as they are concerned, (their intention) to uphold this agreement and to use their best efforts that the terms thereof may be regularly complied with:

(I) The terminus of the lines of the Bagdad Railway is to be Basra. The Bagdad Railway Company has renounced the construction of the branch line from Basra (Zobeir) to the Persian Gulf, provided for in Article 1 of the Bagdad Railway Convention of March 5, 1903, and the construction of a port or a terminal on the Persian Gulf in accordance with Article 23 of the aforesaid Convention.

(II) On the lines of the Bagdad Railway Company, as hitherto, no direct or indirect discrimination in transit facilities or freight rates shall be made in the transportation of goods of the same kind between

---

[1] *Ibid.,* Vol. XXXVIII (1923), pp. 29-35.

the same places, either on account of ownership or on account of origin or destination of the goods or because of any other consideration.

(III) The Bagdad Railway Company agrees that any changes in the conditions of transportation or in freight rates, as set forth in Article 21 of the Specifications (of 1903) always shall be announced two months in advance. The announcement shall be published in the Official Journal of the Imperial Ottoman Government and in the Official Bulletin of the Ottoman Chamber of Commerce in Constantinople.

(IV) Should a branch line be constructed from Basra to the Persian Gulf, appropriate agreements shall be made to facilitate through traffic from and to the railhead of the Bagdad Railway, and full guarantees shall be provided against direct and indirect discriminatory treatment.

(V) The proposed port works in Basra and Bagdad, which were authorized by Article 23 of the Bagdad Railway Convention of March 5, 1903, are to be constructed and administered by a special Ottoman company.

The Port Company shall not collect tolls or duties of any kind or any description from ships or goods, except such as are imposed equally under the same circumstances and in similar cases on all ships and goods, regardless of the nationality of the ships or their owners, or of the owners of the goods, their country of origin or destination, and regardless of the place from which the ships or goods come or whither they are bound. . . .

The rights conferred upon the Port Company shall in no way hinder or interfere with the said Commission in the fulfilment of the tasks conferred upon it by the Anglo-Turkish agreement of July 29, 1913.

(b) The Imperial German Government declares that it will raise no objections to British interests acquiring 40 per cent of the capital of the separate Ottoman Company for the construction and operation of the ports of Basra and Bagdad as mentioned above under (V); or to their being represented on the Board of Directors (*Conseil d'Administration*) of the Port Company in proportion to their participation; or to their sharing in contracts for the construction or maintenance of the port.

Article 3. (a) The Imperial German and His Britannic Majesty's Governments declare that under no circumstances will they support the construction of a branch from Basra (Zobeir) or any other point on the main line of the Bagdad Railway to the Persian Gulf, unless a complete understanding be previously arrived at between the Imperial Ottoman, the Imperial German, and His Britannic Majesty's Governments.

(b) The Imperial German Government declares that it will under no circumstances undertake the construction of a harbor or a railway station on the Persian Gulf or support efforts of any persons or companies directed towards this end, unless a complete agreement be previously arrived at between the Imperial German and His Britannic Majesty's Governments.

(c) His Britannic Majesty's Government declares that under no circumstances will it undertake railway construction on Ottoman territory in direct competition with lines of the Bagdad Railway Company or in contravention of existing rights of this company or support the efforts of any persons or companies directed to this end, unless previously a complete agreement be arrived at between the Imperial German and His Britannic Majesty's Governments. For the provisions of this article the western terminus of the Bagdad Railway lines is considered to be Konia, the eastern terminus, Basra.

Article 4. (a) The Imperial German Government has taken official note of the declaration promulgated by the Imperial Ottoman Government on July 29, 1913, concerning the navigation of the Tigris and Euphrates and declares that it will neither raise objections to the execution of this declaration nor support any action directed against its execution as long as the navigation of these rivers is maintained in accordance with the principal provisions of the declaration.

(b) His Britannic Majesty's Government declares that it will raise no objections if the shareholders of the Bagdad Railway acquire 40 per cent of that part of the capital of the Ottoman River Navigation Company which is to be assigned to Ottoman interests at the first issue (*i.e.*, 20 per cent of the total capital). . . .

Article 5. [Both Powers pledged themselves unreservedly to observe the principle of the economic open door.]

Article 6. The Imperial German and His Britannic Majesty's Governments will together use their good offices with the Imperial Ottoman Government to the end that the Shatt-el-Arab shall be brought into a satisfactory navigable condition and permanently maintained in such condition so that ocean-going ships may always be assured of free and easy access to the port of Basra, and further, that the shipping on the Shatt-el-Arab shall always be open to ocean-going ships, under the same conditions to ships of all nations, regardless of the nationality of the ships or their cargo. . . .

Article 9. Any differences in opinion resulting from this Convention or the Explanatory Note attached thereto are subject to arbitration. If the two governments cannot agree on an arbitrator or a special court of arbitration, the case shall be submitted to the Permanent Court of Arbitration at the Hague.

Article 10. The present Convention and the attached Note shall be ratified and the deeds of ratification shall be exchanged within three months after the date of signature.

In witness whereof the plenipotentiaries on both sides have signed the present Convention and attached their seals.

Made in duplicate in London on the ———————

Initialled in London, on the 15 day of June, 1914.

L. [ichnowsky]

E. [dward] G. [rey]

[In the Explanatory Note, His Britannic Majesty's Government pledged itself to support an increase in the customs duties of the Ottoman Empire from 11% to 15% *ad valorem* and, furthermore, to "raise no objection to the assignment to the Bagdad Railway Company of already existing Turkish State revenues, or of revenues from the intended increase in tariff duties, or of the proposed monopolies or taxes on the consumption of alcohol, petroleum, matches, tinder, cigarette-paper, playing cards, and sugar to the extent necessary for the completion of the Railway."]

53. A GERMAN REACTION TO RUSSIAN WAR REPORTS, 1914

[The nervous tension due to fear of war existing in Europe on the eve of the World War is well shown in the following document, as is also the importance of the action of Germany and England in time of crisis.]

The Imperial Chancellor, Bethmann-Hollweg, to the German Ambassador at London, Prince Lichnowsky, Berlin, June 16, 1914[1]

It will not have escaped your attention that the article in *Birschewija Wjedomosti,* as we know conclusively traced back to the Minister of War, General Sukhomlinoff, has aroused a considerable sensation in Germany. In fact hardly any officially inspired article has ever so brazenly revealed the warlike tendencies of the Russian militarist party as does this utterance of the press. For the purpose of the lasting stimulation of French chauvinism it is indeed too clumsily written. On the other hand, the reactions upon German public opinion are unmistakable and unfortunate.

While up to the present only the most extreme Pan-German and militaristic circles attributed to Russia deliberate preparation for an early attack upon us, now calmer opinion among public men is inclining toward this view. The first consequence is the cry for a new, immediate, and extensive strengthening of the army. Thereby, as things are in Germany, the rivalry of the navy will be aroused, for the latter will never permit itself to be left behind when anything is done for the army. And I may confidentially tell you that since His Majesty the Kaiser has already accustomed himself to this way of thinking, I apprehend for the summer and fall a recurrence of the preparedness fever among us.

Though in the uncertainty of Russian conditions the real aims of Russia cannot with sureness be made out and though we must take into account in our political arrangements that Russia, of all the European Great Powers, will be most inclined to run the risk of a warlike adventure, nevertheless I do not believe that Russia is planning war against us in the near future. Protected as she is by her extensive

---

[1] *Die Grosse Politik,* Vol. XXXIX, pp. 628-630.

military preparations, Russia, one can hardly blame her, wishes to act more forcefully in the event of another Balkan crisis than she did in the last. Whether the situation will then come to a European conflagration will depend exclusively upon the attitude of Germany and England. If we both then combine in guaranteeing European peace, which the obligations of neither the Triple Alliance nor the Entente will not hinder *in so far as we follow this aim in accordance with a common plan from the outset*, war will be prevented. Otherwise any conflict of interests, even a subordinate one, between Russia and Austria-Hungary, can light the torch of war. A foresighted policy must contemplate such an eventuality in time.

Obviously a heightened activity of the German chauvinists and preparedness fanatics would as much hinder German-English coöperation as an undecided attitude of the English Cabinet would encourage French and Russian chauvinism. Germany will never be able to forego an extension of its army corresponding to the increase of its population. An extension of its naval law is not contemplated. But quite within the limits of the naval law, the further bringing into service of foreign cruisers, the arming and manning of battleships, etc., will demand continually mounting expenditures. It makes a great difference, however, whether such measures appear as the necessary consequence of gradual development or whether they are undertaken in a panicky manner under the pressure of an excited public opinion filled with anxiety regarding war.

That Sir Edward Grey has in the Lower House decidedly opposed the rumors of an Anglo-Russian naval convention and underscored his flat denial in the *Westminster Gazette* is altogether gratifying. If these rumors had been confirmed and even so if they only had referred to a formula providing for Anglo-Russian naval coöperation in case of a future war between these two countries and Germany—similar to the agreement which England made with France in the Moroccan crisis —not only would Russian and French chauvinism have been strongly excited, but a disturbance, not unjustified, of our public opinion would have occurred, which would have found expression in a "navy scare" and a renewed poisoning of our gradually improving relations with England. In the midst of this nervous tension in which Europe has found itself in recent years, the further consequences would have been incalculable. At any rate, the idea of the common mission in guarantee of peace of England and Germany in the event of possible complications would have been seriously endangered from the outset.

I respectfully request you to express to Sir Edward Grey my special gratitude for his frank and direct explanations and to add in a casual and cautious manner those general considerations which I have suggested.

I anticipate with special interest your kind report of your reception by Sir Edward Grey.

VON BETHMANN-HOLLWEG

PART II

THE IMMEDIATE ORIGINS OF THE WAR

JUNE–AUGUST, 1914

54. An Account Explaining the Serbian Situation at the Time of the Murder at Serajevo[1]

[Vidov Dan, June 28, the anniversary of the battle of Kossovo in 1389, was celebrated as a national Serb festival, and was the day of the assassination of the Archduke Francis Ferdinand, heir to the Austrian throne. Jovanovič's revelation of the criminal negligence of the Serbian Government, though violently discussed in the Serbian press, has not so far been officially denied, and in the absence of Serbian documents, is generally accepted as accurate.]

At the outbreak of the World War I was Minister for Education in M. Nikola Pašič's Cabinet. I have recently written down some of my recollections and some notes on the events of those days. For the present occasion I have chosen from them a few extracts, because the time is not yet come for everything to be disclosed.

I do not remember whether it was at the end of May or the beginning of June, when one day M. Pašič said to us—he conferred on these matters more particularly with Stojan Protič, who was then Minister of the Interior; but he said this much to the rest of us—that there were people who were preparing to go to Serajevo to kill Francis Ferdinand, who was to go there to be solemnly received on Vidov Dan [St. Vitus's Day.] As they afterward told me, the plot was hatched by a group of secretly organized persons and in patriotic Bosno-Herzegovinian student circles in Belgrade. M. Pašič and the rest of us said, and Stojan agreed, that he should issue instructions to the frontier authorities on the Drina to deny a crossing to the youths who had already set out from Belgrade for that purpose. But the frontier "authorities" themselves belonged to the organization, and did not carry out Stojan's instructions, but reported to him—and he afterward reported to us—that the order had reached them too late, for the young men had already got across.

Thus the endeavor of the Government to prevent the execution of the plot failed, as also did the endeavor made on his own initiative by our Minister in Vienna, M. Joca Jovanovič, in an interview with the Minister Bilinski, to dissuade the Archduke from the fatal journey that he contemplated. And so the attempt at Serajevo was to be carried out,

[1] Ljuba Jovanovič, "More Light on Serajevo," in *The Living Age*, Vol. 325, p. 305ff. May 9, 1925. Translated from *Krv Slovenstava* (The Blood of Slavdom) for the British Institute of International Affairs, and originally published in the Institute's Journal and in the London *National Review* for April, 1925. Reprinted with the permission of *The Living Age*.

in more terrible measure than had been anticipated, and with results that no one could then have pictured even in his wildest dreams. . . .

On the afternoon of Vidov Dan I was in my house on the Senjak. About five o'clock an official telephoned to me from the Press Bureau and told me what had happened at noon at Serajevo. Even though I knew what had been prepared there, nevertheless I felt, as I held the receiver, as though some one had dealt me an unexpected blow; and when a little later the first report was confirmed from other quarters, I began to be overwhelmed with grave anxiety.

Not for a moment did I doubt that Austria-Hungary would make this the occasion for declaring war upon Serbia; and I considered that the position both of the Government and of the country in regard to other States would now become very difficult, and in every way worse than after May 29, 1903 [when King Alexander and Queen Draga were murdered], or during the time of our more recent disputes with Vienna and Budapest. I was afraid that all the European Courts would feel themselves individually the target of Princip's bullets, and would hold aloof from us, with the approval of the monarchist and conservative sections in their countries. And even if it did not quite come to that, who would dare to stand up in our defense? I knew that neither France nor, still less, Russia was in a position to measure herself with Germany and her allies on the Danube, because their preparations were not to be complete before 1917. It was this that more especially filled me with anxiety and fear.

The most terrible thoughts crowded in upon me. This began at five o'clock on the Sunday of Vidov Dan, and continued day and night, except during a few fitful moments of sleep, until Tuesday forenoon. Then my young friend, Major N——, of the Ministry of Education, came to see me. He was uneasy, but he was not in despair as I was. I poured out my apprehensions to him without restraint or reflection. He at once said to me, in the tone usual to him on such occasions, that is to say, pleasantly and quietly, but with complete conviction:—"My dear Minister, I think that it is quite unnecessary to despair. If Austria-Hungary wants to declare war on us—well, let her! It would have had to come to that anyhow sooner or later. The present is a very inconvenient moment for us. But it is not now in our power to choose the moment; and if Austria has chosen it, well, let it be so. It may well turn out badly for us, but who knows? It may perhaps be otherwise."

I was, I think, beside myself at that moment; but these words of his, I declare, quite pulled me together, and I began to recover; and remembering what he had said to me, I little by little began to think clearly, and never afterward was I so overcome by events as during those two days.

My chief concern now was, what echoes of the Serajevo affair would be heard from Europe? Happily, from the Petrograd press—and so far as it was concerned we could assume in advance that it represented the official view—we received the first favorable reports: it took up our defense against the Austria-Hungarian accusations. Russia, then, would not deny us or pass by on the other side. After Russia would come her friends. And so by degrees it turned out. In this respect we were appreciably helped by the 'pogroms' against Serbs, fomented or winked at in Bosnia, Croatia, and Dalmatia. The impartial world could now see how the Serbs, whom the Austria-Hungarian press represented as a people whose turpitude passed all measure, were, on the contrary, themselves the victims of her injustice and her inhumanity.

We could now breathe a little more freely again. But Vienna also began to get to work. It is true that the representatives of the dynasty, and Court circles in general, except those few who were directly stricken, did not greatly mourn the murdered heir apparent and his wife, and made little attempt at concealment, and even, to some extent, paraded their sentiments at his funeral in Vienna. In fact, with the disappearance of Francis Ferdinand, the Imperial House was freed from a serious domestic difficulty and the State from a difficult and involved constitutional problem that threatened seriously to embroil the relations between the Austrian and Hungarian portions of the monarchy and to give rise to endless internal troubles.

For this reason there were, even in Belgrade, people who seriously hoped that our neighbors would, if only for form's sake, cry out a little against us, and then let the matter drop. But, not content with all these favorable consequences of the Serajevo murder, the Austria-Hungarian rulers were evidently bent on exploiting even the event itself and on squeezing the utmost profit out of it, to the detriment of the Serbs and of Serbia, not only in their own country, but also abroad. In particular, they used the greatest efforts through the Vienna Press Bureau to influence the press at home and in Europe, and in fact everywhere.

I was in the same way a witness of the efforts they made to use the event with the greatest profit to their internal situation, and to have the best possible excuse for repressing and even causing damage to Serbs and other similar uncertain elements in their population. In this they found ample assistance among some of the people of our own blood, especially in Bosnia and Herzegovina, but also in Croatia, Slavonia, and Dalmatia. The aim of Vienna still was to create a movement that would draw together all those diverse peoples and unrelated facts which constitute the Hapsburg monarchy, and out of all these to form a single national soul in the face of the enemies of the Imperial House and of the State. This is what Austria-Hungary, above all, lacked. And what she and her friends continually and most of all feared —and we for our part hoped—was that in some great war she would be unable to appear as she appeared in 1866 in the war with Prussia and Italy. I now saw with apprehension how the rulers of our enemy were cleverly repairing this natural defect, and how they were preparing their otherwise patchwork 'people' for unanimous and enthusiastic foreign action, in the first place against Serbia.

It became all the clearer to me what Austria-Hungary had in mind for us. From her side there began to be uttered the word 'war.' There were many signs and events that told me that Germany stood firmly beside Austria-Hungary. I had, however, even before this, become convinced that Germany had determined not to allow Russia and France to complete their preparations for war, upon which Russia was actively working, but to anticipate them in her preparations and herself take the initiative in beginning armed hostilities. That unusual vote of extraordinary military credits to the amount of a milliard marks all pointed in this direction, as indeed the whole world had immediately seen. I myself had the impression in the course of the spring that Germany was beginning to look for a pretext for a quarrel with the French Government; and I was from that moment convinced that Berlin would, out of some trifle or other, manufacture a dispute in which to find occasion for a trial of arms with France and Russia, if she could not find anything more suitable elsewhere.

Princip and his friends had now provided her with such an occasion, and I therefore thought that neither Germany nor Austria would let such an opportunity slip; only that now all the fury of the first attacks would fall, not upon France or some other, but upon Serbia.

My colleagues believed, on the contrary, that war could be avoided, and they therefore decided—altogether in the spirit of the policy of our friends and ourselves—to avoid it. Such satisfaction as must be given to Austria-Hungary should be given to her, and the struggle would thus be postponed until a time when we should again be ready for a fight such as that from which we had issued with glory and great acquisitions the previous summer. The Ministers all worked with this intention. When the Austrian stories arrived from Vienna to the effect that the assassins had received directions in Serajevo from an official of the Serbian Ministry of Public Works, a certain Milan Ciganovič, M. Pašič asked M. Joca Jovanovič, then in charge of that department, who this official of his was; but M. Joca knew nothing about him, nor did anybody in his department. Under pressure from M. Pašič, they at last unearthed Ciganovič in some small clerical post in the railway administration. I remember that somebody, either Stojan or Pašič, said, when Joca told us this: 'There, you see! It is true enough what they say: if any mother has lost her son, let her go and look for him in the railway administration.' After that we heard from M. Joca that Ciganovič had gone off somewhere out of Belgrade. And Stojan set on foot some inquiries from his side. Among other things, there was found at Belgrade post office, *poste restante*, a post card from Serajevo, which one of the conspirators had before Vidov Dan addressed to one of his colleagues in Belgrade.

From all this it might have been expected that Vienna would be unsuccessful in establishing any connection between official Serbia and the event on the Miljacka. M. Pašič therefore hoped that we should somehow pull ourselves through this crisis, and he made efforts, in which he was supported by all the rest of us, to preserve as far as possible the relations which we had so far established, in order that Serbia might get through as cheaply as might be with the unhappy task of giving satisfaction to Austria-Hungary, and that she might recover as quickly as possible from the blows which in such a case were bound in any event to fall upon her.

It is recognized that the Government did not fail to do everything that was possible to show to its friends and to the rest of the world how far removed we were from the Serajevo conspirators. Thus, on the very first evening upon which it was known what Princip had done, Stojan gave orders under which the Belgrade police prohibited music, singing, and every kind of amusement in public places; everything was suspended, and there was, as it were, a period of official mourning. M. Pašič expressed to the Vienna Government our regret at the loss which had befallen a great neighboring Power, and his execration at the deed itself. At the requiem in the Catholic church in the grounds of the Austria-Hungarian Legation on June 20 (July 3), the day upon which the murdered heir apparent and his wife were buried in Vienna, the Government was represented by several Ministers. I myself was of the number. I wished to testify that even I, who more than any of the others might have been thought to approve of Princip's deed, was, on the contrary, entirely in agreement with what our Cabinet was doing. Nevertheless, both my action in going there and the short period during which we were in the church were unpleasant to me. I felt myself among enemies, who did not desire peace with us.

It may be that the root of these feelings and premonitions of mine lay in the thoughts and sentiments which had formed themselves in my mind from my earliest youth. I was all my life taught to look out for evil in everything that Austria did, no matter how or where. I was, therefore, very naturally, in all probability more sensitive to the signs which were likely to betray her and her intentions. Consequently, both there in the church and in every other place, there grew within me the conviction that Austria-Hungary would not be content with any kind of satisfaction, and that she would declare war upon us. She would certainly not let slip this opportunity, as she had—in the opinion of those circles with whom much of the blame for it lay—let slip the opportunity at the time of the annexation crisis (1908-1909) and of the Albanian crisis (1913).

There now befell the sudden death of Nikola Hartwig, Russian Minister to Serbia, which took place in the Austrian Legation itself. His death was a terrible blow to me and to many another Serb also, all the more so as the late Minister and I were intimate, and as I knew how much we owed to him and how much more we might have hoped from him; but Belgrade felt itself especially hit. At first people round about town believed that his host, Baron Giesl, had simply poisoned him, and there arose in consequence a kind of fury against the Baron and the whole Dual Monarchy. No stupidity or infamy on the part of

Austria would have surprised me, but I knew that Hartwig had a very weak heart and took no care of himself, so I asked what the doctors said, and they declared that he had died a natural death. This reassured the more reasonable sections of the public, but the people in the Austria-Hungarian Legation began to be alarmed. They began to complain that demonstrations and assaults and murders were being planned against them and their citizens. Every hour they came to the Ministry to protest and to ask for protection. An attack of this kind was, for example, to be expected on the occasion of Hartwig's funeral, and we took measures to meet any eventuality. I myself, when the procession left the church for the cemetery, kept close beside Giesl— on the one hand, in order that I might by so doing discourage any assassin who might perhaps be sorry for it if I should suffer as well as the Austrian, and on the other hand in order to assure him that there was nothing to be afraid of. All the same, we breathed again when everything passed off without mishap and when Austria-Hungarian lies on the subject had once more been put to shame.

Our enemies, as everybody now knows, concealed their intentions very astutely. When we heard that Kaiser Wilhelm had put out from Kiel on his usual cruise to the North, I hesitated between two opinions: either he was quite sincerely thinking no evil, or, on the contrary, desired to deceive the world, feigning to be unaware of what was being prepared. Immediately after this, Francis Joseph himself made a move and went back to the waters at Ischl, and this also might mean peace. In fact, on that same day there was held in Vienna a council of the 'joint Ministers,' at which the Chief of the General Staff and a representative of the Navy were also present; and Count Berchtold immediately followed the Emperor to Ischl, presumably to submit a report of the meeting. But, in order that this might not be unfavorably interpreted, a *communiqué* was issued in which it was stated that the meeting had been concerned with the preparation of the new Budget, and that the Chief of the General Staff and the representative of the Navy had therefore been summoned in order to report on certain technical questions connected with the Budget. The only effect upon me of such 'candor' on the part of Vienna was, on the contrary, to make me more anxious than ever.

To speak frankly, it is still a marvel to me that serious statesmen of the great friendly Powers could at that time have been so deceived. Sazonov took the whole thing very lightly. Spalajkovic reported to us on July 5 (July 18): 'A few days ago M. Sazonov said to me that he was surprised that the Austria-Hungarian Government had taken no steps to prevent this *sterile* activity on the part of the Vienna press, *which in the long run does no good to anybody* and does harm to Austria-Hungary herself.' One by one he allowed the Imperial Ambassadors in Vienna, Paris, and Berlin to proceed on leave of absence, and he left Hartwig's post unfilled. The French Government in the same way still kept de Kock, a very sick man, as her representative here.

The President of the Republic, Poincaré, made preparations for his visit to the Czar of Russia, and at midnight on July 2 (July 15) set out tranquilly from Paris for Petrograd. In the same way all our friends advised us to remain self-possessed and cool and to moderate our press; and naturally no one gave us any warning to be on the alert and to prepare.

This was a success for the astute Austrian Government, which now at the beginning of July, in contrast to the menacing attitude which it had adopted hitherto, assumed the part of one who harbored no evil designs. The Minister for War and Chief of the General Staff went on leave. At the Ministry for Foreign Affairs they so successfully reassured the Russian Ambassador, Shebeko, that he also went off somewhere for a holiday.

At that time Europe was indeed deaf and blind, and I had a feeling that from Vidov Dan right up to the delivery of the famous ultimatum, 'Europe,' as they say, 'did not exist.' The great Powers—Russia, France, England, and Italy—to whom, it is true, there was no immediate threat of war, took no serious step to prevent that Austria-Hungarian *démarche* in Belgrade, and in fact never had any idea that it was necessary to take any step at all. Today it is perfectly clear that the war might have been prevented if only England had declared herself in good time, and in no uncertain terms, against the projects of our enemies, and if she had threatened Berlin that she would defend France, the ally of Russia, by force of arms. This she did not do, because she would not realize the meaning of the Serbian question and the consequence for the whole world to which it would give birth.

My readers may perhaps reproach me, in writing this, for having gone back to my feelings of ten years ago. They may even have thought that I now regret that there came to pass that struggle that in the end brought unexpected good fortune to our people. But, as may be seen, I have simply recorded what then took place. . . .

55. THE SERBIAN SOCIETY "UNION OR DEATH," ALIAS "THE BLACK HAND"[1]

[The author was Serbian *Chargé d'Affaires* at Berlin.]

The organisation "Union or Death" which was founded in Serbia in 1911, included in its ranks from the outset a large number of members residing in foreign countries such as Turkey and Austria-Hungary. Its object, like that of other Serbian organisations for national propaganda, such as the Narodna Odbrana (National Defense) and Slovenski Jug (The South Slav), was to bring about the reunion of all the Serbs under the domination of the Kingdom of Serbia, the latter being regarded as the Piémont of a "Greater Serbia."

---

[1] Dr. M. Boghitschewitsch, in *Die Kriegsschuldfrage,* Vol. IV, pp. 664-689, September, 1926. Reprinted by permission.

The organisation in question was called into existence because it was thought that the Narodna Odbrana was not working energetically enough for the realisation of this national ideal. From the very start the society exerted a powerful influence on the officers of the Serbian army, in the schools, and above all on a part of the Slav population in Austria. This was natural, as its leaders were the élite of the corps of Serbian officers, the same élite who had paved the way for victory in the two Balkan wars of 1912-1913.

What made these officers so popular was in the main the fact that they were known to be scrupulously honest and uncompromisingly opposed to the system of corruption and graft that had grown up in certain political circles in Serbia,[1] and especially averse to the choice of corrupt and mediocre officials for the newly acquired provinces of Macedonia and Old Serbia. (Note: This opposition provided a dispute between the Minister of the Interior, M. Prositch, and the Officers' Corps.)

There was, however, one outstanding personality who by virtue of his remarkable qualities had more than anyone else gained a preponderating influence over the nationalist youth in the army and in the universities of Serbia and, a fact that should be carefully borne in mind, over the nationalist Serb elements in Turkey and in the Slav provinces in the south of the Austrian monarchy. Colonel Dragoutine Dimitrievitch was the head of the Intelligence Department of the General Staff and the chief instigator in the assassination of the Archduke Francis Ferdinand. He managed to bring about a reunion of the national Serbian elements in Serbia and Austria and succeeded in convincing them of the necessity of intensifying the national movement by terrorist action in all territories inhabited by Serbs living under a foreign administration.

A glance at the list of members of the organisation, whose number was much greater than that given in the statement published by the Serbian Government on the occasion of the Saloniki trial in 1917, shows how important was the organisation and what influence it must have had on social and political life in Serbia. The list, it will be observed, contains a large number of officers of high rank, holding important military positions, high officials in the various State Departments, officials in the Ministry of Foreign Affairs and in the Diplomatic Service. This adequately proves, especially when one remembers that Serbia was a comparatively small state with a population of only 4,000,000, that we are here dealing with a national movement supported by the majority of the nation and one which consequently must also have been supported by the Government itself.

We know today that the Crown Prince, the present King of Jugo-Slavia, helped to establish the journal published in connection with

---

[1] Fostered more especially by the Radical Party at the head of which was M. Pashitch.

this organisation, the *Piémont*, towards the upkeep of which he contributed 20,000 dinars. We also know that some of the members of the association were related to or on terms of close intimacy with the then Ministers of State. These Ministers must consequently have been well aware of the existence of the organisation from its very beginnings. They had even smuggled their secret agents into the organisation, in order to be kept informed in advance of its preparations and activities.

The Minister of Foreign Affairs, the late M. Milovanovitch, from 1911 on, remained in close touch with Colonel Dimitrievitch:

"Place your Black Hand at my disposal, my young friend," he one day said to him, "and you will see what Milovanovitch will accomplish in a short time for the Serbian nation."

And according to Dimitrievitch's own statement,

(Note: I obtained this from Dimitrievitch himself)

he had actually placed at his disposal important sums exclusively for propaganda against Austria-Hungary. The Colonel was also on a very friendly footing with the Chief of the General Staff, the Viovode R. Putnik. Dimitrievitch's close friendship with Colonel Artamanoff, the Russian military attaché at Belgrade, the words pronounced by M. Hartwig, the Russian Minister at Belgrade, in the presence of the Russian journalists in 1913: "The organisation "Union or Death" is the only organisation in Serbia capable of carrying into effect the Serbian national ideal," and finally the declaration made on Feb. 28, 1924, by the comrades of the late Colonel Dimitrievitch who were also sentenced at Saloniki in 1917: "The organisation "Union or Death" was a patriotic organisation whose activities were well known to the competent authorities, activities which were in accord with the intentions of the said authorities,"—all these things compel us to the conclusion that the Serbian Government and Dimitrievitch and his organisation had one and the same aim in view, viz., the creation of a Pan-Serbian state which could only be achieved by a war with Austria-Hungary.

Such being the prevalent state of mind, it is clear that in the case of a war with Austria, no matter on what pretext it might be brought about, Serbia must in any case be regarded as the aggressor.

The most categorical *démentis* on the part of the Serbian government can make no difference. It is quite grotesque for the Serbian government to wish to deny having been aware of the plan and the preparations for the assassination of the Archduke Franz Ferdinand, and it is ridiculous for it to wish to throw the entire responsibility for this crime on the organisation "Union or Death," or, what is even worse, on two of the members of the Central Committee of this organisation, Colonel Dimitrievitch and Commander Tankositch. (Note: As

Professor Stanojevitch does in his pamphlet, "L'Assassinat de l'Archduc François-Ferdinand.")

The statutes of this organisation which we reproduce below were published by the Serbian Government on the occasion of the Saloniki trial, but the Serbian Government in view of its precarious political and military situation at the time took care in order to secure itself a more favourable position in case of a separate peace with Austria and also in order to hide the truth from its allies, as the truth would have opened their eyes as to where lay the real responsibility for the war, to delete from the statutes with minute care all passages relating to propaganda and to terrorist action in foreign countries. The deleted passages are nevertheless of the utmost importance as they demonstrate in connection with the other paragraphs of the statutes that the whole action of the organisation "Union or Death" was directed against the existence and the *status quo* of certain neighbouring states, whose population was partly of Serbian origin, in order to revolutionize and finally to acquire these territories.

To understand the history of these movements one must first be familiar with the Balkan mentality. For if one observes these actions only from the juridical standpoint and through western eyes, one will never succeed in unravelling the causes and consequences of the intrigues woven in this part of Europe. One finds there a lack of logic, a lack of good faith; one meets with moral and juridical obliquities, crimes committed for noble causes, mysticism and relapses into the Middle Ages. In these countries men are at one and the same time heroes, children and criminals who commit crimes in good faith and who have rendered possible by their efforts the realisation of a national ideal but who nevertheless have done so much evil to other countries and to humanity in general.

It is comprehensible enough that the Balkan mode of procedure must from the point of view of western mentality meet with disapproval, but it is incomprehensible and odious that Serbian government circles who possess the same mentality and who were ready to act in exactly the same fashion as the members of the organisation "Union or Death" should deny their complicity and should not dare openly to avow all that these men have done towards the realisation of the national ideal.

It is extraordinary that the Austrian Government of 1914 which has been so justly detested because of its system of political and police espionage should have had no knowledge of the existence of the organisation "Union or Death" or of its influence and its activities. If the famous Austrian Ultimatum of 1914 had commenced with the words "There exists in Serbia a society called "Union or Death" which has as its object the destruction of the Austro-Hungarian Monarchy and whose members are high-placed Serbian military and civil functionaries and to which the Government and even the Crown lend moral and material assistance," I doubt very much whether the Serbian Government would have met with the support which the Entente granted it in 1914. Even the "greatest friends" of Serbia—I am quoting the words M. Poincaré addressed to the Austro-Hungarian ambassador at St. Petersburg, "la Serbie a des grands amis"—would have disapproved of such methods of procedure, unless they had been taken into confidence or were accomplices or authors in the preparation of the war.

EXTRACTS FROM THE STATUTES OF "UNION OR DEATH"

Article 1. This organisation has been created with the object of realising the national ideal: The union of all the Serbs. All Serbs without distinction of sex, religion, place of birth and all who are sincerely devoted to this cause, may become members.

Article 2. This organisation prefers terrorist action to intellectual propaganda and for this reason must be kept absolutely secret from persons who do not belong to it.

Article 3. This organisation bears the name "Union or Death."

Article 4. To accomplish its task, the organisation:

1. Brings influence to bear on Government circles, on the various social classes and on the whole social life of the Kingdom of Serbia, regarded as Piémont.
2. Organises revolutionary action in all territories inhabited by Serbs.
3. Outside the frontiers of Serbia uses every means available to fight the adversaries of this idea.
4. Maintains amicable relations with all states, peoples, organisations and individuals who entertain feelings of friendship towards Serbia and the Serbian element.
5. Lends help and support in every way possible to all peoples and all organisations struggling for their national liberation and for their union.

Article 5. A Central Committee having its headquarters at Belgrade is at the head of this organisation and exercises executive authority. . . .

Article 25. Members of the organisation are not known to each other personally. It is only the members of the Central Committee who are known to one another.

Article 26. In the organisation itself the members are known by numbers. Only the Central Committee at Belgrade is to know their names. . . .

Article 31. Anyone who once enters the organisation may never withdraw from it. . . .

Article 33. When the Central Committee at Belgrade has pronounced penalty of death [on one of the members] the only matter of importance is that the execution take place without fail. . . .

56. Austria's Success in Winning German Support

[When Berchtold had been won over by Conrad to belief in the necessity of using the murder of Francis Ferdinand as an occasion for crushing Serbia, he realized that he must obtain German support. Both the German Ambassador in Vienna and the Austrian Ambassador in Berlin had warned him of the need for the greatest caution. Berchtold accordingly drew up an ambiguous letter (a) for Francis Joseph to sign and send to Emperor William: it was intended to convince both monarchs of Serbia's responsibility for the crime of Serajevo. The Austrian view is well shown in (b) although this document had been completed just prior to the murder. The original draft of Bethmann-Hollweg's telegram giving Germany's official reply (c) to Francis Joseph's letter, had said that Germany would stand by Austria's side "under all circumstances," but the German Chancellor cautiously struck out these words drafted by Zimmermann, Acting Foreign Secretary. The Kaiser's personal reply was similar in tone.]

(a) *The Emperor of Austria to the Emperor of Germany in his own handwriting*[1]

[July 5, 1914]

. . . The perpetration of the assassination of my poor nephew is the direct result of the agitations carried on by the Russian and Serbian Panslavists, the sole object of which is the weakening of the Triple Alliance and the destruction of my realm.

According to all the evidence so far brought to light, the Serajevo affair was not merely the bloody deed of a single individual, but was the result of a well-organized conspiracy, the threads of which can be traced to Belgrade; and even though it will probably prove impossible to get evidence of the complicity of the Serbian Government, there can be no doubt that its policy, directed toward the unification of all the southern-Slav countries under the Serbian flag, is responsible for such crimes, and that the continuation of such a state of affairs constitutes an enduring peril for my house and my possessions.

This peril is increased by the fact that Roumania has contracted a close friendship with Serbia, notwithstanding her existing alliance with us, and permits within her own confines an agitation against us just as hateful as is that tolerated by Serbia.

It is hard for me to doubt the good faith and the good intentions of so old a friend as is Carol of Roumania; yet he has himself twice de-

---

[1] Max Montgelas and Walter Schücking (editors), *Outbreak of the World War, German Documents Collected by Karl Kautsky.* Translated by the Carnegie Endowment for International Peace, Division of International Law. New York, Oxford University Press, 1924. No. 13. (Hereafter cited as *Kautsky Documents.*) Reprinted with the permission of the Carnegie Endowment for International Peace.

clared to my Minister during the course of the last few months that, in the face of the excited and hostile attitude of his people, he would not be in a position to live up to the obligations of his alliance with us in case of need.

At the same time the present Roumanian Government is quite openly supporting the aspirations of the Culture League, is favoring an approach to Serbia, and is striving, with Russian assistance, toward the construction of a new Balkan alliance, which can only be aimed against my dominions.

Even at the beginning of Carol's reign, political fantasies similar to those now being disseminated through the Culture League were disturbing the sound political common sense of Roumanian statesmen, and were putting the Kingdom in danger of becoming the pawn of political gamblers. At that time it was your grandfather of blessed memory who interfered through his Government in energetic and clear-sighted fashion, and set Roumania on the path on which she won to a position of credit in Europe and became a reliable supporter of law and order.

Once again the same danger threatens the Kingdom; I fear that good counsel will not alone avail, and that Roumania can only be retained for the Triple Alliance if, on the one hand, we render the establishment of a Balkan alliance under Russian patronage impossible by binding Bulgaria to the Triple Alliance, and, on the other hand, show Bucharest plainly and clearly that the friends of Serbia can be no friends of ours, and that Roumania can no longer count herself among our allies unless she breaks off her relations with Serbia and suppresses to the extent of her power those agitations aimed at the stability of my realm from within Roumania herself.

The efforts of my government must in the future be directed toward the isolation and diminution of Serbia. The first stage of this journey should be accomplished by the strengthening of the present position of the Bulgarian Government, in order that Bulgaria, whose real interests coincide with our own, may be preserved from a relapse into Russophilism.

When it is recognized in Bucharest that the Triple Alliance is determined not to forego a union with Bulgaria, but would, nevertheless, be willing to persuade Bulgaria to go into partnership with Roumania and guarantee the latter's integrity, perhaps they will retrace there the perilous step to which they have been driven through friendship to Serbia and by the *rapprochement* to Russia.

If this effort should prove successful, we might further attempt to reconcile Greece to Bulgaria and to Turkey; thus there would develop under the patronage of the Triple Alliance a new Balkan alliance whose aim would be to put an end to the advance of the Panslavic flood and to assure peace to our countries.

This can, however, only be possible when Serbia, which at present constitutes the pivot of the Panslavic policy, is eliminated as a factor of political power in the Balkans.

You, too, must be convinced, after the recent frightful occurrence in Bosnia, that a reconciliation of the antagonism that now divides Serbia and ourselves is no more to be thought of, and that the continuance of the peace policy of all European monarchs is threatened as long as this hearth of criminal agitation at Belgrade is left unquenched.

(b) *Memorandum of the Austro-Hungarian Government*[1]

[July 5, 1914]

Confidential

After the great upheavals of the past two years, conditions in the Balkans have cleared up to a point at which it is now possible to review to a certain extent the results of the crisis, and to determine to what extent the interests of the Triple Alliance, especially those of the two Central Powers, have been affected by events, and what conclusions must be drawn to direct the European and Balkan policies of these Powers.

An impartial comparison of the situation as it exists today with that existing previous to the great crisis, compels the conclusion that, when considered as a whole and looked at from the point of view of Austria-Hungary as well as from that of the Triple Alliance, it cannot be described as at all favorable.

It is true that a balancing of the books shows us some items on the credit side of the ledger. It has been possible to create an independent Albanian State to constitute a counterweight against the Serbian pressure—a State which, after a number of years and when its internal organization has been completed, can fairly be reckoned into the calculations of the Triple Alliance as a military factor. The relations of the Triple Alliance with the enlarged and reinvigorated Kingdom of Greece have gradually assumed such a character that Greece, notwithstanding her association with Serbia, need not necessarily be regarded as hostile.

But of greatest importance is the fact that Bulgaria has awakened from the hypnotic spell cast by Russia since the developments that led to the second Balkan war, and cannot be considered today as an executor of Russian policy. On the contrary, the Bulgarian Government is attempting the achievement of a closer relationship with the Triple Alliance.

These favorable considerations are, nevertheless, balanced by others less favorable, which outweigh the former in the scales. Turkey, whose identity of interest with that of the Triple Alliance was self-evident, and which constituted a powerful counterweight to Russia and the

---

[1] *Kautsky Documents*, No. 14.

Balkan States, has been driven almost entirely out of Europe, and has suffered the loss of a material share of her standing as a Great Power. Serbia, whose policy has for years been directed by purposes hostile to Austria-Hungary, and which is wholly subject to Russian influences, has increased in area and population even far beyond its own expectations; the possibility of a further expansion of Serbia by a union with Montenegro is put within reach by its physical neighborhood to Montenegro and by the general spread of the Greater-Serbian idea. And last, during the course of the crisis, Roumania's relation to the Triple Alliance has materially altered.

While the Balkan crisis alone led to results which are in themselves far from favorable to the Triple Alliance, and which contain the germ of further developments especially unwelcome to Austria-Hungary, we can see also that Russian and French diplomacy have instituted a single-minded and systematic line of conduct aiming at the extension of the advantages already won, and at the modification of such results as, from their point of view, are disadvantageous.

A brief review of the European situation shows quite plainly why the Triple Entente—more correctly the Dual Alliance, since England has maintained a reserved attitude ever since the Balkan crisis for comprehensible and very characteristic reasons—could not remain satisfied with the rearrangement of the Balkans that was made in its favor.

While the policy of the two Empires, and, up to a certain point, the policy of Italy, is conservative, and while the character of the Triple Alliance is purely defensive, Russian policy, like that of France, pursues certain paths opposed to the existing status of affairs, and the Franco-Russian alliance, the product of the parallelism of these paths, is, after all, of an offensive character. That the policy of the Triple Alliance has so far been able to maintain itself, and that the peace of Europe has so far been preserved against disturbance by France and Russia, can be laid to the military superiority unquestionably possessed by the armies of the Triple Alliance, particularly of Austria-Hungary and Germany, over those of Russia and France—a situation in which the alliance of Roumania with the Empires constituted a very weighty factor.

The idea of liberating the Christian nations of the Balkans from the dominion of Turkey for the purpose of using them as weapons against Central Europe has been for ages past the actual political mainspring of Russia's traditional interest in these peoples. In latter times there has been developed from this idea the plan—conceived by Russia and intelligently adopted by France—of uniting the Balkan States into a Balkan alliance, in order to eliminate the military superiority of the Triple Alliance. The first requirement necessary to this plan was that Turkey should be driven out of the territories occupied by the Christian Balkan peoples, in order that the strength of those States might be increased and left free to flow westward. This requirement was satisfied, on the whole, by the recent war. On the other hand, there occurred after the completion of the war, a division of the Balkan States into two groups of nearly equal strength, Turkey and Bulgaria on one side, the two Serbian nations, with Greece and Roumania, on the other.

The next task to which France and Russia jointly set themselves, after the conclusion of the crisis, was to patch up this division in order to make use of all the Balkan States, or, at least, of a decisive majority of them, for the upsetting of the European balance of power.

As there already existed an alliance between Serbia and Greece, and as Roumania had declared herself to be in partnership with both of these two nations, at least as far as concerned the results of the peace of Bucharest, the principal business of the Dual Alliance Powers was to heal the deep antagonism of Bulgaria toward Greece, and especially toward Serbia in the matter of the Macedonian question; then to find a basis on which Roumania might be willing to go over completely into the camp of the Dual Alliance and join even with the distrusted Bulgaria in one political combination; finally, if possible, to bring about a peaceful solution of the problem of the islands, in order to bridge the way for an approach toward or a union with the Balkan States on the part of Turkey.

Concerning the basis on which the composition of these antagonisms and rivalries could be attained and the new Balkan alliance be built up, according to the plans of Russian and French diplomacy, there can be no misunderstanding. Under present-day circumstances, inasmuch as a common action against Turkey can no more be considered, an alliance of the Balkan States can only be aimed at Austria-Hungary, and could only be brought into being on the strength of a program the ulterior design of which would be to offer all participants territorial extensions by advancing their frontiers in echelon from east to west. A union of the Balkan States on any other basis is unthinkable; it is not only not precluded on this basis, but is even well on its way to become realized.

It is hardly to be doubted that Serbia would, under pressure from Russia, agree to the admission of Bulgaria into a league aimed against the Monarchy, accepting in the acquisition of Bosnia and its contiguous territories an equivalent for the price to be paid in the form of Macedonia.

The difficulties to be met at Sofia are more serious.

Russia made proposals to Bulgaria on the basis referred to above, even before the second Balkan war, and repeated them after the peace of Bucharest. Bulgaria, plainly thoroughly afraid of a union with Serbia, nevertheless refused to agree to the Russian plans, and has since pursued a policy with any aim rather than that of a peaceful understanding with Serbia under the egis of Russia. But the politicians in St. Petersburg have by no means given up the game for lost. Russian agents are working within the country itself for the overthrow of the present régime, while the diplomacy of the Dual Alliance is at the same time earnestly striving to bring about the isolation of Bulgaria in order to make her susceptible to Russian suggestion.

As Bulgaria sought and found a *rapprochement* to Turkey after the conclusion of peace, and as, on the other hand, the Porte discovered an inclination to form an alliance with Bulgaria and to enter into closer relations with the Triple Alliance, Franco-Russian influence has for some time been busily at work along the Bosphorus to counteract this Turkish policy, to draw Turkey over to the Dual Alliance and in this way to force Bulgaria to a change of face, either by means of a complete isolation or by the coöperative influence of Turkey. Reports from Constantinople, to a certain extent corroborated by Talaat Bey's visit to Livadia, would indicate that these efforts, at least so far as Turkey is concerned, have not been entirely fruitless. By hinting at the alleged plans of other Powers for the partitioning of Turkey's possessions in Asia Minor, and effectually assisted by France's shrewd utilization of Turkey's financial necessities, Russia has so far succeeded in overcoming Turkey's historic distrust of her that Turkish statesmen are earnestly considering a *rapprochement* toward the other group of Powers instead of an association with the Triple Alliance.

It is to the activity of Russian and French diplomacy also that Talaat Bey's journey to Bucharest can be attributed, a visit by which Roumanian mediation in the Island question was to be brought about, and by which, at the same time, the circumscription of Bulgaria was to be promoted through the opening of more friendly relations between Constantinople and Bucharest.

Up to the present time, these efforts at circumscription have had no apparent effect on Bulgarian policy, perhaps because so far Sofia has seen no reason for distrust of Turkish intentions. Nevertheless, Russia's expectation that a complete isolation of Bulgaria in the Balkans as well as in Europe will finally force her to desist from her former policy and submit to the conditions which Russia will impose in order that she may again be received into the Russian fold and under the Russian protection, is fully justified.

Macedonia plays a preëminent rôle both in Bulgaria's internal and external policy. If it should be shown to those who hold her reins of power that the peaceful agreement as proposed by Russia and an alliance with Serbia constitute the only way by which even a portion of Macedonia can be saved to the Bulgarian interest, no Bulgarian government would dare to refuse to agree to this combination, notwithstanding all former disappointments. Only such action as would stiffen Bulgaria's backbone against Russia's threats and cajolery and would secure the nation against isolation, can prevent Bulgaria from finally acceding to the plan for a Balkan alliance.

So far as concerns Roumania, Franco-Russian activities were already moving at full speed even during the Balkan crisis; public opinion had been turned into a current of antagonism toward the Monarchy by astonishing tricks of misrepresentation and by the clever fanning of the Greater-Roumania idea, which is always glowing beneath the surface; while Roumania's foreign policy has been influenced to the point of a military coöperation with Serbia, which was scarcely in consonance with the obligations resulting from the alliance with Austria-Hungary.

These activities have by no means come to a stop since that time; they were and are still being continued to great effect, and by such impressive and demonstrative methods as the visit of the Czar to the Roumanian Court.

An ever-increasing revolution of Roumanian public opinion has been the accompaniment of all this, and it cannot be doubted that today large sections of the army, the intellectuals, and the common people have been won over to a new point of view, which has as its aim "the liberation of the brethren on the other side of the Carpathians." It is evident that the ground is most effectually prepared for the accession of Roumania to a possible future Balkan alliance.

Official Roumania has so far withstood the influence of this popular wave and of the Franco-Russian propaganda, that a public desertion into the camp of the Dual Alliance and a frankly hostile policy against Austria-Hungary cannot as yet be discerned. But it is undeniable that a significant tide in the policy of Roumania has set in, a tide which—without regard to the prospect of its future development in the same direction—has already had a considerable amount of influence on the political and military situation of Austria-Hungary, and even of that of the Triple Alliance as a whole.

Whereas earlier there existed, despite the secrecy of the compact of alliance, no particular and special cause for doubt as to Roumania's fulfilment of the obligations to which she was subject as the result of her understanding with the Triple Alliance Powers, it has several times been publicly asserted of late in authoritative Roumanian quarters that the guiding principle of Roumanian policy was the principle of a free hand—an assertion against which the Triple Alliance Powers were prevented from raising a protest because of the secrecy clause in the compact of alliance. Likewise King Carol has stated to the Imperial and Royal Minister, with the frankness belonging to his high character, that as long as he lived, his efforts would be directed toward preventing the Roumanian army from taking the field against Austria-Hungary, but that he was unable to prevail against the public opinion of the Roumania of today, and that in the case of an attack by Russia on the Monarchy, any operation of Roumania on the side of Austria-Hungary was not to be thought of. The Roumanian Foreign Minister went a step farther—noticeably enough, immediately after the Czar's visit to Constanta—when he openly admitted in an interview that a *rapprochement* between Russia and Roumania had taken place, and that a community of interest existed between the two nations.

The status of Austria-Hungary's relations to Roumania at present can be thus described: the Monarchy stands fast by the terms of the alliance, and is ready today as before, to support Roumania with all its forces in case a *casus fœderis* should develop; while Roumania, for her part, declines to be bound by the terms of her alliance, and offers the Monarchy the sole prospect of an attitude of neutrality. Even Roumania's bare neutrality itself is assured to the Monarchy only by the personal word of King Carol, which is naturally good only for the duration of his reign, and depends, besides, on the King's ability to keep the reins of foreign policy continually and completely in his own hands. That this might prove beyond the power of the Monarch at a time of national excitement throughout the whole country can be denied with all the less assurance since King Carol cites the popular feeling even at the present time as a reason for the impossibility of reliance on Roumania's fulfilling the obligations of her agreement. Nor, finally, must it be forgotten that Roumania is already at the present time bound to the Monarchy's bitterest enemy in the Balkans —to Serbia—by ties of friendship and identical interest.

Up to the present time the Monarchy has restricted itself to friendly discussion of the alteration of the Roumanian policy at Bucharest, not having seen so far any reason to draw serious conclusions from Roumania's constantly and more plainly veering course of action. This attitude of the Vienna Cabinet was originally determined by the fact that the German Government held the opinion that these were transitory divagations, the results of certain misunderstandings at the period of the crisis which would automatically straighten out if they were dealt with peacefully and patiently. But it has been made plain that these tactics of quiet patience and friendly representation have not had the desired effect; that the progress of the estrangement between Austria-Hungary and Roumania has not been checked, but has, on the contrary, been hastened. That no satisfactory result is to be looked for in the future as the effect of these tactics, is proved by the circumstance that the present "free-hand" situation is wholly of advantage to Roumania and only disadvantageous to the Monarchy.

Now we are forced to face the question whether or not Austria-Hungary can restore harmony to her relations with Roumania by bringing the matter to an open exposition, by giving the Kingdom the choice of either breaking off all its connections with the Triple Alliance; or—perhaps through the making public of its affiliation to the Triple Alliance—compel it to give sufficient guaranties that all obligations springing from the Alliance will be fully and completely carried out on its part. Such a solution of the problem would naturally, by reviving a thirty-year-old tradition, best satisfy the desires of Austria-Hungary. But under present circumstances it is not likely that King Carol or any Roumanian government would be willing, even in consideration of a possible extension of the terms of the compact, publicly to announce Roumania as a confederate of the Triple Alliance in the face of the ruling popular feeling. Therefore, a categorical *aut-aut* on the part of the Monarchy might lead to an open break. Vienna is unable to form a competent opinion as to whether or not the German Government might be able to succeed by serious and impressive representations, perhaps combined in the end with an offer such as is referred to above, in getting Roumania to take a stand which could be regarded as a reliable guaranty for her full and lasting good faith toward her allies; but that, too, seems doubtful.

These circumstances appear practically to exclude the possibility of Austria-Hungary being able to build up the compact with Roumania so reliably and securely that it might be used as the pivot of the Monarchy's Balkan policy.

It would not only be useless, but, in consideration of the military and political importance of Roumania, it would be inexcusable carelessness, seriously endangering the power of self-defense, should the Monarchy continue to remain comparatively inactive in the face of the events now coming to light in Roumania, or should it fail to enter without delay upon the military preparations and political activities necessary to counteract, or at least to weaken, the effect of the neutrality and the possible hostility of Roumania.

The military value to the Monarchy of the alliance with Roumania consisted of the fact that, in case of war with Russia, the Monarchy would have been left free from the obligation of military action in the direction of Roumania, inasmuch as a respectable portion of Russia's military power would be tied up by the attack of a flanking Roumanian army. But the present relation between Roumania and the Monarchy, should an armed conflict break out today between Russia and the latter, would practically have a contrary effect. Russia would not now have to fear a Roumanian attack in any case, and would hardly have to line up a single man against Roumania, while Austria-Hungary could not even be sure of Roumanian neutrality, and would therefore be compelled to retain a correspondingly sufficient reserve of troops to guard against a Roumania now threatening *her* flank.

Up to the present, Austria-Hungary's military arrangements for the case of war with Russia have been based on the assumption of the coöperation of Roumania. If this assumption is wrong, if there is not even an absolute assurance against Roumanian aggression, the Monarchy will be forced to make other provisions for the case of war, and plan the construction of fortifications against Roumania.

Our political object should be to show Roumania by our actions that we are able to find other pillars of support for Austria-Hungary's Balkan policy. Any action to be undertaken for this purpose goes hand in hand with the real and timely necessity for devising new methods for counteracting the efforts of the Dual Alliance to erect a new Balkan alliance. Under the circumstances existing in the Balkans today, the only way to accomplish either the one thing or the other is for the Monarchy to accept the offer made a year ago by Bulgaria and repeated several times since, and to enter upon relations with that nation which would practically amount to an alliance. At the same time it should be the policy of the Monarchy to bring about an alliance between Bulgaria and Turkey, a plan to which both nations were up to a short time ago so favorably disposed that a compact was already drawn up, although it was subsequently left unsigned. Here, too, a continuation of the attitude of patient expectation to which the Monarchy was led by a far greater consideration for the alliance than was shown in Bucharest, would prove a great disadvantage impossible to overcome. Further holding off, and particularly the neglect of any counteraction in Sofia, would simply be playing into the hands of the systematic and intensive efforts of France and of Russia. Roumania's attitude actually saddles the Monarchy with the necessity of conceding to Bulgaria that support for which she has for so long been suing, in order to frustrate the otherwise scarcely evitable success of Russia's policy of circumscription. But this must be done as long as the road to Sofia and also to Constantinople still lies open.

The compact with Bulgaria, the definite terms of which will have to be more closely considered, will, of course, in general have to be so drawn up that the Monarchy shall not be placed at odds with the obligations of its alliance with Roumania. Nor should this step on the part of the Monarchy be kept secret, as it indicates no hostility toward Roumania, though it would serve as a solemn warning to the ruling authorities at Bucharest, to bring them to a consciousness of the full significance of a lone and permanent political dependence on Russia.

But before Austria-Hungary enters upon the measures herein mentioned, she deems it of the greatest importance to come to a full understanding with Germany concerning them, not only from considerations arising from tradition and from their close alliance, but particularly for the reason that important interests, both of Germany and of the Triple Alliance, are concerned, and because the successful preservation of those ultimately *common* interests can only be looked for if the equally united action of the Triple Alliance, particularly of Austria-Hungary and the German Empire, is opposed to the united action of France and Russia.

For if Russia, supported by France, is attempting to unite the Balkan States against Austria-Hungary, if she is striving to disturb still further our already ruffled relations with Serbia, this hostility is not being directed alone against the Monarchy as such, not merely against the ally of the German Empire, but against the most easily assailable section of the Central European bloc—greatly exposed both because of its geographical position and its internal structure—which bars Russia's road toward the realization of her aims for world-dominion.

It is the object of the Dual Alliance to break down the military superiority of the two Empires with the aid of Balkan armies, but that is not the ultimate aim of Russia.

While France is striving to weaken the Monarchy because she expects to be able thereby to further her plans for revenge, the intentions of the realm of the Czar go much further.

If one considers the development of Russia during the past two centuries, the constant extension of her territory, the enormous increase of her population, far surpassing that of all other great European Powers; if one considers the tremendous increase in her economic resources and in her military power, and then remembers that this great Empire is almost completely cut off from the open sea by treaties as well as by nature, then one can appreciate the necessity of the immanent and aggressive temper that has always characterized Russian policy from time immemorial.

It does not seem reasonable to impute plans of territorial conquest in the German Empire to Russia; nevertheless, her extraordinary armament and military preparations, the extension of the Russian strategic railways westward, etc., are surely aimed at Germany more than at Austria-Hungary.

For Russia has come to understand that the realization of her designs on both Europe and Asia—designs born of her internal necessities—will, above all, conflict with some of Germany's most important interests, and would therefore meet with Germany's unavoidable opposition.

Russian policy is compelled by conditions that are unalterable, and is therefore constant and far-sighted.

The obvious intention of Russia to circumscribe the Monarchy, which is pursuing no international policy, is aimed at making impossible the opposition of the German Empire to Russia's ultimate aim and her economic and political supremacy.

For all these reasons, those responsible for the foreign policy of Austria-Hungary are convinced that it is no less a matter of common interest for the Monarchy than for Germany to take timely and energetic steps at the present stage of the Balkan crisis against the further developments systematically sought and striven for by Russia, developments which it may later be impossible to prevent. . . .

(c) *The Imperial Chancellor, Bethmann-Hollweg, to the German Ambassador at Vienna, Tschirschky*[1]

Berlin, July 6, 1914

Confidential. For Your Excellency's
personal information and guidance

The Austro-Hungarian Ambassador yesterday delivered to the Emperor a confidential personal letter from the Emperor Franz Joseph, which depicts the present situation from the Austro-Hungarian

---

[1] *Kautsky Documents*, No. 15.

point of view, and describes the measures which Vienna has in view [cf. doc. No. 56 (a)]. A copy is now being forwarded to Your Excellency.

I replied to Count Szögyeny today on behalf of His Majesty that His Majesty sends his thanks to the Emperor Franz Joseph for his letter and would soon answer it personally. In the meantime His Majesty desires to say that he is not blind to the danger which threatens Austria-Hungary and thus the Triple Alliance as a result of the Russian and Serbian Panslavic agitation. Even though His Majesty is known to feel no unqualified confidence in Bulgaria and her ruler, and naturally inclines more toward our old ally Roumania and her Hohenzollern prince, yet he quite understands that the Emperor Franz Joseph, in view of the attitude[1] of Roumania and of the danger of a new Balkan alliance aimed directly at the Danube Monarchy, is anxious to bring about an understanding between Bulgaria and the Triple Alliance. His Majesty will, therefore, direct his minister at Sofia to lend the Austro-Hungarian representative such support as he may desire in any action taken to this end. His Majesty will, furthermore, make an effort at Bucharest, according to the wishes of the Emperor Franz Joseph, to influence King Carol to the fulfilment of the duties of his alliance, to the renunciation of Serbia, and to the suppression of the Roumanian agitations directed against Austria-Hungary.

Finally, as far as concerns Serbia, His Majesty, of course, cannot interfere in the dispute now going on between Austria-Hungary and that country, as it is a matter not within his competence. The Emperor Franz Joseph may, however, rest assured that His Majesty will[2] faithfully stand by Austria-Hungary, as is required by the obligations of his alliance and of his ancient friendship.

BETHMANN-HOLLWEG

57. VON WIESNER'S REPORT, SERAJEVO, JULY 13, 1914, TO THE IMPERIAL AND ROYAL DEPARTMENT OF FOREIGN AFFAIRS[3]

[Dr. Wiesner was a legal counselor of the Austrian Foreign Office who was sent by Berchtold to investigate on the spot Serbian responsibility. His report, absolving the Serbian Government from direct complicity in the crime, though not from responsibility in anti-Austrian agitation, was apparently made little use of, aside from the incorporation of the three demands in the ultimatum. In the brief time at his disposal, Wiesner learned only a small part of what is now known concerning the organization of the plot at Belgrade. The "Narodna Odbrana" (National Defense) was an influential secret society, which had since 1908 been training comitadjis in bomb-throwing and similar activities

---

[1] Originally in the draft: "unhappily evident unreliability," altered by the Imperial Chancellor to "attitude."

[2] Here in the draft, "under all circumstances," was crossed out by the Imperial Chancellor.

[3] *Austrian Red Book* (1919), Pt. I, No. 17.

to be used in guerrilla war against Austria and had been stirring up the people to hatred against Austria by active propagandist agitation.]

Telegram without number. Cipher

It is the firm belief of all persons in authority here that Servia is busily spreading propaganda for Greater Servia—not to speak of the press—through societies and other organisations, and that everything is done with the knowledge and sanction of the Servian government.

Civil and military authorities have given me the material upon which they base their belief; it may be classified as follows:

The material of the time before the assassination contains no proofs that the Servian government promoted propaganda. There is not much, but sufficient material to prove that the movement originates in Servia and is tolerated by the government.

Judicial inquiry on assassination.

There is nothing to prove or even to suppose that the Servian government is accessory to the inducement for the crime, its preparation or the furnishing of weapons. On the contrary, there are reasons to believe that this is altogether out of question.

From evidence of accused persons, ascertained almost indubitably that the crime was resolved upon in Belgrade and that preparations were made with the coercion of Servian state-officials Ciganovic and Major Tankosic, who jointly provided bombs, Brownings, ammunition and prussic acid. Guilt of Pribicevic not ascertained; reports about him based on regrettable misunderstandings on part of examining police organs.

There can be no doubt that bombs came from army stores in Kragujevac, but there is no proof that they were obtained for the crime, as they might have been in the hands of the Komitadschis since the war.

Evidence of accused persons leaves scarcely a doubt that Princip, Cabrinivic, Grabez, with bombs and weapons upon them, were secretly smuggled across the frontier to Bosnia by Servian organs, under the direction of Ciganovic. These organised transports were directed by the frontier-captains Schabatz and Loznica and were contrived by frontier guards. Though it is not ascertained that they knew the purpose of the journey, still they must have accepted secrecy of mission.

Other information gives insight into organisation of propaganda carried on by "Narodna Odbrana." This is valuable material, which will be useful, but has not yet been sifted; will be delivered without loss of time.

If the demands put forth at the time I left, are still valid, the following might be added to what is demanded of Servia:

A. Suppression of government organs' coercion in smuggling persons and goods across frontier.

B. Dismissal of Servian frontier-captains Schabatz and Loznica and the implicated frontier-guards.

C. Prosecution of Ciganovic and Tankosic.

I leave for Vienna this evening, arrive on Tuesday evening and go direct to the Foreign Office.

Verbal explanation necessary.

58. British Knowledge of Austrian Determination to Settle with Serbia[1]

[While the Austrian ultimatum to Serbia was being drafted and until Poincaré should have left Russia on his return to Paris, Berchtold endeavored to allay suspicion as to his real intention of crushing Serbia. His efforts at duping Europe were not so successful as was formerly believed on the basis of the "colored books" of 1914, in which the Entente countries tried to make it appear that the ultimatum came as a surprise to them. The following document, showing that this was not the case, was suppressed from the British Blue Book of 1914.]

Sir M. de Bunsen, British Ambassador in Vienna, to Sir Edward Grey

Telegram. Confidential   Vienna, July 16, 1914

From language held by Minister for Foreign Affairs to a friend of mine, who has repeated it to me, I gather that situation is regarded at the Ministry for Foreign Affairs in a serious light and that a kind of indictment is being prepared against the Servian Government for alleged complicity in the conspiracy which led to assassination of the Archduke. Accusation will be founded on the proceedings in the Serajevo Court. My informant states that the Servian Government will be required to adopt certain definite measures in restraint of nationalist and anarchist propaganda, and that Austro-Hungarian Government are in no mood to parley with Servia, but will insist on immediate unconditional compliance, failing which force will be used. Germany is said to be in complete agreement with this procedure, and it is thought that the rest of Europe will sympathise with Austria-Hungary in demanding that Servia shall adopt in future more submissive attitude.

My informant states that Count Forgach entirely shares these views with his chief and that they are very generally held by all classes in this country.

I asked if Russia would be expected to stand by quietly in the event of force being used against Servia.

My informant said that he presumed that Russia would not wish to protect racial assassins, but in any case Austria-Hungary would go ahead regardless of results. She would lose her position as a Great Power if she stood any further nonsense from Servia.

This language is also held by a portion of the press, including the "Neue Freie Presse," which is now in touch with the Ministry of Foreign Affairs. The official "Fremdenblatt" is more moderate.

---

[1] *British Documents on the Origins of the War, 1898-1914,* **Vol. XI,** No. 50.

I hope to see Minister for Foreign Affairs Friday.
(Repeated to Belgrade.)

59. A Report of Active German Interest[1]

[This famous report of Schoen to Hertling shows that the German
Government did not know half the demands nor the wording of the
ultimatum which had not yet been definitely drawn up, but that it did
know the substance of some of the most important demands, and it
knew that the ultimatum was intended to be so stiff as to preclude
Serbia's yielding. Jagow, German Secretary of State, must therefore
have been "diplomatically lying" when he stated a few days later that
he had no previous knowledge of the Austro-Hungarian Note (see doc.
No. 71). But to later requests of the German Government for information on the subject, Berchtold turned a deaf ear. Only on the evening
of July 22 was Jagow finally shown the text of the ultimatum, which
he then declared was "too sharp" and he reproached the Austrian
Ambassador for presenting him with a virtual *fait accompli*. The
German Government, however, felt that it had to stand back of Austria
because of having given Berchtold a free hand on July 5 (see doc.
No. 56 (c)).]

*The Bavarian Chargé d'Affaires at Berlin to the President of the
Bavarian Ministerial Council*

Report 386   Berlin, July 18, 1914
I have the honor most respectfully to report as follows to Your
Excellency concerning the prospective settlement between the Austro-
Hungarian Government and Serbia, on the basis of conversations I
have had with the Under-Secretary of State Zimmermann, and further
with the Foreign Office reporter for the Balkans and the Triple
Alliance, and with the counselor of the Austro-Hungarian Embassy.
The step which the Vienna Cabinet has decided to undertake at
Belgrade, and which will consist in the presentation of a note, will
take place on the twenty-fifth instant. The reason for the postponement of the action to that date is that they wish to await the departure
of Messrs. Poincaré and Viviani from Petersburg, in order not to
facilitate an agreement between the Dual Alliance Powers on any
possible counter-action. Until then, by the granting of leave of absence
simultaneously to the Minister of War and the Chief of the General
Staff, the Vienna authorities will have the appearance of being peacefully inclined; and they have not failed of success in their attempts to
influence the press and the exchange. It is recognized here that the
Vienna Cabinet has been proceeding quite cleverly in this matter, and
it is only regretted that Count Tisza, who at first is said to have been

[1] *Kautsky Documents*, Supplement IV, No. 2.

against any severe action, has somewhat raised the veil of secrecy by his statement in the Hungarian House of Deputies.

As Mr. Zimmermann told me, the note, so far as has yet been determined, will contain the following demands:

1. The issuing of a proclamation by the King of Serbia which shall state that the Serbian Government has nothing to do with the Greater-Serbia movement, and fully disapproves of it.

2. The initiation of an inquiry to discover those implicated in the murder of Serajevo, and the participation of Austrian officials in this inquiry.

3. Proceedings against all who have participated in the Greater-Serbia movement.

A respite of forty-eight hours is to be granted for the acceptance of these demands.

It is perfectly plain that Serbia cannot accept any such demands, which are incompatible with her dignity as a sovereign state. Thus the result would be war.

Here they are absolutely willing that Austria should take advantage of this favorable opportunity, even at the risk of further complications. But whether they will actually rise to the occasion in Vienna, still seems doubtful to Mr. von Jagow, as it does to Mr. Zimmermann. The Under-Secretary of State made the statement that Austria-Hungary, thanks to her indecision and her desultoriness, had really become the Sick Man of Europe, as Turkey had once been, upon the partition of which, the Russians, Italians, Roumanians, Serbians, and Montenegrins were now waiting. A powerful and successful move against Serbia would make it possible for the Austrians and Hungarians to feel themselves once more to be a national power, would again revive the country's collapsed economic life, and would set foreign aspirations back for years. To judge from the indignation at the bloody deed that was now dominant over the entire Monarchy, it looked as if they could even be sure of the Slav troops. In a few years, with the continuance of the operation of the Slavic propaganda, this would no longer be the case, as even General Conrad von Hötzendorf himself had admitted.

So they are of the opinion here that Austria is face to face with an hour of fate, and for this reason they declared here without hesitation, in reply to an inquiry from Vienna, that we would agree to any method of procedure which they might determine on there, even at the risk of a war with Russia. The blank power of full authority that was given to Count Berchtold's Chief of the Cabinet, Count Hoyos, who came here to deliver a personal letter from the Emperor together with a detailed memorial, went so far that the Austro-Hungarian Government was empowered to deal with Bulgaria concerning her entrance into the Triple Alliance.

In Vienna they do not seem to have expected such an unconditional support of the Danube Monarchy by Germany, and Mr. Zimmermann has the impression that it is almost embarrassing to the always timid and undecided authorities at Vienna not to be admonished by Germany to caution and self-restraint. To what extent they waver in their decisions at Vienna is shown by the circumstances that Count Berchtold, three days after he had had inquiries made here concerning the alliance with Bulgaria, telegraphed that he still had scruples about closing with Bulgaria.

So it would have been liked even better here, if they had not waited so long with their action against Serbia, and the Serbian Government had not been given time to make an offer of satisfaction on its own account, perhaps acting under Russo-French pressure.

What attitude the other Powers will take toward an armed conflict between Austria and Serbia will chiefly depend, according to the opinion here, on whether Austria will content herself with a chastisement of Serbia, or will demand territorial compensation for herself. In the first case, it might be possible to localize the war; in the other case, on the other hand, more serious complications would probably be inevitable.

The administration will, immediately upon the presentation of the Austrian note at Belgrade, initiate diplomatic action with the Powers, in the interest of the localization of the war. It will claim that the Austrian action has been just as much a surprise to it as to the other Powers, pointing out the fact that the Emperor is on his northern journey and that the Prussian Minister of War, as well as the Chief of the Grand General Staff, are away on leave of absence. (As I take the liberty to insert here, not even the Italian Government has been taken into confidence.) It will lay stress upon the fact that it is a matter of interest for all the monarchical Governments that "the Belgrade nest of anarchists" be once and for all rooted out; and it will make use of its influence to get all the Powers to take the view that the settlement between Austria and Serbia is a matter concerning those two nations alone. The mobilization of the German Army is to be refrained from, and they are also going to work through the military authorities to prevent Austria from mobilizing her entire Army, and especially not those troops stationed in Galicia, in order to avoid bringing about automatically a counter-mobilization on the part of Russia, which would force, first ourselves, and then France, to take similar measures and thereby conjure up a European war.

The attitude of RUSSIA will, above all else, determine the question whether the attempt to localize the war will succeed.

If Russia is not determined on war against Austria and Germany, in any case, she can, in that event—and that is the most favorable factor in the present situation—very well remain inactive, and justify herself toward the Serbs by announcing that she approves of the kind of fighting that goes to work with the throwing of bombs and with revolver shots just as little as any of the other civilized nations; this, especially, so long as Austria does not render doubtful Serbia's national independence. Mr. Zimmermann assumes that both England and

France, to neither of whom a war would be acceptable at the present moment, will try to exert a pacifying influence on Russia; besides that, he is counting on the fact that "bluffing" constitutes one of the most favored requisites of Russian policy, and that while the Russian likes to threaten with the sword, he still does not like so very much to draw it in behalf of others at the critical moment.

ENGLAND will not prevent Austria from calling Serbia to account; it is only the destruction of the nation that she would scarcely permit, being far more likely—true to her traditions—to take a stand, even in this case, for the principles of nationality. A war between the Dual Alliance and the Triple Alliance would be unwelcome to England at the present time, if only in consideration of the situation in Ireland. Should it, however, come to that, according to all opinion here, we should find our English cousins on the side of our enemies, in as much as England fears that France, in the event of a new defeat, would sink to the level of a Power of the second class, and that the "balance of power," the maintenance of which England considers to be necessary for her own interests, would be upset thereby.

Italy would take very little pleasure in the correction of Serbia by Austria, the strengthening of whose influence in the Balkans she would in no wise favor. As I was told by Minister von Bergen, reporter for Triple Alliance affairs at the Foreign Office, the relations between Vienna and Rome are anything but friendly again. At Vienna they are said to be in a very bad humor with Aliotti, the Italian Minister in Albania, who appears to have been conducting serious intrigues against Austria; and for this reason Ambassador von Mérey was instructed a few days ago to demand of Italy that she alter her whole policy, as otherwise the continuation of the agreement would be rendered impossible. The instructions were so sharply worded that San Giuliano was quite indignant, and this tension between Austria and Italy constitutes a very serious factor in the situation. Italy would not tolerate, without demanding compensation therefor, the partition of Serbia or even the annexation of the Mount of Lowtschen, which dominates the Bight of Cattaro. It does not seem entirely unlikely that Italy will undertake to call in her reserves, justifying the action by the state of her internal political affairs, for the purpose of occupying Valona, should the occasion offer. Mr. Zimmermann is of the opinion that Austria should not offer any opposition to that, as Valona would constitute for Italy another heel of Achilles, and as the distance between Brindisi and Valona is too great to make it possible for the Italians to close the Adriatic completely.

Perhaps it may be assumed from a statement made by the Counselor of the Austro-Hungarian Embassy, according to which, in his personal opinion, Valona might well be given to the Italians, that in Vienna they are already beginning to familiarize themselves with the idea of Italy's establishing herself firmly in southern Albania.

As I have been told quite confidentially, Prince Stolberg, Counselor of the Embassy at Vienna, who was here a few days ago, was instructed to discuss with Count Berchtold the question of the compensation of Italy, and in so doing to insinuate, in unofficial form, the suggestion that Italy might be permanently won over, once more, if Austria, in the event of her making major extensions to her territory, would agree to the cession to Italy of the southern part of the Trentino, *i.e.*, that portion of the Archbishopric of Trent which had never belonged to the old German Empire. It is, of course, scarcely expected here that the Vienna Cabinet would seriously consider this idea, and it was with intention that the Counselor of the Embassy, and not the Ambassador himself, who is likewise in Vienna, was instructed to bring the Trentino into the conversation, in order to avoid any bad feeling by an official suggestion of that nature.

So far as Bulgaria is concerned, the local Austro-Hungarian Embassy assumes that King Ferdinand would take advantage of the opportunity afforded by the outbreak of a war between Austria and Serbia, also, to attack Serbia, for the purpose of regaining the territory lost under the terms of the Treaty of Bucharest. As the danger would exist that in such an event Roumania, as in the second Balkan war, would turn against Bulgaria—and presumably influences directed toward this end by Russia, which would undertake nothing against Bulgaria directly, would not be lacking this time either,—they have let King Carol, with whose attitude of late they have been far from satisfied, know from here and in no uncertain manner that Germany would place herself at the side of Bulgaria, in case Roumania were unwilling to let Serbia drop. From the answer of the King it is assumed here that Roumania will keep the peace if compensation should be held in prospect for her. The territory around Vidin, the population of which is chiefly composed of Roumanians, would come under consideration as such compensation. Roumania would probably be won over by such action alone to the Triple Alliance, which would thus show itself to be stronger and more useful than the Dual Alliance.

Greece, which would not regard a partition of Serbia with any displeasure, could be compensated in Epirus, and would have to cede Kavala to the Bulgarians in return.

Finally, so far as concerns Montenegro, it is hoped here that the intelligent King Nicholas will find it advantageous to let the Serbs fight alone against Austria. Montenegro could be compensated in northern Albania for the cession of the Lowtschen, which Austria would probably lay claim to for herself on the occasion of so extensive an alteration of the map of the Balkans.

What the fate of the Principality of Albania would be under all these circumstances, can hardly be foreseen today. In the first place, there would be a continuation of the hopeless situation which has been characterized at Paris in the words: *"les caisses sont vides, le trône est Wied, tout est vide,*" and which has fastened on the Prince the nickname *"Prince du Vide."*

Your Excellency will accept, etc.,

v. SCHOEN

60. AUSTRIAN BELIEF IN THE NECESSITY FOR ACTION[1]

[Giesl, formerly Austrian Minister to Montenegro, had been champion of Austrian interests against Serbia during the Balkan wars. To appoint such a well-known Serbophobe to the post of Belgrade was tantamount to throwing a lighted match into a powder magazine. His dispatch is interesting as showing the extreme Austrian point of view. In view of Austrian efforts to deceive Europe, it is revealing to compare this document with Giesl's statement to his English colleague a few days before that "personally he was not in favor of pressing Serbia too hard, since he was convinced that the Serbian Government was ready to take whatever measures can reasonably be demanded of them, and that he did not view the situation in a pessimistic light" (*British Documents,* No. 57).]

Freiherr von Giesl to Count Berchtold, Austro-Hungarian Minister for Foreign Affairs

Belgrade, July 21, 1914

After the lamentable crime of June 28th, I have now been back at my post for some time and I am able to give some judgment as to the tone which prevails here.

After the annexation crisis the relations between the Monarchy and Servia were poisoned on the Servian side by national chauvinism, animosity and an effective propaganda of Great-Servian aspirations carried on in that part of our territory where there is a Servian population; since the last two Balkan Wars, the success of Servia has increased this chauvinism to a paroxysm, the expression of which in some cases bears the mark of insanity.

I may be excused from bringing proof and evidence of this; they can be had easily everywhere among all parties, in political circles as well as among the lower classes. I put it forward as a well-known axiom that the policy of Servia is built up on the separation of the territories inhabited by Southern Slavs, and as a corollary to this on the abolition of the Monarchy as a Great Power; this is its only object.

No one who has taken the trouble to move and take part in political circles here for a week can be blind to this truth.

The hatred against the Monarchy has been further intensified as a result of the latest events which influence political opinion here; among

---

[1] Great Britain. Foreign Office. *Collected Diplomatic Documents Relating to the Outbreak of the European War,* 1915: *Austro-Hungarian Red Book,* No. 6.

them I count the crime of Serajevo, the death of Hartwig and the electoral campaign.

The crime at Serajevo has aroused among the Servians an expectation that in the immediate future the Hapsburg States will fall to pieces; it was this on which they had set their hopes even before; there has been dangled before their eyes the cession of those territories in the Monarchy which are inhabited by the Southern Slavs, a revolution in Bosnia and Herzegovina and the unreliability of the Slav regiments —this is regarded as ascertained fact and had brought system and apparent justification into their nationalist madness.

Austria-Hungary, hated as she is, now appears to the Servians as powerless, and as scarcely worthy of waging war with; contempt is mingled with hatred; she is ripe for destruction, and she is to fall without trouble into the lap of the Great-Servian Empire, which is to be realised in the immediate future.

Newspapers, not among the most extreme, discuss the powerlessness and decrepitude of the neighbouring Monarchy in daily articles, and insult its officials without reserve and without fear of reprimand. They do not even stop short of the exalted person of our ruler. Even the official organ refers to the internal condition of Austria-Hungary as the true cause of this wicked crime. There is no longer any fear of being called to account. For decades the people of Servia has been educated by the press, and the policy at any given time is dependent on the party press; the Great-Servian propaganda and its monstrous offspring, the crime of June 28th, are a fruit of this education.

I pass over the suspicions and accusations with regard to the death of Hartwig, which are on the verge of insanity, and were characterised by "The Times" as "ravings"; I do not mention the lying campaign in the press which, however, might strengthen Servians in the conviction that the Government and the representatives of Austria-Hungary are outlaws, and that appellations such as murderer, rogue, cursed Austrian, etc., are suitable stock epithets for us.

The death of Hartwig and the recognition of the gravity of this loss to the Servian political world, have let loose a fanatical cult of the deceased; in this people were influenced not only by gratitude for the past, but also by anxiety for the future, and outbid one another in servile submissiveness to Russia in order to secure her goodwill in time to come.

As a third factor the electoral campaign has united all parties on a platform of hostility against Austria-Hungary. None of the parties which aspire to office will incur the suspicion of being held capable of weak compliance towards the Monarchy. The campaign, therefore, is conducted under the catchword of hostility towards Austria-Hungary.

For both internal and external reasons the Monarchy is held to be powerless and incapable of any energetic action, and it is believed that the serious words which were spoken by leading men among us are only "bluff."

The leave of absence of the Imperial and Royal Minister of War and Chief of the Staff have strengthened the conviction that the weakness of Austria-Hungary is now obvious.

I have allowed myself to trespass too long on the patience of Your Excellency, not because I thought that in what I have said I could tell you anything new, but because I considered this picture led up to the conclusion which forces itself upon me that a reckoning with Servia, a war for the position of the Monarchy as a Great Power, even for its existence as such, cannot be permanently avoided.

If we delay in clearing up our relations with Servia, we shall share the responsibility for the difficulties and the unfavourable situation in any future war which must, however, sooner or later be carried through.

For any observer on the spot, and for the representative of Austro-Hungarian interests in Servia, the question takes the form that we cannot any longer put up with any further injury to our prestige.

Should we therefore be determined to put forward far-reaching requirements joined to effective control—for this alone could clear the Augean stable of Great-Servian intrigues—then all possible consequences must be considered, and from the beginning there must be a strong and firm determination to carry through the matter to the end.

Half measures, the presentation of demands, followed by long discussions and ending only in an unsound compromise, would be the hardest blow which could be directed against Austria-Hungary's reputation in Servia and her position in Europe.

61. The Austro-Hungarian Ultimatum to Serbia[1]

[This note was presented to Serbia on July 23 at 6 p.m., and was communicated to the Powers the following morning. The time was changed from 5 to 6 p.m. apparently to make certain that Poincaré should have left Russia before the news reached St. Petersburg. The precise terms were approved in a Ministerial Council on July 19, held at Berchtold's private residence to insure secrecy. The minutes of this meeting show that Berchtold was opposed to further postponement of its presentation, because they were already beginning to get nervous in Berlin and news of Austrian intentions had already leaked out at Rome, so that he could not be responsible for undesirable incidents if the matter were further postponed. Tisza, the premier of Hungary, made the consent of his Government contingent upon a declaration at the beginning of the war of Austria's territorial disinterestedness. The ultimatum was actually dispatched to all the Austrian Ambassadors on July 20 without the knowledge of Francis Joseph, who learned of

---

[1] *Kautsky Documents,* Supplement I; another trans. in *Austrian Red Book* (1919), Pt. I, No. 27, where the date is correctly given as July 20th.

the text on July 21. Yet Berchtold still withheld it from Tschirschky, German Ambassador in Vienna, alleging that there were still some corrections to be made in it.]

The Austria-Hungarian Minister for Foreign Affairs, Berchtold, to the Minister at Belgrade, von Giesl

Vienna, *July 22, 1914*

Your Excellency will present the following note to the Royal Government on the afternoon of Thursday, July 23:

On the 31st of March, 1909, the Royal Serbian Minister at the Court of Vienna made, in the name of his Government, the following declaration to the Imperial and Royal Government:

"Serbia recognizes that her rights were not affected by the state of affairs created in Bosnia, and states that she will accordingly accommodate herself to the decisions to be reached by the Powers in connection with Article 25 of the Treaty of Berlin. Serbia, in accepting the advice of the Great Powers, binds herself to desist from the attitude of protest and opposition which she has assumed with regard to the annexation since October last, and she furthermore binds herself to alter the tendency of her present policy toward Austria-Hungary, and to live on the footing of friendly and neighborly relations with the latter in the future."

Now the history of the past few years, and particularly the painful events of the 28th of June, have proved the existence of a subversive movement in Serbia, whose object it is to separate certain portions of its territory from the Austro-Hungarian Monarchy. This movement, which came into being under the very eyes of the Serbian Government, subsequently found expression outside of the territory of the Kingdom in acts of terrorism, in a number of attempts at assassination, and in murders.

Far from fulfilling the formal obligations contained in its declaration of the 31st of March, 1909, the Royal Serbian Government has done nothing to suppress this movement. It has tolerated the criminal activities of the various unions and associations directed against the Monarchy, the unchecked utterances of the press, the glorification of the authors of assassinations, the participation of officers and officials in subversive intrigues; it has tolerated an unhealthy propaganda in its public instruction; and it has tolerated, finally, every manifestation which could betray the people of Serbia into hatred of the Monarchy and contempt for its institutions.

This toleration of which the Royal Serbian Government was guilty, was still in evidence at that moment when the events of the twenty-eighth of June exhibited to the whole world the dreadful consequences of such tolerance.

It is clear from the statements and confessions of the criminal authors of the assassination of the twenty-eighth of June, that the murder at Serajevo was conceived at Belgrade, that the murderers received the weapons and the bombs with which they were equipped from Serbian officers and officials who belonged to the *Narodna Odbrana*, and, finally, that the dispatch of the criminals and of their weapons to Bosnia was arranged and effected under the conduct of Serbian frontier authorities.

The results brought out by the inquiry no longer permit the Imperial and Royal Government to maintain the attitude of patient tolerance which it has observed for years toward those agitations which center at Belgrade and are spread thence into the territories of the Monarchy. Instead, these results impose upon the Imperial and Royal Government the obligation to put an end to those intrigues, which constitute a standing menace to the peace of the Monarchy.

In order to attain this end, the Imperial and Royal Government finds itself compelled to demand that the Serbian Government give official assurance that it will condemn the propaganda directed against Austria-Hungary, that is to say, the whole body of the efforts whose ultimate object it is to separate from the Monarchy territories that belong to it; and that it will obligate itself to suppress with all the means at its command this criminal and terroristic propaganda.

In order to give these assurances a character of solemnity, the Royal Serbian Government will publish on the first page of its official organ of July 26/13, the following declaration:

"The Royal Serbian Government condemns the propaganda directed against Austria-Hungary, that is to say, the whole body of the efforts whose ultimate object it is to separate from the Austro-Hungarian Monarchy territories that belong to it, and it most sincerely regrets the dreadful consequences of these criminal transactions.

"The Royal Serbian Government regrets that Serbian officers and officials should have taken part in the above-mentioned propaganda and thus have endangered the friendly and neighborly relations, to the cultivation of which the Royal Government had most solemnly pledged itself by its declarations of March 31, 1909.

"The Royal Government, which disapproves and repels every idea and every attempt to interfere in the destinies of the population of whatever portion of Austria-Hungary, regards it as its duty most expressly to call attention of the officers, officials and the whole population of the Kingdom to the fact that for the future it will proceed with the utmost rigor against any persons who shall become guilty of any such activities, activities to prevent and to suppress which, the Government will bend every effort."

This declaration shall be brought to the attention of the Royal army simultaneously by an order of the day from His Majesty the King, and by publication in the official organ of the army.

The Royal Serbian Government will furthermore pledge itself:

1. to suppress every publication which shall incite to hatred and contempt of the Monarchy, and the general tendency of which shall be directed against the territorial integrity of the latter;

2. to proceed at once to the dissolution of the *Narodna Odbrana*, to confiscate all of its means of propaganda, and in the same manner to proceed against the other unions and associations in Serbia which occupy themselves with propaganda against Austria-Hungary; the Royal Government will take such measures as are necessary to make sure that the dissolved associations may not continue their activities under other names or in other forms;

3. to eliminate without delay from public instruction in Serbia, everything, whether connected with the teaching corps or with the methods of teaching, that serves or may serve to nourish the propaganda against Austria-Hungary;

4. to remove from the military and administrative service in general all officers and officials who have been guilty of carrying on the propaganda against Austria-Hungary, whose names the Imperial and Royal Government reserves the right to make known to the Royal Government when communicating the material evidence now in its possession;

5. to agree to the coöperation in Serbia of the organs of the Imperial and Royal Government in the suppression of the subversive movement directed against the integrity of the Monarchy;

6. to institute a judicial inquiry against every participant in the conspiracy of the twenty-eighth of June who may be found in Serbian territory; the organs of the Imperial and Royal Government delegated for this purpose will take part in the proceedings held for this purpose;

7. to undertake with all haste the arrest of Major Voislav Tankositch and of one Milan Ciganovitch, a Serbian official, who have been compromised by the results of the inquiry;

8. by efficient measures to prevent the participation of Serbian authorities in the smuggling of weapons and explosives across the frontier; to dismiss from the service and to punish severely those members of the Frontier Service at Schabats and Losnitza who assisted the authors of the crime of Serajevo to cross the frontier;

9. to make explanations to the Imperial and Royal Government concerning the unjustifiable utterances of high Serbian functionaries in Serbia and abroad, who, without regard for their official position, have not hesitated to express themselves in a manner hostile toward Austria-Hungary since the assassination of the twenty-eighth of June;

10. to inform the Imperial and Royal Government without delay of the execution of the measures comprised in the foregoing points.

The Imperial and Royal Government awaits the reply of the Royal Government by Saturday, the twenty-fifth instant, at 6 p.m., at the latest.

A mémoire concerning the results of the inquiry at Serajevo, as far as they concern the functionaries referred to in Points 7 and 8, is appended to this note. . . .

62. AN ENTENTE REACTION TO THE CRISIS[1]

[In a dispatch of July 20 to Buchanan, British Ambassador in St. Petersburg, Grey made a confidential suggestion for "direct conversations" between Vienna and St. Petersburg, and two days later he set forth his idea more fully to the Russian Ambassador in London, Benckendorff. How Poincaré regarded this suggestion may be seen in this document. Poincaré had always wanted the Triple Entente to agree upon their action before any one of them approached Germany or Austria. So now Sazonov and Poincaré proposed counseling moderation at Vienna, but before Grey had acted upon this suggestion, news came that the ultimatum had been presented, and nothing came of the idea. This dispatch was omitted from the British Blue Book of 1914.]

Buchanan to Grey

St. Petersburg, July 22, 1914

Tel. (No. 163)

Servian Minister told me yesterday that he regarded present crisis as most dangerous one through which Servia had passed during the last two years. After repeating to me all that his Government had done to show their readiness to meet any legitimate demands that Austria might address to them, he said that Count Tisza and Count Forgach were inflaming Austrian public opinion so as to force hands of aged Emperor. On my remarking that if Servia adhered to her present correct attitude it would be impossible for Austria to find a pretext for attacking her, Minister replied that she would create some incident that would furnish her with it.

I repeated above to President of the Republic, whom I saw immediately afterwards, and also mentioned what you had said in your telegram No. 336 of 20th July. His Excellency expressed opinion that a conversation *à deux* between Austria and Russia would be very dangerous at present moment, and seemed favourable to moderating counsels by France and England at Vienna.

I also spoke to Minister for Foreign Affairs, whom I met later in the day. His Excellency said that if Austria could prove plot had been hatched in Servia there was no objection to her asking Servian Government to institute judicial enquiry, and this, he believed, Servia was ready to do. He thought, however, it would be advisable for three Governments to counsel moderation at Vienna. This should be done in friendliest manner, and should not take the form of any collective action. He begged me to telegraph to you in this sense, and said he would speak to the President of the Republic today on the subject.

[1] *British Documents on the Origins of the War, 1898-1914.* Vol. XI, No. 76.

63. A NOTE SENT BY BERCHTOLD TO MENSDORFF AT LONDON SUGGESTING HOW TO EXPLAIN TO SIR EDWARD GREY THE NATURE OF AUSTRIA-HUNGARY'S NOTE OF JULY 23 TO SERBIA[1]

Vienna, July 23, 1914

Private

England being that power of the Entente which is most likely to judge our steps in Belgrade in an unprejudiced manner, I will beg you in the conversation to follow the presentation of the circular note of the 24th inst., to remind the Foreign Office that Servia could have avoided the severity of our serious *démarche*, which it must necessarily have expected, by taking the measures for instituting an inquiry in Servia against the Servians who took a part in the crime of the 28th June, and to reveal the connections leading from Belgrade to Sarajevo in the affair of the murderous plot.

The Servian government has to this day, though a number of well-known circumstances point to Belgrade, not only undertaken nothing in this direction, but has even attempted to obliterate some of the important indications.

Thus a telegraphic report of our legation in Belgrade shows that the strongly compromised state-official Ciganovič, whom the murderers accuse of complicity, was still in Belgrade on the day of the murder, but three days later, when the newspapers began to publish his name, had already left the city. The chief of the Servian press at the same time declared that Ciganovič was absolutely unknown in Belgrade.

The short term given to Servia for its answer must be attributed to our experience of Servia's dilatory ways in treating political questions.

We cannot allow the demands, which we have addressed to Servia, and which contain nothing that would not be considered natural between two neighbors, living in peace and harmony, to be made the subject of negotiations and compromises and we owe it to our economical interests, not to consent to political methods, which would allow Servia to prolong the crisis, in which we find ourselves, at its pleasure.

64. GREY'S VIEW OF THE ULTIMATUM

(a) *Grey to Bunsen*[2]

(No. 121)   *Foreign Office, July* 23, 1914

Sir,

Count Mensdorff told me to-day that he would be able to-morrow morning to let me have officially the communication that he understood

---

[1] *Austrian Red Book* (1919), Pt. I, No. 61.

[2] *British Documents on the Origins of the War, 1898-1914,* Vol. XI, No. 86.

was being made to Servia to-day by Austria. He then explained privately what the nature of the demand would be. As he told me that the facts would all be set out in the paper that he would give me to-morrow, it is unnecessary to record them now. I gathered that they would include proof of the complicity of some Servian officials in the plot to murder the Archduke Franz Ferdinand, and a long list of demands consequently made by Austria on Servia.

As regards all this, I said that it was not a matter on which I would make any comment until I received an official communication, and it seemed to me probably a matter on which I should not be able to make any comment at first sight.

But, when Count Mensdorff told me that he supposed there would be something in the nature of a time-limit, which was in effect akin to an ultimatum, I said that I regretted this very much. To begin with, a time-limit might inflame opinion in Russia, and it would make it difficult, if not impossible, to give more time, even if after a few days it appeared that by giving more time there would be a prospect of securing a peaceful settlement and getting a satisfactory reply from Servia. I admitted that if there was no time-limit, the proceedings might be unduly protracted, but I urged that a time-limit could always be introduced afterwards; that if the demands were made without a time-limit in the first instance, Russian public opinion might be less excited, after a week it might have cooled down, and if the Austrian case was very strong it might be apparent that the Russian Government would be in a position to use their influence in favour of a satisfactory reply from Servia. A time-limit was generally a thing to be used only in the last resort, after other means had been tried and failed.

Count Mensdorff said that if Servia, in the interval that had elapsed since the murder of the Archduke, had voluntarily instituted an enquiry on her own territory all this might have been avoided. In 1909 Servia had said in a note that she intended to live on terms of good neighbourhood with Austria; but she had never kept her promise, she had stirred up agitation the object of which was to disintegrate Austria and it was absolutely necessary for Austria to protect herself.

I said that I would not comment upon or criticise what Count Mensdorff had told me this afternoon, but I could not help dwelling upon the awful consequences involved in the situation. Great apprehension had been expressed to me, not specially by M. Cambon and Count Benckendorff, but also by others, as to what might happen, and it had been represented to me that it would be very desirable that those who had influence in St. Petersburg should use it on behalf of patience and moderation. I had replied that the amount of influence that could be used in this sense would depend upon how reasonable were the Austrian demands and how strong the justification that Austria might have discovered for making her demands. The possible consequences of the present situation were terrible. If as many as four Great Powers of Europe—let us say Austria, France, Russia, and Germany—were engaged in war, it seemed to me that it must involve the expenditure of so vast a sum of money and such an interference with trade, that a war would be accompanied or followed by a complete collapse of European credit and industry. In these days, in great industrial States, this would mean a state of things worse than that of 1848, and, irrespective of who were victors in the war, many things might be completely swept away.

Count Mensdorff did not demur to this statement of the possible consequences of the present situation, but he said that all would depend upon Russia.

I made the remark that in a time of difficulties such as this, it was just as true to say that it required two to keep the peace as it was to say, ordinarily, that it took two to make a quarrel. I hoped very much that if there were difficulties, Austria and Russia would be able in the first instance to discuss them directly with each other.

Count Mensdorff said that he hoped this would be possible, but he was under the impression that the attitude in St. Petersburg had not been very favourable recently.

I am, etc.,

E. GREY

(b) Grey to Bunsen[1]

Foreign Office, July 24, 1914

Tel. (No. 148)

Austro-Hungarian Ambassador has communicated to me the note addressed to Servia with the explanation of the Austro-Hungarian Government upon it.

I said that the murder of the Archduke and some of the circumstances stated in the Austro-Hungarian note with regard to Servia naturally aroused sympathy with Austria, but I thought it a great pity that a time-limit, and such a short time-limit, had been introduced at this stage, and the note seemed to me the most formidable document I had ever seen addressed by one State to another that was independent. Demand No. 5 might mean that the Austro-Hungarian Government were to be entitled to appoint officials who should have authority in Servian territory and this would hardly be consistent with the maintenance of independent sovereignty of Servia.

I was not, however, making these comments in order to discuss the merits of the dispute between Austria-Hungary and Servia; that was not our concern. It was solely from the point of view of the peace of

---

[1] British Documents on the Origins of the War, 1898-1914, Vol. XI, No. 91.

Europe that I should concern myself with the matter, and I felt great apprehension.

I must wait to hear the views of other Powers and no doubt we should consult with them to see what could be done to mitigate difficulties.

The Austro-Hungarian Ambassador observed that there had been so much procrastination on the part of Servia that a time-limit was essential. Some weeks had passed since the murder of the Archduke and Servia had made no sign of sympathy or help; if she had held out a hand after the murder the present situation might have been prevented.

I observed that a time-limit could have been introduced at any later stage if Servia had procrastinated about a reply; as it was, the Austro-Hungarian Government not only demanded a reply within forty-eight hours, but dictated the terms of the reply.

65. GERMAN DESIRE TO APPEAR DISINTERESTED

(a) *The German Secretary of State for Foreign Affairs to the German Ambassador at Vienna*[1]

Telegram 134   Berlin, *July 24, 1914*

We consider it desirable to have the declaration of war on Serbia sent directly, and not through our Legation. Our standpoint has to be that the quarrel with Servia is an Austro-Hungarian internal affair, in which it would no more become us to mix than it would others, and for that reason we are advocating the localization of the conflict. Only if Russia should intervene would we be drawn into the conflict. Declaration of war through our Legation would in general, especially to that portion of the public not acquainted with diplomatic customs, appear as though we had HARRIED Austria-Hungary into the war.

JAGOW

(b) *The Under-Secretary of State for Foreign Affairs to the Ambassadors at Paris, London, and St. Petersburg*[2]

Berlin, *July 24, 1914*

In local diplomatic circles the opinion seems to be prevalent that we incited Austria-Hungary to direct a sharp note to Serbia and participated in its composition. Report seems to emanate from Cambon. Kindly refute it there, if necessary. We exercised no influence of any kind with regard to the contents of the note and had as little opportunity as any other Power to adopt an attitude in connection

---

[1] *Kautsky Documents*, No. 142.

[2] *Ibid.*, No. 153.

with it before its publication. That we are now unable to counsel Vienna to retract, since Austria-Hungary has determined on strong speech of her own initiative, goes without saying. Austria-Hungary's prestige, both internal and external, would be completely lost, in case of retraction.

ZIMMERMANN

66. RESULTS OF POINCARÉ'S VISIT TO ST. PETERSBURG[1]

[The part of the British Ambassador's telegram containing the points agreed upon by Poincaré and Sazonov was suppressed from the British Blue Book of 1914. The second of these points was rendered ineffective by Austria's sending the ultimatum before the French and Russian Ambassadors could act. The other two points Paléologue, the French Ambassador in St. Petersburg, treated as a "blank check" promising complete support to Russia in any measures whatsoever.]

Buchanan to Grey

St. Petersburg, July 24, 1914

Tel. (No. 166) Urgent

. . . .

Minister for Foreign Affairs telephoned to me this morning saying that he had just received text of ultimatum presented by Austria at Belgrade yesterday that demands a reply in forty-eight hours. Step thus taken by Austria meant war, and he begged me to meet him at the French Embassy.

Minister for Foreign Affairs and French Ambassador told me confidentially that result of the visit of the President of the French Republic had been to establish the following points:—

1. Perfect community of views on the various problems with which the Powers are confronted as regards the maintenance of general peace and balance of power in Europe, more especially in the East.

2. Decision to take action at Vienna with a view to the prevention of a demand for explanations or any summons equivalent to an intervention in the internal affairs of Servia which the latter would be justified in regarding as an attack on her sovereignty and independence.

3. Solemn affirmation of obligations imposed by the alliance of the two countries.

Minister for Foreign Affairs expressed the hope that His Majesty's Government would proclaim their solidarity with France and Russia. He characterised Austria's conduct as immoral and provocative. Some of the demands which she had presented were absolutely in-

---

[1] *British Documents on the Origins of the War, 1898-1914*, Vol. XI, No. 101.

acceptable, and she would never have acted as she had done without having first consulted Germany. The French Ambassador gave me to understand that France would not only give Russia strong diplomatic support, but would, if necessary, fulfil all the obligations imposed on her by the alliance.

I said that I could not speak in the name of His Majesty's Government, but that I would telegraph all that they had said. I could personally hold out no hope that His Majesty's Government would make any declaration of solidarity that would entail engagement to support France and Russia by force of arms. We had no direct interests in Servia, and public opinion in England would never sanction a war on her behalf. Minister for Foreign Affairs replied that the Servian question was but part of general European question and that we could not efface ourselves.

I said that I gathered that His Excellency wished us to join in telling Austria that we could not tolerate her active intervention in Servian internal affairs. If she paid no attention to our representations and took military action against Servia, did Russia propose to declare war upon her? Minister for Foreign Affairs said that the whole question would be considered by a Council of Ministers to be held this afternoon, but that no decision would be taken till a further Council of Ministers had been held under the presidency of the Emperor, probably tomorrow. He personally thought that Russia would at any rate have to mobilise.

I suggested that the first thing to be done was to try to gain time by bringing our influence to bear to induce Austria to extend term of delay accorded to Servia. The French Ambassador replied that time did not permit of this; either Austria was bluffing or had made up her mind to act at once. In either case a firm and united attitude was our only chance of averting war. I then asked whether it would not be advisable to urge Servian Government to state precisely how far they were prepared to go to meet Austria's wishes. Minister for Foreign Affairs said that some of the demands contained in ultimatum might no doubt be accepted, but that he must first consult his colleagues.

As they both continued to press me to declare our complete solidarity with them, I said that I thought you might be prepared to represent strongly at Vienna and Berlin danger to European peace of an Austrian attack on Serbia. You might perhaps point out that it would in all probability force Russia to intervene, that this would bring Germany and (?France) into the field, and that if war became general, it would be difficult for England to remain neutral. Minister for Foreign Affairs said that he hoped that we would in any case express strong reprobation of Austria's action. If war did break out, we would sooner or later be dragged into it, but if we did not make common cause with France and Russia from the outset we should have rendered war more likely, and should not have played a "beau rôle."

From French Ambassador's language it almost looked as if France and Russia were determined to make a strong stand even if we declined to join them. Language of Minister for Foreign Affairs, however, was not so (?decided) on this subject.

Austrian Government seemed purposely to have presented their ultimatum at moment when President of the French Republic and President of the Council were leaving Russia on their return to France, where they cannot arrive for four or five days.

Towards the close of our interview we were joined by Roumanian Minister, with whom Minister for Foreign Affairs had a private conversation in which His Excellency invited also Roumanian Government to make representations at Vienna.

(Repeated to Paris, 1.20 P.M., No. 217.)

MINUTES [attached by British Foreign Office officials]

The moment has passed when it might have been possible to enlist French support in an effort to hold back Russia.

It is clear that France and Russia are decided to accept the challenge thrown out to them. Whatever we may think of the merits of the Austrian charges against Servia, France and Russia consider that these are the pretexts, and that the bigger cause of Triple Alliance versus Triple *Entente* is definitely engaged.

I think it would be impolitic, not to say dangerous, for England to attempt to controvert this opinion, or to endeavour to obscure the plain issue, by any representation at St. Petersburg and Paris.

The point that matters is whether Germany is or is not absolutely determined to have this war now.

There is still the chance that she can be made to hesitate, if she can be induced to apprehend that the war will find England by the side of France and Russia.

I can suggest only one effective way of bringing this home to the German Government without absolutely committing us definitely at this stage. If, the moment either Austria or Russia begin to mobilize, His Majesty's Government give orders to put our whole fleet on an immediate war footing, this may conceivably make Germany realize the seriousness of the danger to which she would be exposed if England took part in the war.

It would be right, supposing this decision could be taken now, to inform the French and Russian Governments of it, and this again would be the best thing we could do to prevent a very grave situation arising as between England and Russia.

It is difficult not to agree with M. Sazonof that sooner or later England will be dragged into the war if it does come. We shall gain nothing by not making up our minds what we can do in circumstances that may arise to-morrow.

Should the war come, and England stand aside, one of two things must happen:—

(A) Either Germany and Austria win, crush France and humiliate Russia. With the French fleet gone, Germany in occupation of the Channel, with the willing or unwilling coöperation of Holland and Belgium, what will be the position of a friendless England?

(B) Or France and Russia win. What would then be their attitude towards England? What about India and the Mediterranean?

Our interests are tied up with those of France and Russia in this struggle, which is not for the possession of Servia, but one between Germany aiming at a political dictatorship in Europe and the Powers who desire to retain individual freedom. If we can help to avoid the conflict by showing our naval strength, ready to be instantly used, it would be wrong not to make the effort.

Whatever therefore our ultimate decision, I consider we should decide *now* to mobilize the fleet as soon as any other Great Power mobilizes, and that we should announce this decision without delay to the French and Russian Governments.—*E. A. C*[*rowe*], *July 25*

The points raised by Sir Eyre Crowe merit serious consideration, and doubtless the Cabinet will review the situation. Our attitude during the crisis will be regarded by Russia as a test and we must be most careful not to alienate her.—*A. N*[*icolson*]

Mr. Churchill told me today that the fleet can be mobilized in twenty-four hours, but I think it is premature to make any statement to France and Russia yet.—*E. G*[*rey*]

67. RUSSIAN OBJECTION TO A CONFERENCE[1]

[With the Russian attitude toward Grey's mediation proposal should be compared the note of Lichnowsky, German Ambassador in London, to Grey (who was out of town): "My Government accepts your suggested mediation *à quatre*" (*British Documents*, no. 145). Cambon, French Ambassador in London, failed even to report Grey's proposal to his Government. This document was suppressed from the British Blue Book of 1914.]

Grey to Buchanan
Confidential
Sir, Foreign Office, July 25, 1914

I told Count Benckendorff to-day of what I had said to the German Ambassador this morning as to the possibility of Germany, Italy, France, and ourselves working together in Vienna and St. Petersburg to secure peace after Austria and Russia had mobilised.

---

[1] *British Documents on the Origins of the War, 1898-1914*, Vol. XI, No. 132.

Count Benckendorff was very apprehensive that what I said would give Germany the impression that France and England were detached from Russia.

I said that France and ourselves, according to my suggestion, would be no more detached from Russia than Germany would be detached from her ally Austria. I had emphasised to Prince Lichnowsky that the participation of Germany in any such diplomatic mediation was an essential condition, and surely the situation was not made unsatisfactory for Russia if France and England held their hands, provided that Germany also held hers.

Count Benckendorff urged that I should give some indication to Germany to make her think that we would not stand aside if there was a war.

I said that I had given no indication that we would stand aside; on the contrary, I had said to the German Ambassador that, as long as there was only a dispute between Austria and Servia alone, I did not feel entitled to intervene; but that, directly it was a matter between Austria and Russia, it became a question of the peace of Europe, which concerned us all. I had furthermore spoken on the assumption that Russia would mobilise, whereas the assumption of the German Government had hitherto been, officially, that Servia would receive no support; and what I had said must influence the German Government to take the matter seriously. In effect, I was asking that, if Russia mobilised against Austria, the German Government, who had been supporting the Austrian demand on Servia, should ask Austria to consider some modification of her demands, under the threat of Russian mobilisation. This was not an easy thing for Germany to do, even though we would join at the same time in asking Russia to suspend action. I was afraid, too, that Germany would reply that mobilisation with her was a question of hours, whereas with Russia it was a question of days; and that, as a matter of fact, I had asked that if Russia mobilised against Austria, Germany, instead of mobilising against Russia, should suspend mobilisation and join with us in intervention with Austria, thereby throwing away the advantage of time, for, if the diplomatic intervention failed, Russia would meanwhile have gained time for her mobilisation. It was true that I had not said anything directly as to whether we would take any part or not if there was a European conflict, and I could not say so; but there was absolutely nothing for Russia to complain of in the suggestion that I had made to the German Government, and I was only afraid that there might be difficulty in its acceptance by the German Government. I had made it on my own responsibility, and I had no doubt it was the best proposal to make in the interests of peace.

I am, etc.,

E. Grey

68. German View That Russia Was the Key to the European Situation. (Kaiser's Comments Shown)[1]

[Pourtalès was the German Ambassador in St. Petersburg. His interview with Sazonov was a tense one, only accentuating the growing conflict between the view that the Austro-Serbian question should remain "localized" and that it should be Europeanized.]

The German Ambassador at St. Petersburg to the Foreign Office

Telegram 149   St. Petersburg, July 25, 1914

Have just had long interview with Sazonoff at which subject of dispatch 592 figured exhaustively. Minister, who was *very much excited* and gave vent to boundless reproaches against Austria-Hungary, stated in the most determined manner that it would be impossible for Russia to admit that the Austro-Serb quarrel could be settled between the two parties concerned. The obligations which Serbia had assumed after the Bosian crisis and to which the Austrian note refers, were assumed toward Europe, consequently the affair was a European affair, and it was for *Europe* to investigate as to whether Serbia had lived up to these obligations. He therefore proposes that the documents in relation to the inquiry be laid before the Cabinets of the six Powers. Austria could not be both accuser and judge in her own case. Sazonoff announced that he could in no way consider as proven the facts alleged by Austria in her note, that the inquiry, on the other hand, inspired him with the greatest (suspicion). He continued by saying that, in case the facts asserted should be proved to be true, Serbia could give Austria satisfaction in the purely legal questions, but not, on the other hand, in the matter of the demands of a political nature. I called attention to the fact that it was impossible to separate the legal from the political side of the matter, as the assassination was inseparably connected with the Greater-Serbia propaganda.

I promised to lay his ideas before my Government, but did not believe that we would suggest to our ally to submit the results of an inquiry conducted by her *once more to a European tribunal*. Austria would object to this suggestion just as any Great Power would have to refuse to

Marginal notes (Kaiser's comments):

Good.

Rot!

That's a question of the point of view!

Cannot be separated.

Right. Pan-slavistic.

Most certainly not!

---

[1] *Kautsky Documents*, No. 160.

Bravo! Well said!

Not since her fraternizing with the French socialist republic!

Regicide. Very good.

Well, go to it!

That it wants to do, it seems.

Not correct.

submit itself to a court of arbitration in a case in which its vital interests were at stake.

My references to the monarchical principle made little impression on the minister. Russia *knew* what she *owed to the monarchical principle*, with which, however, this case had nothing to do. I requested Sazonoff very seriously, avoiding everything that might have the appearance of a threat, not to let himself be led astray by his hatred of Austria and *"not to defend a bad cause."* Russia could not possibly constitute herself the advocate of *regicides*.

In the course of the conversation Sazonoff exclaimed: "If Austria-Hungary devours Serbia, we will go to war with her." From this it may perhaps be concluded that Russia will only take up arms in the event of Austria's attempting to acquire territory at the expense of Serbia. The expressed desire to Europeanize the question also seems to point to the fact that immediate intervention on the part of Russia is not to be anticipated.

POURTALÈS

69. RUSSIAN ADVICE TO SERBIA[1]

(Copy)

Text of Russia's Plan

On the original his Imperial Majesty was so gracious as to write with his own hand, "agreed to," Tsarkoe Selo, 12 [25] July, 1914. Countersigned: President of the Council of Ministers,
State Secretary Goremykin

Special Journal of the Council of Ministers

11 [24] July, 1914

Subsequent to the declaration made by the Minister of Foreign Affairs regarding the most recent measures taken by the Austro-Hungarian Government against Serbia.

The Minister of Foreign Affairs informed the Council of Ministers that, according to information received by him and according to the announcement made by the Austro-Hungarian Ambassador to the Imperial Court, the Austro-Hungarian Government had turned upon the Serbian Government with demands which appeared, in fact, to be quite unacceptable to the Serbian Government as a sovereign State, and which were drawn up in the form of an ultimatum calling for a

---

[1] R. C. Binkley, "New Light on Russia's War Guilt." Reprinted from the *Current History Magazine,* a periodical published by *The New York Times Company,* Vol. XXIII, pp. 531-533, Jan., 1926.

reply within a definite time, expiring tomorrow, July 12, at 6 o'clock in the evening.

Therefore, foreseeing that Serbia would turn to us for advice, and perhaps also for aid, there arose a need to prepare an answer which might be given to Serbia.

Having considered the declaration made by Marshal Sazonov in its relation to the information reported by the Ministers of War, Marine and Finance concerning the political and military situation, the Council of Ministers decreed:

1—To approve the proposal of the Minister of Foreign Affairs to get in touch with the Cabinets of the Great Powers in order to induce the Austro-Hungarian Government to grant a postponement in the matter of the answer to the ultimatum demands presented by the Austro-Hungarian Government, so that it might be possible for the Governments of the Great Powers to become acquainted with and to investigate the documents on the Sarajevo crime which are in the hands of the Austro-Hungarian Government, and which, according to the declaration of the Austro-Hungarian Ambassador, it is willing to communicate to the Russian Government.

2—To approve the proposal of the Minister of Foreign Affairs to advise the Serbian Government, in case the situation of Serbia should be such that she could not with her own strength protect herself against the possible armed invasion by Austro-Hungary, not to offer armed resistance to the invasion of Serbian territory, if such an invasion should occur, but to announce that Serbia yields to force and that she entrusts her fate to the judgment of the Great Powers.

3—To authorize the Ministers of War and of Marine, in accordance with the duties of their offices, to beg your Imperial Majesty to consent, according to the progress of events, to order the mobilization of the four military districts of Kiev, Odessa, Moscow and Kazan, and the Baltic and Black Sea fleets.

(*Note by the Acting Secretary of the Council:*
"In the original the word 'Baltic' has been added by his Imperial Majesty's own hand, and the word 'fleet' corrected to read 'fleets.' ")

4—To authorize the War Minister to proceed immediately to gather stores of war material.

5—To authorize the Minister of Finance to take measures instantly to diminish the funds of the Ministry of Finance which may be at present in Germany or Austria.

The Council of Ministers considers it its loyal duty to inform your Imperial Majesty of these decisions which it has made.

[The original is signed by the President and Members of the Council and countersigned by the Acting Secretary of the Council.

(The pages from which this translation is made are to be found in mimeographed form in a heavy bound volume: Hoover War Library.

Russia, R. 968, "Vysochaishe utverzhdennye zhurnaly Sovieta Ministrov i Osobykh Sovieshchanii, 1914. Otdielenie 2, K. S. M." The date, July 11, corresponds to July 24, N. S. The journal of the meeting held the following day is to be found in the same volume; thenceforth no meetings are recorded until after the outbreak of the war.)]

70. RUSSIA'S DECISION FOR GENERAL MOBILIZATION[1]

[The "Order concerning preparatory period to war" was defined as the period of diplomatic complications preceding the opening of hostilities, in the course of which all Boards must take the necessary measures of preparation for security and success at the mobilization of the army, the fleet, and the fortresses, as well as for the march of the army to the threatened frontier. Such military measures, which could be ordered by the minister of war without the approval of the Tsar or a public announcement of mobilization, were almost equivalent to mobilization in the frontier districts. There was thus danger that Germany in alarm would resort to counter measures which might lead to a European war. Despite, however, many reports of these Russian preparations along the German frontier, Germany apparently refrained from corresponding preparatory measures until officially notified that Russia had taken the final step by proclaiming general mobilization.]

On original with His Imperial Majesty's own hand written, "Agreed," in Krasnoe Selo July 12 (25), 1914. Countersigned: President of the Council of Ministers, State Secretary Goremykin. Copy. Confidential.

Special Journal of the Council of Ministers
July 12 (25), 1914

Concerning the putting into effect of the Order of February 17 (March 1), 1913, approved by the Tsar about the period preparatory to the war.

On July 12 (25) Your Imperial Majesty approved the special journal of the Council of Ministers of July 11 (24), 1914 in connection with the report of the Minister of Foreign Affairs about aggression of the Austro-Hungarian Government toward Serbia. This journal gives to the Ministers of War and Navy the right to ask the permission of Your Majesty to declare, depending upon the course of events, mobilization of 4 military districts: Kiev, Odessa, Moscow, and Kazan, and of the Baltic and Black Seas navies. And also to hasten immediately the replenishment of the stores of ammunition for the Army.

Now, in accordance with the present state of the diplomatic negotiations, and in order to take all necessary measures to prepare and

[1] Hoover War Library Manuscript.

secure the success of the mobilization of the Army, Navy and Fortresses and the concentration of the Army on the borderland of possible enemies,—the Council of Ministers considers that it is time, beginning July 13 (26) of this year to put into effect throughout the territory of the whole Empire the Order concerning preparatory period to the war in both its parts. Minister of War is authorised to ask permission of Your Imperial Majesty to take measures which have not been foreseen in the Order, but which he [Minister of War], will find necessary, having each time notified the Council of Ministers. According to the art. 2 of the above-mentioned Order, the beginning of the preparatory period to the war is fixed by the decision of the Council of Ministers, approved by the Tzar.

Taking all this into consideration, the Council of Ministers decides as follows: throughout the whole territory of the Empire beginning July 13 (26) of this year the Order of the preparatory period to the war is into effect on the basis indicated in this journal.

About this decision, the Council of Ministers considers it its duty to submit this for Your Majesty's gracious consideration.

Original journal signed, Messrs. President and Members of the Council of Ministers and countersigned by the Executor of the Affairs of the Council of Ministers.

71. AUSTRIAN VIEWS ON LOCALIZATION AND MEDIATION[1]

[See doc. no. 59 for evidence that Jagow was not telling the truth in stating that he had no foreknowledge of the terms of the Austrian ultimatum. Sir H. Rumbold was British Counsellor of Embassy and *Chargé d'Affaires* at Berlin.]

Sir H. Rumbold to Sir Edward Grey

Tel. (No. 90) *Berlin, July 25, 1914*

. . . .

Secretary of State for Foreign Affairs says that on receipt of a telegram at 10 this morning from German Ambassador at London, he immediately instructed German Ambassador at Vienna to pass on to Austrian Minister for Foreign Affairs your suggestion for an extension of time limit, and to "speak to" his Excellency about it. Unfortunately it appeared from press that Count Berchtold is at Ischl, and Secretary of State thought that in these circumstances there would be delay and difficulty in getting time limit extended. Secretary of State said that he did not know what Austria-Hungary had ready on the spot, but he admitted quite freely that Austro-Hungarian Government wished to give the Servians a lesson, and that they meant to

[1] *British Documents on the Origins of the War, 1898-1914,* Vol. XI, No. 122.

take military action. He also admitted that Servian Government could not swallow certain of the Austro-Hungarian demands.

Secretary of State said that a reassuring feature of situation was that Count Berchtold had sent for Russian representative at Vienna and had told him that Austria-Hungary had no intention of seizing Servian territory. This step should, in his opinion, exercise a calming influence at St. Petersburg. I asked whether it was not to be feared that, in taking military action against Servia, Austria would dangerously excite public opinion in Russia. He said he thought not. He remained of opinion that crisis could be localised. I said that telegrams from Russia in this morning's papers did not look very reassuring, but he maintained his optimistic view with regard to Russia. He said that he had given the Russian Government to understand that last thing Germany wanted was a general war, and he would do all in his power to prevent such a calamity. If the relations between Austria and Russia became threatening, he was quite ready to fall in with your suggestion as to the four Powers working in favour of moderation at Vienna and St. Petersburg.

Confidential

Secretary of State again repeated very earnestly that he had had no previous knowledge of contents of Austro-Hungarian note, although he had been accused of knowing all about it. He confessed privately that as a diplomatic document note left much to be desired.

French Ambassador here learns from Vienna that Austrians are ready to act with eight army corps.

72. German Chancellor's Attempt to Hold Back the Kaiser and Allow Mediation to Have Its Effect. (Latter's Comments Are Shown.)[1]

The Imperial Chancellor to the Emperor

Berlin, July 26, 1914

There is a Russian fleet! In the Baltic there are now five Russian torpedo boat flotillas engaged in practice cruises, which as a whole or in part can be at the Belts within six-

As Your Majesty has just been informed by the Admiralty Staff, the naval attaché at London reports that the *English* fleet is discharging its reservists, and giving crews leave according to schedule. In agreement with this fact, I venture most humbly to suggest to Your Majesty to order the High Seas Fleet to remain in Norway for the present, as this would materially lighten the burden of England's proposed

[1] *Kautsky Documents,* No. 221.

teen hours and close them. Port Arthur should be a lesson! My fleet has orders to sail for Kiel, and to Kiel it is going to sail! W.

mediation action at Petersburg, which is *evidently beginning to get shaky.*

BETHMANN-HOLLWEG

Where does he get that idea? *Not* from the material submitted to me.

73. GREY'S PROPOSAL FOR A CONFERENCE[1]

[This proposal was made on the suggestion of Arthur Nicolson, Permanent Under-Secretary in the British Foreign Office. This conference of ambassadors would have been different from that held in London under Grey's leadership during the Balkan wars, as the task was a more delicate one, and as the four less directly interested powers would have been likely to divide three to one against Austria and Germany, since Italy would be likely to side against her ally. This was doubtless one of the chief reasons for Germany's objection to the proposal.]

Sir Edward Grey to Sir F. Bertie

Foreign Office, July 26, 1914

Tel. (No. 232)

Ask Minister for Foreign Affairs if he would be disposed to instruct Ambassador here to join with representatives of Italy, Germany, France, and myself in a conference to be held here at once in order to endeavour to find an issue to prevent complications. With this view representatives at Vienna, St. Petersburg and Belgrade should be authorised in informing Governments to which they are accredited of above suggestion to request that pending results of conference all active military operations shall be suspended.

(Repeated to Vienna, St. Petersburg, and Nish.)

(Sent also to Berlin, and Rome.)

74. REPORTS OF AUSTRO-RUSSIAN DISCUSSION LOOKING TOWARD DIRECT CONVERSATIONS

[The following six documents give us as many accounts of the direct conversations between Russia and Austria. The two by Szápáry (Austrian Ambassador in St. Petersburg) and Sazonov (Russian For-

---

[1] *British Documents on the Origins of the War, 1898-1914,* Vol. XI, No. 140.

eign Minister) are first-hand accounts. The others reported what they heard from the two principals. These parallel accounts offer an instructive problem in the use of historical materials. These conversations, suggested by Pourtalès, German Ambassador in St. Petersburg, were thwarted by the refusal of Austria to consent to any change in her demands, and by her declaration of war on Serbia, planned to forestall any intervention which might prevent Austrian military action against Serbia.]

(a) *The German Ambassador at Petersburg to the German Foreign Office*[1]

Telegram 163   St. Petersburg, July 26, 1914

Count Szápáry had a lengthy conference with Sazonoff this afternoon. Both participants, with whom I talked afterward, emerged from it with the same pleasant impression. The assurances of the Ambassador that Austria-Hungary was contemplating no plan of conquest, and was simply anxious to have the peace kept along its borders, visibly eased the Minister's mind. The Austrian note was quietly discussed by Sazonoff and Count Szápáry. It developed from the discussion that Sazonoff had no objection to a number of the points. Concerning some of the other points, the Minister told me, they might be able to come to an agreement as a result of alterations in their form. Perhaps it was only a matter of words. Austria, he said, made some demands which the Serbian Government could not, as a matter of fact, carry out, without altering the Serbian Constitution, which at the present moment was impossible. But perhaps a method for satisfying Austria might be found without literal compliance with the demands. Sazonoff also touched upon the idea of mediation in his talk with my Austrian colleague, and suggested mediation by the Kings of Italy and England. The Minister also asked me with urgence whether I, too, might not be able to make some proposition. While insisting that I was not empowered to make any proposition and could therefore only suggest my own personal ideas, I replied that the following method might perhaps be feasible. In case the Vienna Cabinet might be found willing to modify to a certain extent the form of certain of the demands, which, from the statements of Count Szápáry, did not seem to be entirely excluded as a possibility, it might be possible to get into immediate touch with Austria-Hungary on this matter. Should an agreement be the result, then Serbia[2] . . . be advised by Russia to accept the demands on the basis agreed upon between Austria and Russia, and to permit Austria to be notified of this through the medium of some third Power. Sazonoff, to whom I again emphatically insisted that I was not speaking in the name of my Government, said that he would immediately telegraph to the Russian Ambassador at Vienna along the lines of my proposal.

---

[1] *Kautsky Documents,* No. 238.

[2] Cipher group lacking here.

I have the impression that Sazonoff, perhaps as the result of information from Paris and London, has lost some of his nerve and is now looking for a way out. Minister earnestly requested of me that the German press be quieted down as much as possible. He promised to see to the same thing here.

POURTALÈS

(b) *M. Paléologue, French Ambassador at St. Petersburgh, to M. Bienvenu-Martin, Acting Minister for Foreign Affairs*[1]

St. Petersburgh, July 26, 1914

The Minister for Foreign Affairs continues with praiseworthy perseverance to seek means to bring about a peaceful solution. "Up to the last moment," he declared to me, "I shall show myself ready to negotiate."

It is in this spirit that he has just sent for Count Szápáry to come to a "frank and loyal explanation." M. Sazonof commented in his presence on the Austro-Hungarian ultimatum, article by article, making clear the insulting character of the principal clauses. "The intention which inspired this document," he said, "is legitimate if you pursued no aim other than the protection of your territory against the intrigues of Servian anarchists; but the procedure to which you have had recourse is not defensible." He concluded: "Take back your ultimatum, modify its form, and I will guarantee you the result."

The Austro-Hungarian Ambassador showed himself moved by this language; however, while awaiting instructions, he reserves the opinion of his Government. Without being discouraged M. Sazonof has decided to propose this evening to Count Berchtold the opening of direct conversations between Vienna and St. Petersburgh on the changes to be introduced into the ultimatum.

This friendly and semi-official interposition of Russia between Austria and Servia has the advantage of being expeditious. I therefore believe it to be preferable to any other procedure and likely to succeed.

PALÉOLOGUE

(c) *Russian Minister for Foreign Affairs, Sazonov, to Russian Ambassador at Vienna, Schebeko*[2]

St. Petersburgh, July 13, (26) 1914

(Telegram)

I had a long and friendly conversation to-day with the Austro-Hungarian Ambassador. After discussing the ten demands addressed

---

[1] *Collected Diplomatic Documents relating to the Outbreak of the European War, 1915, French Yellow Book,* No. 54.

[2] *Ibid.,* No. 25.

to Servia, I drew his attention to the fact that. quite apart from the clumsy form in which they were presented, some of them were quite impracticable, even if the Servian Government agreed to accept them. Thus, for example, points 1 and 2 could not be carried out without recasting the Servian press law and associations law, and to that it might be difficult to obtain the consent of the Skupchtina. As for enforcing points 4 and 5, this might lead to most dangerous consequences, and even to the risk of acts of terrorism directed against the Royal Family and against Pashitch, which clearly could not be the intention of Austria. With regard to the other points it seemed to me that, with certain changes of detail, it would not be difficult to find a basis of mutual agreement, if the accusations contained in them were confirmed by sufficient proof.

In the interest of the maintenance of peace, which, according to the statements of Szápáry, is as much desired by Austria as by all the Powers, it was necessary to end the tension of the present moment as soon as possible. With this object in view it seemed to me most desirable that the Austro-Hungarian Ambassador should be authorised to enter into a private exchange of views in order to redraft certain articles of the Austrian note of the 10th (23rd) July in consultation with me. This method of procedure would perhaps enable us to find a formula which would prove acceptable to Servia, while giving satisfaction to Austria in respect of the chief of her demands. Please convey the substance of this telegram to the Minister for Foreign Affairs in a judicious and friendly manner.

Communicated to Russian Ambassadors in Germany, France, Great Britain, and Italy.

(d) *Sir G. Buchanan to Sir Edward Grey*[1]

Tel. (No. 173)   St. Petersburg, July 27, 1914

Minister for Foreign Affairs had yesterday a long conversation with Austrian Ambassador, in which latter tried to explain away objectionable features of Austria's recent action. Minister for Foreign Affairs said that he perfectly understood Austria's motives, but ultimatum had been drafted in such form as to render it impossible for Servia to accept it as a whole. While some of demands were reasonable enough, others were not only incompatible with Servia's dignity as an independent State, but could not possibly be put into immediate execution, as they entailed revision of her existing laws. Russia, his Excellency added, was object of such suspicion in Austria that it would be useless for her to offer her good offices at Belgrade. He thought, however, England and Italy might be willing to collaborate with Austria with a view to putting an end to present tension. Ambassador promised to inform his Government of what his Excellency had said.

---

[1] *British Documents on the Origins of the War, 1898-1914,* Vol. XI, No. 170.

In reply to question Minister for Foreign Affairs addressed to me, I said that I had in conversation, reported in my telegram No. 166 of 24th July, correctly defined attitude of His Majesty's Government, and that you could not promise to do more. His Excellency was wrong in believing that we should promote cause of peace by telling Germany if she supported Austria by force of arms she would have us to deal with as well as France and Russia. Such a menace would but stiffen her attitude, and it was only by approaching her as a friend anxious to preserve peace that we could induce her to use her influence at Vienna to avert war. If, however, we were to succeed, his Excellency must do nothing to precipitate a conflict, and I therefore trusted that mobilisation ukase would be deferred as long as possible, and that when it was issued troops would not be allowed to cross frontier.

Minister for Foreign Affairs replied that he did not believe that we should succeed in winning over Germany to cause of peace unless we publicly proclaimed our solidarity with France and Russia. No effective steps towards mobilisation could be taken until Imperial ukase was issued, and if it was deferred too long Austria would profit by delay to make her military preparations complete, while Russia could do nothing. Order to mobilise might perhaps be accompanied by a statement that troops would be retained on this side of the frontier. He could not tell me when ukase would be issued, but spoke of day on which Austrian army entered Servia as a likely date.

His Excellency strongly condemned arrest of Servian General Poutnik in Hungary as likely to aggravate present tension.

(e) *Buchanan to Grey*

Tel. (No. 174)   St. Petersburg, July 27, 1914

French Ambassador informs me that since my conversation with Minister for Foreign Affairs, reported in my immediately preceding telegram of to-day, his Excellency has decided to propose direct conversation between Vienna and St. Petersburg as to modifications to be introduced into Austrian demands.

FOREIGN OFFICE MINUTE

This is confusing. In three consecutive days M. Sazonof has made one suggestion and two proposals all differing from each other.

1. The Suggestion.—If Servia were to appeal to the Powers, Russia would stand aside and leave question in hands of England, France, Italy, and Germany. (July 25)

2. July 26.—Proposal to Austrian Ambassador that England and

[1] *British Documents on the Origins of the War, 1898-1914*, Vol. XI, No. 179.

Italy should collaborate with Austria with view to putting an end to present tension.

3. July 27.—Proposal that Russia will converse directly with Vienna.

One really does not know where one is with M. Sazonof and I told Count Benckendorff so this afternoon.—A. N[icholson].

(f) *Austrian Ambassador at St. Petersburg, Count Szápáry, to Berchtold*[1]

Petersburg, July 27, 1914

Telegram. No. 165. Ciphered. Private

Have just had a long conversation with Herr Sazonow.

German ambassador had told me before noon that he had found the minister much more quiet and amenable, when he visited him in the morning. He had advised him to speak with me, whom he knew to be well-disposed towards Russia and filled with regret that our action against Servia met with so little sympathy in Petersburg. Herr Sazonow's reception of me contrasted vastly with his reserved manner last Friday. He told me what Count Pourtalès had said to him and added that if I had not come of my own accord, he would have asked me to visit him, as he was desirous to have open speech with me. Last Friday he had been somewhat surprised and had not quite mastered his temper, besides our conversation was then a purely official one.

I answered that I also wished to be able to speak sincerely with him, as I had the impression, that in Russia a mistaken idea prevailed on the character of our action in Servia. We seemed to be suspected of wanting to get an advance on the Balkans, with a view to marching to Salonica or perhaps even to Constantinople. There were others who regarded our action as a kind of preface to a preventive war against Russia, which Germany was planning. All these suppositions were partly mistaken and partly altogether unreasonable. The aim of our action was self-preservation and defence against a hostile propaganda of word, script and deed, which threatened our integrity. Nobody in all Austria-Hungary was thinking of threatening Russia's interests or seeking a quarrel with that country. We are however firmly resolved to attain the end we have proposed to ourselves and we consider the way we have chosen, the most practicable. As an action of self-defence is in question, I would not conceal from him that every consequence which might arise, had been considered. I was quite clear upon the point, that if a conflict with the Great Powers became unavoidable, the consequences might be tremendous, and the religious, moral and social order of the world might be at stake. In glaring colours I propounded the thought, which also appears to alarm Sir E. Grey, of what might follow, if a European war broke out.

[1] *Austrian Red Book* (1919), Pt. II, p. 131, No. 73.

Herr Sazonow agreed fully and seemed rejoiced that I entertained such thoughts. He repeatedly assured me that in Russia not only he, but all the ministers, and what was still more important, the sovereign himself—all felt the same for Austria-Hungary. He could not deny that in Russia there were some old grudges rankling against Austria-Hungary, he sometimes felt them himself, but these were things of the past, and must not interfere with practical politics. As to the Slavs—he ought not to say as much to the Austro-Hungarian ambassador—he had no heart for the Balkan Slavs. They are a heavy burden for Russia, and we had no conception what Russia has already suffered through them. Our aims, such as I have described them, are perfectly legitimate, but in his opinion the way we were taking for attaining them, was not the safe way. The Note we had presented was not happy in its form. He had studied it since my visit and if I could find time, he would like to look it through with me again. I replied that I held myself at his disposition, but that I was not authorized to discuss the Note or to interpret it. His remarks would of course be full of interest. The minister then one by one discussed all the points of the Note and declared that of the ten points, seven were acceptable without great difficulties, but that the two points referring to the collaboration of Imp. and Roy. functionaries in Servia, and the point in which we demand *ad libitum* the dismissal of officers and officials, which we name, are in their present form altogether unacceptable. With regard to the 5th point I was able to give a full interpretation, having been instructed by your Excellency's telegram No. 172 of the 25th July. With regard to the other two points I said I did not know how my government interpreted them, but that both were absolutely necessary. Herr Sazonow suggested that a consular intervention might have been proposed and as to the dismissal, proofs of the guilt of the persons in question should have been given.

Otherwise King Peter would risk being killed directly. I answered that the minister's view of the case was the best justification of our action in Servia. Herr Sazonow said that we should always remember, that the Karageorgevic dynasty was without any doubt the last Servian dynasty. We surely did not desire the neighbourhood of an anarchist witches' cauldron. I answered that we certainly took an interest in the monarchical form of the Servian State, but the last remark of the minister had again proven, how very necessary a firm attitude was in Servia's case. While recapitulating what had been said, the minister declared that he could not help feeling, that the whole affair was an affair of words, and that it might surely be possible to get over the difficulties as they stood at present. Would we be prepared to accept the mediation of our ally, the King of Italy? Or would we accept the King of England? I answered that I was not in a position to reply to these questions, that I did not know what dispositions my government had already taken, that certain matters were on the move, and that certain things could not be retracted, when once they had been started.

Overmore the Servians had ordered their mobilisation for yesterday and what might have happened since then, was unknown to me.

Herr Sazonow, at the conclusion of the conversation, again in warm words expressed his pleasure at what I had explained to him and declared himself much comforted. He would report to Emperor Nicholas about it, whom he was to see the day after tomorrow, on the day of reception.

Russian politics have travelled over a long distance in two days,— from the discourteous rejection of our plans with regard to Servia, and the hard judgment on our *dossier*, to the proposition of making a European question out of the whole affair, and the search for a mediator. Still we must not overlook the fact, that side by side with this retrograde diplomatic movement, there is energetic military influence at work, which threatens to change the Russian situation in our disfavour.

75. Grey's Request That Germany Urge Moderation at Vienna[1]

Sir Edward Grey to Sir E. Goschen

Tel. (No. 208)   Foreign Office, July 27, 1914

German Ambassador has informed me that German Government accept in principle mediation between Austria and Russia by the four Powers, reserving, of course, their right as an ally to help Austria if attacked. He has also been instructed to request me to use influence in St. Petersburg to localise the war and to keep up the peace of Europe.

I have replied that the Servian reply went further than could have been expected to meet the Austrian demands. German Minister for Foreign Affairs has himself said that there were some things in the Austrian note that Servia could hardly be expected to accept. I assumed that Servian reply could not have gone as far as it did unless Russia had exercised conciliatory influence at Belgrade, and it was really at Vienna that moderating influence was now required. If Austria put the Servian reply aside as being worth nothing and marched into Servia, it meant that she was determined to crush Servia at all costs, being reckless of the consequences that might be involved. Servian reply should at least be treated as a basis for discussion and pause. I said German Government should urge this at Vienna.

I recalled what German Government had said as to the gravity of the situation if the war could not be localised, and observed that if Germany assisted Austria against Russia it would be because, without any reference to the merits of the dispute, Germany could not afford to see Austria crushed. Just so other issues might be raised that would supersede the dispute between Austria and Servia, and would bring

[1] *British Documents on the Origins of the War, 1898-1914*, Vol. XI, No. 176.

other Powers in, and the war would be the biggest ever known; but as long as Germany would work to keep the peace I would keep closely in touch. I repeated that after the Servian reply it was at Vienna that some moderation must be urged.

76. German Advice to Austria in Pursuance of Grey's Request[1]

[By the time Tschirschky, the German Ambassador in Vienna, communicated this telegram of Bethmann-Hollweg's to Berchtold, the latter replied that since the opening of hostilities on Serbia's part and the resulting Austrian declaration of war, England's move was made too late.]

The Imperial Chancellor to the German Ambassador at Vienna

Telegram 169   Berlin, July 27, 1914

Prince Lichnowsky has just telegraphed:

"Sir E. Grey had me call on him just now and requested me to inform Your Excellency as follows:

"The Serbian Chargé d'Affaires had just transmitted to him the text of the Serbian reply to the Austrian note. It appeared from the reply that Serbia had agreed to the Austrian demands to an extent such as he would never have believed possible; except in one point, the participation of Austrian officials in the judicial investigation, Serbia had actually agreed to everything that had been demanded of her. It was plain that this compliance of Serbia's *was to be attributed to the pressure exerted from Petersburg.*

"Should Austria fail to be satisfied with this reply, in other words, should this reply not be accepted at Vienna as a foundation for peaceful negotiations, or should Austria even proceed to the occupation of Belgrade, which lay quite defenseless before her, it would then be absolutely evident that Austria was only seeking an excuse for crushing Serbia. And thus, that Russia and Russian influence in the Balkans were to be struck at through Serbia. It was plain that Russia could not regard such action with equanimity, and would have to accept it as a direct challenge. The result would be the most frightful war that Europe had ever seen, and no one could tell to what such a war might lead.

"We had repeatedly, and even yesterday, stated the Minister, turned to him with the request that he *make a plea for moderation at Petersburg. He had always gladly complied with this request* and during the last crisis had subjected himself to reproaches from Russia to the effect that he was placing himself too much on our side and too little on theirs. Now he was turning to us with the request that we should

[1] *Kautsky Documents*, No. 277.

make use of our influence at Vienna either to get them to accept the reply from Belgrade as satisfactory or as the basis for conferences. He was convinced that it lay in our hands to bring the matter to a settlement by means of the proper representations, and he would regard it as a good augury for the future *if we two should once again succeed in assuring the peace of Europe by means of our mutual influence on our allies.*

"I found the Minister irritated for the first time. He spoke with great seriousness and seemed absolutely to expect that we should successfully make use of our influence to settle the matter. He is also going to make a statement in the House of Commons today in which he is to express his point of view. In any event, I am convinced that in case it should come to war after all, we should no longer be able to count on British sympathy or British support, as every evidence of ill-will would be seen in Austria's procedure."

Since we have already refused one English proposal for a conference, it is impossible for us to waive *a limine* this English suggestion also. By refusing every proposition for mediation, we should be held responsible for the conflagration by the whole world, and be set forth as the original instigators of the war. That would also make our position impossible in our own country, where we must appear as having been forced into the war. Our situation is all the more difficult, inasmuch as Serbia has apparently yielded to a very great degree. Therefore we cannot refuse the mediator's rôle, and must submit the English proposal to the consideration of the Vienna Cabinet, especially as London and Paris continue to make their influence felt in Petersburg. I request Count Berchtold's opinion on the English suggestion, as likewise his views on M. Sazonoff's desire to negotiate directly with Vienna.

BETHMANN-HOLLWEG

77. GERMAN REFUSAL OF GREY'S PROPOSAL OF A CONFERENCE[1]

[Goschen was the British Ambassador in Berlin. Grey's proposal for a conference Jagow and Bethmann-Hollweg did not forward to Vienna; before they could do this they had received Lichnowsky's recommendation that Germany exert influence at Vienna, which they then forwarded instead (see doc. no. 76).]

Sir E. Goschen to Sir Edward Grey

Tel. (No. 96) Berlin, July 27, 1914

Your telegram No. 232 of 26th of July to Paris

Secretary of State for Foreign Affairs says that conference you suggest would practically amount to a court of arbitration and could not, in his opinion, be called together except at the request of Austria and Russia. He could not therefore, desirous though he was to co-

---

[1] *British Documents on the Origins of the War, 1898-1914,* Vol. XI, No. 185.

operate for the maintenance of peace, fall in with your suggestion. I said I was sure that your idea had nothing to do with arbitration, but meant that representatives of the four nations not directly interested should discuss and suggest means for avoiding a dangerous situation. He maintained, however, that such a conference as you proposed was not practicable. He added that news he had just received from St. Petersburg showed that there was an intention on the part of M. Sazonof to exchange views with Count Berchtold. He thought that this method of procedure might lead to a satisfactory result, and that it would be best, before doing anything else, to await outcome of the exchange of views between the Austrian and Russian Governments.

In the course of a short conversation Secretary of State for Foreign Affairs said that as yet Austria was only partially mobilising, but that if Russia mobilised against Germany latter would have to follow suit. I asked him what he meant by "mobilising against Germany." He said that if Russia only mobilised in south Germany would not mobilise, but if she mobilised in north Germany would have to do so too, and Russian system of mobilisation was so complicated that it might be difficult exactly to locate her mobilisation. Germany would therefore have to be very careful not to be taken by surprise. . . .

78. FRENCH FULL SUPPORT OF RUSSIA[1]

[Baron von Schoen was German Ambassador in Paris. France was no more desirous of exerting pressure for peace upon Russia than was Germany upon her ally.]

The Russian Ambassador at Paris, M. Isvolsky, to the Russian Foreign Secretary, M. Sazonov

Telegram. Secret. No. 195   Paris, July 14/27, 1914

Immediately upon my return to Paris, I saw the Minister of Justice [Bienvenu-Martin] in the presence of Abel Ferry and Berthelot. They confirmed the details of the steps taken by the German Ambassador, of which you have been informed by Sevastopoulo's telegrams Nos. 187 and 188. This morning, Baron Schoen confirmed in writing the declaration made by him yesterday, to wit:

1. "Austria has declared to Russia that she is not seeking territorial acquisitions and will respect the integrity of Serbia. Her only aim is to assure her own security;

2. "The prevention of war consequently rests upon Russia;

3. "Germany and France entirely united in the ardent desire to maintain peace, ought to press Russia to be moderate."

In this connection Baron Schoen particularly emphasized the expression "united" [*solidaire*] applied to Germany and France. Accord-

[1] *Un Livre Noir*, Vol. II, p. 281. Reprinted with the permission of the Librairie du Travail.

ing to the conviction of the Minister of Justice, these steps on the part of Germany are taken with the evident object of disuniting Russia and France, of inducing the French Government to make representations at St. Petersburg, and of thus compromising our ally in our eyes, and, in case of war, of throwing the responsibility not on Germany, who is ostensibly making every effort to preserve peace, but on Russia and France. Today, two hours before the steps taken by the Austrian Ambassador reported in my telegram 191, the German Ambassador paid a visit to Abel Ferry and made him, in the name of his Government, a new proposition "of intervention of France and Germany between Russia and Austria." Abel Ferry replied to him that he would bring this proposal to the attention of the Minister of Justice and merely observed that it would be opportune to leave the initiative of intervention to the four Powers, to which Baron Schoen acquiesced. The Minister of Justice has told me that he does not understand the sense of the new proposal of Baron Schoen, but that he viewed it with defiance and proposed to tell him tomorrow that a reply would be given him on the return to Paris of the Minister of Foreign Affairs on Wednesday. Altogether, I am struck by the way the Minister of Justice and his colleagues correctly understand the situation and how firm and calm is their decision to give us the most complete support and to avoid the least appearance of divergence of view between us.

ISVOLSKY

[This dispatch was suppressed from the *Russian Orange Book* of 1914.—EDITORS]

79. SERBIAN REPLY TO THE AUSTRIAN NOTE[1]

[The Serbian Cabinet evinced great diplomatic skill in their reply, winning the approval and sympathy of all the Powers except Austria. Since no Serbian Government could have yielded on every point—a military revolt would have been the consequence—and since Austria was evidently bent on rejecting any reply which did not so yield, Serbia could afford a very conciliatory form which would tend to place Austria in the wrong when she rejected it. Several hours before it was handed to Giesl at the expiration of the time limit, mobilization of the entire Serbian army was ordered, showing that Serbia well knew Austria would not accept her reply. Austria delayed several days in communicating this reply to Germany.]

The Royal Servian Government have received the communication of the Imperial and Royal Government of the 10th instant,[2] and are convinced that their reply will remove any misunderstanding which

---

[1] *Collected Diplomatic Documents relating to the Outbreak of the European War,* 1915, *British Diplomatic Correspondence,* No. 39, July 27, 1914.

[2] Old style.

may threaten to impair the good neighbourly relations between the Austro-Hungarian Monarchy and the Kingdom of Servia.

Conscious of the fact that the protests which were made both from the tribune of the national Skuptchina[1] and in the declarations and actions of the responsible representatives of the State—protests which were cut short by the declarations made by the Servian Government on the 18th[2] March, 1909—have not been renewed on any occasion as regards the great neighbouring Monarchy, and that no attempt has been made since that time, either by the successive Royal Governments or by their organs, to change the political and legal state of affairs created in Bosnia and Herzegovina, the Royal Government draw attention to the fact that in this connection the Imperial and Royal Government have made no representation except one concerning a school book, and that on that occasion the Imperial and Royal Government received an entirely satisfactory explanation. Servia has several times given proofs of her pacific and moderate policy during the Balkan crisis, and it is thanks to Servia and to the sacrifice that she has made in the exclusive interest of European peace that that peace has been preserved. The Royal Government cannot be held responsible for manifestations of a private character, such as articles in the press and the peaceable work of societies—manifestations which take place in nearly all countries in the ordinary course of events, and which, as a general rule, escape official control. The Royal Government are all the less responsible, in view of the fact that at the time of the solution of a series of questions which arose between Servia and Austria-Hungary they gave proof of a great readiness to oblige, and thus succeeded in settling the majority of these questions to the advantage of the two neighbouring countries.

For these reasons the Royal Government have been pained and surprised at the statements, according to which members of the Kingdom of Servia are supposed to have participated in the preparations for the crime committed at Serajevo; the Royal Government expected to be invited to collaborate in an investigation of all that concerns this crime, and they were ready, in order to prove the entire correctness of their attitude, to take measures against any persons concerning whom representations were made to them. Falling in, therefore, with the desire of the Imperial and Royal Government, they are prepared to hand over for trial any Servian subject, without regard to his situation or rank, of whose complicity in the crime of Serajevo proofs are forthcoming, and more especially they undertake to cause to be published on the first page of the "Journal officiel," on the date of the 13th (26th) July, the following declaration:—

"The Royal Government of Servia condemn all propaganda which may be directed against Austria-Hungary, that is to say, all such tendencies as aim at ultimately detaching from the Austro-Hungarian

---

[1] The Servian Parliament.

[2] Old style.

Monarchy territories which form part thereof, and they sincerely deplore the baneful consequences of these criminal movements. The Royal Government regret that, according to the communication from the Imperial and Royal Government, certain Servian officers and officials should have taken part in the above-mentioned propaganda and thus compromised the good neighbourly relations to which the Royal Servian Government was solemnly engaged by the declaration of the 31st March, 1909,[1] which declaration disapproves and repudiates all idea or attempt at interference with the destiny of the inhabitants of any part whatsoever of Austria-Hungary, and they consider it their duty formally to warn the officers, officials, and entire population of the kingdom that henceforth they will take the most rigorous steps against all such persons as are guilty of such acts, to prevent and to repress which they will use their utmost endeavour."

This declaration will be brought to the knowledge of the Royal Army in an order of the day, in the name of His Majesty the King, by his Royal Highness the Crown Prince Alexander, and will be published in the next official army bulletin.

The Royal Government further undertake:—

1. To introduce at the first regular convocation of the Skuptchina a provision into the press law providing for the most severe punishment of incitement to hatred or contempt of the Austro-Hungarian Monarchy, and for taking action against any publication the general tendency of which is directed against the territorial integrity of Austria-Hungary. The Government engage at the approaching revision of the Constitution to cause an amendment to be introduced into article 22 of the Constitution of such a nature that such publication may be confiscated, a proceeding at present impossible under the categorical terms of article 22 of the Constitution.

2. The Government possess no proof, nor does the note of the Imperial and Royal Government furnish them with any, that the "Narodna Odbrana" and other similar societies have committed up to the present any criminal act of this nature through the proceedings of any of their members. Nevertheless, the Royal Government will accept the demand of the Imperial and Royal Government, and will dissolve the "Narodna Odbrana" Society and every other society which may be directing its efforts against Austria-Hungary.

3. The Royal Servian Government undertake to remove without delay from their public educational establishments in Servia all that serves or could serve to foment propaganda against Austria-Hungary, whenever the Imperial and Royal Government furnish them with facts and proofs of this propaganda.

4. The Royal Government also agree to remove from military service all such persons as the judicial enquiry may have proved to be guilty of acts directed against the integrity of the territory of the Austro-

---

[1] New style.

Hungarian Monarchy, and they expect the Imperial and Royal Government to communicate to them at a later date the names and the acts of these officers and officials for the purposes of the proceedings which are to be taken against them.

5. The Royal Government must confess that they do not clearly grasp the meaning or the scope of the demand made by the Imperial and Royal Government that Servia shall undertake to accept the collaboration of the organs of the Imperial and Royal Government upon their territory, but they declare that they will admit such collaboration as agrees with the principle of international law, with criminal procedure, and with good neighbourly relations.

6. It goes without saying that the Royal Government consider it their duty to open an enquiry against all such persons as are, or eventually may be, implicated in the plot of the 15th[1] June, and who happen to be within the territory of the kingdom. As regards the participation in this enquiry of Austro-Hungarian agents or authorities appointed for this purpose by the Imperial and Royal Government, the Royal Government cannot accept such an arrangement, as it would be a violation of the Constitution and of the law of criminal procedure; nevertheless, in concrete cases communications as to the results of the investigation in question might be given to the Austro-Hungarian agents.

7. The Royal Government proceeded, on the very evening of the delivery of the note, to arrest Commandant Voislav Tankossitch. As regards Milan Ziganovitch, who is a subject of the Austro-Hungarian Monarchy and who up to the 15th[2] June was employed (on probation) by the directorate of railways, it has not yet been possible to arrest him.

The Austro-Hungarian Government are requested to be so good as to supply as soon as possible, in the customary form, the presumptive evidence of guilt, as well as the eventual proofs of guilt which have been collected up to the present, at the enquiry at Serajevo for the purposes of the later enquiry.

8. The Servian Government will reinforce and extend the measures which have been taken for preventing the illicit traffic of arms and explosives across the frontier. It goes without saying that they will immediately order an enquiry and will severely punish the frontier officials on the Schabatz-Loznitza line who have failed in their duty and allowed authors of the crime of Serajevo to pass.

9. The Royal Government will gladly give explanations of the remarks made by their officials whether in Servia or abroad, in interviews after the crime which according to the statement of the Imperial and Royal Government were hostile towards the Monarchy, as soon as the Imperial and Royal Government have communicated to them the passages in question in these remarks, and as soon as they have shown

---

[1] Old style.
[2] Old style.

that the remarks were actually made by the said officials, although the Royal Government will itself take steps to collect evidence and proofs.

10. The Royal Government will inform the Imperial and Royal Government of the execution of the measures comprised under the above heads, in so far as this has not already been done by the present note, as soon as each measure has been ordered and carried out.

If the Imperial and Royal Government are not satisfied with this reply, the Servian Government, considering that it is not to the common interest to precipitate the solution of this question, are ready, as always, to accept a pacific understanding, either by referring this question to the decision of the International Tribunal of the The Hague, or to the Great Powers which took part in the drawing up of the declaration made by the Servian Government on the 18th (31st) March 1909.

Belgrade, July 12 (25), 1914

80. Austria's Decision for a Prompt Declaration of War[1]

The German Ambassador at Vienna to the German Foreign Office

Telegram 113   Vienna, July 27, 1914

They have decided here to send out the declaration of war tomorrow, or the day after tomorrow at the latest, chiefly to frustrate any attempt at intervention.

Tschirschky

81. German Attempts to Restrain Austria; The "Pledge Plan"[2]

[The Kaiser had been favorably impressed by the conciliatory tone of the Serbian reply to the Austrian ultimatum. He thereupon wrote to Jagow: "I propose that we say to Austria: Serbia has been forced to retreat in a very humiliating manner, and we offer our congratulations; naturally, as a result, *no more cause for war* exists; but a *guarantee* that the promises *will be carried out*, is probably necessary; that could probably be secured by a temporary military occupation of a portion of Serbia, similar to the way we left troops in France in 1871, until the billions were paid. *On this basis* I am ready to *mediate for peace* with Austria. . . . Submit a proposal to me, along the lines sketched out, to be communicated to Vienna" (*Kautsky Documents*, no. 293). The following telegram of Bethmann's to Tschirschky was the result of the Kaiser's suggestion, but its language was not sufficiently vigorous to be effective in restraining Berchtold. Bethmann-Hollweg did not inform Russia or England of the precise terms of the "pledge plan" until he should learn whether Austria would accept it.

[1] *Kautsky Documents,* No. 257.
[2] *Ibid.,* No. 323.

It was not until sixty hours later that Austria replied, opposing the plan.]

The Imperial Chancellor to the German Ambassador at Vienna

Telegram 174   Berlin, July 28, 1914
Urgent

The Austro-Hungarian Government has distinctly informed Russia that it is not considering any territorial acquisitions in Serbia. This agrees with Your Excellency's report to the effect that neither the Austrian nor the Hungarian statesmen consider the increase of the Slavic element in the Monarchy to be desirable. On the other hand, the Austro-Hungarian Government has left us in the dark concerning its intentions, despite repeated interrogations. The reply of the Serbian Government to the Austrian ultimatum, which has now been received, makes it clear that Serbia has agreed to the Austrian demands to so great an extent that, in case of a completely uncompromising attitude on the part of the Austro-Hungarian Government, it will become necessary to reckon upon the gradual defection from its cause of public opinion throughout all Europe.

According to the statements of the Austrian General Staff, an active military movement against Serbia will not be possible before the 12th of August. As a result, the Imperial Government is placed in the extraordinarily difficult position of being exposed in the meantime to the mediation and conference proposals of the other Cabinets, and if it continues to maintain its previous aloofness in the face of such proposals, it will incur the odium of having been responsible for a world war, even, finally, among the German people themselves. A successful war on three fronts cannot be commenced and carried on on any such basis. It is imperative that the responsibility for the eventual extension of the war among those nations not originally immediately concerned should, under all circumstances, fall on Russia. At Mr. Sazonoff's last conversation with Count Pourtalès the Minister already conceded that Serbia would have to receive her "deserved lesson." At any rate the Minister was no longer so unconditionally opposed to the Austrian point of view as he had been earlier. From this fact it is not difficult to draw the conclusion that the Russian Government might even realize that, once the mobilization of the Austro-Hungarian Army had begun, the very honor of its arms demanded an invasion of Serbia. But it will be all the better able to compromise with this idea if the Vienna Cabinet repeats at Petersburg its distinct declaration that she is far from wishing to make any territorial acquisitions in Serbia, and that her military preparations are solely for the purpose of a temporary occupation of Belgrade and certain other localities on Serbian territory in order to force the Serbian Government to the complete fulfilment of her demands, and for the creation of guaranties of future good behavior—to which Austria-Hungary has an unquestionable claim after the experiences she has had with Serbia. An occupation like the German occupation of French territory after the Peace of Frankfort, for the purpose of securing compliance with the demands for war indemnity, is suggested. As soon as the Austrian demands should be complied with, evacuation would follow. Should the Russian Government fail to recognize the justice of this point of view, it would have against it the public opinion of all Europe, which is now in the process of turning away from Austria. As a further result, the general diplomatic, and probably the military, situation would undergo material alteration in favor of Austro-Hungary and her allies.

Your Excellency will kindly discuss the matter along these lines thoroughly and impressively with Count Berchtold, and instigate an appropriate move at St. Petersburg. You will have to avoid very carefully giving rise to the impression that we wish to hold Austria back. The case is solely one of finding a way to realize Austria's desired aim, that of cutting the vital cord of the Greater-Serbia propaganda, without at the same time bringing on a world war, and, if the latter cannot be avoided in the end, of improving the conditions under which we shall have to wage it, in so far as is possible.

Wire report.

BETHMANN-HOLLWEG

82. AUSTRIA'S INSISTENCE UPON DECLARING WAR ON SERBIA[1]

Bunsen to Grey

Vienna, July 28, 1914

Tel. (No. 115)

As directed by your circular telegram No. 242 of 27th July to Paris, I spoke to Minister for Foreign Affairs today in the sense of your telegram No. 208 of the 27th July to Berlin.[2] I avoided the word "mediation," but said that, as mentioned in your speech, which he had just read to me, you had hopes that conversations in London between the four Powers less interested might yet lead to an arrangement which Austro-Hungarian Government would accept as satisfactory and as rendering actual hostilities unnecessary. I added that you had regarded Servian reply as having gone far to meet just demands of Austria-Hungary; that you thought it constituted a fair base of discussion during which warlike operations might remain in abeyance, and that Austrian [*sic*] Ambassador at Berlin was speaking in this sense. Minister for Foreign Affairs said quietly, but firmly, that no discussion could be accepted on basis of Servian note; that war would be declared today, and that well-known pacific character of Emperor, as well as, he might add, his own, might be accepted as a guarantee that war was both just and inevitable. This was a matter

---

[1] *British Documents on the Origins of the War, 1898-1914,* Vol. XI, No. 230.
[2] Cf. *British Documents,* Vol. XI, No. 176.

that must be settled directly between the two parties immediately concerned. I said that you would hear with regret that hostilities could not now be arrested, as you feared that they might lead to complications threatening the peace of Europe.

In taking leave of his Excellency, I begged him to believe that if in the course of present grave crisis our point of view should sometimes differ from his, this would arise, not from want of sympathy with the many just complaints which Austria-Hungary had against Servia, but from the fact that whereas Austria-Hungary put first her quarrel with Servia, you were anxious in the first instance for peace of Europe. I trusted this larger aspect of the question would appeal with equal force to his Excellency. He said he had it also in mind, but thought that Russia ought not to oppose operations like those impending, which did not aim at territorial aggrandisement and which could no longer be postponed.

83. A German Point of View of the Crisis[1]

[Bethmann-Hollweg's last words to Goschen were omitted from the British Blue Book of 1914.]

Goschen to Grey

Berlin, July 28, 1914
(sent at midnight)

Tel. (No. 99)

Austria and Servia. At the invitation of Imperial Chancellor, I called upon his Excellency this evening. He said that he wished me to say to you that he was most anxious that Germany should work together with England for maintenance of general peace, as they had done successfully in the last European crisis. He had not been able to accept your proposal for a conference of representatives of the Great Powers, because he did not think that it would be effective and because such a conference would in his opinion have had appearance of an "Areopagus" consisting of two Powers of each group sitting in judgment upon the two remaining Powers; but his inability to accept proposed conference must not be regarded as militating against his strong desire for effective coöperation. You could be assured that he was doing his very best both at Vienna and St. Petersburg to get the two Governments to discuss the situation directly with each other and in a friendly way. He had great hopes that such discussions would take place and lead to a satisfactory result, but if the news were true which he had just read in the papers, namely that Russia had mobilised fourteen army corps in the south, he thought situation was very serious and he himself would be in a very difficult position, as in these circumstances it would be out of his power to continue to preach moderation

[1] *British Documents on the Origins of the War, 1898-1914*, Vol. XI, No. 249.

at Vienna. He added that Austria, who as yet was only partially mobilising, would have to take similar measures and if war were to result, Russia would be entirely responsible. I ventured to say that if Austria refused to take any notice of Servian note, which, to my mind, gave way in nearly every point demanded by Austria, and which in any case offered a base for discussion, surely a certain portion of responsibility would rest with her. His Excellency said that he did not wish to discuss Servian note, but that Austria's standpoint, and in this he agreed, was that her quarrel with Servia was a purely Austrian concern with which Russia had nothing to do. His Excellency further said that he resented articles in French press which stated that decision of peace or war rested with German Emperor. This decision rested with Russia and Russia alone. In conclusion his Excellency reiterated his desire to coöperate with England and his intention to do his utmost to maintain general peace. "A war between the Great Powers must be avoided" were his last words.

Austrian colleague said to me today that a general war was most unlikely, as Russia neither wanted nor was in a position to make war. I think that that opinion is shared by many people here.

(Repeated to Embassies.)

84. Russian Gratitude for French Support in View of Inevitability of the War[1]

[For a conflicting version of the French Ambassador's interview with Sazonov, the Russian Minister of Foreign Affairs, see Paléologue, *Memoirs of an Ambassador*, Vol. I, p. 33. Baron Schilling, the Director of the Chancellery of the Russian Foreign Office, says in his *Diary*, p. 43, "The French Ambassador, upon instructions of his Government, informed the Minister of Foreign Affairs of the complete readiness of France to fulfil her obligations as an ally in case of necessity." Whether Paléologue was acting under instruction has been questioned. But *cf.* doc. no. 78.]

Secret Telegram of the Minister of Foreign Affairs to the [Russian] Ambassador at Paris

No. 1551 Urgent   Saint Petersburg, July 29, 1914
Communicate to London

The German Ambassador informed me today of the decision of his Government to mobilize its forces if Russia did not stop its military preparations. Now, these preparations have been begun by us only as a consequence of the mobilization of eight corps which the Austrians have already effected and of the evident unwillingness on the part of the Austrians to accept any means of arriving at a peaceful settle-

---

[1] *Un Livre Noir*, Vol. II, p. 289. Reprinted with the permission of the Librairie du Travail.

ment of their differences with Serbia. As we cannot comply with the wishes of Germany, we have no alternative but to hasten on our own military preparations and to envisage the inevitable eventuality of war. Please inform the French Government and at the same time express to it our sincere gratitude for the declaration which the French Ambassador made to me on its behalf, to the effect that we could count fully upon the support of France. In the present circumstances this declaration is particularly valuable to us. It will be extremely desirable that England join France without loss of time, for only in this way can she succeed in anticipating a dangerous rupture of the European equilibrium.

SAZONOFF

85. A JUSTIFICATION FOR AUSTRIA-HUNGARY AND GERMANY BY A FRENCHMAN[1]

Sir M. de Bunsen to Sir Edward Grey

Vienna, July 29, 1914

Tel. (No. 122)
Confidential

French Ambassador is reporting to French Government that he is convinced by admissions of Servian Minister, with whom he was in close contact till Minister departed 26th July, that growing condition of unrest in Southern Slav provinces of Dual Monarchy was such that Austro-Hungarian Government were compelled either to acquiesce in separation of those provinces or make a desperate effort to retain them by reducing Servia to impotency. Servian Minister always said that time was working for Servia, and he told French Ambassador that within three years Southern Slav provinces would be ready to rise against Austria-Hungary without Servia having to raise her little finger. Austria-Hungary realises she could wait no longer, and determined on war, from which it looks as if nothing would now deter her. French Ambassador thinks this shows that conflict is not due to German instigation and that it does not necessarily show that Germany desires European war, as is thought by many in France.

(Repeated to Embassies.)

86. GERMAN BID FOR BRITISH NEUTRALITY[2]

Goschen to Grey

Tel. (No. 102) Secret
Urgent

Berlin, July 29, 1914

(? Austria and) Servia. Chancellor having just returned from Potsdam sent for me again tonight and made the following strong bid for

---

[1] *British Documents on the Origins of the War, 1898-1914*, Vol. XI, No. 265.
[2] *Ibid.*, Vol. XI, No. 293.

British neutrality in the event of war. He said he was continuing his efforts to maintain peace, but that (group omitted: in the event of) a Russian attack on Austria, Germany's obligation as Austria's ally might, to his great regret, render a European conflagration inevitable, and in that case he hoped Great Britain would remain neutral. As far as he was able to judge key-note of British policy, it was evident that Great Britain would never allow France to be crushed. Such a result was not contemplated by Germany. The Imperial Government was ready to give every assurance to the British Government provided that Great Britain remained neutral that, in the event of a victorious war, Germany aimed at no territorial acquisitions at the expense of France.

In answer to a question from me, his Excellency said that it would not be possible for him to give such an assurance as regards colonies.

Continuing, his Excellency said he was, further, ready to assure the British Government that Germany would respect neutrality and integrity of Holland as long as they were respected by Germany's adversaries.

As regards Belgium, his Excellency could not tell to what operations Germany might be forced by the action of France, but he could state that, provided that Belgium did not take sides against Germany, her integrity would be respected after the conclusion of the war.

Finally, his Excellency said that he trusted that these assurances might form basis of a further understanding with England which, as you well know, had been object of his policy ever since he had been Chancellor.

An assurance of British neutrality in conflict which present crisis might possibly produce would enable him to look forward to a general neutrality agreement between the two countries, the details of which it would, of course, be premature to discuss at the present moment.

His Excellency asked me how I thought you would view his request. I replied that I thought that you would like to retain full liberty of action, and that personally I did not consider it likely that you would care to bind yourself to any course of action at this stage of events.

.   .   .   .

87. The Danger of a Declaration of Position by Britain[1]

[Sir Francis Bertie was the British Ambassador in Paris.]

Bertie to Grey

Private   Paris, July 30, 1914
My dear Grey,

The feeling here is that peace between the Powers depends on England; that if she declare herself *solidaire* with France and Russia there will not be war, for Germany will not face the danger to her of

---

[1] *British Documents on the Origins of the War, 1898-1914,* Vol. XI, No. 320.

her supplies by sea being cut off by the British Fleet at a time when she could not get them from Russia and France and little from Austria who would require all that is available from elsewhere for her own needs.

People do not realize or do not take into account the difficulty for the British Government to declare England *solidaire* with Russia and France in a question such as the Austro-Servian quarrel. The French instead of putting pressure on the Russian Government to moderate their zeal expect us to give the Germans to understand that we mean fighting if war break out. If we gave an assurance of armed assistance to France and Russia now, Russia would become more exacting and France would follow in her wake. . . .

Yours sincerely,
FRANCIS BERTIE

88. GERMAN PRESSURE FOR MODERATION AT VIENNA

[Grey's proposal was welcomed by Bethmann-Hollweg because it included the two points Germany had been urging upon Russia and Austria and because he was alarmed at the possibility of England's not remaining neutral.]

(a) *The Imperial Chancellor to the Ambassador at Vienna*[1]

Telegram 192   Berlin, July 30, 1914
Urgent

The Imperial Ambassador at London [Lichnowsky] telegraphs:

"Sir E. Grey just sent for me again. The Minister was entirely calm, but very grave, and received me with the words that the situation was continuing to grow more acute. Sazonoff had stated that after the declaration of war he will no longer be in a position to negotiate with Austria direct, and *had requested them here to take up the mediation efforts again.* The Russian Government regards the cessation of hostilities for the present as a necessary preliminary to mediation.

"Sir E. Grey repeated his suggestion already reported, that we take part in a mediation *à quatre,* such as we had already accepted in principle. It would seem to him to be a suitable basis for mediation, if Austria, after occupying Belgrade, for example, or other places, should announce her conditions. Should Your Excellency, however, undertake mediation, a prospect I was able early this morning to put before him, this would of course suit him equally well. But *mediation* seemed now to him to be urgently necessary, if *a European catastrophe were not to result.*

"Sir E. Grey then said to me that he had a friendly and private communication to make to me, namely, that he did not want our warm

[1] *Kautsky Documents*, No. 395.

personal relations and the intimacy of our talks on all political matters to lead me astray, and he would *like to spare himself later the reproach (of) bad faith.* The British Government desired now as before to cultivate our previous friendship, and it could *stand aside as long as the conflict remained confined to Austria and Russia. But if we and France* should *be involved,* the situation would immediately be altered, and the British Government would, *under the circumstances, find itself forced to make up its mind quickly.* In that event *it would not be practicable to stand aside and wait for any length of time.* "If war breaks out, it will be *the greatest catastrophe* that the *world has ever seen.*" It was far from his desire to express any kind of a threat; he only wanted to protect me from disappointments and *himself* from the *reproach of bad faith,* and had therefore chosen the form of a private explanation."

As a result we stand, in case Austria refuses all mediation, before a conflagration in which England will be against us; Italy and Roumania to all appearances will not go with us, and we two shall be opposed to four Great Powers. On Germany, thanks to England's opposition, the principal burden of the fight would fall. Austria's political prestige, the honor of her arms, as well as her just claims against Serbia, could all be amply satisfied by the occupation of Belgrade or of other places. She would be strengthening her status in the Balkans as well as in relation to Russia by the humiliation of Serbia. Under these circumstances, we must urgently and impressively suggest to the consideration of the Vienna Cabinet the acceptance of mediation on the above-mentioned honorable conditions. The responsibility for the consequences that would otherwise follow would be an uncommonly heavy one both for Austria and for us.

BETHMANN-HOLLWEG

(b) *The Imperial Chancellor to the German Ambassador at Vienna*[1]
Telegram 193   Berlin, July 30, 1914

Count Pourtalès telegraphs: "Sazonoff informed me . . . meaning any war."[2]

This report does not agree with the impression that Your Excellency gave during the course of the conference of Count Berchtold with Mr. Schebeko. Apparently there is some misunderstanding, which I beg to have cleared up. We can not expect Austria to deal with Serbia, with whom she is at war. The refusal to hold any exchange

---

[1] *Kautsky Documents,* No. 396.

[2] Here was inserted the despatch from Pourtalès of July 29 (*Kautsky Documents,* No. 365) in an abbreviated form, the substance of which was that Sazonoff had informed the German Ambassador that Vienna had refused to deal directly with the Russian Government and that as a result the only thing left to do was to take up Grey's suggestion of a conference à quatre. Pourtalès had said that he felt Russian mobilization to be a great mistake, but Sazonov said it was necessary in view of Austria's action. Mobilization, he said, was far from meaning war.—EDITORS.

of opinions with Petersburg, however, would be a serious error, as it would be direct provocation of Russia's armed interference, which Austria-Hungary is beyond all else interested to prevent.

We are, of course, ready to fulfil the obligations of our alliance, but must decline to be drawn wantonly into a world conflagration by Vienna, without having any regard paid to our counsel. Also, Vienna appears to disregard our advice in regard to the Italian question.[1]

Please talk to Count Berchtold at once with all impressiveness and great seriousness.[2]

BETHMANN-HOLLWEG

(c) *The Imperial Chancellor to the German Ambassador at Vienna*[3]

Telegram 200
Urgent   Berlin, July 30, 1914

If Vienna declines to give in in any direction, especially along the lines of the last Grey proposal (telegram 192), as may be assumed from the telephone conversation of Your Excellency with Mr. von Stumm, it will hardly be possible any longer to place the guilt of the outbreak of a European conflagration on Russia's shoulders. His Majesty undertook intervention at Vienna at the request of the Czar since he could not refuse to do so without creating the incontrovertible suspicion that we wanted war. The success of this intervention is, of course, rendered difficult, inasmuch as Russia has mobilized against Austria. This we have announced to England today, adding that we had already suggested in a friendly tone, both at Paris and Petersburg, the cessation of French and Russian war preparations, so that we could take a new step in this direction only through an ultimatum, which would mean war. We suggested to Sir Edward Grey, nevertheless, that he work energetically along this line at Paris and Petersburg, and have just received through Lichnowsky his assurance to that effect. If England's efforts succeed, while Vienna declines everything, Vienna will be giving documentary evidence that it absolutely wants a war, into which we shall be drawn, while Russia remains free of responsibility. That would place us, in the eyes of our own people, in an untenable situation. Thus we can only urgently advise that Austria accept the Grey proposal, which preserves her status for her in every way.

Your Excellency will at once express yourself most emphatically on this matter to Count Berchtold, perhaps also to Count Tisza.

His Majesty this evening sent the following telegram to the Emperor Franz Joseph: "I did not feel myself able to refuse the personal plea of the Czar that I undertake to attempt mediation for the prevention of a world conflagration and the maintenance of world peace, and had

---

[1] This paragraph was written by von Jagow's hand.
[2] This paragraph was written by the Chancellor.
[3] *Kautsky Documents*, No. 441.

proposals submitted to your Government yesterday and today through my Ambassador. Among other things, they provide that Austria should announce her conditions after occupying Belgrade or other places. I should be honestly obliged to you, if you would favor me with your decision as soon as possible.

"In true friendship,
WILHELM"
v. BETHMANN-HOLLWEG[1]

89. THE SITUATION AS SET FORTH BY THE KAISER TO HIS NAVAL STAFF (IN HIS OWN HANDWRITING)[2]

[The "Willy-Nicky" telegrams between the two monarchs were without effect in preserving peace, though the Kaiser's effort caused the Tsar to suspend the order for general mobilization, but when the Tsar admitted that partial mobilization had been begun "five days before for reasons of defence on account of Austria's preparations," the Kaiser indignantly noted: "I cannot agree to any more mediation, since the Tsar, who requested it, has at the same time secretly mobilized behind my back. It is only a manœuvre, in order to hold us back and increase the start they have already got. My work is at an end." (*Kautsky Documents*, no. 390.)]

For the Guidance of Imperial Naval Office and Admiralty Staff
Absolutely secret   July 31, 1914, 12 o'clock noon

Since yesterday—July 30—Chief Admiralty Staff gave me information of the telegram of the Naval Attaché at London, concerning the interview of Sir E. Grey with Prince Lichnowsky, at which Germany was given to understand that only the betrayal of her ally by not participating in the war against Russia could preserve us from an immediate English attack, there arrived, very soon thereafter, the report of the Ambassador relative to this conversation and corroborating it, sent to me by the Foreign Office without comment. It was plain to me that Sir E. Grey by this held up before me his own King, who had just officially forwarded to me through Prince Henry a plain declaration of neutrality—delivered orally on the 29th—as untruthful. As I am now convinced that the whole crisis was caused by ENGLAND ALONE, and can be dissolved by ENGLAND ALONE (by pressure on the allied Russians and Gauls), I decided to send a telegram of a private nature to the King, who is apparently far from clear as to his rôle and his responsibilities in the crisis. Through Prince Henry I had something like the following telegraphed: I was very much obliged to His Majesty for his declaration of neutrality, which the Prince had been

---

[1] These instructions were canceled later the same day that they were sent because it appeared that the King of England was having success in holding back military preparations in France and Russia. (Cf. *Kautsky Documents*, Nos. 450, 451, 452, 464.)
[2] *Kautsky Documents*, No. 474.

commissioned to bring me. I was very much preoccupied over the situation and working desperately hard to solve it. A continuous telegraphic exchange of opinions between Czar and myself was taking place, as the former had appealed to me to mediate between him and Vienna, which I willingly undertook to do. Unfortunately the Czar had only told me on the twenty-ninth that he had mobilized, whereby it appeared from the date that three days before his appeal to me he had ordered mobilization, without informing me of it. I had called the Czar's attention to the fact that by these unexpected measures he was making my status as mediator illusory, was giving Austria cause to take it as a threat, and was thus taking upon his shoulders the enormous responsibility of a world-conflagration. I was of the opinion that from now on the only possibility of preventing a world-conflagration, which England could not wish for either, lay in London, not in Berlin. Instead of making proposals for conferences, His Majesty the King should order France and Russia, frankly and plainly, at one and the same time—they were HIS ALLIES—to DESIST at once from the mobilization, remain NEUTRAL and await Austria's proposals, which I should immediately transmit as soon as I was informed of them. The FULL RESPONSIBILITY for the most frightful world-conflagration that had ever raged would absolutely rest on HIS SHOULDERS, and he would be misjudged for it by the world and by history. I could do nothing more DIRECT; it was for him to take hold now and prove the honesty of English love for peace. He could feel assured of my loyal and liveliest support. The enclosed telegram from the King is the answer. His proposals are similar to mine, which I suggested to the Vienna Cabinet, which has left us for six days without an answer, and which were likewise telegraphed us as such from Vienna last evening. I transmitted them to London, and the King's reply to Vienna. Diplomatic conferences have at last commenced between Vienna and Peterhof, and Peterhof has also begged London for mediation. In Petersburg, according to today's report from the Ambassador, there is almost NO war enthusiasm, on the contrary a feeling of depression, as yesterday evening there were again violent street fights between revolutionaries and police, and the mood of a sick Tom-cat prevailed at court and in the army, as, coming to their senses, they are getting a scare about what they have done and may do yet with their premature mobilization.

WILHELM I. R.

90. British Cabinet's Denial of Treaty Obligation to Support France[1]

[The words in italics, suppressed from the British Blue Book of 1914, show that Grey realized the truth, but supported France and Russia in

[1] *British Documents on the Origins of the War, 1898-1914*, Vol. XI, No. 367.

their effort to minimize the importance of Russia's step. On July 30 Paul Cambon had appealed to Grey to give a pledge of support to France, recalling their exchange of notes in 1912 (see doc. no. 49) and on July 31, President Poincaré sent a personal entreaty to King George. Nevertheless, Grey refused to give such a pledge (see also Bertie's view in doc. no. 87).]

Grey to Bertie

(No. 513) Foreign Office, July 31, 1914

Sir,

M. Cambon referred today to a telegram that had been shown to Sir Arthur Nicolson this morning from the French Ambassador in Berlin saying that it was the uncertainty with regard to whether we would intervene which was the encouraging element in Berlin, and that, if we would only declare definitely on the side of Russia and France, it would decide the German attitude in favour of peace.

I said that it was quite wrong to suppose that we had left Germany under the impression that we would not intervene. I had refused overtures to promise that we should remain neutral. I had not only definitely declined to say that we would remain neutral; I had even gone so far this morning as to say to the German Ambassador that, if France and Germany became involved in war, we should be drawn into it. That, of course, was not the same thing as taking an engagement to France, and I told M. Cambon of it only to show that we had not left Germany under the impression that we would stand aside.

M. Cambon then asked me for my reply to what he had said yesterday.

I said that we had come to the conclusion, in the Cabinet today, that we could not give any pledge at the present time. The commercial and financial situation was exceedingly serious; there was danger of a complete collapse that would involve us and everyone else in ruin; and it was possible that our standing aside might be the only means of preventing a complete collapse of European credit, in which we should be involved. This might be a paramount consideration in deciding our attitude.

I went on to say to M. Cambon that though we should have to put our policy before Parliament, we could not pledge Parliament in advance. Up to the present moment, we did not feel, and public opinion did not feel, that any treaties or obligations of this country were involved. Further developments might alter this situation and cause the Government and Parliament to take the view that intervention was justified. The preservation of the neutrality of Belgium might be, I would not say a decisive, but an important factor, in determining our attitude. Whether we proposed to Parliament to intervene or not to intervene in a war, Parliament would wish to know how we stood with regard to the neutrality of Belgium, and it might be that I should ask both France and Germany whether each was prepared to undertake an engagement that she would not be the first to violate the neutrality of Belgium.

M. Cambon expressed great disappointment at my reply. He repeated his question of whether we would help France if Germany made an attack on her.

I said that I could only adhere to the answer that, as far as things had gone at present, we could not take any engagement. *The latest news was that Russia had ordered a complete mobilisation of her fleet and army. This, it seemed to me, would precipitate a crisis, and would make it appear that German mobilisation was being forced by Russia.*

M. Cambon urged that Germany had from the beginning rejected proposals that might have made for peace. It could not be to England's interest that France should be crushed by Germany. We should then be in a very diminished position with regard to Germany. In 1870, we had made a great mistake in allowing an enormous increase of German strength; and we should now be repeating the mistake. He asked me whether I could not submit his question to the Cabinet again.

I said that the Cabinet would certainly be summoned as soon as there was some new development, but at the present moment the only answer I could give was that we could not undertake any definite engagement.

I am, &c.

E. GREY

91. ITALIAN REASONS FOR NEUTRALITY

[Von Mérey was Austrian Ambassador in Rome. The Italian Minister of Foreign Affairs in 1914 was San Giuliano.]

(a) *Von Mérey to Count Berchtold*[1]

Telegram   Rome, July 30, 1914

Minister of Foreign Affairs spontaneously brought up today the question of Italy's attitude in the event of a European war.

As the character of the Triple Alliance is purely defensive; as our measures against Servia may precipitate a European conflagration, and finally as we had not previously consulted this government, Italy would not be bound to join us in the war. This, however, does not preclude the alternative that Italy might, in such an event, have to decide for herself whether her interests would best be served by taking sides with us in military operations or by remaining neutral. Personally he feels more inclined to favor the first solution, which appears to him as the more likely one, provided that Italy's interests in the

---

[1] Austro-Hungarian Monarchy. *Diplomatic Documents concerning the Relations of Austria-Hungary with Italy, from July 20, 1914 to May 23, 1915.* No. 17.

Balkan Peninsula are safeguarded and that we do not seek changes likely to give us a predominance detrimental to Italy's interests in the Balkans.

(b) *The German Ambassador at Rome to the German Foreign Office*[1]

Telegram 161   Rome, July 31, 1914

The local Government has discussed, at the Ministerial Council held today, the question of Italy's attitude in the war. Marquis San Giuliano told me that the Italian Government had considered the question thoroughly, and had again come to the conclusion that Austria's procedure against Serbia must be regarded as an act of aggression, and that consequently a *casus fœderis*, according to the terms of the Triple Alliance treaty, did not exist. Therefore Italy would have to declare herself neutral. Upon my violently opposing this point of view, the Minister went on to state that since Italy had not been informed in advance of Austria's procedure against Serbia, she could with less reason be expected to take part in the war, as Italian interests were being directly injured by the Austrian proceeding. All that he could say to me now was that the local Government reserved the right to determine whether it might be possible for Italy to intervene later in behalf of the allies, if, at the time of doing so, Italian interests should be satisfactorily protected. The Minister, who was in a state of great excitement, said in explanation that the entire Ministerial Council, with the exception of himself, had shown a distinct dislike for Austria. It had been all the more difficult for him to contest this feeling, because Austria, as I myself knew, was continuing so persistently with a recognized injury to Italian interests, as to violate Article 7 of the Triple Alliance treaty, and because she was declining to give a guaranty for the independence and integrity of Serbia. He regretted that the Imperial Government had not done more to intervene in this connection to persuade Austria to a timely compliance. I have the impression that it is not yet necessary to give up all hope for the future here, if the Italians should be met halfway with regard to the demands mentioned above, or in other words, if compensation should be offered them. Nevertheless, it cannot be denied that the attitude England has assumed has decidedly diminished the prospects of an active Italian participation in our favor.

In the meanwhile, I pointed out to the Minister in the plainest manner possible the extremely regrettable impression which such an attitude would make on us, and then called to his attention the consequences which might develop for Italy in the future as a result.

FLOTOW

---

[1] *Kautsky Documents*, No. 534.

92. ROUMANIAN DECISION FOR NEUTRALITY[1]

[Count Czernin was Austrian Minister to Roumania.]

Czernin to Berchtold, Aug. 1, 1914

Bucharest

The Prime Minister has just notified me the result of the Cabinet Council. After a warm appeal from the King to bring the treaty into force, the Cabinet Council, with one exception, declared that no party could undertake the responsibility of such action.

The Cabinet Council has resolved that *as Rumania was neither notified nor consulted concerning the Austro-Hungarian action in Belgrade no casus fœderis exists.* The Cabinet Council further resolved that military preparations for the safety of the frontier be undertaken, which would be an advantage for the Austro-Hungarian Monarchy, as several hundred miles of its frontiers would thereby be covered.

The Prime Minister added that he had already given orders to strengthen all military posts, after which by degrees general mobilization would follow.

The government intends only to publish a short *communiqué* relating to the military measures taken for the safety of the country.

93. THE STATEMENT OF THE KING OF GREECE TO THE EMPERORS OF AUSTRIA AND OF GERMANY THAT HE WOULD BE NEUTRAL (THE LATTER'S COMMENTS ARE SHOWN)[2]

Telegram 231   Athens, August 2, 1914

Tell Athens that I have made an alliance with Bulgaria and Turkey for the war against Russia and will treat Greece as an enemy in case she does not join us at once; have just told this myself, personally to Theotoky, while informing him that we are allied with Turkey and Bulgaria.

His Majesty the King has sent me the following telegram for His Majesty the Emperor and King, with the request to transmit it to the Emperor:

Cordial thanks for your telegram and for the promise of your support in our agreement with Turkey. It never came into our minds to help the Serbians. *But it does not seem possible to me, however, for us to associate ourselves with their enemies and attack them,* since, after all, they are our allies. It seems to me that the interests of Greece demand her *absolute neutrality* and the preservation of the *status quo* in the Balkans, as created by the Treaty of Bucharest. If we should sacrifice this point of view, Bulgaria would become enlarged by the annexation of those portions of Macedonia lately won by Serbia, would surround our entire

---

[1] Count Ottokar Czernin. *In the World War*, New York, Harper & Brothers (1920), pp. 14-15. Reprinted with the permission of Curtis Brown, Ltd.

[2] *Kautsky Documents*, No. 702.

northern border as far as Albania, and would constitute an enormous danger for us. I have no assurance that this would not happen. These considerations force us to neutrality and also, *in conjunction with Roumania, to prevent Bulgaria from taking a hand*. You know my opinion of the Slavs and of Russian trusteeship in the Balkans. This opinion is shared by my whole people, and if Bulgaria should attain to such an accretion of power, the balance of power in our part of the world would be destroyed and the domination of the Slavs simply assured. CONSTANTINE.

You have got to March against Russia!

Impossible.

That is no longer to be considered now! The Balkans are marching.

Rubbish!

BASSEWITZ

If Greece does not at once join us, then she will lose her position as a Balkan Power and no longer enjoy our support in her desires but be treated as an enemy. It is not a question of the balance of power in the Balkans, but of coöperation on the part of the Balkan States to free the Balkans from Russia forever! W.

94. GOSCHEN's REPORT ON HIS LAST HOURS IN BERLIN; THE ORIGIN OF THE PHRASE, "A SCRAP OF PAPER"[1]

[The day after Grey's famous speech of August 3 in the House of Commons (doc. no. 99), the Cabinet decided to send an ultimatum to Berlin demanding that the German ultimatum to Belgium be withdrawn, and stating that if a satisfactory reply were not received in London by midnight, Goschen, the British Ambassador in Berlin, would ask for his passports.]

Goschen to Grey. (Received August 19)

Berlin, August 6, 1914

Sir,

In accordance with the instructions contained in your telegram No. 266 of the 4th instant I called upon the Under-Secretary[2] of State for Foreign Affairs that afternoon and enquired in the name of His Majesty's Government whether the Imperial Government would refrain from violating Belgian neutrality. Herr von Jagow at once replied that he was sorry to say that his answer must be "No" as, in consequence of the German troops having crossed the frontier that morning, Belgian neutrality had been already violated. Herr von Jagow again went into the reasons why the Imperial Government had been obliged to take this step—namely that they had to advance into France by the quickest and easiest way—so as to be able to get well ahead with their operations and endeavour to strike some decisive blow as early

---

[1] *British Documents on the Origins of the War, 1898-1914*, Vol. XI, No. 671.
[2] Should be Secretary of State.

as possible. It was a matter of life and death for them, as if they had gone by the more southern route they could not have hoped, in view of the paucity of roads and the strength of the Fortresses, to have got through without formidable opposition entailing great loss of time. This loss of time would have meant time gained by the Russians for bringing up their troops to the German frontier. Rapidity of action was the great German asset while that of Russia was an inexhaustible supply of troops. I pointed out to Herr von Jagow that this *fait accompli* of the violation of the Belgian frontier rendered, as he would readily understand, the situation exceedingly grave and I asked him whether there was not still time to draw back and avoid possible consequences which both he and I would deplore. He replied that for the reasons he had given me it was now impossible for them to draw back.

During the afternoon I received your telegram No. 270 and, in compliance with the instructions therein contained, I again proceeded to the Imperial Foreign Office and informed the Secretary of State for Foreign Affairs that unless the Imperial Government could give the assurance by 12 o'clock that night that they would proceed no further with their violation of the Belgian frontier and stop their advance, I had been instructed to demand my passports and inform the Imperial Government that His Majesty's Government would have to take all steps in their power to uphold the neutrality of Belgium and the observance of a treaty to which Germany was as much a party as themselves.

Herr von Jagow replied that to his great regret he could give no other answer than that which he had given me earlier in the day, namely that the safety of the Empire rendered it absolutely necessary that the Imperial troops should advance through Belgium. I gave his Excellency a paraphrase of your telegram and, pointing out that you had mentioned 12 o'clock as the time when His Majesty's Government would expect an answer, asked him whether, in view of the terrible consequences which would necessarily ensue, it were not possible even at the last moment that their answer should be reconsidered. He replied that if the time given were even twenty-four hours or more his answer must be the same. I said that in that case I should have to demand my passports. This interview would have taken place at about 7 o'clock. In a short conversation which ensued Herr von Jagow expressed his poignant regret at the crumbling of his entire policy and that of the Chancellor, which had been to make friends with Great Britain and then, through Great Britain, to get closer to France. I said that this sudden end to my work in Berlin was to me also a matter of deep regret and disappointment, but that he must understand that under the circumstances and in view of our engagements His Majesty's Government could not possibly have acted otherwise than they had done.

I then said that I should like to go and see the Chancellor as it might be perhaps the last time I should have an opportunity of seeing him. He begged me to do so. I found the Chancellor very agitated. His Excellency at once began a harangue which lasted for about 20 minutes. He said that the step taken by His Majesty's Government was terrible to a degree, just for a word "neutrality" a word which in war time had so often been disregarded—just for a scrap of paper, Great Britain was going to make war on a kindred nation who desired nothing better than to be friends with her. All his efforts in that direction had been rendered useless by this last terrible step, and the policy to which, as I knew, he had devoted himself since his accession to office, had tumbled down like a house of cards. What we had done was unthinkable; it was like striking a man from behind while he was fighting for his life against two assailants. He held Great Britain responsible for all the terrible events that might happen! I protested strongly against that statement and said that in the same way as he and Herr von Jagow wished me to understand that for strategical reasons it was a matter of life and death to Germany to advance through Belgium and violate her neutrality, so I would wish him to understand that it was, so to speak, a matter of "life and death" for the honour of Great Britain that she should keep her solemn engagement to do her utmost to defend Belgium's neutrality if attacked. That solemn compact simply had to be kept, or what confidence could anyone have in engagements given by Great Britain in the future? The Chancellor said, "But at what price will that compact have been kept. Has the British Government thought of that?" I hinted to his Excellency as plainly as I could that fear of consequences could hardly be regarded as an excuse for breaking solemn engagements, but his Excellency was so excited, so evidently overcome by the news of our action and so little disposed to hear reason, that I refrained from adding fuel to the flame by further argument. As I was leaving he said that the blow of Great Britain joining Germany's enemies was all the greater that almost up to the last moment he and his Government had been working with us and supporting our efforts to maintain peace between Austria and Russia. I admitted that that had been the case and said that it was part of the tragedy which saw the two nations fall apart just at the moment when the relations between them had been more friendly and cordial than they had been for years. Unfortunately notwithstanding our efforts to maintain peace between Russia and Austria the war had spread and had brought us face to face with a situation which, if we held to our engagements, we could not possibly avoid, and which unfortunately entailed our separation from our late fellow-workers. He would readily understand that no one regretted this more than I.

After this somewhat painful interview I returned to the embassy and drew up my telegram No. 137. This telegram was handed in at the Central Telegraph Office a little before 9 P.M. It was accepted by that office but apparently never despatched.

At about 9:30 P.M. Herr von Zimmermann, the Under-Secretary of State for Foreign Affairs, came to see me. After expressing his deep regret that the very friendly official and personal relations between us were about to cease, he asked me casually whether a demand for passports was equivalent to a declaration of war. I said that such an authority on international law as he was known to be must know as well, or better than I what was usual in such cases. I added that there were many cases where diplomatic relations had been broken off and nevertheless war had not ensued, but that in this case he would have seen from my instructions of which I had given Herr von Jagow a paraphrase that His Majesty's Government expected an answer to a definite question by 12 o'clock that night, and that in default of a satisfactory answer they would be forced to take such steps as their engagements required. Herr Zimmermann said that that was in fact a declaration of war, as the Imperial Government could not possibly give the assurance required either that night or any other night.

The next morning I demanded my passports in writing.

In the meantime after Herr Zimmermann left me a flying sheet, issued by the "Berliner Tageblatt," was circulated stating that Great Britain had declared war against Germany. The immediate result of this news was the assemblage of an exceedingly excited and unruly mob before His Majesty's Embassy. The small force of police which had been sent to guard the embassy was soon overpowered and the attitude of the mob became more threatening. We took no notice of this demonstration as long as it was confined to noise but when the crash of glass and the landing of cobblestones into the drawing-room where we were all sitting warned us that the situation was getting unpleasant, I telephoned to the Foreign Office an account of what was happening. Herr von Jagow at once informed the Chief of Police, and an adequate force of mounted police sent with great promptness, very soon cleared the street. From that moment on we were well guarded and no more direct unpleasantness occurred. . . .

PART III

THE WAR

1914–1918

95. The German Strategic Plan

[The Schlieffen Plan of German military operation formed the basis of German military movements at the outbreak of the war in August, 1914. To understand the principles which underlay it and their modification is to comprehend the better why Belgium was invaded as it was, why Holland was not invaded, and what the Germans wanted to accomplish by their swift movement upon Paris. While the strategy involved is significant, the effect of the existence of the plan upon German diplomacy is equally so. If war was to come for Germany, it was essential that it come with Russia and France simultaneously. It was apparently thought that England's entry into war might depend upon whether France or Germany violated Belgian neutrality first. Moltke's modifications are given below.]

(a) The Schlieffen Plan[1]

1871

In 1871, after the Franco-Prussian War, the elder Moltke considered the German Army capable of carrying out an offensive campaign on both the French and Russian Fronts in the event of a war with the two Powers. France was exhausted and Russia undeveloped as a fighting power.

PLAN OF 1873

By 1873 France's rapid recovery rendered this impossible, and at that time the plan involved an immediate attack on France and a defensive attitude against Russia.

During the next few years France rendered her eastern frontier from Belfort to Longwy almost impregnable to the armies and weapons of that day by means of a series of fortresses. In front line the Belfort-Epinal group in the south and the Toul-Verdun group in the north, with an intentional gap of 40 miles between, the Trouée de Charmes, which we shall see was used to good purpose by the French on the defensive in 1914.

Behind these lay the Besançon-Langres-Dijon triangle in the south, Rheims and Laon in the north. Still farther in rear were the fortified areas of Lyons and Paris.

[1] Philip Neame, *German Strategy in the Great War*, London, Arnold, 1923, chap. II. Reprinted with the permission of Edward Arnold & Co.

PLAN OF 1879

In consequence of this and after the conclusion of an alliance with Austria, Moltke changed his plan to an offensive against Russia and a defensive against France in the first instance. He proposed to abandon Alsace and Lorraine if necessary, retiring on the Rhine fortresses and fighting a decisive battle in the Mainz-Frankfurt area behind the Rhine when the French armies would be weakened by the investment of Metz, Strassburg, and Mainz and protection of long lines of communication and crossings over the Rhine. If the French came through Belgium he would strike north at their flank and lines of communication. It will appear later that the German armies in 1914 were weakened by just these factors which were not duly appreciated by the great Moltke's nephew, the leader in 1914.

In Russia the Germans were to attack north of the Vistula bend towards the river Narev and the Austrians at the southern end of the front from eastern Galicia. When Italy came into the Triple Alliance Italian troops were to be used in Alsace. (In 1914: two cavalry divisions and three corps.)

Count von Waldersee, Moltke's successor, adhered to these plans, with the modification that a decisive offensive in Russia would be almost impossible in spring or autumn when the roads become impassable.

PLAN OF 1891

Count von Schlieffen became Chief of the Great General Staff in 1891. His character and military career are of great interest, for it was he who conceived the German plan of campaign put into force in 1914. An interesting insight into Schlieffen's character is given by Kuhl in one of his books. Schlieffen made a habit of setting his subordinate Staff Officers holiday tasks on all festive occasions such as Christmas, for he said that then they could devote their brains to the larger military problems undisturbed by routine work. On one occasion Kuhl brought in his appreciation up to time on Boxing Day and was immediately handed out a second problem to be done on New Year's Day.

Schlieffen was once making a tour of inspection in East Prussia when his A.D.C. drew his attention to the beauty of the scenery in a certain valley. Schlieffen looked up and grunted out: "The ground is not suitable for defence, and that river is of no value as a military obstacle," and relapsed into silence again.

He thought of nothing but the German Army and its tasks of war.

Count von Schlieffen retained his predecessor's plan in principle, but changed the front of attack in Russia, as he considered the Austrian and German attacks were too widely separated for decisive results. He proposed combined Austrian and German attacks against the southern and western angle of the Polish salient. It is interesting to compare this decision with the Falkenhayn-Ludendorff controversy on exactly the same subject in 1915, Falkenhayn adhering to Schlieffen's ideas, while Ludendorff was a disciple of the elder Moltke and Waldersee.

SCHLIEFFEN'S FINAL PLAN

In the succeeding years the armies of the Powers increased greatly in size. The areas selected by Moltke in 1879 for the deployment on the west were no longer suitable, and the French might attack in both Lorraine and Belgium instead of in one area only. Considerations of the effect of weather on the operations and supply of vast armies in the east also had greater influence. Schlieffen recognized that a rapid decision against Russia could under no circumstances be reached owing to the lack of vital objectives on the eastern front and the unlimited expanse of territory over which the Russians could retreat if their Field Army was threatened with defeat. An attack in the first instance on Russia with a defence in the west involved a long war and was therefore rejected. It was, therefore, decided to plan a decisive attack in the west as the first operation. The French eastern fortifications still precluded any hope of a rapid advance or victory on the common Franco-German frontier. These fortifications had to be out-flanked. From the German military aspect, the German Army must go through Belgium. The Germans therefore decided to violate ruthlessly the neutrality of Belgium. Actually the Germans still say that their plan was based on the well-founded assumption that France would not respect Belgian neutrality or else that Belgium would join France.

The first plan combined a frontal attack with the turning movement, but as the necessity for a wider and wider envelopment arose to ensure getting round the French flank, the frontal attack was omitted and the northern enveloping armies pivoting on the fortified area Metz-Thionville were increased to the utmost, leaving a small force for defensive duties only in Lorraine. Schlieffen's plan even included an advance through the Maastricht Peninsula of Holland as well as through Belgium. Schlieffen counted for success on strategic surprise in the large numbers deployed, and on the more rapid effect of attack by envelopment as compared with frontal attack. After the Russo-Japanese war the weakness of the Russians allowed the Germans to use nearly their whole force against France, who was now the principal and most threatening enemy. Only the equivalent of thirteen divisions and two cavalry divisions were to face the Russians. The plans of 1905 allotted no less than the equivalent of seventy-eight divisions and eight cavalry divisions to the armies north of Metz-Thionville. This number includes certain *ersatz* divisions formed on mobilization to be sent forward for the investment of Paris. Only nine divisions and three cavalry divisions in addition to fortress garrisons were left to defend Alsace-Lorraine.

Schlieffen is believed to have intended to include an attack on the Verdun-Belfort front in his war plan in addition to the great outflanking move through Belgium and Holland, as soon as he could organize sufficient new formations. His intention was to stage a perfect "Cannæ," complete envelopment on both wings.

In 1906, during the Moroccan crisis, when Schlieffen pressed for war against France, he was dismissed from the post of Chief of General Staff by the Kaiser.

THE PLAN OF 1914

The younger Moltke, a nephew of the Field Marshal of 1870, succeeded Schlieffen as Chief of General Staff. He was chosen by the Kaiser, presumably for the moral effect of his great name, for he had few of the attributes of a great commander.

In 1914 only the equivalent of twelve and a half divisions and one cavalry division were allotted to the eastern frontier. The Germans counted on the slow rate of mobilization of the Russians. This left the equivalent of eighty-eight divisions and ten cavalry divisions for the western front. Moltke adhered to Schlieffen's plan of a great advance through Belgium, but allotted only the equivalent of sixty-one divisions and seven cavalry divisions to the northern or offensive wing, that is, the five armies wheeling north of Thionville. To the two armies south of Metz he gave the equivalent of twenty-seven divisions and three cavalry divisions.

All formations, active, reserve, *landwehr* and *ersatz*, are reduced to the equivalent number of divisions for purposes of comparison. In comparing Schlieffen's and Moltke's figures it is well to remember that Schlieffen had nine less active divisions than Moltke, for nine *ersatz* divisions were organized on an active basis between 1905 and 1914, but Moltke allotted eight of these to his defensive wing.

Moltke, probably quite rightly, omitted an advance through Holland from political considerations. This restricted his lines of advance and may have forced him to reduce the strength of his right wing. The younger Moltke had, therefore, very materially altered Schlieffen's plan of 1905 by weakening the offensive wing by some seventeen divisions. We shall see that he reduced it still further in his conduct of the operations. It is probable that Moltke was aware of Schlieffen's plan for a "Cannæ" by making decisive attacks on both flanks, and he may have considered that in 1914 he had the necessary resources available.

THE PLAN IN DETAIL

In the east the Germans allotted three active and one reserve corps and one reserve division, *i.e.* nine divisions and one cavalry division, for the defense of East Prussia, organized as the Eighth Army under Prittwitz. The remaining troops provided the garrisons of the frontier fortresses such as Posen, Thorn, Danzig, Königsberg, and weak frontier guards along the Polish frontier.

In the west the seven German armies were to concentrate on a front of 250 miles from behind the Dutch frontier in the north down to Neu Breisach in the south. The First Army area was behind the Maastricht Peninsula, Second and Third Armies on the German-Belgium frontier, Fourth Army actually in Luxemburg (a neutral state), Fifth, Sixth and Seventh Armies on the German-French frontier.

The five northern armies were to wheel through Belgium and France, pivoting on the fortified Metz-Thionville area and envelop the left wing of the French armies. Provision was made for seizing Liège by a *coup de main* immediately mobilization was ordered and thus opening the passages across the Meuse. The Belgian Army, in the event of Belgium fighting, was to be dealt with by the First Army and was to be forced away from Antwerp in a westerly direction. The First Army was to be responsible throughout for the protection of the only open flank of the German armies, and the pace of the whole wheel was to be regulated by the rate of advance of the First and Second Armies. As soon as Liège was captured, the right-wing armies were to wheel forward to a line Liège-Thionville, after which orders for the general advance would be issued. The most interesting part of the plan is the forecast of moves up to the 31st day of mobilization. By the 22nd day, actually 23rd August, the armies were expected to be on a line Ghent-Mons-Sedan-Thionville. Four divisions of the right wing were detailed to seize the Channel ports. Owing to other detachments they were not available in 1914. Kluck with the First Army in 1914 actually got rather ahead of the plan. A very interesting point arises out of this. Kluck's leading corps did not complete detrainment in their concentration area before 12th August. They did not and actually could not advance to Aachen till 13th August. The leading troops of the First Army moved 36 miles on 13th, 14th and 15th August, during which time they crossed the Meuse north of Liège. The advance of the German armies depended on the First Army's pace, so it is hard to see that the general advance could have started any earlier. Yet the protagonists of the Belgians and of the defence of Liège have frequently pointed to the priceless value of the delay imposed by Liège. There appears to have been no delay.

By the 31st day of mobilization (1st September) the German armies were to reach the line Amiens-La Fère-Rethel-Thionville. In 1914 all the armies were up to the time-table, and Kluck was hurrying his army forward two days ahead with the bit in his teeth and, as will appear later, with the reins of the Supreme Command pulled out of their hands.

Now the German plan did not attempt a time-table beyond this point. They were prepared, however, for the French to attempt to hold them on the line Verdun-La Fère-R. Oise-Paris, or Verdun-Rheims-R. Marne-Paris. In either case Paris and the positions to the north and east were to be turned by an advance of the fourteen divisions of the First Army round the west side and to the south of Paris, while the Second Army held the French on the Oise or the Marne down to Paris and attacked them by siege warfare methods. In Schlieffen's plan six *ersatz* corps were to follow the First Army to invest Paris on the west and south, while the First Army reinforced by troops withdrawn from the other armies would push forward in the direction of Auxerre and Troyes and drive the French eastwards against the Swiss frontier.

The dispositions of the German railway troops is interesting. Sixty per cent of the Railway Construction and Operation Companies were placed to work in rear of the First and Second Armies. After mobilization, sufficient rolling-stock was held in the area Mainz-Frankfurt to entrain three corps at the same time.

The German plan appears on first examination to be simple, bold and far-reaching, with good prospect of success. It was, moreover, in accordance with the German teaching of strategy, envelopment at all costs.

However, this plan had the effect of bringing Belgium and Great Britain into the scale against them, owing to the violation of Belgian neutrality. Italy remained neutral. In fact, it put Germany in the wrong in the eyes of the world.

OBSERVATIONS REGARDING THE PLAN

It would be of great interest to discover why Moltke strengthened his defensive wing at the expense of his main operation. He thereby went far to ruin the plan prepared by his able predecessor, Schlieffen, described by Ludendorff as "one of the greatest soldiers who ever lived."

Moltke's plan, of course, maintained the neutrality of Holland, which Schlieffen had apparently intended to violate. But the principal difference between the two conceptions lay in Moltke omitting from the right wing the *ersatz* formations intended to follow in rear of the armies and only to reach the front at Paris. Moltke could, probably, have carried these moves out without requiring any greater front to deploy on, and could therefore have maintained the strength of the right wing without marching across the Maastricht Peninsula.

Moltke presumably intended to avoid all risk of invasion of Alsace-Lorraine, but in doing so he violated some of the principles of war—concentration at the decisive point—in that he had not the strength in his offensive wing to envelop the French armies without allowing gaps to arise in his own armies—and economy of force—in that his detachments south of Metz failed to hold the French forces there. It may be considered, judging by after events, that this violation of principles lost the war.

Schlieffen clearly recognized the vital part of his plan, and even as he lay dying, he murmured to his son-in-law, General von Hahnke—"It must come to a fight. Only make the right wing strong!"

The question of the capacity of German Supreme Command to control seven armies on a 300-mile front in the west, and another army with various detachments in the east, is another problem for consideration. It would appear far sounder to have organized the Western Front into two or three army groups and the Eastern Front under one group.

The plan of mobilization and deployment for a great army, once formed, cannot be altered at short notice. When once the Great Powers in 1914 had ordered mobilization, war was inevitable. This is proved by Moltke's argument with the Kaiser on 31st July, 1914. As the result of some misunderstanding the German Ambassador in London wired that England would undertake to keep France out of the war, if Germany would engage not to undertake any hostilities against France. On this the Kaiser said to Moltke: "Now we need only to wage war against Russia. Then we will simply deploy the whole army in the east."

Moltke replied: "Your Majesty, that is impossible; it means a whole laborious year's work, and once settled, cannot be changed. If your Majesty insists on leading the whole army to the east, it will not be an army ready for battle, but a useless agglomeration of dislocated armed men without supplies."

The Kaiser replied, "Your uncle would have given me a different answer." And Moltke records that this hurt him greatly!

However, this conversation shows the Kaiser's ignorance of the larger operations of war, and also that Moltke was prepared to stand up to the "Supreme War Lord."

(b) *A Review of the Schlieffen Plan*[1]

The plan evolved by Graf Schlieffen, the German Chief of the General Staff, in 1904-5, just before he left office, by which France was to be overwhelmed in a few weeks, and the legend of how by departing from this plan—"watering it down" is the favourite expression—his successor, Moltke, failed to deliver the "knock-out blow," have been frequently discussed in the German military books which have been reviewed in these pages. Only short extracts from it and what purported to be summaries of it, often contradictory, have, however, been given, and it has never been published in its entirety. All writers have, however, been in accord that Moltke made the left or defensive wing in Alsace and Lorraine stronger than Schlieffen designed, and that he did so at the expense of the right wing, the decisive one, which in swinging

[1] *The Army Quarterly*, July 1929, Vol. 18, No. 2, pp. 286-290 (unsigned). London, William Clowes & Sons, 94 Jermyn St., St. James's, S. W. Reprinted with the permission of *The Army Quarterly*.

round was to sweep the French Armies against the back of their eastern frontier fortresses and against the Swiss frontier. It has been repeated by many German authorities (*e.g.* General Groener) that Schlieffen made the proportion of one wing to the other 1 to 7, whilst Moltke changed it to 1 to 3, but how these figures are arrived at they do not reveal. According to General Groener in *Das Tastament des Grafen Schlieffen*, the deployment of the troops against France in the 1905 plan and in 1914 were, omitting Landwehr and Ersatz troops, for sieges and L. of C. purposes:

1905	1914	Army
11 corps	8 corps	First and Second
7 Reserve corps	5 Reserve corps	
(line just south of Namur)		
6 corps	6 corps	Third and Fourth
½ Reserve corps	3 Reserve corps	
(line through Mézières)		
8 corps	3 corps	Fifth
5 Reserve corps	2 Reserve corps	
(line through Verdun and Metz)		
3 corps	4 corps	Sixth
1 Reserve corps	1 Reserve corps	
(line through Strasburg)		
nil	2 corps	Seventh
	1 Reserve corps	
41½ (total)	35 (total)	

Schlieffen detailed 10 divisions for the Eastern front; Moltke, 8. Moltke, still less Schlieffen, never had the number of corps and divisions which the Schlieffen plan assumed to exist—the latter's plan was only a "project." But, taking the above figures: in Schlieffen's plan the defensive wing is to the offensive as 4 to 37½ (1 to 9⅜), in Moltke's 8 to 27 (1 to 3⅜); but Schlieffen's with the forces available in 1914, would have been 4 to 31 (1 to 7⅜).

It has been left to Dr. Bredt, a member of the *Reichstag* and of the Parliamentary Committee of Enquiry into the loss of the war, to tell what was the real nature of the plan, how Moltke altered it, and why he did so (J. V. Bredt, *Die Belgische Neutralität und der Schlieffensche Feldzugplan*). His work, which shows a wide acquaintance with war literature, purports to contain portions of the Schlieffen plan of which the public had not yet heard, and which fully justify the reproach that Moltke changed it for the worse, much the worse, but not in the way hitherto imagined. Dr. Bredt, however, points out that Ludendorff was head of the Operations Section of the Great General Staff in 1908-9, at the time of the vital alterations, and from what we know of the First Quartermaster's ruthless methods and ignorance of the world, he probably had more to do with the changes than his courtier chief. Dr. Bredt recalls, what most of us have forgotten, if we ever knew, that in the January, 1909, number of the *Deutsche Revue* Graf Schlieffen anonymously protested against the changes—it was, of course, surmised who wrote the article, and it is now included in his works.

"Graf Schlieffen," says Dr. Bredt, in discussing the plan, "quite realized that an immediate participation of the British on the side of our opponents was to be reckoned with. He did not estimate the value of the British Expeditionary Force very highly, but all the higher the value of the British activity at sea. He insisted in all circumstances on a rapid decision of the war, before the economic consequences of British hostility made themselves felt. For this reason the Franco-British Army must be rapidly and decisively beaten. In the East Graf Schlieffen proposed to remain on the strategic defensive until after the victories in the West. In Alsace-Lorraine the front was to be held with the minimum number of troops, supported by the fortresses of Strasburg and Metz. Should the French succeed in breaking in, so much the better, and it should not cause alarm, for operations there would only absorb the French troops without their serving any useful purpose, and keep them away from the real decisive theatre."

Quoting from the article, he goes on—

"The Germans can feel assured, if they stick to their own operations, that the French will quickly turn about and not north but south of Metz in the direction from which the greater danger threatens. It is therefore imperative that the Germans are as strong as possible on the right wing, for there the decisive battle is to be expected.

"The decision," the author paraphases, "should fall in northern France. The *bataillon carré* on the right flank should be so strong that the French and their Allies can be driven against the rear of their fortress front and against the frontier of Switzerland. Thus by a huge envelopment of the French and British a colossal Cannæ should be prepared. Antwerp and Paris should be invested by Reserve and Ersatz corps, but the decision lies not at these fortresses, but in the surrounding of the field army."

And, quoting Schlieffen again—

"It must be sought throughout to press the French by an attack against their left flank in an easterly direction against the Moselle fortresses, against the Jura, and against Switzerland. The French Army must be annihilated. The essential for the course of the operations as a whole is to form a strong right wing, to win the battles by its help, and in ceaseless pursuit by means of the same strong wing, to force the enemy to give way again and again."

The reasons for strengthening the left wing are given by Dr. Bredt as follows: Moltke could not abandon Alsace, as Schlieffen designed to do, for the Italians might take part on the German side; General Pollio, the Italian Chief of Staff until his death in 1914, had assured him they would. As they were to be brought to Alsace, Moltke considered it necessary to hold that province with two corps. If the

Italians did not appear, then the question of the transport of the two corps to the right wing would arise. As we know, the French attack towards Mülhausen fatally delayed this. These two corps, plus the two corps sent from France to Russia, would, if added to the right wing, have made it as strong as Schlieffen intended.

It emerges incidentally that the Schlieffen plan was worked out for war on the Western front only; for when drawn up Russia was still very weak as a result of the Manchurian War. It also contemplated additions to the army that did not take place. There was only a general statement that in the case of Russia intervening, ten divisions should be withdrawn from the Western front and sent to the East, without altering the proportion of the two wings.

More important than the changes in the technical details was the alteration of the plan politically. In the Schlieffen plan "there was no ultimatum to Belgium, but the German army, without any notification, was first to deploy on the Dutch-Belgian frontier." As the German plan would be divulged by this, it was assumed that the French would take counter measures. These, according to Schlieffen's views, could only be the occupation of the natural defensive position in the Meuse valley south of Namur; and thus the French would themselves violate Belgian neutrality. Such a plan must have been at least considered by the French, and in 1914 the German General Staff took it for granted that they would advance to the Meuse. All this presumed that Belgian neutrality would not be broken by Germany first. Such a step Graf Schlieffen desired, if possible, to avoid. He wished to leave sufficient time so that, in one way or another, the German statesmen would be able to evade the reproach of the violation of Belgian neutrality. "That Liège would always be captured sufficiently soon after the entry of the German army into Belgium, to serve as the railway junction for reinforcements and supply, could be accepted."

This was all changed in the deployment plan of the mobilization year 1908-9, by which Liège was to be captured by a *coup de main*, without artillery preparation, during the mobilization. Dr. Bredt quotes from the mobilization instructions of that year:—

"The weakness of the garrison and armament offers the prospect of a successful attack in which the infantry, without waiting for the artillery to open fire, pushes through the intervals between the forts, obtains possession of the heights surrounding the town, cuts off the bridges and tunnels. The greater the surprise by which it is carried out, and therefore the less time the defenders have been allowed to mobilize the garrison and put the fortress in a state of defence, the better will the prospects be of success by this method of attack. Simultaneously the heavy artillery of the field army should go into position so that it is ready to fire on the night of the break-through. If the infantry columns are detected by the forts, the artillery should draw the fire of the defence as much as possible. It should prove to the enemy, should he delay with surrender, that behind the infantry which has penetrated into the town there is an artillery that is capable of breaking the resistance of the forts. Finally, it should, if the *coup de main* fails, carry out the artillery attack."

There was, Dr. Bredt points out, a further reason in favour of the idea of a *coup de main* against Liège. The German deployment as imagined by Schlieffen would stretch as far north as Crefeld, that is, along the Dutch frontier.

"Schlieffen did not consider it out of the question, in view of the then [1905] political situation, as he judged it, that German diplomacy might succeed on the outbreak of war against England in obtaining from the Netherlands Government by an amicable arrangement (*auf gütlichem Wege*) permission for the German army to cross the Dutch province of Limburg (Maastrich, Roermond). By this means the fortress of Liège would be avoided by passing north of it, and could quickly be brought to surrender by threatening it in the rear."

Moltke did not believe that Holland would give permission to traverse her territory, and dropped the idea of an advance of the German right wing by this route. On the other hand he feared that Liège could not be taken quickly enough by an accelerated artillery attack to prevent a delay in the general advance of the right wing. It was most important not to give the Belgians time to put the fortress in a state of defence, and in particular to construct defences in the intervals between the forts and destroy the important railways passing through Liège. It also appeared to him that it was impossible to march an army between Liège and the Dutch frontier. He therefore decided to take Liège by a *coup de main* carried out by troops of the peace establishment without mobilization immediately on outbreak of war. "Two days and the following night were allowed for the execution of the *coup de main*." (NOTE: As the 5th of August was the first day and the last forts fell on the 16th, the disappointment of the Germans must have been considerable.) . . .

96. THE FRENCH PLAN OF CAMPAIGN: PLAN 17 (FEBRUARY, 1914)[1]

DIRECTIONS FOR THE CONCENTRATION

General Situation

From a careful study of information obtained, it is probable that a great part of the German forces will be concentrated on the common frontier. They may cross this frontier in places before our general operations can be developed.

[1]Brigadier-General J. E. Edmonds, *History of the Great War, Based on Official Documents: Military Operations: France and Belgium, 1914.* London, Macmillan, 1922. Vol. I, Appendix 9. Reprinted with the permission of The Macmillan Company.

Intentions of the Commander-in-Chief

Whatever the circumstances, it is the C.-in-C.'s intention to advance with all forces united to the attack of the German Armies.

The action of the French Armies will be developed in two main operations: one, on the right, in the country between the wooded district of the Vosges and the Moselle below Toul; the other, on the left, north of a line Verdun-Metz.

These two operations will be closely connected by forces operating on the Hauts de Meuse and in the Woëvre.

General distribution of the forces in the theatre of operations

The First and Second Armies will at first operate between the Rhine and the Moselle below Toul, prolonged west of that place by the Marne-Rhine Canal, and the line Vaucouleurs-Gondrecourt.

The Fifth Army and the Cavalry Corps will operate north of the line Verdun-Metz.

The Third Army will act as connecting link between these two operations.

The Fourth Army will be provisionally placed in second line ready to move up either south or north of the Third Army; an alternative detrainment of part of this Fourth Army has consequently to be provided for, and eventually a change in the composition of the other Armies.

The two groups of Reserve divisions which will be at the disposal of the commander-in-chief, are at first to be placed in rear of the wings of the general front.

FIRST ARMY

Five corps. Two cavalry divisions. Five regiments of heavy artillery; two groups at Epinal. [Specific details are omitted here and throughout the transcription of the Plan.]

General idea

This Army will attack in the general direction Baccarat-Sarrebourg-Sarreguemines,—the right of its main body following the crest of the Vosges, and its extreme right advancing into the plains of Alsace, so that the right of the whole battle front may rest on the Rhine.

By this advance it will be able to coöperate with the offensive of the Second Army which is to be made in the direction of Château Salins.

The First Army may be called upon to move out from the Meurthe on the 12th day of mobilization. As a preliminary measure it will as early as possible be in a position to drive back the enemy from the eastern slopes of the Vosges, north of the Schlucht, but at the same time it will avoid becoming engaged with any strong forces in the Alsatian plain.

A part of this Army will advance as early as possible, on the order of the commander-in-chief, into Upper Alsace by the Belfort gap, the pass of the Schlucht and the intermediate passes, in the general direction of Colmar.

Special idea for the group operating in Alsace

The order to advance into Alsace may be given by the commander-in-chief any time after the fourth day of mobilization.

The part of the First Army to carry out this operation will consist of the VII. Corps and the 8th Cavalry Division.

Its special idea is to hold in Alsace, by attacking them, any enemy forces which may attempt to advance on the eastern slopes of the Vosges, and to assist the removal of that part of the population of Alsace that has remained faithful to the cause of France.[1]

97. The Turco-German Alliance, 1914

(a) *The account of its formation by the Governor-General of Constantinople, Djemal Pasha*[2]

The Turco-German alliance was not concluded during the war, as people have believed hitherto. It was certainly signed on August 2nd, 1914, but negotiations had been in progress long before the war.

A few days after my return to Constantinople Talaat Bey said to me:

"What would you say, Pasha, if Germany proposed an alliance with us on such and such terms? Would you accept it? You can see for yourself that we have nothing to hope for from France. As France has declined, would you decline Germany's suggestion too?"

I immediately answered:

"I should not hesitate to accept any alliance which rescued Turkey from her present position of isolation."

During the great military review on July 23rd, which took place on the Levend Tchiflik on the occasion of the national festival, the German Ambassador, Baron von Wangenheim, came up to me.

"Djemal Pasha," he said, "just look at the amazing results achieved by German officers in quite a short time. You have now a Turkish army which can be compared with the best organised armies in the world! All German officers are at one in praising the moral strength of the Turkish soldier, and indeed it has proved itself beyond all expectation.

---

[1] The plan continues with similar details for the Second, Third, Fourth and Fifth Armies, the Reserve Division and the Cavalry.

[2] Djemal Pasha, *Memories of a Turkish Statesman, 1913-1919*, New York, Doran, 1922, pp. 107-115. Reprinted with the permission of Doubleday, Doran & Company, Inc.

We can claim we have won a great victory if we could call ourselves the ally of a Government which has such an army at its disposal!"

In thanking the Ambassador for this compliment I had not the slightest suspicion of the negotiations which had been in progress for a Turco-German alliance. . . .

"The German Government has offered us an alliance," said Enver Pasha, "and as the proposal seems to us in the interests of the country we have signed the compact with Ambassador von Wangenheim today! Now, are you satisfied?"

The importance of the news, for which I was not prepared, moved me to the depths.

"If the terms of the treaty are really in accordance with the interests of the country it may be considered an outstanding political success," I replied.

"It is an agreement which has due regard for the interests of both parties, and secures their rights in a manner which no other Government has yet done," he said.

He went into his cabinet and drew from a drawer in his writing-table the treaty, which comprised several articles. I read it, and saw that it was an excellent compact between two independent Governments on the basis of equality of rights.

"What about Austria?" I asked.

"A few minutes after my colleagues went away, and about half an hour before you came, I received a letter from Ambassador Pallavicini in which he told me that his Government agreed with every point of the compact we had made with Germany. Here's the letter!"

He showed it to me.

"And Italy?" I could not help enquiring.

"As Germany has not yet informed Italy of our entry into the Triple Alliance I have no news for the moment on that point. Germany will first prepare the ground, and we have no doubt that Italy will accept our alliance in the same way that Austria has done."

I could not help asking for what reason it had been thought necessary to keep me out of the negotiations, which must certainly have been in progress for some considerable time to have led to such a conclusion.

The Grand Vizier passed lightly over my question with the remark that he had conducted the negotiations personally, had told his colleagues nothing whatever about them until the affair took definite shape, and that they had only learned of the matter that very day. "Djavid Bey," he added, "still knows nothing about it. I have asked him to come here. He is on his way, and when he arrives I shall show him the treaty."

I asked him whether all the Ministers now knew about the affair.

"As there are individual members of the Ministry who are frightened of a scheme of such importance and might divulge this state secret—

Dardanellenſperre.

THE CLOSING OF THE DARDANELLES

A German gibe at the British upon the occasion of the closing of the Dardanelles by the Turks. *Lustige Blätter*, 39th Yr., No. 41, October, 1914.

a matter which is highly undesirable at the present moment—I thought it my duty to inform only His Highness the Sheik ul Islam, Halil Talaat and Djavid Bey, Enver Pasha, and yourself. The other Ministers have not yet been initiated. Ibrahim Bey and Shukri Bey will be told by Talaat Bey, and the secret is to be kept from the others. You will appreciate that in so delicate a matter we shall have to proceed with the greatest caution. Now you know everything, and you have not even given me your own opinion!" he said by way of conclusion.

"May God make this of real use to the country!" . . . I replied. And that was all I said.

I was not slow to congratulate the Grand Vizier on his success in concluding such an alliance, which undoubtedly represented a fact of the highest historical significance.

The importance of this occurrence gave me much to think about. I may say that I did not sleep a wink that night. I kept the general political situation before my eyes, and asked myself what had been the real motives of the Government, for I saw myself faced with a situation I had never even imagined hitherto.

Judging by all the signs, a terrible conflict at a very early date between the countries of the Alliance and those of the Entente seemed inevitable. If at such a time we were not bound to either side, it would always be possible for us to throw in our lot with the party which offered us the greater advantages. And now we had taken our decision beforehand and chosen our partner. The result was we had deprived ourselves of our freedom of choice. Was the party in whose favour we had decided such as our national aspirations dictated? If we had waited, would not its opponent have made us better, more profitable proposals? By accepting those proposals should we not have rendered our country a greater service?

In spite of every possible outward expression of sympathy, Germany had never actually come to our help, and was always recommending us to maintain the best possible relations with France. Why was she now endeavouring to form an alliance with us? And why an alliance which assigned the same status to the Ottoman Government as to Germany and Austria? What had moved the two Powers to such a sacrifice? All these questions passed through my mind and I found no answer to them.

At length I came to the following conclusion. There is one fact that no one in the world can deny—that Russia is the hereditary enemy of the Ottoman Empire, and that her greatest desire is the possession of Constantinople. It is absolutely impossible to make her abandon that ideal. After the Treaty of Berlin, and Czarism had fully realised that it would be impossible for Russia to get Constantinople, her ambitions had been turned towards India. As the artful policy of England had then blocked her path in that quarter, she turned her eyes to the Far East. But the hand which she stretched out to Port Arthur received a hard knock from the Japanese, and she had to withdraw the bleeding member. Thus her only course was to return to the object of her century-old ambition, and was making her preparations to begin her last mighty onslaught on poor Turkey, the booty for which she had been yearning for hundreds of years. Her allies, so far from opposing her design, were now entirely in agreement with that design. The circumstances prevailing at the time of the Crimean War and the Treaty of Berlin had now wholly changed. England, mistress of Egypt, looked with far more jealous eyes at Germany's economic plans in the Gulf of Basra than at Russia's ambitions with regard to Constantinople and the whole of Anatolia. Russia was to have Constantinople as compensation for Mesopotamia. As for France, she was not of those who would oppose the partition of Turkey so long as she was given a free hand in Syria. . . .

A mighty Empire like Germany was offering us an alliance based on equality of status, we who five or six months before had tried to escape from our isolation and associate ourselves with a group of Powers by making an attempt—a vain attempt—to form an alliance with Bulgaria, from which we promised ourselves great profit.

I myself had followed a policy favourable to the Entente group, but had I found myself personally faced with such an offer would I have discovered the moral force to refuse it? Would such a refusal have been reasonable?

Let us consider the matter frankly and calmly.

What was the position of the two groups of Powers so far as Turkey was concerned?

Among the Entente Powers, England had got Egypt completely in her power, and would undoubtedly strive to possess Mesopotamia, possibly Palestine also, and secure her exclusive influence over the whole of the Arabian Peninsula.

Russia was so utterly anti-Turkish that it was quite unnecessary to look round for proofs.

All this did not exactly suggest benevolent intentions towards Turkey!

As regards the Triple Alliance group, Austria and Italy had nothing more to ask from Turkey. They had already done that country all the harm they possibly could. Thus they coveted no more. The most that could be said was that Italy might be indulging in visions which were in conflict with those of the Entente Governments. (With regard to the coast of Adalia and Phœnicia, for example.)

Germany, whatever else might be said, was the *only* power which desired to see Turkey strong. Germany's interests could be secured by the strengthening of Turkey, and that alone. Germany could not lay hands on Turkey as if she were a colony, for neither the geographical position nor her resources made that possible. The result was that

Germany regarded Turkey as a link in the commercial and trading chain, and thus became her stoutest champion against the Entente Governments which wanted to dismember her, particularly as the elimination of Turkey would mean the final "encirclement" of Germany. Her south-western front remained open thanks to Turkey alone. The only way in which she could escape the pressure of the iron ring was to prevent the dismemberment of Turkey.

Thus we had two groups of Powers before us, the ideal of one of which was to get us in its power, while the aim of the other was to make friendly approaches to us in view of certain prospective advantages, and to conclude an alliance with us based on equal rights and obligations.

Could this offer be rejected?

In the first place, none of the small Balkan States would dare to assert itself with a view to intervening in the domestic affairs of a government which was a member of so powerful an alliance, so that we should, at any rate, be left in peace.

In the second place, no member of the Entente group would venture to lay hands on us for fear of starting a general European war. Above all, Germany's savants, her art and commercial experts, would place their services at the disposal of Turkey in the way she desired. Thus, within a short time we should be able to obtain our release from the bonds of the capitulations.

Although this alliance made us the enemy of the Entente Powers in case of a European war, as long as the conflict was postponed for between five and ten years we should have brought up the fortifications of the Straits and our different coasts to such a standard, made our army so strong, and developed our country to such a degree that we need not hesitate to take our part in such a war.

But if the great war were to break out in a week or two, or a month or two, in view of our weakened condition at the moment should we not find ourselves in a terrible position if we were involved in a war with France, England, and Russia?

Had not Germany made up her mind so quickly to conclude an alliance with us just because she suspected that war would break out in the immediate future?

There can be no doubt about that! To compel Germany to enter into an alliance with us, based upon equality of rights and each and every term of the Triple Alliance compact, she must have been alarmed at the preparations being made by her opponents. She must have been feeling the necessity of strengthening her position in every possible way. Otherwise it was inconceivable that a rationally-minded state should take upon its shoulders such a burden as Turkey merely for the *beaux yeux* of the Turks and from a desire to oblige the Turkish sovereign.

The outbreak of a general European War in the very near future must be regarded as a great misfortune for us.

Yet when the *pros* and *cons* were considered, it would undoubtedly be more profitable for the country not to abandon the scheme. If I had been in my friends' shoes I should have taken that course and done exactly what they did—*i.e.*, accept this alliance without hesitation. At the same time I should have taken good care to insert certain reservations in the treaty. For example, I should have preferred that one stipulation for our acceptance should be that if the European War broke out within two years of the day of signature and the exchange of documents Turkey should merely observe a benevolent neutrality towards the Triple Alliance and enter into an obligation to give it moral support by mobilising her army and closing the Straits to war and trading vessels. If the war lasted more than two years Turkey would intervene in the struggle with the Entente. If a general war were declared more than two years after the signature of the treaty, Turkey would be under an obligation to carry out the terms of the alliance at once.

Of course, I cannot say whether Germany would have accepted these terms or not. . . .

(b) *Text of the Treaty of Alliance between Germany and Turkey*[1]

Constantinople, August 2, 1914

1. The two contracting parties agree to observe strict neutrality in regard to the present conflict between Austria-Hungary and Serbia.

2. In case Russia should intervene with active military measures, and should thus bring about a *casus fœderis* for Germany with relation to Austria-Hungary, this *casus fœderis* would also come into existence for Turkey.

3. In case of war, Germany will leave her military mission at the disposal of Turkey.

The latter, for her part, assures the said military mission an effective influence on the general conduct of the army, in accordance with the understanding arrived at directly between His Excellency the Minister of War and His Excellency the Chief of the Military Mission.

4. Germany obligates herself, if necessary by force of arms . . . [cipher group lacking] Ottoman territory in case it should be threatened.

5. This agreement which has been concluded for the purpose of protecting both Empires from international complications which may result from the present conflict goes into force as soon as it is signed by the above-mentioned plenipotentiaries, and shall remain valid, together with any similar mutual agreements, until December 31, 1918.

6. In case it shall not be denounced by one of the high contracting parties six months before the expiration of the term named above, this treaty shall remain in force for a further period of five years.

---

[1] *Kautsky Documents*, No. 733.

7. This present document shall be ratified by His Majesty the German Emperor, King of Prussia, and by His Majesty the Emperor of the Ottomans, and the ratifications shall be exchanged within a period of one month from the date of its signing.

8. The present treaty shall remain secret and can only be made public as a result of an agreement arrived at between the two high contracting parties.

In testimony whereof, etc.

BARON V. WANGENHEIM
SAID HALIM

With regard to 3: The Turks wished to use this phraseology in view of the fact that His Majesty the Sultan is the Commander in Chief of the Turkish army. General Liman, however, had officially informed me in advance that he had arranged a detailed agreement with the Minister of War Enver which provided the Military Mission with the actual chief command—as required by your telegram 275. . . .

WANGENHEIM

98. ITALY'S DECISION TO REMAIN NEUTRAL

[By the Treaty of Triple Alliance, which had been renewed in 1912 (see doc. no. 46 for full text), Austria-Hungary and Germany had agreed with Italy that there should be no modification of the situation in the Balkans without Italian consent having first been obtained and without satisfaction of Italian interests and claims. By Articles III and IV of the same treaty it was agreed that if one or two of the parties to the treaty should be attacked by two other powers, the *casus fœderis* should arise for all three members of the Alliance; but if one of the members took the offensive, the others needed merely to observe neutrality. The following correspondence shows the attempt to determine Italian obligations in August, 1914. See doc. no. 103.]

(a) *Count Berchtold to von Mérey*[1]

Telegram   Vienna, August 2, 1914

I understand from your telegram of yesterday that the Italian Government is considering the eventuality of an active participation at a later time in the European war.

In consideration of this circumstance I made today the following statement to the Duke of Avarna:

"With a view to avoid any misunderstanding I wish to point out

---

[1] Austria-Hungary. Ministry of Foreign Affairs. *Diplomatic Documents Concerning the Relations of Austria-Hungary with Italy from July 20, 1914, to May 23, 1915*, No. 24.

ARMÉE DE TERRE ET ARMÉE DE MER

ORDRE
DE MOBILISATION GÉNÉRALE

Par décret du Président de la République, la mobilisation des armées de terre et de mer est ordonnée, ainsi que la réquisition des animaux, voitures et harnais nécessaires au complément de ces armées.

Le premier jour de la mobilisation est le *Dimanche deux août 1914*

Tout Français soumis aux obligations militaires doit, sous peine d'être puni avec toute la rigueur des lois, obéir aux prescriptions du **FASCICULE DE MOBILISATION** (pages coloriées placées dans son livret).

Sont visés par le présent ordre **TOUS LES HOMMES** non présents sous les Drapeaux et appartenant :

1° à l'**ARMÉE DE TERRE** y compris les **TROUPES COLONIALES** et les hommes des **SERVICES AUXILIAIRES;**

2° à l'**ARMÉE DE MER** y compris les **INSCRITS MARITIMES** et les **ARMURIERS** de la **MARINE.**

Les Autorités civiles et militaires sont responsables de l'exécution du présent décret.

Le Ministre de la Guerre.   *Le Ministre de la Marine.*

IMPRIMERIE NATIONALE — 1.VII-1914.

FRENCH GENERAL MOBILIZATION ORDER

(Printed with the permission of the directors of the Hoover War Library.)

that our declarations of the 1st instant to the Duke of Avarna concerning the interpretation of Article VII of our Treaty of Alliance were based upon our firm conviction that Italy from the very outset would fulfil her duties as an ally in accordance with Article III of the Treaty of Alliance."

I added that the unjustified Russian mobilization against us and Germany, and in particular the meantime reported incursion of Russian patrols across several points on the Russo-German border line, constituted an ample justification for applying the terms of the alliance.

Please express identical views to the Italian Minister of Foreign Affairs.

I add for your personal information that the Duke of Avarna gave warm expression to his conviction that, even if an intervention by Italy in our favor were not to be deducible from the letter of the Treaty of the Triple Alliance, Italy would be morally bound to side with her allies. He had strongly advocated this course in his reports to his government, but he did not know if his opinion would carry decisive weight.

(b) *Von Mérey to Count Berchtold*[1]

Telegram   Rome, August 2, 1914

The Marchese di San Giuliano has just sent me in the form of a letter his reply concerning Article VII of the Treaty of the Triple Alliance.

Its contents are as follows (translation from the French): "Salandra and I examined yesterday evening the reply of Count Berchtold with regard to Article VII, and I hasten to inform you of the result of our conversation.

"Count Berchtold subordinates the acceptance of our interpretation of Article VII to Italy's attitude in the present crisis. Although any modification of a treaty can be subordinated to this or some other condition, its interpretation cannot be subordinated to any condition. It is not a question of expressing the present will of the contracting parties, but of determining their intentions at the time when the pact was concluded. For instance, Germany subordinates to no condition her interpretation, which is similar to ours, and this is logical.

"In the second place it must be borne in mind that the present crisis is temporary, whereas the Triple Alliance is to last twelve years and can be renewed; it is desirable, I might almost say necessary, that during this long period the policy of Austria-Hungary and Italy regarding Balkan questions should be identical. It is desirable and even necessary that their diplomatic action should develop in thorough

---

[1] *Ibid.*, No. 26.

agreement, trust and mutual friendliness. In order to attain this end it is indispensable that we should be thoroughly agreed as to the interpretation of Article VII. This necessity is clearer than ever in the present crisis, even if we do not participate in the war; we would not be able to lend an unswerving and strong diplomatic support to the military activity of our allies if we were not fully reassured as to the interpretation of Article VII by Austria-Hungary, particularly in anticipation of more complicated situations, when occasions might arise to apply Article VII.

"Furthermore, the acceptance of our interpretation of Article VII, important as it is for determining our diplomatic attitude, will in itself not suffice to eliminate all the very weighty reasons which prevent us, at least for the time being, from joining in the war.

"As a matter of fact, this general statement does not clearly and definitely settle the nature and value of compensation in all cases, nor their relation to the perils and immeasurable sacrifices to which this war might expose us; perils and immense sacrifices which are greater than those to which our allies are exposing themselves. This enormous difference between the perils and sacrifices on the one hand and the advantages on the other is, in fact, the very reason why Austria-Hungary desired a war which she could easily have avoided, whereas we did all in our power to save Europe from this fearful misfortune. Nevertheless, we hope that there will be an opportunity, without our participating in the war, of giving our allies proof of our sincere, friendly sentiments, and we count therefore, on a settlement which will reconcile our respective interests.

"All these considerations, serious as they might be, would not prevent us from doing our duty, were such a duty incumbent upon us; but inasmuch as the *casus fœderis* cannot apply to this war, the Cabinet yesterday evening decided upon neutrality, with the proviso that it might later on come to a decision more in accordance with the wishes of our allies, should this become our duty or should our interests make such a course advisable.

"The balance of power in Europe, in the Balkans and on the sea which surrounds Italy represents a vital interest to our country, and it is not afraid to face any sacrifice or any decision which the protection of its interests and of its existence, should impose upon it.

"Since the day I took over the conduct of the foreign affairs of my country, one of the principal goals of my activities has been to bind ever more closely the ties of mutual friendship between Italy and Austria-Hungary. I shall continue to bend all my energies in this direction, for I consider it essential in the interests of our two nations. In order to attain this goal, their interests must be reconciled and those of each be satisfied without harming those of the other.

"I rely upon Count Berchtold and upon you, my dear Ambassador, to assist me in carrying out this task."

99. Sir Edward Grey's Address to Parliament, August 3, 1914[1]

[Events had moved very fast in Europe during the last days of July and first days of August, so that Parliament was anxious to know just where Great Britain stood on the question of war and peace.

On August 2nd, the Cabinet had given Grey authority to assure the French that if the German Navy came into the North Sea, the British Navy would furnish protection to the French coast. On the same day orders were issued for the organization of the expeditionary force, and as a result, the members of the Cabinet who were out of sympathy with this action, Lord Morley and Mr. John Burns, resigned. Then came news of the German ultimatum to Belgium. Grey met Parliament on the 3rd, explained the situation, and told them that theirs was the decision (see docs. no. 87, 90).]

It now appears from the news I have received today, which has come quite recently—and I am not yet quite sure how far it has reached me in an accurate form—the news is that an ultimatum has been given to Belgium by Germany, the object of which was to offer Belgium friendly relations with Germany on condition that she would facilitate the passage of German troops through Belgium. [Ironical laughter.] Well, Sir, until one has these things absolutely definitely, up to the last moment, I do not wish to say all that one would say if one was in a position to give the House full, complete and absolute information upon the point. Sir, we were sounded once, in the course of last week, as to whether, if a guarantee was given that after the war Belgian integrity would be preserved, that would content us. We replied that we could not bargain away whatever interests or obligations we had in Belgian neutrality. [Cheers.]

Shortly before I reached the House I was informed that the following telegram has been received from the King of the Belgians by our King George:—

"Remembering the numerous proofs of your Majesty's friendship and that of your predecessor, and the friendly attitude of England in 1870 and the proof of friendship you have just given us again, I make a supreme appeal to the diplomatic intervention of your Majesty's Government to safeguard the integrity of Belgium."

Diplomatic intervention took place last week on our part. What can diplomatic intervention do now? We have great and vital interests in the independence, and integrity is the least part of the independence, of Belgium. [Loud cheers.] If Belgium is compelled to submit to allow her neutrality to be violated, of course the situation is clear. Even if,

[1] The London *Times*, Tuesday, August 4, 1914, p. 6. Reprinted with the permission of The London *Times*. Found also in the *Parliamentary Debates, Commons*, Fifth Series, Vol. 65, 1914, p. 1821ff.

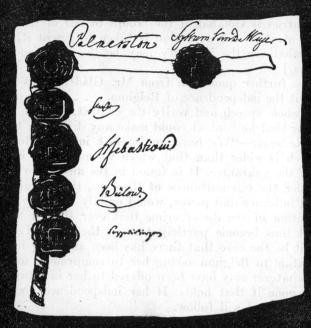

by agreement, she admitted the violation of her neutrality, it is clear she could only do so under duress. The smaller States in that region of Europe, ask but one thing; their one desire is that they shall be left alone and independent. The one thing they fear is, I think, not so much that their integrity, but that their independence should be interfered with. If in this war which is before Europe the neutrality of one of those countries is violated, if the troops of one of the combatants violate its neutrality and no action is taken to resent it, at the end of the war whatever the integrity may be the independence will be gone. [Cheers.]

I have one further quotation from Mr. Gladstone as to what he thought about the independence of Belgium. . . . I have not had time to read the whole speech and verify the context, but the thing seems to me so clear that no context could make any difference to the meaning of it. He said:—"We have an interest in the independence of Belgium which is wider than that which we may have in the literal operation of the guarantee. It is found in the answer to the question whether, under the circumstances of the case, this country, endowed as it is with influence and power, would quietly stand by and witness the perpetration of the direst crime that ever stained the pages of history, and thus become participators in the sin." [Loud cheers.] No, Sir, if it be the case that there has been anything in the nature of an ultimatum to Belgium asking her to compromise or violate her neutrality, whatever may have been offered to her in return, her independence is gone if that holds. If her independence goes, the independence of Holland will follow.

Now, Sir, I ask the House, from the point of view of British interests, to consider what may be at stake. If France is beaten in a struggle of life and death, beaten to her knees, loses her position as a Great Power, becomes subordinate to the will and power of one greater than herself—consequences which I do not anticipate, because I am sure that France has the power to defend herself with all the energy and ability and patriotism which she has shown so often [loud cheers] —still if that were to happen, and if Belgium fell under the same dominating influence, and then Holland and then Denmark, then would not Mr. Gladstone's words come true, that just opposite to us there would be a common interest against the unmeasured aggrandisement of any Power? [Loud cheers.]

It may be said, I suppose, that we might stand aside, husband our strength, and that, whatever happened in the course of this war, at the end of it intervene with effect to put things right and to adjust them to our own point of view. If in a crisis like this we ran away [loud cheers] from those obligations of honour and interest as regards the Belgian Treaty, I doubt whether whatever material force we might have at the end of it would be of very much value in the face of the respect that we should have lost; and, do not believe, whether a Great Power stands outside this war or not, it is going to be in a position

Patience!
Confiance!
Silence!
et vous aiderez nos
héroïques soldats...

à rendre STRASBOURG à la FRANCE!

A French poster calling for public "patience, confidence and silence" in order to aid the French soldiers to secure the return of Strasbourg to France.

(From the Hoover War Library.)

at the end of this war to exert its superior strength. For us, with a powerful Fleet which we believe able to protect our commerce and to protect our shores, and to protect our interests if we are engaged in war, we shall suffer but little more than we shall suffer even if we stand aside. We are going to suffer, I am afraid, terribly in this war, whether we are in it or whether we stand aside. [Cheers.] Foreign trade is going to stop, not because the trade routes are closed, but because there is no trade at the other end. Continental nations engaged in war—all their populations, all their energies, all their wealth, engaged in a desperate struggle—they cannot carry on the trade with us that they are carrying on in times of peace, whether we are parties to the war or whether we are not. At the end of this war, whether we have stood aside or whether we have been engaged in it, I do not believe for a moment—even if we had stood aside and remained aside —that we should be in a position, a material position, to use our force decisively to undo what had happened in the course of the war, to prevent the whole of the west of Europe opposite to us, if that had been the result of the war, falling under the domination of a single Power, and I am quite sure that our moral position would be such— [the rest of the sentence was lost in a loud outburst of cheering].[1]

Now, I can only say that I [have] put the question of Belgium somewhat hypothetically, because I am not yet sure of all the facts; but if the facts turn out to be as they have reached us at present it is quite clear that there is an obligation on this country to do its utmost to prevent the consequences to which those facts will lead if they are undisputed. I have read to the House the only engagements that we have yet taken definitely with regard to the use of force.[2] I think it is due to the House to say that we have taken no engagement yet with regard to sending an expeditionary armed force out of the country. Mobilization of the Fleet has taken place [cheers]; mobilization of the Army is taking place [renewed cheers], but we have as yet taken no engagement, because I do feel that in the case of a European conflagration such as this, without precedent, with our enormous responsibilities in India and other parts of the Empire, or countries in British occupation, with all the unknown factors, we must take very carefully into consideration the use which we make of sending an Expeditionary Force out of the country until we know how we stand.

One thing I would say. The one bright spot in the whole of this terrible situation is Ireland. [Prolonged cheers.] The general feeling throughout Ireland, and I would like this to be clearly understood abroad, does not make that a consideration that we feel we have to take into account. [Cheers.] I have told the House how far we have at present gone in commitments, and the conditions which influence our policy; and I have put and dealt at length to the House upon how vital the condition of the neutrality of Belgium is.

[1] "as to have lost us all respect," are the words omitted.
[2] See Note on p. 418.

„JE EER OF JE LEVEN!"

"L'HONNEUR OU LA VIE"

"YOUR HONOUR OR YOUR LIFE"

YOUR HONOUR OR YOUR LIFE

This illustration of German frightfulness toward the neutral states, Luxemburg and Belgium, is typical of the strongly pro-Entente propaganda from the pen of Louis Raemaekers, the Dutch cartoonist. (Wereld-Wee, Antwerpen, De Neder-lausche Boekhandel. Reproduced in a pamphlet entitled *Raemaekers*, on file in the Hoover War Library.)

What other policy is there before the House? There is but one way in which the Government could make certain at the present moment of keeping outside this war, and that would be that it should immediately issue a proclamation of unconditional neutrality. We cannot do that [cheers] ; we have made a commitment to France, which I have read to the House, which prevents us from doing that. We have got the consideration of Belgium also which prevents us from any unconditional neutrality, and without those conditions absolutely satisfied and satisfactory we are bound not to shrink from proceeding to the use of all the forces in our power. If we [did] take that line by saying that we will have nothing whatever to do with this matter—that no conditions of the Belgium Treaty obligations, the possible position in the Mediterranean, with damage to British interests, and what may happen to France from our failure to support France—if we were to say that all those things mattered nothing, were as nothing, and to say we would stand aside, we should, I believe, sacrifice our respect and good name and reputation before the world, and should not escape the most serious and grave economic consequences. [Cheers and a voice, "No."]

NOTE: Earlier in his address Sir Edward Grey read the following statement of the British commitment to France of August 3, 1914 :—
. . . yesterday afternoon I gave to the French Ambassador the following statement :—

"I am authorized to give an assurance that, if the German Fleet comes into the Channel or through the North Sea to undertake hostile operations against French coasts or shipping, the British Fleet will give all the protection in its power. [Cheers.] This assurance, is, of course, subject to the policy of His Majesty's Government receiving the support of Parliament, and must not be taken as binding His Majesty's Government to take any action until the above contingency or action of the German Fleet takes place."

100. ALLIED WAR AIMS, 1914

(a) *Paléologue to Delcassé, at Bordeaux, Sept. 14, 1914*[1]

Petrograd, Sept. 14, 1914

In cipher
Secret

For the minister alone

During a very friendly conversation, M. Sazonov developed before Sir George Buchanan and me his unofficial ideas on the conduct which Russia, England, and France ought to follow if the present success of

---

[1] *Un Livre Noir*, Vol. III, pp. 11-13. Reprinted with the permission of the Librairie du Travail.

their armies is crowned by a decisive victory. "We ought," he told us, "to work out a project immediately." I said that, in my opinion, the foreign ministers of Russia, France, and England ought to plan among themselves how to fix the general bases of the new order to be established in Europe. They would communicate this basis to their secondary allies—Belgium, Serbia, Montenegro. They would then collectively inform Germany and Austria of them. The project should only establish the basis for fixing conditions of peace and for solving difficulties. M. Savonov, on his side, approved this point of view. Becoming more confidential, M. Sazonov communicated to us, in its main features, his conception of the remaking of the map and the constitution of Europe which the three allies would be interested in effecting.

1. The principal object of the three allies should be to break German power and its claim to military and political domination;

2. Territorial modifications ought to be determined according to the principle of nationality;

3. Russia should annex the lower course of the Niemen and the eastern part of Galicia. She should annex eastern Posnania and Silesia and the western part of Galicia to the kingdom of Poland;

4. France should take back Alsace-Lorraine, adding to it if she likes part of Rhenish Prussia and of the Palatinate;

5. Belgium should obtain in—[words not deciphered] an important increase in territory;

6. Slesvig-Holstein should be restored to Denmark;

7. The kingdom of Hanover should be restored;

8. Austria should constitute a triple monarchy, formed of the empire of Austria, the kingdom of Bohemia, and the kingdom of Hungary. The empire of Austria should include only the "hereditary provinces." The kingdom of Bohemia should include present-day Bohemia and the Slovaks. The kingdom of Hungary should come to an understanding with Roumania on the subject of Transylvania.

9. Serbia should annex Bosnia, Herzegovina, Dalmatia, and northern Albania;

10. Bulgaria should receive from Serbia compensation in Macedonia;

11. Greece should annex southern Albania, with the exception of Valona, which should go to Italy;

12. England, France, and Japan should divide the German colonies;

13. Germany and Austria should pay a war indemnity.

M. Sazonov earnestly begged us, Sir George Buchanan and myself, not to attribute any official importance "to this sketch of a tapestry the woof of which is not yet woven." But a remark which he casually made to me made me understand that he is anxious from now on to put us in touch with his ideas and that he attaches more value than ever to being in close contact with us.

(b) *Izvolsky to Sazonov, Sept. 30/Oct. 13, 1914*[1]

[Paris]

No. 497. Received your no. 2935. *Personal*

I have had occasion of speaking personally, in my own name, with the minister of foreign affairs on the question there touched upon. After having made the reservation that at present it was still early "to count the chickens" ["to sell the bear's skin"], that until today he had avoided all discussion on this subject with his colleagues, Delcassé recognized that it would not be devoid of interest to state precisely in advance among the allies their views and mutual desires. He is convinced that on this point between Russia, France, and England, no misunderstanding can arise. He has often spoken personally and quite sincerely with you, and, as far as I am concerned, I am convinced of the identity of the aims pursued by Russia and by France. For herself, France seeks no territorial acquisition in Europe, with the exception, of course, of the return of Alsace-Lorraine. In Africa, she aspires to no more new acquisitions of territory and will content herself with the suppression of the last vestiges of the act of Algeciras and with the rectification of several colonial frontiers. On the other hand, the essential aim of France—and on this point the three allied powers are entirely agreed—is the destruction of the German Empire and the greatest possible weakening of the military and political power of Prussia. It is essential to act in such a way that the separate German states shall be themselves interested in this aim. It is still too early to speak of the future organization of Germany. England will probably demand the reëstablishment of an autonomous Hanover and it goes without saying that neither Russia nor France will oppose her there. Slesvig and Holstein ought to be returned to Denmark, despite the ambiguous attitude of the Danish government. England seeks no further conquests in Europe, but she demands colonial acquisitions at the expense of Germany, to which France offers no objections. So far as Russia is concerned, her territorial requirements have been stated in their main outlines, and it goes without saying that France gives her consent in advance. In addition, Russia will, it is well understood, claim the freedom of the straits and sufficient guaranties on this subject; here again, Russia will meet with the complete support of France, which can, on this question, act in a way favorable to us at London.

101. British Blockade of Germany

[The German violation of Belgian neutrality and the British blockade of the German coast were actions which, beyond a doubt, were blows at vital spots; but it is also probable that the English, a people depending upon naval power, saw the advance of an army through especially

[1] *Ibid.,* Vol. III, pp. 20-21.

dark-colored spectacles and that the Germans were particularly vehement in their protests against England's action just because their own navy was ineffectual in 1914 and 1915. At the outbreak of the war the British navy eliminated German commerce and seriously restricted neutral commerce with the Continent. Statements regarding this blockade and the sharp protests from the United States are given here. When the German Government placed all food supplies under governmental control Great Britain extended the definition of contraband to cover foodstuffs also. A German interpretation of this is shown in item (d) below.]

(a) British Defense of the Blockade[1]

1. The object of this memorandum is to give an account of the manner in which the sea power of the British Empire has been used during the present war for the purpose of intercepting Germany's imports and exports.

I.—BELLIGERENT RIGHTS AT SEA

2. The means by which a belligerent who possesses a fleet has, up to the time of the present war, interfered with the commerce of his enemy are three in number:—

(i.) The capture of contraband of war on neutral ships.
(ii.) The capture of enemy property at sea.
(iii.) A blockade by which all access to the coast of the enemy is cut off.

3. The second of these powers has been cut down since the Napoleonic wars by the Declaration of Paris of 1856, under which enemy goods on a neutral ship, with the exception of contraband of war, were exempted from capture. Enemy goods which had been loaded on British or Allied ships before the present war were seized in large quantities immediately after its outbreak; but for obvious reasons such shipments ceased, for all practical purposes, after the 4th August, 1914, and this particular method of injuring the enemy may therefore, for the moment, be disregarded.

No blockade of Germany was declared until March, 1915, and therefore up to that date we had to rely exclusively on the right to capture contraband.

II.—CONTRABAND

4. By the established classification goods are divided into three classes:—

[1] Great Britain. *Parliamentary Papers*, 1914-16, Vol. LXXXIV, Cmd. 8145, pp. 2-7. "Statement of the Measures Adopted to Intercept the Sea-borne Commerce of Germany."

(a.) Goods primarily used for warlike purposes.

(b.) Goods which may be equally used for either warlike or peaceful purposes.

(c.) Goods which are exclusively used for peaceful purposes.

5. Under the law of contraband, goods in the first class may be seized if they can be proved to be going to the enemy country; goods in the second class may be seized if they can be proved to be going to the enemy Government or its armed forces; goods in the third class must be allowed to pass free. As to the articles which fall within any particular one of these classes, there has been no general agreement in the past, and the attempts of belligerents to enlarge the first class at the expense of the second, and the second at the expense of the third, have led to considerable friction with neutrals.

6. Under the rules of prize law, as laid down and administered by Lord Stowell, goods were not regarded as destined for an enemy country unless they were to be discharged in a port in that country; but the American prize courts in the Civil War found themselves compelled by the then existing conditions of commerce to apply and develop the doctrine of continuous voyage, under which goods which could be proved to be ultimately intended for an enemy country were not exempted from seizure on the ground that they were first to be discharged in an intervening neutral port. This doctrine, although hotly contested by many publicists, had never been challenged by the British Government, and was more or less recognized as having become part of international law.

7. When the present war broke out it was thought convenient, in order, among other things, to secure uniformity of procedure among all the Allied forces, to declare the principles of international law which the Allied Governments regarded as applicable to contraband and other matters. Accordingly, by the Orders in Council of the 20th August and the 22nd October, 1914, and the corresponding French Decrees, the rules set forth in the Declaration of London were adopted by the French and British Governments with certain modifications. As to contraband, the lists of contraband and free goods in the Declaration were rejected, and the doctrine of continuous voyage was applied, not only to absolute contraband, as the Declaration already provided, but also to conditional contraband, if such goods were consigned to order, or if the papers did not show the consignee of the goods, or if they showed a consignee in enemy territory.

8. The situation as regards German trade was as follows: Direct trade to German ports (save across the Baltic) had almost entirely ceased, and practically no ships were met with bound to German ports. The supplies that Germany desired to import from overseas were directed to neutral ports in Scandinavia, Holland, or (at first) Italy, and every effort was made to disguise their real destination. The

power which we had to deal with this situation in the circumstances then existing was:—

(i.) We had the right to seize articles of absolute contraband if it could be proved that they were destined for the enemy country, although they were to be discharged in a neutral port.

(ii.) We had the right to seize articles of conditional contraband if it could be proved that they were destined for the enemy Government or its armed forces, in the cases specified above, although they were to be discharged in a neutral port.

9. On the other hand, there was no power to seize articles of conditional contraband if they could not be shown to be destined for the enemy Government or its armed forces, or non-contraband articles, even if they were on their way to a port in Germany, and there was no power to stop German exports.

10. That was the situation until the actions of the German Government led to the adoption of more extended powers of intercepting German commerce in March, 1915. The Allied Governments then decided to stop all goods which could be proved to be going to, or coming from, Germany. The state of things produced is in effect a blockade, adapted to the condition of modern war and commerce, the only difference in operation being that the goods seized are not necessarily confiscated. In these circumstances, it will be convenient in considering the treatment of German imports and exports, to omit any further reference to the nature of the commodities in question as, once their destination or origin is established, the power to stop them is complete. Our contraband rights, however, remain unaffected, though they, too, depend on the ability to prove enemy destination.

III.—GERMAN EXPORTS

11. In carrying out our blockade policy great importance was from the outset attached to the stoppage of the enemy's export trade, because it is clear that to the extent that his exports can be stopped, and his power to establish credits for himself in neutral countries curtailed, his imports from such neutral countries will more or less automatically diminish. The identification of articles of enemy origin is, thanks to the system of certificates of origin which has been established, a comparatively simple matter, and the degree to which the policy of stopping German and Austrian oversea exports has been successful can best be judged by looking at the statistics of German and Austrian imports into America.

12. The normal imports into the United States of America from Germany and Austria, before the war, for the seven months March to September inclusive, are valued approximately and in round figures at 124,000,000 dollars (£24,800,000). From March to September

inclusive, this year's imports into the United States of America from those countries were valued at approximately 22,000,000 dollars (£4,-400,000). This sum includes the goods which were already in neutral ports in the way of shipment or in transit when the further measures adopted by the Allied Governments were announced in March, and also a considerable proportion of those which have been allowed to pass in the circumstances mentioned in paragraph 14. A certain amount is also to be accounted for by goods received from Germany and Austria by parcel post, which it was not originally possible to stop effectively. Steps have now been taken to close this channel to enemy exports. The latest returns available, those for September, show that over 92 percent. of the German exports to the United States of America have been stopped.

13. The above figures allow of but one conclusion: the oversea exports of Germany and Austria are very near extinction. It is of special interest to note that in the main these exports have not been merely diverted to the neutral countries adjacent to Germany. The imports which those countries have received from Germany have not in fact exceeded the normal quantities of previous years.

14. The object of the policy being to injure the enemy the Allied Governments have in certain cases permitted the export of goods which had been ordered before the 1st March, and had been either paid for prior to that date or ordered before that date on terms which rendered the neutral purchaser liable to pay whether the goods reached him or not. It is clear that in these cases no harm would be done to the enemy or, pressure put upon him, by not allowing the goods to pass. On the contrary, he would, if that were done, both receive his price and retain the goods and their possible use. The total value of the goods with which the Allied Governments have undertaken not to interfere in such cases up to the end of 1915 is approximately £3,000,000. If the goods allowed to pass under this arrangement were deducted from the total enemy exports to the United States of America, it would be seen that the amount of German exports which serve to increase the resources of the enemy is almost negligible.

IV.—GERMAN IMPORTS

15. As regards German imports, however, the problem is much more complicated. Its central difficulty is that of distinguishing between goods with an enemy destination. A belligerent who makes use of his naval power to intercept the commerce of his enemy has to justify his action in each particular case before a Prize Court, which is bound by international law and not by the ordinary law of the country in which it sits. It is not sufficient for him to stop a neutral vessel and remove from her such articles as he may believe to be intended for his enemy; it is necessary subsequently to demonstrate in a court of law that the

destination of the goods was such as to justify the belligerent in seizing them. If this is not proved, the goods will be released, and damages may be awarded against the captor. It must also be remembered that, in order to justify the seizure of a particular consignment, it is necessary to satisfy the Prize Court of the enemy destination of that consignment and evidence of a general nature, if unaccompanied by proofs directly bearing on a particular case, is not enough. All this applies as much to goods seized as contraband as it does to those seized for breach of blockade.

16. In earlier wars the production of the necessary proof was a comparatively simple matter. Owing to the difficulties of inland transport before the introduction of railways, goods for the enemy country were usually carried to ports in that country and the ship's papers showed their destination. When, therefore, the ship had been captured, the papers found on board were generally sufficient to dispose of the case. In the old cases of contraband, the question at issue was usually not where the goods were in fact going to, but whether their nature was such as to make them liable to condemnation in view of the destination shown on the ship's papers. Even in the American Civil War the difficulty of proving destination was usually not serious, because the neutral harbours through which the supply of goods for the Confederate States was carried on were in normal times ports of comparatively small importance, and it could be shown that in normal times there was no local market for goods of such quantities and character.

17. The case has been far different in the present war. The goods which Germany attempts to import are consigned to neutral ports, and it need hardly be said that the papers on board convey no suggestion as to their ultimate destination. The conditions of modern commerce offer almost infinite opportunities of concealing the real nature of a transaction, and every device which the ingenuity of the persons concerned, or their lawyers, could suggest has been employed to give to shipments intended for Germany the appearance of genuine transactions with a neutral country. The ports to which the goods are consigned, such as Rotterdam and Copenhagen, have in peace time an important trade, which increases the difficulty of distinguishing the articles ultimately intended to reach the enemy country from those which represent importation into the neutral country concerned for its own requirements. If action had to be taken solely on such information as might be gathered by the boarding officer on his visit to the ship, it would have been quite impossible to interfere to an appreciable extent with German imports, and the Allied Governments would therefore have been deprived of a recognised belligerent right.

18. In these circumstances, unless the Allied Governments were prepared to seize and place in the Prize Court the whole of the cargo of every ship which was on her way to a neutral country adjacent to Germany, and to face the consequences of such action, the only course

open to them was to discover some test by which goods destined for the enemy could be distinguished from those which were intended for neutral consumption.

19. The first plan adopted for this purpose is to make use of every source of information available in order to discover the real destination of sea-borne goods, and to exercise to the full the right of stopping such goods as the information obtained showed to be suspect, while making a genuine and honest attempt to distinguish between *bona fide* neutral trade and trade which, although in appearance equally innocent, was in fact carried on with the enemy country.

20. For this purpose a considerable organization has been established in the Contraband Committee, which sits at the Foreign Office, and works in close touch with the Admiralty, Board of Trade, and War Trade Department. Nearly every ship on her way to Scandinavian or Dutch ports comes or is sent into a British port for examination, and every item of her cargo is immediately considered in the light of all the information which has been collected from the various sources open to the Government, and which, after nearly a year and a half of war, is very considerable. Any items of cargo as to which it appears that there is a reasonable ground for suspecting an enemy destination are placed in the Prize Court, while articles as to the destination of which there appears to be doubt are detained pending further investigation.

21. If, however, this were all that could be done, there is little doubt that it would be impossible to effect a complete cutting off of the enemy's supplies. For instance, there are many cases in which it would be difficult to establish in the Prize Court our right to stop goods, although they or their products, perhaps after passing through several hands, would in all probability ultimately reach the enemy. To indicate more plainly the nature of these difficulties would obviously be to assist the enemy and the neutral traders who desire to supply him; but the difficulties exist, and, in order to meet them, it has been necessary to adopt other means by which neutral may be more easily distinguished from enemy trade, and the blockade of Germany made more effective than it would be if we relied solely on the right to stop goods which could be proved to be intended for the enemy.

V.—GUARANTEES BY IMPORTERS

22. Importers in neutral countries adjacent to Germany have found that the exercise of our belligerent rights to some extent impedes the importation of articles which they genuinely need for the requirements of their own country, and consequently they have in many cases shown willingness to make agreements with this country which on the one hand secure their receiving the supplies which they need, while on the other guaranteeing to us that goods allowed to pass under the terms

of the agreement will not reach the enemy. The neutral Governments themselves have as a rule considered it inadvisable to make agreements on such points with His Majesty's Government; they have on the whole confined their action to prohibiting the export of certain articles which it was necessary for them to import from abroad. Inasmuch, however, as in most cases they reserved the right to grant exemptions from such prohibitions, and as trade between the Scandinavian countries themselves was usually excluded from the scope of such measures, the mere fact of the existence of such prohibitions could not be considered a sufficient safeguard that commodities entering the country would not ultimately reach Germany.

23. In some neutral countries, however, agreements have been made by representative associations of merchants, the basis of which is that the associations guarantee that articles consigned to or guaranteed by them, and their products, will not reach the enemy in any form, while His Majesty's Government undertake not to interfere with shipments consigned to the association, subject to their right to institute prize proceedings in exceptional cases where there is evidence that an attempt has been made to perpetrate a fraud upon the association, and to pass the goods ultimately through to Germany. The first of these agreements was made with the Netherlands Oversea Trust, and similar agreements, either general or dealing with particular commodities of special importance, such as rubber and cotton, have been made with bodies of merchants in Sweden, Norway, Denmark, and Switzerland. The details of these agreements it is impossible to give more fully, but the general principle is that the associations, before allowing goods to be consigned to them, require the would-be receivers to satisfy them, by undertakings backed by sufficient pecuniary penalties, that the goods will not leave the country, either in their original shape or after any process of manufacture, and notwithstanding any sales of which they may be the subject.

In some cases these agreements provide that the associations shall themselves be bound to detain or return goods believed by His Majesty's Government to be destined for the enemy; so that it does not follow that cargoes allowed to proceed to neutral ports will necessarily be delivered to the consignees.

24. The existence of such agreements is of great value in connection with the right of seizure, because the fact of articles not being consigned to or guaranteed by the association, or being consigned to it without the necessary consent, at once raises the presumption that they are destined for the enemy.

VI.—AGREEMENTS WITH SHIPPING LINES

25. Delays caused by the elaborate exercise of the belligerent right of visit and search are very irksome to shipping; and many shipping

Forbidden Literature (1916)

The pro-German Dutch cartoonist, Cay, illustrates the way in which he thinks Uncle Sam was led to view the rights of neutrals from a standpoint unusually friendly to the British.

In translation the poster reads: "Forbidden Literature. Grey to Uncle Sam, whom he finds reading the history of the English crimes before and during the English-American war of 1812: 'How dare you, Sam, read in this book!'

"Americans of character were startled when they found that the United States was, and still is, chained to the arch-enemy of their country. 'It is clearly proven,' an English investigator writes, 'that North America is an English colony; that country is not inhabited by an independent nation, but by a de-nationalized people.' The clever English diplomacy had easy work with its *penetration pacifique* in America, and as much as three-quarters of the population of Dollarica has been Anglicized. Uncle Sam has forgotten his fight for life or death in 1776 and in 1812, alas! He thinks his enemies are his friends, and his friends his enemies. When will he wake up from his dead sleep?" (Oorlogs, *Caricaturen* door A. M. Cay. Uitgevers, Nieuwe Maatschappij, Den Haag. 1916.)

Verboden lectuur

Grey tot Uncle Sam, die hij verrast bij het lezen van de geschiedenis der Engelsche wandaden vóór en tijdens den Engelsch-Amerikaanschen oorlog in 1812: „Hoe durf je het wagen, Sam, in dit boek te lezen!"

Amerikanen van karakter stonden ontsteld, toen bleek dat de Vereenigde Staten met lichaam en ziel aan den aartsvijand van hun land waren en nog steeds zijn vastgeketend. „Duidelijk is aangetoond," schrijft een Engelsch onderzoeker, „dat Noord-Amerika een Engelsche kolonie is; geen onafhankelijke natie, doch een gedenationaliseerd volk bewoont dat land." De listige Engelsche diplomatie hat met zijn „pénétration pacifique" in Amerika gemakkelijk werk en Dollárica is dan ook voor driekwart verangliseerd. Uncle Sam heeft helaas zijn strijd op leven en dood van 1776 en 1812 vergeten. Hij ziet zijn vijanden voor vrienden aan en zijn vrienden voor vijanden. Wanneer zal hij uit zijn looden slaap ontwaken?

lines who carry on regular services with Scandinavia and Holland have found it well worth their while to make agreements with His Majesty's Government under which they engage to meet our requirements with regard to goods carried by them, in return for an undertaking that their ships will be delayed for as short a time as possible for examination in British ports. Several agreements of this kind have been made; the general principle of them is that His Majesty's Government obtain the right to require any goods carried by the line, if not discharged in the British port of examination, to be either returned to this country for Prize Court proceedings, or stored in the country of destination until the end of the war, or only handed to the consignees under stringent guarantees that they or their products will not reach the enemy. The companies obtain the necessary power to comply with these conditions by means of a special clause inserted in all their bills of lading, and the course selected by the British authorities is determined by the nature of the goods and the circumstances of the case. In addition to this, some of these companies make a practice, before accepting consignments of certain goods, of enquiring whether their carriage is likely to lead to difficulties, and of refusing to carry them in cases where it is intimated that such would be the case. The control which His Majesty's Government are in a position to exercise under these agreements over goods carried on the lines in question is of very great value.

VII.—BUNKER COAL

26. Much use has been made recently of the power which the British Government are in a position to exercise owing to their ability to refuse bunker coal to neutral ships in ports in the British Empire. Bunker coal is now only supplied to neutral vessels whose owners are willing to comply with certain conditions which ensure that no vessels owned, chartered, or controlled by them trade with any port in an enemy country, or carry any cargo which proceeds from, or is destined for, an enemy country. The number of owners who accept these conditions increases almost daily. The use of this weapon has already induced several shipping lines which before the war maintained regular services between Scandinavian and German Baltic ports to abandon their services.

VIII.—AGREEMENTS IN RESPECT OF PARTICULAR COMMODITIES

27. Special agreements have been made in respect of particular articles the supply of which is mainly derived from the British Empire or over which the British Government are in a position to exercise control. The articles covered by such agreements, the object of which is to secure such control over the supply of these materials as will ensure

that they or their products will not reach the enemy, are rubber, copper, wool, hides, oil, tin, plumbago, and certain other metals.

IX.—RATIONING

28. Though the safeguards already described do much to stop entirely all trade to and from Germany, yet, in spite of all of them, goods may and do reach our enemies, and, on the other hand, considerable inconvenience is caused to genuinely neutral trade. It is to avoid both evils that His Majesty's Government have for months past advocated what is called rationing, as by far the soundest system both for neutrals and belligerents. It is an arrangement by which the import of any given article into a neutral country is limited to the amount of its true domestic requirements. The best way of carrying this arrangement into effect is probably by agreement with some body representing either one particular trade or the whole commerce of the country. Without such an agreement there is always a risk that, in spite of all precautions, the whole rationed amount of imports may be secured by traders who are really German agents. These imports might go straight on to Germany, and there would then be great practical difficulty in dealing with the next imports destined, it may be, for genuine neutral traders. If they were to be stopped, there would be great complaint of injustice to neutrals, and yet unless that be done the system would break down. Accordingly, agreements of this kind have been concluded in various countries, and His Majesty's Government are not without hope that they may be considerably extended in the future. Even so the security is not perfect. An importer may always let his own countrymen go short and reëxport to Germany. The temptation to do so is great, and as our blockade forces prices up is increasing. But the amount that gets through in this way cannot be large, and the system is in its working so simple that it minimises the delays and other inconveniences to neutral commerce inseparable from war. Of the details of these arrangements it is impossible to speak. But their principle appears to offer the most hopeful solution of the complicated problems arising from the necessity of exercising our blockade through neutral countries.

X.—RESULTS

29. As to the results of the policy described in this memorandum, the full facts are not available. But some things are clear. It has already been shown that the export trade of Germany has been substantially destroyed. With regard to imports, it is believed that some of the most important, such as cotton, wool, and rubber, have for many months been excluded from Germany. Others, like fats and oils and dairy produce, can only be obtained there, if at all, at famine prices.

All accounts, public and private, which reach His Majesty's Government agree in stating that there is considerable discontent amongst sections of the German population, and there appear to have been food riots in some of the larger towns. That our blockade prevents any commodities from reaching Germany is not, and under the geographical circumstances cannot, be true. But it is already successful to a degree which good judges both here and in Germany thought absolutely impossible, and its efficiency is growing day by day. It is right to add that these results have been obtained without any serious friction with any neutral Government. There are obvious objections to dwelling on the importance to us of the goodwill of neutral nations; but anyone who considers the geographical, military, and commercial situation of the various countries will certainly not underrate the value of this consideration. There is great danger when dealing with international questions in concentrating attention exclusively on one point in them, even if that point be as vital as is undoubtedly the blockade of Germany.

XI.—CONCLUSION

30. To sum up, the policy which has been adopted in order to enforce the blockade of Germany may be described as follows:—

(i.) German exports to oversea countries have been almost entirely stopped. Such exceptions as have been made are in cases where a refusal to allow the export of the goods would hurt the neutral concerned without inflicting any injury upon Germany.

(ii.) All shipments to neutral countries adjacent to Germany are carefully scrutinised with a view to the detection of a concealed enemy destination. Wherever there is reasonable ground for suspecting such destination, the goods are placed in the Prize Court. Doubtful consignments are detained until satisfactory guarantees are produced.

(iii.) Under agreements in force with bodies of representative merchants in several neutral countries adjacent to Germany, stringent guarantees are exacted from importers, and so far as possible all trade between the neutral country and Germany, whether arising overseas or in the neutral country itself, is restricted.

(iv.) By agreements with shipping lines and by a vigorous use of the power to refuse bunker coal, a large proportion of the neutral mercantile marine which carries on trade with Scandinavia and Holland has been induced to agree to conditions designed to prevent goods carried in these ships from reaching the enemy.

(v.) Every effort is being made to introduce a system of rationing which will ensure that the neutral countries concerned only import such quantities of the articles specified as are normally imported for their own consumption.

(b) *British and French Declarations Prohibiting all Trade with Germany and Statement of Methods to be Used*[1]

The British Ambassador, Mr. Spring Rice, to the Secretary of State

Washington, March 1, 1915

Germany has declared that the English Channel, the north and west coasts of France, and the waters around the British Isles are war area and has officially notified that all enemy ships found in that area will be destroyed and that neutral vessels may be exposed to danger. This is in effect a claim to torpedo at sight, without regard to the safety of the crew or passengers, any merchant vessel under any flag. As it is not in the power of the German Admiralty to maintain any surface craft in these waters, this attack can only be delivered by submarine agency.

The law and custom of nations in regard to attacks on commerce have always presumed that the first duty of the captor of a merchant vessel is to bring it before a prize court where it may be tried, where the regularity of the capture may be challenged and where neutrals may recover their cargoes. The sinking of prizes is in itself a questionable act to be resorted to only in extraordinary circumstances and after provision has been made for the safety of all the crew or passengers, if there are passengers on board. The responsibility for discriminating between neutral and enemy vessels, and between neutral and enemy cargo, obviously rests with the attacking ship, whose duty it is to verify the status and character of the vessel and cargo and to preserve all papers before sinking or even capturing it. So also is the humane duty of providing for the safety of the crews of merchant vessels, whether neutral or enemy, an obligation upon every belligerent.

It is upon this basis that all previous discussions of the law for regulating warfare at sea have proceeded. A German submarine, however, fulfils none of these obligations; she enjoys no local command of the waters in which she operates; she does not take her captures within the jurisdiction of a prize court; she carries no prize crew which she can put on board a prize; she uses no effective means of discriminating between a neutral and enemy vessel; she does not receive on board for safety the crew and passengers of the vessel she sinks; her methods of warfare are therefore entirely outside the scope of any of the international instruments regulating operations against commerce in time of war. The German declaration substitutes indiscriminate destruction for regulated capture. Germany is adopting these methods against peaceful traders and non-combatant crews with the avowed object of preventing commodities of all kinds, including food

---

[1] United States: *Papers Relating to the Foreign Relations of the United States. 1915 Supplement: The World War.* Washington, 1928, p. 127.

for the civil population, from reaching or leaving the British Isles or northern France.

Her opponents are therefore driven to frame retaliatory measures in order in their turn to prevent commodities of any kind from reaching or leaving Germany. These measures will, however, be enforced by the British and French Governments without risk to neutral ships or to neutral or non-combatant life and in strict observance of the dictates of humanity. The British and French Governments will therefore hold themselves free to detain and take into port ships carrying goods of presumed enemy destination, ownership, or origin. It is not intended to confiscate such vessels or cargoes unless they would otherwise be liable to condemnation. The treatment of vessels and cargoes which have sailed before this date will not be affected.

CECIL SPRING RICE

(c) *American Complaints regarding British Violations of International Law*[1]

The Secretary of State to Ambassador W. H. Page

Department of State,
Washington, October 21, 1915

Sir: I desire that you present a note to Sir Edward Grey in the sense of the following:

(1) The Government of the United States has given careful consideration to Your Excellency's notes . . . relating to restrictions upon American commerce by certain measures adopted by the British Government during the present war. This Government has delayed answering the earlier of these notes in the hope that the announced purpose of His Majesty's Government "to exercise their belligerent rights with every possible consideration for the interest of neutrals" and their intention of "removing all causes of avoidable delay in dealing with American cargoes" and of causing "the least possible amount of inconvenience to persons engaged in legitimate trade," as well as their "assurances to the United States Government that they would make it their first aim to minimize the inconveniences" resulting from the "measures taken by the Allied Governments," would in practice not unjustifiably infringe upon the neutral rights of American citizens engaged in trade and commerce. It is, therefore, a matter of regret that this hope has not been realized, but that, on the contrary, interferences with American ships and cargoes destined in good faith to neutral ports and lawfully entitled to proceed have become increasingly vexatious, causing American shipowners and American merchants to complain to this Government of the failure to take steps to prevent an exercise of belligerent power in contravention of their just rights.

---

[1] U. S. Department of State. *Diplomatic Correspondence with Belligerent Governments Relating to Neutral Rights and Duties. European War No. 3*, pp. 25-38.

As the measures complained of proceed directly from orders issued by the British Government, are executed by British authorities, and arouse a reasonable apprehension that, if not resisted, they may be carried to an extent even more injurious to American interests, this Government directs the attention of His Majesty's Government to the following considerations: . . .

(3) *First.* The detentions of American vessels and cargoes which have taken place since the opening of hostilities have, it is presumed, been pursuant to the enforcement of the Orders in Council, which were issued on August 20 and October 29, 1914, and March 11, 1915, and relate to contraband traffic and to the interception of trade to and from Germany and Austria-Hungary. In practice these detentions have not been uniformly based on proofs obtained at the time of seizure, but many vessels have been detained while search was made for evidence of the contraband character of cargoes or of an intention to evade the nonintercourse measures of Great Britain. The question, consequently, has been one of evidence to support a belief of—in many cases a bare suspicion of—enemy destination, or occasionally of enemy origin of the goods involved. Whether this evidence should be obtained by search at sea before the vessel or cargo is taken into port, and what the character of the evidence should be, which is necessary to justify the detention, are the points to which I direct Your Excellency's attention.

(4) In regard to search at sea, an examination of the instructions issued to naval commanders of the United States, Great Britain, Russia, Japan, Spain, Germany, and France from 1888 to the beginning of the present war shows that search in port was not contemplated by the Government of any of these countries. On the contrary, the context of the respective instructions shows that search at sea was the procedure expected to be followed by the commanders. . . .

(7) The British contention that "modern conditions" justify bringing vessels into port for search is based upon the size and seaworthiness of modern carriers of commerce and the difficulty of uncovering the real transaction in the intricate trade operations of the present day. It is believed that commercial transactions of the present time, hampered as they are by censorship of telegraph and postal communication on the part of belligerents, are essentially no more complex and disguised than in the wars of recent years, during which the practice of obtaining evidence in port to determine whether a vessel should be held for prize proceedings was not adopted. . . .

(12) The further contention that the greatly increased imports of neutral countries, adjoining Great Britain's enemies, raise a presumption that certain commodities, such as cotton, rubber, and others more or less useful for military purposes, though destined for those countries, are intended for reexportation to the belligerents who can not import them directly, and that this fact justifies the detention for the purpose of examination of all vessels bound for the ports of those neutral countries, notwithstanding the fact that most of the articles

of trade have been placed on the embargo lists of those countries, can not be accepted as laying down a just or legal rule of evidence. Such a presumption is too remote from the facts and offers too great opportunity for abuse by the belligerent, who could, if the rule were adopted, entirely ignore neutral rights on the high seas and prey with impunity upon neutral commerce. . . .

(15) In view of these considerations, the United States, reiterating its position in this matter, has no other course but to contest seizures of vessels at sea upon conjectural suspicion and the practice of bringing them into port for the purpose, by search or otherwise, of obtaining evidence, for the purpose of justifying prize proceedings, of the carriage of contraband or of breaches of the Order in Council of March 11. Relying upon the regard of the British Government for the principles of justice so frequently and uniformly manifested prior to the present war, this Government anticipates that the British Government will instruct their officers to refrain from these vexatious and illegal practices.

(16) *Second.* The Government of the United States further desires to direct particular attention to the so-called "blockade" measures imposed by the Order in Council of March 11. The British note of July 23, 1915, appears to confirm the intention indicated in the note of March 15, 1915, to establish a blockade so extensive as to prohibit trade with Germany or Austria-Hungary, even through the ports of neutral countries adjacent to them. Great Britain, however, admits that it should not, and gives assurances that it will not, interfere with trade with the countries contiguous to the territories of the enemies of Great Britain. Nevertheless, after over six months' application of the "blockade" order, the experience of American citizens has convinced the Government of the United States that Great Britain has been unsuccessful in her efforts to distinguish between enemy and neutral trade. Arrangements have been made to create in these neutral countries special consignees, or consignment corporations, with power to refuse shipments and to determine when the state of the country's resources requires the importation of new commodities. American commercial interests are hampered by the intricacies of these arrangements, and many American citizens justly complain that their *bona fide* trade with neutral countries is greatly reduced as a consequence, while others assert that their neutral trade, which amounted annually to a large sum, has been entirely interrupted. . . .

(19) The Declaration of Paris in 1856, which has been universally recognized as correctly stating the rule of international law as to blockade, expressly declares that "blockades, in order to be binding, must be effective; that is to say, maintained by force sufficient really to prevent access to the coast of the enemy." The effectiveness of a blockade is manifestly a question of fact. It is common knowledge that the German coasts are open to trade with the Scandinavian countries and that German naval vessels cruise both in the North Sea and the

Baltic and seize and bring into German ports neutral vessels bound for Scandinavian and Danish ports. Furthermore, from the recent placing of cotton on the British list of contraband of war, it appears that the British Government have themselves been forced to the conclusion that the blockade is ineffective to prevent shipments of cotton from reaching their enemies, or else that they are doubtful as to the legality of the form of blockade which they have sought to maintain.

(20) Moreover, it is an essential principle which has been universally accepted that a blockade must apply impartially to the ships of all nations. This was set forth in the Declaration of London, is found in the prize rules of Germany, France, and Japan, and has long been admitted as a basic principle of the law of blockade. This principle, however, is not applied in the present British "blockade," for, as above indicated, German ports are notoriously open to traffic with the ports of Denmark, Norway, and Sweden. . . .

(21) Finally, there is no better settled principle of the law of nations than that which forbids the blockade of neutral ports in time of war. The Declaration of London, though not regarded as binding upon the signatories because not ratified by them, has been expressly adopted by the British Government without modification as to blockade in the British Order in Council of October 29, 1914. . . .

(23) It is incumbent upon the United States Government, therefore, to give the British Government notice that the blockade, which they claim to have instituted under the Order in Council of March 11, can not be recognized as a legal blockade by the United States. . . .

(32) Before closing this note, in which frequent reference is made to contraband traffic and contraband articles, it is necessary, in order to avoid possible misconstruction, that it should be clearly understood by His Majesty's Government that there is no intention in this discussion to commit the Government of the United States to a policy of waiving any objections which it may entertain as to the propriety and right of the British Government to include in their list of contraband of war certain articles which have been so included. The United States Government reserves the right to make this matter the subject of a communication to His Majesty's Government at a later day.

(33) I believe it has been conclusively shown that the methods sought to be employed by Great Britain to obtain and use evidence of enemy destination of cargoes bound for neutral ports and to impose a contraband character upon such cargoes are without justification; that the blockade, upon which such methods are partly founded, is ineffective, illegal, and indefensible; that the judicial procedure offered as a means of reparation for an international injury is inherently defective for the purpose; and that in many cases jurisdiction is asserted in violation of the law of nations. The United States, therefore, can not submit to the curtailment of its neutral rights by these measures, which are admittedly retaliatory, and therefore illegal, in conception and in nature, and intended to punish the enemies of Great

Britain for alleged illegalities on their part. The United States might not be in a position to object to them if its interests and the interests of all neutrals were unaffected by them, but, being affected, it can not with complacence suffer further subordination of its rights and interests to the plea that the exceptional geographic position of the enemies of Great Britain require or justify oppressive and illegal practices.

(34) The Government of the United States desires, therefore, to impress most earnestly upon His Majesty's Government that it must insist that the relations between it and His Majesty's Government be governed, not by a policy of expediency, but by those established rules of international conduct upon which Great Britain in the past has held the United States to account when the latter nation was a belligerent engaged in a struggle for national existence. It is of the highest importance to neutrals not only of the present day but of the future that the principles of international right be maintained unimpaired.

(35) This task of championing the integrity of neutral rights, which have received the sanction of the civilized world against the lawless conduct of belligerents arising out of the bitterness of the great conflict which is now wasting the countries of Europe, the United States unhesitatingly assumes, and to the accomplishment of that task it will devote its energies, exercising always that impartiality which from the outbreak of the war it has sought to exercise in its relations with the warring nations. . . .

I am, etc.,

ROBERT LANSING

(d) German Criticism of the Blockade as a Starvation Measure[1]

The Chancellor asserted that it was the intention of Germany's enemies to extend the war to the women and children of the nation by starving them, and that for this purpose Great Britain and her allies had interfered with the trade of neutrals.

"The American note of Nov. 5, 1915 gave an exact description of British violations of the nations' laws," he continued, "but as far as I know it has not been answered up to this day.

"No fair-minded neutral, no matter whether he favors us or not, can doubt our right to defend ourselves against this war of starvation, which is contrary to international law. No one can ask us to permit our arms of defense to be wrested from our hands. We use them, and must use them. We respect legitimate rights of neutral trade and commerce, but we have a right to expect that this will be appreciated, and that our right and our duty be recognized—to use all means against this policy of starvation, which is a jeering insult not only to all laws of nations, but also the plainest duties of humanity."

[1] The New York Times, April 6, 1916. Extract from the Speech of the German Chancellor, Bethmann-Hollweg, in the Reichstag. Copyrighted by the Associated Press.

102. A Discussion of Some Methods of Modern Warfare[1]

Sir John French's operation orders for the 16th September [1914] ordered the line held by the Army to be strongly entrenched. He still, however, had hopes of being able to push forward eventually and added that it was his intention to assume a general offensive at the first opportunity. His orders proved to be the official notification of the commencement of trench warfare. Next day with the same proviso as before he ordered the line to be strengthened by every available means; and thenceforward, the general situation remaining unaltered, the daily issue of operation orders ceased, and they were prepared only when some considerable change in the situation or a projected attack made them necessary. To those at the front, however, the days on the Aisne seemed a continuous battle which might at any moment develop into a decisive operation and end the war; the apathy of trench warfare had not yet set in on either side. Artillery fire, though intermittent, never ceased for long. By day, sniping made it impossible to move about or to work except under cover; constant vigilance was required to detect enemy infantry attacks in good time. Night was livelier even than day, and was made almost as bright at times by the enemy's flares and light balls; but during darkness working parties and supplies came up, patrols were continually on the move and reliefs were carried out.

There was nothing novel in two armies thus facing each other, entrenched and adding daily to their defences. After the Russo-Japanese war a few writers had forecast that the next war on the Continent would be one of "siege warfare in the field," and, but for the doctrine of the offensive at all costs, held by both the French and German General Staffs, and the generally accepted theory that a war must, for financial and industrial considerations, be short, they had good reason on their side. Measuring the Franco-German frontier as about one hundred and sixty miles in length, or three hundred and twenty miles with the Franco-Belgian frontier added, and counting the heads of the trained men available in the belligerent countries, there were on both sides, for the shorter frontier some 30,000 men, and for the longer nearly 15,000 men, per mile available, nearly twenty or ten to the yard as the case might be. These, entrenched, were ample to hold all national territory—for 2,000 to 4,000 men a mile was the usual estimate for the requirements of a modern fortress—and to provide an enormous reserve to break through at any selected spot.

It is unnecessary to recall the fortified lines of ancient campaigns, when lack of communications made the possession of certain routes indispensable and caused turning movements to be slow and difficult.

---

[1] Brigadier-General J. E. Edmonds. *History of the Great War Based on Official Documents: Military Operations: France and Belgium, 1914.* London, Macmillan, 1922. Vol. I, pp. 374-382. Reprinted with the permission of The Macmillan Company.

Operations of those days, if only from lack of railway and other means of rapid transport, have nothing in common with those of modern warfare. In the American Civil War 1861-65 entrenchments were extensively used by both sides, and after the failure of Grant to force Lee's breastworks in the Wilderness there had been the long period—nine and a half months, 16th June 1864 to 2nd April 1865—of deadlock in the trenches of the Petersburg lines. This genuine trench warfare ended only because the gradual extension of the lines westwards made it impossible for the Confederates to man the trenches in sufficient strength, and they were forced to abandon them, in the hope of keeping the war going elsewhere.

Passing over the extraordinary results obtained by entrenched troops at Plevna in 1877-8, we find that in the Russo-Japanese war, twenty-six years later, both sides took to the spade, and in the four months on the Sha Ho (15th October 1904 to 27th February 1905), assisted by experiences gained at Port Arthur, developed trench warfare to a very high degree.

In the Balkan war the victorious Bulgarians were stopped before the Tchataldja Lines, which they could not turn; the lines it is true had been magnificently sited in the leisure of peace, but were little better than earthworks.

It is remarkable, therefore, that none of the belligerents entered the war prepared for trench warfare on a large scale. Digging had been encouraged by precept in the British Army, but, owing to the rapidity of the course of peace manœuvres, was seldom possible in practice, except on the oft-dug-over soil of the tiny portion of the training ground allotted for the purpose. General Lanrezac has written that so opposed to entrenching was French doctrine in 1914, that when he ordered his corps to dig in before the battle of Charleroi, some evaded the order, and others, to satisfy the written word, threw up just a *bourrelet* of earth: a parapet about the size of a window sandbag, as an Englishman would say.

The Germans naturally had not trained their troops for, and did not expect position warfare, since, as has been already pointed out, their General Staff believed that the decision in France would be reached in 36 to 40 days. They had however prepared for and held exercises in the accelerated attack of fortifications, with a view to dealing quickly with those of Eastern France, or at any rate pretending that they were in a position to do so. They had very carefully studied the Russo-Japanese war from this point of view; and September 1914 found them equipped with heavy guns, trench mortars, rifle-grenades, hand-grenades, searchlights, illuminating pistols and periscopes, designed for the attack of fortresses, but practically comprising all the apparatus of trench warfare. Though, as the German record states, these instruments "in their present form are war-children grown large and perfected in the storms and troubles of the times, yet they had been so far developed in peace that the German Army in

August 1914 achieved great success with them against the Belgian fortresses." As the Germans relied on the suddenness of the attack and never contemplated lengthy operations, such matters as sound ranging, flash spotting and camouflage were absent from their original conception. Of the desirability of scattering batteries, magazines, observation stations, strong points and keeps, and interspersing them with dummies, so as to offer a multiplication of small targets, the Germans were fully cognizant; they had for many years avoided building concrete shell-traps like the self-contained detached forts designed after the war of 1870-71 by Brialmont and Séré de Rivière. The precise nature of shelter necessary to resist heavy artillery had also been decided on. Such matters had been exhaustively studied in the design and layout of the German *Feste*, the super-fortresses of Metz, Thionville, Strasbourg, etc. The arrangement of these permanently fortified areas was, as far as the means available permitted, imitated in field warfare at the front; thus in the course of time the German field defences developed on a definite plan into broad fortified zones.

At the beginning, therefore, the enemy was at a great advantage in his knowledge of trench warfare; and he had the material required for its practice, even if his men had not been generally trained in its use. The improvisation by the British Army of trench warfare implements whilst waiting for them to be manufactured and supplied from home will be told in a later volume of this history; the only engineer stores that reached it on the Aisne, beyond what the engineer companies and bridging trains carried, were small quantities of barbed wire and sandbags, and the only heavy artillery that arrived (apart from the 60-pdrs. which formed part of the divisional artillery) were four batteries of old pattern 6-inch howitzers.

The British could at first do little more than dig cover. Fortunately for them the soil on the slopes of the Aisne valley and on the plateau was easy, and as long as they were in the Aisne district—that is to say before the first frosts—the sides of the trenches, except in one sector of the II. Corps area, stood vertical without revetment; in fact they stood so well that it was even possible to obtain additional cover by undercutting the sides in the South African fashion, thus forming the first "funk holes." The trenches dug at this period were rarely continuous, usually a succession of pits capable of holding a few men. Generally, they were of the narrow type, eighteen inches to two feet wide, with tiny traverses, three to six feet wide. These days were afterward spoken of in jest as the "Augustan Period" (August 1914) of field fortification. The narrow trenches, though giving good cover, proved the graves of some of the defenders, for men were occasionally buried alive in them. In siting fire trenches, when a choice was possible, concealment from the direct observation of hostile artillery became the most important factor; on the slopes of the Aisne valley an extensive field of fire was out of the question, and it soon became evident that a short one, flanked by machine guns, was in reality more effective.

The enemy on the Aisne seemed by his shooting to have such accurate information as to the movements of troops and positions of batteries, that it was for some time suspected that he was being assisted by spies; but experience went to show that the results were due rather to the enterprise of his artillery observers. In one case a German disguised as a farmer was found with a telephone in a house between the lines in direct communication with his countrymen. Several others were caught actually inside the British lines connected by the field telegraph wire to their batteries. One with a week's supply of food was found inside a haystack; another who was concealed in a tree, on being detected by an officer looking up, promptly dropped upon him and, stunning him, escaped.

As regards our own artillery, the difficulties of effectively employing the batteries on the plateau south of the Aisne were at first almost insuperable. In order that they might be defiladed from direct view they were necessarily placed well back from the edge of the heights, where they were four thousand yards or even further from the trenches of the British infantry. In the case of the 3rd Division, however, it was impossible to find positions on the north side of the river. Guns that were visible to ground observation were at once silenced by the German heavy howitzers, and the positions of those which could be approximately identified by their flashes or by aërial observation, were often subjected to a fire which compelled the withdrawal of the detachments. The British field howitzers were occasionally able to reach the German guns, but for the most part only the 60-pdr. batteries were of sufficient power and range to deal with them.

On the 18th September, however, the redistribution of the British aeroplanes and their equipment with wireless enabled the British batteries to reply more effectively to the German. The system of maintaining forward observers was also extended, though the distance of the heavy guns to the rear, the interposition of the river and the incessant fire of the enemy made the laying and maintenance of telephone cables a difficult and dangerous matter; they were continually cut and the labour of repairing them never ceased. Communication was hampered also by the casualties among trained men and by the instruments getting out of order.

As the final weeks on the Aisne witnessed mainly artillery combats and no distinctive battle, some description of the normal conditions of such fighting as did take place may be given here.

In every division an aeroplane with an artillery officer as an observer, went up early each day. The observer noted down the positions of German batteries on a squared map, and sent this map to the divisional artillery commander who settled which objectives his batteries could best engage. When any part of our infantry line was shelled, the batteries most capable of bringing fire to bear on the hostile guns were immediately ordered to search their position. Each "group" of guns and howitzers was under an artillery lieutenant-colonel who was responsible for supporting his portion of the infantry line in case of attack, and was in touch with the infantry brigadier concerned. At certain preconcerted times, a general bombardment by all our batteries was carried out over the whole position of the Germans; our aeroplanes observed this fire, and sent corrections to each group.

Throughout the long series of encounters on the Aisne, the British had the greatest difficulty in finding observation stations, and in maintaining communication between them and the batteries. The Chemin des Dames, being the highest ridge in the neighbourhood, completely defiladed the German positions; for after the first two days, no British soldier overlooked the valley behind it, and it made direct observation impossible, except on a few German infantry trenches; these were dealt with by batteries near the front line. Practically all shooting was done by the map, and ranges, switches and angles of sight were calculated from measures taken from maps.

Attempts were at first made to observe from buildings and sheds, but these were usually knocked down very quickly or set on fire. There remained haystacks and "dug-outs" in the open. These gave cover from view, and deep trenches made near them on the side away from the enemy provided shelter from shrapnel and from machine-gun and rifle fire, but not from heavy shell, which either destroyed them or blew them in. A party of observers did remain nine days in a haystack near the Tour de Paissy, and this only once received a direct hit, though many heavy shells burst close to it. Every precaution had to be taken to prevent any movement from being visible from the front, such as making all orderlies and messengers stop and wait, if possible, one hundred yards short of observation posts, and insisting on absolute immobility when aeroplanes were near.

All batteries were carefully entrenched, covered from view by bushes and straw; dummy batteries were made and teams sent back, as a rule, at least a mile to cover. "Funk holes" were generally to be found ready made in the numerous caves, to which detachments ran when serving their guns became impossible owing to hostile fire, remaining there until the shelling slackened. Replacement of ammunition was generally carried out by hand.

Any change of position found desirable was made during darkness, after reconnaissance had been previously carried out during daylight. Dummy guns made with hop-poles, branches, etc., were left in the old positions when they were vacated.

The deep mud made "switching" for change of target a matter of much labour, and any change of over 15° was impossible. The guns were left at night under a guard, with sufficient men and officers within call to work them in case of attack. Night lines were carefully marked before dark; lamps were used as aiming points, and electric torches employed to read range dials when the batteries were actually firing.

A great many different kinds of shell were fired by the German heavy howitzers. The high-explosive shell burst with a tremendous concussion, and made craters 15-20 feet across and 10 feet deep. Their high-explosive shrapnel, however, though it made a terrific noise, and produced much green and white smoke, was comparatively harmless. Ordinary shrapnel was generally burst too high to be dangerous. A small high-velocity gun shell ("whizz-bang") was very accurate, the burst and report of discharge being practically simultaneous.

Besides using forward observers inside our lines, as already mentioned, the Germans observed artillery fire by means of:

1. Captive sausage-shaped balloons. These were generally kept low and well out of range.

2. Observation posts very near our trenches such as the "Chimney" at the sugar factory on the Chemin des Dames, one half mile northwest of Troyon. This erection, though continually fired on and suffering many direct hits, was never actually demolished.

3. Aeroplanes which continually flew over the whole battle front. If any of our troops moved or any guns fired when these were overhead and able to observe, an accurate heavy crossfire was opened almost at once by the German artillery.

The canals, villages, bridges, and all railways and routes behind our positions were methodically searched by shell each day. Headquarters and roads on which it was known that supplies and ammunition must move received special attention from the enemy.

Nevertheless, the British gunners made their presence felt by the enemy; and the second week of the new warfare saw them competing on less uneven terms with the Germans. The arrival on the 23rd September of the brigade of old pattern 6-inch howitzers tended to reduce the disparity between them, but only to a small degree, for these weapons were of course far inferior to the enemy's 8-inch howitzers. In the matter of anti-aircraft guns, the British ordnance also fell far behind the German. For this service, light quick-firing guns known as pompons were sent out from England early in September. It is sufficient to say that they fired a percussion shell, which, as not one in several hundred ever hit its aërial target, fell to earth, frequently at some point in the British lines, and there burst. Not a single enemy aeroplane was brought down at this period, either by these guns or by rifle fire. Such a state of things, it is needless to say, was neither reassuring nor comfortable.

103. Austria's Attempt to Hold Italy, 1914-15

[At the outbreak of the war Italy announced to the other members of the Triple Alliance that the circumstances under which the war started were such as to justify a position of neutrality on her part (see doc. no. 98). In December of 1914 and during the following months Italy bargained with the Central Powers and with the Entente Allies to see which side would pay the most for her participation. The following documents give the Italian demands and the price which the Central

Powers offered—but too late. Document 104 gives the terms made by the Allies with Italy in order to bring her in on their side.

Sonnino was the Italian Minister for Foreign Affairs. Burián held a similar position in Austria-Hungary, Bülow was on a German mission to Rome at this time, and Macchio was his Austrian colleague.]

(a) *The Minister for Foreign Affairs to the Italian Ambassador at Vienna*[1]

Telegram   Rome, Dec. 9, 1914

I request your Excellency to convey the following verbal communication to Count Berchtold.

The present military advance of Austria-Hungary into Serbia constitutes a fact which cannot avoid becoming the subject of examination by the Italian and Austro-Hungarian Governments on the basis of the stipulations contained in Article VII of the Triple Alliance. The same article places the Austro-Hungarian Government, in the case of even temporary occupations, under the obligation of first coming to an agreement with Italy and also of granting compensation. The Imperial and Royal Government should therefore have consulted us and entered into agreement with us before causing its army to cross the Serbian frontier. To render our attitude effectively clear we must remind the Imperial and Royal Government that basing its actions precisely upon what is set forth in Article VII, it restrained us during our own war against Turkey from carrying out several military operations which would certainly have shortened the duration of that war. The naval operations in the Dardanelles also gave rise to formal reservations on the part of the Imperial and Royal Government. Italy has an interest of the first importance in the preservation of the full integrity and political and economical independence of Serbia. The Austro-Hungarian Government has certainly declared upon several occasions that it has no intention of making acquisitions of territory to the prejudice of Serbia, but a declaration so formulated does not amount to a binding engagement, and assurances of the same general character afforded us by the Imperial and Royal Government on the occasion when Turkey embarked upon war, allow us to foresee the possibility of certain political modifications in the Balkan Peninsula. Moreover the very invasion of Serbia, although this should prove in the end to be no more than temporary, has already sufficed seriously to disturb the equilibrium that prevailed in the Balkan Peninsula and to afford us the right to compensation. It should further be observed that the stipulation of the aforesaid Article VII gives Italy the right to compensation also on the score of advantages other than territorial

---

[1] Italy. *Diplomatic Documents submitted to the Italian Parliament by the Minister for Foreign Affairs (Sonnino). Austria-Hungary.* Session of 20 May, 1915. Published for the Royal Italian Embassy in London by Hodder and Stoughton. (1915) No. 1.

which the Austro-Hungarian Government might secure in the Balkan region. The Italian Government considers that it is necessary to proceed without delay to an exchange of views and thence to a specific treaty with the Imperial and Royal Government concerning this intricate situation which closely affects the most vital political and economical interests of Italy. Unmistakable signs of uneasiness are to be observed in the Italian Parliament and in Italian public opinion, and these clearly manifest the tendency of Italy's national aspirations. The Royal Italian Government is compelled to take this uneasiness and these aspirations seriously into account. The understanding which I earnestly invite upon these grounds between the two Governments would have the result of eliminating in the future all danger of those deplorable incidents arising out of friction and diffidence which are today so painfully frequent, and it would render instead possible and natural between the two nations those relations of cordial and constant friendship which are the common desire of both and without which all official agreement necessarily remains incomplete and barren. Therefore in making clear to Count Berchtold the friendly spirit which has prompted these representations, I beg your Excellency to invite him to make known to us, with the diligence demanded by the case, the point of view of the Imperial and Royal Government.

SONNINO

(b) *The Minister for Foreign Affairs to the Italian Ambassador at Vienna*[1]

Telegram   Rome, 4th March, 1915

I, too, conclude that there is nothing to be expected from the protraction of the discussion with Baron Burián regarding territorial compensation under Article VII. But I think that it may not be without purpose clearly to recapitulate the following settled points in the declarations successively made by us in the course of the interviews:

1. That no military action by Austria-Hungary in the Balkans may be undertaken unless the agreement relating to compensation should antecedently have been carried to its conclusion, we adhering rigidly to the text of Article VII;

2. That any infraction of the above would be considered by us as an open violation of the treaty, in view of which Italy resumes her full liberty of action so as to protect her proper rights and interests;

3. That no proposal to discuss compensation can conduce to any agreement unless it has in view the cession of territories actually possessed by Austria-Hungary;

4. That availing ourselves of the provisions of Article VII, we insist on compensation on the ground of the inception of military action by Austria-Hungary in the Balkans, independently of any result to which

[1] *Ibid.*, No. 35.

such action may lead; not excluding, however, that other indemnities may be stipulated for conditionally and proportionately to the advantages which Austria-Hungary may, in effect, succeed in obtaining;

5. That the fixed quota of compensation correlative to the actual inception of military action independently of its results, far from being kept secret, should be given effect to by the actual transference of the ceded territories and their immediate occupation on the part of Italy;

6. That we do not admit any discussion of compensation on our part regarding the occupation of the Dodecanesus and Valona, and this for various reasons already submitted by your Excellency to Baron Burián.

SONNINO

(c) *Burián to Macchio*[1]

Telegram   Vienna, March 28, 1915

(Translation from the French)

Yesterday I made a proposal to the Italian Ambassador in the matter of an agreement to be concluded between our two governments on the following terms:

Italy shall bind herself to observe toward Austria-Hungary and her allies throughout the duration of the present war a benevolent neutrality in matters political, military and economic.

Within the meaning of this pledge, Italy shall undertake to leave to Austria-Hungary full and unrestrained freedom of action in the Balkans for the entire duration of the present war, and shall renounce beforehand all further claims to compensation for territorial or other advantages which Austria-Hungary may eventually derive from that freedom of action.

This stipulation, however, shall not extend to Albania, in respect of which the existing agreement between Austria-Hungary and Italy, as well as the decisions of the London conference of Ambassadors, shall hold good.

Austria-Hungary on her part will assent to a cession of territories situated in Southern Tyrol, including the city of Trent. The details of delimitation shall be defined in such a manner as to comply with the strategic exigencies created for us by a new frontier, and with the wishes of the population.

This territorial cession on the part of Austria-Hungary shall imply an obligation on Italy's part to take over the proportionate share of

---

[1] Austria-Hungary. Ministry of Foreign Affairs. *Diplomatic Documents Concerning the Relations of Austria-Hungary with Italy from July 20, 1914, to May 23, 1915.* No. 131.

the Austrian public debt incumbent on these territories, as well as their provincial, municipal and other liabilities, inasmuch as the latter are guaranteed by the State. Italy shall also pay to Austria-Hungary a lump sum as an indemnity for all investments made by the State within the territories to be ceded, independently of the purchase of the railroads pertaining to that territory and of collective and individual indemnification for Church properties, entails, pensions of former public officials, etc.

As soon as the fundamental points of the agreement shall have been determined on the above-mentioned basis, Austria-Hungary and Italy will proceed to the discussion of details.

The final agreement resulting from this discussion shall be embodied in a secret convention between Austria-Hungary and Italy.

The transaction referred to will also necessitate the revision of certain treaties which exist between the two Powers, such as those concerning the new junction of railroads, the arrangements relating to border transit trade, navigation on Lake Garda, etc., etc.

The Duke of Avarna observed that Baron Sonnino might find the designation of the object of cession a little vague. I replied that the indication of Southern Tyrol, including the city of Trent, showed clearly the extent of the sacrifice we were prepared to make.

The border-line could not be defined in this initial verbal communication as made today, but I was prepared to do so at our next meeting.

The Ambassador further observed that Baron Sonnino would not assent to the condition of secrecy on the agreement to be concluded; he had expressed the desire for secrecy pending the negotiations but he intended to make the agreement public as soon as it was perfected.

I asked the Duke of Avarna, nevertheless, to communicate my proposal to the Minister, who had promised to confer with me about the declaration he would make in parliament concerning our prospective arrangements. Besides, we could take up this phase of the question in the course of the negotiations.

(d) *Macchio to Burián*[1]

Telegram   Rome, April 14, 1915

Prince Bülow has given me the following information on a conversation he had yesterday with Baron Sonnino:

The two gentlemen went over each individual article of the latest Italian demands together. In the matter of the Trentino, Baron Sonnino admitted that he had included purely German districts but endeavored to excuse this by saying that you in your proposal had retained purely Italian districts for the Dual Monarchy.

Prince Bülow gained the impression that the Italians would be open to negotiations as to the extent of territory to be ceded as well as on the question of the Isonzo border.

---

[1] *Ibid.*, No. 143.

Prince Bülow considered the stipulations about Trieste to be entirely obscure in their disclosures of Baron Sonnino's real aspirations. When Baron Sonnino explained that he had in mind a status similar to that of Hamburg, Prince Bülow retorted that Germany was a confederation of states and that therefore an analogy between the two situations could hardly be established. Moreover, he recapitulated with all his available energy all the reasons why Austria-Hungary could not renounce Trieste.

The most heated conversation ensued on the subject of the Dalmation group of islands. Baron Sonnino admitted that this phase of the proposed cessions involved the entire so-called Adriatic question. The Italian coast in the Adriatic, from Venice to Tarent, did not afford a single suitable port (read: Naval port!). On this account the Italian Navy is in a position of inferiority in the Adriatic Sea. The Minister of Marine and his entire department had exerted pressure upon him on that score and the whole country expected him to bring about an improvement of the situation. The Minister added in a most cynical manner that the present opportunity must be availed of to the best advantage as it would never occur again.

Prince Bülow asked how these exorbitant demands could possibly be brought into harmony with Sonnino's repeatedly asserted desire to create a better basis for the renewal of the Triple Alliance. To this question the Minister replied that it was precisely by the most radical extermination of irredentism that he meant to serve that end!

Referring to Albania, the German Ambassador pointed to the repeated Italian declarations concerning the maintenance of the London decisions and the provisional character of the occupation of Valona. Baron Sonnino became visibly embarrassed as he replied that that matter was only a proposal, open to discussion.

Toward the end of the conversation Baron Sonnino had become more tractable and, in parting said: "I promise you I shall discuss it and shall be very reasonable."

The chief elements which dominate the Italian Government still remain the same: Fear of England, fear of revolution—and at Court revolution seems to be feared even more than war—and on the other hand the uncertainty as to the relative power of the two camps.

(e) Burián to Macchio[1]

Telegram   Vienna, April 22, 1915

The stubborn persistence of the Italian Government in all its demands, as well as the deficient and stale arguments it invariably advances in their support in almost the identical phrases, brings to the fore the question whether Italy is really aiming at an understanding with us, possibly at the price of more extensive sacrifices on the part

[1] *Ibid.*, No. 154.

of Austria-Hungary, or whether she is continuing the conversations only for the sake of appearances and with the concealed motive either to gain time for a later definite decision, or else to join soon the camp of the Entente after having ascertained what our highest offer would be.

In any case you will keep up your conversations with Baron Sonnino by reverting in the most friendly manner to the arguments against the various Italian demands and by endeavouring to explain and rectify any erroneous views entertained by the Italian Government.

(f) *The Minister for Foreign Affairs to the Italian Ambassador at Vienna*[1]

Telegram   Rome, 3rd May, 1915

I beg your Excellency to convey the following communication to the Minister for Foreign Affairs there, of which you will leave him a written copy:

The alliance between Italy and Austria-Hungary proclaimed itself, from the first, to be an element and a guarantee of peace, aiming first of all as the principal object at common defence. In view of subsequent events and of the new situation arising out of them, the two countries found it necessary to propose a new object no less essential, and in course of the successive renewals of the treaty, they devoted themselves to safeguarding the continuity of their alliance, stipulating the principle of preliminary agreements regarding the Balkans, with a view to reconciling the divergent interests and propensities of the two Powers.

It is very evident that these stipulations, loyally observed, would have sufficed as a solid basis for a common and fruitful action. But Austria-Hungary, in the summer of 1914, without coming to any agreement with Italy, without even giving her the least intimation, and without taking any notice of the counsels of moderation addressed to her by the Royal Italian Government, notified to Serbia the ultimatum of the 23rd July, which was the cause and the point of departure of the present European conflagration.

Austria-Hungary by disregarding the obligations imposed by the Treaty profoundly disturbed the Balkan *status quo*, and created a situation from which she alone should profit to the detriment of interests of the greatest importance which her ally had so often affirmed and proclaimed. So flagrant a violation of the letter and the spirit of the Treaty not only justified Italy's refusal to place herself on the side of her allies in a war provoked without previous notice to her, but at the same time deprived the alliance of its essential character and of its *raison d'être*.

Even the compact of friendly neutrality for which the Treaty pro-

---

[1] Italy. *Diplomatic Documents* (1915), *op. cit.*, No. 76.

vides was compromised by this violation. Reason and sentiment alike agree in preventing friendly neutrality from being maintained when one of the allies has recourse to arms for the purpose of realising a programme diametrically opposed to the vital interests of the other ally, interests the safeguarding of which constituted the principal reason of the alliance itself.

Notwithstanding this, Italy exerted herself for several months to create a situation that should be favourable to the reëstablishment between the two States of these friendly relations which constitute the essential foundation of all coöperation in the domain of general policy.

With this aim and in this hope the Royal Italian Government announced its willingness to come to an arrangement having for its basis the satisfaction in an equitable degree of the legitimate national aspirations of Italy and serving at the same time to reduce the disparity existing in the reciprocal position of the two States in the Adriatic.

These negotiations did not lead, however, to any appreciable result.

All the efforts of the Royal Italian Government met with the resistance of the Imperial and Royal Government, which even now, after several months, has consented only to admit the special interests of Italy in Valona, and to promise an insufficient concession of territory in the Trentino, a concession which in no way admits of the normal settlement of the situation, whether from the ethnological, the political or the military point of view.

This concession, moreover, was to be carried into effect only in an indeterminate epoch, namely not until the end of the war.

In this state of things the Italian Government must renounce the hope of coming to an agreement, and sees itself compelled to withdraw all its proposals for a settlement.

It is equally useless to maintain for the alliance a formal appearance which could only serve to dissemble the reality of continual mistrust and daily opposition.

For these reasons Italy, confident of her just rights, affirms and proclaims that she resumes from this moment her complete liberty of action, and declares as cancelled and as henceforth without effect her treaty of alliance with Austria-Hungary.

SONNINO

(g) *Macchio to Burián*[1]

Telegram Rome, May 10, 1915

It appears that the King as well as most of the members of the Cabinet have been systematically misinformed by Baron Sonnino, both as to our concessions and as to the state of feeling in the country. I have heard in particular that the Minister of Foreign Affairs made a

---

[1] Austria-Hungary. *Diplomatic Documents* (1915), *op. cit.*, No. 178.

very incomplete report to the council of ministers concerning my explicit communication (see my telegram dated May 6th), although he had written them down, had read them to me and then had promised expressly to submit them to the council of ministers. For instance, he omitted mention of the concession in regard to the time of putting the cessions into effect.

For the purpose of enlightening the influential personages, of whom some at least are friendly disposed to the Triple Alliance, although they may be influenced by the general distrust, it now seemed necessary to furnish them immediately with a list of the Austro-Hungarian concessions, authenticated by Prince Bülow and myself. In this manner it might be possible to block the political intrigues of Salandra, Sonnino and Martini. This list had to be supplemented so as to leave a margin for further concessions in the spirit of the original Italian demands.

After having drafted the following document with the German Ambassador's assistance, I assumed, in view of the urgency of the situation, the responsibility of signing it jointly with Prince Bülow and to submit it to Sgr. Salandra, Baron Sonnino and other political personages.

(Translation from the French)

Austria-Hungary is willing to make the following concessions to Italy:

1. The entire Tyrol of Italian nationality.
2. The entire western bank of the Isonzo of Italian nationality, including Gradisca.
3. Complete municipal autonomy, Italian university, a free port in Trieste, which will be a free city.
4. Valona.
5. Complete disinterestedness of Austria-Hungary in Albania.
6. Guarantee for the national interests of Italian inhabitants of Austria-Hungary.
7. Amicable examination of demands which Italy may yet propose in connection with the entirety of the questions which form the object of the negotiations (especially Goricia and the Islands).
8. Germany assumes full responsibility for the correct and faithful execution of the agreement to be concluded between Austria-Hungary and Italy.

The Ambassador of Austria-Hungary and the Ambassador of Germany guarantee the authenticity of the above-mentioned propositions.

From the drafting of Article 3 you will see that the idea of granting a suitable title to the city of Trieste has been taken under consideration. Moreover, Articles 6 and 7 are drafted in a manner suggesting our willingness to give further consideration to Italy's wishes.

(h) *Macchio to Burián*[1]

Telegram   Rome, May 23, 1915

In compliance with your telegram of yesterday I reminded Baron Sonnino in a friendly manner that he had not yet sent me his reply to your latest proposals, which he had promised to submit to the Cabinet. Sonnino referred to the demonstrations of the past few days and to the decisive vote in Parliament, which in accord with previous meetings of the Cabinet had pronounced those latest proposals too tardy.

In the spirit of your telegram of today, I responded that I had always been anxious to further the understanding up to the very last, and that I was still prepared to make another proposal to that end. I would undertake to induce my government to take another step forward in the matter of putting the cessions into effect, notwithstanding the latest and very precise definition of time, provided he would agree to accept the last draft of the accord as a whole.

The Minister replied *that it was too late;* he had from the very first looked upon the time of putting the cessions into effect as the pivot of the entire agreement; yet even the latest proposal, where the time was to begin with the ratification of the agreement, was calculated to postpone everything indefinitely.

All my endeavors to continue the discussion were met with the ever-recurring phrase: "It is too late."

(i) *Burián to Macchio*[2]

Telegram   Vienna, May 23, 1915

The Duke of Avarna this afternoon handed to me the following declaration of war:

(Translation from the French)

In compliance with the orders of his noble Sovereign the King, the undersigned Royal Italian Ambassador, has the honor to communicate the following to His Excellency, the Austro-Hungarian Minister of Foreign Affairs:

On the 4th of this month the Austro-Hungarian Government was informed of the grave reasons for which Italy, confident of being in the right, declared that her alliance with Austria-Hungary was null and void, and without effect in future, since this alliance had been violated by the Austro-Hungarian Government, and that Italy resumed her full freedom of action. Fully determined to protect Italian rights and interests with all the means at its disposal, the Italian Government

---

[1] *Ibid.,* No. 203.
[2] *Ibid.,* No. 204.

cannot evade its duty to take such measures as events may impose upon it against all present and future menaces to the fulfillment of Italy's national aspirations. His Majesty the King declares that from tomorrow he will consider himself in a state of war with Austria-Hungary.

The undersigned has the honor at the same time to inform His Excellency, the Minister of Foreign Affairs, that today the Austro-Hungarian Ambassador in Rome will receive his passports, and he would be grateful if His Excellency would hand him likewise his own passports.

104. THE ENTRANCE OF ITALY, 1915

[This treaty is the price paid by the Entente Allies for an alliance with Italy. To realize upon the promises contained within it at the Peace Conference proved to be a very difficult task. (See especially docs. no. 142, 143.)]

(a) Entente Negotiations

Benckendorf to Sazonov, March 12/25, 1915[1]

As I can not yet go out, Cambon came to inform me after having seen Grey concerning the interview which took place today between Grey and Imperiali. Grey dwelt strongly upon the Dalmatian question, invoking above all the necessity for Serbia of a large outlet to the sea and the engagement undertaken to this effect. Imperiali replied that from Venice to Brindisi the Italian coast was completely without natural defence, while the coast and the islands opposite furnished very favorable naval bases. Grey did not contest this point of view and said that in his opinion if the Serbo-Dalmatian coast extended as far as Spalato, the islands facing this coast could be conceded to Italy. As regards Asia, Grey said that questions connected with it had not yet been considered by the Entente powers and he could not discuss them at present. I know besides that Grey is of the opinion that what is left of the Turkish empire in Asia should be preserved, allowing spheres of influence with financial control. I believe also that the British government is very desirous of not meddling in the question of the khalifate which should be reserved to the Moslems and all meddling involving responsibility and friction which he is anxious to avoid.

Isvolsky to Sazonof, March 14/27, 1915[2]

I have received your 1369. Copy to London. I communicated its purport to Delcassé, who already had from Paléologue the text of your

---

[1] *Un Livre Noir*, Vol. III, pp. 92-93. Reprinted with the permission of the Librairie du Travail.

[2] *Ibid.*, Vol. III, pp. 95-96.

memorandum of March 12/25. He told me that, according to information just received from London, from Cambon, Grey had made a compromise proposal, by the terms of which Italy would receive part of the Dalmatian coast from Zara and Spalato and the islands, with the assignment of Spalato to Serbia. Personally, Delcassé is ready to accept this proposal, for he continues to think that the armed intervention of Italy will involve Roumania, Bulgaria, and Greece, and will hasten considerably the end of the war. On returning from Delcassé, I found your telegram no. 1385 in which you insist upon the impossibility of abandoning your point of view, and immediately I communicated its purport to Delcassé in writing.

(b) *Secret Treaty of London, April 26, 1915*[1]

Article 1. A military convention shall be immediately concluded between the General Staffs of France, Great Britain, Italy and Russia. This convention shall settle the minimum number of military forces to be employed by Russia against Austria-Hungary in order to prevent that Power from concentrating all its strength against Italy, in the event of Russia deciding to direct her principal effort against Germany.

This military convention shall settle question of armistices, which necessarily comes within the scope of the Commanders-in-chief of the Armies.

Article 2. On her part, Italy undertakes to use her entire resources for the purpose of waging war jointly with France, Great Britain and Russia against all their enemies.

Article 3. The French and British fleets shall render active and permanent assistance to Italy until such time as the Austro-Hungarian fleet shall have been destroyed or until peace shall have been concluded.

A naval convention shall be immediately concluded to this effect between France, Great Britain and Italy.

Article 4. Under the Treaty of Peace, Italy shall obtain the Trentino, Cisalpine Tyrol with its geographical and natural frontier (the Brenner frontier), as well as Trieste, the counties of Gorizia and Gradisca, all Istria as far as tne Quarnero and including Volosca and the Istrian islands of Cherso and Lussin, as well as the small islands of Plavnik, Unie, Canidole, Palazzuoli, San Pietro di Nembi, Asinello, Gruica, and the neighbouring islets. . . . [Note tracing this frontier in detail]

Article 5. Italy shall also be given the province of Dalmatia within its present administrative boundaries, including to the north [here follow details of boundary].

To be neutralized:—

---

[1] Great Britain, *Parliamentary Papers*, 1920, Vol. LI, Cmd. 671. "Agreement between France, Russia, Great Britain and Italy. Signed in London, April 26, 1915."

(1) The entire coast from Cape Planka on the north to the southern base of the peninsula of Sabbioncello in the south, so as to include the whole of that peninsula; (2) the portion of the coast which begins in the north at a point situated 10 kilometres south of the headland of Ragusa Vecchia extending southward as far as the River Voïussa, in such a way as to include the gulf and ports of Cattaro, Antivari, Dulcigno, St. Jean de Medua and Durazzo, without prejudice to the rights of Montenegro consequent on the declarations exchanged between the Powers in April and May 1909. As these rights only apply to the present Montenegrin territory, they cannot be extended to any territory or ports which may be assigned to Montenegro. Consequently neutralisation shall not apply to any part of the coast now belonging to Montenegro. There shall be maintained all restrictions concerning the port of Antivari which were accepted by Montenegro in 1909; (3) finally, all the islands not given to Italy.

NOTE: The following Adriatic territory shall be assigned by the four Allied Powers to Croatia, Serbia and Montenegro:—

In the Upper Adriatic, the whole coast from the bay of Volosca on the borders of Istria as far as the northern frontier of Dalmatia, including the coast which is at present Hungarian and all the coast of Croatia, with the port of Fiume and the small ports of Novi and Carlopago, as well as the islands of Veglia, Pervichio, Gregorio, Goli and Arbe. And, in the Lower Adriatic, (in the region interesting Serbia and Montenegro) the whole coast from Cape Planka as far as the River Drin, with the important harbours of Spalato, Ragusa, Cattaro, Antivari, Dulcigno and St. Jean de Medua and the islands of Greater and Lesser Zirona, Bua, Solta, Brazza, Jaclian and Calamotta. The port of Durazzo to be assigned to the independent Moslem State of Albania.

Article 6. Italy shall receive full sovereignty over Valona, the island of Saseno and surrounding territory of sufficient extent to assure defence of these points (from the Voïussa to the north and east, approximately to the northern boundary of the district of Chimara on the south).

Article 7. Should Italy obtain the Trentino and Istria in accordance with the provisions of Article 4, together with Dalmatia and the Adriatic islands within the limits specified in Article 5, and the Bay of Valona (Article 6), and if the central portion of Albania is reserved for the establishment of a small autonomous neutralised State, Italy shall not oppose the division of Northern and Southern Albania between Montenegro, Serbia and Greece, should France, Great Britain and Russia so desire. The coast from the southern boundary of the Italian territory of Valona (see Article 6) up to Cape Stylos shall be neutralised.

Italy shall be charged with the representation of the State of Albania in its relations with foreign Powers.

Italy agrees, moreover, to leave sufficient territory in any event to the east of Albania to ensure the existence of a frontier line between Greece and Serbia to the west of Lake Ochrida.

Article 8. Italy shall receive entire sovereignty over the Dodecanese Islands which she is at present occupying.

Article 9. Generally speaking, France, Great Britain and Russia recognise that Italy is interested in the maintenance of the balance of power in the Mediterranean and that, in the event of the total or partial partition of Turkey in Asia, she ought to obtain a just share of the Mediterranean region adjacent to the province of Adalia, where Italy has already acquired rights and interests which formed the subject of an Italo-British convention. The zone which shall eventually be allotted to Italy shall be delimited, at the proper time, due account being taken of the existing interests of France and Great Britain.

The interests of Italy shall also be taken into consideration in the event of the territorial integrity of the Turkish Empire being maintained and of alterations being made in the zones of interest of the Powers.

If France, Great Britain and Russia occupy any territories in Turkey in Asia during the course of the war, the Mediterranean region bordering on the Province of Adalia within the limits indicated above shall be reserved to Italy, who shall be entitled to occupy it.

Article 10. All rights and privileges in Libya at present belonging to the Sultan by virtue of the Treaty of Lausanne are transferred to Italy.

Article 11. Italy shall receive a share of any eventual war indemnity corresponding to her efforts and her sacrifices.

Article 12. Italy declares that she associates herself in the declaration made by France, Great Britain and Russia to the effect that Arabia and the Moslem Holy Places in Arabia shall be left under the authority of an independent Moslem Power.

Article 13. In the event of France and Great Britain increasing their colonial territories in Africa at the expense of Germany, those two Powers agree in principle that Italy may claim some equitable compensation, particularly as regards the settlement in her favour of the questions relative to the frontiers of the Italian colonies of Eritrea, Somaliland and Libya and the neighbouring colonies belonging to France and Great Britain.

Article 14. Great Britain undertakes to facilitate the immediate conclusion, under equitable conditions, of a loan of at least £50,000,-000, to be issued on the London market.

Article 15. France, Great Britain and Russia shall support such opposition as Italy may make to any proposal in the direction of introducing a representative of the Holy See in any peace negotiations or negotiations for the settlement of questions raised by the present war.

Article 16. The present arrangement shall be held secret. The adherence of Italy to the Declaration of the 5th September, 1914, shall alone be made public, immediately upon declaration of war by or against Italy.

After having taken act of the foregoing memorandum the representatives of France, Great Britain and Russia, duly authorised to that effect, have concluded the following agreement with the representative of Italy, also duly authorised by his Government:—

France, Great Britain and Russia give their full assent to the memorandum presented by the Italian Government.

With reference to Articles 1, 2, and 3 of the memorandum which provide for military and naval coöperation between the four Powers, Italy declares that she will take the field at the earliest possible date and within a period not exceeding one month from the signature of these presents.

In faith whereof the undersigned have signed the present agreements and have affixed thereto their seals.

Done at London, in quadruplicate, the 26th day of April, 1915.

(L. S.) E. GREY
(L. S.) IMPERIALI
(L. S.) BENCKENDORFF
(L. S.) PAUL CAMBON

DECLARATION BY WHICH FRANCE, GREAT BRITAIN, ITALY AND RUSSIA UNDERTAKE NOT TO CONCLUDE A SEPARATE PEACE DURING THE COURSE OF THE PRESENT EUROPEAN WAR

The Italian Government, having decided to participate in the present war with the French, British and Russian Governments, and to accede to the Declaration made at London, the 5th September, 1914, by the three above-named Governments,

The undersigned, being duly authorised by their respective Governments, make the following declaration:—

The French, British, Italian and Russian Governments mutually undertake not to conclude a separate peace during the course of the present war.

The four Governments agree that, whenever there may be occasion to discuss the terms of peace, none of the Allied Powers shall lay down any conditions of peace without previous agreement with each of the other Allies.

.   .   .   .   .   .

DECLARATION

The Declaration of the 26th April, 1915, whereby France, Great Britain, Italy and Russia undertake not to conclude a separate peace during the present European war, shall remain secret.

After the declaration of war by or against Italy, the four Powers shall sign a new declaration in identical terms, which shall thereupon be made public.

. . . .

105. ENTENTE NEGOTIATIONS WITH GREECE

[The offers which the Entente Powers made to the Greeks to bring about their participation in the war as allies are made clear in the following extracts. M. Venizelos, the Greek Prime Minister, had to debate the issue with the King, who was the brother-in-law of the German Kaiser. The Gallipoli campaign and the defeat of Serbia made the issue especially vital, but the Entente Allies were not able to procure the help they wanted from Greece until July, 1917.]

(a) *Sir Edward Grey to Sir Francis Elliot, British Minister at Athens, January, 1915*[1]

You are requested to speak non-officially with M. Venizelos, as follows:

As a serious Austrian attempt to crush Serbia is imminent, it is of great importance that the latter should be succoured by any nation which will help her. If Greece ranged herself with Serbia and participated in the war, I know that England, France, and Russia would gladly acknowledge the right of Greece to very considerable compensations on the coast of Asia Minor; and if M. Venizelos is willing to come to a definite understanding on these terms, he may rest assured that any proposal he cares to put forward will be very favourably considered. The matter is urgent, for if Serbia is conquered, although this would not in any way weaken the supposition of the defeat of Austria and Germany, nevertheless certain accomplished facts would supervene during the war in the Balkans which would render difficult, if not impossible, obtaining for Serbia and Greece results as favourable as those contemplated at the present time. . . . The immediate intervention of Greece and Rumania would, on the other hand, render certain a fresh defeat of Austria, would frustrate the attempt to crush Serbia, and would assure to these three States, Greece, Rumania, and Serbia, the realisation of their aspirations and give them control of events which are taking place round them. . . . It is very desirable that Bulgaria should be assured that if the aspirations of Serbia and Greece were satisfied elsewhere, she would receive territorial concessions in Macedonia, on condition that she participated in the war against Turkey, or at least did not maintain an attitude of malevolent neutrality in case she should not decide to fight actively on the side of Serbia. The whole matter especially interests Serbia, and will be the

[1] S. B. Chester, *Life of Venizelos*. London, Constable, 1921, pp. 223-224. Reprinted with the permission of Constable and Company.

subject of *pourparlers* at Nish. You will discuss the question with M. Venizelos only so far as to ask him not to oppose the concessions which Serbia might eventually make to Bulgaria on condition that Serbia realised the Slav objectives on the Adriatic.

(b) *Memoranda submitted to King Constantine by Venizelos*[1]

January 11, 1915

SIRE—I now have the honour to submit to your Majesty the contents of a communication which the British Minister here has made to me by direction of Sir Edward Grey.

Through this communication Greece is again confronted by one of the most critical situations in her national history. Until today, our policy has consisted in the preservation of neutrality, in so far as our engagement with Serbia has not required us to depart from it. We are now called upon to take part in the war, not only in order to carry out a moral duty, but in exchange for compensations, which, if realised, would create a great and powerful Greece, such as not even the boldest optimist could have imagined a few years ago.

In order to obtain these compensations great dangers would inevitably have to be faced. After carefully examining the question, I have formed the opinion that we ought to face the dangers. Even if we were not now to join in the war, and if we contrived to maintain our neutrality to the end, we should still be exposed to peril.

If we allow the new Austro-German invasion to crush Serbia, we have no guarantee whatever that it will stop short at our Macedonian frontier, or that the advance will not be pressed forward as far as Salonica. Assuming that this menace were averted and that Austria, satisfied with the military defeat of Serbia, did not seek to establish herself in Macedonia, is there any doubt possible that Bulgaria, with the approval of Austria, would fail to advance and occupy Serbian Macedonia? We should be obliged, in accordance with the terms of our Treaty of Alliance, to hasten to the aid of Serbia unless we wished to incur the dishonour of disregarding our obligations. If, however, we were indifferent to moral dictates and remained impassive, we should still have to submit to the disturbance of the Balkan equilibrium in favour of Bulgaria, who, thus strengthened, would either attack us immediately or in the near future, when we should stand alone, without an ally or a friend.

If, on the other hand, we had, in the circumstances indicated, to go to the help of Serbia, in order to fulfil the duty incumbent upon us, we should do so under far more unfavourable conditions than if we were to go to her assistance now, because Serbia would already be crushed, and, in consequence, our aid would be of little or no avail. Moreover, by rejecting the overtures of the Powers of the Triple Entente, we should, even in the event of their victory, secure no tangible compensation for our support in their struggle.

[1] *Ibid.*, pp. 224-231.

Let us now examine under what circumstances we ought to take part in the conflict. Above all, we must seek the coöperation not only of Rumania, but if possible, of Bulgaria as well. If we should succeed in obtaining their coöperation, through an alliance of all the Christian States of the Balkans, not only would every serious danger of local defeat be averted, but our participation would bring a most important influence to bear on the struggle of the Entente Powers. It is no exaggeration to say that any such united participation would greatly contribute to the ascendency of England, France, and Russia.

So far we have refused to discuss making any concessions whatever. Further, we have declared that we should emphatically oppose any important concessions by Serbia which might disturb the balance of power established in the Balkans by the Treaty of Bucharest.

Hitherto this policy has been the only one to follow. But now matters have changed. At this instant when visions open out for us the realisation of our national aims in Asia Minor, it is possible to make some concessions in the Balkans. To begin with, we should withdraw our objections to concessions on the part of Serbia to Bulgaria, even if these concessions extended to the right bank of the Vardar. If such concessions neither sufficed to induce Bulgaria to coöperate with her former Allies, nor to extend a benevolent neutrality to them, I would not hesitate, however painful the severance, to recommend the sacrifice of Kavalla, in order to save Hellenism in Turkey, and with a view to the creation of a real Magna Græcia which would include nearly all the provinces where Hellenism flourished through the long centuries of its history.

The sacrifice of Kavalla would not merely be the price of Bulgaria's neutrality, but would be in exchange for her active participation in the war. If the suggestion were accepted, the Entente Powers would guarantee the purchase by Bulgaria of the property of all those inhabitants who wished to emigrate from the ceded district across the boundaries into Greece. At the same time, an agreement could be made to exchange the Greek population living within the boundaries of Bulgaria for the Bulgarian population living within the boundaries of Greece, each State arranging to buy the lands vacated. It would be understood that this interchange of populations and the purchase of their possessions would be carried out by a Commission consisting of five members, one member each to be appointed by England, France, Russia, Greece, and Bulgaria. The actual cession of Kavalla would only take effect after the fulfilment of all these conditions. In this way a definite ethnological system in the Balkans would be reached. The idea of a confederation could be realised or, at any rate, an alliance could be formed with mutual guarantees between the States to enable them to devote themselves to their economic development, without being primarily and almost exclusively absorbed in the task of strengthening their military organization.

As partial compensation, we should demand the Doiran-Ghevgeli district from Serbia, in order to obtain frontier safeguards against Bulgaria to take the place of the present excellent frontier to the East of Greek Macedonia.

Unfortunately, on account of her greed, it is not at all certain that, whatever concessions we offered to make, we should be able to satisfy Bulgaria and lead her to coöperate with her former Allies. If we found it impossible to obtain Bulgaria's coöperation it would then be essential for us to secure Rumania's, for otherwise our joining in the war would be hazardous.

My opinion that we should accede to the request that has been made to us to take part in the war is founded upon various considerations.

Turkey coming unscathed out of the war, which she has dared to wage against three Great Powers, and emboldened by her alliance with Germany, would set to work systematically and without delay to exterminate Hellenism within her frontiers. She would encounter no opposition from her Ally, Germany, but on the contrary, would receive encouragement, as Asia Minor, which Germany covets, would be freed from a competitor. The wholesale expulsion of thousands of Greeks living in Turkey would not only ruin them but would probably drag the whole of Greece to economic disaster.

For all these reasons I have come to the conclusion that our participation in the war is absolutely imperative. As I have already pointed out, this participation must inevitably expose us to grave dangers.

But above all such dangers, there rises a hope, and, as I trust, a well-founded hope, of saving a great proportion of Hellenism now under the Sultan, and of creating a great and powerful Greece. And even in the event of our failure, we should have a clear conscience, knowing that we had fought to free those of our countrymen still held in subjection by Turkey, and knowing that we had fought also for the general interests of humanity and for the independence of small nations, which a Turco-German triumph would jeopardise irreparably. And, finally, we should retain the esteem and friendship of those powerful nations which created Greece and have helped and supported her so many times. While our refusal to carry out the obligations imposed by our Alliance with Serbia would not only destroy our moral existence as a nation, and expose us to the dangers already mentioned, but it would leave us without friends and without credit in the future.

Under such conditions our national life would be endangered.—Your Majesty's most obedient servant,

E. K. VENIZELOS

January 17, 1915

SIRE—Your Majesty is already acquainted with the reply of the Rumanian Government to our proposal relative to common action in favour of Serbia. This reply, as I understand it, signifies that Rumania will refuse us any military coöperation unless Bulgaria also takes part. Even supposing that the Bucharest Government would be satisfied by an official declaration of neutrality from Bulgaria in the event of Greco-Rumanian coöperation with Serbia, it is highly improbable that such a declaration could be obtained. The Staff itself does not consider joint military operations by Greece, Rumania, and Serbia, an absolute guarantee of security, so long as Bulgaria holds aloof, even after a declaration of neutrality. . . .

The members of the General Staff do not seem to be greatly attracted by these considerations; (a) they appear to fear the difficulty of controlling new territories on so vast a scale; and (b) they fear that by our participation in the war we might be more exhausted than the Bulgarians so that the latter would afterwards seize the chance to attack us. No one can minimise the first difficulty, but I do not think it should lead us to abandon the realisation of our national ideals on the unique occasion which is offered to us today. The results of Hellenic administration in Macedonia prove that, in spite of numerous difficulties, the task is not beyond the power of Greece and Hellenism.

The second fear is less justifiable. The Balkan wars prove that we do not become exhausted more quickly than the Bulgarians. It is, nevertheless, true that, for several years, until all our military powers have been organised on the basis of our resources from the recruiting of Greater Greece, we should be obliged, in the event of war in the Balkan Peninsula, to utilise part of our forces in Asia Minor to prevent a local rising. Such a rising would be unlikely, for the Ottoman Empire would have become almost negligible, and our Mussulman subjects would be good and peaceful citizens. However, the army necessary for the purpose could soon be raised from among the Hellenic populations in Asia Minor.

Furthermore, it would be simple to guarantee ourselves against the Bulgarian danger by drawing up for this period a formal agreement with the Powers of the Triple Entente, by virtue of which they would come to our aid in case of attack.

In my opinion, even without such an agreement, we should have nothing to fear from Bulgaria after a successful war in which we had fought side by side. She would be sufficiently occupied by the organisation of the new provinces which she would have acquired. If, however, she were so blind as to wish to attack us, there is no doubt that Serbia would be bound to us both by the obligations of her alliance and by her gratitude.

   .   .   .   .

I must further add that the whole progress of affairs, and the proposal that very wide territorial concessions would be made to us in Asia Minor, prove to me without the slightest doubt that the activities displayed by the New Hellas have attracted the confidence of certain Powers who consider her an important factor in the settlement of the Near East at the moment of the collapse of the Turkish State.

The support of these Powers provides us with the financial and diplomatic means to cope with the inherent difficulties of such a sudden increase of territory. Confident in this support, Greece can follow boldly the new and wonderful paths opening out before her.

To your Majesty, still, happily, in the prime of manhood, it may be given not only to create by your sword the Greater Greece, but to confirm your military success by a complete political organisation of the new State. To you it may thus be given to transmit to your successor, when the fulness of time demands, a work of such magnitude as has been given to few monarchs to achieve.—Your Majesty's most obedient servant,

E. K. VENIZELOS

(c) *An extract from a document discovered in the Russian Foreign Office, describing the relations of the Allies and Greece*[1]

Section I. On November 22, 1914,[2] the Allied Ambassadors at Athens offered Greece South Albania, except Valona, if Greece would immediately join the Allies. M. Venizelos replied demanding guarantees from Rumania that Bulgaria should not attack Greece. This was not given, and the proposal fell through.

Section II. On January 12, 1915, the British Ambassador at Athens told M. Venizelos that if Greece enters the war the Allies will grant her territory on the shores of Asia Minor. On January 20 M. Venizelos gave the Ambassador details of Greece's demands in Asia Minor, but the negotiations were interrupted by the negotiations with Bulgaria to induce her to enter the war on the Allies' side, and in the meantime M. Venizelos resigned. On March 9, M. Gounaris expressed the desire that Greece should continue negotiations. On March 30 the Allied Ambassadors offered Greece the Aidin vilayet (Asiatic Turkey) if Greece would enter the war immediately. On April 1 M. Gounaris declared the willingness of Greece to enter if the Allies would guarantee her territorial integrity, together with North Epirus and the islands for the period of the war and a certain period after it, while the question of territorial acquisitions in Asiatic Turkey was to be a matter for later discussion. No reply was given to this, and on May 1 the Greek Minister declared that since the Allies had apparently no intention to guarantee the territorial integrity of Greece the latter had decided to remain neutral.

---

[1] The *Manchester Guardian*, December 7, 1917. Reprinted with the permission of the *Manchester Guardian*.

[2] The dates given in this memorandum correspond to the Russian calendar. There is a difference of thirteen days.

Section III. On January 20, 1915, M. Venizelos informed the British Ambassador that in agreement with the King he agreed to cede Kavalla to Bulgaria if the latter would enter the war on the side of the Allies. After the resignation of M. Venizelos the attitude of the Greek Government changed, and on May 18 the Government protested against the declaration of the Allied Ambassadors at Sofia to Bulgaria, made on May 16, offering the latter Kavalla. On July 21 the Allied Ambassadors communicated to the Greek Minister that the Allies' offer of Kavalla to Bulgaria was connected with the offer to Greece of large territorial acquisitions in Asiatic Turkey. On July 30 the Greek Government handed to the Allies a Note protesting against ceding Kavalla to Bulgaria.

Section IV. On September 8, 1915, M. Venizelos told the Serbian Ambassador in Athens that if Greece entered the war to assist Serbia the latter must cede the region of Doiran-Gevgelli, and not oppose Greek pretensions to the valley of the Struma. On September 11 the Serbian Government agreed to these claims.

After the resignation of M. Venizelos and the maintenance of Greek neutrality the question was raised in October of the occupation of the Doiran region by Greek troops, but this was not done owing to the desire of Greece not to interfere in the Serbo-Bulgarian war. On October 11 the Greek King declared that Greece did not wish to occupy Doiran-Monastir, and still considered herself the ally of Serbia.

Section V. On October 7, 1915, the British Ambassador in Athens offered Greece the cession of Cyprus if Greece would immediately enter the war. On October 12 the Ambassador informed the Minister that the Cyprus offer was no longer valid since Greece had not entered.

Section VI. On November 6, 1915, the Allied Ambassadors in Athens informed the Greek Government that the Allies would return Salonika and the occupied territories after the war and pay damages.

Section VII. In the beginning of October, 1914, M. Venizelos asked the London Cabinet not to raise objection to the Greek occupation of North Epirus and the Italian occupation of Valona to restore order in these regions without prejudicing a future settlement. The Italian Government agreed, and the occupation was made. On February 14, 1915, the Allied Ambassadors in Athens protested against the Greek seizure of territory in Albania. The latter replied they had no such intention. On March 7, 1916, the Greek Premier Skouloudis declared in the Chamber that North Epirus was part of Greece, and the Government had appointed two prefects in these regions.

On March 13, the Allied Ambassadors in Athens protested against the union of North Epirus to Greece as a breach of the undertaking given in October, 1914. On March 16 the Greek Government answered that it had in view the establishment of a system of government in Epirus more in keeping with Liberal Greek sentiment than that hitherto existing.

106. Note Regarding the Secret Treaty Concerning Constantinople, the Straits and Persia[1]

[Early in 1915 the question of the future of Constantinople arose when the suggestion of an Allied expedition against Constantinople was mooted. Russian dreams seemed about to be realized by the resulting agreement, information concerning which, though not in the form of a treaty, was revealed by the Bolshevists.]

From the Russian Minister of Foreign Affairs to the Russian Ambassador at Paris

March 18, 1915

On February 23 (March 8) the French Ambassador, on behalf of his Government, announced to me that France was prepared to take up a most favourable attitude in the matter of realisation of our desires as set out in my telegram to you, No. 937, in respect of the Straits and Constantinople, for which I charged you to tender Delcassé my gratitude.

In his conversations with you, Delcassé had previously more than once given his assurance that we could rely on the sympathy of France, and only referred to the need of elucidating the question of the attitude of England, from whom he feared some objections, before he could give us a more definite assurance in the above sense. Now the British Government has given its complete consent in writing to the annexation by Russia of the Straits and Constantinople within the limits indicated by us, and only demanded security for its economic interests and a similar benevolent attitude on our part towards the political aspirations of England in other parts.

For me, personally, filled as I am with most complete confidence in Delcassé, the assurance received from him is quite sufficient, but the Imperial Government would desire a more definite pronouncement of France's assent to the complete satisfaction of our desires, similar to that made by the British Government.

(Signed) Sazonoff

107. The Alignment of Roumania

[In August 1914 the Central Powers promised the Roumanian government Bessarabia if they would join their ranks, and Russia offered her Transylvania after the victory. The treaty of 1883 (see doc. no. 5) with the Central Powers was unknown even to the Roumanian parliament at this time. Public sentiment moved first in favor of neutrality and then toward the Triple Entente, especially after the death of King

[1] The *Manchester Guardian*, December 12, 1917. Reprinted with the permission of the *Manchester Guardian*.

Carol, October 10, 1914. On September 23 Roumania signed a treaty with Italy providing for common action; this was renewed the next February. In May Bratianu demanded for neutrality as much as or more than had been promised for participation, but, unable to get it, Roumania remained neutral while Italy joined the Triple Entente. The lack of military success of the Entente Powers made them willing to meet Roumanian terms even at the expense of Serbian desires in Hungary (August 18, 1916). On August 27 the Roumanian government sent the declaration of war cited below to Austria-Hungary and shortly after Germany, Turkey, and Bulgaria declared war on Roumania and overran the country in December.]

(a) *Note Presented to the Austro-Hungarian Government by Roumania, August 27, 1916, giving reasons for a declaration of war*[1]

The Alliance concluded between Germany, Austria-Hungary, and Italy had, according to the declarations of the Governments themselves, only an essentially conservative and defensive character; its principal object was to guarantee the Allied countries against any attack from outside and to consolidate the state of things accepted by previous treaties.

It was with the desire to harmonize her policy with these pacific tendencies that Rumania joined this alliance. Devoted to the work of her internal reconstruction, and faithful to her firm resolution to remain, in the region of the Lower Danube, an element of order and of equilibrium, Rumania has not ceased to contribute to the maintenance of peace in the Balkans.

The last Balkan wars, by destroying the *status quo*, imposed upon her a new line of conduct. Her intervention hastened peace and restored equilibrium. For herself, she was satisfied with a rectification of frontier which gave her greater security against an aggression, and which at the same time repaired the injustice committed to her detriment at the Berlin Congress. But, in the pursuit of this end, Rumania was disappointed to observe that she did not meet from the cabinet of Vienna the attitude which she was entitled to expect.

When the present war broke out Rumania, like Italy, declined to associate herself with the declaration of war by Austria-Hungary, of which she had received no previous notice from the Cabinet of Vienna. In the spring of 1915 Italy declared war on Austria-Hungary; the Triple Alliance no longer existed.

The reasons which had determined the adherence of Rumania to this political system disappeared. At the same time, instead of a grouping of States seeking by common effort to work in agreement in order to assure peace and the maintenance of the situations *de facto* and *de jure* created by treaties, Rumania found herself in presence of

[1] The London *Times*, August 30, 1916. Reprinted with the permission of the London *Times*.

Powers making war with the very object of transforming from top to bottom the old arrangements which had served as a basis for their treaty of Alliance. These profound changes were for Rumania an evident proof that the object which she had pursued in adhering to the Triple Alliance could no longer be attained and that she must direct her views and her efforts towards new paths, the more so as the work undertaken by Austria-Hungary assumed a character threatening the essential interests of Rumania as well as her most legitimate national aspirations.

In presence of so radical a modification of the situation created between the Austro-Hungarian Monarchy and Rumania, the latter resumed her liberty of action. The neutrality of the Royal Government, imposed upon itself in consequence of a declaration of war made without reference to its will and contrary to its interests, had been adopted, in the first instance, as the result of assurances given at the outset by the Imperial and Royal Government that the Monarchy, in declaring war upon Serbia, had not been inspired by a spirit of conquest and that it was in no way aiming at territorial acquisitions.

These assurances have not been realized. Today we find ourselves confronted by situations *de facto* from which may arise great territorial transformations and political changes of a character constituting a grave menace to the security of the future of Rumania. The work of peace which Rumania, faithful to the spirit of the Triple Alliance, had endeavoured to accomplish has thus been rendered fruitless by those very Powers who were called upon to support and defend it.

In adhering in 1883 to the group of the Central Powers Rumania, far from forgetting the ties of blood uniting the populations of the Kingdom with the Rumanian subjects of the Austro-Hungarian Monarchy, had seen in the relations of friendship and alliance which were established between the three Great Powers a precious pledge for her internal tranquillity, as well as for the amelioration of the lot of the Rumanians of Austria-Hungary. In fact, Germany and Italy, who had reconstituted their States on the basis of the principle of nationality, could not but recognize the legitimacy of the foundation on which their own existence rested. As for Austria-Hungary, she found in the friendly relations established between herself and the Kingdom of Rumania assurances for her tranquillity, both in her interior and on our common frontiers—for she was well aware to what an extent the discontent of her Rumanian population found an echo amongst us, threatening every moment to trouble the good relations between the two States.

The hope which we had based from this point of view upon our adhesion to the Triple Alliance was deceived for a period of more than thirty years. The Rumanians of the Monarchy not only have never seen a reform introduced of a nature to give them the semblance of satisfaction, but they have, on the contrary, been treated as an inferior race and condemned to suffer the oppression of a foreign element which constitutes no more than a minority in the midst of the various nationalities of which the Austro-Hungarian State is composed. All the injustices which our brothers were thus made to suffer maintained between our country and the Monarchy a continual state of animosity, which the Governments of the Kingdom only succeeded in appeasing at the cost of great difficulties and of numerous sacrifices.

When the present war broke out it might have been hoped that the Austro-Hungarian Government, at least at the last moment, would end by convincing itself of the urgent necessity of putting an end to this injustice, which endangered not only our relations of friendship but even the normal relations which ought to exist between neighbouring States.

Two years of war, during which Rumania has maintained neutrality, have proved that Austria-Hungary, opposed to all internal reform which could ameliorate the life of the peoples which she governs, has shown herself as ready to sacrifice them as she is powerless to defend them against external attack.

The war in which almost the whole of Europe is taking part raises the gravest problems affecting the national development and the very existence of States. Rumania, moved by the desire to contribute to hasten the end of the conflict and compelled by the necessity of safeguarding her racial interests, sees herself forced to enter into line by the side of those who are able to assure her the realization of her national unity.

For these reasons she considers herself from this moment in a state of war with Austria-Hungary.

(b) *Secret Treaty of Entente Powers with Roumania, August 18, 1916*

(1) *From Mr. Philip Price's summary of the Russian diplomatic documents published at Petrograd*[1]

On the same day (August 8, 1916) the text of an agreement between the Allies and Rumania is prepared, giving satisfaction to all Rumania's claims to the Banat, Transylvania up to the Theiss, and Bukovina up to the Pruth. M. Stürmer, in a memorandum to the Tsar, however, raises the objection that Rumania must not be regarded as on a footing with the Great Powers, and the latter must not be bound to continue the war until all Rumania's territorial claims are realized, since this would cause serious complications over the Constantinople straits. . . . On 12th August the Tsar agrees to all the Rumanian terms. The secret treaty was signed on 18th August, the Salonika advance to take place on 20th August, and the entrance of Rumania on 28th August.

---

[1] The *Manchester Guardian*, February 8, 1918. Reprinted with the permission of the *Manchester Guardian*.

(2) Report of General Polivanov[1]

Since the outbreak of the European War Roumania had officially adopted a neutral attitude, which very frequently and noticeably inclined now to one, now to the other side, according to the course of military operations. This was based upon two main calculations: the wish not to arrive too late for the partition of Austria-Hungary, and the endeavor to earn as much as possible at the expense of the belligerents. Our successes in Galicia and Bukovina in 1914 and early 1915, the capture of Lemberg and Przemysl, and the appearance of our advance guard beyond the Carpathians, brought the question of Roumanian intervention to a head. At the end of May of the same year our retreat from Galicia and Poland took place, and Bukovina was abandoned, and the feelings of leading circles in Roumania correspondingly changed. The negotiations for intervention came of their own accord to a standstill.

At the end of 1915 and early in 1916, after the destruction of Serbia and Bulgaria's intervention, Roumanian policy leaned very noticeably towards the side of our enemies. At that time the Roumanian Government concluded a whole series of very advantageous commercial agreements with Austria-Hungary and Germany. This circumstance forced our military, financial, and commercial authorities to show great caution in the question of the export from Russia to Roumania of war material and various other supplies, such as might fall into the hands of our enemies. In consequence of the brilliant offensive of General Brusilov in the spring and summer, 1916, Roumanian neutrality leant once more to the side of the Entente Powers, and there arose the possibility of renewing the interrupted negotiations for Roumanian intervention. It is to be observed that, from the first, the Chief of Staff, for military reasons, held the neutrality of Roumania to be more advantageous for us than her active intervention in the war. Later on General Alexeiev adopted the point of view of the Allies, who looked upon Roumania's entry as a decisive blow for Austria-Hungary and as the nearing of the war's end.

In August, 1916, a military and political agreement was signed with Roumania, which assigned to her such accessions of territory (Bukovina and all Transylvania) as quite obviously did not correspond to the measure of Roumania's share of military operations; since she had undertaken only to declare war on Austria-Hungary, and had confined herself to operations in Transylvania.

The events which followed showed how greatly our Allies were mistaken, and how they overvalued Roumania's entry. Under the impression of the catastrophe currents arose in Roumania itself, which opposed a continuance of the war and made the early conclusion of peace, even of a separate peace, their aim. The misfortune which overcame Roumania is the natural result of the complete lack of mili-

---

[1] The *New York Evening Post. Full Texts of Secret Treaties as revealed at Petrograd* (pamphlet).

tary preparation under the two-sided policy of Bratianu. Roumania's easy victories in 1913 and her diplomatic success after the Balkan Wars contributed materially to both society and Government exaggerating their own importance. Politically and militarily, the Roumanians greatly overrated themselves, and are now undergoing a bitter disappointment.

From the standpoint of Russian interests, we must be guided by the following considerations in judging the present situation in Roumania. If things had developed in such a way that the military and political agreement of 1916 with Roumania had been fully realized, then a very strong State would have arisen in the Balkans, consisting of Moldavia, Wallachia, the Dobrudja (*i.e.*, the present Roumania), and of Transylvania, the Banat, and Bukovina (acquisitions under the Treaty of 1916), with a population of about 13,000,000. In the future this State could hardly have been friendly disposed towards Russia, and would scarcely have abandoned the design of realizing its national dreams in Bessarabia and the Balkans. Consequently, the collapse of Roumania's plans as a Great Power is not particularly opposed to Russia's interests. This circumstance must be exploited by us in order to strengthen for as long as possible those compulsory ties which link Russia with Roumania. Our successes on the Roumanian front are for us of extraordinary importance, as the only possibility of deciding once for all in the sense we desire the question of Constantinople and the Straits. The events now occurring in Roumania have altered to their very foundation the conditions of the Treaty of 1916. Instead of the comparatively modest military support which Russia was pledged to provide in the Dobrudja, she had to assign the defence of Roumanian territory on all sides almost exclusively to Russian troops. This military aid on the part of Russia has now assumed such dimensions that the promise of territorial compensations to Roumania prescribed in the treaty in return for her entry into the war must undoubtedly be submitted to revision.

(Signed) POLIVANOV

(3) *Political Agreement with Roumania, August 17, 1916*[1]

I. Great Britain, France, Italy and Russia guarantee the territorial integrity of the Kingdom of Roumania within the extent of her present frontiers.

II. Roumania agrees to declare war on and to attack Austria-Hungary according to the conditions stipulated by the military Convention; Roumania likewise agrees to put an end, from the declaration of war, to all economic relations and commercial exchanges with all the enemies of the Allies.

III. Great Britain, France, Italy and Russia recognize the right of

---

[1] Text in French in H. W. V. Temperley, *A History of the Peace Conference of Paris*, Vol. IV, pp. 516-517. Oxford University Press, 1920-24. Reprinted with the permission of the Oxford University Press.

Roumania to annex the territories of the Austro-Hungarian Monarchy stipulated and delimited in article IV.

IV. [Defines the frontier in detail, so as to give to Roumania the Banat, Transylvania up to the Theiss, and Bukovina up to the Pruth.]

V. Great Britain, France, Italy and Russia, for the one part, and Roumania, for the other part, agree not to conclude a separate peace or general peace except conjointly and simultaneously.

Great Britain, France, Italy and Russia, agree likewise that, in the treaty of peace, the territories of the Austro-Hungarian Monarchy, stipulated in article 4, should be annexed to the Crown of Roumania.

VI. Roumania will enjoy the same rights as the Allies in making the preliminaries to the peace negotiations, as well as in the discussion of the questions which shall be submitted to the decision of the Peace Conference.

VII. The contracting Powers agree to keep the present convention secret until the conclusion of general peace.

Made in five copies, at Bucarest, August 4-17, 1916.

(L. S.) G. BARCLAY

(L. S.) SAINT-AULAIRE

(L. S.) FASCIOTTI

(L. S.) S. POKLEVSKI-KOXIELL

(L. S.) JON. J. C. BRATIANU

108. FRANCO-RUSSIAN PLAN FOR THE GERMAN FRONTIERS[1]

[France obtained Russia's consent to redraw the Franco-German boundary line to suit herself and to create a buffer state out of the German territories on the left bank of the Rhine River. This is revealed in the following note sent by the Russian Minister for Foreign Affairs (Pokrovsky) to the French Ambassador (M. Delcassé) at Petrograd, February 14, 1917.]

Note of the Russian Foreign Minister (Pokrovsky) to the French Ambassador at Petrograd, February 14, 1917

In your Note of today's date your Excellency was good enough to inform the Imperial Government that the Government of the Republic was contemplating the inclusion in the terms of peace to be offered to Germany the following demands and guarantees of a territorial nature:

1. Alsace-Lorraine to be restored to France.

2. The frontiers are to be extended at least up to the limits of the former principality of Lorraine, and are to be drawn up at the discretion of the French Government so as to provide for the strategical

---

[1] The *Manchester Guardian*, December 12, 1917. Reprinted with the permission of the *Manchester Guardian*.

needs and for the inclusion in French territory of the entire iron district of Lorraine and of the entire coal district of the Saar Valley.

3. The rest of the territories situated on the left bank of the Rhine which now form part of the German Empire are to be entirely separated from Germany and freed from all political and economic dependence upon her.

4. The territories of the left bank of the Rhine outside French territory are to be constituted an autonomous and neutral State, and are to be occupied by French troops until such time as the enemy States have completely satisfied all the conditions and guarantees indicated in the Treaty of Peace.

Your Excellency stated that the Government of the Republic would be happy to be able to rely upon the support of the Imperial Government for the carrying out of its plans. By order of His Imperial Majesty my most august master, I have the honour, in the name of the Russian Government, to inform your Excellency by the present Note that the Government of the Republic may rely upon the support of the Imperial Government for the carrying out of its plans as set out above.

[Mr. Balfour, in the House of Commons on December 19, 1917, said of this plan:

"We have never expressed our approval of it, nor do I believe it represents the policy of successive French Governments who have held office during the war. Never did we desire, and never did we encourage the idea, that a bit of Germany should be cut off from the parent State and erected into some kind of . . . independent Government on the left bank of the Rhine. His Majesty's Government were never aware that was seriously entertained by any French statesman."

Note that since the Allies undertook, by the Declaration of September 5, 1914, to make peace in common, any arrangement between France and Russia would equally affect Great Britain.]

109. The Stockholm Conference, 1917[1]

[Following the lead of the United States, most of the Allied Governments refused to permit Socialist delegates to attend the Stockholm Conference called by the Russian Council of Workmen's and Soldiers' Delegates to meet in September. Delegates from other countries, already assembled in Stockholm, joined in the following protest.]

Joint Socialist Statement on the Refusal of Passports to Stockholm

The Stockholm conference, called at the instance of the Russian Council of Workmen's and Soldiers' Delegates to discuss and formulate

---

[1] New York *Call*, Sept. 9, 1917.

the basis of a democratic and durable peace between the masses of the peoples, has been postponed because the governments of Italy, France, England and the United States have refused passports to delegates. For this action the American government is largely responsible.

At the entente conference in Paris, it was the Italian government, through Baron Sonnino, which headed the opposition to the Stockholm conference. France also voted no, though the favorable attitude of Petrograd was known. The Russian representative did not vote. England declared herself in favor of allowing Socialists and labor delegates to go to Stockholm.

There remained only the American government, which practically cast the deciding vote. The American government voted no.

We do not understand President Wilson's course of action. When, in the Senate in December, 1916, he addressed the peoples of the world, the Socialists and labor organizations of Europe supported him with all their strength.

In all Wilson's public utterances it has been made perfectly plain that the main obstacle to American peace with Germany is the German political autocracy, and that America's object in the war is to secure the democratization of the German government.

The Stockholm conference is the best and, perhaps, the only opportunity for the representatives of the entente peoples to make clear to the German masses the conditions upon which peace is possible. And yet President Wilson refuses to allow the delegates of American Socialist and Labor groups to come to Stockholm.

The peoples of the world are sick of war, whatever policy their governments see fit publicly to adopt.

In the invitation to the Stockholm conference and its acceptance by democratic political and economic elements in all the belligerent countries is to be seen the first action of the international masses, growing conscious of their power, awakening to the colossal error of unending war and determination that government shall be of, by and for the Social Democracy.

110. Peace Negotiations, 1916-1917

[In less than a week after the fall of Bucharest, and at a time when he must have felt that the position of the Central Powers was so formidable as to make a peace move seem altruistic rather than necessary, Bethmann-Hollweg, the German Chancellor, sent a note (110, a) to the governments of the states which were his enemies suggesting that peace negotiations be started with a view to terminating the war. The reply (110, b) was returned that the Entente Allies had not yet achieved their objectives and could not stop. Wilson made an independent suggestion (110, c) at about this same time that the belligerent powers of both camps announce their war aims and thus, perhaps, open the way for a peace conference. This note was signed by the Secretary of State. The reference in it to the League of Nations is to be noted. The Entente Powers in a general way stated their aims in reply (110, d), but the Central Powers politely reminded Wilson (110, e, f) that they had already suggested a conference.

Early the next March, when German-American relations were disrupted, but a month before the United States entered the war, Austria made a secret peace proposal (110, g) on questions relating to France and Russia, but mentioned nothing of Italy. Prince Sixte, a brother of Empress Zita of Austria, and at the time serving in the Belgian army, carried Emperor Karl's message to President Poincaré. The latter replied that terms must be offered Italy also. Shortly after, the Russian Revolution broke out and Emperor Karl in a letter of March 24, 1917, reserved questions relating to Russia for a later time. He and his government showed willingness to make compromises with Italy and interested Bethmann-Hollweg through the prospect of being able to divert their troops from the South to the Russian frontier. The Austrian note to Italy of August 22 gives the revised terms.

There have been rumors that the Tsarist Government of Russia tried to bring about a separate peace with Austria. The account (110, h) cited below cannot be authenticated, but the proposition of a peace between the monarchs to save themselves from the rising masses is interesting.

The following document (110, i) is a denial on the part of the Russian Provisional (Revolutionary) Government that Russia wanted a separate peace in the spring of 1917; they wanted rather to observe the engagements with the Entente Allies of Russia and urged the latter to work speedily toward a general peace. The British response is included.]

(a) *Proposals for Peace Negotiations Made by Germany, December 12, 1916*[1]

Berlin, December 12, 1916

Mr. Chargé d'Affaires:

The most formidable war known to history has been ravaging for two and a half years a great part of the world. That catastrophe, that the bonds of a common civilization more than a thousand years old could not stop, strikes mankind in its most precious patrimony; it threatens to bury under its ruins the moral and physical progress on which Europe prided itself at the dawn of the twentieth century. In that strife Germany and her allies—Austria-Hungary, Bulgaria,

---

[1] United States. Department of State. *Diplomatic Correspondence with Belligerent Governments Relating to Neutral Rights and Duties. European War, No. 4,* p. 305.

and Turkey—have given proof of their indestructible strength in winning considerable successes at war. Their unshakable lines resist ceaseless attacks of their enemies' arms. The recent diversion in the Balkans was speedily and victoriously thwarted. The latest events have demonstrated that a continuation of the war can not break their resisting power. The general situation much rather justifies their hope of fresh successes. It was for the defense of their existence and freedom of their national development that the four Allied Powers were constrained to take up arms. The exploits of their armies have brought no change therein. Not for an instant have they swerved from the conviction that the respect of the rights of the other nations is not in any degree incompatible with their own rights and legitimate interests. They do not seek to crush or annihilate their adversaries. Conscious of their military and economic strength and ready to carry on to the end, if they must, the struggle that is forced upon them, but animated at the same time by the desire to stem the flood of blood and to bring the horrors of war to an end, the four Allied Powers propose to enter even now into peace negotiations. They feel sure that the propositions which they would bring forward and which would aim to assure the existence, honor, and free development of their peoples, would be such as to serve as a basis for the restoration of a lasting peace.

If notwithstanding this offer of peace and conciliation the struggle should continue, the four Allied Powers are resolved to carry it on to a victorious end, while solemnly disclaiming any responsibility before mankind and history.

The Imperial Government has the honor to ask through your obliging medium the Government of the United States to be pleased to transmit the present communication to the Government of the French Republic, to the Royal Government of Great Britain, to the Imperial Government of Japan, to the Royal Government of Roumania, to the Imperial Government of Russia, and to the Royal Government of Servia. . . .

VON BETHMANN HOLLWEG

(b) *Allied Reply to the German Peace Note*[1]

(Translation)

The Allied Governments of Russia, France, Great Britain, Japan, Italy, Serbia, Belgium, Montenegro, Portugal, and Roumania, united for the defence of the freedom of nations and faithful to their under-

---

[1] Great Britain. *Parliamentary Papers*, 1917-18, Vol. XXXVIII. Cmd. 8467. "Reply to the German Peace Note, communicated by the French Government on behalf of the Allied Powers to the United States Ambassador in Paris, December 30, 1916."

takings not to lay down their arms except in common accord, have decided to return a joint answer to the illusory peace proposals which have been addressed to them by the Governments of the enemy Powers through the intermediary of the United States, Spain, Switzerland, and the Netherlands.

As a prelude to any reply, the Allied Powers feel bound to protest strongly against the two material assertions made in the note from the enemy Powers, the one professing to throw upon the Allies the responsibility of the war, and the other proclaiming the victory of the Central Powers.

The Allies cannot admit a claim which is thus untrue in each particular and is sufficient alone to render sterile all attempts at negotiations.

The Allied nations have for thirty months been engaged in a war which they have done everything to avoid. They have shown by their actions their devotion to peace. This devotion is as strong today as it was in 1914; and after the violation by Germany of her solemn engagements, Germany's promise is no sufficient foundation on which to reëstablish the peace which she broke.

A mere suggestion, without statement of terms, that negotiations should be opened, is not an offer of peace. The putting forward by the Imperial Government of a sham proposal, lacking all substance and precision, would appear to be less an offer of peace than a war manœuvre.

It is founded on a calculated misrepresentation of the character of the struggle in the past, the present, and the future.

As for the past, the German note takes no account of the facts, dates, and figures which establish that the war was desired, provoked, and declared by Germany and Austria-Hungary.

At the Hague Conference it was the German delegate who refused all proposals for disarmament. In July, 1914, it was Austria-Hungary who, after having addressed to Serbia an unprecedented ultimatum, declared war upon her, in spite of the satisfaction which had at once been accorded. The Central Empires then rejected all attempts made by the *Entente* to bring about a pacific solution of a purely local conflict. Great Britain suggested a conference, France proposed an international commission, the Emperor of Russia asked the German Emperor to go to arbitration, and Russia and Austria-Hungary came to an understanding on the eve of the conflict; but to all these efforts Germany gave neither answer nor effect. Belgium was invaded by an Empire which had guaranteed her neutrality and which has had the assurance to proclaim that treaties were "scraps of paper," and that "necessity knows no law."

As for the present these sham offers on the part of Germany rest on a "war map" of Europe alone, which represents nothing more than a superficial and passing phase of the situation, and not the real strength of the belligerents. A peace concluded upon these terms would be only to the advantage of the aggressors, who after imagining that they would reach their goal in two months, discovered after two years that they could never attain it.

As for the future, the disasters caused by the German declaration of war and the innumerable outrages committed by Germany and her allies against both belligerents and neutrals demand penalties, reparation, and guarantees: Germany avoids the mention of any of these.

In reality, these overtures made by the Central Powers are nothing more than a calculated attempt to influence the future course of the war, and to end it by imposing a German peace. The object of these overtures is to create dissension in public opinion in Allied countries. But that public opinion has, in spite of all the sacrifices endured by the Allies, already given its answer with firmness, and has denounced the empty pretence of the declaration of the enemy Powers.

They have the further object of stiffening public opinion in Germany and in the countries allied to her, one and all, already severely tried by their losses, worn out by economic pressure and crushed by the supreme effort which has been imposed upon their inhabitants.

They endeavour to deceive and intimidate public opinion in neutral countries, whose inhabitants have long since made up their minds where the initial responsibility rests, have recognised existing responsibilities, and are far too enlightened to favour the designs of Germany by abandoning the defence of human freedom.

Finally, these overtures attempt to justify in advance in the eyes of the world a new series of crimes: submarine warfare, deportations, forced labour, and forced enlistment of inhabitants against their own countries, and violations of neutrality.

Fully conscious of the gravity of this moment, but equally conscious of its requirements, the Allied Governments, closely united to one another and in perfect sympathy with their peoples, refuse to consider a proposal which is empty and insincere.

Once again the Allies declare that no peace is possible so long as they have not secured reparation of violated rights and liberties, recognition of the principle of nationalities, and of the free existence of small States; so long as they have not brought about a settlement calculated to end once and for all forces which have constituted a perpetual menace to the nations, and to afford the only effective guarantees for the future security of the world.

In conclusion, the Allied Powers think it necessary to put forward the following considerations, which show the special situation of Belgium after two and a half years of war:—

In virtue of international treaties signed by five Great European Powers, of whom Germany was one, Belgium enjoyed, before the war, a special status, rendering her territory inviolable, and placing her, under the guarantee of the Powers, outside all European conflicts.

She was, however, in spite of these treaties, the first to suffer the aggression of Germany. For this reason the Belgian Government think it necessary to define the aims which Belgium has never ceased to pursue, while fighting, side by side with the *Entente* Powers, for right and justice.

Belgium has always scrupulously fulfilled the duties which her neutrality imposed upon her. She has taken up arms to defend her independence and her neutrality violated by Germany, and to show that she remains faithful to her international obligations. On the 4th August, 1914, in the Reichstag the German Chancellor admitted that this aggression constituted an injustice contrary to the laws of nations, and pledged himself, in the name of Germany, to repair it.

During two and a half years this injustice has been cruelly aggravated by the proceedings of the occupying forces which have exhausted the resources of the country, ruined its industries, devastated its towns and villages, and have been responsible for innumerable massacres, executions, and imprisonments. At this very moment, while Germany is proclaiming peace and humanity to the world, she is deporting Belgian citizens by thousands and reducing them to slavery.

Belgium before the war asked for nothing but to live in harmony with all her neighbours. Her King and her Government have but one aim: the reëstablishment of peace and justice. But they only desire a peace which would assure to their country legitimate reparation, guarantees, and safeguards for the future.

December 30, 1916

(c) *Note communicated by the United States Ambassador, December 20, 1916*[1]

The President of the United States has instructed me to suggest to His Majesty's Government a course of action with regard to the present war which he hopes that His Majesty's Government will take under consideration as suggested in the most friendly spirit and as coming not only from a friend but also as coming from the representative of a neutral nation whose interests have been most seriously affected by the war and whose concern for its early conclusion arises out of a manifest necessity to determine how best to safeguard those interests if the war is to continue.

The suggestion which I am instructed to make the President has long had it in his mind to offer. He is somewhat embarrassed to offer it at this particular time because it may now seem to have been prompted by the recent overtures of the Central Powers. It is in fact in no way associated with them in its origin and the President would

[1] Great Britain. *Parliamentary Papers*, 1916, Vol. XXXIV, Cmd. 8431. "Note of President Wilson to the Belligerent Powers Suggesting a Statement of Peace Terms. December 18, 1916."

have delayed offering it until those overtures had been answered but for the fact that it also concerns the question of peace, and may best be considered in connection with other proposals which have the same end in view. The President can only beg that his suggestion be considered entirely on its own merits and as if it had been made in other circumstances.

The President suggests that an early occasion be sought to call out from all the nations now at war such an avowal of their respective views as to the terms upon which the war might be concluded, and the arrangements which would be deemed satisfactory as a guarantee against its renewal or the kindling of any similar conflict in the future as would make it possible frankly to compare them. He is indifferent as to the means taken to accomplish this. He would be happy himself to serve or even to take the initiative in its accomplishment in any way that might prove acceptable, but he has no desire to determine the method or the instrumentality. One way will be as acceptable to him as another if only the great object he has in mind be attained.

He takes the liberty of calling attention to the fact that the objects which the statesmen of the belligerents on both sides have in mind in this war are virtually the same, as stated in general terms to their own people and to the world. Each side desires to make the rights and privileges of weak peoples and small States as secure against aggression or denial in the future as the rights and privileges of the great and powerful States now at war. Each wishes itself to be made secure in the future, along with all other nations and peoples, against the recurrence of wars like this and against aggression of selfish interference of any kind. Each would be jealous of the formation of any more rival leagues to preserve an uncertain balance of power amidst multiplying suspicions; but each is ready to consider the formation of a league of nations to insure peace and justice throughout the world. Before that final step can be taken, however, each deems it necessary first to settle the issues of the present war upon terms which will certainly safeguard the independence, the territorial integrity, and the political and commercial freedom of the nations involved.

In the measures to be taken to secure the future peace of the world the people and the Government of the United States are as vitally and directly interested as the Governments now at war. Their interest, moreover, in the means to be adopted to relieve the smaller and weaker peoples of the world of the peril of wrong and violence is as quick and ardent as that of any other people or Government. They stand ready, and even eager, to coöperate in the accomplishment of these ends, when the war is over, with every influence and resource at their command. But the war must first be concluded. The terms upon which it is to be concluded they are not at liberty to suggest; but the President does feel that it is his right and his duty to point out their intimate interest in its conclusion, lest it should presently be too late to accomplish the greater things which lie beyond its conclusion, lest the situation of neutral nations, now exceedingly hard to endure, be rendered altogether intolerable, and lest, more than all, an injury be done civilization itself which can never be atoned for or repaired.

The President therefore feels altogether justified in suggesting an immediate opportunity for a comparison of views as to the terms which must precede those ultimate arrangements for the peace of the world, which all desire and in which the neutral nations, as well as those at war, are ready to play their full responsible part. If the contest must continue to proceed towards undefined ends by slow attrition until the one group of belligerents or the other is exhausted, if million after million of human lives must continue to be offered up until on the one side or the other there are no more to offer, if resentments must be kindled that can never cool and despairs engendered from which there can be no recovery, hopes of peace and of the willing concert of free peoples will be rendered vain and idle.

The life of the entire world has been profoundly affected. Every part of the great family of mankind has felt the burden and terror of this unprecedented contest of arms. No nation in the civilized world can be said in truth to stand outside its influence or to be safe against its disturbing effects. And yet the concrete objects for which it is being waged have never been definitely stated.

The leaders of the several belligerents have, as has been said, stated those objects in general terms. But, stated in general terms, they seem the same on both sides. Never yet have the authoritative spokesmen of either side avowed the precise objects which would, if attained, satisfy them and their people that the war had been fought out. The world has been left to conjecture what definite results, what actual exchange of guarantees, what political or territorial changes or readjustments, what stage of military success even, would bring the war to an end.

It may be that peace is nearer than we know; that the terms which the belligerents on the one side and on the other would deem it necessary to insist upon are not so irreconcilable as some have feared; that an interchange of views would clear the way at least for conference and make the permanent concord of the nations a hope of the immediate future, a concert of nations immediately practicable.

The President is not proposing peace; he is not even offering mediation. He is merely proposing that soundings be taken in order that we may learn, the neutral nations with the belligerent, how near the haven of peace may be for which all mankind longs with an intense and increasing longing. He believes that the spirit in which he speaks and the objects which he seeks will be understood by all concerned, and he confidently hopes for a response which will bring a new light into the affairs of the world.

United States Embassy, London. December 20, 1916

[LANSING.]

(d) *Reply of the Allied Governments to the Note Communicated by the United States Ambassador on December 20, 1916*[1]

(Translation)

1. The Allied Governments have received the note delivered to them, on the 19th December, in the name of the United States Government. They have studied it with the care enjoined upon them both by their accurate sense of the gravity of the moment and by their sincere friendship for the American people.

2. In general, they make a point of declaring that they pay homage to the loftiness of the sentiments inspiring the American note, and that they associate themselves wholeheartedly with the plan of creating a league of the nations to ensure peace and justice throughout the world. They recognise all the advantages that would accrue to the cause of humanity and civilisation by the establishment of international settlements designed to avoid violent conflicts between the nations, settlements which ought to be attended by the sanctions necessary to assure their execution and thus to prevent fresh aggressions from being made easier by an apparent security.

3. But a discussion of future arrangements designed to ensure a lasting peace presupposes a satisfactory settlement of the present conflict. The Allies feel a desire as deep as that of the United States Government to see ended at the earliest possible moment the war for which the Central Empires are responsible, and which inflicts sufferings so cruel upon humanity. But they judge it impossible today to bring about a peace that shall assure to them the reparation, the restitution, and the guarantees to which they are entitled by the aggression for which the responsibility lies upon the Central Powers, and of which the very principle tended to undermine the safety of Europe; a peace that shall also permit the establishment upon firm foundations of the future of the nations of Europe. The Allied nations are conscious that they are fighting, not for selfish interests, but above all to safeguard the independence of peoples, right, and humanity.

4. The Allies are fully alive to and deplore the losses and sufferings which the war causes neutrals, as well as belligerents, to endure; but they do not hold themselves responsible, since in no way did they desire or provoke this war, and they make every effort to lessen such damage to the full extent compatible with the inexorable requirements of their defence against the violence and the pitfalls of the foe.

5. Hence they note with satisfaction the declaration that as regards its origin the American communication was in no wise associated with that of the Central Powers, transmitted on the 18th December, by

---

[1] Great Britain. *Parliamentary Papers,* 1917-18, Vol. XXXVIII, Cmd. 8468.

the United States Government; neither do they doubt the resolve of that Government to avoid even the appearance of giving any, albeit only moral, support to the responsible authors of the war.

6. The Allied Governments hold themselves bound to make a stand in the friendliest yet in the clearest way against the establishment in the American note of a likeness between the two belligerent groups; this likeness, founded upon the public statements of the Central Powers, conflicts directly with the evidence, both as regards the responsibilities for the past and the guarantees for the future. In mentioning this likeness President Wilson certainly did not mean to associate himself with it.

7. If at this moment there be an established historical fact, it is the aggressive will of Germany and Austria to ensure their mastery over Europe, and their economic domination over the world. By her declaration of war, by the immediate violation of Belgium and Luxembourg, and by the way she has carried on the struggle, Germany has also proved her systematic contempt of every principle of humanity and of all respect for small States; in proportion as the conflict has developed, the attitude of the Central Powers and of their Allies has been a continual challenge to humanity and to civilisation. Need we recall the horrors that accompanied the invasion of Belgium and of Serbia, the atrocious rule laid upon the invaded countries, the massacre of hundreds of thousands of inoffensive Armenians, the barbarities committed against the inhabitants of Syria, the Zeppelin raids upon open towns, the destruction by submarines of passenger steamers and merchantmen, even under neutral flags, the cruel treatment inflicted upon prisoners of war, the judicial murders of Miss Cavell and of Captain Fryatt, the deportation and the reduction to slavery of civil populations?

The accomplishment of such a series of crimes, perpetrated without any regard for the universal reprobation they aroused, amply explains to President Wilson the protest of the Allies.

8. They consider that the note they handed to the United States in reply to the German note answers the question put by the American Government, and forms, according to the words of that Government, "an avowal of their respective views as to the terms on which the war might be concluded."

Mr. Wilson wishes for more: he desires that the belligerent Powers should define, in the full light of day, their aims in prosecuting the war. The Allies find no difficulty in answering this request. Their war aims are well known: they have been repeatedly defined by the heads of their various Governments. These war aims will only be set forth in detail, with all the compensations and equitable indemnities for harm suffered, at the moment of negotiation. But the civilised world knows that they imply, necessarily and first of all, the restoration of

Belgium, Serbia, and Montenegro, with the compensations due to them; the evacuation of the invaded territories in France, in Russia, in Rumania, with just reparation; the reorganisation of Europe, guaranteed by a stable régime, and based at once on respect for nationalities and on the right to full security and liberty of economic development possessed by all peoples, small and great, and at the same time upon territorial conventions and international settlements such as to guarantee land and sea frontiers against unjustified attack; the restitution of provinces formerly torn from the Allies by force or against the wish of their inhabitants; the liberation of the Italians, as also of the Slavs, Rumanes, and Czecho-Slovaks from foreign domination; the setting free of the populations subject to the bloody tyranny of the Turks; and the turning out of Europe of the Ottoman Empire as decidedly foreign to Western civilisation.

9. The intentions of His Majesty the Emperor of Russia in regard to Poland have been clearly indicated by the manifesto he has just addressed to his armies.

10. There is no need to say that, if the Allies desire to shield Europe from the covetous brutality of Prussian militarism, the extermination and the political disappearance of the German peoples have never, as has been pretended, formed part of their designs. They desire above all to ensure peace on the principles of liberty and justice, and upon the inviolable fidelity to international engagements, by which the Government of the United States have ever been inspired.

11. United in the pursuit of this lofty aim, the Allies are determined, severally and jointly, to act with all their power and to make all sacrifices to carry to a victorious end a conflict upon which, they are convinced, depend not only their own welfare and prosperity, but the future of civilisation itself.

Paris, January 10, 1917.

(e) German Reply to President Wilson, December 26, 1916[1]

With reference to the esteemed communication of December 21, Foreign Office No. 15118, the undersigned has the honor to reply as follows: To His Excellency the Ambassador of the United States of America, Mr. James W. Gerard.

The Imperial Government has accepted and considered in the friendly spirit which is apparent in the communication of the President, [the] noble initiative of the President looking to the creation of bases for the foundation of a lasting peace. The President discloses the aim which lies next to his heart and leaves the choice of the way open. A direct exchange of views appears to the Imperial Government as the

---

[1] United States. Department of State. *Diplomatic Correspondence*, etc., *European War, No. 4*, p. 327.

most suitable way of arriving at the desired result. The Imperial Government has the honor, therefore, in the sense of its declaration of the 12th instant, which offered the hand for peace negotiations to propose the speedy assembly, on neutral ground, of delegates of the warring States.

It is also the view of the Imperial Government that the great work for the prevention of future wars can first be taken up only after the ending of the present conflict of exhaustion. The Imperial Government is ready, when this point has been reached, to coöperate with the United States at this sublime task.

The undersigned, while permitting himself to have recourse to good offices of his Excellency the Ambassador in connection with the transmission of the above reply to the President of the United States, avails himself of this opportunity to renew the assurances of his highest consideration.

ZIMMERMANN

(f) *Austro-Hungarian Reply to President Wilson's Peace Note, December 26, 1916*[1]

In reply to the *aide memoire* communicated on the 22d instant by his Excellency the American Ambassador, containing the proposals of the President of the United States of America for an exchange of views among the Powers at present at war for the eventual establishment of peace, the Imperial and Royal Government desires particularly to point out that in considering the noble proposal of the President it is guided by the same spirit of amity and complaisance as finds expression therein.

The President desires to establish a basis for a lasting peace without wishing to indicate the ways and means. The Imperial and Royal Government considers a direct exchange of views among the belligerents to be the most suitable way of attaining this end. Adverting to its declaration of the 12th instant, in which it announced its readiness to enter into peace negotiations, it now has the honor to propose that representatives of the belligerent Powers convene at an early date at some place on neutral ground.

The Imperial and Royal Government likewise concurs in the opinion of the President that only after the termination of the present war will it be possible to undertake the great and desirable work of the prevention of future wars. At an appropriate time it will be willing to coöperate with the United States of America for the realisation of this noble aim.

PENFIELD

[1] United States. Department of State. *Diplomatic Correspondence, etc., European War, No. 4,* p. 328.

(g) *Austria's Peace Offer*[1]

(1) *Memorandum by Prince Sixte de Bourbon-Parma, read by him to the President of the French Republic at Paris, March 5, 1917*

On December 5 and 14 my mother [Duchess of Parma, mother of Empress Zita of Austria] wrote to say that she was particularly anxious to see me. She also sent a letter to the Queen of the Belgians which arrived on December 20, begging her and the King to insist that my brother and I should go to our mother. And, before this letter reached her, the Queen had received a subsequent telegram, sent through the Consulate of Luxembourg, at Berne, in which the Grand Duchess Adelaide of Luxembourg asked her, on my mother's behalf, whether she had received the letter. While all this was happening, we left our Regiment to spend Christmas Eve (December 24, 1916) with the King and Queen. We had the idea of this journey in our minds, and discussed its difficulties with Their Majesties. In the end they gave their consent and we decided to go.

We left the front on January 23 and reached Paris the same evening. We there procured the necessary papers and started again on the evening of the 28th; about noon next day we arrived at the pre-arranged meeting-place in Switzerland. My mother had been there for two days, travelling strictly incognita with my sister Maria-Antonia. She explained to us how much the Emperor wished to see us and to discuss with us directly the possibilities of peace. All arrangements had been made for conveying us with the strictest secrecy to Vienna. The Colonel in charge of the police on the frontier had received instructions from the Emperor to take us by motor to his presence. Absolute secrecy had been observed; but, if we felt that the scheme was impracticable, the Emperor was ready to send a confidential envoy to us in Switzerland, who would communicate his views to us. We considered that the latter course alone was possible, and that only after we had sent word to Paris. Meanwhile, to avert suspicion, we should proceed on the journey into Italy, which we had planned three months earlier, to look after our estates there. The Italian Government knew of this intention.

My mother insisted, in the Emperor's name, that time was of vital importance. She handed us a letter from the Empress, endorsed with a few lines by the Emperor, in which she implored us both most urgently to assist her in realising the ideal of peace which the Emperor had formulated on his accession. In answer to this, I told my mother of the conditions which I, personally, thought fundamental and pre-requisite, on the Entente side, to peace: namely, the restoration to France of the Alsace-Lorraine of 1814, without any colonial or other compensation; the restoration of Belgium, with the Congo; the similar

---

[1] G. de Manteyer (editor). *Austria's Peace Offer, 1916-1917.* London, Constable, 1921, pp. 35-39; 83-84; 233-234. Reprinted with the permission of Constable and Co.

restoration of Serbia, and her eventual extension so as to include Albania; and, lastly, the cession of Constantinople to the Russians. If Austria could manage to conclude a secret armistice with Russia upon these points, that would be a good base for the Peace we all desired.

We left Switzerland on February 1, reached le Pianore next day, and returned to Paris on the morning of Saturday February 10. On the evening of the 12th, at the express wish, as we were told, of the French Government, we both set out again for Switzerland, where at 1.30 on the 13th the Emperor's Envoy was presented to us, bringing with him a letter in which the Empress accredited him to us as the Emperor's representative.

He told us that the Emperor was keenly interested by the first impressions which he had gathered from my mother. He was most anxious for Peace and was prepared to consider it upon the following terms:

1. A secret armistice with Russia in which the question of Constantinople would not be made an issue.

2. Alsace-Lorraine and

3. Belgium to be restored.

4. The formation of a Southern-Slav Monarchy, embracing Bosnia-Herzegovina, Serbia, Albania, and Montenegro. He urgently begged that I would spare no pains to secure Peace upon this footing.

I answered that the situation was enormously complicated by our growing difficulties with America; while I felt that there was no hope of succeeding through diplomatic channels, so long as both Italy and Germany were directly interested in the failure of such a scheme. Austria need show no consideration for Germany, whose interests were quite different from her own, and who might very well abandon her at any moment. It would be preferable to protect the Monarchy by direct action, and only to inform Germany after the event. This direct action would be stimulated by an Imperial Rescript in which Austria, while keeping up an appearance of friendship and alliance with Germany, would offer Peace to her enemies on the terms cited above, except with regard to Serbia, which must be restored *in statu quo* and given a reasonable avenue to the sea by the addition of Albania.

Should the Emperor feel unable to act thus openly, and prefer to attempt to make peace by diplomatic methods, I requested the Envoy to let me have, at the earliest possible moment, the proposals from which the preliminary steps of diplomacy might start. I emphatically insisted that these points would be clearly defined in the document.

The Envoy made a careful note of my requirements, and returned to Vienna. No one else but the Emperor, the Empress and my mother knew of our interview. Count Czernin, the Foreign Minister of the Monarchy, was told no more than that the Emperor had found a means of negotiating with the Entente. On February 21 the Envoy rejoined me. In the interval the Emperor had, by a strongly worded rescript of the 12th, superseded the Archduke Frederick; while on the 13th the Emperor William had come to Vienna; but the Austrian Emperor, in spite of the toasts and other compliments exchanged between them, had declined to sever relations with America, so that the German Emperor went home again without much satisfaction.

The Envoy brought me: (1) a document written in French and signed by himself, but founded on a minute in German, either written or dictated by Count Czernin; (2) a secret and personal message written in German by the Emperor; (3) a letter from my sister Maria-Antonia, written at her dictation to accredit the Envoy; (4) two letters from the Empress; and (5) a long letter from my mother containing many personal details which she had elicited from the Emperor. The Empress, in her two letters, implored me, not only from herself and the Emperor, but also from Count Czernin, to come to Vienna secretly and discuss matters with them there. In Count Czernin's words, "Half an hour's conversation is worth a dozen journeys." In addition to this, I was told again, from the Emperor, how anxious he was to make Peace, not only as an urgent and immediate obligation laid upon him by military conditions, but as his solemn duty, before God, towards the peoples of his Empire and all the belligerents. He repeated his expressions of sympathy for his "dear France," his admiration for the valour of her troops and for the spirit of self-sacrifice and devotion which seemed to prevail throughout the country. I was reminded that I must act with absolute secrecy, into which no one except Count Czernin had been admitted by Their Majesties.

(2) *The text of the Emperor's letter of March 24, published by Clemenceau on April 12, 1918. The Emperor's Autographed Letter*

Laxenburg, March 24, 1917

My dear Sixte—The third anniversary of a war which has plunged the world in mourning is now drawing near. All the peoples of my Empire are united more firmly than ever in the determination to preserve the integrity of the Monarchy, even at the cost of the greatest sacrifices. By virtue of their unity, of the generous collaboration of all the races of my Empire, we have been able to hold out, for nearly three years, against the most fierce attacks. No one can deny the success of my troops in the field, especially in the Balkan Theatre.

France, too, has shown the greatest strength in resisting invasion, and a magnificent vitality. We must all admire without reservation the traditional valour of her gallant army and the willing spirit of sacrifice shown by the whole French people. And I am particularly pleased to note that, although for the time we are in opposite camps, my Empire is not divided from France by any real differences of outlook or of aspiration; while I am justified in hoping that my own keen sympathy for France, supported by the affection which she inspires throughout the Monarchy, will prevent the recurrence at any future time of a state of war for which I myself must disclaim all responsibility. Therefore, and in order that I may express in words what I so strongly feel, I request that you will secretly and unofficially convey to M. Poincaré, the President of the French Republic, my assurance that I will use all my personal influence and every other means in my power to exact from my Allies a settlement of her just claims in Alsace-Lorraine.

As for Belgium, she must be restored in her entirety as a Sovereign State, with the whole of her African possessions, and without prejudice to the compensations she may receive for the losses she has already suffered. Serbia, too, shall be restored as a Sovereign State, and, as a mark of our goodwill towards her, we are prepared to allow her a just and natural approach to the Adriatic, as well as economic concessions on a liberal scale. In return, Austria-Hungary will insist, as a primordial and absolute condition, that the Kingdom of Serbia abandon for the future all relations and suppress all groups or societies whose political object is the disintegration of the Monarchy, and especially the Society called "Narodna Obrana"; and that she take every means in her power loyally to prevent all forms of political agitation, whether within her borders or without, that may tend towards this object, giving us her assurance under a guarantee from the Entente Powers.

Recent events in Russia make it desirable that I should withhold my views with regard to her until such time as a reign of law and order is established there.

Now that I have shown you what I feel, I request that you in your turn, after consultation with France and England, will inform me of their views, so that we may prepare a common ground of mutual understanding on which official negotiations may be based, to the ultimate satisfaction of all parties.

Trusting that we may soon be able to put an end to the sufferings of all the millions of men and all their families, who are now oppressed by sorrow and anxiety, I beg you to be assured of my most warm and brotherly affection.

CHARLES

(3) *Text of the Peace Conditions, communicated to Count Revertera on August 22, 1917*

Belgium.—Complete restitution. Belgium shall be restored in its full extent, and in its independent sovereignty, as it was prior to August 1914.

Complete reparation for all damage done in that country since the beginning of August 1914, to include the payment by Germany of pensions due to the casualties of war, and of Belgium's war-debts.

France.—(A) *Evacuation* of all territory occupied by the enemy. Restitution by Germany of Alsace-Lorraine, as defined by the Treaty of 1814 (with the exception of territories now forming part of the Helvetian Confederation) and free of all charges.

(B) *Reparation* for damage done by the Enemy in occupied territory.

Compensation for the valuables and other wealth taken by him.

Repayment of levies raised by him.

Delivery of coal and wood at an equitable rate pending the restoration of coal-mines and forests.

Payment in compensation for merchant vessels destroyed by his submarines.

Restoration to working order of factories destroyed by the Enemy.

Commissions composed of neutrals shall assess the damages.

(C) *Guarantees.*—Stipulation to refrain from any military activity in the territories on the left bank of the Rhine, which will obviate the possibility of any future aggression. These stipulations need not involve any form of humiliation, their sole object being to render impossible any further act of war on either side.

The Grand Duchy of Luxembourg shall not be included in the German Tariff Union. Its railways shall be withdrawn from any direction or control by Germany.

Heligoland shall be ceded by Germany to an Entente Power.

Rumania.—Rumania shall be restored within her frontiers as prior to the Treaty of Bucharest in 1913.

Serbia.—Serbia shall be restored within the frontiers existing at the end of July 1914, and shall be territorially united with Montenegro. A port on the Adriatic shall be given her.

Balkan Peninsula.—The Powers shall engage in discussion with a view to securing an equitable and lasting Peace in the Balkan Peninsula.

Italy.—Italy shall receive at least the Italian-speaking portion of the Trentino; also Trieste, but full guarantees shall be given to protect Austrian trade.

Poland.—Poland shall be restored within the frontiers of 1772.

Turkey.—The Straits shall be free and open.

The future of the Christian peoples of Turkey and of the inhabitants of Mesopotamia shall be decided so as to guarantee an equitable and lasting Peace in Asia.

Germany.—France is willing to negotiate so that Germany may recover or obtain Colonies by restitution or exchange.

(h) *Rumored Peace Proposals made to the Central Powers by the Russian Court to Save Itself*[1]

When Count Czernin made certain revelations at Vienna on the 11th of last December as to why the war was not promptly concluded by an honorable peace, he said among other things that Austria-Hungary

---

[1] *Pester Lloyd* (Budapest) February 28, 1919 (evening edition), having been reprinted from "an eminent neutral paper." Reprinted with the permission of *Pester Lloyd*.

had never received a peace offer from the Entente. He added: "There were indeed repeated feelers thrown out between Austria-Hungary and the Entente, without these feelers ever resulting in concrete proposals." Taken literally, this may be true. No proposals, so far as we know, were ever actually made by the Entente as a group. We do know definitely, however, that on numerous occasions overtures in favor of peace were made by one or another of the governments forming the Entente and that these overtures for the most part contained concrete and in some cases detailed proposals.

Of the eight instances known to us, of which the first was addressed to the Austro-Hungarian monarchy in July 1915, the most important was the peace tender of Russia, dating from October 1916 to March 1917. Had it been considered, in all probability the war would have been ended in a way quite satisfactory to the Central Powers. . . .

On October 16, 1916, the Russian court let it be known in Berlin and Vienna through neutral channels, that Russia inasmuch as it had made greater sacrifices for the war than it was obliged to make, reserved freedom of action in the matter of peace. It was hinted that an immediate peace could be made. This would depend upon Germany's making concessions in regard to Constantinople. In that case Russia would ask nothing of Austria-Hungary and would restore all the occupied territories without further question. Germany must leave Turkey to its fate, or at least agree that the Dardanelles and a strip five kilometers wide on either side to be neutralized under the control of a sovereign international commission in which all maritime states should be represented. A double representation was to be granted the states having territory on the Black Sea. Stambul was to remain under the immediate jurisdiction of the Sultan and be administered by him. Armenia was to form an autonomous buffer state under international protection with an Armenian at its head. It was to have a local constabulary for which Russia would provide instructors. Russia was willing to grant the Hungarians the boundary line of Midea-Enos, the coast of the Ægean Sea as far as the mouth of the Struma and that part of Macedonia lying between Bulgaria and a line running from Kumanova through Uskub to Kalkandel, including those cities and that part of Dobrudja which was allotted Bulgaria prior to 1913. Bulgaria was to agree to the provisions of the treaty above prescribed in return. Russia made no objections to Poland being erected into an autonomous state under a Polish ruler, under the protection of the three Russian empires. Furthermore, the Tsar was ready to grant Finland complete independence and to limit the relations between Finland and Russia to the original strictly personal union. In Asiatic Turkey Russia would allow the German Empire a free hand south of Diekos on the Bosporus.

Early in November 1916 these proposals were submitted to the Austrian Foreign Office and the Austrian military authorities, the German Foreign Office, the German military authorities and to the

King of Bulgaria. King Ferdinand was in favor of acceptance. The Austrian military authorities were inclined to consider it. The German military authorities absolutely refused.

On January 24, 1917, the Russian court again approached the same neutral intermediary. We quote the following from the document then submitted by the government in Petrograd:

"The fact that the Central Powers do not really wish peace is proved convincingly to any impartial person by its recent peace comedy (the tender of December 12, 1916). For this reason we must continue the war and will do so until the people of Germany appreciate that it is pursuing a course that leads to its own destruction. The sooner Germany learns this the sooner the world will be safe. The Germans refuse to open their eyes to the fact that in a war of exhaustion, the Entente can hold out longer than they can. The only central European power that is not already exhausted is Turkey, but that country lacks skilled leaders to organize it and cannot maintain itself permanently. In regard to human resources the Entente is superior. The Central Powers have no reserves except the Turks. The other governments of that group have no replacement troops. For this reason Turkey must be separated from the Central Powers either by being overwhelmed or surrounded. We can accomplish the latter by winning over Bulgaria and that can be done without much trouble if the war does not end next summer. For this reason we do not ask any sacrifice of Bulgaria, although we are justified in bearing that country great ill will. On the contrary we are ready to recognize the principle of nationality to the extent of granting that people the borders of San Stefano. The peace conditions we have stated to Wilson are perhaps immoderate, but they are not to be taken literally. They are rather to be considered as an appropriate reply in view of the arrogance and over-confidence which Germany continues to show without sufficient guarantees under present conditions. Russia is ready to negotiate on the basis indicated last October but so long as Berlin and Vienna will listen to no mediation it is hopeless.

"Furthermore, we have received from neutral hands, and apparently at the instigation of Berlin and Vienna, peace proposals which we regard as immoderate and unacceptable as the Central Powers regard those made by us, which we submitted to President Wilson. This is particularly true of the conditions proposed in regard to Turkey, Poland, Servia and the colonies. Berlin and Vienna apparently appreciated that fact and for that reason did not publish them in their own peace conditions for fear of losing the support of the neutrals and all their people at home, and of proving that they were not conducting a war of defence but a war of conquest and aggression. If the Central Powers honestly want a reasonable peace, we are ready to negotiate on a basis of our earlier proposals."

These new overtures and proposals were made known to the same higher authorities of the Central Powers on February 11, 1917, that had received the previous proposals in November. The result was identical in both instances. Bulgaria was ready to consider the matter. Vienna and Baden were both indisposed to do so. Berlin did not make an outright refusal but the German higher army command apparently rejected everything.

Meanwhile the continuous intriguing of the British Ambassador, Buchanan, in Russia, supported by his French colleague, had been so successful that the Tsar and his advisors were convinced that the approaching catastrophe could only be avoided by an immediate peace and an agreement with the Central Powers. As a result, court circles in Russia, inspired by Tsar Nicholas, again directed appeals through various channels, among others the same neutral agency which had been employed previously, to the governments at Vienna and Berlin, asking them to consider the Tsar's proposals immediately inasmuch as the interests of Emperor William and Emperor Francis Joseph were vitally affected. This appeal and warning of March 6, 1917, contained the following statements:

"It is clear that the two emperors and the men behind them do not desire peace. The reason for their unfavorable attitude is not clear, although it suggests strongly that personal irritation toward the Tsar and Victor Immanuel is responsible to a large extent.

"Since the common people of all countries want peace, the rulers of those nations may pay dearly for their indulgence in personal sentiment in this matter. The demand for peace from the masses is becoming stronger every day, and the position of the different governments in Europe is becoming increasingly perilous. The situation is especially dangerous in Petrograd. The secret propaganda of the English and French is causing great concern. We have evidence that England is trying to gain control of the whole public machinery of Russia, including the army and navy, using as its agents the intellectuals and the generals whom it has been able to win over to its side. Many of our higher military officers have been corrupted to such an extent that Ambassador Buchanan is now directly promoting a change in rulers, having learned of the resoluted determination of Tsar Nicholas to get peace. The British representatives in Petrograd, like those in Rome and Bucharest, are lavishing money for these purposes. Meantime the Russian Government is not obtaining the allowance promised it for administrative expenses and for the relief of the common people, since these plotters believe that they can thus most rapidly excite the discontent of the masses against the dynasty and the administration.

"The position of ruling families is nowhere a pleasant and secure one today. In this respect our enemies are as badly off as ourselves. If when a balance is struck after the war it shows a serious deficit for the Central Powers, their ruling houses will be far worse off than our own. It is very unfortunate that the Central Powers constantly turn deaf ears to our upright tenders of peace. We urgently advise them to think better of their decision before it is too late. Our only hope is otherwise that the common people of the Central Powers will soon appreciate how sadly they have been betrayed and that further slaughter and devastation is without purpose. Then we may hope that they will force their rulers at last to negotiate with us, for we repeat with emphasis that every day that peace is postponed imperils the position of the ruling houses of the governments of the Central Powers; above all, since America has finally decided to intervene actively to bring matters to a decision.

"For all these reasons the Tsar counsels the monarchs of Germany and Austria-Hungary to listen to reason, and to agree with their governments as to the conditions of peace and to do this without delay before England's intriguing destroys all prospects of success for a long time to come. Russia is ready in case this is done to make some concessions in addition to its peace proposals of last October. The Russian Court believes that it is justified in assuring that as soon as Russia starts to negotiate peace, Italy likewise will follow suit. The preparations for the tenth attack along the Isonzo have revealed many evidences of unsound conditions in that country."

The new conditions proposed were: Restoration of the territorial status existing at the outbreak of the war between Italy and Austria-Hungary; the Italian population in the border territories to be granted the privileges which Austria had promised them before Italy entered the war; the definite and unconditional return of the Libyan colonies to Italy; the complete sovereignty of Italy over the Gulf of Valona and the Island of Sasseno. If necessary, Italy was to exercise this in the capacity of a trustee or lease-holder of a long term for all the Adriatic powers. Restoration of Montenegro and Servia within the boundaries they occupied before the Balkan war. These two countries with the former Sanjak and the department of Skutari were to form a united Serbian Kingdom under the Petrovic family. At the most, Austria-Hungary would be granted concessions in regard to the possession of Lion Mountain that would meet the complaints and claims of the monarch. The rest of Albania was to be divided into three governments, which might be either republics or principalities. The northern or catholic part was to be under the protection of Austria-Hungary, the central part was to be under the protection of the Sultan (and Germany), and the southern or Epirote Republic to be under the protection of Italy.

In return for the complete surrender of Libya to Italy the Turkish Government was to be assured Egypt. The Suez Canal and a territory three kilometers wide on either side and the Straits between Ægæa and Pontus would be internationalized under the administration of a supreme international commission. The Turkish Government was to exercise police control in the name of the commission. In compensation for relinquishing sovereignty over the Straits, the Dodekan Islands were to be ceded to Greece with the exception of seven small islets of which one should be allotted to the European powers and

Turkey as a watch post for the purpose of enforcing international jurisdiction.

Russia would be ready to recognize Poland as an absolutely independent government, subject to the conditions that in this case the Polish speaking territories of Germany and Austria were added, in order that the peace of Europe might not be again imperiled by a Polish irredenta.

This appeal and the proposals accompanying it were conveyed to Vienna, Baden, Berlin and Spa, just as were the previous ones. The King of Bulgaria intervened personally with Emperor Charles in order that the joint action of Austria-Hungary and Bulgaria might be more influential with the German authorities in favor of accepting the Russian proposal. The German higher army command at Spa was unshaken in its opinion that a revolution in Russia would coincide with the interests of the Central Powers, since Russia under such circumstances would be delivered wholly into the hands of Germany and Austria-Hungary.

Hardly a week had elapsed after this urgent action by the Russian court before the revolution predicted occurred. It broke out on the fifteenth of March. The Tsar was forced to abdicate and to intern himself in Tsarsky Selo. Russia probably might have been rescued from the anarchy to which it has fallen a victim and which today constitutes a peril for all Europe, and the war might have been ended if the governing authorities of the Central Powers had been ready to listen to the last desperate appeal of the Russian Court or if they could have reconciled themselves to taking vigorous measures against revolutionary Russia.

There was still one more attempt by Russians which was equally fruitless. On March 26, 1917, certain members of the Russian royal family employed various intermediaries, including the neutral agency already mentioned, in a new appeal to the monarchs of the Central Powers. This document contains the following statement: "Although communication between Petrograd and foreign countries is becoming increasingly difficult and interrupted and possibly may be broken off entirely, we hope that the appeal may reach its destination promptly before everything is lost. The monarch and the royal family of Russia may still be saved if the Central Powers act promptly. A satisfactory peace along the lines proposed will then be certain. The grand dukes and the higher army officers loyal to them still possess a dominant influence and are ready to march upon Petrograd. Thereupon Czar Nicholas, or if it is desired, a new monarch, will officially submit the proposed peace treaty to the Central Powers as soon as a vigorous offensive of the enemy against the northern front has called back the revolutionary troops and permitted the terrorized population of the metropolis to resume control of the city. But it is unconditionally necessary to act immediately before the revolutionary government, which proposed to imprison the royal family and all higher army officers suspected of loyalist sentiment and even to murder them, and the Allies, who are still benumbed by the anticipated turn of events, recover their presence of mind and get firm control. We may rest assured that the revolutionary troops will lay down their arms as soon as they have become convinced by a vigorous advance on the part of the enemy that their cause is lost. The employment of some 700,000 men for a few weeks would be enough to assure the success of this action. We hope that this plan will be adopted at the conference to take place in Berlin shortly between Bethmann-Hollweg, Czernin and Enver Pasha, and have made this proposal with that in mind. We cannot believe that great rulers, although they may for the time being be personal enemies, will find themselves ready to permit a red chaos to rise in Russia the results of which in all probability will endanger themselves. Furthermore, a majority of the Russians, who are returning from banishment, are in favor of a constitutional monarchy under the Romanoffs and of an immediate peace."

This last appeal from Russia likewise received no response. The urgent representations of King Ferdinand to his central European allies not to disregard those warnings and the memorandum which Count Czernin sent to Emperor Charles in 1917 prove that Sophia and Vienna rightly judged the situation. But the German headquarters, which means Ludendorff, obstinately insisted that the Russian revolution would do the cause of the Central Powers more good than harm, and that intervention in this purely domestic affair of Russia's could not be permitted. Consequently nothing was done to bring about a general peace,—a peace that would have resulted very differently for the Central Powers than the one that has actually been proposed.

(i) *Russian Peace Note, 1917*[1]

M. Nabokoff, Russian Chargé d'Affaires, to Mr. Balfour

Russian Embassy, London, May 3, 1917.

Sir,

The Russian Provisional Government published on the 27th March a manifesto to Russian citizens, in which it expressed the views of the Government of free Russia on the objects of the present war. The Minister for Foreign Affairs instructs me to communicate to you this document and to add the following observations. Our enemies have lately endeavoured to sow discord between the Allies by spreading absurd reports regarding the alleged intention of Russia to conclude a separate peace with the Central Monarchies. The text of the annexed document will provide the best refutation of such inventions. The general principles enunciated therein by the Provisional Govern-

---

[1] Great Britain. *Parliamentary Papers,* 1917-18, Vol. XXXVIII, Cmd. 8587. "Note from the Russian Provisional Government and the British Reply respecting the Allied War Aims."

ment are in entire agreement with the lofty ideals which have been repeatedly and recently proclaimed by eminent statesmen of the Allied countries. These principles have also been lucidly expressed in the words of the President of our new Ally, the great American Republic. The Government of the old régime in Russia was certainly not in a position to appreciate and to share these ideas as to the liberating character of the war, the creation of a stable basis for the peaceful coöperation of nations, and the freedom of oppressed peoples. Emancipated Russia can now speak in terms which will be understood by modern democracies, and she hastens to add her voice to those of her Allies. The declarations of the Provisional Government, imbued with this new spirit of a freed democracy, cannot of course afford the least pretext for assuming that the collapse of the old structure has entailed any diminution of Russia's share in the common struggle of all the Allies. On the contrary, the nation's determination to bring the world war to a decisive victory has been accentuated, thanks to the feeling of responsibility which today is incumbent upon us collectively and individually. This tendency has become still more active owing to the fact that it is concentrated on the immediate task, which touches all so closely—of driving back the enemy who has invaded our country's territory.

It is understood, and the annexed document expressly states, that the Provisional Government, in safeguarding the acquired rights of the country, will maintain strict regard for the engagements entered into with Russia's Allies. Firmly convinced of the victorious termination of the present war, and in perfect agreement with its Allies, the Provisional Government is equally sure that the problems raised by this war will find their solution in the creation of some stable basis for a lasting peace, and that, imbued with the same sentiments, the allied democracies will find a means of obtaining the guarantees and penalties necessary for preventing a return of sanguinary wars in the future.

I have, etc.
C. NABOKOFF

Proclamation of the Provisional Government

The Provisional Government, having examined the situation in Russia, has decided, in the name of its duty to the country, to tell the people directly and openly the whole truth. The régime which has now been overthrown left the defence of the country in a gravely disorganised condition. By its culpable inaction and its inept measures it introduced disorganisation into our finances, commissariat, transport, and supply of munitions to the army. It weakened the whole of our economic organisation. The Provisional Government, with the active coöperation of the whole nation, will devote all its energy to repair these grave results of the old régime. But time is pressing. The blood of many sons of the fatherland has been shed freely during

"Marks of Honor for Refined Perfidy"

A parody by the pro-German cartoonist, Cay, throws light upon the pro-Entente propagandist cartoon of his fellow countryman, Raemaekers. (Oorlogs, *Caricaturen* door A. M. Cay. Uitgevers, Nieuwe Maatschappij, den Haag. 1916.)

Translation: Marks of honor for refined perfidy. (Raemaekers, the "neutral" Dutch caricaturist, has been decorated with the cross of the Legion of Honor by the French Government.)

"The Hun"

In order to add lustre to the solemn distribution of the Legion of Honor, the latest creation of the "Raphael of Cruelty," the drawing of the Huns who are devouring children, is being projected on the wall.

Art, how many crimes have been committed in thy name! In the name of art, Poincaré is decorating Raemaekers, because he represents France's enemies as devils. The soiled drawing pencil of this Dutchman has served his principals, the *Telegraph*, the *Daily Mail*, and the *Journal*, extraordinarily well. Medals, ribbons, and other material marks of honor are accepted by Raemaekers graciously. Does the man feel that he is not humiliating the Germans, but that he is striking a blow at the Truth—that his drawings are not caricatures, but sadistic missals? And the inevitable destiny of such talents is becoming visible already—spiritual perversity, artistic insincerity, moral myopia.

Eerbewijzen voor geraffineerde perfidie

(Raemaekers, de „neutrale" Hollandsche caricaturist, is door de Fransche regeering gedecoreerd met het kruis van het Legioen van Eer)

Ter opluistering van de plechtige uitreiking van het Legioen van Eer wordt de nieuwste schepping van den „Rafaël der Ruwheid": de teekening van kinderenverslindende Hunnen, op den muur geprojecteerd.

Kunst, welke misdaden zijn er reeds in Uw naam begaan! In den naam der kunst decoreert Poincaré Raemaekers omdat hij de vijanden van Frankrijk als duivels voorstelt. De besmeurde teekenstift van dezen Hollander heeft buitengewone diensten bewezen aan zijn lastgevers de *Telegraaf*, de *Daily Mail* en het *Journal*. Medaljes, lintjes en andere stoffelijke eerbewijzen neemt Raemaekers gratieus in ontvangst. Voelt de man niet, dat hij niet de Duitschers vernedert, maar de waarheid in 't gezicht slaat — dat zijn teekeningen geen caricaturen, maar sadistische misbaksels zijn? En het onvermijdelijke lot, dat dergelijke talenten treft, wordt reeds zichtbaar — geestelijke perversiteit, artistieke onoprechtheid, moreele bijziendheid.

these two and a half long years of war, but the country, which is now in the very birth-throes of Russian liberty, is still exposed to the attack of the powerful adversary who occupies whole territories of our State and is threatening us with a new and decisive thrust. Whatever be the cost, the defence of our national patrimony and the deliverance of the country from the enemy who has invaded our borders constitutes the principal and vital problem before our soldiers who are defending the liberty of the people. Leaving the definite decision of all questions bearing on the world war and its termination to the will of the people, in close union with our Allies, the Provisional Government deems it its right and its duty to declare forthwith that free Russia does not aim at dominating other peoples, at depriving them of their national patrimony, or at occupying foreign territories by force, but that its object is to establish a durable peace on the basis of the right of nations to decide their own destiny. The Russian people do not lust after the strengthening of their power abroad at the expense of other nations, nor do they aim at subjugating or humbling anyone. In the name of the higher principles of equity they have removed the chains which weighed upon the Polish nation. But the Russian nation will not allow its fatherland to emerge from the great struggle with its vital forces humbled and weakened. These principles will constitute the basis of the foreign policy of the Provisional Government, which is carrying out without fail the popular will and is safeguarding the rights of our fatherland, while observing the engagements entered into with our Allies. The Provisional Government of free Russia has no right to hide the truth from the people. The State is in danger. Every effort must be made to save it. Let the country respond to the truth which has been told, not by useless depression nor by discouragement, but by unanimous vigour with a view to the creation of one national will. This will give us new strength for the struggle and will bring us salvation. In the hour of grave trial, let the whole country find in itself strength to consolidate the freedom won and to devote itself to untiring labour for the welfare of free Russia. The Provisional Government, which has given its solemn oath to serve the people, is firmly confident that, with the general and unanimous support of each and all, it will itself be able to perform its duty to the country till the end.

The President of the Council,

PRINCE LVOV

British Reply to Russian Note regarding the Allied War Aims

On the 3rd May His Majesty's Government received, through the Russian Chargé d'Affaires, a note from the Russian Government declaratory of their war policy.

In the proclamation to the Russian people, enclosed in the note, it is said that "free Russia does not propose to dominate other peoples or to take from them their national patrimony, or forcibly to occupy foreign territory." In this sentiment the British Government heartily concur. They did not enter upon this war as a war of conquest, and they are not continuing it for any such object. Their purpose at the outset was to defend the existence of their country and to enforce respect for international engagements. To those objects has now been added that of liberating populations oppressed by alien tyranny. They heartily rejoice, therefore, that Free Russia has announced her intention of liberating Poland—not only the Poland ruled by the old Russian autocracy, but equally that within the dominion of the Germanic Empires. In this enterprise the British democracy wish Russia God-speed. Beyond everything we must seek for such a settlement as will secure the happiness and contentment of the peoples and take away all legitimate causes of future war.

The British Government heartily joins their Russian Allies in their acceptance and approval of the principles laid down by President Wilson in his historic message to the American Congress. These are the aims for which the British peoples are fighting. These are the principles by which their war policy is and will be guided. The British Government believe that, broadly speaking, the agreements which they have from time to time made with their Allies are conformable to these standards. But if the Russian Government so desire, they are quite ready with their Allies to examine and, if need be, to revise these agreements.

June 8, 1917

111. Events Leading to Unrestricted Submarine Warfare[1]

[In 1919 the German Reichstag appointed a Committee of Inquiry. This body divided itself into four sections to investigate the following:

1. The causes of the war;
2. The reasons for not ending it sooner;
3. The acts of disobedience and disloyalty to political authorities;
4. The cruelties committed during the war.

From the findings of the subcommittee which worked on the second topic named, there is quoted below a brief account of the way in which the military authorities influenced the situation by their decision in favor of unrestricted submarine warfare, and of the bearing of this decision upon the entry of the United States into the war. The Ger-

---

[1] Germany: National Constituent Assembly. *The Reports of the First and Second Subcommittees of the Committee appointed by the National Constituent Assembly to inquire into the responsibility for the war,* etc. Carnegie Endowment for International Peace. New York, Oxford Press, 1923. 2 vols. (English Title: *Official German Documents Relating to the World War.*) Vol. I, pp. 137-138.

man Ambassador at Washington, Bernstorff, protested against the
treatment of Wilson's request for a statement of conditions upon
which Germany might make peace.]

On January 3, 1917, a telegram of Bernstorff of the 29th of December, 1916, was received in Berlin, according to which Colonel
House, acting together with Wilson, asked for confidential information concerning the conditions of peace. It was not until the 7th of
January, 1917—two days before the decision regarding the opening
of an unrestricted U-boat war—that Zimmermann answered this new
appeal. The Ambassador was instructed to handle the question concerning our communication of our peace conditions in a dilatory fashion. He was to state that we were convinced that we were able to bring
the war to a victorious end, both from a military as well as a political
or commercial standpoint. In addition to this, it was to be announced
that we were inclined, after peace was concluded, to take part in a
general conference dealing with the settlement of international legal
questions in which Wilson was interested, and to state that, so far
as Belgium was concerned, we "shall not annex Belgium."

We have reached the point at which it is proper to insert a brief
remark concerning the question of the expediency of communicating
definite peace conditions, because this question frequently played a
prominent part at the hearings. Bethmann-Hollweg in particular took
the ground that either an open or a confidential communication of
definite peace aims would not have been expedient, except in dealing
directly with the enemy himself, because such information would have
disclosed our hand. On the other hand, attention may be called to
the following point: There are circumstances under which it would be
injurious to give full information concerning such conditions if negotiations are just beginning or if the enemy is prepared therefor. If he
is not ready for negotiations, then the real question to be considered
is how he can be brought to the state of mind where he will be ready
for them. One method of bringing about such readiness for negotiation
is precisely the setting out of one's own purpose, the practical working out of which is the end and aim of the negotiations. For the rest,
Bethmann-Hollweg finally, on the 29th of January, 1917, informed
Wilson of the conditions of peace. By doing this, he himself finally
recognized the expediency of giving such information. But already
at the time of answering the telegram of the 29th of December, 1916,
which had arrived on January 3, 1917, Bethmann-Hollweg gives evidence of vacillation. The records contain the draft of a telegram to
Count Bernstorff written by the Chancelor himself on January 4,
1917, giving him power to communicate to House and Wilson, under
the conditions of the most absolute discretion and in limited and
literal outline, the main points of our peace conditions. This instruction was not sent. It was supplanted by Zimmermann's message of

Was koſtet der Krieg?
Was iſt erreicht?

Frontlänge in Europa	Koſten	Geländegewinn

England 170 Klm . . . . 121 Milliarden Mark
Frankreich 545 „ . . . . 85 „ „
Rußland 1889 „ (unſchließlich Rumänien) 103,7 „ „
Italien 240 „ . . . . 23 „ „

332,7 Milliarden Mark

5416 □ Klm

Deutſchland ⎫
Türkei Bulgarien ⎬ Einheitsfront
Oeſterr.-Ung. 2844 Klm ⎭

Mittelmächte 150,9 Milliarden Mark

570278 □ Klm

WHAT DOES THE WAR COST? WHAT HAS BEEN ACCOMPLISHED?

(DECEMBER 1, 1917)

	Length of front lines in Europe	Cost	Land won
England	170 kilometers	121 billion marks	
France	545 "	85 " "	
Russia (including Roumania)	1,889 "	103.7 " "	5,416 square kilometers
Italy	240 "	23 " "	
		332.7 " "	
Germany, Turkey, Bulgaria, and Austria-Hungary, united	2,844 "	150.9 " "	570,278 square kilometers

January 7, 1917, already referred to, according to which here, too, at the instance of the Supreme High Command and at the eleventh hour, the pledge with regard to the provisional restoration of Belgium to which we have referred above was stricken out.

If the German answer of the 7th of January, 1917, avoided the issue of the American endeavors, these tactics do not, in the last analysis, hark back to considerations of expediency of a general order, but to the decision regarding the commencement of the unrestricted U-boat warfare which was imminent. On the 8th of January, 1917, the military leaders had met in council with Hindenburg and had determined unanimously upon the unconditional carrying-out of the unrestricted U-boat warfare. It had been decided that in case the Chancelor would not coöperate, a change of chancelors would be undertaken. On the 9th of January, in Pless, the final determination was formally taken to begin the unrestricted U-boat warfare on the 1st of February. All those who took part saw perfectly clearly that the result of this determination would be war with the United States. "It must be. We are counting on the possibility of war with America and have made all preparations to meet it," are the words of Hindenburg, and he adds: "We are prepared to meet all emergencies." From this point of view, the chief factor to be observed was that the unconditional U-boat warfare should not constitute an operation which "weakens us at any other spot," speaking from the military standpoint. The Chancelor offered no opposition to the resolution reached. Not another word was spent in discussing Wilson's peace move or the fact that it was still in contemplation.

For all practical purposes, Wilson's peace move was destroyed by the adoption of the resolution of January 9, 1917, with regard to the commencement of the unrestricted U-boat warfare. Although the wish had heretofore been entertained to reach peace through a peace move on the part of Wilson, from now on the *casus belli* with America was furnished. This interpretation is voiced by the Emperor's assertion reported on the 16th of January, 1917, that he placed no reliance upon Wilson's peace move, and that in case the break with America was unavoidable, "matters can not be changed; we shall go ahead."

Ambassador Count Bernstorff to the Foreign Office[1]

Washington, January 26, 1917

Telegram No. 238

. . . The commencement of the U-boat war without preliminary negotiations with regard to the above proposals would, in my opinion, put us absolutely in the wrong and make the avoidance of a break impossible on account of personal affront to Wilson.

BERNSTORFF

---

[1] *Ibid.,* Vol. II, p. 1050.

112. The Zimmermann Note, January 19, 1917[1]

[On February 24, 1917, Ambassador Walter Hines Page sent a message to President Wilson revealing to him the text of the note sent by the German Foreign Secretary to the German Minister to Mexico by way of Ambassador Bernstorff in Washington. Page reported that it had been obtained by the British Intelligence Service in Mexico and had been given to him by Balfour. The English translation follows.]

Berlin, January 19, 1917

On the first of February we intend to begin submarine warfare unrestricted. In spite of this, it is our intention to endeavor to keep neutral the United States of America.

If this attempt is not successful, we propose an alliance on the following basis with Mexico: That we shall make war together and together make peace. We shall give general financial support, and it is understood that Mexico is to reconquer the lost territory in New Mexico, Texas, and Arizona. The details are left to you for settlement.

[Mexico to bring in Japan]

You are instructed to inform the President of Mexico of the above in the greatest confidence as soon as it is certain that there will be an outbreak of war with the United States and suggest that the President of Mexico, on his own initiative, should communicate with Japan suggesting adherence at once to this plan; at the same time, offer to mediate between Germany and Japan.

Please call to the attention of the President of Mexico that the employment of ruthless submarine warfare now promises to compel England to make peace in a few months.

ZIMMERMANN

113. Extracts from the Discussion in the Congress of the United States on the Declaration of War

[Wilson gave his reasons for advising the entry of the United States into the war in his address to Congress on April 2, 1917. A portion of this address is here cited. It is followed by a copy of the joint resolution placed before Congress calling for the creation of a state of war and by portions of two typical addresses which formed a part of the debate upon the resolution on April 4th. One of them is by Senator George W. Norris of Nebraska, a "progressive" Republican who saw proposed American entry into the war as essentially a movement to

[1] *Congressional Record,* Vol. 54, March 1, 1917, p. 4596.

protect capital; the other is by Senator Paul O. Husting, a Wisconsin Democrat, who traced the history of the controversy between the American and German Governments over the question of neutral rights on the high seas as brought to a focus by the German use of submarines and the consequent loss of American lives and property. Husting denied that the protection of investments was a cause of entry into the conflict and concluded with the declaration that America must enter the war to safeguard the rights, the lives, the honor, the welfare of this nation. "It will be a war for the democracy of the world."]

(a) *The Address by the President of the United States, April 2, 1917*[1]

I have called the Congress into extraordinary session because there are serious, very serious, choices of policy to be made, and made immediately, which it was neither right nor constitutionally permissible that I should assume the responsibility of making.

On the third of February last I officially laid before you the extraordinary announcement of the Imperial German Government that on and after the first day of February it was its purpose to put aside all restraints of law or of humanity and use its submarines to sink every vessel that sought to approach either the ports of Great Britain and Ireland or the western coasts of Europe or any of the ports controlled by the enemies of Germany within the Mediterranean. That had seemed to be the object of the German submarine warfare earlier in the war, but since April of last year the Imperial Government had somewhat restrained the commanders of its undersea craft in conformity with its promise then given to us that passenger boats should not be sunk and that due warning would be given to all other vessels which its submarines might seek to destroy, when no resistance was offered or escape attempted, and care taken that their crews were given at least a fair chance to save their lives in their open boats. The precautions taken were meagre and haphazard enough, as was proved in distressing instance after instance in the progress of the cruel and unmanly business, but a certain degree of restraint was observed. The new policy has swept every restriction aside. Vessels of every kind, whatever their flag, their character, their cargo, their destination, their errand, have been ruthlessly sent to the bottom without warning and without thought of help or mercy for those on board, the vessels of friendly neutrals along with those of belligerents. Even hospital ships and ships carrying relief to the sorely bereaved and stricken people of Belgium, though the latter were provided with safe conduct through the proscribed areas by the German Government itself and were distinguished by unmistakable marks of identity, have been sunk with the same reckless lack of compassion or of principle.

---

[1] *Congressional Record*, Vol. 55, pp. 102–104.

I was for a little while unable to believe that such things would in fact be done by any government that had hitherto subscribed to the humane practices of civilized nations. International law had its origin in the attempt to set up some law which would be respected and observed upon the seas, where no nation had right of dominion and where lay the free highways of the world. By painful stage after stage has that law been built up, with meagre enough results, indeed, after all was accomplished that could be accomplished, but always with a clear view, at least, of what the heart and conscience of mankind demanded. This minimum of right the German Government has swept aside under the plea of retaliation and necessity and because it had no weapons which it could use at sea except these which it is impossible to employ as it is employing them without throwing to the winds all scruples of humanity or of respect for the understandings that were supposed to underlie the intercourse of the world. I am not now thinking of the loss of property involved, immense and serious as that is, but only of the wanton and wholesale destruction of the lives of non-combatants, men, women, and children, engaged in pursuits which have always, even in the darkest periods of modern history, been deemed innocent and legitimate. Property can be paid for; the lives of peaceful and innocent people cannot be. The present German submarine warfare against commerce is a warfare against mankind.

It is a war against all nations. American ships have been sunk, American lives taken, in ways which it has stirred us very deeply to learn of, but the ships and people of other neutral and friendly nations have been sunk and overwhelmed in the waters in the same way. There has been no discrimination. The challenge is to all mankind. Each nation must decide for itself how it will meet it. The choice we make for ourselves must be made with a moderation of counsel and a temperateness of judgment befitting our character and our motives as a nation. We must put excited feeling away. Our motive will not be revenge or the victorious assertion of the physical might of the nation, but only the vindication of right, of human right, of which we are only a single champion.

When I addressed the Congress on the twenty-sixth of February last I thought that it would suffice to assert our neutral rights with arms, our right to use the seas against unlawful violence. But armed neutrality, it now appears, is impracticable. Because submarines are in effect outlaws when used as the German submarines have been used against merchant shipping, it is impossible to defend ships against their attacks as the law of nations has assumed that merchantmen would defend themselves against privateers or cruisers, visible craft giving chase upon the open sea. It is common prudence in such circumstances, grim necessity indeed, to endeavour to destroy them before they have shown their own intention. They must be dealt with upon sight, if dealt with at all. The German Government denies the right of neutrals to use arms at all within the areas of the sea which it has proscribed, even in the defense of the rights which no modern publicist has ever before questioned their right to defend. The intimation is conveyed that the armed guards which we have placed on our merchant ships will be treated as beyond the pale of law and subject to be dealt with as pirates would be. Armed neutrality is ineffectual enough at best; in such circumstances and in the face of such pretensions it is worse than ineffectual: it is likely only to produce what it was meant to prevent; it is practically certain to draw us into the war without either the rights or the effectiveness of belligerents. There is one choice we cannot make, we are incapable of making: we will not choose the path of submission and suffer the most sacred rights of our nation and our people to be ignored or violated. The wrongs against which we now array ourselves are no common wrongs; they cut to the very roots of human life. With a profound sense of the solemn and even tragical character of the step I am taking and of the grave responsibilities which it involves, but in unhesitating obedience to what I deem my constitutional duty, I advise that the Congress declare the recent course of the Imperial German Government to be in fact nothing less than war against the government and people of the United States; that it formally accept the status of belligerent which has thus been thrust upon it; and that it take immediate steps not only to put the country in a more thorough state of defense but also to exert all its power and employ all its resources to bring the Government of the German Empire to terms and end the war.

What this will involve is clear. It will involve the utmost practicable coöperation in counsel and action with the governments now at war with Germany, and, as incident to that, the extension to those governments of the most liberal financial credits, in order that our resources may so far as possible be added to theirs. It will involve the organization and mobilization of all the material resources of the country to supply the materials of war and serve the incidental needs of the nation in the most abundant and yet the most economical and efficient way possible. It will involve the immediate full equipment of the navy in all respects but particularly in supplying it with the best means of dealing with the enemy's submarines. It will involve the immediate addition to the armed forces of the United States already provided for by law in case of war at least five hundred thousand men, who should, in my opinion, be chosen upon the principle of universal liability to service, and also the authorization of subsequent additional increments of equal force so soon as they may be needed and can be handled in training. It will involve also, of course, the granting of adequate credits to the Government, sustained, I hope, so far as they can equitably be sustained by the present generation, by well-conceived taxation. . . .

While we do these things, these deeply momentous things, let us be very clear, and make very clear to all the world what our motives and our objects are. My own thought has not been driven from its habitual and normal course by the unhappy events of the last two months, and I do not believe that the thought of the nation has been altered or clouded by them. I have exactly the same things in mind now that I had in mind when I addressed the Senate on the twenty-second of January last; the same that I had in mind when I addressed the Congress on the third of February and on the twenty-sixth of February. Our object now, as then, is to vindicate the principles of peace and justice in the life of the world as against selfish and autocratic power and to set up amongst the really free and self-governed peoples of the world such a concert of purpose and of action as will henceforth ensure the observance of those principles. Neutrality is no longer feasible or desirable where the peace of the world is involved and the freedom of its peoples, and the menace to that peace and freedom lies in the existence of autocratic governments backed by organized force which is controlled wholly by their will, not by the will of their people. We have seen the last of neutrality in such circumstances. We are at the beginning of an age in which it will be insisted that the same standards of conduct and of responsibility for wrong done shall be observed among nations and their governments that are observed among the individual citizens of civilized states.

We have no quarrel with the German people. We have no feeling towards them but one of sympathy and friendship. It was not upon their impulse that their government acted in entering this war. It was not with their previous knowledge or approval. It was a war determined upon as wars used to be determined upon in the old, unhappy days when peoples were nowhere consulted by their rulers and wars were provoked and waged in the interest of dynasties or of little groups of ambitious men who were accustomed to use their fellow men as pawns and tools. Self-governed nations do not fill their neighbour states with spies or set the course of intrigue to bring about some critical posture of affairs which will give them an opportunity to strike and make conquest. Such designs can be successfully worked out only under cover and where no one has the right to ask questions. Cunningly contrived plans of deception or aggression, carried, it may be, from generation to generation, can be worked out and kept from the light only within the privacy of courts or behind the carefully guarded confidences of a narrow and privileged class. They are happily impossible where public opinion commands and insists upon full information concerning all the nation's affairs.

A steadfast concert for peace can never be maintained except by a partnership of democratic nations. No autocratic government could be trusted to keep faith within it or observe its covenants. It must be a league of honour, a partnership of opinion. Intrigue would eat its vitals away; the plottings of inner circles who could plan what they would and render account to no one would be a corruption seated at its very heart. Only free peoples can hold their purpose and their

honour steady to a common end and prefer the interests of mankind
to any narrow interest of their own.

Does not every American feel that assurance has been added to our
hope for the future peace of the world by the wonderful and heartening
things that have been happening within the last few weeks in Russia?
Russia was known by those who knew it best to have been always in
fact democratic at heart, in all the vital habits of her thought, in all
the intimate relationships of her people that spoke their natural instinct, their habitual attitude towards life. The autocracy that
crowned the summit of her political structure, long as it had stood
and terrible as was the reality of its power, was not in fact Russian in
origin, character, or purpose; and now it has been shaken off and the
great generous Russian people has been added in all their naïve majesty and might to the forces that are fighting for freedom in the world,
for justice, and for peace. Here is a fit partner for a League of
Honour.

One of the things that has served to convince us that the Prussian
autocracy was not and could never be our friend is that from the very
outset of the present war it has filled our unsuspecting communities
and even our offices of government with spies and set criminal intrigues
everywhere afoot against our national unity of counsel, our peace
within and without, our industries and our commerce. Indeed it is now
evident that its spies were here even before the war began; and it is
unhappily not a matter of conjecture but a fact proved in our courts
of justice that the intrigues which have more than once come perilously
near to disturbing the peace and dislocating the industries of the country have been carried on at the instigation, with the support, and even
under the personal direction of official agents of the Imperial Government accredited to the Government of the United States. Even in
checking these things and trying to extirpate them we have sought to
put the most generous interpretation possible upon them because we
knew that their source lay, not in any hostile feeling or purpose of
the German people towards us (who were, no doubt as ignorant of
them as we ourselves were), but only in the selfish designs of a Government that did what it pleased and told its people nothing. But they
have played their part in serving to convince us at last that that
Government entertains no real friendship for us and means to act
against our peace and security at its convenience. That it means to
stir up enemies against us at our very doors the intercepted note to
the German Minister at Mexico City is eloquent evidence.

We are accepting this challenge of hostile purpose because we
know that in such a government, following such methods, we can never
have a friend; and that in the presence of its organizing power, always
lying in wait to accomplish we know not what purpose, there can be
no assured security for the democratic governments of the world. We
are now about to accept gauge of battle with this natural foe to liberty

and shall, if necessary, spend the whole force of the nation to check and nullify its pretensions and its power. We are glad, now that we see the facts with no veil of false pretence about them, to fight thus for the ultimate peace of the world and for the liberation of its peoples, the German peoples included: for the rights of nations great and small and the privilege of men everywhere to choose their way of life and of obedience. The world must be made safe for democracy. Its peace must be planted upon the tested foundations of political liberty. We have no selfish ends to serve. We desire no conquest, no dominion. We seek no indemnities for ourselves, no material compensation for the sacrifices we shall freely make. We are but one of the champions of the rights of mankind. We shall be satisfied when those rights have been made as secure as the faith and freedom of nations can make them. . . .

(b) *Joint Resolution to create a state of war*[1]

Resolved by the Senate and House of Representatives of the United States of America in Congress assembled, That the state of war between the United States and the Imperial German Government which has thus been thrust upon the United States is hereby formally declared; and that the President be, and he is hereby, authorized and directed to employ the entire naval and military forces of the United States and the resources of the Government to carry on war against the Imperial German Government; and to bring the conflict to a successful determination all of the resources of the country are hereby pledged by the Congress of the United States.

(c) *Speech of Senator Norris on the Joint Resolution (extracts)*[2]

Mr. President, while I am most emphatically and sincerely opposed to taking any step that will force our country into the useless and senseless war now being waged in Europe, yet if this resolution passes I shall not permit my feeling of opposition to its passage to interfere in any way with my duty either as a Senator or as a citizen in bringing success and victory to American arms. I am bitterly opposed to my country entering the war, but if, notwithstanding my opposition, we do enter it, all of my energy and all of my power will be behind our flag in carrying it on to victory.

The resolution now before the Senate is a declaration of war. Before taking this momentous step, and while standing on the brink of this terrible vortex, we ought to pause and calmly and judiciously consider the terrible consequences of the step we are about to take. We ought to consider likewise the route we have recently traveled and

---

[1] *Ibid.,* p. 200.

[2] *Ibid.,* p. 212ff.

ascertain whether we have reached our present position in a way that is compatible with the neutral position which we claimed to occupy at beginning and through the various stages of this unholy and unrighteous war.

No close student of recent history will deny that both Great Britain and Germany have, on numerous occasions since the beginning of the war, flagrantly violated in the most serious manner the rights of neutral vessels and neutral nations under existing international law as recognized up to the beginning of this war by the civilized world.

The reason given by the President in asking Congress to declare war against Germany is that the German Government has declared certain war zones, within which, by the use of submarines, she sinks, without notice, American ships and destroys American lives.

Let us trace briefly the origin and history of these so-called war zones. The first war zone was declared by Great Britain. She gave us and the world notice of it on the 4th day of November, 1914. The zone became effective November 5, 1914, the next day after the notice was given. This zone so declared by Great Britain covered the whole of the North Sea. The order establishing it sought to close the north of Scotland route around the British Isles to Denmark, Holland, Norway, Sweden, and the Baltic Sea. The decree of establishment drew an arbitrary line from the Hebrides Islands along the Scottish coast to Iceland, and warned neutral shipping that it would cross those lines at its peril, and ordered that ships might go to Holland and other neutral nations by taking the English Channel route through the Strait of Dover.

The first German war zone was declared on the 4th day of February, 1915, just three months after the British war zone was declared. Germany gave 15 days' notice of the establishment of her zone, which became effective on the 18th day of February, 1915. The German war zone covered the English Channel and the high sea waters around the British Isles. It sought to close the English Channel route around the British Isles to Holland, Norway, Sweden, Denmark, and the Baltic Sea. The German war zone decreed that neutral vessels would be exposed to danger in the English Channel route, but that the route around the north of Scotland and in the eastern part of the North Sea, in a strip thirty miles wide along the Dutch coast would be free from danger.

It will thus be seen that the British Government declared the north of Scotland route into the Baltic Sea as dangerous and the English Channel route into the Baltic Sea as safe.

The German Government in its order did exactly the reverse. It declared the north of Scotland route into the Baltic Sea as safe and the English Channel route into the Baltic Sea as dangerous.

The order of the British Government declaring the North Sea as a war zone used the following language:

"The British Admiralty gives notice that the waters of the North Sea must be considered a military area. Within this area merchant shipping of all kinds, traders of all countries, fishing craft, and other vessels will be exposed to the gravest danger from mines it has been necessary to lay."

The German Government, by its order declaring its war zone around the south of England, declared that the order would be made effective by the use of submarines.

Thus we have the two declarations of the two Governments, each declaring a military zone and warning neutral shipping from going into the prohibited area. England sought to make her order effective by the use of submerged mines. Germany sought to make her order effective by the use of submarines. Both of these orders were illegal and contrary to all international law as well as the principles of humanity. Under international law no belligerent Government has the right to place submerged mines in the high seas. Neither has it any right to take human life without notice by the use of submarines. If there is any difference on the ground of humanity between these two instrumentalities, it is certainly in favor of the submarines. The submarine can exercise some degree of discretion and judgment. The submerged mine always destroys without notice, friend and foe alike, guilty and innocent the same. In carrying out these two policies, both Great Britain and Germany have sunk American ships and destroyed American lives without provocation and without notice. There have been more ships sunk and more American lives lost from the action of submarines than from English mines in the North Sea; for the simple reason that we finally acquiesced in the British war zone and kept our ships out of it, while in the German war zone we have refused to recognize its legality and have not kept either our ships or our citizens out of its area. If American ships had gone into the British war zone in defiance of Great Britain's order, as they have gone into the German war zone in defiance of the German Government's order, there would have been many more American lives lost and many more American ships sunk by the instrumentality of the mines than the instrumentality of the submarines.

We have in the main complied with the demands made by Great Britain. Our ships have followed the instructions of the British Government in going not only to England but to the neutral nations of the world, and in thus complying with the British order American ships going to Holland, Denmark, Norway, and Sweden have been taken by British officials into British ports, and their cargoes inspected and examined. All the mails we have carried even to neutral countries have been opened and censored, and oftentimes the entire cargo confiscated by the Government. Nothing has been permitted to pass to even the most neutral nations except after examination and with the permission of the officials of the British Government.

I have outlined the beginning of the controversy. I have given in substance the orders of both of these great Governments that constituted the beginning of our controversy with each. There have been other orders made by both Governments subsequent to the ones I have given that interfered with our rights as a neutral Nation, but these two that I have outlined constitute the origin of practically the entire difficulty, and subsequent orders have only been modifications and reproductions of those I have already mentioned. It is unnecessary to cite authority to show that both of these orders declaring military zones were illegal and contrary to international law. It is sufficient to say that our Government has officially declared both of them to be illegal and has officially protested against both of them.

The only difference is that in the case of Germany we have persisted in our protest, while in the case of England we have submitted. What was our duty as a Government and what were our rights when we were confronted with these extraordinary orders declaring these military zones? First, we could have defied both of them and could have gone to war against both of these nations for this violation of international law and interference with our neutral rights. Second, we had the technical right to defy one and to acquiesce in the other. Third, we could, while denouncing them both as illegal, have acquiesced in them both and thus remained neutral with both sides, although not agreeing with either as to the righteousness of their respective orders. We could have said to American shipowners that, while these orders are both contrary to international law and are both unjust, we do not believe that the provocation is sufficient to cause us to go to war for the defense of our rights as a neutral nation and, therefore, American ships and American citizens will go into these zones at their own peril and risk. Fourth, we might have declared an embargo against the shipping from American ports of any merchandise to either one of these Governments that persisted in maintaining its military zone. We might have refused to permit the sailing of any ship from any American port to either of these military zones. In my judgment, if we had pursued this course, the zones would have been of short duration. England would have been compelled to take her mines out of the North Sea in order to get any supplies from our country. When her mines were taken out of the North Sea then the German ports upon the North Sea would have been accessible to American shipping and Germany would have been compelled to cease her submarine warfare in order to get any supplies from our Nation into German North Sea ports.

There are a great many American citizens who feel that we owe it as a duty to humanity to take part in this war. Many instances of cruelty and inhumanity can be found on both sides. Men are often biased in their judgment on account of their sympathy and their interests. To my mind, what we ought to have maintained from the beginning was the strictest neutrality. If we had done this I do not believe we would have been on the verge of war at the present time. We had a right as a nation, if we desired, to cease at any time to be neutral. We had a technical right to respect the English war zone and to disregard the German war zone, but we could not do that and be neutral. I have no quarrel to find with the man who does not desire our country to remain neutral. While many such people are moved by selfish motives and hopes of gain, I have no doubt but that in a great many instances, through what I believe to be a misunderstanding of the real condition, there are many honest, patriotic citizens who think we ought to engage in this war and who are behind the President in his demand that we should declare war against Germany. I think such people err in judgment and to a great extent have been misled as to the real history and the true facts by the almost unanimous demand of the great combination of wealth that has a direct financial interest in our participation in the war. We have loaned many hundreds of millions of dollars to the allies in this controversy. While such action was legal and countenanced by international law, there is no doubt in my mind but the enormous amount of money loaned to the allies in this country has been instrumental in bringing about a public sentiment in favor of our country taking a course that would make every bond worth a hundred cents on the dollar and making the payment of every debt certain and sure. Through this instrumentality and also through the instrumentality of others who have not only made millions out of the war in the manufacture of munitions, etc., and who would expect to make millions more if our country can be drawn into the catastrophe, a large number of the great newspapers and news agencies of the country have been controlled and enlisted in the greatest propaganda that the world has ever known, to manufacture sentiment in favor of war. It is now demanded that the American citizens shall be used as insurance policies to guarantee the safe delivery of munitions of war to belligerent nations. The enormous profits of munition manufacturers, stockbrokers, and bond dealers must be still further increased by our entrance into the war. This has brought us to the present moment, when Congress urged by the President and backed by the artificial sentiment, is about to declare war and engulf our country in the greatest holocaust that the world has ever known. . . .

To whom does war bring prosperity? Not to the soldier who for the munificent compensation of $16 per month shoulders his musket and goes into the trench, there to shed his blood and to die if necessary; not to the broken-hearted widow who waits for the return of the mangled body of her husband; not to the mother who weeps at the death of her brave boy; not to the little children who shiver with cold; not to the babe who suffers from hunger; nor to the millions of mothers and daughters who carry broken hearts to their graves. War brings no prosperity to the great mass of common and patriotic citizens. It increases the cost of living of those who toil and those who already must strain every effort to keep soul and body together. War brings prosperity to the stock gambler on Wall Street—to those who are already in possession of more wealth than can be realized or enjoyed. . . .

Their object in having war and in preparing for war is to make money. Human suffering and the sacrifice of human life are necessary, but Wall Street considers only the dollars and the cents. The men who do the fighting, the people who make the sacrifices, are the ones who will not be counted in the measure of this great prosperity. . . . The stock brokers would not, of course, go to war, because the very object they have in bringing on the war is profit, and therefore they must remain in their Wall Street offices in order to share in that great prosperity which they say war will bring. The volunteer officer, even the drafting officer, will not find them. They will be concealed in their palatial offices on Wall Street, sitting behind mahogany desks, covered up with clipped coupons—coupons soiled with the sweat of honest toil, coupons stained with mothers' tears, coupons dyed in the lifeblood of their fellow men.

We are taking a step today that is fraught with untold danger. We are going into war upon the command of gold. We are going to run the risk of sacrificing millions of our countrymen's lives in order that other countrymen may coin their lifeblood into money. And even if we do not cross the Atlantic and go into the trenches, we are going to pile up a debt that the toiling masses that shall come many generations after us will have to pay. Unborn millions will bend their backs in toil in order to pay for the terrible step we are now about to take. We are about to do the bidding of wealth's terrible mandate. By our act we will make millions of our countrymen suffer, and the consequences of it may well be that millions of our brethren must shed their lifeblood, millions of broken-hearted women must weep, millions of children must suffer with the cold, and millions of babes must die from hunger, and all because we want to preserve the commercial right of American citizens to deliver munitions of war to belligerent nations. . . .

(d) *Speech of Senator Paul O. Husting on the Joint Resolution* *(extracts)*[1]

Mr. President, I would not feel like taking up the time of the Senate this evening were it not for the fact that things have been said here that I feel called upon to try to answer. What I have to say will be more in the nature of a reply to the remarks that have been made upon the floor of the Senate this afternoon and this evening than to offer anything in an affirmative way.

I recognize the right of every Senator—nay, I recognize it as his duty—to have a mind of his own, to formulate his own judgment, and not to surrender it to the Executive or to anybody else; and at the same time I recognize it as a practical proposition that every citizen

[1] *Ibid.,* p. 238ff.

as well as every Senator should give his own Government the benefit of the presumption that it is in the right in its matters of difference with foreign countries. I think every Senator will agree, and I hope it will be subscribed to by every citizen of this country, that this Government of all governments is actuated by no motives of aggression, of ambition, or by anything other than a desire to do justice and to exact justice for itself in return. We must ignore the history of the United States, we must ignore the actions of our Presidents during all its history, we must forget all about the traditions of this country and of its statesmen, if we want to assume that every act of our Government in its present crisis was done from a sinister motive or was inspired by a desire not only to do injustice to friendly nations but to conspire with other nations to undo another.

I want to say that, as far as I am concerned, I am going to proceed upon the presumption that this Government is now acting, as history shows it has always acted, in the interest of right and justice to ourselves and to other nations. Not only that, but I am going to take for granted that President Wilson, whose record and character are beyond dispute, has acted honestly, fairly, patriotically, and in accord with the best and highest traditions of American statesmanship.

There has been some talk here by Senators to the effect that there has been much intolerant language used throughout the land in the discussion of this question. I agree with the statement, but I want to say that most of it has been used by those opposed to the Government. It has been used mostly by the traducers of the President of the United States and slanderers of the Government of the United States. The President has been criticized by citizens, ofttimes of very recent origin—and newspaper scribes began it—as a betrayer of his country and as a tool and ally of a foreign country. He has been held up as a man who is attempting to betray his Government into the hands of a foreign Government and it has been said that we have lost our independence, and that upon our hands and knees we are servilely serving a foreign master.

Such words as those deserve strong words in reply, and those who start the argument in such a manner must expect to receive it back in kind; only in giving it back in kind those that use the words are merely attempting to vindicate their own Government, to defend its honor and good name, while those who attack the Government and the President are doing it in behalf of a foreign Government at the expense and to the degradation of our honor and good name. . . .

I believe that if the people of the United States were asked to vote for war or no war their preference would be against war. I am for no war. The people want no war if they can avoid it, and so I venture to say that if the vote were purely one of peace or war, not only those of the 100,000,000 of people who are old enough to vote, but the President and the Congress, would all vote for peace and against war.

But that is not the question, Mr. President. The question is, Shall the people of the United States suffer Germany to make war on us without defending ourselves? Shall the people of the United States support the President and the Congress of the United States—that is to say, their Government—in whatever course it is concluded best to take in the interest of the people's welfare and safety, even to the extent of going to war? Put this question and I venture to predict that the vote will be overwhelmingly in the affirmative. . . .

I wish that I could vote against this war. It would ease my mind and my conscience to vote against any war. I doubt if there is anyone here who would not feel easier if he were not called upon to settle this question. It would be pleasant to evade responsibility and let things drift and trust to luck to save us. But the question is not whether we want war; the question is, "Shall we suffer war to be made upon us without defending ourselves?" We are not the aggressor. We are not attacking anybody, but we are being attacked. Our ships are being attacked, our citizens and our ships carrying our flag are being sent to the bottom of the sea. In other and even more sinister ways our country has been warred upon for a period of more than two years by agents in the pay of a foreign Government.

Plots have been hatched, conspiracies have been formed, propaganda has been scattered through our country, and the minds of our people have been poisoned against their own Government until they have almost been led to believe that they can not trust their own Government. Men have been led to believe that other and foreign Governments are the abused Governments, and that instead of being in the right, we have been in the wrong. Many men and many newspapers, many societies and conferences and leagues, and what not, have, through the press and upon the forum, attacked the Government of the United States in everything that it has said or done in its controversy with Germany, and justified everything that Germany has done against the United States. According to these pretended loyal supporters of America, America has done nothing that is right, but everything that is wrong, and Germany has done nothing that is wrong, but everything that is right. America can do no right and Germany can do no wrong, according to them. Yet they claim to be loyal, and point with pride to what their brave ancestors or heroes in blood have done for their country in the past. . . .

Now, I want to get down to a discussion of some of the questions that were raised by Senators who have spoken this afternoon and evening. In the first place, it is charged that this Government has been unneutral. It is charged that we have done certain things; that we have tolerated certain things from England that we have not tolerated from Germany. They say that we tolerated a blockade on the part of Great Britain, and it is now said that we should have stopped these violations by Great Britain at the very outset when she first proclaimed her blockade of the North Sea.

Why did we suffer Great Britain to maintain the blockade of the

North Sea? Why did we suffer Germany to establish her first blockade? I claim now, as I have always claimed, that these blockades, at least in part, were illegal. I am sorry they were not stopped. Perhaps that would have ended it all. But, Mr. President, if we are going to go back and consider what should have been done two years ago, then let us go back to the perspective of that time, when these judgments had to be formed. The judgments had to be reached, not in the light of what has happened since but in the light then obtaining. . . .

Going back then to two years ago, we all remember how we hoped to keep out of this war and how everybody wanted the Government to keep out of this war if possible. We argued to ourselves, sometimes like this: Here are several countries at war. This war will not last very long. Europe has gone war mad. These nations do not respect international law any more. The war will soon be over. Whatever they are doing now against us can be paid for in money. Let us not use our Army and our Navy to collect bills; let us not shed the blood of our boys for a few paltry dollars. Let us not put ourselves in a position where we will have to fight with war-mad Europe just because we have lost some business.

So in response to a national sentiment and public opinion, including the approval of those who abhor war and who think war is unjustifiable, and inspired with the hope that the war might end soon, and that we might avoid being drawn in, we adopted the settled policy, which has been adhered to to this day, that we would not make or threaten war on any nation invading our rights in this war so long as the damages we suffered thereby could be compensated in money. Therefore, we filed claims in the nature of suits for every such wrong suffered by us either at the hands of the entente or the Germanic allies, expecting of course, to recover damages when peace returned. Now, it seems to me that this is the reason why Great Britain was suffered to do things against us that she had no right to do and why Germany was suffered to do things against us that she had no right to do. Thus, we adopted the policy of suffering Great Britain and Germany to commit acts upon us that were in violation of international law which we considered susceptible of settlement by way of damages. Now, thus far, in that respect there was no difference in our treatment of Great Britain or of Germany. It has been argued here, however, that the wrong suffered at our hands by both belligerent allies was of equal gravity, and that we had as much reason to war on Great Britain as we had on Germany. It has even been argued that if we felt it necessary to declare war on Germany, we could do no less than to declare war on Great Britain. I have received a great many letters and telegrams along the same line. It is astonishing to find that men who are opposed to war suddenly become so war mad that they suggest that if we enter into war at all we should make war on the whole of Europe. Of course it is absurd to suggest even that we should declare war against the Germanic allies, on the one hand, and the entente allies, on the other, at the same time and thus make it a three-cornered affair.

If these injuries had been confined to pecuniary losses we would not have warred against Great Britain or Germany; we would not have warred at all. We would have remained at peace. Right here the analogy ceases. On February 4, 1915, Germany proclaimed the waters surrounding Great Britain and Ireland, including the whole English Channel, a war zone, and it was further indicated at that time that they intended to ignore the rules of international law requiring visit and search and proposed to sink merchantmen without warning and without providing for the safety of passengers and crew. To this proclamation the United States, on February 10, 1915, protested, pointing out that such action on the part of Germany would endanger the lives of our citizens and it would be in violation of the principles of international law. Notwithstanding this protest Germany proceeded to carry out her threat, resulting in the sinking of the *Lusitania*, where more than 100 Americans lost their lives and many hundreds of noncombatant men, women, and children were sent to a watery grave without warning and without any attempt being made to safeguard their lives. History records no more infamous act than this! The world was horror stricken; the United States was stunned with grief and horror; the people were aflame with wrath. We protested; our protests have not been heeded to this day. Again and again boats were sunk without warning and again and again men, women, and children went down to their death defenseless and undefended. So, in all, 310 American lives have been ruthlessly and wantonly taken. Many American ships, carrying American cargoes, bound from neutral port to neutral port, carrying American mails, are floating phantoms below the surface of the sea, aimlessly and helplessly dragging the bedraggled Stars and Stripes into the depths of the ocean and still carrying the bones and bodies of noncombatant men, women and children, innocent victims of piracy and assassination.

To those who ask what the difference in offenses is, I answer that it is the difference between men and money—the difference between that of life and property. That tells the story. Great Britain says: "We shall stop and seize your ships entering the blockade zone." Germany says: "Here is a dead line. If you cross that line we will kill your people; we will sink your ships; we will destroy your cargoes and your mails. This is a line over which you can not pass and live." Now, not only has Germany said that but she has made good her threat over and over again.

Now, it is said that we have permitted Great Britain to sow mines in the sea, and that there is no difference in principle between laying the mines and the torpedoing of a vessel by a submarine without warning. In addition to her other offenses, let me point out right here that it was Germany who first sowed the mines.

On August 7, 1914, three days after the war began, Germany notified all neutral countries that the trade routes to English ports would be closed by mines.

It has been argued here this evening that Great Britain established mine fields and that we did not make formal protest against it, and having made no formal protest against it, it is contended that we lost our status as a neutral nation. Let me say, in answer to this, first, that the German Government itself never made that argument against us. She recognized our status as a neutral for two years thereafter because it is only recently that diplomatic relations have been severed, and then severed not by Germany, but by us. It would seem difficult, therefore, to understand why any of us should question our neutrality when Germany herself never questioned it. . . .

On April 16, 1916, in presenting the case of the *Sussex* the United States advised Germany that unless its indiscriminate and relentless warfare against vessels of commerce by use of submarines without regard to the sacred and indisputable rules of international law and the universally recognized dictates of humanity ceased, this Government would have no choice but to sever diplomatic relations. In response to this the German Government on May 4, 1916, notified this Government that the German naval forces had received orders that in accordance with the general principles of visit and search and destruction of merchant vessels recognized by international law, such vessels shall not be sunk without warning and without saving human lives unless these ships attempt to escape or offer resistance.

This assurance was withdrawn by the German note of January 31, 1917, and memoranda transmitted therewith, in which the German Government announced that it would forcibly prevent all navigation "that of neutrals included" in a zone around Great Britain, France, and Italy, and in the Mediterranean; that "all ships met within that zone will be sunk," and that "From February 1, 1917, all sea traffic will be stopped with every available weapon and without further notice in certain delimited zones."

In view of this withdrawal of the solemn assurances contained in German note May 4, 1916, this Government on February 3, 1917, notified the German Ambassador that it had no alternative consistent with the dignity and honor of the United States but to take the course it explicitly announced in the *Sussex* note of April 18, 1916, and sever diplomatic relations.

This Government had protested again and again. It must be remembered that the taking of American lives in the manner and form it was done of itself constituted sufficient grounds for war against Germany, but the President was anxious to avoid war if possible. The people clamored for peace each time a new outrage was suffered; a roar of indignation swept over the country only to be quieted down by the calm and patient voice of the President counseling peace. On April 16, 1916, as will appear from the memoranda, in presenting the case of the *Sussex*, the United States advised Germany that unless its indiscriminate and relentless warfare would cease this Government would have no choice but to sever diplomatic relations. You will all remember that then, as now, the cry again was raised, "Keep us out of war." Hundreds of thousands of telegrams poured into Washington praying for peace. These senders did not tell the President how he was to keep us out of war. We had not been the aggressors; we had invaded no rights of any country; we were neither destroying the property nor the lives of the citizens of any foreign country. How, then, did these senders of telegrams want the President to keep us out of war? Clearly, it was only by yielding up our rights and running away. It will be remembered that these telegrams were financed by the "embargo conference," so called; financed by German sympathizers, if not by German money, the purpose of which evidently was not to maintain American rights but to shield German wrongdoing. But the President, standing firm upon the ultimatum which he had sent, found the American way to keep the peace, and that was by persuading Germany to cease her unlawful acts and respect American rights. Wrong yielded to right instead of right yielding to wrong, and it appeared then that the sunshine of peace was to prevail in this country.

Now, like a bolt out of a clear sky, on January 31, 1917, Germany served notice upon this country that she proposed to renew her infamous acts of piracy and assassination upon the high seas and that she intended to extend the dead zone so that it now includes, without counting the forbidden waters of the Mediterranean Sea, an area of no less than one million and a half square miles. Not only that, but she has proceeded to carry out her threats, and American boats manned by American seamen and flying the American flag have been sunk without warning and without attempting to save the lives of Americans on board. Now, what does this mean? It means that we must suffer this and similar outrages in the future in silence, in shame, in cowardice, or we must fight. . . .

So there is a very broad distinction between the things that England has done against us and those which Germany has done against us. The difference is as great as that between human life and money, as great as that between property rights and human rights, and all the sophistry, all the refinement of arguments, all the specious pleading can not change the fact, and fact it is, that Germany has destroyed lives, has committed murder upon our citizens and piracy upon the high seas. The wrongs that we have suffered at Great Britain's hands can and will be compensated for in money.

The President has been charged with vacillation. An analysis of this whole question will show that he has steered a straight and steady course. So long as the wrongs we suffered were capable of being adjusted by the payment of money, though protesting, we refused to go to war about it. From the moment that American lives were being taken and wrongs were being inflicted upon us and upon our honor, which could not be compensated by the payment of money, he served notice upon Germany and upon the world that these wrongs would not be tolerated and, unless abandoned, would mean war.

Mr. President, it has been said upon this floor today that this war would put the dollar sign upon the flag. It has been said that this would be a war by the munitions makers and Wall Street. It has been said that we are a money-mad nation. Let me say that the facts show that for two and one-half years we have been suffering money and commercial losses at the hands of both groups of belligerents. Did we go to war for that? No. It has been only since American lives have been taken that this country has aroused itself and is ready to take the sword in defense of American lives and American honor. This country has refused to use its Army and its Navy or to sacrifice a single American life for the purpose of protecting commerce or property rights either in Mexico or even upon the high seas, but it now shows itself ready to spend its treasure and to sacrifice its blood to protect the lives of its citizens. Are we a money-mad people? . . .

. . . this war, if war comes, will be a war by the American people against the German dynasty. It will be a war, not for profit or pelf, but for the rights, the lives, the honor, the welfare, and the safety of this Nation. It will be a war for the democracy of the world. . . .

114. SOME GERMAN REACTIONS TO THE DECLARATION OF WAR BY THE UNITED STATES[1]

[The British Government printed a Daily Review of the Foreign Press for the confidential use of those in the service of the Government in order that they might be informed upon the utterances of the press in allied, neutral and enemy countries. Other governments printed similar reviews. A study of them all furnishes the student with a variegated picture of the press of the principal countries of the world. See also doc. no. 115.]

The *Frankfurter Zeitung* (Apr. 9):—

Germany to-day is fighting the same war that Athens once fought against the Persians, that the Swiss fought against the Habsburgers, and that the Dutch fought against Spain—a struggle of a minority whose liberty and life are threatened by a brutal, overwhelming majority. The participation of ever new nations in the war proves the truth of the old idea of the gods striking people with blindness. Motives of human reason are not adequate to explain the entry of America into the war. "It is not reason, humaneness, and justice that have driven our enemies into this war, but the lack of them and nationalist passion, the striving for power, the wish to repress and

---

[1] Great Britain. War Office: *Daily Review of the Foreign Press*, April 12, 1917, p. 47.

oppress Germany, and inability to comprehend our perfect right to live and act as a great nation. . . .

". . . In America, where hardly anything is known of war except the sanguinary profits made from supplying war materials, Wilson and Congress are throwing fresh firebrands on to the funeral pile that had died down to a smouldering heap. In Europe all nations are weary of the war. Peace is over-ripe; it depends on our enemies when it comes. Unless we are greatly mistaken the notes blown from the horns of the war men of the Entente no longer resound as they did three months ago; but even should the entry of America reinflame their war zeal we shall yet succeed in achieving our aim."

The *Leipziger Neuste Nachrichten* (extreme Jingo National-Liberal) (Apr. 9) :—

The United States can now be called upon to advance to the impoverished Entente nations the money that will be demanded as an indemnity by the Central Powers. It suggests that Canada should be held by the United States as a mortgage until the money thus advanced is repaid. The declaration of war, which was preceded by a "Parliamentary comedy," means merely that millions of American money will be flung across the ocean in the vain hope of recovering the American millions already lost. The commanders of German submarines will take care that the Americans are taught the frightful seriousness of the war, of which "they have as yet no idea."

The *Fremden-Blatt* (Apr. 9) :—

The Americans will not be more fortunate than were the Italians and Rumanians. The worst is now over, and the sun will soon shine again.

The *Neue Frei Presse* (Apr. 9) :—

America is falling upon Germany without any sufficient reason as an excuse for the rupture of diplomatic relations.

The *Reichspost* (Jingo Clerical) (Apr. 9) :—

The United States is entering the war with the sole object of ensuring the gains resulting from her unneutral attitude pursued hitherto, and generally augmenting the profit made out of the European War. . . . President Wilson never was a philanthropist; the public statements he has made hitherto were deliberately hypocritical and part of a plan conceived long ago.

115. REPORTS OF BETHMANN-HOLLWEG'S SPEECH ON GERMAN POLICY, APRIL, 1917[1]

[Early in 1917, after about four million men had been killed and when war weariness was at its height, two important events took place;

---

[1] Great Britain. War Office: *Daily Review of the Foreign Press*, April 3, 1917, p. 11.

namely, the Russian Revolution and the break between Germany and the United States. At this crisis the German Chancellor spoke as reported below probably to try to win revolutionary Russia to a separate peace and to justify in the sight of his own countrymen the policy which was bringing America into the conflict.]

William Bayard Hale to Hearsts (by wireless) :—

It was a quarter to six o'clock when the tall form of the Chancellor erected itself at the Ministerial table of the Reichstag. His first words were words of thanks for the acceptance of the Budget. He then passed on to discuss the Russian situation. "Momentous events have occurred in Russia," he said. "Czarism has fallen. Now the Entente endeavours to represent that we are interested in the maintenance of Russian Absolutism. This is an absolute lie. Germany was in friendly relations with Russia for some time, but since the death of Alexander II there have not been such relations. Certainly we have had no interest in the maintenance, and we have none in the restoration of Russian Absolutism. It is being said by our enemies that the German spirit is an obstacle to the democratisation of Russia. The truth is that the Kaiser Wilhelm at the end of the Japanese war telegraphed to the Czar Nicholas suggesting that he should give Russia constitutional democratic institutions. The suggestion was neglected. But it alone was sufficient to prove that the German people and Government had no interest in the maintenance of Absolutism in Russia.

"Shortly after, on the heels of his suggestion, came the Serbian plot against our good friend and ally, Austria. Passing to later events, the truth is that Russia was the first to refuse Germany's peace proffer. In spite of all this, it is today immaterial what internal policy Russia adopts. It is only material that eventually we shall find in Russia a permanently friendly neighbour. We Germans desire the utmost well-being of the Russian people and an honourable peace as speedily as is possible."

The Chancellor referred to the relations of Germany with the United States in phrases of the utmost consideration, but he declined to accept on behalf of the German Government responsibility for the present strained situation. "More than once we have suggested to the United States proposals designed to preserve complete understanding. Germany never entertained the least intention to attack America, and has no such intention today. Repeatedly we have endeavoured to make this clear to the President and people. England by its blockade policy has forced us to adopt measures of defence of our own people. These British measures have been by President Wilson and Mr. Lansing described as 'illegal and indefensible.' Nevertheless, the United States has taken no positive and effective action. Therefore, we in defence of our country which is fighting for its existence, have been obliged to adopt special methods. If the United States, with whom the German

people have for more than a century lived peacefully in the exchange
of both material and spiritual advantages, now deems it necessary to
involve itself in a sanguinary struggle and increase the shedding of
blood, then it is not we on whom the responsibility rests. For eight long
months we awaited positive action on the part of America on behalf
of the reëstablishment of peace in a troubled world. No action was
taken in reference to our sincere proposals, which practically were
ignored. Nothing remains but to prosecute to the utmost the exertions
which any Government is bound to make on behalf of its people."

Report of the same Speech by O'Donnell to the *Evening Mail*:—

Von Bethmann-Hollweg in the Reichstag today held forth a hand of
friendship to America, expressing the direst sorrow that events tend
toward hostilities, with a country with which there had been such
long-standing peace. He recalled that, in response to the urgent representations of Wilson, Germany interrupted the U-boat warfare for
eight months, hoping that in that time England would be brought to
her senses and discontinue the illegal blockade. As no results were
forthcoming, it became necessary to apply vigorous reprisals. While
he did not say so, he strongly implied that Germany would be willing
now to abandon the U-boat warfare provided England would return
to the methods prescribed in International Law, and that in the
present circumstances there was no other course to pursue than that
which Germany was adopting.

116. REICHSTAG RESOLUTION ON PEACE TERMS, JULY 19, 1917[1]

[The Resolution was drawn up by Erzberger and had the support of
the Majority Socialists, the Center, and some of the Liberals. It carried by 212 to 126 votes. The Conservatives and National Liberals opposed it. It seemed to mean that Germany would not demand territorial
annexations as a condition of peace if the Entente Powers would also
abandon plans for annexations as well as for economic restrictions and
preferences.]

Fehrenbach, Deputy [of the Center Party]: Gentlemen: By direction of the Center, the Social Democrat, and the Progressive Parties,
I have the honor to present to this distinguished House the following
resolution with the request that it be approved:

"The Reichstag declares: As on August 4, 1914, so now on the
threshold of the fourth year of war, that it approves the words in the
Address from the Throne: 'We are not actuated by lust for conquest.'
For the defense of its freedom and independence, for the inviolability
of its territory, Germany has taken arms.

---

[1] *Verhandlungen des Reichstags*, Vol. 310, *Stenographische Berichte*, 116 Session,
page 3573.

"The Reichstag strives for a peace of understanding and lasting reconciliation of the nations. [Cheers from the Center, the Progressive Peoples' Party and the Social Democrats.] With such a peace, forcible acquisitions of territory and political, economic, or financial coercion are irreconcilable. [Renewed cheers from the Center, the Progressive Peoples' Party and the Social Democrats.] The Reichstag also rejects all plans for the economic isolation and antagonizing of the nations after the War. ['Very true' from the Center, the Progressive Peoples' Party and the Social Democrats.] The Freedom of the seas must be secured. [Approval in the Center, the Progressive Peoples' Party and the Social Democrats.] Only economic peace can prepare the ground for friendly relations among the nations. [Renewed approval from the Center, the Progressive Peoples' Party and the Social Democrats.] The Reichstag will energetically promote the creation of international judicial organizations. [Cheers from the Center, the Progressive Peoples' Party and the Social Democrats.]

"As long, however, as the enemy governments will not enter upon such a peace, as long as they threaten Germany and her allies with conquest and coercion, the German People will stand together as a man [lively approval from the Center, the Progressive Peoples' Party and the Social Democrats], unflinchingly persevere, and fight until their own and their allies' right to life and development are secured. [Cheers from the Center, the Progressive Peoples' Party, and the Social Democrats.] The German People are invincible in their unity. [Lively approval.] The Reichstag knows itself to be in harmony with the men who are defending the Fatherland in heroic struggle. The imperishable gratitude of the entire people is assured them. [Lively agreement from the Center, the Progressive Peoples' Party and the Social Democrats.]"

117. Secret Treaty Partitioning Asiatic Turkey[1]

[This Sykes-Picot Agreement of May 16, 1916, was disclosed by memoranda published in 1917 by the Bolshevists, who repudiated it. It represented a compromise of interests between the British support of the Arab nationalist movement and French imperialist ambitions in Syria.]

Memorandum dated March 6, 1917

As a result of negotiations which took place in London and Petrograd in the Spring of 1916, the Allied British, French and Russian Governments came to an agreement as regards the future delimitation of their respective zones of influence and territorial acquisitions in Asiatic Turkey, as well as the formation in Arabia of an independent

---

[1] *The Manchester Guardian,* January 19, 1918. Reprinted with the permission of *The Manchester Guardian.*

Arab State, or a federation of Arab States. The general principles of the agreement are as follows:

1. Russia obtains the provinces of Erzerum, Trebizond, Van, and Bitlis, as well as territory in the southern part of Kurdistan, along the line Mush-Sert-Ibn-Omar-Amadjie-Persian frontier. The limit of Russian acquisitions on the Black Sea coast will be fixed later on at a point lying west of Trebizond.

2. France obtains the coastal strip of Syria, the vilayet of Adana, and a territory bounded on the south by a line Aintab-Mardin to the future Russian frontier, and on the north by a line Ala-Dagh-Zara-Egin-Kharput.

3. Great Britain obtains the southern part of Mesopotamia with Bagdad, and stipulates for herself in Syria the ports of Haifa and Akka.

4. By agreement between France and England, the zone between the French and the British territories forms a confederation of Arab States, or one independent Arab State, the zones of influence in which are determined at the same time.

5. Alexandretta is proclaimed a free port.

With a view to securing the religious interests of the Entente Powers, Palestine, with the Holy places, is separated from Turkish territory and subjected to a special régime to be determined by agreement between Russia, France and England.

As a general rule the contracting Powers undertake mutually to recognise the concessions and privileges existing in the territories now acquired by them which have existed before the war.

They agree to assume such portions of the Ottoman Debt such as correspond to their respective acquisitions.

118. PEACE PROPOSAL OF POPE BENEDICT XV, AUGUST 1, 1917[1]

[Pope Benedict XV made inquiries in several parts of Europe and on the basis of his findings sent to all of the belligerents the proposal which he hoped would form the basis of an agreement to terminate the war. The proposal is in effect an appeal to the nations to substitute moral law for physical force and return by common consent to the *status quo ante bellum*. The plan seemed to the statesmen of neither side of the conflict to offer a solution of the major problems at issue between them.]

To the Heads of the Belligerent Peoples:

From the beginning of our pontificate, in the midst of the horrors of the terrible war which has been let loose upon Europe, there were three objects above all which we set before ourselves: to maintain a perfect impartiality in regard to all belligerents as is fitting for him

[1] Great Britain. *Parliamentary Papers,* 1919, Vol. LIII. Cmd. 261.

who is the common father, and who loves all his children with a like affection; to strive always to do to all the greatest amount of good possible, and that without distinction of persons, and without difference of nationality or religion, even as is enjoined upon us by the universal law of charity as well as by the supreme spiritual charge entrusted to us by Christ; finally, as is demanded also by our mission of peace, to omit nothing, in so far as may be in our power, which might contribute to hasten the end of this calamity by endeavouring to induce the peoples of the world and their leaders to adopt more moderate resolutions, and to enter into the calm consideration of peace—of a peace "just and durable."

Whoever has followed our work during these last three painful years must surely recognise that, while remaining always faithful to our determination of absolute impartiality and to our humanitarian activities, we have nonetheless continued to exhort the belligerent nations and Governments to resume their brotherhood, although all that we have done to attain this noble object has not become public knowledge.

Towards the end of the first year of the war we addressed the most lively exhortations to the belligerent nations, and we at the same time indicated the road that they should follow, in order to arrive at a stable peace such as would be honourable for all.

Unfortunately our appeal was not regarded; the war has continued pitilessly and with all its horrors for another two years; it has, in truth, increased in cruelty, and spread over the earth, over the sea, and even into the air, and desolation and death have been showered upon defenceless cities, peaceful villages, and innocent populations. No one can now imagine to what extent this universal suffering will be increased and intensified if further months or, worse still, if further years are to be added to the blood-stained period that has elapsed. Is the civilised world then to become no more than a field of death? And is Europe, so glorious and flourishing in the past, to plunge into the abyss, as if driven by some universal madness, and to contrive her own suicide?

In this agonising situation, in the presence of this grave menace, we, who have no private political object, who give ear to the suggestions and interests of no special one of the belligerent parties, but who are inspired solely by the feeling of our supreme duty as common father of the faithful by the prayers of our children who beg for our intervention and for our words of peace, by the voice even of humanity and reason, we again raise a cry of peace and we renew an urgent appeal to those who hold in their hands the destinies of nations. But, in order no longer to confine ourselves to general terms such as circumstances have in the past rendered desirable, we now wish to descend to proposals of a more concrete and practical nature, and to invite the Governments of the belligerent countries to agree upon the following points which we feel should constitute the basis of a just and durable peace while leaving to them the task of defining and completing our proposals.

Before everything the fundamental point must be that the moral force of right should be substituted for the material force of arms. This would entail a just agreement between all countries for the simultaneous and reciprocal reduction of armaments according to rules and under guarantees to be established later, to the extent necessary to, and sufficient for, the maintenance of public order in each country; it would further entail in the place of armies the institution of arbitration with its high pacificatory functions, according to rules and standards to be concerted between the Powers, and subject to sanctions to be employed against whatever State might refuse either to submit international questions to arbitration or to accept the decisions of such arbitration.

When once the supremacy of right has thus been established, all obstacles to the free communications between peoples should be removed by assuring, by means of rules similarly to be established, the true freedom and community of the seas, an ideal which would, on the one hand, eliminate the many causes of conflict, and which would, on the other, open to all new sources of prosperity and progress.

As regards compensation for damages caused and the costs of war, we see no other means of solving this question than by laying down as a general principle a complete and reciprocal condonation, which would, moreover, be justified by the immense benefits which would be secured by disarmament; all the more so as the continuation of this carnage for objects of an economic nature only is not comprehensible. If there exist in certain cases particular reasons against this solution, these reasons should be weighed with justice and equity.

These pacific agreements, with all the immense advantages which they imply, will, however, not be practicable without the reciprocal restitution of the territories at present occupied. There should thus be on the part of Germany a complete evacuation of Belgium with a guarantee of absolute political, military, and economic independence as regards any Power whatsoever; there should also be an evacuation of French territory; as also a similar restitution of the German colonies on the part of the other belligerent Powers.

As regards territorial questions as, for example, those under dispute between Italy and Austria and between Germany and France, there is reason to hope that, in consideration of the immense advantages of a durable peace with disarmament, the opposing parties would be willing to examine them in a conciliatory spirit, taking into account as far as is just and possible, as we said on a former occasion, the aspirations of the peoples concerned, and, when necessary, coördinating particular interests with the general good of human society.

The same spirit of equity and justice should inspire the examination of the other territorial and political questions at issue, and notably those which concern Armenia, the Balkan States, and the territories forming the ancient Kingdom of Poland, whose noble historical traditions and the sufferings endured, especially during the present war, should make a special appeal to the sympathy of the nations.

Such are the principal bases on which we believe that the future reorganisation of States should rest. They are of a nature to render impossible the return of similar conflicts, and to prepare the solution of the economic question, which is so important for the future and the material prosperity of all the belligerent States. In laying them before you, who, at this tragic moment, direct the destinies of nations, we are inspired by the pleasant hope of having them accepted, and of seeing thus this terrible struggle, which appears more and more to be a useless massacre, concluded in the nearest future. On the other hand, the whole world recognises that, on the one side as on the other, military honour has been preserved. Listen therefore to our prayer, accept our fatherly invitation which we address to you in the name of the Divine Redeemer, the Prince of Peace. Reflect upon your very grave responsibility before God and man; on your decisions depend the tranquillity and happiness of numberless families, the lives of thousands of young men—in one word, the felicity of those peoples whose well-being it is your duty to secure. May God inspire you with decisions in harmony with His Holy Will; may Heaven grant that in winning the applause of your contemporaries, you may also assure for yourselves among future generations the fair name of peacemakers.

As regards ourselves, in close unison in prayer and penitence with all the faithful souls who sigh for peace, we implore for you the gift of the Holy Spirit to grant you light and judgment.

BENEDICTUS XV

Vatican, August 1, 1917

119. CZERNIN'S SPEECH ON PEACE TERMS, OCTOBER 2, 1917[1]

[Count Czernin was the Austro-Hungarian foreign minister.]

I feel compelled today to say something in public as to the Austro-Hungarian Government's ideas as regards the restoration of European relationships which have been completely shattered. In broad outlines our programme for the reëstablishment of order in the world (which might more accurately be described as the construction of a new order in the world) has been laid down in our reply to the Peace Note of our Holy Father. The only consideration today, therefore, is to complete this programme, and, above all, to explain the considerations which determine us to set up these principles in opposition to the system hitherto prevailing.

To many people it may appear astonishing and inconceivable that

---

[1] The London *Times*, October 4, 1917, p. 8. Reprinted with the permission of the London *Times*.

the Central Powers, especially Austria-Hungary, desire to make a renunciation in respect of military armament as, after all, in these heavy years, it was only in their military power that they found protection against manifold superiority. The war has not only produced new facts and conditions but has also led to new conceptions which have shaken the foundations of European politics as they existed before. Among many other political theses the one which especially has crumbled is that which held that Austria-Hungary was a moribund State. It was the dogma of the impending dissolution of the monarchy which made our position in Europe difficult and from which sprang all lack of appreciation of our vital needs. By proving ourselves in this war thoroughly sound and at least equal to others the result is that we can now reckon upon a complete understanding of our vital needs in Europe, and hopes that we may be overthrown by force of arms are destroyed. Until the moment came when we had given proof of this we could not give up the protection of our armament and expose ourselves to spiteful treatment on questions vital to us by an Areopagus influenced by the legend of our impending collapse.

Now, however, when this proof has been given, we are in a position simultaneously with our Allies to lay aside our arms and regulate any future conflicts by arbitration and in a peaceful manner. This new conception which has forced its way into the world affords us the opportunity not only of accepting the idea of disarmament and arbitration, but, as you, gentlemen, know, of working as we have done for a considerable time past with all our energy towards its realization. Europe must, without doubt, after this war, be placed on a new basis of right, offering a guarantee of permanence. This basis of right, I believe, must essentially be fourfold: first, it must offer a security that a war of revenge can not occur again on any side. We wish to achieve so much that we may be able to bequeath to our children's children as a legacy that they may be spared the terrors of a terrible time such as we are now passing through. No shifting of power among the belligerent States can attain this end. The only way to attain it is that mentioned—namely, by international disarmament, and by the recognition of arbitration.

It is superfluous to state that this measure of disarmament must never be directed against any particular State, or any particular group of Powers, and that it must of course comprise the land, sea, and air in the same degree. War as an instrument of policy must be combated. On an international basis under international control, universal, equal and gradual disarmament of all the States of the world must take place and the defensive force limited to what is absolutely necessary.

I know very well that this goal is extraordinarily difficult to reach and that the path leading to it is beset with difficulties; that it is long and thorny. Nevertheless, I am convinced that it must be trodden, and it shall be trodden, no matter whether individuals consider it desirable or not. It is a great mistake to believe that the world after this war will begin again where it left off in 1914. Catastrophes such as this war do not pass away without leaving deep traces behind, and the most terrible misfortune that could befall us would be if the competition in armaments were to continue after the conclusion of peace; for it would mean economic ruin for all States. Even before this war our military burdens were oppressive, although we especially should remember that Austria-Hungary was far from being ready in a military sense when she was surprised by the war. Only during the war did she make up for her formerly neglected military equipment. In the event of unrestrained competition in armaments after this war the burden for all States would be simply unbearable.

This war has taught us that we must reckon on a great increase of former armament. In order, after this war, with unrestricted rivalry in armaments, to be adequately equipped, the nations would have to multiply everything by 10. They would need 10 times as many guns, munition factories, ships, and submarines as before and also incomparably more soldiers to man all this apparatus. The military estimates of all the great Powers would amount to milliards. That is impossible. With all the burdens which all the belligerent States after the conclusion of peace would have to bear, this expenditure, I repeat, would mean the ruin of nations. To return, however, to the relatively small armaments prior to 1914 would for any one State be entirely impossible, because it would thereby fall so much behind that its military power would not count, and consequently its expenditure would be completely purposeless. Should, however, a general return to the relatively low armament level of 1914, be brought about, that would, of itself, mean an international reduction of armaments, but there would be no meaning in not going further and actually disarming.

Out of this difficulty there is only one way—namely, complete international disarmament. Gigantic fleets will have no further purpose when the nations of the world guarantee the freedom of the seas, and land armies would have to be reduced to the level required by the maintenance of internal order. Only on an international basis—that is, under international control, is this possible. Every State will have to give up something of its independence for the purpose of ensuring world peace. Probably the present generation will not live to see the end of this great pacific movement in its entirety. It can only be realized slowly but I consider it our duty to place ourselves at the head of this movement and do everything humanly possible to accelerate its realization. At the conclusion of peace its fundamental bases must be laid down.

If its first principle is that of obligatory international arbitration and general disarmament on land, its second principle is that of freedom on the high seas and naval disarmament. I purposely say the high seas for I do not extend the idea to the narrow seas and I freely admit that for sea communications special rules and regulations must obtain. If these two first factors which I have mentioned are made clear then every ground for territorial guarantees disappears and this is the third fundamental principle of a new international basis of right. This is the basis of an idea of the beautiful and sublime Note which the Pope addressed to the whole world. We have not waged war to make conquests and we contemplate no oppression. If the international disarmament which we long for from the bottom of our hearts is accepted by our present enemies and becomes a fact, then we need no territorial guarantees. In this case we can renounce the enlargement of the Austro-Hungarian Monarchy, always provided that the enemy completely evacuates our territory.

The fourth principle which must be observed to ensure the free and pacific development of the world after these evil times is the free economic activity of all and absolute avoidance of future economic war. Economic war must be absolutely eliminated from every future arrangement. Before we conclude peace we must have a positive certainty that our present opponents have relinquished this idea.

These, gentlemen, are the basic principles of the new world order as they are present to my mind, and they are all founded on all-round disarmament. Even Germany, too, in answer to the Papal Note, has most emphatically professed adherence to the idea of all-round disarmament and our present opponents also have made these principles at least in part their own. On most points I am of different opinion from Mr. Lloyd-George, but on the point that there must never again be a war of revenge we are at one.

The question of indemnities which the Entente is always putting forward assumes a remarkable complexion when one considers the devastation which their Armies have wrought in Galicia, the Bukovina, Tyrol, on the Isonzo, in East Prussia, and in the Turkish territories, and the German colonies. Does the Entente intend to compensate us for all this, or is it so completely mistaken in its judgment of our psychology that it hopes for a one-sided indemnification? I could almost believe the latter, judging from the numerous speeches which we have heard.

REUTER

120. ESTABLISHMENT OF THE SUPREME WAR COUNCIL, 1917[1]

[The cause of the Entente Allies was not making the headway on the battlefields in 1917 that the governments and peoples of the Entente countries had hoped it might make. Serious disasters had been en-

[1] *Parliamentary Debates, Commons,* 1917, Vol. XCIX, Nov. 12 to Nov. 29, pp. 893-898.

countered so that strenuous efforts had to be made to put down despair, revive enthusiasm and coördinate efforts so as to avoid working at cross purposes. The establishment of the Supreme War Council was a part of this movement. The British Prime Minister discussed it in the House of Commons in the light of alternative solutions.]

Extract from speech of the Prime Minister, Mr. Lloyd George, Nov. 19, 1917

My right hon. Friend's [Mr. Asquith] speech divided itself, quite naturally, into two parts. The first was the practical, and therefore the most important question. The other half was the presentment of the case. With regard to the first, he examined the proposals in a calm and dispassionate way. I shall follow his example in that respect. I shall deal, before I come to the second part of his speech, with one or two criticisms which he offered on what, after all, is the most important part of what this House has to consider today, and that is the question as to whether it is desirable to secure greater unity of action amongst the Allies, and, if so, whether we have taken the right method to do so. That is far more important than anything I may have had to say either in Paris or anywhere else. With regard to the first part, I am glad that my right hon. Friend has made my task very much easier by practically accepting the premises upon which we based our action. He admits that there is a need for greater coöperation. I do not think he has denied that the mere machinery which has been adopted up to the present, the machinery which was adopted when he was Prime Minister and which I subsequently also adopted—and therefore there is no question of applying any particular blame to any particular Government—the machinery of conference and consultation between the Allies, has proved to be inadequate. What he does say is—and to that I shall come later on—that although the present machinery is inadequate, he does not accept my proposition that the Allies have suffered substantially for that reason. There I shall join issue with him later on. I think we have suffered. We have suffered grievously. We have suffered, as I repeatedly stated in Paris, from no fault of any individual or any staff, but owing to the defects of the system, and that is the reason why I thought the time had come when we ought to effect a complete change in our methods of coördinating our business. My right hon. Friend stated that the enemy had an advantage —an undoubted advantage—from the possession of interior lines. That is a reason why we should do our best to overcome that by coördinating our efforts. Germany has won once through lack of coordination among the Allies. In the case of Frederick the Great his success, in spite of the overwhelming mass of material and men hurled against him, was attributable in the main to the fact that the Allies never coördinated their campaign. It is essential that we should avoid these mistakes of the past, whether in this campaign or elsewhere.

May I just say, first of all, that any criticism upon which I based the action of the Government in proposing a change in our methods of common action, was not directed against any Staffs or any Commanders-in-Chief, either in this or in any other country. It is the business of the Commanders-in-Chief to look after their own particular fronts. It is not their business to survey the whole field of operations throughout Europe, Asia, and Africa. It is quite as much as they can do to look after their own particular fronts. And what is true of General Sir Douglas Haig is true of General Petain, of General Cadorna, and of other Chiefs of Armies in the separate fields of operations. . . . I was simply using the illustration in order to show the same common defect throughout the whole campaign of the Allies during the past three or four years, without any reference to individuals, but purely in order to prove that the lack of coördination amongst the Allies had brought disaster on one or two occasions without any blame being attached to any particular Staff or Commander-in-Chief. For that reason the Allies, after a good deal of consultation, decided that it was desirable to take a step forward in the way of coördinating their activities. Who was the first to suggest the idea? It is rather important that I should inform the House, because there has been a good deal of suggestion . . . that this is an attempt to interfere with the Staffs—an attempt on the part of civilians to interfere with the soldiers. Who was the first to suggest a Council of this kind? Lord Kitchener. I have taken the trouble to look up the records. In 1915 Lord Kitchener proposed it, almost in the very terms in which I recommended it in Paris. That was in 1915, and I have no hesitation in saying if his advice had been carried out—I admit there were difficulties then, and it is easier to do it now than in 1915—but if his advice in 1915 had been carried out by all the Allies, I say, without any hesitation, we should have been further forward. . . .

The second time it was proposed was in July of this year, at a meeting of the Commanders-in-Chief. I forget whether all were there, but all the Chiefs of Staff were. At any rate, Sir William Robertson, General Pershing, General Cadorna, and General Foch were there. They recommended, as a means for dealing with the situation, the setting up of an Inter-Allied Council. Their proposal was "the realisation of unity of action on the Western Front by the help of a permanent Inter-Allied military organisation, which will study and prepare the rapid movement of troops from one theatre to another." When it is suggested that all this is a device on the part of civilians to get control of strategy, I am glad of this opportunity which has been afforded me to quote the authority of these great soldiers, as proof that the initiation of the suggestion came from them in the first instance, and not from politicians.

I come to the second point. Having agreed that it is desirable to get some sort of central authority, in order to coördinate—I use the word my right hon. Friend used: there is no better—what is the best method of doing it? He examined three alternatives. I am in complete agreement with him in his views with regard to the first two. The first has been put forward in very responsible quarters, and that is the appointment of a Generalissimo—a Generalissimo of the whole of the forces of the Allies. I agree with him. Personally I am utterly opposed to that suggestion. . . . It would not work. It would produce real friction, and might really produce not merely friction between the Armies, but friction between the nations and the Government. The second suggestion is a suggestion which finds favour, not merely in France but in America. America, France, Britain, and Italy, have agreed to join in this Allied Council, but as far as I am able to gauge American opinion . . . America would have preferred a Council with executive Powers—with greater powers. That is a criticism in France —the criticism is not that we have gone too far, but that we have not gone far enough. There has been no criticism in any Allied country on the ground that we have gone too far; it has been entirely for a different reason. There are reasons why I think it would be undesirable to set up a Council with full executive authority unless the Allies are absolutely driven to it by the failure of the present experiment. It is undoubtedly a delegation of power from Governments to representatives of theirs sitting, perhaps, in France. I think it would be a mistake to go so far, unless it is found that difficulties are placed in the way of the working of the present experiment; and with good will, and that is essential, with coöperation on the part of all those concerned, with the readiness to throw everything over, to submerge everything to the one desire to win victory for the common cause, I have no doubt that if the first should fail, we should be driven to the second.

What is the last alternative? The last alternative is the one we have adopted, a Council representative of all Allied countries with technical advisers drawn from all the Allied Armies to help the various Governments to coördinate their efforts. That is the present proposal. What are the advantages of the present proposal—what are the advantages of this proposal over the present and existing system? The first is that the information which is at the disposal of each of the Allied Staffs would then be at the disposal of this central council. Nominally that is so now, but only nominally. You have a system of liaison officers. . . . I do not believe that any General Staff would say that it has at its disposal now all the information which is possessed by every General Staff even with regard to their own front, let alone with regard to the enemy. This central body will have distinguished representatives of each Army upon it. Each of these representatives will be supplied with information from his own General Staff. They will, therefore, be able in the first instance, to coördinate information, and information is the basis of good strategy.

What is the second point? They would sit continuously; it would be a permanent body. . . . The present system is a sporadic one, where you have meetings perhaps once every three or four months, barely that—there is only one meeting a year between the whole of the staffs; that has been the rule—for the purpose of settling the strategy of the Allies over the whole of the battle front, which extends over thousands and thousands of miles of front, with millions of men in embattled array upon those fronts. A single day, with perhaps a morning added! No generals, however great their intuition, no generals, whatever their genius, could settle the strategy of a year with a sitting which will only last over five or six hours. Utterly impossible! Therefore, it is an essential part of the scheme that this body should be permanent, that they should sit together day by day, with all the information derived from every front before them, with the view to coördinating the plans of the General Staffs over all the fronts.

The third point is that it will be the duty of this central body to survey the whole field, and not merely a part of it. It may be said that each General Staff does that at the present moment. Well, in a sense they are bound, of course, to consider not merely their own front, but other fronts as well, but it is a secondary matter. They naturally do not devote the same study to it, and there is always a delicacy on the part of any General Staff when it comes to interfere with the sphere of another General Staff and another general. . . .

121. STATEMENT OF BRITISH POLICY IN PALESTINE BY FOREIGN MINISTER BALFOUR, NOVEMBER 8, 1917[1]

His Majesty's Government view with favor the establishment in Palestine of a national home for the Jewish people, and will use their best endeavors to facilitate the achievement of this object, it being clearly understood that nothing shall be done which may prejudice the civil and religious rights of existing non-Jewish communities in Palestine, or the rights and political status enjoyed by Jews in any other country.

I should be grateful if you would bring this declaration to the knowledge of the Zionist Federation.

122. STATEMENT OF BRITISH WAR AIMS BY PRIME MINISTER LLOYD GEORGE, JANUARY 5, 1918[2]

[In a speech to the Trade Unions on January 5, 1918 Lloyd George set forth the war aims of Great Britain more candidly and more fully

---

[1] The London *Times*, November 9, 1917. Reprinted with the permission of the London *Times*.

[2] The London *Times*, January 7, 1918. Reprinted with the permission of the London *Times*.

than had been done before. It will be noted that he had discussed the program he presented with many representative men before making this address, a fact that gave it especial force. As compared with his former pronouncements, it showed much advance toward liberal consideration of the problems that had to be solved, perhaps because the Entente Powers were going through one of their darkest hours at the time he spoke, and because British Labor was making strenuous objection to the war policy of the Government.]

When the Government invited organized labor in this country to assist them to maintain the might of their armies in the field, its representatives are entitled to ask that any misgivings and doubts which any of them may have about the purpose to which this precious strength is to be applied should be definitely cleared, and what is true of organized labor is equally true of all citizens in this country without regard to grade or avocation.

When men by the million are being called upon to suffer and die and vast populations are being subjected to the sufferings and privations of war on a scale unprecedented in the history of the world, they are entitled to know for what cause or causes they are making the sacrifice. It is only the clearest, greatest, and justest of causes, that can justify the continuance even for one day of this unspeakable agony of the nations. And we ought to be able to state clearly and definitely not only the principles for which we are fighting but also their definite and concrete application to the war-map of the world.

We have arrived at the most critical hour in the terrible conflict, and before any Government takes the fateful decision as to the conditions under which it ought either to terminate or continue the struggle, it ought to be satisfied that the conscience of the nation is behind these conditions, for nothing else can sustain the effort which is necessary to achieve a righteous end to this war. I have, therefore, during the last few days, taken special pains to ascertain the views and the attitude of representative men of all sections of thought and opinion in the country. Last week I had the privilege not merely of perusing the declared war aims of the Labour Party, but also of discussing in detail with the Labour Leaders the meaning and intention of that declaration. I have also had an opportunity of discussing this same momentous question with Mr. Asquith and Viscount Grey. Had it not been that the Nationalist Leaders are in Ireland engaged in endeavoring to solve the tangled problem of Irish self-government, I should have been happy to exchange views with them, but Mr. Redmond, speaking on their behalf, with his usual lucidity and force, in many of his speeches, made clear what his ideas are as to the object and purpose of the war. I have also had the opportunity of consulting certain representatives of the great Dominions overseas. I am glad to be able to say as the result of all these discussions that, although the government are alone responsible for the actual language I propose using, there is national agreement as to the character and purpose of our war aims and peace conditions, and in what I say to you today, and through you to the world, I can venture to claim that I am speaking not merely the mind of the government but of the nation and of the empire as a whole.

We may begin by clearing away some misunderstanding and stating what we are *not* fighting for. We are not fighting a war of aggression against the German people. Their leaders have persuaded them that they are fighting a war of self-defense against a league of rival nations bent on the destruction of Germany. That is not so. The destruction or disruption of Germany or the German people has never been a war aim with us from the first day of this war to this day. Most reluctantly and, indeed, quite unprepared for the dreadful ordeal, we were forced to join in this war in self-defense, in defense of a violated public law of Europe and in vindication of the most solemn treaty obligations on which the public system of Europe rested, and on which Germany had ruthlessly trampled in her invasion of Belgium. We had to join in the struggle or stand aside and see Europe go under and brute force triumph over public life and international justice. It was only the realization of that dreadful alternative that forced the British people into the war. And from that original attitude they have never swerved. They have never aimed at the break up of the German peoples or the disintegration of their State or country. Germany has occupied a great position in the world. It is not our wish or intention to question or destroy that position for the future, but rather to turn her aside from hopes and schemes of military domination and to see her devote all her strength to the great beneficent tasks of the world. Nor are we fighting to destroy Austria-Hungary or to deprive Turkey of its capital or of the rich and renowned lands of Asia Minor and Thrace, which are predominantly Turkish in race.

Nor did we enter this war merely to alter or destroy the Imperial constitution of Germany, much as we consider that military autocratic constitution a dangerous anachronism in the twentieth century. Our point of view is that the adoption of a really democratic constitution by Germany would be the most convincing evidence that in her the old spirit of military domination has indeed died in this war, and would make it much easier for us to conclude a broad democratic peace with her. But, after all, that is a question for the German people to decide.

It is now more than a year since the President of the United States, then neutral, addressed to the belligerents a request that they should state clearly the aims for which they were fighting. We and our allies responded by the note of January 10, 1917.

To the President's appeal the Central Empires made no reply and, in spite of many adjurations, both from their opponents and from neutrals, they have maintained a complete silence as to the objects for which they are fighting. Even on so crucial a matter as their intention with regard to Belgium they have uniformly declined to give any trustworthy indication.

On December 25 last, however, Count Czernin, speaking on behalf of Austria-Hungary and her allies, did make a pronouncement of a kind. It is indeed deplorably vague. We are told that "it is not the intention" of the Central Powers "to appropriate forcibly" any occupied territories or "to rob of its independence" any nation which has lost its "political independence" during the war. It is obvious that almost any scheme of conquest and annexation could be perpetrated within the literal interpretation of such a pledge.

Does it mean that Belgium, Serbia, Montenegro and Roumania would be as independent and as free to direct their own destinies as the Germans or any other nation? Or does it mean that all manner of interferences and restrictions, political and economic, incompatible with the status or dignity of a freed, self-respecting people, are to be imposed? If this is the intention then there will be one kind of independence for a great nation and an inferior kind of independence for a small nation. We must know what is meant, for an equality of right amongst nations, small as well as great, is one of the fundamental issues this country and her allies are fighting to establish in this war. Reparation for the wanton damage inflicted on Belgian towns and villages, and their inhabitants, is emphatically repudiated. The rest of the so-called "offer" of the Central Powers, is almost entirely a refusal of all concessions. All suggestions about the autonomy of subject nationalities are ruled out of the peace terms altogether. The question whether any form of self-government is to be given to the Arabs, Armenians, or Syrians, is declared to be entirely a matter for the Sublime Porte. A pious wish for the protection of minorities "in so far as it is practically realizable" is the nearest approach to liberty which the Central statesmen venture to make.

On one point only are they perfectly clear and definite. Under no circumstances will the "German demand" for the restoration of the whole of Germany's colonies be departed from. All principles of self-determination, or, as our earlier phrase goes, government by consent of the governed, here vanish into thin air.

It is impossible to believe that any edifice of permanent peace could be erected on such a foundation as this. Mere lip service to the formula of no annexations and no indemnities or the right of self-determination is useless. Before any negotiation can ever be begun, the Central Powers must realize the essential facts of the situation.

The days of the Treaty of Vienna are long past. We can no longer submit the future of European civilization to the arbitrary decisions of a few negotiators, striving to secure by chicanery or persuasion the interests of this or that dynasty or nation. The settlement of the new Europe must be based on such grounds of reason and justice as will give some promise of stability. Therefore it is that we feel that government with the consent of the governed must be the basis of any territorial settlement in this war. For that reason also, unless treaties be upheld, unless every nation is prepared, at whatever sacrifice, to honor the national signature it is obvious that no Treaty of Peace can be worth the paper on which it is written.

The first requirement, therefore, always put forward by the British Government and their Allies has been the complete restoration, political, territorial, and economic, of the independence of Belgium and such reparation as can be made for the devastation of its towns and provinces. This is no demand for war indemnity such as that imposed on France by Germany in 1871. It is not an attempt to shift the cost of warlike operations from one belligerent to another, which may or may not be defensible. It is no more and no less than an insistence that before there can be any hope for a stable peace, this great breach of the public law of Europe must be repudiated, and, so far as possible, repaired. Reparation means recognition. Unless international right is recognized by insistence on payment for injury done in defiance of its canons, it can never be a reality. Next comes the restoration of Serbia, Montenegro and the occupied parts of France, Italy, and Roumania. The complete withdrawal of the alien armies and the reparation for injustice done is a fundamental condition of permanent peace.

We mean to stand by the French Democracy to the death in the demand they make for a reconsideration of the great wrong of 1871, when, without any regard to the wishes of the population, two French provinces were torn from the side of France and incorporated in the German Empire. This sore has poisoned the peace of Europe for half a century and until it is cured healthy conditions will not have been restored. There can be no better illustration of the folly and wickedness of using a transient military success to violate national right.

I will not attempt to deal with the question of the Russian territories now in German occupation. The Russian policy since the Revolution has passed so rapidly through so many phases that it is difficult to speak without some suspension of judgment as to what the situation will be when the final terms of European peace come to be discussed. Russia accepted the war with all its horrors because, true to her traditional guardianship of the weaker communities of her race, she stepped in to protect Serbia from a plot against her independence. It is this honourable sacrifice which not merely brought Russia into the war but France as well. France, true to the conditions of her treaty with Russia, stood by her Ally in a quarrel which was not her own. Her chivalrous respect for her treaty led to the wanton invasion of Belgium; and the treaty obligations of Great Britain to that little land brought us into the war.

The present rulers of Russia are now engaged, without any reference to the countries whom Russia brought into the war, in separate negotiations, with their common enemy. I am indulging in no reproaches; I am merely stating facts with a view to making it clear why Britain can not be held accountable for decisions taken in her absence and concerning which she has not been consulted or her aid invoked. No one who knows Prussia and her designs upon Russia can for a moment doubt her ultimate intention. Whatever phrases she may use to delude Russia, she does not mean to surrender one of the fair provinces, or cities, of Russia, now occupied by her forces. Under one name or another—and the name hardly matters—these Russian provinces will henceforth be in reality a part of the dominions of Prussia. They will be ruled by the Prussian sword in the interests of Prussian autocracy and the rest of the people of Russia will be partly enticed by specious phrases and partly bullied by the threat of continued war against an impotent army into a condition of complete economic and ultimate political enslavement to Germany. We all deplore the prospect. The democracy of this country mean to stand to the last by the democracies of France and Italy and all our other allies. We shall be proud to fight to the end side by side with the new democracy of Russia, so will America and so will France and Italy, but if the present rulers of Russia take action which is independent of their allies, we have no means of intervening to arrest the catastrophe which is assuredly befalling their country. Russia can only be saved by her own people.

We believe, however, that an independent Poland, comprising all those genuinely Polish elements who desire to form part of it is an urgent necessity for the stability of Western Europe.

Similarly, though we agree with President Wilson that the break-up of Austria-Hungary is no part of our war aims, we feel that unless genuine self-government on true democratic principles is granted to those Austro-Hungarian nationalities who have long desired it, it is impossible to hope for the removal of those causes of unrest in that part of Europe which have so long threatened its general peace.

On the same ground we regard as vital the satisfaction of the legitimate claims of the Italians for union with those of their own race and tongue. We also mean to press that justice be done to men of Roumanian blood and speech in their legitimate aspirations. If these conditions are fulfilled Austria-Hungary would become a Power whose strength would conduce to the permanent peace and freedom of Europe instead of being merely an instrument to the pernicious military autocracy of Prussia that uses the resources of its allies for the furtherance of its own sinister purposes.

Outside Europe we believe that the same principles should be applied. While we do not challenge the maintenance of the Turkish Empire in the homelands of the Turkish race with its capital at Constantinople—the passage between the Mediterranean and the Black

Sea being internationalized and neutralized—Arabia, Armenia, Mesopotamia, Syria, and Palestine are in our judgment entitled to a recognition of their separate national condition.

What the exact form of that recognition in each particular case should be need not here be discussed, beyond stating that it would be impossible to restore to their former sovereignty the territories to which I have already referred.

Much has been said about the arrangements we have entered into with our Allies on this and on other subjects. I can only say that as new circumstances, like the Russian collapse, and the separate Russian negotiations, have changed the conditions under which those arrangements were made, we are, and always have been, perfectly ready to discuss them with our Allies.

With regard to the German colonies, I have repeatedly declared that they are held at the disposal of a Conference whose decisions must have primary regard to the wishes and interests of the native inhabitants of such colonies. None of those territories are inhabited by Europeans. The governing consideration, therefore, in all these cases must be that the inhabitants should be placed under the control of an administration acceptable to themselves, one of whose main purposes will be to prevent their exploitation for the benefit of European capitalists or Governments. The natives live in their various tribal organizations under chiefs and councils who are competent to consult and speak for their tribes and members, and thus to represent their wishes and interests in regard to their disposal.

The general principle of national self-determination is therefore as applicable in their cases as in those of occupied European territories. The German declaration that the natives of the German colonies have, through their military fidelity in the war, shown their attachment and resolve under all circumstances to remain with Germany, is applicable not to the German colonies generally, but only to one of them, and in that case (German East Africa) the German authorities secured the attachment, not of the native population as a whole which is and remains profoundly anti-German but only of a small warlike class from whom their Askaris, or soldiers, were selected. These they attached to themselves by conferring on them a highly privileged position as against the bulk of the native population which enabled these Askaris to assume a lordly and oppressive superiority over the rest of the natives. By this and other means they secured the attachment of a very small and insignificant minority whose interests were directly opposed to those of the rest of the population and for whom they have no right to speak. The German treatment of their native populations in their colonies has been such as amply to justify their fear of submitting the future of those colonies to the wishes of the natives themselves.

Finally there must be reparation for injuries done in violation of international law. The Peace Conference must not forget our seamen and the services they have rendered to and the outrages they have suffered for, the common cause of freedom.

One omission we notice in the proposal of the Central Powers which seems to us especially regrettable. It is desirable, and indeed essential, that the settlement after this war shall be one which does not in itself bear the seed of future war. But that is not enough. However wisely and well we may make territorial and other arrangements, there will still be many subjects of international controversy. Some indeed are inevitable.

The economic conditions at the end of the war will be in the highest degree difficult. Owing to the diversion of human effort to warlike pursuits, there must follow a world shortage of raw materials which will increase the longer the war lasts, and it is inevitable that those countries which have control of the raw materials will desire to help themselves and their friends first.

Apart from this, whatever settlement is made will be suitable only to the circumstances under which it is made, and, as those circumstances change, changes in the settlement will be called for.

So long as the possibility of dispute between nations continues, that is to say, so long as men and women are dominated by passion and ambition and war is the only means of settling a dispute, all nations must live under the burden not only of having from time to time to engage in it, but of being compelled to prepare for its possible outbreak. The crushing weight of modern armaments, the increasing evil of compulsory military service, the vast waste of wealth and effort involved in warlike preparation—these are blots on our civilization of which every thinking individual must be ashamed.

For these and other similar reasons, we are confident that a great attempt must be made to establish by some international organization an alternative to war as a means of settling international disputes. After all, war is a relic of barbarism, and just as law has succeeded violence as the means of settling disputes between individuals, so we believe that it is destined ultimately to take the place of war in the settlement of controversies between nations.

If, then, if we are asked what we are fighting for, we reply, as we have often replied "we are fighting for a just and lasting peace" and we believe that before permanent peace can be hoped for, three conditions must be fulfilled.

First, the sanctity of treaties must be reëstablished; secondly, a territorial settlement must be secured based on the right of self-determination or the consent of the governed; and, lastly, we must seek by the creation of some international organization to limit the burden of armaments and diminish the probability of war.

On these conditions the British Empire would welcome peace; to secure those conditions its peoples are prepared to make even greater sacrifices than those they have yet endured.

123. Address of President Wilson, Delivered at a Joint Session of the Two Houses of Congress, January 8, 1918 (The "14 Points")[1]

[Wilson, on January 8, 1918, put into definite form several conditions of peace that had been left vague' by other spokesmen of the Allied and Associated Powers. The fourteen points he outlined became the basis for negotiations some months later.]

Gentlemen of the Congress:

Once more, as repeatedly before, the spokesmen of the Central Empires have indicated their desire to discuss the objects of the war and the possible bases of a general peace. Parleys have been in progress at Brest-Litovsk between Russian representatives and representatives of the Central Powers to which the attention of all the belligerents has been invited for the purpose of ascertaining whether it may be possible to extend these parleys into a general conference with regard to terms of peace and settlement. The Russian representatives presented not only a perfectly definite statement of the principles upon which they would be willing to conclude peace but also an equally definite programme of the concrete application of those principles. The representatives of the Central Powers, on their part, presented an outline of settlement which, if much less definite, seemed susceptible of liberal interpretation until their specific programme of practical terms was added. That programme proposed no concessions at all either to the sovereignty of Russia or to the preferences of the populations with whose fortunes it dealt, but meant, in a word, that the Central Empires were to keep every foot of territory their armed forces had occupied,—every province, every city, every point of vantage,—as a permanent addition to their territories and their power. It is a reasonable conjecture that the general principles of settlement which they at first suggested originated with the more liberal statesmen of Germany and Austria, the men who have begun to feel the force of their own peoples' thought and purpose, while the concrete terms of actual settlement came from the military leaders who have no thought but to keep what they have got. The negotiations have been broken off. The Russian representatives were sincere and in earnest. They cannot entertain such proposals of conquest and domination.

The whole incident is full of significance. It is also full of perplexity. With whom are the Russian representatives dealing? For whom are the representatives of the Central Empires speaking? Are they speaking for the majorities of their respective parliaments or for the minority parties, that military and imperialistic minority

---

[1] U. S. Serial 7443. Doc. No. 765.

which has so far dominated their whole policy and controlled the affairs of Turkey and of the Balkan states which have felt obliged to become their associates in this war? The Russian representatives have insisted, very justly, very wisely, and in the true spirit of modern democracy, that the conferences they have been holding with the Teutonic and Turkish statesmen should be held within open, not closed, doors, and all the world has been audience, as was desired. To whom have we been listening, then? To those who speak the spirit and intention of the Resolutions of the German Reichstag of the ninth of July last, the spirit and intention of the liberal leaders and parties of Germany, or to those who resist and defy that spirit and intention and insist upon conquest and subjugation? Or are we listening, in fact, to both, unreconciled and in open and hopeless contradiction? These are very serious and pregnant questions. Upon the answer to them depends the peace of the world.

But, whatever the results of the parleys at Brest-Litovsk, whatever the confusions of counsel and of purpose in the utterances of the spokesmen of the Central Empires, they have again attempted to acquaint the world with their objects in the war and have again challenged their adversaries to say what their objects are and what sort of settlement they would deem just and satisfactory. There is no good reason why that challenge should not be responded to, and responded to with the utmost candor. We did not wait for it. Not once, but again and again, we have laid our whole thought and purpose before the world, not in general terms only, but each time with sufficient definition to make it clear what sort of definitive terms of settlement must necessarily spring out of them. Within the last week Mr. Lloyd George has spoken with admirable candor and in admirable spirit for the people and Government of Great Britain. There is no confusion of counsel among the adversaries of the Central Powers, no uncertainty of principle, no vagueness of detail. The only secrecy of counsel, the only lack of fearless frankness, the only failure to make definite statement of the objects of the war, lies with Germany and her Allies. The issues of life and death hang upon these definitions. No statesman who has the least conception of his responsibility ought for a moment to permit himself to continue this tragical and appalling outpouring of blood and treasure unless he is sure beyond a peradventure that the objects of the vital sacrifice are part and parcel of the very life of Society and that the people for whom he speaks think them right and imperative as he does.

There is, moreover, a voice calling for these definitions of principle and of purpose which is, it seems to me, more thrilling and more compelling than any of the many moving voices with which the troubled air of the world is filled. It is the voice of the Russian people. They are prostrate and all but helpless, it would seem, before the grim power of Germany, which has hitherto known no relenting and no pity. Their power, apparently, is shattered. And yet their soul is not subservient. They will not yield either in principle or in action. Their conception of what is right, of what it is humane and honorable for them to accept, has been stated with a frankness, a largeness of view, a generosity of spirit, and a universal human sympathy which must challenge the admiration of every friend of mankind; and they have refused to compound their ideals or desert others that they themselves may be safe. They call to us to say what it is that we desire, in what, if in anything, our purpose and our spirit differ from theirs; and I believe that the people of the United States would wish me to respond, with utter simplicity and frankness. Whether their present leaders believe it or not, it is our heartfelt desire and hope that some way may be opened whereby we may be privileged to assist the people of Russia to attain their utmost hope of liberty and ordered peace.

It will be our wish and purpose that the processes of peace, when they are begun, shall be absolutely open and that they shall involve and permit henceforth no secret understandings of any kind. The day of conquest and aggrandizement is gone by; so is also the day of secret covenants entered into in the interest of particular governments and likely at some unlooked-for moment to upset the peace of the world. It is this happy fact, now clear to the view of every public man whose thoughts do not still linger in an age that is dead and gone, which makes it possible for every nation whose purposes are consistent with justice and the peace of the world to avow now or at any other time the objects it has in view.

We entered this war because violations of right had occurred which touched us to the quick and made the life of our own people impossible unless they were corrected and the world secure once for all against their recurrence. What we demand in this war, therefore, is nothing peculiar to ourselves. It is that the world be made fit and safe to live in; and particularly that it be made safe for every peace-loving nation which, like our own, wishes to live its own life, determine its own institutions, be assured of justice and fair dealing by the other peoples of the world as against force and selfish aggression. All the peoples of the world are in effect partners in this interest, and for our own part we see very clearly that unless justice be done to others it will not be done to us. The programme of the world's peace, therefore, is our programme; and that programme, the only possible programme, as we see it, is this:

I. Open covenants of peace, openly arrived at, after which there shall be no private international understandings of any kind but diplomacy shall proceed always frankly and in the public view.

II. Absolute freedom of navigation upon the seas, outside territorial waters, alike in peace and in war, except as the seas may be closed in whole or in part by international action for the enforcement of international covenants.

III. The removal, so far as possible, of all economic barriers and the establishment of an equality of trade conditions among all the nations consenting to the peace and associating themselves for its maintenance.

IV. Adequate guarantees given and taken that national armaments will be reduced to the lowest point consistent with domestic safety.

V. A free, open-minded, and absolutely impartial adjustment of all colonial claims, based upon a strict observance of the principle that in determining all such questions of sovereignty the interests of the populations concerned must have equal weight with the equitable claims of the government whose title is to be determined.

VI. The evacuation of all Russian territory and such a settlement of all questions affecting Russia as will secure the best and freest coöperation of the other nations of the world in obtaining for her an unhampered and unembarrassed opportunity for the independent determination of her own political development and national policy and assure her of a sincere welcome into the society of free nations under institutions of her own choosing; and, more than a welcome, assistance also of every kind that she may need and may herself desire. The treatment accorded Russia by her sister nations in the months to come will be the acid test of their good will, of their comprehension of her needs as distinguished from their own interests, and of their intelligent and unselfish sympathy.

VII. Belgium, the whole world will agree, must be evacuated and restored, without any attempt to limit the sovereignty which she enjoys in common with all other free nations. No other single act will serve as this will serve to restore confidence among the nations in the laws which they have themselves set and determined for the government of their relations with one another. Without this healing act the whole structure and validity of international law is forever impaired.

VIII. All French territory should be freed and the invaded portions restored, and the wrong done to France by Prussia in 1871 in the matter of Alsace-Lorraine, which has unsettled the peace of the world for nearly fifty years, should be righted, in order that peace may once more be made secure in the interest of all.

IX. A readjustment of the frontiers of Italy should be effected along clearly recognizable lines of nationality.

X. The peoples of Austria-Hungary, whose place among the nations we wish to see safeguarded and assured, should be accorded the freest opportunity of autonomous development.

XI. Rumania, Serbia, and Montenegro should be evacuated; occupied territories restored; Serbia accorded free and secure access to the sea; and the relations of the several Balkan states to one another determined by friendly counsel along historically established lines of allegiance and nationality; and international guarantees of the political and economic independence and territorial integrity of the several Balkan states should be entered into.

XII. The Turkish portions of the present Ottoman Empire should be assured a secure sovereignty, but the other nationalities which are now under Turkish rule should be assured an undoubted security of life and an absolutely unmolested opportunity of autonomous development, and the Dardanelles should be permanently opened as a free passage to the ships and commerce of all nations under international guarantees.

XIII. An independent Polish state should be erected which should include the territories inhabited by indisputably Polish populations, which should be assured a free and secure access to the sea, and whose political and economic independence and territorial integrity should be guaranteed by international covenant.

XIV. A general association of nations must be formed under specific covenants for the purpose of affording mutual guarantees of political independence and territorial integrity to great and small states alike.

In regard to these essential rectifications of wrong and assertions of right we feel ourselves to be intimate partners of all the governments and peoples associated together against the Imperialists. We cannot be separated in interest or divided in purpose. We stand together until the end.

For such arrangements and covenants we are willing to fight and to continue to fight until they are achieved; but only because we wish the right to prevail and desire a just and stable peace such as can be secured only by removing the chief provocations to war, which this programme does remove. We have no jealousy of German greatness, and there is nothing in this programme that impairs it. We grudge her no achievement or distinction of learning or of pacific enterprise such as have made her record very bright and very enviable. We do not wish to injure her or to block in any way her legitimate influence or power. We do not wish to fight her either with arms or with hostile arrangements of trade if she is willing to associate herself with us and the other peace-loving nations of the world in covenants of justice and law and fair dealing. We wish her only to accept a place of equality among the peoples of the world,—the new world in which we now live,—instead of a place of mastery.

Neither do we presume to suggest to her any alteration or modification of her institutions. But it is necessary, we must frankly say, and necessary as a preliminary to any intelligent dealings with her on our part, that we should know whom her spokesmen speak for when they speak to us, whether for the Reichstag majority or for the military party and the men whose creed is imperial domination.

We have spoken now, surely, in terms too concrete to admit of any further doubt or question. An evident principle runs through the whole programme I have outlined. It is the principle of justice to all peoples and nationalities, and their right to live on equal terms of liberty and safety with one another, whether they be strong or weak. Unless this principle be made its foundation no part of the structure of international justice can stand. The people of the United States could act upon no other principle; and to the vindication of this principle they are ready to devote their lives, their honor, and everything that they possess. The moral climax of this the culminating and final war for human liberty has come, and they are ready to put their own strength, their own highest purpose, their own integrity and devotion to the test.

124. ANGLO-FRENCH STATEMENT OF AIMS IN MESOPOTAMIA AND SYRIA, NOVEMBER 7, 1918[1]

The aim of France and Great Britain in carrying on in the Near East the war let loose by Germany's ambitions is the complete and final liberation of the peoples so long oppressed by the Turks and the establishment of governments and administrations deriving their authority from the initiative and the free choice of the native populations.

In view of following out this intention, France and Great Britain are agreed to encourage and help the establishment of native governments and administrations in Syria and Mesopotamia actually liberated by the allies, and in the territories they are now striving to liberate, and to recognize them as soon as effectively established.

Far from seeking to force upon the populations of these countries any particular institution, France and Great Britain have no other concern than to ensure by their support and their active assistance the normal working of the governments and institutions which the populations shall have freely adopted, so as to secure just impartiality for all, and also to facilitate the economic development of the country in arousing and encouraging local initiative by the diffusion of instruction, and to put an end to discords which have too long been taken advantage of by Turkish rule.

Such is the rôle that the two Allied Governments claim for themselves in the liberated territories.

125. EXAMPLES OF NORTHCLIFFE PROPAGANDA DROPPED INTO GERMAN TRENCHES

[Early in 1918 Great Britain established a department of propaganda which seems to have had within its hands a weapon of offense of very telling power. Among its objectives were the break-up of Austria-Hungary through the stimulation of nationalist ambitions and discontent among its peoples, and the creation of the spirit of discouragement and disloyalty in the hearts of the soldiers in the German Army. Some examples of this latter type of literature, printed in England in the German language and dropped from balloons into

---

[1] The *New York Times*, November 8, 1918. Formal statement issued by the British Embassy in Washington by direction of the Foreign Office. From the Associated Press.

the German trenches, are given below and in the illustrations on pages 554-556.]

(a) *What Are You Fighting for, Michel?*[1]

BY BALLOON

They tell you that you are fighting to secure victory for your Fatherland. But have you ever thought about what you are fighting for?

You are fighting for the glory of, and for the enrichment of the Krupps. You are fighting to save the Kaiser, the Junkers and the War Lords who caused the war from the anger of the people.

The Junkers are sitting at home with their bejewelled wives and mistresses. Their bank accounts are constantly growing, accounts to which you and your comrades pay with your lives. For your wives and brides there are no growing bank accounts. They are at home working and starving, sacrifices like yourselves to the greed of the ruling class to whose pipes you have to dance.

What a dance! The dance of death. But yesterday you marched over the corpses of your comrades against the English cannon. To-morrow another German soldier will march over your corpse.

You have been promised victory and peace. You poor fool! Your comrades were also promised these things more than three years ago. Peace indeed they have found—deep in the grave. But victory did not come.

Your Kaiser has adorned the glorious Hindenburg with the Iron Cross with golden beams. What has the Kaiser awarded to you? Ruin, suffering, poverty, hunger for your wives and children, misery, disease, and tomorrow the grave.

It is for the Fatherland, you say, that you go out as a brave patriot to death for the Fatherland.

But of what does your Fatherland consist? Is it the Kaiser with his fine speeches? Is it the Crown Prince with his jolly companions, who sacrificed 600,000 men at Verdun? Is it Hindenburg, who sits with Ludendorf, both covered with medals many kilometers behind you and who plans how he can furnish the English with still more cannon fodder. Is it Frau Bertha Krupp for whom through year after year of war you pile up millions upon millions of marks? Is it the Prussian Junkers who cry out over your dead bodies for annexations?

No, the Fatherland is not any of these. You are the Fatherland, Michel! You and your sisters and your wives and your parents and your children. You, the common people are the Fatherland. And yet it is you and your comrades who are driven like slaves into the hell of English cannon-fire, driven by the command of the feelingless slave-drivers.

---

[1] "Air Post," No. 12 (Hoover War Library files).

When your comrades at home were striking, they were shot at with machine guns. If you, after the war, strike a blow for your rights, the machine guns will be turned upon you, for you are fighting only to increase the power of your lords.

Do you perhaps believe your rulers who love war as you hate it? Of course not. They love war for it brings them advancement, honor, power, profit. The longer the war lasts, the longer they will postpone the revolution.

They promise you that you can compel the English to beg for peace. Do you really believe that? You have advanced a few kilometers but for every Englishman whom you have shot down, six Germans have fallen. And all America is still to come.

Your commanders report to you wonderful stories of English losses. But did they tell you that Germany in the first five days of battle lost 315,000 men?

Arrayed against Germany in battle today stands the entire world because it knows that German rulers caused the war to serve their own greedy ambition. The entire power of the Western World stands behind England and France and America. An army of ten million men is being prepared. Soon it will go forth to battle. Have you thought of that, Michel?

(b) *What a German Soldier Who Recently Has Been Taken Prisoner by the English Told to an English Officer*[1]

BY BALLOON

The German soldier had spent four years in America but had not been naturalized. Shortly before the outbreak of the war he was in London; yet he was able to get back to Germany. There he was busy for a long time with special work, but during the battle of the Somme he had to become a soldier and he fought on various fronts. He relates

THE GREATEST CRIME IN THE WORLD

"This war is the greatest crime that the world has ever seen. The crimes of the French Revolution are nothing in comparison with those brutalities which Germany has committed, and the fault thereof is that the war goes on continually. With the outbreak of the war they were merely thieves and bandits; now they are the bloodiest murderers on a large scale that the world has ever produced. Here on this front the German soldiers are falling like flies. The English artillery is killing them in heaps. Many Germans are being killed by German balls which the German soldiers, driven like cattle into the battle,

---

[1] "Air Post" No. 16 (Hoover War Library files).

Northcliffe Propaganda

In Air Post No. 25, the British propagandist tries to persuade the German soldiers that the price of victory will be their crucifixion upon the Iron Cross at the hands of their officers; in No. 30, that they are being led over the precipice in their pursuit of a "Will-o'-the-Wisp" victory. In No. 36, there is called to the attention of the German soldiers the changed condition of the people due to four years of war, the change in the directors of the state and the substitution of a make-shift victory for a hope of real victory as the objective held up before them. In No. 61, the British try to discourage the enemy by telling of the rapid transshipment of American soldiers.

(Printed with the permission of the directors of the Hoover War Library.)

BY BALLOON.
Durch Luftballon.

A.P. 39.

BY BALLOON.
Durch Luftballon.

A.P. 39.

Amerikanische Soldaten in Frankreich.

Brief von dem Herrn Sekretär Baker an den Präsidenten der Vereinigten Staaten, Washington.

Sehr geehrter Herr Präsident,

Mit dem Zwecke, sich auf den Kriegsschauplatz in Frankreich zu begeben, sind schon über eine Million amerikanische Soldaten an den Hafen dieses Landes eingeschifft.

Indem ich Ihnen diese Tatsache melde, dürfte es wohl auch nicht ohne Interesse sein, etliche Angaben über die Fortschritte unserer Seeeinschiffungen von Mai 1917 bis Ende Juni b.J.

1917.

Monat.	Truppen.	Monat.	Truppen.
Mai	1718	September	32523
Juni	12261	Oktober	38259
Juli	12988	November	23016
August	18323	Dezember	48840

1918.

Monat.	Truppen.	Monat.	Truppen.
Januar	46776	April	117212
Februar	48027	Mai	244345
März	83811	Juni	276372

Seesoldaten eingeschifft · 14644.

Total · · 1019115.

Die Gesamtzahl der Verluste (Dienstunfähige, Getrunkene, Tote oder Verwundete) beläuft sich auf 8165.
Der großartigen Macht der Flotte bezüglich des Transportwesens ist es zuzuschreiben, daß von den Überseetruppen nur 291 durch feindlichen Angriff ertrunken worden sind.

Hochachtungsvoll,
Newton D. Baker.

fire. And why? Only because the Kaiser and his aides, so-called states-men, are afraid of what will happen when our people learn everything. They already know a great deal.

GERMANY AGAINST THE ENTIRE WORLD

Does any sensible German believe that the unavoidable end is to be turned aside if not only the old, but also the new, world fights against Germany? They know very well that America contributes millions of men, billions of dollars, innumerable works and dockyards. They know that America can put hundreds of thousands of fresh troops in the field and that the exhaustion of Germany which is already frightful will become ever more terrible. They know all this, but the beasts which they are let this terrible massacre go on, not in the hope that they will be able to turn aside their fate, but because they fear to look that in the face today which they can put off until tomorrow in spite of the fact that every day costs thousands of good Germans their lives.

The Russians have arisen and broken their chains; but not our people. Our tyrants are too clever; they have enchained not only the bodies, but also the wills. *There has been no free will in Germany since 1870.* The criminals in Berlin have taken all too much care of that. Our people are too well brought up for what they are now doing and are therefore slaves without wills. Germany is today an immense prison full of hungry slaves who may not reach out a hand to help themselves, and it will remain so as long as William the Murderer can buy postponement through the blood of thousands of his slaves. Thank God I am not of it."

GERMAN SOLDIERS, FOLLOW THE RUSSIAN EXAMPLE; CHASE THE TYRANTS TO THE DEVIL!

(c) *American soldiers in France*[1]

BY BALLOON

Letter from Secretary Baker to the President of the United States

Honored Sir: Washington

With the objective of transferring themselves to the battle ground in France, over a million American soldiers have already embarked for the harbors of this country.

It may not be without interest to accompany this report with several facts about the progress of our over-sea military expedition.

Embarkations from May 1917 to the end of June of this year:

[1] "Air Post," No. 61 (Hoover War Library files).

1917

Month	Troops	Month	Troops
May	1 718	September	32 523
June	12 261	October	38 259
July	12 988	November	23 016
August	18 323	December	48 840

1918

Month	Troops	Month	Troops
January	46 776	April	117 212
February	48 027	May	244 345
March	83 811	June	276 372

Naval men sent 14 644

Total 1 019 115

The total losses (incapacitated, drowned, dead or wounded) runs to 8 165.

Due to the wonderful protection afforded to the fleet by the system of transportation, only 291 of the above-mentioned were drowned as a result of attack by the enemy.

Most respectfully,

Newton D. Baker

126. Survey of War-time Propaganda Literature, Principally German[1]

[The British Government had a study made for the confidential use of men in responsible positions of the writers of propaganda literature in Germany, and to a limited extent, in other countries. The purpose of the study seems to have been largely to inform British propagandists of the arguments being used abroad so that counter-arguments or data could be presented to neutralize their effect.]

Objectives of German Propaganda

1. *Control of Home Opinion.*—In modern times it is plain that even the most autocratic ruler cannot hope to conduct a protracted war, or a war that brings a great burden on his people or that sways doubtfully unless public opinion is with him. A very large proportion of German propaganda . . . is for German consumption; it might be interpreted almost as one of the signs of German megalomania, that Germans care much less about convincing other people than about

---

[1] P. Chalmers Mitchell, *Report on the Propaganda Library* (Confidential). Published by the British Ministry of Information, 1917. Selections from Section 23.

convincing themselves. The following are the chief topics of this Home propaganda.

(a) Proclamation of the certainty of German victory, obliteration and explanation of reverses, description of actual and prospective military and naval triumphs, description of economic strength, financial resources, power of organisation, overcoming of the difficulties in the supply of food and raw materials, and so forth. It is notable, however, that as the war has proceeded, this fervour of victory is being replaced by assurances of the German power to endure to the end; the Fronts are now "iron walls" instead of legions marching to victory. "Durchhalten," holding out, is the new motto.

(b) Proclamation that it is a war of Defence.—This theme bulks very large; it is addressed especially to the ordinary German bourgeoisie, who on the whole were mild and peaceful people, to the Socialists, and the commercial classes. The chief points made related to the "encircling policy" of the enemies of Germany, German militarism as a necessary consequence of the position of Germany surrounded by powerful enemies, the Russian danger, and the English jealousy of German commercial success. As it was not easy to square this theory with the actual German plan of campaign, including the invasion of Belgium, the theory was advanced that an offensive was merely the best means of defence. Annexations were to be limited to what might be necessary for future security.

(c) Proclamation of the outrageous conduct of the enemy. The English "starvation plan," violations of laws of war by all the enemies, use of dum-dum bullets, and of black troops, the campaign of calumny of German conduct and aspirations in the neutral Press, and so forth.

(d) Exaltation of Germans. The historic mission, the high culture and civilisation, the real freedom of Germany, the superiority of the Prussian motto "work, order, duty" over "liberty, equality, fraternity," the humanity of the Germans, soldiers and civilians, the order they have brought into occupied territories, etc.

(e) Proclamation that German victory would be for the good of the world.—All the great Empires of the past have expanded and developed for their own selfish purposes. Germany wishes to "free the seas" not for her own selfish objects, but for all the nations, and to open up the world so that all people should be free to develop on their own lines. England, France and Russia have been the great oppressors of smaller nations and races; Germany will liberate them. The unification of Germany was the first stage in a beneficent process which will lead to the formation of a Great Middle Europe and then to a Federation of the whole world.

(f) The Need of Expansion. The Bernhardi and Treitschke doctrine.—This was more prominent in literature written before the war, and in its early stage. It was quickly replaced by a more sober form; the great and expanding German people required land within the

German Empire to which surplus population might go and still remain German. Outlet must be found for German talent, organising capacity, capital, and manufactured products, and the necessary supplies of raw materials must be forthcoming. These objects could have been attained peacefully but for the fact that Germany was a late arrival on the world-scene and her rapid development caused the envy of England in particular, so that German rights had to be secured by force.

(g) Appeals to Cupidity.—The riches, natural resources and possibilities of all the parts of the world in which German influence could be extended or which could be taken by Germany from her enemies, are described elaborately. The growth of the English Empire in particular is described as an accomplishment of successful piracy, to be reprobated because it was accomplished by England who must now be made to disgorge to the younger and stronger pirate.

2. *Control of Neutral Opinion.*—Themes "a," "b," "c," and "e" are repeated just as in the case of Home Opinion. Themes "d" and "f" are treated in a lighter and more careful fashion, and theme "g" is suppressed or disclaimed. Special attention is directed to explaining as necessities of war all those steps which have interfered with the rights of neutrals or have been harmful to them, as for instance, the sinking of neutral vessels, the submarine war, the use of mines. The war aims are presented in the mildest possible fashion, with much stress on the gain that would come to Neutrals from "Freedom of the Seas." Much care is expended in trying to show that the victory of the enemy would be a disaster to Neutrals. . . .

3. *Control of Allied Opinion.*—The Germans fully realised the need of addressing themselves to this task. Themes "a," "b," and "c" were used as in the case of Home opinion; themes "d," "e," "f" and "g" were handled in a minor fashion. . . . Much stress is laid on the common interests of Germany and her Allies, in particular the advantage of Middle Europe for Austria, Bulgaria and Turkey, and of the great future for Turkey as the leader of the Mohammedan world, when by the help of Germany the power of England, France and Russia has been broken.

4. *Control of Enemy Opinion.*—The efforts in this direction may be classed under three main heads.

(a) That the Germans are winning and must win.—More recently this has been replaced by the theme that the Allies cannot win, in fact that the longer they are in realising this, the greater will be their losses.

(b) Attempts to stir up disaffection between the Allies, chiefly by suggesting that they have divergent aims, or that one of them, usually England, is not taking her fair share of the burden. Favorite topics are that England intends to retain Belgium and the northern part of France, that England is using France and Russia merely for her own selfish ends and does not care how much they lose, that the interests of Italy, Greece and the Southern Slavs cannot be reconciled.

(c) Attempts to stir up disaffection or cause trouble within enemy countries.—This has absorbed a large part of the attention of the Germans. Examples in the case of England and Ireland, South Africa, India, Egypt, and Mohammedan countries generally; in the case of Russia, Finland, Baltic Provinces, Lithuania, the Ukraine, Poland, Georgia and Russian Mohammedans; in the case of France chiefly Algeria. Under the same heading come the various attempts to inflame anti-patriotic or revolutionary opinion, and to encourage pacifism in enemy countries.

It is impossible to estimate to what extent the many and varied voices of German propagandists owe their original inspiration to official sources. But it is a clear inference that the bulk of the work, even if not spontaneous in origin, has been accepted heartily, in fact that it represents the views of the German people. Parsons, professors, travellers, traders, novelists, journalists, workingmen and men of leisure, private persons and publicists have all played their part. It is not with the Kaiser or the Chancellor or the Party leaders, but with the German nation itself that we have to reckon. . . .

It is through Neutral countries that attempts to control enemy opinion find their readiest channel. Many of the failures of German propaganda are due to the neglect of this reverberation of propagandist effort. To the present writer it seems of vital importance that those who are engaged in the preparation and useful distribution of propaganda and counter-propaganda should be in close and constant touch with competent observers in Neutral countries. These observers should report at frequent intervals daily or weekly in special circumstances :—

(1) The books, pamphlets and views that appear to be in active circulation.
(2) The methods by which these are being distributed in hotels and clubs and reading-rooms, and circulation through book-sellers and agents who receive special terms.
(3) The reception of these by different classes of the public. . . .

127. The Brest-Litovsk Treaty between Russia and Germany, Austria-Hungary, Bulgaria, and Turkey, Signed March 3, 1918[1]

[The Russian Bolshevists, anxious to end the war, took steps to bring about an armistice as soon as they came into power (November 7, 1917). Because the Entente Allies would not coöperate with them in efforts toward bringing peace, they invited the Central Powers to make

---

[1] [Central Powers (1914-1918).] *Texts of the Russian "Peace."* Washington, D. C., 1918. (Confidential. For Official Use only.) pp. 13-21. Translation from German.

a separate agreement. On December 22, the first peace conference of the war opened. The Russian task was to make peace hurriedly so as to keep pledges made to the soldiers and in order to allow the new communistic experiment to begin, but at the same time it was important that they should not surrender too completely their national interests to the Powers who actually occupied much of Russian territory and who were in a position to take more. The concessions made in order to end the war may be seen in the treaty.]

Article I. Germany, Austria-Hungary, Bulgaria, and Turkey, for the one part, and Russia, for the other part, declare that the state of war between them has ceased. They are resolved to live henceforth in peace and amity with one another.

Article II. The contracting parties will refrain from any agitation or propaganda against the Government or the public and military institutions of the other party. In so far as this obligation devolves upon Russia, it holds good also for the territories occupied by the Powers of the Quadruple Alliance.

Article III. The territories lying to the west of the line agreed upon by the contracting parties which formerly belonged to Russia, will no longer be subject to Russian sovereignty; the line agreed upon is traced on the map submitted as an essential part of this treaty of peace. The exact fixation of the line will be established by a Russo-German commission.

No obligations whatever toward Russia shall devolve upon the territories referred to, arising from the fact that they formerly belonged to Russia.

Russia refrains from all interference in the internal relations of these territories. Germany and Austria-Hungary purpose to determine the future status of these territories in agreement with their population.

Article IV. As soon as a general peace is concluded and Russian demobilization is carried out completely, Germany will evacuate the territory lying to the east of the line designated in paragraph 1 of Article III, in so far as Article VI does not determine otherwise.

Russia will do all within her power to insure the immediate evacuation of the provinces of eastern Anatolia and their lawful return to Turkey.

The districts of Erdehan, Kars, and Batum will likewise and without delay be cleared of the Russian troops. Russia will not interfere in the reorganization of the national and international relations of these districts, but leave it to the population of these districts, to carry out this reorganization in agreement with the neighboring States, especially with Turkey.

Article V. Russia will, without delay, carry out the full demobilization of her army inclusive of those units recently organized by the present Government.

Furthermore, Russia will either bring her warships into Russian ports and there detain them until the day of the conclusion of a general peace, or disarm them forthwith. Warships of the States which continue in the state of war with the Powers of the Qaudruple Alliance, in so far as they are within Russian sovereignty, will be treated as Russian warships.

The barred zone in the Arctic Ocean continues as such until the conclusion of a general peace. In the Baltic sea, and, as far as Russian power extends within the Black sea, removal of the mines will be proceeded with at once. Merchant navigation within these maritime regions is free and will be resumed at once. Mixed commissions will be organized to formulate the more detailed regulations, especially to inform merchant ships with regard to restricted lanes. The navigation lanes are always to be kept free from floating mines.

Article VI. Russia obligates herself to conclude peace at once with the Ukrainian People's Republic and to recognize the treaty of peace between that State and the Powers of the Quadruple Alliance. The Ukrainian territory will, without delay, be cleared of Russian troops and the Russian Red Guard. Russia is to put an end to all agitation or propaganda against the Government or the public institutions of the Ukrainian People's Republic.

Esthonia and Livonia will likewise, without delay, be cleared of Russian troops and the Russian Red Guard. The eastern boundary of Esthonia runs, in general, along the river Narwa. The eastern boundary of Livonia crosses, in general, lakes Peipus and Pskow, to the southwestern corner of the latter, then across Lake Luban in the direction of Livenhof on the Dvina. Esthonia and Livonia will be occupied by a German police force until security is insured by proper national institutions and until public order has been established. Russia will liberate at once all arrested or deported inhabitants of Esthonia and Livonia, and insures the safe return of all deported Esthonians and Livonians.

Finland and the Aaland Islands will immediately be cleared of Russian troops and the Russian Red Guard, and the Finnish ports of the Russian fleet and of the Russian naval forces. So long as the ice prevents the transfer of warships into Russian ports, only limited forces will remain on board the warships. Russia is to put an end to all agitation or propaganda against the Government or the public institutions of Finland.

The fortresses built on the Aaland Islands are to be removed as soon as possible. As regards the permanent non-fortification of these islands as well as their further treatment in respect to military technical navigation matters, a special agreement is to be concluded between Germany, Finland, Russia, and Sweden; there exists an understanding to the effect that, upon Germany's desire, still other countries bordering upon the Baltic Sea would be consulted in this matter.

Article VII. In view of the fact that Persia and Afghanistan are free and independent States, the contracting parties obligate themselves to respect the political and economic independence and the territorial integrity of these States.

Article VIII. The prisoners of war of both parties will be released to return to their homeland. The settlement of the questions connected therewith will be effected through the special treaties provided for in Article XII.

Article IX. The contracting parties mutually renounce compensation for their war expenses, i.e., of the public expenditures for the conduct of the war, as well as compensation for war losses, i.e., such losses as were caused [by] them and their nationals within the war zones by military measures, inclusive of all requisitions effected in enemy country.

Article X. Diplomatic and consular relations between the contracting parties will be resumed immediately upon the ratification of the treaty of peace. As regards the reciprocal admission of consuls, separate agreements are reserved.

Article XI. As regards the economic relations between the Powers of the Quadruple Alliance and Russia the regulations contained in Appendices II-V are determinative. . . .

Article XII. The reëstablishment of public and private legal relations, the exchange of war prisoners and interned civilians, the question of amnesty as well as the question anent the treatment of merchant ships which have come into the power of the opponent, will be regulated in separate treaties with Russia which form an essential part of the general treaty of peace, and, as far as possible, go into force simultaneously with the latter.

Article XIII. In the interpretation of this treaty, the German and Russian texts are authoritative for the relations between Germany and Russia; the German, the Hungarian, and Russian texts for the relations between Austria-Hungary and Russia; the Bulgarian and Russian texts for the relations between Bulgaria and Russia; and the Turkish and Russian texts for the relations between Turkey and Russia.

Article XIV. The present treaty of peace will be ratified. The documents of ratification shall, as soon as possible, be exchanged in Berlin. The Russian Government obligates itself, upon the desire of one of the Powers of the Quadruple Alliance, to execute the exchange of the documents of ratification within a period of two weeks. Unless otherwise provided for in its articles, in its annexes, or in the additional treaties, the treaty of peace enters into force at the moment of its ratification.

In testimony whereof the Plenipotentiaries have signed this treaty with their own hand.

Executed in quintuplicate at Brest-Litovsk, 3 March, 1918.

128. The Organization of Czecho-Slovakia

[The story of the crystallization of the nationalistic spirit among the Czechs is briefly and partially shown through an account of the experiences and activities of the Czech Army in Russia and then through the memoirs of Eduard Beneš, who, with President Masaryk, was outstanding in his leadership in the movement to organize the Czecho-Slovak State.]

(a) *The Czecho-Slovak Army in Siberia*[1]

In view of the curiosity displayed in certain circles as to the origins and aims of the Czecho-Slovak Army holding the Trans-Siberian Railway, we propose to give a brief summary of its origin, development, and movements, so far as it is in our power in the absence of authentic reports about some recent events.

Since the beginning of the war the Czecho-Slovaks sided wholeheartedly with the Allies, but the terrible system of Austrian police espionage and German militarism made it impossible for them successfully to revolt. The only way in which they could render assistance to the Allies was therefore to get as large a number of soldiers as possible to go over to the Allies to form an independent Czecho-Slovak Army which would fight on the side of the Entente for the complete independence of Bohemia. In this task the Czecho-Slovaks have succeeded to a remarkable degree. About 300,000 surrendered to Russia alone. Out of the 70,000 prisoners in Serbia, 35,000 were Czechs. Unfortunately, almost all of these perished during the Serbian retreat. About 20,000 surrendered voluntarily to Italy, and are now fighting shoulder to shoulder with Italian troops.

In Russia there has been a Czecho-Slovak legion from the outbreak of the war, numbering a few thousand, which rendered a valuable service to Russia, especially in scouting. In fact, the famous 28th Regiment of Prague was literally fetched by a few Czech volunteers on the Russian side. It went over to the Russians in a body, including the band, without firing a single shot. The Czech troops were mentioned in the Russian *communqués* of 2 February, 1916, 29 March, 1917, and 2 July, 1917, for bravery. More than a third of them have been decorated with high Russian orders.

The organisation of the Czecho-Slovak prisoners who voluntarily surrendered to Russia into organised army units met with serious obstacles on the part of the old Russian Government. The Czechs who saw in Russia their liberator were sadly disillusioned when they were exposed to harsh treatment on the part of superior German officers in

---

[1] *The New Europe,* July 25, 1918. V. Nosek, "The Czecho-Slovak Army in Siberia." Eyre & Spottiswoode.

the prison camps of Siberia, owing to the ignorance and stupidity of some Russian officials. About 50,000 of them perished from starvation. Being unable to join the Russian ranks to such a degree as they would have liked, and being anxious to assist the Allies, many of them entered the Jugoslav Volunteer Division which was so gallantly fighting in Roumania in October, 1916. These have now been transported and transferred to the Czecho-Slovak Army in France.

It was only after the Russian Revolution, and especially after the arrival of Professor Masaryk in Russia, in May, 1917, that the Czech Legion grew into a brigade, and finally into an army corps, recruited almost exclusively from among prisoners of war. The Czecho-Slovak Brigade especially distinguished itself near Zborow in July, 1917, fighting heroically against vastly superior forces, and taking 4,000 prisoners and a large amount of guns and ammunition. Unfortunately the morale of the Russian troops was already then undermined. The Russians refused to fight, and thus the Czechs, abandoned on both flanks, were compelled to retire.

Some of them were then transported to France, but the bulk, numbering now well over 80,000, remained in Russia. This little army was well trained and disciplined. Its soldiers were all volunteers, with good military experience, educated and full of national ardour and consciousness. Bolshevik propaganda had no effect upon them. They remained determined to fight on for the Allies, from whose victory alone they expect their liberation from the Austrian yoke. Animated by this desire, they kept strict neutrality in all internal Russian disputes. They wanted to assist Russia, but they knew that they could best do so by assisting the Entente's victory. It is true that a few Czechs were involved in the fighting between the Bolsheviks and the Ukrainian Rada at Kiev in January last through a misunderstanding, but all of them were subsequently punished.

When the Bolsheviks came to power and concluded peace with Germany, it was arranged that the Czecho-Slovak Army should leave Russia. Two divisions were to leave Russia immediately, and the rest were to follow. The Bolshevik commander, Muraviev, granted a free passage for these troops through Siberia to Vladivostok on 16 February, and the same has been granted also by the Moscow Soviet. During all this time, up to the end of May, the Czecho-Slovaks were perfectly loyal to the Russian Government. Professor Masaryk rejected every plan directed against the Bolsheviks submitted to him even by such of their adversaries as could not be justly called counter-revolutionaries. He even went so far as to recommend the Allies to be on good terms with the Bolshevik Government, although he himself, of course, never approved of Bolshevik methods and ideas.

Since Russia fell out of the war, and as the Allies have seemed reluctant to undertake armed intervention, the Czecho-Slovaks wished to get *via* Siberia and America to France. At the beginning of March some Czech troops were concentrated near Kiev, on the left bank of the Dnieper, while others were concentrating in Western Siberia, where recruiting from among Czecho-Slovak prisoners was still proceeding. In the middle of April already some Czecho-Slovak detachments (the 5th Regiment, called "Masaryk's Own") reached Vladivostok. About three weeks later, Masaryk himself arrived in America. . . .

[Here follow details of engagements of Czecho-Slovak troops with Bolsheviks.]

There is no doubt that the Czecho-Slovaks have received support from the native population, tired of Bolshevik tyranny. A hopeful sign is also the presence of the troops of Krasnov, Kaledin and Kornilov on the Don, and of Dutov in Ural. As to how far coöperation between these troops and the Czecho-Slovaks will be established remains to be seen. The success with which fortune has favoured the Czecho-Slovaks in Siberia, however, is an encouraging fact which the Allies surely will not fail to exploit in their own, as well as in Russia's, interests. By their courageous enterprise the Czecho-Slovaks have gained for themselves an immortal fame. Let us hope that their success will lead not only to the salvation of Russia, but that it will contribute also towards the triumph of the Allied cause.

(b) *Movement for Czechoslovak Independence*[1]

. . . It seemed to me that the time had now [June, 1918] come to embody the results of everything we had hitherto achieved in the form of a decisive diplomatic document which, from the point of view of international law, would denote the establishment of a State and Government of an independent nation.

This aim was prompted also by our continual endeavour to manage our movement so as to achieve the establishment of a provisional Government before the war had ended, so that we should be actually in existence at the time of the Peace Conference, and thus automatically attend the peace negotiations, not as a section of a defeated State forming the subject of deliberations, but as an Allied nation which had helped to bear the brunt of the war. This was a point which I always emphasized, that we were fighting of our own accord, without guarantees or commitments from the Allies; that we were fighting with our own resources for our independence.

When I survey the details of our political and diplomatic activity abroad during the war, it seems to me that our greatest success lay precisely in the fact that long before the end of the war we managed to achieve full recognition as an Allied and belligerent nation. This proved of enormous advantage to our State as soon as the negotiations for an armistice began, and also later at the Peace Conference.

[1] Eduard Beneš, *My War Memoirs*, Boston, Houghton Mifflin, 1928, pp. 397-399; 407; 416; 440; 441-442; 443; 460-461; 463-464; 485. Reprinted by permission of, and arrangement with, Houghton Mifflin Company.

How great this advantage was can be gauged if we try to imagine what would have happened at the Peace Conference if, the differences of interest and opinion among the Allies being what they were, and in view of the Allied unfamiliarity with conditions in Central Europe, they had negotiated about us and not with us. This danger was particularly great in our case because the whole of our territory was located within the Habsburg Empire. We were thus less favourably situated than the Jugoslavs of Austria-Hungary or the Rumanians of Transylvania with a State behind them, which, when the war ended, would represent and advocate their interests on an internationally legal basis.

The moment which I chose for my negotiations was very favorable. It was the first time that during four years of warfare the Allies were at a decided advantage in the field. The end of July, when I left for London, marked the beginning of the victorious struggle which formed the last momentous episode of the German offensive of March, 1918, and which Marshal Foch regarded as the first step to the military victory of the Allies. In Paris the political circles and all those who had any inside knowledge of the situation breathed a sigh of relief after the second battle of the Marne. . . .

The Foreign Office was thus able to listen to my request at a moment when there was no more doubt that the tide of war had definitely turned in our favour. But the situation was favourable to us in other respects as well. Our troops in Italy had already been engaged at the front, and our French brigade had just been prepared for transfer from Alsace to Gouraud's army in Champagne for the purpose of taking part in the operations on the most difficult sectors of the front. The British Government itself was just negotiating with the Government of the United States and with Japan for the occupation of Siberian territory in the Far East in which Great Britain had special interest. Our army, whose operations were the subject of daily reports in the Press, had gained considerable popularity both for itself and for our cause, and now naturally occupied an important position with the Allied armies also.

Such, then, was the situation, such were my reflections and hopes when, in the last week of June 1918, I called on Mr. Balfour at Downing Street for the second time during the war. . . .

The declaration which, with a special letter from Mr. Balfour, was officially handed to me from the Foreign Office on August 9, 1918, ran as follows:

DECLARATION

Since the beginning of the war the Czechoslovak nation has resisted the common enemy by every means in its power. The Czechoslovaks have constituted a considerable army, fighting on three different battlefields and attempting, in Russia and Siberia, to arrest the Germanic invasion.

In consideration of its efforts to achieve independence, Great Britain regards the Czechoslovaks as an Allied nation, and recognizes the unity of the three Czechoslovak armies as an Allied and belligerent army waging regular warfare against Austria-Hungary and Germany.

Great Britain also recognizes the right of the Czechoslovak National Council as the supreme organ of the Czechoslovak national interest, and, as the present trustee of the future Czechoslovak Government, to exercise supreme authority over this Allied and belligerent army.

A. J. BALFOUR

August 9, 1918

. . . I regard the negotiations which resulted in this declaration as the most important political activity of the National Council during the war. Of all the Allied declarations hitherto, that of Mr. Balfour had the widest scope in its bearings on international law. In this respect it constituted the actual recognition of the independence of our nation (including the Slovaks) while the war was still in progress, and its removal from Austro-Hungarian domination.

. . . matters took a new turn which was of great importance to us. This was the proclamation of the United States Government on September 2, 1918, concerning our liberation movement. This declaration defined our precise position among the Allied States, and solemnly confirmed the assurances which we had received from the European Allies:

WASHINGTON,
September 2, 1918

The Czechoslovak peoples having taken up arms against the German and Austro-Hungarian Empires, and having placed in the field organized armies, which are waging war against those Empires under officers of their own nationality and in accordance with the rules and practices of civilized nations, and Czechoslovaks having in the prosecution of their independence in the present war confided the supreme political authority to the Czechoslovak National Council, the Government of the United States recognizes that a state of belligerency exists between the Czechoslovaks thus organized and the German and Austro-Hungarian Empires.

It also recognizes the Czechoslovak National Council as a *de facto* belligerent Government, clothed with proper authority to direct the military and political affairs of the Czechoslovaks.

The Government of the United States further declares that it is prepared to enter formally into relations with the *de facto* Government thus recognized for the purpose of prosecuting the war against the common enemy, the Empires of Germany and Austria-Hungary.

. . . .

Amid the feverish activity entailed by the organization of the newly recognized State after October 15, 1918, some of the daily papers in Paris published the unexpected news on October 23rd that the Viennese Government had granted permission to the leading Czech politicians to proceed abroad, and even to get in touch with the members of the provisional Czechoslovak Government. At first we could not believe this. We knew, of course, that Austria was in a bad way, and we ourselves had asked for this very step to be taken in Prague, but we had not expected they would allow such a course so soon, and we were therefore not certain what might be behind this decision on the part of the Viennese Government. Later, we ascertained that Vienna, still believing that the Allies were anxious to preserve Austria, hoped that the Entente would bring its influence to bear on the politicians from Prague and on the interim Government at Paris so that the Czechs might be satisfied with autonomy or federalism as a solution of their question. . . . [The delegates from Prague met Beneš and his colleagues in Geneva.]

It seemed to me that on a number of questions the Prague delegates were a little uncertain, and that on the whole they had no very clear idea of our affairs abroad during the war. They were all convinced of the forthcoming collapse of Austria-Hungary. They referred to the desperate economic conditions, the exhaustion of the population, the demoralization of the army, the grim humour prevailing among the Czechs and especially in Prague, the perplexity of Vienna, and the attempts of the Government there to win over the Czech politicians. M. Klofáč told me about his last interview with Karl, from which he discovered that the Emperor's only wish was for everything "to be liquidated peaceably." They all, without exception, however, were alarmed about what might happen at the last moment. M. Habrman expressed this vigorously by saying that, "when the brute was at its last gasp it would lash out and avenge itself on us with terrible butchery." The rest feared that "when breaking point had been reached," German troops would occupy the Czech territories, and that this would be a source of the greatest danger to us. A third serious danger to all consisted of the anarchy of Bolshevism, which was feared not so much among the Czechs, as in Vienna and Budapest. The only remedy lay in rapidly improving the food supplies. . . .

The Prague delegation was so impressed by the documentary and other evidence of what had been achieved by our movement abroad, that on their own initiative they decided to place on record their special recognition of the work done by Masaryk, our troops, and the others who were concerned in our movement. Accordingly, without the knowledge of the Paris delegation, they drew up a statement expressing the sentiments of the nation in this respect. Before my departure to Paris they handed me a signed copy of this manifesto with the request that its contents should be conveyed in a similar form and at the appropriate moment to all those for whom it was intended.

Thus, after having been recognized by the Great Powers, the interim Government at Paris received its final and most important token of recognition from Prague. The unity of our struggle for liberation at home and abroad was in this way solemnly confirmed. . . .

At midday on November 4th a special messenger from the French Foreign Ministry came to the Rue Bonaparte with an official invitation from Pichon for me to attend the plenary meeting of the Supreme War Council which was to be held on the same afternoon at Versailles.

I must confess that I was highly excited when, on the afternoon of November 4th, I took my seat in a motor-car decorated with our flag, and drove through Paris by way of St. Cloud and Sèvres to Versailles. When for the first time I entered the hall at Versailles where all the mighty of this world were assembled—mighty especially at that moment when they were settling the destiny of three Empires in Europe and Asia—and when I took my seat besides Vesnić and Venizelos, I could scarcely believe in the reality of what was happening. Three years previously I had escaped across the frontiers of Bohemia, crawling through the thickets to avoid being seen by the Austrian and Bavarian gendarmes, and staking the whole future on what destiny might bring. Now I was sitting in conference with the representatives of France, Great Britain, United States, Italy, Japan, Serbia, Greece, Belgium, and Portugal, to decide with them as to the fate of the Empires of Wilhelm and Karl, and to sign the terms of their capitulation.

The first meeting on October 31st had been attended only by six States, the four Great Powers (without Japan, which joined the latter meetings), Serbia, and Greece. The proceedings opened with a statement by Marshal Foch on the general situation at the various fronts, in accordance with which the military experts had prepared Armistice conditions to be submitted to the Conference. A discussion on this subject followed immediately, the first topic being the question of an armistice with Austria-Hungary. After certain differences regarding the occupation of Jugoslav areas by the Italian Army, when M. Vesnić expressed his reservation, and acquiesced only after having received an assurance that this arrangement involved no definite commitment with regard to the peace terms, the proposals of the military experts were accepted.

The proceedings continued at the second meeting on November 1st, the subject on this occasion being the Armistice terms for Germany. Belgium also took part in these negotiations. Much of the discussion was concerned with the Allied Note to President Wilson, in which the Allies expressed their two reservations regarding his Fourteen Points, i.e. on the freedom of the seas and on indemnities for areas devastated by the war. . . .

Of the new States, Czechoslovakia was the only one which participated in the Armistice negotiations. Poland was not admitted, and Rumania, although she had resumed hostilities, was also not invited. The Jugoslavs of Austria-Hungary had not yet been recognized as Allies by Italy and the other Great Powers, so that Serbia alone was represented at the Conference. At the meeting on October 31st M. Vesnić raised the question of the recognition of the Austrian Jugoslavs, but in spite of this the Conference took no steps in the matter. From the above account it is clear that we were represented at the Conference on the basis of our juridical recognition and the treaties with the Allies which were signed before the collapse of the Empire. In the interests of historical truth I wish to point out that the events within the Empire and the *coup d'état* at Prague had no influence on this question. This is shown by the examples of the other Austro-Hungarian nationalities, quite apart from the fact that the Allied Governments at that time had no exact information as to the extent of the various upheavals within the Empire, and, from this juridical point of view, did not take them into account. At the meetings themselves not a word was said about the revolutions in Austria-Hungary, and during the discussions concerning the Armistice with Austria the proceedings of the English delegation, for example, were based on the assumption that Vienna might not accept the terms, and that hostilities against Austria would then be continued.

As we shall see, this juridical status of ours was of considerable importance. Our situation was unique and was different from that of the Poles, Rumanians, and Jugoslavs. The Poles were not recognized by the Allies until February, 1919, and the recognition of the Jugoslavs as a unified State was granted only during the signature of the Versailles Peace Treaty. Before our departure from Geneva it had been arranged that I was to transmit the results of our proceedings there not only to the Allies, but also to Masaryk and our military leaders. I also promised to keep in direct touch with Prague, and to supply our people there with the earliest possible news of subsequent events, if necessary, also asking them to communicate their instructions. Having therefore settled the matters connected with the Armistice negotiations, I began to deal with the further points of the Geneva agreement. . . .

On November 20th President Masaryk left New York on his way back to Prague to take up the duties to which the liberated nation had called him. On November 29th he reached England, and spent a few days in London, where he was welcomed as the President of a new State. He took the opportunity of meeting a number of prominent statesmen, such as Mr. Balfour, Mr. Churchill, Lord Milner, Sir Eyre Crowe, Sir William Tyrrell, and others, and then left for Paris, where he arrived on December 7th. Here he visited MM. Poincaré,

Clemenceau, Pichon, and Berthelot, as well as various foreign diplomats, such as Colonel House, Mr. Sharp, Trumbić, Vesnić, Venizelos, Take Jonescu, etc. He remained in Paris for a week. On December 8th he visited our troops at Darney, where they were already preparing to return home. This was at the time when on behalf of the Czechoslovak Government I had participated in the official visit of the French Government to Alsace-Lorraine. After our return to Paris we together went through all the necessary preliminaries to the Peace Conference, and agreed upon our whole procedure. . . .

129. Italo-Jugoslav Agreement, 1918[1]

[After the publication by the Bolshevists of the secret treaty of London, the Jugoslavs in the Austro-Hungarian army fought more zealously against Italy because of the fact that she seemed to be fighting to transfer nearly a million of them to Italian rule. When the harmful consequences of this policy were realized by the Italians, negotiations were begun between Italy and the Jugoslavs which resulted in the "Pact of Rome" of April 1918, which is here given.]

The Resolutions adopted:
The representatives of the nationalities subjected in whole or in part to the rule of Austria-Hungary—the Italians, Poles, Roumanians, Czechs, and Jugo-Slavs—join in affirming their principles of common action as follows:—

1. Each of these peoples proclaims its right to constitute its own nationality and State unity or to complete it and to attain full political and economic independence.

2. Each of these peoples recognises in the Austro-Hungarian Monarchy the instrument of German domination and the fundamental obstacles to the realisation of its aspirations and rights.

3. The assembly recognises the necessity of a common struggle against the common oppressors, in order that each people may attain complete liberation and national unity within a free State unit.

The representatives of the Italian people and of the Jugoslav people in particular agree as follows:—

1. In the relations between the Italian nation and the nation of the Serbs, Croats and Slovenes—known also under the name of the Jugoslav nation—the representatives of the two peoples recognise that the unity and independence of the Jugoslav nation is a vital interest of Italy, just as the completion of Italian national unity is a vital interest of the Jugoslav nation. And therefore the representatives of the two peoples pledge themselves to employ every effort in order that during the war and at the moment of the peace these decisions (*finalità*) of the two nations may be completely attained.

---

[1] *The New Europe*, May 2, 1918, "The Roman Congress of Oppressed Nationalities."

2. They declare that the liberation of the Adriatic Sea and its defence against every present and future enemy is a vital interest of the two peoples.

3. They pledge themselves also in the interest of good and sincere relations between the two peoples in the future, to solve amicably the various territorial controversies on the basis of the principles of nationality and of the right of peoples to decide their own fate, and in such a way as not to injure the vital interests of the two nations, such as shall be defined at the moment of peace.

4. To such racial groups (*nuclei*) of one people as it may be found necessary to include within the frontiers of the other there shall be recognised and guaranteed the right to their language, culture, and moral and economic interests.

130. THE REORGANIZATION OF AUSTRIA-HUNGARY: A MEMORANDUM TO THE DEPARTMENT OF STATE, WASHINGTON[1]

[The conversation notes of George D. Herron, a man who was in confidential communication with Wilson, and whose notes were not unimportant in London and Paris as well, give a glimpse into the situation in Austria-Hungary during that awful period of uncertainty immediately after the armistice had been signed, as the state of affairs was viewed by liberal Austrian statesmen.]

A Visit from Count Windisch-Graetz

Geneva, November 22, 1918

I

I have just received a visit from Count Windisch-Graetz, the last Foreign Minister of the Austro-Hungarian Empire, who very sincerely and impressively set before me his views of the responsibilities resting upon America and England for the reorganization of Europe and the establishment of a permanent peace. Now that we have made ourselves responsible for the destruction of Old Europe, he considers that we cannot escape moral responsibilities for the creation of a Europe that shall be altogether different as well as new.

Personally, Count Windisch-Graetz is a most agreeable and accomplished gentleman. In all that makes up the social amenities and civilities of political intercourse, he differs inconceivably,—as do all Austro-Hungarian politicians and diplomats—from the Germans. Besides that, as a disciple and associate of Professor Lammasch, he was, until the last, an honest and self-sacrificing apostle of Austrian Federalism.

---

[1] Papers of George D. Herron: *Austria*, Document XLIII (Hoover War Library Manuscript).

The Count narrated at considerable length the drama,—the historical tragedy indeed, of the failure of Professor Lammasch and himself
in their program of the New Austria. After the return of Professor
Lammasch from the January conversations with me at the Château
of Dr. Muehlon at Gümligen, and our personal agreement upon the
very Radical program we there discussed,—and which I urged Professor Lammasch to present as imperatively as possible to his Emperor, it seemed, for a few days, as if a great deed were about to be
done—a deed whereby Austria would become the microcosm of the
United States of Europe.

It will be remembered that Professor Lammasch telegraphed that
our conversations and their conclusions had the Emperor's ardent
approval. The program was substantially an adaptation of the Swiss
cantonal system to the six or seven nationalities of the Austrian
Empire, with a plebiscite reserved for the Italian Irredenta, and Trieste
transformed into a free Hanseatic town and port. Under the first
impulse of the report which Professor Lammasch so fervently and
wisely presented, the accordant Emperor asked Count Windisch-
Graetz to prepare a constitution for the new confederation. The Count
had previously prepared the way before Professor Lammasch had
come to Gümligen, by presenting to the Emperor—with all the moral
force he possessed, he said—the necessity of breaking with Germany
and creating the United States of Austria. He told the Emperor,
candidly and insistently, that he must choose between such a course
and the irremediable ruin of Austro-Hungary. It was reconstruction
or dissolution: Kaiser Karl must take the bold and almost Utopian
step proposed or prepare for perdition. In coöperation with Professor
Lammasch, Count Windisch-Graetz wrote a constitution for the expected federation, and the unenacted document is still in writing,
down to the last detail.

But when this constitution was ready for the Emperor's signature
and consequent action, he first asked to reflect for two days; after six
weeks, there was still no answer. Then began a lengthy drama of indecision and vacillation on the part of the Emperor, and treachery and
stupidity on the part of all those about him. One day the Emperor
was under the impulse to sign and decree the constitution—to do
the great deed: the next day, he would defer action; and for six
months this Hamlet-like debate with himself and his ministers proceeded. The opportunity, says Count Windisch-Graetz, was infinitely
greater than the man. It was an action which required the greatest
mental capacity as well as moral heroism; and his Emperor was only
"a poor weak thing," without either mental capacity or adequate
force of character. It was the opportunity that comes once in a
thousand years—an opportunity to change the course of history; and
the man to whom the opportunity came was no match for it.

The tragedy and suffering of those months is written in Count

Windisch-Graetz's face, and the record of the ruin of the Empire is there also.

The great traitor to that opportunity, the Count declares—traitor to his Emperor, to his country and to Europe,—was Czernin.

II

Turning now to the import of this visit, Count Windisch-Graetz expressed some decided opinions as to the Peace Conference and the future of Europe.

A. Having gone as far as we have, America and the Allies cannot compromise as regards the program for the Society of Nations. We must now go the whole length and logic of the liberty we declared ourselves to be fighting for:—it is this or the long ruin of Europe and of modern civilization. We, as well as Germany, must recognize that the Old World is done, and build only according to the pattern of the new. Now that we have proclaimed the right of people to self-disposition, and the principle of free federated nationalities, we must enact these principles throughout the length and breadth of Europe. We must act boldly, without fear or compromise. We have pledged ourselves; the nationalities expect that we keep our pledge; and the results of the war bind us to keep it, and to keep it without grudge or limit.

B. But the basis of this Society of Nations must be freedom of commerce and of intercourse. We must recognize the economic foundations of this Society, and perceive that its only stability, the only certain preventative of war, lies in an inclusive and unrestricted commercial freedom.

Take, for example, the nationalities that formerly composed the Austro-Hungarian Empire; Bohemia is an industrial nation, engaged chiefly in manufacture which requires an abundance of iron. The iron which Bohemia uses comes from German-Austria; the coal which German-Austria must have comes from Bohemia; the wheat upon which they both depend comes from Hungary; the meat which they all consume is largely a Serbian product; other products must come entirely from Galicia and Roumania. If the Society of Nations establishes freedom of commercial intercourse between all these new nations —running up to fifteen or twenty in number, perhaps, before we are done with our recognitions—each can maintain its own political integrity, each live its own life, and all can dwell together in fraternal or even federal relations.

Count Windisch-Graetz agreed that until Germany had paid her just debt for the ruin she had inflicted upon France, Belgium, Serbia, Roumania and Russia, she must be placed in a separate economic or commercial category. She would have to earn her right to free commercial intercourse with the rest of the world, by her manifest repentance and by the full reparation for the wrongs she had done, ere she could be considered fit for membership in the family of nations.

C. But Count Windisch-Graetz was emphatic upon this point—that, in the first instance, the Allies will be forced to decide upon the exterior and to arrange the interior affairs of all these new nationalities, except the Czecho-Slovaks. These people will never agree with each other, nor ever agree among themselves. Such agreement is rendered psychologically impossible by their past history and by their present mentality. It is absurd and perilous to expect them to form stable interior governments or to arrive at mutual concord. The Allies will be obliged to take them in hand and impose upon them the conditions of their existence in the near future. If left to themselves there is nothing but unimaginable anarchy awaiting Europe.

Such is the conviction the Count expresses with greatest earnestness, and which conviction he would lay upon the Allies as the moral and political responsibility which they prepare themselves to assume.

D. So far as German-Austria is concerned, it is only a very small section or party, consisting of those who are called the Old Germans, that desires union with Germany. For the people of German-Austria as a whole, such a union is altogether undesirable: to most Austrians, it is even repulsive, and would be accepted only as a last resort. German-Austrians prefer to constitute themselves an independent state and at last have a chance to live their own political life. Most of them are glad to be rid of the burden and worry that have gone with their dominion over the contending nationalities. They want a chance now to have and to be a real Austria. If they can be assured of commercial freedom, this is the course they will most decidedly take. They will be content to be free of the Slavs, and to pursue their own interior development.

E. As to Hungary, the home of Count Windisch-Graetz, the problem is more difficult. But even here, the difficulties can be removed by free commercial intercourse. If the strictly Hungarian race is to form a state of its own—the Yougo-Slavs and Roumanians and Slovaks taken away—then Hungary must be free to sell her agricultural products to the manufacturing and commercial nations. For Hungarians are altogether an agricultural people, inhabiting a vast and fertile plain, with neither opportunity nor materials for becoming a manufacturing people.

So far as the present so-called Republican or Soviet Government of Hungary is concerned, Count Windisch-Graetz considers that it has no basis or value at all. Count Karolyi is playing with the Bolsheviki, and the new Government consists of a mere handful of men in Budapest, most of them Jews. The people of Budapest tolerate the new order, for the moment, because they have no idea what their future is to be: they do not know how to formulate a program until the Peace Conference has reached some decision. The majority of the peasants are pursuing their way quite ignorant of any change in Budapest.

The great menace to Hungary, as to all the nationalities, is that of a Bolshevist era of plunder, destruction and assassination. It is therefore urgent that Hungary, as well as all the nationalities, know what to expect at the earliest possible moment. The Peace Conference should proceed with the utmost rapidity and precision. All the nations are at a standstill, waiting for the decision of the Conference, and this time of waiting is the golden hour of opportunity for the Bolshevists.

F. Count Windisch-Graetz agrees that the situation in Berlin is critical and ominous. The Emperor has not really abdicated. The armistice was signed by men of insufficient authority—men who can easily be repudiated should an occasion arise that makes repudiation seem promising. The old military régime is still in power, with von Hindenburg as popular and authoritative as ever. The party of Scheidemann is merely a mask for the industrial magnates and the Junkers. Count Windisch-Graetz does not see any sign of a change of mind or manners in the Germany which centres in Berlin.

But he does see a centre of hope in Munich. The new Bavarian Government constitutes, he affirms, the very best that Germany can produce, and is the only centre of hope among the German peoples.

G. Munich and Prague, the Count opines, are the two possible citadels that may withstand the Bolshevist tide. But these two are the only centres of hope in all Europe east of the Rhine. He believes it would be the highest wisdom on the part of the Allies to effect some immediate connection or quasi-alliance with the Bavarian Government, and to place almost unlimited responsibility in the hands of the Czecho-Slovaks, whom he regards as possessing the greatest political capacity of any peoples of Middle or Eastern Europe.

III

Altogether, I was deeply impressed with the words and the manner of the Count. He wrought earnestly and long for a new and federal Austria, he says; and he fought in the trenches against the Allies for three years, always hoping that there would come a time when the states of the Austrian Empire would become the basis of a New Europe. But now the Allies have prevailed, and the Central Empires are in ruin.

But the Count makes no plea for Austro-Hungary: the Empire is ended, he perceives, and ended forever. And it is by the hand of Germany the immedicable ruin was wrought. He is therefore far from wishing any consideration for Germany; he wishes only that the Allies complete the destruction of Germanism, and makes no compromise with the Old Régime.

Windisch-Graetz looks only onward, now; no backward-looking eyes are his. He is consequently urgent that the whole program of President Wilson be carried out, in its full logic without compromise. And he himself would willingly work and sacrifice to that end. There is no choice, he is convinced, between a Europe of entirely free nationalities, based upon economic freedom, united in the Society of Nations, and constituting indeed a world that would seem to the old diplomats a veritable Utopia, or to the early Christians an approach to the kingdom of heaven—there is no choice, he swears, between this, and a Bolshevist régime throughout the Continent, resulting in an unimaginable débâcle of civilization and of all that makes life of men worth while.

Respectfully submitted,

(sgd) George D. Herron

131. A German Discussion of the League of Nations[1]

[When the Germans saw that the end must come shortly, their thoughts turned toward the type of international government which might be set up in Europe and from which they might expect to obtain security. The prophecy here given to the effect that the League of Nations would be a victors' association did not go wrong.]

Propaganda in Germany for a league of nations has been active for a long time. All the social democrats, and the free thinkers, and some of the center, especially Mr. Erzberger, advocate this. Erzberger has published a book on the league of nations which it seems is to determine the policy of the new government. This skillful propaganda has created an impression among a great many people that if Germany entered a league of nations all its troubles will be over, that we can make any concessions with indifference that, under other circumstances, we would have considered as vital as our life and honor, if a league of nations is to be formed. We must warn our readers most emphatically against such ideas. Otherwise they are doomed to a sad disillusion.

A league of nations under the conditions now prevailing is a purely Anglo-Saxon institution. It is a plan for bringing all the nations of the world under Anglo-Saxon control and to leave it in the power of these ruling governments to discriminate in the treatment of the different members. The Anglo-Saxon powers would have the means to enforce their will and moreover the 14 points proposed by Wilson and endorsed by Great Britain are so elastic in interpretation that those two countries can make them mean anything they want to.

Furthermore, the future league of nations will be made up mostly of countries imbued with bitter hate of Germany. It is inconceivable and incredible that so many people should fancy that the minute the war ceases France and Italy and Great Britain and the United States

---

[1] *Hamburger Nachrichten,* Oct. 12, 1918 (Victor S. Clark translation). Reprinted with the permission of the *Hamburger Nachrichten.*

will be inspired suddenly with friendly feeling for the German government. We can be quite assured that the contrary will be true and the result will be that Germany will be the abused slave of the league of nations compelled to put up with any treatment that may come to it.

132. Berne International Resolution Concerning a League of Nations[1]

[Having had experience with "capitalist" national governments, the Socialist International at Berne expressed the hope that through the international government that was in the process of being formed justice as understood by this body might be realized. The *Arbeiter Zeitung* is a Viennese Socialist paper.]

The union of the people in an international society has always been one of the loftiest ideals of the Socialist International. This ideal is in harmony with the solidarity of the proletariat of all countries and also with the final purpose of socialism, which can be realized, not by national, but only by international action. The world war has made this socialist ideal of society of nations one of the most urgent demands of the present, even for public men who are not socialists. It is proved that the high technical development of the military art and of communication make it probable that every war will speedily convert the world into two hostile camps which will fight each other with the most cruel resources and methods at their disposal until utter exhaustion. The late war brought the world to the border of the abyss. The next war will completely destroy it, and even preparations for such a war imperil the safety of human society. The only way of avoiding this calamity will be to create a community of nations. This community should be established through popular representation from every country.

As a basis for such a league of nations, we must have a just peace which does not contain within its provisions the seeds of new international conflicts. The governments composing the league of nations must be based upon free determination of their own people. All members of the community in performing its functions, and such races and peoples as have not yet attained the right of self-determination must be protected until they prove competent to become members of the league of governments.

The first task of the league should be to prevent new wars and new armament. It must create institutions that by mediation and arbitration shall prevent controversies between governments or settle them, and this procedure must be applied also to cases which involve so-called vital questions and questions of honor. The league court must have authority to make changes of frontiers at any time at the request of the people affected, if such seem advisable. The league of

[1] *Arbeiter Zeitung,* Feb. 6, 1919 (Victor S. Clark translation).

nations should abolish standing armies and bring about the complete disarmament of nations. So long as the relations between governments require the existence of armed force, that force shall be under the control of the league of nations. The league of nations must have authority and power to impose economic pressure, to enforce compliance with its judgment, in case of necessity. Customs tariffs shall be subject to the approval of the league of nations. The league shall have direct control of international highways and routes of communication. The league must be authorized and empowered to create such organs as are necessary in order to control and regulate the production and distribution of food and raw materials throughout the world, in order to increase production to the greatest possible extent. Among the powers and obligations of a league of nations shall be the enactment, development, and enforcement of international laws.

A league of nations formed at the present time will be created under pressure of the results of war. Such a league will not develop its full efficiency until later when the pressure is removed, and will not completely attain its great purpose unless the international proletariat throws its whole weight and influence behind it. The more powerful the proletariat agitation in every country the more conscious the proletariat is of its international functions, the more resolutely it opposes all imperialistic movement within its own government, the more it endeavors to bring about a socialist constitution of society and to strengthen the international, the more powerfully, effectively and beneficially the league of nations will be able to perform its functions.

133. An Account of the Work of the Commission for Relief in Belgium by Herbert Hoover[1]

[The Commission for Relief in Belgium was started in October, 1914, as a purely philanthropic enterprise, but later sought and received financial support from the Belgian, British, French, and at a later time from the American Governments. Although it was never incorporated, it carried on a tremendously large business, operating a large fleet of ocean-going vessels, another one of canal boats, having a system of railway transportation, running mills and factories, and even going so far as to provide its ships with its own flag and as to issue passports—a governmental function. The following summary of its activities was written in 1921 by the Chairman of the Commission, Herbert Hoover.]

These statements presented by the auditors represent their summation of the financial operations of the Commission during the six years, from September, 1914, to September, 1920. The detailed ac-

---

[1] The Foreword of *Bulletin: The Commission for Relief in Belgium: Balance Sheet and Accounts*, March, 1921.

counting information covering over 4,000 branch offices of the relief organization will require several volumes for publication and, with the slender resources available, some years may be needed for their issuance.

The great moral responsibility for full accounting was realized by the Commission from its first day. Therefore the precaution was taken to engage one of the leading international firms to audit every ramification of expenditure and receipts, and to make doubly sure they were also engaged to undertake the unusual task of themselves actually keeping the books and furnishing their own accounting staff at all principal branches.

The Commission was born as a purely philanthropic enterprise, dependent upon the charity of the world for support, conceived as a few months' emergency service to defend 10,000,000 people from certain starvation. However, it became evident that the war was not a struggle of months but of years, and that if these 7,500,000 people in Belgium, 2,500,000 in Northern France were to survive, it must be accomplished by much broader operation than public charity. The Commission, therefore, sought and ultimately received financial support from the Belgian, French, British, and later the American Government. These official advances were, by consent of the Belgian and French Governments, debited to them and were finally placed in the Reparations settlement for preferred payment under the indemnity. The organization thus rapidly grew to a great economic engine with an annual budget of over $400,000,000 in all its different ramifications inside and outside of the invaded regions. Carrying on its operations with the moral support of the neutral powers, it came to have many attributes of a government in itself, possessing an agreed immunity from the restrictions placed by belligerent powers during the war, flying its own flag, issuing its own passports, operating a large fleet of ocean vessels, owning and operating a great number of canal boats, extending its offices into many countries, requisitioning the native food supplies, rationing the entire population, making full provision for the destitute, operating mills, factories and transportation, and, in fact, engaged in maintaining the whole economic cycle of a nation.

An understanding of the accounts requires some conception of the method of the organization. A primary division in operations was established between the provisioning of the population and the care of the destitute. The basic theory of administration was to erect a system of food supply with all of its train of handling agencies, stretching from the interior of the United States, the Argentine, Australia, India, and other great food centers, focusing into Rotterdam with a distribution through chains of primary and secondary warehouses, ultimately, through a ration card, reaching to the individual family, which paid for the food supplied at fixed prices. Destitution grew rapidly under the occupation and, of the 10,000,000 people, fully 5,000,000 were wholly or partially destitute before the end of the war. A separate branch of administration was organized for the care of these destitute, giving them assistance to purchase ration cards and by charitable public eating and clothing establishments. Their needs necessarily extended further afield than the provision of imported food and clothing —because bare living requirements necessitated supplies of native foodstuffs, fuel, light, shelter, medical care, as well. The provisioning side was organized in the form of a commercial enterprise, transferring its cash receipts to the benevolent side of the administration for the use of the destitute. This plan of division greatly simplified the accounting and gained the administrative values of a separate personnel more adapted on one hand to commercial administration and on the other to charitable work. It further made possible the exaction of a small profit from the sale of food to those who could afford it, and thus swelled the resources of the benevolent branch.

The whole plan of organization was a continuous chain of decentralization. Purchasers were decentralized into overseas branches. Shipping control was directed from London. Transportation inland to primary warehouses was directed from Rotterdam. A committee was erected in each of the ten Belgian Provinces and six French districts, which may be compared to a wholesale distribution. These committees in turn supplied 4,500 Communal Committees which may be compared to retail distribution, they issuing food under the ration cards issued on a family basis and to the public eating places for certain classes of destitute. The rations were sold for cash by the Communal Committees, who in turn paid cash to the Regional Committees; the Regional Committees paid cash to the National Committees at Brussels and Lille, and these cash receipts were transferred to the benevolent side.

Three methods were employed in benevolent organization. First, existing charitable institutions were supported and, in the case of children, were extended to cover the whole child life of the country. Second, certain professions and trades were assisted to care for the members of their professions. Third, benevolent committees were set up in each Commune for the conduct of public eating places together with provision of ration cards to the destitute, and to supervise other agencies and for the care of those not otherwise reached. Overlaid upon the whole structure were a series of checks and balances to determine the truth as to destitution, to maintain the morale and efficiency of the administration and honesty in accounting.

Thus, keeping in mind this organization, it will be found that the C. R. B. accounts proper show debits to the National Committee at Brussels and Lille for the value of commodities furnished to them and show credits for the amounts allotted to them for benevolent purposes. At this point ends the actual balance sheet of the C. R. B. The National Committees, under the direction and as the agent of the C. R. B., in turn debited commodity values to the Regional and Provincial Committees and credited them with benevolent allowances, and at this point ends the accounting of the National Committees. Again, the Provincial

District and Regional Committees set up the same accounting relation with the Communes. And over the whole the C. R. B. maintained an audit and also maintained membership in the whole committee structure of these organizations which acted as agents of the commission. In later years, the native food supply had to be requisitioned and to be impressed into the system of distribution. These forced purchases were carried out by the Communal Committees for the account of the Provincial and District Committees and where a proven surplus in a given commodity existed in the hands of Regional Committees, it sold its surplus to neighboring Provinces upon the direction of the central organization. Thus, the purchases of native food supplies do not reflect into the C. R. B. balance sheet, although they represent an expenditure of probably $400,000,000. If time and funds permit, a balance sheet of all branch offices will be consolidated and will be of interest from a historical point of view showing gross purchase and sale of foods and clothing of upwards of $1,300,000,000 during the period of operations.

In the balance sheets are shown certain residues of funds remaining in the hands of the relief organization, accruing as a final balance after provision had been made for the care of the destitute. These final residues of funds have been applied at the request of the Belgian and French Governments to the provision of extended foundations for charitable work, to be maintained as a memorial of American help in the time of need offered through the Commission for Relief in Belgium.

The principal officers of the Commission gave their services without salary and in many instances paid the whole of their own incidental and traveling expenses as well. Shipping firms, accountants, insurance agencies, buying agencies, throughout the world gave their services without charge otherwise than the mere out-of-pocket incidentals. The distributing committees of over 55,000 members gave their voluntary services over these many years. 40,000 Belgian and French women dedicated themselves to the saving of the child life of their nations. Never was there greater pressure for economy and efficiency upon an organization.

At no time were the population fed to more than the point of bare subsistence. Every penny saved meant larger food supplies and less suffering. At no time were the finances of the Commission certain for more than a few months, and at different periods its liabilities were in excess of its actual or prospective assets, and the continuous food supply was only maintained through the personal guarantees of the directors and their friends. The total administrative expenditure was held down to less than one-half of one per cent., (exactly 42/100 of 1%) of the entire operation. The record of economy may be extended even further than this, for the changing tides of war often required the diversion of cargoes and sales of foodstuffs outside of Belgium to meet emergency readjustment of purchases or supplies whose shipment or distribution had already been arranged. Upon these and similar transactions entirely outside of Belgium and France a balance of profit of over nine and one-half million dollars was earned, several times greater than all overhead expenditures. From these profits on outside operations the Commission, first, paid its entire administration and overhead expenses; second, paid over to the Benevolent Department some $2,600,000 for charitable distribution in Belgium and France; and third, as at 30th September 1920, still held available for Relief work in those countries and to meet the expense of Liquidation approximately $3,120,000—since that date largely distributed. The economy of operation in the organization has, in fact, even a higher standard of test than this, in that the average prices maintained for food supplies in this occupied territory during the entire period of war will show from 15 to 20 per cent. less than the prices in the Allied countries at the same periods.

No set of accounts or figures can reflect the intense anxiety, the patience and skill required of the 55,000 volunteers who toiled in this complex agency, defending ten million lives. Inspired with humane sympathy for these people, who, having no responsibility for the war, suffered most from its hardships and barbarities, they labored that this service might be done efficiently and with economy. It is due to their unflagging devotion that we are now able to publish exact figures of accountability for funds, and to trace each ton of food from the place of purchase to the ultimate consumer among the civil population of the invaded regions. Surrounded by terror and suffering this multitude had but little concern for the bookkeepers in the back rooms of the 4,000 branch offices of the relief organization. It was of the utmost concern, however, to those in official direction, not only that the work might be effectively performed and presented to the world, but that our honor and the honor of our country in this trusteeship should never be challenged.

HERBERT HOOVER,
Chairman

New York, 1st March, 1921

PART IV

THE SETTLEMENT

1919–1920

134. ORGANIZATION OF THE PEACE CONFERENCE[1]

[Clive Day was the Chief of the Balkan Division of the American Commission to Negotiate Peace.]

The responsible directors of the Powers at war with Germany had realized from the beginning that a study of the terms of peace could not profitably be made in a debating society. Some of the Powers, for example those of Central America, had made contributions so slight and had interests so little affected, that they would certainly not be asked to share in the preliminary deliberations. Some of the Great Powers must as certainly be included. At what point was the line to be drawn? It could readily be seen that France, England, Italy, and the United States would recognize no superior. Was Belgium or Serbia or Japan to be grouped with them above the others? The decision finally announced by the four major Powers, that they would choose but one additional associate, Japan, inevitably gave rise to heart-burnings, and had a material effect on the terms of settlement. It recognized the practical political influence of Japan and neglected such ideal measures as are expressed in national spirit and sacrifice. At least it allowed the Conference to proceed. Two months had passed since the armistice was signed, and the American delegation had already been waiting a month for the beginning of organized business.

The organ of the Conference thus established by informal negotiation of the great Powers was termed the Council, and followed the model of the Supreme Inter-allied War Council that had been acting on matters of military policy at Versailles during the last part of the war. Two representatives of each of the five great Powers, normally the premier and the foreign minister, composed the body and hence it came to be known as the Council of Ten. For more than two months (January 13 to March 25), the Council was recognized as the official source of authority of the Conference. It called the Plenary Assembly into being, regulated the activities, and when it saw fit reviewed the action of that body. It created commissions to study special subjects in detail and prepare them for the consideration of the Conference. It had to face the questions of fact and policy that rose constantly in central and eastern Europe.

As was to be anticipated, the Council was a somewhat formal body. It conducted itself with the ceremony and solemnity which the world would expect of such a gathering. It had a meeting-place worthy of

[1] Clive Day. "The Atmosphere and Organization of the Peace Conference" in House and Seymour, Editors, *What Really Happened at Paris*. N. Y., Scribners, 1921, pp. 16-28. Reprinted with the permission of Clive Day.

its dignity, in the study of the French foreign minister in the palace on the Quai d'Orsay. Double doors on the side entrance prevented the escape of any sound; high windows on the opposite side looked out on a formal lawn, often drenched with rain or covered with snow. Within, all was luxurious comfort. At one end of the room, with his back to an open fire of great logs, sat the presiding officer, Clemenceau, and near him his colleague Pichon; ranged at little tables on their right and facing them were the other delegates; on their left were secretaries and a place where might be stationed officials or representatives who had to address the Council. A second row of chairs about the room gave a place in the background for special secretaries of the different Powers, and for experts who might thus be readily consulted by their principals. Altogether there might be thirty individuals, more or less, in the room.

Much of the business which occupied the attention of the Council was formal in character. The smaller states, excluded from its deliberations, demanded at least the opportunity to present to it their claims, and many hearings were granted to their representatives. Every one knew that the arguments and facts which they stated would soon be printed, and would be turned over for study to specialists, who would sift them critically and so prepare them for the consideration of the principal representatives. Every one recognized the extravagance and unreality of many of the nationalist demands. To illustrate the artificiality of these proceedings may be cited the occasion on which the claims of Albania to national independence were put before the Council. The Albanians are a people apart, who for centuries have lived a free life in their wild country, and to the present day have preserved the virtues and defects of a primitive population. Their spokesman before the Council was a broken-down old Turk who had no interest in Albania, who enjoyed no respect or following there, who got his place at Paris because he was willing to sacrifice the aspirations of the Albanians to the ambitions of Italy to extend her power across the Adriatic. He read from a manuscript which had doubtless been prepared for him, and with the contents of which he was certainly not familiar, for he stopped long at every page until he could find the continuation of his sentence on the next. The reading was lifeless, it seemed interminable. "How much longer is this going on?" asked one of the American plenipotentiaries, very audibly, of the interpreter. And all this took place while almost hourly reports were coming in of war, famine, and pestilence in stricken Europe, and while the people of northern Albania itself were fighting a desperate struggle against the harsh Serbs. Surely no greater contrast is conceivable than that between the idle words which filled M. Pichon's luxurious study in the palace on the Quai d'Orsay and the grim reality of life in the mountains of High Albania, where people were being massacred by thousands.

Such scenes as this appeared, to those who were on the spot as well as to those who viewed them from a distance, unprofitable, but they appeared inevitable. The truth is that people demanded of the Conference something of a show. Even though the meetings of the Council were supposed to be secret sessions, and though the subjects considered and action taken were announced to the public, if at all, only by brief and formal statements, still it was some satisfaction to an aspirant people to know that its representatives had appeared before the Council, to be able later to read the arguments and claims that had been advanced, and to hear something of the manner of their reception.

For spectacles, such as those indicated, the Council was very well fitted. The spectacular, however, is always superficial, and when the Council was called upon for more substantial action, for definite policies, and for vigorous decisions, its weakness became apparent. A survey of the more serious kinds of work which the Conference was called upon to do will make more clear the reasons for a change in its organization.

Some of the questions which came before it for decision did not admit delay. When the term of the armistice expired, the Council must fix the conditions on which it was to be renewed. Marshal Foch was summoned to describe the military situation, and to propose arrangements which would safeguard the interests of the Allies. Throughout central and eastern Europe armies were still in the field, engaged in formal war; the Council must define its attitude toward the interests which they represented, must seek to curb the fighting and to stabilize the political situation. The revolution in Russia presented a whole complex of problems. The Powers found themselves in a labyrinth, in which, turn and twist as they might, they found always the path to the outlet blocked before them. Revolution in Hungary added to their difficulties. Constantly, moreover, they must seek to further the work of salvaging what could be saved from the wreck of Europe. Mr. Hoover would appear before the Council with proposals for relief which involved intricate questions of shipping and finance and raised often also questions of a military and political kind.

The work of the Council cannot be appreciated justly without recognizing the burden of the administrative duties which were imposed upon it. Assembled to draw up terms of peace, it found itself still in the midst of war, and faced by conditions which demanded active treatment if society were to be saved from dissolution. Whether it would or not it had for a time to attempt to govern a large part of Europe, managing affairs which in a modern state are handled by organized departments of foreign affairs, of war, of commerce, of finance. According to general opinion the Council managed this administrative business rather badly. Indeed, there would be occasion for surprise if it had succeeded; even the Council of Four later did not achieve a notable success in this part of its work. Whatever be the critic's judgment on the Conference as an executive he will be unjust if he estimates the merit of its more permanent contributions without taking into account the strain upon its attention of his current business, which constantly distracted it from constructive work.

Besides the questions coming before the Council demanding administrative action, it had, if it were to reach a settlement, to determine problems of two kinds, namely, problems of fact and problems of policy. The principles of settlement had been enunciated by the President, and, with certain modifications, had been accepted both by the Allied Powers and by the Central Powers. Most of these principles, however, were expressed in general terms. Agreement upon them enabled the Powers to stop fighting, but did not enable them to draw up definite terms of peace. What did the President mean, for example, when he said that "a readjustment of the frontiers of Italy should be effected along clearly recognizable lines of nationality?" What *were* these lines, which for an indefinite future were to fix the boundaries of Italy and of neighboring states? The President himself would certainly have refused to define them, if he had been asked to draw them on a map. He would have done as he did later when the question of the Armenian frontiers was referred to him for settlement. He would have assembled experts, whose competence and impartiality he trusted, would have told them to study the region and to draw the best line they could, and when he had satisfied himself by discussion and reflection that this line was the best, he would have proposed it for acceptance.

Even this process would have involved not only a determination of the facts in the region in question, but also a decision on questions of policy. Rarely does a single line present all the advantages of a perfect frontier. Even if nationality be made the only criterion, rarely are the lines of nationality so "clearly recognizable" that they may be said to draw themselves, and still more rarely will such lines, if drawn, satisfy the other desiderata expressed or implied in the President's addresses of a just and lasting peace. A decision on the merits of alternative frontiers involves not merely a knowledge of details, but also a judgment on the relative importance of different human interests, and a prophetic insight into the future of man's development.

If it be difficult for a single individual, supplied with all available knowledge and power, to reach a decision in a matter of this kind, imagine how much the difficulty is intensified when several individuals must agree upon the decision, when each has his individual standard of judgment, when some have views which to the others seem clouded or distorted by individual interests. If agreement is to be reached in these circumstances, it will almost certainly be by a process of compromise, in which A yields his position at one part of the frontier, to get the adherence of B to his line at another part, or A yields his line entire in one part of the world, to get B to accept his line in a distant region. This process of barter is, of course, offensive to the idealist. When the result is analyzed in detail many perversions of justice will appear. The result must be judged as a whole, if it is to be judged fairly. And the critic must also consider not whether the actual decision is as good as one which he might propose, but whether it is better than no decision at all.

For the determination of matters of fact the Council of Ten was manifestly ill adapted. It lacked the technical preparation and intimate acquaintance with detail which were needed for the effective investigation of facts in the many parts of its great field. The Council of Ten proved also unfitted to settle the serious questions of policy, which involved both its administrative and its legislative functions. It could not follow a definite plan in dealing with Russian problems, and it could not clear the way for a settlement of the fundamental territorial and economic problems, until the great Powers had arrived at a common understanding on the issues in which there was grave divergence of view. M. Pichon's study offered a noble setting for a spectacle, but considered as an office for the conduct of practical business it was a failure.

There were too many people in the room. Secretaries and specialists served a useful purpose in the eyes of their principals, but to the eyes of the principals of other countries they appeared as a crowd of hangers-on, unknown to them personally, possibly dishonest or indiscreet, before whom the principals were not inclined to discuss delicate questions with the entire candor that the situation demanded.

There were too many states represented in the Council. The Japanese delegates were diligent in attendance, and, (unlike some others) kept their eyes open, however tedious were the proceedings. When a territorial question was under discussion they peered at their maps with inscrutable gravity. One never knew, however, whether their maps were right side up, and one felt pretty certain, anyway, that it made no difference whether they were or not. The Japanese were not interested in the European questions that composed most of the business. Nor were the Italians equally concerned in all parts of the field. Keenly, sometimes passionately, interested in questions that touched Italy directly, they were complaisant and sometimes almost indifferent when the topic was remote.

There were too many delegates apportioned to each state. The panel system allowed substitutions and a shifting membership, by which individuals were granted the compliment of a seat at the Council, but by which the compactness and the continuity of the Council itself were impaired. Normally the chief of each state was accompanied to the Council meetings by his foreign minister. The arrangement assumed an equality of the two officials which did not in fact exist. The comparison involves no question of the actual merit and ability of the foreign ministers. Sonnino was probably a stronger man than his principal, Orlando, more determined than he to press Italian demands, and certainly better equipped for the business in that he could urge his claims in French or English with equal facility. "Which language shall I speak?" he inquired on one occasion; "it is all the same to me." Balfour appeared, unfortunately, to think that he shared this advantage, but even when he talked French, he presented ideas that were always interesting, if they sometimes inclined to the abstract and doctrinaire. It was a pleasure to hear him analyze and criticize the notion of "autonomy," when that vague concept had crept into the discussion. No one could surpass Lansing in the logic and force with which he could present a legal argument. But ability, even first-rate ability, did not count when it was in the second place in the delegation. Lansing might convince every one else in the room, but if he did not convince Wilson, who had given him his place and who himself was (in the words of the treaty) "acting in his own name and by his own proper authority," his argument profited nothing; it hindered, rather than helped, the progress of deliberation. An observer got the impression that in fact the principal representatives of the American and British delegations were less open to suggestions from their foreign ministers than to those that came from any other source; they appeared openly to resist any appearance of dependence on their colleagues. As to Clemenceau, he did not allow the existence of Pichon to inconvenience him in the slightest degree; he used him and abused him without any recognition of the distinction.

The Council of Ten recognized early that it was not qualified to investigate the intricate facts which underlay most of its problems. Within a fortnight after its opening session it began therefore to establish special commissions, to which it referred questions as they arose, for preliminary study and report. For example, after hearing the claims advanced by the Rumanian representative the Council voted: "The questions raised by the declarations of M. Bratianu on the territorial interests of the Rumanians in the Peace Settlement shall be referred for examination, in the first instance, to a committee of specialists composed of two delegates for each of the following Powers: the United States of America, the British Empire, France, and Italy. The duty of this committee will be to study the questions to be settled, to condense them in as narrow limits as possible and to propose a solution for an equitable settlement. This committee may hear representatives of the peoples concerned."

The advantage of this process, by which the supreme organ of the Conference was relieved of the preliminary processes of investigation and discussion, and could devote itself to the decision of the larger questions, was obvious. Commissions grew rapidly in number. According to the calculation of André Tardieu, fifty-two of them were at work before the treaty with Germany was signed, and these fifty-two commissions held, altogether, one thousand six hundred and forty-six sessions. Dispersed and secluded, these commissions attracted in general little attention. They had no proper authority except that of recommendation. They had, in fact, immense influence on the outcome of the

Conference. Without them the terms of peace would certainly have been very different, if indeed they could have been written at all.

Some of these commissions were intrusted with questions so important that their contributions to the settlement appear positively greater than those of the Council of Ten itself. At the head of the list comes, of course, the commission on the League of Nations. The body which formulated the Covenant of the League had a membership which (unlike that of the Council) was not fixed by any official convention, but was determined by a more personal standard. Under the presidency of Wilson it reached out to include great men of the small Powers, such as Venizelos of Greece and Dmowski of Poland, and men who are recognized as intellectual and moral leaders in the greatest empires, like Lord Robert Cecil, General Smuts, and Léon Bourgeois. If the opinions of those who believe in the future of the League of Nations are to be trusted, the work done by this commission in its sessions at the Hotel Crillon, is destined to be more fruitful, if at the time it seems less decisive, than that accomplished by any other organ of the Conference. Another commission, whose work was essentially constructive, was that on International Legislation on Labor, including such representative spokesmen on the broad and difficult problems that it covered as Gompers of the United States, Barnes of England, and Vandervelde of Belgium. Other commissions studied the reform of international commercial relations, in the case of customs tariffs, shipping regulations, waterways, and railroads. Every student of the history of commerce knows how seriously the world has suffered from the perversions of policy in these matters, and will recognize in the lists of members of the commissions some of the names of those most competent to initiate reform.

Two commissions, those on reparations and on financial questions, occupy a place apart by reason of the peculiar gravity of the questions intrusted to them. Some of the ablest men in banking and in business, some leaders from the academic and some from the official world, were associated in these commissions in the endeavor to determine the damages inflicted on the people of the Allied countries in the war, to decide upon the measure and means of reparation, and to manage the financial questions that were incidental to the restoration of peace. Finally, a whole group of commissions was established to study the territorial questions involved in the peace settlement, with a central committee above them to correlate their work. To these territorial commissions the European states contributed mainly men trained in their foreign offices and in their diplomatic corps; the British Government complimented some of its colonial premiers with seats, and the United States was ordinarily represented by college professors, and the like, who, as members of The Inquiry, had been studying the special questions with a view to the eventual discussion of terms of peace.

135. An Account of the Meetings of the League of Nations Commission[1]

[In 1919 David Hunter Miller was legal adviser in the American Commission to Negotiate Peace. He took an important part in the drafting of the Covenant of the League of Nations, and his account of the proceedings of the League of Nations Commission is authoritative.]

At this point I may give some of my impressions of the meetings as a whole. The discussions were in English and in French. During the first few meetings there were oral translations of the speeches, but this took considerable time, and subsequently interpreters sat behind Delegates who did not understand both languages, and translated as the speeches were made. Thus, Major Bonsal sat behind the President and Colonel House and translated the French to them. Generally speaking the proceedings were most informal. No one rose to speak, although the President was standing during his opening address. The account of the meetings afterwards gotten up by Mr. Shepardson is quite correct as far as it goes. I took some notes generally of the meetings, though not of the first meeting, but my notes are of quite a fragmentary character. While my duties were not expressly defined, I understood them to be of an advisory character, particularly in respect of any question of Constitutionality, and it was accordingly necessary that I should follow the discussions with a care that prevented the taking of notes. I never found difficulty in following discussions in French. In any event, the rather informal nature of the discussions made the taking of notes difficult and in some cases it was even quite difficult with the utmost care to determine the precise language of an amendment which was adopted without dissent, for the language would be read to the meeting and agreed to and discussion commenced of another Article or of a subsequent part of the same Article before it was possible to write down the full language of the amendment. Even after the secretariat was appointed there was considerable difficulty in this regard, although in every case the exact language was finally obtained. In one instance I recall I had to inquire of the President after the close of the meeting as to precisely his understanding of what had been done, and his understanding as stated to me was adopted by the Secretariat as the action of the meeting, although none of the members of the Secretariat had been able to grasp definitely what it was.

The President and Colonel House always spoke in English, although it can hardly be said that Colonel House spoke at all. He never ad-

---

[1] David Hunter Miller, *My Diary at the Conference of Paris with Documents.* Printed for the author by the Appeal Printing Company. "Memorandum regarding the Covenant," Vol. I, pp. 350-355. Reprinted with the permission of David Hunter Miller.

dressed the Commission except at the last meeting when the President was not in attendance. On one occasion before that he made a remark to the President which the President repeated to the conference, commencing "Colonel House suggests." Colonel House sat next to the President on his left, and next to Colonel House were the British Delegation, Lord Robert Cecil and General Smuts. Colonel House, and also the President, conferred frequently during the meetings with Lord Robert Cecil, and sometimes with General Smuts, and indeed the speeches sometimes halted during these conferences.

Lord Robert Cecil spoke usually in English, but sometimes in a rather halting French which he himself described as a jargon, although he understood French perfectly. General Smuts spoke always in English, and I think his understanding of French was not complete. The Japanese delegates seldom spoke, but always in English. I believe that they understood French perfectly, as they never required a translation, but their faces were perfectly impassive, and my belief is perhaps only an assumption.

While only ten powers were represented, M. Reis, delegate from Portugal, sat next to Viscount Chinda. M. Reis was the only delegate who used French and English with equal facility, speaking sometimes in one language and sometimes in the other, and fluently in both. He seemed to me a diplomat of the old school. He was noticeably nearsighted, having to hold papers within two or three inches of his eyes in order to read them, so that the English text of the Covenant, with its very fine print, was peculiarly unfortunate in his case.

M. Vesnitch, of Serbia, sat next to M. Reis, sometimes speaking in an English more fluent than he was disposed to admit. M. Vesnitch preferred to speak, and usually did speak, in French. His English, while accurate, was not of English structure, and at his request I recast the English of some of his proposed amendments.

M. Hymans, of Belgium, spoke and understood English well, but in commenting on amendments always spoke in French, which he obviously preferred, and in which he understood the shades of meaning conveyed by language better than in English. M. Hymans took a very active part in the discussions. He impressed me as being able but not broad. He sometimes let his tongue run away with his discretion, as on one occasion when debating the representation of the small Powers he said that an Executive Council with only two small Powers on it would be the creation of an agreement such as would have been made by the Congress of Vienna. For this I may say he was very promptly, courteously and severely reproved by Lord Robert Cecil, who remarked that he could not imagine any country to which Belgium preferred to submit her case, above Great Britain.

Mr. Koo, delegate from China, always spoke in English. He understood French, and I have heard him speak it a little, though I do not know his fluency in the language. However, he never used it at the meetings. Mr. Koo made a distinct impression by his ability, and on the subject of representation of the small Powers made one of the best speeches of the Commission.

M. Pessôa, delegate from Brazil, spoke only in French. I think he understood English imperfectly, if at all.

Next to M. Pessôa sat the second Italian delegate, Senator Scialoja. Scialoja spoke seldom, and always in French. He did not, I think, understand English. He impressed me as an intelligent scholar, and I assumed that his infrequent speech was due to the presence of Signor Orlando.

Between M. Scialoja and Signor Orlando sat the French delegates, MM. Larnaude, on the right, and Bourgeois, on the left. Neither of these gentlemen speaks English. I think both of them read it, and M. Larnaude at least to some extent understands it. However, the English remarks were interpreted to them. M. Larnaude is a lawyer of distinction. His French was a pleasure to listen to, being elegant and precise, and spoken with great clearness. M. Bourgeois spoke more slowly, and with much greater prolixity. Both he and M. Larnaude were very tenacious of the French view, and frequently they both spoke on the same point, and occasionally, I must say, not with entire consistency.

Signor Orlando sat on the President's right. He does not speak or understand English, and always spoke in French with a little hesitation, and with a distinctly Italian accent. His personality undoubtedly made a deep impression. While speaking with a knowledge of the law, his remarks were always clear and to the point, and his point of view was always that of practical common-sense. President Wilson obviously deferred greatly to Signor Orlando's opinions, and he said openly that he differed with him very rarely, and then with hesitation.

The meetings were greatly dominated by President Wilson. The whole tone of the speeches, when differing from his views, conveyed the aim of convincing him, which indeed they sometimes did. But to his final opinions there was an unmistakable deference, with the possible exception, in some cases, of the French delegates. This was strikingly shown at the last meeting, at which the President was not present, when the meeting was practically unanimous in favor of omitting the paragraph about religious freedom, and yet was unwilling to vote to eliminate it in the absence of the President.

Lord Robert Cecil had also great influence upon the meeting. Not only his views but his manner were obviously those of a statesman of long experience. His patience and his willingness to listen to argument gave his statements in reply to argument great and even convincing weight. . . .

I have said that my duties were not in terms defined, but one of them, or at least one with which I charged myself, was to see that at the beginning of each meeting the text, both in English and French, of the part of the draft agreed upon up to the close of the previous meeting was on the table. This duty did not commence until the meeting of Tuesday, February 4th, when the Commission commenced to consider the text by articles; but from that time on it was most laborious. In doing this work, however, I paid particular attention to the English text, and did not attempt to see that the French text as originally laid before the meeting was correct or not, but simply to see that when changes were made in it they were made in the French. This, of course, sometimes required a translation of an English amendment. At times I translated it myself; at times the translation was done in connection with the work of the Secretariat; and at times it was done by Mlle. Marcou, who was attached to the stenographic staff of Colonel House.

It may be said from a technical point of view that the proceedings of the Commission were really in English. The discussions of the text were of the English text. While amendments were sometimes presented in French, they were always when accepted agreed upon in English. So that despite the fact that the two languages were on equality, English was really the language of the Commission, so far as its actual work was concerned.

136. REPORT OF THE COMMISSION ON BELGIAN AFFAIRS[1]

[This report gives the grounds on which Belgian neutrality was abolished by the Treaty of Versailles. The Belgian claim that she should be given sovereignty over Dutch Flanders on the left bank of the Scheldt and over Dutch Limburg, on the ground that the treaty of 1839 having lapsed, these territories were now necessary for her protection, was referred eventually to direct negotiation between Belgium and Holland. A treaty was finally signed between these two countries, at The Hague, on April 3, 1925, but it had not yet been ratified in 1930.]

The Commission on Belgian Affairs, entrusted by the Supreme Council at its meeting of 26 February, 1919, with the study of the question of the revision of the Treaty of 1839, has arrived at the following conclusions:

(1) In law, the three treaties and all their clauses together constitute a single entity.

The treaty between Belgium and Holland is not separable from the other two.

Without examining the argument that the three agreements may be said to have been terminated by the fact of their violation, the Commission holds that since three of the signatories consider revision necessary, such revision is called for.

(2) In fact, the three treaties which were directed against Belgium

---

[1] American Commission to Negotiate Peace. S-H Bulletin No. 167, April 15, 1919. Commission on Belgian Affairs. "Report to the Supreme Council of the Allies on the Revision of the Treaty of 1839" (Hoover War Library Manuscript).

and imposed upon her and upon Holland by the Great Powers, have not afforded Belgium any of the guarantees which these treaties promised to her, and by their clauses relative to her territory and her rivers have seriously impaired her capacity for defense, and are thus in great measure responsible for the injuries she has sustained. As far as concerns Germany, Austria, and Russia, it is now in fact impossible to give to Belgium the guarantee of the five Great Powers to which she is entitled by the treaties. On this ground, also, the revision of the treaties in their entirety is called for.

(3) In principle, the basis accepted for the Peace Conference contemplates the abandonment of the neutralization of Belgium, which constitutes a limitation upon her full sovereignty. The revision of the treaties is thus a matter of general interest. This neutralization is at present guaranteed to Holland by Great Britain and by France under the treaty between the five powers and Holland. The participation of Holland in the revision of the treaties is thus called for.

The conclusion suggested accordingly is as follows:

(a) The treaties of 1839 should be revised in the entirety of their clauses at the joint request of the Powers which deem their revision necessary.

(b) Holland should take part in this revision.

(c) Those of the guarantor great powers which have fulfilled their obligations should also take part therein.

(d) Similarly the great powers at the Peace Conference whose interests are general should take part therein.

(e) The general object of this revision is, in accordance with the aim of the League of Nations, to free Belgium from that limitation upon her sovereignty which was imposed on her by the treaties of 1839, and, in the interests both of Belgium and of general peace, to remove the dangers and disadvantages arising from the said treaties.

With respect to the procedure to be followed the Commission submits to the Supreme Council the suggestion that:

The Supreme Council entrust the guarantor powers which have been faithful to their obligations with the duty of informing Holland that the Council deems the revision of the Treaties of 1839 to be necessary, and of inviting her to send her representatives to set forth before the Supreme Council the views of the Dutch Government with regard to such revision.

The whole question of the revision of the treaties would then be before the Supreme Council. This revision could be examined with regard to the interests of Belgium and of Holland by the Commission on Belgian affairs, as well as by the Commission of ports, waterways and international communications, on the basis of the investigations carried on by each of these two Commissions.

The provisions of the final treaty would come under the guarantees contemplated by the League of Nations.

The Commission, in support of its conclusions, submits the following note to the Supreme Council.

I. The Present Position

Belgium asks that the treaties of 1839 be revised, and that this revision be undertaken on the initiative of the great powers assembled in the Peace Conference (or at least of France and Great Britain, which are signatories and guarantors of the said treaties).

Without going into the Belgian claims in detail, and confining itself to an examination of the principles involved, the Commission has reviewed in turn:

1. The question of law.
2. The question of fact.

II. The Question of Law

In law, the situation is as follows:

1. The treaties of 1839 constitute an indivisible whole.

These treaties, following on the Treaty of 15 November 1831 (not ratified by Holland), are three in number.

(a) The Treaty of 19 April 1839, between Holland and the five Great Powers, guaranteeing to Holland the entire agreement.

(b) The Treaty of 19 April 1839, between Belgium and Holland.

(c) The Treaty of 19 April 1839, between Belgium and the five Great Powers, guaranteeing to Belgium the entire agreement.

With the exception of the clause containing the guarantee, which occurs only in the treaties signed by the Great Powers, the text of the three treaties is identical.

Moreover, a note presented to the Belgian and Dutch representatives in the course of the negotiations by the five Great Powers declares that: "The articles shall be inserted word for word in a treaty between Holland on the one part and Belgium on the other."

Besides, the treaty between the five Powers and Belgium stipulates (Art. I.): "The articles hereto annexed (Treaty between Belgium and Holland) are deemed to have the same force and effect as if they were set forth at large in the present act and are thus placed under the guarantee of the Five Powers."

Consequently, the three Treaties and all their clauses together constitute an indivisible whole, and the treaty between Belgium and Holland cannot be separated from the other two.

2. The three Treaties have been violated.

What is the actual situation of the seven powers who signed the three treaties?

(a) Of the guarantor Powers, three have failed to fulfill their obligations: Prussia and Austria-Hungary by their aggression in 1914; Russia by the Treaty of Brest-Litowsk.

(b) Of the other guarantor powers two, France and Great Britain, have honored their signatures.

(c) Belgium, attacked in spite of the guarantee of her neutrality, defended herself.

(d) Holland declared her neutrality.

What are the juridical conclusions to be drawn from this situation?

3. The question might be raised whether, from the juridical point of view, the treaties are still in force.

It would be possible to consider whether the treaties of 1839 are not already voided, so that there would be no occasion for their revision.

It may indeed be contended that both in international and in private law a contract is terminated when one of the contracting parties fails of performance, especially if the breach, as is the case here, relates to an essential clause.

This conclusion would then apply to the three treaties and to all their clauses, in their entirety.

It might moreover be supported by the fact that Holland, who is indeed not a guarantor, but is only a signatory of the treaties,

(a) made no protest against the violation of the said treaty but was content to obtain from Germany by negotiation of 3 August, 1914, the promise to respect her integrity.

(b) has been charged with failing to fulfill certain obligations resulting from her neutrality (in the matter of transit allowed to German sand and gravel which were intended for military purposes; and of the passage through Dutch Limburg of 80,000 German troops, with their material in large amount, in November, 1918; etc.).

The Commission desires to express no opinion upon this juridical question.

Moreover, it seems in harmony with the spirit animating the Powers united in Conference at Paris, as well as with the desires of Belgium herself, to refrain from making use of this argument and to adopt another procedure.

4. In any case the revision of the three treaties is called for.

Several of the signatory Powers have in fact given definite expression to their views as to the situation set forth above.

(a) Belgium as early as 26 July, 1917, made the following declaration: "The international statute established 1831-39 in order to guarantee the security of Belgium has become void by reason of the violation of the joint treaty by two of its signatories. It must be revised." She has since renewed this demand before the Peace Conference.

(b) France and Great Britain, signatories and guarantors, have adhered to the Belgian demand for revision.

(c) The United States, not a signatory, has declared that Belgium must be "restored, without any attempt to limit the sovereignty which she enjoys in common with all other free nations."

It is a logical consequence of this unanimity and of the considerations set forth above, that the three treaties should be revised, the revision being undertaken in agreement with Holland, not only by Belgium, but by the Great Powers which are signatories and guarantors thereof.

This revision is fully justified in law and cannot be refused.

III. The Question of Fact

Fully justified in law, revision is indispensable in fact.

(1) The treaties of 1839 were directed against Belgium.

(a) One of the objects of the Congress of Vienna and of the Treaty of Paris had been to restrain France by certain territorial provisions of which that for the union of Belgium with Holland was one of the most important.

The Belgian revolution in 1830 impaired this arrangement at the very time when the French revolution of the same year renewed the former apprehensions.

From that time on it was the object of the makers of the treaties of 1815, as they were not able to preserve them in their integrity, to save what they could, and in particular to weaken Belgium as much as possible since she was suspected of lending support to French ideas and French policy.

(b) The marked feature of the negotiations begun in 1830, which were arrested in August 1831 by the military successes of Holland against Belgium, and which were delayed until 1839 by the refusal of Holland to ratify the treaties, was the rejection in ever increasing measure of the Belgian claims.

On 3 January 1831, in particular, the Belgian Government had said: "The immediate guarantee of the liberty of the Scheldt, the possession of the left bank of that river, the whole of the Province of Limburg, and the Grand Duchy of Luxembourg, are essential to my existence."

In 1839 Belgium received nothing of all this.

(c) The refusal met with by Belgium resulted in the dominating influence of Holland on the Scheldt by which Antwerp was given over to the competition of Rotterdam, and the establishment of the control of the strategic positions in Luxembourg by Germany which opened to her the line of the Meuse.

In exchange for these sacrifices, Belgium received, besides certain provisions with regard to navigation which she has always declared to be ineffective or inadequate, the guarantee of neutrality; this was to be a compensation for the impossibility of defending herself, but it was a compensation "*imposed* upon a restless and unruly nation," which, as one of the participants in the negotiations said, "it seems necessary to *condemn* to a peaceful existence."

In other words the neutrality of Belgium was established as much *against* her interest as *in her behalf.*

(d) The Belgian Government furthermore protested against the Treaty of 1839 in the following statement:

"His Majesty, desiring to spare his people all the misfortunes which the forced execution of the XXIV articles would entail, and desiring to spare Europe a general war, yields to the imperious law of necessity, adheres to the severe and onerous conditions imposed on Belgium by the Conference of London, etc."

2. By the very admission of the guarantor powers, the treaties of 1831-39 were not the outcome of free negotiations between Belgium and Holland but were the result of a decision imposed upon them.

(a) The several clauses (relative to territorial delimitations, to apportionment of the public debt, to waterways, to neutrality and to the guarantee), were discussed and agreed upon as between the Great Powers and not as between Belgium and Holland. It required eight years to secure the ratification of the treaties by Holland and great pressure to secure the ratification of Belgium.

(b) With the protocol of the 20th December, 1830, it became apparent that the purpose was "to adjust the future independence of Belgium to the stipulations of the treaties and to the security of the other Powers."

In this protocol emphasis was laid upon the "irrevocable decisions," upon the "unshakable determination" of the Great Powers.

(c) In other words, the treaties of 1831-39 were inspired by an interest foreign to Belgium and to Holland, that is by a European interest, and these treaties in no wise give effect to any self-determination on the part of Belgium or of Holland.

3. Finally, the Treaties of 1839 have not effectually secured to Belgium what had been promised her, but rather have brought home to her the burden of the sacrifices which they imposed on her.

(a) The whole course of the war from 1914 to 1918 demonstrates this. The course of events has given the lie to the anticipations of 1839.

It was said that Belgium would not be able to defend herself; she has defended herself heroically.

It was said that she would not be called upon to defend herself; in fact she was attacked by the very powers who had undertaken to guarantee her, and for the double error of the old diplomacy she has paid the price known to all.

(b) Indeed under these circumstances, Belgium has suffered for the loss of all of that which the treaties of 1839 took from her in exchange for a guarantee of neutrality which has proved ineffective.

The régime of the Scheldt has prevented the supply and the defense of Antwerp.

Luxembourg has been used as a military base by Germany.

The Meuse could not be effectively held.

Dutch Limburg enabled a part of the German Army to escape capture by the Allies.

(c) In conclusion, German aggression has destroyed that which was the basis of the international existence of Belgium during eighty years, without that basis being of the slightest use to those whom it was intended to guarantee.

The important part, material and moral, which Belgium has played in the war makes it the more incumbent upon the Powers that they should not forget this.

4. Justice demands, on the basis of these facts, the revision of a system which for Belgium has been,

(a) useless.

(b) burdensome.

Furthermore, in such a revision the interests of Belgium cannot be separated from those of the Powers by whose side Belgium has fought since 1914.

137. THE RUSSIAN PROBLEM AT THE PEACE CONFERENCE[1]

[The Russian situation was practically the first problem which the heads of the Allied delegations in Paris considered. On January 16 at a meeting of heads of states, Lloyd George presented three possible policies: military intervention, the establishment of a "cordon sanitaire" between Russia and the rest of Europe, and the British plan of calling the leaders of all the Russian factions to Paris in the hope of bringing them to some agreement among themselves and with the Allies. This last proposal Clemenceau flatly vetoed. Therefore Wilson proposed another place than Paris for such a meeting, and the island of Prinkipo in the Sea of Marmora was eventually fixed upon, but the meeting was never held; the proposal lapsed, in spite of the fact that the Baltic republics had accepted it and that the Soviet Government itself accepted it provided that the powers would undertake to refrain from interference in Russian internal affairs; the reason for its failure lay in the preference of the anti-Bolshevist forces for war. On February 18, William C. Bullitt, a member of the American Commission to Negotiate Peace, received instructions from Secretary of State Lansing, to proceed to Russia for the purpose of studying political and economic conditions. In his evidence before the Foreign Relations Committee of the United States Senate in September 1919, Bullitt testified that he had discussed his mission with Philip Kerr, Lloyd George's private secretary, and had prepared in collaboration with him an outline of possible conditions of peace, and that Kerr said he had discussed the whole matter with Lloyd George and Balfour. Lloyd George called the whole statement "a tissue of lies," but Lansing

---

[1] U. S. serial 7605. Doc. No. 106, pp. 1235-1270, *passim*.

"found it impossible to make an absolute denial." The result was the Bolshevist offer of peace terms, which, however, were not made public at the time, though Lloyd George (according to Bullitt's evidence) urged that it be published. Wilson vetoed that course of action. When the appointed day passed without action having been taken, the Bolshevist offer lapsed. Less than a week later Lloyd George made an equivocal answer in reply to a direct question in the House of Commons, saying: "We have had no approaches at all. . . . There was some suggestion that there was some young American who had come back. . . . But if the President of the United States had attached any value to them he would have brought them before the conference, and he certainly did not."]

Notes on Conversations held in the Office of M. Pichon at the Quai d'Orsay, on January 16, 1919—Preliminary Discussion regarding the situation in Russia

Mr. Lloyd George commenced his statement setting forth the information in the possession of the British Government regarding the Russian situation, by referring to the matter which had been exposed recently in L'Humanité. He stated that he wished to point out that there had been a serious misconception on the part of the French Government as to the character of the proposal of the British Government. The British proposal did not contemplate in any sense whatever, a recognition of the Bolsheviki Government, nor a suggestion that Bolshevik delegates be invited to attend the Conference. The British proposal was to invite all of the different governments now at war within what used to be the Russian Empire, to a truce of God, to stop reprisals and outrages and to send men here to give, so to speak, an account of themselves. The Great Powers would then try to find a way to bring some order out of chaos. These men were not to be delegates to the Peace Conference, and he agreed with the French Government entirely that they should not be made members of the Conference.

Mr. Lloyd George then proceeded to set forth briefly the reasons which had led the British Government to make this proposal. They were as follows:

Firstly, the real facts are not known;

Secondly, it is impossible to get the facts, the only way is to adjudicate the question; and

Thirdly, conditions in Russia are very bad; there is general misgovernment and starvation. It is not known who is obtaining the upper hand, but the hope that the Bolshevik Government would collapse had not been realized. In fact, there is one report that the Bolsheviki are stronger than ever, that their internal position is strong, and that their hold on the people is stronger. Take, for instance, the case of the Ukraine. Some adventurer raises a few men and overthrows the

Government. The Government is incapable of overthrowing him. It is also reported that the peasants are becoming Bolsheviki. It is hardly the business of the Great Powers to intervene either in lending financial support to one side or the other, or in sending munitions to either side.

Mr. Lloyd George stated that there seemed to be three possible policies:

1. Military intervention. It is true there [sic] the Bolsheviki movement is as dangerous to civilization as German militarism, but as to putting it down by the sword, is there anyone who proposes it? It would mean holding a certain number of vast provinces in Russia. The Germans with one million men on their Eastern Front only held the fringe of this territory. If he now proposed to send a thousand British troops to Russia for that purpose, the armies would mutiny. The same applies to U. S. troops in Siberia; also to Canadians and French as well. The mere idea of crushing Bolshevism by a military force is pure madness. Even admitting that it is done, who is to occupy Russia? No one can conceive or understand to bring about order by force.

2. A cordon. The second suggestion is to besiege Bolshevik Russia. Mr. Lloyd George wondered if those present realized what this would mean. From the information furnished him Bolshevik Russia has no corn, but within this territory there are 150,000,000 men, women, and children. There is now starvation in Petrograd and Moscow. This is not an health cordon, it is a death cordon. Moreover, as a matter of fact, the people who would die are just the people that the Allies desire to protect. It would not result in the starvation of the Bolsheviki; it would simply mean the death of our friends. The cordon policy is a policy which, as humane people, those present could not consider.

Mr. Lloyd George asked who was there to overthrow the Bolsheviki? He had been told there were three men, Denekin, Kolchak and Knox. In considering the chances of these people to overthrow the Bolsheviki, he pointed out that he had received information that the Czecho-Slovaks now refused to fight; that the Russian Army was not to be trusted, and that while it was true that a Bolshevik Army had recently gone over to Kolchak it was never certain that just the reverse of this would not take place. If the Allies counted on any of these men, he believed they were building on quicksand. He had heard a lot of talk about Denekin, but when he looked on the map he found that Denekin was occupying a little backyard near the Black Sea. Then he had been told that Denekin had recognized Kolchak, but when he looked on the map, there was a great solid block of territory between Denekin and Kolchak. Moreover, from information received it would appear that Kolchak had been collecting members of the old régime around him, and would seem to be at heart a monarchist. It appeared that the Czecho-Slovaks were finding this out. The sympathies of the Czecho-Slovaks are very democratic, and they are not at all prepared to fight for the restoration of the old conditions in Russia.

Mr. Lloyd George stated that he was informed that at the present time two-thirds of Bolshevik Russia was starving.

Institutions of Bolsheviki are institutions of old Czarist régime. This is not what one would call creating a new world.

3. The third alternative was contained in the British proposal, which was to summon these people to Paris to appear before those present, somewhat in the way that the Roman Empire summoned chiefs of outlying tributary states to render an account of their actions.

Mr. Lloyd George pointed out the fact that the argument might be used that there were already here certain representatives of these Governments; but take, for instance, the case of Sazonov, who claims to represent the Government of Omsk. As a matter of fact, Sassonoff can not speak from personal observation. He is nothing but a partisan, like all the rest. He has never been in contact, and is not now in direct contact with the Government at Omsk.

It would be manifestly absurd for those who are responsible for bringing about the Peace Conference, to come to any agreement and leave Paris when one-half of Europe and one-half of Asia is still in flames. Those present must settle this question or make fools of themselves.

Mr. Lloyd George referred to the objection that had been raised to permitting Bolshevik delegates to come to Paris. It had been claimed that they would convert France and England to Bolshevism. If England becomes Bolshevist, it will not be because a single Bolshevist representative is permitted to enter England. On the other hand, if a military enterprise were started against the Bolsheviki, that would make England Bolshevist, and there would be a Soviet in London. For his part, Mr. Lloyd George was not afraid of Bolshevism if the facts are known in England and the United States. The same applied to Germany. He was convinced that an educated democracy can be always trusted to turn down Bolshevism.

Under all circumstances, Mr. Lloyd George saw no better way out than to follow the third alternative. Let the Great Powers impose their conditions and summon these people to Paris to give an account of themselves to the Great Powers, not to the Peace Conference. . . .

Secretaries' notes of a conversation held in M. Pichon's room at the Quai d'Orsay on Tuesday, January 21, 1919, at 15 hours

Secret

M. Clemenceau said they had met together to decide what could be done in Russia under present circumstances.

President Wilson said that in order to have something definite to discuss, he wished to take advantage of a suggestion made by Mr. Lloyd-George and to propose a modification of the British proposal. He wished to suggest that the various organized groups in Russia should be asked to send representatives, not to Paris, but to some other place, such as Salonika, convenient of approach, there to meet such representatives as might be appointed by the Allies, in order to see if they could draw up a program upon which agreement could be reached.

Mr. Lloyd-George pointed out that the advantage of this would be that they could be brought straight there from Russia through the Black Sea without passing through other countries.

M. Sonnino said that some of the representatives of the various Governments were already here in Paris, for example, M. Sazonoff [sic]. Why should these not be heard?

President Wilson expressed the view that the various parties should not be heard separately. It would be very desirable to get all these representatives in one place, and still better, all in one room, in order to obtain a close comparison of views.

Mr. Balfour said that a further objection to Mr. Sonnino's plan was that if M. Sazonoff was heard in Paris, it would be difficult to refuse to hear the others in Paris also, and M. Clemenceau objected strongly to having some of these representatives in Paris.

M. Sonnino explained that all the Russian parties had some representatives here, except the Soviets, whom they did not wish to hear.

Mr. Lloyd-George remarked that the Bolshevists were the very people some of them wished to hear.

M. Sonnino continuing said that they had heard M. Litvinoff's statements that morning. . . .

The Allies were now fighting against the Bolshevists who were their enemies, and therefore they were not obliged to hear them with the others.

Mr. Balfour remarked that the essence of President Wilson's proposal was that the parties must all be heard at one and the same time.

Mr. Lloyd George expressed the view that the acceptance of M. Sonnino's proposals would amount to their hearing a string of people, all of whom held the same opinion, and all of whom would strike the same note. But they would not hear the people who at the present moment were actually controlling European Russia. In deference to M. Clemenceau's views, they had put forward this new proposal. He thought it would be quite safe to bring the Bolshevist representatives to Salonika, or perhaps to Lemnos. It was absolutely necessary to endeavor to make peace. The report read by President Wilson that morning went to show that the Bolshevists were not convinced of the error of their ways, but they apparently realised the folly of their present methods. Therefore they were endeavouring to come to terms.

President Wilson asked to be permitted to urge one aspect of the case. As M. Sonnino had implied, they were all repelled by Bolshevism, and for that reason they had placed armed men in opposition to them. One of the things that was clear in the Russian situation was that by opposing Bolshevism with arms, they were in reality serving the cause of Bolshevism. The Allies were making it possible for the Bolsheviks to argue that Imperialistic and Capitalistic Governments were endeavouring to exploit the country and to give the land back to the landlords, and so bring about a re-action. If it could be shown that this was not true, and that the Allies were prepared to deal with the rulers of Russia, much of the moral force of this argument would disappear. The allegation that the Allies were against the people and wanted to control their affairs provided the argument which enabled them to raise armies. If, on the other hand, the Allies could swallow their pride and the natural repulsion which they felt for the Bolshevists and see the representatives of all organized groups in one place, he thought it would bring about a marked reaction against Bolshevism.

M. Clemenceau said that, in principle, he did not favour conversation with the Bolshevists; not because they were criminals, but because we would be raising them to our level by saying that they were worthy of entering into conversation with us. The Bolshevist danger was very great at the present moment. Bolshevism was spreading. It had invaded the Baltic Provinces and Poland, and that very morning they received very bad news regarding its spread to Budapesth and Vienna. Italy, also, was in danger. The danger was probably greater there than in France. If Bolshevism, after spreading in Germany, were to traverse Austria and Hungary and so reach Italy, Europe would be faced with a very great danger. Therefore, something must be done against Bolshevism. When listening to the document presented by President Wilson that morning, he had been struck by the cleverness with which the Bolshevists were attempting to lay a trap for the Allies. When the Bolshevists first came into power, a breach was made with the Capitalist Government on questions of principle, but now they offered funds and concessions as a basis for treating with them. He need not say how valueless their promises were, but if they were listened to, the Bolshevists would go back to their people and say: "We offered them great principles of justice and the Allies would have nothing to do with us. Now we offer money, and they are ready to make peace."

He admitted his remarks did not offer a solution. The great misfortune was that the Allies were in need of a speedy solution. After four years of war, and the losses and sufferings they had incurred, their populations could stand no more. Russia also was in need of immediate peace. But its necessary evolution must take time. The signing of the world Peace could not await Russia's final avatar. Had time been available, he would suggest waiting, for eventually sound men representing common-sense would come to the top. But when would that be? He could make no forecast. Therefore they must press for an early solution.

To sum up, had he been acting by himself, he would temporize and erect barriers to prevent Bolshevism from spreading. But he was not alone, and in the presence of his colleagues he felt compelled to make some concession, as it was essential that there should not even be the appearance of disagreement amongst them. The concession came easier after having heard President Wilson's suggestions. He thought that they should make a very clear and convincing appeal to all reasonable peoples, emphatically stating that they did not wish in any way to interfere in the internal affairs of Russia, and especially that they had no intention of restoring Czardom. The object of the Allies being to hasten the creation of a strong Government, they proposed to call together representatives of all parties to a Conference. He would beg President Wilson to draft a paper, fully explaining the position of the Allies to the whole world, including the Russians and the Germans.

Mr. Lloyd George agreed and gave notice that he wished to withdraw his own motion in favour of President Wilson's.

Mr. Balfour said that he understood that all these people were to be asked on an equality. On these terms he thought the Bolshevists would refuse, and by their refusal, they would put themselves in a very bad position.

Mr. Sonnino said that he did not agree that the Bolshevists would not come. He thought they would be the first to come, because they would be eager to put themselves on an equality with the others. He would remind his colleagues that, before the Peace of Brest-Litovsk was signed, the Bolshevists promised all sorts of things, such as to refrain from propaganda, but since that peace had been concluded they had broken all their promises, their one idea being to spread revolution in all other countries. His idea was to collect together all the anti-Bolshevik parties and help them to make a strong Government, provided they pledged themselves not to serve the forces of re-action and especially not to touch the land question, thereby depriving the Bolshevists of their strongest argument. Should they take these pledges, he would be prepared to help them.

Mr. Lloyd George enquired how this help would be given.

Mr. Sonnino replied that help would be given with soldiers to a reasonable degree or by supplying arms, food, and money. For instance, Poland asked for weapons and munitions; the Ukraine asked for weapons. All the Allies wanted was to establish a strong Government. The reason that no strong Government at present existed was that no party could risk taking the offensive against Bolshevism without the assistance of the Allies. He would enquire how the parties of order could possibly succeed without the help of the Allies. President Wilson had said that they should put aside all pride in the matter. He would point out that, for Italy and probably for France also, as M. Clemenceau had stated, it was in reality a question of self-defence. He thought that even a partial recognition of the Bolshevists would strengthen their position, and, speaking for himself, he thought that Bolshevism was already a serious danger in his country.

Mr. Lloyd George said he wished to put one or two practical questions to M. Sonnino. The British Empire now had some 15,000 to 20,000 men in Russia. M. de Scavenius had estimated that some 150,-000 additional men would be required, in order to keep the anti-Bolshevist Governments from dissolution. And General Franchet d'Esperey also insisted on the necessity of Allied assistance. Now Canada had decided to withdraw her troops, because the Canadian soldiers would not agree to stay and fight against the Russians. Similar trouble had also occurred amongst the other Allied troops. And he felt certain that, if the British tried to send any more troops there, there would be mutiny.

M. Sonnino suggested that volunteers might be called for.

Mr. Lloyd George, continuing, said that it would be impossible to raise 150,000 men in that way. He asked, however, what contributions America, Italy and France would make towards the raising of this Army.

President Wilson and M. Clemenceau each said none.

M. Orlando agreed that Italy could make no further contributions.

M. Lloyd George said that the Bolshevists had an army of 300,000 men who would, before long, be good soldiers, and to fight them at least 400,000 Russian soldiers would be required. Who would feed, equip and pay them? Would Italy, or America, or France, do so? If they were unable to do that, what would be the good of fighting Bolshevism? It could not be crushed by speeches. He sincerely trusted that they would accept President Wilson's proposal as it now stood.

M. Orlando agreed that the question was a very difficult one for the reasons that had been fully given. He agreed that Bolshevism consti-tuted a grave danger to all Europe. To prevent a contagious epidemic from spreading, the sanitarians set up a *cordon Sanitaire*. If similar measures could be taken against Bolshevism, in order to prevent its spreading, it might be overcome, since to isolate it meant vanquishing it. Italy was now passing through a period of depression, due to war weariness. But Bolshevists could never triumph there, unless they found a favourable medium, such as might be produced either by a profound patriotic disappointment in their expectations as to the re-wards of the war, or by an economic crisis. Either might lead to revolution, which was equivalent to Bolshevism. Therefore, he would insist that all possible measures should be taken to set up this cordon. Next, he suggested the consideration of repressive measures. He thought two methods were possible; either the use of physical force or the use of moral force. He thought Mr. Lloyd George's objection [to] the use of physical force unanswerable. The occupation of Russia meant the employment of large numbers of troops for an indefinite period of time. This meant an apparent prolongation of the war. There remained the use of moral force. He agreed with M. Clemenceau that no country could continue in anarchy and that an end must eventually come; but they could not wait; they could not proceed to make peace and ignore Russia. Therefore, Mr. Lloyd George's proposal, with the modifications introduced after careful consideration by President Wilson and M. Clemenceau, gave a possible solution. It did not involve entering into negotiations with the Bolsheviks; the proposal was merely an attempt to bring together all the parties in Russia with a view to finding a way out of the present difficulty. He was prepared, therefore, to support it. . . .

President Wilson expressed the view that the emissaries of the Allied Powers should not be authorised to adopt any definite attitude towards Bolshevism. They should merely report back to their Governments the conditions found.

Mr. Lloyd George asked that that question be further considered. He thought the emissaries of the Allied Powers should be able to establish an agreement if they were able to find a solution! For instance, if they succeeded in reaching an agreement on the subject of the organization of a Constituent Assembly, they should be authorised to accept such a compromise without the delay of a reference to the Governments.

President Wilson suggested that the emissaries might be furnished with a body of instructions.

Mr. Balfour expressed the view that abstention from hostile action against their neighbours should be made a condition of their sending representatives to this meeting.

President Wilson agreed.

M. Clemenceau suggested that the manifesto to the Russian parties should be based solely on humanitarian grounds. They should say to the Russians: "You are threatened by famine. We are prompted by humanitarian feelings; we are making peace; we do not want people to die. We are prepared to see what can be done to remove the menace of starvation." He thought the Russians would at once prick up their ears, and be prepared to hear what the Allies had to say. They would add that food cannot be sent unless peace and order were re-established. It should, in fact, be made quite clear that the representatives of all parties should merely be brought together for purely humane reasons. . . .

(It was agreed that President Wilson should draft a proclamation, for consideration at the next meeting, inviting all organized parties in Russia to attend a Meeting to be held at some selected place such as Salonika or Lemnos, in order to discuss with the representatives of the Allied and Associated Great Powers the means of restoring order and peace in Russia. Participation in the Meeting should be conditional on a cessation of hostilities.) . . .

Mr. Bullitt. . . . The French—and particularly the French foreign office, even more than Mr. Clemenceau and you can observe it from that minute were opposed to the idea, and we found that the French foreign office had communicated to the Ukrainian Government and various other antisoviet governments that if they were to refuse the proposal, they would support them and continue to support them, and not allow the Allies, if they could prevent it, or the allied Governments to make peace with the Russian soviet government.

At all events, the time set for the Prinkipos proposal was February 15. At that time nobody had acted in a definite, uncompromising matter [*sic*]. It therefore fell to the ground.

There was a further discussion as to what should be done. The peace conference was still of the opinion that it was impossible to hope to conquer the soviet government by force of arms, because in the latter part of that report . . . there was expressed very forcibly the opinion of Mr. Lloyd-George, that the population at home would not stand it. Therefore they desired to follow up further the line of making peace. . . . On the 19th day of the month, Mr. Clemenceau was shot, and the next day Mr. Lloyd-George telephoned over from London to say that as long as Clemenceau was wounded and was ill, he was boss of the roost, and that anything he desired to veto would be immediately wiped out and therefore it was no use for him and Col. House, as long as Clemenceau was ill, to attempt to renew the Prinkipos proposal, as Clemenceau would simply have to hold up a finger and the whole thing would drop to the ground. Therefore, it was decided that I should go at once to Russia to attempt to obtain from the soviet government an exact statement of the terms on which they were ready to stop fighting. I was ordered if possible to obtain that statement and have it back in Paris before the President returned to Paris from the United States. The plan was to make a proposal to the soviet government which would certainly be accepted. . . . [I was in Russia] for only one week. I was instructed to go in and bring back as quickly as possible a definite statement of exactly the terms the soviet government was ready to accept. The idea in the minds of the British and the American delegation were [*sic*] that if the Allies made another proposal it should be a proposal which we would know in advance would be accepted, so that there would be no chance of another Prinkipos proposal miscarrying. . . . I received on the 14th the following statement from Tchitcherin and Litvinov. . . . Tchitcherin was Peoples' Commissar for Foreign Affairs of the Soviet Republic and Litvinov was the former Soviet Ambassador to London . . . now practically assistant secretary for foreign affairs.

I also had a conference with Lenin. The Soviet Government undertook to accept this proposal provided it was made by the allied and associated Governments not later than April 10, 1919. The proposal reads as follows [reading]:

Text of Projected Peace Proposal by the Allied and Associated Governments

The allied and associated Governments to propose that hostilities shall cease on all fronts in the territory of the former Russian Empire and Finland on[1] and that no new hostilities shall begin after this date, pending a conference to be held at[2] on.[3]

The duration of the armistice to be for two weeks, unless extended by mutual consent, and all parties to the armistice to undertake not to employ the period of the armistice to transfer troops and war material to the territory of the former Russian Empire.

The conference to discuss peace on the basis of the following principles, which shall not be subject to revision by the conference.

1. All existing de facto governments which have been set up on the territory of the former Russian Empire and Finland to remain in full control of the territories which they occupy at the moment when the armistice becomes effective, except in so far as the conference may agree upon the transfer of territories; until the peoples inhabiting the territories controlled by these de facto governments shall themselves determine to change their Governments. The Russian Soviet Government, the other soviet governments and all other governments which have been set up on the territory of the former Russian Empire, the allied and associated Governments, and the other Governments which are operating against the soviet governments, including Finland, Poland, Galicia, Roumania, Armenia, Azerbaidjan, and Afghanistan, to agree not to attempt to upset by force the existing de facto governments which have been set up on the territory of the former Russian Empire and the other Governments signatory to this agreement.[4]

2. The economic blockade to be raised and trade relations between Soviet Russia and the allied and associated countries to be reestablished under conditions which will ensure that supplies from the allied and associated countries are made available on equal terms to all classes of the Russian people.

3. The soviet governments of Russia to have the right of unhindered transit on all railways and the use of all ports which belonged to the former Russian Empire and to Finland and are necessary for the disembarkation and transportation of passengers and goods between their territories and the sea; detailed arrangements for the carrying out of this provision to be agreed upon at the conference.

4. The citizens of the soviet republics of Russia to have the right

---

[1] The date of the armistice to be set at least a week after the date when the allied and associated Governments make this proposal.

[2] The Soviet Government greatly prefers that the conference should be held in a neutral country and also that either a radio or a direct telegraph wire to Moscow should be put at its disposal.

[3] The conference to begin not later than a week after the armistice takes effect and the Soviet Government greatly prefers that the period between the date of the armistice and the first meeting of the conference should be only three days, if possible.

[4] The allied and associated Governments to undertake to see to it that the de facto governments of Germany do not attempt to upset by force the de facto governments of Russia. The de facto governments which have been set up on the territory of the former Russian Empire to undertake not to attempt to upset by force the de facto governments of Germany.

of free entry into the allied and associated countries as well as into all countries which have been formed on the territory of the former Russian Empire and Finland; also the right of sojourn and of circulation and full security, provided they do not interfere in the domestic politics of those countries.[1] Nationals of the allied and associated countries and of the other countries above named to have the right of free entry into the soviet republics of Russia; also the right of sojourn and of circulation and full security, provided they do not interfere in the domestic politics of the soviet republics.

The allied and associated Governments and other governments which have been set up on the territory of the former Russian Empire and Finland to have the right to send official representatives enjoying full liberty and immunity into the various Russian Soviet Republics. The soviet governments of Russia to have the right to send official representatives enjoying full liberty and immunity into all the allied and associated countries and into the non-soviet countries which have been formed on the territory of the former Russian Empire and Finland.

5. The soviet governments, the other Governments which have been set up on the territory of the former Russian Empire and Finland, to give a general amnesty to all political opponents, offenders, and prisoners. The allied and associated governments to give a general amnesty to all Russian political opponents, offenders, and prisoners, and to their own nationals who have been or may be prosecuted for giving help to Soviet Russia. All Russians who have fought in, or otherwise aided the armies opposed to the soviet governments, and those opposed to the other Governments which have been set up on the territory of the former Russian Empire and Finland to be included in this amnesty.

All prisoners of war of non-Russian powers detained in Russia, likewise all nationals of those powers now in Russia to be given full facilities for repatriation. The Russian prisoners of war in whatever foreign country they may be, likewise all Russian nationals, including the Russian soldiers and officers abroad and those serving in all foreign armies to be given full facilities for repatriation.

6. Immediately after the signing of this agreement all troops of the allied and associated Governments and other non-Russian Governments to be withdrawn from Russia and military assistance to cease to be given to antisoviet governments which have been set up on the territory of the former Russian Empire.

The soviet governments and the antisoviet governments which have been set up on the territory of the former Russian Empire and Finland to begin to reduce their armies simultaneously, and at the same rate, to a peace footing immediately after the signing of the agreement. The conference to determine the most effective and just method

---

[1] It is considered essential by the soviet government that the allied and associated Governments should see to it that Poland and all neutral countries extend the same rights as the allied and associated countries.

of inspecting and controlling this simultaneous demobilization and also the withdrawal of the troops and the cessation of military assistance to the antisoviet governments.

7. The allied and associated Governments, taking cognizance of the statement of the soviet government of Russia, in its note of February 4, in regard to its foreign debts, propose as an integral part of this agreement that the soviet governments and the other governments which have been set up on the territory of the former Russian Empire and Finland shall recognize their responsibility for the financial obligations of the former Russian Empire, to foreign States parties to this agreement and to the nationals of such States. Detailed arrangements for the payment of these debts to be agreed upon at the conference, regard being had to the present financial position of Russia. The Russian gold seized by the Czecho-Slovaks in Kazan or taken from Germany by the Allies to be regarded as partial payment of the portion of the debt due from the soviet republics of Russia.

The Soviet Government of Russia undertakes to accept the foregoing proposal provided it is made not later than April 10, 1919. . . .

Mr. Bullitt . . . The fact was that just at this moment, when this proposal was under consideration, Kolchak made a 100-mile advance. There was a revolt of peasants in a district of Russia which entirely cut off supplies from the Bolshevik army operating against Kolchak. Kolchak made a 100-mile advance, and immediately the entire press of Paris was roaring and screaming on the subject, announcing that Kolchak would be in Moscow within two weeks; and therefore everyone in Paris, including, I regret to say, members of the American commission, began to grow very lukewarm about peace in Russia, because they thought Kolchak would arrive in Moscow and wipe out the soviet government. [The proposal was dropped.]

138. POLISH CLAIMS TO UPPER SILESIA[1]

[Upper Silesia is a province which was taken from Austria by the Prussians in the eighteenth century. Any claim of Polish political control had ended in the fifteenth century. It was demanded by Poland on ethnic and economic grounds. It had become highly industrialized in recent decades and its population was predominantly Polish only in the rural sections. The Polish claim that German population statistics were inaccurate has been substantiated by careful studies. The disposition of Upper Silesia was left by the Peace Conference to be decided by a plebiscite on March 20, 1921. When the vote was taken, a large majority was shown to favor union with Germany. This number probably included many Polish votes cast by people who thought it unwise to divide the province. Whether Germany could support itself without this extensive coal and iron area was a grave issue; there was

---

[1] Paris Peace Conference, 1919. Poland. Delegation Propaganda. *Upper Silesia, her Economic Union with other Polish Territories* (Hoover War Library Files).

also a question as to whether Poland could put it to the best use if it were given to her. This selection from the propaganda presented to the Peace Conference is typical of many such documents in its stilted and unidiomatic style. If one looks up Opole in a gazetteer he can see for himself how much importance to attach to its "Chamber of Commerce," the organization responsible for this propaganda.]

The necessity of obtaining for Poland her own base for the production of raw iron.

Besides indisputable ethnographical reasons for the re-union of the Ancient Polish Territory of Upper Silesia to the Polish State, there are others no less sound of a purely economic nature.

A Modern State, desirous of securing her own bases for a free, economic and thriving development, should, in the first place, have possession of her own iron production.

It is certain that, with regard to Germany for example, the intensive development of the iron industry in the years preceding the war was one of the essential causes of her economic scope.

Nauman, whose notable theory on Central Europe is well known, supported the theme in his work, *Neudeutsche Wirtschaftspolitik* (Berlin, 1911, p. 96), that Germany's future depends solely on the iron production. Poland does not hope to lay the foundation of her future thus. She too, however, would be unable to escape the primordial law, to which the economic progress of the last years attests, namely, that a State, unwilling to be at the mercy of her neighbouring countries with regard to the production of machinery and every kind of modern installation, apart from armaments, should possess above all her own necessary foundries for cast-iron. This was the idea which had been germinating for some time in the minds of the people of the Polish State.

When after the Congress of Vienna the Poles were eager to re-establish their artificially amputated State, Lubecki, a man of genius, and the most expert of his time in economic affairs of his Country, strove to secure a greater yield from the mines, and to have foundries established. However, his efforts were not crowned with the success they deserved. The lack of the quality of coal in Congress Poland, Lubecki's sole field of action, rendered the development of the metallurgic industry impossible.

The relative dependence of Russian Poland, Galicia and Posnania on Silesia for oil, coke and raw iron.

Of all Polish territories, Silesia alone (Upper Silesia and Cieszyn Silesia), possesses coal indispensable to the iron industry. Here lies the reason for the inadequate development of the metallurgic industry in the Kingdom of Poland.

In 1912 the Congress Kingdom produced 390,000 tons of raw iron in its foundries, and imported at the same time 156,000 tons. This production, however, responded only to the very restricted needs of the Country. The restriction was due to the political oppression which paralysed its natural economic scope, as

Hungersnot
bedeutet
der Verlust der Ostprovinzen!

Die Hälfte Deiner Brotration stammt aus den Ostprovinzen.
Die Hälfte Deiner Kartoffelration stammt aus den Ostprovinzen.
Willst Du sie Dir von den Polen rauben lassen?
Oberschlesien fördert die Hälfte unserer Kohlen
Ohne Kohle keine Wärme, kein Licht, keine Arbeit, kein Leben!
Deutsche! Rettet den Osten!
Freiwillige vor!
Meldet Euch bei Euren Bezirkskommandos!
Mobile Löhnung und 5 Mrk. tägl. Zulage, freie Verpflegung & Unterkunft.
Lith. und Druck: Wilhelm Greve, Berlin SW68, Ritterstraße 50

UPPER SILESIA PLEBISCITE POST

"Famine is what the loss of the Eastern provinces means. Half of your bread ration comes from the Eastern provinces. Half of your potato ration comes from the Eastern provinces.

"Will you allow the Poles to rob you of them? Upper Silesia furnishes half of your coal; without coal, no warmth, no light, no work, no life!

"Germans! Save the East! Volunteer! Register with your district command! Flexible schedule of pay and 5 marks daily; in addition, free meals and shelter."

(From the private collection of Mr. Ben Hodge, Redlands, Calif.)

well as the industrial and technical progress. The demand for iron in the Kingdom of Poland was 5-8 times less than in other European Countries, not to mention the United States of North America. The consumption of iron in 1910, given per head in cubic cwts. is in:

United States	3,03
Germany	1,34
England	1,12
France	0,92
Belgium	1,31

while the consumption of iron, calculated per head, does not exceed more than 0,19 cub. cwts. in the Kingdom of Poland. It is plain to see what would be the economic dependence, or even the politics of Poland, towards the Country which would furnish her with the necessary iron, if Poland, having regained her independence, but remaining deprived of Silesia, were to start the development of her normal economic life, and attempt the extensive construction of railways, manufactories, refined hygienic installations, canalizations, tramways and the production of armaments for her troops, which would considerably increase the consumption of iron. Not one of the other Polish territories could contribute towards the improvement of this state of things. Galicia produces no raw iron at all, on account of the lack of quality of necessary coal, as well as of the corresponding quantity of iron ore.

With regard to the production of raw iron, Galicia, before the war, was absolutely dependent on the production from Austrian-Silesia and Moravia. Posnania, like Western Prussia, possesses neither raw iron nor coal; these two regions stand in need of the absolutely indispensable materials for the production of iron. Therefore, every attempt to give a new scope for the metallurgic industry in a Poland deprived of Silesia, will place her, of necessity, on the absolute dependence of the State which would have Silesia within its frontiers. The above statements testify clearly that this dependence actually exists.

· · · · · · ·

In this respect, Galicia found herself in still more unfavourable conditions. The importation of coal from Upper Silesia increased uninterruptedly, rising from 449,634 tons in 1900 to 1,909,620 tons in 1913. The importation of coke increased during the same course of time from 24,229 tons to 60,027 tons, and with regard to iron ware, the importation increased from 14,474 tons to 28,408 tons. On the other hand, Western Prussia and Posnania were also exclusively dependent on Upper Silesia for the supply of coal, coke and iron.

The Kingdom of Poland might have evaded, to a certain extent, part of this economic dependence on Silesia, by importing raw iron and iron ware from Russia of which the Kingdom of Poland, from the political point of view, constitutes an integral part. The subjection of the Kingdom of Poland to Russia having ended, a Custom Frontier will be established between the Ancient Kingdom and Russia, which will form an obstacle to the advantageous importation of raw iron and iron ware from Russia. This circumstance will conduce for Poland a still greater economic dependence towards Silesia, or rather, Germany.

This dependence was intolerable for Galicia and the Congress Kingdom, although she was weakened by the amicable relationship that Germany held towards Russia and Austria-Hungary before the War. One must suppose that the necessity for procuring raw iron in a Germany diminished, but possessing Upper Silesia, would be equivalent to Poland, resuscitated by Germany's defeat to her complete economic subjection, and would enforce the nucleus of perpetual armed conflicts. It is to be feared that the danger of such a subjection would only create the necessity for a political reconciliation between Poland and Germany, such as could constitute no durable interest for Poland, and still less for that of the Entente Country.

The economic dependence on Silesia with regard to other parts of Poland. The dependence of the other parts of Poland with regard to Silesia, corresponds reciprocally. We find a convincing and quite impartial proof on the question of this dependence in seven memorandums at least, dedicated to the Germans of Silesia, and delivered to the Chancellor of the Empire, either by the Chamber of Commerce of Opole, or by the Union of the Proprietors of the Upper Silesian mines and foundries, in November 1915; 3rd September, 1916; 24th September, 1916; July, 1917; and September, 1917.

The prominent business men of Upper Silesia prove in all these memorandums, that the closest bonds uniting Upper Silesia to Poland constitute a vital question for this country.

Geographical dependence. In presenting its postulates to the Chancellor, the Chamber of Commerce of Opole mentions amongst other items, in the memorandum of the 24th September, 1916, page 15:

"In the first place we express the desire of liberating Upper Silesia at last from this exclusive encompassment which enforces her geographical and political situation. This encompassment is the chief cause of all eminent complaints in our district. Although one is authorised to hope that, after the conclusion of Peace, the tentatives of an economic union with Austria-Hungary will lead to the reinforcement of the mutual exchange of products between these two countries, it is no less true that the exportation to Austria and Hungary will always be limited by the effort which these two nations will make in order to reëstablish their own industry, and to give it new scope. Thus the exportation to Austria and Hungary could never replace for Silesia and the whole German industry, the exportation to Poland, which, as one may hope, will be of the most importance, considering that the State is still very much behindhand from the point of view of technical progress. For this reason we take the liberty of drawing every attention to this point in our memorandum, of dealing fully with the relationship which has always existed between the commerce and industry of Silesia and Russian Poland. *The future of Upper Silesia depends on the manner in which her relationship with Russian Poland is decided: hence, as the natural consequence of this near relationship we express the wish, in this memorandum, of seeing these countries reunited to Germany as regards economics, or, at least to see the reunion of Germany with the Eastern part bordering on Silesia.*"

Dependence on the importation of victuals. On the other hand, Germany's assertions affirming the impossibility of self-development for the Silesian industry without the importation of raw iron and zinc to the Silesian foundries, wood from Poland to the Silesian mines, and pork, specially imported from Poland, supplying the indispensable need of meat to the Silesian miners, prove how closely the economic relationship unites Silesia with the rest of Poland. In 1912-13, the importation of pork to Silesia from the Kingdom of Poland alone realised 3,075 pieces per week, showing the enormous importance attached to the alimentation of the Silesian workman.

Dependence on the importation of iron ore. Of equal importance is the iron ore from the Kingdom for the Silesian foundries. The iron ore beds of Silesia are already becoming exhausted. Those of the Kingdom, on the contrary, in consequence of the competition with the richer iron ore from South Russia, have been worked only feebly up to the present. The raw iron of the Kingdom does not contain a great quantity of pure iron, but the quality is excellent. For this reason, the authors of the above mentioned memorandum acknowledge that since the occupation of this part of Poland by German troops, the foundries in Upper Silesia hastened to explore these beds in the Kingdom. A special Society, the "Erzverwartungs-Gesellschaft," was formed, which possessed the exclusive privilege for investigation and exploitation of the mines. Through the intermediary of this "Society," the Germans have confiscated 2,000,000 tons of iron ore in the mines and foundries of the Kingdom since the year 1915. In 1916, this same honourable "Society" supplied the Silesian foundries with iron ore from the Kingdom, a quantity valued at 16% of the total consumption, while the production from the Upper Silesian mines supplied only 9.5% of the usual consumption of the local foundries.

The dependence on the importation of victuals. (Sic) The Silesian mines are no less submitted to the other parts of Poland with regard to the importation of wood. According to the data of the above mentioned memorandum, the importation of wood from Galicia and the Kingdom to Silesia amounted to 8,829,242 c.f. per year.

The memorandum states clearly that: "should the importation of wood from the Kingdom have proved disappointing, it would have been impossible to maintain the actual yield in the Silesian mines."

The above quoted facts and information with regard to the business men of Germany prove, as has been pointed out before, how firm an economic relationship binds Silesia to the other Polish territories.

Another memorandum addressed by the Chamber of Commerce of Opole to the Chancellor of Empire in July 1915, likewise makes the same very sincere admission: "In view of the unfavourable situation of the industrial district of Silesia, Poland is, and will continue to be, for the latter, the agent for her all-important and absolutely indispensable development."

There is still a peculiar phenomenon which determines the importance of Poland for the industrial development of Silesia. The conditions for the metallurgic industry in Silesia were less favourable than those of the Rhenish Countries and Westphalia; consequently the products of this industry could not sustain the concurrence of the metallurgic products from Western Germany; either of Germany herself, or on the foreign markets of the West, accustomed to the fixed lower prices for the manufactured products. It was for this reason that the metallurgic and iron production of Silesia was condemned to be drifted away on the Eastern markets where the products always attained a superior price. Russia, even more than Poland, constituted such a market, but in order to take products into Russia, Poland had to be crossed. Poland's present independence creates difficulties for the exportation of products from Upper Silesia to Poland, menacing to reduce to nothing the products of the Silesian industry towards the East. In the German records previously mentioned, this danger is faced, so to say, on every page. We extract from amongst many others the following passage: "We may be certain that Poland will try her utmost to impede German industry and commerce. As we have already shown in previous memorandums, in order to prevent our exportation towards Russia being closed, it is essential to have possession of at least two Polish lines of transit: that of Warsaw-Vienna and the Vistula" (loc. cit., page 8).

In the fear that as a sequel to the reconstruction of an independent Poland, this relationship with Silesia will become completely modified, or even null (what a paradox!), the business men of Upper

The political danger of Germany's retention of Silesia. Silesia resort to the most strange means. Their chief aim is to keep Poland in bondage.

"We must defy the opinion that Poland will become a complete autonomous State independent of Germany, Austria-Hungary and Russia."

That is how the question is treated by the potentates of the German industry, who employ 400,000 Polish workmen.

Should the maintenance of a Poland in slavery prove impossible: "Poland should be made a protectorate State dependent on Germany, in the manner of the provinces of the Ancient Roman Empire. . . . All means of communication, by land or water, must pass into the possession of the German Empire. The same steps are to be taken for post, telegraph and cable services."

Independently of this reprisal of classic examples, so efficacious in Ancient Rome for the potentates of Upper Silesia: ". . . in all circumstances, an absolute economic necessity exists for separating the districts of Bendzin, Wielun-Czestochowa and Olkusz from Poland, and of annexing them to Germany. This, as your Excellency knows, is the principal postulate of Upper Silesia."

How then, do the personal friends of William II picture to themselves the existence of Silesia, in the case of her separation from Poland and Russia? They know pertinently that the supremacy exercised by the lowest majority of plutocrats over the whole Polish population in Silesia is violate and despotic; they fear to lose this hold, and the following are the means they invent:

"To prevent the extension of the Polish agitation on German territory from breaking out afresh and growing stronger, which may be expected after the War, a protective zone must be made along the German frontier, where a purely German population should be established. For this end, Polish residents must be removed further into the Congress Poland, or to colonised territory which should be created to the East of the Congress Poland, and German peasants from Poland should take the place of the expelled Polish proprietors.

"Thus, the dangers of a Polish agitation, and of a powerful prevalence in the German provinces of the East, will be considerably weakened."

Such are the monstrosities of which the Teutonic spirit is capable of bearing. Such is the lot which threatens the Polish population should Silesia remain in German hands.

It is true that the Poles can no longer be driven into what is called by the Germans "Kongrespolen" (provided that this term, which was an insult, no longer bears the same signification after actual Congress), but, we must bear in mind that fact that the political Germany of William, Bismarck and the Commission of Colonization, as also, the experience already sufficient for Germany (revolutionary) of Scheidemann and Noske, have amply proved that the Germans always knew how to find the necessary means for the realisation of their national and imperialistic tendencies.

To leave a thousand Poles under Prussian domination, is to leave a hotbed of discord, where future European oppressions and interminable struggles will germinate.

Apart from the Polish point of view, let us consider further the result should Germany maintain her possession of Upper Silesia.

In the memorandum of 24th September 1916, the Chamber of Commerce of Opole, page 31, the following statement is made: "The Silesian foundries have shown their exceptional importance in the cause for the Country's defence, for the war has proved that the industry of Western Germany is not in a state to furnish the German troops with necessary war material. Without the foundries of Upper Silesia, the manufacture of armaments, munitions and other necessary articles for the armies, would never have been able to sustain the high demands.

Therefore the Silesian industry should be maintained at all costs, especially in the interest of the army."

The conclusions to be drawn from what has been said, are obvious. Prussian militarism must be completely destroyed, and cease to menace the entire civilized world. Poland, in her turn, through her reunion with Silesia, will obtain her own bases for the iron industry, and consequently for the economic reconstruction and rebirth of her technical progress. Upper Silesia, reunited to Poland, already organically forming this technical progress from the national and economic points of view, will become the essential cause for progress and peace. If, on the other hand, the Germans continue to withhold Upper Silesia, the matter will be menace of justice, despotism and even imminent war.

In order to establish the work of Peace on stable assizes, the faults of history must be repaired, even to the uprooting of bygone times.

139. Minutes of the Supreme Council: Poland[1]

[This selection shows how an important question was handled by the Supreme Council. It may be noted here that the attitude of France in the Council and on the commission was extremely favorable to a large and strong Poland; Lloyd George and the British delegation, on the other hand, while committed to the restoration of an independent Poland, were opposed to creating a large pro-French state with contested territories which might prove liabilities. Dmowski was the able Polish Foreign Minister.]

Instructions for the Mission to Poland. 1. M. Clemenceau stated that they had met this morning to examine the instructions for the Commission that was proceeding to Poland. M. Pichon had prepared a text of these instructions and the British Government had suggested certain amendments thereupon. This document, however, proved to be too long, and Mr. Balfour had looked into the matter and curtailed it considerably, and reproduced a further draft instruction which was submitted to the meeting. This draft instruction contained the contents both of the original draft instruction of M. Pichon as well as the amendments made by the British Government.

(The draft instruction as finally drawn up was then read.)

M. Clemenceau thought that the last paragraph of the draft instruction was not suitable, and Mr. Balfour agreed.

(Consequently, it was agreed that the last paragraph should be omitted. For text as finally adopted see Annex A, p. 631.)

Baron Sonnino said that Italy had some Polish prisoners ready to go to Poland and wished to know whether Italy should await the report of this Commission before the soldiers should proceed.

---

[1] Paris Peace Conference. B.C. 15, 29 January, 1919. 11 a.m. Secretary's Notes of a Conversation held in M. Pichon's Room at the Quai d'Orsay, Paris (Hoover War Library Manuscript).

M. Clemenceau was of the opinion that they should wait, particularly as the decision would depend upon what was going to be done with the Polish soldiers in France.

Statement by M. Dmowski. 2. Thereupon M. Dmowski, accompanied by M. Erasme Piltz were called in in order to enlighten the meeting as to the position in Poland.

M. Dmowski wished to know on what particular point he should first attempt to speak, or what points the meeting specially desired information upon.

M. Clemenceau replied that it would perhaps be best that he should say whatever he might have to say so as to place the meeting in a position to consider the question as a whole. It would be possible later on to take the various points in rotation.

President Wilson stated that he was anxious to know the whole case, but that the present object of the Allies was to assist Poland, as far as the Allies could and they were certain that his views on that subject would be most interesting.

M. Dmowski then proceeded to state that the Poles had not been protected to any large extent by the Armistice, but two things did have reference to the situation in Poland. By Article 12 of the Armistice the Germans were obliged to occupy the Eastern Frontier until such time as the Allies should request them to withdraw their troops. And, secondly, Article 16 provided that access should be given the Allies to Poland via Dantzig-Thorn railway. If the German troops had remained, under the terms of the Armistice, in the Eastern Provinces, their presence would have protected the Poles against the Bolsheviks; and if the route through Dantzig had remained open Poland would have been able to have obtained all the arms and ammunition and supplies that she might require. The revolution in Germany had prevented the carrying out of the terms of the Armistice, and the German troops withdrew in a disorderly manner before the Allies had requested them to do so. On their way they were guilty of committing crimes, and they carried away supplies and railway material with them as they went. Dantzig was situated within German territory and was in German possession after the signing of the Armistice. The railway from Dantzig to the Frontier of Poland (a distance of some 100 miles) ran through German territory, and since the conclusion of the Armistice the Germans had shown more and more hostility towards the Poles. Secondly, Article 16 was altogether a dead-letter. In order to make it effective it was absolutely necessary to occupy Dantzig and the railway line running to the Polish Frontier so as to allow of arms, ammunition and supplies being forwarded to Poland. Unless this was done, both Articles would remain a dead-letter.

Situation in German Poland. 3. M. Dmowski next turned to the situation in German-Poland specifically. He stated that, according to German statistics, there were four million Poles in Eastern Posen, Eastern Prussia, Western Prussia and Upper Silesia; but, according to the Polish estimate this number was five million. These Poles were some of the most educated and highly cultured of the nation, with a strong sense of nationality and men of progressive ideas. Even according to the German statement, in these Provinces it was admitted that the Polish farmers and merchants were of a higher standard than the German ones. As soon as the opportunity offered itself to organise themselves, these Poles established a Government by pacific means and then waited until the Peace Conference should have decided upon the status of Poland. All they desired was that Germany should not put anything in the way of their joining up with the other Polish Provinces. But this movement, as showing the aim of the Poles, rather frightened the Germans who immediately proceeded to take steps to suppress it and organised a special corps, known as the "Heinitschutz Ost" (Heimatschütz Oest?), consisting largely of officers, with the idea of crushing this political movement. Troops had been concentrated in the Eastern Provinces waiting for the opportunity to attack. When M. Paderewski came to Posen, he was most enthusiastically received by the population, which remained quite pacific. But the Germans attacked them with machine-guns. In consequence an armed conflict arose and fighting took place in the streets of Posen. The Poles were victorious and occupied the city and the fortress. Once that conflict had begun it was bound to spread, and it spread throughout the whole of the Province until the Germans were practically pushed out of the district. The Poles established a civic government which kept order without doing harm to the inhabitants; conduct very different from that of the Germans, possibly because the Poles were at home, or the Germans were in a foreign territory to them. Further, he reminded the meeting that the Conference had issued a declaration with regard to disputable territory. The Poles in Posen would understand that this declaration and this warning was addressed to them as well, and as it is their desire to stand well with the Allies, they will certainly respect it and it will make a great impression on them. But the Germans certainly will not respect it, but are continuing their organisation against Poland. The result will be that unless the Allies stop both sides (the Germans as well as the Poles), Poland inevitably must be crushed. The Germans have a great respect for the power of the Allies, and M. Dmowski felt that if they received a similar order to cease fighting the possibility was they would accept the same.

M. Dmowski added that German-Poland had as much in the way of supplies as she wanted, in fact more than she required, as the German soldiers, on their return, had requisitioned food along the way to carry themselves on. But the other Polish provinces were starving for want of food. He compared Germany to the god Janus. Germany had one face towards the West, where she had made peace, and the other face towards the East, where she was organising for war. Her troops there were concentrated and out for war. She might have given up the West, but she had not given up her plan for extending her Empire in the East. As regards German-Poland, he made one proposition only, and that was that both sides should discontinue fighting, and should be ordered to stay where they were. The Poles were extremely anxious to keep the rolling stock at present at Posen which the Germans were threatening to take away as they themselves were short of rolling stock.

Russian
Poland.
4. Russian-Poland found itself, after the Armistice, in a most difficult position. The nucleus of the Government, which the Germans had established in 1916, continued until the Armistice, but once the Armistice was concluded it could not stand, on the one hand because it had been established by the Germans, and on the other hand, because it was too conservative. The Government was then handed over to General Pilsudski, a member of the Socialist Party, who had become very popular as he had fought against Russia in the beginning of the war and afterwards had been imprisoned by the Germans. It was perhaps the safest thing for Poland that she now had a Socialist Government, because she had no arms or army to protect herself. On the one side there was a Socialist Revolutionary Government, and on the other, a Democratic Government, which had established a revolution in Germany. Had this not been the case, the Socialistic Government of Pilsudski could not have lasted. As it was, his Government was in great difficulties, as there was a majority against them even in Russian-Poland, but more particularly in German-Poland and also in Austrian-Poland, the two latter provinces being much better organized and more advanced than Russian-Poland. But the greatest weakness of all was that the Pilsudski Government had no money. Inevitably, therefore, attempts were made to overthrow his Government, and even the National Council of the Poles in Paris was approached to aid in this object. The National Council refused because it felt that a Socialistic Government, situated between two extreme Socialistic Governments, was necessary for the safety of Poland at the time, and it concentrated its efforts on arranging a compromise with the Socialists. Consequently, the National Council sent M. Paderewski to Poland in order to establish a Government by compromise, his strong point being that he had so far taken no part in party politics. He was successful and formed a Government representing all portions of the provinces of Poland and also the main parties. He had, perhaps, taken too long to come to this compromise, but the reason was that Socialistic Governments were, from their very nature, not much given to compromise.

External
Situation
Generally.
5. As already mentioned, the German soldiers on returning from the Eastern front committed many crimes, but their worst crime of all was the fact that they assisted the Bolsheviks by leaving them their arms and ammunition, and also by allowing them to follow the Germans up in close succes-

sion. At the same time the German General at Vilna refused passage to the Polish troops. In this way the Germans were advancing the aim of Bolshevism to get into touch with German territory and so to join hands and make a common cause with the Spartacist group inside Germany. Today the Bolshevik troops were threatening Poland and were about 150 miles from Warsaw. The difficulty of Poland was not the lack of men; she had enough to defend herself, but her difficulty was that she had no arms to arm them with or ammunition with which to fight. As evidence of the shortage of ammunition, he stated that the inhabitants of Poland had sent eight million rounds of cartridges to Warsaw in order to assist in defending the country.

Ukraine and Eastern Galicia. 6. The Austrian troops on their return from Eastern Galicia distributed their arms amongst the people, and, at the same time, were guilty of atrocious massacres, particularly of landowners. It was estimated that some 2,000 landowners with their families were murdered in this fashion. In Eastern Galicia, Ukrainian bands actually took Lemberg and held it for a few days, and even though they had been driven out, they were not far from the town.

Summary. M. Dmowski summed up the position by stating that Poland was threatened on three sides; first by the Bolsheviks on the East, second by the Ukrainian bands on the South-East and by the Germans on the North-West. The problem to settle was not the question of supplying Poland with men, but with arms and ammunition and assistance to organise their army. This object could only be attained by using the railway running from Dantzig to the Polish frontier. It was impossible to use the Austro-Hungarian railway system, as that system was not extensive enough and it would take too long, and the question of assistance was extremely urgent. He suggested the temporary occupation by Allied troops of Dantzig and of the railway line between Dantzig and Poland. He further suggested that some agreement should be made with the Germans whereby arms, ammunition and troops could be sent along this railway line and the railway line be occupied by Polish troops. In his opinion it would be much better for the Allies to occupy this line in agreement with the Germans, and if the Poles were to do so the Germans might regard this as an aggressive act of Poland. If Poland could not be assisted and assisted quickly, she must be crushed and submerged by Bolshevism. The only way was to open a means of rapid and sure communication and the only sure and rapid route was that between Dantzig and Thorn. He expressed the opinion that there was not much fear of Bolshevism extending to German and Austrian-Poland because those provinces were well organised and politically sound. In his opinion Bolshevism really was the rule of a despotic organisation representing a well-organised class in a country where all other classes were passive and disorganised. In a country where the various classes were politically organised and enlightened, Bolshevism in the true sense of the word was not a serious danger. It was only possible where a country was passive and disorganised.

Upper Silesia (Teschen). 7. The province of Teschen in Silesia is occupied partly by Czechs and partly by Poles, the latter of whom are in a great majority. It was accordingly agreed in November, 1918, that that portion of the country where the majority of the inhabitants are Poles should be regarded as the Polish sphere, and that portion which is inhabited by the Czechs as the majority, should be the Czech sphere. This agreement, which had been concluded by the local organisations, was approved by the Polish Government, but not by the Czecho-Slovak Government and recently Czech troops had entered this disputed territory. This act was not only one of violence but it was a dangerous act because if the Czech troops continue to remain there bloodshed inevitably must follow and much more harm might be done to the ultimate settlement of this dispute. M. Dmowski urged that the only settlement was that these Czech troops should be withdrawn to the territory as arranged in the terms of the agreement of the 5th of November, pending a settlement by the Peace Conference.

German Policy Towards Poland. 8. M. Dmowski proceeded to direct attention to the Polish policy of the Germans and referred to their anti-Polish laws, their prohibition of the use of the Polish language in the schools and their confiscation of the property of the Poles. He quoted the special and powerful company which had been erected for the special purpose of colonizing portions of Poland with German settlers and in that connection quoted von Bülow's remarks that the whole of Poland is an enemy and pointed out that Germany had employed means to influence both Austria and Russia to adopt the same line of policy. During the war there were two policies, one of annexation of Poland, but this plan was given up because there had been so much difficulty with the five million Poles in the German Eastern provinces, that it was felt to increase the number of recalcitrant subjects would only make matters more difficult. So the other programme was adopted of establishing a small kingdom consisting of some twelve million inhabitants and round it to place two other small states, Lithuania and Ukrainia. The latter two, in case of a German victory, would be completely under German domination, as neither Lithuania nor Ukrainia could, strictly speaking, be said to have reached the stage of nationhood. The national movement in Lithuania was not older than 40 years, and, although the movement had shown great activity, the Lithuanians had not advanced so far yet as to entitle themselves to be called a nation fit to protect themselves and to accept the responsibilities and duties of the state. The same remarks applied to Ukrainia. The aim of this arrangement of establishing two small states was to split up Russia and Poland, both of whom were enemies. The whole idea dominating this programme was that by this means Poland would ultimately be strangled and submerged.

Territorial Claims. 9. M. Dmowski suggested that in reaching the settlement of the territory to belong to Poland, we should start from the date 1772, before the first partition. This did not mean that she must be reconstituted on the same boundaries as then existed, but this must be the point of departure and the boundaries should be rectified according to present conditions. France, Italy, Great Britain and similar countries, owing to the statistics they kept, and to their well-defined boundaries, were able to state immediately what their territory was, and what their people were. But not so with Poland. In settling the boundaries of Poland, the principle of including within those boundaries those territories where the Poles were in a large majority, must not be accepted altogether. In the West, Poland could not be satisfied with the historical boundaries of 1772. For instance, Silesia was lost in the 14th century, but today 90% of the population, owing to the national revival, had kept its language and was strongly Polish. For instance, 15 years ago, Silesia sent a Polish representative to the Austrian Reichsrat. Furthermore, geographically speaking, Silesia falls within the whole territory of Poland.

(The meeting adjourned until 3:30 p.m. in the afternoon.)

29th January, 1919.

AMERICAN COMMISSION TO NEGOTIATE PEACE

BC—15
Annex A

To be appended to notes for January 29, 1919, 11 a.m.

DRAFT OF INSTRUCTION FOR THE DELEGATES OF THE ALLIED GOVERNMENTS IN POLAND

It will be the business of the Delegates of the Allied Governments to convey as early as possible information to their Governments on the present situation in Poland. The Military question and the Food question are the most urgent, but reports on the political and social conditions of the country should be sent without unnecessary delay.

The Polish Government should be warned against adopting a policy of an aggressive character. Any appearance of attempting to prejudge the decisions of the Conference will have the worst possible effect. The Delegates should invite the most earnest consideration of the Polish Government to the declaration recently made on this subject by the representatives of the Powers at Paris.

Every effort should be made to bring to an end the hostilities which are now taking place between the Poles and neighbouring peoples.

Armistices should be arranged wherever possible and the Delegates should use their good offices to bring them about.

In this connection it should be noted that the invasion by the Poles of German territory tends to restore the German military spirit and to delay the break-up of the German army; and it has the further disadvantage of complicating the arrangements for German disarmament which the Allies desire to carry out with the least possible delay.

The Delegates should inquire how far the Polish Government possess the means to maintain order within their existing territory and of preserving it from external aggression whether carried out by Bolshevists or any other forces and they should study and report on the measures necessary to supply any deficiencies which may be found to exist.

The food question will require their earnest attention and they should coöperate with the Mission about to be despatched to Poland by the Supreme Council of Supply and Relief. In order to secure this coöperation the principal Delegates of the Supreme Council of Supply and Relief should be attached to the Delegation whenever questions of food supply have to be dealt with.

January 29th, 1919

Minutes of the Supreme Council: Poland[1]

Territorial Claims. 1. M. Dmowski, resuming his statement, stated furthermore that the whole territory of Eastern Germany was not naturally German but was Germanised, and quoted Von Bülow as saying what Germany had lost in the West as a result of the break-up of the Empire of Charlemagne, she had gained in the East. He quoted Dantzig as an illustration, saying that though, according to the German statistics, only 3 percent of the inhabitants were Poles, he felt certain that at least 40 percent belonged to that nationality. As the Poles were mostly employees, they would be afraid of stating that their nationality was Polish for fear of being dismissed, and he referred to the fact that soon after the Armistice a protest meeting had been held by the Germans against Dantzig being incorporated in Poland. When the petition which had been drawn up at that meeting was circulated for signature, only 16 signators were to be found, and of those 14 were those of officials. Ethnographically, the limits of Poland were irregular, and pointed to the fact that some wrong would have to be done East Prussia. Either a small island of German [people] must be left in the midst of Polish territory, or the large Polish population must remain under Germany. His suggestion was that the small island of German people should be made a republic with

---

[1] Paris Peace Conference. B. C. 16, 29 January, 1919. 3:30 P. M. Secretary's Notes of a Conversation held in M. Pichon's Room at the Quai d'Orsay, Paris (Hoover War Library Manuscript).

its capital at Königsberg. He maintained that it would be more just to expose a small Germanised country to infiltration by Poles, than to deprive all Poland of economic independence and to expose it to German aggression. Summing up the question of what is, or what is not, Polish territory, he said that a rough definition would be that such territory as had been oppressed by anti-Polish laws was Polish territory. From the point of view of the preservation of peace, it was evident that if the coast belonged to one nation and the land to another, there would be mutual tendency to conquest. This had been fully appreciated by the Germans with the result [that it] was apparent in their policy, which had aimed at the gradual absorption of Polish lands, and [he] pointed out the colonisation schemes not only in German Poland but also in Russian Poland, and in this connection he quoted Herr Bebel, the Socialist Democrat, in his work *"Die Frau"*: "Our task is not to colonise Africa, but to colonise the Vistula." It could not be expected that this idea of absorbing Poland would die amongst the Germans. Therefore, he urged that the frontiers should be so arranged that Poland should no longer be exposed to this danger.

Eastern Frontiers of Poland. 2. Polish land reached to the Dnieper and the Dwina when the union of the colonies of Poland and Lithuania took place in the 13th and 14th centuries, but today the bulk of the population of Lithuania was not Polish, though the Lithuanians were closely allied, so he conceded that the Eastern Frontiers of Poland should be curtailed and a large portion remain under Russia. Both Lithuania and Ukrainia he excluded, and did not lay claim to these countries as part of Poland.

Finally, he suggested that the subject of Poland should be viewed from the standpoint of a League of Nations and he defined a nation as a race of men capable of so organising itself as to be able to express collective will and of organising its affairs both externally and internally. In a word, it must be able to govern itself and to oppose oppression. Tested by this test Russia, strictly speaking, was not fit for admission to a League of Nations, nor were the Lithuanians advanced far enough in national unity or ideals to be included amongst the nations. The Ukrainian State at present was really organised anarchy and the Ukrainians were not so far advanced as the Lithuanians on the road to nationality. The great need in Eastern Europe was to have established Governments, able to assure order and to express their will in foreign and in internal policy. It was too early to think of Lithuania or Ukrainia as independent States. Therefore, it would be best that, if organised as separate states they should be united in some other state, and as the Lithuanians were closely allied to the Poles, he suggested Poland as the best state to which they should be united. All that remained East of Poland, he feared, would remain for a long time subject to anarchy. He expressed the opinion that in Russia there would be a despotism for some time to come, because the masses were too indolent and passive. They were able to be ruled but not fit to rule. The red despotism of Bolshevism would last for some time but the reaction would come and a possible return to Czardom with all its vices. In Poland they were afraid to [sic] the anarchy prevalent in the Eastern districts of old historical Poland and, therefore, they were satisfied to renounce these districts for the sake of preserving peace and order within their own borders.

Eastern Galicia. 3. Eastern Galicia was, he admitted, a disputed territory, but he claimed that they were unable to organise a Government and pointed to the fact that in the intellectual professions, excluding small farmers and clergy, there were 400,000 Poles and only 16,000 Ruthenes. They might be entitled to home rule but they were unable to create a separate state.

M. Erasme Piltz wished to associate himself with M. Dmowski as to the danger threatened from the Bolsheviks, and expressed the fear that if troops were sent they would arrive too late. The point he wished to express most forcibly was the urgency of sending help to Poland as soon as possible.

Mr. Balfour remarked that the first portion of M. Dmowski's statement dealt [sic] with the immediate and pressing question of the Polish situation. The latter part dealt [sic] with territorial questions which would have to be discussed later on by the Conference. Today they were only concerned with the first question.

M. Clemenceau said that the Czecho-Slovak representatives were there to deal with the Teschen question, which is disputed territory.

(It was decided that the Czecho-Slovak representatives should be admitted.)

Claims of Czecho-Slovakia to Teschen Province. 4. Dr. Benes, on behalf of Czecho-Slovakia, proceeded to make a statement as to the position of Bohemia, Moravia, and Eastern Silesia.

Mr. Lloyd George said that he was sorry to intervene to point out that the meeting was not dealing with the whole question of Czecho-Slovakia today, but would have to enter into that whole question at a later date. They were dealing today with one narrow point, and that was the territory in dispute between the Czecho-Slovaks and the Poles.

M. Clemenceau said he thought it was necessary to have the whole case of the Czechs as the meeting had had the whole case of Poland.

President Wilson suggested that the only question which [was] the business of the day was information as to the position in Eastern Silesia between the Poles and the Czecho-Slovaks, and suggested that the statement should be confined to that point only.

M. Clemenceau then requested Dr. Benes to confine himself to the dispute between the Czecho-Slovaks and the Poles.

Dr. Benes proceeded to deal with this question at length [of] statistical, ethnological, historical and economic grounds.

(Full details are available in the pamphlet entitled "The Problem of Teschen Silesia" submitted by the Czecho-Slovak delegation. Copies of this pamphlet are obtainable at the office of the Secretary-General.)

Dr. Benes added, as regards the ethnological questions, that his government disputed the correctness of Austrian statistics. For instance in the case of the town of Richvaldt the Austrian statistics gave as the population in 1900: 4,500 Poles against 11 Czechs; and in 1910, 2,900 Czechs against 3,000 Poles. This gives a clear idea of the manner in which Austrian statistics are compiled.

Dr. Kramartz asked to be allowed to emphasise certain points made by Dr. Benes and stated that he had always thought that the points of difference between the Poles and the Czecho-Slovaks would be settled by mutual agreement. To his surprise, the Poles invaded this territory, mobilized the male population, and even went so far as to fix an election day, and settled that the Courts should fall under the Court of Cracow. On representations being made to him by the population of that quarter, his reply was that the Peace Conference must decide the question of disputed territory, and that he had been informed by France and Great Britain that the Czecho-Slovaks were entitled to occupy the historical boundaries of the old Czech Kingdom. He had protested to the Polish Government, and has sent a second protest; but no reply was forthcoming. He was told that if this present condition continued, it was very likely the Bolshevist activity would follow, and therefore he had acted carefully so as to avoid bloodshed.

The second point he emphasised was the fact that the Czecho-Slovak Republic could not exist without the large coal area which was within the disputed area.

In conclusion, he stated that they had always endeavoured to arrive at a private agreement with Poland, but this had failed. Therefore, they now desired to place themselves entirely in the hands of the Peace Conference, in the full confidence that the Great Powers would not forget the great sacrifices which they had made in their cause during the war, and that they would not lose sight of the economic requirements of the country upon which the whole prosperity of the Czecho-Slovak Republic depended.

Mr. Balfour suggested that the representatives of Poland and of the Czecho-Slovaks should meet the members of the Commission appointed by the Peace Conference to investigate Polish questions the following morning at 10 o'clock, so that they could commence that work of pacification and arrangements could be made in Paris immediately.

(This was agreed to.)

M. Clemenceau expressed the wish to hear what M. Dmowski had to say on this subject.

M. Dmowski in a short reply, regretted that apparently the Czecho-Slovak Government had not been fully informed as to what was taking place in Silesia, and stated that it was not the Poles that had invaded

Teschen, but the inhabitants had organised themselves militarily; not a single soldier had been sent from Poland. He suggested that any further movement of the Czecho-Slovak Army should be stopped, pending the decision of the Conference.

Polish Commission to enquire into the Teschen Dispute. 5. Mr. Balfour suggested that the Commission which would meet on the morrow should also consider the question of supplying arms and munitions to Poland.

M. Clemenceau, in summing up, stated that the delegates would meet the representatives of Poland and of Czecho-Slovakia the following morning, Thursday, the 30th January, at 10 o'clock, at the Quai d'Orsay, and would report on the Teschen dispute as well as on the supply of arms and munitions to Poland.

(This was agreed to, and the meeting adjourned until 11 o'clock on Thursday, January 30th.)

29th January, 1919

140. POLAND AT THE PEACE CONFERENCE[1]

[Late in February, 1919, the Supreme Council established the Commission on Polish Affairs, headed by Jules Cambon, French Ambassador in Berlin before the war. Being one of the first territorial commissions, it held more meetings than any other, according to R. L. Lord, Chief of the Polish Division of the American Commission to Negotiate Peace. The commission referred to in doc. no. 139 was not the same but a forerunner of the territorial commission. As regards Eastern Galicia, the population was overwhelmingly Ruthenian and in most districts was Russian in sympathy, but by the Treaty of Riga it was eventually given to Poland.]

Note from the Commission on Polish Affairs asking for instructions regarding the frontiers to be assigned to Poland in Eastern Galicia. M. Cambon said that the following note had been drawn up and distributed to all Members present:—

"The work of the Commission on Polish Affairs in considering the frontiers of Poland has reached the following stage:

"(a) Proposals in regard to the frontier between Poland and Germany were submitted in Report No. 1 dated March 12, 1919;

"(b) Proposals in regard to the frontier between Poland and the Czecho-Slovak State were submitted in the note dated April 6, 1919, which was presented jointly by the Commissions on Polish and Czecho-Slovak Affairs:

"(c) Proposals in regard to the Eastern frontier of Poland north of

---

[1] American Commission to Negotiate Peace. FM—9. Secretary's Notes of a Conversation of the Foreign Ministers, held in M. Pichon's Room at the Quai d'Orsay, Paris, on Saturday, April 26th, 1919, at 3 p. m. (Hoover War Library Manuscript).

the latitude of Kholm were submitted in Report No. 2 dated April 21, 1919. No proposal has been made in regard to a frontier south of this latitude owing to the close connection between this part of the frontier and the frontier to be determined in Eastern Galicia;

"(d) In regard to Eastern Galicia the Commission consider themselves at present debarred from making any definite recommendations as to the frontier in view of the decision taken by the Supreme Council at the meeting on the 19th March, 1919, that the Polish and Ukrainian Representatives should not be heard with regard to their respective claims in Eastern Galicia until the cessation of hostilities between the Polish and Ukrainian troops in that region.

"In view of the constitution at Paris of an Inter-Allied Commission to establish an armistice between the Polish and Ukrainian troops there appear to be grounds for hoping that a truce may be arranged in the near future, and accordingly, that it would be possible for the Commission to undertake the description of the frontier in Eastern Galicia.

"Elsewhere, the Commission has been guided primarily by ethnic considerations modified to a certain extent by various economic factors and the necessities of transport.

"In regard to Galicia, however, if primarily ethnographical considerations were followed it is certain that in spite of the large Polish minority in Eastern Galicia the frontier of Poland would run west of Lemberg, unless an area containing a Ruthenian majority were to be assigned to Poland.

"This question thus introduces problems of general policy involving consequences of the utmost gravity. Several solutions may be considered, namely; the creation of an independent state, the establishment of an autonomous state under the control of the League of Nations, the partition of Eastern Galicia between Poland and the Ukraine. Either of these might, owing to the attraction which Russia would undoubtedly exercise upon a weak Slav State, result in the extension of the Russian frontier to the Carpathians. On the other hand, it may be thought desirable to consider the political advantage which might result from the establishment of a common frontier between Poland and Roumania while securing for Eastern Galicia adequate guarantees in the way of local autonomy.

"The Commission is of opinion that it is not possible to settle the frontiers of Poland in this region without determining at the same time the future status of Eastern Galicia. Considering that this question goes somewhat beyond its original mandate, the Commission respectfully approaches the Supreme Council with the request that it may be given:

"Either explicit instruction as to the basis on which to carry out its work in this region; or a new mandate authorising it to proceed with the study of this question."

Mr. Lansing thought it would be wise for the Commission on Polish Affairs to continue its study with an extension of authority, which would empower it to consider the question not only from the ethnic, economic and strategic point of view, but also from all other standpoints, and since political questions were involved, their deliberations should be especially confidential.

Lord Hardinge said that he did not oppose Mr. Lansing's views, but he thought the question raised was so important as to be too big for a Commission to settle. In his opinion, the Commission could be asked to make a recommendation, but it could not be expected to settle the question.

Mr. Lansing agreed. He had not intended to suggest that the Commission should "settle" the question. In his opinion, the Commission should not even make a recommendation: it should only make a full report clearly indicating the possible solutions, taking into consideration all the different aspects of the case.

Lord Hardinge thought the only objection to that proposal was the great delay that would be incurred, as time was now so short.

M. Cambon explained that no one belonging to the Commission had ever suggested doing more than submitting a report, which would naturally be dealt with in the most confidential manner. The Commission would work as rapidly as possible; but he wished to invite the attention of the Council to the fact that the question under discussion did not concern the Treaty of Peace with Germany. The question related to Austria and Russia. Therefore, without wishing in any way to criticise the work of the Supreme Council, he thought he would be a bold man who would attempt to fix the date when the Russian question would finally come under settlement. For two months he had been trying to obtain permission to interview the Lithuanian representatives in Paris, but so far he had received no mandate.

M. Makino said he was prepared to accept Mr. Lansing's proposal.

(It was agreed to authorise the Commission on Polish Affairs to proceed with the study of the frontier to be assigned to Poland in Eastern Galicia and to submit a full report.)

Note from the Commission on Polish Affairs asking whether it should hear representatives of the Russian Political Conference.

M. Cambon said that the Commission on Polish Affairs had now reached the study of the future frontiers between Poland and Russia. All possible information had been collected, but so far no representative of Russia had been heard. There existed in Paris at the present moment a Russian Political Conference under the presidency of Prince Lvoff, which represented all Anti-Bolshevik parties in Russia. This Conference had asked to be heard, and he was authorised by his Commission to enquire whether this could be done. In this connection he wished to invite attention to the fact that during the last few days an incident had occurred which had a direct bearing on the question he now put to the Council. The Commission on Polish Affairs having advised the Supreme Council that it would be advisable in continuance of its work to hear the Warsaw representatives and that it was not its intention to call them together unless otherwise instructed by the Supreme Council, the Council of Foreign Ministers had decided at their meeting on April 15th to instruct the Commission on Polish Affairs to continue its study of the territorial questions relative to Poland. The Commission on Polish Affairs decided under these conditions that the Sub-Committee specially charged with the preliminary study of the Eastern Frontier of Poland would call before it the Eurasian representatives delegated by the Lithuanian Assembly, namely Dr. Walderman and Mr. Ytchas. These gentlemen had appeared on the 23rd April in compliance with a summons addressed to them. They had immediately read a letter addressed to the President of the Peace Conference which had been circulated. After having taken cognisance of this document the Sub-Committee had unanimously agreed that the hearing of Dr. Walderman and Mr. Ytchas should be postponed and they accordingly withdrew immediately. The Commission on Polish Affairs, therefore, now requested the Supreme Council to instruct them as to the action to be taken in regard to the Lithuanian representatives and as to the answer to be given them. The Commission on Polish Affairs also considered it its duty to call the attention of the Supreme Council to the fact that the work relative to the Eastern Boundaries of Poland would be greatly facilitated by hearing the competent Russian representatives. But the Commission did not consider itself authorised to take a decision on its own account in regard to this matter and begged the Supreme Council to inform it as soon as possible if it might convoke the members of the Russian Political Conference now convened in Paris.

Mr. Lansing enquired what was going to be done about the Lithuanians.

M. Cambon thought that the Commission could only wait until the attitude of the Lithuanians had somewhat changed. The Commission on Polish Affairs had been appointed to consider Polish interests. The Commission was naturally anxious to hear the views of all people surrounding Poland, but the Lithuanians had stated that they were not prepared to give information to the Commission on Polish Affairs, as they wished a special Commission to be appointed to deal only with Lithuanian affairs. He thought under these circumstances, it would be unwise for the Allied and Associated Governments to give way to their pretentions.

M. Pichon said that on the 23rd April, 1919, a letter had been addressed by the Lithuanian Delegation to the President, M. Clemenceau, the concluding paragraph read as follows:—

"In spite of the difficulties above-mentioned the Delegation has decided to send the Members summoned by the Secretary-General of the

Peace Conference with instructions to give to the Commission on Polish Affairs all information relating to the frontiers between Lithovia and Poland."

M. Cambon said that under these circumstances the Commission on Polish Affairs should now proceed to hear the Lithuanians.

Mr. Lansing thought that instructions should be issued to the Commission on Polish Affairs to call in, and obtain the evidence of, any individual Russians that might be able to give information on the subjects under consideration; but the Commission should not give a hearing to any Russian Delegation or Commission, as such.

(It was agreed that the Commission on Polish Affairs should hear the Lithuanian Delegates and also individual Russians who might be able to give information on the question relating to the Eastern Frontiers of Poland.)

Proposals to address a warning in the name of the Conference to the Polish and Lithuanian Governments to refrain from hostilities at Vilna and Grodno.
M. Cambon said that the following report dated April 10th 1919, had been submitted to the Conference by the Commission on Polish Affairs:—

"As a result of recent successes gained over the Bolsheviks, the Polish troops on the one hand, and the Lithuanian troops on the other, are at the present moment, at a short distance from one another. The animosity existing between the Lithuanians and the Poles and the occupation by the latter of a part of the Province of Grodno, which the Lithuanians claimed gave cause to fear that an armed conflict between the two parties might take place. The Commission on Polish Affairs considered that it would be advisable to take steps immediately to relieve a situation which threatened to provoke a serious incident similar to those which had taken place between the Poles and Lithuanians in the region of Lemberg. With a view to avoid such an occurrence, the Commission on Polish Affairs had the honour to recommend to the Supreme Council of the Conference that Marshal Foch be instructed to study means to prevent a conflict between the Lithuanians and Poles, either by bringing about a direct agreement between the Polish and Lithuanian military leaders, or by establishing a line of demarcation which both parties should agree not to cross, or by any other arrangement likely to prevent the outbreak of hostilities between the Poles and Lithuanians and if possible to assure their union against their common adversaries, the Bolsheviks."

Mr. Lansing said he had a decided objection to offer to this question being dealt with as a purely military matter, since, in his opinion, at the present moment, it was far more a political question. An Inter-Allied Military Commission was at present on its way to Warsaw, and its work should now be permitted to proceed without hindrance. In his opinion, the Lithuanian Delegation here in Paris, as well as the Polish Delegates, could be informed that whatever decision might be reached at the present moment would in no way affect the final issue.

Lord Hardinge explained that a few days ago the British Foreign Office had received from Warsaw information similar to that contained in the note read by M. Cambon. Mr. Balfour had asked him to see the Polish representative here in Paris in order to point out to him the grave situation that would be caused by the outbreak of hostilities in Grodno, and to have instructions issued to the Polish Armies. As a result he (Lord Hardinge) had seen M. Zaleski and he had done his utmost to persuade him to approach M. Paderewski in order to put a stop to all hostile operations in the direction of Grodno. The bad effect which the outbreak of any conflicts in that region would have, now that the Polish question had come under discussion at the Peace Conference, was explained to M. Zaleski. If the Polish Government would agree to take action as suggested, he promised that similar warnings would also be issued to the Lithuanians not to attack the Poles in the direction of Vilna, and not to interfere with the transportation of supplies for Poland along the lines of communication between Grodno and Vilna. M. Zaleski had listened with great interest to these remarks and, in reply, had stated that the relations between the Poles and Lithuanians had recently greatly improved. He had agreed to lose no time in placing the matter before M. Paderewski with a recommendation that he should issue the necessary instructions.

Baron Makino said he was prepared to accept Mr. Lansing's proposals.

Mr. Lansing said that his proposal implied that the Council should issue the necessary notifications to the Polish and Lithuanian Delegates here in Paris.

M. Pichon pointed out that similar measures to those indicated by Lord Hardinge had apparently also been taken, independently, by each of the Allied Governments.

Mr. Lansing proposed that in addition to the note to be issued by the Council to the Polish and Lithuanian Delegates in Paris, the Allied and Associated Governments should also notify their respective representatives in Warsaw to use their good offices to obtain the cessation of hostilities, with a view to an agreement being reached between Poles and Lithuanians in the regions of Vilna and Grodno.

(It was agreed that the Council of Foreign Ministers should notify the Polish and Lithuanian representatives in Paris that whatever arrangements might be reached at the present moment in order to avoid hostilities in the regions of Vilna and Grodno, would in no way affect the final decision.

It was also agreed that the Allied and Associated Governments should notify their respective representatives in Warsaw, to use their good offices with a view to an agreement being reached between the Poles and the Lithuanians in the regions of Vilna and Grodno in order to avoid hostilities).

141. REPORT ON THE SLESVIG QUESTION[1]

[This selection illustrates the terms of a plebiscite. It should be noted that the third (southern) zone was later omitted from the terms of the Treaty of Versailles, because the Danish Government was fearful lest the thrifty farmers might try to vote themselves out of the German Empire to escape the fiscal burdens left by the war and would thus form a recalcitrant German-speaking minority when they were once included in Denmark. When the plebiscite was taken, however, the voting proved to follow linguistic rather than economic lines, with the result that the southern zone went to Germany and the northern to Denmark, each by an overwhelming majority. The Slesvig problem was one of the simplest questions the Conference had to deal with, and its solution is generally regarded as just.]

COMPOSITION OF THE COMMITTEE AND TERMS OF REFERENCE

The Supreme Council of the Allies, at its meeting of the 21st February, 1919, charged the Committee on Belgian Affairs with the examination of the question of Slesvig. . . .

The Committee on Belgian Affairs, to which the Supreme Council of the Allies at its meeting of the 21st February, 1919, referred the Danish claims for investigation, had before it for examination the three following demands made by the Danish Government:

1. That the population of Northern Slesvig, taken as a single district, shall be admitted to vote as soon as possible, Yes or No, whether it desires to be again united to Denmark.

2. That the districts of Central Slesvig adjacent to Northern Slesvig, including the town of Flensborg, which may express the desire to do so, shall be summoned to declare by special plebiscite, voting by districts, whether they desire to be united to Denmark.

3. That the conditions necessary to ensure the freedom of the ballot shall be established by the evacuation of the regions in question by the German military forces and by the appointment of an International Commission to prepare and supervise the plebiscite.

ARTICLES PROPOSED FOR INSERTION IN THE PRELIMINARIES OF PEACE

The Committee has the honour to submit the following conclusions which have been unanimously arrived at in the form of articles for insertion in the Preliminaries of Peace:—

---

[1] American Commission to Negotiate Peace. S-H Bulletin No. 167. April 15, 1919. "Report (with Annexes) Presented to the Supreme Council of the Allies by the Committee on Danish Affairs." (Hoover War Library Manuscript.)

Article 1. The frontier between Germany and Denmark will be fixed in conformity with the wishes of the population.

For this purpose the population inhabiting the territories situated to the north of a line which, running from east to west, starts from the mouth of the Schlei (Sli) Schleimündung (Sliminde), goes up the south bank of the Schlei (Sli) to a point south of the town of Schleswig (Slesvig), follows the river Rheiderau (Reideaa) up to and running south of Hollingstedt (Hollingsted), then follows the road going to Husum, which is left to the north of the line, and is continued to the south of the Islands of Nordstrand, Südfall and Süderoog, will be called upon to pronounce by a vote which will be taken under the following conditions:—

1. Within a period not exceeding ten days from the signature of the present Preliminaries of Peace the German troops and authorities . . . shall evacuate the zone lying to the north of the line above fixed.

Within the same period the Workmen's and Soldiers' Councils which have been constituted in this zone will be dissolved; members of such Councils who are natives of another region and are exercising their functions at the date of the present Preliminaries of Peace or who have gone out of office since the 1st March, 1919, will also be evacuated.

The said zone will be immediately placed under the authority of an International Commission, composed of five members, of whom three will be designated by the five great Allied and Associated Powers; the Norwegian and Swedish Governments will each be requested to designate a member; in the event of their failing to do so these two members will be chosen by the five great Allied and Associated Powers.

The Commission will have general powers of administration. In particular, it shall at once provide for filling the places of the evacuated German authorities, and if necessary will itself give orders for their evacuation, and will proceed to fill the places of such local authorities as may be required. It will take all steps which it thinks proper to ensure the freedom, fairness, and secrecy of the vote. It will be assisted by German and Danish technical advisers chosen by it from among the local population. Its decisions will be taken by a majority vote.

One half of the expenses of the International Commission and of the expenditure occasioned by the plebiscite shall be paid by Germany.

2. The right to vote will be given to all persons, male and female, who:—

(a) have completed their twentieth year at the date of the signature of the present Preliminaries of Peace; and

(b) were born in the zone in which the plebiscite is taken, even if they have lost their domicile there, in consequence of their expulsion by the German authorities—or have been domiciled there since a date before the 1st January, 1900.

Every person will vote in the commune (*Gemeinde*) where he is domiciled or of which he is a native.

Military persons, officers, non-commissioned officers and soldiers of the German army, who are natives of the zone of Slesvig in which the plebiscite is taken shall be given opportunity to return to their native place in order to take part in the vote there.

3. In the section of the evacuated zone lying to the north of a line starting from the southern point of the Island of Alsen (Als), following the fjord of Flensburg (Flensborg) as far as Kupfermülde (Kobbermolle), the valley of the river Krusau (Krusaa), passes to the south of Fröslee (Fröslev), so that Pattburg (Padborg) becomes a frontier station, follows the boundary between the administrative districts of Slogs and Kjaer, the brook called Scheidebek (Skelbaek), and then the rivers Süderau (Sönderaa) and Wiedau (Vidaa) to the point where the latter turns to the north, and is continued from this point to the North Sea and to the north of the northern point of the Island of Sylt (Sild), the vote above provided for will be taken within a period not exceeding three weeks after the evacuation of the country by the German troops and authorities.

The result will be determined by the majority of votes cast in the whole of this section. This result will be immediately communicated by the International Commission to the Allied and Associated Governments and proclaimed.

If the vote results in favour of the reincorporation of this territory in the Kingdom of Denmark, the Danish Government in agreement with the International Commission will be entitled to effect its occupation with their military and administrative authorities immediately after the proclamation.

4. In the section of the evacuated zone situated to the south of the preceding section and lying to the north of a line which, passing to the south of the Islands of Amrun and Föhr (För), running along the south bank of the Soholmau (Soholmaa), leaving it to the south of Soholm and continuing in a south-easterly direction to the south of Löwenstedt (Lyngsted) and Ostenau (Ostenaa), turning north-east to Kieracker (Kjaerager), making a bend to the south of Frörup, turning again north-eastwards and winding between Oeversee (Oversö) and Gross-Solt (Store-Solt), between Jarplund and Klein-Wulstrup (Lille-Volstrup), between Tastrup and Weseby (Vesby), between Adelby and Rullschau (Rulskov), between Munkbrarup and Bönstrup, between Ringsberg (Ringsbjaerg) and Langballig (Langballe), reaches the Baltic between Sygum (Sigum) and Langballigholz (Langballeskov), the vote will be taken within a period not exceeding five weeks after the plebiscite has been held in the preceding section.

The result will be determined by communes (*Gemeinden*), according to the majority of the votes cast in each commune (*Gemeinde*).

5. In the section of the evacuated zone situated to the south of the preceding section and to the north of the line which starts from the

mouth of the Schlei (Sli) and ends to the south of the Islands of Nord-strand, Südfall and Süderoog, the vote will be taken within a period not exceeding two weeks after the plebiscite shall have been held in the second section. The result will likewise be determined by communes (*Gemeinden*) in accordance with the majority of the votes cast in each commune (*Gemeinde*).

Article 2. Pending a delimitation on the spot a frontier line will be fixed by the five great Allied and Associated Powers according to a line based on the result of the votes and proposed by the International Commission, and taking into account the particular geographical and economic conditions of the localities in question.

From that time the Danish Government may effect the occupation of these territories with the Danish civil and military authorities, and the German Government may reinstate up to the said frontier line the German civil and military authorities whom it has evacuated.

Germany hereby finally renounces in favour of the Allied and Associated Powers all rights of sovereignty over the territories situated to the north of the frontier line fixed in accordance with the above provisions. The Allied and Associated Powers will hand over the said territories to Denmark.

Article 3. Danish nationality will be acquired as of course by all the inhabitants of the territory which is returned to Denmark. Nevertheless, persons who have taken up their residence on this territory after the 1st October, 1918, will be unable to acquire Danish nationality without special permission.

Article 4. Within two years from the date on which the sovereignty over the whole or part of the territory of Slesvig covered by the plebiscite is returned to Denmark:—

(a) Any person born in the territories which are returned to Denmark, not domiciled in this region, and possessing German nationality, will be entitled to opt for Denmark.

(b) Any person domiciled in the territories returned to Denmark will be entitled to opt for Germany.

The option of a husband covers his wife, and the option of parents covers children less than 18 years old.

All persons who exercise the right of option above provided for must during the following six months become resident in the State in favour of which they have opted. They will be entitled to retain the immovable property which they own in the territory of the other State in which they were domiciled before opting.

They may remove their movable property without paying customs duties in the country for which they have opted.

They may remove their securities and personal property, and will be exempt from export duties or taxes on such securities or property.

Article 5. The Treaty of Peace will settle the proportion and the nature of the financial obligations of Germany which are to be assumed by the Danish Government, and all other questions arising from the return made to it of territory the abandonment of which was imposed upon it by the Treaty of the 3rd October, 1864.

In support of the above conclusions the Committee has the honour to submit to the Supreme Council the following considerations, which have been unanimously agreed to:—

I

Principle of the Plebiscite

The Committee is of the opinion that it is desirable for general reasons and in conformity with the wish expressed by the Danish Government, to place the Danish population of Slesvig in a position to pronounce their opinion on their own future, an opportunity which they are the more entitled to receive by reason of the fact that they can appeal to Article V of the Treaty of Prague of 1866, which expressly guaranteed this right to them, and which Prussia has refused to execute.

II

Northern Slesvig

The Danish Government proposes to divide the voting into two zones. In the first, which it calls Northern Slesvig, it asks that the plebiscite should be taken in the shortest possible period of time, and that the results be considered for the whole of the region together.

The Committee is of opinion that this request should be granted.

In the northern region of Slesvig the population is, in fact, for the larger part, Danish in origin and in customs. It has effectively resisted the attempts at Germanisation, and it is highly probable that it will declare itself by a large majority in favour of reunion to Denmark.

It is desirable to proceed to the voting in the shortest possible period of time, in order to put an end to the uncertainty in which the inhabitants of this district are placed as to their future. The plebiscite accordingly should take place within three weeks following the evacuation of this territory by the troops and authorities of Germany, under conditions which are explained below. This period is also necessary for the arrangements preliminary to taking the vote, as well as to allow for the return of the inhabitants of Slesvig who have been in voluntary or forced exile.

This northern section of Slesvig will be fixed in accordance with the proposals suggested by the Danish Government. It will be bounded by the present Danish-German frontier on the north, and on the south by a line which starts from the southern point of the Island of Alsen (Als), follows the fjord of Flensburg (Flensborg) to Kupfermülde

(Kobbermolle), then the valley of the stream of Krusau (Krusaa), passing to the south of Fröslee (Fröslev) so that Pattburg (Padborg) shall be a frontier station; then follows the boundary between the administrative districts of Slogs and Kjaer, the brook called Scheidebek (Skelbaek), and then the streams Süderau (Sönderaa) and Wiedau (Vidaa), to the point where the latter turns towards the north; and from this point to the North Sea; and then to the north of the northern point of the Isle of Sylt (Sild). (Red line on the map.)

III

Second Zone

South of the northern zone lies a region in which among inhabitants of Danish speech are found many inhabitants of German speech, some of whom indeed are of Danish origin. It is not easy to determine with precision the sympathies of this population, but there is every reason to believe that the Danish sentiment preponderates.

It is for the purpose of giving each of these opposing elements the possibility of freely determining its future that the Danish Government has proposed in this region to ascertain the results of the plebiscite by communes and to fix the frontier on this basis.

The Committee accepts this suggestion, which seems to it to give the most substantial security for the free choice of the people. It is understood, however, that in fixing the frontier account will have to be taken of geographical and economic conditions.

Nevertheless, it has not seemed best to limit the right of voting, as the Danish Government proposes, to those communes which might make a request for it. This procedure would give rise to serious difficulty: it would be necessary to fix a minimum number of petitioners, and it would be impossible to follow this course without reaching arbitrary decisions. Furthermore, there is reason to fear that under the uncertainty which would exist regarding their future, many inhabitants of Slesvig, while desiring to become Danish, would, for fear of exposing themselves to reprisals, in case their commune should remain German, hesitate to give public expression to their sympathies by signing a petition requesting a vote.

Accordingly the Committee is of the opinion that it would be preferable in this portion of Slesvig to admit to the vote all the communes situated south of the first zone and north of a line marking the limit beyond which German speech clearly predominates. In establishing this limit the Committee has likewise taken into consideration the evidence afforded by petitions actually presented, as well as of information in its possession, which enable it to determine the region within which the Danish elements, though not having the same preponderance as in the first zone, are still numerically considerable.

This second zone, situated immediately south of the first, extends as far as a line which, from west to east, passes south of the Islands of

Amrun and Föhr (För), follows the south bank of the Soholmau (Soholmaa), passes to a point south of Soholm, whence it passes to the S.E. as far as Löwenstedt (Lyngsted) and Ostenau (Ostenaa), and leaving these to the north, turns towards the N.E. as far as Kieracker (Kjaerager), making a bend to the south of Frörup, going again N.E. curves between Oeversee (Oversö) and Gross-Solt (Store-Solt), between Jarplund and Klein-Wulstrup (Lille-Volstrup), between Tastrup and Weseby (Vesvy), between Adelby and Rullschau (Rulskov), between Munkbrarup and Bönstrup, between Ringsberg (Ringsbjaerg) and Langballig (Langballe), and reaches the Baltic between Sygum (Sigum) and Langballigholz (Langballeskov). (Green line on the map.)

In this region the plebiscite would take place within a period of five weeks at the latest after the date of the voting in the first zone.

This interval is necessary for several reasons. While in the first zone a plebiscite is expected and all the Danish elements which belong to the district have had time to prepare themselves for voting, in the second zone uncertainty still prevails respecting the decision which will be made on this matter. The result is that the people of Slesvig who have left the country or have been driven out are returning, or preparing to return, into the first zone, whereas many of those who belong to the second zone do not yet know whether they will need to return. At the same time it is desirable to permit these exiles to take part in the voting. It is likewise not undesirable to give those of Danish sympathies in this region an opportunity for recovering their confidence and emancipating themselves from fear which the presence of so large a number of Germans causes among them.

IV

Further Limits of the Plebiscite

Should the consultation of the people be limited to this district?

The Committee is of the opinion that so decisive a test ought to be made complete by including all these parts of Slesvig in which there is any chance of the people becoming conscious of their Danish sympathies, and expressing them by means of a secret ballot.

At the same time it considers it necessary to take this opportunity for finally settling the question of the future of these territories and the character of their population. It appears, however, unnecessary to extend the plebiscite to the whole of Slesvig, the southern part of which beyond the historical line of the Dannevirke has long been clearly German.

Taking into account the historical traditions, as well as the evidence of race and geography, the Committee is of the opinion that there is reason for extending the plebiscite as far as the line which, from east to west, starts from the mouth of the Schlei (Sli) Schleimündung (Sliminde) and ascends the river as far as the town of Schleswig

(Slesvig), which it leaves on the north, follows the stream Rheiderau (Reideaa) as far as Hollingstedt (Hollingsted), which it includes, then the high road going to Husum, which it includes, and continues to the south of the islands of Nordstrand, Südfall, and Süderoog. (Blue line on the map.)

Third Zone

There would thus be established a third zone, within which, as in the second, the results of the plebiscite would be ascertained by communes, and would be used as a basis in fixing the frontier.

In this zone the vote should take place a fortnight after the date on which the plebiscite had been held in the second zone.

This further interval is indispensable. The inhabitants expect a plebiscite even less here than in the second zone; moreover, the influence of the officials and of a more dense German population is strongly exerted here upon the Danes, who are more scattered than in the two other zones, and who, in order that a real expression of opinion may be secured, ought to have time to make up their minds. Indeed, while German is the preponderant language in this zone, it is important to remember that language is not an absolute proof of nationality. Customs, tradition of a common past, in short the aspirations of a people, often survive the disappearance of their original tongue. Thus, many Danes who are apparently Germanised will realise their true individuality when they see the national movement develop, and when at the same time they discover that the evacuation of the country by the German authorities has freed them from the restrictions with which the persistent German oppression has surrounded them.

Furthermore, the plebiscite should be held in this region even if the result in the second zone should show a belt of communes voting for Germany, since, without this, one of the objects proposed would not be attained, namely, the settlement of all dispute regarding the character of the region.

V

Return of Slesvig Soldiers

In accordance with the request of those who are interested, it seems necessary in the Preliminaries of Peace to require from the German Government the immediate discharge and the return to their homes of the officers, non-commissioned officers and privates who belong to the districts of Slesvig in which the voting is to take place.

VI

Evacuation

The whole of the three sections, which in this way are called upon to express their will regarding their future, will have to be evacuated by the German troops within a period which should be as short as possible, since it is important that the plebiscite should take place without delay.

For this purpose the Committee proposes to insert in the Preliminaries of Peace with Germany several clauses designed to secure good order in the country and a genuine expression of opinion. The period for evacution is fixed at ten days. Only small garrisons and a small number of officials are affected.

International Commission

As soon as the evacuation has begun, it will be desirable to entrust the authority in the district and general powers of police to an International Commission authorised to supervise the actual conduct of the plebiscite and to ensure that it shall be properly and honestly carried out. This Commission could sit at Flensborg. Its powers are defined in clauses suggested for the Preliminaries of Peace.

The International Commission should be composed of five members: three nominated by the five Allied and Associated Powers, one Norwegian, and one Swedish member, these last two to be chosen for their knowledge of Scandinavian customs.

It appears desirable that the International Commission should not include any Dane or German, but, on the other hand, it should be able to associate with itself as technical advisers Germans and Danes chosen in the country by the Commission itself.

Naval Forces.

At the same time that the International Commission takes up its quarters at Flensborg, it would be desirable to send to the port of this town either a fairly important man-of-war, or several small war vessels, having on board detachments which could be disembarked in case of need—a few hundred men. The necessary arrangements should at once be taken under consideration. The three Allied Commissioners might proceed to Flensborg on board these vessels.

Method of Voting

It will be the duty of the International Commission to fix the detailed machinery of the voting.

As to the qualifications for voting, they are explained in the clauses suggested for the Preliminaries of Peace and are in agreement with the desires expressed by those who are interested.

They have been so arranged that the people of Slesvig who have been obliged to leave their country should be able to return in order to vote. On the other hand, the mass of Germans who have come into the country during the last twenty years, whilst a policy of persecution was driving away numerous people of Slesvig, are excluded.

Option

In the clauses relating to the option, this privilege has been refused to the numerous Germans who have taken refuge in Slesvig since the beginning of the German revolution and who have no connection with Slesvig; there is no reason to allow the Germanising elements to be reënforced in this way under cover of a Danish label.

Reoccupation of the Country

The Committee has also made provision for the reoccupation of the country by the Danish and German authorities respectively after the frontier has been traced. It seems indispensable to meet the unanimous wish of Denmark and of the Danish inhabitants of Slesvig by deciding that the Danish authorities should be allowed to occupy the northern zone as soon as the result of the plebiscite in this zone has been published. This decision will be welcomed by the Danes of the Kingdom as well as by those of Slesvig.

The Committee hopes that the different measures which it has proposed will enable the wish of the Allied and Associated Powers to be realised, and will finally settle in accordance with the desires of the population the future of the Danish territories which are now held by Germany.

Thus will be rectified the results of the act committed in 1864, an act which inaugurated the policy which for more than fifty years has been the source of the attacks directed against the peaceful evolution of the nations.

(Signed)
A. TARDIEU.
CHARLES H. HASKINS
STANLEY D. EMBICK, Col., U.S.A.
EYRE A. CROWE
J. W. HEADLAM-MORLEY
J. LAROCHE
A. RICCI BUSATTI,
L. VANNUTELLI REY
KATO
SAKUTARO TACHI

March 19, 1919

STATISTICAL INFORMATION

	Area Square kiloms.	Inhabitants.
I.—*First Zone:* To be submitted as a whole to the plebiscite (Section of Northern Slesvig f r o m the present D a n i s h frontier to the red line on the map)	3,994	166,966 (Prussian statistics of 1910.)

II.—*Second Zone:* To be submitted to the plebiscite by communes (from the red to the green line on the map).	1,300	101,500 (Prussian statistics of 1910 for the Tonder district (Amt); Prussian statistics of 1905 for the remainder of the zone)
III.—*Third Zone:* To be submitted to the plebiscite by communes (from the green to the blue line on the map)	1,835	112,213 (Prussian statistics of 1905)
IV.—The whole region to be submitted to the plebiscite (from the present Danish frontier to the blue line on the map)	7,129	380,679

All these figures are approximate.

142. Jugoslav Propaganda on Fiume[1]

[In the "Pact of Rome" of April, 1918 (see doc. no. 129), Italy accepted the agreement of the Congress of Oppressed Austro-Hungarian Nationalities "to solve amicably the various territorial controversies on the basis of the principles of nationality and of the rights of peoples to decide their own fate." The Italians at Fiume formed remote Latin islets in the midst of a great Slavonic sea. To annex the 25,000 Italians at Fiume (33,000 according to the Italian claims) about half a million Jugoslavs would have to be annexed. Fiume was specifically reserved to Croatia in the Treaty of London of 1915. It was undeniably the only practicable port for the new Jugoslav nation, and dominates the great northwestern gateway into the Balkans. The large Fiume claimed by Italy was a different entity from the restricted Fiume represented as containing an Italian majority. Counting the suburb of Sushak, which is an integral part of the city, Fiume has, according to the best statistics available, a Slav majority (26,600 Jugoslavs to 25,800 Italians). Italy's imperialistic claims at Paris are in striking contrast to her acceptance of Wilson's ninth point: "A readjustment of the frontiers of Italy should be effected along clearly recognizable lines of nationality."]

[1] Paris Peace Conference, 1919. Kingdom of the Serbs, Croats and Slovenes. *Memorandum presented to the Peace Conference, in Paris, concerning the claims of the Kingdom of the Serbians, Croatians, and Slovenes.* "The Town of Riyeka (Fiume)" (Hoover War Library Files).

The Town of Riyeka (Fiume)

The Delegation of the Serbo-Croato-Slovene Government begs to expose briefly the reasons on which is based our right on Riyeka, generally known under the Italian name of Fiume.

Ethnical Arguments

It has been said that the last official statistics of 1910 indicated, for the town of Riyeka, the presence of 24,212 Italians, 6,493 Magyars, 2,315 Germans and 15,687 Jugoslavs, which ensures to the Italians a relative preponderance.

But a judicious and equitable critical examination of these statistical figures causes us, first of all, to put the question who were the authorities which effectuated the census and watched its sincerity. It has been made by the municipal office of Fiume, exclusively composed of Italians and Magyars, under the control of the Magyar government. Everybody who knows the proceedings which were in use throughout the whole of the late Austro-Hungarian monarchy, and especially in Hungary, will find, in this simple fact, a reason for suspecting the results of an operation in which the Italo-Magyar political interests were engaged.

The whole situation of Fiume, is, really, for nearly fifty years, dominated by the fact that the Magyars intended to establish in that town an hegemony as jealous as artificial. Impotent to establish themselves and maintain the superiority of numbers, they tried at least to paralyze by alliances or political combinations, the opposition of the only element which they had to fear and the only one with which they ever had had prolonged and serious quarrels, the autochthone [*sic*] Croatian element.

As soon as one leaves, not the agglomeration, but only the town itself of Fiume, to pass into the suburbs, the suburb of Sushak, itself an important urban centre, shows a population of 11,705 Slavs against 658 Italians. And if one advances into the interior of the country, or if one crosses the narrow canal which separates the land from the island of Krk (Veglia), one will find oneself exclusively, with very small exceptions, in Slav country. The suburbs of Fiume, its land outskirts, its sea environs, i.e., all that belongs to the town by a natural and indestructible solidarity, all this is purely Slav and it is superfluous to say that the hinterland is exactly the same.

If we consider, in consequence, the circumstances with a single look and from the simple ethnical point of view, the Italian and Magyar colonies of Fiume leave the impression of an enclosure in the midst of Slav populations, and, as it were, of a foreign body.

We will explain later how the Magyars penetrated into Fiume, where they were, in reality, only represented by functionaries, soldiers, managers of factories, a few shipowners and professors. We must now explain the presence of about 25,000 individuals, in the town itself, who claim to be—according to the official statistics—Italians.

This phenomenon is firstly quite naturally explained by the immigration. Fiume is an industrial and maritime centre close to Italy, which, thanks to the importance of her natality, furnishes workmen to her different neighbours, Switzerland, France, Tunisia, etc.

A convincing proof of the accuracy of this explication can be found in the comparison with anterior statistics. Fiume, whose development is quite recent, had, in 1848, only 12,598 inhabitants, of whom 11,581 were Croatians and 691 Italians. In 1854, according to Kandler, the number of the Italians had already grown, but did not exceed five or six thousands. It is quite natural to coördinate the continuous growing of the Italian colony with the progressive development of the industries of the town, the construction of the railways, the works executed at the port, etc. But this interesting phenomenon, like many other similar ones, from the demographical and industrial point of view, does not prove anything from the national point of view.

Another fact accounts for the place occupied by the "Italian" element, not only among the workmen, but even in the "bourgeoisie" and the commercial classes of Fiume. This phenomenon consists in the fact that a certain number of Slav families have been Italianized in the course of the most recent times. At an epoch when the conscience of the nationality was not yet developed like today, when schools were rare, and when, moreover, the influence of the Italian literature, customs, fashions, was quite naturally exercised from one shore of the Adriatic to the other, many people imagined to distinguish themselves from the populace and to take, by "snobbism," more civilized manners, in adopting the exterior signs of the Italian nationality. That is what explains today—and one could furnish numerous examples of it—that a certain number of more or less ardent protagonists of the "Italianity" of Fiume attest, already by the name they bear, a Slav origin. But this does not prove anything from the national point of view. Still better, such failings show the irresistible character of the *national and democratic* contrary push much better, which has had the result to awaken among the immense majority of the Jugoslavs the conscience that they are an homogeneous nation and which has won them over to the principles of the Entente.

Finally, one must consider that the Magyars, during their mortal fight against the Croatians of Fiume, have tried by all means to make use, for their own profit, of the autonomous tendency, the Italian influence and language, whilst they were suppressing all Croatian schools and were systematically keeping away from the local administration the Croatians. In the midst of a town in which there was no place any more, neither in the State or municipal institutions, nor in any schools whatever, for the Croatian language, but where only Italian and Magyar were admitted for official use, it is not astonishing that among the new generation, a certain number of people, of Slav origin, learn to speak, and perhaps even to think, in Italian and that traces of this phenomenon be found in the census of 1910.

What must especially be remembered in this rapid statement, in the pretended "Italianity" of Fiume—restricted however to the town as such—is the double product of the immigration and different forms of denationalization, imposed upon or consented. And we find the decisive proof hereof in the fact that everywhere, outside the town, where those two artificial factors had not found a favourable ground for their influence, the population has remained purely Slav, so much so, that even the statistics made by the Hungarian government itself completely acknowledged it.

HISTORICAL ARGUMENTS

The town of Fiume which has played an important part in the history of the Habsburg monarchy, and especially in that of Croatia and Hungary, has never had anything to do with the history of Italy, with the only exception of the very brief period, at the beginning of the XVIth century, when Venice exercised there an ephemeral domination.

In the feudal times Fiume and its territory belonged to an ancient family of the Croatian nobility, the Frankopan, and that family ceded their property, in 1465, to Emperor Frederick III. Since that epoch, the town of Fiume formed part of the Federation of the States depending on the Crown of St. Stephen, till the day when Maria Theresia, without separating it from that Crown, declared to annex it direct to Croatia (1775).

The sense and the spirit of this innovation, which had perhaps in view to conciliate the already rival pretensions of Magyars and Croatians, intended to assign to Croatia a juridically intermediate part —it was already such from the double point of view: geographical and economical—between Hungary and that port. Besides, Fiume was enjoying a statute sanctioning certain municipal franchises.

During the revolution of 1848 and the following years Fiume was the theatre of armed conflicts between Croatians and Magyars. The latter, who had succeeded in taking the town for a short time, were turned out by Yelatchitch on the 2nd of December 1849.

When, in 1867, in consequence of the defeat of Sadova, the Habsburg monarchy undertook to reconstitute the State on the Dual system, the special situation of Fiume was the object of negotiations between the representatives of the Croatian and the Hungarian States and one tried to settle it in the text of the compromise (Nagodba), intended to fix the general constitutional relations between Hungary and Croatia. But one only arrived at a postponement of the question, in Art. 66, which became celebrated by the material alteration which the Magyars dared to make on the original of the document, already ratified and signed by the Emperor-King. This article, which simply stated that an understanding had not been possible and that the Hungaro-Croatian negotiations had to be renewed on this particular point, was hidden under a strip of paper whose text stated that Croatia had renounced to Fiume. The document on which this forgery had been committed—forgery discovered only several years later— is kept in Zagreb, in the State archives, and photographical reproductions of the same have been published.

These essential points of the history of Fiume set off a stubborn, rather natural, struggle between the Magyars who, separated from the Adriatic by Croatia, wished to have there a port of their own, and the Croatians who were opposing this pretension, on the base of their geographical and historical right. Italy, which arrived at her own union, only during the last phase of this secular conflict, could only assist as spectator. And even the Italians from Fiume only had the occasion to immix themselves, more or less, in that conflict as allies of the Magyar policy, especially with the aim of conserving, for their own profit, certain municipal franchises, without any relations whatever with the "Irredentism."

When therefore, at the end of 1918, the municipality, mostly Italian, of Fiume and the improvized Italian national council of that town imagined to declare its "annexion" to Italy and to send delegates to Rome with that view, they seem to make a confusion between Municipal Law, expression of an autonomy, reduced to municipal affairs, and Public Law which treats much more important questions of sovereignty and territorial limits. And even if the Latin text, cited from Maria Theresia's rescript and often invoked, which defines Fiume as "separatum sacræ Regni Hungaricæ coronæ adnexum corpus" submits to a controversy, interesting for a judicial exegesis, nothing useful can come out of it today, from the point of view of the devolution of Fiume on the basis of modern Law. The subtilty which had made of Fiume, a century and a half ago, a body, at the same time separated and associated (separatum et adnexum), could be, strictly speaking, explained by the intricacies familiar to the ancient Public Law of the countries submitted to the Habsburg monarchy. But it could not give today the least right to a municipality, elected only for communal affairs, and which remains a stranger to all branches of the State administration as such till the month of October 1918, to invoke the principle of autodisposition for deciding on the destinies of Fiume.

When President Wilson formulated the principle of autodisposition he took good care to add "of the nations," and his thoughts certainly never went as far as the small communities. Besides, the inhabitants of Fiume who are composed, as one has seen, of Italians, Slavs, Magyars, and even Germans, could never pretend to form a nation of their own, neither from the ethnical and juridical, nor the political point of view. Even if they agreed on this pretension—which certainly is not the case—it would be untenable, as its admission would risk to lead the Peace Conference to divide into fragments and to singularly complicate its work of reconstruction on the national basis, as similar pretensions could repeat themselves.

Considering the practical consequences of a dissociation of the town of Fiume alone from the Slav territory in the midst of which it is situated, of the Slav islands which surround it and of the Slav environs which help Fiume and are helped by Fiume to live, one will judge them by the following considerations.

GEOGRAPHICAL AND ECONOMICAL ARGUMENTS

Fiume commands, by the railway Ogouline-Zagreb-Beograd and by its numerous branch-lines, all the basin of the Sava, and, consequently, the accesses to Croatia, Northern Bosnia, Hungary, Northern Serbia, the Banat and the Batchka, in one word to Slav and certain adjacent countries.

All the question is to know if, when this is once established, it is not an imperious necessity that Fiume be maintained within the limits of the territory in which it is incorporated and which it is depending on naturally—or if it is more just to make of it a sort of commercial bridge-head towards the Slav countries and the Balkan Peninsula at the disposition of a foreign Power.

Jugoslav Fiume fulfills a function whose organ ought to be created if it did not exist already; moreover, a necessary function, for, if all Powers, including Italy, agreed that it was right to assure an issue on the Adriatic to pre-war Serbia, such an issue is quite indispensable to Serbia united with the Croatian and Slovene territories whose union makes a State of twelve to thirteen millions of inhabitants. Well, no other Dalmatian or Croatian port, neither Shibenik (Sebenico), nor Split (Spalato), nor Dubrovnik (Ragusa), Kotor (Cattaro), nor Bar (Antivari) fulfills the conditions of geographical situation and especially of railway junction with the interior which would allow it to constitute, from the international point of view, the "issue" required for a State of such an extent, especially because of the mountainous walls which separate Dalmatia, on all her length, from the valley of the Sava.

In the hands of Italy, which possesses a great number of ports, which disposes more particularly in the Adriatic of Venice, Ancona, Bari, Brindisi,—Fiume would only fulfill an artificial function. Italy would use it evidently in order to impose her importations to Slav countries to the detriment of the laws of competition which protect the rights of third parties, and to subordinate their exportations to her own conditions. She could use, towards the State of the Serbians, Croatians and Slovenes, the same means of coercion which former

Austria-Hungary was using without scruple against Serbia on the Danube.

One has made allusion to a system capable of giving commercial guarantees to the States of Central Europe deprived of maritime issues. The Peace Conference has already designated a special Commission in order to study this vast and delicate subject. But, whatever be their conclusions, there is one reflexion which must fix our attention. Out of concern for equity, the liberty and the elimination of causes of conflict between States, the modern tendency is to procure maritime issues to the countries which are confined in the interior of a continent. But, if it is equitable and right to procure, by artificial means, such issues to nations which do not possess them, the more it is right to leave the natural issues to those nations which possess them. It would mean a singular contradiction to deprive the Kingdom of the Serbians, Croatians, and Slovenes of Fiume, of one of its principal accesses to the sea, at the same moment when one erects, to the profit of other, not maritime, States, statutes which are to guarantee them an access to the sea.

In order to separate, politically, Fiume from its hinterland, one would be obliged to disjoin the town not only of its rural environs, to which it is united by a geographical and daily economical solidarity, but also of the suburbs themselves. The suburb of Sushak, to speak only of that, would it also be separated from its hinterland? If yes, one ought to consult the 15,000 Slav inhabitants who have not abdicated their national rights into the hands of the 25,000 Italians or Italianized of Fiume. Otherwise instead of the simply administrative frontier which separated Sushak from Fiume till now, we would have a State frontier, a customs line between hostile powers. In the first case, the Italian vindication is put in question or, better, seems to become more and more fragile, as the statistics for Fiume-town and Sushak united leave the majority to the Slavs. In the second case, one will succeed to create an intolerable situation between a town and its urban prolongations which good sense shows to be destined to form a whole.

In terminating, the Delegation of the Kingdom of the Serbians, Croatians and Slovenes makes a point of stating that guarantees would be given for assuring the liberty to international commerce, destined to pass in transit by Fiume, especially to the profit of the Tcheco-Slovaque State, Poland, and even Hungary, as one of the natural destinations of this port is to serve as issue for these States.

We are equally ready to grant to the town of Fiume all guarantees destined to secure to the inhabitants of Italian tongue the free use and the development of their Italian language and civilization.

This port must belong to an unique Power, if its prosperity has to be increased or even maintained, and this unique State can only be the Serbo-Croatian-Slovene State which concentrates in Fiume its resources and its efforts. Italy, which has numerous ports of commerce, is solicited, in contradictory directions, by the interests of each of them, and she will naturally prefer to grant her protection to these ports than to Fiume. On the other hand, if Fiume did not belong to our State, the Jugoslavs would have no actual interest in favour of that town where their influence has been predominant till now, in the banks, certain branches of commercial activity and especially in maritime industries. From this double abandonment the reapparition of the Magyars or the Germans in Fiume could result at the end, and such an hypothesis, which it is prudent to foresee, is certainly not within the views or the intentions of the Conference.

To conclude, the only solution which is, at the same time, equitable and practical, under the guarantees expressed above, consists in acknowledging that Fiume, already included in the past within the territorial limits of Croatia, forms an integral part, with Croatia together, with the State of the Serbians, Croatians and Slovenes.

143. The Italian Settlement[1]

[The Italians threatened to withdraw from the conference unless their claims to Austro-Hungarian territory were met before the Germans signed the treaty. The Italian premier, Orlando, going beyond the terms of the secret Treaty of London upon the insistence of his political opponents in Italy who forced him to make the most extreme nationalist demands, claimed the city and port of Fiume. The Allies were willing to be bound by the terms of the secret treaty but would not go further. Wilson gave way to the extent of agreeing that Italy's northern frontier should be extended to the Brenner Pass, but he resisted Italian claims on the Adriatic at the expense of Jugoslavia and Albania. As a result of his public letter here given, Orlando and his foreign minister, Sonnino, left Paris for Rome, but returned after the conference had determined to proceed with the German treaty. They reached Paris on May 7, one day too late for the sixth plenary session which approved the draft of the Treaty of Versailles. The Italians were back in the conference but the question of the Adriatic was not settled. After much correspondence in which Wilson took an important part, the Treaty of Rapallo in November, 1920, was signed between Italy and Jugoslavia by which Fiume became a free city, but in 1923 when the exact boundary was determined Italy was allowed to annex Fiume in return for giving Jugoslavia a port in the region.]

(a) Public Statement of President Wilson, April 23, 1919

In view of the capital importance of the questions affected, and in order to throw all possible light upon what is involved in their settle-

---

[1] Ray Stannard Baker, *Woodrow Wilson and World Settlement*, Garden City. Doubleday, Page, 1922. Docs. No. 38, 39. Vol. III, p. 287ff. Reprinted with the permission of Doubleday, Doran & Company, Inc.

ment, I hope that the following statement will contribute to the final formation of opinion and to a satisfactory solution.

When Italy entered the war she entered upon the basis of a definite, but private, understanding with Great Britain and France, now known as the Pact of London. Since that time the whole face of circumstance has been altered. Many other powers, great and small, have entered the struggle, with no knowledge of that private understanding. The Austro-Hungarian Empire, then the enemy of Europe, and at whose expense the Pact of London was to be kept in the event of victory, has gone to pieces and no longer exists. Not only that. The several parts of that Empire, it is now agreed by Italy and all her associates, are to be erected into independent states and associated in a League of Nations, not with those who were recently our enemies, but with Italy herself and the powers that stood with Italy in the great war for liberty. We are to establish their liberty as well as our own. They are to be among the smaller states whose interests are henceforth to be as scrupulously safeguarded as the interests of the most powerful states.

The war was ended, moreover, by proposing to Germany an armistice and peace which should be founded on certain clearly defined principles which should set up a new order of right and justice. Upon those principles the peace with Germany has been conceived, not only, but formulated. Upon those principles it will be executed. We cannot ask the great body of powers to propose and effect peace with Austria and establish a new basis of independence and right in the states which originally constituted the Austro-Hungarian Empire and in the states of the Balkan group on principles of another kind. We must apply the same principles to the settlement of Europe in those quarters that we have applied in the peace with Germany. It was upon the explicit avowal of those principles that the initiative for peace was taken. It is upon them that the whole structure of peace must rest.

If those principles are to be adhered to, Fiume must serve as the outlet and inlet of the commerce, not of Italy, but of the lands to the north and northeast of that port: Hungary, Bohemia, Roumania, and the states of the new Jugo-Slavic group. To assign Fiume to Italy would be to create the feeling that we had deliberately put the port upon which all these countries chiefly depend for their access to the Mediterranean in the hands of a power of which it did not form an integral part and whose sovereignty, if set up there, must inevitably seem foreign, not domestic or identified with the commercial and industrial life of the regions which the port must serve. It is for that reason, no doubt, that Fiume was not included in the Pact of London but there definitively assigned to the Croatians.

And the reason why the line of the Pact of London swept about many of the islands of the eastern coast of the Adriatic and around the portion of the Dalmatian coast which lies most open to that sea was not only that here and there on those islands and here and there on that coast there are bodies of people of Italian blood and connection but also, and no doubt chiefly, because it was felt that it was necessary for Italy to have a foothold amidst the channels of the eastern Adriatic in order that she might make her own coasts safe against the naval aggression of Austria-Hungary. But Austria-Hungary no longer exists. It is proposed that the fortifications which the Austrian government constructed there shall be razed and permanently destroyed. It is part, also, of the new plan of European order which centres in the League of Nations that the new states erected there shall accept a limitation of armaments which puts aggression out of the question. There can be no fear of the unfair treatment of groups of Italian people there because adequate guarantees will be given, under international sanction, of equal and equitable treatment of all racial or national minorities.

In brief, every question associated with this settlement wears a new aspect,—a new aspect given it by the very victory for right for which Italy has made the supreme sacrifice of blood and treasure. Italy, along with the four other great powers, has become one of the chief trustees of the new order which she has played so honourable a part in establishing.

And on the north and northeast her natural frontiers are completely restored, along the whole sweep of the Alps from northwest to southeast to the very end of the Istrian peninsula, including all the great watershed within which Trieste and Pola lie and all the fair regions whose face nature has turned towards the great peninsula upon which the historic life of the Latin people has been worked out through centuries of famous story ever since Rome was first set upon her seven hills. Her ancient unity is restored. Her lines are extended to the great walls which are her natural defence. It is within her choice to be surrounded by friends; to exhibit to the newly liberated peoples across the Adriatic that noblest quality of greatness, magnanimity, friendly generosity, the preference of justice over interest.

The nations associated with her, the nations that know nothing of the Pact of London or of any other special understanding that lies at the beginning of this great struggle, and who have made their supreme sacrifice also in the interest, not of national advantage or defence, but of the settled peace of the world, now unite with her older associates in urging her to assume a leadership which cannot be mistaken in the new order of Europe. America is Italy's friend. Her people are drawn, millions strong, from Italy's own fair countrysides. She is linked in blood as well as in affection with the Italian people. Such ties can never be broken. And America was privileged, by the generous commission of her associates in the war, to initiate the peace we are about to consummate,—to initiate it upon terms she had herself formulated, and in which I was her spokesman. The compulsion is upon her to square every decision she takes a part in with those principles. She can do nothing else. She trusts Italy, and in her trust believes that Italy will ask nothing of her that cannot be made unmistakably consistent with these sacred obligations. Interest is not now in question, but the rights of peoples, of states new and old, of liberated peoples and peoples whose rulers have never accounted them worthy of right; above all, the right of the world to peace and to such settlements of interest as shall make peace secure.

These, and these only, are the principles for which America has fought. These, and these only, are the principles upon which she can consent to make peace. Only upon these principles, she hopes and believes, will the people of Italy ask her to make peace.

(*Signed*) WOODROW WILSON

(b) *Orlando's reply to President Wilson, April 24, 1919*

Yesterday, while the Italian Delegation was assembled discussing an alternative proposal sent them from the British Prime Minister for the purpose of conciliating the opposing tendencies that had shown themselves in regard to Italian territorial aspirations, the newspapers of Paris published a message from the President of the United States, Mr. Wilson, in which he expressed his own opinion in reference to some of the most serious problems that have been submitted to the judgment of the Conference.

The step of making a direct appeal to the different peoples certainly is an innovation in international intercourse. It is not my intention to complain about it, but I do take official notice of it so as to follow this precedent; inasmuch as this new system without doubt will aid in granting the different peoples a broader participation in international questions, and inasmuch as I have always personally been of the opinion that such participation was a sign of a newer era. However, if such appeals are to be considered as being addressed to peoples outside of the Governments that represent them, I should say almost in opposition to their Governments, it is a great source of regret for me to remember that this procedure, which, up to now, has been used only against enemy Governments, is today for the first time being used against a Government which has been, and has tried to be always a loyal friend of the Great American Republic:—against the Italian Government. I could also complain that such a message, addressed to the people, has been published at the very moment when the Allied and Associated Powers were in the middle of negotiations with the Italian Government, that is to say, with the very Government whose participation had been solicited and highly valued in numerous and serious questions which, up to now, had been dealt with in full and intimate faith.

But above all I shall have the right to complain, if the declarations of the presidential message signified opposition to the Italian Government and people, since in that case it would amount to ignoring and denying the high degree of civilization which the Italian nation has attained in these forms of democratic and Liberal rule, in which it is second to no nation on earth.

To oppose, so to speak, the Italian Government and people, would be to admit that this great free nation could submit to the yoke of a will other than its own, and I shall be forced to protest vigorously against such suppositions, unjustly offensive to my country.

I now come to the contents of the presidential message: it is devoted entirely to showing that the Italian claims, beyond certain limits defined in the message, violate the principles upon which the new régime of liberty and justice among nations must be founded. I have never denied these principles, and President Wilson will do me the justice to acknowledge that in the long conversations that we have had together I have never relied on the formal authority of a treaty by which I knew very well that he was not bound. In these conversations I have relied solely on the force of the reason and the justice upon which I have always believed, and upon which I still believe, the aspirations of Italy are solidly based. I did not have the honor of convincing him: I regret it sincerely, but President Wilson himself has had the kindness to recognize, in the course of our conversations, that truth and justice are the monopoly of no one person, and that all men are subject to error, and I add that the error is all the easier as the problems to which the principles apply are more complex. Humanity is such an immense thing, the problems raised by the life of the people are so infinitely complex, that nobody can believe that he has found in a determined number of proposals as simple and sure a way to solve them as if it were a question of determining the dimensions, the volume and the weight of bodies with various units of measure. While remarking that more than once the Conference nearly failed completely when it was a question of applying these principles I do not believe that I am showing disrespect toward this high assembly. On the contrary, these changes have been and still are, the consequence of all human judgment. I mean to say only, that experience has proved the difficulties in the application of these principles of an abstract nature to concrete cases, thus with all deference but firmly, I consider as justified, the application made by President Wilson in his message of his principles to Italian claims. It is impossible for me, in a document of this sort, to repeat the detailed proofs which were produced in great number. I shall only say, one cannot accept without reservation the statement that the downfall of the Austria-Hungarian Empire implies a reduction of the Italian aspirations. It is even permissible to believe the contrary, that is, that at the very moment when all the varied peoples who constituted that empire sought to organize according to their ethnic and national affinities, the essential problem caused by the Italian claims can and must be completely solved. Now this problem is that of the Adriatic in which is summed up all the rights of both the ancient and the new Italy, all her sufferings throughout the centuries and all the benefits she is destined to bring to the great international community.

The Presidential message affirms that with the concessions which she has received, Italy would attain the walls of the Alps, which are her natural defences. This is a grant of vast importance upon condition that the eastern flank of that wall does not remain uncovered and that there be included among the rights of Italy that line from Mount Neveso separating the waters which flow toward the Black Sea from those which empty into the Mediterranean. It is this mountain which the Romans themselves have called the "Limes Italianus" since the very hour when the real figure of Italy appeared to the sentiment and the conscience of the people.

Without that protection a dangerous breach would remain open in that admirable natural barrier of the Alps; and it would mean the rupture of that unquestionable political, historical and economic unity constituted by the peninsula of Istria.

I believe, moreover, that he who can proudly claim that it was he who stated to the world the free right of self-determination of nations, is the very person who must recognize this right for Fiume, ancient Italian city, which proclaimed its Italianness even before the Italian ships were near; to Fiume, admirable example of a national consciousness perpetuated throughout the centuries. To deny it this right for the sole reason that it has to do only with a small community, would be to admit that the criterium of justice toward nations varies according to their territorial expansion. And if, to deny this right, we fall back on the international character of this port, must we not take into account Antwerp, Genoa, Rotterdam,—all of them international ports which serve as outlet for a variety of nations and regions without their being obliged to pay dearly for this privilege by the suppression of their national consciousness?

And can one describe as excessive the Italian aspiration for the Dalmatian Coast, this boulevard of Italy throughout the centuries, which Roman genius and Venetian activity have made noble and great, and whose Italianness, defying all manner of implacable persecution throughout an entire century, today shares with the Italian nation the same emotions of patriotism?—The principle is being adduced with regard to Poland that denationalization obtained by violent and arbitrary methods should not constitute grounds for de jure claims; why not apply the same principle to Dalmatia?

And if we wish to support this rapid synthesis of our good international rights by cold statistical facts, I believe I am able to state that among the various national reorganizations which the Peace Conference has already brought about or may bring about in the future, none of these reorganized peoples will count within its new frontiers, a number of people of a foreign race proportionately less than that which would be assigned to Italy. Why, therefore, is it especially the Italian aspirations that are to be suspected of Imperialistic cupidity?

In spite of all these reasons, the history of these negotiations shall demonstrate that the firmness which was necessary to the Italian Delegation was always associated to a great spirit of conciliation in the research for a general agreement that we all wished for fervently.

The Presidential message ends by a warm declaration of friendship of America towards Italy. I answer in the name of the Italian people and I acclaim with pride this right and this honor which is due me as the man who in the most tragic hour of this war has uttered to the Italian people the cry of resistance at all costs; this cry was listened to and answered with a courage and abnegation of which few examples can be found in the history of the world. And Italy, thanks to the most heroic sacrifices and the purest blood of her children, has been able to climb from an abyss of misfortune to the radiant summit of the most resounding victory. It is therefore, in the name of Italy, that in my turn I express the sentiment of admiration and deep sympathy that the Italian people has for the American people.

(Signed) V. E. Orlando

144. Armenian Claims[1]

[The two parts of Armenia were each represented at Paris: Nubar was head of the delegation of Turkish Armenia; he was a wealthy Egyptian landowner; while Aharoman, the head of the delegation of former subjects of Russian Armenia, was a distinguished poet and novelist. During the war Turkey had massacred or exiled at least one third of the Armenians, with the result that there were no provinces where the majority of the population was clearly Armenian in nationality. By the Paléologue-Sazonov secret treaty, Russia was to be given the four Turkish vilayets of Erzerum, Trebizond, Bitlis, and Van. But since Russia had dropped out, the Treaty of Sèvres provided that Wilson should fix by arbitration the boundaries between Armenia and Turkey, his competence being limited to the four vilayets above-named. This boundary line, however, though drawn, was never in effect. By the treaty of Lausanne these provinces remained Turkish, while Russian Armenia had been included in the dominions of Turkey's ally, the Union of Socialist Soviet Republics. Though the United States was offered a mandate for Armenia by the Peace Conference, the Americans were unwilling to undertake the responsibility.]

In the name of the entire Armenian nation, whose elected delegates from Armenia itself and from all parts of the world are at the present moment assembled in Conference at Paris, the Armenian National Delegation begs to submit to the Peace Conference the present memorandum which sums up the aspirations and claims of the Armenian nation.

[1] Paris. Peace Conference, 1919. Armenia. *The Armenian question before the Peace Conference,* pp. 1-8 (Delegation Propaganda. Hoover War Library Files).

After passing through centuries of oppression and sufferings, our nation at the threshold of the 20th century reached the climax in the universal conflagration, torn and covered with blood, but aspiring with a faith more alive than ever towards its deliberation and the realisation of its national ideal, thanks to the Victory of the Allied and Associated Powers, who have inscribed upon their banners the principles of Right, Justice, and the right of Peoples to dispose of their own lot.

Taking their stand upon these great principles, the Armenian National Delegation, interpreting the unanimous voice of the whole nation, a part of which has already constituted itself into an Independent Republic in the Caucasus, has already proclaimed the independence of Integral Armenia and notified the Allied Governments thereof by a note of 30 November 1918.

Armenia has won its right to independence by its voluntary and spontaneous participation in the war on the three fronts of the Caucasus, Syria and France, and by the myriads of victims in men, women and children through her fidelity to the cause of the Entente looked upon by her from the outset as her own. As a result of these enormous losses on all battlefields, through massacres, and along the paths of deportations she has paid a heavier tribute to Death than any other belligerent nation.

Victory has delivered Armenia from the yoke of her oppressors, and her misfortunes would in themselves suffice to justify her right to Independence; but, as will be proved hereafter, she has other equally and highly legitimate titles of historical, ethnical, political and moral natures.

The policy of the European Powers in respect of Turkey was for long dominated by the dogma of the Integrity of the Ottoman Empire. To reconcile the Integrity of Turkey with the obligations which they had assumed towards the Christian peoples oppressed by the Turks, the Great European Powers advocated "reforms" by which the non-Turkish races would benefit and which would ensure them equality of treatment without distinction of race or religion.

Facts have proved how vain were these hopes. The Turks, Old or Young, have never seen aught in reforms but a means to hoax Europe and have always managed, in practice, by an artful playing off of the rivalries of the Powers against one another, to elude them. The Christian populations, henceforth an object of suspicion to the Porte, became still more wretched than they were at the time when the Turkish power was at its zenith.

The whole history of Armenia under Ottoman domination during six centuries has been but one long martyrdom with periodical massacres; but those persecutions assumed a particularly virulent character in the last 50 years, since, that is, the Armenians have claimed the amelioration of their lot.

The Treaties of San Stefano (1877) [sic] and of Berlin (1878), the

Cyprus Convention, the Reform scheme submitted to the Porte by the Ambassadors in 1895, have been so many international acts intended to reform the abuses of Turkish rule but which have proved as many dead letters, European Diplomacy having always been satisfied with half-measures: whenever Europe spoke of reforms, Turkey replied with massacres and Europe held her peace.

In 1908 the Armenians joined action with the Young Turks with the object of overthrowing the tyrannical power. The Young Turks, in order to obtain Armenian help, had promised them an era of "liberty, equality and fraternity." The Armenians placed faith in these promises. Less than a year afterwards the massacres of Adana took place in which 20,000 Armenians perished; but the policy of the maintenance of the integrity of Turkey prevented once more the Powers from intervening.

It was not till 1912-13, after the Balkan Wars, at the moment when the Conference of London was assembled for the solution of the Balkan problem, that the Great Powers, in response to the appeals of the whole Armenian Nation, intervened and addressed the Porte with the object of obtaining the execution of the reforms stipulated in Article 61 of the Berlin Treaty.

The Ambassadors in Constantinople were instructed to study a project and to draw up same in definite form. Long and laborious were the negotiations to overcome the resistance of the Porte. Finally, however, she was brought to accept a text, but one which was belittled and disfigured by the intervention of Germany, who had never ceased to lend her support to Turkish diplomacy. This agreement, signed on the 8th Feb. 1914, the Young Turks hastened to tear up, as soon as Germany provoked the War. But this did not prevent the Turks from proposing to the Armenians an ignominious compact— they proposed to them that they should make common cause with the Tartars in an insurrection against the Russians and, in exchange, the Porte was to have granted Autonomy to the Armenians. Germany stepped forward as the sponsor of her ally. Need it be said that the Armenians replied with an indignant refusal? The revenge of the Young Turks, coldly premeditated and foreannounced, was terrible.

We will relate neither the massacres, nor the deportations which have been massacres in disguise. The story of them supported by overwhelming evidence is to be found in the Blue Book presented to Parliament by Lord Bryce; in the books by Morgenthau, L. Einstein, and even in pamphlets written by Germans, such as the report of Dr. Niepage, that of Dr. Lepsius, which has just been published in Paris, Mr. Harry Sturmer's book, etc. It is important to recall that we have had many proofs that the work of the extermination of a whole Nation was methodically organised by the Turkish Government whose orders were transmitted by circulars and telegrams to the various Officials in all the Armenian Provinces. Several of these documents have been found since and published.

Nothing was left to chance by the Government, neither assassinations nor pillages, nor tortures, nor rapes, nor compulsory conversions to Mohammedanism, nor death by starvation.

After such deeds the case is settled; the Allies have already, by the solemn declarations of their Statesmen, undertaken to definitely liberate Armenia from a tyranny unparalleled in History. *The War of Peoples, followed by the Peace of Peoples, must needs give Armenia her complete Independence.*

This Independence the Armenians have shed torrents of blood in order to win, not only the blood of their martyrs massacred and deported or put to death after awful tortures, but indeed the blood shed on various battlefields by their volunteers and soldiers who struggled and fought side by side with the Allies for the liberation of their country. Armenians were to be found fighting spontaneously, voluntarily on all fronts. In France, in the "Légion Etrangère," they covered themselves with glory by their bravery. Scarcely a tenth part of their number came through alive. In Syria and Palestine, in the Légion d'Orient, they hurried to the call of the Armenian Delegation. This Légion d'Orient, in which they were by much the dominating element, formed in itself alone more than half the French contingent. They took a no inconsiderable part in the decisive Victory of General Allenby, who paid homage to their valour. Moreover, the Armenians were to be found in the Caucasus, where (not to mention the 150,000 Armenian soldiers who served in the Russian armies on all fronts) thousands of volunteers led by Andranik and an army of 50,000 soldiers uninterruptedly fought since the first days of the war under the supreme command of General Nazarbekian. It was these troops who after the collapse of Russia and the treaty of Brest-Litovsk, deceived and abandoned by the Georgians, and betrayed by the Tartars, who had joined the Turks, defended the front singlehanded and for seven months retarded the Turkish advance. In this manner they rendered a signal service to the British Army in Mesopotamia, as Lord Robert Cecil himself declared in an official letter addressed to Lord Bryce and in a reply to a question in the House of Commons. They also prevented, by their resistance to the Turks up to the signing of the Armistice, the sending of enemy troops to other fronts.

The Armenians have therefore been true belligerents; their losses due to the war, which exceed a million (out of a nation of 4½ million souls) are proportionately much heavier than those of any of the other belligerents.

INTEGRAL ARMENIA

The Armenians, who for centuries had suffered Turkish domination, were spread over all parts of that Empire. A great number too, fleeing from their tyrants, had emigrated to foreign countries, to Russia, to America. It is certain that the majority of those emigrants will return to their fatherland once this latter be liberated. In consequence, the statistics which should have weight are those of before the war, or rather those of before the Hamidian massacres of 1894-96, which not only occasioned 300,000 deaths, but caused also a considerable part of the population to emigrate. It is inadmissible that such crimes should benefit their authors, nor that they should attain the project of their abominable designs,—to assure the majority and supremacy of Mussulmans. THE VOICE OF ALL ARMENIANS LIVING AND DEAD MUST BE HEARD. If Armenians have no absolute majority over the totality of all races in the Armenian Vilayets, yet they are in a majority by comparison with each of them. Before the war, and in spite of the emigrations at the end of the last century, the number of Armenians, in the six Vilayets called Armenian, in the Vilayet of Trebizond, and in Cilicia, was superior to that of the Turks and the Kurds taken separately and even equal to that of Turks and Kurds together. There were 1,403,000 Armenians, against 943,000 Turks and 482,000 Kurds.

On the other hand, the Armenian population was not the only one to have suffered. The Balkanic Wars had already caused heavy losses to the armies of the Sultan, nearly exclusively recruited in Asia. The present War completed the exhaustion of the very sources of recruiting; and even the Turkish civilian population heavily suffered not only in the regions invaded by the Russians, but also throughout their Empire where they were decimated by epidemics which for want of care for the sick and lack of medicaments made terrible ravages among all the Mussulman elements.

However, number is not the sole factor which should serve to determine the granting of our territory and the fixing of its frontiers. One must take into account not only the dead, but also the degree of civilisation and the fact that the Armenians are the sole element capable of actually constituting a State fit for civilisation and progress. The Mussulman and other non-Armenian populations who will find themselves within the Armenian State will enjoy liberties guaranteed by principles admitted by the Peace Conference.

The Kurds are divided into sedentary and nomadic elements. The greater part of the mountaineers who have the reputation of thieves and plunderers, have always in the hands of the Turkish government been the instruments of massacres. Their political evolution has never gone beyond that of tribal government. An important portion of the sedentary Kurds is established in the region generally called Kurdistan, in those parts south of the Vilayets of Diarbekir and Van (Hekkiari). Those regions may be detached from the Armenian State. The rest of the Kurds will live in Armenia under the protection of her laws.

It is however to be noted that among the Kurds there exist a good number who are of Armenian origin, and that, once the Turkish baneful influence is eliminated, it will be easy to establish a community of interest between the two races, Armenians and Kurds, the Armenians having in addition within their power the gift of giving the Kurds the benefits of civilisation, in the mutual interest of both parties.

As to the nomads, special laws will regulate the change of pasture lands in order to guarantee the safety of the country and prevent plunderings.

In accordance with the principles enunciated above, the regions which should form the Armenian State are the following:

1. The 7 Vilayets of Van, Bitlis, Diarbekir, Kharpout, Sivas, Erzeroum and Trebizond (in conformity with the Reform Act of February 1914), excluding the regions situated beyond the South of the Tigris and to the West of the line between Ordou-Sivas.

2. The four Cilician Sandjaks, i.e. Marash, Khozan (Sis), Djebel-Bereket and Adana with Alexandretta.

3. All the territory of the Armenian Republic of the Caucasus, including: the whole province of Erivan, the southerly portion of the former Government of Tiflis, the southwesterly part of the Government of Elisabethopol; the provinces of Kars, with the exception of the region to the north of Ardahan.

When Abdul-Hamid had the administrative boundaries of the vilayets traced, he managed to introduce arbitrarily into each of them non-Armenian regions in such a way as to assure a majority to the Mussulmans. With the same end in view he set up colonies of Circassians and other Mussulmans, immigrated from Russia or from the Balkans, in the midst of regions inhabited by Armenians. A general revision of frontiers will therefore be needed. We request that special Mixed Commissions be charged with this work of rectification and given a mandate to fix all the boundaries of the Armenian State, taking due account of geographical, ethnical, historical, economic and strategical conditions.

The number of Greeks in the vilayet of Trebizond, which was the seat of the ancient Kingdom of Pontus, is superior to that of the Armenians; but the port of Trebizond is the only important outlet from Upper Armenia to the Black Sea. Greece has no designs upon this vilayet which is too far distant from the principal centres which she claims in virtue of the Rights of Peoples, and it is in perfect agreement with the Greek Government, who has looked at this question in a broad spirit of equity to which it gives us pleasure to do justice, that we request the juncture of a part of the Province of Trebizond to the Armenian State. Its Greek population may be certain that respect for their religion and language will be assured by the Armenian Administration under a rule of brotherhood and equal justice.

We desire particularly to declare moreover that on their side the Armenians of such regions as will be returned to Greece will accept in the same spirit of confidence and loyalty the conditions which will be granted to them under the Greek Government.

As to Cilicia or Armenia Minor, need it be said that it is essentially Armenian, having always formed part of Armenia. It was the seat of the last Kingdom of Armenia during nearly four centuries, until the day when, defeated by the Arabs, its last King Leon V was carried away captive into Egypt, then liberated, coming at last to Paris to end his life. He was buried at the Basilica of Saint-Denis where his tomb is still to be seen.

The region of Zeitoun, whereof the inhabitants of warlike and proud race are so attached to their national rights, has always and under all forms of governments enjoyed a semi-independence. Let it be also remembered that at all times and to this day the Catholicos of Sis, religious supreme head of Cilicia, has had his seat at Sis, capital of Cilicia.

The population of Cilicia is Armenian and Turkish. The Arab element figures in it only in a very small proportion. Before the war, there were only 20,000 Syrians in Cilicia, whereas the number of the Armenians was as much as 200,000 or over, in spite of the enormous emigration of 1909 caused by the massacres of Adana. Further on there will be found, in the historical part, other proofs of our incontestable rights over Cilicia. We cannot conceive therefore in virtue of what principle does the Syrian Committee extend the frontier on the north as far as the Taurus mountains, thus claiming Cilicia as part of Syria, as shown on the map and published under the care of the Syrian Committee and presented to the Congress of Marseilles. No Atlas, either of the Modern World or of the Ancient, includes Cilicia in Syria, of which the northern boundaries are the Amanus near Alexandretta and NOT the Taurus Mountains. We will not insist upon the fact that the term Syria has never been a political expression, and there has not been a Kingdom of Syria. The Kingdom of the Seleucides founded by Seleucus, one of Alexander's generals, was Greek and had no Syrian national character.

The Armenian people, deprived of Cilicia, separated from the natural ports of Mersina and Youmourtalik (Ayas), would be condemned to languish in the mountains, without intercourse with the Mediterranean world, without the power to breathe, and, to use an expression oft used, Armenia would thus be deprived of her lungs. Her life and future are on the Mediterranean.

The views of the Syrian Committee cannot moreover be reconciled with the agreements between the French Government and the Armenian National Delegation, when in 1916 the latter was notified of the clause relating to Armenia in the Convention which the Great Allied Powers had just concluded with regard to Turkey-in-Asia. Acceding at that moment with gratitude to the desire of the Allies, who promised the liberation of Cilicia and the three western vilayets from the Turkish yoke, the Delegation hastened to furnish Armenian volunteers to contribute to the deliverance of their Fatherland. More than 5,000 Armenians, enlisted in the "Légion d'Orient" in which the Syrians did not count more than 3 or 400 fighting men, took part in the decisive Victory of Palestine, to which Victory Syria owes her liberation.

We only recall these facts in order to enable the Peace Conference to come to a decision with a thorough knowledge of the matter and according to the principles of nationalities, a bed-rock for all their deliberations.

If there exists, as it is apparent, some divergence of the boundary lines between Armenians and Syrians, we must none the less say that our sentiments of friendship and solidarity towards the Syrians, cemented by centuries of equal sufferings, could not suffer from those differences, and that none more than we can wish the constitution of a free and strong Syria as neighbour to the Armenian State.

We request that Armenia, with boundaries as aforesaid, be placed under the collective guarantee of the Allied and Associated Powers or under that of the League of Nations, who will guarantee the integrity and inviolability of her territory. They will in addition delegate one of the Powers to give to the new State during the first few years an assistance in the organisation of the Country and its economic and financial conditions. This assistance should in no way take the form of a protectorate, not even a provisional one, and should be exercised so as to promote the interests of the Armenian Nation, and in such a way that the Sovereignty of the State be not impaired.

ARMENIAN CLAIMS

The programme of our National claims may be summarised as follows:

1. The recognition of an Independent Armenian State, formed by the union of the seven vilayets and of Cilicia with the territories of the Armenian Republic of the Caucasus.

That boundary-fixing Missions, composed of Delegates from the guarantor Powers, and assisted by Armenian Commissioners, should be charged with the fixing on the spot of the definite boundaries of Armenia; such Missions to have full powers to settle without appeal all difficulties which may arise with bordering countries, at the time when the outlines, as traced on the map, are fixed on the ground itself.

2. That the Armenian State, thus constituted, be placed under the collective guarantee of the Allied Powers and the United States or under that of the League of Nations of which she requests that she may form a part.

3. That Special Mandate be given by the Peace Conference to one of the Powers to lend the necessary assistance to Armenia during a period of transition. The Armenian Conference, gathered at the present moment in Paris, and representing the whole Armenian Nation,

should be consulted about the choice of the Mandatory Power. The mandate to be of a maximum duration of twenty years.

4. That an indemnity be fixed by the Peace Conference for making good the damages of all kinds suffered by the Armenian Nation through massacres, deportations, spoliations, and devastations of the Country.

5. That the assisting Power have particularly as her mandate:—

a) To oblige the Turkish, Tartar, and other authorities who still occupy these territories to evacuate them.

b) To carry out the general disarmament of the population.

c) To expel and to punish those who have participated in the massacres, done violences to the population, taken part in plunders or benefited from the spoils of the victims.

d) To drive out of the country the elements of disturbance and disorder; and to expel the nomadic tribes.

e) To send away the mouhadjirs, Mussulman colonists, implanted under the Hamidian rule and that of the Young Turks.

f) Lastly to have all necessary steps taken everywhere, in Armenia and outlying districts, for the return to their former Christian Faith of all women, young girls, children and others converted by force to Islamism or kept captive in Harems.

Armenia will be ready to bear her share of the Ottoman Public Debt, consolidated before the War. Turkey should likewise undertake to pay the equivalent value of all requisitions made by her, and to restore with fair indemnity to the Armenians having rights thereto real properties situated in her own territory, as well as all churches, schools, monasteries with their dependencies, lands and goods, which were taken away from the Armenian community in any form whatever.

As to any national or private landed estates of Armenians which are liable to escheat in Turkey, the religious Armenian Authorities in Constantinople should have right to dispose of them, to sell them, and to devote the proceeds to the needs of their flocks.

Every person, of Armenian origin, domiciled in a foreign country or naturalised, will enjoy during a term of five years the option, either in his own name or in that of his children they being minors, of the new Nationality and of becoming an Armenian citizen, by informing beforehand and in writing the competent authorities of the two countries concerned.

The Armenians rely entirely upon the spirit of justice of the Peace Conference and feel confident that she will sanction this programme of their national claims. The Powers, who are by now acquainted with the Armenians, whose national sentiments, vitality and warlike virtues have been powerfully revealed in the course of the present war, may repose confidence in us. Moreover, the Powers should also note the energy, love for work, and many aptitudes in all human activities of a race always eager for higher culture and progress and which is in addition remarkably prolific.

The Powers may rest assured that with such elements as these, Armenia, under a rule of peace, justice and liberty and thanks to the patronage of the League of Nations and the help of the Mandatory Power, will rapidly become a flourishing and prosperous State, and will be one of the most powerful factors of peace and civilisation in the East.

The Armenian question is not solely a local and national one; it concerns the Peace of Europe, and upon its solution depends the pacification, the progress and the prosperity of the Near East.

Paris, 12th February, 1919

A. AHARONIAN,

President of the delegation from the Armenian
Republic to the Peace Conference

BOGHOS NUBAR,

President of the Armenian National Delegation

145. KING-CRANE REPORT ON THE NEAR EAST (EXTRACTS)[1]

[After long, complicated, and spirited discussions of Syria at the Peace Conference, it was agreed that the situation in Syria should be examined on the spot by an international commission of inquiry. This commission never assembled, but the American members, King and Crane, went to Syria in the summer of 1919, and inquired into the wishes of the inhabitants. The King-Crane report had no influence on the course of events, and was not made public until December, 1922. On April 25, 1920, at San Remo, the Supreme Council of the Allies agreed that France should receive the mandate for Syria, and by the Treaty of Lausanne, 1923, Turkey recognized formally her loss of Syria. The report of the American members in favor of giving the mandate to the United States or to Great Britain in preference to France is significant in view of the successive Syrian revolts against the French administration.]

RECOMMENDATIONS

The recommendations, dealing with mandates in the Asia Minor portion of the former Ottoman Empire, follow naturally upon the preceding discussions of pertinent action already taken by the Peace Conference; of dangers arising from a selfish division and exploitation of Turkey; of considerations looking to a proper division of Turkey; and of problems naturally resulting. For the recommendations built

---

[1] *Editor and Publisher.* December 2, 1922, Vol. LV, No. 27, Second Section. Reprinted with the permission of *Editor and Publisher.*

directly on foundations already laid by the Peace Conference. They aim to prevent a selfish exploitation and division of Turkey. They intend not less surely to ground such division of Turkey as is recommended solely upon considerations of justice and the good of all men. And in this spirit they endeavor honestly to face the grave problems arising, and to seek their solution in the light of the full discussion which precedes. That discussion has been so full, that the Recommendations of the Commissioners need do little more than summarize conclusions, except upon two points—the reasons for a general American Mandate, and the conditions upon which such a mandate might be taken by America.

The Commissioners Recommend:

1. The formation, under a Mandatory, of an Armenian State, completely separated from Turkey, as defined in the preceding section of the report, for reasons already fully given.

It is consequently recommended that Cilicia should not be separated from Anatolia at present.

2. The similar formation, under a Mandatory, of an International Constantinopolitan State, completely separated from Turkey, as defined in the preceding section, also for reasons already fully given.

3. The appointment of a Mandatory for the continued Turkish State, in line with the apparent wishes of the majority of the Turkish people; the major terms of the Mandate to be defined by the Peace Conference or the League of Nations, and further adjustments to be arranged between the Mandatory and Turkey. The reasons for the Mandate and its necessary scope have been already fully given.

4. That, for the reasons already stated, no independent territory be set off for the Greeks; though local autonomy be granted to that portion of the Sanjak of Smyrna which has a decided majority of Greeks, but under the general mandate for Turkey.

5. That a commission or commissions on boundaries in Asia Minor be appointed to study on the ground and to exactly define the boundaries of the states named in the first three recommendations, and the precise limits of any locally autonomous area in Smyrna. The definition of the boundaries of the Turkish State would require the study and definition of the northern boundaries of Syria and Mesopotamia as well, with special reference to allowing to the Kurds a measure of autonomy under close mandatory rule, possibly in connection with Mesopotamia, and with the clear understanding that the rights of the Syrian, Chaldean, and Nestorian Christian minorities in this whole region shall be carefully guarded.

6. A general single mandate for the whole of Asia Minor (not assigned to Mesopotamia or Syria) to include under it the mandate for Armenia, the mandate for the Constantinopolitan State, and the mandate for the continued Turkish State, each with a gov-

ernor of its own to insure full attention to its particular interests, besides a governor-general over the whole. The various interrelations and common concerns of the constituent states would thus be studied and cared for, as well as their individual needs. The reasons for such a general mandate have been fully given and need not be repeated here.

7. That the United States of America be asked to take this general single mandate, together with its inclusive mandates for the Armenian State, the Constantinopolitan State, and the continued Turkish State. This recommendation is made for the following reasons which need to be developed in full:

(1) As already pointed out, it seems to be generally desired that America should take the mandate for Armenia. In this, both the Armenians and the Allies seem agreed—and even the Turks, if there must be an Armenian State at all. Nevertheless, America cannot wisely take this mandate without at the same time taking a mandate for the rest of Asia Minor as well.

For, in the first place, this Armenian mandate would be in many respects the most difficult of all: because it would begin in relations of bitter hostility; because the State would have to [be] built from the bottom under most peculiar circumstances; and because the mandate would have to be prolonged against the impatience of the Armenians. And these difficulties would all be accentuated, if the surrounding conditions could not be determined. It concerns the world that this Armenian State should clearly succeed; its mandatory should not be needlessly handicapped.

In the second place, the problems of the different States in Asia Minor are too closely related to be wisely entrusted to entirely different Powers, with different ideals and methods. That situation would inevitably tend to produce friction, waste, and bad feeling, and unsatisfactory conditions in one state would naturally spread to other states also.

In the third place, if the rest of Turkey, outside of a modest Armenian State, were divided into spheres of influence and exploitation areas, the direct hindrance to the working out of a truly conceived mandate in Armenia would be well nigh insuperable.

The American mandate for Armenia, thus, calls for a general mandate over all of Asia Minor.

(2) America is also the most natural Power to take the mandate for the International Constantinopolitan State, as well as for Armenia; for the simple reason that she is the only Great Power territorially and strategically disinterested. The mandatory for this international state should be herself strong, to discourage any further intrigue for control of the Straits; disinterested, to command the confidence of all the nations concerned; and in unmistakably earnest sympathy with the aim of such a state, and with those international means by which this aim is to be achieved,—the League of Nations and its mandatory system. These needed qualifications are best met by America. Now

the full fruits of such an international state cannot be secured, unless the rest of Asia Minor is made a fit environment for such a state, practically embodying the same great principles.

The mandate for the Constantinopolitan State also calls for a general mandate over all Asia Minor.

(3) It is to be added that America is also the most natural Power for the mandate over the new Turkish State, because the Turkish people want her, and generally trust her, as the evidence previously given indicates; and because America is peculiarly prepared to meet the needs of the Turkish people in this crisis in their history, as the reasons to be given for a general American mandate will later bring out.

The desired American mandate for the new Turkish State, then, calls also for a general mandate over all Asia Minor.

(4) The best solution for mandates in Asia Minor would seem then to be, to combine all three mandates in a composite mandate, which would be put in the hands of America as the single mandatory.

The general reasons for a single mandatory for all Asia Minor, already given, are not to be lightly regarded. They give solid grounds for a composite supervisory mandate.

The further direct reasons for making America that single mandatory should now be considered. To begin with, there is the recognized fact that all the other Great Allies are already heavily loaded with colonial responsibilities, which of itself suggests a special obligation here for America. But the positive reasons—if there are any—lie necessarily in some special fitness of America for the particular task in hand—a fitness growing naturally out of her experience as a great growing democracy, largely freed hitherto from European entanglements. Those reasons, that is, lie inevitably in certain dominant national convictions of America; in a certain idealistic international faith; in her record in these international relations; and in the indications of her duty at this critical point in human history. All of these considerations concern the Turkish situation.

In the first place, we have found both the Syrian and Turkish peoples recognizing that at the foundation of the common life of America were to be found certain great dominant convictions. They saw that she had a passion for peace and for the possibility of its attainment, in spite of all sordid manifestations to the contrary, and that to bring such a righteous peace nearer, she entered this war. They saw that she had a passion for democracy, for the common man everywhere, in spite of inconsistencies at home and abroad, and could treat men of all races with a genuine respect born of some insight into their own individual gifts. They felt sure that she would not go into any situation simply to dominate, and to stamp American customs on a people. They knew that, because she really believed in democracy, she had also a passion for universal education, as possible for the rank and file of every nation, and as absolutely essential to a democracy. They believed, therefore, that as a mandatory she would gird herself to help a people fulfill its own highest possibilities. They believed, indeed, that she had a passion for the development of a national spirit in every people, not as narrow conceit, but as faith in a divine individuality, to which the people must be true, if they were to be significant members of that larger fellowship of nations for which the world longs. They instinctively felt, thus, that she combined in a way fairly unique, educational emphasis with respect for the values of another people. They knew, too, that with a high religious idealism, America somehow combined belief in the principle of the separation of Church and State in governmental administration, for the highest good both of religion and of the state, and was thus especially fitted to render help to a state like Turkey at so peculiarly critical a point in her transition from an imperialistic to a democratic state on modern lines and with complete religious liberty.

In the second place, with these mastering convictions, the Syrians and Turkish people believed that America combined a certain idealistic international faith, in her stubborn belief in the League of Nations and in the possibilities of its mandatory system, when honestly carried out. She was naturally prepared, therefore, they believed, to throw herself into the responsibilities of a mandate; steadfastly to seek to train the people entrusted to her care into self-government and into economic independence; and promptly to withdraw when that task was complete; for she would measure the success of her stewardship by both the completeness and the promptness with which her task was accomplished.

In the third place, both the Syrian and the Turkish people, in expressing their desire for an American mandate, have laid steady emphasis upon the assurance which came from America's record in dealing with other peoples. They believed in her unselfish aims in the war, and that she was now seeking for no share in the spoils of the war. They believed that she had no territorial or imperialistic ambitions. They believed in her high and unselfish aims in dealing with Cuba and the Philippines. They believed that she was not involved in any joint plan for an exploiting division of either Syria or Turkey. They believed in the high quality of her relief service and especially of her educational service in both countries—a service so fine, that so competent and impartial an observer as Ramsey can say: "I firmly believe that Robert College has done more to render possible a safe solution of the 'Eastern Question' in Turkey than all the ambassadors of all the European Powers have succeeded in doing to render that solution difficult." They believed that, so far was America from scheming to obtain a mandate in Asia, she was honestly reluctant to undertake such a mandate of any kind.

In the fourth place, America is peculiarly fitted to be the single Mandatory Power for all Asia Minor, not only because of her national convictions, her international faith, and her record, but also because the course of duty for her would seem to lie in this direction.

It is no part of the task of the commissioners to determine whether America is now willing to accept the general single mandate for Turkey, with its three involved subordinate mandates. It is their business to point out where, in their honest judgment, that mandate belongs (if proper conditions can be fulfilled), and so give an opportunity to the Peace Conference to put the resulting obligation squarely up to the American people.

Can America deny all obligation in this matter of a mandate for Turkey? She has believed perhaps more than any other people, in the high possibilities of the League of Nations; but, if the League of Nations is not to be a sham and a delusion, all nations must be willing to bear their share in the resulting responsibilities. America, certainly, cannot be an exception. She came into the war, too, with the ardent faith and hope that a more democratic world might result. Is she willing to carry those war purposes through to the end? Here in Turkey is an unrivaled opportunity to try these purposes out, for the good not only of a single people, but of the entire world; for here in Turkey has been through centuries a center of intrigue and strife that has engulfed all nations in its consequences. Moreover, America's intervention in the war went far to determine the war's issue. Was that intervention justified? America must still do her utmost to complete the proof.

But America's obligation goes still deeper, in this desperate hour of human need. Men still need peace—long deferred. They need far better provision for bodily wants. They need simple, homely happiness. But beneath all this, they need renewed faith in one another and in one another's honest purposes of good.

The war destroyed that faith between the hostile forces; the settlements of the war, it is to be feared, have gone far to destroy that faith among the Allies themselves. It is not roseate dreaming, but practical politics of the most imperative sort, to do something to bring back men's faith in men. If we can see the radical necessity of such faith, to prevent or break a financial panic, are we to see less clearly in times like these, of a moral world panic? Cynicism and disillusionment, as we have seen, are rife. Can they be conquered? Only by indisputable examples to the contrary. It may be doubtful, then, if America could do anything so significant for the human race today, as to prove that she had not forgotten her own ideals and purposes in the war, but was willing to give a new and even greater proof of them in undertaking unselfishly a difficult and distasteful, but highly important and far-reaching task—by taking on the general mandate for Turkey (as well as for Syria, if the Peace Conference thought best). In fidelity to herself does not America owe that demonstration to the world? It is hard to estimate the immense effect of so important a mandate under the League of Nations being carried through with absolutely honest unselfishness. It would make a reality of the League of Nations; it would make a reality of the mandatory system. It would set a new standard in international relations. It would renew men's faith in one another. It would help to save America herself from a disastrous reaction from her genuinely high aims in the war.

Nothing has been said of America's ample means for the economic development of Turkey's large resources; though it is not suggested that the financial relations of Turkey to America should be finally other than those of self-respecting independence. Turkey's present condition, however, is so necessitous in a thousand ways, that very large amounts of capital would be initially required, and returns at first would be small and slow. But before the mandate ended, a fair return on capital, put into direly needed public improvements and the development of natural resources, might properly be expected, at the same time that Turkey's own interests were guarded against selfish and monopolistic exploitation. America should not come into the Turkish Mandate with the expectation of large financial profits. But if even so favorable a result as that indicated proved quite impossible, America might well spend millions to insure relations of peace and good will among nations, rather than the billions required for another war, sure to come if the present cynical national selfishness and lack of good will are not checked.

As against the considerations now presented, it might be urged that the very suggestion of so large and significant a mandate for America is itself proof that America too is grasping imperialistic power. The answer is, that America's idea of a mandate is emphatically that a mandate is for a limited term; so that even if a mandate for Syria were added to the mandate for Turkey the whole would mean no long retention of power by America, except as the League of Nations should continue her as mandatory over the Constantinopolitan State; that she literally does not want this mandate, except to meet her fair share of responsibility in the world today; that she would have to be persuaded by a campaign of education to take it on; and that she ought not to take it at all, if certain important conditions cannot be fulfilled.

(5) Considerations on which America would be justified in taking a composite general mandate for Asia Minor. Those conditions are: That she is really wanted by the Turkish people; that Turkey should give evidence that she is ready to do justice to the Armenians, not only by the allotment of the territory within her borders, recommended for the Armenian State, but also by encouraging the repatriation of Armenians, and by seeing that all possible just reparation is made to them as they return to their homes; that Turkey should also give evidence that she is ready to become a modern constitutional state, and to abolish military conscription; that Russia should be ready to renounce all claims upon Russian Armenia; that the Allies should cordially welcome America's help in the difficult situation in Turkey; and especially that all plans for cutting up Turkey, for the benefit

of outside peoples, into spheres of influence and exploitation areas should be abandoned.

These conditions are necessary to a successful solution of the Turkish problem. Unless they are fulfilled, America ought not to take the mandate for Asia Minor. And the Commissioners do not recommend that the mandate be given to America if these conditions cannot be essentially met.

Respectfully submitted,

HENRY C. KING,

CHARLES R. CRANE

CONFIDENTIAL APPENDIX

Prepared by the Commission for use of Americans only

Since the Commission was the American Section of a projected international Commission on Mandates in the Turkish Empire, it has seemed best to prepare the report in such form that copies could be furnished to representatives of all the Allied Powers, if that were desired. The body of the report, therefore, though trying squarely to face all the facts, has been written with that possibility in mind.

At the same time there was material involving criticism of our Allies, that ought not to come into a report to be put into their hands, and yet that the American Delegation to the Peace Conference and our own State Department ought to have, as involved in a complete statement of the case. That material prepared by Dr. Lybyer has been gathered into this Confidential Appendix.

The opportunity has also been taken to bring in some supplementary discussions that treat with a little more detail certain important aspects of our inquiry and so throw light on the broader bearings of our report. . . .

Arab Feeling Toward the French

While the Commission was prepared beforehand for some disinclination toward France in Syria, the strength, universality and persistency of anti-French feeling among practically all Moslems and non-Catholic Christians (except a division of the Greek Orthodox), came as a distinct surprise.

Friends of the French affirmed that it is due to German and Turkish, succeeded by Arab and British propaganda, and that it is not deepseated. The Commission went to great pains in testing these affirmations by questioning. Germans and Turks did conduct a vigorous propaganda during the war against the French, and against the other Allies as well. There was no evidence found of direct propaganda by the British against the French, and frequent denials were made that the Arabs had worked thus.

It was said several times that the French had themselves conducted an anti-French propaganda by their actions since the Armistice. On the other hand, it was charged that some Arabs were working against the French, and also against the British and all foreigners. Friends of France say that the Moslems of Syria resent the just punishment which the French gave them in 1860, and their disposition to treat the native Christians as fully equal to the Moslems, an attitude which the British do not take in Egypt and India.

Apart from the questions of process and recency, the anti-French feeling does seem to be deep-rooted in a large proportion of the Syrian population. This appears in an examination of the principal reasons given by the Syrians for their opposition to all French interference in their affairs. They say:

i. The French are enemies of religion, having none at home, and supporting Roman Catholics abroad for purely political motives.

ii. They disapprove of the French attitude toward women.

iii. The French education is superficial and inferior in character-building to the Anglo-Saxon. It leads to familiarity with that kind of French literature which is irreligious and immoral. The Moslems recognize that the time has come for the education of their women, and they say that those who receive French education tend to become uncontrollable.

iv. The French have not treated the natives as equals in Algeria and Tunisia, but have imposed differences in officeholding and in various civil rights. This argument was presented very often and developed in some detail.

v. The French have shown a marked tendency to give an undue proportion of offices, concessions, and the like, to the Christians of Syria. Non-Catholics complain that the same discrimination is shown in favor of Catholics and Maronites.

vi. By this discrimination, and by various intrigues since the occupation, the French have increased the religious divisions in Syria, which had been reduced greatly during the war. They thus endanger the possibility of Syrian nationalism on a non-religious basis.

vii. The French are inclined to a policy of colonization, by which they wish to substitute the use of the French language for native tongues, and make the people into Frenchmen. The Syrians wish to preserve the use of the Arabic language, and to retain their separateness. Furthermore, it is inherent in this policy that the French would never leave Syria.

viii. The French have lost so many men in the war that they are unable to give needful protection or adequate administration. This is illustrated by the few soldiers and the inferior type of French officers and officials now in Syria. (Friends of the French deny that France lacks good officials, and blame the French foreign office for choosing badly those who were sent out. Again, while for the English the Eastern service is a career and draws the best of the young men, for the French it seems a kind of exile and the best prefer to remain at home.)

It was affirmed that bribery and intrigue are worse in the French area now than under the Turks.

ix. The French have suffered financially in the war to such an extent that they have not the means to restore France itself or to develop what possessions they have already. They cannot therefore give Syria the financial and economic support she needs.

x. The French are inclined toward financial exploitation of subject areas, and would govern Syria not for its own development, but for the profit of Frenchmen.

It is not necessary here to try to estimate the measure of truth that lies behind these statements. It is sufficient to note that most of the Syrians believe substantially the whole of this, and are therefore very strongly against French control of the country.

Much feeling persists in connection with the execution of Arabs by Jemal Pasha, and this acts against the French. Despite the fact that France was intriguing with the Arabs against the Turks before the Great War, the knowledge that M. Picot, upon leaving his position as Consul in 1914, failed to secure his correspondence, so that fatal evidence fell into Turkish hands, has played into position so that France is held responsible for the hangings. Every reference to the "Arab Martyrs," by subscriptions for their orphans, exhibitions of these children, meetings of the relatives—the "Unfortunate Syrians," now not only strengthens the sentiment for Arab independence, but stirs feeling against France. . . .

SPECIAL DISCUSSIONS

1. French Feeling Toward the British

It is evident that the French feel resentment toward the British as not having played a fair game in the Syrian area. Without going into historical details, the Sykes-Picot agreement provided that France should have ownership or influence in a large area, including Damascus and Cilicia, and extending to Sivas and Harpoot, while England should be in a similar position toward the former Turkish area southeast of this. At the present moment, France is threatened with the loss of all her sphere, while England complacently holds all that was then assigned to her, and extends her influence toward much of the rest.

America, by showing interest in Armenia, and even by the sending of the Commission on Mandates to Syria, seems to the French to be an accomplice of England in despoiling France. The French feel that the English took advantage of their dire necessity, by reason of which they were obliged to keep practically all of their men in France, to occupy more than a due share of Syria, and to seduce the affection of the Arabs.

They also resent the payment by the English to the Emir Feisal of a large monthly subsidy, which they claim covers a multitude of bribes, and enables the British to stand off and show clean hands while Arab agents do dirty work in their interest. They feel that in arming the Arabs the British are again working against the French. They claim further that the British are more or less directly responsible for the undeniably strong anti-French feeling shown by practically all the Moslem and non-Catholic Christian elements of Syria. They feel that Britain has been unable to resist the desire to connect Egypt with Mesopotamia under one control as a bulwark of India, and as a new field for profitable commercial exploitation.

It cannot be denied that some of the French contentions are difficult of refutation, and that the whole situation is such that British honor would seem cleaner if Britain were to withdraw wholly from Syria. Yet the aversion of the people to France, however it may have arisen, is so great and deep-seated that England cannot leave Syria to France without seeming to abandon her friends to their enemies, a process which would probably react strongly in Egypt and elsewhere in the Moslem world. There is good reason for the position of many Englishmen, who are strongly desirous that America should take the whole situation off their hands, including with the French and Arab entanglements the promises to Zionism. . . .

146. Lloyd George's Memorandum on Peace[1]

[Lloyd George's memorandum contained the aims to which he committed himself after three months' experience at the Peace Conference. The points in this program which he failed to secure may be summarized thus: (1) his idea of reconciling Russia to the League of Nations and the Peace Conference; (2) general disarmament previous to the signature of the Covenant or Germany's early admission to the League; (3) the Germans and Magyars ceded more territory and population, and the Turks less, than he desired; (4) the Penalties on War Criminals have not been effective and the Guarantee Treaties have not been ratified; (5) the settlement of Germany's economic conditions was not made and the problem of Reparations long remained unsolved. Nevertheless, he achieved some results, for it was due to Lloyd George that the Germans signed the treaty; in this connection his insistence upon the plebiscite being applied in Upper Silesia and his solution of the Danzig problem were important. The reasons for the defeat of his views are to be found partly in a telegram said to have been signed by 370 Members of Parliament, which forced him to disclaim moderation with reference to Reparation; but more important was the influence of France, which demanded guarantees for France. Lloyd George himself declared in 1920: "Quite apart from Germany's deserts, the peace that we signed at Versailles was the

---

[1] Great Britain. *Parliamentary Papers,* 1922, Vol. XXIII, Cmd. 1614. "Memorandum circulated by the Prime Minister on March 25, 1919."

minimum that France would have accepted. . . . Should England have stood out of the peace as America did?"]

Some Considerations for the Peace Conference Before They Finally Draft Their Terms

I. When nations are exhausted by wars in which they have put forth all their strength and which leave them tired, bleeding and broken, it is not difficult to patch up a peace that may last until the generation which experienced the horrors of the war has passed away. Pictures of heroism and triumph only tempt those who know nothing of the sufferings and terrors of war. It is therefore comparatively easy to patch up a peace which will last for 30 years.

What is difficult, however, is to draw up a peace which will not provoke a fresh struggle when those who have had practical experience of what war means have passed away. History has proved that a peace, which has been hailed by a victorious nation as a triumph of diplomatic skill and statesmanship, even of moderation in the long run, has proved itself to be shortsighted and charged with danger to the victor. The peace of 1871 was believed by Germany to ensure not only her security but her permanent supremacy. The facts have shown exactly the contrary. France itself has demonstrated that those who say you can make Germany so feeble that she will never be able to hit back are utterly wrong. Year by year France became numerically weaker in comparison with her victorious neighbour, but in reality she became ever more powerful. She kept watch on Europe; she made alliance with those whom Germany had wronged or menaced; she never ceased to warn the world of its danger and ultimately she was able to secure the overthrow of the far mightier power which had trampled so brutally upon her. You may strip Germany of her colonies, reduce her armaments to a mere police force and her navy to that of a fifth-rate power; all the same in the end if she feels that she has been unjustly treated in the peace of 1919 she will find means of exacting retribution from her conquerors. The impression, the deep impression, made upon the human heart by four years of unexampled slaughter will disappear with the hearts upon which it has been marked by the terrible sword of the great war. The maintenance of peace will then depend upon there being no causes of exasperation constantly stirring up the spirit of patriotism, of justice or of fair play. To achieve redress our terms may be severe, they may be stern and even ruthless, but at the same time they can be so just that the country on which they are imposed will feel in its heart that it has no right to complain. But injustice, arrogance, displayed in the hour of triumph, will never be forgotten or forgiven.

For these reasons I am, therefore, strongly averse to transferring more Germans from German rule to the rule of some other nation than can possibly be helped. I cannot conceive any greater cause of future war than that the German people, who have certainly proved themselves one of the most vigorous and powerful races in the world, should be surrounded by a number of small states, many of them consisting of people who have never previously set up a stable government for themselves, but each of them containing large masses of Germans clamouring for reunion with their native land. The proposal of the Polish Commission that we should place 2,100,000 Germans, under the control of a people which is of a different religion and which has never proved its capacity for stable self-government throughout its history must, in my judgment, lead sooner or later to a new war in the East of Europe. What I have said about the Germans is equally true of the Magyars. There will never be peace in South Eastern Europe if every little state now coming into being is to have a large Magyar Irredenta within its borders. I would therefore take as a guiding principle of the peace that as far as is humanly possible the different races should be allocated to their motherlands, and that this human criterion should have precedence over considerations of strategy or economics or communications, which can usually be adjusted by other means. Secondly, I would say that the duration for the payments of reparation ought to disappear if possible with the generation which made the war.

But there is a consideration in favour of a long-sighted peace which influences me even more than the desire to leave no causes justifying a fresh outbreak 30 years hence. There is one element in the present condition of nations which differentiates it from the situation as it was in 1815. In the Napoleonic war the countries were equally exhausted, but the revolutionary spirit had spent its force in the country of its birth, and Germany had satisfied the legitimate popular demands for the time being by a series of economic changes which were inspired by courage, foresight and high statesmanship. Even in Russia the Czar had effected great reforms which were probably at that time even too advanced for the half-savage population. The situation is very different now. The revolution is still in its infancy. The extreme figures of the Terror are still in command in Russia. The whole of Europe is filled with the spirit of revolution. There is a deep sense not only of discontent, but of anger and revolt, amongst the workmen against pre-war conditions. The whole existing order in its political, social and economic aspects is questioned by the masses of the population from one end of Europe to the other. In some countries, like Germany and Russia, the unrest takes the form of open rebellion; in others, like France, Great Britain and Italy, it takes the shape of strikes and of general disinclination to settle down to work—symptoms which are just as much concerned with the desire for political and social change as with wage demands.

Much of this unrest is healthy. We shall never make a lasting peace by attempting to restore the conditions of 1914. But there is a danger that we may throw the masses of the population throughout Europe into the arms of the extremists whose only idea for regenerating mankind is to destroy utterly the whole existing fabric of society. These men have triumphed in Russia. They have done so at a terrible price. Hundreds of thousands of the population have perished. The railways, the roads, the towns, the whole structural organisation of Russia has been almost destroyed, but somehow or other they seem to have managed to keep their hold upon the masses of the Russian people, and what is much more significant, they have succeeded in creating a large army which is apparently well directed and well disciplined, and is, as to a great part of it, prepared to die for its ideals. In another year Russia, inspired by a new enthusiasm, may have recovered from her passion for peace and have at her command the only army eager to fight, because it is the only army that believes that it has any cause to fight for.

The greatest danger that I see in the present situation is that Germany may throw in her lot with Bolshevism and place her resources, her brains, her vast organising power at the disposal of the revolutionary fanatics whose dream it is to conquer the world for Bolshevism by force of arms. This danger is no mere chimera. The present Government in Germany is weak; it has no prestige; its authority is challenged; it lingers merely because there is no alternative but the spartacists, and Germany is not ready for spartacism, as yet. But the argument which the spartacists are using with great effect at this very time is that they alone can save Germany from the intolerable conditions which have been bequeathed her by the war. They offer to free the German people from indebtedness to the Allies and indebtedness to their own richer classes. They offer them complete control of their own affairs and the prospect of a new heaven and earth. It is true that the price will be heavy. There will be two or three years of anarchy, perhaps of bloodshed, but at the end the land will remain, the people will remain, the greater part of the houses and the factories will remain, and the railways and the roads will remain, and Germany, having thrown off her burdens, will be able to make a fresh start.

If Germany goes over to the spartacists it is inevitable that she should throw in her lot with the Russian Bolshevists. Once that happens all Eastern Europe will be swept into the orbit of the Bolshevik revolution and within a year we may witness the spectacle of nearly three hundred million people organised into a vast red army under German instructors and German generals equipped with German cannon and German machine guns and prepared for a renewal of the attack on Western Europe. This is a prospect which no one can face with equanimity. Yet the news which came from Hungary yesterday shows only too clearly that this danger is no fantasy. And what are the reasons alleged for this decision? They are mainly the belief that large numbers of Magyars are to be handed over to the control of others. If we are wise, we shall offer to Germany a peace, which, while just, will be preferable for all sensible men to the alternative of Bolshevism. I would, therefore, put it in the forefront of the peace that once she accepts our terms, especially reparation, we will open to her the raw materials and markets of the world on equal terms with ourselves, and will do everything possible to enable the German people to get upon their legs again. We cannot both cripple her and expect her to pay.

Finally, we must offer terms which a responsible Government in Germany can expect to be able to carry out. If we present terms to Germany which are unjust, or excessively onerous, no responsible Government will sign them; certainly the present weak administration will not. If it did, I am told that it would be swept away within 24 hours. Yet if we can find nobody in Germany who will put his hand to a peace treaty, what will be the position? A large army of occupation for an indefinite period is out of the question. Germany would not mind it. A very large number of people in that country would welcome it as it would be the only hope of preserving the existing order of things. The objection would not come from Germany, but from our own countries. Neither the British Empire nor America would agree to occupy Germany. France by itself could not bear the burden of occupation. We should therefore be driven back upon the policy of blockading the country. That would inevitably mean spartacism from the Urals to the Rhine, with its inevitable consequence of a huge red army attempting to cross the Rhine. As a matter of fact I am doubtful whether public opinion would allow us deliberately to starve Germany. If the only difference between Germany and ourselves were between onerous terms and moderate terms, I very much doubt if public opinion would tolerate the deliberate condemnation of millions of women and children to death by starvation. If so the Allies would have incurred the moral defeat of having attempted to impose terms on Germany which Germany had successfully resisted.

From every point of view, therefore, it seems to me that we ought to endeavour to draw up a peace settlement as if we were impartial arbiters, forgetful of the passions of the war. This settlement ought to have three ends in view. First of all it must do justice to the Allies by taking into account Germany's responsibility for the origin of the war and for the way in which it was fought. Secondly, it must be a settlement which a responsible German Government can sign in the belief that it can fulfil the obligations it incurs. Thirdly, it must be a settlement which will contain in itself no provocations for future wars, and which will constitute an alternative to Bolshevism, because it will commend itself to all reasonable opinion as a fair settlement of the European problem.

II. It is not, however, enough to draw up a just and far-sighted peace with Germany. If we are to offer Europe an alternative to Bolshevism we must make the League of Nations into something which will be both a safeguard to those nations who are prepared for fair dealing with their neighbours and a menace to those who would trespass on the rights of their neighbours, whether they are imperialist empires or imperialist Bolshevists. An essential element, therefore, in the peace settlement is the constitution of the League of Nations as the effective guardian of international right and international liberty throughout the world. If this is to happen the first thing to do is that the leading members of the League of Nations should arrive at an understanding between themselves in regard to armaments. To my mind it is idle to endeavour to impose a permanent limitation of armaments upon Germany unless we are prepared similarly to impose a limitation upon ourselves. I recognize that until Germany has settled down and given practical proof that she has abandoned her imperialist ambitions, and until Russia has also given proof that she does not intend to embark upon a military crusade against her neighbours, it is essential that the leading members of the League of Nations should maintain considerable forces both by land and sea in order to preserve liberty in the world. But if they are to present an united front to the forces both of reaction and revolution, they must arrive at such an agreement in regard to armaments among themselves as would make it impossible for suspicion to arise between the members of the League of Nations in regard to their intentions towards one another. If the League is to do its work for the world it will only be because the members of the League trust it themselves and because there are no rivalries and jealousies in the matter of armaments between them. The first condition of success for the League of Nations is, therefore, a firm understanding between the British Empire and the United States of America and France and Italy that there will be no competitive building up of fleets or armies between them. Unless this is arrived at before the Covenant is signed the League of Nations will be a sham and a mockery. It will be regarded, and rightly regarded, as a proof that its principal promoters and patrons repose no confidence in its efficacy. But once the leading members of the League have made it clear that they have reached an understanding which will both secure to the League of Nations the strength which is necessary to enable it to protect its members and which at the same time will make misunderstanding and suspicion with regard to competitive armaments impossible between them its future and its authority will be ensured. It will then be able to ensure as an essential condition of peace that not only Germany, but all the smaller States of Europe undertake to limit their armaments and abolish conscription. If the small nations are permitted to organise and maintain conscript armies running each to hundreds of thousands, boundary wars will be inevitable and all Europe will be drawn in. Unless we secure this universal limitation we shall achieve neither lasting peace, nor the permanent observance of the limitation of German armaments which we now seek to impose.

I should like to ask why Germany, if she accepts the terms we consider just and fair, should not be admitted to the League of Nations, at any rate as soon as she has established a stable and democratic Government. Would it not be an inducement to her both to sign the terms and to resist Bolshevism? Might it not be safer that she should be inside the League than that she should be outside it?

Finally, I believe that until the authority and effectiveness of the League of Nations has been demonstrated, the British Empire and the United States ought to give to France a guarantee against the possibility of a new German aggression. France has special reason for asking for such a guarantee. She has twice been attacked and twice invaded by Germany in half a century. She has been so attacked because she has been the principal guardian of liberal and democratic civilisation against Central European autocracy on the Continent of Europe. It is right that the other great Western democracies should enter into an undertaking which will ensure that they stand by her side in time to protect her against invasion, should Germany ever threaten her again or until the League of Nations has proved its capacity to preserve the peace and liberty of the world.

III. If, however, the Peace Conference is really to secure peace and prove to the world a complete plan of settlement which all reasonable men will recognize as an alternative preferable to anarchy, it must deal with the Russian situation. Bolshevik imperialism does not merely menace the States on Russia's borders. It threatens the whole of Asia and is as near to America as it is to France. It is idle to think that the Peace Conference can separate, however sound a peace it may have arranged with Germany, if it leaves Russia as it is today. I do not propose, however, to complicate the question of the peace with Germany by introducing a discussion of the Russian problem. I mention it simply in order to remind ourselves of the importance of dealing with it as soon as possible. . . .

147. Smuts' Note on Reparation[1]

[Of the many difficult problems with which the Paris Peace Conference had to deal none was more thorny than the question of reparations. A Reparations Commission was established to deal with it; this was divided into three subcommissions. No. 1 dealt with the question of categories of damage: here the American principle was adopted, that war costs were to be excluded. No. 2 dealt with the German capacity to pay and the question of how payments should be made. Lloyd George and Clemenceau were opposed to fixing the amount for fear of losing their political power if they accepted a lump sum, since any such fixed sum was sure to be far below the amount hoped for by the French and the British voters. The problem of just what constituted "damage done to the civilian population" was hotly contested: the British delegation said it included the actual costs of war; this conten-

---

[1] H. W. V. Temperley, *A History of the Peace Conference of Paris,* Vol. V, pp. 372-374. Reprinted with the permission of the Oxford University Press.

tion was supported by the French. House of the American Commission wirelessed to Wilson who was then on the ocean returning to the United States; Wilson replied supporting the point of view of the American delegation, and the other heads of state withdrew their contention. On the question of whether pensions were to be included, Smuts' argument convinced Wilson. These amounted to probably about fifteen billion dollars. Smuts was a British delegate from South Africa.]

The extent to which reparation can be claimed from Germany depends in the main on the meaning of the last reservation made by the Allies in their note to President Wilson, November, 1918. That reservation was agreed to by President Wilson and accepted by the German Government in the armistice negotiations, and was in the following terms:

"Further, in the conditions of peace laid down in his address to Congress on January 8, 1918, the President declared that invaded territories must be restored, as well as evacuated and made free. The Allied Governments feel that no doubt ought to be allowed to exist as to what this provision implies. By it they understand that compensation will be made by Germany for all damage done to the civilian population of the Allies and to their property by the aggression of Germany by land, by sea, and from the air."

In this reservation, a careful distinction must be made between the quotation from the President, which refers to the evacuation and restoration of the invaded territories, and the implication which the Allies find in that quotation and which they proceed to enunciate as a principle of general applicability. The Allies found in the President's provision for restoration of the invaded territories a general principle implied of far-reaching scope. This principle is that of compensation for all damage to the civilian population of the Allies in their persons or property, which resulted from the German aggression, and whether done on land or sea or from the air. By accepting this comprehensive principle (as the German Government did), they acknowledged their liability to compensation for all damage to the civilian population or their property wherever and however arising, so long as it was the result of German aggression. The President's limitation to restoration of the invaded territories only of some of the Allies was clearly abandoned.

The next question is how to understand the phrase "civilian population" in the above reservation, and it can be most conveniently answered by an illustration. A shopkeeper in a village in northern France lost his shop through enemy bombardment, and was himself badly wounded. He would be entitled as one of the civilian population to compensation for the loss of his property and for his personal disablement. He subsequently recovered completely, was called up for military service, and after being badly wounded and spending some time in the hospitals was discharged as permanently unfit. The expense he was to the French Government during this period as a soldier (his pay and maintenance, his uniform, rifle, ammunition, his keep in the hospital, etc.) was not damage to a civilian, but military loss to his Government, and it is therefore arguable that the French Government cannot recover compensation for such expense under the above reservation. His wife, however, was, during this period, deprived of her bread-winner, and she therefore suffered damage as a member of the civilian population, for which she would be entitled to compensation. In other words, the separation allowances paid to her and her children during this period by the French Government would have to be made good by the German Government, as the compensation which the allowances represent was their liability. After the soldier's discharge as unfit, he rejoins the civilian population, and as for the future he cannot (in whole or in part) earn his own livelihood, he is suffering damage as a member of the civilian population, for which the German Government are again liable to make compensation. In other words, the pension for disablement which he draws from the French Government is really a liability of the German Government, which they must under the above reservation make good to the French Government. It could not be argued that as he was disabled while a soldier he does not suffer damage as a civilian after his discharge if he is unfit to do his ordinary work. He does literally suffer as civilian after his discharge, and his pension is intended to make good this damage, and is therefore a liability of the German Government. If he had been killed in active service, his wife as a civilian would have been totally deprived of her breadwinner, and would be entitled to compensation. In other words, the pension she would draw from the French Government would really be a liability of the German Government under the above reservation, and would have to be made good by them to the French Government.

The plain, common-sense construction of the reservation therefore leads to the conclusion that, while direct war expenditure (such as the pay and equipment of soldiers, the cost of rifles, guns, and ordinance and all similar expenditures) could perhaps not be recovered from the Germans, yet disablement pensions to discharged soldiers, or pensions to widows and orphans, or separation allowances paid to their wives and children during the period of their military service are all items representing compensation to members of the civilian population for damage sustained by them, for which the German Government are liable. What was spent by the Allied Governments on the soldier himself, or on the mechanical appliances of war, might perhaps not be recoverable from the German Government under the reservation, as not being in any plain and direct sense damage to the civilian population. But what was, or is, spent on the citizen before he became a soldier or after he has ceased to be a soldier or at any time on his family, represents compensation for damage done to civilians and must be made good by the German Government under any fair interpretation of the above reservation. This includes all war pensions and separation allowances, which the German Government are liable to make good, in addition to reparation or compensation for all damage done to property of the Allied peoples.

(Signed)   J. C. SMUTS

Paris, March 31, 1919

148. REPORT PRESENTED TO THE PRELIMINARY PEACE CONFERENCE BY THE COMMISSION ON THE RESPONSIBILITY OF THE AUTHORS OF THE WAR AND ON ENFORCEMENT OF PENALTIES[1]

[The Preliminary Peace Conference at the plenary session of January 25, 1919, created a commission composed of fifteen members to inquire into the responsibility for the war. Among the prominent members of this commission were Robert Lansing and James Brown Scott for the United States, and André Tardieu for France. Though the American members presented a dissenting opinion, they concurred in the conclusions here given as well as in the process of reasoning by which they were reached and justified. This report became the basis of the article (231) of the Treaty of Versailles which placed responsibility for the war upon the Central Powers, and has been subjected to serious criticism by "revisionists." This selection should be compared with documents in Part II. The footnotes given are a part of the report.]

CHAPTER I.—RESPONSIBILITY OF THE AUTHORS OF THE WAR

On the question of the responsibility of the authors of the war, the Commission, after having examined a number of official documents relating to the origin of the World War, and to the violations of neutrality and of frontiers which accompanied its inception, has determined that the responsibility for it lies wholly upon the Powers which declared war in pursuance of a policy of aggression, the concealment of which gives to the origin of this war the character of a dark conspiracy against the peace of Europe.

This responsibility rests first on Germany and Austria, secondly on Turkey and Bulgaria. The responsibility is made all the graver by reason of the violation by Germany and Austria of the neutrality of Belgium and Luxemburg, which they themselves had guaranteed. It is

---

[1] *German White Book Concerning the Responsibility of the Authors of the War,* New York, Oxford Press, 1924, pp. 15-21. Reprinted with the permission of the Carnegie Endowment for International Peace.

READINGS IN EUROPEAN

increased, with regard to both France and Serbia, by the violation of their frontiers before the declaration of war.

I. Premeditation of the War

A. Germany and Austria

Many months before the crisis of 1914 the German Emperor had ceased to pose as the champion of peace. Naturally believing in the overwhelming superiority of his Army, he openly showed his enmity towards France. General von Moltke said to the King of the Belgians: "This time the matter must be settled." In vain the King protested. The Emperor and his Chief of Staff remained no less fixed in their attitude.[1]

On the 28th of June, 1914, occurred the assassination at Serajevo of the heir-apparent of Austria. "It is the act of a little group of madmen," said Francis Joseph.[2] The act, committed as it was by a subject of Austria-Hungary on Austro-Hungarian territory, could in no wise compromise Serbia, which very correctly expressed its condolences[3] and stopped public rejoicings in Belgrade. If the Government of Vienna thought that there was any Serbian complicity, Serbia was ready[4] to seek out the guilty parties. But this attitude failed to satisfy Austria and still less Germany, who, after their first astonishment had passed, saw in this royal and national misfortune a pretext to initiate war.

At Potsdam a "decisive consultation" took place on the 5th of July, 1914.[5] Vienna and Berlin decided upon this plan: "Vienna will send to Belgrade a very emphatic ultimatum with a very short limit of time."[6]

The Bavarian Minister, von Lerchenfeld, said in a confidential dispatch dated the 18th of July, 1914, the facts stated in which have never been officially denied: "It is clear that Serbia can not accept the demands, which are inconsistent with the dignity of an independent state."[7] Count Lerchenfeld reveals in this report that, at the time it was made, the ultimatum to Serbia had been jointly decided upon by the Governments of Berlin and Vienna; that they were waiting to send it until President Poincaré and Mr. Viviani should have left for St. Petersburg; and that no illusions were cherished, either at Berlin or Vienna, as to the consequences which this threatening measure would involve. It was perfectly well known that war would be the result.

---

[1] Yellow Book; Mr. Cambon to Mr. Pichon, Berlin, November 22, 1913.
[2] Message to his people.
[3] Serbian Blue Book, p. 30.
[4] Yellow Book, No. 15; Mr. Cambon to Mr. Bienvenu-Martin, July 21, 1914.
[5] Lichnowsky memoir.
[6] Dr. Muehlon's memoir.
[7] Report of July 18, 1914.

The Bavarian Minister explains, moreover, that the only fear of the Berlin Government was that Austria-Hungary might hesitate and draw back at the last minute, and that on the other hand Serbia, on the advice of France and Great Britain, might yield to the pressure put upon her. Now, "the Berlin Government considers that war is necessary." Therefore, it gave full powers to Count Berchtold, who instructed the Ballplatz on the 18th of July, 1914, to negotiate with Bulgaria to induce her to enter into an alliance and to participate in the war.

In order to mask this understanding, it was arranged that the Emperor should go for a cruise in the North Sea, and that the Prussian Minister of War should go for a holiday, so that the Imperial Government might pretend that events had taken it completely by surprise.

Austria suddenly sent Serbia an ultimatum that she had carefully prepared in such a way as to make it impossible to accept. Nobody could be deceived; "the whole world understands that this ultimatum means war."[1] According to Mr. Sazonoff, "Austria-Hungary wanted to devour Serbia."[2]

Mr. Sazonoff asked Vienna for an extension of the short time-limit of forty-eight hours given by Austria to Serbia for the most serious decision in its history.[3] Vienna refused the demand. On the 24th and 25th of July, England and France multiplied their efforts to persuade Serbia to satisfy the Austro-Hungarian demands. Russia threw in her weight on the side of conciliation.[4]

Contrary to the expectation of Austria-Hungary and Germany, Serbia yielded. She agreed to all the requirements of the ultimatum, subject to the single reservation that, in the judicial inquiry which she would commence for the purpose of seeking out the guilty parties, the participation of Austrian officials would be kept within the limits assigned by international law. "If the Austro-Hungarian Government is not satisfied with this," Serbia declared she was ready "to submit to the decision of the Hague Tribunal."[5]

"A quarter of an hour before the expiration of the time-limit," at 5.45 on the 25th, Mr. Pashitch, the Serbian Minister for Foreign Affairs, delivered this reply to Baron Giesl, the Austro-Hungarian Minister.

On Mr. Pashitch's return to his own office he found awaiting him a letter from Baron Giesl saying that he was not satisfied with the reply. At 6.30 the latter had left Belgrade and even before he had arrived at Vienna, the Austro-Hungarian Government had handed his passports

---

[1] Lichnowsky memoir.
[2] Austro-Hungarian Red Book, No. 16.
[3] Blue Book, No. 26.
[4] Yellow Book, No. 36; Blue Book, Nos. 12, 46, 55, 65, 94, 118.
[5] Yellow Book, No. 46.

to Mr. Yovanovitch, the Serbian Minister, and had prepared the thirty-three mobilization proclamations, which were published on the following morning in the *Budapest Kozlöni*, the official gazette of the Hungarian Government. On the 27th Sir Maurice de Bunsen telegraphed to Sir Edward Grey: "This country has gone wild with joy at the prospect of war with Serbia."[1] At midday on the 28th Austria declared war on Serbia. On the 29th the Austrian army commenced the bombardment of Belgrade, and made its dispositions to cross the frontier.

The reiterated suggestions of the Entente Powers with a view to finding a peaceful solution of the dispute only produced evasive replies on the part of Berlin or promises of intervention with the Government of Vienna without any effectual steps being taken.

On the 24th of July Russia and England asked that the Powers should be granted a reasonable delay in which to work in concert for the maintenance of peace. Germany did not join in this request."[2]

On the 25th of July Sir Edward Grey proposed mediation by four Powers (England, France, Italy and Germany). France[3] and Italy[4] immediately gave their concurrence. Germany[5] refused, alleging that it was not a question of mediation but of arbitration, as the conference of the four Powers was called to make proposals, not to decide.

On the 26th of July Russia proposed to negotiate directly with Austria. Austria refused.[6]

On the 27th of July England proposed a European conference. Germany refused.[7]

On the 29th of July Sir Edward Grey asked the Wilhelmstrasse to be good enough to "suggest any method by which the influence of the four Powers could be used together to prevent a war between Austria and Russia."[8] She was asked herself to say what she desired.[9] Her reply was evasive.[10]

On the same day, the 29th of July, the Czar dispatched to the Emperor William II a telegram suggesting that the Austro-Serbian problem should be submitted to the Hague Tribunal. This suggestion received no reply. This important telegram does not appear in the German White Book. It was made public by the Petrograd *Official Gazette* (January, 1915).

The Bavarian Legation, in a report dated the 31st of July, de-

---

[1] Blue Book, No. 41.
[2] Russian Orange Book, No. 4; Yellow Book, No. 43.
[3] Yellow Book, No. 70.
[4] *Ibid.*, No. 72; Blue Book, No. 49.
[5] Blue Book, No. 43.
[6] Yellow Book, No. 54.
[7] *Ibid.*, Nos. 68 and 73.
[8] *Ibid.*, No. 97; Blue Book, No. 84.
[9] Blue Book, No. 111.
[10] Yellow Book, Nos. 97, 98 and 109.

clared its conviction that the efforts of Sir Edward Grey to preserve peace would not hinder the march of events.[1]

As early as the 21st of July German mobilization had commenced by the recall of a certain number of classes of the reserve,[2] then of German officers in Switzerland,[3] and finally of the Metz garrison on the 25th of July.[4] On the 26th of July the German Fleet was called back from Norway.[5]

The Entente did not relax its conciliatory efforts, but the German Government systematically brought all its attempts to nought. When Austria consented for the first time on the 31st of July to discuss the contents of the Serbian note with the Russian Government and the Austro-Hungarian Ambassador received orders to "converse" with the Russian Minister of Foreign Affairs,[6] Germany made any negotiation impossible by sending her ultimatum to Russia. Prince Lichnowsky wrote that "a hint from Berlin would have been enough to decide Count Berchtold to content himself with a diplomatic success and to declare that he was satisfied with the Serbian reply, but this hint was not given. *On the contrary they went forward towards war.*"[7]

On the 1st of August the German Emperor addressed a telegram to the King of England[8] containing the following sentence: "The troops on my frontier are, at this moment, being kept back by telegraphic and telephonic orders from crossing the French frontier." Now, war was not declared till two days after that date, and as the German mobilization orders were issued on that same day, the 1st of August, it follows that, as a matter of fact, the German Army had been mobilized and concentrated in pursuance of previous orders.

The attitude of the Entente nevertheless remained still to the very end so conciliatory that at the very time at which the German fleet was bombarding Libau, Nicholas II gave his word to William II that Russia would not undertake any aggressive action during *pourparlers*,[9] and that when the German troops commenced their march across the French frontier Mr. Viviani telegraphed to all the French Ambassadors "we must not stop working for accommodation."

On the 3rd of August Mr. von Schoen went to the Quai d'Orsay with the declaration of war against France. Lacking a real cause of complaint, Germany alleged, in her declaration of war, that bombs had been dropped by French aeroplanes in various districts in Germany. This statement was entirely false. Moreover, it was either later ad-

---

[1] Second report of Count Lerchenfeld, Bavarian plenipotentiary at Berlin, published on the instructions of Kurt Eisner.

[2] Yellow Book, No. 15.

[3] July 23, *ibid.*, No. 60.

[4] *Ibid.*, No. 106.

[5] *Ibid.*, No. 58.

[6] Blue Book, No. 133; Red Book, No. 55.

[7] Lichnowsky memoir, p. 41.

[8] White Book, Annex 32; Yellow Book, Annex II *bis*, No. 2.

[9] Telegram from Nicholas II to William II; Yellow Book, No. 6, Annex V.

mitted to be so[1] or no particulars were ever furnished by the German Government.

Moreover, in order to be manifestly above reproach, France was careful to withdraw her troops ten kilometers from the German frontier. Notwithstanding this precaution, numerous officially established violations of French territory preceded the declaration of war.[2]

The provocation was so flagrant that Italy, herself a member of the Triple Alliance, did not hesitate to declare that in view of the aggressive character of the war the *casus fœderis* ceased to apply.[3]

B. Turkey and Bulgaria

The conflict was, however, destined to become more widespread and Germany and Austria were joined by allies.

Since the Balkan War the Young Turk Government had been drawing nearer and nearer Germany, whilst Germany on her part had constantly been extending her activities at Constantinople.

A few months before war broke out, Turkey handed over the command of her military and naval forces to the German General Liman von Sanders and the German Admiral Souchon.

In August, 1914, the former, acting under orders from the General Headquarters at Berlin, caused the Turkish army to begin mobilizing.[4]

Finally, on the 4th of August, the understanding between Turkey and Germany was definitely formulated in an alliance.[5] The consequence was that when the *Gœben* and the *Breslau* took refuge in the Bosphorus, Turkey closed the Dardanelles against the Entente squadrons and war followed.

On the 14th of October, 1915, Bulgaria declared war on Serbia, which country had been at war with Austria since the 28th of July, 1914, and had been attacked on all fronts by a large Austro-German Army since the 6th of October, 1915. Serbia had, however, committed no act of provocation against Bulgaria.

Serbia never formulated any claim against Bulgaria during the negotiations which took place between the Entente Powers and Bulgaria prior to the latter's entry into the war. On the contrary, she was

---

[1] Statement of the municipality of Nüremburg, dated April 3, 1916.

[2] (a) Patrols of various strengths crossed the French frontier at fifteen po'ts, one on the 30th of July at Xures, eight on the 2nd of August, and the others on the 3rd of August, before war was declared.

The French troops lost one killed and several wounded. The enemy left on French territory four killed, one of whom was an officer, and seven prisoners. (b) At Suarce, on the 2nd of August, the enemy carried off nine inhabitants, twenty-five horses, and three carriages. (c) Four incursions by German dirigibles took place between the 25th of July and the 1st of August. (d) Finally, German aeroplanes flew over Lunéville on the 3rd of August, before the declaration of war, and dropped six bombs (Yellow Book, Nos. 106, 136, 139, etc.).

[3] Yellow Book, No. 124.

[4] H. Morgenthau, *Secrets of the Bosphorus* (London, 1918), pp. 39, 40. ,

[5] Greek White Book, 1913, 1917, Nos. 19 and 20.

offering herself ready to make certain territorial concessions to Bulgaria in order to second the efforts of the Entente Powers to induce Bulgaria to join them. According to Count Lerchenfeld's reports, however, Bulgaria had begun negotiations with the Central Powers as early as the 18th of July, 1914, with a view to entering the war on their side. In April, 1915, the Bulgars made an armed attack against Serbia near Valandovo and Struvmitza, where a real battle was fought on Serbian territory. Being defeated, the Bulgars retired, ascribing this act of aggression to some comitadjis. An international commission (composed of representatives of the Entente) discovered, however, that there had been Bulgarian regular officers and soldiers among the dead and the prisoners.[1]

On the 6th of September, 1915, Bulgaria and Austria-Hungary concluded a treaty which recited that they had agreed to undertake common military action against Serbia and by which Austria-Hungary guaranteed to Bulgaria certain accretions of territory at Serbia's expense, and also agreed, jointly with Germany, to make to the Bulgarian Government a war loan of fr. 200,000,000, to be increased if the war lasted more than four months.[2] Even after this, Mr. Malinoff, one of the former Prime Ministers of Bulgaria, took part in the negotiations with the Entente, and, while these negotiations were continuing, Bulgaria, on the 23rd of September, mobilized, ostensibly to defend her neutrality.

No sooner had the army been mobilized and concentrated and Bulgarian forces massed on the whole length of the Serbian frontier, than the Bulgarian Government openly and categorically repudiated Mr. Malinoff, stating that he was in no way qualified to commit Bulgaria, and that he deserved "to be subjected to the utmost rigor of his country's laws for his conduct on that occasion." Some days later, Austro-German troops crossed the Danube and began to invade Serbia.

As soon as the Serbian troops began to retire, the Bulgars, on the pretext that the former had violated their frontier, launched the attack which eventually led to the complete subjugation of Serbia.

Two documents in the possession of the Serbian Government prove that this incident on the frontier was "arranged" and represented as a Serbian provocation. On the 10th of October, 1915, the Secretary General of the Foreign Office at Sofia, at the request of the Bulgarian Minister for Foreign affairs, sent the following communication to Count Tarnowsky, Austro-Hungarian Minister at Sofia: "In order to divest the attack on Serbia of the appearance of a preconceived plot, we shall, this evening or tomorrow morning, provoke a frontier incident in some uninhabited region."[3] Also, on the 12th of October, 1915, Count Tarnowsky sent the following telegram to Vienna: "The com-

---

[1] Memorandum I of the Serbian delegation, chap. II, par. c.

[2] Treaty between Bulgaria and Austria-Hungary, dated August 24/September 6, 1915 (furnished by the Serbian delegation).

[3] Memorandum I of the Serbian delegation, chap. II, par. c.

manding general informs me that the desired incident on the Serbian frontier was arranged yesterday."[1]

Bulgaria, in fact, first attacked on October 12, 1915, two days before the declaration of war on Serbia, which took place on October 14, 1915. That this was the case does not prevent Bulgaria from asserting that the Serbs first crossed her frontier.

The above sequence of events proves that Bulgaria had premeditated war against Serbia, and perfidiously brought it about.

By means of German agents Enver Pasha and Talaat Pasha had, since the spring of 1914, been aware of the Austro-German plan, *i.e.*, an attack by Austria against Serbia, the intervention by Germany against France, the passage through Belgium, the occupation of Paris in a fortnight, the closing of the Straits by Turkey, and the readiness of Bulgaria to take action. The Sultan acknowledged this plot to one of his intimates. It was indeed nothing but a plot engineered by heads of four States against the independence of Serbia and the peace of Europe.[2]

CONCLUSIONS

1. *The war was premeditated by the Central Powers together with their Allies, Turkey and Bulgaria, and was the result of acts deliberately committed in order to make it unavoidable.*

2. *Germany, in agreement with Austria-Hungary, deliberately worked to defeat all the many conciliatory proposals made by the Entente Powers and their repeated efforts to avoid war.*

149. GERMAN VIEW OF THE TREATY OF VERSAILLES[3]

[On May 7, 1919, the treaty was presented to the German delegates, who under the leadership of Brockdorff-Rantzau, German Foreign Minister, had arrived at Versailles on April 29. The delegates were informed that they would have three weeks in which to make written observations on the terms, but that no oral discussions with the Allied delegates would be permitted. The counter proposals, amounting to 443 pages, reached the Council of Four on May 29. They were at once turned over to ten inter-allied committees of experts, and on June 16 the Allied reply granted a few concessions, especially in regard to the Polish frontier, and required Germany to declare her willingness to sign the treaty within five days on penalty of termination of the armistice. Feeling in Germany was very bitter, the Scheidemann government resigned rather than sign, and a new government was formed. Because

---

[1] *Ibid.*

[2] Basri Bey, *L'Orient debalkanisé et l'Albanie*, chap. II (Paris, 1919).

[3] Germany. Peace Conference Delegations, 1919. *The German Counter Proposals to the Draft of the Versailles Peace Treaty*, pp. 3-27.

of this political crisis, the time limit was extended two days, when the Germans finally consented to sign.]

I have the honour to transmit herewith the observations of the German Delegation on the Draft of the Treaty of Peace. We had come to Versailles in the expectation of receiving a proposal of peace founded on the basis actually agreed upon. We had the firm intention of doing everything in our power to fulfil the heavy obligations which have been assumed by us. We hope to get the Peace of Right which has been promised us. We were aghast when, in reading that document, we learned what demands Might Triumphant has raised against us. The deeper we penetrated into the spirit of this Treaty, the more we became convinced of its impracticability. The demands raised go beyond the power of the German Nation.

For the purpose of the reëstablishment of the Polish Empire we are to renounce territory uncontestedly German, that is to say, almost the whole of the Province of West Prussia prevailingly German, German parts of Pomerania, the genuine German city of Danzig; we are to allow the old Hanseatic town to be converted into a "Free City" under Polish suzerainty. We are to give our consent to East Prussia's being amputated from the organism of the state, to its being condemned to decay and to its being deprived of its northern part with the pure German town of Memel. In favour of Poland and the Czecho-Slovak State we are to surrender Upper Silesia in spite of its being, since upwards of 750 years, in close political union with Germany, of its pulsing with German life and of its constituting the foundation for the industry in the whole of Eastern Germany. Districts with a German majority are to be ceded to Belgium by way of a plebiscite, only subsequently to be entered upon and without sufficient guarantees for its unbiased character. The genuine German Saar-District is to be severed from our Empire and its subsequent incorporation into France is to be prepared, although we do not owe France human beings, but merely coals.

Rhineland is to be occupied for fifteen years, and after this time the Allies are to be in a position of refusing to restore the territory; in the meantime they can do everything to sever the economic and moral relations with the mother-country and finally to forge the mind of the native population.

A Germany thus mutilated and weakened is, although her adversaries expressly renunciated any claim to a restitution of the costs of war, to declare her readiness in principle to charge herself with all the costs of war of all the adversaries, sums which would exceed several times the entire public and private wealth of Germany. For the present the adversaries demand, going beyond the basis agreed upon, compensation for the damages caused to the civilian population, Germany being moreover held answerable for her Allies too. The sum to be paid is to be assessed in a one-sided manner by the adversaries alone and is to be subject to ulterior changes and augmentations. The productive capacity of the German Nation is to set the limit, graduated not according to its standard of living, but solely according to its capability of satisfying by its work the exactions of the enemies. The German Nation would, therefore, be condemned to perpetual slave-work.

In spite of such monstrous demands the rebuilding of our economic system is at the same time made impossible. We are to surrender our merchant fleet. We are to give up all foreign interests. We are to transfer to our opponents the property of all German undertakings abroad, even of those situated in countries allied to us. Even after the conclusion of peace the enemy states are to be empowered to confiscate all German property. No German merchant will then, in their countries, be safe from such war measures. We are to completely renounce our colonies, not even in these are German missionaries to have the right of exercising their profession. We are, in other words, to renounce every kind of political, economic and moral activity.

But more than this, we are also to resign the right of self-determination in domestic affairs. Dictatorial powers are conferred on the International Reparation Commission over our whole national life in economic and cultural matters, its power by far exceeding those ever enjoyed within the German Empire by the Emperor, the German Federal Council and the Reichstag put together. This Commission has the unrestrained power of disposal over the economic system of the state, of the municipalities and of private individuals. All matters of education and public health likewise depend on it. The Commission is able to keep the whole German Nation in intellectual slavery. It can, in order to augment the payments of Serfdom, inhibit the whole system of social care for the working classes in Germany.

Also in other respects Germany's right of sovereignty is abrogated. Her principal rivers are placed under international administration, she is obliged to build on her own territory the canals and railways desired by the enemy, she must, without knowing the contents, assent to agreements which her adversaries intend concluding with the new states in the East and which affect Germany's own boundaries. The German people is excluded from the League of Nations to which all common work of the world is confided.

Thus a whole nation is called upon to sign its own proscription, yea, even its own death warrant.

Germany knows that she must make sacrifices in order to come to Peace. Germany knows that she has promised such sacrifices by agreement and wishes to carry them through to the utmost limit she can possibly go to.

1. Germany offers to take the lead before all other nations in disarming herself, in order to show that she is willing to help them in bringing forth the new era of the Peace of Right. She will give up compulsory service and will, apart from transitory provisions, dimin-

ish her army to 100,000 men. She is even prepared to surrender the battleships which her opponents intend leaving her. But she hereby acts on the assumption that she will be immediately admitted, as a state with equal rights, into the League of Nations. She presumes that a genuine League of Nations is to be formed, comprising all nations that are of good will, also the enemies of today. The League must be based on a sense of responsibility towards mankind and must be equipped with compulsory powers, strong and reliable enough to defend the boundaries of its members.

2. In territorial questions Germany unreservedly endorses the Wilson programme. She renounces her sovereignty in Alsace-Lorraine, desires, however, a free plebiscite to be carried through there. She cedes to Poland the greatest part of the province of Posnania, the districts incontestably inhabited by Poles, as well as the capital, Posen. She is ready to grant to the Poles a free and secure access to the sea under international guaranty, through conceding free ports in Danzig, Königsberg and Memel, through a Vistula shipping-act and through special railway conventions. Germany is prepared to assure France's being supplied with coals, chiefly from the Saar-territory, till the French mines have been restored to working-order. The prevailingly Danish districts of Sleswig will be handed over to Denmark on the basis of a plebiscite. Germany demands that the right of self-determination be respected also in favour of the Germans in Austria and Bohemia.

She is prepared to submit her entire colonies to the joint administration of the League of Nations on condition of being recognised as its mandatory.

3. Germany is prepared to make the payments incumbent on her according to the programme of Peace agreed upon, up to the maximum amount of a hundred milliard marks gold, namely, twenty milliard marks gold until May 1, 1926, the remaining eighty milliard marks gold afterwards, by annual instalments bearing no interest. The principle is acknowledged that these instalments are to constitute a definite percentage of the revenues of the German Empire and those of its federal states. The instalment will nearly come up to the budget of former peace times. During the first ten years the instalment is not to exceed one milliard marks gold every time. The German taxpayer is to be burdened no less than the taxpayer of the most highly charged state represented on the Reparation Commission.

In conceding this, Germany acts on the assumption that she will have to make no further sacrifices of territory beyond the above mentioned ones, and that she will again be granted freedom of action at home and abroad.

4. Germany is ready to devote her entire economic power to the work of reparation. She is desirous of actively coöperating in the restoration of the devastated territories in Belgium and Northern France. In compensation for the deficiency of output of the destroyed

mines in Northern France, up to twenty million tons of coal a year are to be supplied during the first five years, up to eight million tons of coal a year during the next five years. Germany will contrive to deliver further supplies of coals for France, Belgium, Italy and Luxemburg.

Furthermore, Germany is ready to effectuate considerable deliveries of benzol, coal-tar, sulphide of ammonia, dye-stuffs and medicines.

5. Finally, Germany offers to contribute her entire tonnage of merchant ships to a world-pool, to place at the opponents' disposal part of the freights for being credited to the reparation account, and to build tonnage for them in German yards for a number of years, to an amount exceeding their demands.

．　．　．　．　．　．　．

7. Germany deems the granting of participation in industrial concerns, principally in coal-mines to assure the supplies of coal, the appropriate ways and means for the accelerated fulfilment of her duty of indemnification.

8. Germany, in unison with the will of the organized workmen of the whole world, wants to see the workmen in all countries free and endowed with equal rights. She means to secure for them in the Treaty of Peace the right of decisive co-determination in all questions of social politics and social insurance.

9. The German Delegation again raise their demand for a neutral inquiry into the question of responsibility for the war and of guilt during the war. An impartial commission should have the right of inspecting the archives of all belligerent countries and examining, as in a court of law, all chief actors of the war.

Only the confidence that the question of guilt will be examined in an unbiased manner, can give the nations non-hostile to each other, the disposition of mind necessary to build up the League of Nations.

These are merely the most important proposals which we have to make. As regards further extensive sacrifices to be made by Germany and the details, the Delegation refers to the enclosed memorandum, and the annex thereto.

The time-limit set us for the elaboration of this memorandum was so short that it has not been possible to exhaust all questions. A fruitful and enlightening treatment of the matter could only be attained through oral discussions. This Peace is to be the greatest treaty-work in history. There exists no example of so complex negotiations having been carried through solely by exchange of written notes. The feeling of the nations that have brought such immense sacrifices demands that their fate be settled in an open, unreserved exchange of views, on the principle: "Open covenants of peace, openly arrived at, after which there shall be no private international understandings of any kind, but diplomacy shall proceed always frankly and in the public view."

Germany is asked to set her name under the Treaty presented to her and to fulfil this Treaty. Even in her distress, she deems right too sacred than that she could assent to accept conditions for the fulfilment of which she could not pledge herself. It is true that the treaties concluded by the great powers in the history of the last decades have over and again proclaimed the right of the more powerful. But every one of those treaties is to be counted among the authors and prolongators of the world-war. Wherever in this war the victor has spoken to the vanquished, in Brest-Litowsk and Bukarest, his words of might were only a seed-corn for future strife. The high aims which our adversaries were the first to establish for their warfare, the new era of a just and durable Peace, demand a Treaty of a different mind. Only a coöperation of all nations, a coöperation of hands and intellects, can bring about a permanent peace. We are not under a misapprehension as to the intensity of hatred and bitterness that is caused by this war; and yet the forces at work for the union of mankind are now stronger than ever. It is the historical task of the Peace Conference of Versailles to bring about this union.

Accept, Sir, the assurance of my high esteem.

(signed) BROCKDORFF-RANTZAU

COMMENTS BY THE GERMAN DELEGATION ON THE CONDITIONS OF PEACE

First Part

1. General Remarks

I. Legal Basis of the Negotiations of Peace.

The German Delegation has entered into the task of concluding peace in the legitimate conviction that the essential contents of the Treaty of Peace to be concluded are in principle outlined by the events preceding it, and that thereby a sure platform is established for the negotiations at Versailles. This conviction is founded upon the following facts:

On the 5th of October 1918, the German Government requested President Wilson to take into his hands the task of establishing peace on the basis of the 14 points contained in his message to Congress of January 8th, 1918 and on the basis of his subsequent proclamations, especially his speech of September 27th 1918,—to invite all belligerent powers to send delegates for the purpose of entering into negotiations and to bring about the immediate conclusion of a general armistice.

On the 8th of October 1918, President Wilson asked if the German Government accepted his 14 points and if the object of their discussion would be only to agree upon practical details of their application. The German Government expressly confirmed this and at the same time said it expected that also the Allied Goverments stood on the platform of President Wilson's proclamations. Besides that, it declared its readiness to evacuate the occupied territories, this being demanded by President Wilson as a condition for bringing about the armistice.

After further correspondence President Wilson on the 23rd of October 1918 notified that he was willing to take up with the Allied Governments the question of an armistice, making known at the same time that in carrying out this intention he had transmitted to the Allies his correspondence with the German Government and had suggested, in case the Allies agreed to the terms and principles of peace accepted by Germany, to point out through their military advisers the terms for an armistice, as would be fit to safeguard or to enforce the details of the peace to which the German Government had agreed. Germany, thus it was expressly said, could by the acceptance of such terms of armistice afford the best concrete evidence that she accepted the fundamental terms and principles of the whole treaty of peace.

The German Government having in its answer of the 27th of October given satisfactory information concerning further matters of inner politics which President Wilson had touched upon in his last-mentioned note of October 23rd, President Wilson notified the German Government on the 3rd of November that he had, in answer to the correspondence with the German Government transmitted by him, received from the Allied Governments a memorandum as follows:

"The Allied Governments have given careful consideration to the correspondence which has passed between the President of the United States and the German Government. Subject to the qualifications which follow they declare their willingness to make peace with the Government of Germany on the terms of peace laid down in the President's address to Congress of January the 8th 1918 and the principles of settlement enunciated in his subsequent addresses. They must point out, however, that what is usually described as the freedom of the seas admits various interpretations, some of which they could not accept. They must therefore reserve to themselves complete freedom of this subject when they enter the peace conference.

"Further in the conditions of peace laid down in his address to Congress of January the 8th 1918 the President declared that the invaded territories must be restored as well as evacuated and freed. The Allied Governments feel that no doubt ought to be allowed to exist as to what this provision implies. By it they understand that compensation will be made by Germany for all damage done to the civilian population of the Allies and their property by the aggression of Germany by land, by sea and from the air."

On the 11th of November 1918, armistice was concluded. From the correspondence that led to this armistice, the following points become evident:

1. As a basis of peace, Germany has expressly accepted nothing but President Wilson's 14 points and his subsequent proclamations. Any other bases have been demanded neither by President Wilson nor after him by any of the Allied Governments.

2. The acceptance of the terms of armistice was, according to President Wilson's own assurance, to be the best evidence for the unequivocal acceptance of the above mentioned fundamental terms and principles of peace on the part of Germany. Germany has accepted the terms of armistice and thereby furnished the proof demanded by President Wilson. Beyond that she has with all her might endeavoured to fulfil those terms in spite of their great severity.

3. The Allies also have accepted Wilson's 14 points and his subsequent proclamations as a basis of peace.

4. A solemn agreement as to the basis of peace therefore exists between the two Contracting Parties. Germany has a right to this basis of peace. By forsaking it, the Allies would break an international legal agreement.

The historical facts stated show that between the German Government on the one hand and the Governments of the Allied and Associated Powers on the other a pactum de contrahendo has been concluded which is, without doubt, legally binding and whereby the basis for the peace to be worked out is for both parties unalterably fixed.

The practical application of the principles agreed upon must, according to President Wilson's own words, be negotiated upon. Germany has a right to a discussion of the terms of peace. This discussion can only extend to the application of the 14 points and of the subsequent proclamations of Wilson. If a peace of different character were to be forced upon Germany, that would be the breach of a solemn pledge.

II. The contradiction between the draft of the treaty on the one hand and the legal basis, agreed upon, the previous assurances of the enemy statesmen and the general ideas of international law on the other hand

Relying on the legal basis agreed upon for the negotiations of peace, the German people laid down arms. In this confidence the German people felt all the more safe as it saw the agreement merely comprising the fundamental ideas which previously had over and over again been expressed by the enemy statesmen. Our enemies have repeatedly professed that they do not make war against the German people but against an imperialistic and irresponsible Government. Our enemies repeated again and again that this war without parallel should be followed by a new order of peace, a peace of right and no peace of might. A new spirit should emanate from this peace and should be embodied in a League of Nations, a member of which also Germany was to be. Germany's position amongst the nations should not be destroyed, and the right of self-determination should be recognized for all nations.

All these principles were comprised in President Wilson's 14 points and his subsequent declarations.

The conditions of peace put before us are an obvious contradiction to all such assurances from the mouth of the enemy statesmen.

．　　．　　．　　．　　．　　．　　．

Today, after the radical political subversions that have taken place in Germany in the late autumn 1918, the enemies no more face an irresponsible German Government but the German people ruling its future itself. The new constitution of the German Empire, the structure of its popular government are adapted to the most rigorous principles of democracy, the abandonment of the militaristic spirit is evident also in the fact that the Statute for a League of Nations proposed by Germany contains an agreement concerning the restriction of armaments, which establishes greater securities than the corresponding provisions of the Statute for a League of Nations as contained in the draft of the Treaty of Peace.

But these facts like others have been utterly disregarded in the draft of the Treaty of Peace. It cannot be imagined, what harder terms could have been imposed upon an imperialistic government.

2. No Peace of Might, but a Peace of Right

The peace to be concluded with Germany was to be a peace of right, no peace of might.

．　　．　　．　　．　　．　　．　　．

The document of peace shows that none of these repeated solemn assurances have been kept.

To begin with the territorial questions:

In the West, a purely German territory on the Saar with a population of at least 650,000 inhabitants is to be separated from the German Empire for at least fifteen years merely for the reason that claims are asserted to the coal abounding there.

The other cessions in the West, German-Austria and German-Bohemia will be mentioned in connection with the right of self-determination of the nations.

In Schleswig, the line of demarcation for voting has been traced through purely German districts and goes farther than Denmark herself wished.

In the East, Upper-Silesia is to be separated from Germany and conveyed to Poland, although it has been in no political connexion with Poland for the last 750 years. Contrary to this, the provinces of Posnania and almost the whole of West-Prussia are to be separated from the German Empire in consideration of the former extension of the ancient Polish realm, although millions of Germans are living there. Again the district of Memel is separated quite regardless of its historical past in the obvious attempt at economically separating Germany from Russia. For the purpose of securing to Poland a free access to the sea, East-Prussia is to be utterly cut off from the Bulk of the Empire and thereby to be condemned to economical and national decay. The purely German city of Danzig is to become a Free State under the suzerainty of Poland. Such terms are no more founded on any principle of justice. At random, here the idea of an imprescribable historical right, there the idea of the ethnographical state of possession, there the standpoint of economical interest is to prevail, in every case the decision being in disfavour of Germany.

The settlement of the colonial question is equally contradictory to a peace of justice.

For the essence of activity in colonial work does not consist in economical exploitation of a less developed human race, but in raising peoples of a lower standard to a superior civilization. This gives the Powers advanced in culture a natural claim to take part in colonial work. Germany also whose colonial accomplishments cannot be denied, has this natural claim, which is not realized by a treaty of peace that deprives Germany of each and all of her colonies.

Not only the settlement of the territorial questions but each and every provision of the Treaty of Peace is governed by the ill-renowned word: "Might above Right"! A few illustrations:

Under the provisions of Article 117 Germany is to recognize beforehand the full force of all treaties or agreements which may be entered into by her enemies with the states created or to be created in any part of the former Russian Empire, even with respect to her own frontiers.

According to the provisions of international law as understood on the Continent, the economical war ought to have been deemed unlawful and private property ought to have been left untouched, even while the war was being carried on. In spite of this, the instrument of peace does not confine itself to vindicate for the public claims of restitution against Germany the total of German private property liquidated by the enemies within their territories, but monstrously the hostile governments reserve to themselves a right, for an indefinite period after the coming into force of the Treaty of Peace, to liquidate all German property within their territories without real equivalent and independent of the time of its importation or to submit the same to other measures of war at their discretion; this to include German property even in the German colonies, in Alsace-Lorraine and in the other districts to be ceded.

The claim is asserted to hand over German citizens to Courts of the enemy Powers, instead of a new solution, borne by the idea of the peace of justice, being sought by appointing an impartial authority that should ascertain all violations of international law that have occurred in this war.

Although President Wilson in his speech of October 20th 1916 has acknowledged that no single fact caused the war, but that lastly the whole European system is in a deeper sense responsible for the war, its combination of alliances and understandings, a complicated texture of intrigues and espionage that unfailingly caught the whole family of nations in its meshes, that the present war is not so simply to be explained and that its roots reach deep into the dark soil of history, Germany is to acknowledge, that Germany and her Allies are responsible for all damages which the enemy governments or their subjects have incurred by her and her Allies' aggression. This appears all the less tolerable as it is an indisputable historical fact that several of the enemy Powers, as Italy and Roumania, on their part entered into the war for the object of territorial conquests. Thus there is no incontestable legal foundation for the obligation of reparation imposed upon Germany, and beyond that, the amount of such compensation is to be determined by a commission nominated solely by the enemies of Germany, Germany taking no part in the findings of the commission. The powers of this commission plainly come to administrate Germany like a big bankrupt's estate.

As there are innate rights of Man, so there are innate rights of Nations. The inalienable fundamental right of every state is the right of self-preservation and self-determination. With this fundamental right the insinuation here proposed to Germany is incompatible. Germany is to submit to an obligation to restitute damages, the amount of which at present is not even stated. The German rivers are to be placed under an international authority of control, in which Germany's delegates are always to be but the smallest minority. On Germany's soil, canals and railroads are to be built at the discretion of foreign authorities.

These few instances show that that is not the peace of justice we were promised, not the peace "the very principle of which," according to a word of President Wilson, "is equality and the common participation in a common benefit. The equality of nations upon which peace must be founded if it is to last must be an equality of rights."

3. The Spirit of the League of Nations

In such a peace the solidarity of human interests which was to find its expression in a League of Nations, would have been respected. How often Germany has been given the promise that this League of Nations would unite the belligerents, conquerors as well as conquered, in a permanent system of common rights.

．　．　．　．　．　．　．

These manifestations made it appear as a matter of course to the German people that it would, from the beginning, participate in the establishing of the League of Nations. But in contradiction to them, the statute of the League of Nations has been established without the coöperation of Germany. Nay, still more: Germany does not even stand on the list of those States that have been invited to join the

München, 11. März 1919   Preis 1 K   23. Jahrgang Nr. 50

SIMPLICISSIMUS

Bezugspreis vierteljährlich 12 K
Nur Rechte vorbehalten

Begründet von Albert Langen und Th. Th. Heine

Bezugspreis vierteljährlich 12 K
Copyright 1919 by Simplicissimus-Verlag G.m.b.H. & Co., München

Die Grundlage für den Völkerbund

(Th. Th. Heine)

„Nur so kann Deutschland darin geduldet werden!"

"THE BASIS FOR THE LEAGUE OF NATIONS"

"Only thus can Germany be tolerated in it." (March 11, 1919.) [At the start, the League of Nations was a league of victors.]

League of Nations. To be sure, Germany may apply for admission which, however, is made dependent on "effective guarantees," the extent and tenor of which she does not even know.

The importance of Germany is independent of her temporary military or political power; therefore, without her being admitted, a true "League of Nations" cannot be spoken of. What the treaty of peace proposes to establish, is rather a continuance of the enemy coalition not deserving the name of "League of Nations." The inner structure, too, does not realise the true League of Nations. Instead of the dreamt-of holy alliance of the nations, there reappears in it the fatal idea of the holy alliance of 1815, the belief as though it were possible to secure to the world a peace from above by way of diplomatic conferences with diplomatic organs. We miss proper technical authorities and impartial tribunals beside the select committee controlled by the Great Powers which may submit the whole civilized world to its control at the expense of the independence and equality of rights of the smaller States. The maintenance of the old political system with its tricks and rivalries based on force is thus not rendered impossible!

4. Will the Position of Germany be Destroyed?

Again and again the enemies of Germany have assured the whole world that they did not aim at a destruction of Germany.

"Who has ever desired," avowed Prime Minister Lloyd George on September 19th 1916 in the House of Commons, "to put an end to the national existence of Germany or her free national development?" On February 20th, 1918, Lord Milner, member of the English Council of War, said: "We are not fighting to destroy Germany . . . we are not fighting to deprive the German people of their independence or of their fair share in the trade and intercourse of the world."

. . . .

In contradiction to this, the peace document shows that Germany's position as a world power is to be destroyed by all means. Germans abroad are deprived of the possibility of keeping up their old relations in foreign countries and of regaining for Germany a share in international economy, their property confiscated and liquidated so far being used for reparation instead of being restored to them.

In like manner, it is made impossible to every German to acquire for his country a share in the world's trade, if—even after the peace treaty has been signed—all German property in foreign countries, for an indefinite period, may remain subject to measures of war and, therefore, be liable to confiscation and liquidation. Apart from this, Germans in the enemies' countries are not to enjoy the same personal legal position to which they would be entitled in Germany. The desire of shutting out and eliminating Germany from the world's trade manifests itself also in the confiscation of her cables.

As an addition to this comes the destruction of German economic life in the interior, which is shown at some other place.

Such stipulations amount to a complete denial of that idea of international law according to which every people has a claim to life. This supreme benefit must not be taken from it in favour of the economic interests of other nations.

5. Right of Self-Determination of Nations

In this war, a new fundamental law has arisen which the statesmen of all belligerent peoples have again and again acknowledged to be their aim: the right of self-determination of nations. To make the putting into practice of this privilege possible to all nations, was just meant to be one achievement of the war.

．．．．．．．．．

Neither the above described treatment of the inhabitants of the Saar region as accessories to the pits nor the public form of consulting the population in the districts of Eupen, Malmédy and Prussian Moresnet—which, in addition to it, shall not take place before their having been put under Belgian sovereignty—comply in the least with such a solemn recognition of the right of self-determination.

The same is also true with regard to Alsace-Lorraine. If Germany has pledged herself "to right the wrong of 1871," this does not mean any renunciation of the right of self-determination of the inhabitants of Alsace-Lorraine. A cession of the country without consulting the population would be a new wrong, if for no other reason, because it would be inconsistent with the recognised principle of peace.

On the other hand, it is incompatible with the idea of national self-determination if $2\frac{1}{2}$ million Germans are to be torn away from their native land against their own will. By the intended demarcation of the boundary unmistakably German territories are disposed of in favour of their Polish neighbours. Thus, from the Central Silesian districts of Guhrau and Militsch certain portions are to be wrenched off in which, besides 44,900 Germans, reside at the utmost 3700 Poles. The same may be said with reference to the towns of Schneidemühl and Bromberg of which the latter has, at the utmost, 18% Polish inhabitants, whereas in the rural district of Bromberg the Poles do not form even 40% of the population. Of the Netze district now assigned to Poland, Wilson in his book *The State* . . . page 255, has explicitly recognised that an absolutely German territory was in question. The demarcation of the boundary between Poland on the one, Central Silesia, Brandenburg and West Prussia on the other hand has been based on strategic considerations. These, however, are absolutely untenable in an age in which property rights are internationally safeguarded by the League of Nations. How arbitrary in every respect the frontiers drawn in the East are, may also be inferred from the fact that the Upper-Silesian districts of Leobschütz and Ratibor are assigned to the Czecho-Slovak

State although Leobschütz has 7,6% Ratibor 39,7% Czecho-Moravian population. Likewise the demarcation of the districts in southern East Prussia comprises purely German regions, e.g., Angerburg and Oletzko. Most grossly this disrespect of the right of self-determination is shown in the fact that Danzig is to be separated from the German Empire and turned into a free state. Neither historical rights nor the present ethnographical conditions of ownership of the Polish people can be held up against the German past and the German character of that city. A free access to the sea satisfying the economic wants of Poland can be secured by means of guarantees founded on international law, by creating ports. Likewise the cession of the commercial town of Memel which is to be exacted from Germany stands in no relation whatever to such a right of self-determination of nations. The same may be said with reference to the fact that millions of Germans in German Austria are to be denied the union with Germany as desired by them, and that further millions of Germans dwelling along our frontiers are to be forced to remain part of the newly created Czecho-Slovak State.

Even as regards that part of the national territory that is to be left to Germany, the promised right of self-determination is not observed. A commission nominated in order to carry out the compensations shall be the highest instance for the whole national organism. Our enemies have alleged to have fought for the great aim of the democratisation of Germany. To be sure, the issue of the war has delivered us from our former authorities, but instead of them we shall take in exchange a foreign, dictatorial power whose aim can and must be only to exploit the working-power of the German people for the benefit of the creditor states. Such a surrender of its independence may not be inflicted upon any State. The right of self-preservation of a State means above all an unrestricted disposing of the inner organisation of its existence; a restriction of this freedom of Germany is a violation of the fundamental laws of nations.

III. The Results

All this shows that this draft of a peace treaty as submitted to the German Government stands in full and irreconcilable conflict to the basis agreed upon for a lasting peace of right. Scarcely a single stipulation of the draft corresponds with the conditions agreed upon, and with regard to the territorial questions, the draft demands the annexation of purely German territory and the suppression of the German nationality.

It involves the utter destruction of German economic life. It leads the German people into a financial thraldom unknown in history up to the present day. Therefore, in the session of the National Assembly on the 12th of May it was characterised as being beyond the reach of realisation, by the Government as well as by all the parties. The putting into practice of this draft of a treaty would be equivalent to a new disaster for the whole world.

Did not the former President Roosevelt on October 10th 1914 warn: "A destruction or even mere crippling of Germany apt to lead to its political powerlessness, would be a catastrophe for mankind." This would make itself felt first in the sphere of economics. From an economically pauperised Germany, as would be the inevitable result of such a peace, her creditors cannot obtain those immense sums which Germany is to pay to them. The disadvantageous consequences of such a peace would range far beyond any diminution of the enemies' demands. The economic prosperity of the world is, taking everything into account, dependent on the total sum of the produced goods. The entire elimination of Germany from the world's trade may, to be sure, oust an obnoxious competitor: as a result from the economic breakdown of Germany, the world as a whole must become infinitely poorer. Such a lasting damage done to the welfare of the world is doubly disastrous because the war has devoured a large portion of the national wealth of most of the belligerents.

What the world is in need of is an international community of labour in all domains.

The age of international economy requires the political organization of the civilized world. The German Government agrees with the Governments of the Allied and Associated Powers in the conviction that the horrible devastations involved by this war, require the establishment of a new regulation of the world, a regulation of "effective authority of the principles of international law" and of "just and honourable relations between the nations." The restoration and consolidation of inter-state regulation in the world is only safeguarded if the existing authorities, in a new spirit, succeed in realising the great idea of democracy, if, as President Wilson uttered on the 4th of July, 1918, "the settlement of every question" is brought about ". . . upon the basis of the free acceptance of that settlement by the people immediately concerned. . . ." Only the nations that live in free self-responsibility according to right, may give each other the guarantee of just and honourable relations. But their fairness and honour also require that they warrant each other freedom and life as the most sacred and inalienable fundamental laws.

There is no evidence of these principles being reflected in the peace document as laid before us. Expiring theories of existence emanating from imperialistic and capitalistic tendencies celebrate in it their last horrible triumph. As opposed to these views that have brought unspeakable disaster upon the world we appeal to the innate right of men and nations, under whose token the English State developed, the Dutch People freed itself, the North American Nation established her independence, France shook off absolutism. This right cannot be denied by the bearers of such hallowed traditions to the German people that now for the first time acquired in its inner politics the possibility of living in harmony with its free will to right. A Treaty such as has been proposed to Germany appears not to be compatible with the respect for this innate right.

150. Activities of the Supreme Economic Council

[The Supreme Economic Council was established February 8, 1919, at the instance of Wilson. Its first meeting was held February 17, when it was decided to coördinate all former war boards and to direct them as sections of its own organization. Accordingly, food and relief were under Herbert Hoover, who had been chairman of the Commission for Relief in Belgium. Under the chairmanship of Robert Cecil the Supreme Economic Council became one of the most important international bodies directing the reorganization of Europe. It continued to meet till February 1920.]

(a) *Review of Relief Measures effected by Entente Powers during March, 1919, by the Director General, Herbert Hoover*[1]

The total value of supplies distributed during the month was approximately $111,280,000 of which all but about $3,350,000 was furnished on a basis of deferred payment.

Poland

The Supplies distributed were:

Breadstuffs	35,715,000	kilos
Fats	13,902,000	"
Condensed milk	1,668,000	"
Gift clothing	460,000	"
Total	51,745,000	"

The arrangements for shipment through Dantzig under the terms of the Armistice have proceeded with great smoothness and dispatch of as high as 4,500 tons a day by rail from Dantzig to Warsaw have been reached. All the sections of critical famine condition are now under successful relief.

Finland

During the month the arrivals in Finland were as follows:

Breadstuffs	25,414,000	kilos
Peas and beans	127,000	"
Fats	753,000	"
Condensed milk	50,000	"
Total	26,344,000	"

[1] *Documents of the Supreme Economic Council* (American Relief Administration Archives, Hoover War Library); Minutes of the 12th Meeting of the Supreme Economic Council, April 14, 1919. Doc. 83.

About 10,000 tons of these supplies were furnished under replacement agreements with Northern Neutrals. Distribution is gradually spreading into outlying points and the straw bread formerly in use is rapidly disappearing. Some difficulties have been met from ice and mines, one ship having been lost and another badly crushed.

Baltic States

Preliminary measures for the establishment of regular supplies to the coastal areas in the Baltic States have been undertaken.

2,750,000 kilos of breadstuffs were actually delivered during the month.

Czecho-Slovakia

The following amounts of overseas foodstuffs were delivered into Czecho-Slovakia during the month:

Breadstuffs	26,280,000	kilos
Peas and Beans	283,000	"
Fats	2,429,000	"
Condensed milk	463,000	"
Miscellaneous	456,000	"
TOTAL	29,911,000	"

Distribution has been less during the month than was hoped for owing to difficulties of railway transportation from the Adriatic. As a further security to regularity of supplies arrangements have been made for shipment through Hamburg via the Elbe into Bohemia. The first shipments from Hamburg were dispatched on the third of April.

German-Austria

The total deliveries from Allied sources during the month of March were:

Breadstuffs	32,951,000	kilos
Peas and beans	68,000	"
Rice	4,138,000	"
Fats	240,000	"
Condensed milk	759,000	"
TOTAL	38,156,000	"

Supplies amounting to about 10,000 tons were also made under replacement arrangements from neighbouring countries. German-Austria suffered also during the month from difficulties of railway transportation from the Adriatic, but the situation is rapidly improving. The difficulties in financing supplies for this state have been overcome by the joint action of the four governments. The situation at Vienna is extremely bad and measures have been taken to increase the arrivals to 2,000,000 kilos per diem, if transportation permits.

Greater Serbia

The relief of the entire area of Jugo-Slavia, Montenegro and Serbia is conducted as a single unit. The total distribution during the month amounted to:

Breadstuffs	28,922,000 kilos
Fats	5,000,000 "
TOTAL	33,922,000 "

Surplus of supplies existing in the Banat and Northern counties of Jugo-Slavia have so far enabled the relief of the interior section of this area to be accomplished without heavy shipments far inland.

Roumania

The total deliveries during the month were 26,967,000 kilos of breadstuffs. The inland transportation owing to ice in the Danube and the reduction in railway rolling stock from about 1,000 locomotives under pre-war conditions to only 100 actually in use during the month rendered adequate distribution impossible. Again by the energetic coöperation of all the Allied Governments, this situation is in course of remedy and supplies during the month of April from overseas should show considerable improvement.

Turkey

2,298,000 kilos of foodstuffs have been distributed during the month in Constantinople. In addition further supplies are being distributed inland by the military authorities, but again inland transportation conditions make any relief extremely unsatisfactory.

Armenia

There were supplied from the Relief Administration 4,521,000 kilos of breadstuffs, and 731,000 kilos of condensed milk. In addition to these, three shiploads of food, clothing and medical supplies have been delivered for the Far Eastern Relief Commission. Again, the difficulties of inland transportation render assistance extremely difficult.

Belgium

The following supplies were delivered during the month:

Breadstuffs	113,173,000 kilos
Peas and beans	7,575,000 "
Rice	8,382,000 "
Fats	9,230,000 "
Clothing	3,710,000 "
Misc. food	3,534,000 "
TOTAL	145,604,000 "

The energetic development of the Belgian Food Ministry has rendered it possible for the government to undertake at an early date her own purchase of supplies and transportation; although, of course, Belgium must continue to receive financial and tonnage support from the Associated Governments.

Northern France

The progressive resumption of the ravitaillement of the occupied regions by the French Food Ministry has proceeded so far as to render it possible to gradually withdraw the relief measures which have been continuous over four and a half years and such withdrawal should be complete by the first of May. During the month of March, a total of 6,906,000 kilos of foodstuffs and clothing were delivered into devastated areas.

Germany

The financial, tonnage and food arrangements were completed at Brussels on March 14th. The first German ships arrived at Allied ports about March 22nd, and on March 25th foodstuffs were actually delivered inside German territory, consisting of,

Breadstuffs	6,787,000 kilos
Fats	743,000 "

The available supplies from all quarters should permit the import into Germany of approximately 200,000,000 kilos during the month of April.

Other Areas

Relief has been inaugurated in further directions including Bulgaria, Russian prisoners in Germany, refugees from South Russia, etc., the quantitative results of which will be included in April returns.

Organisation

A great deal of progress has been made during the month in the organisation of the Allied Food Missions, in the various countries under relief, and the very complex port, railway, and distribution administrations have been greatly advanced by the coöperation of the Associated Governments and the countries under relief.

Under action taken by the Supreme War Council on March 10th, authority was given the Director General of Relief, acting through the Communication Section of the Economic Council, over railway movements in the old Austrian Empire. The improvements have been marked, as evidenced by the fact that the average railway shipments from Trieste for the first fifteen days of March average less than 600 tons per diem, whereas they have averaged over 2,500 per diem during the ten days ending April 5th.

Considerable has been accomplished during the month in the exchange of supplies between various States in Central Europe, whose political and economic relations require friendly intervention to secure necessary exchanges. These measures will proceed on an increasing scale in the future.

Child Feeding

In order to cope with the very large amount of malnutrition in the liberated areas of Central and Eastern Europe, plans are under way involving medical examination of the children of the poor and provision for the regular and systematic feeding from special canteens. These measures will involve the direct care of between 500,000 and 1,000,000 children. The large expenditure involved places such wholesale measures beyond the capacities of the various charitable associations and bodies operating in Europe. It is felt that if child life is to be preserved it can only be done by large and systematic measures of this character. Some subventions have been arranged from some of the Associated Governments added to by the local Governments concerned.

During March this work was initiated in Finland, Poland and Roumania, and it is hoped that during the month of April it will be established generally over the liberated countries. It is hoped that charitable support to relief in Europe can be directed into those channels as the financial burden will be of very large dimensions.

General

It has been solely due to the coöperation of the Food, Financial and Transportation officials of the eighteen governments involved that these results have been possible.

(b) The Feeding of Germany[1]

1. On grounds of humanity, the Associated Governments reiterate their decision to deliver to Germany the food now available in Europe for which payment has been arranged as soon as Germany shows her genuine intention to carry out her obligations, by sending to sea for that purpose the ships to be selected by the Associated Governments, and the Associated Governments will themselves provide (as quickly as transportation can be arranged) or will give permits for import from neighbouring neutrals for the balance of the month's supply, that is, of 270,000 tons agreed on, as soon as at least —— ships have been similarly sent to sea, and as soon as payment for such food has been arranged.

2. She may import up to (300,000) tons of breadstuffs and (70,-000) tons of fats monthly until September 1st.

3. She must pay for this food and may pay in any of the following ways:

---

[1] *Documents of the Supreme Economic Council* (American Relief Administration Archives, Hoover War Library); Minutes of the 7th Meeting, March 10, 1919. Doc. **27.**

(a) By the hire of ships.

(b) By the export of commodities and the sale of cargoes of German ships now in neutral countries.

(c) By credits in neutral countries.

(d) By the outright sale of foreign securities or properties.

(e) By the arrangement of advances against the use of foreign securities or properties as collateral.

(f) Further gold also may be used as collateral for loans to be released as other means of payment provide means of liquidating such loans.

The methods of payment provided in (d), (e), (f) shall not be resorted to beyond the sum of $200,000,000 (in addition to the financial arrangements already agreed upon in payment of the first 270,000 tons of food), until in the judgment of the Supreme Economic Council the possibilities of payment under (a), (b) and (c) have proved inadequate.

The outright sale of gold can only be permitted in the event of its being agreed by the Associated Powers that the above named means of payment are inadequate.

4. She may export commodities (except those on a black list) to any neutral or other agreed destination. The proceeds from these exports must, however, be converted into payments for foodstuffs.

5. A definite amount of the shipping handed over will be continuously available to transport food to Germany until next harvest.

6. She may purchase and import foodstuffs within the limits above stated, from neutrals who will, when necessary, be allowed to re-import equivalent quantities.

7. It is understood that the declaration of the Associated Governments under this communication will be null and void, should Germany break the terms of the Armistice.

(c) *The Feeding of Austria: Hoover's Proposal as finally amended and accepted by the Council of Ten*[1]

(a) All the States of the old Austrian Empire, including the areas held by the Italians on the Adriatic, should be called upon to furnish a definite contribution of railway rolling stock;

(b) This rolling stock should be marked as belonging to the Relief Administration and will be given priority for that purpose;

(c) The Director General of Relief *working through the Communications Section of the Supreme Economic Council*, should be made the Mandatory for the disposition of this rolling stock;

(d) A regular train service should be established under his direction

---

[1] *Documents of the Supreme Economic Council* (American Relief Administration Archives, Hoover War Library); Minutes of the 7th meeting of the Supreme Economic Council, March 10, 1919. Doc. 26, Annex B.

that will carry out the necessary programmes of food to the different localities;

(e) This service should have entire freedom of movement over all railways regardless of political boundaries and in complete priority to other services except military; and within the Italian frontier this will be carried out in coöperation with the Italian Authorities;

(f) The Railway Servants of any nationality may be employed in operations over any territory within the old Austrian Empire, regardless of nationality or political boundaries;

(g) The Italian Authorities will assign definite portions of port facilities to the Relief Administration at Trieste and Fiume for the consummation of these ends;

(h) In general the rolling stock should not be demanded by any of the Allied Governments until this service is completely equipped without prejudice to the ultimate ownership thereof;

(i) The Railway Officials of each State and Port Officials in each Port will coöperate in maintenance of this service.

Paris,
March 7, 1919

(d) *Typhus Relief in Eastern Europe, 1919. By Herbert Hoover*[1]

The Council will recollect that during the last Spring the typhus situation in Eastern Europe was raised in the Council by myself and after discussion it was determined to appeal to the Red Cross Societies of the world to undertake a special campaign in this particular. This appeal was made and in consequence of it some discussion of the matter took place at the Conference held in Cannes, from which were finally organised the League of Red Cross Societies. The League of Red Cross Societies addressed themselves directly to the Heads of States for financial assistance and these gentlemen referred the matter back again to the Supreme Economic Council for consideration.

The Council instructed me, together with my colleagues in charge of relief on behalf of the various Governments (Sir William Goode, Mr. Caetani, Major Fillioux) to interest ourselves in assisting the matter. A considerable number of discussions were held with the representatives of the League of Red Cross Societies and it was pointed out to them that the only assistance the Council could bring to bear would be to enlist the interest of the various armies in the disposal of their surplus supplies and in the lending of their personnel, and urgent representations in the matter were made by us to the American, British and French military authorities.

The League of Red Cross Societies raised the question of the

---

[1] *Documents of the Supreme Economic Council* (American Relief Administration Archives, Hoover War Library); Minutes of the 29th Meeting of the Supreme Economic Council, August 1 and 2, 1919. Doc. 253.

authority that would be given to them by the Governments of Eastern Europe. They considered that it was necessary that they should have a practically complete police authority in order to make effectual the results of their efforts. They also stated that they had no resources otherwise than for purposes of general organisation, that while under the resources they possessed they could mobilize enterprises of this character, the entire expenditure would have to be met from governmental quarters. We decided that the best method of procedure would be to ask the Polish Minister of Health to come to Paris for consultation with the League of Red Cross Societies which was done and conferences were held early in July.

At these conferences, the League of Red Cross Societies stated that they could not take the responsibility for such a campaign unless they were given very large authorities by the Ministry of Health and the Polish Minister felt that he could justifiably surrender the control of health conditions internally in Poland, in view of the very large amount of work already being carried on by the Polish Government and his own responsibility. A number of conferences appeared to have taken place between the Polish Minister of Health and the Red Cross Societies by which ultimately they decided that their best services would be performed by recruiting personnel for the Ministry of Health and at the expense of the Polish Government. The matter appeared to be making but little progress as the Polish Minister of Health informed me that he was not able to find the necessary expenditures to cover the problem. It was therefore resolved by your committee that they should appeal directly to the Armies of the various governments to assist the Polish Ministry of Health with Army personnel and at the same time further urgent representations were made to the various Liquidation Boards with regard to a liberal attitude towards Poland in the matter of Army supplies available for combatting typhus.

Ultimately, the President of the United States and the Secretary of War delegated personnel from the American Army to be placed at my disposal for the Polish Ministry of Health and at the expense of the American Army. With the intervention of the President I also arranged with the American Liquidation Board to sell several million dollars' worth of supplies and material at a nominal figure to the Polish Government and I undertook for the Relief Administration to secure the expense of transportation.

Our British colleagues arranged also to secure appropriation for a large quantity of medical supplies and the transfer of certain Army equipment to the Polish Ministry of Health and have now arranged for further contributions from the British Red Cross. A note on these supplies is being furnished by the British delegates.

Colonel H. L. Gilchrist of the American Army has been delegated, together with a personnel of some 500 members, to proceed to Poland to assist the Polish Government. . . .

The principle underlying these arrangements has been in accord with policies of the Council in all of its measures; that is, to build up and strengthen existing government departments among the new governments rather than to impose authority over them. Any other measures must be short lived and the only hope of permanent solutions is by the development of local efficiency. . . .

151. TREATY OF VERSAILLES[1]

[The treaty was prepared by committees of the Paris Peace Conference. All controversial questions were settled by the Supreme Council ("Big Ten" replaced by "Big Four") and approval by the Plenary Conference was merely perfunctory. It was then presented to the German delegation at Versailles on May 7. (For the German criticism see doc. no. 149.) In response to German protests two important modifications in the draft were made: Upper Silesia was not ceded outright to Poland, but a plebiscite was provided for; and the plebiscite area in Slesvig was reduced in size; other changes were minor. Smuts was outspoken in his criticism on the occasion of its final signature, and the Chinese delegates refused to sign as a protest against the Shantung provisions. Ratifications were exchanged January 10, 1920, thus bringing the treaty into effect, but the United States Senate refused to approve. The state of war between the United States and Germany was terminated by a joint resolution of the Senate and House, signed by the President July 2, 1921, by which the United States accepted all the treaty except Part I (the Covenant of the League), Parts II and III (territorial changes in Europe), Part IV, sections 2-8 (renunciation of German rights in China, Siam, etc.), and Part XIII (labor clauses).]

PART I

THE COVENANT OF THE LEAGUE OF NATIONS

THE HIGH CONTRACTING PARTIES,

In order to promote international co-operation and to achieve international peace and security

by the acceptance of obligations not to resort to war,
by the prescription of open, just and honourable relations between nations,

---

[1] Great Britain. *Parliamentary Papers*, 1919. Vol. LIII. Cmd. 153. "Treaty of Peace between the Allied and Associated Powers and Germany, signed at Versailles, 28th of June, 1919" (Extracts), except that the Covenant of the League of Nations is reprinted from *The Assembly of the League of Nations*, Bull. No. 6, September, 1930, League of Nations Association, Research Committee, Geneva Office. Amendments adopted before 1931 are shown in italics.

by the firm establishment of the understandings of international law as the actual rule of conduct among Governments,
and by the maintenance of justice and a scrupulous respect for all treaty obligations in the dealings of organised peoples with one another,

Agree to this Covenant of the League of Nations.

Article 1. 1. The original Members of the League of Nations shall be those of the Signatories which are named in the Annex to this Covenant and also such of those other States named in the Annex as shall accede without reservation to this Covenant. Such accession shall be effected by a Declaration deposited with the Secretariat within two months of the coming into force of the Covenant. Notice thereof shall be sent to all other Members of the League.

2. Any fully self-governing State, Dominion or Colony not named in the Annex may become a Member of the League if its admission is agreed to by two-thirds of the Assembly, provided that it shall give effective guarantees of its sincere intention to observe its international obligations, and shall accept such regulations as may be prescribed by the League in regard to its military, naval and air forces and armaments.

3. Any Member of the League may, after two years' notice of its intention so to do, withdraw from the League, provided that all its international obligations and all its obligations under this Covenant shall have been fulfilled at the time of its withdrawal.

Article 2. The action of the League under this Covenant shall be effected through the instrumentality of an Assembly and of a Council, with a permanent Secretariat.

Article 3. 1. The Assembly shall consist of Representatives of the Members of the League.

2. The Assembly shall meet at stated intervals and from time to time as occasion may require at the Seat of the League or at such other place as may be decided upon.

3. The Assembly may deal at its meetings with any matter within the sphere of action of the League or affecting the peace of the world.

4. At meetings of the Assembly, each Member of the League shall have one vote, and may have not more than three Representatives.

Article 4. 1. The Council shall consist of Representatives of the Principal Allied and Associated Powers, together with Representatives of four other Members of the League. These four Members of the League shall be selected by the Assembly from time to time in its discretion. Until the appointment of the Representatives of the four Members of the League first selected by the Assembly, Representatives of Belgium, Brazil, Spain and Greece shall be members of the Council.

2. With the approval of the majority of the Assembly, the Council may name additional Members of the League whose Representatives

shall always be Members of the Council; the Council with like approval may increase the number of Members of the League to be selected by the Assembly for representation on the Council.[1]

2bis. *The Assembly shall fix by a two-thirds majority the rules dealing with the election of the non-permanent Members of the Council, and particularly such regulations as relate to their term of office and the conditions of re-eligibility.*

3. The Council shall meet from time to time as occasion may require, and at least once a year, at the Seat of the League, or at such other place as may be decided upon.

4. The Council may deal at its meetings with any matter within the sphere of action of the League or affecting the peace of the world.

5. Any Member of the League not represented on the Council shall be invited to send a Representative to sit as a member at any meeting of the Council during the consideration of matters specially affecting the interests of that Member of the League.

6. At meetings of the Council, each Member of the League represented on the Council shall have one vote, and may have not more than one Representative.

Article 5. 1. Except where otherwise expressly provided in this Covenant or by the terms of the present Treaty, decisions at any meeting of the Assembly or of the Council shall require the agreement of all the Members of the League represented at the meeting.

2. All matters of procedure at meetings of the Assembly or of the Council, including the appointment of Committees to investigate particular matters shall be regulated by the Assembly or by the Council and may be decided by a majority of the Members of the League represented at the meeting.

3. The first meetings of the Assembly and the first meeting of the Council shall be summoned by the President of the United States of America.

Article 6. 1. The permanent Secretariat shall be established at the Seat of the League. The Secretariat shall comprise a Secretary-General and such secretaries and staff as may be required.

2. The first Secretary-General shall be the person named in the Annex; thereafter the Secretary-General shall be appointed by the Council with the approval of the majority of the Assembly.

3. The secretaries and staff of the Secretariat shall be appointed by the Secretary-General with the approval of the Council.

4. The Secretary-General shall act in that capacity at all meetings of the Assembly and of the Council.

5. *The expenses of the League shall be borne by the Members of the League in the proportion decided by the Assembly.*

Article 7. 1. The Seat of the League is established at Geneva.

---

[1] An Assembly resolution of September 25, 1922, increased the non-permanent members of the Council from four to six; and by resolution of September 8, 1926, the elected members were extended to nine.

2. The Council may at any time decide that the Seat of the League shall be established elsewhere.

3. All positions under or in connection with the League, including the Secretariat, shall be open equally to men and women.

4. Representatives of the Members of the League and officials of the League when engaged on the business of the League shall enjoy diplomatic privileges and immunities.

5. The buildings and other property occupied by the League or its officials or by Representatives attending its meetings shall be inviolable.

Article 8. 1. The Members of the League recognise that the maintenance of peace requires the reduction of national armaments to the lowest point consistent with national safety and the enforcement by common action of international obligations.

2. The Council, taking account of the geographical situation and circumstances of each State, shall formulate plans for such reduction for the consideration and action of the several Governments.

3. Such plans shall be subject to reconsideration and revision at least every ten years.

4. After these plans shall have been adopted by the several Governments, the limits of armaments therein fixed shall not be exceeded without the concurrence of the Council.

5. The Members of the League agree that the manufacture by private enterprise of munitions and implements of war is open to grave objections. The Council shall advise how the evil effects attendant upon such manufacture can be prevented, due regard being had to the necessities of those Members of the League which are not able to manufacture the munitions and implements of war necessary for their safety.

6. The Members of the League undertake to interchange full and frank information as to the scale of their armaments, their military, naval and air programmes and the conditions of such of their industries as are adaptable to warlike purposes.

Article 9. A permanent Commission shall be constituted to advise the Council on the execution of the provisions of Articles 1 and 8 and on military, naval and air questions generally.

Article 10. The Members of the League undertake to respect and preserve as against external aggression the territorial integrity and existing political independence of all Members of the League. In case of any such aggression or in case of any threat or danger of such aggression the Council shall advise upon the means by which this obligation shall be fulfilled.

Article 11. 1. Any war or threat of war, whether immediately affecting any of the Members of the League or not, is hereby declared a matter of concern to the whole League, and the League shall take any action that may be deemed wise and effectual to safeguard the peace of nations. In case any such emergency should arise the Secretary-General shall on the request of any Member of the League forthwith summon a meeting of the Council.

2. It is also declared to be the friendly right of each Member of the League to bring to the attention of the Assembly or of the Council any circumstance whatever affecting international relations which threatens to disturb international peace or the good understanding between nations upon which peace depends.

Article 12. 1. The Members of the League agree that if there should arise between them any dispute likely to lead to a rupture they will submit the matter either to arbitration *or judicial settlement* or to enquiry by the Council, and they agree in no case to resort to war until three months after the award by the arbitrators *or the judicial decision* or the report by the Council.

2. In any case under this Article the award of the arbitrators' *or the judicial decision* shall be made within a reasonable time, and the report of the Council shall be made within six months after the submission of the dispute.

Article 13. 1. The Members of the League agree that whenever any dispute shall arise between them which they recognise to be suitable for submission to arbitration *or judicial settlement,* and which cannot be satisfactorily settled by diplomacy, they will submit the whole subject-matter to arbitration *or judicial settlement.*

2. Disputes as to the interpretation of a treaty, as to any question of international law, as to the existence of any fact which, if established would constitute a breach of any international obligation, or as to the extent and nature of the reparation to be made for any such breach, are declared to be among those which are generally suitable for submission to arbitration *or judicial settlement.*

3. *For the consideration of any such dispute, the court to which the case is referred shall be the Permanent Court of International Justice, established in accordance with Article 14, or any tribunal agreed on by the parties to the dispute or stipulated in any convention existing between them.*

4. The Members of the League agree that they will carry out in full good faith any award *or decision* that may be rendered, and that they will not resort to war against a Member of the League which complies therewith. In the event of any failure to carry out such an award *or decision,* the Council shall propose what steps should be taken to give effect thereto.

Article 14. The Council shall formulate and submit to the Members of the League for adoption plans for the establishment of a Permanent Court of International Justice. The Court shall be competent to hear and determine any dispute of an international character which the parties thereto submit to it. The Court may also give an advisory opinion upon any dispute or question referred to it by the Council or by the Assembly.

Article 15. 1. If there should arise between Members of the League any dispute likely to lead to a rupture, which is not submitted to arbitration *or judicial settlement* in accordance with Article 13, the Members of the League agree that they will submit the matter to the Council. Any party to the dispute may effect such submission by giving notice of the existence of the dispute to the Secretary-General, who will make all necessary arrangements for a full investigation and consideration thereof.

2. For this purpose the parties to the dispute will communicate to the Secretary-General, as promptly as possible, statements of their case with all the relevant facts and papers, and the Council may forthwith direct the publication thereof.

3. The Council shall endeavour to effect a settlement of the dispute, and if such efforts are successful, a statement shall be made public giving such facts and explanations regarding the dispute and the terms of settlement thereof as the Council may deem appropriate.

4. If the dispute is not thus settled, the Council either unanimously or by a majority vote shall make and publish a report containing a statement of the facts of the dispute and the recommendations which are deemed just and proper in regard thereto.

5. Any Member of the League represented on the Council may make public a statement of the facts of the dispute and of its conclusions regarding the same.

6. If a report by the Council is unanimously agreed to by the members thereof other than the Representatives of one more of the parties to the dispute, the Members of the League agree that they will not go to war with any party to the dispute which complies with the recommendations of the report.

7. If the Council fails to reach a report which is unanimously agreed to by the members thereof, other than the Representatives of one or more of the parties to the dispute, the Members of the League reserve to themselves the right to take such action as they shall consider necessary for the maintenance of right and justice.

8. If the dispute between the parties is claimed by one of them, and is found by the Council, to arise out of a matter which by international law is solely within the domestic jurisdiction of that party, the Council shall so report, and shall make no recommendation as to its settlement.

9. The Council may in any case under this Article refer the dispute to the Assembly. The dispute shall be so referred at the request of either party to the dispute provided that such request be made within fourteen days after the submission of the dispute to the Council.

10. In any case referred to the Assembly, all the provisions of this Article and of Article 12 relating to the action and powers of the Council shall apply to the action and powers of the Assembly, provided that a report made by the Assembly, if concurred in by the Representatives of those Members of the League represented on the Council and of a majority of the other Members of the League, exclusive in each case of the Representatives of the parties to the dispute, shall have the same force as a report by the Council concurred in by

all the members thereof other than the Representative of one or more of the parties to the dispute.

Article 16. 1. Should any Member of the League resort to war in disregard of its covenants under Articles 12, 13 or 15, it shall *ipso facto* be deemed to have committed an act of war against all other Members of the League, which hereby undertake immediately to subject it to the severance of all trade or financial relations, the prohibition of all intercourse between their nationals and the nationals of the covenant-breaking State, and the prevention of all financial, commercial or personal intercourse between the nationals of the covenant-breaking State and the nationals of any other State, whether a Member of the League or not.

2. It shall be the duty of the Council in such case to recommend to the several Governments concerned what effective military, naval or air force the Members of the League shall severally contribute to the armed forces to be used to protect the covenants of the League.

3. The Members of the League agree, further that they will mutually support one another in the financial and economic measures which are taken under this Article, in order to minimise the loss and inconvenience resulting from the above measures, and that they will mutually support one another in resisting any special measures aimed at one of their number by the covenant-breaking State, and that they will take the necessary steps to afford passage through their territory to the forces of any of the Members of the League which are cooperating to protect the covenants of the League.

4. Any Member of the League which has violated any covenant of the League may be declared to be no longer a Member of the League by a vote of the Council concurred in by the Representatives of all the other Members of the League represented thereon.

Article 17. 1. In the event of a dispute between a Member of the League and a State which is not a Member of the League, or between States not Members of the League, the State or States not Members of the League shall be invited to accept the obligations of membership in the League for the purposes of such dispute, upon such conditions as the Council may deem just. If such invitation is accepted, the provisions of Articles 12 to 16 inclusive shall be applied with such modifications as may be deemed necessary by the Council.

2. Upon such invitation being given the Council shall immediately institute an inquiry into the circumstances of the dispute and recommend such action as may seem best and most effectual in the circumstances.

3. If a State so invited shall refuse to accept the obligations of membership in the League for the purposes of such dispute, and shall resort to war against a Member of the League, the provisions of Article 16 shall be applicable as against the State taking such action.

4. If both parties to the dispute when so invited refuse to accept the obligations of membership in the League for the purposes of such

dispute, the Council may take such measures and make such recommendations as will prevent hostilities and will result in the settlement of the dispute.

Article 18. Every treaty or international engagement entered into hereafter by any Member of the League shall be forthwith registered with the Secretariat and shall as soon as possible be published by it. No such treaty or international engagement shall be binding until so registered.

Article 19. The Assembly may from time to time advise the reconsideration by Members of the League of treaties which have become inapplicable and the consideration of international conditions whose continuance might endanger the peace of the world.

Article 20. 1. The Members of the League severally agree that this Covenant is accepted as abrogating all obligations or understandings *inter se* which are inconsistent with the terms thereof, and solemnly undertake that they will not hereafter enter into any engagements inconsistent with the terms thereof.

2. In case any Member of the League shall, before becoming a Member of the League, have undertaken any obligations inconsistent with the terms of this Covenant, it shall be the duty of such Member to take immediate steps to procure its release from such obligations.

Article 21. Nothing in this Covenant shall be deemed to affect the validity of international engagements, such as treaties of arbitration or regional understandings like the Monroe doctrine, for securing the maintenance of peace.

Article 22. 1. To those colonies and territories which as a consequence of the late war have ceased to be under the sovereignty of the States which formerly governed them and which are inhabited by peoples not yet able to stand by themselves under the strenuous conditions of the modern world, there should be applied the principle that the well-being and development of such peoples form a sacred trust of civilisation and that securities for the performance of this trust should be embodied in this Covenant.

2. The best method of giving practical effect to this principle is that the tutelage of such peoples should be entrusted to advanced nations who by reason of their resources, their experience or their geographical position can best undertake this responsibility, and who are willing to accept it, and that this tutelage should be exercised by them as Mandatories on behalf of the League.

3. The character of the mandate must differ according to the stage of the development of the people, the geographical situation of the territory, its economic conditions and other similar circumstances.

4. Certain communities formerly belonging to the Turkish Empire have reached a stage of development where their existence as independent nations can be provisionally recognised subject to the rendering of administrative advice and assistance by a Mandatory until such

time as they are able to stand alone. The wishes of these communities must be a principal consideration in the selection of the Mandatory.

5. Other peoples, especially those of Central Africa, are at such a stage that the Mandatory must be responsible for the administration of the territory under conditions which will guarantee freedom of conscience and religion, subject only to the maintenance of public order and morals, the prohibition of abuses such as the slave trade, the arms traffic and the liquor traffic, and the prevention of the establishment of fortifications or military and naval bases and of military training of the natives for other than police purposes and the defence of territory, and will also secure equal opportunities for the trade and commerce of other Members of the League.

6. There are territories, such as South-West Africa and certain of the South Pacific Islands, which, owing to the sparseness of their population, or their small size, or their remoteness from the centres of civilisation, or their geographical contiguity to the territory of the Mandatory, and other circumstances, can be best administered under the laws of the Mandatory as integral portions of its territory, subject to the safeguards above mentioned in the interest of the indigenous population.

7. In every case of mandate, the Mandatory shall render to the Council an annual report in reference to the territory committed to its charge.

8. The degree of authority, control or administration to be exercised by the Mandatory shall, if not previously agreed upon by the Members of the League, be explicitly defined in each case by the Council.

9. A permanent Commission shall be constituted to receive and examine the annual reports of the Mandatories and to advise the Council on all matters relating to the observance of the mandates.

Article 23. Subject to and in accordance with the provisions of international conventions existing or hereafter to be agreed upon, the Members of the League:

    (*a*) will endeavour to secure and maintain fair and humane conditions of labour for men, women, and children, both in their own countries and in all countries to which commercial and industrial relations extend, and for that purpose will establish and maintain the necessary international organisations;

    (*b*) undertake to secure just treatment of the native inhabitants of territories under their control;

    (*c*) will entrust the League with the general supervision over the execution of agreements with regard to the traffic in women and children, and the traffic in opium and other dangerous drugs;

    (*d*) will entrust the League with the general supervision of the trade in arms and ammunitions with the countries in which the control of this traffic is necessary in the common interest;

(*e*) will make provision to secure and maintain freedom of communications and of transit and equitable treatment for the commerce of all Members of the League. In this connection, the special necessities of the regions devastated during the war of 1914-1918 shall be borne in mind;

(*f*) will endeavour to take steps in matters of international concern for the prevention and control of disease.

Article 24. 1. There shall be placed under the direction of the League all international bureaux already established by general treaties if the parties to such treaties consent. All such international bureaux and all commissions for the regulation of matters of international interest hereafter constituted shall be placed under the direction of the League.

2. In all matters of international interest which are regulated by general conventions but which are not placed under the control of international bureaux or commissions, the Secretariat of the League shall, subject to the consent of the Council and if desired by the parties, collect and distribute all relevant information and shall render any other assistance which may be necessary or desirable.

3. The Council may include as part of the expenses of the Secretariat the expenses of any bureau or commission which is placed under the direction of the League.

Article 25. The Members of the League agree to encourage and promote the establishment and co-operation of duly authorised voluntary national Red Cross organisations having as purposes the improvement of health, the prevention of disease and the mitigation of suffering throughout the world.

Article 26. 1. Amendments to this Covenant will take effect when ratified by the Members of the League whose Representatives compose the Council and by a majority of the Members of the League whose Representatives compose the Assembly.

2. No such amendments shall bind any Member of the League which signifies its dissent therefrom but in that case it shall cease to be a Member of the League.

ANNEX

I. Original Members of the League of Nations Signatories

Of the Treaty of Peace

United States of America, Belgium, Bolivia, Brazil, British Empire, (Canada, Australia, South Africa, New Zealand, India), China, Cuba, Ecuador, France, Greece, Guatemala, Haiti, Hedjaz, Honduras, Italy, Japan, Liberia, Nicaragua, Panama, Peru, Poland, Portugal, Roumania, Serb-Croat-Slovene State, Siam, Czecho-Slovakia, Uruguay.

States Invited to Accede to the Covenant

Argentine Republic, Chile, Colombia, Denmark, Netherlands, Norway, Paraguay, Persia, Salvador, Spain, Sweden, Switzerland, Venezuela.

II. First Secretary General of League of Nations

The Honourable Sir James Eric Drummond, K.C.M.G., C.B.

PART II

BOUNDARIES OF GERMANY

[Omitted]

PART III

POLITICAL CLAUSES FOR EUROPE

SECTION I: BELGIUM

Article 31. Germany, recognizing that the Treaties of April 19, 1839, which established the status of Belgium before the war, no longer conform to the requirements of the situation, consents to the abrogation of the said treaties and undertakes immediately to recognize and to observe whatever conventions may be entered into by the Principal Allied and Associated Powers, or by any of them, in concert with the Governments of Belgium and of the Netherlands, to replace the said Treaties of 1839. If her formal adhesion should be required to such conventions or to any of their stipulations, Germany undertakes immediately to give it.

Article 32. Germany recognizes the full sovereignty of Belgium over the whole of the contested territory of Moresnet (called *Moresnet neutre*).

Article 33. Germany renounces in favour of Belgium all rights and title over the territory of Prussian Moresnet situated on the west of the road from Liège to Aix-la-Chapelle; the road will belong to Belgium where it bounds this territory.

Article 34. Germany renounces in favour of Belgium all rights and title over the territory comprising the whole of the *Kreise* of Eupen and of Malmédy.

During the six months after the coming into force of this Treaty, registers will be opened by the Belgian authorities at Eupen and Malmédy in which the inhabitants of the above territory will be entitled to record in writing a desire to see the whole or part of it remain under German sovereignty.

The results of this public expression of opinion will be communicated by the Belgian Government to the League of Nations, and Belgium undertakes to accept the decision of the League.

Article 35. A Commission of seven persons, five of whom will be appointed by the Principal Allied and Associated Powers, one by Germany and one by Belgium, will be set up fifteen days after the coming into force of the present Treaty to settle on the spot the new frontier line between Belgium and Germany, taking into account the economic factors and the means of communication.

Decisions will be taken by a majority and will be binding on the parties concerned.

Article 36. When the transfer of the sovereignty over the territories referred to above has become definitive, German nationals habitually resident in the territories will definitively acquire Belgian nationality *ipso facto*, and will lose their German nationality.

Nevertheless, German nationals who became resident in the territories after August 1, 1914, shall not obtain Belgian nationality without a permit from the Belgian Government.

Article 37. Within the two years following the definitive transfer of the sovereignty over the territories assigned to Belgium under the present Treaty, German nationals over 18 years of age habitually resident in those territories will be entitled to opt for German nationality.

Option by a husband will cover his wife, and option by parents will cover their children under 18 years of age.

Persons who have exercised the above right to opt must within the ensuing twelve months transfer their place of residence to Germany.

They will be entitled to retain their immovable property in the territories acquired by Belgium. They may carry with them their movable property of every description. No export or import duties may be imposed upon them in connection with the removal of such property.

Article 38. The German Government will hand over without delay to the Belgian Government the archives, registers, plans, title deeds and documents of every kind concerning the civil, military, financial, judicial or other administrations in the territory transferred to Belgian sovereignty.

The German Government will likewise restore to the Belgian Government the archives and documents of every kind carried off during the war by the German authorities from the Belgian public administrations, in particular from the Ministry of Foreign Affairs at Brussels.

Article 39. The proportion and nature of the financial liabilities of Germany and of Prussia which Belgium will have to bear on account of the territories ceded to her shall be fixed in conformity with Articles 254 and 256 of Part IX (Financial Clauses) of the present Treaty.

. . . .

SECTION III: LEFT BANK OF THE RHINE

Article 42. Germany is forbidden to maintain or construct any fortifications either on the left bank of the Rhine or on the right bank to the west of a line drawn 50 kilometres to the East of the Rhine.

Article 43. In the area defined above the maintenance and the assembly of armed forces, either permanently or temporarily, and military manœuvres of any kind, as well as the upkeep of all permanent works for mobilization, are in the same way forbidden.

Article 44. In case Germany violates in any manner whatever the provisions of Articles 42 and 43, she shall be regarded as committing a hostile act against the Powers signatory of the present Treaty and as calculated to disturb the peace of the world.

SECTION IV: SAAR BASIN

Article 45. As compensation for the destruction of the coal-mines in the north of France and as part payment towards the total reparation due from Germany for the damage resulting from the war, Germany cedes to France in full and absolute possession, with exclusive rights of exploitation, unencumbered and free from all debts and charges of any kind, the coal-mines situated in the Saar Basin as defined in Article 48.

Article 46. In order to assure the rights and welfare of the population and to guarantee to France complete freedom in working the mines, Germany agrees to the provisions of Chapters I and II of the Annex hereto.

Article 49. Germany renounces in favour of the League of Nations, in the capacity of trustee, the government of the territory defined above. . . .

Article 50. The stipulations under which the cession of the mines in the Saar Basin shall be carried out, together with the measures intended to guarantee the rights and the well-being of the inhabitants and the government of the territory, as well as the conditions in accordance with which the plebiscite hereinbefore provided for is to be made, are laid down in the Annex hereto. This Annex shall be considered as an integral part of the present Treaty, and Germany declares her adherence to it.

. . . .

SECTION V: ALSACE-LORRAINE

The High Contracting Parties, recognising the moral obligation to redress the wrong done by Germany in 1871 both to the rights of

France and to the wishes of the population of Alsace and Lorraine, which were separated from their country in spite of the solemn protest of their representatives at the Assembly of Bordeaux,

Agree upon the following Articles:

Article 51. The territories which were ceded to Germany in accordance with the Preliminaries of Peace signed at Versailles on February 26, 1871, and the Treaty of Frankfort of May 10, 1871, are restored to French sovereignty as from the date of the Armistice of November 11, 1918.

The provisions of the Treaties establishing the delimitation of the frontiers before 1871 shall be restored.

Article 52. The German Government shall hand over without delay to the French Government all archives, registers, plans, titles and documents of every kind concerning the civil, military, financial, judicial or other administrations of the territories restored to French sovereignty. If any of these documents, archives, registers, titles, or plans have been misplaced, they will be restored by the German Government on the demand of the French Government.

Article 53. Separate agreements shall be made between France and Germany dealing with the interests of the inhabitants of the territories referred to in Article 51, particularly as regards their civil rights, their business and the exercise of their professions, it being understood that Germany undertakes as from the present date to recognise and accept the regulations laid down in the Annex hereto regarding the nationality of the inhabitants or natives of the said territories, not to claim at any time or in any place whatsoever as German nationals those who shall have been declared on any ground to be French, to receive all others in her territory, and to conform, as regards the property of German nationals in the territories indicated in Article 51, with the provisions of Article 297 and the Annex to Section IV of Part X (Economic Clauses) of the present Treaty.

Those German nationals who without acquiring French nationality shall receive permission from the French Government to reside in the said territories shall not be subjected to the provisions of the said Article.

Article 54. Those persons who have regained French nationality in virtue of paragraph 1 of the Annex hereto will be held to be Alsace-Lorrainers for the purposes of the present Section.

The persons referred to in paragraph 2 of the said Annex will from the day on which they have claimed French nationality be held to be Alsace-Lorrainers with retroactive effect as from November 11, 1918. For those whose application is rejected, the privilege will terminate at the date of the refusal.

Such juridical persons will also have the status of Alsace-Lorrainers as shall have been recognised as possessing this quality, whether by the French administrative authorities or by a judicial decision.

. . . .

Article 80. Germany acknowledges and will respect strictly the independence of Austria, within the frontiers which may be fixed in a Treaty between that State and the Principal Allied and Associated Powers; she agrees that this independence shall be inalienable, except with the consent of the Council of the League of Nations.

SECTION VII: CZECHO-SLOVAK STATE

Article 81. Germany, in conformity with the action already taken by the Allied and Associated Powers, recognizes the complete independence of the Czecho-Slovak State which will include the autonomous territory of the Ruthenians to the south of the Carpathians. Germany hereby recognizes the frontiers of this State as determined by the Principal Allied and Associated Powers and the other interested States.

.   .   .   .

SECTION VIII: POLAND

Article 87. Germany, in conformity with the action already taken by the Allied and Associated Powers, recognizes the complete independence of Poland, and renounces in her favour all rights and title over the territory [of Poland]. . . .

The boundaries of Poland not laid down in the present Treaty will be subsequently determined by the Principal Allied and Associated Powers.

A Commission consisting of seven members, five of whom shall be nominated by the Principal Allied and Associated Powers, one by Germany and one by Poland, shall be constituted fifteen days after the coming into force of the present Treaty to delimit on the spot the frontier line between Poland and Germany.

The decisions of the Commission will be taken by a majority of votes and shall be binding upon the parties concerned.

Article 88. In the portion of Upper Silesia included within the boundaries described below, the inhabitants will be called upon to indicate by a vote whether they wish to be attached to Germany or to Poland. . . .

The régime under which this plebiscite will be taken and given effect to is laid down in the Annex hereto.

The Polish and German Governments hereby respectively bind themselves to conduct no prosecutions on any part of their territory and to take no exceptional proceedings for any political action performed in Upper Silesia during the period of the régime laid down in the Annex hereto and up to the settlement of the final status of the country.

Germany hereby renounces in favour of Poland all rights and title over the portion of Upper Silesia lying beyond the frontier line fixed by the Principal Allied and Associated Powers as the result of the plebiscite.

1. Within fifteen days from the coming into force of the present Treaty the German troops and such officials as may be designated by the Commission set up under the provisions of paragraph 2 shall evacuate the plebiscite area. Up to the moment of the completion of the evacuation they shall refrain from any form of requisitioning in money or in kind and from all acts likely to prejudice the material interests of the country.

Within the same period the Workmen's and Soldiers' Councils which have been constituted in this area shall be dissolved. Members of such Councils who are natives of another region and are exercising their functions at the date of the coming into force of the present Treaty, or who have gone out of office since March 1, 1919, shall be evacuated.

All military and semi-military unions formed in the said area by inhabitants of the district shall be immediately disbanded. All members of such military organizations who are not domiciled in the said area shall be required to leave it.

2. The plebiscite area shall be immediately placed under the authority of an International Commission of four members to be designated by the following Powers: the United States of America, France, the British Empire and Italy. It shall be occupied by troops belonging to the Allied and Associated Powers, and the German Government undertakes to give facilities for the transference of these troops to Upper Silesia.

3. The Commission shall enjoy all the powers exercised by the German or the Prussian Government, except those of legislation or taxation. It shall also be substituted for the government of the province and the *Regierungsbezirk*.

It shall be within the competence of the Commission to interpret the powers hereby conferred upon it and to determine to what extent it shall exercise them, and to what extent they shall be left in the hands of the existing authorities.

Changes in the existing laws and the existing taxation shall only be brought into force with the consent of the Commission.

The Commission will maintain order with the help of the troops which will be at its disposal, and, to the extent which it may deem necessary, by means of gendarmerie recruited among the inhabitants of the country.

The Commission shall provide immediately for the replacement of the evacuated German officials and, if occasion arises, shall itself order the evacuation of such authorities and proceed to the replacement of such local authorities as may be required.

It shall take all steps which it thinks proper to ensure the freedom, fairness and secrecy of the vote. In particular, it shall have the right to order the expulsion of any person who may in any way have attempted to distort the result of the plebiscite by methods of corruption or intimidation.

The Commission shall have full power to settle all questions arising from the execution of the present clauses. It shall be assisted by technical advisers chosen by it from among the local population.

The decisions of the Commission shall be taken by a majority vote.

4. The vote shall take place at such date as may be determined by the Principal Allied and Associated Powers, but not sooner than six months or later than eighteen months after the establishment of the Commission in the area.

The right to vote shall be given to all persons without distinction of sex who:

(a) Have completed their twentieth year on the 1st January of the year in which the plebiscite takes place;

(b) Were born in the plebiscite area or have been domiciled there since a date to be determined by the Commission, which shall not be subsequent to the 1st January, 1919, or who have been expelled by the German authorities and have not retained their domicile there.

Persons convicted of political offences shall be enabled to exercise their right of voting.

Every person will vote in the commune where he is domiciled or in which he was born, if he has not retained his domicile in the area.

The result of the vote will be determined by communes according to the majority of votes in each commune.

5. On the conclusion of the voting, the number of votes cast in each commune will be communicated by the Commission to the Principal Allied and Associated Powers, with a full report as to the taking of the vote and a recommendation as to the line which ought to be adopted as the frontier of Germany in Upper Silesia. In this recommendation regard will be paid to the wishes of the inhabitants as shown by the vote, and to the geographical and economic conditions of the locality.

6. As soon as the frontier has been fixed by the Principal Allied and Associated Powers, the German authorities will be notified by the International Commission that they are free to take over the administration of the territory which it is recognised should be German; the said authorities must proceed to do so within one month of such notification and in the manner prescribed by the Commission.

Within the same period and in the manner prescribed by the Commission, the Polish Government must proceed to take over the administration of the territory which it is recognised should be Polish.

When the administration of the territory has been provided for by the German and Polish authorities respectively, the powers of the Commission will terminate.

The cost of the army of occupation, and expenditure by the Commission, whether in discharge of its own functions or in the administration of the territory, will be a charge on the area.

Article 89. Poland undertakes to accord freedom of transit to persons, goods, vessels, carriages, wagons, and mails in transit between East Prussia and the rest of Germany over Polish territory, including territorial waters, and to treat them at least as favourably as the persons, goods, vessels, carriages, wagons and mails respectively of Polish or of any other more favoured nationality, origin, importation, starting point, or ownership as regards facilities, restrictions and all other matters.

Goods in transit shall be exempt from all customs or other similar duties.

Freedom of transit will extend to telegraphic and telephonic services. . . .

Article 90. Poland undertakes to permit for a period of fifteen years the exportation to Germany of the products of the mines in any part of Upper Silesia transferred to Poland in accordance with the present Treaty.

Such products shall be free from all export duties or other charges or restrictions on exportation.

Poland agrees to take such steps as may be necessary to secure that any such products shall be available for sale to purchasers in Germany on terms as favourable as are applicable to like products sold under similar conditions to purchasers in Poland or in any other country.

Article 91. German nationals habitually resident in territories recognised as forming part of Poland will acquire Polish nationality *ipso facto* and will lose their German nationality.

German nationals, however, or their descendants who became resident in these territories after January 1, 1908, will not acquire Polish nationality without a special authorisation from the Polish State.

Within a period of two years after the coming into force of the present Treaty, German nationals over 18 years of age habitually resident in any of the territories recognised as forming part of Poland will be entitled to opt for German nationality.

Poles who are German nationals over 18 years of age and habitually resident in Germany will have a similar right to opt for Polish nationality.

Option by a husband will cover his wife and option by parents will cover their children under 18 years of age.

Persons who have exercised the above right to opt may within the succeeding twelve months transfer their place of residence to the State for which they have opted.

They will be entitled to retain their immovable property in the territory of the other State where they had their place of residence before exercising the right to opt.

They may carry with them their movable property of every description. No export or import duties or charges may be imposed upon them in connection with the removal of such property.

Within the same period Poles who are German nationals and are in a foreign country will be entitled, in the absence of any provisions to the contrary in the foreign law, and if they have not acquired the foreign nationality, to obtain Polish nationality and to lose their German nationality by complying with the requirements laid down by the Polish State. . . .

Article 93. Poland accepts and agrees to embody in a Treaty with the Principal Allied and Associated Powers such provisions as may be deemed necessary by the said Powers to protect the interests of inhabitants of Poland who differ from the majority of the population in race, language or religion.

Poland further accepts and agrees to embody in a Treaty with the said Powers such provisions as they may deem necessary to protect freedom of transit and equitable treatment of the commerce of other nations.

. . . .

SECTION X: MEMEL

Article 99. Germany renounces in favour of the Principal Allied and Associated Powers all rights and title over the territories included between the Baltic, the north-eastern frontier of East Prussia as defined in Article 28 of Part II (Boundaries of Germany) of the present Treaty and the former frontier between Germany and Russia.

Germany undertakes to accept the settlement made by the Principal Allied and Associated Powers in regard to these territories, particularly in so far as concerns the nationality of the inhabitants.

SECTION XI: FREE CITY OF DANZIG

. . . .

Article 101. A Commission composed of three members appointed by the Principal Allied and Associated Powers, including a High Commissioner as President, one member appointed by Germany and one member appointed by Poland, shall be constituted within fifteen days of the coming into force of the present Treaty for the purpose of delimiting on the spot the frontier of the territory as described above, taking into account as far as possible the existing communal boundaries.

Article 102. The Principal Allied and Associated Powers undertake to establish the town of Danzig, together with the rest of the territory described in Article 100, as a Free City. It will be placed under the protection of the League of Nations.

Article 103. A constitution for the Free City of Danzig shall be drawn up by the duly appointed representatives of the Free City in agreement with a High Commissioner to be appointed by the League of Nations. This constitution shall be placed under the guarantee of the League of Nations.

The High Commissioner will also be entrusted with the duty of dealing in the first instance with all differences arising between Poland and the Free City of Danzig in regard to this Treaty or any arrangements or agreements made thereunder.

The High Commissioner shall reside at Danzig.

Article 104. The Principal Allied and Associated Powers undertake to negotiate a Treaty between the Polish Government and the Free City of Danzig, which shall come into force at the same time as the establishment of the said Free City, with the following objects:

(1) To effect the inclusion of the Free City of Danzig within the Polish Customs frontiers, and to establish a free area in the port;

(2) To ensure to Poland without any restriction the free use and service of all waterways, docks, basins, wharves and other works within the territory of the Free City necessary for Polish imports and exports;

(3) To ensure to Poland the control and administration of the Vistula and of the whole railway system within the Free City, except such street and other railways as serve primarily the needs of the Free City, and of postal, telegraphic and telephonic communication between Poland and the port of Danzig;

(4) To ensure to Poland the right to develop and improve the waterways, docks, basins, wharves, railways and other works and means of communication mentioned in this Article, as well as to lease or purchase through appropriate processes such land and other property as may be necessary for these purposes;

(5) To provide against any discrimination within the Free City of Danzig to the detriment of citizens of Poland and other persons of Polish origin or speech;

(6) To provide that the Polish Government shall undertake the conduct of the foreign relations of the Free City of Danzig as well as the diplomatic protection of citizens of that city when abroad.

PART IV

GERMAN RIGHTS AND INTERESTS OUTSIDE GERMANY

Article 118. In territory outside her European frontiers as fixed by the present Treaty, Germany renounces all rights, titles and privileges whatsoever in or over territory which belonged to her or to her allies, and all rights, titles and privileges whatever their origin which she held as against the Allied and Associated Powers.

Germany hereby undertakes to recognise and to conform to the measures which may be taken now or in the future by the Principal Allied and Associated Powers, in agreement where necessary with third Powers, in order to carry the above stipulation into effect.

In particular Germany declares her acceptance of the following Articles relating to certain special subjects:

SECTION I: GERMAN COLONIES

Article 119. Germany renounces in favour of the Principal Allied and Associated Powers all her rights and titles over her oversea possessions.

·　·　·　·　·　·　·　·

SECTION V: MOROCCO

Article 141. Germany renounces all rights, titles and privileges conferred on her by the General Act of Algeciras of April 7, 1906, and by the Franco-German Agreements of February 9, 1909, and November 4, 1911. All treaties, agreements, arrangements and contracts concluded by her with the Sherifian Empire are regarded as abrogated as from August 3, 1914.

In no case can Germany take advantage of these instruments and she undertakes not to intervene in any way in negotiations relating to Morocco which may take place between France and the other Powers.

·　·　·　·　·　·　·

SECTION VIII: SHANTUNG

Article 156. Germany renounces, in favour of Japan, all her rights, title and privileges—particularly those concerning the territory of Kiaochow, railways, mines and submarine cables—which she acquired in virtue of the Treaty concluded by her with China on March 6, 1898, and of all other arrangements relative to the Province of Shantung.

All German rights in the Tsingtao-Tsinanfu Railway, including its branch lines, together with its subsidiary property of all kinds, stations, shops, fixed and rolling stock, mines, plant and material for the exploitation of the mines, are and remain acquired by Japan, together with all rights and privileges attaching thereto.

The German State submarine cables from Tsingtao to Shanghai and from Tsingtao to Chefoo, with all the rights, privileges and properties attaching thereto, are similarly acquired by Japan, free and clear of all charges and encumbrances.

·　·　·　·　·　·　·

PART V

In order to render possible the initiation of a general limitation of the armaments of all nations, Germany undertakes strictly to observe the military, naval and air clauses which follow.

SECTION I: MILITARY CLAUSES

CHAPTER I: EFFECTIVES AND CADRES OF THE GERMAN ARMY

Article 159. The German military forces shall be demobilized and reduced as prescribed hereinafter.

Article 160. (1) By a date which must not be later than March 31, 1920, the German Army must not comprise more than seven divisions of infantry and three divisions of cavalry.

After that date the total number of effectives in the Army of the States constituting Germany must not exceed one hundred thousand men, including officers and establishments of depots. The Army shall be devoted exclusively to the maintenance of order within the territory and to the control of the frontiers.

The total effective strength of officers, including the personnel of staffs, whatever their composition, must not exceed four thousand.

(2) Divisions and Army Corps headquarters staffs shall be organised in accordance with Table No. 1 annexed to this Section.

The number and strengths of the units of infantry, artillery, engineers, technical services and troops laid down in the aforesaid Table constitute maxima which must not be exceeded.

The following units may each have their own depot:

An Infantry regiment;

A Cavalry regiment;

A regiment of Field Artillery;

A battalion of Pioneers.

(3) The divisions must not be grouped under more than two army corps headquarters staffs.

The maintenance or formation of forces differently grouped or of other organisations for the command of troops or for preparation for war is forbidden.

The Great German General Staff and all similar organisations shall be dissolved and may not be reconstituted in any form.

The officers, or persons in the position of officers, in the Ministries of War in the different States in Germany and in the Administrations attached to them, must not exceed three hundred in number and are included in the maximum strength of four thousand laid down in the third sub-paragraph of paragraph (1) of this Article.

. . . .

CHAPTER IV: FORTIFICATIONS

Article 180. All fortified works, fortresses and field works situated in German territory to the west of a line drawn fifty kilometres to the east of the Rhine shall be disarmed and dismantled.

Within a period of two months from the coming into force of the present Treaty such of the above fortified works, fortresses and field works as are situated in territory not occupied by Allied and Associated troops shall be disarmed, and within a further period of four months they shall be dismantled. Those which are situated in territory occupied by Allied and Associated troops shall be disarmed and dismantled within such periods as may be fixed by the Allied High Command.

The construction of any new fortification, whatever its nature and importance, is forbidden in the zone referred to in the first paragraph above.

The system of fortified works of the southern and eastern frontiers of Germany shall be maintained in its existing state.

SECTION II: NAVAL CLAUSES

Article 181. After the expiration of a period of two months from the coming into force of the present Treaty the German naval forces in commission must not exceed:

6 battleships of the *Deutschland* or *Lothringen* type,
6 light cruisers,
12 destroyers,
12 torpedo boats,

or an equal number of ships constructed to replace them as provided in Article 190.

No submarines are to be included.

All other warships, except where there is provision to the contrary in the present Treaty, must be placed in reserve or devoted to commercial purposes.

. . . .

Article 191. The construction or acquisition of any submarine, even for commercial purposes, shall be forbidden in Germany.

Article 198. The armed forces of Germany must not include any military or naval air forces.

Germany may, during a period not extending beyond October 1, 1919, maintain a maximum number of one hundred seaplanes or flying boats, which shall be exclusively employed in searching for submarine mines, shall be furnished with the necessary equipment for this purpose, and shall in no case carry arms, munitions or bombs of any nature whatever.

In addition to the engines installed in the seaplanes or flying boats above mentioned, one spare engine may be provided for each engine of each of these craft.

No dirigible shall be kept.

SECTION IV: INTER-ALLIED COMMISSIONS OF CONTROL

Article 203. All the military, naval and air clauses contained in the present Treaty, for the execution of which a time-limit is prescribed, shall be executed by Germany under the control of Inter-Allied Commissions specially appointed for this purpose by the Principal Allied and Associated Powers.

Article 204. The Inter-Allied Commissions of Control will be specially charged with the duty of seeing to the complete execution of the delivery, destruction, demolition and rendering things useless to be carried out at the expense of the German Government in accordance with the present Treaty.

They will communicate to the German authorities the decisions which the Principal Allied and Associated Powers have reserved the right to take, or which the execution of the military, naval and air clauses may necessitate.

Article 205. The Inter-Allied Commissions of Control may establish their organisations at the seat of the central German Government.

They shall be entitled as often as they think desirable to proceed to any point whatever in German territory, or to send sub-commissions, or to authorize one or more of their members to go, to any such point.

Article 206. The German Government must give all necessary facilities for the accomplishment of their missions to the Inter-Allied Commissions of Control and to their members.

It shall attach a qualified representative to each Inter-Allied Commission of Control for the purpose of receiving the communications which the Commission may have to address to the German Government and of supplying or procuring for the Commission all information or documents which may be required.

The German Government must in all cases furnish at its own cost all labour and material required to effect the deliveries and the works of destruction, dismantling, demolition, and of rendering things useless, provided for in the present Treaty.

. . . .

PART VII

PENALTIES

Article 227. The Allied and Associated Powers publicly arraign William II of Hohenzollern, formerly German Emperor, for a supreme offence against international morality and the sanctity of treaties.

A special tribunal will be constituted to try the accused, thereby assuring him the guarantees essential to the right of defence. It will be composed of five judges, one appointed by each of the following Powers: namely, the United States of America, Great Britain, France, Italy and Japan.

In its decision the tribunal will be guided by the highest motives of international policy, with a view to vindicating the solemn obligations of international undertakings and the validity of international morality. It will be its duty to fix the punishment which it considers should be imposed.

The Allied and Associated Powers will address a request to the Government of the Netherlands for the surrender to them of the ex-Emperor in order that he may be put on trial.

. . . . .

PART VIII

REPARATION

SECTION I: GENERAL PROVISIONS

Article 231. The Allied and Associated Governments affirm and Germany accepts the responsibility of Germany and her allies for causing all the loss and damage to which the Allied and Associated Governments and their nationals have been subjected as a consequence of the war imposed upon them by the aggression of Germany and her allies.

Article 232. The Allied and Associated Governments recognize that the resources of Germany are not adequate, after taking into account permanent diminutions of such resources which will result from other provisions of the present Treaty, to make complete reparation for all such loss and damage.

The Allied and Associated Governments, however, require, and Germany undertakes, that she will make compensation for all damage done to the civilian population of the Allied and Associated Powers and to their property during the period of the belligerency of each as an Allied or Associated Power against Germany by such aggression by land, by sea and from the air, and in general all damage as defined in Annex I hereto.

In accordance with Germany's 'pledges, already given, as to complete restoration for Belgium, Germany undertakes, in addition to the compensation for damage elsewhere in this Part provided for, as a consequence of the violation of the Treaty of 1839, to make reimbursement of all sums which Belgium has borrowed from the Allied and Associated Governments up to November 11, 1918, together with interest at the rate of five per cent. (5%) per annum on such sums. This amount shall be determined by the Reparation Commission, and the German Government undertakes thereupon forthwith to make a special issue of bearer bonds to an equivalent amount payable in marks gold, on May 1, 1926, or, at the option of the German Government, on May 1 in any year up to 1926. Subject to the foregoing, the form of such bonds shall be determined by the Reparation Commission. Such bonds shall be handed over to the Reparation Commission, which has authority to take and acknowledge receipt thereof on behalf of Belgium.

．　．　．　．　．　．　．

SECTION II: SPECIAL PROVISIONS

Article 245. Within six months after the coming into force of the present Treaty the German Government must restore to the French Government the trophies, archives, historical souvenirs or works of art carried away from France by the German authorities in the course of the war of 1870-1871 and during this last war, in accordance with a list which will be communicated to it by the French Government; particularly the French flags taken in the course of the war of 1870-1871 and all the political papers taken by the German authorities on October 10, 1870, at the château of Cerçay, near Brunoy (Seine-et-Oise) belonging at the time to Mr. Rouher, formerly Minister of State.

Article 246. Within six months from the coming into force of the present Treaty, Germany will restore to His Majesty the King of the Hedjaz the original Koran of the Caliph Othman, which was removed from Medina by the Turkish authorities and is stated to have been presented to the ex-Emperor William II.

Within the same period Germany will hand over to His Britannic Majesty's Government the skull of the Sultan Mkwawa which was removed from the Protectorate of German East Africa and taken to Germany.

The delivery of the articles above referred to will be effected in such

place and in such conditions as may be laid down by the Governments
to which they are to be restored.

. . . .

PART IX

FINANCIAL CLAUSES

Article 248. Subject to such exceptions as the Reparation Commission may approve, a first charge upon all the assets and revenues
of the German Empire and its constituent States shall be the cost of
reparation and all other costs arising under the present Treaty or
any treaties or agreements supplementary thereto or under arrangements concluded between Germany and the Allied and Associated
Powers during the Armistice or its extensions.

Up to May 1, 1921, the German Government shall not export or
dispose of, and shall forbid the export or disposal of, gold without the
previous approval of the Allied and Associated Powers acting through
the Reparation Commission.

. . . .

PART XII

SECTION II: CHAPTER III

Clauses Relating to the Elbe, the Oder, the Niemen (Russstrom-Memel-
Niemen` and the Danube.

(1)—*General Clauses*

Article 331. The following rivers are declared international:
> the Elbe (*Labe*) from its confluence with the Vltava (*Moldau*),
> and the Vltava (*Moldau*) from Prague;
> the Oder (*Odra*) from its confluence with the Oppa;
> the Niemen (*Russstrom-Memel-Niemen*) from Grodno;
> the Danube from Ulm;

and all navigable parts of these river systems which naturally provide
more than one State with access to the sea, with or without transshipment from one vessel to another; together with lateral canals and
channels constructed either to duplicate or to improve naturally navigable sections of the specified river systems, or to connect two naturally navigable sections of the same river.

The same shall apply to the Rhine-Danube navigable waterway,
should such a waterway be constructed under the conditions laid down
in Article 353.

. . . .

PART XIII

LABOUR

Whereas the League of Nations has for its object the establishment of universal peace, and such a peace can be established only if it is based upon social justice;

And whereas conditions of labour exist involving such injustice, hardship and privation to large numbers of people as to produce unrest so great that the peace and harmony of the world are imperilled; and an improvement of those conditions is urgently required: as, for example, by the regulation of the hours of work, including the establishment of a maximum working day and week, the regulation of the labour supply, the prevention of unemployment, the provision of an adequate living wage, the protection of the worker against sickness, disease and injury arising out of his employment, the protection of children, young persons and women, provision for old age and injury, protection of the interests of workers when employed in countries other than their own, recognition of the principle of freedom of association, the organisation of vocational and technical education and other measures;

Whereas also the failure of any nation to adopt humane conditions of labour is an obstacle in the way of other nations which desire to improve the conditions in their own countries;

The High Contracting Parties, moved by sentiments of justice and humanity, as well as by the desire to secure the permanent peace of the world, agree to the following:

CHAPTER I: ORGANISATION

Article 387. A permanent organisation is hereby established for the promotion of the objects set forth in the Preamble.

The original Members of the League of Nations shall be the original Members of this Organisation, and hereafter membership of the League of Nations shall carry with it membership of the said organisation.

Article 388. The permanent organisation shall consist of:

(1) a General Conference of Representatives of the Members and,

(2) an International Labour Office controlled by the Governing Body described in Article 393.

. . . .

Article 392. The International Labour Office shall be established at the seat of the League of Nations as part of the organisation of the League.

. . . .

Article 396. The functions of the International Labour Office shall include the collection and distribution of information on all subjects relating to the international adjustment of conditions of industrial life and labour, and particularly the examination of subjects which it is proposed to bring before the Conference with a view to the conclusion of international conventions, and the conduct of such special investigations as may be ordered by the Conference.

It will prepare the agenda for the meetings of the Conference.

It will carry out the duties required of it by the provisions of this Part of the present Treaty in connection with international disputes.

It will edit and publish in French and English, and in such other languages as the Governing Body may think desirable, a periodical paper dealing with problems of industry and employment of international interest.

Generally, in addition to the functions set out in this Article, it shall have such other powers and duties as may be assigned to it by the Conference.

.   .   .   .

PART XIV

GUARANTEES.

SECTION I: WESTERN EUROPE

Article 428. As a guarantee for the execution of the present Treaty by Germany, the German territory situated to the west of the Rhine, together with the bridgeheads, will be occupied by Allied and Associated troops for a period of fifteen years from the coming into force of the present Treaty.

Article 429. If the conditions of the present Treaty are faithfully carried out by Germany, the occupation referred to in Article 428 will be successively restricted as follows:

(1) At the expiration of five years there will be evacuated: the bridgehead of Cologne and the territories north of a line running along the Ruhr, then along the railway Jülich, Duren, Euskirchen, Rheinbach, thence along the road Rheinbach to Sinzig, and reaching the Rhine at the confluence with the Ahr; the roads, railways and places mentioned above being excluded from the area evacuated.

(2) At the expiration of ten years there will be evacuated: the bridgehead of Coblenz and the territories north of a line to be drawn from the intersection between the frontiers of Belgium, Germany and Holland, running about 4 kilometres south of Aix-la-Chapelle, then to and following the crest of Forst Gemünd, then east of the railway of the Urft Valley, then along Blankenheim, Valdorf, Dreis, Ulmen to and following the Moselle from Bremm to Nehren, then passing by Kappel and Simmern, then following the ridge of the heights between Simmern

and the Rhine and reaching this river at Bacharach; all the places, valleys, roads and railways mentioned above being excluded from the area evacuated.

(3) At the expiration of fifteen years there will be evacuated: the bridgehead of Mainz, the bridgehead of Kehl and the remainder of the German territory under occupation.

If at that date the guarantees against unprovoked aggression by Germany are not considered sufficient by the Allied and Associated Governments, the evacuation of the occupying troops may be delayed to the extent regarded as necessary for the purpose of obtaining the required guarantees.

Article 430. In case either during the occupation or after the expiration of the fifteen years referred to above the Reparation Commission finds that Germany refuses to observe the whole or part of her obligations under the present Treaty with regard to reparation, the whole or part of the areas specified in Article 429 will be reoccupied immediately by the Allied and Associated forces.

Article 431. If before the expiration of the period of fifteen years Germany complies with all the undertakings resulting from the present Treaty, the occupying forces will be withdrawn immediately.

Article 432. All matters relating to the occupation and not provided for by the present Treaty shall be regulated by subsequent agreements, which Germany hereby undertakes to observe.

152. TREATY OF SÈVRES, AUGUST 10, 1920 (NOT RATIFIED)[1]

[The treaty of Sèvres, imposed upon a vanquished Turkey by the victors, was never ratified. As the Nationalist movement gained force and power it became evident that the distant Allies could never enforce a treaty which the Turkish Nationalist Government refused to sign. The first step taken by the Turks to modify the terms of the treaty was in the Angora Agreement, 1921, with France by which Turkey got back Alexandretta and Cilicia. Mustapha Kemal then turned to Smyrna and recaptured it and threatened to take Constantinople. The Allies were ready to make concessions after the Greek armies of occupation in the Smyrna region were routed in the summer of 1922. The Mudania armistice a month later permitted the Nationalists to retain Smyrna and to assume the administration of Constantinople. It was followed by negotiations at Lausanne, where a treaty was finally signed. The provision of the treaty given below should be compared with the final settlement of Lausanne (see doc. no. 169). By a supplementary tripartite agreement signed the same date as the treaty of Sèvres, between England, France, and Italy, these nations agreed to coöperate in the Near East, to divide control of the Bagdad and Ana-

---

[1] Great Britain. *Parliamentary Papers*, 1920, Vol. LI, Cmd. 964. "Treaty of Peace with Turkey signed at Sèvres, August 10, 1920" (Extracts).

tolian railways, and to recognize the special interests of Italy in southern Anatolia, including the Heraclea coal basin, and of France in Cilicia and Kurdistan.]

PART III

POLITICAL CLAUSES

SECTION I: CONSTANTINOPLE

Article 36. Subject to the provisions of the present Treaty, the High Contracting Parties agree that the rights and title of the Turkish Government over Constantinople shall not be affected, and that the said Government and His Majesty the Sultan shall be entitled to reside there and to maintain there the capital of the Turkish State.

Nevertheless, in the event of Turkey failing to observe faithfully the provisions of the present Treaty, or of any treaties or conventions supplementary thereto, particularly as regards the protection of the rights of racial, religious or linguistic minorities, the Allied Powers expressly reserve the right to modify the above provisions, and Turkey hereby agrees to accept any dispositions which may be taken in this connection.

SECTION II: STRAITS

Article 37. The navigation of the Straits, including the Dardanelles, the Sea of Marmora and the Bosphorus, shall in future be open, both in peace and war, to every vessel of commerce or of war and to military and commercial aircraft, without distinction of flag.

These waters shall not be subject to blockade, nor shall any belligerent right be exercised nor any act of hostility be committed within them, unless in pursuance of a decision of the Council of the League of Nations.

Article 38. The Turkish Government recognizes that it is necessary to take further measures to ensure the freedom of navigation provided for in Article 37, and accordingly delegates, so far as it is concerned, to a Commission to be called the "Commission of the Straits," and hereinafter referred to as "the Commission," the control of the waters specified in Article 39.

The Greek Government, so far as it is concerned, delegates to the Commission the same powers and undertakes to give it in all respects the same facilities.

Such control shall be exercised in the name of the Turkish and Greek Governments respectively, and in the manner provided in this Section.

Article 39. The authority of the Commission will extend to all the waters between the Mediterranean mouth of the Dardanelles and the

Black Sea mouth of the Bosphorus, and to the waters within three miles of each of these mouths.

This authority may be exercised on shore to such extent as may be necessary for the execution of the provisions of this Section.

Article 40. The Commission shall be composed of representatives appointed respectively by the United States of America (if and when that Government is willing to participate), the British Empire, France, Italy, Japan, Russia (if and when Russia becomes a member of the League of Nations), Greece, Roumania, and Bulgaria and Turkey (if and when the two latter States become members of the League of Nations). Each Power shall appoint one representative. The representatives of the United States of America, the British Empire, France, Italy, Japan and Russia shall each have two votes. The representatives of Greece, Roumania, and Bulgaria and Turkey shall each have one vote. Each Commissioner shall be removable only by the Government which appointed him.

. . . . . .

SECTION III: KURDISTAN

Article 62. A Commission sitting at Constantinople and composed of three members appointed by the British, French and Italian Governments respectively shall draft within six months from the coming into force of the present Treaty a scheme of local autonomy for the predominantly Kurdish areas lying east of the Euphrates, south of the southern boundary of Armenia as it may be hereafter determined, and north of the frontier of Turkey with Syria and Mesopotamia as defined in Article 27, II (2) and (3). If unanimity cannot be secured on any question, it will be referred by the members of the Commission to their respective Governments. The scheme shall contain full safeguards for the protection of the Assyro-Chaldeans and other racial or religious minorities within these areas, and with this object a Commission composed of British, French, Italian, Persian and Kurdish representatives shall visit the spot to examine and decide what rectifications, if any, should be made in the Turkish frontier where, under the provisions of the present Treaty, that frontier coincides with that of Persia.

. . . . . .

Article 69. The city of Smyrna and the territory defined in Article 66 remain under Turkish sovereignty. Turkey however transfers to the Greek Government the exercise of her rights of sovereignty over the city of Smyrna and the said territory. In witness of such sovereignty the Turkish flag shall remain permanently hoisted over an outer fort in the town of Smyrna. The fort will be designated by the Principal Allied Powers.

Article 70. The Greek Government will be responsible for the administration of the city of Smyrna and the territory defined in Article 66, and will effect this administration by means of a body of officials which it will appoint specially for the purpose.

Article 72. A local parliament shall be set up with an electoral system calculated to ensure proportional representation of all sections of the population, including racial, linguistic and religious minorities. Within six months from the coming into force of the present Treaty the Greek Government shall submit to the Council of the League of Nations a scheme for an electoral system complying with the above requirements; this scheme shall not come into force until approved by a majority of the Council.

The Greek Government shall be entitled to postpone the elections for so long as may be required for the return of the inhabitants who have been banished or deported by the Turkish authorities, but such postponement shall not exceed a period of one year from the coming into force of the present Treaty.

．　　．　　．　　．　　．　　．　　．

SECTION V: GREECE

Article 84. Without prejudice to the frontiers of Bulgaria laid down by the Treaty of Peace signed at Neuilly-sur-Seine on November 27, 1919, Turkey renounces in favour of Greece all rights and title over the territories of the former Turkish Empire in Europe situated outside the frontiers of Turkey as laid down by the present Treaty.

The islands of the Sea of Marmora are not included in the transfer of sovereignty effected by the above paragraph.

Turkey further renounces in favour of Greece all her rights and title over the islands of Imbros and Tenedos. The decision taken by the Conference of Ambassadors at London in execution of Articles 5 of the Treaty of London of May 17/30, 1913, and 15 of the Treaty of Athens of November 1/14, 1913, and notified to the Greek Government on February 13, 1914, relating to the sovereignty of Greece over the other islands of the Eastern Mediterranean, particularly Lemnos, Samothrace, Mytilene, Chios, Samos and Nikaria, is confirmed, without prejudice to the provisions of the present Treaty relating to the islands placed under the sovereignty of Italy and referred to in Article 122, and to the islands lying less than three miles from the coast of Asia.

Nevertheless, in the portion of the zone of the Straits and the islands, referred to in Article 178, which under the present Treaty are placed under Greek sovereignty, Greece accepts and undertakes to observe, failing any contrary stipulation in the present Treaty, all the obligations which, in order to assure the freedom of the Straits, are imposed by the present Treaty on Turkey in that portion of said zone, including the islands of the Sea of Marmora, which remains under Turkish sovereignty.

.   .   .   .

SECTION VI: ARMENIA

Article 88. Turkey, in accordance with the action already taken by the Allied Powers, hereby recognises Armenia as a free and independent State.

Article 89. Turkey and Armenia as well as other High Contracting Parties agree to submit to the arbitration of the President of the United States of America the question of the frontier to be fixed between Turkey and Armenia in the Vilayets of Erzerum, Trebizond, Van and Bitlis, and to accept his decision thereupon, as well as any stipulations he may prescribe as to access for Armenia to the sea, and as to the demilitarisation of any portion of Turkish territory adjacent to the said frontier.

.   .   .   .

SECTION VII: SYRIA, MESOPOTAMIA, PALESTINE

Article 94. The High Contracting Parties agree that Syria and Mesopotamia shall, in accordance with the fourth paragraph of Article 22, Part I (Covenant of the League of Nations), be provisionally recognised as independent States subject to the rendering of administrative advice and assistance by a Mandatory until such times as they are able to stand alone.

A Commission shall be constituted within fifteen days from the coming into force of the present Treaty to trace on the spot the frontier line described in Article 27, II (2) and (3). This Commission will be composed of three members nominated by France, Great Britain and Italy respectively, and one member nominated by Turkey; it will be assisted by a representative of Syria for the Syrian frontier, and by a representative of Mesopotamia for the Mesopotamian frontier.

The determination of the other frontiers of the said States, and the selection of the Mandatories, will be made by the Principal Allied Powers.

Article 95. The High Contracting Parties agree to entrust, by application of the provisions of Article 22, the administration of Palestine, within such boundaries as may be determined by the Principal Allied Powers, to a Mandatory to be selected by the said Powers. The Mandatory will be responsible for putting into effect the declaration originally made on November 2, 1917, by the British Government and adopted by the other Allied Powers, in favour of the establishment in Palestine of a national home for the Jewish people, it being clearly understood that nothing shall be done which may prejudice the civil and religious rights of existing non-Jewish communities in Palestine, or the rights and political status enjoyed by Jews in any other country.

The Mandatory undertakes to appoint as soon as possible a special Commission to study and regulate all questions and claims relating to the different religious communities. In the composition of this Commission the religious interests concerned will be taken into account. The Chairman of the Commission will be appointed by the Council of the League of Nations.

．．．．．．．．

SECTION VIII: HEDJAZ

Article 98. Turkey, in accordance with the action already taken by the Allied Powers, hereby recognises the Hedjaz as a free and independent State, and renounces in favour of the Hedjaz all rights and titles over the territories of the former Turkish Empire situated outside the frontiers of Turkey as laid down by the present Treaty, and comprised within the boundaries which may ultimately be fixed.

Cyprus

Article 115. The High Contracting Parties recognise the annexation of Cyprus proclaimed by the British Government on November 5, 1914.

．．．．．．．．

SECTION XIII: GENERAL PROVISIONS

Article 136. A Commission composed of four members, appointed by the British Empire, France, Italy and Japan respectively, shall be set up within three months from the coming into force of the present Treaty, to prepare, with the assistance of technical experts representing the other capitulatory Powers, Allied or neutral, who with this object will each be invited to appoint an expert, a scheme of judicial reform to replace the present capitulatory system in judicial matters in Turkey. This Commission may recommend, after consultation with the Turkish Government, the adoption of either a mixed or an unified judicial system.

The scheme prepared by the Commission will be submitted to the Governments of the Allied and neutral Powers concerned. As soon as the Principal Allied Powers have approved the scheme they will inform the Turkish Government, which hereby agrees to accept the new system.

The Principal Allied Powers reserve the right to agree among themselves, and if necessary with the other Allied or neutral Powers concerned, as to the date on which the new system is to come into force.

PART V

REORIENTATION

153. Organizing the League of Nations

[The establishment of the League of Nations and the Permanent Court of International Justice were among the momentous events of the years immediately following the war. The organization of the various related bodies and the initiation of the functions of all bodies are shown by extracts from the *Official Journal* of the League of Nations. In the case of the International Labor Office, a report from the 1929 meeting is included in conjunction with Lord Curzon's address before the first meeting in order to explain more adequately the nature of the services of this office.]

(a) *Second Public Meeting of the Council*[1]

Held in London at St. James's Palace, on Friday, 13th February, 1920, at 12 noon.

The Members of the Council of the League of Nations were represented as follows:—

The British Empire........By the Rt. Hon. A. J. Balfour
(President)
Belgium..........................By M. Paul Hymans
Brazil...........................By M. Gastâo da Cunha
France..........................By M. Léon Bourgeois
Greece..................By M. Demetrius Caclamanos
Italy...................By M. Maggiorino Ferraris
Japan..........................By M. M. K. Matsui
Spain........................By M. Quinones de Léon
Secretary General: Sir Eric Drummond.

Mr. Balfour: Ladies and Gentlemen, you will remember that when we met on Wednesday last in public session, I explained the procedure that we proposed to follow, which consisted of a preliminary meeting open to the public, then private discussions in Committee terminated by other public meetings, at which formal decisions regarding the subjects on the Agenda will be taken. The Council have agreed that the final stage of their decisions shall be taken in public and this procedure, which we have deliberately adopted, will be carried out at these meetings.

It is unnecessary for me to occupy your time by any lengthy re-

---

[1] League of Nations, *Official Journal*, March, 1920, pp. 32-33.

marks before we begin our discussions, or, rather, the statement of the conclusions at which we have arrived regarding the various items in our programme. That statement will be made by my colleagues on the Council, each one taking in turn the subject of which he is the appointed rapporteur. He will explain the decisions to which we have come and we shall formally ratify them.

Perhaps before calling upon His Excellency M. Bourgeois to begin our strictly business proceedings I may be allowed to say this one word of preface. We are a very young institution; this is the second time that we have met and it is perhaps the first time on which it may be said that we have had before us a general programme of international business. It is too early to forecast our future, but I may say that, if the experience of the last few days and hours is any guide or indication of what that future will be, I look forward to it with the utmost confidence. In Paris the greater part of the work was as you know done and had to be done by the representatives of the Great Powers; they were assisted by representatives of the other Allies on certain rare special and fixed occasions. Here we have for the first time not merely representatives of the, I am sorry to say in this case, four not five Great Powers, but also representatives of the other Allied Powers, and more important perhaps than all, more novel, at all events, than all, we have the valuable assistance of representatives of Neutral countries. This is a great and, I believe, happy and beneficent innovation, and if the nations of the world, not merely those who were engaged in hostilities, but those—not very many after all—who were not involved in this world cataclysm are able in the future to meet together and discuss in the same business-like, friendly and conciliatory spirit which has marked our proceedings during the past two days, I do not doubt that the service which the League of Nations is capable of rendering in the future to mankind is almost incalculable and certainly is beyond computation at the present moment.

.   .   .   .

(b) *Rules of Procedure of the Council*[1]

Resolved at the Meeting of the Council in Rome on 17th May, 1920

Article 1.—The Council will meet as occasion may require, and at least once a year, at the seat of the League. In special circumstances the Council may be convened at such other place as the Council may appoint or the President deem suitable, after consultation, if possible, with the other Representatives on the Council.

The Council will be convened by the President by means of a letter addressed by the Secretary-General to the regularly accredited Repre-

---

[1] League of Nations, *Official Journal*, July-August, 1920, pp. 272-274.

sentatives of each Government through their respective Governments. This letter must be sent at least 20 days before the first meeting of each session.

The letter will state the items on the Agenda, and will, as far as possible, be accompanied by the necessary documents.

Should important circumstances so demand, the President may reduce the time-limit mentioned in the second paragraph, as far as the situation may require and permit.

The Council shall be convened within reasonable time on the demand of any Member of the League represented on the Council, or of three Members of the League not represented on the Council. Every demand for a meeting of the Council shall be sent to the Secretary-General.

The rules laid down in the foregoing paragraphs shall in no wise affect the provisions concerning the cases referred to in paragraphs 1 and 2 of Article 2, and in paragraph 1 of Article 15 of the Covenant.

Article 2.—The Council will decide on the items which it desires to see placed on the Agenda of the next session, and may appoint a reporter for each subject.

Should a Member of the League, in the interval between two sessions of the Council, request that a subject be considered at the next session, the Secretary-General will place this subject on the Agenda. This also applies to any subject which may have been referred to the Council in the interval between two sessions, and which the Secretary-General, in agreement with the President, may deem to require consideration.

In all cases where the Council has not appointed a reporter for any subject on the Agenda, he may be appointed by the President.

New items not on the Agenda may be added in the course of a session if a majority of the Members of the Council represented at the meeting give their consent. The Council shall, however, take no decision in respect of these matters until 48 hours after they have been placed on the Agenda, and after a report upon them has been presented.

Article 3.—At the beginning of each session the Secretary-General will present a written report upon the steps taken to give effect to decisions previously adopted, and upon the progress achieved in respect of matters submitted to the Council, and in respect of matters that may have come directly under his cognisance since the preceding session.

Article 4.—The President and the Vice-President will be elected by the Council from amongst its Members by secret ballot and by a majority. They will hold office for one year.

If the President or Vice-President ceases, for any reason, to be a Representative on the Council of the League of Nations, the Council will hold a fresh election.

The Representative on the Council who has filled the office of President or of Vice-President for one year is not eligible in the following year either as President or as Vice-President.

Article 5.—Unless the Council decides to the contrary, the reading of the reports presented by the reporters, the final discussions, and the voting on the resolutions which have been proposed, shall take place at public meetings. The Council will sit in private for the preliminary discussion of the items on the Agenda.

Every item on the Agenda shall be reviewed and put to the vote at a public meeting, unless the Council decides otherwise.

Article 6.—The President shall declare the meeting open as soon after the hour fixed in the letter of convocation, or at a previous meeting, as there shall be present a majority of the Representatives of the Members entitled to representation under paragraphs 1 and 2 of Article 4 of the Covenant. He will declare the meeting closed or suspended if the number of Representatives present falls below this majority.

Article 7.—The Secretary-General or his Deputy shall keep the minutes of the meetings. Copies thereof will be supplied as soon as possible to the Representatives on the Council. The text of minutes which have not been approved in the course of the meeting will be sent by the Secretary-General to the Representatives on the Council within a fortnight after the closing of the session, either to the permanent address of the Representative, or any other address he may indicate.

These texts will be deemed final if, within 20 days of the communication of copies, no objection is raised by a Representative on the Council.

All resolutions must receive approval in their final form before the close of the session.

Copies of the final texts will be distributed to the Representatives on the Council and to the Members of the League.

Article 8.—Except where otherwise expressly provided in the Covenant, or by the terms of a Treaty, decisions at any meeting of the Council shall require the agreement of all the Members of the League represented at the meeting.

All matters of procedure at meetings of the Council, including the appointment of Committees to investigate particular matters, shall be regulated by the Council, and may be decided by a majority of the Members of the League represented at the meeting.

Voting shall be by show of hands, or by calling over the names of Members should one of the Representatives on the Council demand it.

Article 9.—All decisions relating to individuals will be taken by means of a secret vote, taken at a private sitting. If at this voting there is at first no clear majority in favour of any individual, an entirely new ballot shall be taken; if still no individual obtains a clear majority, a third ballot shall be taken, but on this occasion the voting shall be only on the two candidates who obtained the highest number of votes at the second ballot. In case of equality of votes between several candidates, the third ballot shall be taken on the two oldest candidates only. Should there be equality, the elder candidate shall be elected.

In case of equality in any other voting in which a majority is required, a second vote shall be taken in the course of the next meeting. This meeting shall be held within 48 hours from the date on which the first vote was taken, and it shall be expressly mentioned on the Agenda that a second vote will then be taken on the matter in question. Unless there is at this subsequent meeting a majority in favour of the motion, it shall be treated as lost.

Article 10.—Expert advisers and officials of the League may be admitted to the meetings, in order to supply information or give assistance if required.

Each Member of the Council may bring two advisers or secretaries.

Article 11.—Before the last quarter of each year the Secretary-General will present a draft budget for the following year, for approval by the Council.

The Council will present, as soon as possible, the draft budget it has approved together with its report, for final approval by the Assembly.

Should it be impossible to obtain in time, the final approval of the budget by the Assembly, the Council may declare the budget it has passed applicable and effective from the beginning of the year, pending approval by the Assembly. This approval must be applied for as soon as circumstances permit.

Article 12.—At the close of every financial period the Council will appoint two of its Members to examine the accounts and to draw up a report thereon, preliminary to their being presented for approval.

The Secretary-General will present the Members so appointed with all documents necessary for their report four months at most after the close of every financial period.

The Members so appointed may avail themselves of the assistance of the financial experts of a Government which shall be designated by the Council from among the Members of the League of Nations.

Article 13.—In conformity with the provisions of the Covenant, these Rules of Procedure may at any time be modified by a majority decision of the Members of the League represented on the Council. Should the proposed modification not have been inserted in the letter of convocation, it must be duly considered in accordance with the stipulation of paragraph 4 of Article 2.

Article 14.—These Rules of Procedure shall come into force at the close of the session of the Council at Rome, from 14th to 19th May, 1920. As regards, however, the nomination of the President and Vice-President these Rules shall only take effect after adoption of a special resolution by the Council.

(c) *Secretariat*[1]

Staff of the Secretariat

Report presented by the British Representative, Mr. A. J. Balfour

In dealing with the subject which has been entrusted to me, namely the course to be adopted by the Council as regards the Secretariat of the League, it will probably be convenient if I begin with a brief historical explanation:—

The Secretary-General of the League was appointed by the Treaty of Versailles, and not only was the office then established, but its first occupant was mentioned by name; he is the present holder of the post. His duties are not only of immense importance, but he is the servant of two masters. He serves the Council of the League of Nations; he also serves the Assembly of the League of Nations—the two representative bodies who are entrusted with the general guidance of the policy of the League. When I remind you that on his shoulders has fallen the chief burden of organising the Secretariat in the first days of our still infant institution, you will be able to measure the importance of the responsibilities which he has to bear.

Soon after the appointment was thus made by Treaty, the Peace Conference, acting in plenary session, appointed a Committee to deal with the first stages of organisation. The Committee represented the nine Powers who send Representatives to the Council: Monsieur Pichon, then Foreign Minister of France, presided. They gave authority to the Secreary-General to make the necessary arrangements for the appointment of a staff, and they also fixed the amount of his remuneration. This remuneration, therefore, is the only one which so far has been made by the full authority of the Powers assembled in Paris.

As soon as these preliminary steps were accomplished, the Secretary-General set to work to collect the nucleus of his staff. At the moment, this appeared to be a matter of pressing necessity, for the general anticipation was that the Treaty of Versailles would be ratified soon after its signature, and as soon as the ratification took place the responsibilities of the League, and of its Secretariat, would immediately begin.

As you are all aware, these sanguine hopes were disappointed, and while the Treaty was signed on the 28th June, 1919, it was not ratified until the 10th January, 1920. For this reason, the foresight and energy of the Secretary-General led to the creation of a staff somewhat in anticipation of the duties which it had to perform. The blame, if blame there be, for this result falls evidently not upon him, but upon the complex conditions which produced a most regrettable delay.

[1] League of Nations, *Official Journal*, June, 1920, pp. 136-139.

By the terms of the Treaty, the duty of selecting the staff falls upon the Secretary-General, just as the duty of approving it falls upon the Council. In making his appointments, he had primarily to secure the best available men and women for the particular duties which had to be performed; but in doing so, it was necessary to have regard to the great importance of selecting the officials from various nations. Evidently, no one nation or group of nations ought to have a monopoly in providing the material for this international institution. I emphasise the word "International," because the members of the Secretariat once appointed are no longer the servants of the country of which they are citizens, but become for the time being the servants only of the League of Nations. Their duties are not national but international.

One further point of importance in this connection has to be noted. The International Labour Office is intimately connected by its constitution and origin with the League of Nations. Its Director and the Secretary-General are both alive to the immense importance of maintaining the closest coöperation between these two international organs and an agreement has been reached by which certain of the central services shall be common to both institutions.

I need hardly go into details as to the constitution of the Secretariat. So far, it has not been found necessary to create more than 10 separate sections, dealing with the various duties entrusted to the League by the Covenant, which forms part of the Treaty of Versailles; but there can be no doubt that, as our work increases, so the number of these sections will undergo corresponding augmentation.

The question of remuneration is one of considerable difficulty. This arises in part from the problems of exchange which are so deeply exercising the minds of all those who are concerned with International Finance, but it partly depends upon more permanent causes. The problem is to find a scale of pay appropriate to the members of an organisation who are drawn from different countries, between which there prevails a great difference in the ordinary scale of remuneration. It is clear on the one side that objection may be felt to paying any member of the staff a much higher salary than he would receive for work of equal difficulty and responsibility in his own country, and on the other hand, it would be most unfortunate if the scale of salaries were fixed at a rate which made it impossible to obtain first-class talent from those countries where the ordinary rate of remuneration is above the general average. While the final solution of this problem is not yet decided upon, and must receive further examination, I propose that the Council should approve the scale of salaries provisionally arranged by the Secretary-General until the confirmation of the budget by the Assembly.

One or two points of importance still remain to be mentioned.

I suggest that the Council should confirm the appointment of the members of the staff for five years. At the end of this period, a considerable number of them will probably be reappointed, and in many cases, no doubt, be promoted to higher posts. This seems to be necessary if only to secure smoothness and continuity of administration, but at the same time it is most desirable that at the end of the quinquennial period a certain infusion of new blood should be secured. This will obviate any danger of the Staff of the League of Nations becoming as it were a separate bureaucratic caste, divided by their duties from the life of any particular community. It will also give room for the citizens of nations not at present represented on the staff, to obtain in their turn the intimate knowledge of the working of the League which would be invaluable not only to the League as a whole but to the various nations which compose it.

I shall presently propose Resolutions covering, so far as is necessary, these various points, but I shall also propose two other Resolutions dealing with temporary or subsidiary matters which have a certain interest or importance. In the first of these Resolutions, I shall ask the Council to approve that the provisional seat of the Secretariat shall remain in London until the Assembly of the League comes to a decision as to the date of transfer. It seems quite clear that to remove the League from its provisional seat before the Assembly meets would be very detrimental to its efficiency. The amount of preliminary work which the meeting of the Assembly will throw upon it is very great, and it would be neither wise nor fair to add to these necessary labours the quite unnecessary exertions involved in a change of residence. This requires in itself a considerable organising effort, and if confusion is to be wholly avoided, it would certainly be wise to await the meeting of the Assembly and its decision as to the dates on which the movement of the Secretariat should take place.

My last Resolution touches what might at first sight seem to be only a personal issue, but I think it is of some importance. I shall propose that no member of the Secretariat, during his or her term of office, shall accept any honour or decoration except for services rendered prior to the appointment. The reasons for this proposal are fairly clear; they commend themselves, I know, to my colleagues, and I hope they will commend themselves to the public. The members of the staff carry out, as I have explained, not national but international duties. Nothing should be done to weaken the sense of their international allegiance; the acceptance of special marks of distinction or favour, either from their own or from any other country, militates in our view against the general spirit of the Covenant.

In accordance with these preliminary observations, I now beg to propose the four Resolutions whose general character and intentions I have endeavoured to explain.

RESOLUTIONS ADOPTED BY THE COUNCIL OF THE LEAGUE OF NATIONS

I.—That in accordance with Article 6 of the Covenant by which the secretaries and staff of the Secretariat shall be appointed by the Secretary-General with the approval of the Council, the Council approve the provisional appointments made by the Secretary-General acting under the authority of the Organisation Committee of the League of Nations. This approval is given for a period of five years, dating from the day of appointment if made after the coming into force of the Treaty, and for the other appointments from the date of the coming into force of the Treaty.

II.—That the salaries provisionally allotted by the Secretary-General be approved by the Council until the budget has been confirmed by the Assembly.

III.—That the continuance of the Secretariat in London, where the present provisional seat is established, be authorised, and that the date of a transfer to the permanent seat be decided by the Council after the Assembly has had the opportunity of discussion.

IV.—That no member of the International Secretariat during the term of his or her appointment accept any honour or decoration (except for services rendered prior to such appointment).

(d) *Registration of Treaties*[1]

THE REGISTRATION AND PUBLICATION OF TREATIES AS PRESCRIBED UNDER
ARTICLE 18 OF THE COVENANT OF THE LEAGUE OF NATIONS

Memorandum Approved by the Council of the League of Nations,
Meeting in Rome, on 19th May, 1920

1. One of the important innovations in International Law established by the Covenant of Members of the League of Nations consists in the registration and publication of every Treaty or International Engagement entered into by any Member of the League.

Article 18 of the Covenant of the League of Nations, by which this has been provided for, reads as follows:—

"Every Treaty or International Engagement entered into hereafter by any Member of the League shall be forthwith registered with the Secretariat and shall as soon as possible be published by it. No such Treaty or International Engagement shall be binding until so registered."

It is hardly necessary to dwell on the importance of an arrangement whereby publicity of Treaties and other International Engagements— and, as a preliminary thereto, their registration—will be secured.

[1] League of Nations, *Official Journal*, June, 1920, pp. 154-157.

Publicity has for a long time been considered as a source of moral strength in the administration of National Law. It should equally strengthen the laws and engagements which exist *between nations*. It will promote public control. It will awaken public interest. It will remove causes for distrust and conflict. Publicity alone will enable the League of Nations to extend a moral sanction to the contractual obligations of its Members. It will, moreover, contribute to the formation of a clear and indisputable system of International Law.

Since the satisfactory execution of the principles of Article 18 of the Covenant depends in the first place on the coöperation of the Governments of the Members of the League of Nations, the Secretary-General begs to present to the Members of the League in the following memorandum some suggestions whereby, in his opinion, the application of Article 18 may best be secured. The arrangements suggested have, of course, only a provisional character. Experience may, in the future, suggest modification and revision.

2. If the application of Article 18 is to conform to the best advantage with the objects of the League of Nations, an extensive interpretation of its provisions should be adopted. The details of its applications have accordingly been worked out with this principle in view.

The aim of the following suggestions is to establish as far as possible a complete and reliable survey of the whole system of Treaties and International Engagements entered into after the coming into force of the Covenant of the League.

3. The provision that "every Treaty or International Engagement shall be forthwith registered with the Secretariat" leads to the following conclusions as regards the material which requires registration.

This material comprises not only every formal Treaty of whatsoever character and every International Convention, but also any other International Engagement or act by which nations or their Governments intend to establish legal obligations between themselves and another State, Nation or Government.

Agreements regarding the revision or the prolongation of Treaties form separate international engagements; they also should be registered under Article 18.

It is proposed, moreover, that the denunciation of any Treaty or Agreement should, if only for the sake of completeness, be included in the scheme of registration.

4. Article 18 refers to Treaties, etc., entered into "hereafter." It is thereby understood that registration is necessary for *all* Treaties, etc., which become, or *have* become finally binding so far as the acts between the Parties *inter se* are concerned, after the date of the coming into force of the Covenant (January 10, 1920).

Treaties or Engagements which have finally come into force at an earlier date are not included; but the International Secretariat is authorised, if this appear desirable to the Contracting Parties, to extend the system of Treaty Registration so as to include Treaties and Engagements of an earlier date.

5. As no Treaties or International Engagements will be binding until registration with the International Secretariat has taken place, the latest date at which they should be presented for registration will be the date when, so far as the acts of the Parties *inter se* are concerned, they receive final binding force, and are intended to come into operation. It may prove convenient, however, for various reasons, for the Parties to present a Treaty or International Engagement for Registration as soon as the text has been finally decided upon, even if exchange of ratifications between them still has to take place at a later date. The Secretary-General will, of course, have to see that, if a Treaty or Engagement be published at this stage, it is made clear that the Parties have not yet finally entered into the Treaty or Engagement.

In the event of a Treaty or Engagement being presented for registration before it is finally entered into, the Parties will no doubt inform the Secretariat of the later act by which they definitely bring the Treaty into force.

6. It is suggested as a general principle that the Parties presenting a Treaty or Engagement for registration should do so by depositing a textual and complete copy thereof with all appurtenant declarations, protocols, ratifications, etc., at the Treaty Registration Bureau of the International Secretariat, accompanying it with an authentic statement that this text represents the full contents of the Treaty or Engagement into which the Parties intend to enter.

In case of necessity, the contents of a Treaty or Engagement can of course be transmitted to the International Secretariat by other means—for instance, by telegram—so long as it is established that the text is indisputably the one agreed upon between the Parties.

7. A certificate of Registration will be delivered to the Parties concerned, under the signature of the Secretary-General of the League of Nations, or of his Deputy. . . .

8. Treaties or International Engagements may be presented for Registration by one Party only, either in the name of all the Parties at the same time, or of that Party alone, as long as it is established that the text is that which has been agreed upon between the Parties.

9. Publication of a Treaty or Engagement registered with the Secretariat will be secured automatically and as soon as possible, by its inclusion in the Treaty Part of the League of Nations Journal. Copies of this Journal will be regularly forwarded to the Governments of all States Members of the League.

It is intended to give that part of the Journal in which the publication of Treaties and Engagements is effected a special form, convenient for placing separately in Law Libraries and in private studies.

The separate index for this Treaty Part of the League of Nations Journal will be published at regular intervals.

10. The Secretary-General of the League proposes to organise his system of Registration in the following manner, hoping that it may prove convenient alike to the Parties and to all those interested in the contents of Treaties and the relevant details.

A Register will be kept in chronological order, stating, with regard to each Treaty or other Engagement or International Act, the Parties between which it has been concluded, the title (short title if any), the date of signature, ratification and presentation for registration, and finally, the number under which it has been registered.

The actual texts presented to the Secretariat will be kept as an annex to this Register, each text being marked *ne varietur* by the Secretary-General or his Deputy.

Apart from the chronological Register, a second Register will be kept which will form to some extent an *état civil* of all Treaties and Engagements concerned. For every Treaty or Engagement a special page will be set apart as in a ledger, where all the data concerning it will be noted—including not only the Parties' signatures and ratifications, but also later adhesions, denunciations, etc. Notes relative to preparatory matter, discussions, and internal legislation arising out of the Treaties, etc., may also be added.

The Secretariat may on occasion be requested to deliver to States, Courts of Justice or private persons interested, certified extracts from this Register, attesting the existence and the status of International Treaties and Engagements, the moment of their coming into force, their ratification, their denunciations, the reservations entered in respect of them, etc., etc. The Secretary-General intends to make the Treaty Registration Office available for this purpose, but no legal liability for the contents of such extracts can be assumed by the Secretariat.

A general Index will be made to the Collection of Treaties and Engagements. It will be arranged in a way convenient for consultation.

11. The Treaty Registers of the International Secretariat will, moreover, include a special series of those Treaties and Conventions which, by some special provision or with some special object in view, are placed under the care of the Secretary-General. An instance of such a provision will be found in Article 405 in the Treaty of Versailles, according to which Draft Labour Conventions will be deposited with the Secretariat. The same applied to Labour Recommendations.

To these may be added other Draft Conventions and Recommendations which may be made by analogous organisations under the League of Nations.

12. It should be noted that by the provisions of Article 18 not only Treaties between Members of the League of Nations have to be registered, but also Treaties or Engagements entered into by a Member of the League with a State which has not yet been admitted into the League.

13. In connection with this last point, it has been suggested that the system of Registration of Treaties by the Secretariat of the League of Nations should from the beginning be so extended as to admit of the Registration of Treaties, etc., made by and between States or Communities that have not yet been admitted as Members of the League of Nations. This would serve to complete the Registration of Treaties and the public collection of Treaties which will be formed by the Treaty Part of the League of Nations Journal. The Secretary-General therefore proposes, although the Registration will be for this part absolutely voluntary, to accept applications for the Registration of Treaties, etc., even if none of the Parties is at the time a Member of the League of Nations.

The Secretary-General of the League of Nations trusts that experience may show that the system of Registration and Publication of Treaties on the lines suggested in this Memorandum will work satisfactorily. He will be glad to receive suggestions for possible modifications of the present scheme.

(e) *League of Nations Assembly*[1]

MEETING OF THE ASSEMBLY

Report presented by the Greek Representative, M. Coromilas

Two classes of States have the right of entering the League of Nations as original Members: first, those who are signatories of the Treaty of Versailles; second, those who are invited to notify their accession to the Covenant within two months from the coming into force of the Treaty.

The latter class includes the 13 most important countries which, during the war, remained neutral. By the 10th March last all these, without exception, had made a declaration of adhesion to the League. Of the signatory States, by far the greater number have ratified the Covenant. At the present moment, therefore, the following thirty-seven countries and Dominions are Members of the League of Nations:—

Argentine Republic	Chile	Netherlands
Belgium	Colombia	Norway
Bolivia	Czecho-Slovakia	Panama
Brazil	Denmark	Paraguay
British Empire	France	Persia
Canada	Greece	Peru
Australia	Guatemala	Poland
South Africa	Italy	Portugal
New Zealand	Japan	Roumania
India	Liberia	Salvador

[1] League of Nations, *Official Journal*, June, 1920, pp. 125-127.

Serb-Croat-Slovene	Spain	Uruguay
State	Sweden	Venezuela
Siam	Switzerland	

Under Article 2 of the Covenant, the action of the League is effected through the instrumentality of an Assembly and a Council, with a Permanent Secretariat.

The Permanent Secretariat and, shortly afterwards, the Council began their work, and both have been for several months in full operation; the Council has decided many questions which have been submitted to it, and has already taken the preliminary steps in the establishment of certain very important organisations referred to in the Covenant and the Treaty of Versailles, or of organisations which are indispensable to their execution. In order that the work of the League may develop to the maximum of power and usefulness, it remains for the Assembly of States, which is its most comprehensive organ, to be summoned.

The Council of the League of Nations fully appreciates how essential it is that all Members of the League should, in accordance with the terms of the Covenant, share in its work; and has, therefore, in the present Meeting, considered the circumstances in which the Assembly could begin its work. The Council does not wish to delay the meeting of the Assembly for a day longer than is strictly necessary. Those Members who are not represented on the Council rightly desire to take a full share in the work of the League, and this work can only increase in value and importance by the active coöperation of all. Moreover, a certain number of new States have requested admission, and as to this the Assembly alone can decide.

Now that the Council has prepared the way and taken the necessary preliminary measures in order to enable the Assembly to deal usefully with several questions of the very greatest importance—such as the Permanent Court of International Justice, the Permanent Health Organisation, the General Conference on Communications and Transit —the date of the meeting of the Assembly can be fixed. And this date should be fixed so that the Governments of States, Members of the League, may have time to receive and consider all documents and all information bearing on the questions which will be discussed at the Assembly, and so that their Delegates may have sufficient time to reach the meeting place which is chosen.

In view of the distance of certain States, the Council thinks that the most suitable date would be the first fortnight in November, and has, therefore, despatched to President Wilson—whose privilege it is under Article V of the Covenant, to convene the first meeting of the Assembly —a telegram asking him if he would be prepared to summon it for this date; the meeting to be held in some European town, which will ultimately be chosen, upon the Council's proposal, and after a further exchange of views.

(f) *Relations Between Technical Organisations and the Council and Assembly of the League*[1]

Resolution Adopted by the Council of the League of Nations.

With a view to defining the relations between the technical organisations of the League of Nations and the Council and the Assembly of the League, the Council agrees to the following Resolution, subject to the approval of the Assembly. The Resolution will be forwarded to the secretariat of all technical organisations, and those secretariats must in all cases be administered by the Secretary-General of the League.

The technical organisations of the League now in process of formation are established for the purpose of facilitating the task of the Assembly and the Council by the setting up of technical sections on the one hand and on the other to assist the Members of the League, by establishing direct contact between their technical representatives in the various spheres, to fulfil their international duties.

With this double object, they must keep enough independence and flexibility to make them effectively useful to the Members of the League, and yet they must remain under the control of the responsible organisations which conduct the general business of the League, with a view to verifying whether the proposals are in conformity with the principles and spirit of the Covenant, in accordance with Articles 19 and 20.

The two following principles will serve as a guide:

(a) *The interior working of the various organisations should be independent.*

They will prepare their own agenda, and communicate it to the Council of the League before discussion thereon takes place.

(b) *Their relations with the Members of the League should be under control.*

Before any communication of the results or proposals of the technical organisations is made to the Members, and before any action concerning a Member is taken, the Council of the League must be immediately informed in order that they may be able to exercise their power of control, if necessary.

In this case, the Council may decide that the communication or action in question shall be postponed and request the technical organisation concerned either to withdraw the question from its agenda or to submit it to further consideration.

The technical organisation may, however, request that the decision taken by the Council shall be discussed at the next meeting of the Assembly.

The Assembly of the League should be informed of all questions

---

[1] League of Nations, *Official Journal*, June, 1920, pp. 151-152.

dealt with in the interval between its meetings by the Council, in the exercise of its power of control defined above. It may either be informed of such questions by the Council on its own initiative, or on the proposal of any one of its Members, or at the request of one of the technical organisations of the League.

(g) World Court[1]

Report on the Organisation of a Permanent Court of International Justice

M. Bourgeois:

The League of Nations, like a group of individuals, can only exist if the rights of each member are scrupulously respected. Its aim is to establish a reign of Justice in a world which has been convulsed by the most murderous of wars; the League must be founded on Justice.

If Justice is to reign, it must have a permanent instrument to its hand—it must take some tangible form which will make its existence felt among the peoples and give the support of its powerful, impartial and supreme authority to those whose weakness is only too often undefended.

In each State private individuals know where to find judges to whom they can submit their grievances, and who will settle justly the questions on which there is conflict. In addition to *national* Courts of Law, whose duty it is to administer the laws of each State within its territorial limits, there is room for an *international tribunal* entrusted with the important task of administering *international law* and enforcing among the nations the *cuique suum* which is the law which governs human intercourse. This international tribunal will take the form of a Permanent Court of International Justice, the early establishment of which is provided for in the Covenant of the League of Nations, though the preparations for the Court are left to the Council of the League.

"The Council," runs Article 14 of the Covenant, "shall formulate and submit to the members of the League plans for the establishment of a Permanent Court of International Justice. This Court shall be competent to hear and determine any dispute of an international character which the parties thereto submit to it. The Court may also give an advisory opinion upon any dispute or question referred to it by the Council or by the Assembly."

This court of justice which is about to be established, whose general jurisdiction has thus been briefly described, has already been invested with certain definite powers by the Peace Treaty of Versailles and the other Treaties modelled upon it. For instance, Articles 336, 337 and 386 of the Treaty of Versailles entrust to the tribunal set up by the League of Nations the investigation and solution of various problems concerning international waterways. Articles 415 to 420 and

---

[1] League of Nations, *Official Journal*, March, 1920, pp. 33-38.

423 on the organisation of labour bring within the jurisdiction of the Court a matter which is still more important.

In order to give full effect to these stipulations, and to curtail the temporary measures which are considered to be necessary (see Articles 425 and 426), it is essential that consideration shall be given without delay to the formation of the Permanent Court of International Justice. For this reason the Council has been called upon to study this problem at its meeting today.

The idea of entrusting to a supreme tribunal the peaceable settlement of disputes between nations and between governments is of the greatest antiquity. But until now this tribunal has engaged only in arbitration, which alone seems consistent with the sovereignty of States. In early days princes and towns in France and Italy submitted their differences to trusted arbitrators whose decisions they accepted in advance.

In the Middle Ages, not to mention the Greek Amphictyonic Councils and the Courts of Ancient Rome, interesting examples of international arbitration could be found. Kings of France, Saint Louis amongst them, Popes, jurists of the School of Bologna, were often chosen as arbitrators in the Courts of that period.

In the last half-century particularly arbitration achieved its most valuable conquests. The settlement by arbitration at Geneva in 1872 of the dispute between Great Britain and the United States in the Alabama affair is within the memory of many of us; and subsequent settlements between 1872 and 1899 have happily put an end to dangerous disagreements which appeared incapable of solution but by the force of arms.

While becoming more and more frequent, arbitration was still only an incident in the life of nations; it knew no law but the convenience of States which, sure of their right or distrustful of their military strength, would consent to accept its verdict. Free as they were to accept or refuse the arbitrator's services, wholly free to select who those arbitrators should be, the Powers were no less free to settle the order of procedure suitable for the settlement of their disputes; there were times, indeed, when they found this liberty truly embarrassing.

The appointment of one or of several arbitrators, the constitution of a court of arbitration, the drawing up of the procedure to be followed in any particular suit, involved delicate negotiations and raised difficulties before which the States at variance often recoiled: a tendency which threatened to discredit the very principle of arbitration.

The Institute of International Law in 1874 and 1875 prepared draft rules of procedure for arbitration courts. The important conventions on the peaceable settlement of international disputes signed at The Hague in 1899 and again in 1907, went further. Though they left the disputing parties entirely free to apply, as before, to arbitrators of their own selection (Convention of 1899, Article 21; Convention of 1907, Article 42), they put at their disposal an organized body of arbitrators ready to take up their duties and, according to a procedure carefully laid down beforehand, to deal with grievances submitted to them. This is the Permanent Court of Arbitration, with its seat at The Hague. Article 20 of the Convention of 1899, reproduced in Article 41 in the Convention of 1907, defines clearly the part assigned to the new tribunal: "In order to facilitate *immediate* appeal to arbitration for international disputes which diplomacy has failed to settle, the signatory Powers undertake to set up a Permanent Court of Arbitration, available at all times and operating, unless otherwise desired by the contending parties, according to the rules of procedure in the present Convention."

The Permanent Court of The Hague does not consist of a fixed number of magistrates invested with public duties, sitting periodically, if not continuously, waiting for litigants, and always ready, as national courts are, to decide disputes submitted to them. As a matter of fact, the only permanent feature of the Court is the International Office, which acts as its registry and as the necessary channel for all communications concerning its meetings and general work.

There is also a governing body composed of diplomatic representatives of the contracting Powers, accredited to The Hague, and presided over by the Minister of Foreign Affairs of the Netherlands. It is the duty of this Council to draw up the rules necessary to ensure the satisfactory working of the Court of Arbitration, and the International Office is placed under its direction and control. The Court, properly so called, consists of a panel or list of men of the highest moral standing—not more than four from each State—from amongst whom the contending parties are permitted to make their own free choice of the members of the tribunal to give judgment in their disputes, without the slightest obligation to limit their selection in any way to the official arbitrators proposed to them.

The Court of The Hague is not, therefore, really a permanent tribunal and has not the special character of a Court of Justice. It has, nevertheless, made considerable progress on the previous system of arbitration.

No one would wish to belittle a system of international justice which has already brilliantly justified its existence, nor restrict the field of arbitration, and close the doors of the Court of The Hague. But as early as 1907 the attention of the Peace Conference was drawn to the advisability of creating a really Permanent Tribunal, working either as a part of the Court already set up at The Hague, or side by side with it, with the object of giving to the future decisions of international judges the unity and the stability which the awards of arbitrators had hitherto lacked. The United States suggested that a Court should be set up entirely separate from that of 1899, sitting in regular and continuous session. This scheme, which was adopted by the conference, may be thus briefly described:—

The Court of Justice consists of a *small number* of judges and deputy-judges nominated for twelve years; they shall be eminent lawyers of the highest reputation, of recognised authority on questions of international law. They will be required to take an oath or make a solemn declaration, and will receive remuneration for their services. The Court shall have its seat at The Hague and will meet once a year. A delegation of three judges, appointed annually by the Court, will deal with urgent matters requiring prompt settlement, and will, if necessary, conduct inquiries. Further, the scheme of 1907 leaves a purely optional authority to the Court for whose organisation it is responsible: it maintains, in its general outline, the procedure fixed in 1899 for the arbitration tribunals, but it is careful to lay down that the decisions of the new tribunal shall be based on the evidence of reason.

On all these points agreement was easy; it was not so, however, when it became necessary to decide how the members of the Court should be appointed. The number of judges had necessarily to be restricted, and there could be no question of giving a representative to each of the forty-four States which had taken part in the work of the conference. How was a choice to be made between Powers of equal sovereignty, equally jealous of their prerogatives? Should the selected judges, to the number of, say, fifteen or seventeen, be chosen for their ability and without distinction of nationality by the General Assembly of the Court of Arbitration or by the representatives of the States? Should they be drawn by lot for each case from amongst representatives nominated by each of the forty-four States invited to the conference? Would a rotation-roll be possible, as was proposed by the United States and decided for the International Prize Court, each of the Great Powers to have a permanent judge, whilst the others would have a judge only for a number of years commensurate with their importance? On this question, which threatened the very principle of the legal equality of nations, the conference could arrive at no definite conclusion: it therefore gave up the idea of organising the Court itself, the principle of which it approved, and contented itself with inserting in the final report of its labours a hope expressed in these words: "The conference recommends to the Signatory Powers the adoption of the annexed convention and scheme for the establishment of a Court of Justice by Arbitration and for its putting into force as soon as an agreement has been reached on the nomination of judges and the constitution of the Court."

It rests with the League of Nations, the outcome of the War of Nations, to realise today this hope which the Institute of International

Law expressed at its meeting at Christiania in 1912. Moreover, circumstances are singularly favourable for its immediate realisation. From all parts of the devastated and tormented world rises a cry for justice. The military and moral unity which for five years has held the free peoples together, and concentrated their efforts in the defence of the right, must survive with our victory; it can find no nobler expression nor a more splendid symbol than the establishment of a *Permanent Court of International Justice.* This instrument of the League of Nations, this Court, however composed, will be free from all national preoccupations, particularly the exercise of its sovereign jurisdiction; and the intervention of the Council or even of the Assembly, in the choice of its members will be calculated to remove all anxieties and guarantee against all attack the guardian principle of the equality of nations. How is this problem to be solved? How shall the Permanent Court be organised? How shall its members be nominated? In what country, in what city, shall this new tribunal have its seat? Is it possible to specify now the rule of procedure to be followed in the investigation and trial of the cases to be brought before it, or shall this duty be left to the Court itself? Such, amongst many others, are the principal problems set before us by the mandate which Article 14 of the Covenant of the League of Nations has entrusted to us. It seems that the study of them may usefully be entrusted to a commission of legal experts, whose conclusions will be brought up and discussed at one of our next meetings. The duty assigned to our collaborators will be facilitated by the extensive researches initiated in various countries by the unfinished work of The Hague. The reports at the Conference to which the problems of the composition and procedure of the Permanent Court often gave rise in 1907 will form the natural point of departure for their enquiry. This enquiry will lead them to prepare a scheme designated to satisfy absolute justice, to conciliate the legitimate interests of nations, to crown in the happiest manner possible the evolution of centuries whose history we have related. . . . [Here follows a list of twelve names of men proposed as justices for the Permanent Court.]

Mr. Balfour: Before I come to the next resolution let me just say that it will not have escaped the notice of anybody who has heard the list that in it is included the distinguished name of Mr. Root, the well-known American lawyer. It may be that Mr. Root for one reason or another will not find it possible immediately to accept, but the Council desires formally to put on record that Mr. Root will always be welcome at whatever stage of our proceedings he feels it within his power to add to our deliberations the great weight of his learning and his name.

I ought to make our proceedings in this very important matter quite clear, and I think I should read the letter of instructions which the Council proposes to send to each of the distinguished jurists whose names you have heard:—

"Sir,—I am instructed by the Council of the League of Nations to inform you that it has been decided to invite certain distinguished international lawyers to form themselves into a Committee, to be convened at an early date, to prepare plans for the establishment of the Permanent Court of International Justice and to ask you to be a member thereof. The Article of the Covenant of the League of Nations under which the Committee is to be established is as follows:—

I will not read the Article but it will appear in the letter.

"The duties which will fall to the Court will cover a wide sphere, and will be of the very highest importance. The Council in no way underrates the sacrifice which it asks you to make in devoting a period of what will no doubt be arduous labour to helping to plan and create it; nor does it fail to realise that the work which it is asking you to interrupt is itself of very great importance. But the Court is a most essential part of the Organization of the League of Nations. If it is established on sound and statesmanlike principles, it can contribute perhaps more than any other single institution to maintain the peace of the world and the supremacy of right amongst the nations. It must be established as soon as possible after the coming into effect of the Covenant; and it is hoped that this Committee may find it possible to present its report to the Council of the League in sufficient time for that body to be able to submit it to an early meeting of the Assembly. It is understood that the question of a Permanent Court of International Justice has been carefully examined by certain of the countries named in the Annex to the Covenant, some of which have already forwarded plans for the constitution of the Court to the Secretary General. It is therefore suggested that the Committee should consider these plans and should also invite the other countries named in the Annex to forward any proposals they may have prepared."

Now comes a paragraph which is of special importance and to which I hope due attention will be paid:—

"You are no doubt aware that both the Austrian and the German Governments have made certain proposals for the composition of the Court, and that the Allied and Associated Governments have promised that these proposals would be submitted for detailed consideration to the Council of the League of Nations when it prepares a plan for the establishment of a Permanent Court in accordance with Article 14 of the Covenant. The Council suggests, therefore, that the Committee of which you are invited to be a member should not overlook these assurances in preparing plans for the establishment of the Permanent Court of International Justice. Invitations to join the Committee are also being sent to the following gentlemen," and so on.

.   .   .   .

(h) *Limitation of Armaments*[1]

PERMANENT ADVISORY ARMAMENTS COMMISSION DEALING WITH
MILITARY, NAVAL AND AIR QUESTIONS

Report presented by the French Representative, M. Léon Bourgeois

The Council of the League of Nations, at its meetings held in Paris
on 10th and 12th April, 1920, decided to place on the agenda of its
Rome meeting the Constitution of the Permanent Commission which,
under Article 9 of the Covenant, is to advise the Council on the execution of the provisions of Articles 1 and 8 and on military, naval and
air questions generally.

The text of Articles 1 and 8 need not be quoted here.

The stipulations of these two articles deal with two entirely different
matters. Article 1 defines the regulations which must be accepted by
States, not included in the list of original Members of the League of
Nations, which are seeking admission to the League. Article 8 defines
the general obligations accepted by the original Members of the
League which have agreed to the Covenant.

Article 1 deals with one particular question. The States referred to
in that article, several of which have already transmitted to the
Secretary-General their request for admission to the League, "shall
accept, provisionally, such regulations as may be prescribed by the
League in regard to its military, naval and air forces."

The framing of these regulations is our urgent duty and their study
should be the first and immediate task of the Commission referred to
in Article 9 of the Covenant.

In addition to this special and immediate work, the Commission is
entrusted with duties of a general kind; that is, the execution of
Article 8 of the Covenant.

Under this Article the Members of the League "recognise that the
maintenance of peace requires the reduction of national armaments to
the lowest point consistent with national safety and the enforcement
by common action of international obligations."

Under paragraph 4, the States Members of the League agree to
interchange full and frank information as to the scale of their armaments, their military, naval and air programmes, and the condition of
such of their industries as are adaptable to warlike purposes.

By paragraph 2, the Council undertakes to formulate plans for the
reduction of armaments and to advise on the measures to be taken in
order to limit the manufacture, by private enterprise, of munitions and
implements of war.

The Council of the League has no more important duty than that

[1] League of Nations, *Official Journal*, June, 1920, pp. 131-136.

defined in Article 8 of the Treaty, namely, to constitute at the earliest possible moment the Permanent Commission, whose investigations will enable the Council to determine the military, naval and air situation in the various States, Members of the League. No action of the League could be of greater value for the maintenance of peace; no decision of the Council in other matters could be really effective if it did not carry out these duties, with the execution of which it has been expressly entrusted.

It is this question, above all others, which interests public opinion. To postpone the discussion of so important a problem would be to disappoint the most confident hopes of the peoples of the world.

We are fully aware of the difficulties with which this Commission will be faced from the outset. It will be difficult to draw up a practical scheme and to determine the military situation of the world as long as the conditions of the Treaty of Peace, regarding the disarmament of the Central Empires, have not been fulfilled. The troubled condition of Eastern Europe makes the situation still more obscure. Our present duty, however, is not to take final decisions, but to prepare the work and to outline the future policy of the Council. The technical work of the Permanent Commission should begin at once in order to enable the Council to take the final decision when part of the stipulations of the Treaty of Peace have been carried out and when the conditions of Europe will be such as to make it possible to discover a solution of the problems.

We should therefore determine, at this meeting, the organisation of the Permanent Commission, whose technical advice will enable us to lay down the general plan with which we are entrusted.

It must be noted, moreover, that apart from the stipulations of Article 8, the Council of the League of Nations may need the advice of the Permanent Commission regarding the carrying out of other terms of the Covenant and of the Treaty of Peace.

Article 16 stipulates that if any State Member of the League disregards its Covenants under Article 12, 13, or 15, it shall be the duty of the Council to "recommend to the several Governments concerned what effective military, naval or air force the Members of the League shall severally contribute to the armed forces to be used to protect the Covenants of the League."

Moreover, Article 23, paragraph (d), entrusts the League "with the general supervision of the trade in arms and ammunition with the countries in which the control of this traffic is necessary in the common interest."

Attention should be called to the Convention regarding the trade in arms and ammunition which was signed on 10th September, 1919, by the Allied and Associated Powers, other Powers being invited to adhere thereto. The object the Signatory Powers had in view was to establish a system of restriction and, in some cases even, of prohibition of the export of arms. They instituted a Central International Organ which is placed under the authority of the League of Nations. This office shall collect information and statistics on the quantity and destination of exported arms and ammunition. Although this Convention has not yet been ratified by the Signatory Powers, it is to be observed that the Signatory Governments declared in the final Protocol that: "It would be contrary to the intentions of the Signatory Powers and to the spirit of the Convention should one of the Signatory Powers take measures inconsistent with the terms of the Convention pending its coming into force."

In view of the carrying out of Article 23 (d) of the Covenant and of the subsequent ratification of the Convention, it would seem necessary immediately to entrust the Permanent Commission with obtaining from the Governments Signatories to the Convention, and from the States Members of the League of Nations, all relevant information on the export of and trade in arms and ammunition, thus enabling the Commission, after due consideration, to submit recommendations to the Council for the establishment of a central international office for the trade in arms and ammunition.

Further, it must be remembered that, under Article 213 of the Treaty, Germany has undertaken to give every facility for any investigation which the Council of the League of Nations, acting if need be, by majority, may consider necessary, with regard to carrying out the Military Regulations imposed by the Treaty.

Here again it is important that the technical commission should be organised beforehand so as to be able to intervene effectively should it be considered necessary to do so.

We have outlined the duties with which the Permanent Commission is to be entrusted under Article 9. No rule is laid down in the Covenant as regards the constitution of the Commission, but due consideration of the nature of its task will make it possible to determine the general outline of the plan according to which it should be constituted and carry out its duties.

1. The Commission should consist of national representatives, responsible to their respective Governments and General Staffs—that is to say, they shall be in a position to present the true wishes and plans of their respective nations at the discussions and enquiries of the Commission. If constituted in this manner, the Permanent Commission will be a living organisation well-informed and qualified, on the one hand, to prepare the way for the decisions of the Council of the League, without giving offence to the Governments concerned, and on the other hand, to prepare the way for the decisions of those Governments in accordance with the spirit of the League.

2. The Commission should be permanent. Its members should therefore not be too numerous. It is essential, however, that all the States Members of the Council shall be represented on it from the beginning, pending the final decision of the Assembly on this question.

3. It should be clearly understood, however, that other nations will

be invited to send representatives to the Conference when questions which interest them directly are under discussion.

4. As regards the number of members of each national delegation, it must be remembered that it will have to be capable of dealing with naval, military or air problems alike.

This makes it essential to set up, in the Commission, three separate sections; and each State should therefore be entitled to send three, at most, delegates, one of whom is competent to deal with each of these three special kinds of problem. The voting power, in the Commission, of each delegation would, of course, remain the same whatever the number of delegates.

5. The secretariat of the Armaments Commission shall be organised by the Secretariat-General in accordance with the rule which must govern all technical organisations of the League in order to ensure uniformity of action.

If these general principles are adopted, the following resolutions may be submitted to the Council:—

RESOLUTIONS ADOPTED BY THE COUNCIL OF THE LEAGUE OF NATIONS MEETING IN ROME, ON 19TH MAY, 1920

Article 1.—The Commission prescribed by Article 9 of the Covenant shall be entitled: "The Permanent Advisory Commission for Military, Naval and Air Questions." The Commission shall be formed of representatives from each nation represented on the Council of the League as follows:—

> 1 military representative,
> 1 naval representative,
> 1 air representative.

The same representative may combine the duties of more than one of the above, if his Government so desires.

Article 2.—Any other States which are Members of the League may be invited to send a similar number of representatives to sit on the Commission temporarily when a question directly affecting them is under discussion.

Article 3.—Whatever the number of representatives from any nation attending the Meetings of the Commission, or of the Sub-Commissions referred to in Article 6, no national delegation shall be allowed more than one vote.

Article 4.—The representatives laid down in Article 1 may be joined by such number of officers as may be necessary according to circumstances, or may call in any "Service" or civil experts whose experience may be useful. In order, however, to facilitate the accommodation of the Commission, the Governments concerned are recommended not to attach more than two officers for each of the Sub-Commissions laid down in Article 6 as permanent assistants of the above-mentioned representatives.

Article 5.—The representatives of each State, together with the officers permanently attached, shall constitute the "national delegation" of each State. This delegation shall be placed at the disposal of the Council of the League in order to give advice as laid down in Article 9 of the Covenant, and in accordance with the procedure given below.

The ordinary pay and allowances of the officers of the Commission will be furnished by their respective Governments.

Article 6.—The Commission shall be divided into three Sub-Commissions, entitled:

The Military Sub-Commission
The Naval Sub-Commission
The Air Sub-Commission.

Article 7.—Each Sub-Commission shall nominate a Chairman for six months in the alphabetical order following that of the Treaty of Versailles.

When a meeting of the Commission is necessary, the three Chairmen of the Sub-Commissions shall select one of their number to preside at the sitting (or sittings) at which any particular question is to be discussed.

Article 8.—Representatives of a State which has been newly admitted to the Council of the League shall not be called to the chairmanship of the Commission or Sub-Commissions before six months have elapsed from the date of admission.

Article 9.—The Commission or Sub-Commissions shall meet on the demand either of the Council of the League or of one of their own members.

Article 10.—In principle, reports of the Sub-Commissions shall be forwarded to the Council by the full Commission with its remarks. The Council or the full Commission may, however, decide that a question raised by either, respectively, is of a purely technical nature, and within the competence of one Sub-Commission only. In such case, the report of the Sub-Commission shall be addressed to the Council direct.

Article 11.—Representatives who are absent, or who are prevented from attending, may depute an assistant to represent them.

Article 12.—The secretarial work of the Commission shall be carried out by three technical officers (an army officer for the Military Sub-Commission, a naval officer for the Naval Sub-Commission, an air officer for the Air Sub-Commission). These officers shall be nominated by the Secretary-General and placed by him at the disposal of the three Sub-Commissions. Together, these officers will form the secretariat of the whole Commission.

The Secretaries shall, as a rule, be appointed for one year, and may, at the wish of a Sub-Commission, be continued in their appointments for periods of six months, provided that the total duration of such an appointment shall not exceed three years.

The remuneration of the Secretariat and all expenses connected with it shall be met by the League of Nations.

NOTE.—In order to promote coöperation and to facilitate the exchange of information as laid down in Article 8 of the Covenant of the League, it is desirable that the technical experts (military, naval and air) should be accommodated in the same building or in buildings situated as closely as possible to each other.

The Council of the League of Nations instructs the Permanent Advisory Commission for Military, Naval and Air Questions to begin immediately the study of such technical questions as are required for the execution of Articles 1 and 8 of the Covenant, and in particular:—
(1) To consider and draft regulations in accordance with Article 1 of the Covenant in regard to the military, naval and air forces and armaments of the following States, which have applied for admission to the League:—

> Esthonian Republic,
> Republic of Georgia,
> Iceland,
> Luxemburg,
> Republic of San Marino,
> Ukrainian Republic,

and to forward a report to the Council on this subject.
(2) To request the Governments signatories of the Arms Traffic Convention of 10th September, 1919, and other States Members of the League, to furnish all necessary information regarding the export of arms and munitions, in accordance with the principles laid down in Article 23, paragraph (d), of the Arms Traffic Convention, including the final Protocol, and to submit to the Council proposals for the formation of a Central International Office.

(i) The International Labor Office

(1) Extract from an address by Lord Curzon delivered before the first meeting of the Council of the League of Nations, Paris, January 16, 1920.[1]

The League is an association of sovereign States whose purpose it is to reconcile divergent interests and to promote international coöperation in questions which affect—or may affect—the world at large. How valuable such international coöperation can be is proved by the Labour Conference which took place recently at Washington [October 29 to November 29, 1919].

---

[1] League of Nations, *Official Journal,* February, 1920, p. 21.

Here, for the first time, an attempt was made to bring together, under the auspices of the League of Nations, representatives of Governments, of employers, and of Labour. In spite of many adverse circumstances, delegates attended from thirty-nine nations in every part of the world, and the result has been a great advance towards the general betterment of world labour conditions. Employers and Labour, brought face to face, found that there was a large extent of common ground on which they could meet. Instead of the violent conflict of class interests, which was predicted by some, agreement was reached on many questions, such as that of the eight-hour day, and the forty-eight-hour week, which had led to bitter disputes in the past. In a single month there were drafted and passed, in most cases with a full measure of agreement, six conventions and six recommendations. There is every hope that within twelve months, the provisions of these instruments will be placed on the statute-books of most, if not all, of the countries concerned.[1] If this hope is fulfilled, there will have been achieved in one year, through the machinery created by the Treaty of Versailles, an advance exceeding the results of the entire work of the previous quarter of a century in the field of international action in industrial questions.

The success of the Labour Conference is of good augury for the future of the League of Nations, and in particular it has demonstrated the use and the power of public debate in one field of international action. The peoples of all countries have now learnt that foreign affairs are their vital concern, and they are demanding, with ever-increasing insistence, that international obligations shall not be incurred without their knowledge and behind their backs. Their eyes have been opened to the necessity for coöperation between all nations, but they ask that it shall be open coöperation. . . .

(2) Report of the Twelfth Session of the International Labor Conference. 1929.[2]

Fifty of the fifty-five States Members of the International Labour Organisation were represented at the Twelfth Session of the International Labour Conference, which took place at Geneva from 30 May until 21 June. This is the largest number of States which have yet been represented at the Conference. For the first time, China sent a complete delegation. There was also a complete delegation from Brazil, which, although it is no longer a Member of the League of Nations, thus once more manifested its desire to maintain its collaboration with the International Labour Organization. Turkey,

---

[1] [The 1925 *Year Book* of the League of Nations, World Peace Foundation Pamphlet, Vol. VIII, Nos. 8-9 lists the adoptions.]

[2] *Monthly Summary of the International Labour Organisation*, July, 1929, pp. 35-39. (Published by the International Labour Office.)

though not a Member of the Organisation, once more sent an observer this year.

The importance of the questions which the Conference had before it amply justified the interest manifested by the various States Members. As Mr. Arthur Fontaine, Chairman of the Governing Body, pointed out: "All the questions which were discussed, numerous and difficult as they were, have been settled in a definite way. This will facilitate the work of the Governing Body as well as that of future Conferences, and will expedite the progress of the social reforms which the workers are awaiting." The Twelfth Session may thus be regarded as having been particularly successful.

The President of the Conference was Dr. Heinrich Brauns, German Government Delegate, and former German Minister of Labour. The Vice-Presidents were Mr. Duzmans, Government Delegate of Latvia; Mr. Čurčin, Employers' Delegate of the Serb-Croat-Slovene Kingdom; and Mr. Thorberg, Workers' Delegate of Sweden.

It will be remembered that there were four items on the agenda:

(1) Prevention of industrial accidents.
(2) Protection against accidents of workers engaged in loading or unloading ships.
(3) Forced labour.
(4) Hours of work of salaried employees.

The Conference was only asked to take final decisions on the first two questions, which had previously been considered at last year's Session. The third and fourth questions came up for preliminary consideration this year under the double discussion procedure which is followed by the Conference.

The decisions arrived at may be summarised as follows:

Prevention of Industrial Accidents

The Conference adopted four decisions on this subject, which relates to the organisation of what Mr. Albert Thomas calls "the international Red Cross on the battlefield of labour": (1) a Recommendation concerning general principles for the prevention of industrial accidents; (2) a Draft Convention concerning the marking of the weight on heavy packages transported by vessels; (3) a Recommendation concerning responsibility for the protection of power-driven machinery; (4) a Resolution concerning industrial accident statistics.

The general Recommendation concerning the prevention of accidents was adopted by 100 votes to 12. It includes four parts. The first part relates to the problem of enquiry into the causes of accidents and the methods of preventing them. The second deals with the part to be played by the State, the employers and the workers in accident prevention, and gives definite indications as to the methods which may be adopted for that purpose. The third relates principally to the legal obligations imposed on employers and workers for the purpose of accident prevention. It suggests that before Governments issue regulations for any particular industry, opportunity should be given to the representative organisations of employers and workers in the industry to submit their views. The Recommendation suggests by way of example that workers should take part in the inspection of factories. The fourth part contains various suggestions relating to insurance companies as a factor in accident prevention.

The Draft Convention concerning the marking of the weight on heavy packages transported by vessel was adopted by 98 votes to 24. Its purpose is to protect workers against certain kinds of accidents which are particularly frequent. When the weight is not marked on packages or heavy objects which it is necessary to load or unload by mechanical means, it may happen that the cranes which are used have not been constructed to bear so heavy a load, and may therefore break, thus causing serious accidents. The Draft Convention, which applies both to maritime and inland navigation, accordingly lays down the principle that packages which are to be transported by water must be marked with their weight if this is a thousand kilograms or over.

The Recommendation concerning responsibility for the protection of power-driven machinery is intended to provide an additional safeguard for workers. The Recommendation suggests that, without prejudice to the responsibility for protecting machinery, which should in any case rest on the employer, this should be supplemented by placing responsibility on the person who, within the territory of the country, supplies or installs the machinery in the undertaking. This would increase the probability that national safety regulations were properly observed.

A Recommendation on this subject was adopted by 87 votes to 28.

Finally, the Conference unanimously adopted a Resolution requesting the Governing Body of the International Labour Office to consider the desirability of convening a Conference or Commission of experts in accident prevention and accident statistics, to consider the possibility of laying down uniform bases for the compilation of such statistics.

Protection against Accidents of Workers Engaged in Loading or Unloading Ships

The Eleventh Session of the Conference, which discussed the general problem of accident prevention, considered it necessary, in addition to the measures of a general character referred to above, to establish special international regulations for work in ports. The transport workers' organisations also expressed a strong desire for regulations of this kind. The Twelfth Session of the Conference accordingly adopted a Draft Convention concerning the protection against accidents of workers engaged in loading or unloading ships. The Draft Convention, which was adopted by 84 votes to 22, does not confine itself to laying down general principles, but contains a number of detailed provisions.

The Draft Convention covers all work of loading or unloading, whether performed on shore or on board any ship, whether engaged in maritime or inland navigation, with the single exception of ships of war. It lays down the measures to be adopted in connection with approaches over docks, wharves, quays, or similar premises, with a view to the safety of workers. It also lays down the measures to be taken for the protection of the ways of access.

There are also provisions dealing with hoisting machinery and gear both on shore and on board ship. All such machinery and gear must be periodically inspected. Safeguards are laid down for engines, transmission gear, electric cables, cranes, derricks, etc. Certain dangerous methods of work are prohibited, and the means of ensuring that first aid for the injured is rapidly available are provided. There are also provisions intended to ensure efficient inspection and the imposition of penalties.

This important Draft Convention is supplemented by two Recommendations. The first, which was adopted by 101 votes to nil, draws the attention of States Members to the desirability of concluding reciprocal agreements. The second, which was adopted by 88 votes to nil, refers to the consultation of the employers' and workers' organisations concerned with a view to the establishment of regulations for the safety of workers engaged in loading and unloading ships. The Conference also unanimously adopted a Resolution inviting the Governing Body of the International Labour Office to set up an international technical Committee to work out a model set of regulations which might guide Governments in framing or modifying their respective regulations with a view to putting them into agreement with the Draft Convention.

Forced Labour

The other two questions which were placed on the agenda of the Conference—that of forced labour and that of hours of work of salaried employees—did not come up for final decision this year. Under the double discussion procedure, the Conference was simply asked to decide whether the questions should be placed on the agenda of the 1930 Session, and, if so, to adopt questionnaires with a view to the second discussion, by means of which the Governments would be asked whether they considered international regulations on the subjects desirable, and what provisions should be included. The Conference will be in a position to adopt Draft Conventions or Recommendations in 1930 on the basis of the Governments' replies.

In dealing with the question of forced labour, the International Labour Conference entered a new field. The question affects millions of persons, and is connected with the great problem of colonisation, the relations between civilised and backward or primitive peoples, and the exploitation of natural wealth which is an indispensable factor in the economic life of the world. It will be remembered that the question of forced labour was laid before the International Labour Organisation as a result of the Slavery Convention adopted by the Sixth Assembly of the League of Nations. The ground was prepared for the Conference by a Committee of Experts on Native Labour set up in connection with the International Labour Office.

After full discussion, the Conference decided by 101 votes to 15 to place the question of forced labour on the agenda of the 1930 Session. It adopted by 83 votes to 17 a questionnaire for Governments which deals with all aspects of the problem and the possible solutions. This may lead to the adoption next year of a Draft Convention for the abolition of forced labour, or at any rate for its limitation, and the prevention of abuses in connection with it. Without going into details, it may be said that there was unanimous agreement that forced labour for private individuals should be abolished, and that forced labour for public purposes should be regulated with a view to the ultimate total abolition of a system which has justly been called a survival of slavery.

The Draft Questionnaire drawn up by the Committee was amended by the Conference, at the suggestion of the Workers' Group, in three important respects—right of association for native workers, a maximum eight-hour day in the case of forced labour, and the institution of a permanent Committee of Experts on Forced Labour in connection with the Office.

The nature of the proposals which will be laid before the next Session of the Conference will of course depend on the Governments' replies, but there can be no doubt that great progress has been accomplished and that the International Labour Conference has done important humanitarian work on this question.

It should also be noted that the Conference, by 64 votes to 21, adopted a Resolution asking the Office to undertake, with a view to future action, a study of various problems connected with forced labour, and in particular of penal sanctions in connection with indentured contract labour.

Hours of Work of Salaried Employees

The Conference decided by 103 votes to 17 to place the question of hours of work of salaried employees on the agenda of the 1930 Session. By 92 votes to 15 it adopted a questionnaire by means of which Governments will be asked to supply full information with a view to the decision to be taken at the 1930 Session in the form of a Draft Convention or Recommendation.

The questionnaire deals with the various ways of determining the scope of the future Convention or Recommendation. Governments are asked whether the scope should include all salaried employees if it is found possible to establish a general definition of that term, or whether, in the absence of such a definition, the classes of workers to be covered should be enumerated. Governments are asked whether in any case the Convention or Recommendation should include persons employed in commercial undertakings of whatever kind, undertakings which are both industrial and commercial in so far as they are not treated by national law as industrial undertakings (and as such already covered by the Washington Hours Convention), in undertakings and public administrative services in which the staff is mainly engaged in office work, in institutions for the preventive and curative treatment of the sick, infirm, destitute and mentally unfit, in theatres and places of public amusement, in hotels, clubs, cafés, restaurants and other refreshment houses. Governments are also asked to indicate any other kinds of undertaking which they wish to propose. They are also asked whether the Convention or Recommendation should apply to all undertakings of the kind specified, whether they are public or private, whether they are secular or religious and whether or not they are carried on for profit. Governments would also be requested to state whether they consider that undertakings in which only members of the employer's family are employed should be excluded.

A subsequent question relates to the definition of the term "hours of work." Reference is made to a general weekly maximum of 48 hours and a daily maximum of eight hours for all persons employed in the undertakings to be covered. There is also a question relating to various methods of distributing hours of work.

Unemployment

Although the question of unemployment was not placed on the agenda of this year's Session with a view to the adoption of decisions, the Conference nevertheless devoted special attention to the subject. It may be remembered that it had before it a report by the International Labour Office relating more particularly to the effect of certain important factors of an international character on the unemployment situation in recent years.

The Conference set up a special Committee to study the report of the Office and two draft Resolutions on the subject of unemployment submitted by Mr. Schurch and Mr. Mertens respectively. As the conclusion of its discussions, the Committee decided to propose a Resolution dealing with various aspects of the unemployment problem.

In this Resolution, which was adopted by the Conference, satisfaction was expressed at the setting up in association with the Financial Committee of the League of Nations of a Committee of experts to examine the causes of fluctuations in the purchasing power of gold and their effect on the economic life of the nations. The Office is asked to offer its assistance to the Committee of experts in the investigation of the effects of monetary fluctuations on the economic situation of the workers, to communicate to that Committee the results which have already been obtained by its studies concerning the effects of monetary fluctuations and the stability of employment of the workers, and, if possible in coöperation with the Committee of experts, to undertake further investigations concerning the effects of these fluctuations on the standard of living of the workers, on their efficiency, their hours of work, the relations between employers and workers and the general development of legislation for the protection of workers.

The Resolution goes on to invite the Governing Body of the International Labour Office to study the best means of bringing about the adoption of measures, either nationally or internationally, which may be thought desirable for the reduction of unemployment among workers in coal mines. It also invites the Office to continue its investigations on the problem of unemployment in the textile industries and to undertake similar investigations in the case of other industries, not excluding agriculture.

The Office is further invited to pursue investigations on the development of public employment agencies and their administrative organisation.

Finally, the Governing Body of the International Labour Office is invited to examine, after consideration of the activities of the League of Nations in connection with the coal industry, the desirability of placing the question of unemployment among miners on the agenda of a forthcoming Session of the Conference, preferably the 1930 Session.

Resolutions.

Unanimously or by large majorities the Conference adopted Resolutions submitted by individual delegates in favour of the consideration by the Governing Body of the following questions for possible discussion at future Sessions of the Conference:

(1) The organisation of work in sheet-glass factories on a shift basis which would ensure to the workers a regular weekly rest;
(2) Insurance against old age, invalidity and death, and the rights of foreign workers in connection therewith;
(3) The underground work of women and young persons;
(4) Equality of treatment between national and coloured foreign workers. . . .

154. The Upper Silesian Question Before the Council of the League[1]

[The Peace Conference decided that a plebiscite should be held, the results to be reported to the Supreme Council of the Allies by the Inter-Allied Commission which had been authorized to conduct the

---

[1] League of Nations, *Official Journal*, December, 1921, pp. 1224-1225; 1228-1229.

plebiscite. But no decision as to the disposition of the area could be made and the whole matter was referred to the Council of the League of Nations on August 12, 1921. This body appointed a commission representative of Belgium, Brazil, China, and Spain to study the question, and returned the following report to the Supreme Council of the Allies (see doc. no. 138).]

RECOMMENDATION

The question of Upper Silesia was submitted to the Council of the League of Nations in a letter dated August 12th and signed by M. Briand on behalf of the Supreme Council of the Principal Allied Powers.

The letter announced the decision which had been arrived at by the Supreme Council "in pursuance of Article 11, paragraph 2 of the Covenant, to submit to the Council of the League of Nations the difficulties attending the fixing of the frontier between Germany and Poland in Upper Silesia, and to request it to be so good as to inform the Supreme Council of the solution which it recommends as to the delimitation of the frontier which the Principal Allied and Associated Powers should adopt."

In a Note on the history of the question, dated August 24th, M. Briand added that: ". . . each of the Governments represented on the Supreme Council had, in the course of the discussions, formally undertaken to accept the solution recommended by the Council of the League."

The Council, at its meeting on August 29th, decided to accept this invitation. It has made the weighty problem which was submitted to it the subject of long deliberations and thorough investigation. It has endeavoured to interpret faithfully and in an equitable spirit the provisions of the Treaty of Versailles with regard to Upper Silesia. The Council, being convinced that its duty was above all to endeavour to find a solution in conformity with the wishes of the inhabitants, as expressed by the plebiscite, while taking into account the geographical and economic situation of the various districts, has been led to the conclusion that it is necessary to divide the industrial region of Upper Silesia. Owing to the geographical distribution of the population and the mixture of the racial elements, any division of this district must inevitably result in leaving relatively large minorities on both sides of the line and in separating important interests.

In these circumstances, the Council considered that it would be desirable to take measures to guarantee, during a provisional period of readjustment, the continuity of the economic life of this region, which, owing to the density of its population, the number of its industrial undertakings, the closely-woven network of its means of communication, possesses the character of a vast agglomeration. It was also of the opinion that it would be desirable to provide for the protection of minorities.

Such are the general principles by which the Council was governed.

The Council carefully examined various solutions for giving accurate and faithful expression to the results of the plebiscite.

It recognised that solutions based on calculations of the proportion of votes would give results which would constitute an injustice for one side or the other, and it endeavoured to find a system which, when applied, would assign to each State a number of electors not differing appreciably from the total number of votes given in its favour, and which would, at the same time, as far as possible equalise and reduce the minorities.

Guided by the above considerations, as well as by the geographical and economic considerations referred to in the Treaty, the Council came to the conclusion that the most equitable solution would be obtained by the frontier line which is described in Appendix No. 1, and the adoption of which it unanimously decided to recommend.

The measures which the Council considers necessary in order to ensure the continuity of the economic and social existence of Upper Silesia, and to reduce to a minimum the inconveniences of the period of readjustment, are chiefly designed with the following objects:—

To preserve, for a certain time, for the industries of the territory separated from Germany their former markets, and to ensure the supplies of raw material and manufactured products which are indispensable to these industries; to avoid the economic disturbances which would be caused by the immediate substitution of the Polish mark for the German mark as the sole legal currency in the territory assigned to Poland; to prevent the working of the railways serving Upper Silesia from being affected by the shifting of the political frontier; to regulate the supplies of water and electricity; to maintain freedom of movement for individuals across the new frontier; to guarantee respect for private property; to guarantee, as far as possible, to the workers that they shall not lose in the portion of territory assigned to Poland the advantages which were secured to them by German social legislation and by their Trades Union organisation; and, finally, to ensure the protection of minorities upon the basis of an equitable reciprocity.

The solution of these problems should be achieved by means of arrangements effected under the form of a general Convention between Germany and Poland. The Treaty of Versailles has provided, in several analogous cases, for Conventions of this kind. As regards Upper Silesia, the Treaty has regulated certain questions by means of special provisions.

Article 92 stipulated, moreover, that "further agreements shall regulate all questions arising out of the cession of the above territory which are not regulated by the present Treaty."

The conclusion between the parties of a general Convention which will place Upper Silesia under a special régime during the transitional period seems to correspond to the intentions already expressed by the States concerned. Both Germany and Poland have, indeed, already considered establishment of special institutions for this region.

With a view to facilitating the preparation and to supervising the application of the temporary measures, of which a summary has been given above, and which should be incorporated in a general Convention, the Council considers that it is necessary to set up a Commission composed of an equal number of Germans and Poles from Upper Silesia, and of a President of another nationality, who might be designated by the Council of the League of Nations. This Commission might be called the "Upper Silesian Mixed Commission." It would be essentially an advisory organ.

Further, it would also be expedient to constitute an arbitral tribunal to settle any private disputes which might be occasioned by the application of the temporary measures.

All disputes in connection with the carrying out and the interpretation of the general Convention should be settled in conformity with the provisions of this Convention and, where necessary, with the Covenant of the League of Nations.

A certain time will elapse before the temporary régime referred to above can be definitively adopted and put in force. It will be for the Principal Allied Powers to take all measures necessitated by this preliminary period.

A Frontier Delimitation Commission should mark out the course of the frontier on the spot. It will be the duty of the Inter-Allied Commission already in existence to take the necessary measures for the maintenance of order during this preliminary period.

Finally, it is important that the Mixed Commission referred to above should be appointed without delay in order that it may give its assistance to the Inter-Allied Commission, which, taking into account the provisions of paragraph 6 of the Annex to Article 88 of the Treaty of Versailles, will take measures for preparing the transition from the present situation to the provisional régime.

DECISION OF THE CONFERENCE OF AMBASSADORS

. . . E. *Customs Régime.*—The customs frontier will be made to coincide with the new political frontier as soon as the latter has been fixed.

The German and Polish Customs law and Customs tariffs shall be applied, with the following exceptions:—

1. During a period of six months, goods coming from other countries destined for the plebiscite area, on which the Customs duties levied at the German or Polish frontier have been paid before the date of the partition of Upper Silesia, shall cross the frontier free of duty.

2. During a period of fifteen years the natural products which originate in and come from one of the two zones of the plebiscite area, and are destined for consumption or use in the other zone, shall cross the frontier free of duty.

3. (a) During a period of six months, raw, half-manufactured and unfinished products of the industrial establishments of one of the two zones of the plebiscite area, destined to be used or finished in the industrial establishments of the other zone, shall cross the frontier free of duty. The permits issued for the entry of these products shall mention the names of the consignors and consignees.

(b) During a period of fifteen years, raw, half-manufactured and unfinished products originating in and coming from the industrial establishments of one of the two zones of the plebiscite area, which are to be finished in the industrial establishments of the other zone, shall cross the frontier free of duty when these products are intended for re-importation into the country of origin. The permits issued for the entry of these products shall mention the names of the consignors and the consignees.

4. In conformity with Article 268 of the Treaty of Versailles, natural or manufactured products which originate in and come from the Polish zone of the plebiscite area shall, on importation into German Customs territory, be exempt from all Customs duty during a period of three years. The period of three years shall be reckoned from the notification of the delimitation of the frontier to Germany and to Poland.

With regard to the export regulations, the two countries shall undertake to facilitate during a period of fifteen years the export from their respective territories of such products as are indispensable for the industry of either zone of the plebiscite area, by supplying the necessary export licenses and by authorising the execution of contracts entered into between private individuals, it being understood that the entrance duties shall be paid by these goods upon their importation into German or Polish territory, apart from the exceptions detailed in the foregoing paragraphs.

Any arrangement with regard to the Customs régime on the new Polono-German frontier in Upper Silesia, which is not an application of the principle stated above, shall be considered as an ordinary commercial agreement between Poland and Germany.

F. *Coal. Products of the Mines.*—In conformity with Article 90 of the Treaty of Versailles, Poland shall permit for a period of 15 years, dating from the definitive allocation of the territory, the exportation to Germany of the products of the mines in the Polish zone of the plebiscite area.

As regards coal, account shall be taken in the application of this

Article of the provisions of the different Treaties of Peace, and of the international decisions and agreements, between Germany, Poland and the countries directly or indirectly concerned in the importation of coal from Upper Silesia, which impose obligations on Germany and Poland in respect to coal.

Germany shall permit for a period of 15 years the exportation, to the Polish zone of the plebiscite area, of the products of the mines in its territory, under the conditions laid down in Article 90 of the Treaty of Versailles. The quantities of the products of the mines to which this provision shall apply shall be calculated on the basis of the average exchange of these products in the years 1911 to 1913.

. . . .

155. Mandates

[As a result of their defeat, the Germans had to relinquish their overseas possessions and the Turks most of their Arab lands. These areas were placed under the mandatory system by the Peace Conference, to be administered by the League of Nations in the interests of the inhabitants. Class "A" mandates included those territories whose stage of development made it probable that they could be self-governing if put under the protection of a stronger state. Classes "B" and "C" needed, respectively, more supervision. There are cited below as illustrative of the system the terms under which Great Britain accepted from the League of Nations a Class "A" and a Class "C" mandate and also an agreement drawn by the British and Feisal, King of Iraq, to illustrate the type of arrangement which the mandatory made with the mandate, in this case with a Class "A" mandate, and one which presented special difficulties. See also doc. no. 156.]

(a) Terms of a Class "A" Mandate: Mesopotamia[1]

The Council of the League of Nations:

Whereas by Article 132 of the Treaty of Peace signed at Sèvres on the tenth day of August, 1920, Turkey renounced in favour of the Principal Allied Powers all rights and title over Mesopotamia, and whereas by Article 94 of the said treaty the High Contracting Parties agreed that Mesopotamia should, in accordance with the fourth paragraph of Article 22 of Part I (Covenant of the League of Nations), be provisionally recognised as an independent State, subject to the rendering of administrative advice and assistance by a Mandatory until such time as it is able to stand alone, and that the determination of the frontiers of Mesopotamia, other than those laid down in the

---

[1] Great Britain. *Parliamentary Papers*, 1921, Vol. XLIII, Cmd. 1500. "Final Drafts of the Mandates for Mesopotamia and Palestine for the Approval of the Council of the League of Nations."

said treaty, and the selection of the Mandatory would be made by the Principal Allied Powers; and

Whereas the Principal Allied Powers have selected His Britannic Majesty as Mandatory for Mesopotamia; and

Whereas the terms of the Mandate in respect of Mesopotamia have been formulated in the following terms and submitted to the Council of the League for approval; and

Whereas His Britannic Majesty has accepted the Mandate in respect of the said territories and undertaken to exercise it on behalf of the League of Nations in conformity with the following provisions;

Hereby approves the terms of the said Mandate as follows:—

Article 1. The Mandatory will frame within the shortest possible time, not exceeding three years from the date of the coming into force of this Mandate, an Organic Law for Mesopotamia, which shall be submitted to the Council of the League of Nations for approval, and shall, as soon as possible, be published by it. This Organic Law shall be framed in consultation with the native authorities, and shall take account of the rights, interests and wishes of all the populations inhabiting the mandated territory. It shall contain provisions designed to facilitate the progressive development of Mesopotamia as an independent State. Pending the coming into effect of the Organic Law, the administration of Mesopotamia shall be conducted in accordance with the spirit of this Mandate.

Article 2. The Mandatory may maintain armed forces in the territories under his Mandate for the defence of these territories. Until the entry into force of the Organic Law and the reëstablishment of public security, he may organise and employ local forces necessary for the maintenance of order and for the defence of these territories. Such local forces may only be recruited from the inhabitants of the territories under the Mandate.

The said local forces shall thereafter be responsible to the local authorities, subject always to the control to be exercised over these forces by the Mandatory. The Mesopotamian Government shall not employ them for other than the above-mentioned purposes, except with the consent of the Mandatory.

Nothing in this article shall preclude the Mesopotamian Government from contributing to the cost of the maintenance of any forces maintained by the Mandatory in Mesopotamia.

The Mandatory shall be entitled at all times to use the roads, railways, and ports of Mesopotamia for the movement of armed forces and the carriage of fuel and supplies.

Article 3. The Mandatory shall be entrusted with the control of the foreign relations of Mesopotamia, and the right to issue exequaturs to consuls appointed by foreign Powers. It shall also be entitled to afford diplomatic and consular protection to citizens of Mesopotamia when outside its territorial limits.

Article 4. The Mandatory shall be responsible for seeing that no

Mesopotamian territory shall be ceded or leased to or in any way placed under the control of the Government of any foreign Power.

Article 5. The immunities and privileges of foreigners, including the benefits of consular jurisdiction and protection as formerly enjoyed by Capitulation or usage in the Ottoman Empire, are definitely abrogated in Mesopotamia.

Article 6. The Mandatory shall be responsible for seeing that the judicial system established in Mesopotamia shall safeguard (*a*) the interests of foreigners; (*b*) the law, and (to the extent deemed expedient) the jurisdiction now existing in Mesopotamia with regard to questions arising out of the religious beliefs of certain communities (such as the laws of Wakf and personal status). In particular the Mandatory agrees that the control and administration of Wakf shall be exercised in accordance with religious law and the dispositions of the founders.

Article 7. Pending the making of special extradition agreements with foreign Powers relating to Mesopotamia, the extradition treaties in force between foreign Powers and the Mandatory shall apply to Mesopotamia.

Article 8. The Mandatory will ensure to all complete freedom of conscience and the free exercise of all forms of worship, subject only to the maintenance of public order and morals. No discrimination of any kind shall be made between the inhabitants of Mesopotamia on the ground of race, religion or language. Instruction in and through the medium of the native languages of Mesopotamia shall be promoted by the Mandatory.

The right of each community to maintain its own schools for the education of its own members in its own language (while conforming to such educational requirements of a general nature as the Administration may impose) shall not be denied or impaired.

Article 9. Nothing in this Mandate shall be construed as conferring upon the Mandatory authority to interfere with the fabric or the management of the sacred shrines, the immunities of which are guaranteed.

Article 10. The Mandatory shall be responsible for exercising such supervision over missionary enterprise in Mesopotamia as may be required for the maintenance of public order and good government. Subject to such supervision, no measures shall be taken in Mesopotamia to obstruct or interfere with such enterprise or to discriminate against any missionary on the ground of his religion or nationality.

Article 11. The Mandatory must see that there is no discrimination in Mesopotamia against the nationals of any State member of the League of Nations (including companies incorporated under the laws of such State) as compared with the nationals of the Mandatory or of any foreign State in matters concerning taxation, commerce or navigation, the exercise of industries or professions, or in the treatment of merchant vessels or civil aircraft. Similarly, there shall be no discrimination in Mesopotamia against goods originating in or destined for any of the said States, and there shall be freedom of transit under equitable conditions across the mandated area.

Subject as aforesaid the Mesopotamian Government may on the advice of the Mandatory impose such taxes and customs duties as it may consider necessary and take such steps as it may think best to promote the development of the natural resources of the country and to safeguard the interests of the population.

Nothing in this article shall prevent the Mesopotamian Government on the advice of the Mandatory, from concluding a special customs arrangement with any State, the territory of which in 1914 was wholly included in Asiatic Turkey or Arabia.

Article 12. The Mandatory will adhere on behalf of Mesopotamia to any general international conventions already existing or that may be concluded hereafter with the approval of the League of Nations respecting the slave traffic, the traffic in arms and ammunition, and the traffic in drugs, or relating to commercial equality, freedom of transit and navigation, laws of aërial navigation, railways and postal, telegraphic and wireless communication, or artistic, literary or industrial property.

Article 13. The Mandatory will secure the coöperation of the Mesopotamian Government, so far as social, religious and other conditions may permit, in the execution of any common policy adopted by the League of Nations for preventing and combating disease, including diseases of plants and animals.

Article 14. The Mandatory will secure the enactment within twelve months from the coming into force of this Mandate, and will ensure the execution of a Law of Antiquities, based on the contents of Article 421 of Part XIII of the Treaty of Peace with Turkey. This law shall replace the former Ottoman Law of Antiquities, and shall ensure equality of treatment in the matter of archæological research to the nationals of all States, members of the League of Nations.

Article 15. Upon the coming into force of the Organic Law an arrangement shall be made between the Mandatory and the Mesopotamian Government for settling the terms on which the latter will take over Public Works and other services of a permanent character, the benefit of which will pass to the Mesopotamian Government. Such arrangement shall be communicated to the Council of the League of Nations.

Article 16. Nothing in this Mandate shall prevent the Mandatory from establishing a system of local autonomy for predominantly Kurdish areas in Mesopotamia as he may consider suitable.

Article 17. The Mandatory shall make to the Council of the League of Nations an annual report as to the measures taken during the year to carry out the provisions of the Mandate. Copies of all laws and regulations promulgated or issued during the year shall be communicated with the report.

Article 18. The consent of the Council of the League of Nations is required for any modification of the terms of the present Mandate, provided that in the case of any modification proposed by the Mandatory such consent may be given by a majority of the Council.

Article 19. If any dispute whatever should arise between the members of the League of Nations relating to the interpretation or the application of these provisions which cannot be settled by negotiation, this dispute shall be submitted to the Permanent Court of International Justice provided for by Article 14 of the Covenant of the League of Nations.

Article 20. In the event of the termination of the Mandate conferred upon the Mandatory by this Declaration, the Council of the League of Nations shall make such arrangements as may be deemed necessary for securing under the guarantee of the League that the Mesopotamian Government will fully honour the financial obligations legally incurred by the Mandatory during the period of the Mandate, including the rights of public servants to pensions or gratuities.

The present copy shall be deposited in the archives of the League of Nations. Certified copies shall be forwarded by the Secretary-General of the League of Nations to all Powers Signatories of the Treaty of Peace with Turkey.

Made at   the   day of

(b) *Terms of a Class "C" Mandate: Certain German Islands*[1]

The Council of the League of Nations:

Whereas by article 119 of the Treaty of Peace with Germany signed at Versailles on the 28th June, 1919, Germany renounced in favour of the Principal Allied and Associated Powers all her rights over her overseas possessions, including therein German New Guinea and the groups of islands in the Pacific Ocean lying south of the equator other than German Samoa and Nauru; and

Whereas the Principal Allied and Associated Powers agreed that, in accordance with article 22, part I (Covenant of the League of Nations), of the said treaty, a mandate should be conferred upon His Britannic Majesty, to be exercised on his behalf by the Government of the Commonwealth of Australia, to administer New Guinea and the said islands, and have proposed that the mandate should be formulated in the following terms; and

Whereas His Britannic Majesty, for and on behalf of the Government of the Commonwealth of Australia, has agreed to accept the mandate in respect of the said territory and has undertaken to exercise it on behalf of the League of Nations in accordance with the following provisions; and

---

[1] Great Britain. *Parliamentary Papers*, 1921, Vol. XLIII, Cmd. 1201. "Mandate for German Possessions in the Pacific Ocean Situated South of the Equato⁻ Other Than German Samoa and Nauru."

Whereas, by the aforementioned article 22, paragraph 8, it is provided that the degree of authority, control or administration to be exercised by the Mandatory, not having been previously agreed upon by the members of the League, shall be explicitly defined by the Council of the League of Nations:

Confirming the said mandate, defines its terms as follows:

Article 1. The territory over which a mandate is conferred upon His Britannic Majesty for and on behalf of the Government of the Commonwealth of Australia (hereinafter called the mandatory) comprises the former German colony of New Guinea and the former German islands situated in the Pacific Ocean and lying south of the equator, other than the islands of the Samoan group and the island of Nauru.

Article 2. The mandatory shall have full power of administration and legislation over the territory subject to the present mandate as an integral portion of the Commonwealth of Australia, and may apply the laws of the Commonwealth of Australia to the territory, subject to such local modifications as circumstances may require.

The mandatory shall promote to the utmost the material and moral well-being and the social progress of the inhabitants of the territory subject to the present mandate.

Article 3. The mandatory shall see that the slave trade is prohibited, and that no forced labour is permitted, except for essential public works and services, and then only for adequate remuneration.

The mandatory shall also see that the traffic in arms and ammunition is controlled in accordance with principles analogous to those laid down in the convention relating to the control of the arms traffic, signed on the 10th September, 1919, or in any convention amending the same.

The supply of intoxicating spirits and beverages to the natives shall be prohibited.

Article 4. The military training of the natives, otherwise than for purposes of internal police and the local defence of the territory, shall be prohibited. Furthermore, no military or naval bases shall be established or fortifications erected in the territory.

Article 5. Subject to the provisions of any local law for the maintenance of public order and public morals, the mandatory shall ensure in the territory freedom of conscience and the free exercise of all forms of worship, and shall allow all missionaries, nationals of any State member of the League of Nations, to enter into, travel and reside in the territory for the purpose of prosecuting their calling.

Article 6. The mandatory shall make to the Council of the League of Nations an annual report to the satisfaction of the Council, containing full information with regard to the territory, and indicating the measures taken to carry out the obligations assumed under articles 2, 3, 4 and 5.

Article 7. The consent of the Council of the League of Nations is required for any modification of the terms of the present mandate.

The mandatory agrees that, if any dispute whatever should arise between the mandatory and another member of the League of Nations relating to the interpretation or the application of the provisions of the mandate, such dispute, if it cannot be settled by negotiation, shall be submitted to the Permanent Court of International Justice provided for by article 14 of the Covenant of the League of Nations.

The present declaration shall be deposited in the archives of the League of Nations. Certified copies shall be forwarded by the Secretary-General of the League of Nations to all Powers signatories of the Treaty of Peace with Germany.

Made at Geneva the 17th day of December, 1920.

Certified true copy.

ERIC DRUMMOND,
Secretary-General

(c) *A British Solution of the Problem of Relations with a Mandate: Iraq*[1]

Article I. At the request of His Majesty the King of Iraq, His Britannic Majesty undertakes subject to the provisions of this Treaty to provide the State of Iraq with such advice and assistance as may be required during the period of the present Treaty, without prejudice to her national sovereignty. His Britannic Majesty shall be represented in Iraq by a High Commissioner and Consul-General assisted by the necessary staff.

Article II. His Majesty the King of Iraq undertakes that for the period of the present Treaty no gazetted official of other than Iraq nationality shall be appointed in Iraq without the concurrence of His Britannic Majesty. A separate agreement shall regulate the numbers and conditions of employment of British officials so appointed in the Iraq Government.

Article III. His Majesty the King of Iraq agrees to frame an Organic Law for presentation to the Constituent Assembly of Iraq and to give effect to the said law, which shall contain nothing contrary to the provisions of the present Treaty and shall take account of the rights, wishes and interests of all populations inhabiting Iraq. This Organic Law shall ensure to all complete freedom of conscience and the free exercise of all forms of worship, subject only to the maintenance of public order and morals. It shall provide that no discrimination of any kind shall be made between the inhabitants of Iraq on the ground of race, religion or language, and shall secure that the right of each community to maintain its own schools for the education of its own members in its own language, while conforming to such

[1] Great Britain. *Parliamentary Papers*, 1922, session 2, Vol. IV, Cmd. 1757. "Iraq. Treaty with King Feisal."

educational requirements of a general nature as the Government of Iraq may impose, shall not be denied or impaired. It shall prescribe the constitutional procedure, whether legislative or executive, by which decisions will be taken on all matters of importance, including those involving questions of fiscal, financial and military policy.

Article IV. Without prejudice to the provisions of Article XVII and XVIII of this Treaty, His Majesty the King of Iraq agrees to be guided by the advice of His Britannic Majesty tendered through the High Commissioner on all important matters affecting the international and financial obligations and interests of His Britannic Majesty for the whole period of this Treaty. His Majesty the King of Iraq will fully consult the High Commissioner on what is conducive to a sound financial and fiscal policy and will ensure the stability and good organisation of the finances of the Iraq Government so long as that Government is under financial obligations to the Government of His Britannic Majesty.

Article V. His Majesty the King of Iraq shall have the right of representation in London and in such other capitals and places as may be agreed upon by the High Contracting Parties. Where His Majesty the King of Iraq is not represented he agrees to entrust the protection of Iraq nationals to His Britannic Majesty. His Majesty the King of Iraq shall himself issue exequaturs to representatives of Foreign Powers in Iraq after His Britannic Majesty has agreed to their appointment.

Article VI. His Britannic Majesty undertakes to use his good offices to secure the admission of Iraq to membership of the League of Nations as soon as possible.

Article VII. His Britannic Majesty undertakes to provide such support and assistance to the armed forces of His Majesty the King of Iraq as may from time to time be agreed by the High Contracting Parties. A separate agreement regulating the extent and conditions of such support and assistance shall be concluded between the High Contracting Parties and communicated to the Council of the League of Nations.

Article VIII. No territory in Iraq shall be ceded or leased or in any way placed under the control of any Foreign Power; this shall not prevent His Majesty the King of Iraq from making such arrangements as may be necessary for the accommodation of foreign representatives and the fulfilment of the provisions of the preceding Article.

Article IX. His Majesty the King of Iraq undertakes that he will accept and give effect to such reasonable provisions as His Britannic Majesty may consider necessary in judicial matters to safeguard the interests of foreigners in consequence of the non-application of the immunities and privileges enjoyed by them under capitulation or usage. These provisions shall be embodied in a separate agreement, which shall be communicated to the Council of the League of Nations.

Article X. The High Contracting Parties agree to conclude separate agreements to secure the execution of any treaties, agreements or undertakings which His Britannic Majesty is under obligation to see carried out in respect of Iraq. His Majesty the King of Iraq undertakes to bring in any legislation necessary to ensure the execution of these agreements. Such agreements shall be communicated to the Council of the League of Nations.

Article XI. There shall be no discrimination in Iraq against the nationals of any State, members of the League of Nations, or of any State to which His Britannic Majesty has agreed by treaty that the same rights should be ensured as it would enjoy if it were a member of the said League (including companies incorporated under the laws of such State) as compared with British nationals or those of any foreign State in matters concerning taxation, commerce or navigation, the exercise of industries or professions, or in the treatment of merchant vessels or civil aircraft. Nor shall there be any discrimination in Iraq against goods originating in or destined for any of the said States. There shall be freedom of transit under equitable conditions across Iraq territory.

Article XII. No Measure shall be taken in Iraq to obstruct or interfere with missionary enterprise or to discriminate against any missionary on the ground of his religious belief or nationality, provided that such enterprise is not prejudicial to public order and good government.

Article XIII. His Majesty the King of Iraq undertakes to cooperate, in so far as social, religious and other conditions may permit, in the execution of any common policy adopted by the League of Nations for preventing and combating disease, including diseases of plants and animals.

Article XIV. His Majesty the King of Iraq undertakes to secure the enactment, within twelve months of the coming into force of this Treaty, and to ensure the execution of a law of Antiquities based on the rules annexed to Article 421 of the Treaty of Peace signed at Sèvres on the 10th August, 1920. This Law shall replace the former Ottoman Law of Antiquities, and shall ensure equality of treatment in the matter of archæological research to the nationals of all States members of the League of Nations, and of any State to which His Britannic Majesty has agreed by treaty that the same rights should be ensured as it would enjoy if it were a member of the said League.

Article XV. A separate agreement shall regulate the financial relations between the High Contracting Parties. It shall provide, on the one hand, for the transfer by His Britannic Majesty's Government to the Government of Iraq of such works of public utility as may be agreed upon and for the rendering by His Britannic Majesty's Government of such financial assistance as may from time to time be considered necessary for Iraq, and, on the other hand, for the progressive liquidation by the Government of Iraq of all liabilities thus incurred.

Such agreement shall be communicated to the Council of the League of Nations.

Article XVI. So far as is consistent with his international obligations His Britannic Majesty undertakes to place no obstacle in the way of the association of the State of Iraq for customs or other purposes with such neighbouring Arab States as may desire it.

Article XVII. Any difference that may arise between the High Contracting Parties as to the interpretation of the provisions of this Treaty shall be referred to the Permanent Court of International Justice provided for by Article 14 of the Covenant of the League of Nations. In such case, should there be any discrepancy between the English and Arabic texts of this Treaty, the English shall be taken as the authoritative version.

Article XVIII. This Treaty shall come into force as soon as it has been ratified by the High Contracting Parties after its acceptance by the Constituent Assembly, and shall remain in force for twenty years, at the end of which period the situation shall be examined, and if the High Contracting Parties are of opinion that the Treaty is no longer required it shall be terminated. Termination shall be subject to confirmation by the League of Nations unless before that date Article VI of this Treaty has come into effect, in which case notice of termination shall be communicated to the Council of the League of Nations. Nothing shall prevent the High Contracting Parties from reviewing from time to time the provisions of this Treaty, and those of the separate Agreements arising out of Articles VII, X and XV, with a view to any revision which may seem desirable in the circumstances then existing, and any modification which may be agreed upon by the High Contracting Parties shall be communicated to the Council of the League of Nations.

The ratifications shall be exchanged at Baghdad.

The present Treaty has been drawn up in English and Arabic. One copy in each language will remain deposited in the archives of the Iraq Government, and one copy in each language in those of the Government of His Britannic Majesty.

In Witness of which the respective Plenipotentiaries have signed the present Treaty and have affixed thereto their seals. Done at Baghdad in duplicate this tenth day of October, One thousand nine hundred and twenty-two of the Christian Era, corresponding with the nineteenth day of Safar, One thousand three hundred and forty Hijrah.

P. Z. Cox,
His Britannic Majesty's High Commissioner in Iraq

'Abd-Ur-Rahman,
Naqib-al-Ashraf of Baghdad and Prime Minister of the Iraq Government

156. British Mandate for Iraq: Report for 1925[1]

[The foregoing treaty, though signed October 10, 1922, was not ratified until 1924, when the term of the treaty was reduced from twenty to four years after the ratification of peace with Turkey (August 6, 1924), and the provision was made that the treaty would lapse if Iraq became a member of the League of Nations. Subsequently in another treaty (of December, 1927), the British Government formally recognized Iraq as an independent state and agreed to support her candidature for admission to the League of Nations in 1932.]

I. Survey of the Period

1. outline of political developments

Position at the Opening of the Year 1925

Visit of the League of Nations Frontier Commission

The year under review in this report is a period of steady progress during which a determined effort has been made to solve the financial and administrative problems which clog the feet of every newly established state. In 1924, the Constituent Assembly had accepted the treaty with Great Britain for a maximum period of four years dating from the ratification of peace between Great Britain and Turkey. It had also passed the Organic and Electoral Laws, thus providing the basis for a stable and constitutional government. The crucial question of the northern frontier, involving a claim by the Turkish Government to the whole of the former Mosul Wilayat, remained in dispute and was the dominant interest of the year 1925.

. . . .

In the early part of the year the chief preoccupation was the visit of the Commission appointed by the Council of the League of Nations to advise it regarding the solution of the frontier question. This Commission reached Baghdad on 16th January, 1925. It was composed of three eminent nationals of Sweden, Belgium and Hungary, M. de Wirsen, the President, Colonel Paulis and Count Teleki, together with two Secretaries, Italian and Swiss, and three Assistant Secretaries. The Commission was provided with a Turkish Assessor, Jevad Pasha, who had previously been in command of Turkish forces on the frontier. A British Assessor, Mr. R. F. Jardine, was also appointed and was

---

[1] Great Britain. Colonial Office. *Report by His Majesty's Government to the Council of the League of Nations on the Administration of Iraq for the Year 1925*, pp. 7-20 (Extracts).

accompanied by Sabih Beg, a former Minister of Communications and Works, as the representative of the 'Iraq Government. Unfortunately an element of discord had been introduced in the persons of three Turkish "experts," two of whom were former inhabitants of 'Iraq and well known there. The first, Nadhim Beg Naftji Zadah, had been one of the leading members of the Turkish Committee in Kirkuk and had been closely implicated in a comprehensive scheme for the capture of Kirkuk and Arbil by Shaikh Mahmud of Sulaimaniya in the beginning of 1923. He had subsequently fled to Angora. The second, Fattah Beg, was Shaikh Mahmud's brother-in-law, and since 1921 had been his agent in correspondence with the Turks. Both had been put forward as representatives at Angora of the Mosul Wilayat, but their pretensions had been exposed by Sir Percy Cox at the Constantinople Conference in 1924. In accepting the proposal of the Turkish Government that they should accompany him, the President of the Commission had been unaware of their antecedents, but their presence not unnaturally caused indignation among 'Iraqis: the Prime Minister lodged a protest with the High Commissioner; and there was considerable apprehension lest these individuals should be assaulted by young and hot-headed nationalists. The problem of securing their safety, while not impinging on their free circulation, was a difficult one.

The Commission remained in Baghdad until 26th January and during its stay interviewed all leading persons in the town, Ministers, Government officials, and representatives of every class and community. They arrived at Mosul on 27th January, to find popular feeling running very high. Two days previously there had been formed a Committee of National Defence which proceeded at once to organize demonstrations in Mosul and establish branches in all the local towns. The protection of the two Turkish assessors was a matter of great delicacy, while organized demonstrations roused the suspicions of the Commission. The Ministry of Interior warned the Mutasarrif that the Nationalists were prejudicing the 'Iraq cause and, on 7th February, the High Commissioner flew up to Mosul in a snowstorm to dispel the misunderstandings which had arisen. It was arranged that the Commission should break up into groups in order to get through their work in time to present their report to the League in June and subsequently reunite at Sulaimaniya, Arbil, Kirkuk and Mosul. This programme was carried out successfully; the Turkish "experts" were, however, regarded with suspicion and, in Sulaimaniya, Fattah Beg thought it more prudent not to leave his house.

The Turkish Government had demanded that a plebiscite should be taken. This had been resisted by the British Government on the ground that no machinery could be devised with which to carry it out. The Commissioners finally decided to proceed by studying the racial, geographic and economic features of the problem, and made secret enquiries among all sections of the population in the territories under dispute as to which government they would prefer, that of 'Iraq or Turkey. These secret enquiries, necessary as they may have been, tended, inevitably, to undermine the authority of the 'Iraq administration among the unruly tribes of the frontier districts and to aggravate the unrest naturally created by the state of uncertainty regarding the frontier itself.

One of the chief matters of concern to the Commission was the future of the Christians of Mosul and especially that of the Assyrian refugees, numbering some 20,000 souls, who, as related in former reports, had been settled temporarily on vacant 'Iraq lands near Amadia, while some had been encouraged to filter back to their deserted villages further north, only to be expelled once more by the Turkish incursion of September, 1924. It was largely in order to provide suitable homes for these people that the British Government had claimed for 'Iraq a part of the mountainous region lying north of the Brussels line, though this northernmost frontier, while regarded by the military authorities as strategically most defensible, did not include the whole of the area occupied by the Assyrians before the war. The Assyrians were united in a determination never again to submit themselves to Turkish rule, but were also suspicious of the 'Iraq administration as a predominantly Moslem Government. The Arabs and Kurds, on the other hand, were inclined to resent any signs of special favor shown to the Assyrians by the British, and it has been the task of the High Commissioner to allay this mutual mistrust. The 'Iraq Government had, however, pledged itself officially to provide lands for such of the Assyrians as might be dispossessed of their homes in consequence of the final settlement of the frontier question and already, in 1924, had come to the aid of those who had been re-expelled by the Turks. As its report showed, the Frontier Commission fully appreciated the danger which would await not only the Assyrians, but the large Christian community of every denomination, if the former Wilayat of Mosul were handed back to Turkey.

The Commission terminated its labours in the third week of March: the Turkish "experts" returned by Jazirat ibn 'Umar and the European members, with Jevad Pasha, left Mosul on 23rd March, travelling through Syria. Its report could not be prepared in time for the June session of the League and was held over till September.

Election of the First Parliament

The 'Iraq Government now addressed itself to the holding of its first parliament. . . . It was further considered inadvisable to proceed with elections until the Frontier Commission had finished its work. The promulgation of the Organic Law, passed by the Constituent Assembly in July, 1924, was consequently delayed, so as to avoid an interregnum between the close of Cabinet Government and the introduction of a parliamentary régime. The Law was officially issued on 21st March, 1925, amid widespread rejoicings, and orders were given for the initiation of elections.

Measures Passed by the Cabinet of Yasin Pasha

During this interval the Cabinet of Yasin Pasha had passed four notable measures vital to the future prosperity and stability of 'Iraq. In January, 1925, an agreement was signed with the Anglo-Persian Oil Company for the dredging of the bar at the mouth of the Shatt al Arab, so as to allow vessels of heavy draught to enter the port of Basra. A trade transit convention with Syria was signed and came into effect on 1st April. In March, the Turkish Petroleum Company was granted a concession for the development of oil throughout 'Iraq except the "Transferred Territories" (i.e. transferred from Persia to Turkey in 1913) and the region formerly the vilayet of Basra, the exact limits of the concession area to be defined as soon as the territorial limits of 'Iraq had been determined. . . . The fourth measure, decided upon by the Cabinet in March, 1925, was an undertaking to offer long term contracts to British advisers and officials whose experience and devoted industry were thus secured for 'Iraq throughout the first and most difficult stage of her career as a quasi-independent state. Fifty-eight contracts for ten years and seven for five years were confirmed by Royal Irada during the next few months; nine more ten-year contracts have been approved and there are still other vacancies to be filled, nominations for which are under discussion. At the same time it was agreed to grant special contracts for short periods; the terms of these contracts have not yet been finally settled, but ten have been agreed upon in principle.

Visit of the Financial Mission

In February, His Majesty's Government proposed to send a Financial Mission to 'Iraq to study the financial situation. The offer was gladly accepted by the 'Iraq Government and the Mission, consisting of Commander Hilton Young, M.P., and Mr. Vernon, then an Assistant Secretary in the Middle East Department of the Colonial Office, arrived in March, 1925, and completed its Report by 25th April.

The Mission, while taking a favourable view of the future of the country, recommended the strictest economy on the part of the 'Iraq Government, and on the part of His Majesty's Government the cancellation of certain claims in respect of works of public utility transferred to 'Iraq. The Report was the cause of much satisfaction in 'Iraq and contributed to the election to the first 'Iraq Parliament of a majority of deputies actuated by the friendliest feelings towards the British Alliance.

Visit of the Secretaries of State for the Colonies and Air

Another factor which affected the general situation very favourably was the visit to 'Iraq in the first half of April, 1925, of the Secretaries of State for the Colonies and Air, Mr. Amery and Sir Samuel Hoare. Their presence cheered and encouraged those whose minds had been troubled by the uncertainty regarding the frontier and convinced the Government and people of 'Iraq of the steadfast interest of Great Britain in their affairs. It gave a unique opportunity to His Majesty King Faisal and the leading personages in 'Iraq, to bring their various difficulties and anxieties fully and frankly before the British Government, and the substitution of personal discussion for paper impersonalities had the happiest effect. Particularly valuable were the discussions which took place between Mr. Amery and King Faisal and his Prime Minister as to the prerogatives and duties of the King under the newly-promulgated Constitution, a question which urgently needed discussion, since His Majesty King Faisal had been inclined to withdraw more than was desirable from influencing the conduct of affairs of State after the coming into force of the Organic Law. The main preoccupation of the two Secretaries of State was, however, the more rapid improvement and training of the 'Iraq Army. Many conferences were held on this subject and, before the Secretaries of State left, a scheme had been accepted which should enable the 'Iraq Army in a short time to take the principal part in the maintenance of internal security and the control of the 'Iraq frontiers. This should relieve the British Exchequer of its burden on this account, which at present amounts to something over £3,000,000 a year. . . .

Acceptance of the Conditions Laid Down in the Report of the Frontier Commission

Meantime, in August, 1925, the report of the Frontier Commission had been published. Before it could be translated *in extenso* the Prime Minister explained to the Chamber that it was proposed, if all the Mosul Wilayat were to be retained, that the relation of 'Iraq to Great Britain should be prolonged for a period of about 25 years. He added that there was no one who did not recognize the value of the existing relations with Great Britain and the advantages to the country which had accrued therefrom. There was a striking unanimity in both Houses in favour of prolonging these relations and when the Council of the League met in September and Mr. Amery accepted on the part of the British Government the terms proposed by the Commission, both Chambers telegraphed to thank him for his defence of the rights of 'Iraq. It had indeed alarmed the ultra-nationalist party to find a section of the British press averse from the extension of the alliance. It was even suggested as a possible explanation that these British papers were in the pay of the Turkish Government. Though the settlement which had been hoped for was not reached at the September meeting, owing to the reference of certain legal points to the Permanent Court of International Justice at The Hague, the speeches of Mr. Amery and Mr. Baldwin had a most reassuring effect on public opinion and it was never doubted by the large majority of 'Iraqis that Great Britain would support their rights.

Deportation of Christians and Kurds by the Turks and Appointment of a New Frontier Commission by the League

In January, 1925, a protest had been lodged with the Turkish Government, through His Britannic Majesty's Representative in Constantinople, against violation of the *status quo* boundary. In May, a police patrol was ambushed south of the "Brussels" line by a band under Turkish instigation and, in June, enquiries were addressed by His Majesty's Government to the Turkish Government as to the reason for the large concentration of troops in the area north of the 'Iraq frontier, since it had been officially declared that the Kurdish rebellion had been suppressed. At the same time reports began to come in that the Turks were taking vengeance on the Christians and Kurds of Goyan, who had testified to the Frontier Commission their desire to be included in 'Iraq, and some 500 refugees arrived at Zakho. Early in September, reports began to be received of atrocities committed on Chaldean villages north and also south of the provisional frontier. The villagers, though they had never taken part against Turkey during the war, were being systematically removed from the neighbourhood of the frontier and transported into the interior, but many escaped, in a pitiable state of destitution, and reached Zakho with tales of massacre and violence. The 'Iraq Ministry of Interior placed a sum of money at the disposal of the Mutasarrif of Mosul for the relief of these unfortunate people. Mr. Amery brought the matter in strong terms before the Council of the League at the meeting in September 1925, the Turkish delegate equally hotly denied the accusations; and the Secretary of State requested the Council to send an impartial commission to report on the matter and also on charges and counter-charges as to the violation of the provisional frontier. The Council entrusted the task to a distinguished Esthonian, General Laidoner, and the Commission arrived on 26th October. The Turkish Government refused to allow General Laidoner to pursue enquiries north of the "Brussels" line, so that the Commission had access to such evidence only as could be gathered within 'Iraq territory. Immediately before its arrival the refugee camps were visited by the General Secretary of the Friends of Armenia Society, who satisfied himself that the 'Iraq authorities were diligent in their efforts to succour the refugees, but that owing to their number and their desperate plight, help from outside was required. He sent telegrams to various Christian societies and communities, and a committee was formed in London to collect funds which were despatched to the High Commission and distributed through a committee of three British officers well acquainted with conditions on the frontier. In December Colonel Fergusson, a member of the King's Bodyguard, was sent out by the British committee to administer all moneys collected.

Work of the Laidoner Commission

General Laidoner and his colleagues made a careful examination of the frontier and the relief camps, at the close of which the General telegraphed to the League, stating that the Turks had undoubtedly deported Christians from south of the "Brussels" line, that the deportees deposed that they had been removed by force and violence, and that the Turks had committed crimes, atrocities and massacres. He added that without means of enquiry on the Turkish side of the frontier, it was impossible to define the true reasons for the deportations of Christians, but that these deportations might well have results deserving the attention of the Council. As for the charges brought by either side of violation of the "Brussels" line, he had ascertained that the villages which the British Government claimed as belonging to 'Iraq were actually south of the provisional frontier, but that, owing to errors in the maps, such misunderstandings were inevitable, and should not influence the League.

General Laidoner and part of the Commission left 'Iraq on 23rd November, but two members remained at Mosul to examine any further complaints which might arise. The full reports of the mission were presented to the Council of the League during the meeting in December, 1925. . . .

Advisory Opinion of the Permanent Court of International Justice at the Hague

The opinion of the Hague Court was received some ten days after his Majesty's return. It was to the effect that the "decision to be taken" by the League Council would be in the nature of an arbitral award binding on both parties, that this decision must be unanimous, and that though both Great Britain and Turkey had the right to be represented and to vote, such votes, if adverse to the otherwise unanimous opinion of the Council of the League, would not be taken into account. This opinion was formally adopted by the League Council on 8th December. . . .

Decision of the Council of the League on the Frontier Question

The decision of the Council of the League on the frontier question was published in Baghdad on 17th December. The Council unanimously decided that the Turco-'Iraq frontier should be the "Brussels line" on condition that Great Britain undertook by mean of a new treaty with 'Iraq to continue her present relations with 'Iraq for a period of 25 years, unless before the expiry of that period 'Iraq were admitted to membership of the League. Further provisions dealt with the measures to be taken to secure for the Kurds in 'Iraq the guarantees in regard to local administration recommended by the Frontier Commission, measures to afford equal protection to all elements of the population and such commercial measures as were indicated in the special recommendations of the report of the Commission.

The Turkish delegate refused to recognize the arbitral authority of the League Council and was not present at the meeting. At its close, Sir Austen Chamberlain expressed the hope that the situation between Great Britain and Turkey would be regulated by friendly agreement between the two governments. This proposal is being followed up.

King Faisal telegraphed to King George his sincere thanks and gratitude. The Prime Minister telegraphed to Mr. Baldwin and the Secretary-General of the League, and Mr. Amery was the recipient of many grateful messages. All through 'Iraq there was a general sense of deep relief, and of hope that the stability thus attained would be reflected in the prosperity which the country would now be able to achieve.

Initiation of Discussions in Regard to the New Anglo-'Iraq Treaty

Conversations with regard to the new treaty were begun before the end of the year. The King and the Cabinet showed the utmost willingness to comply with the request of Mr. Amery that the terms of the alliance should be accepted by 'Iraq before the reassembling of the British Parliament in the beginning of February, 1926. On the part of the Opposition, now definitely constituted under the name of the People's Party, with Yasin Pasha as leader, doubts were expressed as to the advantage to 'Iraq of the extension of the 1922 Treaty for 25 years, and more particularly of the similar extension of the subsidiary Agreements; but it was clear from the first that the majority, both inside the 'Iraq Parliament and outside, agreed that the permanent welfare of 'Iraq was bound up with her connection with her ally. To this was added the consideration that the period of the new instrument of alliance might, and most probably would, as Mr. Amery had stated, be reduced by the entrance of 'Iraq into the League of Nations, a step which the British Government would be as anxious as that of

'Iraq to bring about, since it would relieve Great Britain of the responsibilities imposed by the treaty.

Position at the Close of the Year 1925

Thus the close of the period under report saw the termination of doubts as to the integrity of the 'Iraq State, an uncertainty which had hung, since the initiation of self-government, as a dread over the future, impeding progress and the development of the sense of national unity. It witnessed an 'Iraq prepared to accept the terms laid down by the League of Nations, trusting in the policy from which her ally had never deviated, that of helping her to become an independent state, and, at the earliest opportunity, a member of the community of civilized nations. Constitutional Government as laid down in the Organic Law, has now been tested for eighteen months; the first Parliament has proved its capacity for dealing wisely and conscientiously with the measures brought before it; and the past year has given the country a sense of consolidated and established government which there is every ground to hope may increase with each successive year. It should therefore be possible for 'Iraq to satisfy the League of Nations, at no very distant time, of her fitness to become a member of the League. It remains for the British Government to secure an amicable settlement with Turkey and the delimitation of the western frontier with Syria, and the year ends with the hopeful anticipation that these conditions may shortly be accomplished.

2. GENERAL RELATIONS WITH FOREIGN POWERS.

The 'Iraq Ministry of Foreign Affairs

In March, 1925, an 'Iraq Ministry of Foreign Affairs was created, with the concurrence of the High Commissioner, who pointed out, however, that 'Iraq could have no direct relations with Powers which had not explicitly recognized her existence, and that even when 'Iraq had been formally recognized and an accredited representative had been appointed by at least one party, direct correspondence on the part of the 'Iraq Ministry of Foreign Affairs must in every case be subject to prior consultation with the High Commissioner. He called attention to Article 1 of the decision of the Council of the League in September, 1924, by which His Britannic Majesty's Government is held responsible for the fulfilment by 'Iraq of the provisions of the Anglo-'Iraq Treaty in her relations with foreign powers. The portfolio has been held in two successive Cabinets by the Prime Minister.

'Iraq Representative in London

As yet the only representative of the 'Iraq Government abroad is Ja 'far Pasha el 'Askeri, who was sent to London in July, 1925. His official title is " 'Iraq Diplomatic Agent in London." While his formal relations are with the Foreign Office, in practice he transacts official business with the Colonial Office direct. He was present at Geneva during the meetings of the Council of the League in September and December, 1925.

Recognition of 'Iraq by Foreign Powers

As regards the recognition of the 'Iraq State by foreign powers, whenever foreign governments express a desire to appoint a consular representative in 'Iraq, they are requested to apply through His Britannic Majesty's Government for His Majesty King Faisal's exequatur on the Consular Commissions and it is explained to them that such an application in itself constitutes *de jure* recognition of 'Iraq. In this way King Faisal has granted exequaturs to consular representatives of France, Italy, Norway and Sweden and these governments are therefore held to have recognized the 'Iraq State. The Persian Government has always maintained consuls in 'Iraq, and these have been allowed to carry on their functions, while 'Iraqi subjects in Persia have resort to the British consular service.

157. Work of the Permanent Mandates Commission of the League of Nations

[During the war prominent French and British statesmen made promises of independence to the peoples of Syria, Palestine, and Arabia in order to weaken Turkey. (See doc. no. 124.) Britain promised also to make a home for Jews in Palestine after the war. (See doc. no. 121.) When this time came, this latter promise made trouble, for a very large majority of the inhabitants in the area were non-Jewish. Moreover, the promises of independence were remembered by the inhabitants when Britain and France tried to assume the responsibilities of mandatories. Civil strife and bloodshed were the results. Britain eventually granted to the peoples a considerable degree of autonomy, limited immigration of Jews, showed no enmity toward Moslems, and thus won the country back to peaceful rule. France was not so fortunate in Syria.]

(a) Observations on Palestine[1]

GENERAL OBSERVATIONS.

The Commission desires to record its special appreciation of the valuable report by the former High Commissioner, the Right Honourable Sir Herbert Samuel, on the administration of Palestine from

---

[1] League of Nations Permanent Mandates Commission. *Minutes of the Seventh Session,* held at Geneva from October 19th to October 30th, 1925, pp. 212-214; 218-220.

1920-1925, copies of which were placed at its disposal by the British Government.

In the report on its Fifth Session, the Commission referred at length to the special problems which confront the mandatory Power in Palestine in view of its duty not only to safeguard the civil and religious rights of all the inhabitants of the country, irrespective of race and religion, but to place the country under such political, administrative and economic conditions as will secure the establishment of a National Home for the Jewish people.

The Commission was impressed with the broadminded view of the relations between the different racial and religious groups which was presented to it by the mandatory Power. The Commission understands the causes of existing difficulties, but it regrets that certain elements of the population do not appear to recognise that the essential principles embodied in the mandate, the observation of which is the sole care of the Mandates Commission, provide the only substantial basis for the economic and political development of the country. It is glad to learn from the accredited representative that political agitation in the territory has diminished, and it trusts that the experience born of the contact between individuals of the different religious groups in working out the problems of everyday life will help to bring about a larger measure of mutual understanding and confidence, so that an extension of coöperation, particularly in the conduct of municipal and district affairs, may be found possible in the near future. The Commission will be interested to receive the report of the special commission which has been considering the question of the development of local government, and it is glad to note that, in the opinion of the accredited representative, the enactment of the Palestinian Citizenship Order-in-Council should do much to strengthen a sense of Palestinian nationality.

The Commission notes with satisfaction that the population, both Jewish and Arab, is increasing, and that there is no unemployment of any account in the country. That these favourable conditions, so far as the Jewish element is concerned, are dependent for the present in large measure on funds from abroad seems evident, and it is to be hoped that they may still continue when these funds are no longer available.

It is glad to note that attention which is being paid by the Administration to the regulation of Jewish immigration so that Palestine will readily be able to absorb the numbers admitted and offer them employment for which they are suited. The Commission appreciates the reasons which have prevented these immigrants from settling more rapidly on the land, and notes that the Mandatory Power is, in accordance with Article 6 of the Mandate, ready to give its very special attention to any requests which may be made by or on behalf of such settlers for the acquisition of any State or waste lands which may be made available without prejudice to the rights of those belonging to other sections of the population. The Commission desires to be kept informed of the progress made in carrying out the survey of the country, which is considered by the mandatory Power as a necessary preliminary to the allocation of Government lands, and of the exact methods used or contemplated by the Government for disposing of any of these lands.

SPECIAL OBSERVATIONS

1. *Transjordan.*—The Commission desires to be kept fully informed of any progress which may be made toward the determination or delimitation of the various frontiers of Transjordan.

It learned with interest from the accredited representative that the next report would contain much fuller information on this territory. Explanations as regards the relative powers of the chief British Representative, the Emir and the Executive Council, as well as regarding the administration of justice, public health and education, would be particularly appreciated.

2. *Land Tenure.*—The Commission notes that a scheme of systematic land settlement which has been prepared by Sir Ernest Dowson will be communicated to it.

3. *Immigration.*—Although appreciating the more complete information given in the report for 1924 concerning the immigrants admitted to the country, the Commission desires to have fuller details so far as they can be supplied.

4. *Freedom of Conscience.*—The Commission notes with satisfaction that, in accordance with the remarks concerning the interpretation of Article 2 of the mandate made by the accredited representative in connection with the complaints of the Ashkenasic Community, the mandatory Power has no intention of depriving any community of complete religious freedom and complete liberty of conscience.

5. *Military Organisation.*—The Commission notes with satisfaction that the peace and order existing in Palestine has enabled the mandatory Power to maintain only a very small armed force in the territory.

6. *Slavery.*—The Commission asks to be informed whether a law formally abolishing the legal status of slavery in Transjordan has been promulgated.

7. *Labour.*—The Commission would like to find in future reports more information concerning conditions of labour in Palestine. In view of the increase in industrial activity in that country, it considers that the information supplied is meagre and hopes that greater progress in the field of legislative and administrative action for the protection of the workers and particularly for the regulation and control of child labour may be evident.

It would welcome information concerning the constitution and labours of the Committee which, according to the report, was appointed in 1924 to consider these matters, and would particularly enquire whether the adequacy or otherwise of the present law in regard to trade unions and their activities is included among the questions to be examined by this Committee.

8. *Education.*—The full information in the report on educational facilities in Palestine was received with satisfaction by the Commission, which hopes that, when the financial situation improves, the Government will be able to provide larger funds both for continuing its policy of creating village schools in the Arab communities, and also that more substantial assistance may be given to Jewish schools in view of the constantly increasing number of school-children. Information as to the prospects for opening an agricultural school for the Arabs would also be welcomed.

9. *Public Health.*—The Commission notes that the health condition of the population is improving as shown by the vital statistics. It also desires to express its appreciation of the important contribution made by the Hadassah Medical Organisation (Jewish) not only professionally, but socially and politically by reason of the services which it renders to all sections of the population. The reduction in the public health budget of the Government is, it is hoped, only temporary, for the Commission cannot believe that the mandatory Power could intend to effect permanent economies in this direction.

10. *Public Finance.*—The Commission would appreciate in future reports a comprehensive statement in a clear form of all financial operations of a public character concerning such matters as payments for the upkeep of the armed forces and the British gendarmerie, the Ottoman Debt, the agricultural loans from the Anglo-Egyptian Bank, and various railway and monopoly accounts. It would also be useful to have a separate table showing the funds advanced, loaned or given gratuitously to the Palestine Government by the British Government year by year since it assumed control as mandatory Power.

•   •   •   •   •   •   •

OBSERVATIONS OF THE PERMANENT MANDATES COMMISSION ON THE
PETITIONS EXAMINED AT ITS SEVENTH SESSION

At its seventh session, the Commission considered five petitions from individuals and communities in mandated territories; these petitions were forwarded through the Government of the mandatory Power, whose observations upon them were also transmitted to the Commission. . . .

A. Palestine

1. *Petition from the Ashkenasic Community in Jerusalem*
The report submitted by M. Orts at the Commission's sixth session . . . the conclusions of which were adopted by the Commission on

June 29th, 1925, sets forth in detail the history of the Ashkenasic Community's petition up to that date.

In compliance with the Commission's request, which was approved by the Council, the British Government, in a letter dated October 2nd, 1925, commented upon certain points in the petition.

As was stated in M. Orts' report, the Ashkenasic Community at Jerusalem objects to certain administrative regulations now in force by which it is affected, and also to a draft ordinance for the organisation of the Jewish communities in Palestine.

A. The Commission regrets that the mandatory Power had not furnished it with any explanations concerning the present situation which would enable it to consider the complaints of the petitioners with regard to certain administrative regulations which it is alleged have been actually put into force by the Government of Palestine. These complaints concern in particular:

(a) The arrangements for the slaughtering of animals ("kosher");
(b) The tax on unleavened bread;
(c) Failure to give them official recognition and the privileges resulting therefrom;
(d) Refusal to allow them to use the name "Council (Waad Hair) of the Jewish Ashkenasic Community."

The Commission is grateful to the accredited representative for his offer to secure explanations from the authorities in Palestine in regard to these points, and in order that there may be complete liberty of conscience it would ask the mandatory Power to ensure their careful examination by the responsible authorities in the country without waiting for such decisions as may eventually be reached with reference to the proposed legislative regulations.

B. As regards the proposed ordinance and regulations which will affect the future legal status of Jewish communities in Palestine, the Commission notes the statement of the mandatory Power that it is prepared to give the utmost consideration to the wishes of the Ashkenasic Community for complete liberty in religious matters. In recalling the provisions of Articles 2 and 15 of the Palestine mandate, the Commission notes the declaration of the accredited representative that the mandatory Power has no intention of interfering in any way with the religious freedom of the different groups of inhabitants of the country. In the opinion of the Commission, the provisions of the Mandate would not appear to oblige the Mandatory to recognise only one Jewish religious community in Palestine. The Commission trusts that an arrangement satisfactory to all groups may be found, and will follow future developments with close attention.

2. *Two communications from the Executive Committee of the Palestine Arab Congress*, dated April 8th and 12th, 1925, forwarded to the

Secretary-General with a letter from the British Government dated September 18th, 1925.

In view of the fact that in the first petition the very principle of the Palestine Mandate was contested, the Commission has decided not to take it into consideration.

As regards the second petition, the Commission has discussed the matter at length, first in the presence of the accredited representative of the mandatory Power and then *in camera* after he had left. In spite of the very numerous allegations made and the information contained in this petition and in the report and comments of the mandatory Power, and in spite of the supplementary information given by the accredited representative, the Commission has not been able to reach a unanimous and final decision concerning the numerous questions raised. Indeed, the Commission doubts whether it can make any adequate recommendation on so complex and delicate a subject on the sole basis of written documents, even by examining these documents in conjunction with the accredited representative of the mandatory Power against whom the petitioners feel they have cause for complaint.

In view of this difficulty and of the information received that further petitions will shortly be submitted to it by the same persons, the Commission has decided to postpone its final decision.

3. *Letter dated September 1st, with two memoranda on the development of the Jewish National Home in Palestine, submitted by the Zionist Organisation* and forwarded to the Secretary-General with a letter from the British Government dated October 19th, 1925.

The memoranda and letter from the Zionist Organisation were forwarded to the Commission in accordance with the procedure in force in regard to petitions; in addition to three definite complaints, they contain much useful information which calls for no comment. The Commission availed itself of the presence of the Hon. W. Ormsby-Gore, the accredited representative of the mandatory Power, to obtain from him further information on several subjects dealt with in these papers.

The three complaints formulated by the Zionist Organisation are the following:

(a) The Zionist Organisation complains of the uncertain position in which it is placed by the present regulations regarding petitions. The Permanent Mandates Commission is particularly anxious to remove this difficulty because this is not the first occasion on which it has arisen. The Commission recommends that the Council should authorise it to place upon the term "petition" in the regulations governing the above procedure, a wider interpretation which will enable it to include under that term memoranda and memorials of all kinds relating to the administration of mandated territories. The Commission also considers that there is no objection to the Zionist Organisation continuing the procedure it has followed this year in communicating through the mandatory Power all documents which it wishes to bring to the notice of the Permanent Mandates Commission. As this latter procedure also appears acceptable to the mandatory Power, there is no need to make any recommendation on this point.

(b) The Zionist Organisation complains that Article 6 of the Palestine Mandate has not yet been effectively applied. The former High Commissioner, the Right Hon. Sir Herbert Samuel, in his report on the administration of Palestine for 1920-1925, has already pointed out that the administration of Palestine has not yet considered it possible to encourage "the close settlement by Jews on the land, including State lands and waste lands not required for public purposes" without "prejudicing the rights and position of other sections of the population." In its observations the mandatory Power explains the difficulties which have hitherto prevented the application of these provisions. The Permanent Mandates Commission cannot, of course, recommend the allocation to Jewish immigrants of land which is already held by the indigenous population. If, however, after the present land survey has been completed, the Government has at its disposal land which could be handed over to the Jewish immigrants for cultivation without thereby prejudicing the rights and position of other sections of the population, the Permanent Mandates Commission feels sure that the mandatory Power will do its utmost to give full effect to Article 6.

(c) As regards the Zionist Organisation's complaint that only 3 per cent of the sum set aside from public funds appropriated for education has been used to subsidise Jewish schools in Palestine, the Commission is of opinion that the explanation given on this subject by the mandatory Power is sufficient.

(b) *Suggested Content for Mandate Reports*[1]

B AND C MANDATES

LIST OF QUESTIONS WHICH THE PERMANENT MANDATES COMMISSION
DESIRES SHOULD BE DEALT WITH IN THE ANNUAL REPORTS OF
THE MANDATORY POWERS

The attached document replaces the former *questionnaires* for B and C mandated territories. It has been drawn up with a view to facilitating the preparation of the annual reports which, under the terms of article 22 of the Covenant, mandatory Powers are required to furnish to the Council with regard to the territories for which they are responsible.

The document indicates, in the form of questions, the principal

[1] Great Britain. *Parliamentary Papers*, 1926, Vol. XXX, Cmd. 2767. "Papers Respecting the Work of the Permanent Mandates Commission of the League of Nations." (League of Nations, Geneva, June 25, 1926.)

points upon which the Permanent Mandates Commission desires that information should be given in the annual reports.

Without asking that its questions should be necessarily reproduced in the reports, the commission considers it desirable that the reports should be drawn up in accordance with the general plan of the *questionnaire*.

(A)—*Status of the Territory*

1. Is there any organic law in which the mandatory Power has laid down and defined the status of the mandated territory? Please forward such changes as have been made in this organic law.
2. To what extent is the territory financially and administratively autonomous?

(B)—*Status of the Native Inhabitants of the Territory*

3. Has a special national status been granted to the native inhabitants? If so, what is the legal or current term used to describe this special status?
4. Do natives of the territory enjoy the same guarantees as regards the protection of their persons and property in the territory of the mandatory Power and in its Colonies, Protectorates and Dependencies as the native inhabitants of each or any of the latter? If not, what treatment do they receive in this respect?

(C)—*International Relations*

5. What international treaties or conventions (general or special) apply to the territory?
6. How fully has effect been given, as a consequence of the stipulations of the Mandate, to the principle of economic equality for all members of the League of Nations?

(D)—*General Administration*

7. To what extent have legislative and executive powers been delegated to the chief administrative officer of the territory?
8. Does the chief administrative officer exercise these powers with the assistance of legislative, executive or advisory councils? If so, what are the powers of these councils? How are they constituted and do they include unofficial members and native members?
9. What are the different Government departments? How are they organised?
10. Into what administrative districts is the country divided? How are they organised?

11. How many officials are there? How are they divided between the central administration, technical services (agriculture, public health, public works, etc.) and district administrations? What is their origin and their nationality? What are the conditions required for appointment? What is the status of the officials? Are they entitled to a pension? Are advantages reserved to officials with a knowledge of the native languages?

12. Do natives take part in the general administration, and, if so, to what extent? Are any posts in the public service open to natives? Have any councils of native notables been created?

13. Are there any native communities organised under native rulers and recognised by the Government? What degree of autonomy do they possess and what are their relations with the Administration? Do village councils exist?

(E)—Public Finance

14. Please forward the detailed budget of revenue and expenditure for the current fiscal year, and a similar statement for the last completed year of account. Please attach a comparative table of the total revenue and expenditure, section by section, for each of the past five years.

15. Has the territory a public debt? If so, attach figures for the last five years.

16. Has the ordinary and extraordinary expenditure been covered by budgetary revenue or in some other way—either by public loans, or by advances or free grants by the mandatory Government?

In the latter cases, state the conditions of the financial transactions involved.

17. Please give the annual and total amounts of advances and grants-in-aid by the mandatory Power to the mandated territory.

(F)—Direct Taxes

18. What direct taxes—such as capitation, or income, or land taxes—are imposed—

        (a) On natives?
        (b) On non-natives?

19. Are the native direct taxes paid individually or collectively? Are they applicable to all natives without distinction or only to able-bodied male adults? Is the rate of taxation the same throughout the territory, or does it vary in different districts? Can a native pay in kind or only in money?

20. Is compulsory labour exacted in default of the payment of taxes in cash or kind? If so, on what basis is the equivalent calculated?

21. What methods are employed to assess and collect the native taxes?

22. Is any portion of this tax handed over to the native chiefs or communities? Are chiefs salaried by the Administration?

23. Are the native chiefs allowed to exact tribute or other levies in cash or in kind or in labour? If so, is this tribute in addition to the Government taxes?

(G)—Indirect Taxes

24. What is the tariff of import and export duties? Are transit and statistical duties charged?

25. Are there any indirect taxes in force other than import, export and transit duties?

26. Does the territory form part of a customs union with neighbouring Colonies and Dependencies of the mandatory Power? If so, how are the customs receipts and expenses divided?

27. Are the products of the mandated territory given preferential treatment when imported into the territory of the mandatory Power, its Colonies or Dependencies, or do they pay the same duties as similar products from foreign countries?

(H)—Trade Statistics

28. Please forward comparative statistics concerning the general and special trade of the territory, showing both imports and exports for the past five years. (Please indicate the amount of imports and exports of Government material and store.)

(I)—Judicial Organisation

29. Please give a description of the judicial organisation, both civil and criminal.

30. How are the courts and tribunals of the various instances constituted?

31. Do they recognise native customary law, and if so, in what cases and under what conditions?

32. Are natives entitled to officiate in the courts and tribunals: for example, as assessors or members of the jury?

33. Does the judicial organisation include tribunals exclusively composed of natives? Are these tribunals under direct or indirect control of the mandatory Power? What powers do they exercise? Can they inflict punishments for which the law makes no provision? How are their sentences carried out?

34. Does the law inflict the penalties of corporal punishment, forced residence and deportation? If so, under what conditions and limitations?

35. Does the penitentiary system obviate the necessity of sending prisoners long distances for confinement?

(J)—Police

36. Is there any police force apart from the armed forces proper? If so, what is its strength?

37. Are the police concentrated in centres under direct European/ Japanese authority or distributed in detachments in the villages under native subalterns only?

(K)—Defence of the Territory

38. Are any military forces maintained for the defence of the territory? If so, how are they recruited, organised and armed? What is the period of service? What proportion of Europeans or Japanese do they include? What is their strength? Is it provided that discharged soldiers are called up as reservists in case of an emergency?

39. If the territory has no armed forces of its own, what are the arrangements for its defence?

40. If military expenditure and expenditure on the police are included under the same item of the budget, please indicate separately by the expenditure on each.

(L)—Arms and Ammunition

41. What measures have been adopted to control the importation of arms and ammunition?

42. What number of arms, and quantity of ammunition of the different categories have been imported during the year, and what approximately is the number of such arms and the quantity of ammunition in the country?

43. Is the importation (with or without restrictions) allowed of "trade guns" (flint locks) and "trade powder" for self-defence, or for the protection of crops against wild animals, or for any other harmless purpose?

(M)—Social, Moral and Material Condition of the Natives

44. What, generally speaking, are the measures adopted to promote the moral, social and material welfare of the natives?

As an indication, please state approximately the total revenue derived from the natives by taxation and the total amount of the expenditure on their welfare (education, public health, etc.).

45. Is the native population divided into distinct social castes? If so, does the law recognise these distinctions and the privileges which may be attached thereto by native tradition and custom?

46. Does the slave trade or slave-dealing exist in any form? If so, what

measures are taken for their suppression and what has been the success of these measures?

47. Does slavery still exist and, if so, in what form—

        (a) In Moslem districts?
        (b) In other districts?

Can a slave be emancipated under native customary law?

48. What measures are being taken to suppress slavery? What have been the results of these measures?

49. Do any of the following practices exist in the territory:—
Acquisition of women by purchase disguised as payment of dowry or of presents to parents?
Purchase of children under the guise of adoption?
Pledging of individuals as security for debt?
Slavery for debts?
Are these practices penalised by law?

50. What is the status of freed slaves, especially women and children, in the native social organisation?

51. What is the social status of women? In particular, are polygamy and concubinage universal or prevalent? Are they recognised by law?

52. Can a native move about freely throughout the entire territory? Are there any regulations in regard to such movement? Is vagrancy a penal offence? If so, how is it defined?

(N)—Conditions and Regulations of Labour

53. Have measures been taken in accordance with Part XIII of the Treaty of Versailles to ensure the application of conventions or recommendations of the International Labour Conference?
Please indicate such local circumstances, if any, as render these provisions inapplicable or ineffective.

54. Does the local supply of labour, in quantity, physical powers of resistance and aptitude for industrial and agricultural work conducted on modern lines appear to indicate that it is adequate, as far as can be foreseen, for the economic development of the territory? Or does the Government consider it possible that sooner or later a proper care for the preservation and development of the native races may make it necessary to restrict for a time the establishment of new enterprises or the extension of existing enterprises and to spread over a longer term of years the execution of such large public works as are not of immediate and urgent necessity?

55. Are there any laws and regulations regarding labour, particularly concerning—
Labour contracts and penalties to which employers and employed are liable in the case of their breach?
Rates of wages and methods of payments?

Hours of work?

Disciplinary powers possessed by employers?

Housing and sanitary conditions in the camps or villages of workers?

Inspection of factories, workshops and yards?

Medical inspection before and on completion of employment: medical assistance to workers?

Compensation in the event of accident, disease or incapacity arising out of, and in the course of, employment?

Insurance against sickness, old age or unemployment?

56. Do labourers present themselves freely in sufficient numbers to satisfy the local demand for labour? Or has recruiting to be carried out in native centres more or less distant to make good shortage of labour?

57. Does the Administration recruit labour for the service of the Administrations of other territories or for private employers? If so, under what conditions and safeguards?

58. Are private recruiting organisations or agents of employers permitted to recruit labour within the territory for service in the territory itself at a distance from the place of recruiting or in another country? If so, under what conditions and safeguards?

59. Please give a table showing the number of workers of each sex recruited (a) for Government work, (b) for private enterprise.

60. Indicate the nature of the work for which recruiting has taken place during the year (e.g., mines, porterage, agriculture, construction of railways, roads, etc.). Give, where possible, mortality and morbidity statistics among the workers.

61. Does the existing law provide for compulsory labour for essential public works and services?

What authority is competent to decide what are public works and services, the essential nature of which justifies recourse to compulsory labour?

What payment is made to the workers?

May such compulsory labour be commuted for a money payment?

Are all classes of the population liable to such labour?

For what period can this labour be exacted?

62. How is the recruiting and supervision of compulsory labour organised?

63. Are any workers recruited from outside the territory? If so, by whom and under what conditions?

64. Are the contracts of such workers signed before departure from their native country? Give a specimen contract.

65. Is there any special officer charged with the duty of looking after those workers on arrival, allocating them to employers, seeing that the employer fulfils his obligations through the period of contract, and arranging for their repatriation or reëngagement?

66. Are they segregated, in camps, compounds or otherwise? What

are the regulations in this matter? Has their presence in the territory given rise to any trouble with the native inhabitants?

67. Are these workers encouraged to bring their wives with them, and do they do so? Are they allowed to settle in the territory if they so wish?

68. Give the nationality of imported workers, the numbers of new arrivals, repatriations, deaths and the total present at the end of the year (men and women).

69. Are there any trade unions in the territory? If so have these unions put forward any protests or demands?

(O)—Liberty of Conscience and Worship

70. Is freedom of exercise of all forms of worship and religious instruction ensured?

71. Has it been considered necessary, in the interest of public order and morality, to impose restrictions on the free exercise of worship, or to enact regulations on the subject?

72. Are there any restrictions on missionaries, who are nationals of States not members of the League of Nations?

(P)—Education[1]

73. State the general policy and principles adopted in regard to the education of the natives. How do the methods in use illustrate the application of the different characteristics of these principles?

74. Please give a brief analysis of the education budget indicating the amounts allocated respectively to—

> Government schools.
> Non-Government schools.
> Inspection of educational institutions.

75. Is official authorisation necessary for opening non-Government educational institutions? If so, under what conditions is such authorisation granted?

76. Are non-Government educational institutions subject to a compulsory official inspection, and, if so, how is it carried out?

77. What conditions are attached to any grants-in-aid made to non-Government schools? On what basis are the grants made?

78. Please give a table showing the number of boys' schools of the different grades in the following categories:—

> Government schools.
> Non-Government schools subsidised by the government.
> Non-Government schools not subsidised.

---

[1] Questions 73 to 84 refer only to the education of the natives.

State the numbers enrolled and the average attendance in each category of schools.

79. Please give the same information regarding girls' schools.

80. Is any vocational training, or instruction in agriculture, or domestic science given in the territory?

81. Are there any normal classes or training institutions for the education of native teachers?

82. Give some general indication of the curricula in each class of school mentioned above.

Do they include the teaching of a European or Japanese language, and, if so, how far does this teaching go?

Does the curriculum in Government schools include religious instruction (compulsory or optional)?

83. What language is used as a medium of instruction?

84. What are the numbers of the teaching staff (Government and non-Government, certificated and uncertificated)? How are they distributed among the different categories of schools?

85. Are there any schools for non-natives?

(Q)—*Alcohol, Spirits and Drugs*

86. Are the natives much addicted to the use of alcohol and spirits?

87. What is the accepted definition of the terms "liquor traffic" and "trade spirits"?

88. Have legal methods concerning the liquor traffic been enacted to give effect to the mandates and the Convention of Saint-Germain of the 10th September, 1919?

89. Is there any licensing system for the sale of imported alcoholic liquors?

90. What are the import duties on (a) spirituous liquors, (b) wines, (c) beer and other fermented beverages? Has any limit of strength of (b) and (c) been adopted?

Are the duties higher or lower than those in the neighbouring countries?

91. What are the quantities of each class imported each year for the last five years, and what are the principal countries of origin?

92. What steps are taken to prevent smuggling and the illicit traffic in imported alcohol and spirits?

93. Is the process of distillation known to the natives? Have any measures been taken to restrict (a) the manufacture, (b) the sale, (c) the consumption of intoxicants manufactured by the natives?

94. Is any encouragement given to communities or associations which, for religious or other reasons, are trying to suppress the use of these intoxicants?

95. Is the population of the territory addicted to the use of drugs (including hashish and hemp)? If so, what measures are in force to prohibit or regulate their use?

(R)—Public Health

96. What health organisation is in charge of research work and the prevention, control and treatment of disease? State the work done by this organisation and the results observed.

97. Does this organisation train natives as medical and sanitary assistants, or women as midwives and as nurses? What is the method adopted?

98. How many doctors, both official and private, are there in the territory? Has official and private action as regards sanitation and preventive and curative medicine been coördinated?

99. What progress has been made in inducing the natives, especially the chiefs, to adopt sanitary reforms in the towns and villages?

100. What endemic or epidemic diseases have been responsible for the greatest mortality? Are there statistics regarding the morbidity and death rate attributable to these diseases? If no general statistics exist, please supply any which have been compiled for certain centres or certain specified areas.

101. Give any other information of importance from the epidemiological point of view, particularly as regards the spread of dangerous diseases, such as sleeping-sickness, etc., which are not covered by the preceding question.

102. Does the health organisation deal with the supervision of prostitution? What is the position with regard to prostitution?

(S)—Land Tenure

103. Is the Government's policy directed towards the exploitation of the arable land by the establishment of large agricultural undertakings under foreign management, or by the development of the system of native small-holdings?

104. What are the various classes of property which, in view of their nature, origin or use, constitute the domain of the territory?

Under what item of the local budget do the revenues of this domain appear, or, in the case of the sale of such property, the sum realised? Under what items of the local budget do the costs of exploiting such domain appear?

Are the recruiting and employment of the labour required for the exploitation of this domain regulated by the common law?

105. Does the law provide a definition of the term "vacant lands"? What authority is competent to decide whether land is vacant?

Does the law recognise the rights of use and enjoyment that may be exercised by the natives in the "vacant lands" (the right of gathering produce, cutting wood, grazing, hunting, fishing, etc.)?

106. Has the mandatory Power acquired on its own account (and not

in its capacity as mandatory) any property or rights whatsoever in the territory? If so, what property or rights?

On what basis does the State's proprietary title rest?

Is this property subject to the same dues and charges as the property of private individuals?

Is the State subject to the ordinary regulations regarding the recruiting and employment of the labour needed for the exploitation of these lands?

How is the revenue of these lands employed?

107. What is the system of land registration in force? Is it applicable to land owned or occupied by natives? Is there a land registry department?

108. What is the native system of land tenure? Is it uniform through the territory? Have the natives any notion of the right of individual property?

Does the law recognise the right of natives to hold property as individuals?

109. Do the authorities exercise control over land transactions with a view to safeguarding the customary rights of the natives on such land?

What is the maximum term of land-leases to non-natives?

Does the law reserve land for the natives or native communities, from which they cannot be dispossessed for the benefit of non-natives?

110. Have the native chiefs the power of dispossessing existing occupiers and of granting the land to third parties? If so, have the persons dispossessed the right of appeal to the authorities?

111. What is the (approximate) proportion in the whole territory of—

> Native land,
> State land,
> Land leased or sold to non-natives (including any property of the mandatory Power referred to in Section 106)?

112. What are the regulations with regard to expropriation for reasons of public utility? How is the compensation determined?

(T)—Forests

113. State the main provisions of the forest law (if any). Does it provide for the protection of forests and for afforestation of cleared or waste lands?

(U)—Mines

114. Is any legislation in force with regard to mines? What are the main provisions? If there is no special legislation on this subject, does the State claim the ownership of the sub-soil?

115. What mineral resources (a) are known to exist, (b) have been leased, (c) are actually exploited by the State or privately?

(V)—*Population*

116. What is the population of the territory in natives, coloured persons other than natives, Asiatics, Europeans and Americans? Are the figures supplied the result of a census or are they merely an estimate?
117. Please supply, if possible, quinquennial or decennial comparative statistics of the population.
118. Is there any considerable emigration from, or immigration into, the territory? If so, what are the causes?
What are the countries of destination or origin of emigrants and immigrants, respectively?

158. HUMANITARIAN WORK OF THE LEAGUE

[At the close of the war there were soldiers of many nationalities stranded in parts of Europe remote from their homes. In most cases they had been prisoners of war and were without means of transportation. Their presence was not only undesired by the people among whom they found themselves, but they were a social menace. What is more, they were needed in their own countries and wanted to be there. The League of Nations, under the leadership of Dr. Fridjof Nansen, the Arctic explorer, undertook the task of moving these large groups of men for the good of Europe in general.

This task was not completed when an appeal came to the League to find places of refuge and habitation for the thousands of Russian refugees who were cast upon certain neighboring peoples and who were the source of much distress as well as being in dire need themselves. Then came the war between Greece and Turkey and the call from the Greek and Armenian refugees on the coast of Asia Minor who were in need of food, habitations, and protection. Dr. Nansen took upon himself, under the authority of the League, the work of financing and carrying out the project of establishing refugee camps, of preventing the spread of disease, and of assisting in the rehabilitation of these unnumbered thousands of people.]

(a) *Repatriation of Prisoners of War*
Report of the High Commissioner, Dr. Nansen, submitted to the Council, September 1, 1922[1]

(1) The High Commissioner is happy to be able to report to the Members of the Assembly and the Members of the League that he has been able to bring to a satisfactory conclusion the work which he has

---

[1] League of Nations *Official Journal*, November, 1922, p. 1223ff.

carried out on behalf of the League for the repatriation of prisoners of war.

The Members of the Assembly will remember that at the last session the High Commissioner informed them that he still had to repatriate large numbers of prisoners from the Black Sea and a considerable number from Russia through the Baltic.

(2) For the evacuation of the prisoners who were collected in the Black Sea ports he sent vessels which made a number of voyages between those ports and Trieste in the autumn of 1921. By this means he was able to repatriate at a small cost approximately 12,000 prisoners and a number of civilians.

(3) During the winter months the numbers of prisoners who were repatriated through the Baltic continued to be comparatively large, but in the spring transports became less frequent and their importance diminished. The High Commissioner gave instructions for the work to be carried on into the summer months in order to enable those who were too weak and too ill-clothed to travel during the winter months to avail themselves of the opportunity of repatriation under better climatic conditions. By the middle of June, however, the number availing themselves of the means which he placed at their disposal was so reduced that he thought it right to close the work down altogether at the end of that week. The whole work of repatriation has therefore been brought to an end, and the liquidation of the entire organisation is being rapidly put through.

(4) The High Commissioner has to report that the number of prisoners who have been brought to their homes during the course of the last two years is 427,886; and annexed to this report is a note showing in detail how this great total is made up.

(5) The High Commissioner is at present engaged in drawing up a full account of the monies which have been placed at his disposal for the carrying out of his work. He hopes shortly to be able to present these accounts for audit and for the examination of the Governments which have lent him the funds which he has used and the Governments on whose behalf he has used these funds.

(6) The High Commissioner wishes to take this last opportunity of expressing once more his deep indebtedness to all those organisations and individuals which have helped him in this task. He feels that he should make a very special mention of the assistance given him by the International Committee of the Red Cross, without whose coöperation and practical help the whole work could scarcely have been carried out so rapidly and at such small cost.

Total Number of Prisoners of War Repatriated by the High Commissioner of the League of Nations, with the assistance of the International Committee of the Red Cross, from May 1920 to July 1922.

(a) Prisoners Repatriated from Russia and Siberia

(1) *Via Baltic and Overland*

Austrians	16,961	Japanese	1
Americans	7	Italians	1,417
Armenians	2	Letts	11
Belgians	9	Lithuanians	11
British	20	Poles	7,961
Bulgarians	50	Roumanians	18,140
Czechoslovaks	27,120	Russians	55
Danes	14	Swedes	18
Esthonians	11	Swiss	1,162
French	8	Turks	113
Germans	33,903	Ukranians	134
Greeks	4	Yugoslavs	11,159
Hungarians	36,097		
		Total	154,388

(2) *Via Black Sea*

Argentinians	8	Italians	133
Austrians	630	Letts	61
Belgians	12	Poles	1,746
British	20	Roumanians	901
Czechoslovaks	2,048	Russians	20
Esthonians	5	Spaniards	2
French	36	Swedes	5
Germans	1,997	Swiss	65
Hungarians	1,475	Yugoslavs	621
		Total	9,785
		Russian refugees from Constantinople	2,406
		Total	12,191

(b) Prisoners Repatriated from Vladivostok

Austrians	814	Lithuanians	10
Belgians	3	Poles	874
Bulgarians	1	Roumanians	649
Czechoslovaks	1,178	Turks	19
Germans	57	Yugoslavs	637
Hungarians	2,596		
Letts	13	Total	6,851

(c) Prisoners Repatriated to Russia

(1) *Via Baltic and Overland*

Russian prisoners of war	198,486
Interned members of Soviet army	47,712
In addition a certain number of Esthonians, Letts, Lithuanians and Poles, of Russian prisoners from Czechoslovakia, Austria and Hungary, and of Hungarian communists, were repatriated, making a grand total of	251,703

(2) *Via Vladivostok*

Russians... 2,753

Total: Via Baltic Sea and overland............................. 406,091
        via Black Sea.. 12,191
        via Vladivostok.......................................   9,604
                                                                ———————
        Grand total.. 427,886

(b) *Russian Refugees. Report by Dr. Nansen, submitted to the Council, July 7, 1923*[1]

I have the honour to submit for the information of the Council the following report on the work accomplished by the High Commissariat on behalf of the Russian refugees since its last meeting.

1. IDENTITY CERTIFICATES FOR REFUGEES

I am very glad to be able to report exceedingly good progress in the arrangements for the issue of identity certificates to Russian refugees in various countries. Almost all the Members of the League interested in the question have adopted the identity certificate system, and the German Government, which at present affords hospitality to some hundreds of thousands of refugees, has also adhered to the system. The great advantages to the refugees of possessing these documents are too many and too obvious to need emphasis in this report, and a detailed memorandum on the subject has already been circulated for the information of the States Members. I am happy to announce that since the issue of this statement, the Governments of Poland, Albania, Denmark, Luxemburg, Japan and Mexico have formally adhered to the arrangement or adopted it in principle, and Hungary has also notified me unofficially of her proposed adhesion. China, which is very closely concerned in the refugee question, has not yet adopted the system, and I make a special appeal to the Chinese representative on the Council. I very much hope that his Government's adhesion will not be long delayed.

As a result of representations made by the High Commissariat to the British, French and Italian delegations at the Lausanne Conference, Signor Mondana obtained a verbal promise from the Turkish Delegation that its Government would deliver identity certificates to the refugees remaining in Constantinople on the model recommended by the Geneva Conference. This promise has since been confirmed verbally to my representative in Constantinople, who is now endeavouring to bring the matter to a satisfactory formal conclusion.

[1] League of Nations *Official Journal*, August, 1923, p. 1040ff.

2. THE SITUATION OF RUSSIAN REFUGEE CHILDREN IN VARIOUS COUNTRIES

The High Commissariat has continued to maintain a particular interest in the welfare of these unfortunate children, not only because the interests of children make a special appeal to all, but particularly because of the exceedingly unhappy situation of the Russian refugee children. A special effort has been made on behalf of the Russian refugee children who were in Constantinople because of the urgent necessity of evacuating all the refugees possible from that city, and I venture to think that, on the whole, our efforts in this direction have met with a moderate amount of success. The transfer to Belgium of the Bebek Orphanage and the St. George's Institute has been effected with our assistance, and a grant has been made to the former orphanage to enable it to be established in that country. The transfer has further been secured of considerable groups of children to France, where arrangements for their adoption and welfare have been undertaken by the "Placement Familial" and other responsible French organisations. In addition, some hundreds of children transferred from Constantinople to Bulgaria, have been maintained and educated from funds made available by the Bulgarian Government and the High Commissariat. These funds are now practically exhausted, and the future of these children therefore becomes in the highest degree critical.

It is estimated that there are at least 400,000 Russian refugee children in Europe, the majority of whom are totally unprovided for.

3. SITUATION OF RUSSIAN REFUGEE INVALIDS IN VARIOUS COUNTRIES

It is not necessary for me to emphasise the deplorable situation of these unfortunate people and the great claim they have on the sympathy of the relief organisations and on the benevolent attitude of the public in general. The High Commissariat has arranged for the transfer of upwards of 800 invalids from Constantinople and Egypt to Bulgaria, where grants have been made to the Russian Red Cross for their maintenance. In addition, 693 invalids under the care of General Baratoff were evacuated to the Kingdom of the Serbs, Croats and Slovenes during February, and not only were their travelling expenses granted but an establishment grant of £2 per invalid was made to General Baratoff. Similar arrangements were made for the transfer of the Canlidja Sanatorium to the Kingdom of the Serbs, Croats and Slovenes, and in this case a grant of 2,400 dinars per head for establishment expenses was made.

4. SITUATION OF RUSSIAN REFUGEES IN THE EAST

In December 1922 I was asked by the Russian Red Cross to consider the question of the legal protection and material aid of about

22,000 Russian refugees who had fled from Vladivostok and established themselves on the coasts of China, Korea and Japan. In response to this request, I immediately got into touch with representatives of the Japanese and Chinese Governments, from whom I received assurances that everything possible was being done by official and private bodies to improve the situation of these unfortunate people. Both Governments emphasised, however, that the presence of these refugees in the respective territories presented a difficulty which required outside help in order to reach a satisfactory solution. The Japanese Government particularly emphasised that the present situation could not be allowed to continue indefinitely, and that, in the near future, the Japanese Government would be obliged to terminate it either with the assistance of neighbouring countries or the League of Nations.

The situation of the refugees in China would appear to be more difficult still. As many of the refugees concerned are men who have recently been engaged in military activities against the Soviet Government, it is to be hoped that the Chinese Government will not insist upon their repatriation except against approved guarantees for their protection.

5. CONSTANTINOPLE

It is hardly necessary for me to remind the Council that the High Commissariat had no responsibility for the material welfare of the refugees either in Constantinople or elsewhere. Nevertheless, in view of the exceedingly hard situation of the refugees in that city, the High Commissariat has, from time to time, been compelled to offer them material relief as an exceptional measure. For example, towards the end of 1921, when various relief organisations working for the refugees in Constantinople withdrew their support, the High Commissariat fed some thousands of the refugees to save them from starvation.

As a result of the appeal which I made to the Council in May of last year, I received about £11,700 from various Members of the League. This amount was supplemented by a most generous contribution of £15,000 from the American Red Cross, making a total of £26,700. It is doubtful whether this sum would have been sufficient to secure the evacuation of even the destitute refugees, but the changed political situation involving the imminent departure of the Allies from Constantinople necessitated emergency assistance for the evacuation of some thousands of refugees who up to that time had been self-supporting, and the High Commissariat saw no alternative but to take the matter actively in hand.

Briefly, the High Commissariat has been instrumental in securing the evacuation of over 20,000 refugees in all to 44 different countries at a cost of about £50,000. Of this amount, £26,700 was provided as mentioned above, leaving £23,300 to be provided by the High Commissariat from private funds.

Despite the liquidation by the League of its obligation to the refugees, who were receiving rations from the American Relief Administration, the Constantinople office has continued to evacuate Russian refugees from Constantinople to countries where they will be enabled to live in conditions of greater security and where they will have more chance of economic settlement and political security.

From January 1st until June 15th this year, the total evacuated as a result of the diplomatic and financial activities of the League is approximately 4,400.

When it is realised that practically every country in the world has stringent regulations against the admission of refugees and that most of the refugees themselves are practically destitute, some idea can be obtained of the diplomatic and financial difficulties which had to be overcome in order to attain this result.

(a) *Serbian Evacuation.*—Special features which should be noted are the evacuation to Serbia of 1,424 Russian refugees whose previous political associations were such as to render dangerous their presence in Constantinople after the evacuation of that town by the Allies.

Amongst groups thus sent to the Kingdom of the Serbs, Croats and Slovenes are convoys of disbanded regiments of General Wrangel who had been employed by Allied forces at Kelia and were evacuated on the representations of General Wrangel's representative in Constantinople. It is interesting to note that with the evacuation of these persons to employment in the Kingdom of the Serbs, Croats and Slovenes, the last phase is satisfactorily concluded of the great tragedy which occurred in Constantinople in the latter part of November 1920, when General Wrangel's army of approximately 90,000 men suddenly arrived in the port as the result of the Crimean evacuation.

(b) *Bulgarian Evacuation.*—As a result of the visa payment scheme arranged by the High Commissariat with the Bulgarian Government, some 500 Russian refugees able to produce the small sum necessary for their journey to Bulgaria have been provided with visas for Bulgaria and evacuated to that country by League machinery.

(c) *Further Evacuations.*—Fifty-three orphan boys between the ages of 12 and 17 have been evacuated to France, where they were received by the League's delegate and handed over to the French organisation known as the "Placement Familial." A convoy of 142 ex-Russian soldiers from Gallipoli has also been evacuated to Hungary, where work has been found for them.

(d) *Coöperation with American Organisations.*—Coöperation with the great American relief organisations continues to constitute as important a feature of the work of this office as before. The sittings of the High Commissariat Refugee Coördination Committee continue to form a medium for the discussion and solution of the various refugee evacuation problems as they arise. More tangible evidence of the successful coöperation of the High Commissariat with the American Red Cross and the American Relief Administration is afforded by the fact that, as a result of the united efforts of these two organisations and the League, 598 refugees were sent to America by the High Commissariat's individual departure scheme. The success of this experiment in coöperation and the excellent reports received from the refugees evacuated as to their successful absorption in America encouraged the three organisations concerned to endeavour to send another 1,200 who should enter America in the quota opening July 1st. Towards the cost of this, the High Commissariat will pay £3 per head. The rest of the expense is met by practically equal contributions by the American Relief Administration and the American Red Cross and by the refugees themselves. The scheme has been successfully begun, and two convoys amounting to 205 persons have already been sent under it. Reception is arranged by the Russian Refugee Relief Society of America. A pledge is given by the refugee for repayment of sums advanced. Any sums thus returned are held by the Russian Refugee Relief Society for America in trust for disposal, as the result of an agreement between the American Red Cross and the American Relief Association.

. . . .

(c) Refugee's Certificate of Identity and Origin[1]

In accordance with the proposal dated.................made to the Governments interested, by the League of Nations' High Commissioner for Russian Refugees.

We.....................................certify that the bearer of this certificate, a refugee to...................territory, whose photograph, description and signature appear hereinafter, claims and has been ascertained to be one.................................. a national of*.........................according to the law of* ....in force before August 1st, 1914.

We hereby request that he (she) may be permitted and assisted to travel and to enter and remain for all lawful purposes to and in any country other than*..........................as though he (she) were the bearer of a passport duly issued and recognised, notwithstanding that he (she) may not hold such passport, subject always to the laws and regulations in force concerning the admission and residence of foreign nationals.

We, therefore, request that this certificate may, to this end, be treated as susceptible of receiving a visa in the manner as a passport issued by a duly recognised government.

This certificate is valid for . . . years from its date and may at its expiration, be renewed by us or by the consuls under our authority abroad, subject to the regulations in force at the date of expiration.

------

[1] League of Nations *Official Journal*, May, 1922, p. 399.

This certificate shall cease to be valid if the bearer shall at any time enter the territory of*...............................

Given at ....
The ....day of ....19..
Signed ....

* Insert name of the country of which the person in question would be a national, according to the law of that country in force before August 1, 1914.

(d) *Relief Measures for Refugees in Greece and Asia Minor. Report by Dr. Nansen, High Commissioner of the League of Nations. November 18, 1922*[1]

1. Immediately after the close of the session of the Assembly of the League of Nations I proceeded to Constantinople to carry out the enquiries into the problem of the refugees in the Near East with which the Assembly had charged me.

From Constantinople I proceeded on a journey of inspection through Eastern Thrace and from there to Athens.

In Constantinople, Salonica and Athens I had the advantage of establishing close contact on the problem of refugees with all the competent authorities of the Turkish and Greek Governments and with the leaders of the relief organisations which have already begun to bring assistance to the refugees. The conclusions which I venture to present to the Council of the League of Nations in this report are therefore based on a close study of the actual situation, and are arrived at after careful consideration of the problems which it raised.

2. Although I was prepared to make a journey in Asia Minor, I was unfortunately not able to carry this intention into effect. I have had therefore to rely for my information concerning the situation in Asia Minor upon what I have been able to learn from official sources and from relief workers on the spot. I am satisfied, however, from what they have told me there has been real distress on a large scale among a great number of the population inhabiting the area in which the military operations of September last were carried out. I endeavoured to do what I could to assist the authorities of the Turkish Red Crescent in alleviating this distress. I despatched to Smyrna 200 tons of flour, bought with the funds placed at my disposal by the Assembly of the League. I also provided transport for a number of Turkish refugees from Constantinople to reach their homes on the shores of Asia Minor in time to carry through autumn cultivation of their fields. Colonel Gauthier, the representative of the League of Nations Epidemic Commission, was able to come to the aid of the Turkish Red Crescent with medical supplies, especially vaccine and serum. The International Red Cross has also brought a certain amount of relief and a number of blankets to Smyrna, and the American Red Cross

[1] League of Nations *Official Journal*, January, 1923, p. 133ff.

and the Near East Relief are carrying out work of assistance on a generous scale.

Nevertheless it is clear, from the evidence which I have received, that the situation of the population in this area of Asia Minor, although undoubtedly serious, is one with which the Turkish authorities are in a position to deal without great assistance from outside, and I do not think that the problem there is comparable in gravity with that of the refugees in Greece.

3. There are already within the frontiers of Greece refugees of Greek and Armenian race amounting, according to information received, to not less than 900,000. The collection of exact statistics is still a matter of great difficulty, but it appears that at least 50,000 and probably a greater number of these refugees are Armenians. To these Armenians the Greek Government is with great generosity extending hospitality and relief.

It is calculated that, of the 900,000 refugees, approximately 300,-000 are from Eastern Thrace and the remainder from Asia Minor. Those from Eastern Thrace who left their homes after the conclusion of the Armistice of Mudania are in comparatively good condition. They were able to bring away with them at least some of their movable possessions, including for the most part their cattle, wagons, clothing and in some cases their agricultural implements. Although they were obliged to leave behind the abundant crops which they had reaped this year, they have nevertheless, generally speaking, a certain amount of money.

The refugees from Asia Minor, on the other hand, have left their homes with such precipitation that they have no other possessions of any kind than the light summer clothes which they wear. They urgently require not only shelter but also winter clothing and blankets to enable them to face the severity of the coming winter; they are also without any money with which to supply themselves with food.

The Greek Government has made great efforts to distribute these refugees throughout the country in such a way as to permit of their absorption by the local population.

For the refugees from Eastern Thrace who are agriculturists this absorption is less difficult, and a certain measure of success has already been achieved in placing them on the vacant lands in Macedonia and Western Thrace, where they will be able to grow for next year the crops which they will require to enable them to live. For the whole of the refugees from Asia Minor, however, and for the town population from Eastern Thrace, the difficulties are far greater. In spite of the great efforts which have been made by the Greek Government and people and by the various relief agencies, the situation of these refugees is very grave.

4. It is not possible to give in this report a detailed account of the work which is being done and the problems that are being dealt with

by the relief agencies. I will on a later occasion give a detailed account to the Council of the use which I have made of the funds placed at my disposal. I succeeded in acquiring a considerable quantity of flour with the least possible delay, which was used to meet a difficult situation on the islands of Samos and Chios. League representatives are now carrying out direct relief in Western Thrace. I venture to appeal urgently and insistently to the Governments of the Members of the League to provide the further contributions which are required to enable me to acquire the whole of the £50,000 promised by the British Government when a similar sum has been contributed by the other Members of the League.

I am very happy to be able to say that the American Red Cross, under the able leadership of Dr. Ross Hill, has come into the field and is now bringing help in the form of food and other direct relief which will go far to solve the most immediate problems. The American people, through the agency of the American Red Cross, are thus about to add another chapter to their already long record of great acts of charity. It may be hoped that if the response to the appeal for charity from other quarters of the world is equally generous, and if there is no further influx of refugees into Greece, the problem of feeding the refugees during the next few months may be satisfactorily solved. This result can only be achieved, however, if the charitable organisations of other countries make a response corresponding in degree to that of the American Red Cross.

5. Even if the problem of food for the next few months is solved, there remain other difficulties to be overcome which are not less grave. Hundreds of thousands of the refugees are without any proper shelter. The provision of tents, hutments and elementary building material (wood and roofing) is of urgent importance, and I venture to appeal to the charitable organisations and to the Governments to make any provision of this sort which may be within their power.

In addition a vast quantity of clothing and blankets is required to enable the refugees to face the hardships of the winter months. Unless supplies of these articles are forthcoming in great quantities and without delay, vast numbers of mothers and little children must inevitably die. The mortality among the babies and mothers whose children have been born in refugee camps during the last month is already very great.

6. In addition, the presence of this great number of refugees in temporary camps gives rise to a grave danger of serious epidemics. In some camps smallpox has already broken out. In all of them dysentery is more or less common. Typhoid, cholera and, above all, typhus may be expected. It is therefore extremely important that every step which is possible should be taken to assist the Greek civil authorities to combat this great danger. I have been fortunate enough to secure for this work the services of the Epidemic Commission of the League of

Nations, which has done such good work in Poland and the border States of Russia. Representatives of the Commission have already arrived in Greece and are carrying out investigations into the situation. They are of the opinion that the possibility of epidemics is one which threatens not only Greece alone but the whole of Southern Europe. As a preliminary measure the Epidemic Commission has already provided some hundred thousand doses of vaccine for inoculating refugees against diseases, and it is preparing further large quantities. I venture therefore to appeal to the Governments of the Members of the League and to their Red Cross Societies to provide the Epidemic Commission with the resources—whether in the form of money or in the form of disinfecting apparatus and other medical supplies—which will enable them to bring effective assistance to the Greek authorities.

7. I need not draw the attention of the Council of the League in any detail to the serious results which the situation I have described must entail for the Greek State. It inevitably imposes a terrible strain upon its financial, economic and moral resources. If the food supply for this vast influx of refugees were to break down it might threaten the whole social and economic stability not only of Greece itself but even of the neighboring countries in the Near East. . . .

It is clear that for those of the refugees who are agriculturists—the estimate of the number of agriculturists is about 550,000—the obvious solution is to place them on the vacant lands of Greece. This can no doubt be done, and if it is done it will bring to Greece a great new source of wealth, but it can only be done if substantial capital is found. To establish an agricultural population on vacant land requires great quantities of all building materials, animals, ploughs, seed and food. In addition, the settlement of the vacant lands of Macedonia necessitates the carrying out of great works of sanitation to remove the sources of malaria which at present decimate any new population which settles there. Much capital is required, and this capital the Greek people alone are not in a position at present to provide. . . .

In my opinion the only way in which the necessary capital can be found is by some form of international loan. I believe it is in the interests of the other Members of the League that such an international loan should be granted to the Greek people to enable them to reëstablish on a firm footing their national economy. I venture to hope that the Governments, acting through the Council of the League of Nations or otherwise as they may think fit, may find it possible to study this urgent question at the earliest possible moment. There is no need to add that the Greek Government would be prepared to allocate revenues for the payment of the interest and the amortisation of the capital of such a loan.

8. Even if the capital required for the scheme of agricultural settlement be found, all the difficulties of the situation will not be solved. In the first place it must be mentioned that the refugees from Asia

Minor consist principally of women and children and old men. Even if they are in a great part agriculturists it would be extremely difficult to settle these people on the land without any men to help them to build their temporary huts or houses and to open up the fields.

In the second place it is much harder to deal with the town population, which amounts to 35% or 40% of the whole. It must be hoped that the great immigration countries across the ocean will consent to receive some of these refugees. Others no doubt can be absorbed into the industries of Greece, but it is evident that for some time to come a great amount of direct relief will be required to enable these refugees to be maintained. There is therefore a wide field for the assistance of the whole world.

9. I have hitherto only spoken of the situation as it actually exists at the moment at which I write, November 10th, 1922. There are certain grounds, however, for fearing that the situation may be rendered still more acute by a new great influx of refugees from Asia Minor. There is evidence that within the last few days a large number of refugees have arrived from the Black Sea ports of Anatolia, and they all report that a great new movement of the Greek and Armenian population from Anatolia has begun. They allege that at least 100,000 Armenians and 250,000 Greeks are now moving towards the coast to take refuge in Europe. These new refugees are arriving in the same condition as the first refugees from Asia Minor, that is to say with nothing but the clothes they wear. There are therefore strong grounds for fearing that some quarter of a million additional refugees are to be thrown upon Europe for support. We may still hope that the reports of these refugees who have recently arrived may be untrue, or that something may be done to avert this new tragic exodus from Asia Minor. If, however, it takes place, the consequences to which it will lead will be grave in the extreme. It is more than probable that such an exodus will be followed by a further exodus of the Greek and Armenian population from Constantinople. If such an event occurs, the burden of immediate relief thrown upon Greece would be one which it could not possibly support. The movement of refugees which followed immediately the military operation of September has already put a terrible strain upon Greek resources. If the number of refugees is to be more than trebled by the events which have followed the conclusion of hostilities, the situation will be one which will affect the peace and prosperity of the whole of Europe.

I cannot too strongly insist that the support and the assistance of the world at large will be necessary to cope with these desperate problems.

[EDITORS' NOTE: On February 2, 1923, Dr. Nansen reported to the Council of the League of Nations that conditions in the Near East were worse than he stated in his November report. It is to be noted that in October of 1924 there were still 500,000 refugees waiting to be helped to the means of earning a livelihood.

For the conditions upon which the Bank of England made a loan to the Greek Government of £1,000,000, see the League of Nations *Official Journal*, 4th Year, No. 10, October, 1923, pp. 1142-1145.]

(e) *Plan for Rehabilitating Refugees in Near East as stated in the Report of Dr. Nansen, High Commissioner for Refugees, submitted to the Council of the League of Nations, April 23rd, 1923*[1]

In my last report to the Council, reference was made to the establishment of feeding camps and settlements in Western Thrace and Macedonia and to the attempt to organize these on a constructive and self-supporting basis. A survey of the development of these settlements for upwards of 10,000 refugees, within the last six months, from an indiscriminate mass of humanity sheltered, if at all, under inadequate tents, in old stables and improvised barracks, into organized communities engaged in productive labour, constitutes a record of constructive and enduring work.

The following report from Colonel Proctor, the Deputy High Commissioner for Refugees at Constantinople, who initiated this scheme, merits the attention of the Council. Colonel Proctor is in attendance and would be pleased to amplify the information contained in this report:

.   .   .   .

"Our plan may be briefly summarised as follows:

"(1) The guiding principle was not indiscriminate charity, which tends to the degeneration of the refugees, but to encourage them to work for themselves and thus become producers of wealth and independent citizens as soon as possible.

"(2) The main plan was, first, to establish village settlements under canvas for about 10,000 refugees, and later, with the assistance of the Greek Government, to enable the settlers to build houses and thus release the tents for still further settlers.

"(3) The refugees were to be fed, organised and their general welfare in other ways cared for until their crops could be reaped (about the end of next July) or until such earlier date as they could become self-supporting.

"(4) To organise skilled and general workers and to establish them in such occupations as their previous life and training fitted them, such as farming, charcoal burning, brick making, carpet and blanket weaving, lace making, fishing, etc.

[1] League of Nations *Official Journal*, June, 1923, p. 696ff.

"(5) To maintain a hospital for the care of the refugees and to work for the maintenance of a high standard of health.

"(6) To arrange for the provision of fodder for the working cattle, which is an absolute necessity.

"In October 1922, many of the refugees evacuated by the High Commissariat from Asia Minor and Eastern Thrace arrived in Western Thrace, for the most part in a state of utter destitution. As a preliminary relief measure, a series of feeding stations and dispensaries, with rations for 10,000 refugees for a period of three months, was immediately organized by the High Commissariat of the League of Nations, and on November 23rd, a hospital and base camp for 10,000 persons was despatched to Western Thrace. The hospital consisted of 120 beds, complete with supplies of drugs for a period of three months. The money for it was raised by Lady Rumbold. This hospital now serves all the refugees in an area of 500 square miles. . . ."

159. A RUSSIAN VIEW OF THE LEAGUE[1]

[In 1920-1921 Poland was at war with Bolshevist Russia in an endeavour to obtain the 1772 boundaries on the East. Because the states members of the League of Nations were more friendly in general to Poland than to Russia—although it must be said that these states did not support all the Polish ambitions—Lenin published this tirade against the League of Nations. It was printed in America, undoubtedly to arouse American interest in the Russian cause.]

The so-called League of Nations has become in reality a plague of nations. Born of the hatred engendered by four years of world war, ruled by the unscrupulous, moribund servants of greedy imperialism and capitalism, this organization is doing its utmost to prolong the sufferings of humanity. This so-called League of Nations is sending to slaughter British workers in Mesopotamia and India, French in Syria, Polish workers in Russia, and Turkish nationalists and Greeks thruout Asia Minor. It is starving to death the innocent children of Vienna, even the Lord Mayor of the City of Cork in the Tower of London.

Above all, this Plague of Nations is blockading, starving and fighting openly and secretly the peasants and workers of Soviet Russia. The anti-Bolshevist Polish nationalists, Pilsudski and Paderewski, have openly stated that it was this Plague of Nations ("League of Nations") which prevented them from concluding early peace with Soviet Russia. It is this same Plague of Nations again which is threatening Soviet Russia with new ultimata and injecting itself between

---

[1] Nicolai Lenin, *Against the Plague of Nations: An Address to Thinking People on the Polish Question*. Published by The Toiler Publishing Association, Cleveland, Ohio (n.d.) [1920-21].

the Poles and Russians at the present peace parleys at Minsk. It is this same Plague of Nations which is sending munitions, officers and aviators to the Polish front, thus clearly demonstrating the "neutrality" of that decrepit imperialism. Great Britain, the most elusive and most powerful member of the League, is being kept at bay by its revolutionary working class organizations demanding immediate lifting of the blockade and recognition of Soviet Russia. This explains the wavering and double-cross attitude toward Soviet Russia on the part of Lloyd George, who is supporting General Wrangel with ships and munitions while asserting His Majesty's neutrality towards that German baron bandit.

Italy has been forced by its working class revolutionary organizations to abandon all attacks against Soviet Russia and virtually to recognize the Soviet Government of the peasants and workers of Russia.

France remains the sworn enemy of every progress, especially in Russia. Her generals, her officers, guns, munitions and airplanes have been fighting the Soviet armies on the Polish front ever since the beginning of the present offensive against Soviet Russia. France has recognized General Wrangel as the government of All Russia. France is bent upon destroying the Soviets by starvation, hatred and violence.

There are still other governments supporting Poland morally and immorally, with empty words and promises.

These wanton onslaughts against the peaceful Republic of Soviet Russia have aroused the workers of the world to the highest pitch of indignation. They have become conscious of the fact that poverty, disease and starvation cannot be eradicated from the face of the earth unless Russia, this giant nation, is permitted to rehabilitate itself. The imperialistic policy of capitalist governments is calculated to prolong the sufferings of Russia and of the workers the world over.

Here is the toll of epidemics exacted from the workers of Petrograd during the single week from May 30 to June 5, 1920:

246 cases of Spotted Typhus
88 " " Repeated Typhus
10 " " Smallpox
18 " " Dysentery
10 " " Acute Diarrhœa
45 " " Other Diseases

Total 417 cases of needless suffering caused by filth and starvation imposed upon the Russian people by the horrible blockade of the Plague of Nations.

The Poles are spreading false stories about alleged atrocities of the Soviet Armies. We need not say much to refute their falsehoods. The massacres perpetrated upon the Jewish population by the Poles have been established beyond a scintilla of doubt by the most anti-Bolshevist investigators, by the High Commissioner of Great Britain, Sir Samuel himself. The inhuman treatment accorded by the Poles to the conquered nations was not confined to the Jews alone. They have maimed and killed peaceful peasants, even cattle, which they could not take with them. Upon the capture of Kiev they destroyed a freight depot, a sugar refinery and were about to burn the railroad station offices which they were prevented from doing by the employees. They blew up the palace of the former governor-general, his church, the Girls' Gymnasium with the church, four bridges, waterworks, railroad cars, houses, and the big Georgiev Works, taking the machinery to Warsaw. The Ukranian Executive Committee of the local communes have addressed a solemn protest to the People's Commissar of Foreign Affairs of Soviet Russia, G. Chicherin, against the Polish atrocities perpetrated before the evacuation by them of the captured cities. They mention the destruction of the famous Cathedral of St. Vladimir in Kiev, a relic of antiquity as old as the famous Rheims Cathedral in France. They protest against the complete destruction of the town of Borisov by Polish artillery.

There is system in the madness of the henchmen of the Allied managers of the Plague of Nations. Their aim is to so weaken and dishearten the workers of Russia as to compel them to submit to the dictates of greedy imperialism and capitalism. But the Soviet Government and its leaders have risen to the occasion. Their wits are more than a match for the war lords' dying Plague. The gradual disorganization and decomposition of the League is taking place before our eyes. The Soviet Government on the other hand, is gathering its forces and straining every nerve to unite and to strengthen the power of resistance and the morale of the People of Soviet Russia. It is hoped that the workers in other countries will realize the world-wide significance of the battles going on at the Polish front, that they will give their moral and material support to the Soviet Republic of Russia in its darkest hour of trial.

The remarks of Comrade Lenin, chairman of the Council of the People's Commissars of the Soviet Republic, before a recent conference of Rural Commissars of Soviet Russia may well serve as an inspiration for the gigantic task facing the Soviet Republic and the proletariat of all countries.

160. BOLSHEVIST PROGRAM OF WORLD REVOLUTION[1]

[One of the outstanding factors in recent international relations has been the fear of the spread of Russian communist propaganda. It has been as much feared as was once French republicanism. The following statement is an exposition of the propagandist's point of view.]

[1] U. S. Department of State. *Memorandum on Certain Aspects of the Bolshevist Movement in Russia.* Washington, 1919, Appendix, pp. 45-46.

XVII

World Revolution

(Bolshevist Program, from Chapter XIX of Pamphlet entitled "Program of Communists," by N. Bukharin; July 24, 1918.)

The program of the Communist Party is the program not only of liberating the proletariat of one country; it is the program of liberating the proletariat of the world, for such is the program of the "International Revolution." At the same time it is the program of liberating all smaller, oppressed countries and peoples. Those robbers, the "Great Powers" (England, Germany, Japan, and America) have stolen an immense quantity of lands and peoples. They divided the world between themselves. It is not surprising that in these stolen countries the workmen and toilers are suffering under double pressure, under the pressure of their own bourgeois[ie] as well as under the pressure of the conquerors. The Tsar's Russia also stole many countries and peoples; that is why our "empire" is so enormous. Therefore among many of our so-called "aliens" and also among some of the non-Russian proletariat there was no faith in the Great-Russians. . . . For the definite victory of the workmen's revolution a complete mutual confidence between the different parts of the proletariat is all-important. It must be pointed out and proved that the proletariat of the oppressing nation was a faithful ally of the proletariat of other nations. In Russia the dominant nation was the Great-Russian, who conquered the Finns, Tartars, Little-Russians, Armenians, Georgians, Poles, and many other peoples. It is natural that even among the proletariat of these peoples there exists a wrong conception concerning every Russian. They have been accustomed to see how the Tsar forcibly used Russians, and because of that have believed all Russians, even the members of the proletariat, to be of the kind.

Therefore, in order to create a brotherly union between the different divisions of the proletariat, the communist program announces the right of working classes of every nation to complete separation. That is to say, the Russian workman who has the power, says to the workmen of other peoples living in Russia: "Comrades, if you do not care to become members of our Soviet Republic, if you desire to form your own Soviet Republic, do so. We give you the full right to do so. We do not wish to hold you by force a single minute."

Only by such tactics it is possible to win the confidence of the whole proletariat. We have only to imagine what would happen in case the Great-Russian Soviets should keep in subjection the working classes of other nations, and the latter should protect themselves with arms. It is evident that this would mean the entire failure of the proletarian movement, the complete collapse of the revolution. It is impossible to act in this way, for, we repeat, a brotherly union of proletarians is the one guarantee of victory.

We do not speak of the right of self-determination of nations (i.e., of their bourgeoisie [sic] and their workmen), but only of the right of the working classes. Therefore, the so-called "will of the nation" is not sacred for us. Should we wish to learn the will of the nation, we would be forced to call a Constituent Assembly of the nation. For us, the will of the proletariat and of the semiproletarian masses is sacred. . . . During the dictatorship of the proletariat, not the will of the Constituent Assembly, but the will of the Soviets of the working people decides the question. And if at the same time in two different parts of Russia two assemblies should be called, a Constituent Assembly and a Congress of Soviets, and the former should against the will of the latter proclaim a "separation," we will defend the latter with all means, using armed force if necessary.

That is the manner in which the proletarian party decides the question of different peoples of the same country. But then comes up the broader question of its international program. The way is clear here. It is the way of the world-wide support of the international revolution, of revolutionary propaganda, of strikes and rebellions in imperialistic countries, of uprisings in the colonies of these countries.

In the imperialistic countries (and such are all of them, except Russia, where the workmen have smashed the rule of capital) that section of the Social-Democrats which stands for the defense of the country is one of the most serious obstacles. It is even now setting forth the idea of defending the country (robbers' country), telling different lies to the wide working classes. It pursues our friends, the German, Austrian, and English Bolsheviks, who are the only ones who contemptuously reject the idea of defending the bourgeois [sic] countries. It wails over the decomposition of the (robber) army. The situation of the Soviet Republic is quite an exceptional one. It is the only state organization of the proletariat in the whole world, among the robber organizations of the bourgeoisie [sic]. Therefore it alone has the right to be defended. Moreover, it must be regarded as the fighting weapon of the universal proletariat against the universal bourgeoisie [sic]. The fighting slogan of this struggle is quite clear now. It is the International Soviet Republic.

The overthrowing of imperialistic governments by armed uprisings and the organization of an International Soviet Republic is the way of the international dictatorship of the working class.

The most forceful way to maintain the international revolution is by the organization of the armed forces of revolution. All workmen of all countries, who are not blinded by traitor Socialists, by their Socialist-Revolutionaries and their Mensheviks (and these are found in each country) see in the workmen's revolution in Russia and in the

Soviet authority their own cause. Why? Because they see that the Soviet authority is the authority of the workmen themselves. It would be quite different if the bourgeoisie, assisted by the Mensheviks and the Socialist-Revolutionaries, should overthrow the Soviets, should call the Constituent Assembly and through it should recreate the bourgeois authority, for example, as it existed before the October revolution. Then the working class would lose its country for it would lose its power. Then inevitably the banks would be returned to bankers, the factories to manufacturers, the land to the landowners. The land of "profits" would then revive. And the workmen would have no interest to protect such a country. On the other hand, the workmen of Western Europe would be unable to find in bourgeois Russia a lighthouse, which lights them in their hard struggle. The development of the international revolution would be checked.

On the other hand, the strengthening of the Soviet authority, the organization of armed forces of the workmen and poorest peasants, the organization of resistance to international robbers who are going against Soviet Russia as enemies, because they are members of different classes, such as landowners and capitalists, like a band of "hangmen of the workmen's revolution," and finally the organization of the Red Army would strengthen the revolutionary movement in European countries. The better we are organized, the stronger the armed detachments of workmen and peasants, the more powerful the dictatorship of the proletariat in Russia, the more quickly will the international revolution come.

This revolution will inevitably come, despite the efforts of German, Austrian, French and English Mensheviks. The working masses in Russia have cut all relations with the compromisers. The workmen of all Europe will do, and in fact are already doing, the same. The slogan of overthrowing robber governments and of the dictatorship of workmen is winning more and more sympathy. Sooner or later we will have the International Republic of Soviets.

This International Soviet Republic will liberate from oppression hundreds of millions of inhabitants of colonies. The "civilized" robber powers tortured the population of colonial countries by a régime of terror. European civilization was maintained by exploitation and by stealing small peoples in distant countries. The latter will be liberated only by the dictatorship of the proletariat. Just as the Russian Soviet authority has actually proved that it is not willing to continue the colonial policy (for instance Persia) so the European workmen, after overthrowing the rule of the bankers, will give complete freedom to the exploited and oppressed classes. Therefore, the program of our party, which is the program of international revolution, is at the same time the program of complete liberation of the weak and oppressed. The great class—the working class—sets itself great tasks. It is also solving these tasks in a bloody, torturing and heroic fight.

161. ANGLO-RUSSIAN RELATIONS

[The Russians were exhausted following the war and the revolution and set out in 1920-21 to establish relations which would make possible an increase of foreign trade. The first state to sign an agreement with them was Great Britain. The increasing strength of the Labor Party and the need of reviving British trade were factors which helped to bring about this step. The memorandum by Lord Curzon, British Foreign Secretary, shows that Anglo-Russian relations were not entirely satisfactory; but with the advent of the MacDonald Government in December, 1923, there was an attempt to improve the situation, and *de jure* recognition was accorded Russia on February 1, 1924. A new commercial treaty was made (1924) but the succeeding Baldwin Government failed to ratify it. Early in 1927 the British Government again complained to Russia of communist propaganda and broke off relations, but these were resumed December 20, 1929.]

(a) *The Anglo-Russian Trade Agreement, 1921*[1]

Whereas it is desirable in the interests both of Russia and of the United Kingdom that peaceful trade and commerce should be resumed forthwith between these countries, and whereas for this purpose it is necessary pending the conclusion of a formal general Peace Treaty between the Governments of these countries by which their economic and political relations shall be regulated in the future that a preliminary Agreement should be arrived at between the Government of the United Kingdom and the Government of the Russian Socialist Federal Soviet Republic, hereinafter referred to as the Russian Soviet Government.

The aforesaid parties have accordingly entered into the present Agreement for the resumption of trade and commerce between the countries.

The present Agreement is subject to the fulfilment of the following conditions, namely:—

(a) That each party refrains from hostile action or undertakings against the other and from conducting outside of its own borders any official propaganda direct or indirect against the institutions of the British Empire or the Russian Soviet Republic respectively, and more particularly that the Russian Soviet Government refrains from any attempt by military or diplomatic or any other form of action or propaganda to encourage any of the peoples of Asia in any form of hostile action against British interests or the British Empire, especially in India and in the Independent State of Afghanistan. The

[1] Great Britain. *Parliamentary Papers*, 1921, Vol. XLIII, Cmd. 1207. "Russian Trade Agreement."

British Government gives a similar particular undertaking to the Russian Soviet Government in respect of the countries which formed part of the former Russian Empire and which have now become independent.

(b) That all British subjects in Russia are immediately permitted to return home, and that all Russian citizens in Great Britain or other parts of the British Empire who desire to return to Russia are similarly released.

It is understood that the term "conducting any official propaganda" includes the giving by either party of assistance or encouragement to any propaganda conducted outside its own borders.

The parties undertake to give forthwith all necessary instructions to their agents and to all persons under their authority to conform to the stipulations undertaken above.

I

Both parties agree not to impose or maintain any form of blockade against each other and to remove forthwith all obstacles hitherto placed in the way of the resumption of trade between the United Kingdom and Russia in any commodities which may be legally exported from or imported into their respective territories to or from any other foreign country, and not to exercise any discrimination against such trade, as compared with that carried on with any other foreign country or to place any impediments in the way of banking, credit and financial operations for the purpose of such trade, but subject always to legislation generally applicable in the respective countries. It is understood that nothing in this Article shall prevent either party from regulating the trade in arms and ammunition under general provisions of law which are applicable to the import of arms and ammunition from, or their export to foreign countries.

Nothing in this Article shall be construed as overriding the provisions of any general International Convention which is binding on either party by which the trade in any particular article is or may be regulated (as for example, the Opium Convention).

. . . .

IV

Each party may nominate such number of its nationals as may be agreed from time to time as being reasonably necessary to enable proper effect to be given to this Agreement, having regard to the conditions under which trade is carried on in its territories, and the other party shall permit such persons to enter its territories, and to sojourn and carry on trade there, provided that either party may restrict the admittance of any such persons into any specified areas, and may refuse admittance to or sojourn in its territories to any individual who is *persona non grata* to itself, or who does not comply with this Agreement or with the conditions precedent thereto.

Persons admitted in pursuance of this Article into the territories of either party shall, while sojourning therein for purposes of trade, be exempted from all compulsory services whatsoever, whether civil, naval, military or other, and from any contributions whether pecuniary or in kind imposed as an equivalent for personal service and shall have right of egress.

They shall be at liberty to communicate freely by post, telegraph and wireless telegraphy, and to use telegraph codes under the conditions and subject to the regulations laid down in the International Telegraph Convention of St. Petersburg, 1875 (Lisbon Revision of 1908).

Each party undertakes to account for and to pay all balances due to the other in respect of terminal and transit telegrams and in respect of transit letter mails in accordance with the provisions of the International Telegraph Convention and Regulations and of the Convention and Regulations of the Universal Postal Union respectively. The above balances when due shall be paid in the currency of either party at the option of the receiving party.

Persons admitted into Russia under this Agreement shall be permitted freely to import commodities (except commodities, such as alcoholic liquors, of which both the importation and the manufacture are or may be prohibited in Russia), destined solely for their household use or consumption to an amount reasonably required for such purposes.

. . . . . .

XIII

The present Agreement shall come into force immediately and both parties shall at once take all necessary measures to give effect to it. It shall continue in force unless and until replaced by the Treaty contemplated in the Preamble so long as the conditions laid down both in the Articles of the Agreement and in the Preamble are observed by both sides. Provided that at any time after the expiration of twelve months from the date on which the Agreement comes into force either party may give notice to terminate the provisions of the preceding Articles, and on the expiration of six months from the date of such notice those Articles shall terminate accordingly.

Provided also that if as the result of any action in the Courts of the United Kingdom dealing with the attachment or arrest of any gold, funds, securities, property or commodities not being identifiable as the exclusive property of a British subject, consigned to the United Kingdom by the Russian Soviet Government or its representatives, judgment is delivered by the Court under which such gold, funds, securities, property or commodities are held to be validly attached on account of obligations incurred by the Russian Soviet Government or by any previous Russian Government before the date of the signature of this Agreement, the Russian Soviet Government shall have the right to terminate the Agreement forthwith.

Provided also that in the event of the infringement by either party at any time of any of the provisions of this Agreement or of the conditions referred to in the Preamble, the other party shall immediately be free from the obligations of the Agreement. Nevertheless it is agreed that before taking any action inconsistent with the Agreement the aggrieved party shall give the other party a reasonable opportunity of furnishing an explanation or remedying the default.

It is mutually agreed that in any of the events contemplated in the above provisos, the parties will afford all necessary facilities for the winding up in accordance with the principles of the Agreement of any transactions already entered into thereunder, and for the withdrawal and egress from their territories of the nationals of the other party and for the withdrawal of their movable property.

As from the date when six months' notice of termination shall have been given under this Article, the only new transactions which shall be entered into under the Agreement shall be those which can be completed within the six months. In all other respects the provisions of the Agreement will remain fully in force up to the date of termination.

XIV

This Agreement is drawn up and signed in the English language. But it is agreed that as soon as may be a translation shall be made into the Russian language and agreed between the Parties. Both texts shall then be considered authentic for all purposes.

Signed at London, this sixteenth day of March, nineteen hundred and twenty-one.

R. S. HORNE
L. KRASSIN

DECLARATION OF RECOGNITION OF CLAIMS

At the moment of signature of the preceding Trade Agreement both parties declare that all claims of either party or of its nationals against the other party in respect of property or rights or in respect of obligations incurred by the existing or former Governments of either country shall be equitably dealt with in the formal general Peace Treaty referred to in the Preamble.

In the meantime and without prejudice to the generality of the above stipulation the Russian Soviet Government declares that it recognises in principle that it is liable to pay compensation to private persons who have supplied goods or services to Russia for which they have not been paid. The detailed mode of discharging this liability shall be regulated by the Treaty referred to in the Preamble.

The British Government hereby makes a corresponding declaration.

It is clearly understood that the above declarations in no way imply that the claims referred to therein will have preferential treatment in the aforesaid Treaty as compared with any other classes of claims which are to be dealt with in that Treaty.

Signed at London this sixteenth day of March, nineteen hundred and twenty-one.

R. S. HORNE

L. KRASSIN

(b) *Lord Curzon's Review of Anglo-Russian Relations, 1921-1923*[1]

MEMORANDUM

1. The tone and character of the notes recently received by the British agent at Moscow from the Russian Commissariat for Foreign Affairs, in reply to certain representations made by the former under instructions from His Majesty's Government have imposed upon His Majesty's Government the duty, which has perhaps been already too long delayed, of considering carefully, and *seriatim*, in relation to a large number of similar incidents, whether it is desirable, or indeed possible, that the relations of the two Governments should remain any longer upon so anomalous and indeed unprecedented a footing, and whether His Majesty's Government can with due self-respect continue to ignore the repeated challenges which the Soviet Government has thought fit with apparent deliberation to throw down. His Majesty's Government have therefore decided that the moment has arrived to address to the Soviet Government a considered statement of their views with the desire to arrive at a definite conclusion

2. It is now just over two years since His Majesty's Government signed a trade agreement with the Soviet Government, with a view to promoting commercial relations between the two countries, the question of political relations being postponed until the above agreement had been tested in practice, and until the Soviet Government had satisfied certain indispensable conditions. In taking this step, which was in advance of any similar action by any other foreign Government, His Majesty's Government not only signified their willingness to establish a friendly understanding with the Russian Government and the Russian people, but they made a material contribution to the stability and prosperity of the Russian State. At the same time, they were careful to prefix to the agreement the stipulation, incumbent upon both parties, to refrain from hostile action or propaganda, the one against

[1] Great Britain. *Parliamentary Papers,* 1923. Vol. XXV. Cmd. 1869. pp. 6-13. "Correspondence between His Majesty's Government and the Soviet Government Respecting the Relations between the Two Governments." Enclosure in No. 5.

the other. This undertaking, which has been loyally and scrupulously observed by His Majesty's Government, has from the start been consistently and flagrantly violated by the Soviet Government, and correspondence between the two Governments in the autumn and winter of 1921, which has been published, sufficiently indicate the grounds of complaint of His Majesty's Government, as well as the nature of the Russian reply. After this, there was some slight curtailment of the activities of Russian agents in Asia, the Soviet authorities apparently realising that the Trade Agreement, from which they derived such substantial advantage, might be imperilled by unduly rash conduct. More recently these pernicious activities have been vigorously resumed. It would be easy to fill many pages with a narrative of these proceedings resting upon unimpeachable authority. Such a narrative would doubtless provoke, as it did before, an indignant denial from the Soviet Government with allegations as to false information and spurious documents. His Majesty's Government have no intention to embark upon any such controversy. They are content to rely exclusively upon communications which have passed in the last few months between the Russian Government and its agents, and which are in their possession, and upon the recorded acts of members of the Soviet Government itself.

3. Among the most useful bases for Russian anti-British propaganda has always been the area which comprises Persia, Afghanistan and the Indian border.

I.—Persia

4. The Russian Minister at Tehran has been the most tireless, though not always the most successful, operator in this field. He has housed Indian seditionists within his hospitable walls, and has sped them on their mission to India. His Majesty's Government know the exact sums which have been sent to him from time to time by the Russian Government largely for the purpose of anti-British intrigue; and they have seen instructions that have passed between him and his superiors, and between him and his subordinate agents, with a view to stirring up anti-British movements and rebellion in that part of the world. The activities of this agent have even extended to the neighbouring territory of Irak; and Kermanshah, where there is a Soviet consul, the instructions to whom are known to His Majesty's Government, has been made the active centre of these benevolent intentions. That these activities are well known to, and have been authorised by, the Soviet Government at Moscow is demonstrated by a report from M. Shumiatsky, the Russian representative at Tehran to the Commissariat for Foreign Affairs, in February 1923, which contains the following interesting paragraph: "Our mission, in carrying out the instructions which your telegram amplifies, had decided on this politi-

cal line of action, especially in North Persia and Tehran; a good group of workers has been organized who can act in an anti-British direction with real activity. . . . If the Commissary for Foreign Affairs will agree to the plan of the mission, for the first expenditure 300,000 tomans will be necessary as a credit to enable us to work."

II.—Afghanistan

5. Afghanistan affords an even more favourable base for enterprise, owing to its proximity to the turbulent tribes within the India border. Here M. Raskolnikov, the Soviet representative in Kabul, has distinguished himself by exceptional zeal. On the 17th February, 1923, he informed the Soviet authorities in Tashkent that every possible means should be used "to aggravate the undoubted existing crisis by making a breach between Afghanistan and the English," and that "the immediate delivery of arms and money would have an immense significance." The Russian Commissariat for Foreign Affairs will no doubt recognise the following communication dated the 21st February, 1923, which they received from M. Raskolnikov: "I am making arrangements for giving help to Waziristan, probably to the extent of the outlay of 3,000 roubles and ten boxes of cartridges"; and a further communication dated the 17th March, in which M. Raskolnikov implored the Commissariat not to curtail his work for "Indian work and extraordinary expenses," as this would cause "an irretrievable loss to the work of the Legation in its most vital spheres." These extraordinary expenses for the year October 1922 to October 1923 were estimated by M. Raskolnikov in November 1922 at 800,000 out of a total Legation expenditure of about 1,200,000, Kabul rupees.

6. The Commissariat for Foreign Affairs will also doubtless recognise a communication received by them from Kabul, dated the 8th November, 1922, to the following effect: "Your instructions as regards the caution with which our intelligence and propaganda work should be done are being complied with exactly. Special attention is now being given to the region north of Peshawar, among the Mohmands, but in this respect we cannot do much owing to the insufficiency of funds."

7. Nor will they have forgotten a communication, dated the 16th March, 1923, from M. Karakhan, the Assistant Commissary for Foreign Affairs, to M. Raskolnikov, in which he said: "Bring with you a concrete proposal with regard to the form the coöperation in assisting the tribes should take. On the settlement of this question will depend the question of the delivery of arms. Please inform us of your ideas as to the form of coöperation necessary to ensure local supervision in the distribution of the arms."

8. These communications throw an interesting light on some recent events in the Indian Borderland.

III.—India

9. The Soviet Government ha also not failed to carry its activities further into India. Already, in November 1922, seven Indians, who had been trained as Communist agitators at Tashkent and, after the conclusion of the Russian Trade Agreement, at Moscow, were arrested on their arrival in India from Moscow, whence they had travelled under the charge of Russian civil and military officials by a circuitous and very difficult route, in order to avoid detection.

10. In the same year a number of banknotes of 100 l each, issued through Lloyd's Bank and the Russian Commercial and Industrial Bank in London to Nikolai Klishko, Assistant Official Agent of the Soviet Government in London in June 1921, were cashed in India on behalf of a revolutionary Panjabi in touch with other Indian seditionaries who are known to have been closely associated with the Russian representative in Kabul.

11. In the light of these incidents, it is not surprising to learn that in a recent communication to M. Karakhan, M. Raskolnikov thus expressed himself: "I consider it most important to maintain personal touch with and render at least the minimum amount of assistance to Indian revolutionaries. At the very lowest it is necessary to assign at least 25,000 gold roubles. Failing this, the existing organisation will collapse."

12. In their note of the 27th September, 1921, the Soviet Government indignantly repudiated any connection between themselves and the mischievous body known as the Third International. It is singularly unfortunate, if this be the case, that a member of the Soviet Government, M. Sokolnikov, People's Commissary for Finance, and presumably a responsible official, should at a meeting of the Financial Commission of the Fourth Congress of the Third International held at Moscow on the 25th November, 1922, have been one of the body of three by whom the sums of 80,000 l and 120,000 l were allotted to the British and Indian Communist parties respectively. Of this sum 75,000 l had arrived in England by the beginning of January 1923. A little earlier, in September 1922, the Soviet Government had borne the expense of equipping and despatching to India and other Eastern countries sixty-two Oriental students trained in propaganda schools under the Third International.

13. The above paragraphs contain but a few selected examples among many scores of similar incidents, covering in their wide ambit Egypt, Turkey, the British Dominions, and even Great Britain, which testify to the consistent manner in which the Soviet Government has flouted and infringed the preliminary condition upon which the Trade Agreement was signed. It is clearly impossible that an arrangement should be perpetuated which is faithfully observed by one party and as systematically violated by the other. Unless such acts are repudiated

and apologised for, and unless the officials who have been responsible
for them are disowned and recalled from the scene of their maleficent
labours, it is manifestly impossible to persevere with an agreement
which is so one-sided in its operation.

IV.—Outrages on British Subjects

14. Nor do these cases stand alone. They have been accompanied
or supplemented by a series of outrages inflicted upon British subjects
in the past few years, for which no apology has been offered and no
compensation given. The most conspicuous of these cases are the murder of Mr. C. F. Davison, in January 1920, and the arrest and imprisonment on a false charge of Mrs. Stan Harding in the summer of
the same year. A prolonged correspondence has taken place on both
of these subjects and has been published in both countries. It has produced the most painful impression in the British Parliament and in the
press of this country, where public opinion is at a loss to understand
how such treatment as that accorded to these unfortunate persons
should be meted out by a Government to which the British Government has gone out of its way to extend a friendly hand, or how the
latter Government can consistently with its own dignity and with the
adequate protection of legitimate British interests acquiesce in the
continuance of such a scandal.

.   .   .   .

V.—Treatment of British Trawlers

19. The feelings aroused in this country by the above treatment of
British subjects, without justification, and so far without redress,
have been greatly aggravated during the past year by a series of acts
perpetrated by the Russian authorities in contravention of the generally accepted conventions of international law, and involving a
wholly indefensible interference with British shipping and acts of
indignity against British subjects. Prolonged correspondence has
taken place upon the arrest of the steam trawler "Magneta," while fishing about 9 miles off the Murman coast on the 31st January, 1922, the
trawler, while under Soviet compulsion, being subsequently wrecked
and the crew of ten men drowned; and also upon the arrest of the
steam trawler "St. Hubert" on the 3rd March, 1922, when fishing more
than 12 miles from the coast, that vessel being confiscated by the
Soviet authorities and being still detained in the harbour at Mur-
mansk. The reiterated demands of His Majesty's Government for the
admission of liability and the grant of compensation in these two cases
have been persistently refused by the Soviet Government. More recently, another flagrant case has occurred, the steam trawler "James
Johnson" having been seized in March while fishing in the same waters,

the vessel and the catch confiscated by the Soviet Government and the master sentenced to forced labour.

20. It is time that the Soviet Government should be made aware that it cannot with impunity behave towards British subjects and British shipping in this arbitrary and intolerable manner. His Majesty's Government are compelled to insist upon (a) the grant of compensation to the owners and relatives for the loss of the "Magneta" and the death of the crew; (b) the release of the "St. Hubert" and "James Johnson," as well as the crew of the latter, with the grant of suitable compensation; and (c) an assurance that British fishing vessels will not be interfered with in future outside the 3-mile limit.

VI.—Return of Notes Relating to Religious Persecution

21. During the past year a series of events have occurred in Russia involving the trial, the condemnation, and, in more than one case, the execution of prominent Russian ecclesiastics, occupying a high place in the hierarchy of the Orthodox or Catholic churches in that country. In July 1922 the Metropolitan Benjamin of Petrograd and ten other priests were tried and condemned to death, and, it is believed, executed for opposing the confiscation of church property. At the end of March 1923 Archbishop Cieplak and Mgr. Butkevitch, the leading Roman Catholic prelates in Russia, were tried for alleged acts of hostility to the Soviet Government, and were condemned, the former to ten years' solitary confinement and the latter to death, the sentences being duly carried out. The Catholicos of Georgia and the Bishop of Kutais, in the Caucasus, are under arrest in Tiflis and awaiting trial. The Patriarch Tikhon, of the Russian Orthodox Church, was in May 1922 placed under close arrest and is shortly to be tried (the trial having apparently been only temporarily postponed) on a charge of counter-revolutionary activity.

22. His Majesty's Government have refrained from expressing an opinion upon the nature or validity of the charges brought against these ecclesiastics, conceiving that that is a matter on which they are not called upon to pronounce. No attempt, however, is made in Russia itself to deny that these prosecutions and executions are part of a deliberate campaign undertaken by the Soviet Government, with the definite object of destroying all religion in Russia, and enthroning the image of godlessness in its place. As such they have excited the profound consternation and have provoked the indignant remonstrance of the civilized world. When Mgr. Butkevitch was sentenced to death, appeals were made to the Soviet Government from Governments and religious bodies in many countries. It was in sympathy with this outburst of the affronted moral sentiment of mankind that on the 30th March the British representative at Moscow, acting under instructions from His Majesty's Government, approached M. Chicherin with

a "submission that the execution of the sentence cannot fail to produce throughout the civilised world a feeling of horror and indignation which the Russian Government can hardly wish to invite" and "with an earnest and final appeal to that Government for a stay of execution." On the following day Mr. Hodgson received a reply signed by M. Weinstein claiming the undeniable right of Russia to pass sentences in conformity with its own laws, and declaring that "every attempt from outside to interfere with this right and to protect spies and traitors in Russia is an unfriendly act." Further, M. Weinstein proceeded in the same letter to make an irrelevant and insulting reference to a communication received by M. Chicherin from the alleged representative of a so-called Irish Republic in France. This note, unexampled in the case of Governments affecting to be on friendly terms, was at once and rightly returned by Mr. Hodgson, at the same time that he repudiated all desire to interfere with the right of the Russian Government to exercise jurisdiction within its own territory. On the 4th April, Mr. Hodgson received a further reply from M. Weinstein couched in terms even more offensive. Mr. Hodgson returned no answer. But the Soviet Government, in accordance with a practice which usage has now rendered familiar, published the correspondence to the world.

23. It must be clear that the exchange of correspondence conducted by one of the two parties in the above temper and language is not merely inconsistent with that standard of courtesy which ordinarily prevails in the relations between Governments, but places the continuance of those relations in grave jeopardy. When, further, it is remembered that this is only the latest incident in the long series of studied affronts which have been recorded in this memorandum, it seems difficult to arrive at any other conclusion than that the Soviet Government are either convinced that His Majesty's Government will accept any insult sooner than break with Soviet Russia, or that they desire themselves to bring relations created by the Trade Agreement to an end.

24. His Majesty's Government would on general grounds, and in the interest of the economic recovery of a country with whose people (as they have recently had many opportunities of testifying in a practical way) they have genuine ties of sympathy and old alliance, much regret that an abrupt termination should be made to an experiment which was entered into by them in sincerity, and has been pursued with undeviating loyalty and good faith. But it is not possible for them to acquiesce in a continuance of the treatment which has been summarised in this memorandum and which is incompatible alike with national dignity and with mutual respect.

25. In the above note have been stated the requests which His Majesty's Government feel constrained to make. They are requests for:—

1. The actions and assurances by the Soviet Government with re-

gard to propaganda and hostile action which are contained in paragraph 13.

2. The admission of liability by the Soviet Government and the undertaking to pay compensation in the case of the British subjects and the British ships are demanded in paragraphs 17 and 20.

3. The unequivocal withdrawal of the two communications signed by M. Weinstein which have been described in paragraph 22.

26. His majesty's Government have no desire or intention to enter into a prolonged and possibly acrimonious controversy on any of those subjects; but, unless, within ten days of the receipt of the above communication by the Commissariat for Foreign Affairs, the Soviet Government has undertaken to comply fully and unconditionally with the requests which it contains, His Majesty's Government will recognise that that Government does not wish the existing relations between them to be maintained. In that case His Majesty's Government, on their part, will, in view of the manifest infringement of the Trade Agreement by the Soviet Government, as set forth in the earlier part of the present memorandum, consider themselves immediately free from the obligation of that agreement, in accordance with the provisions of the third paragraph of its thirteenth article.

162. RUSSO-GERMAN RELATIONS, 1922

[While the representatives of the European states—except Russia—were meeting at Genoa, discussing the question of debts, the German delegates consummated a treaty with Soviet Russia. Its announcement made the public conscious of a hostile community of interest existing beween the two great debtor nations.]

(a) *Russo-German Treaty* [*of Rapallo*], *16th April, 1922*[1]

The Government of the Russian Socialistic Federal Soviet Republic, represented by the People's Commissary for Foreign Affairs, George Tchitcherin, and by the Vice-Commissary for Foreign Affairs, Maxim Litvinoff, and the German Government, represented by [Rathenau] have come to an agreement regarding the following provisions:—

Article I. The two Governments agree that the settlement between German and the Russian S.F.S.R. of the questions arising from the period of the state of war between Germany and Russia is to be regulated on the following basis:—

(a) Germany and the R.S.F.S.R. mutually renounce compensation for their war expenditure as well as compensation for war damages, i.e., the damages which have been caused to them and their nationals

---

[1] Great Britain. *Parliamentary Papers*, 1922, Vol. XXIII., Cmd. 1667. "Papers Relating to International Economic Conference, Genoa, April-May 1922."

in the war area by military measures, including all requisitions in enemy territory. Both parties likewise renounce compensation for civil damages which have been caused to the nationals of one party under the so-called special war legislation or by the forcible measures of the State authorities, of the other party:

(b) The public and private legal relationships affected by the state of war, including the question of the treatment of vessels of the mercantile marine which have fallen into the hands of the other party, shall be settled on the basis of reciprocity;

(c) Germany and Russia mutually renounce their claims to reimbursement of their respective expenditure on behalf of prisoners of war. The German Government likewise waives its claim to reimbursement of its expenditure in connection with the soldiers of the Red Army interned in Germany. The Russian Government, on its part, renounces claim to the proceeds of the sale by Germany of the military material brought by the interned soldiers of the Red Army into Germany.

Article II. Germany renounces claims which have arisen through the application up to the present of the laws and measures of the R.S.F.S.R. to German nationals or to their private rights as well as to the rights of Germany and its constituent States against Russia, or from the measures otherwise adopted by the R.S.F.S.R. or its officials against German nationals or their private rights, provided that the Government of the R.S.F.S.R. does not satisfy similar claims of other States.

Article III. Diplomatic and Consular relations between Germany, and the R.S.F.S.R. will immediately be resumed. The admission of Consuls of the two parties shall be governed by a special agreement.

Article IV. The two Governments further agree that as regards the general legal position of nationals of the one party in the territory of the other, and the general regulation of mutual commercial and economic relations, the principle of the most-favoured-nation treatment shall apply. The most-favoured-nation principle does not extend to the privileges and facilities which the R.S.F.S.R. grants to any Soviet Republic or to a State which previously formed part of the former Russian Empire.

Article V. The two Governments shall mutually assist, in a spirit of good will, in supplying the economic requirements of the two countries. In the event of this question being settled in principle on an international basis, they will exchange views as above. The German Government declares itself ready to support, as far as possible, the agreements contemplated by private firms, which have recently been communicated to it, and to facilitate their execution.

Article VI. Article I, para. b, and 4 of the present Treaty shall enter into force on ratification; the other provisions at once.

Signed in duplicate at Rapallo, April 16, 1922.

(*Signed*) RATHENAU (*Signed*) TCHITCHERIN

(b) *Allied Note to the German Delegation*[1]

Genoa, April 18, 1922

Mr. President,

The undersigned Powers have learned with astonishment that in the first stage of the Genoa Conference, Germany, without reference to the other Powers assembled there, has secretly concluded a treaty with the Soviet Government.

The questions covered by this treaty are at present the subject of negotiations between the representatives of Russia and those of all the other Powers invited to the Conference, including Germany; and the German Chancellor himself declared at the opening session only a week ago that the German Delegation would coöperate with the other Powers for the solution of these questions in a spirit of genuine loyalty and fellowship.

The undersigned Powers have therefore to express to the German Delegation in the frankest terms their opinion that the conclusion of such an agreement, while the Conference is in session, is a violation of the conditions to which Germany pledged herself in entering the Conference.

By inviting Germany to Genoa and by offering representation to her in every Commission on equal terms with themselves, the inviting Powers proved their readiness to waive the memories of war and granted Germany the opportunity of honest coöperation with her former enemies in the European tasks of the Conference. To that offer of good will and fellowship Germany has replied with an act which destroys that spirit of mutual confidence which is indispensable to international coöperation and the establishment of which is the chief aim of this Conference.

At all conferences unofficial conversations between the parties are permissible and often desirable. They are helpful so long as they are designed to facilitate the common task and so long as the results are brought to the Conference table for common discussion and decision. But that is not what the German delegates have done.

Whilst the Conference was sitting and whilst Germany was represented on the Commission and sub-Commission charged with the negotiation of the European peace with Russia on the basis of the Cannes stipulations, the German representatives on that Commission have, behind the backs of their colleagues, concluded in secret a treaty with Russia on the very questions which they had undertaken to consider in loyal conjunction with the representatives of other nations. This treaty is not subject to any examination or sanction by the Conference. We understand that it is final and that it is not proposed to

---

[1] *Idem.*

submit it to the judgment of the Conference. It is, in fact, a violation of some of the principles on which the Conference is based.

In these circumstances the undersigned do not consider it fair or equitable that Germany, having effected her own arrangement with Russia, should enter into the discussion of the conditions of an arrangement between their countries and Russia; and they therefore assume that the German Delegates have by their action renounced further participation in the discussion of the conditions of an agreement between Russia and the various countries represented at the Conference.

Please accept, Mr. President, the assurance of our high consideration.

(Signed)

D. LLOYD GEORGE	LOUIS BARTHOU
FACTA K. ISHII	G. THEUNIS
EDOUARD BÊNES	C. SKIRMUNT
M. NINCIC	CONST. DIAMONDY
M. TEIXEIRA-GOMES	

To the President of the German Delegation, Genoa Conference, 18th April, 1922.

(c) *Note from the German Delegation in Reply to Note of 18th April*[1]

German Delegation,
Genoa, 21st April, 1922

Mr. President,

In reply to the note of the 18th inst., signed by yourself and by the Presidents of the French, British, Japanese, Belgian, Czecho-Slovak, Polish, Serb-Croat-Slovene, Roumanian, and Portuguese Delegations, I have the honour to submit the following observations.

Germany recognised the Russian Soviet Republic several years ago. Before normal diplomatic relations could be established, however, it was necessary for the two countries to conclude an agreement to liquidate the consequences of the war. The negotiations entered into by the two Governments in this connection had already, several weeks ago, reached a sufficiently advanced stage to allow of the conclusion of an agreement.

The agreement with Russia was especially important for Germany in that it placed her upon a peace footing, without involving the prospect of indefinite indebtedness, with one of the great nations which had taken part in the war, and permitted the establishment of friendly relations unhampered by the burdens of the past.

Germany came to Genoa, earnestly desiring to coöperate with all nations in the reconstruction of a suffering Europe, and relying upon an international spirit of solidarity in matters of mutual concern.

---

[1] *Idem.*

The proposals set forth in the London programme ignored German
interests. Their acceptance would have led to oppressive demands for
reparation from Russia. Several of the provisions would have resulted
in laying upon Germany alone the whole burden of the consequences
of the legislation promulgated under the Czarist régime during
the war.

In the course of the detailed discussion which had taken place, the
German delegation has, on more than one occasion, drawn the atten-
tion of members of the delegations of the inviting Powers to these
grave difficulties. Their observations, however, have led to no result.
On the other hand, the German Delegation learnt that the inviting
Powers had initiated separate negotiations with Russia. From in-
formation received regarding these negotiations, it seemed that an
agreement was about to be reached, in which the legitimate desires of
Germany were not considered. Under these circumstances the German
Delegation was clearly forced to safeguard its interests by direct
means. It would otherwise have been confronted, at the meeting of the
Commission, with a scheme which, while not acceptable to Germany,
would already have been approved by the majority of the members.
For this reason the Treaty with Russia was signed on Sunday evening,
in exact conformity with the draft of several weeks previously, and
was immediately made public.

These facts clearly prove that the German Delegation entered into
negotiations with Russia, not with any sentiment of disloyalty, but
under constraint. It is also clear that the German Delegation has made
every endeavour to prevent its action assuming a secret character.

It would be in entire conformity with the wishes of the German
Delegation if the Conference succeeded in arriving at a general settlement of the Russian problem, and in including the German-Russian
Treaty within the bounds of possibility. The Treaty does not in any
way affect the relations of third Powers with Russia. Moreover, each
of its stipulations is based upon the principle which you have justly
stated to be the chief aim of the Conference, namely, that of regarding
the past as definitely closed and of seeking to lay a foundation for the
common work of peaceful reconstruction.

As regards subsequent discussions of Russian questions by the Conference, the German Delegation itself also considers it fitting that, unless its collaboration is particularly desired, it should take no further
part in the deliberations of the First Commission on questions similar
to those already settled between Germany and Russia. On the other
hand, the German Delegation is still interested in all questions assigned to the First Commission which do not relate to the points
settled in the German-Russian Treaty.

The German Delegation has followed the progress of the work of
the Commissions with satisfaction. It is in full sympathy with the spirit
of solidarity and mutual confidence which inspired these labours. Far
from wishing to withdraw from European coöperation, it is prepared

to collaborate in the tasks to be performed by the Genoa Conference with the object of the reconciliation of nations and the adjustment of the interests of East and West.

Please accept, Mr. President, the assurance of my highest consideration.

(Signed) WIRTH

(d) *Note in Reply to German Note of April 21, 1922*[1]

Genoa, April 23rd, 1922

Mr. President,

The undersigned desire to acknowledge the receipt of your reply to their note of April the 18th, indicating the attitude which they felt bound to adopt in view of the treaty concluded between the Russian and German Delegations. They note with satisfaction that the German Delegation realises that the conclusion of a separate treaty with Russia on matters falling within the purview of the Conference renders it undesirable that that Delegation should participate in future in the discussion of the conditions of an agreement between Russia and the various countries represented at the Conference.

The undersigned would have preferred to refrain from further correspondence on the subject. There are, however, certain statements in your letter which they feel it their duty to correct.

Your letter suggests that the German Delegation have been forced to conclude a separate agreement with Russia by the refusal of members of the Delegations of the Inviting Powers to consider the grievous difficulties which the proposals formulated by their experts in London would have created for Germany. The undersigned representatives of the Inviting Powers have made enquiries of the members of their respective Delegations and find that there is no shadow of justification for this statement.

On various occasions members of the German Delegation have met and talked with members of the Delegations of the Inviting Powers, but never has it been suggested that the London proposals afforded no basis for discussion in Conference, and that the German Delegation were about to conclude a separate Treaty with Russia.

The allegation that the informal discussions with the Russians on the subject of the recognition of debts, exposed the Delegation to the risk of being confronted with a scheme unacceptable to Germany but already approved by the majority of the Members of the Commission is equally unfounded. No scheme would or could have been accepted by the Conference without the fullest opportunity for discussion in the competent committees and sub-committees, and in these Germany was represented on a footing of equality with other Powers.

A misconception of the scope of the experts' proposals or misunder-

[1] *Idem.*

standing of the informal conversations with the Russians might well have justified a request for full discussion in the Committees of the Conference. They can provide no justification for the action which has now been taken, and the undersigned can only regret that your note should have attempted in this way to impose on the other Powers the responsibility for a proceeding so contrary to the spirit of loyal coöperation which is essential to the restoration of Europe.

The undersigned expressly reserve for their Governments the right to declare null and void any clauses in the Russo-German Treaty which may be recognised as contrary to existing Treaties.

The incident may now be regarded as closed.

Please accept, Mr. President, the assurance of our high consideration.

(Signed)

D. LLOYD GEORGE
FACTA
G. THEUNIS
C. SKIRMUNT
CONST. DIAMONDY

LOUIS BARTHOU
K. ISHII
EDOUARD BÊNES
M. NINCIC
M. TEIXIRA-GOMES

To the
    President of the German Delegation.
        Genoa Conference.

163. EDITORIAL ON THE ANGLO-FRENCH OIL AGREEMENT AT SAN REMO, APRIL 25TH, 1920[1]

[At the end of 1918 Great Britain controlled three-fourths or more of the stock of the Turkish Petroleum Company. This control was limited by the San Remo Agreement by which France was allowed to have the interests that had been taken over from Germany in December of 1918. It may be added for the sake of interest that this agreement elicited a vigorous protest from the American Government in 1920, for it looked as if a monopolistic control of Mesopotamian oil was being created which would close the door to American capital. The British have tried to satisfy particular American interests by taking them into their operations, but the solution has been very hard to find.]

THE OIL AGREEMENT

Among the many details necessarily introduced into it, it is possible that the general bearing of the oil agreement between England and France may be overlooked. It may be misunderstood or misrepresented,

---

[1] The *Manchester Guardian Weekly*, July 24, 1920. Editorial. Reprinted with the permission of the *Manchester Guardian*.

especially in America, where there is a vigorous Standard Oil propaganda. America has not much reason to complain, for I believe that between the States and Mexico she controls something like sixty percent of the present oil supply of the world, and by commercial arrangements a good deal more, perhaps amounting to eighty percent—almost to a world monopoly. As to the agreement published tonight, which mainly concerns Mesopotamia oil, I give below the Government interpretation of it.

Essentially the agreement is to give France the option either of taking twenty-five percent of the oil obtained at market prices if the development is done by Government action, or alternatively of taking up twenty-five percent of the shares in any development by private companies. In the latter case they have to give twenty percent of the twenty-five percent to the Arab State, which would leave them with twenty percent of the whole capital.

For the rest the agreement is simply an arrangement between England and France not to compete with each other. In view of the American virtual monopoly there can be no question of a Franco-British corner in oil. Generally speaking, it is urged, the agreement is designed to protect the industrial and economic interests of France, who herself controls no oil. She needs oil like every one else, and this agreement is to reassure her. Whatever form of development may be adopted, we are told, Mesopotamia is to get its profit out of it. The first consideration is to be the interest of Mesopotamia.

This is the Government interpretation of the agreement.[1]

164. THE WASHINGTON CONFERENCE, 1922

[The Washington Conference was called into existence by the American president, Harding, to settle four major problems or sets of problems: those dealing with China and Chinese rights, those bearing upon the balance of power in the Pacific, the question of a substitute for the Anglo-Japanese Alliance which had lost its *raison d'être* since the fall of both Russia and Germany, and those bearing upon disarmament. As a result of its deliberations, the Conference put forth a nine-power treaty guaranteeing Chinese rights, a four-power treaty having to do with insular possessions in the Pacific Ocean, and a five-power pact calling for drastic reductions in naval armament.]

(a) *Report of the American Delegation*[2]

The Anglo-Japanese Alliance

It may be stated without reservation that one of the most important factors in the Far Eastern situation was the Anglo-Japanese

---

[1] For text of this agreement see *Manchester Guardian*, July 24, 1920.
[2] U. S. serial 7975. Doc. No. 125, pp. 43-54.

Alliance. This Alliance has been viewed by the people of the United States with deep concern. Originally designed as a measure of protection in view of the policies of Russia and Germany in Far Eastern affairs, the continuance of the Alliance after all peril from those sources had ceased could not fail to be regarded as seriously prejudicial to our interests. Without reviewing the reasons for this disquietude, it was greatly increased by the "state of international tension" which had arisen in the Pacific area. The question constantly recurred: The original sources of danger having been removed, against whom and for what purposes was the Alliance maintained? The difficulty lay in the fact that the Treaty was not one that had to be renewed. It ran until it was formally denounced by one of the two parties. Great Britain accordingly found itself, as Mr. Balfour has expressed it, "between the possibilities of two misunderstandings—a misunderstanding if they retained the Treaty, a misunderstanding if they denounced the Treaty."

It was, therefore, a matter of the greatest gratification that the American Delegation found that they were able to obtain an agreement by which the Anglo-Japanese Alliance should be immediately terminated. No greater step could be taken to secure the unimpeded influence of liberal opinion in promoting peace in the Pacific region.

The Four-Power Treaty

This agreement between the United States, British Empire, France, and Japan, which was signed on December 13, 1921, provided as follows:

I

"The High Contracting Parties agree as between themselves to respect their rights in relation to their insular possessions and insular dominions in the region of the Pacific Ocean.

"If there should develop between any of the High Contracting Parties a controversy arising out of any Pacific question and involving their said rights which is not satisfactorily settled by diplomacy and is likely to affect the harmonious accord now happily subsisting between them, they shall invite the other High Contracting Parties to a joint conference to which the whole subject will be referred for consideration and adjustment.

II

"If the said rights are threatened by the aggressive action of any other Power, the High Contracting Parties shall communicate with one another fully and frankly in order to arrive at an understanding as to the most efficient measures to be taken, jointly or separately, to meet the exigencies of the particular situation.

III

"This Treaty shall remain in force for ten years from the time it shall take effect, and after the expiration of said period it shall continue to be in force subject to the right of any of the High Contracting Parties to terminate it upon twelve months' notice.

IV

"This Treaty shall be ratified as soon as possible in accordance with the constitutional methods of the High Contracting Parties and shall take effect on the deposit of ratifications, which shall take place at Washington, and thereupon the agreement between Great Britain and Japan, which was concluded at London on July 13, 1911, shall terminate."

It was accompanied by the following statement signed at the same time:

"In signing the Treaty this day between The United States of America, The British Empire, France, and Japan it is declared to be the understanding and intent of the Signatory Powers:

"1. That the Treaty shall apply to the Mandated Islands in the Pacific Ocean; provided, however, that the making of the Treaty shall not be deemed to be an assent on the part of The United States of America to the mandates and shall not preclude agreements between The United States of America and the Mandatory Powers respectively in relation to the mandated islands.

"2. That the controversies to which the second paragraph of Article I refers shall not be taken to embrace questions which according to principles of international law lie exclusively within the domestic jurisdiction of the respective Powers."

Accordingly, the signing of the Treaty on the part of the United States was subject to the making of a convention with Japan concerning the status of the Island of Yap and what are termed the mandated islands in the Pacific Ocean north of the Equator, the negotiations in regard to which have been concluded, and also to the reservations with respect to what are termed the mandated islands in the Pacific Ocean south of the Equator. The position of the United States in regard to mandates is not in any way affected by this Treaty.

Further, it is distinctly stated that the controversies to which the Treaty refers do not embrace questions which, according to principles of international law, lie exclusively within the domestic jurisdiction of the respective Powers. Illustrations of questions of this sort are immigration and tariff matters, so far as they are unaffected by existing treaties.

It will be observed that the Treaty relates only to "insular possessions and insular dominions." It contains no provision with respect to continental territory either in the East or in the West.

Under Article I, the parties do not agree to give any support to claims, but only to respect rights that actually exist. When controversies arise of the character stated in the Article, the Powers merely agree to confer together concerning them. No Power binds itself to anything further; and any consents or agreements must be reached in accordance with its constitutional methods. The reference to "consideration and adjustment" does not imply that any agreement can be made at a conference relating to a controversy which would be binding upon the United States, unless that agreement is made by constitutional authority. The present Treaty promises not an agreement of any sort, but merely consultation. The same is true of the provision in Article II.

As Senator Lodge said, in communicating the terms of the Treaty to the Conference:

"To put it in a few words, the treaty provides that the four signatory powers will agree as between themselves to respect their insular possessions and dominions in the region of the Pacific, and that if any controversy should arise as to such rights, all the high contracting parties shall be invited to a joint conference looking to the adjustment of such controversy. They agree to take similar action in the case of aggression by any other power upon these insular possessions or dominions. The agreement is to remain in force for 10 years, and after ratification under the constitutional methods of the high contracting parties the existing agreement between Great Britain and Japan, which was concluded at London on July 13, 1911, shall terminate. And that is all. Each signer is bound to respect the rights of the others and before taking action in any controversy to consult with them. There is no provision for the use of force to carry out any of the terms of the agreement, and no military or naval sanction lurks anywhere in the background or under cover of these plain and direct clauses."

This statement was made in open Conference, in the presence of all the Delegates who signed the Treaty, and must be regarded as an authoritative and accepted exposition of its import.

A question arose whether the main islands of Japan were within the scope of the Treaty. This had been considered while the Treaty was being negotiated, and it had been understood that they had been included. The words "insular possessions and insular dominions" were deemed comprehensively to embrace all islands of the respective powers in the region described.

The American Delegation did not regard it as important whether the main islands of Japan were included or excluded, save that it was understood that their exclusion might give rise to difficulties with respect to the position of Australia and New Zealand. After the Treaty was signed, it became apparent that in view of the sentiment both in this country and in Japan, it would be preferable to exclude the main islands of Japan from the Treaty, and it was ascertained that Australia and New Zealand would not object to this course.

It was thought desirable that specific mention should be made of the Japanese islands to which the Treaty should apply.

Accordingly, on February 6, 1922, the Four Powers signed a Treaty, supplementary to the Treaty of December 13, 1921, providing—

"the term 'insular possessions and insular dominions' used in the aforesaid Treaty, shall, in its application to Japan, include only Karafuto (or the southern portion of the island of Sakhalin), Formosa and the Pescadores, and the islands under the mandate of Japan."

It was further provided that this agreement should have the same force and effect as the Treaty to which it was supplementary, and thus it is subject to the reservations made at the time the Treaty of December 13, 1921, was signed.

The Shantung Controversy

The most acute question, perhaps, in the Far East was that relating to Shantung, and it was also apparently the most difficult to settle satisfactorily.[1]

.   .   .   .

The question could not be brought, technically, before the Washington Conference, as all the nations represented at the Conference table, save the United States, China, and The Netherlands, were bound by the Treaty of Versailles. Japan could, of course, at once oppose any action by any of these Powers at the Conference which could be regarded as a departure from the terms of that Treaty.

. . . In order that the parties might be brought together, the good offices of Mr. Balfour and Mr. Hughes, individually, were tendered to both parties, with their consent, and conversations looking to a settlement were begun. These conversations continued for many weeks and had the happy result of complete agreement, which was embodied in a Treaty signed on the part of China and Japan on February 4, 1922. The main outlines of this Treaty are as follows:

"Japan will, within six months from the date of the Treaty, restore to China the former German leased territory of Kiaochow, and all public properties therein, without charge except for such additions and improvements as may have been made by Japan during the period of her occupation;

"All Japanese troops are to be withdrawn as soon as possible—from the line of the Railway within six months at the latest, and from the leased territory not later than 30 days from the date of its transfer to China;

"The customhouse at Tsingtao is at once to be made an integral part of the Chinese Maritime Customs;

---

[1] Mr. Lodge then gave an historical review of the Shantung question.

"The Shantung (Tsingtao-Tsinanfu) Railway and appurtenant properties are to be transferred to China, the transfer to be completed within 9 months, at the latest, from the date of coming into force of the Treaty; the value of the property to be determined by a commission upon the basis of approximately 53,000,000 gold marks, already assessed against Japan by the Reparations Commission as the value of the railway property taken by Japan from Germany in 1914; the value fixed being paid by China to Japan by Chinese Government treasury notes, secured on the properties and revenues of the Railway, and running for a period of 15 years, but redeemable either in whole or in part at any time after 5 years from the date of payment; pending the complete redemption of such treasury notes, the Chinese Government to employ a Japanese subject as traffic manager, and a Japanese subject as one of two joint chief accountants, under the authority and control of the Chinese managing director of the railway;

"The rights in the construction of two extensions of the Shantung Railway, reserved in 1914 for German enterprise, and subsequently granted to a Japanese syndicate, are to be opened to the activities of an international financial group on terms to be arranged between China and that group;

"The coal and iron mines formerly owned by the German Shantung Railway Company are to be handed over to a company to be formed under a special charter of the Chinese Government, in which Japanese capital may participate equally with Chinese capital;

"Japan relinquishes its claim to the establishment of an exclusive Japanese settlement in the leased territory, and China opens the whole of that territory to foreign trade, undertaking to respect all valid vested rights therein;

"China is enabled to purchase, for incorporation in its Government salt monopoly, the salt fields now operated in the leased territory by Japanese subjects, on the understanding that it will allow the export on reasonable terms of salt to meet the shortage in Japan;

"Japan relinquishes to China all claims with respect to the Tsingtao-Chefoo and Shanghai cables, except such portions as were utilized by Japan during the war for the laying of the cable from Tsingtao to Sasebo;

"Japan is to transfer to China for fair compensation the wireless stations at Tsingtao and Tsinanfu;

"Japan renounces all preferential rights in respect of foreign assistance in persons, capital, and material stipulated in the Kiaochow Convention of 1898 between China and Germany."

Wei-Hai-Wei

On the announcement to the Conference of the conclusion of the agreement relating to Shantung, Mr. Balfour, on behalf of the British

Government, proposed to restore Wei-Hai-Wei to China. Mr. Balfour said:

"The circumstances under which Weihaiwei thus came under the control of Britain have now not only provisionally changed, but they have altogether disappeared. The rest of the Province of Shantung is now handed back under suitable conditions to the complete sovereignty of China. Under like suitable conditions I have to announce that Great Britain proposes to hand back Weihaiwei to the country within whose frontiers it lies.

"It has so far been used merely as a sanatorium or summer resort for ships of war coming up from the tropical or more southern portions of the China station. I doubt not that arrangements can be made under which it will remain available for that innocent and healthful purpose in time to come. But Chinese sovereignty will now be restored, as it has been restored in other parts of the Province, and we shall be largely guided in the arrangements that we propose at once to initiate by the example so happily set us by the Japanese and Chinese negotiators in the case of Shantung. They have received from this great assembly unmistakable proof of your earnest approval, and most surely they deserve it."

Principles and Policies in Relation to China

The work of the Conference in connection with Far Eastern matters was largely devoted to the effort to give new vigor and reality to the coördinated principles of territorial and administrative integrity of China and of the "Open Door" or equality of opportunity for all nations in China. These principles have been called coördinate, but they are, in fact, different aspects of the same principle. For any impairment of the sovereignty of China must affect the rights and interests of other powers in relation to China; and any attempt to establish a particularistic and exclusive system in favor of any foreign nation thereby creates conditions prejudicial to China's freedom of action in relation to other Powers. The distinction between the two phases of this question would therefore seem to be one of relative emphasis rather than of kind.

As the foundation of its work in relation to China, the Conference adopted the following fundamental principles, in agreeing:

"(1) To respect the sovereignty, the independence, and the territorial and administrative integrity of China;

"(2) To provide the fullest and most unembarrassed opportunity to China to develop and maintain for herself an effective and stable government;

"(3) To use their influence for the purpose of effectually establishing and maintaining the principle of equal opportunity for the commerce and industry of all nations throughout the territory of China;

"(4) To refrain from taking advantage of conditions in China in order to seek special rights or privileges which would abridge the rights of subjects or citizens of friendly States and from countenancing action inimical to the security of such States."

Thus were reaffirmed the postulates of American policy which were no longer to be left to the exchanges of diplomatic notes, but were to receive the sanction of the most solemn undertaking of the Powers.

This statement was supplemented by the agreement that the Powers attending the Conference "would not enter into any treaty, agreement, arrangement or understanding, either with one another, or individually, or collectively, with any Power or Powers, which would infringe or impair these principles."

In the light of experience, it was deemed important that there should be a more definite statement of what was connoted by the "Open Door" or the principle of equal opportunity, and accordingly the Conference adopted the following resolutions:

"I. With a view to applying more effectually the principles of the Open Door or equality of opportunity in China for the trade and industry of all nations, the Powers other than China represented at this Conference agree—

"(a) Not to seek or to support their nationals in seeking any arrangement which might purport to establish in favor of their interests any general superiority of rights with respect to commercial or economic development in any designated region of China;

"(b) Not to seek or to support their nationals in seeking any such monopoly or preference as would deprive other nationals of the right of undertaking any legitimate trade or industry in China or of participating with the Chinese Government or with any local authority in any category of public enterprise, or which by reason of its scope, duration or geographical extent is calculated to frustrate the practical application of the principle of equal opportunity.

"It is understood that this agreement is not to be so construed as to prohibit the acquisition of such properties or rights as may be necessary to the conduct of a particular commercial, industrial or financial undertaking or to the encouragement of invention and research.

"II. The Chinese Government takes note of the above agreement and declares its intention of being guided by the same principles in dealing with applications for economic rights and privileges from Governments and nationals of all foreign countries whether parties to that agreement or not."

There still remained the efforts of nationals, as distinguished from governments, in derogation of the Open Door principle, to create for themselves spheres of influence in China in order to enjoy mutually exclusive opportunities. This sort of endeavor the Powers agreed to restrain by resolving:

"*Resolved*, That the Signatory Powers will not support any agreements by their respective nationals with each other designed to create Spheres of Influence or to provide for the enjoyment of mutually exclusive opportunities in designated parts of Chinese territory."

It was also apparent, in connection with the particular subject of railways, that safeguards should be erected against practices of unjust discrimination, although there was no intent to intimate that any unfair discrimination lay at the door of China. Accordingly the Conference took action as follows:

"The Chinese Government declares that throughout the whole of the railways in China it will not exercise or permit any unfair discrimination of any kind. In particular, there shall be no discrimination whatever, direct or indirect, in respect of charges or of facilities on the ground of the nationality of passengers or the countries from which or to which they are proceeding, or the origin or ownership of goods or the country from which or to which they are consigned, or the nationality or ownership of the ship or other means of conveying such passengers or goods before or after their transport on the Chinese railways.

"The other Powers represented at this Conference take note of the above declaration and make a corresponding declaration in respect of any of the aforesaid railways over which they or their nationals are in a position to exercise any control in virtue of any concession, special agreement, or otherwise."

The agreements evidenced by these Resolutions, and constituting a Magna Charta for China, were embodied in the Treaty signed on February 6, 1922.

In this Treaty it was also provided that the Contracting Powers agreed fully to respect Chinese rights as a neutral in time of war to which China is not a party, and China declared that when she was a neutral she would observe the obligations of neutrality.

Again, in order to aid the carrying out of these stipulations of the Treaty, provision was made for consultation among the Powers concerned with respect to their application. It was provided:

"The Contracting Powers agree that, whenever a situation arises which in the opinion of any one of them involves the application of the stipulations of the present Treaty, and renders desirable discussion of such application, there shall be full and frank communication between the Contracting Powers concerned."

This involves no impairment of national sovereignty, no sacrifice of national interests, no provision for agreements reached apart from the constitutional methods of the respective Powers, but a simple opportunity for consultation, examination, and expression of views whenever any question under the specified stipulations of the Treaty may arise.

It is believed that through this Treaty the Open Door in China has at last been made a fact.

(b) *A Treaty between the United States of America, the British Empire, France, Italy and Japan, Limiting Naval Armament*[1]

CHAPTER I

GENERAL PROVISIONS RELATING TO THE LIMITATION OF
NAVAL ARMAMENT

Article I. The Contracting Powers agree to limit their respective naval armament as provided in the present Treaty.

Article II. The Contracting Powers may retain respectively the capital ships which are specified in Chapter II, Part I. On the coming into force of the present Treaty, but subject to the following provisions of this Article, all other capital ships, built or building, of the United States, the British Empire and Japan shall be disposed of as prescribed in Chapter II, Part 2.

In addition to the capital ships specified in Chapter II, Part 1, the United States may complete and retain two ships of the *West Virginia* class now under construction. On the completion of these two ships the *North Dakota* and *Delaware* shall be disposed of as prescribed in Chapter II, Part 2.

The British Empire may, in accordance with the replacement table in Chapter II, Part 3, construct two new capital ships not exceeding 35,000 tons (35,560 metric tons) standard displacement each. On the completion of the said two ships the *Thunderer, King George V, Ajax* and *Centurion* shall be disposed of as prescribed in Chapter II, Part 2.

Article III. Subject to the provisions of Article II, the Contracting Powers shall abandon their respective capital-ship building programs, and no new capital ships shall be constructed or acquired by any of the Contracting Powers except replacement tonnage which may be constructed or acquired as specified in Chapter II, Part 3.

Ships which are replaced in accordance with Chapter II, Part 3, shall be disposed of as prescribed in Part 2 of that Chapter.

Article IV. The total capital ship replacement tonnage of each of the Contracting Powers shall not exceed in standard displacement, for the United States 525,000 tons (533,400 metric tons); for the British Empire 525,000 tons (533,400 metric tons); for France 175,000 tons (177,800 metric tons); for Italy 175,000 tons (177,800 metric tons); for Japan 315,000 tons (320,040 metric tons).

Article V. No capital ship exceeding 35,000 tons (35,560 metric tons) standard displacement shall be acquired by, or constructed by, for, or within the jurisdiction of, any of the Contracting Powers.

Article VI. No capital ship of any of the Contracting Powers shall carry a gun with a calibre in excess of 16 inches (406 millimetres).

---

[1] *Ibid.*, pp. 93-97.

Article VII. The total tonnage for aircraft carriers of each of the Contracting Powers shall not exceed in standard displacement, for the United States 135,000 tons (137,160 metric tons); for the British Empire 135,000 tons (137,160 metric tons); for France 60,000 tons (60,960 metric tons); for Italy 60,000 tons (60,960 metric tons); for Japan 81,000 tons (82,296 metric tons).

Article VIII. The replacement of aircraft carriers shall be effected only as prescribed in Chapter II, Part 3, provided, however, that all aircraft carrier tonnage in existence or building on November 12, 1921, shall be considered experimental, and may be replaced, within the total tonnage limit prescribed in Article VII, without regard to its age.

Article IX. No aircraft carrier exceeding 27,000 tons (27,432 metric tons) standard displacement shall be acquired by, or constructed by, for or within the jurisdiction of, any of the Contracting Powers.

However, any of the Contracting Powers may, provided that its total tonnage allowance of aircraft carriers is not thereby exceeded, build not more than two aircraft carriers, each of a tonnage of not more than 33,000 tons (33,528 metric tons) standard displacement, and in order to effect economy any of the Contracting Powers may use for this purpose any two of their ships, whether constructed or in course of construction, which would otherwise be scrapped under the provisions of Article II. The armament of any aircraft carriers exceeding 27,000 tons (27,432 metric tons) standard displacement shall be in accordance with the requirements of Article X, except that the total number of guns to be carried in case any of such guns be of a calibre exceeding 6 inches (152 millimetres), except anti-aircraft guns and guns not exceeding 5 inches (127 millimetres), shall not exceed eight.

Article X. No aircraft carrier of any of the Contracting Powers shall carry a gun with a calibre in excess of 8 inches (203 millimetres). Without prejudice to the provisions of Article IX, if the armament carried includes guns exceeding 6 inches (152 millimetres) in calibre the total number of guns carried, except anti-aircraft guns and guns not exceeding 5 inches (127 millimetres), shall not exceed ten. If alternatively the armament contains no guns exceeding 6 inches (152 millimetres) in calibre, the number of guns is not limited. In either case the number of anti-aircraft guns and of guns not exceeding 5 inches (127 millimetres) is not limited.

Article XI. No vessel of war exceeding 10,000 tons (10,160 metric tons) standard displacement, other than a capital ship or aircraft carrier, shall be acquired by, or constructed by, for, or within the jurisdiction of, any of the Contracting Powers. Vessels not specifically built as fighting ships nor taken in time of peace under government control for fighting purposes, which are employed on fleet duties or as troop transports or in some other way for the purpose of assisting in the prosecution of hostilities otherwise than as fighting ships, shall not be within the limitations of this Article.

No vessel of war of any of the Contracting Powers, hereafter laid down, other than a capital ship, shall carry a gun with a calibre in excess of 8 inches (203 millimetres).

Article XIII. Except as provided in Article IX, no ship designated in the present Treaty to be scrapped may be reconverted into a vessel of war.

Article XIV. No preparations shall be made in merchant ships in time of peace for the installation of warlike armaments for the purpose of converting such ships into vessels of war, other than the necessary stiffening of decks for the mounting of guns not exceeding 6 inch (152 millimetres) calibre.

Article XV. No vessel of war constructed within the jurisdiction of any of the Contracting Powers for a non-Contracting Power shall exceed the limitations as to displacement and armament prescribed by the present Treaty for vessels of a similar type which may be constructed by or for any of the Contracting Powers; provided, however, that the displacement for aircraft carriers constructed for a non-Contracting Power shall in no case exceed 27,000 tons (27,432 metric tons) standard displacement.

Article XVI. If the construction of any vessel of war for a non-Contracting Power is undertaken within the jurisdiction of any of the Contracting Powers, such Power shall promptly inform the other Contracting Powers of the date of the signing of the contract and the date on which the keel of the ship is laid; and shall also communicate to them the particulars relating to the ship prescribed in Chapter II, Part 3, Section I (b), (4) and (5).

Article XVII. In the event of a Contracting Power being engaged in war, such Power shall not use as a vessel of war any vessel of war which may be under construction within its jurisdiction for any other Power, or which may have been constructed within its jurisdiction for another Power and not delivered.

Article XVIII. Each of the Contracting Powers undertakes not to dispose by gift, sale or any mode of transfer of any vessel of war in such a manner that such vessel may become a vessel of war in the Navy of any foreign Power.

Article XIX. The United States, the British Empire and Japan agree that the *status quo* at the time of the signing of the present Treaty, with regard to fortifications and naval bases, shall be maintained in their respective territories and possessions specified hereunder:

(1) The insular possessions which the United States now holds or may hereafter acquire in the Pacific Ocean, except (a) those adjacent to the coast of the United States, Alaska and the Panama Canal Zone, not including the Aleutian Islands, and (b) the Hawaiian Islands;

(2) Hongkong and the insular possessions which the British Em-

pire now holds or may hereafter acquire in the Pacific Ocean, east of the meridian 110 east longitude, except (a) those adjacent to the coast of Canada, (b) the Commonwealth of Australia and its Territories, and (c) New Zealand;

(3) The following insular territories and possessions of Japan in the Pacific Ocean, to wit: the Kurile Islands, the Bonin Islands, Amami-Oshima, the Loochoo Islands, Formosa and the Pescadores, and any insular territories or possessions in the Pacific Ocean which Japan may hereafter acquire.

The maintenance of the *status quo* under the foregoing provisions implies that no new fortifications or naval bases shall be established in the territories and possessions specified, that no measures shall be taken to increase the existing naval facilities for the repair and maintenance of naval forces, and that no increase shall be made in the coast defences of the territories and possessions above specified. This restriction, however, does not preclude such repair and replacement of worn-out weapons and equipment as is customary in naval and military establishments in time of peace.

Article XX. The rules for determining tonnage displacement prescribed in Chapter II, Part 4, shall apply to the ships of each of the Contracting Powers.

[Chapter II, "Rules relating to the execution of the treaty—definition of terms," is omitted.]

(c) *British and French Views on the Submarine Question*[1]

Fifth Meeting, Committee on Limitation of Armament, December 22, 1921

LORD LEE (the British Empire): . . . The view of the British Government and the British Empire delegation was that what was required was not merely restriction on submarines, but their total and final abolition. In explaining the position he wished to make it clear that the British Empire delegation had no unworthy or selfish motives. He would first like to reply in advance, since this might be his only opportunity of doing so, to the arguments of the friends of the submarine. He understood their first contention to be that the submarine was the legitimate weapon of the weaker powers and was an effective and economical means of defense for an extensive coast line and for maritime communications. Both these standpoints could be contested on technical grounds and, as he would show, were clearly disproved by recent history. If some weak country possessed an exposed coast line, it would, of course, desire to defend it against bombardment or the disembarkation of a military force.

. . . The British people lived in a crowded island whose soil only produced two-fifths of its supply of food. For the remaining three-

---
[1] U. S. serial 7976, Doc. No. 126, pp. 265-271.

fifths they relied upon sea communications. On an average only seven weeks' stocks were maintained in the country. By far the greatest anxiety which the British Government had felt during the war was to prevent the reserves of food falling to zero. Was it surprising, therefore, if, with a danger in front of them as great as any to which Mr. Briand had so eloquently explained France was subject, the British people protested against a weapon which was the negation of humanity, chivalry, and civilization itself? There were some people who said it was this vulnerability of Great Britain which justified the retention of the submarine, since it was by these means alone that the British Empire could be stricken down. The late war had shown, however, that the British Empire was not easily stricken down, and, if war should ever come again, he imagined that means would be found for Great Britain to save itself from starvation. But, it might be claimed, if the U-boat had begun its operations earlier or had had better luck, the result might have been different. To this he would reply that the British Navy had constituted the keystone of the allied arch; but for the British Navy France would have been ruined, Belgium and Holland would have been overrun, and even the United States of America, self-contained, self-supporting, with all its vast resources would have been impotent to intervene and might have had to abandon its Army and all that it had in France, or else to make a humiliating peace. . . .

The average number of German submarines operating at any one time on the Atlantic approaches to France and Great Britain during the late war had not been more than nine or ten, but Great Britain had had to maintain an average of no less than 3,000 anti-submarine surface craft in order to deal with these. It could be seen, therefore, that is was a very expensive form of war for the defender. The British Empire delegation were anxious to contribute toward the ideals of the present conference. They desired not only a limitation of armaments but also a limitation of expenditures, which constituted so great burden in time of peace. That was why Great Britain, which had the tradition of possessing the greatest navy, had welcomed the proposals for curbing capital ships. What would be gained, however, if this competition were merely transferred to submarines? . . .

To show the earnestness of the British Government in this matter, Lord Lee pointed out that Great Britain possessed the largest and probably the most efficient submarine navy in the world, composed of 100 vessels of 80,000 tons. She was prepared to scrap the whole of this great fleet, to disband the personnel, provided the other powers would do the same. That was the British offer to the world, and he believed it was a greater contribution to the cause of humanity than even the limitation of capital ships. . . .

MR. SARRAUT . . . read the following declaration of the views of the French Government: . . .

"France believes that the submarine is the only weapon which at present permits a nation scantily supplied with capital ships to defend itself at sea. For France, therefore, the submarine is an essential means of preserving her independence which she can not give up, especially in view of the sacrifices to which she has been asked to consent in the matter of capital ships. Moreover, in the present state of the development of naval science, the submarine can not suffice to assure the control of the seas to a belligerent, even if that belligerent possesses a great superiority in submarines. It is not, therefore, a weapon making for supremacy.

"The French Government believes that every method of warfare may or may not be employed in conformity with the laws of war, and that the inhuman and barbarous use made of the submarine by a belligerent in the late war is a reason for condemning that belligerent, but not for condemning the submarine.

"As submarines are particularly subject to withdrawal from service in war time, the restriction within a certain limit of the total tonnage of these vessels which a maritime nation may build would have, to a lesser degree, the same effect as their total abolition, and should be declined for the same reasons.

"The French Government has already stated that it can not accept an agreement based on the principle that the total tonnage of submarines which a nation may build should be in direct proportion to the capital ship tonnage of that nation. In its opinion, the contrary point of view is the rational one, since a nation would be deprived of the protection which would be afforded her by capital ships.

"The French Government believes that it is possible to reconcile the use of submarines with the laws of humanity. From this point of view, large submarines have the advantage of being able to rescue the crews of torpedoed vessels or to furnish prize crews to captured vessels.

"The French Government is obliged to assume eventually the defense of its numerous colonies, some of which are far distant from the mother country. In view of this fact, and also in order to safeguard its lines of communication with the colonies, it must possess submarines with a very large cruising radius, and consequently with appropriate dimensions.

"For these reasons the French Government can not consent to accept either abolition of submarines or a reduction of the total tonnage of submarines which it considers to be the irreducible minimum necessary to assure the safety of the territories for which it is responsible, or a limitation of the individual tonnage of submarines."

· · · · · · · · · · ·

165. ITALO-GREEK DISPUTE (CORFU) 1923[1]

[In this affair the League was for the first time called upon to deal with an international crisis which directly involved one of the great

---

[1] League of Nations, *Monthly Summary*, Vol. III, 1923, pp. 212-215.

Powers. The matter was eventually settled by the Council of Ambassadors, which made an important modification in the League's proposal in respect to the indemnity. Instead of being decided by the Permanent Court of International Justice, this question was to be settled immediately by the Council of Ambassadors. When on September 22 an Inter-Allied commission reported that the persons guilty of the crime had not been discovered, the ambassadors on the 26th ordered Greece to pay 50,000,000 lire to the Italian government. This sum, which Greece had already deposited in the Swiss National Bank, was thereupon paid and Italy evacuated Corfu on September 27. While the League did not settle the question, it undoubtedly helped bring about a speedy solution partly by serving as an instrument for expressing the collective opinion of the world, which indisputably was influential in changing Mussolini's mind.]

SUMMARY OF THE ITALO-GREEK DISPUTE

The dispute between Italy and Greece occurred just as the Council was meeting for its twenty-sixth Session and the Assembly for its fourth session.

This dispute arose out of the murder, on August 27th, on Greek soil, of General Tellini, Major Corti, Lieutenant Bonaccini and the chauffeur, Farnetti, all Italians, and their interpreter, an Albanian. The murdered men were members of the International Commission for Delimitation of the Albanian frontier, who were acting on behalf of the Conference of Ambassadors to delimit the frontier between Greece and Albania. They were proceeding by automobile to carry out this task, when their passage was blocked by a large tree thrown across the road, and they themselves were shot, either in their car or attempting to escape into the adjoining woods.

Two days later, the Italian Government presented a Note to the Greek Government demanding full apologies and reparations. On the following day, the 30th, Greece replied accepting some of these demands and refusing others. On August 31st, the Italian naval authorities occupied the Island of Corfu, stating at the same time that the occupation was purely temporary and a guarantee for the execution by Greece of the reparations demand. On that same day, the Conference of Ambassadors, whose representatives the murdered men had been, also sent a Note to Greece requesting an immediate enquiry and reserving the right of considering penalties.

On the following morning, September 1st, the question of the Italian demands was first brought before the League of Nations, by a Note, dated August 31st, from the Greek Government requesting its consideration by the Council under Article XII and XV of the Covenant. This request was considered at a session that same afternoon, when Greece, as an interested State, sat as a Member of the Council in accordance with the Covenant provisions. At that meeting, after some discussion, and on the request of the Italian representative for post-ponement in order that he might have time to receive instructions, the Council passed a Resolution which, in assenting to a short adjournment for the further consideration of the question, expressed the confident hope that in the meantime the two States concerned would commit no act which might aggravate the situation.

The Council met again on September 4th and agreed that its next meetings on this question should be held in public. M. Politis, the Greek representative, took the occasion to make certain definite suggestions in addition to those previously made by Greece concerning the judicial enquiry already undertaken by the Greek authorities, and declared that the Greek Government would deposit 50 million Italian lire in a Swiss bank as guarantee of the immediate payment of whatever indemnity might be decided upon.

On the following day, September 5th, M. Salandra, Italian representative, stating that he had received instructions from his Government, made a declaration asking that the Council should not proceed to take action in this matter, invoking several reasons based on the fact that the Conference of Ambassadors, a directly interested party, had already begun consideration of the matter, and on an interpretation of certain clauses of the Covenant. M. Politis replied to this statement wholly disagreeing with the points raised regarding the interpretation of the Covenant, but declaring that the Greek Government had recognised by its Note of September 2nd that it owed reparations and explanations to the Conference of Ambassadors, the verdict of which Greece had agreed to accept. Lord Robert Cecil then asked to have read Articles X, XII, and XV of the Treaty of Versailles and stated that if the terms of these treaties should be disregarded, the whole settlement of new Europe would be shaken.

On September 6th, the Council met again, when it had before it a telegram from the Conference of Ambassadors stating that it had considered the Greek reply to its communication, had noted Greece's willingness, if her responsibility were proved, to make any reparation which the Conference might regard as just, and that it had at once considered how the enquiry should be conducted. M. Quinones de Leon, the Spanish representative, then submitted to the Council a draft reply to the Conference of Ambassadors containing seven suggested points agreed upon by certain Members of the Council as forming a just basis of settlement of the dispute between Greece and Italy. As the Italian representative could not agree to the Council's entering into the substance of the question, and as the French representative asked for delay in order that he might have instructions from his Government, it was finally decided briefly to acknowledge the Note from the Conference of Ambassadors and to send to the Conference that night the minutes of this session of the Council.

The interpretation given by M. Salandra to certain articles of the Covenant was further discussed at this meeting and several important declarations made with regard to it. Lord Robert Cecil (Great Britain), M. Hymans (Belgium), Mr. Branting (Sweden), and M. Guani (Uruguay), declared that they held a contrary opinion to that advanced by the Italian representative. It was generally agreed that, while this aspect of the matter was of the greatest importance to the future of the League, it would be wise to postpone its further discussion until the actual dispute had been further advanced towards settlement.

The Council met again on September 10th to consider a telegram from the Conference of Ambassadors, dated September 7th, acknowledging the receipt of the verbatim record of the Council's session on September 6th, stating that it had examined, with the greatest care, the opinions advanced by various Members of the Council at that meeting, and thanking the Council for having supplied it with valuable material, which had greatly assisted it in forming a judgment. Appended to this telegram was a Note to the Greek Government, observing that Greece had agreed, if her responsibilities were proved, to make any reparation the Conference might regard as just, and setting forth seven conditions, which the Conference of Ambassadors had agreed that Greece should fulfil in reparation for the murder. The Council, in acknowledging receipt of this communication, asked to be kept informed of any further discussions on the subject. At this same meeting also, M. Politis, Greek representative, read a Note from his Government to the effect that the 50 million Italian lire had actually been deposited in a Swiss bank.

In conformity with a decision taken at this meeting of the Council, Viscount Ishii, as President of the Council, made a statement to the Assembly session of September 12th to the effect that the dispute between Italy and Greece was still under examination by the Council and that important negotiations were also in progress which it was hoped would lead to a satisfactory conclusion. He expressed the conviction that, in view of these facts, the delegates to the Assembly would desire to refrain for the moment from any discussion of this important matter. Jonkheer Loudon (Netherlands) in reply, stated that he thought he would be voicing the opinion of most of his colleagues in stating that that Assembly had confidence that the Council would make another communication to the Assembly before the close of the session.

On September 17th, the Council met again to consider a further communication from the Conference of Ambassadors announcing the settlement of the dispute between Italy and Greece, and enclosing a new and more detailed Note from the Conference of Ambassadors to Greece. The Council welcomed the fact that this communication put an end to a situation which had aroused intense anxiety. Mr. Branting, while declaring his satisfaction at the solution and at the services performed by the Council of the League, expressed his anxiety as to the questions raised concerning the interpretation of the Covenant, and especially as to the precedent created by the occupation of Corfu, which he felt was contrary to the Covenant. Lord Robert Cecil then made a detailed analysis of the juridical questions involved both as regards the general relationship of the Council to the dispute and as regards the interpretation of the Covenant. In conclusion, M. Politis, Greek representative, in declaring the Italo-Greek dispute at an end, expressed his gratitude to the Council for the manner in which it had acquitted itself of a very difficult task, to the Italian Government for the spirit of conciliation which it had shown, and to M. Salandra personally. M. Salandra, in his turn, while reserving till the following day his reply to the legal points involved, thanked M. Politis for the aid which he had given to the Council in bringing the dispute to a satisfactory conclusion, and noted with pleasure that the dispute was now definitely settled.

On the day following, namely, the 18th, M. Salandra, in reply to the statements made by Mr. Branting and Lord Robert Cecil, made a declaration on the legal points involved, emphasising that pacific reprisals and occupation of territory as security were measures which had often been sanctioned in international practice and stressing the point that Italy's attitude was based particularly on Article XIII of the Covenant which made recourse to the League obligatory only if diplomatic negotiations failed, which had not happened in this case.

The immediate question of the Italo-Greek difficulty having thus been declared as closed, the Council proceeded to a consideration of the interpretation of certain articles of the Covenant and other questions of international law which had arisen during the discussions.

During the following sessions of the Council, the various legal points involved were discussed both by the Council and by a special Committee of Jurists who were invited to help the Council. Unanimous agreement was finally reached by all Members of the Council both as to the actual questions to be settled and as to the procedure to be adopted.

Accordingly, on September 28th, the day before the Assembly was to rise, Viscount Ishii, as President of the Council, made the following statement to the Assembly:

At its meeting of the 22nd September, 1923, the Council asked a Committee of Jurists to formulate questions with regard to certain points concerning the interpretation of the Covenant and other matters of international law, which the Council had had under consideration.

The Committee submitted to the Council on the 26th September, the following questions:

Question 1.—Is the Council, when seized at the instance of a Member of the League of Nations of a dispute submitted in accordance with the terms of Article XV of the Covenant, by such a Member as "likely to lead to a rupture," bound, either at the request of the other party or on its own authority, and before inquiring into any point, to decide whether in fact such description is well-founded?

Question 2.—Is the Council, when seized of a dispute in accordance with Article XV, paragraph 1, of the Covenant, at the instance of a Member of the League of Nations bound, either at the request of a party, or on its own authority, to suspend its enquiry into the dispute, when, with the consent of the parties, the settlement of the dispute is being sought through some other channel?

Question 3.—Is an objection founded on Article XV, paragraph 8, of the Covenant the only objection based on the merits of the dispute on which the competence of the Council to make an enquiry can be challenged?

Question 4.—Are measures of coercion which are not meant to constitute acts of war consistent with the terms of Article XII and XV of the Covenant when they are taken by one Member of the League of Nations against another Member of the League without prior recourse to the procedure laid down in those articles?

Question 5.—In what circumstances and to what extent is the responsibility of a State involved by the commission of a political crime in its territory?

The Members of the Council being in agreement that any dispute between Members of the League likely to lead to a rupture is within the sphere of action of the League, and that if such dispute cannot be settled by diplomacy, arbitration or judicial settlement, it is the duty of the Council to deal with it in accordance with the terms of Article XV of the Covenant; the Council decides that these questions shall be referred to a Special Commission of Jurists for an opinion as to the answers to be given.

The Council resolves that the Report of the Special Commission of Jurists shall be submitted to it in time for consideration at its meeting in December. Each Member of the Council may nominate within a period of 15 days a Jurist to be a Member of the Commission. The Members thus nominated, together with the Director of the Legal Section of the Secretariat, will constitute the Special Commission of Jurists.

166. French View of the Reparations Problem[1]

[By 1922 the French had spent a large sum of money in reconstruction and pensions and were receiving from Germany a much smaller amount. They were therefore anxious that German reparation payments should in no way be delayed, and when the Germans asked for a moratorium they occupied the Ruhr industrial district (January 11, 1923) to enforce their demands. Because they did this against British

---

[1] *Le Temps*, December 17, 1922. "Why We Occupy the Ruhr" by Raymond Poincaré (Extract).

PEACE-WORK.

FRITZ: "AH! THAT'S WHAT I WAS TRYING TO DO ALL THROUGH THE WAR—AND NOW THEY'RE DOING IT FOR ME!"

From *Punch*, August 22, 1923
(Reprinted by arrangements with the proprietors of *Punch*.)

advice they broke the solidarity of the Allied nations which had but recently been so highly prized. After a period of passive resistance the Germans saw that payments were necessary. The Dawes Plan put the whole reparations question upon a new footing. (See doc. no. 173.)]

The speech delivered in the Chamber on December 16 by the Premier, during the debate upon Reparations

You will recall that the Reparations Commission went to Berlin some weeks ago. It has not obtained anything. On November 13, Wirth's Cabinet sent the Commission a note which the new Chancellor, Cuno, has accepted as his own. It may be summarized in a very few words: We can do nothing until we have placed our currency on a stable footing; to stabilize our currency we must have a reduction or—as they say by way of euphemism—a revision and a definite statement of the amount that we owe. We demand that we be freed for a period of three or four years from all deliveries in kind and all payments of money for which we are at present held. We will make an exception for the devastated regions, subject to one condition; that we shall not be called upon to pay more than we can raise by ordinary taxes and internal loans—which means practically nothing. Finally, we demand the calling of an international financial conference to ascertain what sum is necessary to put Europe and Germany on their feet—that is to say, how much banking credit can be placed at the disposal of Germany.

This was what Germany told us on November 13. We were therefore faced with the question of revising, or, in other words, of overturning and abolishing the scheme of payments agreed upon in May 1921. We were asked to grant a moratorium of three or four years. In return Germany did not promise to carry out a single one of the reforms that the Reparations Commission asked her for: to stop padding her government expenses, to collect all the taxes due her from her citizens, and to correct the inaccuracies in the statistics showing her foreign-trade balance.

The first condition laid down by Germany was that her debts should be scaled down to some definite figure. This is a favorite proposal with many financiers on both sides of the Atlantic. But this places France in a most unhappy situation. By the end of this year she will have advanced one hundred billion francs against her bill on Germany, and she has collected scarcely anything on that bill. It will be impossible for her to continue this policy longer, without receiving substantial payments.

Furthermore, during the long course of the war France incurred heavy debts in the common cause, toward America and toward England. These debts have not been paid. I cannot tell you their exact amount, but they are approximately the equivalent of thirteen billion gold marks due the United States, and ten billion gold marks due

England. On the other hand, Belgium, Russia, Serbia, Rumania, and other Allied Countries owe us five or six billion marks. In the aggregate, England is the creditor of France, Italy, and other countries to the amount of twenty-three billion marks, and the United States is the creditor of Europe to the extent of forty-one billion marks. If we add together all the sums due the various creditor nations of Europe, we find they total about seventy-two billion gold marks.

Are we justified in making any comparison between this war debt and the debt of Germany to the Allies? Certainly they have nothing in common. Our war debts were contracted by certain Allies toward other Allies, in order to win our common victory. They represent purchases of arms, ammunition, war materials, and food for troops who fought shoulder to shoulder. They represent practically the whole cost of the war, a collective cost. When the Allies were thus assisting each other, they were all in a critical situation. They might hope—they had the right to hope—that the day would come when these war costs that they thus shared among themselves would be shifted to the shoulders of vanquished Germany.

But what happened when we signed the Peace Treaty? (The Premier read paragraphs 231 and 232 of that treaty.) You see the victorious nations renounced their claim against Germany for the total amount of their losses and expenses—speaking generally, for the cost of the war. They limited themselves to claiming merely compensation for injury done to private persons and property. What does that mean? It means that these injuries to persons and property constitute in the minds of the Allies a claim taking priority to war expenses. Well, then, are these war costs, which it was agreed stood second to Reparations, and which were not demanded of Germany, to be collected by the Allies from each other even before Germany has paid a cent? In other words, are friends to be treated worse than the enemies of yesterday? That would certainly seem to be the strangest and most intolerable injustice.

So, gentlemen, we have always said to our creditor Allies: "We have no intention of disputing our debt. We recognize that debt. But in neither justice nor fact can we pay that debt until we have received what Germany owes us."

However, we have not wished to stop with a mere negative declaration. As early as last June and July I informed the two Chambers that we were ready to transfer to England and the United States in payment of our debts a corresponding share of what Germany owes us, in the form of such German obligations as the Reparations Commission may later authorize. . . .

Coming to the question of rehabilitating Germany's finances, the neutral experts that the German Government recently consulted are in full agreement with the Reparations Commission. The Chamber will recall that these experts divided into two groups—some presented findings more indulgent for Germany, others presented findings more severe. The first group consisted of Messrs. Brandt, Cassel, Jenks, and Keynes. The second was composed of Messrs. Wissering, Dubois, and Kamenka. But both groups were equally emphatic as to the need of a serious effort by Germany to better her condition.

The first experts said: The stabilization of the mark must be brought about in the first instance by the efforts of Germany herself and with her own resources, through the vigorous action of her Government. Germany should have her own policy of reconstruction. Such a policy may involve certain risks, but it is the only path to pursue.

The other experts said: It is necessary to enforce the strictest economy in public expenditures, to reduce the number of employees in government offices and government services, and gradually to abolish direct or indirect subventions for keeping down the cost of food.

It is perfectly evident that without these reforms and without the organization of some instrument of control, any attempt to stabilize the mark will be illusory. It will be more harmful than beneficial, and will precipitate the formidable crisis that now threatens Germany. This control ought to be exercised by the Reparations Commission and the Committee upon Guaranties. It goes without saying that this Commission and this Committee would not take the place of the German administrative authorities. They would not assume any responsibility that they should not assume. But they should have powers of investigation that would enable them to unmask trickery and prevent fraud, and the right to veto lavish and wasteful appropriations and new issues of paper money.

Coming to the next point, gentlemen, the Germans demanded a new moratorium. What should our reply be to this?

In this case, likewise, it is well to review a little recent history. The fact is that ever since January, 1922, Germany has been enjoying a moratorium. She has not been paying, as we know to our sorrow, what she should pay under the London agreement. On March 21, the Reparations Commission concluded that Germany ought to pay this year seven hundred and twenty million marks in gold, and one billion, four hundred and fifty million marks in goods, or a total of two billion, one hundred and seventy million gold marks.

Of the seven hundred and twenty million gold marks only four hundred and fifty millions have been paid, and the two hundred and seventy millions which should have been paid beginning August 15 have been converted, as you know, into six months' notes.

The deliveries in kind were to be divided this way: nine hundred and fifty millions for France and five hundred millions for the other Allies. Unhappily, they are far from reaching this figure.

That is where we stand at the close of 1922. . . .

Well, then, finding ourselves faced with this prospect of a total or partial failure in the payments due us, we have stated to Parliament and to the country: If Germany will not pay up, the Treaty of Versailles affords us a remedy. Article 248 gives the Allies a priority claim against all the property and resources of the German Empire and the German States. Is this article to remain a dead letter?

Certainly not. Its meaning is very clear. All the national wealth of Germany, and all the wealth of the Federal States that compose the Commonwealth, can be seized by the creditors of the Commonwealth. I know quite well that the English word does not correspond exactly with the French word. In English the Treaty reads 'a first charge,' and not 'a mortgage.' But France has taken the position that the French text shall be decisive, and, so far as I am concerned, I shall stick to the French text. Furthermore, international law as well as civil law recognizes the elementary principle that all the property of a debtor is everywhere and under all conditions security for the creditor.

France is not seeking, and has not sought, and will never seek remedies primarily military. She does not design to punish Germany or impose punitive sanctions. She simply wishes her money in the full measure that it can be collected . . . and believes that she should lay hands upon German property where that property really is. . . .

167. THE DARIAC REPORT

[In 1922 President Poincaré sent M. Dariac, President of the Finance Commission of the Chamber of Deputies, into the Ruhr, the Rhineland, and the Saar Basin, to report upon the economic and industrial conditions there as they were related to French interests. The report was not adopted by the French Government, but does represent, in all probability, the point of view of many Frenchmen toward the situations created by the occupation of these previously German areas. The report was dated May 28, 1922.]

(a) The Rhineland[1]

The following is the full text of the report presented recently to the French Government by M. Dariac, who was sent by M. Poincaré as a Commissioner to report on the economics and the industry of the Rhine province.

TEXT OF THE REPORT

It will be remembered that the occupation of the Düsseldorf bridgehead was provoked by the ill will which Germany showed in meeting her engagements in 1921. It was after the London agreement of May 5, 1921, and the ultimatum which resulted from it, that it was decided to adopt the military sanctions consisting of the occupation of Düsseldorf, Duisburg, Ruhrort, and the neighbouring region, and the eco-

---

[1] The *Manchester Guardian Weekly*, November 3, 1922. Reprinted with the permission of the *Manchester Guardian*.

nomic sanctions consisting of the control of the Rhenish Customs and the establishment of a Customs barrier at the limit of our zone of occupation. The economic sanctions were dropped in September, 1921, following the German acceptance of the ultimatum; but the military sanctions have remained in force as a means of pressure on our former enemies.

A PLEDGE OF THE FIRST IMPORTANCE

The feature of this region of occupation is its very accentuated industrial character, which makes of it a pledge in our hands of quite the first importance for the recovery of the sums which Germany has undertaken to pay us.

In existing circumstances, indeed, the Ruhr, and in particular the region of Düsseldorf, Duisburg, Ruhrort, which we are occupying, and which forms its head, constitutes the principal element of German wealth, which is based entirely on iron and coal, their transformations and their derivatives. The majority of the Great German consortiums have been formed there, have their headquarters and their establishments there, and the ten or twelve industrialists who direct them rule, directly or indirectly, but absolutely, the economic destinies of Germany. (Metallurgy, coal, coal derivatives, dyestuffs, manures, shipping companies, import and export of raw materials or manufactured goods.)

. . . .

As regards her general trade, Germany exported annually, out of a total of ten milliard gold marks, more than 700 millions' worth of coal, coke, and briquettes.

Her exports of cast-iron were about a million tons.

Her exports of steel (various steel products) were six to seven million tons, of which the money value amounted roughly to—

Steel products, nearly 1,900 million gold marks;
Various machines, about 950 millions.

The remainder of the exports was made up largely of dyestuffs, pharmaceutical products, perfumes, etc., derived from coal.

FRENCH PRE-WAR PRODUCTIONS

The figures for the whole of the French production before the war are obviously unable to compare with the production of the Ruhr, the extent of which, however, does not equal that of a small French Department. We recall them below:—

Coal, 40 million tons (reduced today to 25 millions).
Coke, 3,500,000 tons.

Tar, 300,000 to 400,000 tons.
Sulphate of ammonia, 50,000 tons.
Cast-iron, 5 to 6 million tons.
Steel, 4 to 5 million tons.

It may suffice to set against these figures those of the production of a single one of the consortiums of the Ruhr, the Stinnes group:—

Coal, 18,300,000 tons.
Coke, 4,565,000 tons.
Tar, 129,000 tons.
Sulphate of ammonia, 59,000 tons.
Steel, 2,600,000 tons.
Cast iron, 2,119,200 tons.

It is this industrial power alone which has made the greatness and the prosperity of Germany; from the agricultural point of view, before the war, and despite an intensive culture unrivalled in Europe; Germany bought abroad nearly three milliard gold marks' worth of foodstuffs of every sort (wheat, barley, rice, maize, coffee, fruits, wine, oils, cattle, etc.). This means in effect that Germany's food supply was only assured through the production of her industries, (coal, dyestuffs, metals, chemical and textile industries, etc.).

"In Germany," as Vogler, Stinnes's chief-lieutenant, has said, "the potato is a coal by-product."

The large-scale industry, the "heavy industry" of the Ruhr, concentrated entirely in the hands of a few individuals, is thus called to play a decisive part in the events which will unfold themselves in Germany's future.

THE GREAT INDUSTRIALISTS

In this field the Stinnes, the Thyssens, the Krupps, the Haniels, the Kloeckners, the Funkes, the Mannesmanns, and some three or four others play in Germany an economic rôle analogous to that of the Carnegies, the Rockefellers, the Harrimans, the Vanderbilts, and the Goulds in America; they also carry on a political activity unknown among the American billionaires.

From the point of view of reparations they have already offered to substitute themselves for the German State for carrying out the payment of the Allied claims, or at all events the first ones, but on conditions which have been adjudged unacceptable.

From their account they alone are capable, through their continually growing transactions, through the credit which foreigners do not fail to grant them, to provide the German State, by way of loan, with the gold and securities and foreign bills which it would itself never be able to obtain by means of a depreciated mark.

In other words, they generously offer to lend to the State, at a good rate of interest, the sums which the fiscal authorities would have a right to demand from them without further ado after the voting of taxes.

And, in fact, if the paper mark plunges down day after day, the means of production of the Stinnes and Thyssens and Krupps and Haniels and their colleagues remain intact and are worth gold. This is what gives value to our occupation of the country.

No doubt we do not hold the whole of the Ruhr, but by our simple occupation at present we hold in reality the whole of its industrial production under our domination.

"WE CAN UTTERLY DISORGANISE THEIR INDUSTRY"

We occupy, indeed, the greater part of the basin, in which there have been established the blast furnaces which produce the cast-iron, as well as the ports of the Ruhr and the Rhine through which these blast furnaces are supplied with ores. Thus we cut in two the metallurgical establishments; we can, when we wish, separate from their coal, their ore, their cast-iron and steel production, the connected and complementary establishments which only complete their products in unoccupied Germany; we can utterly disorganise the industry of the potentates of Düsseldorf, Duisburg, and Ruhrort. . . .

THE FRENCH ADVANTAGE

So long as we maintain our present position on the Rhine we shall thus constitute a constant menace for the ten or twelve masters of German industry, who are in reality financially the masters of Germany.

From this point of view it is very regrettable that we have been led to abandon the economic sanctions which accompanied our occupation of Düsseldorf in 1921; the Customs barrier established between the occupied zone and free Germany, if it did not give great results in immediate return, nevertheless was in its simple presence a reminder that the circulation of the products between the factories producing crude metal and the factories working upon it was at our mercy, and that we could, by a simple raising of tariffs, either levy a virtually unlimited tithe upon the German metal industry or completely disorganise it.

And this perspective alone would have been of a sort which would suggest to the German Government, or its councils, suitable means for facilitating the rapid payment of its war debt.

But recriminations avail nothing.

In the existing circumstances, how can we profit by the pledge which we thus hold?

THE PLEDGE MUST NOT BE ABANDONED

To begin with, there is one question which should be outside all debate: we cannot dream of abandoning this pledge.

At the moment the German State is unable to pay us from its normal resources; the systematic squandering in which it has indulged for a year past, its fiduciary inflation, now reaching 155 milliards, are material facts which no one can alter.

But there are in Germany coal syndicates, iron, steel, dyestuffs syndicates, etc. If any Germany is to pay us it will be that of the Stinnes and Thyssens and Krupps and of the great syndicates, the true holders of German capital: the Germany of the great consortiums will find abroad all the credits it desires. We must therefore retain at all costs our means of eventual action against this producing Germany, which has succeeded in organising itself. At present we can destroy it or utilise it by controlling it; it feels this permanent menace weighing upon it; and from now onwards we see all the shapes which can be taken by the utilisation of this pledge.

To begin with, it is possible that the mere menace will inspire the German Government, counselled and assisted by the industrialists of the Ruhr, themselves desirous of evading a constraint of which they feel that we alone are the masters, with proposals which would be of a nature to give us satisfaction for the moment. But let us not be deceived; if the great industrialists concede to the German Government credits and facilities for the payment of the first arrears of its debt —a thing they will not do without good guarantees secured on the railways or other State property,—it will be in order to endeavour to rid themselves of the Nessus' shirt which the occupation of the Düsseldorf bridgehead constitutes for them.

Three years' experience has shown us how little confidence we can place in German good will; let us beware, then, of abandoning a pledge which we can have available for exploiting if this good will, always uncertain, should begin to flag.

SUGGESTED CUSTOMS AND CAPITAL LEVY

In the case of the insolvency of Germany we can still, while leaving full scope to the functioning of the German metal industry, reëstablish the Customs barrier between our bridgeheads and the unoccupied territory, and levy on inward and outward goods duties which, suitably graduated, would replenish the reparations chest. This would be a levy on the profits of a limited category of producers, easy to collect, and, in view of the universal employment of coal and its derivatives, would inevitably be borne in the last analysis by the mass of the German people.

As to the rate of this levy, it would be for the Allies to fix it in proportion to the greater or less good will of Germany to acquit herself by other means.

One of these means, which we might suggest to the German Government if it took too long over thinking of it, should be to impose a participation of the State in the profits of the exploitation of the capital represented by the great industries; the compulsory creation of shares representing for each enterprise one-fourth or one-fifth of its capital, and their assignment to the German Government, under the control of our Committee of Guarantees, would, for example, constitute an easy levy on the capital of these industries, of which we should then have every interest in facilitating the development. Another conceivable method would be for these securities to serve as the basis of an international loan, which would at once relieve the finances of the Allies simultaneously with those of the Germans.

It is clear how the possession of the pledge which we hold in the Ruhr invests our action of persuasion or constraint with suppleness.

A POSSIBLE COLLABORATION

And finally, without employing constraint, is it not possible to imagine a utilisation of the Ruhr by a collaboration, a friendly *entente* between France and the Allies on the one part and Germany on the other, with permanent control of its means of production?

The Rhine separates two great metallurgical regions; on one side the Ruhr, with its nine million tons of cast-iron (1913 yield), absorbing annually 18 to 25 million tons of ore; on the other side, the Lorraine region (including the Saar), the productive capacity of which is also nine million tons of cast-iron.

The ironmasters of the Ruhr have available (in times of normal production) indefinite quantities of coal, but quite insufficient quantities of ore, since the new Germany produces no more than seven to eight million tons, for a consumption which before the war amounted to 48 million tons and would still easily reach 30 millions.

On the other hand, the ironmasters in the Lorraine group have available twice as much ore as they can work. Before the war Lorraine, France, Algeria, and Tunisia produced normally 45 million tons of iron ore; now our industrialists work up nine millions, and they will work up 25 millions when all the blast furnaces (including those of Lorraine and the Saar) are in full working; on the other hand, they absolutely require for their blast furnaces the coke of the Ruhr.

Hackneyed conclusion, a hundred times repeated: the French metal industry cannot live without the German coke, the German metal industry can only reach half its full development if it is deprived of French ore.

At present the German metal industry is creating new means of production, building the foundations of its recovery, and organising its future. The industrialists who have lost their establishments in Lorraine have been liberally indemnified by the German Government; they have diverted their capital to the right bank of the Rhine to reconstitute in the Ruhr establishments destined to replace those which they have lost in Lorraine. The enlargements recently built by Thyssen and those which we have seen under construction at Homburg are significant.

And, despite some partial strikes, all these factories are fully at work, and at costs which the exchange renders ludicrous. But that will only last so long as there remain raw materials in the country; no doubt there are heaps of ore in reserve, and it continues to arrive daily from Spain, Sweden, etc.—but at what prices?

Cannot France envisage the exchange of German metallurgical coke and French ore as a friendly exploitation offering the bases of a true industrial association?

"A Control of German Production."

We cannot demand that Germany shall pay enormous sums for 35 years, and on the other hand, we are afraid of seeing her industries develop in the proportion which would permit her to assure the payment of the debts which she has acknowledged. But so long as we are on the right bank of the Rhine and are masters of 45 million tons a year of ore we shall be in a position to play a decisive part in the German metal industry, demanding a control of production in return.

And no doubt this will be the solution of the future. So long as the Committee of Guarantees limits itself to controlling the German finances it will do no more than periodically report a series of monetary disasters which it will be impotent to alter. The day when it has the power to control Germany's industrial production we shall be in a position to profit by her economic prosperity.

As soon, moreover, as we have control of a share in the German capital we shall have an interest in seeing it as fruitful as possible; for money payments and supplies in kind are at the bottom of every system of payment, and one may discern the whole series of economic agreements, wider in scope than those of Wiesbaden, which may result.

· · · · · · ·

The German industrialists profess openly that the union of German coke and French ore would have great results, and that if the two peoples could conclude directly with one another, reparation agreements of which those of Wiesbaden are but the prelude, all problems would simplify themselves rapidly.

Our occupation of the Düsseldorf bridgehead should lead us, with a little skill, to the realisation of the only two methods of payment which will give us real satisfaction; a German loan, secured on German capital, and the recovery of economic life.

FRENCH POLICY IN THE RHINELAND

The Rhinelander certainly does not love the Prussian, a greedy and disagreeable functionary, installed in this kindly country, with his concern for strict discipline and his spirit of authority.

There is a Rhenish psychology, complex enough and yet easily unravelled. These marches have been the prize of every victory, the ransom of every defeat; men at arms have heavily trampled down their soil. The troops of Louis XIV., of Louis XV., of Napoleon succeeded one another there, and were replaced by those of Frederick the Great or of Blücher. Geographically, intellectually their pole is on the west. Acts of force, the great disasters of the end of the Empire, cast them politically into the Prussian system.

Reluctantly the populations accepted it; but this Prussian system has presented itself to them under the aspect of ordered progress, of economic prosperity, of various reforms, and if its unpleasing rigidity was at first revolting to these people of semi-Latin culture, who had lived in the secular anarchy of a historical subdivision but had been immersed in belles-lettres and had experienced the sweetness of a beneficent liberty and of perhaps uncertain but still real democratic aspirations, they forgave these martinets with their barrack-room methods and their dry discipline in consideration of an unprecedented prosperity which seemed to secure the hegemony of Europe to Prussian Germany.

There came the great catastrophe of 1918. In the first months of 1919 the Rhineland expected modifications in its national status. It anticipated French annexation, or autonomy, and if the first of these eventualities awakened, if not resistance—the Rhenish populations are sufficiently malleable to accept the decisions of force—at least disquietude, the second appeared, on the whole, to be desired. The Versailles peace arrived at a third solution: inter-Allied occupation for five, ten, or fifteen years, but with the maintenance of the Rhineland within the German unit. The most that has been done has been to impose certain inter-Allied organisations on the solid texture of the administrative organisation of the Reich; the Prussian functionary has remained, and with him the perspective of a future in no way differing from the past.

STRONG WORDS AND FEEBLE ACTIONS

Instead of the autonomy which was within a few months to find expression in the adventure of Dr. Dorten, it was in the main a case of the *status quo*, and if the Rhinelanders saw French, British, American, or Belgian soldiers mounting guard along their great river, they were regarded as temporary and inconvenient guests, encamped purely in order to assure the observation of the peace treaty.

There followed the events of 1920-21: the desire of Germany to escape from her engagements; conferences, arrangements, ultimatums; formal declarations from the French Government that it would not evacuate the left bank of the Rhine until the Versailles Treaty was executed in full; the threat of the occupation of the Ruhr.

The Rhenish populations attentively followed the development of the crisis; anxious as to their destinies, they awaited French statements which might define them. If the military occupation was to be prolonged, they foresaw certain collaborations, which would be very difficult if this occupation was to be precarious.

Forcible words were followed by feeble actions; the hand fell without gripping the shoulder of the perjured Germany; the London Conference reduced our rights, curtailed our claim, gave the populations of Rhenish Prussia or of the Bavarian palatinate the clear impression that our country had embarked on the path of concessions, that France, though unpaid, would not realise the pledge which she held in her hand, this Rhineland prepared to adapt herself to fresh formulæ, but prudent and insufficiently heroic to break with her lord of yesterday, who, once our soldiers were gone, would remain her lord of tomorrow. May, 1921, was for us, from Mainz to Cologne, the painful period in which our policy of abandonment made its appearance.

Prussian propaganda was encouraged by this bankruptcy.

It redoubled in intensity; it affirmed that, with the bad times over, the Reich was soon to recover the mastery of its western provinces.

In face of this campaign the Rhinelanders drew back more, and since then the situation has become more delicate. The French Government therefore owes it to itself, as, indeed, the High Commissariat has understood, to practise a Rhenish policy based on collaboration in the economic field, a policy of conciliation and of *rapprochement* towards the populations.

RIGHT OF CONTINUED OCCUPATION

The whole of French policy in the Rhineland is at all times subordinate to one primary condition, the prolonged maintenance of our army of the Rhine in the occupied territories. Without this assurance this policy is disastrously precarious. The populations, as we have seen, do not wish to compromise themselves for a cause of which the weakness is obvious since it is limited in time—and limited by a fixed date—and uncertain in regard to its means of action.

In the life of a nation five, ten, or fifteen years count for little. If we had to withdraw at the end of these short periods our rôle must be limited to an occupation by way of military guarantee. Must we, on the contrary, remain? All sorts of possibilities open out before us. In this matter the Governments which have succeeded one another in France since 1919 have on many occasions declared plainly that following on the failure of Germany to carry out her engagements the limitations of this occupation were suspended—but the foreclosure has not been formally proclaimed as an irrevocable decision.

The judicial thesis of the foreclosure, the right of the unpaid creditor to enter upon the property which he holds from his debtor as guarantee, was applicable here. France as creditor had received from Germany as debtor the Rhineland as security. Payment not having been made, she retained it and administered it (*l'aménageait*)—and conveyed her decision to the populations concerned.

Certainly she envisaged no compulsion of the latter, no form of annexation direct or indirect, avowed or disguised. She simply affirmed the necessity of remaining on the Rhine so long as she failed to receive the legitimate satisfaction to which she was entitled under the treaties —the necessity of retaining a military *glacis* for her pledge. At the same time she freed the Rhinelanders from the fear of an early return to the Prussian rod, and consolidated their future. The possibility of disposing freely of themselves appeared to them thenceforth as disengaged from the anxiety which falsified their opinion. France thus disengaged the policy of autonomy which should be ours, and which, after this gesture, became relatively easy, whereas until then it had been impossible.

A RHENISH POLICY.

The first act of this policy is the financial organisation of the Rhineland; a Customs barrier placed on the east facing Germany and razed on the west facing France, to avoid the economic strangulation which would result from a double fiscal wall diminishing the exchange of goods and compromising the industrial life of the Rhinelands; a budget separate from that of the Reich; the substitution of a healthy currency for the damaged mark.

The second act is the replacement of Prussian by Rhenish functionaries.

The third is the extension of the powers of the High Commission and the convocation of an elected assembly.

These are doubtless ambitious projects, but if executed wisely and discerningly in proportion as Germany slips out of her engagements they would be amply justified. It is a long-drawn-out policy, in which a well-considered diplomacy must apply one after another the successive links of a well-thought-out course of action which, little by little, will detach from Germany a free Rhineland under the military guard of France and Belgium.

(b) *The Saar Territory*[1]

THE FRENCH TROOPS IN THE SAAR

Surrounded on the east, north, and north-west by the wooded heights of the Hardt, the Palatinate, and the Hochwald, the Saar territory, with a population of over 700,000, forms an undulating prolongation of the plateau of Lorraine.

The shortest route to Mainz from Metz or Nancy passes through Saarbrücken; for this reason the Saar assumes, from the strategic point of view, an importance of the first rank.

The military interest presented by the numerous means of communication which traverse the Saar territory is reinforced for us by the not less considerable interest of the economic resources existing along their track, arising out of the recent development of the coal mines, which make this one of the most important industrial basins in Europe.

Under the Treaty of Versailles the territory of the Saar was placed under the government of the League of Nations, the Imperial German mines were allotted to the French State in compensation for the mines destroyed in the north of France, and French capital was authorised to take a large share in the various industries of the country. A Governing Commission, consisting of five members chosen by the Council of the League of Nations, governs and administers the territory in the name of the League of Nations. This Commission comprises at present a French member as president, a Danish member, a Belgian, a Saarlander, and a Canadian.

When the Governing Commission entered upon its duties in February, 1920, it asked that the French troops should be maintained as a garrison in the Saar. The maintenance was based on the necessity of assuring the safety of property and persons in the territory as well as of the communications of the French army of the Rhine, pending the creation of a local gendarmery as provided by the treaty.

The constitution of this gendarmery has met with insurmountable difficulties; the Governing Commission considers that its effectives should be at least 4,000 men, including 500 horse, in order to be able effectively to fulfil its mission.

On June 30, 1920, it decided to create the first nucleus of this local police force, making use of the gendarmery elements already existing, sifted and reinforced by new recruits. The corps of gendarmery thus constituted comprises 144 "Saarlandjäger," commanded by a "Saarlandjägerrat" and placed under the authority and the direct control of the Director of Public Safety in the Government. These Landjäger are distributed in small groups throughout the Saar territory in the communes and important agglomerations (rural gendarmery) a larger contingent being maintained in Saarbrücken (mobile gendarmery).

[1] The *Manchester Guardian*, March 5, 1923.

The attempts subsequently made to add to this first nucleus have remained fruitless for the following reasons: First, the difficulty of recruiting an effective force of 4,000 men in the Saar, where the population is attracted by the remunerative wages in mine and factory. It proved also that this mounted police presented the drawbacks inherent in police forces recruited locally; it must not be forgotten that the municipal police and rural gendarmery coöperated in August, 1920, in the strike of officials and deserted their posts. Finally, there was the financial difficulty; to maintain even the 144 "Saarlandjäger" is costing 900,000 francs per annum.

Faced with these insuperable obstacles, the Governing Commission decided unanimously, in the first months of 1921, to maintain the French troops placed at their disposition up to then by the French Government.

The French troops in the Saar do not, therefore, constitute an occupying force but a garrison, absolutely distinct from the French army of the Rhine. Their head has to comply with all the requests of the president of the Governing Commission.

Their presence cannot be considered as contrary to the dispositions of section 4 of the Peace Treaty (annex, paragraph 30), which reads as follows:—

"There will be no military service, whether compulsory or voluntary, in the territory of the Saar basin, and the construction of fortifications therein is forbidden. Only a local gendarmery for the maintenance of order may be established. It will be the duty of the Governing Commission to provide in all cases for the protection of persons and property in the Saar basin."

The German Government has relied on this article in protesting vehemently and repeatedly against the maintenance of the French troops.

But this article simply means that the Governing Commission has not the right to constitute a local army; it contains nothing against the sojourn of French troops in the Saar; nothing in the text of the treaty, indeed, restricts the powers of the Governing Commission in the choice of the means which will enable it to assure the protection of persons and property. Finally, from the French point of view, article 428 of the Peace Treaty gives the troops of the Allied Powers the right to occupy the German territories situated to the west of the Rhine for a period of fifteen years, and this article, absolutely general in scope, is not subjected to the slightest qualifications elsewhere. In order to be able to support the contention that the presence of the French troops in the Saar constitutes a violation of the treaty, it would have been necessary for article 428 to except the territory of the Saar basin from the general rule, or for the article dealing with the construction of the local gendarmery to lay down precisely that in any case no troops of the Allied Powers shall be stationed in the Saar territory.

Nothing of the sort is stated in the treaty, and the League of Nations, which has not to read limitations into clauses expressed in very clear and precise terms, has on two occasions, February 13, 1920, and June 20, 1921, had before it the German claim and recognised the soundness of the case for the maintenance of the French troops in the Saar.

As to policing properly so termed, it is exercised (1) by the State police, (a) the Saarbrücken town police, (b) the Saar gendarmery instituted in execution of the annex to section 4 of the Peace Treaty; (2) by communal police, existing in each commune or communal group, under the direction of a police commissioner and under the authority of the "burgomaster," who is himself a functionary appointed by the Government; (3) by the French gendarmery. The French gendarmery brigades distributed over the Saar territory are placed at the disposition of the Governing Commission for the execution of the requisitions addressed to it by the president of the said Commission in the interest of the public safety.

The effectives kept in the Saar have been determined by the strategic importance of the territory occupied, which arises (a) from its communications, which are precisely those of the French army of the Rhine, and (b) from the wooded heights which these communications have to traverse north of Saarbrücken.

The safety of the former can only be secured by a sufficient contingent permanently on the spot; the safety of the wooded range can be confided to foreign elements, subject always to their admixture with special nuclei and units drawn from the garrison of the country.

At the end of 1919 the French troops stationed in the Saar were war units; they comprised the 127th Division of Infantry and elements from the communications of the French army of the Rhine. In 1920 the intervention of the League of Nations with the French Government led to the dissolution of the 127th Division and its replacement by a detachment of all arms stationed in the Saar territory, and to the compression of the elements of the communications of the French army of the Rhine.

We have found that Rhineland coal merchants have offered coal to the Saar troops at a price below that at which they obtain coal from the Saarbrücken mines; there is a mystery to be elucidated here. Probably owing to the debasement of the mark the cost price of Ruhr coal, including transport, is below that of Saar coal, the Saar miners being paid in francs.

This points to the vice of our control of the finances of the Reich; the German Budget is being pillaged by the public enterprises and in particular by the railways which, under the pretext of a working deficit, in reality receive enormous subventions from the Government, whence comes a deficit in the Budget, met by more and more enormous inflation and a more and more accentuated downward movement of the mark.

Meanwhile, whatever the value of the mark, transport rates remain unchanged, so that industry and commerce and even private individuals benefit, in all the public services, from prices which have nothing in common with the real cost of the services. The purpose is always the same: the impoverishment of the State to the point of bankruptcy, but the enrichment of private individuals in Germany.

A single example will illustrate this. Our railway ticket from Cologne to the Saar frontier, via Trèves, costs us 340 marks, for a distance of about 180 kilometres. The journey across the Saar, via Saarbrücken and Sarreguemines, came to 420 marks for a distance of 70 kilometres. It is true that the Saar railways require payment in francs for tickets.

THE ECONOMIC IMPORTANCE OF THE SAAR BASIN

The Versailles Treaty gave to France, in compensation for the destruction of the mines in the Nord, the entire and absolute ownership, free of all debts and burdens, of all the coal seams situated in the basin of the Saar.

The average production of the basin before the war was below its potentialities; in 1913 it was 13 millions of tons (18 millions, if the annexed part of Lorraine be included). The French administration of the mines considers that within ten years the figure can be brought up to 20 millions.

After a period of stagnation on the morrow of the war the Saar mines, now French State mines, rapidly increased their output. Despite the general economic crisis they have already regained the level up to which the Germans had brought them in the most prosperous period of their pre-war administration.

The State mines are now subdivided into twelve inspectorates, occupying a numerous staff of French engineers and more than 70,000 Saar workers. There are 30 main centres, with 67 working shafts and 65 air shafts.

The coal extracted has increased from 20,000 tons a day in 1918 to 40,000 in 1921. These figures will be greatly exceeded in the near future. The results already obtained by the French administration are a guarantee of the success of the coming improvements which it proposes to introduce in the various services.

The localities in which the miners and the workers in the subsidiary industries are grouped form a continuous zone of agglomerations, more than 30 kilometres in length, in the valley of the Sulz from Saarbrücken to Neunkirchen. They have an indigenous population of 100,000, to which must be added a floating population of equal number, attracted from the country districts of St. Ingbert, St. Wendel, Ottweiler, and the Palatinate, by the opportunity of remunerative work in mine or factory. The total mining population of the Saar basin may thus be estimated at 200,000.

Around these areas of coal extraction there has grown up an important metal industry. There are great iron and steel works at Saarbrücken and in its neighbourhood. In other localities there are metal works specialising in the production of manufactured goods.

The heavy iron and steel industry consists of five principal undertakings: the Brebach, Dillinger, Neunkirchen, Saarbrücken, and Burbach works, with 30 blastfurnaces. Around these great firms there gravitates numberless iron-working factories. The number of Saar metal workers is about 60,000.

Finally, alongside the extraction of coal and the production of iron and steel, various industries occupy an important place in the Saar basin.

1. The Saar glassworks produce annually 30,000,000 bottles of all patterns and a considerable quantity of glass sheets; they occupy 2,200 workers. The principal factories are the Sulzbach works (900 workers), the St. Ingbert works (400), the Stockheim works at Homburg (525), and the Oldenburg works at Friedrichsthal (350).

2. China and earthenware, cement, etc. The tile works and earthenware works of the Saar are represented by famous firms; the Villeroy and Boch works at Mettlach (1,300 workers), the works at Walderfangen (600), those at Merzig (600), etc.

3. Other industries. Among the small industries which provide a livelihood for the numerous working populations must be mentioned the chemical industry, producing considerable quantities of sulphuric acid, hydrochloric acid, etc.; the explosive factories, 150 workers; the paper mills, some employing over 200, etc.

Besides the large industries, local industries spreading even into the villages and the country districts support a very dense population throughout the territory.

According to the latest figures, the industrial population of the Saar is 500,000 or two-thirds of the total. The remainder is composed of about 70,000 traders (including their families), 70,000 officials and State and municipal employees (and families), 40,000 peasants, and 50,000 persons of private means, engineers, teachers, etc.

THE POLITICAL SITUATION

We recalled above that the administration of the Saar territory was vested in a Governing Commission placed under the authority of the League of Nations.

It is worth while to examine impartially the conditions under which the Governing Commission is functioning at present, and at the same time to point to the causes of the purely political agitation lately observed in the principal centres in the Saar.

The Governing Commission, which has its headquarters at Saarbrücken, has all the powers of government hitherto belonging to the German Empire, Prussia or Bavaria, including the appointment and dismissal of officials and the creation of such administrative and representative bodies as it may deem necessary. It has full powers to administer and operate the railways, canals, and the different public services. It has the sole power of levying taxes and dues. Justice is rendered in its name. It ensures, by such means and under such conditions as it deems suitable, the protection abroad of the inhabitants of the territory of the Saar. (It has confided the task of such protection to the Government of the French Republic.) Its decisions are taken by a majority.

The laws and regulations in force in the territory on November 11, 1918, except those enacted in consequence of the state of war, continue to apply. But the Governing Commission may, if it deems it necessary, modify this legislation, on condition that it first consults the elected representatives of the inhabitants. The inhabitants retain their local assemblies, their schools, language, and nationality.

The Governing Commission has established equality between all the inhabitants of the territory, irrespective of nationality. The quality of inhabitant of the Saar can be acquired by anyone domiciled three years in the territory and inscribed on the roll of taxpayers. This period can be reduced in certain cases to one year.

In 1935 the population of the territory will be called upon to indicate their desires in the following manner. A vote will take place by communes or burgomasters' areas on the three following alternatives: —(a) Maintenance of the régime established by the Versailles Treaty: (b) reunion with France: (c) union with Germany.

THE FRENCH POLICY IN THE SAAR

The French policy in the Saar should be one of methodical and prudent action, without premature rashness or excessive timidity.

In this region the German-speaking Lorraine elements, which represent the autochthonous and secular race, are submerged by other elements of Prussian origin established after the treaties of 1815, a numerous colony from the North—miners, officials who have founded families, traders long established in the industrial zone. These constitute, above the mass of the Lorraine peasants, a more active class, better organised, attached to the memory of Greater Germany, and with an ingrained hostility to the action of France.

The official is in general hostile to us; the teacher retains the German culture and transmits it to the new generations; the clergy, in a country predominantly Catholic, shows a prudent reserve explainable by the uncertainty of the morrow.

A delicate, prudent, sustained policy is essential: the progressive replacement of these Pan-German officials, the conquest of the school, alliance with this clergy whose national sentiment is easily dominated by a preoccupation with adaptation to the forms of a new régime, the utilisation of the press, the organisation of the working classes into

trade unions with a defined tendency being problems which offer themselves to our meditations.

It is in this complex country that elections are to be held shortly
with universal and unrestricted suffrage, women having the right to
vote, and with a single ballot list for the whole of the territory.

From the Armistice until now the political life of the Saar territory
was reduced to a minimum. Seven rural districts (Saarbrücken rural
area, Saarlouis, Merzig, Ottweiler, St. Wendel, St. Ingbert, and Homburg) and one urban district (the town of Saarbrücken) elect for
three years a district council (Kreistag) by universal suffrage with
proportional representation.

Each commune elects its municipal council, again by universal
suffrage. The communes in the Prussian part of the territory are
grouped into burgomasters' areas, with a council comprised of the
mayors of the communes so grouped and of delegates elected by each
municipal council.

Municipal councils and district councils, with greater powers than
ours, these were the only organs to which the electors in the Saar could
send their representatives. Over them there was the Governing Commission.

Under an ordinance dated March 24 the latter enacted the setting
up of a Consultative Council of 30 members, elected by universal
suffrage, equal, direct, and secret, on a single ballot paper, in conformity with the principle of proportional representation.

The electors in the territory are grouped into a single electoral
college.

Undoubtedly this Consultative Council can, on pain of nullity, deliberate on no other objects than those which, in the application of
paragraphs 23 and 26 of chapter 2 of the annex to section 4 of the
Peace Treaty, should be submitted for the advice of the elected representatives of the inhabitants.

Undoubtedly all deliberations, motions, or resolutions tending either
directly or indirectly to do injury to the legal conditions created by
the Peace Treaty of Versailles or to subsequent ordinances of the Governing Commission will be null and void.

But can one prevent an elected assembly, on pain of nullity, from
passing resolutions, from bringing them to the attention of public
opinion, of opinion in the Saar, in Germany, in Allied countries?

The fact is that for the first time the power of speech has been
restored to the Saar populations, which will have to pronounce for or
against France.

An eventuality full of dangers.

It is true that if all the electors domiciled in the Saar are going to
have the right to vote, only those aged over 25 and born within the
frontiers of the State will be eligible. It is an insufficient limitation,
ostracising certain professional politicians recently imported for the
special benefit of the German cause, but not extended to numbers of

sons of Prussian immigrants, officials or traders, born in the Saar territory, of recent origin, and of equivocal attitude, who see in a consultation of the electorate not simply the return of a lost liberty but the possibility of a public profession of faith in the future of the Saar.

Who will prevent these people, if they throw down the gage, from giving to the elections the air of a plebiscite, and, under the modest pretext of choosing a consultative assembly, interrogating the people of the Saar concerning their destinies? And if, instead of taking refuge in abstention, the German caucuses put at the head of their programme this fidelity to the cause of the Reich, what means will there be of opposition to their propaganda and its pernicious results?

After all, what imperious necessity was there, under the pretext of rendering closer the collaboration of the Rhenish populations with the Governing Commission, to provoke a premature popular consultation, in advance of the expiration of the fifteen years prescribed by the Peace Treaty? (Paragraph 34 of the annex to section 4.)

Did not Mr. Wellington Koo, the Chinese delegate to the League of Nations, who reported on the project for his Committee, hint at fears of the possibility that grave consequences might accrue to the authority of the Governing Commission from the creation of a Consultative Council for the Saar, even if the powers and competence of this Council were to be strictly limited?

It looks like creating difficulties for no reason. The elections are to take place on a single list for the whole country. It is not a piecemeal consultation by districts, in which it would be possible to avoid a great current of opinion, to split it up in some way. The whole of the people of the Saar is going to vote for competing lists. One of them may have an absolute majority. It is precisely a plebiscite to which we are committed. If it turns out well, what a success! But if the German candidates carry the day, what a setback!

A strong agitation, moreover, is under way throughout the territory. A press campaign and a campaign of meetings have been commenced to secure from the Governing Commission the extension of the terms of eligibility and also of the powers of the Consultative Council. The Governing Commission, by means of posters, has had to put things right, and in doing so has added fuel to the fire.

The future of our Saar policy is at stake. It would be puerile to deny it, and it would be lamentable to fail to take every possible step to conjure the peril.

The question, moreover, is no longer entirely local; it was raised recently before the Genoa Conference, and if the French delegates succeeded for the moment in securing the rejection of the demands of certain Saar organisations, the problem as a whole is placed before the opinion of the world.

The decision of March 24 accentuated an agitation which challenges the very rights which we secured under the treaties.

It is for the Government to take, in these circumstances, such initiative as shall attenuate the consequences of such a decision.

168. THE BALFOUR NOTE ON INTER-ALLIED DEBTS, 1922[1]

[In August, 1922, with the United States demanding payments from Great Britain, with the economic life of his country in a serious condition, with German credit, both external and internal, almost worthless, and with a German demand for a moratorium at hand and a French refusal of this demand, Balfour proposed to the French Government something very different from that for which the latter had been striving. Perhaps all debts could be wiped away and a new start made. There has been great difference of opinion as to how this scheme would have worked had it received approval.]

The Earl of Balfour to the French Ambassador

Foreign Office, August 1, 1922

Your Excellency,

As your Excellency is aware, the general question of the French debt to this country has not as yet been the subject of any formal communication between the two Governments, nor are His Majesty's Government anxious to raise it at the present moment. Recent events, however, leave them little choice in the matter, and they feel compelled to lay before the French Government their views on certain aspects of the situation created by the present condition of international indebtedness.

Speaking in general terms, the war debts, exclusive of interest, due to Great Britain at the present moment amount in the aggregate to about £3,400,000,000 of which Germany owes £1,450,000,000; Russia £650,000,000; and our allies £1,300,000,000. On the other hand, Great Britain owes the United States about a quarter of this sum—say £850,000,000, at par exchange, together with interest accrued since 1919.

No international discussion has yet taken place on the unexampled situation partially disclosed by these figures; and, pending a settlement which would go to the root of the problem, His Majesty's Government have silently abstained from making any demands upon their allies, either for the payment of interest or the repayment of capital. But, if action in the matter has hitherto been deemed inopportune, this is not because His Majesty's Government either underrate the evils of the present state of affairs, or because they are reluctant to make large sacrifices to bring it to an end. On the contrary, they are prepared, if such a policy formed part of a satisfactory international

---

[1] Great Britain, *Parliamentary Papers*, 1922, Vol. XXIII, Cmd. 1737. "Despatch to the Representatives of France, Italy, Serb-Croat-Slovene State, Roumania, Portugal and Greece at London respecting War Debts."

settlement, to remit all the debts due to Great Britain by our allies in respect of loans, or by Germany in respect of reparations.

Recent events, however, make such a policy difficult of accomplishment. With the most perfect courtesy, and in the exercise of their undoubted rights, the American Government have required this country to pay the interest accrued since 1919 on the Anglo-American debt, to convert it from an unfunded to a funded debt, and to repay it by a sinking fund in twenty-five years. Such a procedure is clearly in accordance with the original contract. His Majesty's Government make no complaint of it; they recognise their obligations and are prepared to fulfil them. But evidently they cannot do so without profoundly modifying the course which, in different circumstances, they would have wished to pursue. They cannot treat the repayment of the Anglo-American loan as if it were an isolated incident in which only the United States of America and Great Britain had any concern. It is but one of a connected series of transactions, in which this country appears sometimes as debtor, sometimes as creditor, and, if our undoubted obligations as a debtor are to be enforced, our not less undoubted rights as a creditor cannot be left wholly in abeyance.

His Majesty's Government do not conceal the fact that they adopt this change of policy with the greatest reluctance. It is true that Great Britain is owed more than it owes, and that, if all inter-Allied war debts were paid, the British Treasury would, on balance, be a large gainer by the transaction. But can the present world situation be looked at only from this narrow financial standpoint? It is true that many of the Allied and Associated Powers are, as between each other, creditors or debtors, or both. But they were, and are, much more. They were partners in the greatest international effort ever made in the cause of freedom; and they are still partners in dealing with some, at least, of its results. Their debts were incurred, their loans were made, not for the separate advantage of particular States, but for a great purpose common to them all, and that purpose has been, in the main, accomplished.

To generous minds it can never be agreeable, although, for reasons of State, it may perhaps be necessary, to regard the monetary aspect of this great event as a thing apart, to be torn from its historical setting and treated as no more than an ordinary commercial dealing between traders who borrow and capitalists who lend. There are, moreover, reasons of a different order, to which I have already referred, which increase the distaste with which His Majesty's Government adopt so fundamental an alteration in method of dealing with loans to allies. The economic ills from which the world is suffering are due to many causes, moral and material, which are quite outside the scope of this despatch. But among them must certainly be reckoned the weight of international indebtedness, with all its unhappy effects upon credit and exchange, upon national production and international trade. The peoples of all countries long for a speedy return to the normal. But how can the normal be reached while conditions so abnormal are permitted to prevail? And how can these conditions be cured by any remedies that seem at present likely to be applied?

For evidently the policy hitherto pursued by this country of refusing to make demands upon its debtors is only tolerable so long as it is generally accepted. It cannot be right that one partner in the common enterprise should recover all that she has lent, and that another, while recovering nothing, should be required to pay all that she has borrowed. Such a procedure is contrary to every principle of natural justice and cannot be expected to commend itself to the people of this country. They are suffering from an unparalleled burden of taxation, from an immense diminution in national wealth, from serious want of employment, and from the severe curtailment of useful expenditure. These evils are courageously borne. But were they to be increased by an arrangement which, however legitimate, is obviously one-sided, the British taxpayer would inevitably ask why he should be singled out to bear a burden which others are bound to share.

To such a question there can be but one answer, and I am convinced that Allied opinion will admit its justice. But while His Majesty's Government are thus regretfully constrained to request the French Government to make arrangements for dealing to the best of their ability with Anglo-French loans, they desire to explain that the amount of interest and repayment for which they ask depends not so much on what France and other Allies owe to Great Britain as on what Great Britain has to pay America. The policy favoured by His Majesty is, as I have already observed, that of surrendering their share of German reparation, and writing off, through one great transaction, the whole body of inter-Allied indebtedness. But, if this be found impossible of accomplishment, we wish it to be understood that we do not in any event desire to make a profit out of any less satisfactory arrangement. In no circumstances do we propose to ask more from our debtors than is necessary to pay to our creditors. And, while we do not ask for more, all will admit that we can hardly be content with less. For it should not be forgotten, though it sometimes is, that our liabilities were incurred for others, not for ourselves. The food, the raw material, the munitions required by the immense naval and military efforts of Great Britain and half the £2,000,000,000 advanced to allies were provided, not by means of foreign loans, but by internal borrowing and war taxation. Unfortunately, a similar policy was beyond the power of other European nations. Appeal was therefore made to the Government of the United States; and under the arrangement then arrived at the United States insisted, in substance, if not in form, that, though our allies were to spend the money, it was only on our security that they were prepared to lend it. This coöperative effort was of infinite value to the common cause, but it cannot be said that the rôle assigned in it to this country was one of special privilege or advantage.

Before concluding I may be permitted to offer one further observation in order to make still clearer the spirit in which His Majesty's Government desire to deal with the thorny problem of international indebtedness.

In an earlier passage of this despatch I pointed out that this, after all, is not a question merely between allies. Ex-enemy countries also are involved; for the greatest of all international debtors is Germany. Now His Majesty's Government do not suggest that, either as a matter of justice or expediency, Germany should be relieved of her obligation to the other allied States. They speak only for Great Britain; and they content themselves with saying once again that, so deeply are they convinced of the economic injury inflicted on the world by the existing state of things that this country would be prepared (subject to the just claims of other parts of the Empire) to abandon all further right to German reparations and all claims to repayment by allies, provided that this renunciation formed part of a general plan by which this great problem could be dealt with as a whole and find a satisfactory solution. A general settlement would, in their view, be of more value to mankind than any gains that could accrue even from the most successful enforcement of legal obligations.

I have, etc.,

BALFOUR

169. THE TREATY OF LAUSANNE, 1923[1]

[The inclusion of Turkish delegates made this the only one of the treaties ending the war which was negotiated and not dictated. The conference opened in Lausanne on November 20, but the Turkish delegates refused to sign the treaty as presented on January 31, 1923, because of certain economic and judicial clauses. The conference was broken up, but on April 24 resumed its sessions. During the next three months the Allies yielded on enough points to satisfy the Turks and the Treaty was signed. The selections here given should be compared with the Treaty of Sèvres (doc. no. 152). Turkey thus obtained nearly everything for which the nationalists had fought: ethnographic frontiers, freedom from international servitudes, and national independence.]

Article 27. No power or jurisdiction in political, legislative or administrative matters shall be exercised outside Turkish territory by the Turkish Government or authorities, for any reason whatsoever, over the nationals of a territory placed under the sovereignty or protectorate of the other powers signatory of the present Treaty, or over the nationals of a territory detached from Turkey. It is understood that

[1] Great Britain, *Parliamentary Papers*, 1923, Vol. XXV, Cmd. 1929. "Treaty of Peace with Turkey and other Instruments signed at Lausanne on July 24, 1923."

the spiritual attributions of the Moslem religious authorities are in no way infringed. . . .

SECTION III: PROTECTION OF MINORITIES

Article 37. Turkey undertakes that the stipulations contained in Articles 38 to 44 shall be recognised as fundamental laws, and that no laws, no regulation, nor official action shall conflict or interfere with these stipulations, nor shall any law, regulation, nor official action prevail over them.

Article 38. The Turkish Government undertakes to assure full and complete protection of life and liberty to all inhabitants of Turkey without distinction of birth, nationality, language, race or religion.

All inhabitants of Turkey shall be entitled to free exercise, whether in public or private, of any creed, religion or belief, the observance of which shall not be incompatible with public order and good morals.

Non-Moslem minorities will enjoy full freedom of movement and of emigration, subject to the measures applied, on the whole or on part of the territory, to all Turkish nationals, and which may be taken by the Turkish Government for national defence, or for the maintenance of public order.

Article 39. Turkish nationals belonging to non-Moslem minorities will enjoy the same civil and political rights as Moslems.

All the inhabitants of Turkey, without distinction of religion, shall be equal before the law.

Differences of religion, creed or confession shall not prejudice any Turkish national in matters relating to the enjoyment of civil or political rights, as, for instance, admission to public employments, functions and honours, or the exercise of professions and industries.

No restrictions shall be imposed on the free use by any Turkish national of any language in private intercourse, in commerce, religion, in the press, or in publications of any kind or at public meetings.

Notwithstanding the existence of the official language, adequate facilities shall be given to Turkish nationals of non-Turkish speech for the oral use of their own language before the Courts.

Article 40. Turkish nationals belonging to non-Moslem minorities shall enjoy the same treatment and security in law and in fact as other Turkish nationals. In particular, they shall have an equal right to establish, manage and control at their own expense, any charitable, religious and social institutions, any schools and other establishments for instruction and education, with the right to use their own language and to exercise their own religion freely therein.

Article 41. As regards public instruction, the Turkish Government will grant in those towns and districts, where a considerable proportion of non-Moslem nationals are resident, adequate facilities for ensuring that in the primary schools the instruction shall be given to the children of such Turkish nationals through the medium of their own language. This provision will not prevent the Turkish Government from making the teaching of the Turkish language obligatory in the said schools.

In towns and districts where there is a considerable proportion of Turkish nationals belonging to non-Moslem minorities, these minorities shall be assured an equitable share in the enjoyment and application of the sums which may be provided out of public funds under the State, municipal or other budgets for educational, religious, or charitable purposes.

The sums in question shall be paid to the qualified representatives of the establishments and institutions concerned.

Article 42. The Turkish Government undertakes to take, as regards non-Moslem minorities, in so far as concerns their family law or personal status, measures permitting the settlement of these questions in accordance with the customs of those minorities.

These measures will be elaborated by special Commissions composed of representatives of the Turkish Government and of representatives of each of the minorities concerned in equal number. In case of divergence, the Turkish Government and the Council of the League of Nations will appoint in agreement an umpire chosen from amongst European lawyers.

The Turkish Government undertakes to grant full protection to the churches, synagogues, cemeteries, and other religious establishments of the above-mentioned minorities.

All facilities and authorisation will be granted to the pious foundations, and to the religious and charitable institutions of the said minorities at present existing in Turkey, and the Turkish Government will not refuse, for the formation of new religious and charitable institutions, any of the necessary facilities which are guaranteed to other private institutions of that nature.

Article 43. Turkish nationals belonging to non-Moslem minorities shall not be compelled to perform any act which constitutes a violation of their faith or religious observances, and shall not be placed under any disability by reason of their refusal to attend Courts of Law or to perform any legal business on their weekly day of rest.

This provision, however, shall not exempt such Turkish nationals from such obligations as shall be imposed upon all other Turkish nationals for the preservation of public order.

Article 44. Turkey agrees that, in so far as the preceding Articles of this Section affect non-Moslem nationals of Turkey, these provisions constitute obligations of international concern and shall be placed under the guarantee of the League of Nations. They shall not be modified without the assent of the majority of the Council of the League of Nations. The British Empire, France, Italy and Japan hereby agree not to withhold their assent to any modification in these Articles which is in due form assented to by a majority of the Council of the League of Nations.

Turkey agrees that any Member of the Council of the League of Nations shall have the right to bring to the attention of the Council any infraction or danger of infraction of any of these obligations, and that the Council may thereupon take such action and give such directions as it may deem proper and effective in the circumstances.

Turkey further agrees that any difference of opinion as to questions of law or of fact arising out of these Articles between the Turkish Government and any one of the other Signatory Powers or any other Power, a member of the Council of the League of Nations, shall be held to be a dispute of an international character under Article 14 of the Covenant of the League of Nations. The Turkish Government hereby consents that any such dispute shall, if the other party thereto demands, be referred to the Permanent Court of International Justice. The decision of the Permanent Court shall be final and shall have the same force and effect as an award under Article 13 of the Covenant. . . .

Article 51. The rights conferred by the provisions of the present Section of the non-Moslem minorities of Turkey will be similarly conferred by Greece on the Moslem minority in her territory. . . .

Article 59. Greece recognises her obligation to make reparation for the damage caused in Anatolia by the acts of the Greek army or administration which were contrary to the laws of war.

On the other hand, Turkey, in consideration of the financial situation of Greece resulting from the prolongation of the war and from its consequences, finally renounces all claims for reparation against the Greek Government. . . .

CONVENTION RELATING TO THE RÉGIME OF THE STRAITS

Article 1. The High Contracting Parties agree to recognise and declare the principle of freedom of transit and of navigation by sea and by air in the Strait of the Dardanelles, the Sea of Marmora and the Bosphorus, hereinafter comprised under the general term of the "Straits."

ANNEX

Rules for the Passage of Commercial Vessels and Aircraft, and of War Vessels and Aircraft through the Straits

Article 1. . . .

(b.) In Time of War, Turkey Being Neutral.

Complete freedom of navigation and passage by day and by night under the same conditions as above. The duties and rights of Turkey as a neutral Power cannot authorise her to take any measures liable to interfere with navigation through the Straits, the waters of which, and the air above which, must remain entirely free in time of war, Turkey being neutral, just as in time of peace.

Pilotage remains optional.

(c.) In Time of War, Turkey Being a Belligerent.

Freedom of navigation for neutral vessels and neutral non-military aircraft, if the vessel or aircraft in question does not assist the enemy, particularly by carrying contraband, troops or enemy nationals. Turkey will have the right to visit and search such vessels and aircraft, and for this purpose aircraft are to alight on the ground or on the sea in such areas as are specified and prepared for this purpose by Turkey. The rights of Turkey to apply to enemy vessels the measures allowed by international law are not affected.

Turkey will have full power to take such measures as she may consider necessary to prevent enemy vessels from using the Straits. These measures, however, are not to be of such a nature as to prevent the free passage of neutral vessels, and Turkey agrees to provide such vessels with either the necessary instructions or pilots for the above purpose. . . .

Article 4. The zones and islands indicated below shall be demilitarised:

1. Both shores of the Straits of the Dardanelles and the Bosphorus over the extent of the zones delimited below.

Convention Concerning the Exchange of Greek and Turkish Populations

Signed at Lausanne, January 30, 1923

The Government of the Grand National Assembly of Turkey and the Greek Government have agreed upon the following provisions:—

Article 1. As from the 1st May, 1923, there shall take place a compulsory exchange of Turkish nationals of the Greek Orthodox religion established in Turkish territory, and of Greek nationals of the Moslem religion established in Greek territory.

These persons shall not return to live in Turkey or Greece respectively without the authorisation of the Turkish Government or of the Greek Government respectively.

Article 2. The following persons shall not be included in the exchange provided for in Article 1:—

(a.) The Greek inhabitants of Constantinople.

(b.) The Moslem inhabitants of Western Thrace.

All Greeks who were already established before the 30th October, 1918, within the areas under the Prefecture of the City of Constantinople, as defined by the law of 1912, shall be considered as Greek inhabitants of Constantinople.

All Moslems established in the region to the east of the frontier line laid down in 1913 by the Treaty of Bucharest shall be considered as Moslem inhabitants of Western Thrace.

Article 3. Those Greeks and Moslems who have already, and since the 18th October, 1912, left the territories the Greek and Turkish inhabitants of which are to be respectively exchanged, shall be considered as included in the exchange provided for in Article 1.

The expression "emigrant" in the present Convention includes all physical and juridical persons who have been obliged to emigrate or have emigrated since the 18th October, 1912.

Article 4. All able-bodied men belonging to the Greek population, whose families have already left Turkish territory, and who are now detained in Turkey, shall constitute the first instalment of Greeks sent to Greece in accordance with the present Convention.

Article 5. Subject to the provisions of Article 9 and 10 of the present Convention, the rights of property and monetary assets of Greeks in Turkey or Moslems in Greece shall not be prejudiced in consequence of the exchange to be carried out under the present Convention.

Article 6. No obstacle may be placed for any reason whatever in the way of the departure of a person belonging to the populations which are to be exchanged. In the event of an emigrant having received a definite sentence of imprisonment, or a sentence which is not yet definitive, or of his being the object of criminal proceedings, he shall be handed over by the authorities of the prosecuting country to the authorities of the country whither he is going, in order that he may serve his sentence or be brought to trial.

Article 7. The emigrants will lose the nationality of the country which they are leaving, and will acquire the nationality of the country of their destination, upon their arrival in the territory of the latter country.

Such emigrants as have already left one or other of the two countries and have not yet acquired their new nationality, shall acquire that nationality on the date of the signature of the present Convention.

Article 8. Emigrants shall be free to take away with them or to arrange for the transport of their movable property of every kind, without being liable on this account to the payment of any export or import duty or any other tax.

Similarly, the members of each community (including the personnel of mosques, tekkes, meddresses, churches, convents, schools, hospitals, societies, associations and juridical persons, or other foundations of any nature whatever) which are to leave the territory of one of the Contracting States under the present Convention, shall have the right to take away freely or to arrange for the transport of the movable property belonging to their communities.

The fullest facilities for transport shall be provided by the authorities of the two countries, upon the recommendation of the Mixed Commission provided for in Article 11.

Emigrants who may not be able to take away all or part of their movable property can leave it behind. In that event, the local authorities shall be required to draw up, the emigrant in question being given an opportunity to be heard, an inventory and valuation of the property left by him. *Procès-verbaux* containing the inventory and the valuation of the movable property left by the emigrant shall be drawn up in four copies, one of which shall be kept by the local authorities, the second transmitted to the Mixed Commission provided for in Article 11 to serve as the basis for the liquidation provided for by Article 9, the third shall be handed to the Government of the country to which the emigrant is going, and the fourth to the emigrant himself.

Article 9. Immovable property, whether rural or urban, belonging to emigrants, or to the communities mentioned in Article 8, and the movable property left by these emigrants or communities, shall be liquidated in accordance with the following provisions by the Mixed Commission provided for in Article 11.

Property situated in the districts to which the compulsory exchange applies and belonging to religious or benevolent institutions of the communities established in a district to which the exchange does not apply, shall likewise be liquidated under the same conditions.

170. TREATY OF ALLIANCE AND FRIENDSHIP BETWEEN FRANCE AND CZECHOSLOVAKIA, SIGNED AT PARIS JANUARY 25, 1924[1]

[This treaty is quoted as typical of the various treaties of anti-German alliances which France formed in carrying out her policy of encirclement. In October, 1923, Masaryk, the president, and Beneš, the foreign minister, of Czechoslovakia, visited Paris; the conferences then held resulted in the drafting of the terms of the following treaty. It is interesting to compare the extent to which this treaty takes arbitration into account (Article 6) with the lack of such provisions in the Bismarckian system. This group of French security treaties included agreements between France, Czechoslovakia, Belgium, Poland, Rumania, and Jugoslavia. These in turn had still other treaty connections which broadened the base of the French security system.]

Article 1. The Governments of the French Republic and of the Czechoslovak Republic undertake to concert their action in all matters of foreign policy which may threaten their security or which may tend to subvert the situation created by the Treaties of Peace of which both parties are signatories.

Article 2. The High Contracting Parties shall agree together as to

---

[1] Ratified March 4, 1924; registered March 15, 1924. League of Nations, *Treaty Series*, Vol. XXIII, p. 164ff.

THE BENEVOLENT DEBTOR.

M. Poincaré *(distributing largesse to the Little Entente and other new friends)*. "THERE YOU ARE, MY BOYS. NOW GO AND BUY YOURSELVES SOME SOLDIERS AND GUNS."

[France has recently lent some eight hundred millions of francs to Poland, Roumania and Yugo-Slavia, to be expended in war-material. The French war-debt to this country, including accrued interest, now amounts to about six hundred millions sterling.]

From *Punch*, January 9, 1924
(Reprinted by arrangements with the proprietors of *Punch*.)

the measures to be adopted to safeguard their common interests in case the latter are threatened.

Article 3. The High Contracting Parties, being fully in agreement as to the importance, for the maintenance of the world's peace, of the political principles laid down in Article 88 of the Treaty of Peace of St. Germain-en-Laye of September 10, 1919, and in the Protocols of Geneva dated October 4, 1922, of which instruments they both are signatories, undertake to consult each other as to the measures to be taken in case there should be any danger of an infraction of these principles.

Article 4. The High Contracting Parties, having special regard to the declarations made by the Conference of Ambassadors on February 3, 1920, and April 1, 1921, on which their policy will continue to be based, and to the declaration made on November 10, 1921, by the Hungarian Government to the Allied diplomatic representatives, undertake to consult each other in case their interests are threatened by a failure to observe the principles laid down in the aforesaid declarations.

Article 5. The High Contracting Parties solemnly declare that they are in complete agreement as to the necessity, for the maintenance of peace, of taking common action in the event of any attempt to restore the Hohenzollern dynasty in Germany, and they undertake to consult each other in such a contingency.

Article 6. In conformity with the principles laid down in the Covenant of the League of Nations, the High Contracting Parties agree that if in the future any dispute should arise between them which cannot be settled by friendly agreement and through diplomatic channels, they will submit such dispute either to the Permanent Court of International Justice or to such other arbitrator or arbitrators as they may select.

Article 7. The High Contracting Parties undertake to communicate to each other all Agreements affecting their policy in Central Europe which they may have previously concluded, and to consult one another before concluding any further Agreements. They declare that, in this matter, nothing in the present Treaty is contrary to the above Agreements, and in particular to the Treaty of Alliance between France and Poland, or to the Conventions and Agreements concluded by Czechoslovakia with the Federal Republic of Austria, Roumania, the Kingdom of the Serbs, Croats and Slovenes, or to the Agreement effected by an exchange of notes on February 8, 1921, between the Italian Government and the Czechoslovak Government.

Article 8. The present Treaty shall be communicated to the League of Nations in conformity with Article 18 of the Covenant.

The present Treaty shall be ratified and the instruments of ratification shall be exchanged at Paris as soon as possible.

In faith whereof the respective plenipotentiaries, duly empowered for this purpose, have signed the present Treaty and have thereto affixed their seals.

Done at Paris, in duplicate, on January 25, 1924.

R. POINCARÉ

DR. EDUARD BENEŠ

171. GRÆCO-BULGARIAN AFFAIR, 1925[1]

[Clashes along the Jugoslav-Bulgarian and Græco-Bulgarian frontiers have repeatedly occurred during the post-war period, largely because of the Macedonian problem. This dispute of 1925 would almost unquestionably have led to war without the able assistance of the League. In settling the matter the Council laid down the general principle that "where territory is violated without sufficient cause, reparation is due, even if at the time of the occurrence it was believed by the party committing the act of violation that circumstances justified the action."]

EXTRAORDINARY (THIRTY-SIXTH) SESSION OF THE COUNCIL.

The Græco-Bulgarian Incident

At the request of the Bulgarian Government, which on October 23rd had invoked Articles X and XI of the Covenant, the Secretary-General convened the Council to meet in extraordinary session on October 26th in Paris.

The events which led to the Bulgarian appeal may be summarised as follows:

During the day of October 19th shots were exchanged on the frontier to the north-east of Salonica between Bulgarians and Greek sentries. A sentry was killed, as stated by Bulgarian telegrams, on Bulgarian territory, and, according to Greek despatches, a Greek officer was killed. Prolonged firing and movements of troops ensued.

Between the telegrams dealing with these events, addressed to the Council by the Governments concerned, there were divergencies and contradictions.

The Bulgarian Government proposed to the Greek Government that a mixed commission should be appointed to fix the responsibilities. The Greek Government, on the other hand, sent a Note to the Bulgarian Government, demanding apologies, the punishment of the officers responsible, and the payment of an indemnity to the families of the victims.

Meanwhile hostile acts continued. The Greek Government having instructed its military command to take all measures it considered necessary for the defence of its territory and the security of its troops, Greek detachments had entered Bulgarian territory in the neighbour-

---

[1] League of Nations, *Monthly Summary*, October, 1925, Vol. V, pp. 256-261.

hood of Petrich. On the other hand, according to telegrams from the Greek Government, Bulgarian detachments had penetrated Greek territory. The Bulgarian Government, in asking for a meeting of the Council, stated that it had given instructions to its military command that no resistance should be offered to the Greek troops. The appeal of the Bulgarian Government was received by the Secretary-General early in the morning of the 23rd. A few hours later, the Secretary-General summoned an extraordinary session of the Council. After consulting the acting President, M. Briand, he fixed the meeting for October 26th in Paris. In the afternoon of the same day, M. Briand sent a telegram, reminding both Governments of the "solemn obligations undertaken by them as Members of the League of Nations under Article XII of Covenant not to resort to war, and of grave consequences which Covenant lays down for breaches thereof"; he therefore exhorted the two Governments to give immediate instructions that pending consideration [of] dispute by Council not only no further military movements should be undertaken but that the troops should at once retire behind their respective frontiers.

On the same day the appeal of the Bulgarian Government, the convocation of the Council and M. Briand's telegram were communicated telegraphically to all States Members of the League and to the press.

Three days later the Council, including representatives of Greece and Bulgaria, met in public session in Paris, one of its members arriving by air. All the meetings were public.

CESSATION OF HOSTILITIES AND EVACUATION OF OCCUPIED TERRITORIES

For the Council two distinct questions arose. The first which involved ascertaining the facts and responsibilities, and, if necessary, fixing the amount of reparation due, demanded time and care. The second was urgent, as it concerned the cessation of hostilities and the immediate withdrawal of the Bulgarian and Greek troops to their respective territories.

Accordingly, at the first meeting of the Council, on October 26th, M. Briand asked the representatives of the parties, M. Marfoff (Bulgaria) and M. Carapanos (Greece), what action had been taken on his recommendation with regard to the cessation of hostilities and the withdrawal of troops, and what was the present situation.

M. Marfoff (Bulgaria) declared that at no moment and at no point had Greek territory been invaded or occupied by Bulgarian troops. M. Carapanos (Greece) stated that, as his Government had already made known, the Greeks were ready to evacuate Bulgarian soil as soon as the Bulgarians had withdrawn from Greek territory and that his Government was ready to accept the Council's decision.

The Council, on the report of Mr. Chamberlain, then decided to request the representatives of both States to inform it within twenty-four hours, that the Bulgarian and Greek Governments had given unconditional orders to their troops to withdraw behind their respective national frontiers, and, within sixty hours, that all troops had been withdrawn within the national frontiers, that hostilities had ceased, and that all troops had been warned that the resumption of firing would be visited with severe punishment.

The Council requested the French, British and Italian Governments to direct officers within reach to repair immediately to the region where the conflict had broken out, and to report direct to the Council on the execution of its decision. The Bulgarian and Greek Governments were so notified telegraphically in the evening of the 26th, the period fixed by the Council for the execution of its decision beginning at that moment.

On October 27th the Greek representative mentioned certain suggestions for agreement between Greece and Bulgaria and the consequent evacuation of the territory occupied; the President of the Council said that what was now hoped for was the full acceptance of the Council's proposals. Both nations were given the opportunity of stating their case in full.

In the morning of the 28th the Bulgarian representative informed the Council that, in accordance with its decision, strict orders had been given to Bulgarian troops to abstain from all military action; and to the Bulgarian military command to withdraw any Bulgarian troops which might be on Greek territory.

M. Carapanos (Greece) said that his Government had, on receipt of the telegram notifying the Council's decision, repeated and confirmed instructions previously given with a view to the cessation of hostilities and the withdrawal of its troops.

The first part of the Council's decision of the 26th had therefore been executed. Orders had been given by both parties for the cessation of hostilities and for the evacuation of occupied territory.

As regards the execution of these orders, the Greek Government, on October 29th, informed the Council that it was neglecting no steps to ensure that the Bulgarian territory would be evacuated by the time fixed. This information was confirmed that same day by a report from the British, French and Italian military attachés at Belgrade, who had already arrived at the scene of action. The report stated that both parties had given formal assurances that the Council's decision would be executed, that calm reigned on the whole front, and that the arrangements made gave reason to hope that no incident was to be feared.

The Council was notified later by telegrams from the attachés and from the Greek Minister of Foreign Affairs that the Greek troops had entirely evacuated Bulgarian territory on October 28th, at midnight, that is to say, eight hours before the time-limit fixed by the Council, and that the evacuation had given rise to no incident of any kind.

·   ·   ·   ·   ·   ·   ·

At the public meetings of the Council, the Acting President, M. Briand, and the Rapporteur, Mr. Chamberlain, made several important declarations, which were unanimously approved by their colleagues.

On October 26th Mr. Chamberlain drew attention to the fact that the frontier incident with which the Council had to deal had arisen between two States Members of the League of Nations, both of which had accepted the obligations of the Covenant, in particular, Articles X and XI. He continued:

Such incidents as that which has caused our present meeting have sometimes had very serious consequences in the past, where there was no machinery such as that offered by the League for their peaceful adjustment and for securing justice to both parties; but it would be an intolerable thing—I go so far as to say that it would be an affront to civilisation—if, with all the machinery of the League at their disposal and with the good offices of the Council immediately available— as this meeting shows—such incidents should now lead to warlike operations instead of being submitted at once for peaceful and amicable adjustment by the countries concerned to the Council, which will always have regard to their honour and to the safety and security of their nations.

The Greek representative observed on different occasions that his country had been called upon to take rapid steps for its legitimate defence. On October 28th the President of the Council, M. Briand, said that it was essential that such ideas should not take root in the minds of Members of the League and become a kind of jurisprudence.

Under the pretext of legitimate defence, he said, disputes might arise which, though limited in extent, were extremely unfortunate owing to the damage they entailed. These disputes, once they had broken out, might assume such proportions that the Government, which started them under a feeling of legitimate defence, would be no longer able to control them.

The League of Nations, through its Council, and through all the methods of conciliation which were at its disposal, offered the nations a means of avoiding such deplorable events. The nations had only to appeal to the Council. It had been shown that the criticisms which had been brought against the League of Nations to the effect that its machinery was cumbersome and that it found it difficult to take action in circumstances which required an urgent solution, were unjustified. It had been proved that a nation which appealed to the League, when it felt that its existence was threatened, could be sure that the Council would be at its post ready to undertake its work of conciliation.

The rapporteur said that the declaration of M. Briand as to the rôle which the League could play in such cases as that before the Council, and as to the restraint which nations might be expected to exercise in view of the fact that the Council could be immediately convened and use its good offices, was of such consequences for the moral position of the League of Nations and for the guidance of its Members, that he would like, on behalf of his Government, to express his complete concurrence in all that the President had said.

The other Members of the Council, one by one, approved M. Briand's declaration, laying particular emphasis on the importance of the solemn undertaking entered into by all States under Article X—which M. Hymans (Belgium) considered as the "soul of the Covenant and the essence of the international engagements it embodied"—and upon the promptitude with which the Council had acted.

M. Guani (Uruguay) and M. de Mello Franco (Brazil) were of opinion that the results achieved by the Council would have a very considerable effect in the countries of Latin-America. In this connection, it may be mentioned that seven Latin-American countries—Cuba, Guatemala, Honduras, Nicaragua, Peru, Salvador and Venezuela— addressed telegrams to the Secretary-General, acknowledging the notification of the Bulgarian appeal and the convocation of the Council, and stating the interest they attached to a pacific settlement of the question.

Similar telegrams were received from Australia, Hungary, Luxemburg, Siam and Switzerland.

CONSTITUTION OF A COMMISSION OF INVESTIGATION AND SETTLEMENT

As soon as the Council was satisfied that the territories occupied had been evacuated and that hostilities had ceased, it considered the measures to be taken for a complete and final solution of the difficulties which had necessitated its intervention.

On October 27th, it heard the representatives of the parties, who described the incident from the Bulgarian and the Greek point of view, at the same time stating their demands.

The Bulgarian representative declared that his Government, as soon as it had received news of the incident, had proposed that a mixed commission of inquiry should be appointed. He added that at no time and on no point had Greek territory been occupied by Bulgarian troops and that it was not possible to speak of an aggression on the part of Bulgaria. He recalled that Articles X, XI, XII and XV of the Covenant absolutely precluded the use of force by the Members of the League, and that Bulgaria, in virtue of the Treaty of Neuilly, was a disarmed country, the provisions of this Treaty having been faithfully carried out. To conclude, the Bulgarian representative demanded an investigation and reparation for damages. He also requested that the Bulgarians taken prisoner by the Greeks should be set free.

The Greek representative said that the measures taken by his Government were necessary for the defence of Greek territory. The Greek advance only took place after the violation of Greek territory by Bulgarians, and had technically a defensive character.

The Greek representative asserted that the Bulgarian proposal for an inquiry had only been made after the Bulgarian troops had been beaten. He ascribed the various incidents to the activity of the comitadji organisations, and to the fact that the Bulgarian Government had not been able to enforce the application of the military clauses of the Treaty of Neuilly. He requested the Council to investigate the local causes which had led to the incident of the Græco-Bulgarian frontier, in particular the existence of a Bulgarian army corps ready to take the field on any occasion.

The Bulgarian representative said that his Government consented to the question of the comitadji being elucidated in the course of the inquiry.

From these declarations it appeared that both the Bulgarian and the Greek Government wished the Council to investigate the origin and the underlying causes of the incident which occurred on their common frontier, to establish responsibilities and to consider whether indemnities or reparations were due. The Council accepted this task and undertook moreover to seek means of eliminating in the future the likelihood of such incidents as gave rise to the recent trouble. On the report of Mr. Chamberlain, the Council decided, on October 29th, to appoint a Commission to proceed to a thorough investigation of the incidents which had arisen on the Græco-Bulgarian frontier to the north-east of Salonica.

The Commission was instructed, in particular, to establish the facts enabling the responsibility to be fixed and to supply the necessary material for the determination of any indemnity or reparation. Further, in order that the Council might be in a position to make suitable recommendations to the Governments concerned, the Commission was requested to submit to the Council, either in its report or subsequently, any suggestions as to measures which, in its opinion, would eliminate or minimise the general causes of such incidents and prevent their recurrence.

The Commission was constituted as follows: Sir Horace Rumbold, British Ambassador at Madrid, Chairman; a French officer; an Italian officer; a civilian of Swedish nationality, and a civilian of Dutch nationality.

The Commission will meet at Geneva on November 6th and will proceed to the scene of the incident with the utmost dispatch. It will be entitled to conduct its investigation both on the spot and at the seats of the two Governments concerned. Pending its arrival, the military attachés of France, Great Britain and Italy, who are at present on the scene of the incident, will remain in touch with the situation, and, on the arrival of the Commission, put at its disposal all the information they may have collected.

The Commission was requested to submit its report before the end of November, in order that the Council might examine it in December.

The representatives of both parties accepted this decision, declaring moreover that they accepted in advance any other decisions the Council might take in the matter. They also gave formal assurances that any prisoners who might have been captured by their troops should be at once set free and transferred at the expense of the Government having captured them, to their national territory, and that any movable property, cattle, etc., that might have been seized should be forthwith restored, or, if that was not possible, that suitable compensation should be made, the figure to be fixed eventually by the Commission.

.   .   .   .

At the last meeting of the session, several members of the Council made statements on the Græco-Bulgarian affair and the Locarno agreements from the point of view of the spirit and work of the League.

On hearing that the decision of the Council had been completely executed, the President, M. Briand, thanked the Bulgarian and Greek representatives for the rapidity with which their Governments had complied with the invitation of the Council. He continued:

Throughout this affair which ends in so fortunate a manner there is neither victor nor vanquished. There are two nations which, forming part of the same great family of peace, have shown their desire for conciliation by agreeing immediately to accord to reason and justice in the dispute in which they were engaged. . . . It is composed of nations great and small, all equal and all sure of finding within the League the same justice for every member. . . . In this case the League of Nations has not failed to fulfil either the spirit which inspired its foundation or the purpose for which it was intended.

Mr. Chamberlain observed that the importance of the work which had been done by the Council lay above all in the fact that the Council was building up the jurisprudence of the League of Nations. He added:

Thanks to the readiness with which the two Powers concerned immediately submitted their case to the Council, thanks to the promptitude with which the President and the Secretary-General acted before a dangerous situation had got out of control, the Council has met, and, with the willing assent of both parties to the dispute, has brought to a close—a happy close—the incidents which immediately threatened the peace of those nations, and has put in the way of friendly settlements, the further questions which remained to be considered.

We have here an example of the conduct which may be expected of nations, Members of the League, between whom some unfortunate dispute arises, which threatens the peace of the world; and we have an example of the manner in which the Council of the League will use the authority of the powers entrusted to it by the Covenant of the League for conciliation, for restoring friendly relations between nations, between whom a dispute has arisen, for removing, if possible, those causes of dispute in the future, and above all for preserving the peace of the world.

Now that we are all bound together in the League and by the conditions of the Covenant, a threat of war anywhere is a menace which comes home to us all, and which affects us all. . . .

172. League Assistance in Rehabilitation of Ex-enemy States

(a) *Financial Reconstruction of Hungary*[1]

OBJECTS AND RESULTS OF THE RECONSTRUCTION PLAN

The causes which made it necessary for Hungary to ask the League of Nations for assistance in 1923 have been admirably stated in the preface to the documents relating to the reconstruction plan, which were issued by the League of Nations in April 1924. Briefly summarised, they are as follows:

Disorganisation caused by the war and consequent loss of territory, political difficulties, internal and external, which followed the Armistice, the undetermined liability for reparations and the difficulty of reorganising a political and commercial establishment designed for a much larger country presented obstacles which could not be overcome. The budget became unbalanced, current expense was met from note inflation, which produced a continually increasing depreciation of the currency, and the only means of arresting it became a foreign loan to meet the budget deficit during the period necessary for financial reorganisation. The League entrusted the preparation of a suitable plan to its Financial Committee. The entire success of this experiment depended upon the preparation of the plan and too much praise cannot be given to the Financial Committee of the League for the ability shown in this task. The Committee had the wisdom and courage to prepare a plan based upon sound financial principles which had been tested under normal conditions. Many people doubted the efficacy of such a plan under the abnormal conditions which prevailed at that time in Hungary, but the Committee rejected many of the theories which were then being put forward as necessary to correct abnormal conditions and preferred to rely upon principles which had stood the test of time. The result has vindicated the judgment of the Committee.

The principal features of the plan were:

(1) Definite settlement of the reparation liability for 20 years, which was obtained through a decision of the Reparation Commission, fixing annual payments on account of reparations until 1944, at an average rate of 10 million gold crowns a year.

(2) The stoppage of inflation through the creation of a central bank of issue, with the exclusive privilege of issuing banknotes, divorced

---

[1] Twenty-Fifth (Final) Report by the Commissioner-General [Jeremiah Smith, Jr.] of the League of Nations for Hungary, June 30, 1926. League of Nations, *Official Journal*, September, 1926, p. 1176ff.

from political control and forbidden to loan money to the State or any of its subdivisions without adequate security. The ultimate adoption of the free exchange of notes for gold is contemplated by this plan.

(3) The issue of an international loan, secured on some of the most productive revenues of the State, for the purpose of covering budget deficits until June 30th, 1926, when it was expected that the budget would be in a state of permanent equilibrium.

(4) The preparation of a budget covering the period up to June 30th, 1926, and the appointment of a Commissioner-General to supervise the execution of the whole programme and to control the expenditure of the proceeds of the Loan as well as the revenues pledged to secure the service of the Loan, with power to regulate expenditure and revenue in case the Government should fall behind the reconstruction programme.

(5) The adoption of a centralised system of Treasury receipts and disbursements, which would give exact knowledge of the cash position of the Treasury at all times.

The execution of the plan has proved even more successful than anticipated. As was expected, there was a large deficit for the financial year ending June 30th, 1924, which was met from the proceeds of the Reconstruction Loan. Since July 1st, 1924, the budget has been in a state of equilibrium, and it has been unnecessary to expend any of the proceeds of the Reconstruction Loan for budgetary deficits. This surprising result is not due to reductions in expenditure—for none was contemplated by the plan—but to unexpected increases in the estimated revenue of the State over the conservative estimates of the plan due to the stabilisation of the currency and the increased confidence which followed it. The currency has been stable since the National Bank was opened on June 24th, 1924, and the Bank has ample reserves for the maintenance of the currency.

It should not be forgotten that the Financial Committee of the League, in its original report, pointed out that the problem which confronted Hungary was a double one: financial and budgetary on the one hand and economic on the other. It further pointed out that the responsibility of the League should be expressly limited to remedying the budgetary and financial position. "The necessary economic adaptation must be effected by Hungary itself; the essential contribution (of the League) is to give a stable basis on which this adaptation can take place." The League has now done all that it undertook to do—i.e., to create a sound budgetary and financial position, which is necessary to establish a firm foundation for the future upon which the complete economic recovery of Hungary can take place. Economic conditions have slowly and steadily improved since the plan became effective, and if the present position is maintained by Hungary itself, the economic conditions should continue to improve until they reach at least the normal pre-war conditions.

(b) *The Financial Reconstruction of Austria*[1]

This is the last time I shall have the honour of appearing at the Council table, where I have so often had occasion to describe the financial position of Austria.

In a few weeks I shall have left the work which for three and a half years has taken up all my time and energy.

I do not think that the time has yet come to pass a final judgment on the work that is now coming to an end, for some degree of perspective is essential if we are to see things in their true light. Nevertheless, it is already possible to record certain encouraging facts. Naturally, in an enterprise which was subject to the influences of international politics as well as of internal politics, nobody could have had the illusion that all his hopes would be fully realised; but the concrete results which have been achieved are sufficiently important to justify the optimism and foresight of those who, in the autumn of 1922, laid the foundations of Austria's recovery.

At the present juncture we may note the following facts:

First: The currency has remained absolutely stable for nearly four years, and that despite the grave crisis on the stock exchange in 1924, despite the economic crisis from which the country is still suffering, despite all the political and economic events which have supervened in many European countries, and despite the violent fluctuations which have occurred, and are still occurring, in the currencies of several States.

The situation of the National Bank is sound. It has always been in a position to satisfy any demand for foreign currencies that has arisen; it has ample and secure cover for its notes, and the circulation has for a long time past been at an approximately constant level, proportionate to the legitimate requirements of the national economy.

The stability of the currency has provided a solid basis for public finance, for economic enterprise, and for the reconstitution of capital.

Secondly: The ordinary budget is balanced, and, in addition, a considerable part of the productive expenditure is met by current revenue. This state of affairs is chiefly due to the unexpected rapidity of the increase in revenue, which rapidly reacted to the reform of the existing taxes and the introduction of certain new ones.

Another reason for the increase in revenue was the stabilisation of the crown. It revealed the enormous recuperative effect, hitherto unsuspected, of the restoration of a stable monetary unit. The receipts derived from taxes, Customs, State monopolies and industrial enterprises increased as soon as payments ceased to be made in a depreciated currency, inferior in real value at the time of payment, to the amount

---

[1] Speech by the Commissioner-General [Dr. Zimmermann] at the Meeting of the Council of the League of Nations, June 9, 1926. League of Nations, *Official Journal,* September, 1926, pp. 1164-1165.

of the debt at the time those payments were ordered. A strong movement of readjustment set in throughout the whole business world. Private incomes and capital felt the effects, and several of the large fortunes which had been transferred abroad returned to the country. Austria was found to be much richer than she had been presumed to be at the outset of the process of reconstitution, and the city of Vienna, in particular, proved to be an asset of the highest importance in the financial reconstruction of the State.

Consequently, the deficit on current administration had already disappeared by November of 1923, *i.e.*, by the tenth month of control. This enabled the budget to support the "personnel" charges, which have increased very considerably, and unemployment relief, which requires much larger funds than had been estimated. Austria's wealth and taxable capacity have therefore proved in excess of the most sanguine expectations.

Thirdly: A stricter system has been introduced in the administration of public finances, which is once more following the principles of order and accuracy. The supervision of the Finance Ministry over other departments has been restored and the powers of the Audit Office have been increased. The management of State funds has been centralised.

Fourthly: The budget is supporting without difficulty the interest and redemption charges of the international loan, and the assigned revenues cover four times the service of the debt. Out of the total yield of the loan it has been possible to employ large sums in productive expenditure and a considerable balance is still available; only 13 percent has been used to meet current deficits, which proves that, for the stabilisation of currency, the actual figure of the loan is of less importance than the confidence inspired by the reconstructive effect. The bonds of this loan, issued under the auspices of the League of Nations, are quoted in all countries which have a stable currency at considerably above par.

I feel that the facts which I have stated justify a confident view of the future. They show that Austria, which was on the brink of an abyss and had by many been given up for lost, is now leading a normal life and is in a better financial position than many other countries.

There can be no doubt that these successes would not have been achieved but for the intervention of the League of Nations, and we can say without reserve that the League's action has been a boon to Austria and will not have been wasted, whatever developments may be in store.

In brief, the results which I have set forth—and on which I must congratulate the Government as well as the Director of the National Bank—have shown that Austria is financially sound, even in her present economic condition.

The Council has on several occasions been told that the economic condition is not satisfactory. The forthcoming Economic Conference will afford an opportunity of discussing remedies for this situation.

It has, of course, many causes, both general and specific. Among these are the exhausted condition of Europe after the war, the diversion of world trade, and the falling-off in the total exports of the Continent of Europe. I may further point out that the absence of any general stabilisation of currency values provides an opening for competition on unequal terms and for every kind of restriction on free trade. Another aggravating factor is the Customs policy in force over the greater part of Europe.

Finally, it will have to be considered to what extent the public burdens imposed on production can be reduced.

I know that the Austrian Government does not look upon the removal of control as meaning the termination of the process of reform and economy in the public services, and that it realises the necessity of continuing that policy. Only a few days ago, the Federal Chancellor, replying to a delegation of officials, said that the taxes and duties at their present level contributed to reducing Austria's economic capacity to compete in foreign markets. It is quite true that, in the coming years, the countries which will best be able to sustain competition will be those whose economic life is the least heavily burdened by public charges. That the Government will succeed in this policy with the help of all the factors in its favour is the sincere wish of all who have Austria's prosperity at heart. . . .

173. THE DAWES REPORT, 1924

[In 1921-22 the powers could come to no agreement with Germany as to the amount of reparation payments that the latter state would be asked to make. The Ruhr occupation by the French followed and German passive resistance brought on a deadlock which was broken only when the Germans put forward on June 7, 1923, the suggestion that had been made by Charles Evans Hughes that a committee of experts be appointed to study the reparations question. France reluctantly agreed to the proposal and in November the Reparation Commission decided to appoint such a body. On January 14, 1924, it began its work. It was composed of two representatives each from the United States, Great Britain, France, Italy, and Belgium. Charles G. Dawes of the United States was made chairman. The plan went into effect in September, 1924.]

(a) Letter from the Chairman to the Reparation Commission[1]

April 9th, 1924

Your Committee of Experts has unanimously adopted a report upon the means of balancing the budget of Germany and the measures to be taken to stabilize its currency, which I now have the honour to submit.

---

[1] Great Britain. *Parliamentary Papers*, 1924, Vol. XXVII, Cmd. 2105. "Reports of the Expert Committees Appointed by the Reparation Commission."

Deeply impressed by a sense of its responsibility to your Commission and to the universal conscience, the Committee bases its plan upon those principles of justice, fairness and mutual interest, in the supremacy of which not only the creditors of Germany and Germany herself, but the world, has a vital and enduring concern.

With these principles fixed and accepted in that common good faith which is the foundation of all business, and the best safeguard for universal peace, the recommendations of the Committee must be considered not as inflicting penalties, but as suggesting means for assisting the economic recovery of all the European peoples and the entry upon a new period of happiness and prosperity unmenaced by war.

Since, as a result of the war, the creditors of Germany are paying taxes to the limit of their capacity, so also must Germany pay taxes from year to year to the limit of her capacity. This is in accord with that just and underlying principle of the Treaty of Versailles, reaffirmed by Germany in her note of May 29th, 1919, that the German scheme of taxation must be "fully as heavy proportionately as that of any of the Powers represented on the Commission." More than this limit could not be expected, and less than this would relieve Germany from the common hardship and give her an unfair advantage in the industrial competition of the future. This principle the plan embodies.

The plan has been made to include flexible adjustments which, from the very beginning, tend to produce the maximum of contributions consistent with the continued and increasing productivity of Germany. The conservative estimates of payments to be made in the near future are dictated by business prudence in outlining the basis of a loan, and should not destroy perspective as to the effects to be registered in the aggregate of eventual payments, which will annually increase. With normal economic conditions and productivity restored in Germany, most hopeful estimates of amounts eventually receivable will be found to be justified. Without such restoration, such payments as can be obtained will be of little value in meeting the urgent needs of creditor nations.

To ensure the permanence of a new economic peace between the Allied Governments and Germany, which involves the economic readjustments presented by the plan, there are provided the counterparts of those usual economic precautions against default recognised as essential in all business relations involving expressed obligations. The existence of safeguards in no way hampers or embarrasses the carrying out of ordinary business contracts. The thorough effectiveness of these safeguards should not embarrass the normal economic functioning of Germany, and is of fundamental importance to her creditors and to Germany.

Great care has been taken in fixing conditions of supervision over Germany's internal organisation so as to impose the minimum of interference consistent with proper protection. This general plan, fair and reasonable in its nature, if accepted, leads to an ultimate and lasting peace. The rejection of these proposals by the German Government means the deliberate choice of a continuance of economic demoralisation, eventually involving her people in hopeless misery.

In the preparation of this report, the Committee has carefully and laboriously covered the broad field of investigation. It has had the constant coöperation of able staffs of experts, gathering information, digesting it and presenting it. It conducted, on the ground, an examination of the officials of the German Government and representatives of its labour, agriculture, and industry. It received from the German Government and its representatives voluminous and satisfactory answers in response to its written enquiries. In connection with various features of its report, both for gathering information and for advice, it has called to its assistance outside experts of international reputation. The published reports and statements of economists of worldwide standing have been in its hands. It has had the benefit of the accumulated information heretofore gathered by your Commission.

In its work, the full Committee has held, since January 14th, 1924, 54 meetings; the sub-committee on the stabilisation of the currency, composed of Monsieur Parmentier, Sir Robert Kindersley, Monsieur Francqui and Professor Flora, assisted by Mr. H. M. Robinson, under the chairmanship of Mr. Owen D. Young, has held 81 meetings; and the sub-committee on the balancing of the budget, composed of Professor Allix, Baron Houtart and Monsieur Pirelli, under the chairmanship of Sir Josiah Stamp, has held 63 meetings. They have had the assistance of Mr. Andrew McFadyean, the General Secretary. Again, the time of the Committee, outside of that consumed by the meetings, has been given largely to investigation and study.

In speaking of my colleagues and as bearing upon the value of this report, I feel that I should make it known to your Commission and to the world, that their governments have in no case limited their complete independence of judgment and action, either before or after their appointment by you. Limited only by the powers granted by your Commission, each has performed his arduous and responsible work as a free agent. These men, searching for truth and advice thereon, were answerable only to conscience. In granting this freedom, the governments have but followed your own spirit and intent in constituting the Committee, but in so doing, they have paid the highest tribute which governments can bestow: complete confidence in a time of crisis in human affairs. In their vision—in their independence of thought—and above all, in their spirit of high and sincere purpose, which rises above the small things over which the small so often stumble, my colleagues have shown themselves worthy of this trust. That their work, which I now place in your hands, may assist you in the discharge of your great responsibilities, is their prayer, and the knowledge hereafter, that it has done so, will be their full reward.

(Signed) CHARLES G. DAWES,
Chairman

(b) *Summary of Report from the First Committee of Experts*[1]

I.—The Attitude of the Committee.

(a) The standpoint adopted has been that of business and not politics.
(b) Political factors have been considered only in so far as they affect the practicability of the plan.
(c) The recovery of debt, not the imposition of penalties, has been sought.
(d) The payment of that debt by Germany is her necessary contribution to repairing the damage of the war.
(e) It is in the interest of all parties to carry out this plan in that good faith which is the fundamental of all business. Our plan is based upon this principle.
(f) The reconstruction of Germany is not an end in itself; it is only part of the larger problem of the reconstruction of Europe.
(g) Guarantees proposed are economic, not political.

II.—German Economic Unity

For success in stabilising currency and balancing budgets, Germany needs the resources of German territory as defined by the Treaty of Versailles, and free economic activity therein.

III.—Military Aspects.—Contingent Sanctions and Guarantees

(a) Political guarantees and penalties are outside our jurisdiction.
(b) The military aspect of this problem is beyond our terms of reference.
(c) Within the unified territory, the plan requires that, when it is in effective operation:
   1. if any military organisation exists, it must not impede the free exercise of economic activities;
   2. there shall be no foreign economic control or interference other than that proposed by the plan.
(d) But adequate and productive guarantees are provided.

IV.—The Committee's Task

(a) Stabilisation of currency and the balancing of budgets are interdependent, though they are provisionally separable for examination.
(b) Currency stability can only be maintained if the budget is normally balanced; the budget can only be balanced if a stable and reliable currency exists.

---

[1] *Idem.*

(c) Both are needed to enable Germany to meet her internal requirements and Treaty payments.

V.—Economic Future of Germany

(a) Productivity is expected from increasing population, technical skill, material resources and eminence in industrial science.
(b) Plant capacity has been increased and improved since the war.

VI.—Currency and a Bank of Issue

(a) All classes will benefit from stabilised currency, especially labour.
(b) Under present conditions, rentenmark stability is only temporary.
(c) A new Bank is set up or the Reischsbank reorganised.
(d) The main characteristics of the Bank will be:
   (1) to issue notes on a basis stable in relation to gold, with an exclusive privilege;
   (2) to serve as a Banker's Bank, establishing the official rate of discount;
   (3) to act as the Government Banker, but free of Government Control;
   (4) advances to Government to be strictly limited;
   (5) to hold on deposit Reparation payments;
   (6) the capital of the Bank will be 400 million gold marks;
   (7) it will be directed by a German President and Managing Board, who can be assisted by a German consultative Committee;
   (8) the due observance of its statutes will be further safeguarded by a General Board, of which half of the members, including a Commissioner, will be foreign.

VII.—Budget and Temporary Reparation Relief

Balancing the German budget requires:
(a) Full economic and fiscal sovereignty, subject to the supervision provided for in this report;
(b) a stable currency;
(c) temporary relief from charges on the budget for Treaty obligations;
(d) such relief not to suspend essential deliveries in kind.

VIII.—The Basic Principles of Germany's Annual Burden

(a) Treaty obligations and continuity of balanced budgets.
   (1) Balancing the budget does not entail merely provision for internal administrative expenditure.

(2) Germany must also provide within the utmost limit of her capacity for her external Treaty obligations.

(3) the budget can be balanced without necessarily dealing with the total capital debt of Germany.

(4) It cannot be continuously balanced, unless the annual charge is fixed for a considerable period, on a basis clearly prescribed in advance.

(b) Commensurate taxation:

(1) Government internal debt has been practically extinguished by the depreciation of the currency.

(2) New debt charge ought to be met, commensurate with the burden of the French, English, Italian and Belgian taxpayer.

(3) The Treaty recognises this principle.

(4) It is morally sound.

(5) It is economically just in its influence on costs of production.

(6) This principle has been applied to the full limit of practicability.

(c) Allies' share in Germany's prosperity.

(1) Germany's creditors must share in the improvement in Germany's prosperity.

(2) This will be secured by an index of prosperity.

(d) There is an important difference between the German's capacity to pay taxes and Germany's capacity to transfer wealth abroad.

IX.—Normal Resources from Which Payments Are Made

Germany will pay Treaty charges from three sources:—A. Taxes; B. Railways; C. Industrial debentures.

A. From her ordinary budget:

(1) 1924-25 Budget may be balanced if it is free from Peace Treaty charges.

(2) 1925-26 Budget receiving 500 million gold marks from special Sources, may pay that sum for reparation.

(3) 1926-27, 110 million gold marks.

(4) 1927-28, 500 million gold marks.

(5) 1928-29, 1,250 million gold marks. This is considered a normal year and a standard payment; thereafter additional payments will be made, depending on prosperity.

B. From Railways:

(1) Railway Bonds—

(a) eleven milliards of first-mortgage railway bonds against a capital cost of twenty-six milliards will be created for reparations;

(b) these bonds bear 5 per cent interest and 1 per cent sinking fund per annum;

(c) In view of reorganisation, interest is accepted as follows: 1924-25: three hundred and thirty million gold marks;

1925-26: four hundred and sixty-five million gold marks;
1926-27: five hundred and fifty million gold marks;
1927-28: and thereafter: six hundred and sixty million gold
marks.

Behind the Bonds, there will be created:

2 milliards of preference shares to be reserved for sale to the
public and

13 milliards of common stock.

¾ of the proceeds of the preference shares will be applied, as
required, to the payment of debt and for capital expenditure of the railways. The remaining 500 milliards of preference shares and all the common shares go to the German
Government.

(2) Transport Tax.

After 1925-26, 290 million gold marks per annum for reparation, and balance to German Government.

C. Industrial debentures.

(1) Five milliards of industrial debentures are provided for reparation.

(2) The resulting charge on industry is less than that existing
before the war and now wiped out by depreciation.

(3) These bonds bear five per cent. interest and one per cent. sinking fund, *i.e.*, 300 million gold marks per annum.

(4) Pending economic restoration, interest and sinking fund are
accepted as follows:

First year.—Nothing.

Second year.—One hundred and twenty-five million gold
marks.

Third year.—Two hundred and fifty million gold marks.

Thereafter.—Three hundred million gold marks.

X.—Summary of Provision for Treaty Payment

(a)   1. *Budget Moratorium Period*

First year.—From foreign loans and part interest on railway bonds.
Total of 1,000 million gold marks.

Second year.—From part interest on railway bonds, and on industrial
debentures, budget contribution, through sale of 500 million gold
mark railway shares.
Total of 1,220 million gold marks.

2. *Transition Period*

Third year.—From interest on railway bonds and on industrial debentures, from transport tax and from budget.

Total of 1,200 million gold marks (subject to contingent addition or reduction of 250 million gold marks).

Fourth year.—From interest on railway bonds and on industrial debentures, from transport tax and from budget.

Total of 1,750 million gold marks (subject to contingent addition or reduction of 250 million gold marks).

3. *Standard Year*

Fifth year.—From interest on railway bonds and on industrial debentures, from transport tax and from budget.

Total of 2,500 million gold marks.

Thereafter, 2,500 millions plus a supplement computed on the index of prosperity.

Interest on the securities, but not the proceeds of their sale, is included in these figures.

(b) The first year will begin to run from the date when the plan shall have been accepted and put into effective execution.

XI.—Inclusive Amounts and Deliveries in Kind

(a) The above sums cover all amounts for which Germany may be liable to the Allied and Associated Powers.

(b) Deliveries in kind are to be continued, but are paid for out of balances in the Bank.

XII.—How the Annual Payments Are Made by Germany

(a) The amounts will be raised in gold marks and paid into the Bank.

(b) These payments cover Germany's annual obligation.

XIII.—How the Payments Are Received by the Creditors

(a) Germany's creditors will use these moneys in Germany or convert them into foreign currencies.

(b) Experience will show the rate and extent to which the conversion can safely take place.

(c) Danger to stability through excessive remittances is obviated by a Transfer Committee.

(d) Sums not remitted accumulate, but with a limitation of amount.

XIV.—Guarantees, in Addition to Railway and Industrial Bonds

(a) The following revenues are pledged as collateral security for budget contributions and other payments:—

(i) Alcohol.

(ii) Tobacco.
(iii) Beer.
(iv) Sugar.
(v)   Customs.
(b) The yield of these revenues is estimated to be substantially in excess of required payments.
(c) The excess is returned to the German Government.

XV.—External Loan—Its Conditions and Purpose

Foreign loan of 800 million gold marks meets a double purpose.
(a) Requirements of gold reserve of the new Bank.
(b) Internal payments for essential Treaty purposes in 1924-25.

XVI.—Organisation

The Organisation consists of:
(a) A Trustee for railway and industrial bonds:
(b) Three Commissioners of (1) Railways, (2) the Bank, (3) Controlled Revenues;
(c) An Agent for Reparation Payments, who will coördinate the activities of the above and will preside over the Transfer Committee.

XVII.—The Nature of the Plan

(a) The plan is an indivisible unit.
(b) The aim of the plan is:
  (1) to set up machinery to provide the largest annual payments from Germany;
  (2) to enable maximum transfers to be made to Germany's creditors;
  (3) to take the question of "what Germany can pay" out of the field of speculation and put it in the field of practical demonstration;
  (4) to facilitate a final and comprehensive agreement upon all the problems of reparations and connected questions, as soon as circumstances make this possible.

174. The Geneva Protocol, 1924[1]

[In 1923 the Fourth Assembly of the League of Nations had unanimously adopted a draft Treaty of Mutual Assistance. But when circulated it was unacceptable to twelve states, who criticized the lack of

---

[1] Great Britain. *Parliamentary Papers*, 1924, Vol. XXVII, Cmd. 2273. "League of Nations. Fifth Assembly. Arbitration, Security and Reduction of Armaments. Protocol and Resolutions adopted by the Assembly, and Report by the First and Third Committees of the Assembly."

definition of what constituted aggression. When in 1924, therefore, socialist governments were in power in both France and England, Herriot and MacDonald decided to coöperate in working for peace and security through the League. Consequently in September, 1924, the two Prime Ministers submitted to the Fifth Assembly a joint resolution reopening the question of disarmament and security, but linking with these two elements a third feature—arbitration. This move resulted in the Geneva Protocol for the Pacific Settlement of International Disputes. This document, though passed unanimously by the Assembly, failed of adoption because many states feared the increase of their international obligations which it entailed. But it proved to be a step toward Locarno.]

Protocol for the Pacific Settlement of International Disputes, adopted by the Assembly, October 2, 1924, and opened for Signature by all States Members and Non-Members of the League of Nations

Animated by the firm desire to ensure the maintenance of general peace and the security of nations whose existence, independence or territories may be threatened;

Recognising the solidarity of the members of the international community;

Asserting that a war of aggression constitutes a violation of this solidarity and an international crime;

Desirous of facilitating the complete application of the system provided in the Covenant of the League of Nations for the pacific settlement of disputes between States and of ensuring the repression of international crimes; and

For the purpose of realising, as contemplated by article 8 of the Covenant, the reduction of national armaments to the lowest point consistent with national safety and the enforcements by common action of international obligations;

The undersigned, duly authorised to that effect, agree as follows:—

Article 1. The signatory States undertake to make every effort in their power to secure the introduction into the Covenant of amendments on the lines of the provisions contained in the following articles.

They agree that, as between themselves, these provisions shall be binding as from the coming into force of the present Protocol and that, so far as they are concerned, the Assembly and the Council of the League of Nations shall thenceforth have power to exercise all the rights and perform all the duties conferred upon them by the Protocol.

Article 2. The signatory States agree in no case to resort to war either with one another or against a State which, if the occasion arises, accepts all the obligations hereinafter set out, except in case of resistance to acts of aggression or when acting in agreement with the Council or the Assembly of the League of Nations in accordance with the provisions of the Covenant and of the present Protocol.

Article 3. The signatory States undertake to recognise as compulsory, *ipso facto* and without special agreement, the jurisdiction of the Permanent Court of International Justice in the cases covered by paragraph 2 of article 36 of the Statute of the Court, but without prejudice to the right of any State, when acceding to the special Protocol provided for in the said article and opened for signature on the 16th December, 1920, to make reservations compatible with the said clause.

Accession to this special Protocol, opened for signature on the 16th December, 1920, must be given within the month following the coming into force of the present Protocol.

States which accede to the present Protocol, after its coming into force, must carry out the above obligation within the month following their accession.

Article 4. With a view to render more complete the provisions of paragraphs 4, 5, 6 and 7 of article 15 of the Covenant, the signatory States agree to comply with the following procedure:—

1. If the dispute submitted to the Council is not settled by it as provided in paragraph 3 of the said article 15, the Council shall endeavour to persuade the parties to submit the dispute to judicial settlement or arbitration.

2. (a.) If the parties cannot agree to do so, there shall, at the request of at least one of the parties, be constituted a Committee of Arbitrators. The Committee shall so far as possible be constituted by agreement between the parties.

(b.) If within the period fixed by the Council the parties have failed to agree, in whole or in part, upon the number, the names and the powers of the arbitrators and upon the procedure, the Council shall settle the points remaining in suspense. It shall with the utmost possible despatch select in consultation with the parties the arbitrators and their President from among persons who by their nationality, their personal character and their experience, appear to it to furnish the highest guarantees of competence and impartiality.

(c.) After the claims of the parties have been formulated, the Committee of Arbitrators, on the request of any party, shall through the medium of the Council request an advisory opinion upon any points of law in dispute from the Permanent Court of International Justice, which in such case shall meet with the utmost possible despatch.

3. If none of the parties asks for arbitration, the Council shall again take the dispute under consideration. If the Council reaches a report which is unanimously agreed to by the members thereof other than the representatives of any of the parties to the dispute, the signatory States agree to comply with the recommendations therein.

4. If the Council fails to reach a report which is concurred in by all its members, other than the representatives of any of the parties to the dispute, it shall submit the dispute to arbitration. It shall itself determine the composition, the powers and the procedure of the Committee of Arbitrators and, in the choice of the arbitrators, shall bear in

mind the guarantees of competence and impartiality referred to in paragraph 2 (b) above.

5. In no case may a solution, upon which there has already been a unanimous recommendation of the Council accepted by one of the parties concerned, be again called in question.

6. The signatory States undertake that they will carry out in full good faith any judicial sentence or arbitral award that may be rendered and that they will comply, as provided in paragraph 3 above, with the solutions recommended by the Council. In the event of a State failing to carry out the above undertakings, the Council shall exert all its influence to secure compliance therewith. If it fails therein, it shall propose what steps should be taken to give effect thereto, in accordance with the provision contained at the end of article 13 of the Covenant. Should a State in disregard of the above undertakings resort to war, the sanctions provided for by article 16 of the Covenant, interpreted in the manner indicated in the present Protocol, shall immediately become applicable to it.

7. The provisions of the present article do not apply to the settlement of disputes which arise as the result of measures of war taken by one or more signatory States in agreement with the Council or the Assembly.

Article 5. The provisions of paragraph 8 of article 15 of the Covenant shall continue to apply in proceedings before the Council.

If in the course of an arbitration, such as is contemplated in article 4 above, one of the parties claims that the dispute, or part thereof, arises out of a matter which by international law is solely within the domestic jurisdiction of that party, the arbitrators shall on this point take the advice of the Permanent Court of International Justice through the medium of the Council. The opinion of the Court shall be binding upon the arbitrators, who, if the opinion is affirmative, shall confine themselves to so declaring in their award.

If the question is held by the Court or by the Council to be a matter solely within the domestic jurisdiction of the State, this decision shall not prevent consideration of the situation by the Council or by the Assembly under article 11 of the Covenant.

Article 6. If in accordance with paragraph 9 of article 15 of the Covenant a dispute is referred to the Assembly, that body shall have for the settlement of the dispute all the powers conferred upon the Council as to endeavouring to reconcile the parties in the manner laid down in paragraphs 1, 2 and 3 of article 15 of the Covenant and in paragraph 1 of article 4 above.

Should the Assembly fail to achieve an amicable settlement:

If one of the parties asks for arbitration, the Council shall proceed to constitute the Committee of Arbitrators in the manner provided in sub-paragraphs (a), (b) and (c) of paragraph 2 of article 4 above.

If no party asks for arbitration, the Assembly shall again take the dispute under consideration and shall have in this connection the same powers as the Council. Recommendations embodied in a report of the Assembly, provided that it secures the measure of support stipulated at the end of paragraph 10 of article 15 of the Covenant, shall have the same value and effect, as regards all matters dealt with in the present Protocol, as recommendations embodied in a report of the Council adopted as provided in paragraph 3 of article 4 above.

If the necessary majority cannot be obtained, the dispute shall be submitted to arbitration and the Council shall determine the composition, the powers and the procedure of the Committee of Arbitrators as laid down in paragraph 4 of article 4.

Article 7. In the event of a dispute arising between two or more signatory States, these States agree that they will not, either before the dispute is submitted to proceedings for pacific settlement or during such proceedings make any increase of their armaments or effectives which might modify the position established by the Conference for the Reduction of Armaments provided for by article 17 of the present Protocol, nor will they take any measure of military, naval, air, industrial or economic mobilisation, nor, in general, any action of a nature likely to extend the dispute or render it more acute.

It shall be the duty of the Council, in accordance with the provisions of article 11 of the Covenant, to take under consideration any complaint as to infraction of the above undertakings which is made to it by one or more of the States parties to the dispute. Should the Council be of opinion that the complaint requires investigation, it shall, if it deems it expedient, arrange for enquiries and investigations in one or more of the countries concerned. Such enquiries and investigations shall be carried out with the utmost possible despatch and the signatory States undertake to afford every facility for carrying them out.

The sole object of measures taken by the Council as above provided is to facilitate the pacific settlement of disputes and they shall in no way prejudge the actual settlement.

If the result of such enquiries and investigations is to establish an infraction of the provisions of the first paragraph of the present article, it shall be the duty of the Council to summon the State or States guilty of the infraction to put an end thereto. Should the State or States in question fail to comply with such summons, the Council shall declare them to be guilty of a violation of the Covenant or of the present Protocol, and shall decide upon the measures to be taken with a view to end as soon as possible a situation of a nature to threaten the peace of the world.

For the purposes of the present article decisions of the Council may be taken by a two-thirds majority.

Article 8. The signatory States undertake to abstain from any act which might constitute a threat of aggression against another State.

If one of the signatory States is of opinion that another State is making preparations for war, it shall have the right to bring the matter to the notice of the Council.

The Council, if it ascertains that the facts are as alleged, shall proceed as provided in paragraphs 2, 4 and 5 of article 7.

Article 9. The existence of demilitarised zones being calculated to prevent aggression and to facilitate a definite finding of the nature provided for in article 10 below, the establishment of such zones between States mutually consenting thereto is recommended as a means of avoiding violations of the present Protocol.

The demilitarised zones already existing under the terms of certain treaties or conventions, or which may be established in future between States mutually consenting thereto, may at the request and at the expense of one or more of the conterminous States, be placed under a temporary or permanent system of supervision to be organized by the Council.

Article 10. Every State which resorts to war in violation of the undertakings contained in the Covenant or in the present Protocol is an aggressor. Violation of the rules laid down for a demilitarised zone shall be held equivalent to resort to war.

In the event of hostilities having broken out, any State shall be presumed to be an aggressor, unless a decision of the Council, which must be taken unanimously, shall otherwise declare:—

1. If it has refused to submit the dispute to the procedure of pacific settlement provided by articles 13 and 15 of the Covenant as amplified by the present Protocol, or to comply with a judicial sentence or arbitral award or with a unanimous recommendation of the Council, or has disregarded a unanimous report of the Council, a judicial sentence or an arbitral award recognising that the dispute between it and the other belligerent State arises out of a matter which by international law is solely within the domestic jurisdiction of the latter State; nevertheless, in the last case the State shall only be presumed to be an aggressor if it has not previously submitted the question to the Council or the Assembly, in accordance with article 11 of the Covenant.

2. If it has violated provisional measures enjoined by the Council for the period while the proceedings are in progress as contemplated by article 7 of the present Protocol.

Apart from the cases dealt with in paragraphs 1 and 2 of the present article, if the Council does not at once succeed in determining the aggressor it shall be bound to enjoin upon the belligerents an armistice, and shall fix the terms, acting, if need be, by a two-thirds majority and shall supervise its execution.

Any belligerent which has refused to accept the armistice or has violated its terms shall be deemed an aggressor.

The Council shall call upon the signatory States to apply forthwith against the aggressor the sanctions provided by article 11 of the present Protocol, and any signatory State thus called upon shall thereupon be entitled to exercise the rights of a belligerent.

Article 11. As soon as the Council has called upon the signatory States to apply sanctions, as provided in the last paragraph of article

10 of the present Protocol, the obligations of the said States, in regard to the sanctions of all kinds mentioned in paragraphs 1 and 2 of article 16 of the Covenant, will immediately become operative in order that such sanctions may forthwith be employed against the aggressor.

Those obligations shall be interpreted as obliging each of the signatory States to coöperate loyally and effectively in support of the Covenant of the League of Nations, and in resistance to any act of aggression, in the degree which its geographical position and its particular situation as regards armaments allow.

In accordance with paragraph 3 of article 16 of the Covenant the signatory States give a joint and several undertaking to come to the assistance of the State attacked or threatened, and to give each other mutual support by means of facilities and reciprocal exchanges as regards the provision of raw materials and supplies of every kind, openings of credits, transport and transit, and for this purpose to take all measures in their power to preserve the safety of communications by land and by sea of the attacked or threatened State.

If both parties to the dispute are aggressors within the meaning of article 10, the economic and financial sanctions shall be applied to both of them.

Article 12. In view of the complexity of the conditions in which the Council may be called upon to exercise the functions mentioned in article 11 of the present Protocol concerning economic and financial sanctions, and in order to determine more exactly the guarantees afforded by the present Protocol to the signatory States, the Council shall forthwith invite the economic and financial organisations of the League of Nations to consider and report as to the nature of the steps to be taken to give effect to the financial and economic sanctions and measures of coöperation contemplated in article 16 of the Covenant and in article 11 of this Protocol.

When in possession of this information, the Council shall draw up through its competent organs:—

(1.) Plans of action for the application of the economic and financial sanctions against an aggressor State;

(2.) Plans of economic and financial coöperation between a State attacked and the different States assisting it; and shall communicate these plans to the members of the League and to the other signatory States.

Article 13. In view of the contingent military, naval and air sanctions provided for by article 16 of the Covenant and by article 11 of the present Protocol, the Council shall be entitled to receive undertakings from States determining in advance the military, naval and air forces which they would be able to bring into action immediately to ensure the fulfilment of the obligations in regard to sanctions which result from the Covenant and the present Protocol.

Furthermore, as soon as the Council has called upon the signatory States to apply sanctions, as provided in the last paragraph of article

10 above, the said States may, in accordance with any agreements which they may previously have concluded, bring to the assistance of a particular State, which is the victim of aggression, their military, naval and air forces.

The agreements mentioned in the preceding paragraph shall be registered and published by the Secretariat of the League of Nations. They shall remain open to all States members of the League which may desire to accede thereto.

Article 14. The Council shall alone be competent to declare that the application of sanctions shall cease and normal conditions be reestablished.

Article 15. In conformity with the spirit of the present Protocol, the signatory States agree that the whole cost of any military, naval or air operations undertaken for the repression of an aggression under the terms of the Protocol, and reparation for all losses suffered by individuals, whether civilians or combatants, and for all material damage caused by the operations of both sides, shall be borne by the aggressor State up to the extreme limit of its capacity.

Nevertheless, in view of article 10 of the Covenant, neither the territorial integrity nor the political independence of the aggressor State shall in any case be affected as the result of the application of the sanctions mentioned in the present Protocol.

Article 16. The signatory States agree that in the event of a dispute between one or more of them and one or more States which have not signed the present Protocol and are not members of the League of Nations, such non-member States shall be invited, on the conditions contemplated in article 17 of the Covenant, to submit, for the purpose of a pacific settlement, to the obligations accepted by the States signatories of the present Protocol.

If the State so invited, having refused to accept the said conditions and obligations, resorts to war against a signatory State, the provisions of article 16 of the Covenant, as defined by the present Protocol, shall be applicable against it.

Article 17. The signatory States undertake to participate in an International Conference for the Reduction of Armaments which shall be convened by the Council, and shall meet at Geneva on Monday, the 15th June, 1925. All other States, whether members of the League or not, shall be invited to this conference.

In preparation for the convening of the Conference, the Council shall draw up with due regard to the undertakings contained in articles 11 and 13 of the present Protocol a general programme for the reduction and limitation of armaments, which shall be laid before the Conference and which shall be communicated to the Governments at the earliest possible date, and at the latest three months before the Conference meets.

If by the 1st May, 1925, ratifications have not been deposited by at least a majority of the permanent members of the Council and ten other members of the League, the Secretary-General of the League shall immediately consult the Council as to whether he shall cancel the invitations or merely adjourn the Conference to a subsequent date to be fixed by the Council so as to permit the necessary number of ratifications to be obtained.

Article 18. Wherever mention is made in article 10, or in any other provision of the present Protocol, of a decision of the council, this shall be understood in the sense of article 15 of the Covenant, namely that the votes of the representatives of the parties to the dispute shall not be counted when reckoning unanimity or the necessary majority.

Article 19. Except as expressly provided by its terms, the present Protocol shall not affect in any way the rights and obligations of members of the League as determined by the Covenant.

Article 20. Any dispute as to the interpretation of the present Protocol shall be submitted to the Permanent Court of International Justice.

Article 21. The present Protocol, of which the French and English texts are both authentic, shall be ratified.

The deposit of ratifications shall be made at the Secretariat of the League of Nations as soon as possible.

States of which the seat of government is outside Europe will be entitled merely to inform the Secretariat of the League of Nations that their ratification has been given; in that case, they must transmit the instrument of ratification as soon as possible.

So soon as the majority of the permanent members of the Council and ten other members of the League have deposited or have effected their ratifications, a *procès-verbal* to that effect shall be drawn up by the Secretariat.

After the said *procès-verbal* has been drawn up, the Protocol shall come into force as soon as the plan for the reduction of armaments has been adopted by the Conference provided for in article 17.

If within such period after the adoption of the plan for the reduction of armaments as shall be fixed by the said Conference, the plan has not been carried out, the Council shall make a declaration to that effect; this declaration shall render the present Protocol null and void.

The grounds on which the Council may declare that the plan drawn up by the International Conference for the Reduction of Armaments has not been carried out, and that in consequence the present Protocol has been rendered null and void, shall be laid down by the Conference itself.

A signatory State which, after the expiration of the period fixed by the Conference, fails to comply with the plan adopted by the Conference, shall not be admitted to benefit by the provisions of the present Protocol.

In faith whereof the undersigned, duly authorised for this purpose, have signed the present Protocol.

Done at Geneva on the ―――― day of October, 1924, in a single copy, which will be kept in the archives of the Secretariat of the League and registered by it on the date of its coming into force.

175. Personal Reflections on the Locarno Negotiations[1]

[Hugh Spender is Central European correspondent at Geneva for the *Christian Science Monitor*.]

Locarno, October [1925]

Last night the lake was lit up with a brilliant display of fireworks, the rockets illuminating the mountains, as they burst into showers of golden rain, while the sound of the explosions reëchoed like the thunder of artillery. The noise was perhaps a little too reminiscent of an air raid to be altogether enjoyable, but it was natural that Locarno, which has entertained us so well, should rejoice that the work of peace had received its seal at the court of justice on that eventful day, October 16th, when M. Briand and Herr Luther appeared at the window of the Conference room with clasped hands amid the frantic plaudits of the crowd. Protocol, pact and arbitration treaties were, as Mr. Chamberlain reminded us, only the beginning of a new era, but the foundations had been well laid in the firm agreement and good will of all the statesmen concerned.

The last fortnight has been one of the most interesting experiences of my life. There were many difficulties to be overcome, but after listening to the views which Mr. Chamberlain expounded to the representatives of the British Press in his private room, and finding that his good will and determination to succeed were shared by Herr Stresemann and M. Briand, I had no doubt that a settlement would be reached. The excellent spirit which animated all the Foreign Ministers, all desiring to forget the bitterness of the past, concession on the one side being accepted as an argument for concession on the other, and none desiring to triumph over the other, but all aiming at a settlement based on the common good, was the best of all auguries for the final success of the Conference. But there were critical moments when it needed a united effort on the part of Mr. Chamberlain and M. Briand, assisted by M. Vandervelde, the Belgian Foreign Minister, and Signor Scialoja, the Italian (who showed an extraordinary ingenuity in devising formulas to settle differences), to prevent a deadlock in the negotiations with the Germans. It was at such critical moments that the jurists, who had already cleared away a formidable obstacle to agreement by adjusting the different points of view as to the form which the arbitration treaties should take, justified the reliance which was placed in their skill. They would work for hours at a stretch to find, not a formula which would conceal differences of opinion, but a form of words which would embody

[1] Hugh F. Spender. "Notes from Locarno," *Fortnightly Review*, December, 1925. Vol. CXVIII, pp. 755-68. By permission of the Leonard Scott Publishing Company.

an agreement. Never let us be tempted to scoff at lawyers again, for in the arrangement of the family quarrel of the European nations the jurists performed a really admirable service. Again and again Sir Cecil Hurst, M. Fromageot, M. Rollin and Signor Pilotti brought the disputants back to reason, in the sound judgments which they delivered on the problems which were submitted to them. They, like clever doctors, found the right prescription for restoring sanity to the nations, so long incarcerated in the madhouse of fears and suspicions.

But these physicians would not by themselves have performed this miracle, if the patients had not desired to be cured, and if Mr. Chamberlain and M. Briand had not been such skilful students of international psychology. It was they who were the master alienists who were to grasp the fact that Germany was *seelenkrank* and *nervenkrank*, as Dr. Stresemann said, and that her fears and suspicions had to be treated with respect and not dismissed as hallucinations.

Thus Mr. Chamberlain and M. Briand treated the German fears as to the effect of Article 16 of the Covenant on their position as prospective members of the League in a sympathetic spirit, although the German Government had been given to understand that Germany must make no conditions as to her entry into the League. Nor were the German Ministers debarred from raising the question of the evacuation of Cologne and the mitigation of the Rhineland *régime*, although they had been informed in the reply to their last Note that these questions were outside the scope of the Conference.

Since Germany, as Mr. Chamberlain insisted from the first, was to be treated on a perfect footing of equality, it became impossible to draw a line and declare that her representatives at Locarno must not speak their mind on questions in which they were interested. The conversations at the Conference table roamed over the whole field of controversy, and one of the great advantages of bringing the Foreign Ministers face to face was that the barriers between Germany and her former enemies were broken down. Thus, with their *amour propre* no longer wounded by the restriction on their right to express their opinions freely, the Germans shook off their cramped, nervous attitude and opened their minds to the healing influence of human fellowship. In this atmosphere good will responded to good will, and gradually the miasma of fear and suspicion was dispelled by the kindly light of a more friendly spirit, in which a bond of common interest uniting former enemies was discovered.

It is unnecessary to ascribe a sudden and improbable saintliness to the statesmen who sat round the long table in the Conference hall at Locarno. If they were animated by a greater desire than is usually to be found in a conclave of Foreign Ministers to arrive at a settlement, they were bent at the same time on doing their best for their respective countries, which now and again led to sharp collisions of opinion. But the arguments on either side were always advanced with perfect courtesy, and although the differences might for the moment seem insurmountable, there was always the underlying resolve to overcome them.

Dr. Luther and Herr Stresemann had the most difficult task to perform, for they were faced all the time with factious opposition of a section of their own supporters, the German Nationalists, forming part of the coalition which had sent them to Locarno. Herr Stresemann was in particular the *bête noire* of the extreme Nationalists, and he was warned to leave the train at Bellinzona and to motor to Locarno in order to escape an alleged plot against his life. He was guarded by a strong force of detectives, for every day almost he received threatening letters. After the murder of Rathenau and Erzberger, who endeavoured to improve the relations of Germany with her former enemies, these threats could not be altogether ignored.

I found Herr Stresemann looking far from well, the victim of a feverish cold, and my talk with him impressed me with the grave difficulties which he had to face. Even moderate opinion in Germany was suspicious about Germany's entry into the League, the good name of which, as Dr. Stresemann explained to me, had been gravely compromised by the Upper Silesian decision, which, in spite of the plebiscite, gave the most important industrial districts to Poland. Then there was the administration of the Saar district, which is regarded in Germany as a further proof of the hopelessness of expecting fair play from the League, while just before the Conference met at Locarno the League gave a decision against Danzig in favour of Poland on a question connected with postal facilities in Danzig. This seemed a minor matter, but it was widely regarded in Germany as a final proof that no German could expect justice from Geneva. I suggested to Herr Stresemann that all this was an argument for Germany's entry into the League, for once on the Council she would be able to present her case far more effectively at Geneva. Moreover, if the Council proved unsympathetic, Germany would be able to ventilate her grievances in the Assembly of the League, which was the sounding-board of the world. I do not think that Herr Stresemann had any real doubt as to the advantages which Germany would gain from entering the League, which he knew was absolutely necessary if the Rhineland Pact was to be signed. If Germany refused to enter the League, not only would the Pact of Security be sacrificed, but the League would tend to become more and more of a partial and lopsided institution, and, finally, Europe would be divided into hostile camps again. It seemed to me that Germany had the power to make the League a success and to convert it into a real instrument of peace. "Let Germany come into the League," I pleaded, "and loyally work with it for the good of the world; she will have nothing to fear and much to gain in the new atmosphere of confidence and good will which will be created."

I remember speaking with all the emphasis which I could command, for at that moment the most vital issues for the peace of Europe hung on the decision of the German Government. Dr. Stresemann assured me that if he could obtain certain modifications to Article 16, in other words to the conditions governing Germany's entry into the League, he was fully prepared to face the opposition in his own camp. He impressed me not only with his courage and sincerity, but as a statesman with a wide vision and a deep insight into European problems. Although insisting that the German view as to the impossibility of entering the League must be respected if Article 16 of the Covenant, the Sanctions Article, with its obligation of the economic boycott and the right-of-way through Germany as the territory of a member of the League, were not amended, he had the League spirit to a far greater degree than some of the extreme champions of the League, who will have it that the League, even as at present constituted, can do no wrong. . . .

Fortunately, Dr. Stresemann and Dr. Luther responded to this effort to convince them that their former enemies were sincere in their desire to make a new *entente* with Germany. Mr. Chamberlain played his *rôle* of conciliator with such admirable tact and discretion that he really astonished the Germans, who had the idea that he was the type of a stiff and self-conscious Englishman who viewed the world through the cold and haughty stare of an eyeglass. At the same time, M. Briand charmed everyone by his *bonhomie*. At the long table in the Conference room, which was adorned by the Mayor of Locarno with a fresh bouquet of flowers every day, all the Ministers were on a footing of equality. Arguments were put without heat, but lost none of their force for that reason, and when the tussle became severe, as it did on certain questions, Mr. Chamberlain would relax the tension by summing up the points on both sides and by suggesting that concessions on one side should be met by concessions on the other, while M. Briand would dispel the dark clouds by the lightning flashes of his humour.

Thus did the days pass, the jurists working feverishly to tide over the difficulties which the Conference could not solve and to find the right form of words to express a real agreement.

Let us look at the chief actors in this great drama a little more closely, for the success of the Locarno Conference depended on their skill and characters and on the play of mind on mind. Of Mr. Chamberlain I have already spoken. His achievement as Conciliator-in-Chief was very remarkable. He was never discouraged, never over-elated, but steered his course on an even keel. He deserves the highest recognition, for he established such a reputation for fairness, that when it came to the tussle between the Germans and the Poles on questions connected with their arbitration treaty and the French guarantee, both sides went to Mr. Chamberlain, who called in the aid of Sir Cecil Hurst.

It was Mr. Chamberlain's idea to commission the boat called the *Orange Blossom*, in which he and M. Briand, Dr. Luther and Dr. Stresemann sailed one Saturday to find a solution to the vexed question of the conditions which should govern Germany's entry into the League. The day was happily chosen, for it was Mrs. Chamberlain's birthday, and she accompanied these master mariners in their adventurous voyage in the *Orange Blossom*, presiding at the tea-table in the cabin as the genius of this romantic occasion. I watched the Ministers return to Locarno, where they were greeted with acclamation, for the good news had spread abroad that they had reached an agreement.

Briand's broad-shouldered figure, with its stooping gait, reminded me of honest Jacques Bonhomme, the very embodiment of a shrewd but kindly nature. Stresemann, so typically German with his square head and military figure, had a genial twinkle in his blue eyes. In him the Prussian and the romantic temperament are combined. He loved the old order, with its pomp and ceremony, but since he is also a philosopher, with a clear vision into the needs of the world today and a sincere desire for peace, he has turned his back on Prussianism. He is a man of undoubted genius for the task which he has to perform, which is to lead the German democracy out of its prison-house of fears and suspicions, and to teach it the hopelessness of relying on force. But, like all men of genius, he is very susceptible to the impression of the moment.

Luther, who is less expansive, has the stronger character of the two, following the course which he has mapped out for himself with great determination. That day he walked along deep in thought, hardly heeding the greetings of the crowd. Chamberlain looked, on the contrary, the picture of cheerfulness.

The voyage of the *Orange Blossom* was a fitting sequel to the meeting of M. Briand and Herr Luther in the wayside inn at Ascona, a romantic little town near Locarno. Here a few days previously, under the pergola of the trailing vines, the two statesmen met to talk over the difficulties which still separated their countries. The talk was very frank and the meeting prepared the way for the settlement of the problem of Germany's entry into the League. How this was settled may be seen in the declaration attached in the form of a "Collective Allies' Note" at the end of the Locarno treaties. This is a clear indication that the Great Powers will use their influence at Geneva to obtain an amendment of the Sanctions Article of the Covenant which will meet the German objections to the obligation, to impose an economic boycott against an aggressor nation, and to the necessity of giving a right of way through their territory. Since a member of the League will henceforth be able to plead that its military situation and geographical position should be taken into account in meeting its moral obligation to render assistance to the League, the effect of the proposal will be to place all sanctions on a footing compatible with the power of a nation to carry them out. The important result, from the German point of view, of such an amendment of Article 16 is that Germany will no longer be in danger of being drawn in her present disarmed condition into war with Russia by being obliged to impose economic sanctions. The fear of the *durchmarsch* is removed, although it never existed to the extent that the Germans imagined, for it is obvious that no French general would march an army through Germany without the consent of the German Government. As to military assistance, this is already limited to a recommendation by the Council as to what each member State of the League should contribute. Germany, therefore, has nothing to fear, and other nations may also rejoice that they will escape from the obligation to impose the economic blockade. This is indeed no small gain, from the British point of view, for it is on Great Britain above all others that the duty of making the blockade effective would fall, and this might have most embarrassing results for this country in its relations with America and other Powers. . . .

176. LOCARNO TREATIES, 1925[1]

[The German Foreign Minister, Stresemann, offered France a pact of guarantee: the proposal suggested a pact by which all the powers interested in the Rhine should guarantee the existing territorial status of the Rhine; while Germany would recognize the loss of Alsace-Lorraine, France would renounce a French frontier on the Rhine together with the possibility of another invasion of the Ruhr. During the exchange of notes which followed the German proposal, France admitted the possibility of such an agreement if Germany became a member of the League and if nothing in the pact prevented France from going to the aid of Poland or the Allies from acting in accordance with the Covenant of the League. In September drafts were prepared by Allied and German experts meeting in London. These served as the basis for the Locarno negotiations which lasted only a brief two weeks. Here for the first time since the war Germany met the Allies on an equal footing.]

No. 1

FINAL PROTOCOL OF THE LOCARNO CONFERENCE, 1925

(Translation)

The representatives of the German, Belgian, British, French, Italian, Polish and Czechoslovak Governments, who have met at Locarno, from the 5th to 16th October, 1925, in order to seek by common agreement means for preserving their respective nations from the scourge of war and for providing for the peaceful settlement of disputes of every nature which might eventually arise between them,

Have given their approval to the draft treaties and conventions which respectively affect them and which, framed in the course of the present conference, are mutually interdependent:

Treaty between Germany, Belgium, France, Great Britain and Italy (Annex A).

---

[1] Great Britain. *Parliamentary Papers*, 1925, Vol. XXXI, Cmd. 2525. "Final Protocol of the Locarno Conference, 1925 (with Annexes), together with Treaties between France and Poland, and France and Czechoslovakia, Locarno, October 16, 1925."

Arbitration Convention between Germany and Belgium (Annex B).
Arbitration Convention between Germany and France (Annex C).
Arbitration Treaty between Germany and Poland (Annex D).
Arbitration Treaty between Germany and Czechoslovakia (Annex E).

These instruments, hereby initialled *ne varietur*, will bear today's date, the representatives of the interested parties agreeing to meet in London on the 1st December next, to proceed during the course of a single meeting to the formality of the signature of the instruments which affect them.

The Minister for Foreign Affairs of France states that as a result of the draft arbitration treaties mentioned above, France, Poland and Czechoslovakia have also concluded at Locarno draft agreements in order reciprocally to assure to themselves the benefit of the said treaties. These agreements will be duly deposited at the League of Nations, but M. Briand holds copies forthwith at the disposal of the Powers represented here.

The Secretary of State for Foreign Affairs of Great Britain proposes that, in reply to certain requests for explanations concerning article 16 of the Covenant of the League of Nations presented by the Chancellor and the Minister for Foreign Affairs of Germany, a letter, of which the draft is similarly attached (Annex F), should be addressed to them at the same time as the formality of signature of the above-mentioned instruments takes place. This proposal is agreed to.

The representatives of the Governments represented here declare their firm conviction that the entry into force of these treaties and conventions will contribute greatly to bring about a moral relaxation of the tension between nations, that it will help powerfully towards the solution of many political or economic problems in accordance with the interests and sentiments of peoples, and that, in strengthening peace and security in Europe, it will hasten on effectively the disarmament provided for in article 8 of the Covenant of the League of Nations.

They undertake to give their sincere coöperation to the work relating to disarmament already undertaken by the League of Nations and to seek the realisation thereof in a general agreement.

Done at Locarno, the 16th October, 1925.

> LUTHER
> STRESEMANN
> EMILE VANDERVELDE
> ARI. BRIAND
> AUSTEN CHAMBERLAIN
> BENITO MUSSOLINI
> AL. SKRZYNSKI
> EDUARD BENEŠ

ANNEX A

Treaty of Mutual Guarantee between Germany, Belgium, France, Great Britain and Italy. (Initialled at Locarno, October 16, 1925)

(Translation)

The President of the German Reich, His Majesty the King of the Belgians, the President of the French Republic, and His Majesty the King of the United Kingdom of Great Britain and Ireland and of the British Dominions beyond the Seas, Emperor of India, His Majesty the King of Italy;

Anxious to satisfy the desire for security and protection which animates the peoples upon whom fell the scourge of the war of 1914-18;

Taking note of the abrogation of the treaties for the neutralisation of Belgium, and conscious of the necessity of ensuring peace in the area which has so frequently been the scene of European conflicts;

Animated also with the sincere desire of giving to all the signatory Powers concerned supplementary guarantees within the framework of the Covenant of the League of Nations and the treaties in force between them;

Have determined to conclude a treaty with these objects, and have appointed as their plenipotentiaries: . . .

Who, having communicated their full powers, found in good and due form, have agreed as follows:

Article 1. The high contracting parties collectively and severally guarantee, in the manner provided in the following articles, the maintenance of the territorial *status quo* resulting from the frontiers between Germany and Belgium and between Germany and France and the inviolability of the said frontiers as fixed by or in pursuance of the Treaty of Peace signed at Versailles on the 28th June, 1919, and also the observance of the stipulations of articles 42 and 43 of the said treaty concerning the demilitarised zone.

Article 2. Germany and Belgium, and also Germany and France, mutually undertake that they will in no case attack or invade each other or resort to war against each other.

This stipulation shall not, however, apply in the case of—

1. The exercise of the right of legitimate defence, that is to say, resistance to a violation of the undertaking contained in the previous paragraph or to a flagrant breach of articles 42 or 43 of the said Treaty of Versailles, if such breach constitutes an unprovoked act of aggression and by reason of the assembly of armed forces in the demilitarised zone immediate action is necessary.

2. Action in pursuance of article 16 of the Covenant of the League of Nations.

3. Action as the result of a decision taken by the Assembly or by the Council of the League of Nations or in pursuance of article 15, paragraph 7, of the Covenant of the League of Nations, provided that in this last event the action is directed against a State which was the first to attack.

Article 3. In view of the undertakings entered into in article 2 of the present treaty, Germany and Belgium and Germany and France undertake to settle by peaceful means and in the manner laid down herein all questions of every kind which may arise between them and which it may not be possible to settle by the normal methods of diplomacy:

Any question with regard to which the parties are in conflict as to their respective rights shall be submitted to judicial decision, and the parties undertake to comply with such decision.

All other questions shall be submitted to a conciliation commission. If the proposals of this commission are not accepted by the two parties, the question shall be brought before the Council of the League of Nations, which will deal with it in accordance with article 15 of the Covenant of the League.

The detailed arrangements for effecting such peaceful settlement are the subject of special agreements signed this day.

Article 4. 1. If one of the high contracting parties alleges that a violation of article 2 of the present treaty or a breach of articles 42 or 43 of the Treaty of Versailles has been or is being committed, it shall bring the question at once before the Council of the League of Nations.

2. As soon as the Council of the League of Nations is satisfied that such violation or breach has been committed, it will notify its finding without delay to the Powers signatory of the present treaty, who severally agree that in such case they will each of them come immediately to the assistance of the Power against whom the act complained of is directed.

3. In case of a flagrant violation of article 2 of the present treaty or of a flagrant breach of articles 42 or 43, of the Treaty of Versailles by one of the high contracting parties, each of the other contracting parties hereby undertakes immediately to come to the help of the party against whom such a violation or breach has been directed as soon as the said Power has been able to satisfy itself that this violation constitutes an unprovoked act of aggression and that by reason either of the crossing of the frontier or of the outbreak of hostilities or of the assembly of armed forces in the demilitarised zone immediate action is necessary. Nevertheless, the Council of the League of Nations, which will be seized of the question in accordance with the first paragraph of this article, will issue its findings, and the high contracting parties undertake to act in accordance with the recommendations of the Council

provided that they are concurred in by all the members other than the representatives of the parties which have engaged in hostilities.

Article 5. The provisions of article 3 of the present treaty are placed under the guarantee of the high contracting parties as provided by the following stipulations:

If one of the Powers referred to in article 3 refuses to submit a dispute to peaceful settlement or to comply with an arbitral or judicial decision and commits a violation of article 2 of the present treaty or a breach of articles 42 or 43 of the Treaty of Versailles, the provisions of article 4 shall apply.

Where one of the Powers referred to in article 3 without committing a violation of article 2 of the present treaty or a breach of articles 42 or 43 of the Treaty of Versailles, refuses to submit a dispute to peaceful settlement or to comply with an arbitral or judicial decision, the other party shall bring the matter before the Council of the League of Nations, and the Council shall propose what steps shall be taken; the high contracting parties shall comply with these proposals.

Article 6. The provisions of the present treaty do not affect the rights and obligations of the high contracting parties under the Treaty of Versailles or under arrangements supplementary thereto, including the agreements signed in London on the 30th August, 1924.

Article 7. The present treaty, which is designed to ensure the maintenance of peace, and is in conformity with the Covenant of the League of Nations, shall not be interpreted as restricting the duty of the League to take whatever action may be deemed wise and effectual to safeguard the peace of the world.

Article 8. The present treaty shall be registered at the League of Nations in accordance with the Covenant of the League. It shall remain in force until the Council, acting on a request of one or other of the high contracting parties notified to the other signatory Powers three months in advance, and voting at least by a two-thirds' majority, decides that the League of Nations ensures sufficient protection to the high contracting parties; the treaty shall cease to have effect on the expiration of a period of one year from such decision.

Article 9. The present treaty shall impose no obligation upon any of the British dominions, or upon India, unless the Government of such dominion, or of India, signifies its acceptance thereof.

Article 10. The present treaty shall be ratified and the ratifications shall be deposited at Geneva in the archives of the League of Nations as soon as possible.

It shall enter into force as soon as all the ratifications have been deposited and Germany has become a member of the League of Nations.

The present treaty, done in a single copy, will be deposited in the archives of the League of Nations, and the Secretary-General will be requested to transmit certified copies to each of the high contracting parties.

In faith whereof the above-mentioned plenipotentiaries have signed the present treaty.

Done at Locarno, the 16th October, 1925.

LUTHER
STRESEMANN
EMILE VANDERVELDE
A. BRIAND
AUSTEN CHAMBERLAIN
BENITO MUSSOLINI

ANNEX B

Arbitration Convention between Germany and Belgium
(Initialled at Locarno, October 16, 1925)

(Translation)

The undersigned duly authorised,

Charged by their respective Governments to determine the methods by which, as provided in article 3 of the treaty concluded this day between Germany, Belgium, France, Great Britain and Italy, a peaceful solution shall be attained of all questions which cannot be settled amicably between Germany and Belgium,

Have agreed as follows:—

PART I

Article 1. All disputes of every kind between Germany and Belgium with regard to which the parties are in conflict as to their respective rights, and which it may not be possible to settle amicably by the normal methods of diplomacy, shall be submitted for decision either to an arbitral tribunal or to the Permanent Court of International Justice, as laid down hereafter. It is agreed that the disputes referred to above include in particular those mentioned in article 13 of the Covenant of the League of Nations.

This provision does not apply to disputes arising out of events prior to the present convention and belonging to the past.

Disputes for the settlement of which a special procedure is laid down in other conventions in force between Germany and Belgium shall be settled in conformity with the provisions of those conventions.

Article 2. Before any resort is made to arbitral procedure or to procedure before the Permanent Court of International Justice, the dispute may, by agreement between the parties, be submitted, with a view to amicable settlement, to a permanent international commission styled the Permanent Conciliation Commission, constituted in accordance with the present convention.

Article 3. In the case of a dispute the occasion of which, according to the municipal law of one of the parties, falls within the competence of the national courts of such party, the matter in dispute shall not be submitted to the procedure laid down in the present convention until a judgment with final effect has been pronounced, within a reasonable time, by the competent national judicial authority.

Article 4. The Permanent Conciliation Commission mentioned in article 2 shall be composed of five members, who shall be appointed as follows, that is to say: the German Government and the Belgian Government shall each nominate a commissioner chosen from among their respective nationals, and shall appoint, by common agreement, the three other commissioners from among the nationals of third Powers; these three commissioners must be of different nationalities, and the German and Belgian Governments shall appoint the president of the commission from among them.

The commissioners are appointed for three years, and their mandate is renewable. Their appointment shall continue until their replacement and, in any case, until the termination of the work in hand at the moment of the expiry of their mandate.

Vacancies which may occur as a result of death, resignation or any other cause shall be filled within the shortest possible time in the manner fixed for the nominations.

Article 5. The Permanent Conciliation Commission shall be constituted within three months from the entry into force of the present convention.

If the nomination of the commissioners to be appointed by common agreement should not have taken place within the said period, or, in the case of the filling of a vacancy, within three months from the time when the seat falls vacant, the President of the Swiss Confederation shall, in the absence of other agreement, be requested to make the necessary appointments.

Article 6. The Permanent Conciliation Commission shall be informed by means of a request addressed to the president by the two parties acting in agreement or, in the absence of such agreement, by one or other of the parties.

The request, after having given a summary account of the subject of the dispute, shall contain the invitation to the commission to take all necessary measures with a view to arrive at an amicable settlement.

If the request emanates from only one of the parties, notification thereof shall be made without delay to the other party.

Article 7. Within fifteen days from the date when the German Government or the Belgian Government shall have brought a dispute before the Permanent Conciliation Commission either party may, for the examination of the particular dispute, replace its commissioner by a person possessing special competence in the matter.

The party making use of this right shall immediately inform the other party: the latter shall in that case be entitled to take similar action within fifteen days from the date when the notification reaches it.

Article 8. The task of the Permanent Conciliation Commission shall be to elucidate questions in dispute, to collect with that object all necessary information by means of enquiry or otherwise, and to endeavour to bring the parties to an agreement. It may, after the case has been examined, inform the parties of the terms of settlement which seem suitable to it, and lay down a period within which they are to make their decision.

At the close of its labours the commission shall draw up a report stating, as the case may be, either that the parties have come to an agreement and, if need arises, the terms of the agreement, or that it has been impossible to effect a settlement.

The labours of the commission must, unless the parties otherwise agree, be terminated within six months from the day on which the commission shall have been notified of the dispute.

Article 9. Failing any special provision to the contrary, the Permanent Conciliation Commission shall lay down its own procedure, which in any case must provide for both parties being heard. In regard to enquiries the commission, unless it decides unanimously to the contrary, shall act in accordance with provisions of Chapter III (International Commissions of Enquiry) of the Hague Convention of the 18th October, 1907, for the Pacific Settlement of International Disputes.

Article 10. The Permanent Conciliation Commission shall meet, the absence of agreement by the parties to the contrary, at a place selected by its president.

Article 11. The labours of the Permanent Conciliation Commission are not public, except when a decision to that effect has been taken by the commission with the consent of the parties.

Article 12. The parties shall be represented before the Permanent Conciliation Commission by agents, whose duty it shall be to act as intermediary between them and the commission; they may, moreover, be assisted by counsel and experts appointed by them for that purpose, and request that all persons whose evidence appears to them useful should be heard.

The commission, on its side, shall be entitled to request oral explanations from the agents, counsel and experts of the two parties, as well as from all persons it may think useful to summon with the consent of their Government.

Article 13. Unless otherwise provided in the present convention, the decisions of the Permanent Conciliation Commission shall be taken by a majority.

Article 14. The German and Belgian Governments undertake to facilitate the labours of the Permanent Conciliation Commission, and particularly to supply it to the greatest possible extent with all relevant documents and information, as well as to use the means at their disposal to allow it to proceed in their territory and in accordance with their law to the summoning and hearing of witnesses or experts, and to visit the localities in question.

Article 15. During the labours of the Permanent Conciliation Commission each commissioner shall receive salary, the amount of which shall be fixed by agreement between the German and Belgian Governments, each of which shall contribute an equal share.

Article 16. In the event of no amicable agreement being reached before the Permanent Conciliation Commission the dispute shall be submitted by means of a special agreement either to the Permanent Court of International Justice under the conditions and according to the procedure laid down by its statute or to an arbitral tribunal under the conditions and according to the procedure laid down by The Hague Convention of the 18th October, 1907, for the Pacific Settlement of International Disputes.

If the parties cannot agree on the terms of the special agreement after a month's notice one or other of them may bring the dispute before the Permanent Court of International Justice by means of an application.

PART II

Article 17. All questions on which the German and Belgian Governments shall differ without being able to reach an amicable solution by means of the normal methods of diplomacy the settlement of which cannot be attained by means of a judicial decision as provided in article 1 of the present convention, and for the settlement of which no procedure has been laid down by other conventions in force between the parties, shall be submitted to the Permanent Conciliation Commission, whose duty it shall be to propose to the parties an acceptable solution and in any case to present a report.

The procedure laid down in articles 6-15 of the present convention shall be applicable.

Article 18. If the two parties have not reached an agreement within a month from the termination of the labours of the Permanent Conciliation Commission the question shall, at the request of either party, be brought before the Council of the League of Nations, which shall deal with it in accordance with article 15 of the Covenant of the League.

GENERAL PROVISION

Article 19. In any case, and particularly if the question on which the parties differ arises out of acts already committed or on the point of commission, the Conciliation Commission or, if the latter has not been notified thereof, the arbitral tribunal or the Permanent Court of International Justice, acting in accordance with article 41 of its statute, shall lay down within the shortest possible time the provisional measures to be adopted. It shall similarly be the duty of the Council of the League of Nations, if the question is brought before it, to ensure that suitable provisional measures are taken. The German and Belgian Governments undertake respectively to accept such measures, to abstain from all measures likely to have a repercussion prejudicial to the execution of the decision or to the arrangements proposed by the Conciliation Commission or by the Council of the League of Nations, and in general to abstain from any sort of action whatsoever which may aggravate or extend the dispute.

Article 20. The present convention continues applicable as between Germany and Belgium, even when other Powers are also interested in the dispute.

Article 21. The present convention shall be ratified. Ratifications shall be deposited at Geneva with the League of Nations at the same time as the ratifications of the treaty concluded this day between Germany, Belgium, France, Great Britain and Italy.

It shall enter into and remain in force under the same conditions as the said treaty.

The present convention, done in a single copy, shall be deposited in the archives of the League of Nations, the Secretary-General of which shall be requested to transmit certified copies to each of the two contracting Governments.

Done at Locarno the 16th October, 1925.

STR.   E. V.

ANNEX C

Arbitration Convention between Germany and France
(Initialled at Locarno, October 16, 1925)

Substance of Annex C and Annex B is identical

No. 2

TREATY BETWEEN FRANCE AND POLAND

(Translation)

The President of the French Republic and the President of the Polish Republic;

Equally desirous to see Europe spared from war by a sincere observance of the undertakings arrived at this day with a view to the maintenance of general peace;

Have resolved to guarantee their benefits to each other reciprocally by a treaty concluded within the framework of the Covenant of the League of Nations and of the treaties existing between them;

And have to this effect nominated for their plenipotentiaries:

. . . .

Who, after having exchanged their full powers, found in good and due form, have agreed on the following provisions:

Article 1. In the event of Poland or France suffering from a failure to observe the undertakings arrived at this day between them and Germany with a view to the maintenance of general peace, France, and reciprocally Poland, acting in application of article 16 of the Covenant of the League of Nations, undertake to lend each other immediately aid and assistance, if such a failure is accompanied by an unprovoked recourse to arms.

In the event of the Council of the League of Nations, when dealing with a question brought before it in accordance with the said undertakings, being unable to succeed in making its report accepted by all its members other than the representatives of the parties to the dispute, and in the event of Poland or France being attacked without provocation, France, or reciprocally Poland, acting in application of article 15, paragraph 7, of the Covenant of the League of Nations, will immediately lend aid and assistance.

Article 2. Nothing in the present treaty shall affect the rights and obligations of the high contracting parties as members of the League of Nations, or shall be interpreted as restricting the duty of the League to take whatever action may be deemed wise and effectual to safeguard the peace of the world.

Article 3. The present treaty shall be registered with the League of Nations, in accordance with the Covenant.

Article 4. The present treaty shall be ratified. The ratifications will be deposited at Geneva with the League of Nations at the same time as the ratification of the treaty concluded this day between Germany, Belgium, France, Great Britain and Italy, and the ratification of the treaty concluded at the same time between Germany and Poland.

It will enter into force and remain in force under the same conditions as the said treaties.

The present treaty done in a single copy will be deposited in the archives of the League of Nations, and the Secretary-General of the League will be requested to transmit certified copies to each of the high contracting parties.

Done at Locarno the 16th October, 1925.

No. 3

Substance is identical with that of Treaty between France and Poland

177. THE ADMISSION OF GERMANY TO THE LEAGUE OF NATIONS, 1926

[A note from Germany expressing the desire to enter the League of Nations was presented to the Secretary-General on February 12, 1926. It had been presented by Stresemann to the German Cabinet and had received unanimous approval. The Assembly of the League was called to meet in special session on March 8, but an attempt was made before that date by the Locarno group of statesmen to reach a settlement of the critical problems which had been raised by Germany's proposal. Germany's request for a permanent seat on the Council of the League had been followed by no less than six others of like nature. No progress was apparent until the Council created a Committee on the Constitution of the Council, composed of one member from each of the ten states represented on the Council and one each from Argentina, China, Germany, Poland, and Switzerland. This Committee met from May 10 to 17, 1926. The report of Motta of Switzerland, chairman, shows the decisions reached by this body.]

(a) *Text of the Report Adopted by the First Committee*[1]

Geneva, March 11, 1926

The request of the German Government for admission to the League of Nations has been examined by the Sub-Committee of the First Committee of the Assembly.

The Sub-Committee was agreed that the ordinary precedent should be followed, according to which the following questions would have to be considered:

1. Is the application of the German Government for admission to the League of Nations in order?
2. Is the German Government recognised *de jure* or *de facto* and by what States?
3. Does the country possess a stable Government and well-defined frontiers?
4. Is it fully self-governing?

---

[1] League of Nations, *Journal of the Special Assembly of the League of Nations,* Geneva, March, 1926. No. 5, p. 26ff.

5. What have been the acts and the declarations of the German Government regarding:
   (a) its international engagements;
   (b) the stipulations of the League with regard to armaments?

The Sub-Committee was unanimously agreed that the reply to the first question was in the affirmative and that no doubt could be entertained in regard to questions 2, 3 and 4.

As regards the fifth question, the Council, acting under Article 9 of the Covenant, obtained the opinion of the Permanent Advisory Commission for Military, Naval and Air Questions, copy of which is annexed to this report. [The substance of the opinion was: "The question of the status of the military, naval and air forces of Germany is regulated by the Treaty of Versailles of June 28th, 1919, and does not require to be considered by this Commission."] Further, in accordance with precedent, the Sub-Committee intended to obtain from the competent authority a statement regarding the execution by the German Government of its international obligations arising out of the Treaty of Versailles. But in anticipation of a request of this nature, the Ambassadors' Conference in Paris had already been good enough to communicate to the Secretary-General the document, copy of which is annexed. [Declaration: "The Conference of Ambassadors declares that, as far as it is concerned and to the best of its knowledge, Germany is now giving effective guarantees of her sincere intention to discharge her obligations under the Treaty of Peace of June 28th, 1919, and the instruments connected therewith. . . ."]

In view of the evidence thus afforded, the Sub-Committee was unanimous in considering that an affirmative reply could be returned to all the above questions, and in recommending the First Committee to propose to the Assembly that Germany should be admitted to the League of Nations under Article I of the Covenant.

(b) *Proposal of the General Committee of the Assembly relative to the German request for admission into the League of Nations and the question of the composition of the Council*[1]

The President [M. Nintchitch]:

Translation: There has been distributed to the delegations a document containing the proposals which the General Committee decided to submit to the Assembly concerning Questions 11 and 12 on the agenda and the Council's resolution of September 4th communicated to the Assembly at its meeting on the afternoon of September 6th.

The proposals of the General Committee are as follows:

"The General Committee of the Assembly proposes that there should be a plenary meeting of the Assembly on Wednesday, September 8th,

[1] League of Nations, *Official Journal, Special Supplement* No. 44, 1926. Fourth Plenary Meeting. Admission of Germany, pp. 31-36.

at 10 o'clock, with the following agenda, which comprises Questions 11 and 12 on the agenda of the Assembly:

"1. Consideration of the report of the First Committee of the special session of the Assembly on the request of the German Government for admission to the League of Nations.

"2. Consideration of the resolution adopted by the Council of September 4th, 1926, in regard to:

(a) The nomination of Germany as a permanent Member of the Council.

(b) The increase to nine of the number of non-permanent seats on the Council.

"3. Consideration of the proposals made by the Committee instructed to study the question of the composition of the Council as regards the method of election and tenure of the non-permanent seats.

"The General Committee proposes that the Assembly should determine, in accordance with Rule 14, paragraph 2, of its Rules of Procedure, to decide on Items 1 and 2 on the above agenda without reference to a Committee.

"The General Committee proposes that Question 3 on the above agenda should be referred to the First Committee with the request that a report on the subject be presented to the full Assembly at the earliest possible date.

"The General Committee has asked M. Motta, delegate of Switzerland, to present its proposal to the Assembly."

M. Motta, first delegate of Switzerland, will address the Assembly.

M. Motta (Switzerland):

Translation: Mr. President, ladies and gentlemen—The General Committee of the Assembly has entrusted me with the task of giving you a verbal report on the proposals which I have the honour to submit to you on its behalf.

My task, though perhaps not difficult, is extremely delicate. I therefore feel that I should at the outset claim your indulgence and your sympathy.

With your permission I will divide my report into two parts. I will first deal with certain questions of procedure and then briefly with the fundamental question involved.

As regards procedure, the General Committee suggests that you should employ the most direct and expeditious means of attaining our object. It asks you to consider the matter yourselves without referring it to one of the Committees. It is true that under the Rules of Procedure all matters coming up for decision by the Assembly should first be considered by one of the Committees. Rule 14, paragraph 2, of the Rules of Procedure, however, lays down that the Assembly, by a majority of two-thirds, may take up and debate any subject directly, that is to say, without referring it previously to one of the Committees. We ask you to make use of this power. We ask this because the usual procedure would seem in this case to be unnecessary. The summary procedure would rather seem to be called for in the circumstances.

If the employment of the summary procedure were in any way to interfere with the liberty of the Assembly, the General Committee would not have made this proposal. Indeed, we consider that the complete liberty and authority of the Assembly are necessary for the discussion of questions of principle which are raised.

There are three things to be considered. First, the admission of Germany to the League; secondly, the granting to her of a permanent seat on the Council, in ratification of the unanimous decision already adopted by the Council itself; and, thirdly, the simultaneous increase of the number of non-permanent, i.e., elective, seats from six to nine.

The first of these questions is more than ripe; it is much over ripe. The First Committee of the special session of the Assembly held in March presented on March 11th a unanimous report proposing the admission of Germany to the League. The Rapporteur was the first delegate of the British Empire, our distinguished colleague, Sir Austen Chamberlain. You all know how the March Assembly was prevented from completing the task for which it was convened.

The allocation of a permanent seat on the Council is one of the conditions laid down by Germany in submitting her request for admission to the League. It is obvious that these two questions—admission to the League and the allocation of a permanent seat—must be considered *pari passu.*

The third point in the proposals submitted to you is, as I have said, the increase in the number of non-permanent seats on the Council.

The President of the Council, who gave the General Committee all necessary explanations at its meeting yesterday, stated that in the intention of the Council the allocation of a permanent seat to Germany and the increase from six to nine in the number of non-permanent seats constituted two inter-locking actions. The resolution therefore forms a single whole.

If the two questions had had to be separated, it was by no means certain that the necessary unanimity would be obtained in the Council. It is not, therefore, possible, speaking politically, to refer to a Committee the question of the non-permanent seats without referring to it the other two questions at the same time.

I would point out that these two questions are quite distinct and should not be confused; I refer to the question of the increase from six to nine in the number of non-permanent Members of the Council and that of the rules to be applied by the Assembly in the election of these non-permanent Members.

This last question is referred to the First Committee, which will give it most careful consideration and will shortly present its report with its proposals.

To sum up: the immediate procedure is indicated, but this will not interfere with the Assembly's liberty of discussion. I hope you will accept the General Committee's views.

I have still a few remarks to make on the fundamental question involved. This forms the second part of my report. I will be as brief as possible.

The admission of Germany to the League has, in my opinion, always been a vital necessity. This feeling has been strengthened year by year. It is no longer questioned by anyone. That is one of the most striking proofs of the great impulse which the establishment of the League of Nations gave to ideals of peace, conciliation and arbitration.

The admission of Germany to the League will realise one of the dearest wishes of the Swiss people, which I have the great honour to represent here among you. I venture to add that I humbly rejoice no less on this account.

The allocation of a permanent seat to Germany is one of those ideas which have in public opinion the force of elementary truth. Whether it is right or not that the Covenant should *de jure* grant permanent seats to great Powers is an open question.

The discussion of this subject, although closed today, may perhaps be resumed at some more or less distant date. The pros and cons of the question are very evenly balanced.

I am not so devoid of all sense of political reality as to ignore the full weight of the reasons that militate in favour of permanent seats, but it is none the less true that the theory of permanent seats is not altogether in conformity with democratic doctrines as we conceive them or with the theory of equality among nations.

However, I do not propose to discuss that question today. This is neither the hour nor the place for such a discussion. It is obvious that if the great Powers are given permanent seats, Germany, being beyond all doubt a great Power, could not, cannot, enter the League except upon the condition that she also obtains a permanent seat on the Council.

The question of the increase in the number of non-permanent seats, however, is another matter. I am prompted to make this observation by my sense of justice and equity in debate. This question may be, indeed has been, the subject of much controversy. I realise only too well the reasons which militate both against an increase in the number of the non-permanent seats and against an excessive increase in that number.

The great honour of presiding over the Committee on the Composition of the Council fell to me. I considered it my duty, since that Committee was in a position to examine all the aspects, all the facets, of the problem, to indicate what, in my view, were the reasons against an increase.

There are two reasons which I do not propose to dwell upon or to develop particularly, but which I wish to indicate in order to show you that the problem before us has been considered in the necessary atmosphere of calm and tranquillity.

One of the reasons against increasing the number of the non-permanent seats is the danger lest the Council, were it to become too large, should be tempted to assume too great a measure of power, with the result that the Assembly would suffer—though quite unintentionally as far as the Council was concerned—a loss of prestige and authority.

If—as I trust will be the case, and as I urge you to decide—the number of permanent seats is increased, we shall have to see that the Assembly's sovereignty remains inviolate, for we must never forget that it is in the Assembly, especially when unanimous, that the pulse of the world beats.

The second reason is that an unduly large Council might, in view of the rule demanding unanimity, be hampered or handicapped in its working and actions.

These are, I think, the two principal reasons which may reasonably be adduced against an increase in the number of the non-permanent seats and, in general, against too large a Council.

But there are also weighty, and at the present time—in my opinion—conclusive, reasons in favour of an increase.

When I say that these reasons are conclusive, I must admit that I too have had to make an effort of mind and conscience—as I trust every delegate will do—to weigh and decide, with a full knowledge of the facts, the reasons which conscience and mind show to be conclusive.

The chief reason in favour of the increase is that we must in future strike a more equitable balance between the interests of the different continents. Latin America has no permanent seat, and you know that it has not been possible to satisfy the desire expressed by one of the Latin-American States. Since this continent has no permanent seat, it seems only fair that we should be generous towards it in the allocation of non-permanent seats, and this is the reason why first the Committee, and then the Council, proposed, and are now proposing to you, to give three non-permanent seats to Latin America.

The experience of past years, moreover, has shown us how painful it was for the Assembly to vote each year a recommendation addressed to itself, inviting it to take into account the big geographical divisions of the world, and each year to find it morally impossible to fulfil the obligation it had thus imposed upon itself. Thus, one of the largest Asiatic States was unable to gain election to the Council, though we all thought at the time that she ought in fairness to be represented there.

The second reason for increasing the number of non-permanent seats is the necessity for reconciling the principle of rotation, by which all, or almost all, the States of the Assembly will one day be able to take their seat on the Council, with the need which may exist, which does exist, and which has existed, as we all realise, to take into account the political exigencies, the meritorious services and the aspirations of certain States in particular circumstances.

That is why the Committee and the Council, while proposing to increase the number of non-permanent seats, have also recommended greater flexibility in the system of rotation by providing, subject to a two-thirds majority of the Assembly, for exceptions to the rule by which a State whose period of reëlection to the Council has come to an end is no longer reëligible.

Finally, the third reason which, apart from all purely academic theories, militates in favour of increasing the number of the non-permanent seats, the reason which statesmen regard as conclusive, is that it was imperative to put an end to the crisis. If for this purpose it was necessary to sacrifice some preferences, some opinions, some views, it was impossible, if we were to find a solution, to refuse to make the necessary sacrifice on the altar of the common weal.

There is a proverb which may be aptly quoted here: *primum vivere deinde philosophare*. The question of the best constitution for the Council could be discussed to the end of time, but the best solution will always be that which obtains the unanimous suffrages of the Assembly. The goodwill and the spirit of conciliation which prevailed in the Committee and later in the Council will, I hope, I trust, I beg of you, prevail in the Assembly also. This will be a historic day. Discussion of internal organisation will cease for a time, and the League will be able to devote its energies to the concrete tasks that await it—international collaboration in every field, the codification of law, the development of pacific methods for the solution of disputes, disarmament. Today will be a day of reconciliation and justice. The work of Locarno that prospered in the sunlit little city to which I am so deeply attached—since it is one of the jewels of my homeland, the little Canton of Ticino—will at length be fully and effectively safeguarded for all time.

From my student days I call to mind some lines of the poet Lucretius. They occur in his great poem *De Rerum Natura*. At the opening of the poem Lucretius invokes the Goddess of Love and Life:

"Terrible the sufferings of Rome from war, but the sky at length has cleared."

"*Placatumque nitet effuso lumine cælum.*"

For many years past the sky of Europe has been overcast with grief and darkened with the lowering clouds of anxiety. May God in His goodness at length restore to us, through the medium of the League of Nations, the quickening sun of peace and justice!

The President:
Translation: M. Loudon, first delegate of the Netherlands, will address the Assembly.

M. Loudon (Netherlands):
Translation: Mr. President, ladies and gentlemen—The General Committee of the Assembly, adopting the resolution of the Council, proposes that, in conformity with the second paragraph of Article 14

of the Rules of Procedure, we should now agree to take a decision on Items 1 and 2 of the agenda of the present meeting without first referring them to a Committee of the Assembly.

As regards the first question, namely, the admission of Germany to the League, there can be no objection, since her admission was unanimously voted by the Committee of the special session of the Assembly appointed to examine the matter in March of this year.

Nor shall I, in the present circumstances, oppose the adoption of the second item. I should, however, be lacking in frankness if I did not declare that in my opinion, despite what has just been said by the Rapporteur, M. Motta, it is a mistake to link the question of a permanent seat on the Council for Germany—which no one, as we all know, has any desire to refuse—with the question of an increase in the number of non-permanent seats, a matter on which opinions are divided.

I consider that such a procedure amounts to forcing the Assembly's hand, and that even if we agree to it as an exceptional measure, with the sole object of avoiding fresh complications, the Assembly has a right, and indeed is morally bound, to express its profound disappointment.

I did not come to this platform to raise objections; I realise too well the difficulties with which we are faced. At the same time, those of you who were present at the meeting of the third session of the Assembly on September 25th, 1922, will not be surprised to hear the delegate of the Netherlands declare himself opposed to the principle of an increase in the number of Members of the Council. On the occasion to which I refer, we alone voted against the proposal for an additional two seats. My late colleague, Professor Struycken, explained the reasons for our vote in the following terms:

"The solidarity and collective responsibility of the Council will diminish."

And his concluding words were:

"If this year we admit a radical transformation of the principal organ of the League . . . by reason of the aspirations of political groups . . . what guarantee have we that . . . every year the composition of the Council will not be determined in accordance with the ephemeral state of affairs at the moment?"

The Assembly ignored his arguments, and by 44 votes to 1 (that of the Netherlands delegation) increased the Members of the Council by two. The suggestion now before us is that it should be increased by no less than four!

In the space of four years, therefore, we shall have increased the number of seats from eight to fourteen. Consider what danger this involves for the League, for the maintenance of a proper balance between the Assembly and the Council, for that unanimity, which is so necessary in the Council! Consider what difficulties may arise whenever it becomes necessary to convene the Council suddenly, if some political question calls for immediate decision!

These objections were clearly set forth in the Committee of Fifteen; the Minutes of its proceedings show how forcibly M. Scialoja, M. Sjöborg and M. Le Breton opposed any further extension of the Council. M. Scialoja's concluding words were: "The smaller the increase the better; best of all would be no increase at all."

Nevertheless, the opponents of the scheme, acting in a spirit of conciliation and desirous of amending the rather painful situation which arose out of what has too often been called the "crisis in the League," have finally agreed on the proposed compromise, by which the number of non-permanent seats is raised to nine.

The Netherlands delegation will adopt the same course, and for the same reasons. We desire to state, however, that we still maintain all our previous objections to the extension of the Council. If it were feasible, we would even urge that the number of non-permanent seats should again be reduced to four, the number existing up to 1922, even if our country itself were never to have a seat on the Council; for as I declared with the most profound conviction at the Assembly in March of this year, the spirit which should, in my opinion, animate the League —but which, as we have seen to our regret, does not always do so— should place the interests of the community above the *amour-propre* of individual Members.

The Netherlands delegation, constrained by circumstances, is thus prepared to support this further proposal to increase the number of non-permanent seats. We accept it as a temporary expedient, with the sole object of surmounting the difficulties which have arisen.

Having said so much, we now proclaim our satisfaction—a feeling which is, I know, shared by the whole Assembly—that this day should witness a further step in the application of that principle of universality so essential to the evolution of the League by the admission of another great Power—Germany—and that this proposal should be passed not merely by a majority, but by the unanimous vote of the Assembly.

The President:

Translation: Dr. Nansen, first delegate of Norway, will address the Assembly.

Dr. Nansen (Norway):

Mr. President, ladies and gentlemen—The Norwegian Government is very happy that we have at last come so far, that there is a very near prospect of Germany entering the League and taking her proper place amongst its Members. That the prospect of this happy result is so very much better now than it was even in March, is due to the work of the special Committee on the Composition of the Council. Our Government recognises that immense difficulties have been overcome by that Committee and that it has deeply changed the situation for the better by its well-ordered debates and by the methods of publicity which it has brought to bear on all the aspects of the question.

We are also convinced that the proposal of the General Committee of the Assembly, which is now before us, is inspired by the desire to settle this question as soon as possible, to end this unhappy period and to open the way for the League to proceed with its proper work of reconstruction. No one can be more anxious than the Norwegian Government and the Norwegian delegation that this should be achieved at the earliest possible moment.

Having said this, I am, however, bound to say that my Government has the gravest misgivings about some parts of the proposal. These misgivings arise from the fact that during all the past difficult period there have been serious departures from the proper constitutional methods of the League. Of the lamentable events in March, I need say nothing. Everybody in this hall regrets them as much as we do and, if we have learnt nothing from them, our bitter disappointment will have been in vain. Yet even now part of what has been done and certain of the proposals made do not seem to us to be quite constitutional.

For instance, on Saturday last the Council decided to grant a permanent seat among its Members to a State which was not a Member of the League. We rejoice in that decision on every ground except one. We believe that it was not consistent with the strict terms of Article 4 of the Covenant and on the grounds of constitutional principles alone, therefore, we regret that it could not have been done otherwise.

Similarly, we deeply regret the proposal of the General Committee of the Assembly that the questions of the permanent seat and the increase in the number of non-permanent seats are linked together and that they should both have been dealt with without the usual reference to a Committee. For our part, we have to admit that the explanation given in this connection does not appear conclusive. The explanation given just now by the Rapporteur, that the permanent seat on the Council might not be given to Germany unless this Assembly raised the number of non-permanent Members to nine, surprised us, and we sincerely hope that it may be based upon some misunderstanding. We deeply deplore that these two questions, being thus linked together, prevented us from voting freely on them separately as we desired.

We entirely agree with every word of the views which have just been expressed by our honourable colleague, the delegate for the Netherlands, on this subject. Ever since the beginning of the League, the granting of a permanent seat to Germany has always seemed to practically every Member of the League as right and inevitable.

The increase in the number of the non-permanent Members is an entirely different matter. It is a new proposal which no one ever heard of until a few months ago and of which most of the Members of the Assembly have only had formal notification this morning. It is a proposal which we consider to be of vital importance for the future of the League. A similar proposal for an increase from four to six was discussed for weeks in the First Committee and in Sub-Committee before it was adopted by the full Assembly.

This new proposal, which is infinitely more serious, because it increases the size of the Council to the unwieldy number of fourteen, we are now asked to accept without any similar discussion, and without any chance of debating the matter on its merits. I wish to emphasise that only fifteen Members out of fifty-five have had any opportunity of expressing an opinion on this particular proposal, whether in the special Committee, which the Council set up, or in the Council itself, or by written communication. Forty Members of the League have had no opportunity until this morning of expressing their views and yet we are asked to accept this very serious increase without any time for consideration and practically at sight. We understand the reasons of those who urge this procedure, but we nevertheless feel that it involves an infringement of the full liberty of the Members of the Assembly and that, if it were accepted as a precedent, it might constitute a very serious menace to the future working of the League.

I will not develop other points on which I might dwell. We do not propose to move any counter proposal; we do not propose to take any action which will prevent a rapid solution of the problem or which will disturb the full harmony which ought to mark the entry of Germany into the League.

We only want to make this declaration, and we want it to be considered as the most solemn protest we can make against any form of unconstitutional procedure. We desire, finally, to make a fervent appeal to the Members of the Council, and to other leaders of the League, to uphold with scrupulous care the sound and constitutional methods which have proved satisfactory in the past and to help in every way to safeguard the rights of the Assembly which is and must be the supreme organ of the League, and thus to build up its authority and prestige. We make this appeal because we are absolutely convinced that only these methods can create the true League spirit of coöperation and confidence which is vital to its future success.

The President:

Translation: M. Löfgren, delegate of Sweden, will address the Assembly.

M. Löfgren (Sweden):

Mr. President, ladies and gentlemen—After what has been said by the Rapporteur and by the previous speaker, I have only to make a declaration in order to express the views of my Government and of the Swedish delegation on the question now before us.

It has been proposed by the President that the admission of Germany to the League, the granting to Germany of a permanent seat on the Council, and the question of increasing the number of the non-permanent Members from six to nine—all these questions should be treated as one question and should not be referred to a Committee. I feel bound, on principle, to join in certain reservations already made to this procedure, although I do not wish under the present circumstances to ask for a division on the question.

I also respectfully submit that the granting to Germany of a permanent seat on the Council has, as a matter of procedure, no material connection with the creation of new non-permanent seats. The admission of Germany as a permanent Member of the Council has, from the outset, been made an integral condition of her membership and has thus been known to all the Members of the Assembly and has in fact, if not in form, been already agreed to by all of us here present.

On the other hand, the creation of three new non-permanent seats has hitherto not been considered in any way. This question, moreover, is in its turn intimately connected with the regulations proposed by the Committee, regulations which are entirely within the sole competence of the Assembly.

It is true that certain countries, like my own, had the privilege of studying the whole of this problem in the Committee appointed by the Council. While loyally collaborating for the purpose of reaching an agreement, we have thus had the opportunity of expressing our serious doubts as to the wisdom of the proposed increase in the Council and of formulating the conditions which we for our part felt bound to attach to the acceptance of a scheme which we considered fraught with certain dangers for the future development of the League. While now agreeing to the proposed extension of the Council, we do this for the purpose of saving the League from what is, perhaps, the gravest crisis that has occurred in its short existence.

In my view, however, all the other Members of the League who have not been members of the Committee should not have been deprived of their right and freedom to deliberate on this vital problem in accordance with the ordinary procedure of the League. I feel, therefore, that, whereas the question of Germany's permanent seat on the Council, which is universally accepted, could be decided at once, the question of the increase in the number of the non-permanent seats should have been referred separately to a Committee together with the proposed regulations.

I venture very respectfully to think it a mistake, when dealing with a problem of this magnitude, not to have had sufficient confidence in the political judgment of the Assembly to enable it to treat the question laid before it by the Council in accordance with its ordinary procedure.

In conclusion, I express the fervent hope that the present exception which has been made in the ordinary procedure of the Assembly will not be considered as a precedent for the future.

The President:

Translation: The Assembly has before it the proposal submitted by M. Motta on behalf of the General Committee of the Assembly. Before asking you to take a decision on the procedure to be followed in regard to these proposals, I would remind you that the General Committee suggests that one of them—the third—should be referred to the First Committee, which will be asked to report on it. The third proposal reads as follows:

"Consideration of the proposals made by the Committee instructed to study the question of the composition of the Council as regards the method of election and tenure of the non-permanent seats."

I think the Assembly will agree that there is no objection to the reference of this resolution to the First Committee without further formality.

Question 3 was referred to the First Committee.

As regards the first proposal made by M. Motta on behalf of the General Committee, the Assembly must decide first of all whether it desires to discuss it forthwith.

If no one wishes to speak, I declare that, in accordance with Article 14, paragraph 2, of the Rules of Procedure, the Assembly, without taking a vote, unanimously decides to discuss this proposal immediately. [Assent.]

The Assembly having decided upon the immediate discussion of the first proposal submitted by M. Motta, I will now read the following draft resolution:

Subject to the approval of the Council resolution mentioned in Point 2 of the agenda of the present meeting, the Assembly approves the report of the First Committee of the special session of the Assembly on the request of the German Government for admission to the League of Nations.

According to the conclusions of the report, therefore, the Assembly will now have to take a decision regarding the admission of Germany to the League of Nations.

Under the second paragraph of Article 1 of the Covenant, the Assembly must take its decision on this admission by a two-third majority.

The vote will be taken by roll-call. The name of each delegation will be called out, and one of its members will answer either "yes," or "no," or "I abstain from voting." The result of the vote will be duly registered and announced.

[The vote was taken by roll-call.]

The President:

Translation: The result of the voting is as follows:

Number of States voting: 48.

All the delegations have voted in favour of the admission of Germany to the League.

I therefore proclaim that Germany is admitted to the League of Nations by a unanimous decision of the Assembly.

I think we may congratulate ourselves upon the step that has just been taken. It vindicates those who, last March, never lost heart despite the difficulties which we all deplored—difficulties which could not have been foreseen and which may always rise to stop any great measure of progress.

By this vote we have accomplished one of the most necessary and at the same time one of the most difficult and important tasks with which the League has been faced—one, too, which is of momentous importance for its future. I feel sure I shall be voicing the unanimous feeling of the Assembly in expressing my joy, my very justifiable satisfaction, at the step which the Assembly has just taken, and also in expressing the hope that the representatives of Germany will take their places among us as soon as possible.

I will now ask you to take a decision on the second draft resolution proposed by M. Motta on behalf of the General Committee of the Assembly.

The draft resolution reads as follows:

The Assembly approves the proposals put forward by the Council in its resolution of September 4th, 1926, regarding:

(a) *The nomination of Germany as a permanent Member of the Council.*

(b) *The increase in the number of non-permanent seats, which shall be brought up to nine.*

In accordance with the second paragraph of Article 4 of the Covenant, the Assembly is asked to approve the Council's proposals by a simple majority.

The second paragraph of Article 4 of the Covenant reads as follows:

"With the approval of the majority of the Assembly, the Council may name additional Members of the League whose representatives shall always be Members of the Council; the Council with like approval may increase the number of Members of the League to be selected by the Assembly for representation on the Council."

If there is no objection, I will at once proceed with the roll-call for the second proposal. The vote will be taken in accordance with Article 20 of the Rules of Procedure.

Dr. Nansen (Norway):

Is it decided that we are not to refer the matter to a Committee?

The President:

Translation: That has already been decided. We voted for immediate discussion.

The roll-call will now be taken.

[The vote was taken by roll-call.]

The President:

Translation: The result of the vote is as follows:

Number of States voting: 48.

All the delegations voted in favour of the resolution.

I therefore declare that the second resolution has been unanimously adopted.

The Assembly having approved the Council's proposals by the necessary majority, the conditions laid down in the second paragraph of Article 4 of the Covenant have been fulfilled. Accordingly, Germany is now included among the Members of the League which are permanently represented on the Council, and the number of Members of the League to be elected by the Assembly for representation on the Council has been raised to nine.

178. THE WORLD COURT

[A permanent world court of law was an institution envisaged at the beginning of the twentieth century but made possible only when a world assembly came into being to make practicable the selection of judges. The Peace Conference made provision for the court in Article 14 of the Covenant of the League of Nations and at its first meeting the Council of the League named a commission to plan the Court. Upon the acceptance of the plan by the Assembly and the Council, 15 judges were elected and the Court got under way. By January, 1930, it had averaged about two meetings a year and had rendered sixteen judgments and sixteen advisory opinions.

The reasons for non-adherence by the United States to the Court may be inferred from the conditions laid down by the Senate for acceptance by the other members of the Court before the United States should join. When the other members did not find it possible to meet all of these conditions, Mr. Elihu Root worked out a plan whereby the United States might preserve the essential points in its reservations and still join the Court.]

(a) *Statute for the Permanent Court of International Justice*[1]

Art. 1. A Permanent Court of International Justice is hereby established in accordance with Article 14 of the Covenant of the League of Nations. This Court shall be in addition to the Court of Arbitration organised by the Conventions of The Hague of 1899 and 1907, and to the special Tribunals of Arbitration to which States are always at liberty to submit their disputes for settlement.

Art. 2. The Permanent Court of International Justice shall be composed of a body of independent judges, elected regardless of their nationality from amongst persons of high moral character, who possess the qualifications required in their respective countries for appointment

---

[1] League of Nations Secretariat, Information Section. *The Permanent Court of International Justice,* pp. 44-59, selections.

to the highest judicial offices, or are jurisconsults of recognised competence in international law.

Art. 3. The Court shall consist of fifteen members: eleven judges and four deputy-judges. The number of judges and deputy-judges may hereafter be increased by the Assembly, upon the proposal of the Council of the League of Nations, to a total of fifteen judges and six deputy judges.

Art. 4. The members of the Court shall be elected by the Assembly and by the Council from a list of persons nominated by the national groups in the Court of Arbitration, in accordance with the following provisions. . . .

Art. 22. The seat of the Court shall be established at The Hague. The President and Registrar shall reside at the seat of the Court.

Art. 23. A session of the Court shall be held every year. . . .

Art. 34. Only States or Members of the League of Nations can be parties in cases before the Court. . . .

Art. 38. The Court shall apply:

1. International conventions, whether general or particular, establishing rules expressly recognised by the contesting States;

2. International custom, as evidence of a general practice accepted as law;

3. The general principles of law recognised by civilised nations;

4. Subject to the provisions of Article 59, judicial decisions and the teachings of the most highly qualified publicists of the various nations, as subsidiary means for the determination of rules of law.

This provision shall not prejudice the power of the Court to decide a case *ex æquo et bono,* if the parties agree thereto.

Art. 39. The official languages of the Court shall be French and English. If the parties agree that the case shall be conducted in French, the judgment will be delivered in French. If the parties agree that the case shall be conducted in English, the judgment will be delivered in English.

In the absence of an agreement as to which language shall be employed, each party may, in the pleadings, use the language which it prefers; the decision of the Court will be given in French and English. In this case the Court will at the same time determine which of the two texts shall be considered as authoritative. . . .

Art. 46. The hearing in Court shall be public, unless the Court shall decide otherwise, or unless the parties demand that the public be not admitted. . . .

Art. 55. All questions shall be decided by a majority of the judges present at the hearing.

In the event of an equality of votes, the President or his deputy shall have a casting vote.

Art. 60. The judgment is final and without appeal. In the event of dispute as to the meaning or scope of the judgment, the Court shall construe it upon the request of any party.

(b) *Examples of a Judgment and an Advisory Opinion*[1]

Third Session (Ordinary), 1923.

Case of the S.S. *Wimbledon*. The case of the S.S. *Wimbledon* is of special interest, being the first occasion in history on which one party to an inter-State dispute summoned the other to appear before an international court for judgment by unilateral arraignment. It was also the first occasion upon which the Permanent Court of International Justice had to deliver a judgment; previously it had given only advisory opinions.

In March 1921 the British S.S. *Wimbledon*, chartered by a French company and carrying a cargo of munitions consigned to Poland, arrived at the entrance to the Kiel Canal en route for Danzig and was refused access by the Director of Canal Traffic. This official, acting under instructions, cited in support of his refusal the German Neutrality Regulations.

According to Article 380 of the Treaty of Versailles, the Kiel Canal and its approaches are to be maintained free and open to the vessels of commerce and war of all nations at peace with Germany on terms of entire equality.

The French Embassy at Berlin having failed to obtain the withdrawal of this refusal, the *Wimbledon* was ordered to proceed via the Danish Straits, thus undergoing delay and deviation. The question was submitted to the Conference of Ambassadors, but that body did not succeed in effecting an agreement. During the ensuing negotiations the German Government was the first to suggest that the case should be submitted to the Court. Subsequently, it was the Allied Governments—France, Great Britain, Italy and Japan—who took the initiative of instituting proceedings against Germany before the Court. As it was provided in the Statute that, if in a given case the Court did not include upon the Bench a judge of the nationality of one of the parties, that party might select one, Germany appointed a national judge. Poland availed herself of the right to intervene which she possessed as a signatory of the Peace Treaty.

The judgment of the Court as fixed by a majority of nine judges was delivered on August 17th. It was to the effect that the German authorities were wrong in refusing passage to the S.S. *Wimbledon*, and that therefore the German Government was bound to make good the prejudice sustained (estimated by the Court at 140,000 French francs) as the result of this action. Two judges were unable to concur in the judgment of the majority, and made use of their right to deliver a

---

[1] *Ibid.*, pp. 27-28; 36-37.

separate opinion. The same course was adopted by the German national judge.

Sixth Session (Extraordinary).

Exchange of Greek and Turkish populations (Advisory opinion). This was the case which rendered necessary the convocation of an extraordinary session. It arose out of the following facts:

One of the agreements forming part of the Lausanne peace settlement provided for the compulsory exchange of the Turkish population of Greece and the Greek population of Turkey, with certain exceptions, *inter alia*, the Greek inhabitants of Constantinople "established" before a given date. Difficulties having arisen between the two interested Governments with regard to the meaning of the word "established," the authority set up to deal with the problems arising out of the exchange —a Mixed Commission—eventually accepted an offer by the Council of the League to obtain the opinion of the Court on the point at issue.

This opinion, which was delivered on February 21st, 1925, defined the notion of "establishment" as used in the Lausanne Convention, and gave indications according to which the Mixed Commission would be able to decide whether in a given case a person was liable to exchange or not.

The dispute was subsequently settled by an agreement concluded between the two Governments concerned on the basis of the Court's opinion.

(c) *U. S. Senate Reservations on the World Court, 1926*[1]

Whereas the President, under date of February 24, 1923, transmitted a message to the Senate, accompanied by a letter from the Secretary of State, dated February 17, 1923, asking the favorable advice and consent of the Senate to the adherence on the part of the United States to the protocol of December 16, 1920, of signature of the statute for the Permanent Court of International Justice, set out in the said message of the President (without accepting or agreeing to the optional clause for compulsory jurisdiction contained therein), upon the conditions and understandings hereafter stated, to be made a part of the instrument of adherence: Therefore be it

Resolved (Two-Thirds of the Senators Present Concurring), That the Senate advise and consent to the adherence on the part of the United States to the said protocol of December 16, 1920, and the adjoined statute for the Permanent Court of International Justice (without accepting or agreeing to the optional clause for compulsory jurisdiction contained in said statute), and that the signature of the United States be affixed to the said protocol, subject to the following reserva-

---

[1] *Congressional Record*, Vol. 67, pp. 2824-2825. (January 27, 1926.)

tions and understandings, which are hereby made a part and condition of this resolution, namely:

1. That such adherence shall not be taken to involve any legal relation on the part of the United States to the League of Nations or the assumption of any obligations by the United States under the treaty of Versailles.

2. That the United States shall be permitted to participate, through representatives designated for the purpose and upon an equality with the other states, members, respectively, of the Council and Assembly of the League of Nations, in any and all proceedings of either the council or the assembly for the election of judges or deputy judges of the Permanent Court of International Justice or for the filling of vacancies.

3. That the United States will pay a fair share of the expenses of the court as determined and appropriated from time to time by the Congress of the United States.

4. That the United States may at any time withdraw its adherence to the said protocol and that the statute for the Permanent Court of International Justice adjoined to the protocol shall not be amended without the consent of the United States.

5. That the court shall not render any advisory opinion except publicly after due notice to all states adhering to the court and to all interested states and after public hearing or opportunity for hearing given to any state concerned; nor shall it, without the consent of the United States, entertain any request for an advisory opinion touching any dispute or question in which the United States has or claims an interest.

The signature of the United States to the said protocol shall not be affixed until the powers signatory to such protocol shall have indicated, through an exchange of notes, their acceptance of the foregoing reservations and understandings as a part and a condition of adherence by the United States to the said protocol.

Resolved Further, As a part of this act of ratification that the United States approve the protocol and statute hereinabove mentioned, with the understanding that recourse to the Permanent Court of International Justice for the settlement of differences between the United States and any other state or states can be had only by agreement thereto through general or special treaties concluded between the parties in dispute; and

Resolved Further, That adherence to the said protocol and statute hereby approved shall not be so construed as to require the United States to depart from its traditional policy of not intruding upon, interfering with, or entangling itself in the political questions of policy or internal administration of any foreign state; nor shall adherence to the said protocol and statute be construed to imply a relinquishment by the United States of its traditional attitude toward purely American questions.

(d) *Root Formula for American Entrance into the World Court, 1929*[1]

The Court shall not, without the consent of the United States of America, render an advisory opinion touching any dispute to which the United States is a party.

The Court shall not, without the consent of the United States, render an advisory opinion touching any dispute to which the United States is not a party, but in which it claims an interest, or touching any question other than a dispute in which the United States claims an interest.

The manner in which it shall be made known whether the United States claims an interest and gives or withholds its consent shall be as follows:

Whenever in contemplation of a request for an advisory opinion it seems to them desirable, the Council or the Assembly may invite an exchange of views with the United States and such exchange of views shall proceed with all convenient speed.

Whenever a request for an advisory opinion comes to the Court, the Registrar shall notify the United States thereof among other States mentioned in the now existing Article LXXIII of the rules of the Court, stating that a reasonable time limit would be fixed by the President within which a written statement by the United States concerning the request will be received.

In case the United States shall, within the time fixed, advise the Court in writing that the request touches a dispute or a question in which the United States has an interest, and that the United States has not consented to the submission of the question, thereupon all proceedings upon the question shall be stayed to admit of an exchange of views between the United States and the proponents of the request, and such exchange of views shall proceed with all convenient speed.

If, after such exchange of views, either while a question is in contemplation, or after a question has gone to the Court, it shall appear (1) that no agreement can be reached as to whether the question does touch an interest of the United States within the true meaning of the second paragraph of this article; and (2) that submission of the question is still insisted upon after attributing to the objection of the United States the same force and effect as attaches to a vote against asking for the opinion given by a member of the League of Nations either in Assembly or Council; and if it also appears that the United States has not been able to find the submission of the question so important for the general good as to call upon the United States to forego its objection, in that particular instance leaving the request to be acted upon by the Court without in any way binding the United States, then it shall be deemed that owing to material difference of view

---

[1] The *New York Times*, September 5, 1929. Reprinted with the permission of the New York Times Company.

regarding the proper scope or practice of requesting advisory opinions, the arrangement now agreed upon is not yielding satisfactory results, and that exercise of powers of withdrawal provided in Article VII hereof will follow naturally without any imputation of unfriendliness to coöperate generally for peace and good will.

(NOTE: Article VII of the 1926 protocol, referred to in the last sentence of the formula, provides that the United States may at any time notify the Secretary General of the League of Nations that it is withdrawing from its adherence to the World Court.)

179. BRITISH IMPERIAL CONFERENCE, 1926[1]

[As a result of war experiences, it was recognized in Great Britain and elsewhere that because matters relating to foreign relations were of common concern to the Empire as a whole, they could not longer be settled in London, but must necessarily be passed upon by an Imperial body. The Conferences of 1923 and 1926, composed of Prime Ministers of Great Britain, the Dominions and India, worked out a plan for this action. Decisions are reached in these meetings by unanimous vote only, and must be approved by the several parliaments. All matters of common concern may be presented to an Imperial Conference for discussion. This procedure has brought a revolutionary change to the nature of the British Empire.]

STATUS OF GREAT BRITAIN AND THE DOMINIONS

The Committee are of opinion that nothing would be gained by attempting to lay down a Constitution for the British Empire. Its widely scattered parts have very different characteristics, very different histories, and are at very different stages of evolution; while considered as a whole, it defies classification and bears no real resemblance to any other political organisation which now exists or has ever yet been tried.

There is, however, one most important element in it which, from a strictly constitutional point of view, has now, as regards all vital matters, reached its full development—we refer to the group of self-governing communities composed of Great Britain and the Dominions. Their position and mutual relation may be readily defined. *They are autonomous Communities within the British Empire, equal in status, in no way subordinate one to another in any aspect of their domestic or external affairs, though united by a common allegiance to the Crown, and freely associated as members of the British Commonwealth of Nations.*

A foreigner endeavouring to understand the true character of the British Empire by the aid of this formula alone would be tempted to

---

[1] Great Britain. *Parliamentary Papers,* 1926. Vol. XI, Cmd. 2768, "Imperial Conference, 1926. Summary of Proceedings," pp. 14, 15 and 20-26.

think that it was devised rather to make mutual interference impossible than to make mutual coöperation easy.

Such a criticism, however, completely ignores the historic situation. The rapid evolution of the Oversea Dominions during the last fifty years has involved many complicated adjustments of old political machinery to changing conditions. The tendency towards equality of status was both right and inevitable. Geographical and other conditions made this impossible of attainment by way of federation. The only alternative was by the way of autonomy; and along this road it has been steadily sought. Every self-governing member of the Empire is now the master of its destiny. In fact, if not always in form, it is subject to no compulsion whatever.

But no account, however accurate, of the negative relations in which Great Britain and the Dominions stand to each other can do more than express a portion of the truth. The British Empire is not founded upon negations. It depends essentially, if not formally, on positive ideals. Free institutions are its life-blood. Free coöperation is its instrument. Peace, security, and progress are among its objects. Aspects of all these great themes have been discussed at the present Conference; excellent results have been thereby obtained. And, though every Dominion is now, and must always remain, the sole judge of the nature and extent of its coöperation, no common cause will, in our opinion, be thereby imperilled.

Equality of status, so far as Britain and the Dominions are concerned, is thus the root principle governing our Inter-Imperial Relations. But the principles of equality and similarity, appropriate to *status*, do not universally extend to function. Here we require something more than immutable dogmas. For example, to deal with questions of diplomacy and questions of defence, we require also flexible machinery—machinery which can, from time to time, be adapted to the changing circumstances of the world. This subject also has occupied our attention. The rest of this Report will show how we have endeavoured not only to state political theory, but to apply it to our common needs.

. . . .

RELATIONS WITH FOREIGN COUNTRIES

From questions specially concerning the relations of the various parts of the British Empire with one another, we naturally turned to those affecting their relations with foreign countries. In the latter sphere, a beginning had been made towards making clear those relations by the Resolution of the Imperial Conference of 1923 on the subject of the negotiation, signature, and ratification of treaties. But it seemed desirable to examine the working of that Resolution during the past three years and also to consider whether the principles laid down with regard to Treaties could not be applied with advantage in a wider sphere.

(a) Procedure in Relation to Treaties

We appointed a special Sub-Committee under the Chairmanship of the Minister of Justice of Canada (The Honourable E. Lapointe, K.C.) to consider the question of treaty procedure.

The Sub-Committee, on whose report the following paragraphs are based, found that the Resolution of the Conference of 1923 embodied on most points useful rules for the guidance of the Governments. As they became more thoroughly understood and established, they would prove effective in practice.

Some phases of treaty procedure were examined however in greater detail in the light of experience in order to consider to what extent the Resolution of 1923 might with advantage be supplemented.

Negotiation.

It was agreed in 1923 that any of the Governments of the Empire contemplating the negotiation of a treaty should give due consideration to its possible effect upon other Governments and should take steps to inform Governments likely to be interested of its intention.

This rule should be understood as applying to any negotiations which any Government intends to conduct, so as to leave it to the other Governments to say whether they are likely to be interested.

When a Government has received information of the intention of any other Government to conduct negotiations, it is incumbent upon it to indicate its attitude with reasonable promptitude. So long as the initiating Government receives no adverse comments and so long as its policy involves no active obligations on the part of the other Governments, it may proceed on the assumption that its policy is generally acceptable. It must, however, before taking any steps which might involve the other Governments in any active obligations, obtain their definite assent.

Where by the nature of the treaty it is desirable that it should be ratified on behalf of all the Governments of the Empire, the initiating Government may assume that a Government which has had full opportunity of indicating its attitude and has made no adverse comments will concur in the ratification of the treaty. In the case of a Government that prefers not to concur in the ratification of a treaty unless it has been signed by a plenipotentiary authorised to act on its behalf, it will advise the appointment of a plenipotentiary so to act.

Form of Treaty

Some treaties begin with a list of the contracting countries and not with a list of Heads of States. In the case of treaties negotiated under the auspices of the League of Nations, adherence to the wording of the Annex to the Covenant for the purpose of describing the contracting party has led to the use in the preamble of the term "British Empire" with an enumeration of the Dominions and India if parties to the Convention but without any mention of Great Britain and Northern Ireland and the Colonies and Protectorates. These are only included by virtue of their being covered by the term "British Empire." This practice, while suggesting that the Dominions and India are not on a footing of equality with Great Britain as participants in the treaties in question, tends to obscurity and misunderstanding and is generally unsatisfactory.

As a means of overcoming this difficulty it is recommended that all treaties (other than agreements between Governments) whether negotiated under the auspices of the League or not should be made in the name of Heads of States, and, if the treaty is signed on behalf of any or all of the Governments of the Empire, the treaty should be made in the name of the King as the symbol of the special relationship between the different parts of the Empire. The British units on behalf of which the treaty is signed should be grouped together in the following order: Great Britain and Northern Ireland and all parts of the British Empire which are not separate members of the League, Canada, Australia, New Zealand, South Africa, Irish Free State, India. A specimen form of treaty as recommended is attached as an appendix to the Committee's Report.

In the case of a treaty applying to only one part of the Empire it should be stated to be made by the King on behalf of that part.

The making of the treaty in the name of the King as the symbol of the special relationship between the different parts of the Empire will render superfluous the inclusion of any provision that its terms must not be regarded as regulating *inter se* the rights and obligations of the various territories on behalf of which it has been signed in the name of the King. In this connection it must be borne in mind that the question was discussed at the Arms Traffic Conference in 1925, and that the Legal Committee of that Conference laid it down that the principle to which the foregoing sentence gives expression underlies all international conventions.

In the case of some international agreements the Governments of different parts of the Empire may be willing to apply between themselves some of the provisions as an administrative measure. In this case they should state the extent to which and the terms on which such provisions are to apply. Where international agreements are to be applied between different parts of the Empire, the form of a treaty between Heads of States should be avoided.

Full Powers

The plenipotentiaries for the various British units should have Full Powers, issued in each case by the King on the advice of the Government concerned, indicating and corresponding to the part of the Empire for which they are to sign. It will frequently be found convenient, particularly where there are some parts of the Empire on which it is not contemplated that active obligations will be imposed, but where the position of the British subjects belonging to these parts will be affected, for such Government to advise the issue of Full Powers on their behalf to the plenipotentiary appointed to act on behalf of the Government or Governments mainly concerned. In other cases provision might be made for accession by other parts of the Empire at a later date.

Signature

In the cases where the names of countries are appended to the signatures in a treaty, the different parts of the Empire should be designated in the same manner as is proposed in regard to the list of plenipotentiaries in the preamble to the treaty. The signatures of the plenipotentiaries of the various parts of the Empire should be grouped together in the same order as is proposed above.

The signature of a treaty on behalf of a part of the Empire should cover territories for which a mandate has been given to that part of the Empire, unless the contrary is stated at the time of the signature.

Coming into Force of Multilateral Treaties

In general, treaties contain a ratification clause and a provision that the treaty will come into force on the deposit of a certain number of ratifications. The question has sometimes arisen in connection with treaties negotiated under the auspices of the League whether, for the purpose of making up the number of ratifications necessary to bring the treaty into force, ratifications on behalf of different parts of the Empire which are separate Members of the League should be counted as separate ratifications. In order to avoid any difficulty in future, it is recommended that, when it is thought necessary that a treaty should contain a clause of this character, it should take the form of a provision that the treaty should come into force when it has been ratified on behalf of so many separate Members of the League.

We think that some convenient opportunity should be taken of explaining to the other Members of the League the changes which it is desired to make in the form of treaties and the reasons for which they are desired. We would also recommend that the various Governments of the Empire should make it an instruction to their representatives at International Conferences to be held in future that they should use their best endeavours to secure that effect is given to the recommendations contained in the foregoing paragraphs.

(b) Representation at International Conferences

We also studied, in the light of the Resolution of the Imperial Conference of 1923 to which reference has already been made, the question of the representation of the different parts of the Empire at International Conferences. The conclusions which we reached may be summarised as follows:—

1. No difficulty arises as regards representation at conferences con-

vened by, or under the auspices of, the League of Nations. In the case of such conferences all members of the League are invited, and if they attend are represented separately by separate delegations. Coöperation is ensured by the application of paragraph I.1. (c) of the Treaty Resolution of 1923.

2. As regards international conferences summoned by foreign Governments, no rule of universal application can be laid down, since the nature of the representation must, in part, depend on the form of invitation issued by the convening Government.

(a.) In conferences of a technical character, it is usual and always desirable that the different parts of the Empire should (if they wish to participate) be represented separately by separate delegations, and where necessary efforts should be made to secure invitations which will render such representation possible.

It is for each part of the Empire to decide whether its particular interests are so involved, especially having regard to the active obligations likely to be imposed by any resulting treaty, that it desires to be represented at the conference, or whether it is content to leave the negotiation in the hands of the part or parts of the Empire more directly concerned and to accept the result.

If a Government desires to participate in the conclusion of a treaty, the method by which representation will be secured is a matter to be arranged with the other Governments of the Empire in the light of the invitation which has been received.

Where more than one part of the Empire desires to be represented, three methods of representation are possible:—

(i.) By means of a common plenipotentiary or plenipotentiaries, the issue of Full Powers to whom should be on the advice of all parts of the Empire participating.

(ii.) By a single British Empire delegation composed of separate representatives of such parts of the Empire as are participating in the conference. This was the form of representation employed at the Washington Disarmament Conference of 1921.

(iii.) By separate delegations representing each part of the Empire participating in the conference. If, as a result of consultation, this third method is desired, an effort must be made to ensure that the form of invitation from the convening Government will make this method of representation possible.

(b.) Conferences of a political character called by a foreign Government must be considered on the special circumstances of each individual case.

Certain non-technical treaties should, from their nature, be concluded in a form which will render them binding upon all parts of the Empire, and for this purpose should be ratified with the concurrence of all the Governments. It is for each Government to decide to what extent its concurrence in the ratification will be facilitated by its participation in the conclusion of the treaty, as, for instance, by the appointment of a common plenipotentiary. Any question as to whether the nature of the treaty is such that its ratification should be concurred in by all parts of the Empire is a matter for discussion and agreement between the Governments.

(c) General Conduct of Foreign Policy

We went on to examine the possibility of applying the principles underlying the Treaty Resolution of the 1923 Conference to matters arising in the conduct of foreign affairs generally. It was frankly recognised that in this sphere, as in the sphere of defence, the major share of responsibility rests now, and must for some time continue to rest, with His Majesty's Government in Great Britain. Nevertheless, practically all the Dominions are engaged to some extent, and some to a considerable extent, in the conduct of foreign relations, particularly those with foreign countries on their borders. A particular instance of this is the growing work in connection with the relations between Canada and the United States of America which has led to the necessity for the appointment of a Minister Plenipotentiary to represent the Canadian Government in Washington. We felt that the governing consideration underlying all discussions of this problem must be that neither Great Britain nor the Dominions could be committed to the acceptance of active obligations except with the definite assent of their own Government. In the light of this governing consideration, the Committee agreed that the general principle expressed in relation to Treaty negotiations in Section V (a) of this Report, which is indeed already to a large extent in force, might usefully be adopted as a guide by the Governments concerned in future in all negotiations affecting foreign relations falling within their respective sphere.

180. Italo-Albanian Treaty, 1926[1]

[Italy's long interest in the eastern coast of the Adriatic culminated in this Treaty of Tirana by which she secured the virtual protectorate over Albania which Italian nationalists had been seeking ever since the outbreak of the World War. Excitement in Jugoslavia was intense, and relations between Jugoslavia and Albania became strained and as a result of a frontier incident were broken off. Thereupon Jugoslavia resorted to a diplomatic counter move by signing a treaty of coöperation with France, and a few days later Italy retaliated by signing a twenty-year defensive alliance with Albania in which each agreed that "when all the means of conciliation have been exhausted," it would come to the aid of the other in case of unprovoked attack. Relations between the two countries gradually became better. Meanwhile internal

---

[1] Foreign Policy Association, *Information Service*, Vol. III, No. 1, March 16, 1927. Reprinted with the permission of the Foreign Policy Association.

improvements have been carried out in Albania with Italian supervision and financial assistance.]

ANNEX I

Text of the Italo-Albanian Treaty of Tirana, November 27, 1926

Italy and Albania, with a view to reënforcing their mutual relations of friendship and security in regard to their geographical position and with a view to contributing to the consolidation of peace, animated by the desire to maintain the political, juridical, and territorial *status quo* of Albania within the framework of the treaties to which both parties are signatories and of the Covenant of the League of Nations, have decided to conclude the present pact of friendship and security and for the purpose have designated as their plenipotentiaries the following. . .

Article I. Italy and Albania recognize that any disturbance directed against the political, juridical, and territorial *status quo* of Albania is opposed to their reciprocal political interest.

Article II. To safeguard the above-mentioned interest, the High Contracting Parties undertake to give their mutual support and cordial collaboration; they likewise undertake not to conclude with other Powers political or military agreements prejudicial to the interests of the other Party as defined in the present pact.

Article III. The High Contracting Parties undertake to submit to a special procedure of conciliation and of arbitration questions which may arise between them and which can not be settled through regular diplomatic channels.

The conditions of this procedure of peaceful settlement will be the object of a special convention to be concluded as soon as possible.

Article IV. The present pact shall remain in force for five years, and may be denounced or renewed one year before the expiry.

Article V. The present pact shall be ratified and afterwards registered with the League of Nations. The ratification shall be exchanged at Rome.

Done at Tirana, November 27, 1926.

Signed:

POMPEO ALOISI
H. VRIONI

181. "THE OUTLAWRY OF WAR"

[The French Foreign Minister, Aristide Briand, with motives which were possibly both humanitarian and French, made a public gesture toward winning America's perpetual friendship and received a warm response from the United States; but before a treaty was concluded, the American Secretary of State, Frank B. Kellogg, had pressed for and received a broader application of the principle of the renunciation of war as an instrument of national policy. As a consequence of this, a multilateral treaty, with certain qualifying interpretations, replaced the proposed pact of friendship and was accepted by France, the United States, and a large number of the other nations of the world. The treaty was signed by the representatives of fifteen states, including Germany, at the Quai d'Orsay on August 27, 1928, and within a few months it was accepted by Russia, the United States, and almost all other states. Much credit for its initiation must be given to J. T. Shotwell.]

(a) *Extract from M. Briand's Message to the American People on the occasion of the tenth anniversary of the entry of the United States into the World War*[1]

Now in the problems of peace, France and America are following different roads, but each toward the same goal. Disarmament can come about only by the will to peace among all nations. In that the thought of America will ever be certain to find sympathetic accord in the thought of France.

If there were need of it between the two great democracies in order to give high testimony of their desire for peace and to furnish a solemn example to other peoples, France would be willing to enter into an engagement with America mutually outlawing war, to use your way of expressing it.

The renunciation of war as an instrument of national policy is a conception already familiar to the signatories of the League Covenant and the Locarno Treaties. Any engagement subscribed to in the same spirit by the United States toward another nation, such as France, should greatly contribute in the eyes of the world to enlarge and fortify the foundation on which the international policy of peace is being erected. Thus the two great friendly nations, equally devoted to the cause of peace, would furnish the world the best illustration of the truth that the condition immediately to be obtained is not disarmament but the practice of peace. . . .

(b) *Draft of pact of perpetual friendship between France and the United States. Transmitted to the Secretary of State by M. Briand through the American Ambassador at Paris*[2]

June 20, 1927

The President of the French Republic and the President of the United States of America,

---

[1] The *New York Times*, April 6, 1927, p. 5. From the Associated Press.

[2] *Notes Exchanged between the United States and Other Powers on the Subject of a Multilateral Treaty for the Renunciation of War, June 20, 1927-June 23, 1928*, Washington, 1928.

Equally desirous of affirming the solidarity of the French people and the people of the United States of America in their wish for peace and in their renunciation of a recourse to arms as an instrument of their policy towards each other,

And having come to an agreement to consecrate in a solemn act these sentiments as much in accord with the progress of modern democracies as with the mutual friendship and esteem of two nations that no war has ever divided and which the defense of liberty and justice has always drawn closer,

Have to this end designated for their plenipotentiaries, to wit:

The President of the French Republic: ———————————————
The President of the United States of America: ———————————

Who, after having exchanged their powers, recognized in good and due form, have agreed upon the following provisions:

Article I. The high contracting powers solemnly declare, in the name of the French people and the people of the United States of America, that they condemn recourse to war and renounce it respectively as an instrument of their national policy towards each other.

Article II. The settlement or the solution of all disputes or conflicts, of whatever nature or of whatever origin they may be, which may arise between France and the United States of America, shall never be sought by either side except by pacific means.

Article III. The present act shall be ratified. The ratifications thereof shall be exchanged at ———————————— as soon as possible and from that time it shall have full force and value.

In witness whereof the above-named plenipotentiaries have signed the present act and have thereunto set their seal.

Done at ———————————— in two copies (each drawn up both in French and English and having equal force), the ————————————
————————————————, nineteen hundred and twenty-seven.

(Signatures and seals)

(c) *The Multilateral Treaty for the Renunciation of War (Briand-Kellogg Pact) 1928*[1]

Note of the Government of the United States to the Governments of Australia, Belgium, Canada, Czechoslovakia, France, Germany, Great Britain, India, Irish Free State, Italy, Japan, New Zealand, Poland, and South Africa, June 23, 1928

It will be recalled that, pursuant to the understanding reached between the Government of France and the Government of the United States, the American Ambassadors at London, Berlin, Rome and Tokyo transmitted on April 13, 1928, to the Governments to which they were respectively accredited the text of M. Briand's original proposal of

———————
[1] *Ibid.*

June 20, 1927, together with copies of the notes subsequently ex-changed by France and the United States on the subject of a multi-lateral treaty for the renunciation of war. At the same time the Government of the United States also submitted for consideration a preliminary draft of a treaty representing in a general way the form of treaty which it was prepared to sign, and inquired whether the Governments thus addressed were in a position to give favorable con-sideration thereto. The text of the identic notes of April 13, 1928, and a copy of the draft treaty transmitted therewith, were also brought to the attention of the Government of France by the American Ambassa-dor at Paris.

It will likewise be recalled that on April 20, 1928, the Government of the French Republic circulated among the other interested govern-ments, including the Government of the United States, an alterna-tive draft treaty, and that in an address which he delivered on April 28, 1928, before the American Society of International Law, the Secretary of State of the United States explained fully the construc-tion placed by my Government upon the treaty proposed by it, refer-ring as follows to the six major considerations emphasized by France in its alternative draft treaty and prior diplomatic correspondence with my Government:

(1) *Self-defense.* There is nothing in the American draft of an anti-war treaty which restricts or impairs in any way the right of self-defense. That right is inherent in every sovereign state and is implicit in every treaty. Every nation is free at all times and regardless of treaty provisions to defend its territory from attack or invasion and it alone is competent to decide whether circumstances require recourse to war in self-defense. If it has a good case, the world will applaud and not condemn its action. Express recognition by treaty of this inalien-able right, however, gives rise to the same difficulty encountered in any effort to define aggression. It is the identical question approached from the other side. Inasmuch as no treaty provision can add to the natural right of self-defense, it is not in the interest of peace that a treaty should stipulate a juristic conception of self-defense since it is far too easy for the unscrupulous to mold events to accord with an agreed definition.

(2) *The League Covenant.* The Covenant imposes no affirmative primary obligation to go to war. The obligation, if any, is secondary and attaches only when deliberately accepted by a state. Article 10 of the Covenant has, for example, been interpreted by a resolution sub-mitted to the Fourth Assembly but not formally adopted owing to one adverse vote to mean that "it is for the constitutional authorities of each member to decide, in reference to the obligation of preserving the independence and the integrity of the territory of members, in what degree the member is bound to assure the execution of this obligation by employment of its military forces." There is, in my opinion, no necessary inconsistency between the Covenant and the idea of an

unqualified renunciation of war. The Covenant can, it is true, be construed as authorizing war in certain circumstances but it is an authorization and not a positive requirement.

(*3*) *The treaties of Locarno.* If the parties to the treaties of Locarno are under any positive obligation to go to war, such obligation certainly would not attach until one of the parties has resorted to war in violation of its solemn pledges thereunder. It is therefore obvious that if all the parties to the Locarno treaties become parties of the multilateral antiwar treaty proposed by the United States, there would be a double assurance that the Locarno treaties would not be violated by recourse to arms. In such event it would follow that resort to war by any state in violation of the Locarno treaties would also be a breach of the multilateral antiwar treaty and the other parties to the antiwar treaty would thus as a matter of law be automatically released from their obligations thereunder and free to fulfil their Locarno commitments. The United States is entirely willing that all parties to the Locarno treaties should become parties to its proposed antiwar treaty either through signature in the first instance or by immediate accession to the treaty as soon as it comes into force in the manner provided in Article 3 of the American draft, and it will offer no objection when and if such a suggestion is made.

(*4*) *Treaties of neutrality.* The United States is not informed as to the precise treaties which France has in mind and cannot therefore discuss their provisions. It is not unreasonable to suppose, however, that the relations between France and the states whose neutrality she has guaranteed are sufficiently close and intimate to make it possible for France to persuade such states to adhere seasonably to the antiwar treaty proposed by the United States. If this were done no party to the antiwar treaty could attack the neutralized states without violating the treaty and thereby automatically freeing France and the other powers in respect of the treaty-breaking state from the obligations of the antiwar treaty. If the neutralized states were attacked by a state not a party to the antiwar treaty, the latter treaty would of course have no bearing and France would be as free to act under the treaties guaranteeing neutrality as if she were not a party to the antiwar treaty. It is difficult to perceive, therefore, how treaties guaranteeing neutrality can be regarded as necessarily preventing the conclusion by France or any other power of a multilateral treaty for the renunciation of war.

(*5*) *Relations with a treaty-breaking state.* As I have already pointed out, there can be no question as a matter of law that violation of a multilateral antiwar treaty through resort to war by one party thereto would automatically release the other parties from their obligations to the treaty-breaking state. Any express recognition of this principle of law is wholly unnecessary.

(*6*) *Universality.* From the beginning it has been the hope of the United States that its proposed multilateral antiwar treaty should be world-wide in its application, and appropriate provision therefor was made in the draft submitted to the other governments on April 13. From a practical standpoint it is clearly preferable, however, not to postpone the coming into force of an antiwar treaty until all the nations of the world can agree upon the text of such a treaty and cause it to be ratified. For one reason or another a state so situated as to be no menace to the peace of the world might obstruct agreement or delay ratification in such manner as to render abortive the efforts of all the other powers. It is highly improbable, moreover, that a form of treaty acceptable to the British, French, German, Italian and Japanese Governments, as well as to the United States, would not be equally acceptable to most, if not all, of the other powers of the world. Even were this not the case, however, the coming into force among the above-named six powers of an effective antiwar treaty and their observance thereof would be a practical guaranty against a second world war. This in itself would be a tremendous service to humanity and the United States is not willing to jeopardize the practical success of the proposal which it has made by conditioning the coming into force of the treaty upon prior universal or almost universal acceptance.

The British, German, Italian and Japanese Governments have now replied to my Government's notes of April 13, 1928, and the Governments of the British Dominions and of India have likewise replied to the invitations addressed to them on May 22, 1928, by my Government pursuant to the suggestion conveyed in the note of May 19, 1928, from His Majesty's Government in Great Britain. None of these Governments has expressed any dissent from the above-quoted construction, and none has voiced the least disapproval of the principle underlying the proposal of the United States for the promotion of world peace. Neither has any of the replies received by the Government of the United States suggested any specific modification of the text of the draft treaty proposed by it on April 13, 1928, and my government, for its part, remains convinced that no modification of the text of its proposal for a multilateral treaty for the renunciation of war is necessary to safeguard the legitimate interests of any nation. It believes that the right of self-defense is inherent in every sovereign state and implicit in every treaty. No specific reference to that inalienable attribute of sovereignty is therefore necessary or desirable. It is no less evident that resort to war in violation of the proposed treaty by one of the parties thereto would release the other parties from their obligations under the treaty towards the belligerent state. This principle is well recognized. So far as the Locarno treaties are concerned, my Government has felt from the very first that participation in the antiwar treaty by the powers which signed the Locarno agreements, either through signature in the first instance or thereafter, would meet every practical requirement of the situation, since in such event no state could resort to war in violation of the Locarno treaties without simultaneously violating the antiwar treaty, thus leaving the other parties thereto free, so far as the treaty-breaking state is concerned. As your excellency knows, the Government of the United States has welcomed the idea that all parties to the treaties of Locarno should be among the original signatories of the proposed treaty for the renunciation of war and provision therefor has been made in the draft treaty which I have the honor to transmit herewith. The same procedure would cover the treaties guaranteeing neutrality to which the Government of France has referred. Adherence to the proposed treaty by all parties to these other treaties would completely safeguard their rights since subsequent resort to war by any of them or by any party to the anti-war treaty would violate the latter treaty as well as the neutrality treaty, and thus leave the other parties to the antiwar treaty free, so far as the treaty-breaking state is concerned. My Government would be entirely willing, however, to agree that the parties to such neutrality treaties should be original signatories of the multilateral anti-war treaty, and it has no reason to believe that such an arrangement would meet with any objection on the part of the other Governments now concerned in the present negotiations.

While my Government is satisfied that the draft treaty proposed by it on April 13, 1928, could be properly accepted by the powers of the world without change except for including among the original signa-tories the British Dominions, India, all parties to the treaties of Locarno and, it may be, all parties to the neutrality treaties mentioned by the Government of France, it has no desire to delay or complicate the present negotiations by rigidly adhering to the precise phraseology of that draft, particularly since it appears that by modifying the draft in form though not in substance, the points raised by other Governments can be satisfactorily met and general agreement upon the text of the treaty to be signed be promptly reached. The Government of the United States has therefore decided to submit to the fourteen other Governments now concerned in these negotiations a revised draft of a multilateral treaty for the renunciation of war. The text of this revised draft is identical with that of the draft proposed by the United States on April 13, 1928, except that the preamble now provides that the British Dominions, India, and all parties to the treaties of Locarno are to be included among the powers called upon to sign the treaty in the first instance, and except that the first three paragraphs of the preamble have been changed to read as follows:

Deeply sensible of their solemn duty to promote the welfare of mankind;

Persuaded that the time has come when a frank renunciation of war as an instrument of national policy should be made to the end that the peaceful and friendly relations now existing between their peoples may be perpetuated;

Convinced that all changes in their relations with one another should be sought only by pacific means and be the result of a peaceful and orderly process, and that any signatory power which shall hereafter seek to promote its national interests by resort to war should be denied the benefits furnished by this treaty;

The revised preamble thus gives express recognition to the principle that if a state resorts to war in violation of the treaty, the other contracting parties are released from their obligations under the treaty to that state; it also provides for participation in the treaty by all parties to the treaties of Locarno, thus making it certain that resort to war in violation of the Locarno treaties would also violate the present treaty and release not only the other signatories of the Locarno treaties but also the other signatories to the antiwar treaty from their obligations to the treaty-breaking state. Moreover, as stated above, my Government would be willing to have included among the original signatories the parties to the neutrality treaties referred to by the Government of the French Republic, although it believes that the interests of those states would be adequately safeguarded if, instead of signing in the first instance, they should choose to adhere to the treaty.

In these circumstances I have the honor to transmit herewith for the consideration of your excellency's Government a draft of a multilateral treaty for the renunciation of war containing the changes outlined above. I have been instructed to state in this connection that the Government of the United States is ready to sign at once a treaty in the form herein proposed, and to express the fervent hope that the Government of _____ will be able promptly to indicate its readiness to accept, without qualification or reservation, the form of treaty now suggested by the United States. If the Governments of Australia, Belgium, Canada, Czechoslovakia, France, Germany, Great Britain, India, the Irish Free State, Italy, Japan, New Zealand, Poland, South Africa and the United States can now agree to conclude this antiwar treaty among themselves, my Government is confident that the other nations of the world will, as soon as the treaty comes into force, gladly adhere thereto, and that this simple procedure will bring mankind's age-long aspirations for universal peace nearer to practical fulfilment than ever before in the history of the world.

I have the honor to state in conclusion that the Government of the United States would be pleased to be informed at as early a date as may be convenient whether your excellency's Government is willing to join with the United States and other similarly disposed Governments in signing a definitive treaty for the renunciation of war in the form transmitted herewith.

[Enclosure]

Text of draft treaty

The President of the United States of America, the President of the French Republic, His Majesty the King of the Belgians, the President of the Czechoslovak Republic, His Majesty the King of Great Britain, Ireland and the British Dominions beyond the Seas, Emperor of India, the President of the German Reich, His Majesty the King of Italy, His Majesty the Emperor of Japan, the President of the Republic of Poland;

Deeply sensible of their solemn duty to promote the welfare of mankind;

Persuaded that the time has come when a frank renunciation of war as an instrument of national policy should be made to the end that the peaceful and friendly relations now existing between their peoples may be perpetuated;

Convinced that all changes in their relations with one another should be sought only by pacific means and be the result of a peaceful and orderly process, and that any signatory power which shall hereafter seek to promote its national interests by resort to war should be denied the benefits furnished by this treaty;

Hopeful that, encouraged by their example, all the other nations of the world will join in this humane endeavor and by adhering to the present treaty as soon as it comes into force bring their peoples within the scope of its beneficent provisions, thus uniting the civilized nations of the world in a common renunciation of war as an instrument of their national policy;

Have decided to conclude a treaty and for that purpose have appointed as their respective plenipotentiaries:

The President of the United States of America: _____

The President of the French Republic: _____

His Majesty the King of the Belgians: _____

The President of the Czechoslovak Republic: _____

His Majesty the King of Great Britain, Ireland and the British Dominions beyond the Seas, Emperor of India:

For Great Britain and Northern Ireland and all parts of the British Empire which are not separate members of the League of Nations: _____

For the Dominion of Canada: _____

For the Commonwealth of Australia: _____

For the Dominion of New Zealand: _____

For the Union of South Africa: _____

For the Irish Free State: _____

For India: _____

The President of the German Reich: _____

His Majesty the King of Italy: _____

His Majesty the Emperor of Japan: _____

The President of the Republic of Poland: _____

Who, having communicated to one another their full powers found in good and due form have agreed upon the following articles:

Article 1. The high contracting parties solemnly declare in the names of their respective peoples that they condemn recourse to war for the solution of international controversies, and renounce it as an instrument of national policy in their relations with one another.

Article 2. The high contracting parties agree that the settlement or solution of all disputes or conflicts of whatever nature or of whatever origin they may be, which may arise among them, shall be never sought except by pacific means.

Article 3. The present treaty shall be ratified by the high contracting parties named in the preamble in accordance with their respective constitutional requirements, and shall take effect as between them as soon as all their several instruments of ratification shall have been deposited at _____.

This treaty shall, when it has come into effect as prescribed in the preceding paragraph, remain open as long as may be necessary for adherence by all the other powers of the world. Every instrument evidencing the adherence of a power shall be deposited at _____ and the treaty shall immediately upon such deposit become effective as between the power thus adhering and the other powers parties hereto.

It shall be the duty of the Government of _____ to furnish each Government named in the preamble and every Government subsequently adhering to this treaty with a certified copy of the treaty and of every instrument of ratification or adherence. It shall also be the duty of the Government of _____ telegraphically to notify such Governments immediately upon the deposit with it of each instrument of ratification or adherence.

In faith whereof the respective plenipotentiaries have signed this treaty in the French and English languages, both texts having equal force, and hereunto affix their seals.

Done at _____ the _____ day of _____ in the year of our Lord one thousand nine hundred and twenty _____.

182. The Italo-Vatican Agreement, 1929[1]

[The Pope had always refused to recognize the Law of Papal Guarantees of 1871 because it was a unilateral arrangement, being a simple legislative act of the Italian government, instead of a concordat. A sort of *modus vivendi*, however, was reached, though the Roman question still existed. Steps looking to its settlement were taken in October, 1926, negotiations were begun, and on February 11, 1929, three documents were signed: a treaty of international importance, a concordat concerned only with the relations between the Vatican and the Italian kingdom, and a financial convention. On June 7 ratifications were exchanged, and a papal nuncio was at once appointed to the Quirinal and an Italian ambassador to the Holy See. A little later the Pope left the Vatican for the first time since he had declared himself a prisoner in 1871, and the Roman question was apparently settled.]

---

[1] *Current History*, Vol. XXX, July, 1929, pp. 552-566. Reprinted from the *Current History* Magazine, a periodical published by the New York Times Company.

THE POLITICAL TREATY

Whereas the Holy See and Italy have both recognized the desirability of eliminating every cause of disagreement existing between them by coming to a definite understanding of their mutual relations which shall be in accordance with justice and compatible with the dignity of the two High Contracting Parties and which, by assuring permanently to the Holy See a status of fact and of right that shall guarantee to it absolute independence in the exercise of its mission in the world, allows the said Holy See to acknowledge as settled definitively and irrevocably the "Roman Question" which arose in 1870 with the annexation of Rome to the Kingdom of Italy under the dynasty of the House of Savoy;

And whereas, for the purpose of assuring to the Holy See absolute and visible independence and of guaranteeing to it undisputed sovereignty in the field of international relations also, it has been deemed necessary to establish the City of the Vatican, recognizing, so far as the said City is concerned, complete ownership, exclusive and absolute power and sovereign jurisdiction on the part of the Holy See;

His Holiness, the Sovereign Pontiff, Pius XI, and His Majesty, Victor Emmanual III, King of Italy, have resolved to make a treaty, appointing for this purpose two Plenipotentiaries, namely, on the part of His Holiness, His Eminence, Cardinal Pietro Gasparri, His Secretary of State, and on the part of His Majesty, His Excellency, Signor Cavaliere Benito Mussolini, Prime Minister and Leader of the Government. These Plenipotentiaries, having exchanged their respective credentials, which were found to be duly and properly executed, have agreed to the following articles:

1. Italy recognizes and reaffirms the principle set forth in Article I of the Constitution of the Kingdom of Italy of March 4, 1848, whereby the Roman Catholic and Apostolic Religion is the sole religion of the State.

2. Italy recognizes the sovereignty of the Holy See in the field of international relations as an attribute that pertains to the very nature of the Holy See, in conformity with its traditions and with the demands of its mission in the world.

CREATION OF VATICAN CITY

3. Italy recognizes full possession and exclusive and absolute power and sovereign jurisdiction of the Holy See over the Vatican, as at present constituted, with all its appurtenances and endowments. Thus the Vatican City is established for the special purposes and with the provisions which are laid down in the present Treaty. The confines of

said Vatican City are indicated on a plan which constitutes the first appendix to the present Treaty, of which it forms an integral part.[1]

It is agreed, however, that the Piazza di San Pietro (St. Peter's Square), although forming part of Vatican City, will continue ordinarily to be open to the public and subject to the police powers of the Italian authorities. The jurisdiction of these authorities shall not extend beyond the foot of the steps leading to the Basilica, although the latter continues to serve for public worship. The police, therefore, will refrain from ascending the steps and entering the Basilica unless they are requested by competent authority to intervene.

When the Holy See, in connection with special functions, shall deem it necessary to close St. Peter's Square to the public temporarily, the Italian police, unless requested by the proper authorities to remain, shall withdraw beyond the outer limits of the Bernini colonnade and their prolongation.

4. The sovereignty and exclusive jurisdiction which Italy recognizes on the part of the Holy See with regard to the Vatican City implies that there cannot be any interference whatsoever on the part of the Italian Government, and that within the said City there shall be no other authority than that of the Holy See.

5. For the execution of that which is set forth in the preceding article, before the present Treaty goes into effect, the Italian Government shall see to it that the territory constituting Vatican City is made free from all liens and closed to any and all tenants in the future. The Holy See will provide for closing the approaches by inclosing the open parts, except St. Peter's Square. It is agreed, however, that regarding property therein belonging to religious institutions or organizations, the Holy See will arrange directly to determine its relations with these, the Italian State taking no part in these arrangements.

VATICAN CITY COMMUNICATIONS

6. Italy undertakes to furnish through agreement with interested organizations assurance to the Vatican City of an adequate water supply within the territory. It will also provide for communication with the Italian State Railways by constructing a railroad station within the Vatican City at a location marked on the annexed plan,[2] as well as for the movement of the Vatican's coaches on the Italian railroads. It will provide, moreover, for the linking up, directly with other States, also, of the telegraph, telephone, radio-telegraph, radio-telephone and postal services within the Vatican City. It will, besides, provide for the coördination of other public utilities.

The Italian State will furnish the above at its own expense within one

---

[1] It embraces the territory lying within the area bounded by the Vatican walls, the Via di Porta Angelica, the Piazza di San Pietro, the Via and Piazza della Sagrestia and the Via Teutonica.

[2] That is within the Vatican walls, between Porta Pertusa and Porta Fabbrica (both walled up for many years), near the new building of the Vatican Seminary.

year from the date the present Treaty goes into effect. The Holy See will arrange at its own expense for systematizing the present approaches to the Vatican as well as others which it may be found advisable to open in the future. Agreements will be made between the Holy See and the Italian Government for the circulation in the latter's territory of the vehicles and aircraft of the Vatican City.

7. In territory adjoining the Vatican City the Italian Government pledges itself not to allow the construction of new buildings that shall overlook the said City. Likewise, it will provide for the partial demolition of such buildings as now overlook the Vatican City, specifically those near the Porta Cavalleggeri and along the Via Aurelia and the Viale Vaticano.

In conformity with the regulations of international law, aircraft of any kind are prohibited from flying over Vatican territory. In the Piazza Rusticucci and in the zones adjacent to the colonnade, to which the ex-territoriality mentioned in Article 15 does not extend, any building or street changes in which the Vatican City might be interested shall be made by mutual agreement.

INVIOLABILITY OF THE POPE'S PERSON

8. Italy, considering the person of the Sovereign Pontiff as sacred and inviolable, declares attempts against said person, as well as any incitement to commit such, punishable by the same penalties as attempts against the person of the King or incitement to commit same. Public offenses or insults committed in Italian territory against the person of the Sovereign Pontiff, whether by deed or by spoken or written word, punishable by the same penalties as similar offenses and injuries against the person of the King.

9. In conformity with the provision of international law, all persons having a fixed residence in Vatican City are subject to the sovereignty of the Holy See. Such residence is not lost by the simple fact of temporary domicile elsewhere unless such domicile entails the giving up of one's habitation in Vatican City or is accompanied by other circumstances which make it clear that the individual concerned has abandoned his residence therein.

Ceasing to be subject to the sovereignty of the Holy See, the persons mentioned in the preceding paragraph, when, according to the provisions of Italian law, and independently of the circumstances actually provided for above, they are not to be regarded as enjoying the privileges of citizenship elsewhere, shall in Italy be considered as Italian citizens without further investigation.

The same persons, while subject to the sovereignty of the Holy See, will be subject in Italian territory—even in matters in which personal law must be observed (when these are not regulated by provisions of the Holy See)—to Italian legislation; and in cases where they are believed to be citizens of other countries, they shall be subject to the laws of the State to which they belong.

EXEMPTION FROM MILITARY SERVICE

10. Dignitaries of the Church and persons attached to the Pontifical Court, who will be designated in a list to be agreed upon by the High Contracting Parties, even when they are not citizens of the Vatican, shall always and in every case, so far as Italy is concerned, be exempt from military service, from jury duty and from all services of a personal character. This rule will also be applied to chancery officials declared by the Holy See to be indispensable, who are permanently attached with fixed stipends to the offices of the Holy See and to the tribunals and offices which are mentioned below in Articles 13, 14, 15, and 16, and which are located outside Vatican City. Such functionaries will be named in a second list, to be agreed upon as stipulated above, which will be brought up to date annually by the Holy See.

Ecclesiastics who, in the performance of the duties of their office, are occupied in the execution of the acts of the Holy See shall not be subjected on account of such execution to any hindrance, investigation or molestation on the part of the Italian authorities.

Every foreigner invested with ecclesiastical office in Rome shall enjoy the same personal guarantees as belong to Italian citizens by virtue of the laws of the Kingdom.

11. The central corporate entities of the Catholic Church are exempt from all interference on the part of the Italian State (except for the provisions of Italian law concerning the acquisitions of moral entities) and also from appropriation with regard to real estate.

RIGHTS OF DIPLOMATIC RELATIONS

12. Italy recognizes the right of the Holy See to send and to receive diplomatic representatives according to the general provisions of international law. Envoys of foreign governments to the Holy See will continue to enjoy in the Kingdom of Italy all the privileges and immunities which pertain to diplomatic agents according to international law. Their embassies or legations may still be located in Italian territory, possessing the immunity due to them according to the provisions of international law, even though their governments may not have diplomatic relations with Italy. It is understood that Italy guarantees always and in every case to allow free correspondence from all nations, including belligerents, to the Holy See and *vice versa*, and to permit free access of bishops from all parts of the world to the Apostolic See.

The High Contracting Parties pledge themselves to establish regular diplomatic relations with one another by the accrediting of an Italian Ambassador to the Holy See and of a Papal Nuncio to Italy, who will be dean of the diplomatic corps according to the customary provision sanctioned by the Congress of Vienna with the Act of June 9, 1815.

By reason of the recognized sovereignty, and without prejudice to what is set forth in Article 19 below, the diplomatic representatives of the Holy See and emissaries dispatched in the name of the Sovereign Pontiff enjoy in Italian territory, even in times of war, the same treatment as is due to the diplomatic representatives and secret emissaries of other foreign States according to the provisions of international law.

．　．　．　．　．　．　．

26. The Holy See maintains that with the agreements signed today adequate assurance is guaranteed as far as is necessary for the said Holy See to provide, with due liberty and independence, for the pastoral régime of the Diocese of Rome and of the Catholic Church in Italy and the world. The Holy See declares the "Roman Question" definitively and irrevocably settled and, therefore, eliminated; and recognizes the Kingdom of Italy under the dynasty of the House of Savoy with Rome as the capital of the Italian State.

Italy, in turn, recognizes the State of the Vatican City under the sovereignty of the Supreme Pontiff.

The Law of May 15, 1871, No. 214, is abrogated, as well as any other decree or decision contrary to the present Treaty.

27. The present Treaty will be submitted to the Sovereign Pontiff and to the King of Italy for ratification within four months from the date of signing and will become effective immediately on the exchange of ratification.

Rome, Feb. 11, 1929.

Signed: PIETRO, CARD. GASPARRI
Signed: BENITO MUSSOLINI

THE CONCORDAT

Whereas, from the very beginning of the negotiations between the Holy See and Italy for the settlement of the "Roman Question," the Holy See itself proposed that the Treaty dealing with this question should be accompanied by a Concordat planned to regulate the status of Religion and of the Church in Italy, which Concordat should form a necessary complement of the Treaty; and

Whereas, the Treaty for the settlement of the "Roman Question" has been concluded and signed today;

His Holiness, the Sovereign Pontiff, Pius XI, and His Majesty, Victor Emmanuel III, King of Italy, have agreed to make a Concordat and for this purpose have appointed the same Plenipotentiaries as were named for the drawing up of the Treaty, namely, for His Holiness, His Eminence, Cardinal Pietro Gasparri, His Secretary of State, and for His Majesty, His Excellency, Signor Cavaliere Mussolini, Prime

Minister and Leader of the Government. These Plenipotentiaries, having exchanged their respective credentials, which were found to be duly and properly executed, have agreed to the following articles:

1. Italy, according to the terms of Article 1 of the Treaty, guarantees to the Catholic Church free exercise of spiritual power, free and public exercise of worship, as well as jurisdiction in ecclesiastical matters, in conformity with the provisions of the present Concordat; and, where it shall be necessary for the carrying out of their spiritual ministry, grants to ecclesiastics protection on the part of its authorities.

In consideration of the sacred character of the Eternal City, episcopal see of the Sovereign Pontiff, centre of the Catholic world, and goal of pilgrimages, the Italian Government will take precautions to prevent the occurrence in Rome of everything that might be contrary to this sacred character.

2. The Holy See communicates and corresponds freely with the Bishops, the clergy and the whole Catholic world, without any interference on the part of the Italian Government. Bishops, likewise, in everything that concerns their pastoral office, communicate and correspond freely with their clergy and with all the Faithful.

Both the Holy See and the Bishops may freely publish and post either within, or on the external portals of, buildings that are set aside for worship and offices used for the business of their ministry such instructions, ordinances, pastoral letters, diocesan bulletins and other notices concerning the spiritual direction of the Faithful as they may see fit to issue within the province of their competency. Such publications and notices and, in general, all decrees and documents dealing with the spiritual direction of the Faithful are exempt from revenue tax.

So far as the Holy See is concerned, the above-mentioned publications may be issued in any language. Those emanating from the Bishops are to be printed in Italian or Latin; but alongside the Italian text the ecclesiastical authorities may add a translation in other languages.

The ecclesiastical authorities may, without any interference on the part of the civil authorities, take up collections both within the churches and at the portals of the same, as well as in the buildings which belong to them.

MILITARY SERVICE OF PRIESTS

3. Students in theology, those preparing for the priesthood who are in the last two years of study preliminary to theology and novices in religious institutes may, on their own request, put off from year to year, up to the age of 26, the fulfillment of the obligations of military service.

Ordained clerics *in sacris* and religious who have taken their vows are exempt from military service except in case of general mobilization. In such a case the priests join the armed forces of the State but retain their clerical garb in order that they may exercise their sacred ministry among the troops under the ecclesiastical jurisdiction of the Military Ordinary according to the provisions of Article 14. The other clerics or religious will be assigned preferably to the sanitary branch of the service.

However, even when general mobilization is ordered, priests who are entrusted with the care of souls are exempt from the obligation of answering to the call. Bishops, parish priests, assistant parish priests or coadjutors, vicars and permanent rectors of churches which are open to public worship are included in this category.

4. Ecclesiastics and religious are exempt from jury duty.

5. No ecclesiastic may be employed or remain in the employment or service of the Italian State or of any of the public departments subordinate to the same without the express permission of his diocesan Bishop. The revocation of this permission deprives the ecclesiastic of power to continue exercising the duty or office assumed.

In any case apostate priests or those who have incurred censure cannot be employed or retained in a teaching post, or in an office or an employment in which they are brought into immediate contact with the public.

6. Stipends and other emoluments enjoyed by ecclesiastics by reason of their office are exempt from charges and liens in the same way as the stipends and salaries of the employes of the State.

7. Ecclesiastics cannot be requested by magistrates or other authorities to give information regarding persons or matters which has come to their knowledge through the exercise of their sacred ministry.

PUNISHMENT OF ECCLESIASTICS

8. When it happens that an ecclesiastic or a religious is brought before a penal magistrate because of some crime the State's Attorney must immediately inform the Ordinary of the diocese in whose territory he exercises jurisdiction and he must take pains to transmit officially to him the preliminary decision in the case and, if issued, the final sentence both of the court of first instance and of the court of appeal.

In case of arrest, the ecclesiastic or religious is to be treated with the respect due to his calling and to his clerical status. In case an ecclesiastic or religious is convicted he is to serve his sentence, if possible, in quarters separate from those intended for laymen unless the Ordinary to whose jurisdiction he belongs has unfrocked the offender.

. . . .

SELECTION OF BISHOPS

19. The selection of Archbishops and Bishops pertains to the Holy See. Before proceeding to the nomination of an Archbishop, a Bishop or a Coadjutor with the right of succession, the Holy See will com-

municate the name of the person chosen to the Italian Government in order to be sure that the latter has no objection from a political standpoint against the nomination. The formalities required will be carried out with all possible care and with every precaution so that secrecy may be maintained with regard to the person selected until his nomination is formally announced.

20. Bishops before taking possession of their dioceses shall take an oath of loyalty at the hands of the Head of the State according to the following formula:

"Before God and on the Holy Gospels I swear and promise, as becomes a Bishop, loyalty to the Italian State. I swear and promise to respect, and to make my clergy respect, the King and the Government established according to the constitutional laws of the State. I swear and promise, moreover, that I shall not participate in any agreement or take part in any discussion that might be injurious to the Italian State or detrimental to public order and that I shall not permit my clergy to take part in such. Being mindful of the welfare and of the interests of the Italian State, I shall endeavor to ward off any danger that may threaten it."

21. The awarding of ecclesiastical benefices pertains to ecclesiastical authority. The competent ecclesiastical authority will communicate confidently [sic] to the Italian Government the names of those who are invested with parochial benefices, and the investiture can have no effect until after thirty days from the date of the said communication. During this period, the Italian Government, if grave reasons against the appointment exist, may make these reasons known confidentially to ecclesiastical authority, and this authority, if no agreement can be reached, shall refer the case to the Holy See.

Wherever serious reasons arise which might render undesirable the continuance of an ecclesiastic in a particular parochial benefice, the Italian Government will communicate these reasons to the Ordinary who, after an understanding with the Government, shall take appropriate measures within three months. In case of disagreement between the Ordinary and the Government, the Holy See will entrust the settlement of the difficulty to two ecclesiastics of its own choice who, after coming to an agreement with two delegates of the Italian Government, will render a decision that shall be final.

ITALIAN BENEFICES LIMITED TO ITALIAN CITIZENS

22. Ecclesiastics who are not Italian citizens cannot be appointed to Italian benefices. Moreover, the Bishops of the dioceses and the rectors of parishes must speak Italian. If necessary, they must have assistants who, in addition to Italian, also understand and speak the local dialect in order that they may give religious assistance to the faithful in their own language according to the rules of the Church.

.   .   .   .

MARRIAGE LAWS

34. The Italian State, desirous of restoring to the institution of marriage, which is the foundation of the family, the dignity that belongs to it according to the Catholic traditions of its people, recognizes the civil effects of the sacrament of matrimony as administered according to the regulations of the Canon Law. The banns of marriage as defined above will be published both in the parish church and in the city or town hall. Immediately after the celebration of a marriage, the parish priest will explain to the married couple the civil effects of the marriage, reading the articles of the Civil Code which have to do with the rights and duties of husbands and wives, and will make a record of the ceremony. Within five days he will send a complete copy of this record to the municipal building in order that it may be transcribed in the register of the civil authorities.

Questions having to do with the nullification of marriage and with the dispensation of a marriage *ratum et non consummatum* are reserved to the jurisdiction of ecclesiastical tribunals and courts. The findings and relative opinions when they have become final, will be conveyed to the Supreme Tribunal of the Segnatura, which will decide whether the regulations of the Canon Law with regard to the competency of the judge, the summons, and the legitimate representation or contumacy of the parties have been observed. These findings and final opinions, together with the decrees of the Supreme Tribunal of the Segnatura relating thereto, will be transmitted to the Civil Court of Appeal having local jurisdiction, which court, by means of an order issued in council, will make the decrees effective with regard to the civil effects and will give orders to have them recorded in the civil register alongside the record of the marriage.

As regards cases of personal separation, the Holy See is willing that the same shall be judged by the civil judicial authority.

35. For the schools of secondary education maintained by ecclesiastical or religious organizations the policy of the state examinations remains in force, the candidates from these schools taking the examinations on exactly the same conditions as are prescribed for the candidates from schools maintained by the institutions of the Government.

RELIGIOUS TEACHING IN THE SCHOOLS

36. Italy considers the teaching of Christian doctrine, according to the form handed down by Catholic tradition, as the foundation and capstone of public education. Therefore, Italy agrees that the religious instruction now given in the public elementary schools shall be further developed in the secondary schools according to a program to be agreed upon by the Holy See and the State. This instruction is to be given by teachers and professors who are priests or religious approved by eccle-

siastical authority, and who will be aided by lay teachers and professors holding for this purpose proper certificates of fitness and capacity, these certificates to be issued by the diocesan Bishop. Revocation of the certificate by the Bishop immediately deprives the individual of the right to teach. No texts will be adopted for this religious instruction in the public schools except such as are approved by ecclesiastical authority.

37. The Directors of State associations for physical education, for pre-military instruction, as well as the directors of the Avanguardisti and the Ballila, in order to facilitate the religious instruction and care of the youth entrusted to their charge, will so arrange their programs that they will not interfere with the young people's fulfillment of their religious duties on Sundays and holy days of obligation. The officials of the public schools will make similar provisions in the matter of arranging the classes to be held on holy days.

. . . .

44. If, in the future, any difficulty should arise with regard to the interpretation of the present Concordat, the Holy See and Italy will proceed with mutual understanding to an amicable solution.

45. The present Concordat will be effective upon the exchange of ratifications simultaneously with the Treaty made by the two High Contracting Parties by which the "Roman Question" is eliminated.

As soon as the present Concordat goes into effect the provisions of the obsolete Concordats of the ex-Italian States will cease to be applicable in Italy. The Austrian laws, as well as the actually existing laws, regulations, ordinances and decrees of the Italian State which are contrary to the provisions of the present Concordat, are understood to be abrogated when said Concordat goes into effect.

In order that the present Concordat may be put into effect without delay, a commission made up of individuals chosen by the two High Contracting Parties will be appointed immediately after the Concordat is signed.

Rome, Feb. 11, 1929.

Signed: PIETRO CARD. GASPARRI
Signed: BENITO MUSSOLINI

183. SUMMARY OF THE "YOUNG PLAN" OF REPARATIONS TO BE MADE BY GERMANY. 1929[1]

[The Dawes Committee did not set a figure which would represent the total of the reparation payments Germany would be asked to make. By 1928 at least three things became apparent: that such a figure must be set, that the schedules of 1924 (see doc. no. 173) needed adjustment, and that there must be set up some international machinery to transfer

---

[1] *Federal Reserve Bulletin*, July, 1929, pp. 458-464. Reprinted with the permission of the Federal Reserve Board.

payments from Germany to the allied nations. In September, 1928, the six nations interested appointed a new commission of experts to study the problem of reparation payments. As in 1924, an American was made chairman, this time Owen D. Young. The new plan was adopted on June 7, 1929.]

.   .   .   .

Creation of committee and terms of reference.—The committee of experts was appointed in accordance with the decision of the Belgian, British, French, German, Italian, and Japanese Governments to entrust to independent experts the task of drawing up proposals for a complete and final settlement of the reparations problem. The Belgian, British, French, Italian, and Japanese experts were appointed by the Reparation Commission upon the nomination of their respective Governments; the German experts were appointed by the German Government, and the experts who were citizens of the United States were appointed by the Reparation Commission conjointly with the German Government. Six members of the present committee, including the chairman, had been members of the Dawes committee of 1924, and several others had been associated with the practical working of the Dawes plan. An important difference between the present committee of experts and the Dawes committee is that representatives of Germany were members of the present committee, whereas their status with reference to the Dawes committee was that of witnesses. Mr. Owen D. Young, one of the American members of the committee, was elected chairman. The first regular meeting of the committee was held in Paris on February 11, and it was in practically continuous session over a period of 17 weeks after that date.

The terms of reference of the committee of experts were as follows:

The Belgian, British, French, German, Italian, and Japanese Governments, in pursuance of the decision reached at Geneva on September 16, 1928, whereby it was agreed to set up a committee of independent financial experts, hereby entrust to the committee the task of drawing up proposals for a complete and final settlement of the reparation problem.

These proposals shall include a settlement of the obligations resulting from the existing treaties and agreements between Germany and the creditor powers. The committee shall address its report to the Governments which took part in the Geneva decision and also to the Reparation Commission.

These terms of reference giving broad power to propose a complete and final settlement of the reparation problem may be contrasted with the terms in which the Dawes committee of 1924 was invited by the Reparation Commission. That committee was asked to "consider the means of balancing the German budget and the measures to be taken to stabilize German currency."

The report of the committee, having received the unanimous approval of the experts, must now be submitted to the respective Governments for their approval. Since the United States is not a party to the proposed settlement, the report as a whole does not require the approval of the American Government, which must, however, approve the proposed schedule of payments to this country. Until the report shall have been approved by the Governments concerned, the arrangements under which reparations have been paid since September 1, 1924, continue in effect. The proposal contemplates that the proposed plan, if ratified in time, should go into effect on September 1, 1929, at the close of the fifth year under the Dawes plan and the first year under the standard annuity.

Quotations from 1924 report of experts.—At the outset the report of the committee quotes and adopts from the Dawes report the following statement of point of view and method of procedure:

We have approached our task as business men anxious to obtain effective results. We have been concerned with the technical and not the political aspects of the problem presented to us. We have recognized, indeed, that political considerations necessarily set certain limits within which a solution must be found if it is to have any chance of acceptance. To this extent, and to this extent only, we have borne them in mind.

The report ends also with a quotation from the Dawes report, as follows:

We regard our report as an indivisible whole. It is not possible, in our opinion, to achieve any success by selecting certain of our recommendations for adoption and rejecting the others, and we would desire to accept no responsibility for the results of such a procedure, nor for undue delay in giving execution to our plan.

Schedule of payments.—In making out a schedule of annual payments, the committee adopted the following three principles: (1) A division of the annuity into an unconditional part and a postponable part; (2) the necessity for continuing deliveries in kind for a few years; and (3) the arrangement of suitable conditions for the postponable part in times of exceptional difficulty.

The unconditional part of the annuity consists of 660,000,000 reichsmarks ($157,212,000) payable in foreign currencies in equal monthly installments without any right of postponement of any kind. The remainder of the annual payments, also payable in foreign currencies, is subject to certain postponements of transfer and of payment under prescribed conditions. The committee states, however, that "the total amount of the annuity proposed . . . is one which they have every reason to believe can in fact be both paid and transferred by Germany."

Under the proposed plan the maximum amount of the annuities and the maximum period during which they are to run are fixed. In the first full annuity year (April 1, 1930-March 31, 1931) the annuity proposed is 1,707,900,000 reichsmarks ($406,821,780). In the following year the annuity is slightly less; but thereafter it rises practically without interruption to a maximum of 2,428,800,000 reichsmarks ($578,540,160) in 1965-66. Average payments to the creditor powers during the first 37 years are to be 1,988,800,000 reichsmarks ($473,-732,160), to which are to be added installments on the international loan floated after the adoption of the Dawes plan, bringing the total average up to 2,050,600,000 reichsmarks ($488,452,920) per year. Payments for the following 22 years are then sharply reduced to approximately the amount necessary to cover "outpayments" of the creditor countries as set forth in the special memorandum on outpayments which accompanies the report. The outpayments rise from 965,-100,000 reichsmarks ($229,886,820) in 1930-31 to 1,573,700,000 reichsmarks ($374,855,340) in 1965-66; attain a maximum of 1,703,-300,000 reichsmarks ($405,726,060) in 1983-84; and drop to approximately 900,000,000 reichsmarks ($214,380,000) annually in the last three years.

Concurrently with the execution of the plan proposed by the experts, Germany, France, Great Britain, Italy, and Belgium executed an agreement, which is not part of the plan itself nor an annex to it, and which was not signed by the American experts, who considered it a matter for these powers alone to deal with. Under the terms of this agreement during the first 37 years two-thirds of "any relief which any creditor power may effectively receive in respect of its net outward payments on account of war debts" shall be passed on to Germany in the form of a reduction of annuity payments, and one-third shall accrue to the creditor power. So long, however, as any German liability remains on the final 22 payments, the creditor power concerned will receive only one-fourth of the net relief, and the difference between one-fourth and one-third will be paid in to the Bank for International Settlements to accumulate toward meeting the final 22 payments. During the last 22 years the entire relief from outpayments shall be applied to the reduction of Germany's liabilities. In addition, certain funds accumulated by the Bank for International Settlements, including the funds mentioned above, are to be utilized to assist Germany in meeting the final 22 annuities.

It is apparent, therefore, that in the new plan the maximum amounts and maximum time period of the German payments are determined, while the actual amounts to be paid are subject to reduction.

The payments under the present proposal may be compared with those under the Dawes plan. Under the Dawes plan Germany is obliged to pay a standard annuity of 2,500,000,000 gold marks ($595,000,-000). No limit is set to the number of years the annuity is to run. Furthermore, there is the possibility that a supplementary annuity may be required; for beginning with the annuity year 1929-30 Germany is obligated under the Dawes plan to pay an additional percentage equivalent to the percentage by which the "prosperity index" for the last calendar year exceeds the base period 1927-1929. There is also a provision permitting an alteration of both the standard and the supplementary annuities in case of a 10 percent change in the general purchasing power of gold as compared with 1928. Thus under the Dawes plan there is no definite limit fixed either for the number of years that the annuity is to be paid or for the amount of the annual payments.

Distribution of annuities.—The distribution of the annuities among the creditor powers is set forth in Annex VII. During the period 1929-1965 France will receive an annual average amount of 1,046,500,000 reichsmarks ($249,276,300); the British Empire, 409,000,000 reichsmarks ($97,423,800); Italy, 213,700,000 reichsmarks ($50,903,340); Belgium, 115,500,000 reichsmarks ($27,512,100); the United States, 66,100,000 reichsmarks ($15,745,020); and other countries 138,-000,000 reichsmarks ($32,871,600). The distribution of payments after 1965 will be approximately in the same proportion.

The experts of the principal creditor Governments have agreed that there shall be assigned to France out of the unconditional annuity 500,000,000 reichsmarks ($119,100,000) annually, in order to allow her to mobilize a substantial part of her share in the total annuity. Out of the remainder of the unconditional annuity, after allowing for the service of the Dawes loan, 42,000,000 reichsmarks ($10,004,400) will be apportioned to Italy; and the balance will be distributed among the other powers. In view of the large portion assigned to France, and in order to protect the other powers in case transfer of their shares is postponed, machinery is proposed by which France will guarantee to the other powers the shares they would have received had the non-postponable annuity been distributed in the same proportions as the total annuity.[1]

Sources of payments.—The payments are to be derived from two sources—the German Railway Company and the general budget. The bonds of the railway company, amounting to 11,000,000,000 reichsmarks ($2,620,200,000) imposed under the Dawes plan, are to be canceled according to the experts' proposal, and the railway is to assume instead the obligation to pay a 660,000,000 reichsmarks ($157,-212,000) annual tax, equivalent to the service payable on the railway bonds now outstanding. The tax on the railways is to cease after three years.

Outside of 660,000,000 reichsmarks to be raised from the railroads, the payments are to come directly and entirely out of the German budget. The 5,000,000,000 reichsmarks ($1,191,000,000) of bonds imposed upon industry and agriculture are to be canceled. The contribution from the budget is to increase by an average amount of 24,000,000 reichsmarks ($5,716,800) a year.

---

[1] See revisions made at The Hague, page 1028.

Removal of controls.—The committee proposes to remove most of the foreign controls now operative in Germany. Under the Dawes plan there were created, in addition to the Agent General, various commissioners and trustees—for example, commissioners of the Reichsbank, German railways, and controlled revenues, and trustees for the German railway bonds and the industrial debentures. For the most part these offices were rendered necessary by reason of the number of sources from which reparations payments were to be drawn. The committee now proposes to abolish these offices and to place full responsibility upon the German Government for meeting the reparation payments as due. As regards the revenues assigned under the Dawes plan to meet the budget payment, the committee's language is as follows:

"We have also considered the position with regard to the assigned revenues and, having regard to the fact that these revenues are pledged as collateral security for the service of the German external loan of 1924, we feel it is impossible to recommend the release thereof.

"Nevertheless, we are of the opinion that it would be suitable for the German Government to discuss with the trustees for the bond holders of that loan the possibility of simplifying, as far as possible, the existing machinery and that the creditor Governments for their part should accept a similar arrangement.

"Apart from these special questions the committee desires to record its view that the basis of security for the payment of annuities is the solemn undertaking of the German Government, to which no further guarantee can add anything whatsoever."

Deliveries in kind.—The plan provides for a temporary continuance of deliveries in kind in decreasing amounts, chiefly for the purpose of maintaining a transitional period, and to avoid any possible shock to existing economic conditions in Germany. Deliveries in kind are to continue for a period of 10 years and are to absorb each year a decreasing amount of the postponable portion of the annuity. During the first year deliveries in kind are to amount to about 750,000,000 reichsmarks ($178,650,000) and this amount is to diminish by 50,000,000 until the tenth year, when it is to be 300,000,000 reichsmarks ($71,460,-000). These deliveries in kind are to be adapted to the actual annuities of the new plan without increasing the total.[1]

Conditions of postponement.—In order to protect Germany against the danger of having the annual payments disorganize the German currency, there is a provision under which transfers, and even payments, may be postponed. The German Government is given the right to bring about a postponement of transfers by giving at least 90 days' previous notice, the postponement to be for a maximum period of two years and not to be applicable to the unconditional part of the annuity. In case Germany claims a postponement in any one year, the transfers falling due in any second year can be postponed by no more than one year. At a time when postponement of transfers is in effect,

---

[1] See revisions made at The Hague, page 1028.

but not until one year after it has become effective, the German Government has the right to postpone payment for one year of 50 per cent any sum the transfer of which is then susceptible of postponement. This percentage may be increased upon the recommendation of the advisory committee provided for in the experts' plan. Funds of which the transfer has been postponed shall be utilized in a manner agreed upon between the Reichsbank and the Bank for International Settlements. Special arrangements about additional deliveries in kind may be made to supplement payments in any year when a portion of the annuity is postponed. Transfers or payments which have been postponed and which have not been invested or utilized for deliveries in kind shall bear interest at $5\frac{1}{2}$ percent or at a rate 1 percent above the prevailing discount rate at the Reichsbank, whichever is lower.

Under the Dawes plan the annuities are payable in gold marks, and it is the duty of a transfer committee acting under the Agent General for Reparations to transfer the marks into foreign currencies "without threatening the stability of the German currency." If necessary, transfers by the committee may be postponed. Now that the German Government is to be made responsible for effecting the transfers, it is given a similar right to postpone. But in case this right is exercised, payment of the annuities must still be made in marks in Germany, except to the extent noted above, and the liability of the German Government is not extinguished until the transfer into foreign currencies has finally been effected.

Advisory committee.—On the declaration of any postponement the Bank for International Settlements shall convene a special advisory committee. This committee shall make full investigation of Germany's position in regard to her obligations under the plan and, after having satisfied itself that the German authorities have used every effort in their power to fulfill their obligations, the committee shall recommend to the Governments and the bank what in their opinion are the measures that should be taken with reference to the application of the present plan. The committee shall act in a purely consultative capacity, shall play no part in respect to the unconditional annuity, and shall consist of seven ordinary and four coöpted members. The seven regular members shall be the governors of the six central banks and of a Federal Reserve bank of the United States or some other agreed American financial institution. These members shall, when they so desire, elect four more members, which are to be the coöpted members.

Convertibility and content of the reichsmark.—The fact that the annuities are payable in foreign currencies but are defined in reichsmarks gave rise during the deliberations of the committee to a question as to the interpretation to be attached to the word "reichsmark." Under section 31 of the bank law of August 30, 1924, the Reichsbank is obligated to redeem its notes in gold or gold exchange, thereby assuring the stable value of the reichsmark. But under section 52 of the same law the coming into force of section 31 requires concurrent resolutions of the Reichsbank managing board and of the general council. These concurrent resolutions have not yet been made, but the president of the Reichsbank, a representative of Germany on the committee, has undertaken in a letter that is incorporated in the report to introduce the necessary resolutions. To avoid possible misunderstanding a statement is inserted in the plan to the effect that "the German Government undertakes for the purpose of the present provisions, as well as for the general purposes of the plan, that the reichsmark shall have and shall retain its convertibility into gold or devisen as contemplated in section 31 of the present Reichsbank law and that for these purposes the reichsmark shall have and shall retain a mint parity of 1/2790 kilograms of fine gold as defined in the German coinage law of August 30, 1924."

Provision for bond issues.—Upon that portion of the annuities which is not postponable and which is not required for service of the Dawes loan, the German Government may at any time be required by the Bank for International Settlements to create issuable bonds. The Bank for International Settlements is under obligation to make this demand upon the request of the creditor Governments only if it considers such a course opportune. If, however, a creditor Government is desirous of undertaking internal issues of German bonds, in connection with conversion operations, the bank is obliged to accede to its request. Such bonds, however, are to be quoted only on the market of the country for which they were issued. Bonds representing the postponable portion of the annuities can be created only with the consent of the German Government.

Bank for International Settlements.—As the proposed plan does away with the office of the Agent General for Reparation Payments, and with the Reparation Commission, so far as Germany is concerned, it became necessary to devise some plan for handling reparation payments and deliveries in kind, and for this purpose the plan proposes the organization of the Bank for International Settlements, which will have two sets of functions; its primary and compulsory function will be to receive and disburse reparation payments, effect transfers in certain contingencies, and handle deliveries in kind as long as they are made; its secondary and permissive function will authorize it to act as a bank for other central banks. At the outset the bank will have a capital equivalent to $100,000,000, of which $25,000,000 will be paid up. Shares will be issued in equal amounts to the seven countries to which members of the experts' committee belong—that is, Belgium, France, Germany, Great Britain, Italy, Japan, and the United States; and the percentage of the total shares issued in these countries shall never fall below 55. The shares will carry no voting rights; but voting rights corresponding to the number of shares originally issued in each country will be exercised by the central bank of that country. In section 12 of Annex 1 the term "central bank," as used in the report is defined and certain alternatives are indicated:

"If in any country there is more than one bank of issue, the term 'central bank' as used in this outline shall be interpreted to mean the bank of issue situated and operating in the principal financial market of that country.

"If in the process of organizing the bank or in the performance of its functions after establishment it is found that the central bank of any country or its governor is unable to act officially or unofficially in any or all of the capacities provided for in this outline, or refrains from so acting, alternative arrangements not inconsistent with the laws of that country shall be made.

"In particular, the governors of the central banks of the countries whose nationals are members of the present committee, or as many of them as are qualified to act, may invite to become members of the board of directors of the bank two nationals of any country, the central bank of which is eligible under this outline to take part in forming the board of the bank but does not do so. The two nationals of that country, upon acceptance of the invitation, shall be qualified to act in the full capacity of directors of the bank as provided in this outline.

"Further, the directors of the bank shall be authorized to appoint, in lieu of any central bank not exercising any or all of the functions, authorities, or privileges which this outline provides that central banks may or shall exercise, any bank or banking house of widely recognized standing and of the same nationality.

"Such bank or banking house, upon appointment and acceptance, shall be entitled to act in the place of the central bank in any or all capacities appropriate to central banks under this outline, provided only that such action is not inconsistent with the laws of the country in question."

Organization committee of bank.—The plan provides for an organization committee to put the bank in operation. This committee is to be appointed by the governors of the central banks of the seven countries represented at the conference, each governor to appoint two members. In case any governor fails to appoint, the remaining governors can select two of his nationals as members of the organization committee.

Directorate.—The entire administrative control of the bank is vested in the board of directors, which in the first instance is composed of the governors of the central banks of the seven countries mentioned above and their appointees to the number of seven. During the period of the German annuities the governor of the Bank of France and the president of the Reichsbank may each appoint one additional director of his own nationality representative of industry or commerce. Nine remaining directors are to be elected by the original group from a list furnished by governors of the central banks of each of the other countries participating in the share ownership of the bank. "The functions of a director," the report says, "are incompatible with those involving national political responsibilities."

Power to receive deposits.—The bank will have authority to receive deposits. This power is limited, by the condition that the "deposits must be of a nature consistent with the bank's functions with respect to the facilitation of international settlements or in connection with the German annuities." The board of directors or the executive committee shall have the right to consider applications to open deposit accounts, which may include a variety of classes: (1) Deposits on annuity account; (2) deposits from central banks; (3) deposits on clearing account; (4) deposits originating in connection with the German annuities; (5) deposits in connection with the guarantee fund and relative to the mobilization of the unconditional annuity; (6) special deposits of the German Government.

The bank shall have the right to pay interest on deposits that are not susceptible of withdrawal until at least one month from the time of deposit. The rate of interest shall be determined by the board of directors or by the executive committee.

Reserve requirements.—Definite reserve requirements are placed against deposits. Against clearing accounts, which constitute in effect a gold settlement fund representing gold delivered by central banks or earmarked by them for account of the Bank for International Settlements, the whole amount of the gold so deposited must be held. Against deposits payable in 15 days or less a minimum reserve of 40 per cent must be held in gold or in foreign exchange on gold standard or gold exchange standard countries. Against deposits of longer maturity than 15 days a reserve of 25 per cent in gold or foreign exchange must be held.

Powers of the bank.—The bank has the power (1) to buy and sell gold, earmark gold, and make advances on gold; (2) to buy and sell bills of exchange and other obligations of prime liquidity; (3) to open and maintain deposit accounts with central banks; (4) to rediscount for central banks bills taken from their portfolios, to make loans to them on security of such bills, or to make advances to them against the pledge of other securities; (5) to buy and to sell intermediate or long-term securities up to the amount of its capital and reserve funds; (6) to invest in Germany reichsmark funds standing to the credit of the bank at the Reichsbank, which are not transferable, owing to a declaration of transfer postponement; against funds so invested the bank has authority to issue counter obligations and to sell them in non-German markets and to distribute the proceeds of such sales in the same way as in the case of normal transfers; (7) to issue its own obligations at long or short term, secured or unsecured, for the purpose of relending to any central bank—in each case upon the specific decision of the board of directors by two-thirds vote. The injunction is laid down, however, that "the investment powers of the bank shall never be used in such a way as to exercise a predominant influence over business interests in any country"; and the bank is permitted to conduct operations in any country only with the consent of the central bank of that country, and consistently with the policy of such bank.

Distribution of profits.—With regard to the annuity payments, not only will the bank carry out all the necessary operations involved in administering them as trustee, but to some extent its profits will be employed in assisting the German Government to cover the annuities for the last 22 years. How important this assistance becomes will depend upon the volume of profits remaining after prior claims have been met. At the outset the bank is expected to pay a 6 per cent dividend on paid-up share capital and to make heavy contributions to reserves. Thereafter the dividend will gradually be increased to 12 per cent, if earnings permit, and the contributions to reserves will be diminished. Of the profits remaining after the payment of dividends and the transfers to reserves, 75 per cent will be distributed "to Governments or central banks or creditor countries or of Germany which maintain time deposits at the bank withdrawable in not less than five years from the time of deposit and, after four years, on not less than one year's notice." The other 25 per cent is to go to the German Government alone, to aid it in paying the last 22 annuities, providing it elects to make a long-term deposit of the kind just described and amounting to 400,000,000 reichsmarks ($95,280,000). If the deposit is smaller, Germany's share in the profits will be proportionately smaller. Aside from sharing in profits, the deposit is to carry compound interest at the maximum current rate paid by the bank on time deposits. If the fund comes to exceed the amount required to pay the last 22 annuities the balance is to be distributed among the creditor Governments in proportion to their outpayments during the period. The provisions as to the distribution of profits do not release the German Government from its absolute liability to pay the prescribed annuities, whether any profits exist or not.

Broad view of bank's functions.—That the committee does not regard the bank solely as a factor in facilitating the payment of reparations is indicated by the following statement:

"It will be seen that the essential reparation functions of the bank were such as to form a solid reason for its existence; but the committee were led inevitably to add to those reasons the auxiliary, but none the less material, advantages that it might have in the general position of present international finance. . . . The character of the annuities and the magnitude of the payments to be transferred over the exchanges provide at once the opportunity and the need for supplementing with additional facilities the existing machinery for carrying on international settlements and, within limitations, of the sound use of credit to contribute to the stability of international finance and the growth of world trade. . . . Especially it is to be hoped that it will become an increasingly close and valuable link in the coöperation of central banking institutions generally—a coöperation essential to the continuing stability of the world's credit structure."

Complete settlement recommended.—In connection with the adoption of the proposed plan, the committee urges that there shall be a general liquidation of the other financial questions arising out of the war and the subsequent treaty of peace within one year from the coming into force of the plan. It recommends that this liquidation take place in a broad spirit of mutual concession, with the general object of confining payments to those outlined in the plan.

Belgian marks.—An annex to the plan provides for machinery of a separate adjustment between Germany and Belgium in connection with the German marks issued in Belgium at the time of German occupation, which are now held by the National Bank of Belgium. The experts "recognize that the new plan can not become operative until the Belgian and German Governments have come to an internationally binding agreement on the mark claim."

Organization committee.—In addition to the organization committee for the Bank for International Settlements, which has already been mentioned, the experts' report provides for other committees to put the other parts of the plan into effect. Each of these other committees is to consist of the same number of representatives of the creditors and of the debtors, with a neutral chairman to be called in case of disagreement. The committees are to deal respectively, with the adaptation of the German loan set up under the Dawes plan, with the handling of the securities assigned to the Dawes plan, with the adaptation of the German banking law, and with the adaptation of the German railway law. When the Governments have approved the plan, it is contemplated that a special committee be organized to do the administrative work for setting up the organization provided for by the plan and for handing over to it the functions of existing organizations. The task of transferring the functions of the existing organizations to the Bank for International Settlements is to be conferred upon a small special committee composed of two members of the organization committee of the Bank for International Settlements, as well as of representatives of the German Government, the Agent General, and the Reparation Commission, an equitable representation being assured to the powers represented on the present committee.

Additional Agreements Relative to the Experts' Plan (Young Plan) made at The Hague, August 6-31, 1929[1]

The powers represented at The Hague were: Germany, Belgium, Great Britain, Canada, Australia, South Africa, New Zealand, India, France, Greece, Italy, Japan, Poland, Roumania, the Kingdom of the

---
[1] Summarized from *Federal Reserve Bulletin*, Dec. 1929, pp. 792-796.

Serbs, Croats and Slovenes, Czechoslovakia, and the United States (through observers). The Prime Minister of Belgium acted as president of the conference. The revisions cited below were made with a view to satisfying the British delegate, Mr. Snowden, who objected to the distribution of annuities under the proposed Young Plan.

1. The balance of unconditional annuities, it was agreed, should be distributed as follows:

The British Empire	55,000,000 reichsmarks
Japan	6,600,000
Serbs, Croats, Slovenes	6,000,000
Portugal	2,400,000

2. The Belgian and French Governments guarantee without reserve to pay to Great Britain in addition to the annuities allocated to her by the experts' report 19,800,000 reichsmarks for 37 years as from 1929. France and Belgium would agree between themselves as to the source of this sum. Italy guaranteed 9,000,000 reichsmarks for the same period.

3. Of the total amount of deliveries in kind, it is agreed by the Belgian, British, French, Italian and Japanese Governments that the British quota is to be 23.05% and the French quota 4.95%.

The allocations to Italy of deliveries in kind are fixed at 52,500,000 reichsmarks instead of varying between 30 and 75 million reichsmarks a year. This limits the amount of coal Italy can buy from Germany to this figure (52,500,000). Italy agrees to buy a million tons of coal yearly for three years from Great Britain (November 1929-1932), and not to take reparation coal by sea in excess of one and one-half million tons per year for the ten-year period. Deliveries in kind due France are to start at 430,900,000 reichsmarks for the first year and are to be diminished at about 32 million reichsmarks a year so that France will receive the equivalent of 140,800,000 reichsmarks for the tenth year.

4. The costs of the Armies of Occupation are to be paid from a reserve fund of 60 million reichsmarks, one half of which is to be paid in a lump sum by Germany; the responsibility for the balance is to be divided between France (35%), Britain (12%) and Belgium (3%).

[NOTE.—To convert reichsmarks to dollars, multiply by .2382.]